Lord Macaulay's Essays ; And, Lays of Ancient Rome

You are holding a reproduction of an original work that is in the public domain in the United States of America, and possibly other countries.You may freely copy and distribute this work as no entity (individual or corporate) has a copyright on the body of the work.This book may contain prior copyright references, and library stamps (as most of these works were scanned from library copies).These have been scanned and retained as part of the historical artifact.

This book may have occasional imperfections such as missing or blurred pages, poor pictures, errant marks, etc. that were either part of the original artifact, or were introduced by the scanning process. We believe this work is culturally important, and despite the imperfections, have elected to bring it back into print as part of our continuing commitment to the preservation of printed works worldwide. We appreciate your understanding of the imperfections in the preservation process, and hope you enjoy this valuable book.

LORD MACAULAY'S

ESSAYS

AND

LAYS OF ANCIENT ROME

COMPLETE EDITION

LONDON
GEORGE ROUTLEDGE AND SONS, Limited
Broadway, Ludgate Hill
MANCHESTER AND NEW YORK
1892

20472.25.7

HARVARD COLLEGE LIBRARY
GIFT OF
PROF. JOHN TUCKER MURRAY
JUNE 13, 1938

CONTENTS.

ESSAYS FROM THE EDINBURGH REVIEW.

	PAGE
MILTON	1
MACHIAVELLI	36
HALLAM'S CONSTITUTIONAL HISTORY	55
SOUTHEY'S COLLOQUIES ON SOCIETY	105
MR. ROBERT MONTGOMERY'S POEMS	131
CIVIL DISABILITIES OF THE JEWS	143
MOORE'S LIFE OF LORD BYRON	151
SAMUEL JOHNSON	170
JOHN BUNYAN	196
JOHN HAMPDEN	204
BURGHLEY AND HIS TIMES	235
WAR OF THE SUCCESSION IN SPAIN	251
HORACE WALPOLE	281
HISTORY OF THE EARL OF CHATHAM	303
HISTORY OF THE REVOLUTION	329
LORD BACON	368
SIR WILLIAM TEMPLE	439
GLADSTONE ON CHURCH AND STATE	490
LORD CLIVE	524
VON RANKE	571
LEIGH HUNT	593
LORD HOLLAND	621
WARREN HASTINGS	627
FREDERIC THE GREAT	692
MADAME D'ARBLAY	736
THE LIFE AND WRITINGS OF ADDISON	769
THE EARL OF CHATHAM	814

LAYS OF ANCIENT ROME 861

ESSAYS.

MILTON.

Joannis Miltoni, Angli, de Doctrinâ Christiana libri duo posthumi. A Treatise on Christian Doctrine, compiled from the Holy Scriptures alone. By JOHN MILTON. *Translated from the original by Charles R. Sumner, M.A., &c., &c.* 1825.

TOWARDS the close of the year 1823 Mr. Lemon, Deputy Keeper of the State Papers, in the course of his researches among the presses of his office, met with a large Latin manuscript. With it were found corrected copies of the foreign despatches written by Milton, while he filled the office of Secretary, and several papers relating to the Popish Trials and the Rye House Plot. The whole was wrapped up in an envelope, superscribed "*To Mr. Skinner, Merchant.*" On examination, the large manuscript proved to be the long lost Essay on the Doctrines of Christianity, which, according to Wood and Toland, Milton finished after the Restoration, and deposited with Cyriac Skinner. Skinner, it is well known, held the same political opinions with his illustrious friend. It is, therefore, probable, as Mr. Lemon conjectures, that he may have fallen under the suspicions of the Government during that persecution of the Whigs which followed the dissolution of the Oxford Parliament, and that, in consequence of a general seizure of his papers, this work may have been brought to the office in which it has been found. But whatever the adventures of the manuscript may have been, no doubt can exist that it is a genuine relic of the great poet.

Mr. Sumner, who was commanded by his Majesty to edit and translate the treatise, has acquitted himself of his task in a manner honourable to his talents and to his character. His version is not, indeed, very easy or elegant; but it is entitled to the praise of clearness and fidelity. His notes abound with interesting quotations, and have the rare merit of really elucidating the text. The preface is evidently the work of a sensible and candid man, firm in his own religious opinions, and tolerant towards those of others.

The book itself will not add much to the fame of Milton. It is, like all his Latin works, well written—though not exactly in the style of the Prize essays of Oxford and Cambridge. There is no elaborate imitation of classical antiquity, no scrupulous purity, none of the ceremonial cleanness which characterizes the diction of our academical Pharisees. He does not attempt to polish and brighten his composition into the Ciceronian gloss and brilliancy. He does not, in short, sacrifice sense and spirit to pedantic refinements. The nature of his subject compelled him to use many words

"That would have made Quintilian stare and gasp."

But he writes with as much ease and freedom as if Latin were his mother tongue; and where he is least happy, his failure seems to arise from the carelessness of a native, not from the ignorance of a foreigner. What Denham with great felicity says of Cowley may be applied to him. He wears the garb, but not the clothes of the ancients.

Throughout the volume are discernible the traces of a powerful and independent mind, emancipated from the influence of authority, and devoted to the search of truth. He professes to form his system from the Bible alone;

and his digest of Scriptural texts is certainly among the best that have appeared. But he is not always so happy in his inferences as in his citations.

Some of the heterodox opinions which he avows seem to have excited considerable amazement; particularly his Arianism, and his notions on the subject of polygamy. Yet we can scarcely conceive that any person could have read the Paradise Lost without suspecting him of the former; nor do we think that any reader, acquainted with the history of his life, ought to be much startled at the latter. The opinions which he has expressed respecting the nature of the Deity, the eternity of matter, and the observation of the Sabbath might, we think, have caused more just surprise.

But we will not go into the discussion of these points. The book, were it far more orthodox, or far more heretical than it is, would not much edify or corrupt the present generation. The men of our time are not to be converted or perverted by quartos. A few more days, and this essay will follow the Defensio Populi to the dust and silence of the upper shelf. The name of its author, and the remarkable circumstances attending its publication, will secure to it a certain degree of attention. For a month or two it will occupy a few minutes of chat in every drawing-room, and a few columns in every magazine; and it will then, to borrow the elegant language of the play-bills, be withdrawn, to make room for the forthcoming novelties.

We wish, however, to avail ourselves of the interest, transient as it may be, which this work has excited. The dexterous Capuchins never choose to preach on the life and miracles of a saint, till they have awakened the devotional feelings of their auditors by exhibiting some relic of him—a thread of his garment, a lock of his hair, or a drop of his blood. On the same principle, we intend to take advantage of the late interesting discovery, and while this memorial of a great and good man is still in the hands of all, to say something of his moral and intellectual qualities. Nor, we are convinced, will the severest of our readers blame us if, on an occasion like the present, we turn for a short time from the topics of the day, to commemorate, in all love and reverence, the genius and virtues of John Milton, the poet, the statesman, the philosopher, the glory of English literature, the champion and the martyr of English liberty.

It is by his poetry that Milton is best known; and it is of his poetry that we wish first to speak. By the general suffrage of the civilized world his place has been assigned among the greatest masters of the art. His detractors, however, though out-voted, have not been silenced. There are many critics, and some of great name, who contrive in the same breath to extol the poems and to decry the poet. The works, they acknowledge, considered in themselves, may be classed among the noblest productions of the human mind. But they will not allow the author to rank with those great men who, born in the infancy of civilization, supplied, by their own powers, the want of instruction, and, though destitute of models themselves, bequeathed to posterity models which defy imitation. Milton, it is said, inherited what his predecessors created; he lived in an enlightened age; he received a finished education; and we must, therefore, if we would form a just estimate of his powers, make large deductions for these advantages.

We venture to say, on the contrary, paradoxical as the remark may appear, that no poet has ever had to struggle with more unfavourable circumstances than Milton. He doubted, as he has himself owned, whether he had not been born, "an age too late." For this notion Johnson has thought fit to make him the butt of his clumsy ridicule. The poet, we believe, understood the nature of his art better than the critic. He knew that his poetical genius derived no advantage from the civilization which surrounded him, or from the learning which he had acquired; and he looked back with something like regret to the ruder age of simple words and vivid impressions.

We think that, as civilization advances, poetry almost necessarily declines. Therefore, though we admire those great works of imagination which have appeared in dark ages, we do not admire them the more because they have appeared in dark ages. On the contrary, we hold that the most wonderful and splendid proof of genius is a great poem produced in a civilized age. We cannot understand why those who believe in that most orthodox article of literary faith, that the earliest poets are generally the best, should wonder at the rule as if it were the exception. Surely the uniformity of the phenomenon indicates a corresponding uniformity in the cause.

The fact is that common observers reason from the progress of the experimental sciences to that of the imitative arts. The improvement of the former is gradual and slow. Ages are spent in collecting materials, ages more in separating and combining them. Even when a system has been formed, there is still something to add, to alter, or to reject. Every generation enjoys the use of a vast hoard bequeathed to it by antiquity, and transmits it, augmented by fresh acquisitions, to future ages. In these pursuits, therefore, the first speculators lie under great disadvantages, and, even when they fail, are entitled to praise. Their pupils, with far inferior intellectual powers, speedily surpass them in actual attainments. Every girl who has read Mrs. Marcet's little Dialogues on Political Economy could teach Montague or Walpole many lessons in finance. Any intelligent man may now, by resolutely applying himself for a few years to mathematics, learn more than the great Newton knew after half a century of study and meditation.

But it is not thus with music, with painting, or with sculpture. Still less is it thus with poetry. The progress of refinement rarely supplies these arts with better objects of imitation. It may, indeed, improve the instruments which are necessary to the mechanical operations of the musician, the sculptor, and the painter. But language, the machine of the poet, is best fitted for his purpose in its rudest state. Nations, like individuals, first perceive and then abstract. They advance from particular images to general terms. Hence the vocabulary of an enlightened society is philosophical, that of a half-civilized people is poetical.

This change in the language of men is partly the cause and partly the effect of a corresponding change in the nature of their intellectual operations, a change by which science gains and poetry loses. Generalisation is necessary to the advancement of knowledge, but particularly in the creations of the imagination. In proportion as men know more and think more, they look less at individuals and more at classes. They therefore make better theories and worse poems. They give us vague phrases instead of images, and personified qualities instead of men. They may be better able to analyse human nature than their predecessors. But analysis is not the business of the poet. His office is to pourtray, not to dissect. He may believe in a moral sense, like Shaftesbury. He may refer all human actions to self-interest, like Helvetius, or he may never think about the matter at all. His creed on such subjects will no more influence his poetry, properly so called, than the notions which a painter may have conceived respecting the lachrymal glands, or the circulation of the blood, will affect the tears of his Niobe, or the blushes of his Aurora. If Shakespeare had written a book on the motives of human actions, it is by no means certain that it would have been a good one. It is extremely probable that it would have contained half so much able reasoning on the subject as is to be found in the Fable of the Bees. But could Mandeville have created an Iago? Well as he knew how to resolve characters into their elements, would he have been able to combine those elements in such a manner as to make up a man,—a real, living, individual man?

Perhaps no person can be a poet, or can even enjoy poetry, without a certain unsoundness of mind, if anything which gives so much pleasure ought to be called unsoundness. By poetry we mean not, of course, all writing in verse, nor even all good writing in verse. Our definition excludes many metrical compositions which, on other grounds, deserve the highest praise. By poetry, we mean the art of employing words in such a manner as to produce an illusion on the imagination, the art of doing by means of words what the painter does by means of colours. Thus the greatest of poets has described it, in lines universally admired for the vigour and felicity of their diction, and still more valuable on account of the just notion which they convey of the art in which he excelled:—

> "As imagination bodies forth
> The forms of things unknown, the poet's pen
> Turns them to shapes, and gives to airy nothing
> A local habitation and a name."

These are the fruits of the "fine frenzy" which he ascribes to the poet,—a fine frenzy, doubtless, but still a frenzy. Truth, indeed, is essential to poetry; but it is the truth of madness. The reasonings are just; but the premises are false. After the first suppositions have been made, everything ought to be consistent; but those first suppositions require a degree of credulity which almost amounts to a partial and temporary derangement of the intellect. Hence, of all people, children are the most imaginative. They abandon themselves without reserve to every illusion. Every image which is strongly presented to their mental eye produces on them the effect of reality. No man, whatever his sensibility may be, is ever affected by Hamlet or Lear as a little girl is affected by the story of poor Red Riding-Hood. She knows that it is all false, that wolves cannot speak, that there are no wolves in England. Yet, in spite of her knowledge, she believes; she weeps, she trembles; she dares not go into a dark room lest she should feel the teeth of the monster at her throat. Such is the despotism of the imagination over uncultivated minds.

In a rude state of society men are children with a greater variety of ideas. It is, therefore, in such a state of society that we may expect to find the poetical temperament in its highest perfection. In an enlightened age there will be much intelligence, much science, much philosophy, abundance of just classification and subtle analysis, abundance of wit and eloquence, abundance of verses, and even of good ones,—but little poetry. Men will judge and compare; but they will not create. They will talk about the old poets, and comment on them, and to a certain degree enjoy them. But they will scarcely be able to conceive the effect which poetry produced on their ruder ancestors, the agony, the ecstasy, the plenitude of belief. The Greek Rhapsodists, according to Plato, could not recite Homer without almost falling into convulsions.* The Mohawk hardly feels the scalping knife while he shouts his death-song. The power which the ancient bards of Wales and Germany exercised over their auditors seems to modern readers almost miraculous. Such feelings are very rare in a civilized community, and most rare among those who participate most in its improvements. They linger longest among the peasantry.

Poetry produces an illusion on the eye of the mind, as a magic lantern produces an illusion on the eye of the body. And, as the magic lantern acts best

---

* See the Dialogue between Socrates and Io.

in a dark room, poetry effects its purpose most completely in a dark age. As the light of knowledge breaks in upon its exhibitions, as the outlines of certainty become more and more definite, and the shades of probability more and more distinct, the hues and lineaments of the phantoms which it calls up grow fainter and fainter. We cannot unite the incompatible advantages of reality and deception, the clear discernment of truth and the exquisite enjoyment of fiction.

He who, in an enlightened and literary society, aspires to be a great poet, must first become a little child. He must take to pieces the whole web of his mind. He must unlearn much of that knowledge which has perhaps constituted hitherto his chief title to superiority. His very talents will be a hinderance to him. His difficulties will be proportioned to his proficiency in the pursuits which are fashionable among his contemporaries; and that proficiency will in general be proportioned to the vigour and activity of his mind. And it is well if, after all his sacrifices and exertions, his works do not resemble a lisping man, or a modern ruin. We have seen in our own time great talents, intense labour, and long meditation employed in this struggle against the spirit of the age, and employed, we will not say absolutely in vain, but with dubious success and feeble applause.

If these reasonings be just, no poet has ever triumphed over greater difficulties than Milton. He received a learned education. He was a profound and elegant classical scholar: he had studied all the mysteries of Rabbinical literature: he was intimately acquainted with every language of modern Europe from which either pleasure or information was then to be derived. He was, perhaps, the only great poet of later times who has been distinguished by the excellence of his Latin verse. The genius of Petrarch was scarcely of the first order: and his poems in the ancient language, though much praised by those who have never read them, are wretched compositions. Cowley, with all his admirable wit and ingenuity, had little imagination: nor, indeed, do we think his classical diction comparable to that of Milton. The authority of Johnson is against us on this point. But Johnson had studied the bad writers of the middle ages till he had become utterly insensible to the Augustan elegance, and was as ill qualified to judge between two Latin styles as a habitual drunkard to set up for a wine-taster.

Versification in a dead language is an exotic, a far-fetched, costly, sickly imitation of that which elsewhere may be found in healthful and spontaneous perfection. The soils on which this rarity flourishes are in general as ill suited to the production of vigorous native poetry as the flower-pots of a hothouse to the growth of oaks. That the author of the Paradise Lost should have written the Epistle to Manso was truly wonderful. Never before were such marked originality and such exquisite mimicry found together. Indeed, in all the Latin poems of Milton the artificial manner indispensable to such works is admirably preserved, while, at the same time, the richness of his fancy and the elevation of his sentiments give to them a peculiar charm, an air of nobleness and freedom, which distinguishes them from all other writings of the same class. They remind us of the amusements of those angelic warriors who composed the cohort of Gabriel:—

> "About him exercised heroic games
> The unarmed youth of heaven. But o'er their heads
> Celestial armoury, shield, helm, and spear,
> Hung bright, with diamond flaming and with gold."

We cannot look upon the sportive exercises for which the genius of Milton ungirds itself, without catching a glimpse of the gorgeous and terrible panoply which it is accustomed to wear. The strength of his imagination triumphed over every obstacle. So intense and ardent was the fire of his mind that it not only was not suffocated beneath the weight of its fuel, but penetrated the whole superincumbent mass with its own heat and radiance.

It is not our intention to attempt anything like a complete examination of the poetry of Milton. The public has long been agreed as to the merit of the most remarkable passages, the incomparable harmony of the numbers, and the excellence of that style which no rival has been able to equal, and no parodist to degrade, which displays in their highest perfection the idiomatic powers of the English tongue, and to which every ancient and every modern language has contributed something of grace, of energy, or of music. In the vast field of criticism on which we are entering, innumerable reapers have already put their sickles. Yet the harvest is so abundant that the negligent search of a straggling gleaner may be rewarded with a sheaf.

The most striking characteristic of the poetry of Milton is the extreme remoteness of the associations by means of which it acts on the reader. Its effect is produced, not so much by what it expresses, as by what it suggests, not so much by the ideas which it directly conveys, as by other ideas which are connected with them. He electrifies the mind through conductors. The most unimaginative man must understand the Iliad. Homer gives him no choice, and requires from him no exertion; but takes the whole upon himself, and sets his images in so clear a light that it is impossible to be blind to them. The works of Milton cannot be comprehended or enjoyed unless the mind of the reader co-operate with that of the writer. He does not paint a finished picture or play for a mere passive listener. He sketches, and leaves others to fill up the outline. He strikes the key-note, and expects his hearer to make out the melody.

We often hear of the magical influence of poetry. The expression in general means nothing, but, applied to the writings of Milton, it is most appropriate. His poetry acts like an incantation. Its merit lies less in its obvious meaning than in its occult power. There would seem, at first sight, to be no more in his words than in other words. But they are words of enchantment. No sooner are they pronounced than the past is present and the distant near. New forms of beauty start at once into existence, and all the burial places of the memory give up their dead. Change the structure of the sentence; substitute one synonym for another, and the whole effect is destroyed. The spell loses its power; and he who should then hope to conjure with it would find himself as much mistaken as Cassim in the Arabian tale, when he stood crying "Open Wheat," "Open Barley," to the door which obeyed no sound but "Open Sesame!" The miserable failure of Dryden in his attempt to re-write some parts of the Paradise Lost is a remarkable instance of this.

In support of these observations, we may remark that scarcely any passages in the poems of Milton are more generally known, or more frequently repeated, than those which are little more than muster-rolls of names. They are not always more appropriate or more melodious than other names. But they are charmed names. Every one of them is the first link in a long chain of associated ideas. Like the dwelling-place of our infancy revisited in manhood, like the song of our country heard in a strange land, they produce upon us an effect wholly independent of their intrinsic value. One transports us back to a remote period of history. Another places us among the moral scenery and manners of a distant country. A third evokes all the dear classical recollections of childhood, the school-room, the dog-eared Virgil, the holiday, and the prize. A fourth brings before us the splendid phantoms of chivalrous romance, the trophied lists, the embroidered housings, the quaint devices, the haunted forests, the enchanted gardens, the achievements of enamoured knights, and the smiles of rescued princesses.

In none of the works of Milton is his peculiar manner more happily displayed than in the Allegro and the Penseroso. It is impossible to conceive that the mechanism of language can be brought to a more exquisite degree of perfection. These poems differ from others as ottar of roses differs from ordinary rose water, the close-packed essence from the thin diluted mixture. They are, indeed, not so much poems as collections of hints from each of which the reader is to make out a poem for himself. Every epithet is a text for a canto.

The Comus and the Samson Agonistes are works which, though of very different merit, offer some marked points of resemblance. They are both lyric poems in the form of plays. There are, perhaps, no two kinds of composition so essentially dissimilar as the drama and the ode. The business of the dramatist is to keep himself out of sight, and to let nothing appear but his characters. As soon as he attracts notice to his personal feelings the illusion is broken. The effect is as unpleasant as that which is produced on the stage by the voice of a prompter, or the entrance of a scene-shifter. Hence it was that the tragedies of Byron were his least successful performances. They resemble those pasteboard pictures invented by the friend of children, Mr. Newberry, in which a single movable head goes round twenty different bodies; so that the same face looks out upon us successively from the uniform of a hussar, the furs of a judge, and the rags of a beggar. In all the characters, patriots and tyrants, haters and lovers, the frown and sneer of Harold were discernible in an instant. But this species of egotism, though fatal to the drama, is the inspiration of the ode. It is the part of the lyric poet to abandon himself, without reserve, to his own emotions.

Between these hostile elements many great men have endeavoured to effect an amalgamation; but never with complete success. The Greek drama, on the model of which the Samson was written, sprung from the ode. The dialogue was ingrafted on the chorus, and naturally partook of its character. The genius of the greatest of the Athenian dramatists co-operated with the circumstances under which tragedy made its first appearance. Æschylus was, head and heart, a lyric poet. In his time the Greeks had far more intercourse with the East than in the days of Homer; and they had not yet acquired that immense superiority in war, in science, and in the arts which, in the following generation, led them to treat the Asiatics with contempt. From the narrative of Herodotus it should seem that they still looked up, with the veneration of disciples, to Egypt and Assyria. At this period, accordingly, it was natural that the literature of Greece should be tinctured with the Oriental style. And that style, we think, is clearly discernible in the works of Pindar and Æschylus. The latter often reminds us of the Hebrew writers. The book of Job, indeed, in conduct and diction, bears a considerable resemblance to some of his dramas. Considered as plays, his works are absurd; considered as choruses, they are above all praise. If, for instance, we examine the address of Clytemnestra to Agamemnon on his return, or the description of the seven Argive chiefs, by the principles of dramatic writing, we shall instantly condemn them as monstrous. But if we forget the characters and think only of the poetry, we shall admit that it has never been surpassed in energy and magnificence. Sophocles made the Greek drama as dramatic as was consistent with its original form. His portraits of men have a sort of similarity; but it is the similarity not of a painting, but of a bas-relief. It suggests a resemblance; but it does not produce an illusion. Euripides attempted to carry the reform further. But it was a task far beyond his powers, perhaps beyond any powers. Instead of correcting what was bad, he destroyed what was excellent. He substituted crutches for stilts, bad sermons for good odes.

Milton, it is well known, admired Euripides highly; much more highly than, in our opinion, he deserved. Indeed the caresses which this partiality leads him to bestow on "sad Electra's poet," sometimes remind us of the beautiful Queen of Fairyland kissing the long ears of Bottom. At all events, there can be no doubt that his veneration for the Athenian, whether just or not, was injurious to the Samson Agonistes. Had he taken Æschylus for his model, he would have given himself up to the lyric inspiration, and poured out profusely all the treasures of his mind, without bestowing a thought on those dramatic proprieties which the nature of the work rendered it impossible to preserve. In the attempt to reconcile things in their own nature inconsistent he has failed, as every one else must have failed. We cannot identify ourselves with the characters, as in a good play. We cannot identify ourselves with the poet, as in a good ode. The conflicting ingredients, like an acid and an alkali mixed, neutralize each other. We are by no means insensible to the merits of this celebrated piece, to the severe dignity of the style, the graceful and pathetic solemnity of the opening speech, or the wild and barbaric melody which gives so striking an effect to the choral passages. But we think it, we confess, the least successful effort of the genius of Milton.

The Comus is framed on the model of the Italian masque, as the Samson is framed on the model of the Greek tragedy. It is certainly the noblest performance of the kind which exists in any language. It is as far superior to the Faithful Shepherdess as the Faithful Shepherdess is to Aminta, or the Aminta to the Pastor Fido. It was well for Milton that he had here no Euripides to mislead him. He understood and loved the literature of modern Italy. But he did not feel for it the same veneration which he entertained for the remains of Athenian and Roman poetry, consecrated by so many lofty and endearing recollections. The faults, moreover, of his Italian predecessors were of a kind to which his mind had a deadly antipathy. He could stoop to a plain style, sometimes even to a bald style; but false brilliancy was his utter aversion. His Muse had no objection to a russet attire: but she turned with disgust from the finery of Guarini, as tawdry and as paltry as the rags of a chimney-sweeper on May-day. Whatever ornaments *she* wears are of massive gold, not only dazzling to the sight, but capable of standing the severest test of the crucible.

Milton attended in the Comus to the distinction which he neglected in the Samson. He made it what it ought to be, essentially lyrical, and dramatic only in semblance. He has not attempted a fruitless struggle against a defect inherent in the nature of that species of composition; and he has, therefore, succeeded, wherever success was not impossible. The speeches must be read as majestic soliloquies; and he who so reads them will be enraptured with their eloquence, their sublimity, and their music. The interruptions of the dialogue, however, impose a constraint upon the writer, and break the illusion of the reader. The finest passages are those which are lyrics in form as well as in spirit. "I should much commend," says the excellent Sir Henry Wotton in a letter to Milton, "the tragical part, if the lyrical did not ravish me with a certain dorique delicacy in your songs and odes, whereunto, I must plainly confess to you, I have seen yet nothing parallel in our language." The criticism was just. It is when Milton escapes from the shackles of the dialogues, when he is discharged from the labour of uniting two incongruous styles, when he is at liberty to indulge his choral raptures without reserve, that he rises even above himself. Then, like his own good genius bursting from the earthly form and weeds of Thyrsis, he stands forth in celestial freedom and beauty; he seems to say exultingly,

"Now my task is smoothly done,
I can fly or I can run,"

to skim the earth, to soar above the clouds, to bathe in the Elysian dew of the rainbow, and to inhale the balmy smells of nard and cassia, which the musky wings of the zephyr scatter through the cedared alleys of the Hesperides.*

There are several of the minor poems of Milton on which we would willingly make a few remarks. Still more willingly would we enter into a detailed examination of that admirable poem, the Paradise Regained, which, strangely enough, is scarcely ever mentioned except as an instance of the blindness of that parental affection which men of letters bear towards the offspring of their intellects. That Milton was mistaken in preferring this work, excellent as it is, to the Paradise Lost, we must readily admit. But we are sure that the superiority of the Paradise Lost to the Paradise Regained is not more decided than the superiority of the Paradise Regained to every poem which has since made its appearance. But our limits prevent us from discussing the point at length. We hasten on to that extraordinary production which the general suffrage of critics has placed in the highest class of human compositions.

The only poem of modern times which can be compared with the Paradise Lost is the Divine Comedy. The subject of Milton, in some points, resembled that of Dante; but he has treated it in a widely different manner. We cannot, we think, better illustrate our opinion respecting our own great poet than by contrasting him with the father of Tuscan literature.

The poetry of Milton differs from that of Dante as the Hieroglyphics of Egypt differed from the picture-writing of Mexico. The images which Dante employs speak for themselves; they stand simply for what they are. Those of Milton have a signification which is often discernible only to the initiated. Their value depends less on what they directly represent than on what they remotely suggest. However strange, however grotesque may be the appearance which Dante undertakes to describe, he never shrinks from describing it. He gives us the shape, the colour, the sound, the smell, the taste; he counts the numbers; he measures the size. His similes are the illustrations of a traveller. Unlike those of other poets, and especially of Milton, they are introduced in a plain, business-like manner, not for the sake of any beauty in the objects from which they are drawn, not for the sake of any ornament which they may impart to the poem, but simply in order to make the meaning of the writer as clear to the reader as it is to himself. The ruins of the precipice which led from the sixth to the seventh circle of hell were like those of the rock which fell into the Adige on the south of Trent. The cataract of Phlegethon was like that of Aqua Cheta at the monastery of St. Benedict. The place where the heretics were confined in burning tombs resembled the vast cemetery of Arles!

---
* "There eternal summer dwells,
And west winds, with musky wing,
About the cedared alleys fling
Nard and cassia's balmy smells:
Iris there with humid bow
Waters the odorous banks, that blow
Flowers of more mingled hue
Than her purfled scarf can show,
And drenches with Elysian dew
(List, mortals, if your ears be true)
Beds of hyacinths and roses,
Where young Adonis oft reposes,
Waxing well of his deep wound."

Now let us compare with the exact details of Dante the dim intimations of Milton. We will cite a few examples. The English poet has never thought of taking the measure of Satan. He gives us merely a vague idea of vast bulk. In one passage the fiend lies stretched out, huge in length, floating many a rood, equal in size to the earth-born enemies of Jove, or to the sea monster which the mariner mistakes for an island. When he addresses himself to battle against the guardian angels, he stands like Teneriffe or Atlas; his stature reaches the sky. Contrast with these descriptions the lines in which Dante has described the gigantic spectre of Nimrod. "His face seemed to me as long and as broad as the ball of St. Peter's at Rome; and his other limbs were in proportion; so that the bank, which concealed him from the waist downwards, nevertheless showed so much of him that three tall Germans would in vain have attempted to reach to his hair." We are sensible that we do no justice to the admirable style of the Florentine poet. But Mr. Cary's translation is not at hand; and our version, however rude, is sufficient to illustrate our meaning.

Once more, compare the lazar-house in the eleventh book of the Paradise Lost with the last ward of Malebolge in Dante. Milton avoids the loathsome details, and takes refuge in indistinct but solemn and tremendous imagery; Despair hurrying from couch to couch to mock the wretches with his attendance, Death shaking his dart over them, but in spite of supplications, delaying to strike. What says Dante? "There was such a moan there as there would be if all the sick who, between July and September, are in the hospitals of Valdichiana, and of the Tuscan swamps, and of Sardinia, were in one pit together; and such a stench was issuing forth as is wont to issue from decayed limbs."

We will not take upon ourselves the invidious office of settling precedency between two such writers. Each in his own department is incomparable; and each, we may remark, has, wisely or fortunately, taken a subject adapted to exhibit his peculiar talent to the greatest advantage. The Divine Comedy is a personal narrative. Dante is the eye-witness and ear-witness of that which he relates. He is the very man who has heard the tormented spirits crying out for the second death, who has read the dusky characters on the portal within which there is no hope, who has hidden his face from the terrors of the Gorgon, who has fled from the hooks and the seething pitch of Barbariccia and Diaghignazzo. His own hands have grasped the shaggy sides of Lucifer. His own feet have climbed the mountain of expiation. His own brow has been marked by the purifying angel. The reader would throw aside such a tale in incredulous disgust, unless it were told with the strongest air of veracity, with a sobriety even in its horrors, with the greatest precision and multiplicity in its details. The narrative of Milton in this respect differs from that of Dante as the adventures of Amadis differ from those of Gulliver. The author of Amadis would have made his book ridiculous if he had introduced those minute particulars which give such a charm to the work of Swift, the nautical observations, the affected delicacy about names, the official documents transcribed at full length, and all the unmeaning gossip and scandal of the court, springing out of nothing, and tending to nothing. We are not shocked at being told that a man who lived, nobody knows when, saw many very strange sights, and we can easily abandon ourselves to the illusion of the romance. But when Lemuel Gulliver, surgeon, now actually resident at Rotherhithe, tells us of pygmies and giants, flying islands and philosophizing horses, nothing but such circumstantial touches could produce for a single moment a deception on the imagination.

Of all the poets who have introduced into their works the agency of supernatural beings, Milton has succeeded best. Here Dante decidedly yields to him. And as this is a point on which many rash and ill-considered judgments have been pronounced, we feel inclined to dwell on it a little longer. The most fatal error which a poet can possibly commit in the management of his machinery is that of attempting to philosophize too much. Milton has been often censured for ascribing to spirits many functions of which spirits must be incapable. But these objections, though sanctioned by eminent names, originate, we venture to say, in profound ignorance of the art of poetry.

What is spirit? What are our own minds, the portion of spirit with which we are best acquainted? We observe certain phenomena. We cannot explain them into material causes. We therefore infer that there exists something which is not material. But of this something we have no idea. We can define it only by negatives. We can reason about it only by symbols. We use the word; but we have no image of the thing; and the business of poetry is with images, and not with words. The poet uses words indeed; but they are merely the instruments of his art, not its objects. They are the materials which he is to dispose in such a manner as to present a picture to the mental eye. And if they are not so disposed, they are no more entitled to be called poetry than a bale of canvas and a box of colours to be called a painting.

Logicians may reason about abstractions. But the great mass of mankind can never feel an interest in them. They must have images. The strong tendency of the multitude in all ages and nations to idolatry can be explained on no other principle. The first inhabitants of Greece, there is every reason to believe, worshipped one invisible Deity. But the necessity of having something more definite to adore produced, in a few centuries, the innumerable crowd of gods and goddesses. In like manner the ancient Persians thought it impious to exhibit the Creator under a human form. Yet even these transferred to the sun the worship which, speculatively, they considered due only to the Supreme Mind. The history of the Jews is the record of a continued struggle between pure theism, supported by the most terrible sanctions, and the strangely fascinating desire of having some visible and tangible object of adoration. Perhaps none of the secondary causes which Gibbon has assigned for the rapidity with which Christianity spread over the world, while Judaism scarcely ever acquired a proselyte, operated more powerfully than this feeling. God, the uncreated, the incomprehensible, the invisible, attracted few worshippers. A philosopher might admire so noble a conception: but the crowd turned away in disgust from words which presented no image to their minds. It was before Deity embodied in a human form, walking among men, partaking of their infirmities, leaning on their bosoms, weeping over their graves, slumbering in the manger, bleeding on the cross, that the prejudices of the synagogue, and the doubts of the academy, and the pride of the portico, and the fasces of the lictor, and the swords of thirty legions, were humbled in the dust! Soon after Christianity had achieved its triumph, the principle which had assisted it began to corrupt it. It became a new paganism. Patron saints assumed the offices of household gods. St. George took the place of Mars. St. Elmo consoled the mariner for the loss of Castor and Pollux. The Virgin Mother and Cecilia succeeded to Venus and the Muses. The fascination of sex and loveliness was again joined to that of celestial dignity; and the homage of chivalry was blended with that of religion. Reformers have often made a stand against these feelings; but never with more than apparent and partial success. The men who demolished the images in cathedrals have not always been able to demolish those which were enshrined in their minds. It would not be difficult to show that in politics the same rule holds good. Doctrines we are afraid, must generally be *embodied* before they can excite a strong public feeling. The multitude is more easily interested for the most unmeaning badge, or the most insignificant name, than for the most important principle.

From these considerations we infer that no poet who should affect that metaphysical accuracy for the want of which Milton has been blamed would escape a disgraceful failure. Still, however, there was another extreme which, though far less dangerous, was also to be avoided. The imaginations of men are, in a great measure, under the control of their opinions. The most exquisite art of poetical colouring can produce no illusion when it is employed to represent that which is at once perceived to be incongruous and absurd. Milton wrote in an age of philosophers and theologians. It was necessary, therefore, for him to abstain from giving such a shock to their understandings as might break the charm which it was his object to throw over their imaginations. This is the real explanation of the indistinctness and inconsistency with which he has often been reproached. Dr. Johnson acknowledges that it was absolutely necessary for him to clothe his spirits with material forms. "But," says he, "he should have secured the consistency of his system by keeping immateriality out of sight, and seducing the reader to drop it from his thoughts." This is easily said; but what if he could not seduce the reader to drop it from *his* thoughts? What if the contrary opinion had taken so full a possession of the minds of men as to leave no room even for the *quasi-belief* which poetry requires? Such we suspect to have been the case. It was impossible for the poet to adopt altogether the material or the immaterial system. He therefore took his stand on the debatable ground. He left the whole in ambiguity. He has doubtless, by so doing, laid himself open to the charge of inconsistency. But, though philosophically in the wrong, we cannot but believe that he was poetically in the right. This task, which almost any other writer would have found impracticable, was easy to him. The peculiar art which he possessed of communicating his meaning circuitously, through a long succession of associated ideas, and of intimating more than he expressed, enabled him to disguise those incongruities which he could not avoid.

Poetry which relates to the beings of another world ought to be at once mysterious and picturesque. That of Milton is so. That of Dante is picturesque, indeed, beyond any that ever was written. Its effect approaches to that produced by the pencil or the chisel. But it is picturesque to the exclusion of all mystery. This is a fault, indeed, on the right side, a fault inseparable from the plan of his poem, which, as we have already observed, rendered the utmost accuracy of description necessary. Still it is a fault. His supernatural agents excite an interest; but it is not the interest which is proper to supernatural agents. We feel that we could talk with his ghosts and demons without any emotion of unearthly awe. We could, like Don Juan, ask them to supper, and eat heartily in their company. His angels are good men with wings. His devils are spiteful ugly executioners. His dead men are merely living men in strange situations. The scene which passes between the poet and Facinata is justly celebrated. Still Facinata in the burning tomb is exactly what Facinata would have been at an *auto-da-fé*. Nothing can be more touching than the first interview of Dante and Beatrice. Yet what is it but a lovely woman chiding, with sweet, austere composure, the lover for whose affection she is grateful, but whose vices she reprobates? The feelings which give the passage its charm would suit the streets of Florence as well as the summit of the Mount of Purgatory.

The spirits of Milton are unlike those of almost all other writers. His fiends, in particular, are wonderful creations. They are not metaphysical abstractions. They are not wicked men. They are not ugly beasts. They have no horns, no tails, none of the fee-faw-fum of Tasso and Klopstock. They have just enough in common with human nature to be intelligible to human beings. Their characters are, like their forms, marked by a certain dim resemblance to those of men, but exaggerated to gigantic dimensions, and veiled in mysterious gloom.

Perhaps the gods and demons of Æschylus may best bear a comparison with the angels and devils of Milton. The style of the Athenian had, as we have remarked, something of the vagueness and tenor of the Oriental character; and the same peculiarity may be traced in his mythology. It has nothing of the amenity and elegance which we generally find in the superstitions of Greece. All is rugged, barbaric, and colossal. His legends seem to harmonize less with the fragrant groves and graceful porticos in which his countrymen paid their vows to the God of Light and Goddess of Desire than with those huge and grotesque labyrinths of eternal granite in which Egypt enshrined her mystic Osiris, or in which Hindoostan still bows down to her seven-headed idols. His favourite gods are those of the elder generations—the sons of heaven and earth, compared with whom Jupiter himself was a stripling and an upstart,—the gigantic Titans and the inexorable Furies. Foremost among his creations of this class stands Prometheus, half fiend, half redeemer, the friend of man, the sullen and implacable enemy of heaven. He bears undoubtedly a considerable resemblance to the Satan of Milton. In both we find the same impatience of control, the same ferocity, the same unconquerable pride. In both characters also are mingled, though in very different proportions, some kind and generous feelings. Prometheus, however, is hardly superhuman enough. He talks too much of his chains and his uneasy posture: he is rather too much depressed and agitated. His resolution seems to depend on the knowledge which he possesses that he holds the fate of his torturer in his hands, and that the hour of his release will surely come. But Satan is a creature of another sphere. The might of his intellectual nature is victorious over the extremity of pain. Amidst agonies which cannot be conceived without horror he deliberates, resolves, and even exults. Against the sword of Michael, against the thunder of Jehovah, against the flaming lake, and the marl burning with solid fire, against the prospect of an eternity of unintermittent misery, his spirit bears up unbroken, resting on its own innate energies, requiring no support from anything external, nor even from hope itself!

To return for a moment to the parallel which we have been attempting to draw between Milton and Dante, we would add that the poetry of these great men has, in a considerable degree, taken its character from their moral qualities. They are not egotists. They rarely obtrude their idiosyncracies on their readers. They have nothing in common with those modern beggars for fame who extort a pittance from the compassion of the inexperienced by exposing the nakedness and sores of their minds. Yet it would be difficult to name two writers whose works have been more completely, though undesignedly, coloured by their personal feelings.

The character of Milton was peculiarly distinguished by loftiness of thought; that of Dante by intensity of feeling. In every line of the Divine Comedy we discern the asperity which is produced by pride struggling with misery. There is perhaps no work in the world so deeply and uniformly sorrowful. The melancholy of Dante was no fantastic caprice. It was not, as far as at this distance of time can be judged, the effect of external circumstances. It was from within. Neither love nor glory, neither the conflicts of earth nor the hope of heaven could dispel it. It twined every consolation and every pleasure into its own nature. It resembled that noxious Sardinian soil of which the intense

and full of valuable information, but has also an air of dignity and sincerity which makes even the prejudices and errors with which it abounds respectable. Hume, from whose fascinating narrative the great mass of the reading public are still contented to take their opinions, hated religion so much that he hated liberty for having been allied with religion—and has pleaded the cause of tyranny with the dexterity of an advocate, while affecting the impartiality of a judge.

The public conduct of Milton must be approved or condemned according as the resistance of the people to Charles I. shall appear to be justifiable or criminal. We shall, therefore, make no apology for dedicating a few pages to the discussion of that interesting and most important question. We shall not argue it on general grounds; we shall not recur to those primary principles from which the claim of any government to the obedience of its subjects is to be deduced; it is a vantage-ground to which we are entitled; but we will relinquish it. We are, on this point, so confident of superiority that we have no objection to imitate the ostentatious generosity of those ancient knights who vowed to joust without helmet or shield against all enemies, and to give their antagonists the advantage of sun and wind. We will take the naked constitutional question. We confidently affirm that every reason which can be urged in favour of the Revolution of 1688 may be urged with at least equal force in favour of what is called the Great Rebellion.

In one respect only, we think, can the warmest admirers of Charles venture to say that he was a better sovereign than his son. He was not, in name and profession, a Papist; we say in name and profession,—because both Charles himself and his miserable creature Laud, while they abjured the innocent badges of Popery, retained all its worst vices, a complete subjection of reason to authority, a weak preference of form to substance, a childish passion for mummeries, an idolatrous veneration for the priestly character, and above all, a stupid and ferocious intolerance. This, however, we wave. We will concede that Charles was a good Protestant; but we say that his Protestantism does not make the slightest distinction between his case and that of James.

The principles of the Revolution have often been grossly misrepresented, and never more than in the course of the present year. There is a certain class of men who, while they profess to hold in reverence the great names and great actions of former times, never look at them for any other purpose than in order to find in them some excuse for existing abuses. In every venerable precedent, they pass by what is essential, and take only what is accidental; they keep out of sight what is beneficial, and hold up to public imitation all that is defective. If in any part of any great example there be anything unsound, these flesh-flies detect it with an unerring instinct, and dart upon it with a ravenous delight. They cannot always prevent the advocates of a good measure from compassing their end; but they feel, with their prototype, that

"Their labours must be to pervert that end,
And out of good still to find means of evil."

To the blessings which England has derived from the Revolution these people are utterly insensible. The expulsion of a tyrant, the solemn recognition of popular rights, liberty, security, toleration, all go for nothing with them. One sect there was, which, from unfortunate temporary causes, it was thought necessary to keep under close restraint. One part of the empire there was, so unhappily circumstanced, that at that time its misery was necessary to our happiness, and its slavery to our freedom! These are the parts of the Revolution which the politicians of whom we speak love to contemplate, and which seem to them, not indeed to vindicate, but in some degree to palliate the good which it has produced. Talk to them of Naples, of Spain, or of South America! they stand forth, zealots for the doctrine of Divine Right—which has now come back to us, like a thief from transportation, under the *alias* of Legitimacy. But mention the miseries of Ireland! Then William is a hero. Then Somers and Shrewsbury are great men. Then the Revolution is a glorious era! The very same persons who, in this country, never omit an opportunity of reviving every wretched Jacobite slander respecting the Whigs of that period, have no sooner crossed St. George's Channel than they begin to fill their bumpers to the glorious and immortal memory. They may truly boast that they look not at men but at measures. So that evil be done, they care not who does it—the arbitrary Charles or the liberal William, Ferdinand the Catholic or Frederick the Protestant! On such occasions their deadliest opponents may reckon upon their candid construction. The bold assertions of these people have of late impressed a large portion of the public with an opinion that James II. was expelled simply because he was a Catholic, and that the Revolution was essentially a Protestant Revolution.

But this certainly was *not* the case. Nor can any person who has acquired more knowledge of the history of those times than is to be found in Goldsmith's Abridgment, believe that, if James had held his own religious opinions without wishing to make proselytes, or if, wishing even to make proselytes, he had contented himself with exerting only his constitutional influence for that purpose, the Prince of Orange would ever have been invited over. Our ancestors, we suppose, knew their own meaning. And, if we may believe them, their hostility was *primarily* not to popery but to *tyranny*. They did not drive out a tyrant because he was a Catholic; but they excluded Catholics from the crown because they thought them likely to be tyrants. The ground on which they, in their famous resolution, declared the throne vacant was this, "that James had broken the fundamental laws of the kingdom." Every man, therefore, who approves of the Revolution of 1688 must hold that *the breach of fundamental laws on the part of the sovereign* justifies resistance. The question, then, is this: Had Charles I. broken the fundamental laws of England?

No person can answer in the negative, unless he refuses credit, not merely to all the accusations brought against Charles by his opponents, but to the narratives of the warmest Royalists, and to the confessions of the king himself. If there be any truth in *any* historian of *any* party who has related the events of that reign, the conduct of Charles, from his accession to the meeting of the Long Parliament, had been a continued course of oppression and treachery. Let those who applaud the Revolution and condemn the Rebellion mention one act of James II. to which a parallel is not to be found in the history of his father. Let them lay their fingers on a single article in the Declaration of Right, presented by the two Houses to William and Mary, which Charles is not acknowledged to have violated. He had, according to the testimony of his own friends, usurped the functions of the legislature, raised taxes without the consent of Parliament, and quartered troops on the people in the most illegal and vexatious manner. Not a single session of Parliament had passed without some unconstitutional attack on the freedom of debate. The right of petition was grossly violated. Arbitrary judgments, exorbitant fines, and unwarranted imprisonments, were grievances of daily and hourly occurrence. If these things do not justify resistance, the Revolution was treason: if they do, the Great Rebellion was laudable.

But, it is said, why not adopt milder measures? Why, after the king had consented to so many reforms, and renounced so many oppressive prerogative did the Parliament continue to rise in their demands at the risk of provoking a civil war? The Ship-money had been given up. The Star Chamber had been abolished. Provision had been made for the frequent convocation and secure deliberation of Parliaments. Why not pursue an end confessedly good, by peaceable and regular means? We recur again to the analogy of the Revolution. Why was James driven from the throne? Why was he not retained upon conditions? He too had offered to call a free Parliament, and to submit to its decision all the matters in dispute. Yet we praise our forefathers, who preferred a revolution, a disputed succession, a dynasty of strangers, twenty years of foreign and intestine war, a standing army, and a national debt, to the rule, however restricted, of a tried and proved tyrant. The Long Parliament acted on the same principle, and is entitled to the same praise. They could not trust the king. He had, no doubt, passed salutary laws. But what assurance had they that he would not break them? He had renounced oppressive prerogatives. But where was the security that he would not resume them? They had to deal with a man whom no tie could bind; a man who made and broke promises with equal facility, a man whose honour had been a hundred times pawned, and never redeemed.

Here, indeed, the Long Parliament stands on still stronger ground than the Convention of 1688. No action of James can be compared, for wickedness and impudence, to the conduct of Charles with respect to the Petition of Right. The Lords and Commons present him with a bill in which the constitutional limits of his power are marked out. He hesitates; he evades; at last he bargains to give his assent, for five subsidies. The bill receives his solemn assent. The subsidies are voted. But no sooner is the tyrant relieved than he returns at once to all the arbitrary measures which he had bound himself to abandon, and violates all the clauses of the very act which he had been paid to pass.

For more than ten years the people had seen the rights which were theirs by a double claim, by immemorial inheritance and by recent purchase, infringed by the perfidious king who had recognised them. At length circumstances compelled Charles to summon another Parliament: another chance was given them for liberty. Were they to throw it away as they had thrown away the former? Were they again to be cozened by *le roi le veut?* Were they again to advance their money on pledges which had been forfeited over and over again? Were they to lay a second Petition of Right at the foot of the throne, to grant another lavish aid in exchange for another unmeaning ceremony, and then to take their departure till, after ten years more of fraud and oppression, their prince should again require a supply, and again repay it with a perjury? They were compelled to choose whether they would *trust* a tyrant or *conquer* him. We think that they chose wisely and nobly.

The advocates of Charles, like the advocates of other malefactors against whom overwhelming evidence is produced, generally decline all controversy about the facts, and content themselves with calling testimony to character. He had so many private virtues! And had James II. no private virtues? Was even Oliver Cromwell, his bitterest enemies themselves being judges, destitute of private virtues? And what, after all, are the virtues ascribed to Charles? A religious zeal, not more sincere than that of his son, and fully as weak and narrow-minded, and a few of the ordinary household decencies which half the tomb stones in England claim for those who lie beneath them. A good father! A good husband! Ample apologies indeed for fifteen years of persecution, tyranny, and falsehood?

We charge him with having broken his coronation-oath—and we are told that he kept his marriage-vow! We accuse him of having given up his people to the merciless inflictions of the most hot-headed and hard-hearted of prelates—and the defence is that he took his little son on his knee and kissed him! We censure him for having violated the articles of the Petition of Right, after having, for good and valuable consideration, promised to observe them—and we are informed that he was accustomed to hear prayers at six o'clock in the morning! It is to such considerations as these, together with his Vandyke dress, his handsome face, and his peaked beard, that he owes, we verily believe, most of his popularity with the present generation.

For ourselves, we own that we do not understand the common phrase, a good man but a bad king. We can as easily conceive a good man and an unnatural father, or a good man and a treacherous friend. We cannot, in estimating the character of an individual, leave out of our consideration his conduct in the most important of all human relations. And if, in that relation, we find him to have been selfish, cruel, and deceitful, we shall take the liberty to call him a bad man, in spite of all his temperance at table and all his regularity at chapel.

We cannot refrain from adding a few words respecting a topic on which the defenders of Charles are fond of dwelling. If, they say, he governed his people ill, he at least governed them after the example of his predecessors. If he violated their privileges, it was because those privileges had not been accurately defined. No active oppression has ever been imputed to him which has not a parallel in the annals of the Tudors. This point Hume has laboured, with an art which is as discreditable in a historical work as it would be admirable in a forensic address. The answer is short, clear, and decisive. Charles had assented to the Petition of Right. *He had renounced* the oppressive powers said to have been exercised by his predecessors, and he had renounced them for money. He was not entitled to set up his antiquated claims against his own recent release.

These arguments are so obvious that it may seem superfluous to dwell upon them. But those who have observed how much the events of that time are misrepresented and misunderstood will not blame us for stating the case simply. It is a case of which the simplest statement is the strongest.

The enemies of the Parliament, indeed, rarely choose to take issue on the great points of the question. They content themselves with exposing some of the crimes and follies to which public commotions necessarily give birth. They bewail the unmerited fate of Strafford. They execrate the lawless violence of the army. They laugh at the Scriptural names of the preachers. Major-generals fleecing their districts; soldiers revelling on the spoils of a ruined peasantry; upstarts, enriched by the public plunder, taking possession of the hospitable firesides and hereditary trees of the old gentry; boys smashing the beautiful windows of cathedrals; Quakers riding naked through the market-place; Fifth-monarchy-men shouting for King Jesus; agitators lecturing from the tops of tubs on the fate of Agag—all these, they tell us, were the offspring of the Great Rebellion.

Be it so. We are not careful to answer in this matter. These charges, were they infinitely more important, would not alter our opinion of an event which alone has made us to differ from the slaves who crouch beneath the sceptres of Brandenburgh and Braganza. Many evils, no doubt, *were* produced by the civil war. They were the price of our liberty. Has the acquisition been worth the sacrifice? It is the nature of the Devil of tyranny to tear and rend the body which he leaves. Are the miseries of continued possession less horrible than the struggles of the tremendous exorcism?

If it were possible that a people brought up under an intolerant and arbitrary system could subvert that system without acts of cruelty and folly, half the objections to despotic power would be removed. We should, in that case, be compelled to acknowledge, that it at least produces no pernicious effects on the intellectual and moral character of a people. We deplore the outrages which accompany revolutions. But the more violent the outrages, the more assured we feel that *a revolution was necessary*. The violence of those outrages will always be proportioned to the ferocity and ignorance of the people : and the ferocity and ignorance of the people will be proportioned to the oppression and degradation under which they have been accustomed to live. Thus it was in our civil war. The rulers in the Church and State reaped only that which they had sown. They had prohibited free discussion ; they had done their best to keep the people unacquainted with their duties and their rights. The retribution was just and natural. If they suffered from popular ignorance, it was because they had themselves taken away the key of knowledge. If they were assailed with blind fury, it was because they had exacted an equally blind submission.

It is the character of such revolutions that we always see the worst of them at first. Till men have been for some time free, they know not how to use their freedom. The natives of wine countries are always sober. In climates where wine is a rarity intemperance abounds. A newly liberated people may be compared to a northern army encamped on the Rhine or the Xeres. It is said that when soldiers in such a situation first find themselves able to indulge without restraint in such a rare and expensive luxury nothing is to be seen but intoxication. Soon, however, plenty teaches discretion ; and after wine has been for a few months their daily fare, they become more temperate than they had ever been in their own country. In the same manner, the final and permanent fruits of liberty are wisdom, moderation, and mercy. Its immediate effects are often atrocious crimes, conflicting errors, scepticism on points the most clear, dogmatism on points the most mysterious. It is just at this crisis that its enemies love to exhibit it. They pull down the scaffolding from the half-finished edifice : they point to the flying dust, the falling bricks, the comfortless rooms, the frightful irregularity of the whole appearance ; and then ask in scorn where the promised splendour and comfort is to be found ? If such miserable sophisms were to prevail, there would never be a good house or a good government in the world.

Ariosto tells a pretty story of a fairy who, by some mysterious law of her nature, was condemned to appear, at certain seasons, in the form of a foul and poisonous snake. Those who injured her during the period of her disguise were for ever excluded from participation in the blessings which she bestowed. But to those who, in spite of her loathsome aspect, pitied and protected her, she afterwards revealed herself in the beautiful and celestial form which was natural to her, accompanied their steps, granted all their wishes, filled their houses with wealth, made them happy in love and victorious in war.[*] Such a spirit is Liberty. At times she takes the form of a hateful reptile. She grovels, she hisses, she stings. But woe to those who, in disgust, shall venture to crush her ! And happy are those who, having dared to receive her in her degraded and frightful shape, shall at length be rewarded by her in the time of her beauty and her glory !

There is only one cure for the evils which newly acquired freedom produces —and that cure is *freedom !* When a prisoner first leaves his cell he cannot bear the light of day : he is unable to discriminate colours, or recognize faces. But the remedy is, not to remand him into his dungeon, but to accustom him to the rays of the sun. The blaze of truth and liberty may at first

---

[*] Orlando Furioso, canto 43.

dazzle and bewilder nations which have become half blind in the house of bondage. But let them gaze on, and they will soon be able to bear it. In a few years men learn to reason. The extreme violence of opinions subsides. Hostile theories correct each other. The scattered elements of truth cease to conflict, and begin to coalesce. And at length a system of justice and order is educed out of the chaos.

Many politicians of our time are in the habit of laying it down as a self-evident proposition that no people ought to be free till they are fit to use their freedom. The maxim is worthy of the fool in the old story, who resolved not to go into the water till he had learnt to swim! If men are to wait for liberty till they become wise and good in slavery, they may indeed wait for ever.

Therefore it is that we decidedly approve of the conduct of Milton and the other wise and good men who, in spite of much that was ridiculous and hateful in the conduct of their associates, stood firmly by the cause of public liberty. We are not aware that the poet has been charged with personal participation in any of the blamable excesses of that time. The favourite topic of his enemies is the line of conduct which he pursued with regard to the execution of the king. Of that celebrated proceeding we by no means approve. Still we must say, in justice to the many eminent persons who concurred in it, and in justice more particularly to the eminent person who defended it, that nothing can be more absurd than the imputations which, for the last hundred and sixty years, it has been the fashion to cast upon the regicides. We have throughout abstained from appealing to first principles; we will not appeal to them now. We recur again to the parallel case of the Revolution. What essential distinction can be drawn between the execution of the father and the deposition of the son? What constitutional maxim is there which applies to the former and not to the latter? The king can do no wrong. If so, James was as innocent as Charles could have been. The minister only ought to be responsible for the acts of the sovereign. If so, why not impeach Jeffries and retain James? The person of a king is sacred. Was the person of James considered sacred at the Boyne? To discharge cannon against an army in which a king is known to be posted, is to approach pretty near to regicide. Charles too, it should always be remembered, was put to death by men who had been exasperated by the hostilities of several years, and who had never been bound to him by any other tie than that which was common to them with all their fellow citizens. Those who drove James from his throne, who seduced his army, who alienated his friends, who first imprisoned him in his palace, and then turned him out of it, who broke in upon his very slumbers by imperious messages, who pursued him with fire and sword from one part of the empire to another, who hanged, drew, and quartered his adherents, and attainted his innocent heir, were his nephew and his two daughters! When we reflect on all these things, we are at a loss to conceive how the same persons who, on the fifth of November thank God for wonderfully conducting his servant King William, and for making all opposition fall before him until he became our king and governor, can, on the thirtieth of January, contrive to be afraid that the blood of the Royal Martyr may be visited on themselves and their children.

We do not, we repeat, approve of the execution of Charles; not because the constitution exempts the king from responsibility, for we know that all such maxims, however excellent, have their exceptions; nor because we feel any peculiar interest in his character, for we think that his sentence describes him with perfect justice as "a tyrant, a traitor, a murderer, and a public enemy;" but because we are convinced that the measure was most injurious to the cause of freedom. He whom it removed was a captive and a hostage:

His heir, to whom the allegiance of every Royalist was instantly transferred, was at large. The Presbyterians could never have been perfectly reconciled to the father. They had no such a rooted enmity to the son. The great body of the people, also, contemplated that proceeding with feelings which, however unreasonable, no government could safely venture to outrage.

But though we think the conduct of the regicides blamable, that of Milton appears to us in a very different light. The deed was done. It could not be undone. The evil was incurred; and the object was to render it as small as possible. We censure the chiefs of the army for not yielding to the popular opinion: but we cannot censure Milton for wishing to change that opinion. The very feeling which would have restrained us from committing the act would have led us, after it had been committed, to defend it against the ravings of servility and superstition. For the sake of public liberty we wish that the thing had not been done while the people disapproved of it. But, for the sake of public liberty, we should also have wished the people to approve of it when it was done. If anything more were wanting to the justification of Milton, the book of Salmasius would furnish it. That miserable performance is now with justice considered only as a beacon to word-catchers who wish to become statesmen. The celebrity of the man who refuted it, the "Æneæ magni dextra," gives it all its fame with the present generation. In that age the state of things was different. It was not then fully understood how vast an interval separates the mere classical scholar from the political philosopher. Nor can it be doubted that a treatise which, bearing the name of so eminent a critic, attacked the fundamental principles of all free governments must, if suffered to remain unanswered, have produced a most pernicious effect on the public mind.

We wish to add a few words relative to another subject on which the enemies of Milton delight to dwell—his conduct during the administration of the Protector. That an enthusiastic votary of liberty should accept office under a military usurper seems, no doubt, at first sight, extraordinary. But all the circumstances in which the country was then placed were extraordinary. The ambition of Oliver was of no vulgar kind. He never seems to have coveted despotic power. He at first fought sincerely and manfully for the Parliament, and never deserted it till it had deserted its duty. If he dissolved it by force, it was not till he found that the few members who remained, after so many deaths, secessions, and expulsions, were desirous to appropriate to themselves a power which they held only in trust, and to inflict upon England the curse of a Venetian oligarchy. But even when thus placed by violence at the head of affairs, he did not assume unlimited power. He gave the country a constitution far more perfect than any which had at that time been known in the world. He reformed the representative system in a manner which has extorted praise even from Lord Clarendon. For himself he demanded, indeed, the first place in the Commonwealth; but with powers scarcely so great as those of a Dutch stadtholder, or an American president. He gave the Parliament a voice in the appointment of ministers, and left to it the whole legislative authority—not even reserving to himself a veto on its enactments. And he did not require that the chief magistracy should be hereditary in his family. Thus far, we think, if the circumstances of the time, and the opportunities which he had of aggrandizing himself be fairly considered, he will not lose by comparison with Washington or Bolivar. Had his moderation been met by corresponding moderation, there is no reason to think that he would have overstepped the line which he had traced for himself. But when he found that his Parliaments questioned the authority under which they met, and that he was in danger of being deprived of the restricted power which was absolutely necessary to his personal safety, then, it must be acknowledged, he adopted a more arbitrary policy.

Yet, though we believe that the intentions of Cromwell were at first honest, though we believe that he was driven from the noble course which he had marked out for himself by the almost irresistible force of circumstances, though we admire, in common with all men of all parties, the ability and energy of his splendid administration, we are not pleading for arbitrary and lawless power, even in his hands. We know that a good constitution is infinitely better than the best despot. But we suspect that, at the time of which we speak, the violence of religious and political enmities rendered a stable and happy settlement next to impossible. The choice lay, not between Cromwell and liberty, but between Cromwell and the Stuarts. That Milton chose well no man can doubt who fairly compares the events of the Protectorate with those of the thirty years which succeeded it—the darkest and most disgraceful in the English annals. Cromwell was evidently laying, though in an irregular manner, the foundations of an admirable system. Never before had religious liberty and the freedom of discussion been enjoyed in a greater degree. Never had the national honour been better upheld abroad, or the seat of justice better filled at home. And it was rarely that any opposition, which stopped short of open rebellion, provoked the resentment of the liberal and magnanimous usurper. The institutions which he had established, as set down in the Instrument of Government, and the Humble Petition and Advice, were excellent. His practice, it is true, too often departed from the theory of these institutions. But, had he lived a few years longer, it is probable that his institutions would have survived him, and that his arbitrary practice would have died with him. His power has not been consecrated by ancient prejudices. It was upheld only by his great personal qualities. Little, therefore, was to be dreaded from a second protector, unless he were also a second Oliver Cromwell. The events which followed his decease are the most complete vindication of those who exerted themselves to uphold his authority; for his death dissolved the whole frame of society. The army rose against the Parliament, the different corps of the army against each other. Sect raved against sect. Party plotted against party. The Presbyterians, in their eagerness to be revenged on the Independents, sacrificed their own liberty, and deserted all their old principles. Without casting one glance on the past, or requiring one stipulation for the future, they threw down their freedom at the feet of the most frivolous and heartless of tyrants.

Then came those days, never to be recalled without a blush—the days of servitude without loyalty, and sensuality without love, of dwarfish talents and gigantic vices, the paradise of cold hearts and narrow minds, the golden age of the coward, the bigot, and the slave. The king cringed to his rival that he might trample on his people, sunk into a viceroy of France, and pocketed, with complacent infamy, her degrading insults and her more degrading gold. The caresses of harlots and the jests of buffoons regulated the measures of a government which had just ability enough to deceive and just religion enough to persecute. The principles of liberty were the scoff of every grinning courtier, and the Anathema Maranatha of every fawning dean. In every high place worship was paid to Charles and James—Belial and Moloch; and England propitiated those obscene and cruel idols with the blood of her best and bravest children. Crime succeeded to crime, and disgrace to disgrace, till the race accursed of God and man was a second time driven forth, to wander on the face of the earth, and to be a by-word and a shaking of the head to the nations.

Most of the remarks which we have hitherto made on the public character of Milton apply to him only as one of a large body. We shall proceed to notice some of the peculiarities which distinguished him from his contemporaries. And, for that purpose, it is necessary to take a short survey of the parties into which the political world was at that time divided. We must premise that our observations are intended to apply only to those who adhered, from a sincere preference, to one or to the other side. At a period of public commotion, every faction, like an oriental army, is attended by a crowd of camp followers, an useless and heartless rabble, who prowl round its line of march in the hope of picking up something under its protection, but desert it in the day of battle, and often join to exterminate it after a defeat. England, at the time of which we are treating, abounded with such fickle and selfish politicians, who transferred their support to every government as it rose; who kissed the hand of the king in 1640, and spit in his face in 1649; who shouted with equal glee when Cromwell was inaugurated in Westminster Hall, and when he was dug up to be hanged at Tyburn; who dined on calves' head or on broiled rumps, and cut down oak-branches or stuck them up as circumstances altered, without the slightest shame or repugnance. These we leave out of the account. We take our estimate of parties from those who really deserved to be called partisans.

We would speak first of the Puritans, the most remarkable body of men, perhaps, which the world has ever produced. The odious and ridiculous parts of their character lie on the surface. He that runs may read them; nor have there been wanting attentive and malicious observers to point them out. For many years after the Restoration they were the theme of unmeasured invective and derision. They were exposed to the utmost licentiousness of the press and of the stage, at the time when the press and stage were most licentious. They were not men of letters; they were as a body unpopular; they could not defend themselves; and the public would not take them under its protection. They were, therefore, abandoned, without reserve, to the tender mercies of the satirists and dramatists. The ostentatious simplicity of their dress, their sour aspect, their nasal twang, their stiff posture, their long graces, their Hebrew names, the Scriptural phrases which they introduced on every occasion, their contempt of human learning, their detestation of polite amusements were, indeed, fair game for the laughers. But it is not from the laughers alone that the philosophy of history is to be learnt. And he who approaches this subject should carefully guard against the influence of that potent ridicule which has already misled so many excellent writers.

"Ecco il fonte del riso, ed ecco il rio
Che mortali perigli in se contiene;
Hor qui tener a fren nostro desio,
Ed esser cauti molto a noi conviene."*

Those who roused the people to resistance, who directed their measures through a long series of eventful years, who formed, out of the most unpromising materials, the finest army that Europe had ever seen, who trampled down king, church, and aristocracy,—who, in the short intervals of domestic sedition and rebellion, made the name of England terrible to every nation on the face of the earth, were no vulgar fanatics. Most of their absurdities were mere external badges, like the signs of freemasonry or the dresses of friars. We regret that these badges were not more attractive. We regret that a body to whose courage and talents mankind has owed inestimable obligations had not the lofty elegance which distinguished some of the adherents of Charles I., or the easy good-breeding for which the court of

---

* Gerusalemme Liberata, xv. 57.

Charles II. was celebrated. But, if we must make our choice, we shall, like Bassanio in the play, turn from the specious caskets which contain only the Death's head and the Fool's head, and fix our choice on the plain leaden chest which conceals the treasure.

The Puritans were men whose minds had derived a peculiar character from the daily contemplation of superior beings and eternal interests. Not content with acknowledging, in general terms, an overruling Providence, they habitually ascribed every event to the will of the Great Being, for whose power nothing was too vast, for whose inspection nothing was too minute. To know him, to serve him, to enjoy him, was with them the great end of existence. They rejected with contempt the ceremonious homage which other sects substituted for the pure worship of the soul. Instead of catching occasional glimpses of the Deity through an obscuring veil, they aspired to gaze full on the intolerable brightness, and to commune with him face to face. Hence originated their contempt for terrestrial distinctions. The difference between the greatest and meanest of mankind seemed to vanish when compared with the boundless interval which separated the whole race from him on whom their own eyes were constantly fixed. They recognized no title to superiority but his favour; and, confident of that favour, they despised all the accomplishments and all the dignities of the world. If they were unacquainted with the works of philosophers and poets, they were deeply read in the oracles of God. If their names were not found in the registers of heralds, they felt assured that they were recorded in the Book of Life. If their steps were not accompanied by a splendid train of menials, legions of ministering angels had charge over them. Their palaces were houses not made with hands; their diadems, crowns of glory which should never fade away! On the rich and the eloquent, on nobles and priests they looked down with contempt; for they esteemed themselves rich in a more precious treasure and eloquent in a more sublime language; nobles by the right of an earlier creation, and priests by the imposition of a mightier hand. The very meanest of them was a being to whose fate a mysterious and terrible importance belonged—on whose slightest action the spirits of light and darkness looked with anxious interest, who had been destined, before heaven and earth were created, to enjoy a felicity which should continue when heaven and earth should have passed away. Events which short-sighted politicians ascribed to earthly causes had been ordained on his account. For his sake empires had risen, and flourished, and decayed. For his sake the Almighty had proclaimed his will by the pen of the Evangelist and the harp of the prophet. He had been wrested by no common deliverer from the grasp of no common foe. He had been ransomed by the sweat of no vulgar agony, by the blood of no earthly sacrifice. It was for him that the sun had been darkened, that the rocks had been rent, that the dead had arisen, that all nature had shuddered at the sufferings of her expiring God!

Thus the Puritan was made up of two different men, the one all self-abasement, penitence, gratitude, passion; the other proud, calm, inflexible, sagacious. He prostrated himself in the dust before his Maker: but he set his foot on the neck of his king. In his devotional retirement he prayed with convulsions, and groans, and tears. He was half maddened by glorious or terrible illusions. He heard the lyres of angels or the tempting whispers of fiends. He caught a gleam of the Beatific Vision, or woke screaming from dreams of everlasting fire. Like Vane, he thought himself intrusted with the sceptre of the millennial year. Like Fleetwood, he cried in the bitterness of his soul that God had hid his face from him. But, when he took his seat in the council, or girt on his sword for war, these tempestuous workings of the soul had left no perceptible trace behind them. People who saw nothing of the godly but their uncouth visages, and heard nothing from them but their groans and their whining hymns, might laugh at them. But those had little reason to laugh who encountered them in the hall of debate, or in the field of battle. These fanatics brought to civil and military affairs a coolness of judgment and an immutability of purpose which some writers have thought inconsistent with their religious zeal, but which were, in fact, the neccessary effects of it. The intensity of their feelings on one subject made them tranquil on every other. One overpowering sentiment had subjected to itself pity and hatred, ambition and fear. Death had lost its terrors, and pleasure its charms. They had their smiles and their tears, their raptures and their sorrows, but not for the things of this world. Enthusiasm had made them Stoics, had cleared their minds from every vulgar passion and prejudice, and raised them above the influence of danger and of corruption. It sometimes might lead them to pursue unwise ends, but never to choose unwise means. They went through the world like Sir Artegale's iron man Talus with his flail, crushing and trampling down oppressors, mingling with human beings, but having neither part nor lot in human infirmities; insensible to fatigue, to pleasure, and to pain; not to be pierced by any weapon, not to be withstood by any barrier.

Such we believe to have been the character of the Puritans. We perceive the absurdity of their manners. We dislike the sullen gloom of their domestic habits. We acknowledge that the tone of their minds was often injured by straining after things too high for mortal reach: and we know that, in spite of their hatred of popery, they too often fell into the worst vices of that bad system, intolerance and extravagant austerity—that they had their anchorites and their crusades, their Dunstans and their De Montforts, their Dominics and their Escobars. Yet, when all circumstances are taken into consideration, we do not hesitate to pronounce them a brave, a wise, an honest and an useful body.

The Puritans espoused the cause of civil liberty mainly because it was the cause of religion. There was another party, by no means numerous, but distinguished by learning and ability, which co-operated with them on very different principles. We speak of those whom Cromwell was accustomed to call the Heathens, men who were, in the phraseology of that time, doubting Thomases or careless Gallios with regard to religious subjects, but passionate worshippers of freedom. Heated by the study of ancient literature, they set up their country as their idol, and proposed to themselves the heroes of Plutarch as their examples. They seem to have borne some resemblance to the Brissotines of the French Revolution. But it is not very easy to draw the line of distinction between them and their devout associates, whose tone and manner they sometimes found it convenient to affect, and sometimes, it is probable, imperceptibly adopted.

We now come to the Royalists. We shall attempt to speak of them, as we have spoken of their antagonists, with perfect candour. We shall not charge upon a whole party the profligacy and baseness of the horseboys, gamblers, and bravoes, whom the hope of licence and plunder attracted from all the dens of Whitefriars to the standard of Charles, and who disgraced their associates by excesses which, under the stricter discipline of the Parliamentary armies, were never tolerated. We will select a more favourable specimen. Thinking, as we do, that the cause of the king was the cause of bigotry and tyranny, we yet cannot refrain from looking with complacency on the character of the honest old Cavaliers. We feel a national pride in comparing them with the instruments which the despots of other countries are compelled to employ, with the mutes who throng their antichambers, and the janissaries who mount guard at their gates. Our royalist countrymen were not heartless, dangling courtiers, bowing at every step and simpering at every word. They were not mere machines for destruction dressed up in uniforms, caned into skill, intoxicated into valour, defending without love, destroying without hatred. There was a freedom in their subserviency, a nobleness in their very degradation. The sentiment of individual independence was strong within them. They were, indeed, misled, but by no base or selfish motive. Compassion and romantic honour, the prejudices of childhood, and the venerable names of history, threw over them a spell potent as that of Duessa; and, like the Red-Cross Knight, they thought that they were doing battle for an injured beauty, while they defended a false and loathsome sorceress. In truth, they scarcely entered at all into the merits of the political question. It was not for a treacherous king or an intolerant church that they fought; but for the old banner which had waved in so many battles over the heads of their fathers, and for the altars at which they had received the hands of their brides. Though nothing could be more erroneous than their political opinions, they possessed, in a far greater degree than their adversaries, those qualities which are the grace of private life. With many of the vices of the Round Table, they had also many of its virtues, courtesy, generosity, veracity, tenderness and respect for women. They had far more both of profound and of polite learning than the Puritans. Their manners were more engaging, their tempers more amiable, their tastes more elegant, and their households more cheerful.

Milton did not strictly belong to any of the classes which we have described. He was not a Puritan. He was not a free-thinker. He was not a Cavalier. In his character the noblest qualities of every party were combined in harmonious union. From the Parliament and from the Court, from the conventicle and from the Gothic cloister, from the gloomy and sepulchral circles of the Roundheads, and from the Christmas revel of the hospitable Cavalier, his nature selected and drew to itself whatever was great and good, while it rejected all the base and pernicious ingredients by which those finer elements were defiled. Like the Puritans, he lived

"As ever in his great task-master's eye."

Like them he kept his mind continually fixed on an Almighty Judge and an eternal reward. And hence he acquired their contempt of external circumstances, their fortitude, their tranquillity, their inflexible resolution. But not the coolest sceptic or the most profane scoffer was more perfectly free from the contagion of their frantic delusions, their savage manners, their ludicrous jargon, their scorn of science, and their aversion to pleasure. Hating tyranny with a perfect hatred, he had nevertheless all the estimable and ornamental qualities which were almost entirely monopolized by the party of the tyrant. There was none who had a stronger sense of the value of literature, a finer relish for every elegant amusement, or a more chivalrous delicacy of honour and love. Though his opinions were democratic, his tastes and his associations were such as harmonize best with monarchy and aristocracy. He was under the influence of all the feelings by which the gallant Cavaliers were misled. But of those feelings he was the master and not the slave. Like the hero of Homer, he enjoyed all the pleasure of fascination; but he was not fascinated. He listened to the song of the Syrens; yet he glided by without being seduced to their fatal shore. He tasted the cup of Circe; but he bore about him a sure antidote against the effects of its bewitching sweetness. The illusions which captivated his imagination never impaired his reasoning powers. The statesman was proof against the splendour, the solemnity, and the romance which enchanted the poet. Any person who will contrast the sentiments expressed in his Treatises on Prelacy with the exquisite lines on Ecclesiastical architecture and music in the Penseroso, which was published about the same time, will understand our meaning. This is an inconsistency which, more than anything else, raises his character in our estimation; because it shows how many private tastes and feelings he sacrificed in order to do what he considered his duty to mankind. It is the very struggle of the noble Othello. His heart relents; but his hand is firm. He does naught in hate, but all in honour. He kisses the beautiful deceiver before he destroys her.

That from which the public character of Milton derives its great and peculiar splendour still remains to be mentioned. If he exerted himself to overthrow a foresworn king and a persecuting hierarchy, he exerted himself in conjunction with others. But the glory of the battle which he fought for that species of freedom which is the most valuable, and which was then the least understood, the freedom of the human mind, is all his own. Thousands and tens of thousands among his contemporaries raised their voices against Ship-money and the Star Chamber. But there were few indeed who discerned the more fearful evils of moral and intellectual slavery, and the benefits which would result from the liberty of the press and the unfettered exercise of private judgment. These were the objects which Milton justly conceived to be the most important. He was desirous that the people should think for themselves as well as tax themselves, and be emancipated from the dominion of prejudice as well as from that of Charles. He knew that those who, with the best intentions, overlooked these schemes of reform, and contented themselves with pulling down the king and imprisoning the malignants, acted like the heedless brothers in his own poem, who, in their eagerness to disperse the train of the sorcerer, neglected the means of liberating the captive. They thought only of conquering when they should have thought of disenchanting.

"Oh, ye mistook ! Ye should have snatched the wand !
Without the rod reversed,
And backward mutters of dissevering power,
We cannot free the lady that sits here
Bound in strong fetters, fixed and motionless."

To reverse the rod, to spell the charm backward, to break the ties which bound a stupefied people to the seat of enchantment was the noble aim of Milton. To this all his public conduct was directed. For this he joined the Presbyterians—for this he forsook them. He fought their perilous battle; but he turned away with disdain from their insolent triumph. He saw that they, like those whom they had vanquished, were hostile to the liberty of thought. He therefore joined the Independents, and called upon Cromwell to break the secular chain, and to save free conscience from the paw of the Presbyterian wolf.* With a view to the same great object, he attacked the licensing system, in that sublime treatise which every statesman should wear as a sign upon his hand, and as frontlets between his eyes. His attacks were, in general, directed less against particular abuses than against those deeply seated errors on which almost all abuses are founded, the servile worship of eminent men, and the irrational dread of innovation.

That he might shake the foundation of these debasing sentiments more effectually, he always selected for himself the boldest literary services. He never came up in the rear when the outside works had been carried, and the

---

* Sonnet to Cromwell.

breach entered. He pressed into the forlorn hope. At the beginning of the changes he wrote with incomparable energy and eloquence against the bishops. But when his opinion seemed likely to prevail, he passed on to other subjects, and abandoned prelacy to the crowd of writers who now hastened to insult a falling party. There is no more hazardous enterprise than that of bearing the torch of truth into those dark and infected recesses in which no light has ever shone. But it was the choice and the pleasure of Milton to penetrate the noisome vapours and to brave the terrible explosion. Those who most disapprove of his opinions must respect the hardihood with which he maintained them. He, in general, left to others the credit of expounding and defending the popular parts of his religious and political creed. He took his own stand upon those which the great body of his countrymen reprobated as criminal, or derided as paradoxical. He stood up for divorce and regicide. He ridiculed the Eikon. He attacked the prevailing systems of education. His radiant and beneficent career resembled that of the god of light and fertility.

" Nitor in adversum ; nec me, qui caetera, vincit
Impetus, et rapido contrarius evehor orbi."

It is to be regretted that the prose writings of Milton should, in our time, be so little read. As compositions, they deserve the attention of every man who wishes to become acquainted with the full power of the English language. They abound with passages compared with which the finest declamations of Burke sink into insignificance. They are a perfect field of cloth of gold. The style is stiff, with gorgeous embroidery. Not even in the earlier books of the Paradise Lost has he ever risen higher than in those parts of his controversial works in which his feelings, excited by conflict, find a vent in bursts of devotional and lyric rapture. It is, to borrow his own majestic language, " a sevenfold chorus of hallelujahs and harping symphonies." *

We had intended to look more closely at these performances, to analyze the peculiarities of the diction, to dwell at some length on the sublime wisdom of the Areopagitica, and the nervous rhetoric of the Iconoclast, and to point out some of those magnificent passages which occur in the Treatise of Reformation, and the Animadversions on the Remonstrant. But the length to which our remarks have already extended renders this impossible.

We must conclude. And yet we can scarcely tear ourselves away from the subject. The days immediately following the publication of this relic of Milton appear to be peculiarly set apart and consecrated to his memory. And we shall scarcely be censured if, on this his festival, we be found lingering near his shrine, how worthless soever may be the offering which we bring to it. While this book lies on our table, we seem to be contemporaries of the great poet. We are transported a hundred and fifty years back. We can almost fancy that we are visiting him in his small lodging ; that we see him sitting at the old organ beneath the faded green hangings ; that we can catch the quick twinkle of his eyes, rolling in vain to find the day ; that we are reading in the lines of his noble countenance the proud and mournful history of his glory and his affliction ! We image to ourselves the breathless silence in which we should listen to his slightest word ; the passionate veneration with which we should kneel to kiss his hand and weep upon it ; the earnestness with which we should endeavour to console him, if, indeed, such a spirit could need consolation for the neglect of an age unworthy of his talents and his virtues ; the eagerness with which we should contest with his daughters, or with his Quaker friend Elwood, the privilege of reading Homer to him, or of taking down the immortal accents which flowed from his lips.

* The Reason of Church Government urged against Prelatcy, Book II.

These are, perhaps, foolish feelings. Yet we cannot be ashamed of them; nor shall we be sorry if what we have written shall in any degree excite them in other minds. We are not much in the habit of idolizing either the living or the dead. And we think that there is no more certain indication of a weak and ill-regulated intellect than that propensity which, for want of a better name, we will venture to christen *Boswellism*. But *there are* a few characters which have stood the closest scrutiny and the severest tests, which have been tried in the furnace and have proved pure, which have been weighed in the balance and have not been found wanting, which have been declared sterling by the general consent of mankind, and which are visibly stamped with the image and superscription of the Most High. These great men we trust that we know how to prize; and of these was Milton. The sight of his books, the sound of his name, are refreshing to us. His thoughts resemble those celestial fruits and flowers which the Virgin Martyr of Massinger sent down from the gardens of Paradise to the earth, distinguished from the productions of other soils, not only by their superior bloom and sweetness, but by their miraculous efficacy to invigorate and to heal. They are powerful, not only to delight, but to elevate and purify. Nor do we envy the man who can study either the life or the writings of the great poet and patriot without aspiring to emulate, not indeed the sublime works with which his genius has enriched our literature, but the zeal with which he laboured for the public good, the fortitude with which he endured every private calamity, the lofty disdain with which he looked down on temptations and dangers, the deadly hatred which he bore to bigots and tyrants, and the faith which he so sternly kept with his country and with his fame.

MACHIAVELLI.

Œuvres complètes de MACHIAVEL, traduites par J. V. PÉRIER. Paris, 1825.

THOSE who have attended to the practice of our literary tribunal are well aware that, by means of certain legal fictions similar to those of Westminster Hall, we are frequently enabled to take cognizance of cases lying beyond the sphere of our original jurisdiction. We need hardly say, therefore, that, in the present instance, M. Périer is merely a Richard Roe—that his name is used for the sole purpose of bringing Machiavelli into court—and that he will not be mentioned in any subsequent stage of the proceedings.

We doubt whether any name in literary history be so generally odious as that of the man whose character and writings we now propose to consider. The terms in which he is commonly described would seem to import that he was the Tempter, the Evil Principle, the discoverer of ambition and revenge, the original inventor of perjury; that, before the publication of his fatal Prince, there had never been a hypocrite, a tyrant, or a traitor, a simulated virtue or a convenient crime. One writer gravely assures us that Maurice of Saxony learned all his fraudulent policy from that execrable volume. Another remarks that, since it was translated into Turkish, the sultans have been more addicted than formerly to the custom of strangling their brothers. Our own foolish Lord Lyttelton charges the poor Florentine with the manifold treasons of the House of Guise and the massacre of St. Bartholomew. Several authors have hinted that the Gunpowder Plot is to be primarily attributed to his doctrines, and seem to think that his effigy ought to be substituted for that of Guy Faux in those processions by which the ingenuous youth of England annually commemorate the preservation of the Three Estates. The Church of Rome has pronounced his works accursed things. Nor have our own countrymen been backward in testifying their opinion of his merits. Out of his surname they have coined an epithet for a knave—and out of his Christian name a synonym for the Devil.*

It is, indeed, scarcely possible for any person not well acquainted with the history and literature of Italy to read, without horror and amazement, the celebrated treatise which has brought so much obloquy on the name of Machiavelli. Such a display of wickedness, naked, yet not ashamed, such cool, judicious, scientific atrocity seem rather to belong to a fiend than to the most depraved of men. Principles which the most hardened ruffian would scarcely hint to his most trusted accomplice, or avow, without the disguise of some palliating sophism, even to his own mind, are professed without the slightest circumlocution and assumed as the fundamental axioms of all political science.

It is not strange that ordinary readers should regard the author of such a book as the most depraved and shameless of human beings. Wise men, however, have always been inclined to look with great suspicion on the angels and demons of the multitude: and in the present instance several circumstances have led even superficial observers to question the justice of the vulgar decision. It is notorious that Machiavelli was, through life, a zealous republican. In the same year in which he composed his manual of King-craft he suffered imprisonment and torture in the cause of public liberty. It seems inconceivable that the martyr of freedom should have designedly acted as the apostle of tyranny. Several eminent writers have, therefore, endeavoured to detect, in this unfortunate performance, some concealed meaning, more consistent with the character and conduct of the author than that which appears at the first glance.

One hypothesis is that Machiavelli intended to practise on the young Lorenzo de Medici a fraud similar to that which Sunderland is said to have employed against our James the Second—that he urged his pupil to violent and perfidious measures, as the surest means of accelerating the moment of deliverance and revenge. Another supposition, which Lord Bacon seems to countenance, is that the treatise was merely a piece of grave irony, intended to warn nations against the arts of ambitious men. It would be easy to show that neither of these solutions is consistent with many passages in the Prince itself. But the most decisive refutation is that which is furnished by the other works of Machiavelli. In all the writings which he gave to the public, and in all those which the research of editors has, in the course of three centuries, discovered, in his comedies, designed for the entertainment of the multitude, in his Comments on Livy, intended for the perusal of the most enthusiastic patriots of Florence, in his History, inscribed to one of the most amiable and estimable of the popes in his public despatches, in his private memoranda, the same obliquity of moral principle for which the Prince is so severely censured is more or less discernible. We doubt whether it would be possible to find, in all the many volumes of his compositions, a single expression indicating that dissimulation and treachery had ever struck him as discreditable.

After this it may seem ridiculous to say that we are acquainted with few writings which exhibit so much elevation of sentiment, so pure and warm a zeal for the public good, or so just a view of the duties and rights of citizens as those of Machiavelli. Yet so it is. And even from the Prince itself we

* Nick Machiavel had ne'er a trick,
Tho' he gave his name to our old Nick.
Hudibras, Part iii., canto i
But, we believe, there is a schism on this subject among the antiquarians.

could select many passages in support of this remark. To a reader of our age and country this inconsistency is, at first, perfectly bewildering. The whole man seems to be an enigma—a grotesque assemblage of incongruous qualities—selfishness and generosity, cruelty and benevolence, craft and simplicity, abject villany and romantic heroism. One sentence is such as a veteran diplomatist would scarcely write in cipher for the direction of his most confidential spy; the next seems to be extracted from a theme composed by an ardent schoolboy on the death of Leonidas. An act of dexterous perfidy, and an act of patriotic self-devotion, call forth the same kind and the same degree of respectful admiration. The moral sensibility of the writer seems at once to be morbidly obtuse and morbidly acute. Two characters altogether dissimilar are united in him. They are not merely joined, but interwoven. They are the warp and the woof of his mind; and their combination, like that of the variegated threads in shot silk, gives to the whole texture a glancing and ever-changing appearance. The explanation might have been easy if he had been a very weak or a very affected man. But he was evidently neither the one nor the other. His works prove, beyond all contradiction, that his understanding was strong, his taste pure, and his sense of the ridiculous exquisitely keen.

This is strange—and yet the strangest is behind. There is no reason whatever to think that those amongst whom he lived saw anything shocking or incongruous in his writings. Abundant proofs remain of the high estimation in which both his works and his person were held by the most respectable among his contemporaries. Clement the Seventh patronized the publication of those very books which the Council of Trent, in the following generation, pronounced unfit for the perusal of Christians. Some members of the democratical party censured the secretary for dedicating the Prince to a patron who bore the unpopular name of Medici. But to those immoral doctrines which have since called forth such severe reprehensions no exception appears to have been taken. The cry against them was first raised beyond the Alps—and seems to have been heard with amazement in Italy. The earliest assailant, as far as we are aware, was a countryman of our own, Cardinal Pole. The author of the Anti-Machiavelli was a French Protestant.

It is, therefore, in the state of moral feeling among the Italians of those times that we must seek for the real explanation of what seems most mysterious in the life and writings of this remarkable man. As this is a subject which suggests many interesting considerations, both political and metaphysical, we shall make no apology for discussing it at some length.

During the gloomy and disastrous centuries which followed the downfall of the Roman Empire Italy had preserved, in a far greater degree than any other part of Western Europe, the traces of ancient civilization. The night which descended upon her was the night of an Arctic summer: the dawn began to reappear before the last reflection of the preceding sunset had faded from the horizon. It was in the time of the French Morovingians and of the Saxon Heptarchy that ignorance and ferocity seemed to have done their worst. Yet even then the Neapolitan provinces, recognizing the authority of the Eastern empire, preserved something of Eastern knowledge and refinement. Rome, protected by the sacred character of its pontiffs, enjoyed at least comparative security and repose. Even in those regions where the sanguinary Lombards had fixed their monarchy there was incomparably more of wealth, of information, of physical comfort, and of social order than could be found in Gaul, Britain, or Germany.

That which most distinguished Italy from the neighbouring countries was the importance which the population of the towns, from a very early period, began to acquire. Some cities, founded in wild and remote situations by fugitives who had escaped from the rage of the barbarians, preserved their freedom by their obscurity, till they became able to preserve it by their power. Others seem to have retained, under all the changing dynasties of invaders, under Odoacer and Theodoric, Narses and Alboin, the municipal institutions which had been conferred on them by the liberal policy of the Great Republic In provinces which the central government was too feeble either to protect or to oppress these institutions first acquired stability and vigour. The citizens, defended by their walls and governed by their own magistrates and their own by-laws, enjoyed a considerable share of republican independence. Thus a strong democratic spirit was called into action. The Carlovingian sovereigns were too imbecile to subdue it. The generous policy of Otho encouraged it. It might, perhaps, have been suppressed by a close coalition between the Church and the empire. It was fostered and invigorated by their disputes. In the twelfth century it attained its full vigour, and, after a long and doubtful conflict, triumphed over the abilities and courage of the Swabian princes.

The assistance of the ecclesiastical power had greatly contributed to the success of the Guelfs. That success would, however, have been a doubtful good, if its only effect had been to substitute a moral for a political servitude, to exalt the popes at the expense of the Cæsars. Happily the public mind of Italy had long contained the seeds of free opinions, which were now rapidly developed by the genial influence of free institutions. The people of that country had observed the whole machinery of the Church, its saints and its miracles, its lofty pretensions and its splendid ceremonial, its worthless blessings and its harmless curses too long and too closely to be duped. They stood behind the scenes on which others were gazing with childish awe and interest. They witnessed the arrangement of the pullies and the manufacture of the thunders. They saw the natural faces and heard the natural voices of the actors. Distant nations looked on the pope as the vicegerent of the Almighty, the Oracle of the All-wise, the umpire from whose decisions, in the disputes either of theologians or of kings, no Christian ought to appeal. The Italians were acquainted with all the follies of his youth, and with all the dishonest arts by which he had attained power. They knew how often he had employed the keys of the Church to release himself from the most sacred engagements, and its wealth to pamper his mistresses and nephews. The doctrines and rites of the established religion they treated with decent reverence. But though they still called themselves Catholics, they had ceased to be papists. Those spiritual arms which carried terror into the palaces and camps of the proudest sovereigns excited only their contempt. When Alexander commanded our Henry II. to submit to the lash before the tomb of a rebellious subject, he was himself an exile. The Romans, apprehending that he entertained designs against their liberties, had driven him from their city; and, though he solemnly promised to confine himself for the future to his spiritual functions, they still refused to readmit him.

In every other part of Europe a large and powerful privileged class trampled on the people and defied the government. But, in the most flourishing parts of Italy the feudal nobles were reduced to comparative insignificance. In some districts they took shelter under the protection of the powerful commonwealths which they were unable to oppose, and gradually sank into the mass of burghers. In others they possessed great influence, but it was an influence widely different from that which was exercised by the chieftains of the Transalpine kingdoms. They were not petty princes, but eminent citizens. Instead of strengthening their fastnesses among the mountains, they embellished their palaces in the market-place. The state of society in the Neapolitan dominions and in some parts of the Ecclesiastical State more nearly resembled that which existed in the great monarchies of Europe. But the governments of Lombardy and Tuscany, through all their revolutions, preserved a different character. A people when assembled in a town is far more formidable to its rulers than when dispersed over a wide extent of country. The most arbitrary of the Cæsars found it necessary to feed and divert the inhabitants of their unwieldy capital at the expense of the provinces. The citizens of Madrid have more than once besieged their sovereign in his own palace, and extorted from him the most humiliating concessions. The sultans have often been compelled to propitiate the furious rabble of Constantinople with the head of an unpopular vizier. From the same cause there was a certain tinge of democracy in the monarchies and aristocracies of Northern Italy.

Thus liberty, partially, indeed, and transiently, revisited Italy; and with liberty came commerce and empire, science and taste, all the comforts and all the ornaments of life. The Crusades, from which the inhabitants of other countries gained nothing but relics and wounds, brought the rising commonwealths of the Adriatic and Tyrrhene seas a large increase of wealth, dominions, and knowledge. Their moral and their geographical position enabled them to profit alike by the barbarism of the West and by the civilization of the East. Their ships covered every sea. Their factories rose on every shore. Their money-changers set their tables in every city. Manufactures flourished. Banks were established. The operations of the commercial machine were facilitated by many useful and beautiful inventions. We doubt whether any country of Europe, our own, perhaps, excepted, have at the present time reached so high a point of wealth and civilization as some parts of Italy had attained four hundred years ago. Historians rarely descend to those details from which alone the real state of a community can be collected. Hence posterity is too often deceived by the vague hyperboles of poets and rhetoricians, who mistake the splendour of a court for the happiness of a people. Fortunately, John Villani has given us an ample and precise account of the state of Florence in the earlier part of the fourteenth century. The revenue of the Republic amounted to three hundred thousand florins, a sum which, allowing for the depreciation of the precious metals, was at least equivalent to six hundred thousand pounds sterling; a larger sum than England and Ireland, two centuries ago, yielded annually to Elizabeth—a larger sum than, according to any computation which we have seen, the Grand Duke of Tuscany now derives from a territory of much greater extent. The manufacture of wool alone employed two hundred factories and thirty thousand workmen. The cloth annually produced sold, at an average, for twelve hundred thousand florins; a sum fairly equal, in exchangeable value, to two millions and a half of our money. Four hundred thousand florins were annually coined. Eighty banks conducted the commercial operations, not of Florence only, but of all Europe. The transactions of these establishments were sometimes of a magnitude which may surprise even the contemporaries of the Barings and the Rothschilds. Two houses advanced to Edward III. of England upwards of three hundred thousand marks, at a time when the mark contained more silver than fifty shillings of the present day, and when the value of silver was more than quadruple of what it now is. The city and its environs contained a hundred and seventy thousand inhabitants. In the various schools about ten thousand children were taught to read; twelve hundred studied arithmetic; six hundred received a learned education. The progress of elegant literature and of the fine arts was proportioned to that of the public prosperity. Under the despotic successors of Augustus all the fields of the intellect had been turned into arid wastes, still marked out by formal boundaries, still retaining the traces of old cultivation, but yielding neither flowers nor fruit. The deluge of barbarism came. It swept away all the landmarks. It obliterated all the signs of former tillage. But it fertilised while it devastated. When it receded, the wilderness was as the garden of God, rejoicing on every side, laughing, clapping its hands, pouring forth, in spontaneous abundance, everything brilliant, or fragrant, or nourishing. A new language, characterized by simple sweetness and simple energy, had attained its perfection. No tongue ever furnished more gorgeous and vivid tints to poetry: nor was it long before a poet appeared who knew how to employ them. Early, in the fourteenth century came forth the Divine Comedy, beyond comparison the greatest work of imagination, which had appeared since the poems of Homer. The following generation produced, indeed, no second Dante; but it was eminently distinguished by general intellectual activity. The study of the Latin writers had never been wholly neglected in Italy. But Petrarch introduced a more profound, liberal, and elegant scholarship; and communicated to his countrymen that enthusiasm for the literature, the history, and the antiquities of Rome which divided his own heart with a frigid mistress and a more frigid Muse. Boccaccio turned their attention to the more sublime and graceful models of Greece.

From this time the admiration of learning and genius became almost an idolatry among the people of Italy. Kings and republics, cardinals and doges, vied with each other in honouring and flattering Petrarch. Embassies from rival states solicited the honour of his instructions. His coronation agitated the Court of Naples and the people of Rome as much as the most important political transaction could have done. To collect books and antiques, to found professorships, to patronize men of learning, became almost universal fashions among the great. The spirit of literary research, allied itself to that of commercial enterprise. Every place to which the merchant princes of Florence extended their gigantic traffic, from the bazaars of the Tigris to the monasteries of the Clyde, was ransacked for medals and manuscripts. Architecture, painting, and sculpture were munificently encouraged. Indeed, it would be difficult to name an Italian of eminence, during the period of which we speak, who, whatever may have been his general character, did not at least affect a love of letters and of the arts.

Knowledge and public prosperity continued to advance together. Both attained their meridian in the age of Lorenzo the Magnificent. We cannot refrain from quoting the splendid passage, in which the Tuscan Thucydides describes the state of Italy at that period :—" Ridotta tutta in somma pace e tranquillità, coltivata non meno ne' luoghi più montuosi e più sterili che nelle pianure e regioni più fertili, nè sottoposta ad altro imperio che de' suoi medesimi, non solo era abbondantissima d'abitatori e di ricchezze ; ma illustrata sommamente dalla magnificenza di molti principi, dallo splendore di molte nobilissime e bellissime città, dalla sedia e maestà della religione, fioriva d' uomini prestantissimi nell' amministrazione delle cose pubbliche, e d'ingegni molto nobili in tutte le scienze, ed in qualunque arte preclara ed industriosa." * When we peruse this just and splendid description we can scarcely persuade ourselves that we are reading of times in which the annals of England and France present us only with a frightful spectacle of poverty, barbarity, and ignorance. From the oppressions of illiterate masters and the sufferings of a brutalized peasantry, it is delightful to turn to the opulent and enlightened States of Italy—to the vast and magnificent cities, the ports, the arsenals, the villas, the museums, the libraries, the marts filled with every

---

* Guicciardini, lib. i.

article of comfort or luxury, the manufactories swarming with artisans, the Apennines covered with rich cultivation up to their very summits, the Po wafting the harvests of Lombardy to the granaries of Venice, and carrying back the silks of Bengal and the furs of Siberia to the palaces of Milan. With peculiar pleasure every cultivated mind must repose on the fair, the happy, the glorious Florence; on the halls which rang with the mirth of Pulci; the cell where twinkled the midnight lamp of Politian, the statues on which the young eye of Michael Angelo glared with the frenzy of a kindred inspiration, the gardens in which Lorenzo meditated some sparkling song for the May-day dance of the Etrurian virgins. Alas, for the beautiful city! Alas, for the wit and the learning, the genius and the love!

> "Le donne, i cavalier, gli affanni, gli agi,
> Che ne'nvogliava amore e cortesia,
> La dove i cuor son fatti si malvagi."†

A time was at hand when all the seven vials of the Apocalypse were to be poured forth and shaken out over those pleasant countries—a time of slaughter, famine, beggary, infamy, slavery, despair!

In the Italian States, as in many natural bodies, untimely decrepitude was the penalty of precocious maturity. Their early greatness and their early decline are principally to be attributed to the same cause—the preponderance which the towns acquired in the political system.

In a community of hunters or of shepherds every man easily and necessarily becomes a soldier. His ordinary avocations are perfectly compatible with all the duties of military service. However remote may be the expedition on which he is bound, he finds it easy to transport with him the stock from which he derives his subsistence. The whole people is an army; the whole year a march. Such was the state of society which facilitated the gigantic conquests of Attila and Timour.

But a people which subsists by the cultivation of the earth is in a very different situation. The husbandman is bound to the soil on which he labours. A long campaign would be ruinous to him. Still his pursuits are such as give to his frame both the active and the passive strength necessary to a soldier. Nor do they, at least in the infancy of agricultural science, demand his uninterrupted attention. At particular times of the year he is almost wholly unemployed, and can, without injury to himself, afford the time necessary for a short expedition. Thus the legions of Rome were supplied during its earlier wars. The season during which the farms did not require the presence of the cultivators sufficed for a short inroad and a battle. These operations, too frequently interrupted to produce decisive results, yet served to keep up among the people a degree of discipline and courage which rendered them, not only secure, but formidable. The archers and billmen of the middle ages, who, with provisions for forty days at their backs, left the fields for the camp, were troops of the same description.

But when commerce and manufactures begin to flourish a great change takes place. The sedentary habits of the desk and the loom render the exertions and hardships of war insupportable. The occupations of traders and artisans require their constant presence and attention. In such a community there is little superfluous time; but here is generally much superfluous money. Some members of the society are, therefore, hired to relieve the rest from a task inconsistent with their habits and engagements.

The history of Greece is, in this, as in many other respects, the best commentary on the history of Italy. Five hundred years before the Christian era

---

* Dante Purgatorio, xiv.

the citizens of the republics round the Ægean Sea formed perhaps the finest militia that ever existed. As wealth and refinement advanced, the system underwent a gradual alteration. The Ionian States were the first in which commerce and the arts were cultivated—and the first in which the ancient discipline decayed. Within eighty years after the battle of Platæa mercenary troops were everywhere plying for battles and sieges. In the time of Demosthenes it was scarcely possible to persuade or compel the Athenians to enlist for foreign service. The laws of Lyurcgus prohibited trade and manufactures. The Spartans, therefore, continued to form a national force long after their neighbours had begun to hire soldiers. But their military spirit declined with ther singular institutions. In the second century Greece contained only one nation of warriors, the savage highlanders of Ætolia, who were at least ten generations behind their countrymen in civilization and intelligence.

All the causes which produced these effects amongst the Greeks, acted still more strongly on the modern Italians. Instead of a power like Sparta, in its nature warlike, they had amongst them an ecclesiastical state, in its nature pacific. Where there are numerous slaves every freeman is induced by the strongest motives to familiarize himself with the use of arms. The commonwealths of Italy did not, like those of Greece, swarm with thousands of these household enemies. Lastly, the mode in which military operations were conducted during the prosperous times of Italy was peculiarly unfavourable to the formation of an efficient militia. Men covered with iron from head to foot, armed with ponderous lances, and mounted on horses of the largest breed, were considered as composing the strength of an army. The infantry was regarded as comparatively worthless, and was neglected till it became really so. These tactics maintained their ground for centuries in most parts of Europe. That foot soldiers could withstand the charge of heavy cavalry was thought utterly impossible, till, towards the close of the fifteenth century, the rude mountaineers of Switzerland dissolved the spell, and astounded the most experienced generals by receiving the dreaded shock on an impenetrable forest of pikes.

The use of the Grecian spear, the Roman sword, or the modern bayonet might be acquired with comparative ease. But nothing short of the daily exercise of years could train the man at arms to support his ponderous panoply, and manage his unwieldy weapon. Throughout Europe this most important branch of war became a separate profession. Beyond the Alps, indeed, though a profession, it was not generally a trade. It was the duty and the amusement of a large class of country gentlemen. It was the service by which they held their lands, and the diversion by which, in the absence of mental resources, they beguiled their leisure. But in the Northern States of Italy, as we have already remarked, the growing power of the cities, where it had not exterminated this order of men, had completely changed their habits. Here, therefore, the practice of employing mercenaries became universal at a time when it was almost unknown in other countries.

When war becomes the trade of a separate class the least dangerous course left to a government is to form that class into a standing army. It is scarcely possible that men can pass their lives in the service of a single state without feeling some interest in its greatness. Its victories are their victories. Its defeats are their defeats. The contract loses something of its mercantile character. The services of the soldier are considered as the effects of patriotic zeal, his pay as the tribute of national gratitude. To betray the power which employs him, to be even remiss in its service, are in his eyes the most atrocious and degrading of crimes.

When the princes and commonwealths of Italy began to use hired troops, their wisest course would have been to form separate military establishments. Unhappily this was not done. The mercenary warriors of the Peninsula, instead of being attached to the service of different powers, were regarded as the common property of all. The connexion between the state and its defenders was reduced to the most simple and naked traffic. The adventurer brought his horse, his weapons, his strength, and his experience into the market. Whether the King of Naples or the Duke of Milan, the pope or the Signory of Florence struck the bargain, was to him a matter of perfect indifference. He was for the highest wages and the longest term. When the campaign for which he had contracted was finished, there was neither law nor punctilio to prevent him from instantly turning his arms against his late masters. The soldier was altogether disjoined from the citizen and from the subject.

The natural consequences followed. Left to the conduct of men who neither loved those whom they defended nor hated those whom they opposed—who were often bound by stronger ties to the army against which they fought than the state which they served—who lost by the termination of the conflict, and gained by its prolongation, war completely changed its character. Every man came into the field of battle impressed with the knowledge that, in a few days, he might be taking the pay of the power against which he was then employed and fighting by the side of his enemies against his associates. The strongest interest and the strongest feelings concurred to mitigate the hostility of those who had lately been brethren in arms, and who might soon be brethren in arms once more. Their common profession was a bond of union not to be forgotten even when they were engaged in the service of contending parties. Hence it was that operations, languid and indecisive beyond any recorded in history, marches and countermarches, pillaging expeditions and blockades, bloodless capitulations and equally bloodless combats, make up the military history of Italy during the course of nearly two centuries. Mighty armies fight from sunrise to sunset. A great victory is won. Thousands of prisoners are taken; and hardly a life is lost! A pitched battle seems to have been really less dangerous than an ordinary civil tumult.

Courage was now no longer necessary even to the military character. Men grew old in camps, and acquired the highest renown by their warlike achievements, without being once required to face serious danger. The political consequences are too well known. The richest and most enlightened part of the world was left, undefended, to the assaults of every barbarous invader—to the brutality of Switzerland, the insolence of France, and the fierce rapacity of Arragon. The moral effects which followed from this state of things were still more remarkable.

Among the rude nations which lay beyond the Alps valour was absolutely indispensable. Without it none could be eminent; few could be secure. Cowardice was, therefore, naturally considered as the foulest reproach. Among the polished Italians, enriched by commerce, governed by law, and passionately attached to literature, everything was done by superiority of intelligence. Their very wars, more pacific than the peace of their neighbours, required rather civil than military qualifications. Hence, while courage was the point of honour in other countries, ingenuity became the point of honour in Italy.

From these principles were deduced, by processes strictly analogous, two opposite systems of fashionable morality. Through the greater part of Europe the vices which peculiarly belong to timid dispositions, and which are the natural defence of weakness, fraud and hypocrisy, have always been most disreputable. On the other hand, the excesses of haughty and daring spirits have been treated with indulgence, and even with respect. The Italians regarded with corresponding lenity those crimes which require self-command, address, quick observation, fertile invention, and profound knowledge of human nature.

Such a prince as our Henry V. would have been the idol of the North. The follies of his youth, the selfish and desolating ambition of his manhood, the Lollards roasted at slow fires, the prisoners massacred on the field of battle, the expiring lease of priestcraft renewed for another century, the dreadful legacy of a causeless and hopeless war bequeathed to a people who had no interest in its event, everything is forgotten but the victory of Agincourt! Francis Sforza, on the other hand, was the model of the Italian hero. He made his employers and his rivals alike his tools. He first overpowered his open enemies by the help of faithless allies; he then armed himself against his allies with the spoils taken from his enemies. By his incomparable dexterity, he raised himself from the precarious and dependent situation of a military adventurer to the first throne of Italy. To such a man much was forgiven—hollow friendship, ungenerous enmity, violated faith. Such are the opposite errors which men commit, when their morality is not a science, but a taste; when they abandon eternal principles for accidental associations.

We have illustrated our meaning by an instance taken from history. We will select another from fiction. Othello murders his wife; he gives orders for the murder of his lieutenant; he ends by murdering himself. Yet he never loses the esteem and affection of a Northern reader—his intrepid and ardent spirit redeeming everything. The unsuspecting confidence with which he listens to his adviser, the agony with which he shrinks from the thought of shame, the tempest of passion with which he commits his crimes and the haughty fearlessness with which he avows them, give an extraordinary interest to his character. Iago, on the contrary, is the object of universal loathing. Many are inclined to suspect that Shakespeare has been seduced into an exaggeration unusual with him, and has drawn a monster who has no archetype in human nature. Now we suspect that an Italian audience in the fifteenth century would have felt very differently. Othello would have inspired nothing but detestation and contempt. The folly with which he trusts to the friendly professions of a man whose promotion he had obstructed—the credulity with which he takes unsupported assertions and trivial circumstances for unanswerable proofs, the violence with which he silences the exculpation till the exculpation can only aggravate his misery, would have excited the abhorrence and disgust of the spectators. The conduct of Iago they would assuredly have condemned; but they would have condemned it as we condemn that of his victim. Something of interest and respect would have mingled with their disapprobation. The readiness of his wit, the clearness of his judgment, the skill with which he penetrates the dispositions of others and conceals his own, would have insured to him a certain portion of their esteem.

So wide was the difference between the Italians and their neighbours. A similar difference existed between the Greeks of the second century before Christ and their masters the Romans. The conquerors, brave and resolute, faithful to their engagements, and strongly influenced by religious feelings, were, at the same time, ignorant, arbitrary, and cruel. With the vanquished people were deposited all the art, the science, and the literature of the western world. In poetry, in philosophy, in painting, in architecture, in sculpture, they had no rivals. Their manners were polished, their perceptions acute, their invention ready; they were tolerant, affable, humane. But of courage and sincerity they were almost utterly destitute. The rude warriors who had subdued them consoled themselves for their intellectual inferiority by remarking that knowledge and taste seemed only to make men atheists, cowards, and slaves. The distinction long continued to be strongly marked, and furnished an admirable subject for the fierce sarcasms of Juvenal.

The citizen of an Italian commonwealth was the Greek of the time of Juvenal and the Greek of the time of Pericles joined in one. Like the former he was timid and pliable, artful and unscrupulous. But, like the latter, he had a country. Its independence and prosperity were dear to him. If his character were degraded by some mean crimes, it was, on the other hand, ennobled by public spirit and by an honourable ambition.

A vice sanctioned by the general opinion is merely a vice. The evil terminates in itself. A vice condemned by the general opinion produces a pernicious effect on the whole character. The former is a local malady, the latter a constitutional taint. When the reputation of the offender is lost he too often flings the remains of his virtue after it in despair. The Highland gentleman who, a century ago, lived by taking black mail from his neighbours, committed the same crime for which Wild was accompanied to Tyburn by the huzzas of two hundred thousand people. But there can be no doubt that he was a much less depraved man than Wild. The deed for which Mrs. Brownrigg was hanged sinks into nothing when compared with the conduct of the Roman who treated the public to a hundred pair of gladiators. Yet we should probably wrong such a Roman if we supposed that his disposition was so cruel as that of Mrs. Brownrigg. In our own country a woman forfeits her place in society by what, in a man, is too commonly considered as an honourable distinction, and, at worst, as a venial error. The consequence is notorious. The moral principle of a woman is frequently more impaired by a single lapse from virtue than that of a man by twenty years of intrigue. Classical antiquity would furnish us with instances stronger, if possible, than those to which we have referred.

We must apply this principle to the case before us. Habits of dissimulation and falsehood, no doubt, mark a man of our age and country as utterly worthless and abandoned. But it by no means follows that a similar judgment would be just in the case of an Italian of the middle ages. On the contrary, we frequently find those faults which we are accustomed to consider as certain indications of a mind altogether depraved, in company with great and good qualities, with generosity, with benevolence, with disinterestedness. From such a state of society Palamedes, in the admirable dialogue of Hume, might have drawn illustrations of his theory as striking as any of those with which Fourli furnished him. These are not, we well know, the lessons which historians are generally most careful to teach, or readers most willing to learn. But they are not therefore useless. How Philip disposed his troops at Chæronea, where Hannibal crossed the Alps, whether Mary blew up Darnley, or Siquier shot Charles XII., and ten thousand other questions of the same description, are in themselves unimportant. The inquiry may amuse us, but the decision leaves us no wiser. He alone reads history aright who, observing how powerfully circumstances influence the feelings and opinions of men, how often vices pass into virtues, and paradoxes into axioms, learns to distinguish what is accidental and transitory in human nature from what is essential and immutable.

In this respect no history suggests more important reflections than that of the Tuscan and Lombard commonwealths. The character of the Italian statesman seems, at first sight, a collection of contradictions, a phantom as monstrous as the portress of Hell in Milton, half divinity, half snake, majestic and beautiful above, grovelling and poisonous below. We see a man whose thoughts and words have no connexion with each other; who never hesitates at an oath when he wishes to seduce, who never wants a pretext when he is inclined to betray. His cruelties spring, not from the heat of blood, or the insanity of uncontrolled power, but from deep and cool meditation. His passions, like well-trained troops, are impetuous by rule, and in their most headstrong fury never forget the discipline to which they have been accustomed. His whole soul is occupied with vast and complicated schemes of ambition: Yet his aspect and language exhibit nothing but philosophic moderation. Hatred and revenge eat into his heart.—Yet every look is a cordial smile, every gesture a familiar caress. He never excites the suspicion of his adversary by petty provocations. His purpose is disclosed only when it is accomplished. His face is unruffled, his speech is courteous, till vigilance is laid asleep, till a vital point is exposed, till a sure aim is taken; and then he strikes —for the first and last time. Military courage, the boast of the sottish German, the frivolous and prating Frenchman, the romantic and arrogant Spaniard, he neither possesses nor values. He shuns danger—not because he is insensible to shame, but because, in the society in which he lives, timidity has ceased to be shameful. To do an injury openly is, in his estimation, as wicked as to do it secretly—and far less profitable. With him the most honourable means are the surest, the speediest, and the darkest. He cannot comprehend how a man should scruple to deceive him whom he does not scruple to destroy. He would think it madness to declare open hostilities against a rival whom he might stab in a friendly embrace, or poison in a consecrated wafer.

Yet this man, black with vices which *we* consider as most loathsome—traitor, hypocrite, coward, assassin—was by no means destitute even of those virtues which we generally consider as indicating superior elevation of character. In civil courage, in perseverance, in presence of mind, those barbarous warriors who were foremost in the battle or the breach were far his inferiors. Even the dangers which he avoided with a caution almost pusillanimous never confused his perceptions, never paralysed his inventive faculties, never wrung out one secret from his ready tongue and his inscrutable brow. Though a dangerous enemy and a still more dangerous accomplice, he was a just and beneficent ruler. With so much unfairness in his policy, there was an extraordinary degree of fairness in his intellect. Indifferent to truth in the transactions of life, he was honestly devoted to the pursuit of truth in the researches of speculation. Wanton cruelty was not in his nature. On the contrary, where no political object was at stake, his disposition was soft and humane. The susceptibility of his nerves and the activity of his imagination inclined him to sympathize with the feelings of others and to delight in the charities and courtesies of social life. Perpetually descending to actions which might seem to mark a mind diseased through all its faculties, he had, nevertheless, an exquisite sensibility, both for the natural and the moral sublime, for every graceful and every lofty conception. Habits of petty intrigue and dissimulation might have rendered him incapable of great general views, but that the expanding effect of his philosophical studies counteracted the narrowing tendency. He had the keenest enjoyment of wit, eloquence, and poetry. The fine arts profited alike by the severity of his judgment and the liberality of his patronage. The portraits of some of the remarkable Italians of those times are perfectly in harmony with this description. Ample and majestic foreheads, brows strong and dark, but not frowning, eyes of which the calm, full gaze, while it expresses nothing, seems to discern everything; cheeks pale with thought and sedentary habits, lips formed with feminine delicacy, but compressed with more than masculine decision, mark out men at once enterprising and apprehensive; men equally skilled in detecting the purposes of others, and in concealing their own; men who must have been formidable enemies and unsafe allies; but men, at the same time, whose tempers were mild and equable, and who possessed an amplitude and subtlety of mind which would have rendered them eminent either in active or in contemplative life, and fitted them either to govern or to instruct mankind.

Every age and every nation has certain characteristic vices, which prevail almost universally, which scarcely any person scruples to avow, and which even rigid moralists but faintly censure. Succeeding generations change the fashion of their morals, with their hats and their coaches; take some other kind of wickedness under their patronage, and wonder at the depravity of their ancestors. Nor is this all. Posterity, that high court of appeal, which is never tired of eulogizing its own justice and discernment, acts, on such occasions, like a Roman dictator after a general mutiny. Finding the delinquents too numerous to be all punished, it selects some of them at hazard, to bear the whole penalty of an offence in which they are not more deeply implicated than those who escape. Whether decimation be a convenient mode of military execution, we know not; but we solemnly protest against the introduction of such a principle into the philosophy of history.

In the present instance the lot has fallen on Machiavelli; a man whose public conduct was upright and honourable, whose views of morality, where they differed from those of the persons around him, seemed to have differed for the better, and whose only fault was that, having adopted some of the maxims then generally received, he arranged them more luminously and expressed them more forcibly than any other writer.

Having now, we hope, in some degree cleared the personal character of Machiavelli, we come to the consideration of his works. As a poet, he is not entitled to a very high place. The Decennali are merely abstracts of the history of his own times in rhyme. The style and versification are sedulously modelled on those of Dante. But the manner of Dante, like that of every other great original poet, was suited only to his own genius, and to his own subject. The distorted and rugged diction which gives to his unearthly imagery a yet more unearthly character, and seems to proceed from a man labouring to express that which is inexpressible, is at once mean and extravagant when misemployed by an imitator. The moral poems are in every point superior. That on Fortune, in particular, and that on Opportunity exhibit both justness of thought and fertility of fancy. The Golden Ass has nothing but the name in common with the Romance of Apuleius—a book which, in spite of its irregular plan and its detestable style, is among the most fascinating in the Latin language, and in which the merits of Le Sage and Radcliffe, Bunyan and Crébillon, are singularly united. The poem of Machiavelli, which is evidently unfinished, is carefully copied from the earlier cantos of the Inferno. The writer loses himself in a wood. He is terrified by monsters and relieved by a beautiful damsel. His protectress conducts him to a large menagerie of emblematical beasts, whose peculiarities are described at length. The manner, as well as the plan, of the Divine Comedy is carefully imitated. Whole lines are transferred from it. But they no longer produce their wonted effect. Virgil advises the husbandman who removes a plant from one spot to another to mark its bearings on the cork, and to place it in the same position with regard to the different points of the heaven in which it formerly stood. A similar care is necessary in poetical transplantation. Where it is neglected we perpetually see the flowers of language which have bloomed on one soil wither on another. Yet the Golden Ass is not altogether destitute of merit. There is considerable ingenuity in the allegory and some vivid colouring in the description.

The Comedies deserve more attention. The Mandragola, in particular, is superior to the best of Goldoni, and inferior only to the best of Molière. It is the work of a man who, if he had devoted himself to the drama, would probably have attained the highest eminence, and produced a permanent and salutary effect on the national taste. This we infer, not so much from the degree as from the kind of its excellence. There are compositions which indicate still greater talent, and which are perused with still greater delight, from which we should have drawn very different conclusions. Books quite worthless are quite harmless. The sure sign of the general decline of an art is the frequent occurrence, not of deformity, but of misplaced beauty. In general, tragedy is corrupted by eloquence, and comedy by wit.

The real object of the drama is the exhibition of the human character. This, we conceive, is no arbitrary canon, originating in local and temporary associations, like those which regulate the number of acts in a play, or of syllables in a line. It is the very essence of a species of composition in which every idea is coloured by passing through the medium of an imagined mind. To this fundamental law every other regulation is subordinate. The situations which most signally develop character form the best plot. The mother tongue of the passions is the best style.

This principle, rightly understood, does not debar the poet from any grace of composition. There is no style in which some man may not, under some circumstances, express himself. There is, therefore, no style which the drama rejects, none which it does not occasionally require. It is in the discernment of place, of time, and of person that the inferior artists fail. The brilliant rhodomontade of Mercutio, the elaborate declamation of Antony, are, where Shakespeare has placed them, natural and pleasing. But Dryden would have made Mercutio challenge Tybalt in hyperboles as fanciful as those in which he describes the chariot of Mab. Corneille would have represented Antony as scolding and coaxing Cleopatra with all the measured rhetoric of a funeral oration.

No writers have injured the comedy of England so deeply as Congreve and Sheridan. Both were men of splendid wit and polished taste. Unhappily they made all their characters in their own likeness. Their works bear the same relation to the legitimate drama which a transparency bears to a painting: no delicate touches: no hues imperceptibly fading into each other: the whole is lighted up with an universal glare. Outlines and tints are forgotten in the common blaze which illuminates all. The flowers and fruits of the intellect abound; but it is the abundance of a jungle, not of a garden—unwholesome, bewildering, unprofitable from its very plenty, rank from its very fragrance. Every fop, every boor, every valet is a man of wit. The very butts and dupes, Tattle, Urkwould, Puff, Acres, outshine the whole Hotel de Rambouillet. To prove the whole system of this school absurd it is only necessary to apply the test which dissolved the enchanted Florimel—to place the true by the false Thalia, to contrast the most celebrated characters which have been drawn by the writers of whom we speak, with the Bastard in King John or the nurse in Romeo and Juliet. It was not surely from want of wit that Shakespeare adopted so different a manner. Benedick and Beatrice throw Mirabel and Millamant into the shade. All the good sayings of the facetious hours of Absolute and Surface might have been clipped from the single character of Falstaff without being missed. It would have been easy for that fertile mind to have given Bardolph and Shallow as much wit as Prince Hal, and to have made Dogberry and Verges retort on each other in sparkling epigrams. But he knew, to use his own admirable language, that such indiscriminate prodigality was "*from* the purpose of playing, whose end, both at the first and now, was, and is, to hold, as it were, the mirror up to Nature."

This digression will enable our readers to understand what we mean when we say that, in the Mandragola, Machiavelli has proved that he completely understood the nature of the dramatic art and possessed talents which would have enabled him to excel in it. By the correct and vigorous delineation of human nature, it produces interest without a pleasing or skilful plot, and laughter without the least ambition of wit. The lover, not a very delicate or generous lover, and his adviser the parasite are drawn with spirit. The hypocritical confessor is an admirable portrait. He is, if we mistake not, the original of Father Dominic, the best comic character of Dryden. But old Nicias is the glory of the piece. We cannot call to mind anything that resembles him. The follies which Molière ridicules are those of affectation, not those of fatuity. Coxcombs and pedants, not simpletons, are his game. Shakespeare has, indeed, a vast assortment of fools; but the precise species of which we speak is not, if we remember right, to be found there. Shallow is a fool. But his animal spirits supply, to a certain degree, the place of cleverness. His talk is to that of Sir John what soda-water is to champagne. It has the effervescence, though not the body or the flavour. Slender and Sir Andrew Aguecheek are fools, troubled with an uneasy consciousness of their folly, which, in the latter, produces a most edifying meekness and docility, and in the former, awkwardness, obstinacy, and confusion. Cloten is an arrogant fool; Osric a foppish fool, Ajax a savage fool; but Nicias is, as Thersites says of Patroclus, a fool positive. His mind is occupied by no strong feeling; it takes every character, and retains none; its aspect is diversified, not by passions, but by faint and transitory semblances of passion, a mock joy, a mock fear, a mock love, a mock pride, which chase each other like shadows over its surface, and vanish as soon as they appear. He is just idiot enough to be an object, not of pity or horror, but of ridicule. He bears some resemblance to poor Calandrino, whose mishaps, as recounted by Boccaccio, have made all Europe merry for more than four centuries. He, perhaps, resembles still more closely Simon de Villa, to whom Bruno and Buffalmacco promised the love of the Countess Civillari.* Nicias is, like Simon, of a learned profession, and the dignity with which he wears the doctoral fur renders his absurdities infinitely more grotesque. The old Tuscan is the very language for such a being. Its peculiar simplicity gives even to the most forcible reasoning and the most brilliant wit an infantine air, generally delightful, but to a foreign reader sometimes a little ludicrous. Heroes and statesmen seem to lisp when they use it. It becomes Nicias incomparably, and renders all his silliness infinitely more silly.

We may add that the verses with which the Mandragola is interspersed appear to us to be the most spirited and correct of all that Machiavelli has written in metre. He seems to have entertained the same opinion; for he has introduced some of them in other places. The contemporaries of the author were not blind to the merits of this striking piece. It was acted at Florence with the greatest success. Leo X. was among its admirers, and by his order it was represented at Rome.†

The Clizia is an imitation of the Casina of Plautus, which is itself an imitation of the lost κληρούμενοι of Diphilus. Plautus was, unquestionably, one of the best Latin writers. His works are copies; but they have, in an extraordinary degree, the air of originals. We infinitely prefer the slovenly

* Decameron, Giorn. viii. Nov. 9.
† Nothing can be more evident than that Paulus Jovius designates the Mandragola under the name of the Nicias. We should not have noticed what is so perfectly obvious, were it not that this natural and palpable misnomer has led the sagacious and industrious Bayle into a gross error.

exuberance of his fancy and the clumsy vigour of his diction to the artfully disguised poverty and elegant languor of Terence. But the Casina is by no means one of his best plays; nor is it one which offers great facilities to an imitator. The story is as alien from modern habits of life as the manner in which it is developed from the modern fashion of composition. The lover remains in the country, and the heroine is locked up in her chamber during the whole action, leaving their fate to be decided by a foolish father, a cunning mother, and two knavish servants. Machiavelli has executed his task with judgment and taste. He has accommodated the plot to a different state of society, and has very dexterously connected it with the history of his own times. The relation of the trick put on the doting old lover is exquisitely humorous. It is far superior to the corresponding passage in the Latin comedy, and scarcely yields to the account which Falstaff gives of his ducking.

Two other comedies without titles, the one in prose, the other in verse, appear among the works of Machiavelli. The former is very short, lively enough, but of no great value. The latter we can scarcely believe to be genuine. Neither its merits nor its defects remind us of the reputed author. It was first printed in 1796, from a manuscript discovered in the celebrated library of the Strozzi. Its genuineness, if we have been rightly informed, is established solely by the comparison of hands. Our suspicions are strengthened by the circumstance that the same manuscript contained a description of the plague of 1527, which has also, in consequence, been added to the works of Machiavelli. Of this last composition, the strongest external evidence would scarcely induce us to believe him guilty. Nothing was ever written more detestable, in matter and manner. The narrations, the reflections, the jokes, the lamentations, are all the very worst of their respective kinds, at once trite and affected,—threadbare tinsel from the Rag Fairs and Monmouth Streets of literature. A foolish schoolboy might, perhaps, write it, and, after he had written it, think it much finer than the incomparable introduction of the Decameron. But that a shrewd statesman, whose earliest works are characterized by manliness of thought and language, should, at nearly sixty years of age, descend to such puerility is utterly inconceivable.

The little novel of Belphegor is pleasantly conceived and pleasantly told. But the extravagance of the satire, in some measure, injures its effect. Machiavelli was unhappily married; and his wish to avenge his own cause and that of his brethren in misfortune carried him beyond even the licence of fiction. Jonson seems to have combined some hints taken from this tale, with others from Boccaccio, in the plot of The Devil is an Ass—a play which, though not the most highly finished of his compositions, is, perhaps, that which exhibits the strongest proofs of genius.

The political correspondence of Machiavelli, first published in 1767, is unquestionably genuine and highly valuable. The unhappy circumstances in which his country was placed during the greater part of his public life gave extraordinary encouragement to diplomatic talent. From the moment that Charles VIII. descended from the Alps the whole character of Italian politics was changed. The governments of the Peninsula ceased to form an independent system. Drawn from their old orbit by the attraction of the larger bodies which now approached them, they became mere satellites of France and Spain. All their disputes, internal and external, were decided by foreign influence. The contests of opposite factions were carried on, not as formerly, in the Senate-house, or in the market-place, but in the antichambers of Louis and Ferdinand. Under these circumstances, the prosperity of the Italian States depended far more on the ability of their foreign agents than on the conduct of those who were intrusted with the domestic administration. The ambassador had to discharge functions far more delicate than transmitting orders of knighthood, introducing tourists, or presenting his brethren with the homage of his high consideration. He was an advocate to whose management the dearest interests of his clients were intrusted, a spy clothed with an inviolable character. Instead of consulting the dignity of those whom he represented by a reserved manner and an ambiguous style, he was to plunge into all the intrigues of the court at which he resided, to discover and flatter every weakness of the prince who governed his employers, of the favourite who governed the prince, and of the lacquey who governed the favourite. He was to compliment the mistress and bribe the confessor, to panegyrize or supplicate, to laugh or weep, to accommodate himself to every caprice, to lull every suspicion, to treasure every hint, to be everything, to observe everything, to endure everything. High as the art of political intrigue had been carried in Italy, these were times which required it all.

On these arduous errands a Machiavelli was frequently employed. He was sent to treat with the King of the Romans and with the Duke of Valentinois. He was twice ambassador at the Court of Rome, and thrice at that of France. In these missions, and in several others of inferior importance, he acquitted himself with great dexterity. His despatches form one of the most amusing and instructive collections extant. We meet with none of the mysterious jargon so common in modern state-papers, the flash language of political robbers and sharpers. The narratives are clear and agreeably written; the remarks on men and things clever and judicious. The conversations are reported in a spirited and characteristic manner. We find ourselves introduced into the presence of the men who, during twenty eventful years, swayed the destinies of Europe. Their wit and their folly, their fretfulness and their merriment, are exposed to us. We are admitted to overhear their chat, and to watch their familiar gestures. It is interesting and curious to recognize, in circumstances which elude the notice of historians, the feeble violence and shallow cunning of Louis XII.; the bustling insignificance of Maximilian, cursed with an impotent pruriency for renown; rash, yet timid; obstinate, yet fickle; always in a hurry, yet always too late; the fierce and haughty energy which gave dignity to the eccentricities of Julius; the soft and graceful manners which masked the insatiable ambition and the implacable hatred of Borgia.

We have mentioned Borgia. It is impossible not to pause for a moment on the name of a man in whom the political morality of Italy was so strongly personified, partially blended with the sterner lineaments of the Spanish character. On two important occasions Machiavelli was admitted to his society; once, at the moment when his splendid villainy achieved its most signal triumph, when he caught in one snare and crushed at one blow all his most formidable rivals; and again when, exhausted by disease and overwhelmed by misfortunes which no human prudence could have averted, he was the prisoner of the deadliest enemy of his house. These interviews between the greatest speculative and the greatest practical statesman of the age are fully described in the correspondence, and form perhaps the most interesting part of it. From some passages in the Prince, and perhaps also from some indistinct traditions, several writers have supposed a connexion between those remarkable men much closer than ever existed. The envoy has even been accused of prompting the crimes of the artful and merciless tyrant. But from the official documents it is clear that their intercourse, though ostensibly amicable, was in reality hostile. It cannot be doubted, however, that the imagination of Machiavelli was strongly impressed and his speculations on government coloured by the observations which he made on the singular character and equally singular fortunes of a man who, under such disadvantages, had achieved such exploits; who, when sensuality, varied through innumerable forms, could no longer stimulate his sated mind, formed a more powerful and durable excitement in the intense thirst of empire and revenge; who emerged from the sloth and luxury of the Roman purple, the first prince and general of the age; who, trained in an unwarlike profession, formed a gallant army out of the dregs of an unwarlike people; who, after acquiring sovereignty by destroying his enemies, acquired popularity by destroying his tools; who had begun to employ for the most salutary ends the power which he had attained by the most atrocious means; who tolerated within the sphere of his iron despotism no plunderer or oppressor but himself; and who fell at last amidst the mingled curses and regrets of a people of whom his genius had been a wonder and might have been the salvation. Some of those crimes of Borgia which to us appear the most odious would not, from causes which we have already considered, have struck an Italian of the fifteenth century with equal horror. Patriotic feeling also might induce Machiavelli to look with some indulgence and regret on the memory of the only leader who could have defended the independence of Italy against the confederate spoilers of Cambray.

On this subject Machiavelli felt most strongly. Indeed, the expulsion of the foreign tyrants and the restoration of that golden age which had preceded the irruption of Charles VIII. were projects which, at that time, fascinated all the master-spirits of Italy. The magnificent vision delighted the great but ill-regulated mind of Julius. It divided with manuscripts and sauces, painters and falcons, the attention of the frivolous Leo. It prompted the generous treason of Morone. It imparted a transient energy to the feeble mind and body of the last Sforza. It excited for one moment an honest ambition in the false heart of Pescara. Ferocity and insolence were not among the vices of the national character. To the discriminating cruelties of politicians, committed for great ends on select victims, the moral code of the Italians was too indulgent. But though they might have recourse to barbarity as an expedient, they did not require it as a stimulant. They turned with loathing from the atrocity of the strangers who seemed to love blood for its own sake, who, not content with subjugating, were impatient to destroy; who found a fiendish pleasure in razing magnificent cities, cutting the throats of enemies who cried for quarter, or suffocating an unarmed people by thousands in the caverns to which they had fled for safety. Such were the scenes which daily excited the terror and disgust of a people amongst whom, till lately, the worst that a soldier had to fear in a pitched battle was the loss of his horse, and the expense of his ransom. The swinish intemperance of Switzerland, the wolfish avarice of Spain, the gross licentiousness of the French, indulged in violation of hospitality, of decency, of love itself, the wanton inhumanity which was common to all the invaders, had rendered them objects of deadly hatred to the inhabitants of the Peninsula.* The wealth which had been accumulated during centuries of prosperity and repose was rapidly melting away. The intellectual superiority of the oppressed people only rendered them more keenly sensible of their political degradation. Literature and taste, indeed, still disguised with a flush of hectic loveliness and brilliancy the ravages of an incurable decay. The iron had not yet entered into the soul.

---

* The opening stanzas of the Fourteenth Canto of the Orlando Furioso give a frightful picture of the state of Italy in those times. Yet, strange to say, Ariosto is speaking of the conduct of those who called themselves allies.

The time was not yet come when eloquence was to be gagged, and reason to be hoodwinked—when the harp of the poet was to be hung on the willows of Arno, and the right hand of the painter to forget its cunning. Yet a discerning eye might even then have seen that genius and learning would not long survive the state of things from which they had sprung—that the great men whose talents gave lustre to that melancholy period had been formed under the influence of happier days, and would leave no successors behind them. The times which shine with the greatest splendour in literary history are not always those to which the human mind is most indebted. Of this we may be convinced by comparing the generation which follows them with that which preceded them. The first fruits which are reaped under a bad system often spring from seed sown under a good one. Thus it was, in some measure, with the Augustan age. Thus it was with the age of Raphael and Ariosto, of Aldus and Vida.

Machiavelli deeply regretted the misfortunes of his country, and clearly discerned the cause and the remedy. It was the military system of the Italian people which had extinguished their valour and discipline, and rendered their wealth an easy prey to every foreign plunderer. The secretary projected a scheme, alike honourable to his heart and to his intellect, for abolishing the use of mercenary troops, and organizing a national militia.

The exertions which he made to effect this great object ought alone to rescue his name from obloquy. Though his situation and his habits were pacific, he studied with intense assiduity the theory of war. He made himself master of all its details. The Florentine government entered into his views. A council of war was appointed. Levies were decreed. The indefatigable minister flew from place to place in order to superintend the execution of his design. The times were, in some respects, favourable to the experiment. The system of military tactics had undergone a great revolution. The cavalry was no longer considered as forming the strength of an army. The hours which a citizen could spare from his ordinary employments, though by no means sufficient to familiarize him with the exercise of a man-at-arms, might render him an useful foot-soldier. The dread of a foreign yoke, of plunder, massacre, and conflagration might have conquered that repugnance to military pursuits which both the industry and the idleness of great towns commonly generate. For a time the scheme promised well. The new troops acquitted themselves respectably in the field. Machiavelli looked with parental rapture on the success of his plan; and began to hope that the arms of Italy might once more be formidable to the barbarians of the Tagus and the Rhine. But the tide of misfortune came on before the barriers which should have withstood it were prepared. For a time, indeed, Florence might be considered as peculiarly fortunate. Famine and sword and pestilence had devastated the fertile plains and stately cities of the Po. All the curses denounced of old against Tyre seemed to have fallen on Venice. Her merchants already stood afar off, lamenting for their great city. The time seemed near when the sea-weed should overgrow her silent Rialto, and the fisherman wash his nets in her deserted arsenal. Naples had been four times conquered and reconquered by tyrants equally indifferent to its welfare and equally greedy for its spoils. Florence, as yet, had only to endure degradation and extortion, to submit to the mandates of foreign powers, to buy over and over again, at an enormous price, what was already justly her own, to return thanks for being wronged, and to ask pardon for being in the right. She was at length deprived of the blessings even of this infamous and servile repose. Her military and political institutions were swept away together. The Medici returned, in the train of foreign invaders, from their long exile.

The policy of Machiavelli was abandoned; and his public services were requited with poverty, imprisonment, and torture.

The fallen statesman still clung to his project with unabated ardour. With the view of vindicating it from some popular objections, and of refuting some prevailing errors on the subject of military science, he wrote his seven books on the Art of War. This excellent work is in the form of a dialogue. The opinions of the writer are put into the mouth of Fabrizio Colonna, a powerful nobleman of the Ecclesiastical State, and an officer of distinguished merit in the service of the King of Spain. He visits Florence on his way from Lombardy to his own domains. He is invited to meet some friends at the house of Cosimo Rucellai, an amiable and accomplished young man, whose early death Machiavelli feelingly deplores. After partaking of an elegant entertainment, they retire from the heat into the most shady recesses of the garden. Fabrizio is struck by the sight of some uncommon plants. His host informs him that, though rare in modern days, they are frequently mentioned by the classical authors, and that his grandfather, like many other Italians, amused himself with practising the ancient methods of gardening. Fabrizio expresses his regret that those who, in later times, affected the manners of the old Romans, should select for imitation their most trifling pursuits. This leads to a conversation on the decline of military discipline, and on the best means of restoring it. The institution of the Florentine militia is ably defended; and several improvements are suggested in the details.

The Swiss and the Spaniards were, at that time, regarded as the best soldiers in Europe. The Swiss battalion consisted of pikemen, and bore a close resemblance to the Greek phalanx. The Spaniards, like the soldiers of Rome, were armed with the sword and the shield. The victories of Flaminius and Æmilius over the Macedonian kings seem to prove the superiority of the weapons used by the legions. The same experiment had been recently tried with the same result at the battle of Ravenna, one of those tremendous days into which human folly and wickedness compress the whole devastation of a famine or a plague. In that memorable conflict the infantry of Arragon, the old companions of Gonsalvo, deserted by all their allies, hewed a passage through the thickest of the imperial pikes, and effected an unbroken retreat, in the face of the gend-armerie of De Foix and the renowned artillery of Esté. Fabrizio, or rather Machiavelli, proposes to combine the two systems, to arm the foremost lines with the pike, for the purpose of repulsing cavalry, and those in the rear with the sword, as being a weapon better adapted for every purpose. Throughout the work the author expresses the highest admiration of the military science of the ancient Romans, and the greatest contempt for the maxims which had been in vogue amongst the Italian commanders of the preceding generation. He prefers infantry to cavalry, and fortified camps to fortified towns. He is inclined to substitute rapid movements and decisive engagements for the languid and dilatory operations of his countrymen. He attaches very little importance to the invention of gunpowder. Indeed, he seems to think that it ought scarcely to produce any change in the mode of arming or of disposing troops. The general testimony of historians, it must be allowed, seems to prove that the ill-constructed and ill-served artillery of those times, though useful in a siege, was of little value on the field of battle.

Of the tactics of Machiavelli we will not venture to give an opinion: but we are certain that his book is most able and interesting. As a commentary on the history of his times, it is invaluable. The ingenuity, the grace, and the perspicuity of the style, and the eloquence and animation of particular passages must give pleasure even to readers who take no interest in the subject.

The Prince and the Discourses on Livy were written after the fall of the Republican Government. The former was dedicated to the young Lorenzo de Medici. This circumstance seems to have disgusted the contemporaries of the writer far more than the doctrines which have rendered the name of the work odious in later times. It was considered as an indication of political apostasy. The fact, however, seems to have been that Machiavelli, despairing of *the liberty* of Florence, was inclined to support any government which might preserve her *independence*. The interval which separated a democracy and a despotism, Soderini and Lorenzo, seemed to vanish when compared with the difference between the former and the present state of Italy, between the security, the opulence, and the repose which it had enjoyed under its native rulers, and the misery in which it had been plunged since the fatal year in which the first foreign tyrant had descended from the Alps. The noble and pathetic exhortation with which the Prince concludes shows how strongly the writer felt upon the subject.

The Prince traces the progress of an ambitious man, the Discourses the progress of an ambitious people. The same principles on which, in the former work, the elevation of an individual is explained are applied, in the latter, to the longer duration and more complex interests of a society. To a modern statesman the form of the Discourses may appear to be puerile. In truth, Livy is not a historian on whom much reliance can be placed, even in cases where he must have possessed considerable means of information. And his first Decade, to which Machiavelli has confined himself, is scarcely entitled to more credit than our chronicle of British kings who reigned before the Roman invasion. But his commentator is indebted to him for little more than a few texts which he might as easily have extracted from the Vulgate or the Decameron. The whole train of thought is original.

On the peculiar immorality which has rendered the Prince unpopular, and which is almost equally discernible in the Discourses, we have already given our opinion at length. We have attempted to show that it belonged rather to the age than to the man, that it was a partial taint, and by no means implied general depravity. We cannot, however, deny that it is a great blemish and that it considerably diminishes the pleasure which, in other respects, those works must afford to every intelligent mind.

It is, indeed, impossible to conceive a more healthful and vigorous constitution of the understanding than that which these works indicate. The qualities of the active and the contemplative statesman appear to have been blended, in the mind of the writer, into a rare and exquisite harmony. His skill in the details of business had not been acquired at the expense of his general powers. It had not rendered his mind less comprehensive; but it had served to correct his speculations, and to impart to them that vivid and practical character which so widely distinguishes them from the vague theories of most political philosophers.

Every man who has seen the world knows that nothing is so useless as a general maxim. If it be very moral and very true, it may serve for a copy to a charity-boy. If, like those of Rochefoucault, it be sparkling and whimsical, it may make an excellent motto for an essay. But few, indeed, of the many wise apophthegms which have been uttered from the time of the Seven Sages of Greece to that of Poor Richard have prevented a single foolish action. We give the highest and the most peculiar praise to the precepts of Machiavelli, when we say that they may frequently be of real use in regulating conduct—not so much because they are more just, or more profound, than those which might be culled from other authors as because they can be more readily applied to the problems of real life.

There are errors in these works. But they are errors which a writer situated like Machiavelli, could scarcely avoid. They arise, for the most part, from a single defect which appears to us to pervade his whole system. In his political scheme the means had been more deeply considered than the ends. The great principle, that societies and laws exist only for the purpose of increasing the sum of private happiness, is not recognized with sufficient clearness. The good of the body, distinct from the good of the members, and sometimes hardly compatible with it, seems to be the object which he proposes to himself. Of all political fallacies, this has had the widest and the most mischievous operation. The state of society in the little commonwealths of Greece, the close connection and mutual dependence of the citizens, and the severity of the laws of war tended to encourage an opinion which, under such circumstances, could hardly be called erroneous. The interests of every individual were inseparably bound up with those of the state. An invasion destroyed his corn-fields and vineyards, drove him from his home, and compelled him to encounter all the hardships of a military life. A peace restored him to security and comfort. A victory doubled the number of his slaves. A defeat, perhaps, made him a slave himself. When Pericles, in the Peloponnesian war, told the Athenians that, if their country triumphed, their private losses would speedily be repaired; but that, if their arms failed of success, every individual amongst them would probably be ruined,* he spoke no more than the truth. He spoke to men whom the tribute of vanquished cities supplied with food and clothing, with the luxury of the bath and the amusements of the theatre, on whom the greatness of their country conferred rank, and before whom the members of less prosperous communities trembled; and to men who, in case of a change in the public fortunes, would, at least, be deprived of every comfort and every distinction which they enjoyed. To be butchered on the smoking ruins of their city, to be dragged in chains to a slave-market, to see one child torn from them to dig in the quarries of Sicily, and another to guard the harems of Persepolis—those were the frequent and probable consequences of national calamities. Hence, among the Greeks patriotism became a governing principle, or rather an ungovernable passion. Both their legislators and their philosophers took it for granted that, in providing for the strength and greatness of the state, they sufficiently provided for the happiness of the people. The writers of the Roman empire lived under despots into whose dominion a hundred nations were melted down, and whose gardens would have covered the little commonwealths of Phlius and Platæa. Yet they continued to employ the same language, and to cant about the duty of sacrificing everything to a country to which they owed nothing.

Causes similar to those which had influenced the disposition of the Greeks operated powerfully on the less vigorous and daring character of the Italians. They, too, were members of small communities. Every man was deeply interested in the welfare of the society to which he belonged—a partaker in its wealth and its poverty, in its glory and its shame. In the age of Machiavelli this was peculiarly the case. Public events had produced an immense sum of money to private citizens. The Northern invaders had brought want to their boards, infamy to their beds, fire to their roofs, and the knife to their throats. It was natural that a man who lived in times like these should overrate the importance of those measures by which a nation is rendered formidable to its neighbours, and undervalue those which make it prosperous within itself.

Nothing is more remarkable in the political treatises of Machiavelli than

---

* Thucydides, ii. 6s.

the fairness of mind which they indicate. It appears where the author is in the wrong almost as strongly as where he is in the right. He never advances a false opinion because it is new or splendid, because he can clothe it in a happy phrase, or defend it by an ingenious sophism. His errors are at once explained by a reference to the circumstances in which he was placed. They evidently were not sought out; they lay in his way, and could scarcely be avoided. Such mistakes must necessarily be committed by early speculators in every science.

In this respect it is amusing to compare the Prince and the Discourses with the Spirit of Laws. Montesquieu enjoys, perhaps, a wider celebrity than any political writer of modern Europe. Something he doubtless owes to his merit, but much more to his fortune. He had the good luck of a valentine. He caught the eye of the French nation at the moment when it was waking from the long sleep of political and religious bigotry ; and, in consequence, he became a favourite. The English, at that time, considered a Frenchman who talked about constitutional checks and fundamental laws as a prodigy not less astonishing than the learned pig or the musical infant. Specious but shallow, studious of effect, indifferent to truth, eager to build a system, but careless of collecting those materials out of which alone a sound and durable system can be built, he constructed theories as rapidly and as slightly as card houses, no sooner projected than completed, no sooner completed than blown away, no sooner blown away than forgotten. Machiavelli errs only because his experience, acquired in a very peculiar state of society, could not always enable him to calculate the effect of institutions differing from those of which he had observed the operation. Montesquieu errs because he has a fine thing to say, and is resolved to say it. If the phenomena which lie before him will not suit his purpose, all history must be ransacked. If nothing established by authentic testimony can be raked or chipped to suit his Procrustean hypothesis, he puts up with some monstrous fable about Siam, or Bantam, or Japan, told by writers compared with whom Lucian and Gulliver were veracious—liars by a double right, as travellers and as Jesuits

Propriety of thought and propriety of diction are commonly found together. Obscurity and affectation are the two greatest faults of style. Obscurity of expression generally springs from confusion of ideas; and the same wish to dazzle at any cost which produces affectation in the manner of a writer is likely to produce sophistry in his reasonings. The judicious and candid mind of Machiavelli shows itself in his luminous, manly, and polished language. The style of Montesquieu, on the other hand, indicates in every page a lively and ingenious, but an unsound mind. Every trick of expression, from the mysterious conciseness of an oracle to the flippancy of a Parisian coxcomb, is employed to disguise the fallacy of some positions and the triteness of others. Absurdities are brightened into epigrams ; truisms are darkened into enigmas. It is with difficulty that the strongest eye can sustain the glare with which some parts are illuminated, or penetrate the shade in which others are concealed.

The political works of Machiavelli derive a peculiar interest from the mournful earnestness which he manifests whenever he touches on topics connected with the calamities of his native land. It is difficult to conceive any situation more painful than that of a great man, condemned to watch the lingering agony of an exhausted country, to tend it during the alternate fits of stupefaction and raving which precede its dissolution, to see the symptoms of vitality disappear one by one, till nothing is left but coldness, darkness, and corruption. To this joyless and thankless duty was Machiavelli called. In the energetic language of the prophet, he was "mad for the sight of his eyes which he saw"—disunion in the council, effeminacy in the camp, liberty extinguished, commerce decaying, national honour sullied, an enlightened and flourishing people given over to the ferocity of ignorant savages. Though his opinions had not escaped the contagion of that political immorality which was common among his countrymen, his natural disposition seems to have been rather stern and impetuous than pliant and artful. When the misery and degradation of Florence and the foul outrage which he had himself sustained raised his mind, the smooth craft of his profession and his nation is exchanged for the honest bitterness of scorn and anger. He speaks like one sick of the calamitous times and abject people among whom his lot is cast. He pines for the strength and glory of ancient Rome, for the fasces of Brutus and the sword of Scipio, the gravity of the curule chair, and the bloody pomp of the triumphal sacrifice. He seems to be transported back to the days when eight hundred thousand Italian warriors sprung to arms at the rumour of a Gallic invasion. He breathes all the spirit of those intrepid and haughty patricians, who forgot the dearest ties of nature in the claims of public duty, who looked with disdain on the elephants and on the gold of Pyrrhus, and listened with unaltered composure to the tremendous tidings of Cannæ. Like an ancient temple deformed by the barbarous architecture of a later age, his character acquires an interest from the very circumstances which debase it. The original proportions are rendered more striking by the contrast which they present to the mean and incongruous additions.

The influence of the sentiments which we have described was not apparent in his writings alone. His enthusiasm, barred from the career which it would have selected for itself, seems to have found a vent in desperate levity. He enjoyed a vindictive pleasure in outraging the opinions of a society which he despised. He became careless of those decencies which were expected from a man so highly distinguished in the literary and political world. The sarcastic bitterness of his conversation disgusted those who were more inclined to accuse his licentiousness than their own degeneracy, and who were unable to conceive the strength of those emotions which are concealed by the jests of the wretched, and by the follies of the wise.

The historical works of Machiavelli still remain to be considered. The life of Castruccio Castracani will occupy us for a very short time, and would scarcely have demanded our notice had it not attracted a much greater share of public attention than it deserves. Few books, indeed, could be more interesting than a careful and judicious account, from such a pen, of the illustrious Prince of Lucca, the most eminent of those Italian chiefs who, like Pisistratus and Gelon, acquired a power felt rather than seen, and resting, not on law or on prescription, but on the public favour and on their great personal qualities. Such a work would exhibit to us the real nature of that species of sovereignty, so singular and so often misunderstood, which the Greeks denominated *tyranny*, and which, modified in some degree by the feudal system, reappeared in the commonwealths of Lombardy and Tuscany. But this little composition of Machiavelli is in no sense a history. It has no pretensions to fidelity. It is a trifle, and not a very successful trifle. It is scarcely more authentic than the novel of Belphegor, and is very much duller.

The last great work of this illustrious man was the history of his native city. It was written by the command of the pope, who, as chief of the house of Medici, was at that time sovereign of Florence. The characters of Cosmo, of Piero, and of Lorenzo are, however, treated with a freedom and impartiality equally honourable to the writer and to the patron. The miseries and humiliations of dependence, the bread which is more bitter than every other food, the stairs which are more painful than every other ascent,* had not broken the spirit of Machiavelli. The most corrupting post in a corrupting profession had not depraved the generous heart of Clement.

The history does not appear to be the fruit of much industry or research. It is unquestionably inaccurate. But it is elegant, lively, and picturesque beyond any other in the Italian language. The reader, we believe, carries away from it a more vivid and a more faithful impression of the national character and manners than from more correct accounts. The truth is, that the book belongs rather to ancient than to modern literature. It is in the style, not of Davila and Clarendon, but of Herodotus and Tacitus: and the classical histories may almost be called romances founded in fact. The relation is, no doubt, in all its principal points, strictly true. But the numerous little incidents which heighten the interest, the words, the gestures, the looks, are evidently furnished by the imagination of the author. The fashion of later times is different. A more exact narrative is given by the writer. It may be doubted whether more exact notions are conveyed to the reader. The best portraits are those in which there is a slight mixture of caricature; and we are not aware that the best histories are not those in which a little of the exaggeration of fictitious narrative is judiciously employed. Something is lost in accuracy; but much is gained in effect. The fainter lines are neglected; but the great characteristic features are imprinted on the mind for ever.

The history terminates with the death of Lorenzo de Medici. Machiavelli had, it seems, intended to continue it to a later period. But his death prevented the execution of his design; and the melancholy task of recording the desolation and shame of Italy devolved on Guicciardini.

Machiavelli lived long enough to see the commencement of the last struggle for Florentine liberty. Soon after his death monarchy was finally established—not such a monarchy as that of which Cosmo had laid the foundations deep in the constitution and feelings of his countrymen, and which Lorenzo had embellished with the trophies of every science and every art; but a loathsome tyranny, proud and mean, cruel and feeble, bigoted and lascivious. The character of Machiavelli was hateful to the new masters of Italy; and those parts of his theory which were in strict accordance with their own daily practice afforded a pretext for blackening his memory. His works were misrepresented by the learned, misconstrued by the ignorant, censured by the Church, abused, with all the rancour of simulated virtue, by the minions of a base despotism and the priests of a baser superstition. The name of the man whose genius had illuminated all the dark places of policy, and to whose patriotic wisdom an oppressed people had owed their last chance of emancipation and revenge, passed into a proverb of infamy. For more than two hundred years his bones lay undistinguished. At length, an English nobleman paid the last honours to the greatest statesman of Florence. In the church of Santa Croce a monument was erected to his memory, which is contemplated with reverence by all who can distinguish the virtues of a great mind through the corruptions of a degenerate age; and which will be approached with still deeper homage when the object to which his public life was devoted shall be attained—when the foreign yoke shall be broken, when a second Proccita shall avenge the wrongs of Naples, when a happier Rienzi shall restore the good estate of Rome, when the streets of Florence and Bologna shall again resound with their ancient war cry—*Popolo; popolo!; muoiano i tiranni!*

---

* Dante Paradiso, canto xvii.

HALLAM'S CONSTITUTIONAL HISTORY.

The Constitutional History of England, from the Accession of Henry VII. to the Death of George II. By HENRY HALLAM. In 2 vols. 1827.

HISTORY, at least in its state of imaginary perfection, is a compound of poetry and philosophy. It impresses general truths on the mind by a vivid representation of particular characters and incidents. But, in fact, the two hostile elements of which it consists have never been known to form a perfect amalgamation; and, at length, in our own time, they have been completely and professedly separated. Good histories, in the proper sense of the word, we have not. But we have good historical romances, and good historical essays. The imagination and the reason, if we may use a legal metaphor, have made partition of a province of literature of which they were formerly seised *per my et per tout;* and now they hold their respective portions in severalty, instead of holding the whole in common.

To make the past present, to bring the distant near—to place us in the society of a great man or on the eminence which overlooks the field of a mighty battle, to invest with the reality of human flesh and blood beings whom we are too much inclined to consider as personified qualities in an allegory, to call up our ancestors before us with all their peculiarities of language, manners, and garb, to show us over their houses, to seat us at their tables, to rummage their old-fashioned wardrobes, to explain the uses of their ponderous furniture,—these parts of the duty which properly belongs to the historian have been appropriated by the historical novelist. On the other hand, to extract the philosophy of history, to direct our judgment of events and men, to trace the connection of causes and effects, and to draw from the occurrences of former times general lessons of moral and political wisdom has become the business of a distinct class of writers.

Of the two kinds of composition into which history has been thus divided, the one may be compared to a map, the other to a painted landscape. The picture, though it places the object before us, does not enable us to ascertain with accuracy the form and dimensions of its component parts, the distances, and the angles. The map is not a work of imitative art. It presents no scene to the imagination; but it gives us exact information as to the bearings of the various points, and is a more useful companion to the traveller or the general than the painting could be, though it were the grandest that ever Rosa peopled with outlaws, or the sweetest over which Claude ever poured the mellow effulgence of a setting sun.

It is remarkable that the practice of separating the two ingredients of which history is composed has become prevalent on the Continent as well as in this country. Italy has already produced a historical novel of high merit and of still higher promise. In France the practice has been carried to a length somewhat whimsical. M. Sismondi publishes a grave and stately history, very valuable, and a little tedious. He then sends forth as a companion to it a novel, in which he attempts to give a lively representation of characters and manners. This course, as it seems to us, has all the disadvantages of a division of labour, and none of its advantages. We understand the expediency of keeping the functions of cook and coachman distinct—the dinner will be better dressed, and the horses better managed. But where the two situations are united, as in the Maître Jacques of Molière, we do not see that the matter

* Edinburgh Review, Vol. xlviii. September, 1828, p. 96.

is much mended by the solemn form with which the pluralist passes from one of his employments to the other.

We manage these things better in England. Sir Walter Scott gives us a novel; Mr. Hallam a critical and argumentative history. Both are occupied with the same matter. But the former looks at it with the eye of a sculptor. His intention is to give an express and lively image of its external form. The latter is an anatomist. His task is to dissect the subject to its inmost recesses and to lay bare before us all the springs of motion and all the causes of decay.

Mr. Hallam is, on the whole, far better qualified than any other writer of our time for the office which he has undertaken. He has great industry and great acuteness. His knowledge is extensive, various, and profound. His mind is equally distinguished by the amplitude of its grasp and by the delicacy of its tact. His speculations have none of that vagueness which is the common fault of political philosophy. On the contrary, they are strikingly practical. They teach us not only the general rule, but the mode of applying it to solve particular cases. In this respect they often remind us of the discourses of Machiavelli.

The style is sometimes harsh, and sometimes obscure. We have also here and there remarked a little of that unpleasant trick which Gibbon brought into fashion, the trick, we mean, of narrating by implication and allusion. Mr. Hallam, however, has an excuse which Gibbon had not. His work is designed for readers who are already acquainted with the ordinary books on English history, and who can, therefore, unriddle these little enigmas without difficulty. The manner of the book is, on the whole, not unworthy of the matter. The language, even when most faulty, is weighty and massive, and indicates strong sense in every line. It often rises to an eloquence, not florid or impassioned, but high, grave, and sober; such as would become a state paper, or a judgment delivered by a great magistrate, a Somers, or a D'Aguesseau.

In this respect the character of Mr. Hallam's mind corresponds strikingly with that of his style. His work is eminently judicial. Its whole spirit is that of the bench, not that of the bar. He sums up with a calm, steady impartiality, turning neither to the right nor to the left, glossing over nothing, exaggerating nothing, while the advocates on both sides are alternately biting their lips to hear their conflicting misstatements and sophisms exposed. On a general survey, we do not scruple to pronounce the Constitutional History the most impartial book that we ever read. We think it the more incumbent on us to bear this testimony strongly at first setting out, because, in the course of our remarks, we shall think it right to dwell principally on those parts of it from which we dissent.

There is one peculiarity about Mr. Hallam which, while it adds to the value of his writings, will, we fear, take away something from their popularity. He is less of a worshipper than any historian whom we can call to mind. Every political sect has its esoteric and its exoteric school; its abstract doctrines for the initiated; its visible symbols, its imposing forms, it mythological fables, for the vulgar. It assists the devotion of those who are unable to raise themselves to the contemplation of pure truths by all the devices of pagan or papal superstition. It has its altars and its deified heroes, its relics and pilgrimages, its canonized martyrs and confessors, its festivals and its legendary miracles. Our pious ancestors, we are told, deserted the high altar of Canterbury, to lay all their oblations on the shrine of St. Thomas. In the same manner the great and comfortable doctrines of the Tory creed, those particularly which relate to restrictions on worship and on trade, are adored by squires and rectors in Pitt Clubs, under the name of a minister who was as bad a representative of the system which has been christened after him as Becket of the spirit of the Gospel. And, on the other hand, the cause for which Hampden bled on the field and Sydney on the scaffold is enthusiastically toasted by many an honest radical who would be puzzled to explain the difference between Ship-money and the Habeas Corpus Act. It may be added that, as in religion, so in politics, few even of those who are enlightened enough to comprehend the meaning latent under the emblems of their faith can resist the contagion of the popular superstition. Often, when they flatter themselves that they are merely feigning a compliance with the prejudices of the vulgar, they are themselves under the influence of those very prejudices. It probably was not altogether on grounds of expediency that Socrates taught his followers to honour the gods whom the state honoured, and bequeathed a cock to Esculapius with his dying breath. So there is often a portion of willing credulity and enthusiasm in the veneration which the most discerning men pay to their political idols. From the very nature of man it must be so. The faculty by which we inseparably associate ideas which have often been presented to us in conjunction is not under the absolute control of the will. It may be quickened into morbid activity. It may be reasoned into sluggishness. But in a certain degree it will always exist. The almost absolute mastery which Mr. Hallam has obtained over feelings of this class is perfectly astonishing to us; and will, we believe, be not only astonishing but offensive to many of his readers. It must particularly disgust those people who, in their speculations on politics, are not reasoners but fanciers; whose opinions, even when sincere, are not produced, according to the law of intellectual births, by induction or inference, but are equivocally generated by the heat of fervid tempers out of the overflowing of tumid imaginations. A man of this class is always in extremes. He cannot be a friend to liberty without calling for a community of goods, or a friend to order without taking under his protection the foulest excesses of tyranny. His admiration oscillates between the most worthless of rebels and the most worthless of oppressors, between Marten, the scandal of the High Court of Justice, and Laud, the scandal of the Star Chamber. He can forgive anything but temperance and impartiality. He has a certain sympathy with the violence of his opponents, as well as with that of his associates. In every furious partisan he sees either his present self or his former self, the pensioner that is or the Jacobin that has been. But he is unable to comprehend a writer who, steadily attached to principles, is indifferent about names and badges,— and who judges of characters with equable severity, not altogether untinctured with cynicism, but free from the slightest touch of passion, party spirit, or caprice.

We should probably like Mr. Hallam's book more if, instead of pointing out with strict fidelity the bright points and the dark spots of both parties, he had exerted himself to whitewash the one and to blacken the other. But we should certainly prize it far less. Eulogy and invective may be had for the asking. But for cold, rigid justice—the one weight and the one measure—we know not where else we can look.

No portion of our annals has been more perplexed and misrepresented by writers of different parties than the history of the Reformation. In this labyrinth of falsehood and sophistry the guidance of Mr. Hallam is peculiarly valuable. It is impossible not to admire the even-handed justice with which he deals out castigation to right and left on the rival persecutors.

It is vehemently maintained by some writers of the present day that the government of Elizabeth persecuted neither Papists nor Puritans as such; and occasionally that the severe measures which it adopted were dictated, not by religious intolerance, but by political necessity. Even the excellent account of those times which Mr. Hallam has given, has not altogether imposed silence on the authors of this fallacy. The title of the queen, they say, was annulled by the pope; her throne was given to another; her subjects were incited to rebellion; her life was menaced; every Catholic was bound in conscience to be a traitor; it was, therefore, against traitors, not against Catholics, that the penal laws were enacted.

That our readers may be the better able to appreciate the merits of this defence, we will state, as concisely as possible, the substance of some of these laws.

As soon as Elizabeth ascended the throne, and before the least hostility to her government had been shown by the Catholic population, an act passed prohibiting the celebration of the rites of the Romish Church, on pain of forfeiture for the first offence, of a year's imprisonment for the second, and of perpetual imprisonment for the third.

A law was next made in 1562, enacting that all who had ever graduated at the Universities, or received holy orders, all lawyers, and all magistrates, should take the oath of supremacy when tendered to them, on pain of forfeiture and imprisonment during the royal pleasure. After the lapse of three months it might again be tendered to them; and if it were again refused, the recusant was guilty of high treason! A prospective law, however severe, framed to exclude Catholics from the liberal professions, would have been mercy itself compared with this odious act. It is a retrospective statute; it is a retrospective penal statute; it is a retrospective penal statute against a large class. We will not positively affirm that a law of this description must always, and under all circumstances, be unjustifiable. But the presumption against it is most violent; nor do we remember any crisis, either in our own history or in the history of any other country, which would have rendered such a provision necessary. In the present case, what circumstances called for extraordinary rigour? There might be disaffection among the Catholics. The prohibition of their worship would naturally produce it. But it is from their situation, not from their conduct; from the wrongs which they had suffered, not from those which they had committed, that the existence of discontent among them must be inferred. There were libels, no doubt, and prophecies, and rumours, and suspicions,—strange grounds for a law inflicting capital penalties, *ex post facto*, on a large body of men.

Eight years later the bull of Pius deposing Elizabeth produced a third law. This law, to which alone, as we conceive, the defence now under our consideration can apply, provides that, if any Catholic shall convert a Protestant to the Romish Church, they shall both suffer death as for high treason.

We believe that we might safely content ourselves with stating the fact and leaving it to the judgment of every plain Englishman. Recent controversies have, however, given so much importance to this subject that we will offer a few remarks on it.

In the first place, the arguments which are urged in favour of Elizabeth apply with much greater force to the case of her sister Mary. The Catholics did not, at the time of Elizabeth's accession, rise in arms to seat a pretender on her throne. But before Mary had given, or could give, provocation, the most distinguished Protestants attempted to set aside her rights in favour of the Lady Jane. That attempt, and the subsequent insurrection of Wyatt, furnished at least as good a plea for the burning of Protestants as the conspiracies against Elizabeth furnished for the hanging and embowelling of Papists.

The fact is that both pleas are worthless alike. If such arguments are to pass current, it will be easy to prove that there was never such a thing as religious persecution since the creation. For there never was a religious persecution in which some odious crime was not, justly or unjustly, said to be obviously deducible from the doctrines of the persecuted party. We might say that the Cæsars did not persecute the Christians; that they only punished men who were charged, rightly or wrongly, with burning Rome, and with committing the foulest abominations in their assemblies; and that the refusal to throw frankincense on the altar of Jupiter was not the crime, but only evidence of the crime. We might say that the massacre of St. Bartholomew was intended to extirpate, not a religious sect, but a political party. For, beyond all doubt, the proceedings of the Huguenots, from the conspiracy of Amboise to the battle of Moncontour, had given much more trouble to the French monarchy than the Catholics have ever given to the English since the Reformation; and that too, with much less excuse.

The true distinction is perfectly obvious. To punish a man because he has committed a crime, or is believed, though unjustly, to have committed a crime, is not persecution. To punish a man because we infer from the nature of some doctrine which he holds, or from the conduct of other persons who hold the same doctrines with him, that he will commit a crime, is persecution; and is, in every case, foolish and wicked.

When Elizabeth put Ballard and Babington to death, she was not persecuting. Nor should we have accused her government of persecution for passing any law, however severe, against overt acts of sedition. But to argue that, because a man is a Catholic, he must think it right to murder a heretical sovereign, and that because he thinks it right he will attempt to do it,—and then to found on this conclusion a law for punishing him as if he had done it, is plain persecution.

If, indeed, all men reasoned in the same manner on the same data, and always did what they thought it their duty to do, this mode of dispensing punishment might be extremely judicious. But as people who agree about premises often disagree about conclusions, and as no man in the world acts up to his own standard of right, there are two enormous gaps in the logic by which alone penalties for opinions can be defended. The doctrine of reprobation, in the judgment of many very able men, follows by syllogistic necessity from the doctrine of election. Others conceive that the Antinomian and Manichean heresies directly follow from the doctrine of reprobation; and it is very generally thought that licentiousness and cruelty of the worst description are likely to be the fruits, as they often have been the fruits, of Antinomian and Manichean opinions. This chain of reasoning, we think, is as perfect in all its parts as that which makes out a Papist to be necessarily a traitor. Yet it would be rather a strong measure to hang the Calvinists, on the ground that, if they were spared, they would infallibly commit all the atrocities of Matthias and Knipperdoling. For, reason the matter as we may, experience shows us that a man may believe in election without believing in reprobation, that he may believe in reprobation without being an Antinomian, and that he may be an Antinomian without being a bad citizen. Man, in short, is so inconsistent a creature that it is impossible to reason from his belief to his conduct, or from one part of his belief to another.

We do not believe that every Englishman who was reconciled to the Catholic Church would, as a necessary consequence, have thought himself justified in deposing or assassinating Elizabeth. It is not sufficient to say that the convert must have acknowledged the authority of the pope and that the pope had issued a bull against the queen. We know through what strange loopholes the human mind contrives to escape when it wishes to avoid a disagreeable inference from an admitted proposition. We know how long the Jansenists contrived to believe the pope infallible in matters of doctrine, and at the same time to believe doctrines which he pronounced to be heretical. Let it pass, however, that every Catholic in the kingdom thought that Elizabeth might be lawfully murdered. Still the old maxim that what is the business of everybody is the business of nobody is particularly likely to hold good in a case in which a cruel death is the almost inevitable consequence of making any attempt.

Of the ten thousand clergymen of the Church of England there is scarcely one who would not say that a man who should leave his country and friends to preach the Gospel among savages, and who should, after labouring indefatigably without any hope of reward, terminate his life by martyrdom, would deserve the warmest admiration. Yet we doubt whether ten of the ten thousand ever thought of going on such an expedition. Why should we suppose that conscientious motives, feeble as they are constantly found to be in a good cause, should be omnipotent for evil? Doubtless there was many a jolly Popish priest in the old manor-houses of the northern couuties, who would have admitted, in theory, the deposing power of the pope, but who would not have been ambitious to be stretched on the rack, even though it were to be used, according to the benevolent proviso of Lord Burleigh, "as charitably as such a thing can be," or to be hanged, drawn, and quartered, even though, by that rare indulgence which the queen, of her special grace, certain knowledge, and mere motion, sometimes extended to very mitigated cases, he were allowed a fair time to choke before the hangman began to grabble in his entrails.

But the laws passed against the Puritans had not even the wretched excuse which we have been considering. In this case the cruelty was equal, the danger infinitely less. In fact, the danger was created solely by the cruelty. But it is superfluous to press the argument. By no artifice of ingenuity can the stigma of persecution, the worst blemish of the English Church, be effaced or patched over. Her doctrines, we well know, do not tend to intolerance. She admits the possibility of salvation out of her own pale. But this circumstance, in itself honourable to her, aggravates the sin and the shame of those who persecuted in her name. Dominic and De Montfort did not, at least, murder and torture for differences of opinion which they considered as trifling. It was to stop an infection which, as they believed, hurried to perdition every soul which it seized, that they employed their fire and steel. The measures of the English government with respect to the Papist and Puritans sprang from a widely different principle. If those who deny that the founders of the Established Church were guilty of religious persecution mean only that they were not influenced by any religious motive, we perfectly agree with them. Neither the penal code of Elizabeth nor the more hateful system by which Charles II. attempted to force episcopacy on the Scotch, had an origin so noble. Their cause is to be sought in some circumstances which attended the Reformation in England—circumstances of which the effects long continued to be felt, and may in some degree be traced even at the present day.

In Germany, in France, in Switzerland, and in Scotland the contest against the Papal power was essentially a religious contest. In all those countries, indeed, the cause of the Reformation, like every other great cause, attracted to itself many supporters influenced by no conscientious principle,—many who quitted the Established Church only because they thought her in danger,— many who were weary of her restraints,—and many who were greedy for her spoils. But it was not by these adherents that the separation was there conducted. They were welcome auxiliaries; their support was too often purchased by unworthy compliances, but, however exalted in rank or power, they were not the leaders in the enterprise. Men of a widely different description, men who redeemed great infirmities and errors by sincerity, disinterestedness, energy, and courage; men who, with many of the vices of revolutionary chiefs and of polemic divines, united some of the highest qualities of apostles, were the real directors. They might be violent in innovation and scurrilous in controversy. They might sometimes act with inexcusable severity towards opponents, and sometimes connive disreputably at the vices of powerful allies. But fear was not in them, nor hypocrisy, nor avarice, nor any petty selfishness. Their one great object was the demolition of the idols and the purification of the sanctuary. If they were too indulgent to the failings of eminent men from whose patronage they expected advantage to the Church, they never flinched before persecuting tyrants and hostile armies. If they set the lives of others at naught in comparison of their doctrines, they were ready to throw away their own. Such were the authors of the great schism on the Continent and in the northern part of this island. The Elector of Saxony and the Landgrave of Hesse, the Prince of Condé and the King of Navarre, Moray and Morton, might espouse the Protestant opinions, or might pretend to espouse them;— but it was from Luther, from Calvin, from Knox, that the Reformation took its character.

England has no such names to show; not that she wanted men of sincere piety, of deep learning, of steady and adventurous courage. But these were thrown into the background. Elsewhere, men of this character were the principals. Here they acted a secondary part. Elsewhere, worldliness was the tool of zeal. Here zeal was the tool of worldliness. A king, whose character may be best described by saying that he was despotism itself personified, unprincipled ministers, a rapacious aristocracy, a servile Parliament,—such were the instruments by which England was delivered from the yoke of Rome. The work which had been begun by Henry, the murderer of his wives, was continued by Somerset, the murderer of his brother, and completed by Elizabeth, the murderer of her guest. Sprung from brutal passion,—nurtured by selfish policy,—the Reformation in England displayed little of what had, in other countries, distinguished it,—unflinching and unsparing devotion, boldness of speech, and singleness of eye. These were indeed to be found; but it was in the lower ranks of the party which opposed the authority of Rome, in such men as Hooper, Latimer, Rogers, and Taylor. Of those who had any important share in bringing the alteration about, Ridley was perhaps the only person who did not consider it as a mere political job. Even Ridley did not play a very prominent part. Among the statesmen and prelates who principally gave the tone to the religious changes, there is one, and one only, whose conduct partiality itself can attribute to any other than interested motives. It is not strange, therefore, that his character should have been the subject of fierce controversy. We need not say that we speak of Cranmer.

Mr. Hallam has been severely censured for saying, with his usual placid severity, that, "if we weigh the character of this prelate in an equal balance, he will appear far indeed removed from the turpitude imputed to him by his enemies; yet not entitled to any extraordinary veneration." We will venture to expand the sense of Mr. Hallam, and to comment on it thus :—If we consider Cranmer merely as a statesman, he will not appear a much worse man than Wolsey, Gardiner, Cromwell, or Somerset. But when an attempt is made to set him up as a saint, it is scarcely possibly for any man of sense who knows the history of the times to preserve his gravity. If the memory of the archbishop had been left to find its own place, he would have soon been lost among the crowd which is mingled

"A quel cattivo coro
Degli angeli, che non furon ribelli,
Nè fur fedeli a Dio, ma per sè furo."

And the only notice which it would have been necessary to take of his name would have been

"Non ragioniam di lui ; ma guarda, e passa."

But, since his admirers challenge for him a place in the noble army of martyrs, his claims require fuller discussion.

The origin of his greatness, common enough in the scandalous chronicles of courts, seems strangely out of place in a hagiology. Cranmer rose into favour by serving Henry in the disgraceful affair of his first divorce. He promoted the marriage of Anne Boleyn with the king. On a frivolous pretence, he pronounced that marriage null and void. On a pretence, if possible, still more frivolous, he dissolved the ties which bound the shameless tyrant to Anne of Cleves. He attached himself to Cromwell while the fortunes of Cromwell flourished. He voted for cutting off his head without a trial, when the tide of royal favour turned. He conformed backwards and forwards as the king changed his mind. While Henry lived, he assisted in condemning to the flames those who denied the doctrine of transubstantiation. When Henry died, he found out that the doctrine was false. He was, however, not at a loss for people to burn. The authority of his station and of his grey hairs was employed to overcome the disgust with which an intelligent and virtuous child regarded persecution.

Intolerance is always bad. But the sanguinary intolerance of a man who thus wavered in his creed excites a loathing to which it is difficult to give vent without calling foul names. Equally false to political and religious obligations, he was first the tool of Somerset, and then the tool of Northumberland. When the Protector wished to put his own brother to death, without even the semblance of a trial, he found a ready instrument in Cranmer. In spite of the canon law, which forbade a churchman to take any part in matters of blood, the archbishop signed the warrant for the atrocious sentence. When Somerset had been in his turn destroyed, his destroyer received the support of Cranmer in a wicked attempt to change the course of the succession.

The apology made for him by his admirers only renders his conduct more contemptible. He complied, it is said, against his better judgment, because he could not resist the entreaties of Edward. A holy prelate of sixty, one would think, might be better employed by the bedside of a dying child than in committing crimes at the request of his disciple. If he had shown half as much firmness when Edward requested him to commit treason as he had before shown when Edward requested him not to commit murder, he might have saved the country from one of the greatest misfortunes that it ever underwent. He became, from whatever motive, the accomplice of the worthless Dudley. The virtuous scruples of another young and amiable mind were to be overcome. As Edward had been forced into persecution, Jane was to be seduced into usurpation. No transaction in our annals is more unjustifiable than this. If a hereditary title were to be respected, Mary possessed it. If a parliamentary title were preferable, Mary possessed that also. If the interest of the Protestant religion required a departure from the ordinary rule of succession, that interest would have been best served by raising Elizabeth to the throne. If the foreign relations of the kingdom were considered, still stronger reasons might be found for preferring Elizabeth to Jane. There was great doubt whether Jane or the Queen of Scotland had the better claim ; and that doubt would, in all probability, have produced a war both with Scotland and with France, if the project of Northumberland had not been blasted in its infancy. That Elizabeth had a better claim than the Queen of Scotland was indisputable. To the part which Cranmer, and unfortunately some better men than Cranmer, took in this most reprehensible scheme, much of the severity with which the Protestants were afterwards treated must in fairness be ascribed.

The plot failed; Popery triumphed; and Cranmer recanted. Most people look on his recantation as a single blemish on an honourable life, the frailty of an unguarded moment. But, in fact, it was in strict accordance with the system on which he had constantly acted. It was part of a regular habit. It was not the first recantation that he had made; and, in all probability, if it had answered its purpose, it would not have been the last. We do not blame him for not choosing to be burned alive. It is no very severe reproach to any person that he does not possess heroic fortitude. But surely a man who liked the fire so little should have had some sympathy for others. A persecutor who inflicts nothing which he is not ready to endure deserves some respect. But when a man who loves his doctrines more than the lives of his neighbours loves his own little finger better than his doctrines, a very simple argument *à fortiori* will enable us to estimate the amount of his benevolence.

But his martyrdom, it is said, redeemed everything. It is extraordinary that so much ignorance should exist on this subject. The fact is that, if a martyr be a man who chooses to die rather than to renounce his opinions, Cranmer was no more a martyr than Dr. Dodd. He died solely because he could not help it. He never retracted his recantation till he found he had made it in vain. The queen was fully resolved that, Catholic or Protestant, he should burn. Then he spoke out, as people generally speak out when they are at the point of death and have nothing to hope to or to fear on earth. If Mary had suffered him to live, we suspect that he would have heard mass and received absolution, like a good Catholic, till the accession of Elizabeth, and that he would then have purchased, by another apostasy, the power of burning men better and braver than himself.

We do not mean, however, to represent him as a monster of wickedness. He was not wantonly cruel or treacherous. He was merely a supple, timid, interested courtier, in times of frequent and violent change. That which has always been represented as his distinguishing virtue, the facility with which he forgave his enemies, belongs to the character. Those of his class are never vindictive, and never grateful. A present interest effaces past services and past injuries from their minds together. Their only object is self-preservation; and for this they conciliate those who wrong them, just as they abandon those who serve them. Before we extol a man for his forgiving temper, we should inquire whether he is above revenge, or below it.

Somerset, with as little principle as his coadjutor, had a firmer and more commanding mind. Of Henry, an orthodox Catholic, excepting that he chose to be his own pope, and of Elizabeth, who certainly had no objection to the theology of Rome, we need say nothing. These four persons were the great authors of the English Reformation. Three of them had a direct interest in the extension of the royal prerogative. The fourth was the ready tool of any who could frighten him. It is not difficult to see from what motives, and on what plan, such persons would be inclined to remodel the Church. The scheme was merely to rob the Babylonian enchantress of her ornaments, to transfer the full cup of her sorceries to other hands, spilling as little as possible by the way. The Catholic doctrines and rites were to be retained in the Church of England. But the king was to exercise the control which had formerly belonged to the Roman pontiff. In this Henry for a time succeeded. The extraordinary force of his character, the fortunate situation in which he stood with respect to foreign powers, and the vast resources which the suppression of the monasteries placed at his disposal, enabled him to oppress both the religious factions equally. He punished with impartial severity those who renounced the doctrines of Rome, and those who acknowledged her jurisdiction. The basis, however, on which he attempted to establish his power was too narrow to be durable. It would have been impossible even for him long to persecute both persuasions. Even under his reign there had been insurrections on the part of the Catholics, and signs of a spirit which was likely soon to produce insurrection on the part of the Protestants. It was plainly necessary, therefore, that the government should form an alliance with one or with the other side. To recognize the Papal supremacy, would have been to abandon the whole design. Reluctantly and sullenly it at last joined the Protestants. In forming this junction, its object was to procure as much aid as possible for its selfish undertaking, and to make the smallest possible concessions to the spirit of religious innovation.

From this compromise the Church of England sprung. In many respects, indeed, it has been well for her that, in an age of exuberant zeal, her principal founders were mere politicians. To this circumstance she owes her moderate articles, her decent ceremonies, her noble and pathetic liturgy. Her worship is not disfigured by mummery. Yet she has preserved, in a far greater degree than any of her Protestant sisters, that art of striking the senses and filling the imagination in which the Catholic Church so eminently excels. But, on the other hand, she continued to be, for more than a hundred and fifty years, the servile handmaid of monarchy, the steady enemy of public liberty. The divine right of kings, and the duty of passively obeying all their commands, were her favourite tenets. She held them firmly through times of oppression, persecution, and licentiousness; while law was trampled down; while judgment was perverted; while the people were eaten as though they were bread. Once, and but once,—for a moment, and but for a moment,—when her own dignity and property were touched, she forgot to practise the submission which she had taught.

Elizabeth clearly discerned the advantages which were to be derived from a close connection between the monarchy and the priesthood. At the time of her accession, indeed, she evidently meditated a partial reconciliation with Rome. And, throughout her whole life, she leaned strongly to some of the most obnoxious parts of the Catholic system. But her imperious temper, her keen sagacity, and her peculiar situation, soon led her to attach herself completely to a Church which was all her own. On the same principle on which she joined it, she attempted to drive all her people within its pale by persecution. She supported it by severe penal laws, not because she thought conformity to its discipline necessary to salvation; but because it was the fastness which arbitrary power was making strong for itself;—because she expected a more profound obedience from those who saw in her both their civil and their ecclesiastical chief, than from those who, like the Papists, ascribed spiritual authority to the Pope, or from those who, like some of the Puritans, ascribed it only to Heaven. To dissent from her establishment was to dissent from an institution founded with an express view to the maintenance and extension of the royal prerogative.

The great queen and her successors, by considering conformity and loyalty as identical, at length made them so. With respect to the Catholics, indeed, the rigour of persecution abated after her death. James soon found that they were unable to injure him, and that the animosity which the Puritan party felt towards them drove them of necessity to take refuge under his throne. During the subsequent conflict, their fault was anything but disloyalty. On the other hand, James hated the Puritans with more than the hatred of Elizabeth. Her aversion to them was political; his was personal. The sect had plagued him in Scotland, where he was weak; and he was determined to be even with them in England, where he was powerful. Persecution gradually changed a sect into a faction. That there was anything in the religious opinions of the Puritans which rendered them hostile to monarchy has never been proved to our satisfaction. After our civil contests, it became the fashion to say that Presbyterianism was connected with Republicanism; just as it has been the fashion to say, since the time of the French Revolution, that infidelity is connected with Republicanism. It is perfectly true that a Church, constituted on the Calvinistic model, will not strengthen the hands of the sovereign so much as a hierarchy which consists of several ranks, differing in dignity and emolument, and of which all the members are constantly looking to the government for promotion. But experience has clearly shown that a Calvinistic Church, like every other Church, is disaffected when it is persecuted, quiet when it is tolerated, and actively loyal when it is favoured and cherished. Scotland has had a Presbyterian establishment during a century and a half. Yet her general assembly has not, during that period, given half so much trouble to the government as the convocation of the Church of England gave to it during the thirty years which followed the Revolution. That James and Charles should have been mistaken in this point is not surprising. But we are astonished, we must confess, that men of our own time, men who have before them the proof of what toleration can effect, —men who may see with their own eyes that the Presbyterians are no such monsters when government is wise enough to let them alone, should defend the old persecutions on the ground that they were indispensable to the safety of the Church and the throne.

How persecution protects churches and thrones was soon made manifest. A systematic political opposition, vehement, daring, and inflexible, sprang from a schism about trifles altogether unconnected with the real interests of religion or of the state. Before the close of the reign of Elizabeth this opposition began to show itself. It broke forth on the question of the monopolies. Even the imperial lioness was compelled to abandon her prey, and slowly and fiercely to recede before the assailants. The spirit of liberty grew with the growing wealth and intelligence of the people. The feeble struggles and insults of James irritated instead of suppressing it; and the events which immediately followed the accession of his son portended a contest of no common severity between a king resolved to be absolute, and a people resolved to be free.

The famous proceedings of the third Parliament of Charles and the tyrannical measures which followed its dissolution are extremely well described by Mr. Hallam. No writer, we think, has shown, in so clear and satisfactory a manner, that at that time the government entertained a fixed purpose of destroying the old parliamentary constitution of England, or at least of reducing it to a mere shadow. We hasten, however, to a part of his work which, though it abounds in valuable information and in remarks well deserving to be attentively considered,—and though it is, like the rest, evidently written in a spirit of perfect impartiality, appears to us, in many points, objectionable.

We pass to the year 1640. The fate of the short Parliament held in that year clearly indicated the views of the king. That a Parliament so moderate in feeling should have met after so many years of oppression is truly wonderful. Hyde extols its loyal and conciliatory spirit. Its conduct, we are told, made the excellent Falkland in love with the very name of Parliament. We think, indeed, with Oliver St. John, that its moderation was carried too far, and that the times required sharper and more decided councils. It was for innate, however, that the king had another opportunity of showing that hatred of the liberties of his subjects which was the ruling principle of all his conduct. The sole crime of this assembly was that, meeting after a long intermission of Parliaments, and after a long series of cruelties and illegal imposts, they seemed inclined to examine grievances before they would vote supplies. For this insolence they were dissolved almost as soon as they met.

Defeat, universal agitation, financial embarrassments, disorganization in every part of the government, compelled Charles again to convene the Houses before the close of the same year. Their meeting was one of the great eras in the history of the civilized world. Whatever of political freedom exists either in Europe or in America, has sprung, directly or indirectly, from those institutions which they secured and reformed. We never turn to the annals of those times without feeling increased admiration of the patriotism, the energy, the decision, the consummate wisdom, which marked the measures of that great Parliament, from the day on which it met to the commencement of civil hostilities.

The impeachment of Strafford was the first, and perhaps the greatest blow. The whole conduct of that celebrated man proved that he had formed a deliberate scheme to subvert the fundamental laws of England. Those parts of his correspondence which have been brought to light since his death place the matter beyond a doubt. One of his admirers has, indeed, offered to show "that the passages which Mr. Hallam has invidiously extracted from the correspondence between Laud and Strafford, as proving their design to introduce a thorough tyranny, refer not to any such design, but to a thorough reform in the affairs of state, and the thorough maintenance of just authority." We will recommend two or three of these passages to the especial notice of our readers.

All who know anything of those times know that the conduct of Hampden in the affair of the Ship-money met with the warm approbation of every respectable Royalist in England. It drew forth the ardent eulogies of the champions of the prerogative and even of the Crown lawyers themselves. Clarendon allows his demeanour through the whole proceeding to have been such that even those who watched for an occasion against the defender of the people were compelled to acknowledge themselves unable to find any fault in him. That he was right in the point of law is now universally admitted. Even had it been otherwise, he had a fair case. Five of the judges, servile as our courts then were, pronounced in his favour. The majority against him was the smallest possible. In no country retaining the slightest vestige of constitutional liberty can a modest and decent appeal to the laws be treated as a crime. Strafford, however, recommends that, for taking the sense of a legal tribunal on a legal question, Hampden should be punished, and punished severely, "whipt," says the insolent apostate, "whipt into his senses. If the rod," he adds, "be so used that it smarts not, I am the more sorry." This is the maintenance of just authority.

In civilized nations, the most arbitrary governments have generally suffered justice to have a free course in private suits. Strafford wished to make every cause in every court subject to the royal prerogative. He complained that in Ireland he was not permitted to meddle in cases between party and party. "I know very well," says he, "that the common lawyers will be passionately against it, who are wont to put such a prejudice upon all other professions, as if none were to be trusted or capable to administer justice, but themselves; yet how well this suits with monarchy, when they monopolise all to be governed by their year-books, you in England have a costly example." We are really curious to know by what arguments it is to be proved that the power of interfering in the law-suits of individuals is part of the just authority of the executive government.

It is not strange that a man so careless of the common civil rights, which even despots have generally respected, should treat with scorn the limitations which the Constitution imposes on the royal prerogative. We might quote pages: but we will content ourselves with a single specimen:—"The debts of the Crown being taken off, *you may govern as you please*; and most resolute I am that may be done without borrowing any help forth of the king's lodgings."

Such was the theory of that thorough reform in the state which Strafford meditated. His whole practice, from the day on which he sold himself to the court, was in strict conformity to his theory. For his accomplices various excuses may be urged, ignorance, imbecility, religious bigotry. But Wentworth had no such plea. His intellect was capacious. His early prepossessions were on the side of popular rights. He knew the whole beauty and value of the system which he attempted to deface. He was the first of the Rats,—the first of those statesmen whose patriotism has been only the coquetry of political prostitution, and whose profligacy has taught governments to adopt the old maxim of the slave-market, that it is cheaper to buy than to breed, to import defenders from an opposition than to rear them in a ministry. He was the first Englishman to whom a peerage was not an addition of honour, but a sacrament of infamy—a baptism into the communion of corruption. As he was the earliest of the hateful list, so was he also by far the greatest;—eloquent, sagacious, adventurous, intrepid, ready of invention, immutable of purpose, in every talent which exalts or destroys nations pre-eminent, the lost Archangel, the Satan of the apostasy. The title for which, at the time of his desertion, he exchanged a name honourably distinguished in the cause of the people, reminds us of the appellation which, from the moment of the first treason, fixed itself on the fallen Son of the Morning,

"———; so call him now.—His former name
Is heard no more in heaven."

The defection of Strafford from the popular party contributed mainly to draw on him the hatred of his contemporaries. It has since made him an object of peculiar interest to those whose lives have been spent, like his, in proving that there is no malice like the malice of a renegade. Nothing can be more natural or becoming than that one turncoat should eulogise another.

Many enemies of public liberty have been distinguished by their private virtues. But Strafford was the same throughout. As was the statesman, such was the kinsman, and such the lover. His conduct towards Lord Mountmorris is recorded by Clarendon. For a word which can scarcely be called rash, which could not have been made the subject of an ordinary civil action, he dragged a man of high rank, married to a relative of that saint about whom he whimpered to the Peers, before a tribunal of slaves. Sentence of death was passed. Everything but death was inflicted. Yet the treatment which Lord Ely experienced was still more scandalous. That nobleman was thrown into prison, in order to compel him to settle his estate in a manner agreeable to his daughter-in-law, whom, as there is every reason to believe, Strafford had debauched. These stories do not rest on vague report. The historians most partial to the minister admit their truth, and censure them in terms which, though too lenient for the occasion, are still severe. These facts are alone sufficient to justify the appellation with which Pym branded him:— "the wicked Earl."

In spite of all his vices, in spite of all his dangerous projects, Strafford was certainly entitled to the benefit of the law;—but of the law in all its rigour; of the law according to the utmost strictness of the letter, which killeth. He was not to be torn in pieces by a mob, or stabbed in the back by an assassin. He was not to have punishment meted out to him from his own iniquitous measure. But if justice, in the whole range of its wide armoury, contained one weapon which could pierce him, that weapon his pursuers were bound, before god and man, to employ.

> "If he may
> Find mercy in the law, 'tis his; if none,
> Let him not seek't of us."

Such was the language which the Parliament might justly use.

Did, then, the articles against Strafford strictly amount to high treason? Many people, who know neither what the articles were nor what high treason is, will answer in the negative, simply because the accused person, speaking for his life, took that ground of defence. The journals of the Lords show that the judges were consulted. They answered, with one accord, that the articles on which the earl was convicted amounted to high treason. This judicial opinion, even if we suppose it to have been erroneous, goes far to justify the Parliament. The judgment pronounced in the Exchequer Chamber has always been urged by the apologists of Charles in defence of his conduct respecting Ship-money. Yet on that occasion there was but a bare majority in favour of the party at whose pleasure all the magistrates composing the tribunal were removable. The decision in the case of Strafford was unanimous; as far as we can judge, it was unbiassed; and though there may be room for hesitation, we think on the whole that it was reasonable. "It may be remarked," says Mr. Hallam, "that the fifteenth article of the impeachment, charging Strafford with raising money by his own authority, and quartering troops on the people of Ireland in order to compel their obedience to his unlawful requisitions, upon which, and upon one other article, not upon the whole matter, the Peers voted him guilty, does, at least, approach very nearly, if we may not say more, to a substantive treason within the statute of Edward III., as a levying of war against the king." This most sound and just exposition has provoked a very ridiculous reply. "It should seem to be an Irish construction this," says an assailant of Mr. Hallam, "which makes the raising money for the king's service, with his knowledge, and by his approbation, to come under the head of levying war on the king, and therefore to be high treason." Now, people who undertake to write on points of constitutional law should know what every attorney's clerk and every forward schoolboy on an upper form knows, that by a fundamental maxim of our polity, the king can do no wrong; that every court is bound to suppose his conduct and his sentiments to be, on every occasion, such as they ought to be, and that no evidence can be received for the purpose of setting aside this loyal and salutary presumption. The Lords, therefore, were bound to take it for granted that the king considered arms which were unlawfully directed against his people, as directed against his own throne.

The remarks of Mr. Hallam on the bill of attainder, though, as usual, weighty and acute, do not perfectly satisfy us. He defends the principle, but objects to the severity of the punishment. That on great emergencies, the State may justifiably pass a retrospective act against an offender, we have no doubt whatever. We are acquainted with only one argument on the other side, which has in it enough of reason to bear an answer. Warning, it is said, is the end of punishment. But a punishment inflicted, not by a general rule, but by an arbitrary discretion, cannot serve the purpose of a warning; it is, therefore, useless, and useless pain ought not to be inflicted. This sophism has found its way into several books on penal legislation. It admits, however, of a very simple refutation. In the first place, punishments *ex post facto* are not altogether useless even as warnings. They are warnings to a particular class which stand in great need of warnings, to favourites and ministers. They remind persons of this description that there may be a day of reckoning for those who ruin and enslave their country in all the forms of law. But this is not all. Warning is, in ordinary cases, the principal end of punishment; but it is not the only end. To remove the offender, to preserve society from those dangers which are to be apprehended from his incorrigible depravity, is often one of the ends. In the case of such a knave as Wild, or such a ruffian as Thurtell, it is a very important end. In the case of a powerful and wicked statesman it is infinitely more important; so important as alone to justify the utmost severity, even though it were certain that his fate would not deter others from imitating his example. At present, indeed, we should think it extremely pernicious to take such a course, even with a worse minister than Strafford—if a worse could exist; for, at present, Parliament has only to withhold its support from a Cabinet to produce an immediate change of hands. The case was widely different in the reign of Charles I. That prince had governed during eleven years without any Parliament; and, even when Parliament was sitting, had supported Buckingham against its most violent remonstrances.

Mr. Hallam is of opinion that a bill of pains and penalties ought to have been passed against Strafford; but he draws a distinction less just, we think, than his distinctions usually are. His opinion, so far as we can collect it, is this—that there are almost insurmountable objections to retrospective laws for capital punishment; but that, where the punishment stops short of death, the objections are comparatively trifling. Now, the practice of taking the severity of the penalty into consideration, when the question is about the mode of procedure and the rules of evidence, is no doubt sufficiently common. We often see a man convicted of a simple larceny on evidence on which he would not be convicted of a burglary. It sometimes happens that a jury, when there is strong suspicion, but not absolute demonstration, that an act, unquestionably amounting to murder, was committed by the prisoner before them, will find him guilty of manslaughter, but this is surely very irrational. The rules of evidence no more depend on the magnitude of the interests at stake than the rules of arithmetic. We might as well say that we have a greater chance of throwing a size when we are playing for a penny than when we are playing for a thousand pounds, as that a form of trial which is sufficient for the purposes of justice, in a matter affecting liberty and property, is insufficient in a matter affecting life. Nay, if a mode of proceeding be too lax for capital cases, it is, *à fortiori*, too lax for all others; for, in capital cases, the principles of human nature will always afford considerable security. No judge is so cruel as he who indemnifies himself for scrupulosity in cases of blood by licence in affairs of smaller importance. The difference in tale on the one side far more than makes up for the difference in weight on the other.

If there be any universal objection to retrospective punishment, there is no more to be said. But such is not the opinion of Mr. Hallam. He approves of the mode of proceeding. He thinks that a punishment, not previously affixed by law to the offences of Strafford, should have been inflicted; that he should have been degraded from his rank, and condemned to perpetual banishment by act of Parliament; but he sees strong objections to the taking away of his life. Our difficulty would have been at the first step, and there only. Indeed, we can scarcely conceive that any case which does not call for capital punishment, can call for retrospective punishment. We can scarcely conceive a man so wicked and so dangerous that the whole course of law must be disturbed in order to reach him; yet not so wicked as to deserve the severest sentence, nor so dangerous as to require the last and surest custody —that of the grave. If we had thought that Strafford might be safely suffered to live in France, we should have thought it better that he should continue to live in England than that he should be exiled by a special act. As to degradation, it was not the earl, but the general and the statesman, whom the people had to fear. Essex said on that occasion, with more truth than eloquence, "Stone-dead hath no fellow." And often during the civil wars the Parliament had reason to rejoice that an irreversible law and an impassable barrier protected them from the valour and capacity of Strafford.

It is remarkable that neither Hyde nor Falkland voted against the bill of attainder. There is, indeed, reason to believe that Falkland spoke in favour of it. In one respect, as Mr. Hallam has observed, the proceeding was honourably distinguished from others of the same kind. An act was passed to relieve the children of Strafford from the forfeiture and corruption of blood which were the legal consequences of the sentence. The Crown had never shown equal generosity in a case of treason. The liberal conduct of the Commons has been fully and most appropriately repaid. The house of Wentworth has since that time been as much distinguished by public spirit as by power and splendour, and may at the present moment boast of members with whom Say and Hampden would have been proud to act.

It is somewhat curious that the admirers of Strafford should also be, without a single exception, the admirers of Charles; for, whatever we may think of the conduct of the Parliament towards the unhappy favourite, there can be no doubt that the treatment which he received from his master was disgraceful. Faithless alike to his people and to his tools, the king did not scruple to play the part of the cowardly approver, who hangs his accomplice. It is good that there should be such men as Charles in every league of villainy. It is for such men that the offer of pardon and reward which appears after a murder is intended. They are indemnified, remunerated, and despised. The very magistrate who avails himself of their assistance looks on them as wretches more degraded than the criminal whom they betray. Was Strafford innocent? was he a meritorious servant of the Crown? If so, what shall we think of the prince who, having solemnly promised him that not a hair of his head should be hurt, and possessing an unquestioned constitutional right to save him, gave him up to the vengeance of his enemies? There were some points which we know that Charles would not concede, and for which he was willing to risk the chances of civil war. Ought not a king, who will make a stand for anything, to make a stand for the innocent blood? Was Strafford guilty? Even on this supposition, it is difficult not to feel disdain for the partner of his guilt, the tempter turned punisher. If, indeed, from that time forth, the conduct of Charles had been blameless, it might have been said that his eyes were at last opened to the errors of his former conduct, and that, in sacrificing to the wishes of his Parliament a minister whose crime had been a devotion too zealous to the interests of his prerogative, he gave a painful and deeply humiliating proof of the sincerity of his repentance. We may describe his behaviour on this occasion in terms resembling those which Hume has employed when speaking of the conduct of Churchill at the Revolution. It acquired ever after the most rigid justice and sincerity in his dealings with his people to vindicate it. His subsequent dealings with his people, however, clearly showed, that it was not from any respect for the Constitution, or from any sense of the deep criminality of the plans in which Strafford and himself had been engaged, that he gave up his minister to the axe. It became evident that he had abandoned a servant who, deeply guilty as to all others, was guiltless to him alone, solely in order to gain time for maturing other schemes of tyranny, and purchasing the aid of other Wentworths. He, who would not avail himself of the power which the laws gave him to save a friend to whom his honour was pledged, soon showed that he did not scruple to break every law and forfeit every pledge in order to work the ruin of his opponents.

"Put not your trust in princes!" was the expression of the fallen minister, when he heard that Charles had consented to his death. The whole history of the times is a sermon on that bitter text. The defence of the Long Parliament is comprised in the dying words of its victim.

The early measures of that Parliament Mr. Hallam in general approves. But he considers the proceedings which took place after the recess in the summer of 1641 as mischievous and violent. He thinks that, from that time, the demands of the Houses were not warranted by any imminent danger to the Constitution, and that in the war which ensued they were clearly the aggressors. As this is one of the most interesting questions in our history, we will venture to state, at some length, the reasons which have led us to form an opinion on it contrary to that of a writer whose judgment we so highly respect.

We will premise that we think worse of King Charles I. than even Mr. Hallam appears to do. The fixed hatred of liberty which was the principle of the king's public conduct, the unscrupulousness with which he adopted any means which might enable him to attain his ends; the readiness with which he gave promises, the impudence with which he broke them, the cruel indifference with which he threw away his useless or damaged tools, rendered him—at least till his character was fully exposed and his power shaken to its foundations,—a more dangerous enemy to the Constitution than a man of far greater talents and resolution might have been. Such princes may still be seen,—the scandals of the southern thrones of Europe;—princes false alike to the accomplices who have served them and to the opponents who have spared them;—princes who, in the hour of danger, concede everything, swear everything,—hold out their cheeks to every smiter,—give up to punishment every minister of their tyranny, and await with meek and smiling implacability the blessed day of perjury and proscription.

We will pass by the instances of oppression and falsehood which disgraced the early part of the reign of Charles. We will leave out of the question the whole history of his third Parliament,—the price which he exacted for assenting to the Petition of Right,—the perfidy with which he violated his engagements,—the death of Eliot,—the barbarous punishments inflicted by the Star Chamber,—the Ship-money, and all the measures now universally condemned, which disgraced his administration from 1630 to 1640. We will admit that it might be the duty of the Parliament, after punishing the most guilty of his creatures,—after abolishing the inquisitorial tribunals which had been the instruments of his tyranny,—after reversing the unjust sentences of his victims, to pause in its course. The concessions which had been made were great, the evils of civil war obvious—the advantages even of victory doubtful. The former errors of the king might be imputed to youth,—to the pressure of circumstances,—to the influence of evil counsel,—to the undefined state of the law. We firmly believe that, if even at this eleventh hour, Charles had acted fairly towards his people, if he had even acted fairly towards his own partisans, the House of Commons would have given him a fair chance of retrieving the public confidence. Such was the opinion of Clarendon. He distinctly states that the fury of opposition had abated,—that a reaction had begun to take place,—that the majority of those who had taken part against the king were desirous of an honourable and complete reconciliation, and that the more violent, or, as it soon appeared, the more judicious members of the party, were fast declining in credit. The remonstrance had been carried with great difficulty. The uncompromising antagonists of the court, such as Cromwell, had begun to talk of selling their estates and leaving England. The event soon showed that they were the only men who really understood how much inhumanity and fraud lay hid under the constitutional language and gracious demeanour of the king.

The attempt to seize the five members was undoubtedly the real cause of the war. From that moment the loyal confidence with which most of the popular party were beginning to regard the king was turned into hatred and incurable suspicion. From that moment the Parliament was compelled to surround itself with defensive arms;—from that moment the city assumed the appearance of a garrison;—from that moment it was that, in the phrase of Clarendon, the carriage of Hampden became fiercer, that he drew the sword and threw away the scabbard. For, from that moment, it must have been evident to every impartial observer, that in the midst of professions, oaths, and smiles, the tyrant was constantly looking forward to an absolute sway and to a bloody revenge.

The advocates of Charles have very dexterously contrived to conceal from their readers the real nature of this transaction. By making concessions apparently candid and ample, they elude the great accusation. They allow that the measure was weak and even frantic,—an absurd caprice of Lord Digby, absurdly adopted by the king. And thus they save their client from the full penalty of his transgression, by entering a plea of guilty to the minor offence. To us his conduct appears at this day as at the time it appeared to the Parliament and the city. We think it by no means so foolish as it pleases his friends to represent it, and far more wicked.

In the first place, the transaction was illegal from beginning to end. The impeachment was illegal. The process was illegal. The service was illegal. If Charles wished to prosecute the five members for treason, a bill against them should have been sent to a grand jury. That a commoner cannot be tried for high treason by the Lords, at the suit of the Crown, is part of the very alphabet of our law. That no man can be arrested by a message or verbal summons of the king, with or without a warrant from a responsible magistrate, is equally clear. This was an established maxim of our jurisprudence in the time of Edward IV. "A subject," said Chief Justice Markham to that prince, "may arrest for treason: the king cannot; for, if the arrest be illegal, the party has no remedy against the king."

The time at which Charles took this step also deserves consideration. We have already said that the ardour which the Parliament had displayed at the time of its first meeting had considerably abated, that the leading opponents of the Court were desponding, and that their followers were in general inclined to milder and more temperate measures than those which had hitherto been pursued. In every country, and in none more than in England, there is a disposition to take the part of those who are unmercifully run down and who seem destitute of all means of defence. Every man who has observed the ebb and flow of public feeling in our own time will easily recall examples to illustrate this remark. An English statesman ought to pay assiduous worship to Nemesis,—to be most apprehensive of ruin when he is at the height of power and popularity, and to dread his enemy most when most completely prostrated. The fate of the coalition ministry of 1784 is perhaps the strongest instance in our history of the operation of this principle. A few weeks turned the ablest and most extended ministry that ever existed into a feeble opposition, and raised a king who was talking of retiring to Hanover, to a height of power which none of his predecessors had enjoyed since the Revolution. A crisis of this description was evidently approaching in 1642. At such a crisis a prince of a really honest and generous nature, who had erred, who had seen his error, who had regretted the lost affections of his people, who rejoiced in the dawning hope of regaining them, would be peculiarly careful to take no step which could give occasion of offence, even to the unreasonable. On the other hand, a tyrant, whose whole life was a lie, who hated the Constitution the more because he had been compelled to feign respect for it, and to whom his honour and the love of his people were as nothing, would select such a crisis for some appalling violation of law, for some stroke which might remove the chiefs of an opposition, and intimidate the herd. This Charles attempted. He missed his blow;—but so narrowly that it would have been mere madness in those at whom it was aimed to trust him again.

It deserves to be remarked that the king had, a short time before, promised the most respectable Royalists in the house of Commons, Falkland, Colepepper, and Hyde, that he would take no measure in which that House was concerned, without consulting them. On this occasion he did not consult them. His conduct astonished them more than any other members of the Assembly. Clarendon says that they were deeply hurt by this want of confidence, and the more hurt, because, if they had been consulted, they would have done their utmost to dissuade Charles from so improper a proceeding. Did it never occur to Clarendon,—will it not at least occur to men less partial,—that there was good reason for this? When the danger to the throne seemed imminent, the king was ready to put himself for a time into the hands of those who, though they disapproved of his past conduct, thought that the remedies had now become worse than the distempers. But we believe that in his heart he regarded both the parties in the Parliament with feelings of aversion which differed only in the degree of their intensity, and that the awful warning which he proposed to give, by immolating the principal supporters of the remonstrance, was partly intended for the instruction of those who had concurred in censuring the Ship-money and in abolishing the Star Chamber.

The Commons informed the king that their members should be forthcoming to answer any charge legally brought against them. The Lords refused to assume the unconstitutional office with which he attempted to invest them. And what was then his conduct? He went, attended by hundreds of armed men, to seize the objects of his hatred in the House itself. The party opposed to him more than insinuated that his purpose was of the most atrocious kind. We will not condemn him merely on their suspicions. We will not hold him answerable for the sanguinary expressions of the loose brawlers who composed his train. We will judge of his act by itself alone. And we say, without hesitation, that it is impossible to acquit him of having meditated violence, and violence which might probably end in blood. He knew that the legality of his proceedings was denied; he must have known that some of the accused members were not men likely to submit peaceably to an illegal arrest. There was every reason to expect that he would find them in their places, that they would refuse to obey his summons, and that the House would support them in their refusal. What course would then have been left to him? Unless we suppose that he went on this expedition for the sole purpose of making himself ridiculous, we must believe that he would have had recourse to force. There would have been a scuffle; and it might not, under such circumstances, have been in his power, even if it had been in his inclination, to prevent a scuffle from ending in a massacre. Fortunately for his fame, unfortunately, perhaps, for what he prized far more, the interests of his hatred and his ambition, the affair ended differently. The birds, as he said, were flown, and his plan was disconcerted. Posterity is not extreme to mark abortive crimes; and thus the king's advocates have found it easy to represent a step which, but for a trivial accident, might have filled England with mourning and dismay, as a mere error of judgment, wild and foolish, but perfectly innocent. Such was not, however, at the time, the opinion of any party. The most zealous Royalists were so much disgusted and ashamed that they suspended their opposition to the popular party, and, silently at least, concurred in measures of precaution so strong as almost to amount to resistance.

From that day, whatever of confidence and loyal attachment had survived the misrule of seventeen years was, in the great body of the people, extinguished, and extinguished for ever. As soon as the outrage had failed, the hypocrisy recommenced. Down to the very eve of this flagitious attempt, Charles had been talking of his respect for the privileges of Parliament and the liberties of his people. He began again in the same style on the morrow; but it was too late. To trust him now would have been, not moderation, but insanity. What common security would suffice against a prince who was evidently watching his season with that cold and patient hatred which, in the long run, tires out every other passion?

It is certainly from no admiration of Charles that Mr. Hallam disapproves of the conduct of the Houses in resorting to arms. But he thinks that any attempt on the part of that prince to establish a despotism would have been as strongly opposed by his adherents as by his enemies, and that therefore the Constitution might be considered as out of danger, or, at least, that it had more to apprehend from the war than from the king. On this subject Mr. Hallam dilates at length, and with conspicuous ability. We will offer a few considerations which lead us to incline to a different opinion.

The Constitution of England was only one of a large family. In all the monarchies of western Europe, during the middle ages, there existed restraints on the royal authority, fundamental laws, and representative assemblies. In the fifteenth century the government of Castile seems to have been as free as that of our own country. That of Arragon was beyond all question more so. In France the sovereign was more absolute. Yet, even in France, the States-General alone could constitutionally impose taxes; and, at the very time when the authority of those assemblies was beginning to languish, the Parliament of Paris received such an accession of strength as enabled it, in some measure, to perform the functions of a legislative assembly. Sweden and Denmark had constitutions of a similar description.

Let us overleap two or three hundred years, and contemplate Europe at the commencement of the eighteenth century. Every free constitution, save one, had gone down. That of England had weathered the danger, and was riding in full security. In Denmark and Sweden the kings had availed themselves of the disputes which raged between the nobles and the commons, to unite all the powers of government in their own hands. In France the institution of the States was only mentioned by lawyers as a part of the ancient theory of their government. It slept a deep sleep, destined to be broken by a tremendous waking. No person remembered the sittings of the three orders, or expected ever to see them renewed. Louis the Fourteenth had imposed on his Parliament a patient silence of sixty years. His grandson, after the War of the Spanish Succession, assimilated the constitution of Arragon to that of Castile and extinguished the last feeble remains of liberty in the Peninsula.

In England, on the other hand, the Parliament was infinitely more powerful than it had ever been. Not only was its legislative authority fully established; but its right to interfere, by advice almost equivalent to command, in every department of the executive government, was recognized. The appointment of ministers, the relations with foreign powers, the conduct of a war or a negotiation, depended less on the pleasure of the prince than on that of the two Houses.

What then made us to differ? Why was it that, in that epidemic malady of constitutions, ours escaped the destroying influence; or rather that, at the very crisis of the disease, a favourable turn took place in England, and in England alone? It was not surely without a cause that so many kindred systems of government, having flourished together so long, languished and expired at almost the same time.

It is the fashion to say, that the progress of civilization is favourable to liberty. The maxim, though on the whole true, must be limited by many qualifications and exceptions. Wherever a poor and rude nation, in which the form of government is a limited monarchy, receives a great accession of wealth and knowledge, it is in imminent danger of falling under arbitrary power.

In such a state of society as that which existed all over Europe during the middle ages it was not from the king but from the nobles that there was danger. Very slight checks sufficed to keep the sovereign in order. His means of corruption and intimidation were scanty. He had little money, little patronage,—no military establishment. His armies resembled juries. They were drafted out of the mass of the people: they soon returned to it again: and the character which was habitual prevailed over that which was occasional. A campaign of forty days was too short, the discipline of a national militia too lax, to efface from their minds the feelings of civil life. As they carried to the camp the sentiments and interests of the farm and the shop, so they carried back to the farm and the shop the military accomplishments which they had acquired in the camp. At home the soldier learned how to value his rights—abroad how to defend them.

Such a military force as this was a far stronger restraint on the regal power than any legislative assembly. Resistance to an established government, in modern times so difficult and perilous an enterprise, was, in the fourteenth and fifteenth centuries the simplest and easiest matter in the world. Indeed, it was far too simple and easy. An insurrection was got up then almost as easily as a petition is got up now. In a popular cause, or even in an unpopular cause, favoured by a few great nobles, a force of ten thousand armed men was raised in a week. If the king were, like our Edward II. and Richard II., generally odious, he could not procure a single bow or halbert. He fell at once and without an effort. In such times a sovereign like Louis the Fifteenth or the Emperor Paul, would have been pulled down before his misgovernment had lasted for a month. We find that all the fame and influence of our Edward III. could not save his Madame de Pompadour from the effects of the public hatred.

Hume and many other writers have hastily concluded that, in the fifteenth century, the English Parliament was altogether servile, because it recognized, without opposition, every successful usurper. That it was not servile, its conduct on many occasions of inferior importance is sufficient to prove. But surely it was not strange that the majority of the nobles, and of the deputies chosen by the commons, should approve of revolutions which the nobles and commons had effected. The Parliament did not blindly follow the event of war, but participated in those changes of public sentiment on which the event of war depended. The legal check was secondary and auxiliary to that which the nation held in its own hands. There have always been monarchies in Asia in which the royal authority has been tempered by fundamental laws, though no legislative body exists to watch over them. The guarantee is the opinion of a community of which every individual is a soldier. Thus, the king of Cabul, as Mr. Elphinstone informs us, cannot augment the land revenue, or interfere with the jurisdiction of the ordinary tribunals.

In the European kingdoms of this description there were representative assemblies. But it was not necessary, that those assemblies should meet very frequently, that they should interfere with all the operations of the executive government, that they should watch with jealousy, and resent with prompt indignation, every violation of the laws which the sovereign might commit. They were so strong that they might safely be careless. He was so feeble that he might safely be suffered to encroach. If he ventured too far, chastisement and ruin were at hand. In fact, the people suffered more from his weakness than from his authority. The tyranny of wealthy and powerful subjects was the characteristic evil of the times. The royal prerogatives were not even sufficient for the defence of property and the maintenance of police.

The progress of civilization introduced a great change. War became a science, and, as a necessary consequence, a separate trade. The great body of the people grew every day more reluctant to undergo the inconveniences of military service, and better able to pay others for undergoing them. A new class of men, therefore, dependent on the Crown alone, natural enemies of those popular rights which are to them as the dew to the fleece of Gideon—slaves among freemen—freemen among slaves—grew into importance. That physical force, which in the dark ages, had belonged to the nobles and the commons, and had, far more than any charter or any assembly, been the safeguard of their privileges, was transferred entire to the king. Monarchy gained in two ways. The sovereign was strengthened, the subjects weakened. The great mass of the population, destitute of all military discipline and organization, ceased to exercise any influence by force on political transactions. There have, indeed, during the last hundred and fifty years, been many popular insurrections in Europe; but all have failed, except those in which the regular army has been induced to join the disaffected.

Those legal checks which had been adequate to the purpose for which they were designed while the sovereign remained dependant on his subjects were now found wanting. The dikes which had been sufficient while the waters were low were not high enough to keep out the spring-tide. The deluge passed over them; and according to the exquisite illustration of Butler, the formal boundaries which had excluded it, now held it in. The old constitutions fared like the old shields and coats of mail. They were the defences of a rude age; and they did well enough against the weapons of a rude age. But new and more formidable means of destruction were invented. The ancient panoply became useless; and it was thrown aside to rust in lumber-rooms, or exhibited only as part of an idle pageant.

Thus absolute monarchy was established on the Continent. England escaped; but she escaped very narrowly. Happily our insular situation, and the pacific policy of James, rendered standing armies unnecessary here, till they had been for some time kept up in the neighbouring kingdoms. Our public men had, therefore, an opportunity of watching the effects produced by this momentous change in form of governments which bore a close analogy to that established in England. Everywhere they saw the power of the monarch increasing, the resistance of assemblies which were no longer supported by a national force gradually becoming more and more feeble, and at length altogether ceasing. The friends and the enemies of liberty perceived with equal clearness the causes of this general decay. It is a favourite theme of Strafford. He advises the king to procure from the judges a recognition of his right to raise an army at his pleasure. "This place well fortified," says he, "for ever vindicates the monarchy at home from under the conditions and restraints of subjects." We firmly believe that he was in the right. Nay; we believe that, even if no deliberate scheme of arbitrary government had been formed by the sovereign and his ministers, there was great reason to apprehend a natural extinction of the Constitution. If, for example, Charles had played the part of Gustavus Adolphus—if he had carried on a popular war for the defence of the Protestant cause in Germany—if he had gratified the national pride by a series of victories—if he had formed an army of forty or fifty thousand devoted soldiers,—we do not see what chance the nation would have had of escaping from despotism. The judges would have given as strong a decision in favour of Camp-money as they gave in favour of Ship-money. If they had scrupled it would have made little difference. An individual who resisted would have been treated as Charles treated Eliot, and as Strafford wished to treat Hampden. The Parliament might have been summoned once in twenty years, to congratulate a king on his accession, or to give solemnity to some great measure of state. Such had been the fate of legislative assemblies as powerful, as much respected, as high-spirited, as the English Lords and Commons.

The two Houses, surrounded by the ruins of so many free constitutions overthrown or sapped by the new military system, were required to intrust the command of an army, and the conduct of the Irish war to a king who had proposed to himself the destruction of liberty as the great end of his policy. We are decidedly of opinion that it would have been fatal to comply. Many of those who took the side of the king on this question would have cursed their own loyalty, if they had seen him return from war at the head of twenty thousand troops, accustomed to carnage and free quarters in Ireland.

We think, with Mr. Hallam, that many of the Royalist nobility and gentry were true friends to the Constitution, and that, but for the solemn protestations by which the king bound himself to govern according to the law for the future, they never would have joined his standard. But surely they underrated the public danger. Falkland is commonly selected as the most respectable specimen of this class. He was indeed a man of great talents and of great virtues; but, we apprehend, infinitely too fastidious for public life. He did not perceive that, in such times as those on which his lot had fallen, the duty of a statesman is to choose the better cause and to stand by it, in spite of those excesses by which every cause, however good in itself, will be disgraced. The present evil always seemed to him the worst. He was always going backward and forward; but it should be remembered to his honour that it was always from the stronger to the weaker side that he deserted. While Charles was oppressing the people, Falkland was a resolute champion of liberty. He attacked Strafford. He even concurred in strong measures against Episcopacy. But the violence of his party annoyed him, and drove him to the other party, to be equally annoyed there. Dreading the success of the cause which he had espoused, sickened by the courtiers of Oxford, as he had been sickened by the patriots of Westminster, yet bound by honour not to abandon them, he pined away, neglected his person, went about moaning for peace, and at last rushed desperately on death, as the best refuge in such miserable times. If he had lived through the scenes that followed, we have little doubt that he would have condemned himself to share the exile and beggary of the royal family; that he would then have returned to oppose all their measures; that he would have been sent to the Tower by the Commons as a disbeliever in the Popish Plot, and by the king as an accomplice in the Rye-House Plot; and that, if he had escaped being hanged, first by Scroggs, and then by Jefferies, he would, after manfully opposing James II. through his whole reign, have been seized with a fit of compassion at the very moment of the Revolution, have voted for a regency, and died a non-juror.

We do not dispute that the royal party contained many excellent men and excellent citizens. But this we say,—that they did not discern those times. The peculiar glory of the Houses of Parliament is that, in the great plague and mortality of constitution, they took their stand between the living and the dead. At the very crisis of our destiny, at the very moment when the fate which had passed on every other nation was about to pass on England, they arrested the danger.

Those who conceive that the parliamentary leaders were desirous merely to maintain the old constitution and those who represent them as conspiring to subvert it are equally in error. The old constitution, as we have attempted to show, could not be maintained. The progress of time, the increase of wealth, the diffusion of knowledge, the great change in the European system of war, rendered it impossible that any of the monarchies of the middle ages should continue to exist on the old footing. The prerogative of the Crown was constantly advancing. If the privileges of the people were to remain absolutely stationary, they would relatively retrograde. The monarchical and democratical parts of the government were placed in a situation not unlike that of the two brothers in the Fairy Queen, one of whom saw the soil of his inheritance daily washed away by the tide and joined to that of his rival. The portions had at first been fairly meted out. By a natural and constant transfer, the one had been extended: the other had dwindled to nothing. A new partition, or a compensation, was necessary to restore the original equality.

It was now absolutely necessary to violate the formal part of the constitution, in order to preserve its spirit. This might have been done, as it was done at the Revolution, by expelling the reigning family, and calling to the throne princes who, relying solely on an elective title, would find it necessary to respect the privileges and follow the advice of the assemblies to which they owed everything, to pass every bill which the Legislature strongly pressed upon them, and to fill the offices of state with men in whom it confided. But, as the two Houses did not choose to change the dynasty, it was necessary that they should do directly what at the Revolution was done indirectly. Nothing is more usual than to hear it said that, if the Long Parliament had contented itself with making such a reform in the government under Charles as was afterwards made under William, it would have had the highest claim to national gratitude; and that in its violence it overshot the mark. But how was it possible to make such a settlement under Charles? Charles was not, like William and the princes of the Hanoverian line, bound by community of interests and dangers to the two Houses. It was, therefore, necessary that he should be bound by treaty and statute.

Mr. Hallam reprobates, in language which has a little surprised us, the nineteen propositions into which the Parliament digested its scheme. We will ask him whether he does not think that if James II. had remained in the island, and had been suffered,—as he probably would in that case have been suffered—to keep his crown, conditions to the full as hard would have been imposed on him? On the other hand, if the Long Parliament had pronounced the departure of Charles from London an abdication, and had called Essex or Northumberland to the throne, the new prince might have safely been suffered to reign without such restrictions. His situation would have been a sufficient guarantee. In the nineteen propositions we see very little to blame except the articles against the Catholics. These, however, were in the spirit of that age; and to some sturdy churchmen in our own they may seem to palliate even the good which the Long Parliament effected. The regulation with respect to new creations of peers is the only other article about which we entertain any doubt.

One of the propositions is that the judges shall hold their offices during good behaviour. To this surely no exception will be taken. The right of directing the education and marriage of the princes was most properly claimed by the Parliament, on the same ground on which, after the Revolution, it was enacted that no king, on pain of forfeiting his throne, should espouse a Papist. Unless we condemn the statesmen of the Revolution, who conceived that England could not safely be governed by a sovereign married to a Catholic queen, we can scarcely condemn the Long Parliament because, having a sovereign so situated, they thought it necessary to place him under strict restraints. The influence of Henrietta Maria had already been deeply felt in political affairs. In the regulation of her family, in the education and marriage of her children, it was still more likely to be felt. There might be another Catholic queen; possibly, a Catholic king. Little as we are disposed to join in the vulgar clamour on this subject, we think that such an event ought to be, if possible, averted; and this could only be done, if Charles was to be left on the throne, by placing his domestic arrangements under the control of Parliament.

A veto on the appointment of ministers was demanded. But this veto Parliament has virtually possessed ever since the Revolution. It is no doubt very far better that this power of the Legislature should be exercised as it is now exercised, when any great occasion calls for interference, than that at every change it should have to signify its approbation or disapprobation in form. But, unless a new family had been placed on the throne, we do not see how this power could have been exercised as it is now exercised. We again repeat that no restraints which could be imposed on the princes who reigned after the Revolution could have added to the security which their title afforded. They were compelled to court their Parliaments. But from Charles nothing was to be expected which was not set down in the bond.

It was not stipulated that the king should give up his negative on acts of Parliament. But the Commons had certainly shown a strong disposition to exact this security also. "Such a doctrine," says Mr. Hallam, "was in this country as repugnant to the whole history of our laws as it was incompatible with the subsistence of the monarchy in anything more than a nominal preeminence." Now this article has been as completely carried into effect by the Revolution as if it had been formally inserted in the Bill of Rights and the Act of Settlement. We are surprised, we confess, that Mr Hallam should attach so much importance to a prerogative which has not been exercised for a hundred and thirty years, which probably will never be exercised again, and which can scarcely, in any conceivable case, be exercised for a salutary purpose.

But the great security, the security without which every other would have been insufficient, was the power of the sword. This both parties thoroughly understood. The Parliament insisted on having the command of the militia and the direction of the Irish war. "By God, not for an hour!" exclaimed the king. "Keep the militia," said the queen, after the defeat of the royal party; "Keep the militia; that will bring back everything." That, by the old constitution, no military authority was lodged in the Parliament, Mr. Hallam has clearly shown. That it is a species of power which ought not to be permanently lodged in large and divided assemblies, must, we think, in fairness be conceded. Opposition, publicity, long discussion, frequent compromise: these are the characteristics of the proceedings of such bodies. Unity, secrecy, decision, are the qualities which military arrangements require. This undoubtedly was an evil. But on the other hand, at such a crisis, to trust such a king with the very weapon which, in hands less dangerous, had destroyed so many free constitutions, would have been the extreme of rashness. The jealousy with which the oligarchy of Venice and the States of Holland regarded their generals and armies induced them perpetually to interfere in matters of which they were incompetent to judge. This policy secured them against military usurpation, but placed them under great disadvantages in war. The uncontrolled power which the king of France exercised over his troops enabled him to conquer his enemies, but enabled him also to oppress his people. Was there any intermediate course? None, we confess, altogether free from objection. But, on the whole, we conceive that the best measure would have been that which the Parliament over and over proposed—that for a limited time the power of the sword should be left to the two Houses, and that it should revert to the Crown when the constitution should be firmly established, and when the new securities of freedom should be so far strengthened by prescription that it would be difficult to employ even a standing army for the purpose of subverting them.

Mr. Hallam thinks that the dispute might easily have been compromised, by enacting that the king should have no power to keep a standing army on foot without the consent of Parliament. He reasons as if the question had been merely theoretical—and as if at that time no army had been wanted. "The kingdom," he says, "might have well dispensed, in that age, with any military organization." Now, we think that Mr. Hallam overlooks the most important circumstance in the whole case. Ireland was at that moment in rebellion: and a great expedition would obviously be necessary to reduce that kingdom to obedience. The Houses had, therefore, to consider, not an abstract question of law, but an urgent practical question, directly involving the safety of the state. They had to consider the expediency of immediately giving a great army to a king who was at least as desirous to put down the Parliament of England as to conquer the insurgents of Ireland.

Of course we do not mean to defend all their measures. Far from it. There never was a perfect man. It would, therefore, be the height of absurdity to expect a perfect party or a perfect assembly. For large bodies are far more likely to err than individuals. The passions are inflamed by sympathy; the fear of punishment and the sense of shame are diminished by partition. Every day we see men do for their faction what they would die rather than do for themselves.

No private quarrel ever happens, in which the right and the wrong are so exquisitely divided that all the right lies on one side, and all the wrong on the other. But here was a schism which separated a great nation into two parties. Of these parties, each was composed of many smaller parties. Each contained many members, who differed far less from their moderate opponents than from their violent allies. Each reckoned among its supporters many who were determined in their choice by some accident of birth, of connection, or of local situation. Each of them attracted to itself in multitudes those fierce and turbid spirits, to whom the clouds and whirlwinds of the political hurricane are the atmosphere of life. A party, like a camp, has its sutlers and camp-followers, as well as its soldiers. In its progress it collects round it a vast retinue, composed of people who thrive by its custom or are amused by its display, who may be sometimes reckoned, in an ostentatious enumeration, as forming part of it, but who give no aid to its operations, and take but a languid interest in its success, who relax its discipline and dishonour its flag by their irregularities, and who, after a disaster, are perfectly ready to cut the throats and rifle the baggage of their companions.

Thus it is in every great division; and thus it was in our civil war. On both sides there was, undoubtedly, enough of crime and enough of error to disgust any man who did not reflect that the whole history of the species is, nothing but a comparison of crimes and errors. Misanthropy is not the temper which qualifies a man to act in great affairs, or to judge of them.

"Of the Parliament," says Mr. Hallam, "it may be said, I think, with not greater severity than truth, that scarce two or three public acts of justice, humanity, or generosity, and very few of political wisdom or courage, are recorded of them, from their quarrel with the king, to their expulsion by Cromwell." Those who may agree with us in the opinion which we have expressed as to the original demands of the Parliament will scarcely concur in this strong censure. The propositions which the Houses made at Oxford, at Uxbridge, and at Newcastle were in strict accordance with these demands. In the darkest period of the war they showed no disposition to concede any vital principle. In the fulness of their success they showed no disposition to encroach beyond these limits. In this respect we cannot but think that they showed justice and generosity, as well as political wisdom and courage.

The Parliament was certainly far from faultless. We fully agree with Mr. Hallam in reprobating their treatment of Laud. For the individual, indeed, we entertain a more unmitigated contempt than for any other character in our history. The fondness with which a portion of the Church regards his memory can be compared only to that perversity of affection which sometimes leads a mother to select the monster or the idiot of the family as the object of her especial favour. Mr. Hallam has incidentally observed that, in the correspondence of Laud with Strafford there are no indications of a sense of duty towards God or man. The admirers of the archbishop have, in consequence, inflicted upon the public a crowd of extracts designed to prove the contrary. Now, in all those passages, we see nothing which a prelate as wicked as Pope Alexander or Cardinal Dubois might not have written. They indicate no sense of duty to God or man, but simply a strong interest in the prosperity and dignity of the order to which the writer belonged; an interest which, when kept within certain limits, does not deserve censure, but which can never be considered as a virtue. Laud is anxious to accommodate satisfactorily the disputes in the University of Dublin. He regrets to hear that a church is used as a stable and that the benefices of Ireland are very poor. He is desirous that, however small a congregation may be, service should be regularly performed. He expresses a wish that the judges of the court before which questions of tithe are generally brought should be selected with a view to the interest of the clergy. All this may be very proper; and it may be very proper that an alderman should stand up for the tolls of his borough, and an East India director for the charter of his company. But it is ridiculous to say that these things indicate piety and benevolence. No primate, though he were the most abandoned of mankind, could wish to see the body with the consequence of which his own consequence was identical degraded in the public estimation by internal dissensions, by the ruinous state of its edifices, and by the slovenly performance of its rites. We willingly acknowledge that the particular letters in question have very little harm in them; a compliment which cannot often be paid either to the writings or to the actions of Laud.

Bad as the archbishop was, however, he was not a traitor within the statute. Nor was he by any means so formidable as to be a proper subject for a retrospective ordinance of the Legislature. His mind had not expansion enough to comprehend a great scheme, good or bad. His oppressive acts were not, like those of the Earl of Strafford, parts of an extensive system. They were the luxuries in which a mean and irritable disposition indulges itself from day to day—the excesses natural to a little mind in a great place. The severest punishment which the two Houses could have inflicted on him would have been to set him at liberty and send him to Oxford. There he might have stayed, tortured by his own diabolical temper, hungering for Puritans to pillory and mangle, plaguing the Cavaliers, for want of somebody else to plague, with his peevishness and absurdity, performing grimaces and antics in the cathedral, continuing that incomparable diary, which we never see without forgetting the vices of his heart in the abject imbecility of his intellect, minuting down his dreams, counting the drops of blood which fell from his nose, watching the direction of the salt, and listening for the note of the screech-owls. Contemptuous mercy was the only vengeance which it became the Parliament to take on such a ridiculous old bigot.

The Houses, it must be acknowledged, committed great errors in the conduct of the war, or rather one great error, which brought their affairs into a condition requiring the most perilous expedients. The Parliamentary leaders of what may be called the first generation, Essex, Manchester, Northumberland, Hollis, even Pym—all the most eminent men, in short, Hampden excepted, were inclined to half measures. They dreaded a decisive victory almost as much as a decisive overthrow. They wished to bring the king into a situation which might render it necessary for him to grant their just and wise demands, but not to subvert the Constitution or to change the dynasty. They were afraid of serving the purposes of those fierce and determined enemies of monarchy who now began to show themselves in the lower ranks of the party. The war was, therefore, conducted in a languid and inefficient manner. A resolute leader might have brought it to a close in a month. At the end of three campaigns, however, the event was still dubious; and that it had not been decidedly unfavourable to the cause of liberty was principally owing to the skill and energy which the more violent Roundheads had displayed in subordinate situations. The conduct of Fairfax and Cromwell at Marston had exhibited a remarkable contrast to that of Essex at Edgehill, and to that of Waller at Lansdowne.

If there be any truth established by the universal experience of nations, it is this,—that to carry the spirit of peace into war is a weak and cruel policy. The time for negociation is the time for deliberation and delay. But when an extreme case calls for that remedy which is in its own nature most violent, and which, in such cases, is a remedy only because it is violent, it is idle to think of mitigating and diluting. Languid war can do nothing which negociation or submission will not do better; and to act on any other principle is, not to save blood and money, but to squander them.

This the Parliamentary leaders found. The third year of hostilities was drawing to a close; and they had not conquered the king. They had not obtained even those advantages which they had expected from a policy obviously erroneous in a military point of view. They had wished to husband their resources. They now found that in enterprises like theirs parsimony is the worst profusion. They had hoped to effect a reconciliation. The event taught them that the best way to conciliate is to bring the work of destruction to a speedy termination. By their moderation many lives and much property had been wasted. The angry passions which, if the contest had been short, would have died away almost as soon as they appeared, had fixed themselves in the form of deep and lasting hatred. A military caste had grown up

Those who had been induced to take up arms by the patriotic feelings of citizens had begun to entertain the professional feelings of soldiers. Above all, the leaders of the party had forfeited its confidence. If they had, by their valour and abilities, gained a complete victory, their influence might have been sufficient to prevent their associates from abusing it. It was now necessary to choose more resolute and uncompromising commanders. Unhappily the illustrious man who alone united in himself all the talents and virtues which the crisis required, who alone could have saved his country from the present dangers without plunging her into others, who alone could have united all the friends of liberty in obedience to his commanding genius and his venerable name, was no more. Something might still be done. The Houses might still avert that worst of all evils, the triumphant return of an imperious and unprincipled master. They might still preserve London from all the horrors of rapine, massacre, and lust. But their hopes of a victory as spotless as their cause,—of a reconciliation which might knit together the hearts of all honest Englishmen for the defence of the public good,—of durable tranquillity,—of temperate freedom, were buried in the grave of Hampden.

The self-denying ordinance was passed, and the army was remodelled. These measures were undoubtedly full of danger. But all that was left to the Parliament was to take the less of two dangers. And we think that, even if they could have accurately foreseen all that followed, their decision ought to have been the same. Under any circumstances, we should have preferred Cromwell to Charles. But there could be no comparison between Cromwell and Charles victorious,—Charles restored, Charles enabled to feed fat all the hungry grudges of his smiling rancour and his cringing pride. The next visit of his majesty to his faithful Commons would have been more serious than that with which he last honoured them; more serious than that which their own general paid them some years after. The king would scarce have been content with praying that the Lord would deliver him from Vane, and collaring Martin. If, by fatal mismanagement, nothing was left to England but a choice of tyrants, the last tyrant whom she should have chosen was Charles.

From the apprehension of this worst evil the Houses were soon delivered by their new leaders. The armies of Charles were everywhere routed, his fastnesses stormed, his party humbled and subjugated. The king himself fell into the hands of the Parliament; and both the king and the Parliament soon fell into the hands of the army. The fate of both the captives was the same. Both were treated alternately with respect and with insult. At length the natural life of one and the political life of the other were terminated by violence; and the power for which both had struggled was united in a single hand. Men naturally sympathize with the calamities of individuals; but they are inclined to look on a fallen party with contempt rather than with pity. Thus misfortune turned the greatest of Parliaments into the despised Rump, and the worst of kings into the Blessed Martyr.

Mr. Hallam decidedly condemns the execution of Charles; and in all that he says on that subject we heartily agree. We fully concur with him in thinking that a great social schism, such as the civil war, is not to be confounded with an ordinary treason, and that the vanquished ought to be treated according to the rules, not of municipal, but of international law. In this case the distinction is of the less importance, because both international and municipal law were in favour of Charles. He was a prisoner of war by the former, a king by the latter. By neither was he a traitor. If he had been successful, and had put his leading opponents to death, he would have deserved severe censure; and this without reference to the justice or injustice of his cause. Yet the opponents of Charles, it must be admitted, were technically guilty of treason.

He might have sent them to the scaffold without violating any established principle of jurisprudence. He would not have been compelled to overturn the whole Constitution in order to reach them. Here his own case differed widely from theirs. Not only was his condemnation in itself a measure which only the strongest necessity could vindicate; but it could not be procured without taking several previous steps every one of which would have required the strongest necessity to vindicate it. It could not be procured without dissolving the government by military force, without establishing precedents of the most dangerous description, without creating difficulties which the next ten years were spent in removing, without pulling down institutions which it soon became necessary to reconstruct, and setting up others which almost every man was soon impatient to destroy. It was necessary to strike the House of Lords out of the Constitution, to exclude members of the House of Commons by force, to make a new crime, a new tribunal, a new mode of procedure. The whole legislative and judicial systems were trampled down for the purpose of taking a single head. Not only those parts of the Constitution which the Republicans were desirous to destroy, but those which they wished to retain and exalt, were deeply injured by these transactions. High Courts of Justice began to usurp the functions of juries. The remaining delegates of the people were soon driven from their seats by the same military violence which had enabled them to exclude their colleagues.

If Charles had been the last of his line, there would have been an intelligible reason for putting him to death. But the blow which terminated his life at once transferred the allegiance of every Royalist to an heir, and an heir who was at liberty. To kill the individual was truly, under such circumstances, not to destroy, but to release the king.

We detest the character of Charles; but a man ought not to be removed by a law *ex post facto*, even constitutionally procured, merely because he is detestable. He must also be very dangerous. We can scarcely conceive that any danger which a state can apprehend from any individual could justify the violent measures which were necessary to procure a sentence against Charles. But in fact the danger amounted to nothing. There was indeed danger from the attachment of a large party to his office. But this danger his execution only increased. His personal influence was little indeed. He had lost the confidence of every party. Churchmen, Catholics, Presbyterians, Independents, his enemies, his friends, his tools, English, Scotch, Irish, all divisions and subdivisions of his people had been deceived by him. His most attached councillors turned away with shame and anguish from his false and hollow policy, plot intertwined with polt, mine sprung beneath mine, agents disowned, promises evaded, one pledge given in private, another in public.—"Oh, Mr. Secretary," says Clarendon, in a letter to Nicholas, "those stratagems have given me more sad hours than all the misfortunes in war which have befallen the king, and look like the effects of God's anger towards us."

The abilities of Charles were not formidable. His taste in the fine arts was indeed exquisite. He was as good a writer and speaker as any modern sovereign has been. But he was not fit for active life. In negociation he was always trying to dupe others, and duping only himself. As a soldier, he was feeble, dilatory, and miserably wanting, not in personal courage, but in the presence of mind which his station required. His delay at Gloucester saved the parliamentary party from destruction. At Naseby, in the very crisis of his fortune, his want of self-possession spread a fatal panic through his army. The story which Clarendon tells of that affair reminds us of the excuses by which Bessus and Bobadil explain their cudgellings. A Scotch nobleman, it seems, begged the king not to run upon his death, took hold of his bridle, and turned his horse round. No man who had much value for his life would have tried to perform the same friendly office on that day for Oliver Cromwell. One thing, and one alone, could make Charles dangerous,—a violent death. His tyranny could not break the high spirit of the English people. His arms could not conquer, his arts could not deceive them; but his humiliation and his execution melted them into a generous compassion. Men who die on a scaffold for political offences almost always die well. The eyes of thousands are fixed upon them. Enemies and admirers are watching their demeanour. Every tone of voice, every change of colour, is to go down to posterity. Escape is impossible. Supplication is vain. In such a situation pride and despair have often been known to nerve the weakest minds with fortitude adequate to the occasion. Charles died patiently and bravely: not more patiently or bravely, indeed, than any other victims of political rage; not more patiently or bravely than his own judges, who were not only killed, but tortured; or than Vane, who had always been considered as a timid man. However, his conduct during his trial and at his execution made a prodigious impression. His subjects began to love his memory as heartily as they had hated his person; and posterity has estimated his character from his death rather than from his life.

To represent Charles as a martyr in the cause of Episcopacy is absurd. Those who put him to death cared as little for the Assembly of Divines as for the Convocation, and would, in all probability, only have hated him the more if he had agreed to set up the Presbyterian discipline; and in spite of the opinion of Mr. Hallam, we are inclined to think that the attachment of Charles to the Church of England was altogether political. Human nature is, indeed, so capricious that there may be a single sensitive point in a conscience which everywhere else is callous. A man without truth or humanity may have some strange scruples about a trifle. There was one devout warrior in the royal camp whose piety bore a great resemblance to that which is ascribed to the king. We mean Colonel Turner. That gallant Cavalier was hanged, after the Restoration, for a flagitious burglary. At the gallows he told the crowd that his mind received great consolation from one reflection: he had always taken off his hat when he went into a church. The character of Charles would scarcely rise in our estimation, if we believed that he was pricked in conscience after the manner of this worthy loyalist, and that, while violating all the first rules of Christian morality, he was sincerely scrupulous about Church government. But we acquit him of such weakness. In 1641 he deliberately confirmed the Scotch Declaration, which stated that the government of the Church by archbishops and bishops was contrary to the Word of God. In 1645 he appears to have offered to set up Popery in Ireland. That a king who had established the Presbyterian religion in one kingdom, and who was willing to establish the Catholic religion in another, should have insurmountable scruples about the ecclesiastical constitution of the third, is altogether incredible. He himself says in his letters that he looks on Episcopacy as a stronger support of monarchical power than even the army. From causes which we have already considered, the Established Church had been, since the Reformation, the great bulwark of the prerogative. Charles wished, therefore, to preserve it. He thought himself necessary both to the Parliament and to the army. He did not foresee, till too late, that, by paltering with the Presbyterians, he should put both them and himself into the power of a fiercer and more daring party. If he had foreseen it, we suspect that the royal blood which still cries to Heaven, every thirtieth of January, for judgments only to be averted by salt-fish and egg-sauce, would never have been shed. One who had swallowed the Scotch Declaration would scarcely strain at the Covenant.

The death of Charles and the strong measures which led to it raised Cromwell to a height of power fatal to the infant Commonwealth. No men occupy so splendid a place in history as those who have founded monarchies on the ruins of republican institutions. Their glory, if not of the purest, is assuredly of the most seductive and dazzling kind. In nations broken to the curb, in nations long accustomed to be transferred from one tyrant to another, man without eminent qualities may easily gain supreme power. The defection of a troop of guards, a conspiracy of eunuchs, a popular tumult, might place an indolent senator or a brutal soldier on the throne of the Roman world. Similar revolutions have often occurred in the despotic states of Asia. But a community which has heard the voice of truth and experienced the pleasures of liberty—in which the merits of statesmen and of systems are freely canvassed,—in which obedience is paid, not to persons, but to laws,—in which magistrates are regarded, not as the lords, but as the servants of the public,—in which the excitement of a party is a necessary of life,—in which political warfare is reduced to a system of tactics;—such a community is not easily reduced to servitude. Beasts of burden may easily be managed by a new master. But will the wild ass submit to the bonds? Will the unicorn serve and abide by the crib? Will leviathan hold out his nostrils to the hook? The mythological conqueror of the East, whose enchantments reduced the wild beasts to the tameness of domestic cattle, and who harnessed lions and tigers to his chariot, is but an imperfect type of those extraordinary minds which have thrown a spell on the fierce spirits of nations unaccustomed to control, and have compelled raging factions to obey their reins and swell their triumph. The enterprise, be it good or bad, is one which requires a truly great man. It demands courage, activity, energy, wisdom, firmness, conspicuous virtues, or vices so splendid and alluring as to resemble virtues.

Those who have succeeded in this arduous undertaking form a very small and a very remarkable class. Parents of tyranny, but heirs of freedom, kings among citizens, citizens among kings, they unite in themselves the characteristics of the system which springs from them, and of the system from which they have sprung. Their reigns shine with a double light, the last and dearest rays of departing freedom mingled with the first and brightest glories of empire in its dawn. Their high qualities lend to despotism itself a charm drawn from the institutions under which they were formed, and which they have destroyed. They resemble Europeans who settle within the tropics, and carry thither the strength and the energetic habits acquired in regions more propitious to the constitution. They differ as widely from princes nursed in the purple of imperial cradles as the companions of Gama from their dwarfish and imbecile progeny, which, born in a climate unfavourable to its growth and beauty, degenerates more and more, at every descent, from the qualities of the original conquerors.

In this class three men stand pre-eminent, Cæsar, Cromwell, and Bonaparte. The highest place in this remarkable triumvirate belongs undoubtedly to Cæsar. He united the talents of Bonaparte to those of Cromwell, and he possessed also what neither Cromwell nor Bonaparte possessed, learning, taste, wit, eloquence, the sentiments and the manners of an accomplished gentleman.

Between Cromwell and Napoleon Mr. Hallam has instituted a parallel scarcely less ingenious than that which Burke has drawn between Richard Cœur de Lion and Charles XII. of Sweden. In this parallel, however, and indeed throughout his work, we think that he hardly gives Cromwell fair measure. "Cromwell," says he, "far unlike his antitype, never showed any signs of a legislative mind, or any desire to place his renown on that noblest basis, the amelioration of social institutions." The difference in this respect, we conceive, was not in the characters of the men, but in the characters of the revolutions by means of which they rose to power. The civil war in England had been undertaken to defend and restore; the republicans of France set themselves to destroy. In England the principles of the common law had never been disturbed, and most even of its forms had been held sacred. In France, the law and its ministers had been swept away together. In France, therefore, legislation became the first business of the first settled government which rose on the ruins of the old system. The admirers of Inigo Jones have always maintained that his works are inferior to those of Sir Christopher Wren, only because the great fire of London gave to the latter such a field for the display of his powers as no architect in the history of the world ever possessed. Similar allowance must be made for Cromwell. If he erected little that was new, it was because there had been no general devastation to clear a space for him. As it was, he reformed the representative system in a most judicious manner. He rendered the administration of justice uniform throughout the island. We will quote a passage from his speech to the Parliament in September, 1656, which contains, we think, stronger indications of a legislative mind than are to be found in the whole range of orations delivered on such occasions before or since.

"There is one general grievance in the nation. It is the law. . . . . I think, I may say it, I have as eminent judges in this land as have been had, or that the nation has had for these many years. Truly, I could be particular as to the executive part, to the administration; but that would trouble you. But the truth of it is, there are wicked and abominable laws that will be in your power to alter. To hang a man for sixpence, threepence, I know not what— to hang for a trifle, and pardon murder, is in the ministration of the law, through the ill framing of it. I have known in my experience abominable murders quitted; and to see men lose their lives for petty matters! This is a thing that God will reckon for; and I wish it may not lie upon this nation a day longer than you have an opportunity to give a remedy; and I hope I shall cheerfully join with you in it."

Mr. Hallam truly says that, though it is impossible to rank Cromwell with Napoleon as a general, yet "his exploits were as much above the level of his contemporaries, and more the effects of an original uneducated capacity." Bonaparte was trained in the best military schools; the army which he led to Italy was one of the finest that ever existed. Cromwell passed his youth and the prime of his manhood in a civil situation. He never looked on war till he was more than forty years old. He had first to form himself, and then to form his troops. Out of raw levies he created an army, the bravest and the best disciplined, the most orderly in peace, and the most terrible in war, that Europe had seen. He called this body into existence. He led it to conquest. He never fought a battle without gaining a victory. He never gained a victory without annihilating the force opposed to him. Yet his triumphs were not the highest glory of his military system. The respect which his troops paid to property, their attachment to the laws and religion of their country, their submission to the civil power, their temperance, their intelligence, their industry, are without parallel. It was after the Restoration that the spirit which their great leader had infused into them was most signally displayed. At the command of the established government, a government which had no means of enforcing obedience, fifty thousand soldiers, whose backs no enemy had ever seen, either in domestic or in continental war, laid down their arms, and retired into the mass of the people, thenceforward to be distinguished only by superior diligence, sobriety, and regularity in the pursuits of peace, from the other members of the community which they had saved.

In the general spirit and character of his administration, we think Cromwell far superior to Napoleon. "In civil government," says Mr. Hallam, "there can be no adequate parallel between one who had sucked only the dregs of a besotted fanaticism, and one to whom the stores of reason and philosophy were open." These expressions, it seems to us, convey the highest eulogium on our great countryman. Reason and philosophy did not teach the conqueror of Europe to command his passions, or to pursue, as a first object, the happiness of his people. They did not prevent him from risking his fame and his power in a frantic contest against the principles of human nature and the laws of the physical world, against the rage of the winter and the liberty of the sea. They did not exempt him from the influence of that most pernicious of superstitions, a presumptuous fatalism. They did not preserve him from the inebriation of prosperity, or restrain him from indecent querulousness in adversity. On the other hand, the fanaticism of Cromwell never urged him on impracticable undertakings, or confused his perception of the public good. Inferior to Bonaparte in invention, he was far superior to him in wisdom. The French Emperor is among conquerors what Voltaire is among writers, a miraculous child. His splendid genius was frequently clouded by fits of humour as absurdly perverse as those of the pet of the nursery, who quarrels with his food, and dashes his playthings to pieces. Cromwell was emphatically a man. He possessed, in an eminent degree, that masculine and full-grown robustness of mind, that equally diffused intellectual health, which, if our national partiality does not mislead us, has peculiarly characterised the great men of England. Never was any ruler so conspicuously born for sovereignty. The cup which has intoxicated almost all others sobered him. His spirit, restless from its buoyancy in a lower sphere, reposed in majestic placidity as soon as it had reached the level congenial to it. He had nothing in common with that large class of men who distinguish themselves in lower posts, and whose incapacity becomes obvious as soon as the public voice summons them to take the lead. Rapidly as his fortunes grew, his mind expanded more rapidly still. Insignificant as a private citizen, he was a great general; he was a still greater prince. The manner of Napoleon was a theatrical compound, in which the coarseness of a revolutionary guard-room was blended with the ceremony of the old Court of Versailles. Cromwell, by the confession even of his enemies, exhibited in his demeanour the simple and natural nobleness of a man neither ashamed of his origin nor vain of his elevation, of a man who had found his proper place in society, and who felt secure that he was competent to fill it. Easy, even to familiarity, where his own dignity was concerned, he was punctilious only for his country. His own character he left to take care of itself; he left it to be defended by his victories in war and his reforms in peace. But he was a jealous and implacable guardian of the public honour. He suffered a crazy Quaker to insult him in the midst of Whitehall, and revenged himself only by liberating him and giving him a dinner. But he was prepared to risk the chances of a war to avenge the blood of a private Englishman.

No sovereign ever carried to the throne so large a portion of the best qualities of the middling orders—so strong a sympathy with the feelings and interests of his people. He was sometimes driven to arbitrary measures; but he had a high, stout, honest, English heart. Hence it was that he loved to surround his throne with such men as Hale and Blake. Hence it was that he allowed so large a share of political liberty to his subjects, and that, even when an opposition dangerous to his power and to his person almost compelled him to govern by the sword, he was still anxious to leave a germ from which, at a more favourable season, free institutions might spring. We firmly believe that, if his first Parliament had not commenced its debates by disputing his title, his government would have been as mild at home as it was energetic and able abroad. He was a soldier—he had risen by war. Had his ambition been of an impure or selfish kind, it would have been easy for him to plunge his country into continental hostilities on a large scale, and to dazzle the restless factions which he ruled, by the splendour of his victories. Some of his enemies have sneeringly remarked, that in the successes obtained under his administration he had no personal share; as if a man who had raised himself from obscurity to empire solely by his military talents could have any unworthy reason for shrinking from military enterprise. This reproach is his highest glory. In the success of the English navy he could have no selfish interest. Its triumphs added nothing to his fame; its increase added nothing to his means of overawing his enemies; its great leader was not his friend. Yet he took a peculiar pleasure in encouraging that noble service which, of all the instruments employed by an English government, is the most impotent for mischief, and the most powerful for good. His administration was glorious, but with no vulgar glory. It was not one of those periods of overstrained and convulsive exertion which necessarily produce debility and languor. Its energy was natural, healthful, temperate. He placed England at the head of the Protestant interest, and in the first rank of Christian powers. He taught every nation to value her friendship and to dread her enmity. But he did not squander her resources in a vain attempt to invest her with that supremacy which no power, in the modern system of Europe, can safely affect, or can long retain.

This noble and sober wisdom had its reward. If he did not carry the banners of the Commonwealth in triumph to distant capitals, if he did not adorn Whitehall with the spoils of the Stadthouse and the Louvre, if he did not portion out Flanders and Germany into principalities for his kinsmen and his generals, he did not, on the other hand, see his country overrun by the armies of nations which his ambition had provoked. He did not drag out the last years of his life an exile and a prisoner, in an unhealthy climate and under an ungenerous gaoler, raging with the impotent desire of vengeance, and brooding over visions of departed glory. He went down to his grave in the fulness of power and fame; and he left to his son an authority which any man of ordinary firmness and prudence would have retained.

But for the weakness of that foolish Ishbosheth, the opinions which we have been expressing would, we believe, now have formed the orthodox creed of good Englishmen. We might now be writing under the government of his Highness Oliver V. or Richard IV., Protector, by the Grace of God, of the Commonwealth of England, Scotland, and Ireland, and the dominions thereto belonging. The form of the great founder of the dynasty, on horseback, as when he led the charge at Naseby, or on foot, as when he took the mace from the table of the Commons, would adorn our squares and overlook our public offices from Charing Cross; and sermons in his praise would be duly preached on his lucky day, the third of September, by court-chaplains, guiltless of the abomination of the surplice.

But, though his memory has not been taken under the patronage of any party, though every device has been used to blacken it, though to praise him would long have been a punishable crime, truth and merit at last prevail. Cowards who had trembled at the very sound of his name, tools of office who, like Downing, had been proud of the honour of lacqueying his coach, might insult him in loyal speeches and addresses. Venal poets might transfer to the king the same eulogies, little the worse for wear, which they had bestowed on the Protector. A fickle multitude might crowd to shout and scoff round the gibbeted remains of the greatest prince and soldier of the age. But when the Dutch cannon startled an effeminate tyrant in his own palace, when the conquests which had been made by the armies of Cromwell were sold to pamper the harlots of Charles, when Englishmen were sent to fight under the banners of France against the independence of Europe and the Protestant religion, many honest hearts swelled in secret at the thought of one who had never suffered his country to be ill used by any but himself. It must indeed have been difficult for any Englishman to see the salaried Viceroy of France, at the most important crisis of his fate, sauntering through his harem, yawning and talking nonsense over a despatch, or beslobbering his brother and his courtiers in a fit of maudlin affection,* without a respectful and tender remembrance of him before whose genius the young pride of Louis and the veteran craft of Mazarin had stood rebuked, who had humbled Spain on the land and Holland on the sea, and whose imperial voice had arrested the victorious arms of Sweden and the persecuting fires of Rome. Even to the present day his character, though constantly attacked, and scarcely ever defended, is popular with the great body of our countrymen.

The most questionable act of his life was the execution of Charles. We have already strongly condemned that proceeding; but we by no means consider it as one which attaches any peculiar stigma of infamy to the names of those who participated in it. It was an unjust and injudicious display of violent party spirit; but it was not a cruel or perfidious measure. It had all those features which distinguish the errors of magnanimous and intrepid spirits from base and malignant crimes.

We cannot quit this interesting topic without a few words on a transaction which Mr. Hallam has made the subject of a severe accusation against Cromwell; and which has been made by others the subject of a severe accusation against Mr. Hallam. We conceive that both the Protector and the historian may be vindicated. Mr. Hallam tells us that Cromwell sold fifty English gentlemen as slaves in Barbadoes. For making this statement he has been charged with two high literary crimes. The first accusation is, that, from his violent prejudice against Oliver, he has calumniated him falsely. The second, preferred by the same accuser, is, that from his violent fondness for the same Oliver, he has hidden his calumnies against him, at the fag end of a note, instead of putting them into the text. Both these imputations cannot possibly be true, and it happens that neither is so. His censors will find, when they take the trouble to read his book, that the story is mentioned in the text as well as in the notes; and they will also find, when they take the trouble to read some other books with which speculators on English history ought to be acquainted, that the story is true. If there could have been any doubt about the matter, Burton's Diary must have set it at a rest. But, in truth, there was abundant and superabundant evidence, before the appearance of that valuable publication. Not to mention the authority to which Mr. Hallam refers, and which alone is perfectly satisfactory, there is Slingsby Bethel's account of the proceedings of Richard Cromwell's Parliament, published immediately after its dissolution. He was a member; he must, therefore, have known what happened: and violent as his prejudices were, he never could have been such an idiot as to state positive falsehoods with respect to public transactions which had taken place only a few days before.

It will not be quite so easy to defend Cromwell against Mr. Hallam as to

---

* These particulars, and many more of the same kind, are recorded by Pepys.

defend Mr. Hallam against those who attack his history. But the story is certainly by no means so bad as he takes it to be. In the first place, this slavery was merely the compulsory labour to which every transported convict is liable. Nobody acquainted with the language of the last century can be ignorant that such convicts were generally termed slaves, until discussions about another species of slavery, far too miserable and altogether unmerited, rendered the word too odious to be applied even to felons of English origin. These persons enjoyed the protection of the law during the term of their service, which was only five years. The punishment of transportation has been inflicted, by almost every government that England has ever had, for political offences. After Monmouth's insurrection, and after the rebellions in 1715 and 1745, great numbers of the prisoners were sent to America. These considerations ought, we think, to free Cromwell from the imputation of having inflicted on his enemies any punishment which in itself is of a shocking and atrocious character.

To transport fifty men, however, without a trial is bad enough. But let us consider, in the first place, that some of these men were taken in arms against the government, and that it is not clear that they were not all so taken. In that case Cromwell or his officers might, according to the usage of those unhappy times, have put them to the sword, or turned them over to the provost-marshal at once. This, we allow, is not a complete vindication; for execution by martial law ought never to take place but under circumstances which admit of no delay; and if there is time to transport men, there is time to try them.

The defenders of the measure stated in the House of Commons that the persons thus transported not only consented to go, but went with remarkable cheerfulness. By this we suppose it is to be understood, not that they had any violent desire to be bound apprentices in Barbadoes, but that they considered themselves as, on the whole, fortunate and leniently treated, in the situation in which they had placed themselves.

When these considerations are fairly estimated, it must, we think, be allowed that this selling into slavery was not, as it seems at first sight, a barbarous outrage, unprecedented in our annals, but merely a very arbitrary proceeding, which, like most of the arbitrary proceedings of Cromwell, was rather a violation of positive law than of any great principle of justice and mercy. When Mr. Hallam, declares it to have been more oppressive than any measures of Charles II., he forgets, we imagine, that under the reign of that prince, and during the administration of Lord Clarendon, many of the Roundheads were, without any trial, imprisoned at a distance from England, merely in order to remove them beyond the reach of the great liberating writ of our law. But, in fact, it is not fair to compare the cases. The government of Charles was perfectly secure. The "*res dura et regni novitas*" is the great apology of Cromwell.

From the moment that Cromwell is dead and buried, we go on in almost perfect harmony with Mr. Hallam to the end of his book. The times which followed the Restoration peculiarly require that unsparing impartiality which is his most distinguishing virtue. No part of our history, during the last three centuries, presents a spectacle of such general dreariness. The whole breed of our statesmen seems to have degenerated; and their moral and intellectual littleness strikes us with the more disgust because we see it placed in immediate contrast with the high and majestic qualities of the race which they succeeded. In the great civil war even the bad cause had been rendered respectable and amiable by the purity and elevation of mind which many of its friends displayed. Under Charles II. the best and noblest of ends was disgraced by means the most cruel and sordid. The rage of faction succeeded to the love of liberty. Loyalty died away into servility. We look in vain among the leading politicians of either side for steadiness of principle, or even for that vulgar fidelity to party which, in our time, it is esteemed infamous to violate. The inconsistency, perfidy, and baseness which the leaders constantly practised, which their followers defended, and which the great body of the people regarded, as it seems, with little disapprobation, appear in the present age almost incredible. In the age of Charles I. they would, we believe, have excited as much astonishment.

Man, however, is always the same. And when so marked a difference appears between two generations it is certain that the solution may be found in their respective circumstances. The principal statesmen of the reign of Charles II. were trained during the civil war and the revolutions which followed it. Such a period is eminently favourable to the growth of quick and active talents. It forms a class of men, shrewd, vigilant, inventive; of men whose dexterity triumphs over the most perplexing combinations of circumstances, whose presaging instinct no sign of the times, no incipient change of public feelings, can elude. But it is an unpropitious season for the firm and masculine virtues. The statesman who enters on his career at such a time can form no permanent connections, can make no accurate observations on the higher parts of political science. Before he can attach himself to a party, it is scattered. Before he can study the nature of a government, it is overturned. The oath of abjuration comes close on the oath of allegiance. The association which was subscribed yesterday is burned by the hangman to-day. In the midst of the constant eddy and change self-preservation becomes the first object of the adventurer. It is a task too hard for the strongest head to keep itself from becoming giddy in the eternal whirl. Public spirit is out of the question. A laxity of principle, without which no public man can be eminent or even safe, becomes too common to be scandalous; and the whole nation looks coolly on instances of apostasy which would startle the foulest turncoat of more settled times.

The history of France since the Revolution affords some striking illustrations of these remarks. The same man was minister of the Republic, of Bonaparte, of Louis XVIII., of Bonaparte again after his return from Elba, of Louis again after his return from Ghent. Yet all these manifold treasons by no means seemed to destroy his influence, or even to fix any peculiar stain of infamy on his character. We, to be sure, did not know what to make of him; but his countrymen did not seem to be shocked; and in truth they had little right to be shocked: for there was scarcely one Frenchman, distinguished in the state or in the army, who had not, according to the best of his talents and opportunities, emulated the example. It was natural, too, that this should be the case. The rapidity and violence with which change followed change in the affairs of France towards the close of the last century had taken away the reproach of inconsistency, unfixed the principles of public men, and produced in many minds a general scepticism and indifference about principles of government.

No Englishman who has studied attentively the reign of Charles II. will think himself entitled to indulge in any feelings of national superiority over the *Dictionnaire des Girouettes*. Shaftesbury was surely a far less respectable man than Talleyrand; and it would be injustice even to Fouché to compare him with Lauderdale. Nothing, indeed, can more clearly show how low the standard of political morality had fallen in this country than the fortunes of the men whom we have named. The government wanted a ruffian to carry on the most atrocious system of misgovernment with which any nation was ever cursed, to extirpate Presbyterianism by fire and sword, the drowning of women, the frightful torture of the boot. And they found him among the chiefs of the rebellion and the subscribers of the Covenant. The opposition looked for a chief to head them in the most desperate attacks ever made, under the forms of the Constitution, on any English administration: and they selected the minister who had the deepest share in the worst parts of that administration,—the soul of the Cabal,—the counsellor who had shut up the exchequer and urged on the Dutch war. The whole political drama was of the same cast. No unity of plan, no decent propriety of character and costume, could be found in the wild and monstrous harlequinade. The whole was made up of extravagant transformations and burlesque contrasts; Atheists turned Puritans; Puritans turned Atheists; Republicans defending the divine right of kings; prostitute courtiers clamouring for the liberties of the people; judges inflaming the rage of mobs; patriots pocketing bribes from foreign powers; a Popish prince torturing Presbyterians into Episcopacy in one part of the island; Presbyterians cutting off the heads of Popish noblemen and gentlemen in the other. Public opinion has its natural flux and reflux. After a violent burst, there is commonly a reaction. But vicissitudes so extraordinary as those which mark the reign of Charles II. can only be explained by supposing an utter want of principle in the political world. On neither side was there fidelity enough to face a reverse. Those honourable retreats from power which, in later days, parties have often made, with loss, but still in good order, in firm union, with unbroken spirit and formidable means of annoyance, were utterly unknown. As soon as a check took place a total route followed: arms and colours were thrown away. The vanquished troops, like the Italian mercenaries of the fourteenth and fifteenth centuries, enlisted, on the very field of battle, in the service of the conquerors. In a nation proud of its sturdy justice and plain good sense, no party could be found to take a firm middle stand between the worst of oppositions and the worst of courts. When, on charges as wild as Mother Goose's tales, on the testimony of wretches who proclaimed themselves to be spies and traitors, and whom everybody now believes to have been also liars and murderers, the offal of gaols and brothels, the leavings of the hangman's whip and shears, Catholics guilty of nothing but their religion were led like sheep to the Protestant shambles, where were the loyal Tory gentry and the passively obedient clergy? And where, when the time of retribution came, when laws were strained and juries packed to destroy the leaders of the Whigs, when charters were invaded, when Jefferies and Kirke were making Somersetshire what Lauderdale and Graham had made Scotland, where were the ten thousand brisk boys of Shaftesbury, the members of ignoramus juries, the wearers of the Polish medal? All-powerful to destroy others, unable to save themselves, the members of the two parties oppressed and were oppressed, murdered and were murdered, in their turn. No lucid interval occurred between the frantic paroxysms of two contradictory illusions.

To the frequent changes of the government during the twenty years which had preceded the Revolution this unsteadiness is, in a great measure, to be attributed. Other causes had also been at work. Even if the country had been governed by the house of Cromwell or by the remains of the Long Parliament, the extreme austerity of the Puritans would necessarily have produced a revulsion. Towards the close of the Protectorate many signs indicated that a time of licence was at hand. But the restoration of Charles II. rendered the change wonderfully rapid and violent. Profligacy became a test of orthodoxy and loyalty, a qualification for rank and office. A deep and general taint infected the morals of the most influential classes, and spread itself through every province of letters. Poetry inflamed the passions; philosophy undermined the principles; divinity itself, inculcating an abject reverence for the Court, gave additional effect to its licentious example. We look in vain for those qualities which lend a charm to the errors of high and ardent natures, for the generosity, the tenderness, the chivalrous delicacy, which ennoble appetites into passions, and impart to vice itself a portion of the majesty of virtue. The excesses of that age remind us of the humours of a gang of footpads, revelling with their favourite beauties at a flash-house. In the fashionable libertinism there is a hard, cold ferocity, an impudence, a lowness, a dirtiness, which can be paralleled only among the heroes and heroines of that filthy and heartless literature which encouraged it. One nobleman of great abilities wanders about as a Merry-Andrew. Another harangues the mob stark naked from a window. A third lays an ambush to cudgel a man who has offended him. A knot of gentlemen of high rank and influence combine to push their fortunes at Court by circulating stories intended to ruin an innocent girl, stories which had no foundation, and which, if they had been true, would never have passed the lips of a man of honour.* A dead child is found in the palace, the offspring of some maid of honour by some courtier, or perhaps by Charles himself. The whole flight of panders and buffoons pounce upon it, and carry it in triumph to the royal laboratory, where his majesty, after a brutal jest, dissects it for the amusement of the assembly, and probably of its father among the rest. The favourite Duchess stamps about Whitehall, cursing and swearing. The ministers employ their time at the council-board in making mouths at each other and taking off each other's gestures for the amusement of the king. The Peers at a conference begin to pommel each other and to tear collars and periwigs. A speaker in the House of Commons gives offence to the Court. He is waylaid by a gang of bullies, and his nose is cut to the bone. This ignominious dissoluteness, or, rather, if we may venture to designate it by the only proper word, blackguardism of feeling and manners, could not but spread from private to public life. The cynical sneers, the epicurean sophistry, which had driven honour and virtue from one part of the character, extended their influence over every other. The second generation of the statesmen of this reign were worthy pupils of the schools in which they had been trained, of the gaming-table of Grammont, and the tiring-room of Nell. In no other age could such a trifler as Buckingham have exercised any political influence. In no other age could the path to power and glory have been thrown open to the manifold infamies of Churchill.

The history of that celebrated man shows, more clearly, perhaps, than that of any other individual, the malignity and extent of the corruption which had eaten into the heart of the public morality. An English gentleman of family attaches himself to a prince who has seduced his sister, and accepts rank and wealth as the price of her shame and his own. He then repays by ingratitude the benefits which he has purchased by ignominy, betrays his patron in a manner which the best cause cannot excuse, and commits an act, not only of private treachery, but of distinct military desertion. To his conduct at the crisis of the fate of James no service in modern times has, as far as we remember, furnished any parallel. The conduct of Ney, scandalous enough no doubt, is the very fastidiousness of honour in comparison of it. The perfidy of Arnold approaches it most nearly. In our age and country no talents, no services, no party attachments, could bear any man up under such mountains of infamy. Yet, even before Churchill had performed those great actions

---

* The manner in which Hamilton relates the circumstances of the atrocious plot against poor Anne Hyde, is, if possible, more disgraceful to the Court, of which he may be considered as a specimen, than the plot itself.

which in some degree redeem his character with posterity, the load lay very lightly on him. He had others in abundance to keep him in countenance. Godolphin, Orford, Danby, the trimmer Halifax, the renegade Sunderland, were all men of the same class.

Where such was the political morality of the noble and the wealthy, it may easily be conceived that those professions which, even in the best times, are peculiarly liable to corruption, were in a frightful state. Such a bench and such a bar England has never seen. Jones, Scroggs, Jefferies, North, Wright, Sawyer, Williams, Shower, are to this day the spots and blemishes of our legal chronicles. Differing in constitution and in situation,—whether blustering or cringing,—whether persecuting Protestants or Catholics—they were equally unprincipled and inhuman. The part which the Church played was not equally atrocious; but it must have been exquisitely diverting to a scoffer. Never were principles so loudly professed, and so flagrantly abandoned. The Royal prerogative had been magnified to the skies in theological works. The doctrine of passive obedience had been preached from innumerable pulpits. The University of Oxford had sentenced the works of the most moderate constitutionalists to the flames. The accession of a Catholic king, the frightful cruelties committed in the west of England, never shook the steady loyalty of the clergy. But did they serve the king for naught? He laid his hand on them, and they cursed him to his face. He touched the revenue of a college and the liberty of some prelates; and the whole profession set up a yell worthy of Hugh Peters himself. Oxford sent its plate to an invader with more alacrity than she had shown when Charles I. requested it. Nothing was said about the wickedness of resistance till resistance had done its work, till the anointed vicegerent of Heaven had been driven away, and till it had become plain that he would never be restored, or would be restored at least under strict limitations. The clergy went back, it must be owned, to their old theory, as soon as they found that it would do them no harm.

To the general baseness and profligacy of the times Clarendon is principally indebted for his high reputation. He was, in every respect, a man unfit for his age,—at once too good for it and too bad for it. He seemed to be one of the ministers of Elizabeth, transplanted at once to a state of society widely different from that in which the abilities of such statesmen had been serviceable. In the sixteenth century the royal prerogative had scarcely been called in question. A minister who held it high was in no danger, so long as he used it well. That attachment to the Crown, that extreme jealousy of popular encroachments, that love, half religious, half political, for the Church, which, from the beginning of the Long Parliament, showed itself in Clarendon, and which his sufferings, his long residence in France, and his high station in the Government served to strengthen, would, a hundred years earlier, have secured to him the favour of his sovereign without rendering him odious to the people. His probity, his correctness in private life, his decency of deportment, and his general ability would not have misbecome a colleague of Walsingham and Burleigh. But, in the times on which he was cast, his errors and his virtues were alike out of place. He imprisoned men without trial. He was accused of raising unlawful contributions on the people for the support of the army. The abolition of the Triennial Act which ensured the frequent holding of Parliaments was one of his favourite objects. He seems to have meditated the revival of the Star Chamber and the High Commission Court. His zeal for the prerogative made him unpopular; but it could not secure to him the favour of a master far more desirous of ease and pleasure than of power. Charles would rather have lived in exile and privacy, with abundance of money, a crowd of mimics to amuse him, and a score of mistresses, than have purchased the absolute dominion of the world by the privations and exertions to which Clarendon was constantly urging him. A councillor who was always bringing him papers and giving him advice, and who stoutly refused to compliment Lady Castlemaine and to carry messages to Miss Stewart, soon became more hateful to him than ever Cromwell had been. Thus, considered by the people as an oppressor, by the Court as a censor, the minister fell from his high office with a ruin more violent and destructive than could ever have been his fate if he had either respected the principles of the Constitution or flattered the vices of the king.

Mr. Hallam has formed, we think, a correct estimate of the character and administration of Clarendon. But he scarcely makes a sufficient allowance for the wear and tear which honesty almost necessarily sustains in the friction of political life, and which, in times so rough as those through which Clarendon passed, must be very considerable. When these are fairly estimated, we think that his integrity may be allowed to pass muster. A high-minded man he certainly was not, either in public or in private affairs. His own account of his conduct in the affair of his daughter is the most extraordinary passage in autobiography. We except nothing even in the Confessions of Rousseau. Several writers have taken a perverted and absurd pride in representing themselves as detestable; but no other ever laboured hard to make himself despicable and ridiculous. In one important particular Clarendon showed as little regard to the honour of his country as he had shown to that of his family. He accepted a subsidy from France for the relief of Portugal. But this method of obtaining money was afterwards practised to a much greater extent, and for objects much less respectable, both by the Court and by the Opposition.

These pecuniary transactions are commonly considered as the most disgraceful part of the history of those times; and they were, no doubt, highly reprehensible. Yet, in justice to the Whigs and to Charles himself, we must admit that they were not so shameful or atrocious as at the present day they appear. The effect of violent animosities between parties has always been an indifference to the general welfare and honour of the State. A politician, where factions run high, is interested not for the whole people, but for his own section of it. The rest are, in his view, strangers, enemies, or rather pirates. The strongest aversion which he can feel to any foreign power is the ardour of friendship, when compared with the loathing which he entertains towards those domestic foes with whom he is cooped up in a narrow space, with whom he lives in a constant interchange of petty injuries and insults, and from whom, in the day of their success, he has to expect severities far beyond any that a conqueror from a distant country would inflict. Thus, in Greece it was a point of honour for a man to leave his country and cleave to his party. No aristocratical citizen of Samos or Corcyra would have hesitated to call in the aid of Lacedæmon. The multitude, on the contrary, looked to Athens. In the Italian States of the thirteenth and fourteenth centuries, from the same cause, no man was so much a Florentine or a Pisan as a Ghibeline or a Guelf. It may be doubted whether there was a single individual who would have scrupled to raise his party from a state of depression by opening the gates of his native city to a French or an Arragonese force. The Reformation, dividing almost every European country into two parts, produced similar effects. The Catholic was too strong for the Englishman, the Huguenot for the Frenchman. The Protestant statesmen of Scotland and France accordingly called in the aid of Elizabeth; and the Papists of the League brought a Spanish army into the very heart of France. The commotions to which the French Revolution gave rise were followed by the same consequences. The Republicans in every part of Europe were eager to see the armies of the National Convention and the Directory appear among them, and exulted in defeats which distressed and humbled those whom they considered as their worst enemies, their own rulers. The princes and nobles of France, on the other hand, did their utmost to bring foreign invaders to Paris. A very short time has elapsed since the Apostolical party in Spain invoked, too successfully, the support of strangers.

The great contest which raged in England during the seventeenth century and the earlier part of the eighteenth, extinguished, not indeed in the body of the people, but in those classes which were most actively engaged in politics, almost all national feelings. Charles II. and many of his courtiers had passed a large part of their lives in banishment, serving in foreign armies, living on the bounty of foreign treasuries, soliciting foreign aid to re-establish monarchy in their native country. The oppressed Cavaliers in England constantly looked to France and Spain for deliverance and revenge. Clarendon censures the continental governments with great bitterness for not interfering in our internal dissensions. During the Protectorate, not only the Royalists, but the disaffected of all parties, appear to have been desirous of assistance from abroad. It is not strange, therefore, that, amidst the furious contests which followed the Restoration, the violence of party feeling should produce effects which would probably have attended it even in an age less distinguished by laxity of principle and indelicacy of sentiment. It was not till a natural death had terminated the paralytic old age of the Jacobite party that the evil was completely at an end. The Whigs long looked to Holland,—the High Tories to France. The former concluded the Barrier Treaty;—some of the latter entreated the Court of Versailles to send an expedition to England. Many men who, however erroneous their political notions might be, were unquestionably honourable in private life, accepted money without scruple from the foreign powers favourable to the Pretender.

Never was there less of national feeling among the higher orders than during the reign of Charles II. That prince, on the one side, thought it better to be the deputy of an absolute king than the king of a free people. Algernon Sydney, on the other hand, would gladly have aided France in all her ambitious schemes, and have seen England reduced to the condition of a province, in the wild hope that a foreign despot would assist him to establish his darling republic. The king took the money of France to assist him in the enterprise which he meditated against the liberty of his subjects with as tle scruple as Frederic of Prussia or Alexander of Russia accepted our subsidies in time of war. The leaders of the Opposition no more thought themselves disgraced by the presents of Louis than a gentleman of our own time thinks himself disgraced by the liberality of powerful and wealthy members of his party who pay his election bill. The money which the king received from France had been largely employed to corrupt members of Parliament. The enemies of the Court might think it fair, or even absolutely necessary, to encounter bribery with bribery. Thus they took the French gratuities, the needy among them for their own use, the rich probably for the general purposes of the party, without any scruple. If we compare their conduct, not with that of English statesmen in our own time, but with that of persons in those foreign countries which are now situated as England then was, we shall probably see reason to abate something of the severity of censure with which it has been the fashion to visit those proceedings. Yet, when every allowance is made, the transaction is sufficiently offensive. It is satisfactory to find that Lord Russell stands free from any imputation of personal participation in the spoil. An age so miserably poor in all the moral qualities which render public characters respectable can ill spare the credit which it derives from a man, not indeed conspicuous for talents or knowledge, but honest even in

E

his errors, respectable in every relation of life, rationally pious, steadily and placidly brave.

The great improvement which took place in our breed of public men is principally to be ascribed to the Revolution. Yet that memorable event, in a great measure, took its character from the very vices which it was the means of reforming. It was assuredly a happy revolution, and a useful revolution; but it was not, what it has often been called, a glorious revolution. William, and William alone, derived glory from it. The transaction was, in almost every part, discreditable to England. That a tyrant who had violated the fundamental laws of the country, who had attacked the rights of its greatest corporations, who had begun to persecute the established religion of the state, who had never respected the law either in his superstition or in his revenge, could not be pulled down without the aid of a foreign army, is a circumstance not very grateful to our national pride. Yet this is the least degrading part of the story. The shameless insincerity, the warm assurances of general support which James received, down to the moment of general desertion, indicate a meanness of spirit and a looseness of morality most disgraceful to the age. That the enterprise succeeded, at least that it succeeded without bloodshed or commotion, was principally owing to an act of ungrateful perfidy such as no soldier had ever before committed, and to those monstrous fictions respecting the birth of the Prince of Wales which persons of the highest rank were not ashamed to circulate. In all the proceedings of the Convention, in the conference particularly, we see that littleness of mind which is the chief characteristic of the times. The resolutions on which the two Houses at last agreed were as bad as any resolutions for so excellent a purpose could be. Their feeble and contradictory language was evidently intended to save the credit of the Tories, who were ashamed to name what they were not ashamed to do. Through the whole transaction no commanding talents were displayed by any Englishman; no extraordinary risks were run; no sacrifices were made, except the sacrifice which Churchill made of honour, and Anne of natural affection.

It was in some sense fortunate, as we have already said, for the Church of England, that the Reformation in this country was effected by men who cared little about religion. And, in the same manner, it was fortunate for our civil government that the Revolution was, in a great measure, effected by men who cared little about their political principles. At such a crisis, splendid talents and strong passions might have done more harm than good. There was far greater reason to fear that too much would be attempted, and that violent movements would produce an equally violent reaction, than that too little would be done in the way of change. But narrowness of intellect and flexibility of principle, though they may be serviceable, can never be respectable.

If in the Revolution itself there was little that can properly be called glorious, there was still less in the events which followed. In a Church which had, as one man, declared the doctrine of resistance unchristian, only four hundred persons refused to take the oath of allegiance to a government founded on resistance. In the preceding generation both the Episcopal and the Presbyterian clergy, rather than concede points of conscience not more important, had resigned their livings by thousands.

The churchmen, at the time of the Revolution, justified their conduct by all those profligate sophisms which are called Jesuitical, and which are commonly reckoned amongst the peculiar sins of Popery, but which in fact are everywhere the anodynes employed by minds rather subtle than strong, to quiet those internal twinges which they cannot but feel and which they will not obey. As their oath was in the teeth of their principles, so was their conduct in the teeth of their oath. Their constant machinations against the Government to which they had sworn fidelity brought a reproach on their order and on Christianity itself. A distinguished churchman has not scrupled to say that the rapid increase of infidelity at that time was principally produced by the disgust which the faithless conduct of his brethren excited in men not sufficiently candid or judicious to discern the beauties of the system amidst the vices of its ministers.

But the reproach was not confined to the Church. In every political party, in the Cabinet itself, duplicity and perfidy abounded. The very men whom William loaded with benefits, and in whom he reposed most confidence, with his seals of office in their hands, kept up a correspondence with the exiled family. Orford, Carmarthen, and Shrewsbury were guilty of this odious treachery. Even Devonshire is not altogether free from suspicion. It may well be conceived that, at such a time, such a nature as that of Marlborough would riot in the very luxury of baseness. His former treason, thoroughly furnished with all that makes infamy exquisite, placed him under the disadvantage which attends every artist from the time that he produces a masterpiece. Yet his second great stroke may excite wonder, even in those who appreciate all the merit of the first. Lest his admirers should be able to say that at the time of the Revolution he had betrayed his king from any other than selfish motives, he proceeded to betray his country. He sent intelligence to the French Court of a secret expedition intended to attack Brest. The consequence was that the expedition failed, and that eight hundred British soldiers lost their lives from the abandoned villainy of a British general. Yet this man has been canonized by so many eminent writers that to speak of him as he deserves may seem scarcely decent. To us he seems to be the very San Ciappelletto of the political calendar.

The reign of William III., as Mr. Hallam happily says, was the nadir of the national prosperity. It was also the nadir of the national character. During that period was gathered in the rank harvest of vices sown during thirty years of licentiousness and confusion; but it was also the seed-time of great virtues.

The press was emancipated from the censorship soon after the Revolution; and the Government fell immediately under the censorship of the press. Statesmen had a scrutiny to endure which was every day becoming more and more severe. The extreme violence of opinions abated. The Whigs learned moderation in office; the Tories learned the principles of liberty in opposition. The parties almost constantly approximated, often met, sometimes crossed each other. There were occasional bursts of violence; but, from the time of the Revolution, those bursts were constantly becoming less and less terrible. The severity with which the Tories, at the close of the reign of Anne, treated some of those who had directed public affairs during the war of the Grand Alliance, and the retaliatory measures of the Whigs, after the accession of the House of Hanover, cannot be justified; but they were by no means in the style of the infuriated parties whose alternate murders had disgraced our history towards the close of the reign of Charles II. At the fall of Walpole far greater moderation was displayed. And from that time it has been the practice,— a practice not strictly according to the theory of our Constitution, but still most salutary,—to consider the loss of office, and the public disapprobation as punishments sufficient for errors in the administration not imputable to personal corruption. Nothing, we believe, has contributed more than this lenity to raise the character of public men. Ambition is of itself a game sufficiently hazardous and sufficiently deep to inflame the passions, without adding property, life, and liberty to the stake. Where the play runs so desperately high as in the seventeenth century, honour is at an end. Statesmen, instead of being as they should be, at once mild and steady, are at once ferocious and inconsistent. The axe is for ever before their eyes. A popular outcry sometimes unnerves them, and sometimes makes them desperate; it drives them to unworthy compliances, or to measures of vengeance as cruel as those which they have reason to expect. A minister in our times need not fear either to be firm or to be merciful. Our old policy in this respect was as absurd as that of the king in the Eastern tales who proclaimed that any physician who pleased might come to Court and prescribe for his diseases, but that if the remedies failed the adventurer should lose his head. It is easy to conceive how many able men would refuse to undertake the cure on such conditions; how much the sense of extreme danger would confuse the perceptions, and cloud the intellect, of the practitioner, at the very crisis which most called for self-possession, and how strong his temptation would be, if he found that he had committed a blunder, to escape the consequences of it by poisoning his patient.

But, in fact, it would have been impossible, since the Revolution, to punish any minister for the general course of his policy, with the slightest semblance of justice; for since that time no minister has been able to pursue any general course of policy without the approbation of the Parliament. The most important effects of that great change were, as Mr. Hallam has most truly said and most ably shown, those which it indirectly produced. Thenceforward it became the interest of the executive government to protect those very doctrines which an executive government is in general inclined to persecute. The sovereign, the ministers, the courtiers, at last even the universities and the clergy, were changed into advocates of the right of resistance. In the theory of the Whigs, in the situation of the Tories, in the common interest of all public men, the Parliamentary constitution of the country found perfect security. The power of the House of Commons, in particular, has been steadily on the increase. By the practice of granting supplies for short terms, and appropriating them to particular services, it has rendered its approbation as necessary in practice to all the measures of the executive government as it is in the theory of a legislative act.

Mr. Hallam appears to have begun with the reign of Henry VII., as the period at which what is called modern history, in contradistinction to the history of the middle ages, is generally supposed to commence. He has stopped at the accession of George III., "from unwillingness," as he says, "to excite the prejudices of modern politics, especially those connected with personal character." These two eras, we think, deserved the distinction on other grounds. Our remote posterity, when looking back on our history in that comprehensive manner in which remote posterity alone can, without much danger of error, look back on it, will probably observe those points with peculiar interest. They are, if we mistake not, the beginning and the end of an entire and separate chapter in our annals. The period which lies between them is a perfect cycle, a great year of the public mind.

In the reign of Henry VII. all the political differences which had agitated England since the Norman conquest seemed to be set at rest. The long and fierce struggle between the Crown and the barons had terminated. The grievances which had produced the rebellions of Tyler and Cade had disappeared. Villanage was scarcely known. The two royal houses, whose conflicting claims had long convulsed the kingdom, were at length united. The claimants whose pretensions, just or injust, had disturbed the new settlement, were overthrown. In religion there was no open dissent, and probably very little secret heresy. The old subjects of contention, in short, had vanished those which were to succeed had not yet appeared.

Soon, however, new principles were announced; principles which were destined to keep England during two centuries and a half in a state of commotion. The Reformation divided the people into two great parties. The Protestants were victorious.* They again subdivided themselves. Political systems were engrafted on theological doctrines. The mutual animosities of the two parties gradually emerged into the light of public life. First came conflicts in Parliament; then civil war; then revolutions upon revolutions, each attended by its appurtenance of proscriptions, and persecutions, and tests; each followed by severe measures on the part of the conquerors; each exciting a deadly and festering hatred in the conquered. During the reign of George II. things were evidently tending to repose. At the close of it the nation had completed the great revolution which commenced in the early part of the sixteenth century, and was again at rest. The fury of sects had died away. The Catholics themselves practically enjoyed toleration; and more than toleration they did not yet venture even to desire. Jacobitism was a mere name. Nobody was left to fight for that wretched cause, and very few to drink for it. The Constitution, purchased so dearly, was on every side extolled and worshipped. Even those distinctions of party which must almost always be found in a free state could scarcely be traced. The two great bodies which, from the time of the Revolution, had been gradually tending to approximation were now united in emulous support of that splendid administration which smote to the dust both the branches of the House of Bourbon. The great battle for our ecclesiastical and civil polity had been fought and won. The wounds had been healed. The victors and the vanquished were rejoicing together. Every person acquainted with the political writers of the last generation will recollect the terms in which they generally speak of that time. It was a glimpse of a golden age of union and glory,—a short interval of rest, which had been preceded by centuries of agitation, and which centuries of agitation were destined to follow.

How soon faction again began to ferment is well known. In the letters of Junius, in Burke's Thoughts on the Cause of the Discontents, and in many other writings of less merit, the violent dissensions which speedily convulsed the country are imputed to the system of favouritism which George III. introduced, to the influence of Bute, or to the profligacy of those who called themselves the king's friends. With all deference to the eminent writers to whom we have referred, we may venture to say that they lived too near the events of which they treated to judge correctly. The schism which was then appearing in the nation, and which has been from that time almost constantly widening, had little in common with those which had divided it during the reigns of the Tudors and the Stuarts. The symptoms of popular feeling, indeed, will always be in a great measure the same; but the principle which excited that feeling was here new. The support which was given to Wilkes, the clamour for reform during the American war, the disaffected conduct of large classes of people at the time of the French Revolution, no more resembled the opposition which had been offered to the government of Charles II. than that opposition resembled the contest between the Roses.

In the political, as in the natural body, a sensation is often referred to a part widely different from that in which it really resides. A man whose leg is cut off fancies that he feels a pain in his toe. And in the same manner the people, in the earlier part of the late reign, sincerely attributed their discontent to grievances which had been effectually lopped off. They imagined that the prerogative was too strong for the Constitution, that the principles of the Revolution were abandoned, that the system of the Stuarts was restored. Every impartial man must now acknowledge that these charges were groundless. The proceedings of the government with respect to the Middlesex election would have been contemplated with delight by the first generation of Whigs. They would have thought it a splendid triumph of the cause of liberty that the king and the Lords should resign to the House of Commons a portion of the legislative power, and allow it to incapacitate without their consent. This, indeed, Mr. Burke clearly perceived. "When the House of Commons," says he, "in an endeavour to obtain new advantages at the expense of the other orders of the state, for the benefit of the commons at large, have pursued strong measures, if it were not just, it was at least natural; that the constituents should connive at all their proceedings; because we ourselves were ultimately to profit. But when this submission is urged to us in *a contest between the representatives and ourselves*, and where nothing can be put into their scale which is not taken from ours, they fancy us to be children when they tell us that they are our representatives, our own flesh and blood, and that all the stripes they give us are for our good." These sentences contain, in fact, the whole explanation of the mystery. The conflict of the seventeenth century was maintained by the Parliament against the Crown. The conflict which commenced in the middle of the eighteenth century, which still remains undecided, and in which our children and grandchildren will probably be called to act or to suffer, is between a large portion of the people on the one side, and the Crown and the Parliament united on the other.

The privileges of the House of Commons, those privileges which, in 1642, all London rose in arms to defend, which the people considered as synonymous with their own liberties, and in comparison of which they took no account of the most precious and sacred principles of English jurisprudence, have now become nearly as odious as the rigours of martial law. That power of committing which the people anciently loved to see the House of Commons exercise, is now, at least when employed against libellers, the most unpopular power in the Constitution. If the Commons were to suffer the Lords to amend money-bills, we do not believe that the people would care one straw about the matter. If they were to suffer the Lords even to originate money-bills, we doubt whether such a surrender of their constitutional rights would excite half so much dissatisfaction as the exclusion of strangers from a single important discussion. The gallery in which the reporters sit has become a fourth estate of the realm. The publication of the debates, a practice which seemed to the most liberal statesmen of the old school full of danger to the great safeguards of public liberty, is now regarded by many persons as a safeguard tantamount, and more than tantamount, to all the rest together.

Burke, in a speech on parliamentary reform, which is the more remarkable because it was delivered long before the French Revolution, has described, in striking language, the change in public feeling of which we speak. "It suggests melancholy reflections," says he, "in consequence of the strange course we have long held, that we are now no longer quarrelling about the character, or about the conduct of men, or the tenor of measures; but we are grown out of humour with the English Constitution itself; this is become the object of the animosity of Englishmen. This Constitution in former days used to be the envy of the world; it was the pattern for politicians; the theme of the eloquent; the meditation of the philosopher in every part of the world. As to Englishmen, it was their pride,—their consolation. By it they lived, and for it they were ready to die. Its defects, if it had any, were partly covered by partiality, and partly borne by prudence. Now all its excellences are forgot, its faults are forcibly dragged into day, exaggerated by every artifice of misrepresentation. It is despised and rejected of men; and every device and invention of ingenuity or idleness is set up in opposition, or in preference to it." We neither adopt nor condemn the language of reprobation which the great orator here employs. We call him only as a witness to the fact. That the revolution of public feeling which he described was then in progress is indisputable; and it is equally indisputable, we think, that it is in progress still.

To investigate and classify the causes of so great a change would require far more thought, and far more space, than we at present have to bestow. But some of them are obvious. During the contest which the Parliament carried on against the Stuarts, it had only to check and complain. It has since had to govern. As an attacking body, it could select its points of attack, and it naturally chose those on which it was likely to receive public support. As a ruling body, it has neither the same liberty of choice nor the same motives to gratify the people. With the power of an executive government, it has drawn to itself some of the vices, and all the unpopularity of an executive government. On the House of Commons above all, possessed as it is of the public purse, and consequently of the public sword, the nation throws all the blame of an ill-conducted war, of a blundering negociation, of a disgraceful treaty, of an embarrassing commercial crisis. The delays of the Court of Chancery, the misconduct of a judge at Van Diemen's Land, anything, in short, which in any part of the administration any person feels as a grievance, is attributed to the tyranny, or at least to the negligence, of that all-powerful body. Private individuals pester it with their wrongs and claims. A merchant appeals to it from the courts of Rio Janeiro or St. Petersburgh. A painter who can find nobody to buy the acre of spoiled canvas, which he calls a historical picture, pours into its sympathizing ear the whole story of his debts and his jealousies. Anciently the Parliament resembled a member of opposition, from whom no places are expected, who is not required to confer favours and propose measures, but merely to watch and censure, and who may, therefore, unless he is grossly injudicious, be popular with the great body of the community. The Parliament *now* resembles the same person put into office, surrounded by petitioners whom twenty times his patronage would not satisfy; stunned with complaints, buried in memorials, compelled by the duties of his station to bring forward measures similar to those which he was formerly accustomed to observe and to check, and perpetually encountered by objections similar to those which it was formerly his business to raise.

Perhaps it may be laid down as a general rule that a legislative assembly, not constituted on democratical principles, cannot be popular long after it ceases to be weak. Its zeal for what the people, rightly or wrongly, conceive to be their interest, its sympathy with their mutable and violent passions, are merely the effects of the particular circumstances in which it is placed. As long as it depends for existence on the public favour, it will employ all the means in its power to conciliate that favour. While this is the case, defects in its constitution are of little consequence. But, as the close union of such a body with the nation is the effect of an identity of interest not essential but accidental, it is in some measure dissolved from the time at which the danger which produced it ceases to exist.

Hence, before the Revolution, the question of Parliamentary reform was of very little importance. The friends of liberty had no very ardent wish for it. The strongest Tories saw no objections to it. It is remarkable that Clarendon loudly applauds the changes which Cromwell introduced; changes far stronger than the Whigs of the present day would in general approve. There is no reason to think, however, that the reform effected by Cromwell made any great difference in the conduct of the Parliament. Indeed, if the

House of Commons had, during the reign of Charles II., been elected by universal suffrage, or if all the seats had been put up to sale, as in the French Parliaments, it would, we suspect, have acted very much as it did. We know how strongly the Parliament of Paris exerted itself in favour of the people on many important occasions; and the reason is evident. Though it did not emanate from the people, its whole consequence depended on the support of the people. From the time of the Revolution the House of Commons has been gradually becoming what it now is,—a great council of state, containing many members chosen freely by the people, and many others anxious to acquire the favour of the people; but, on the whole, aristocratical in its temper and interest. It is very far from being an illiberal and stupid oligarchy; but is equally far from being an express image of the general feeling. It is influenced by the opinion of the people, and influenced powerfully, but slowly and circuitously. Instead of outrunning the public mind, as before the Revolution it frequently did, it now follows with slow steps and at a wide distance. It is, therefore, necessarily unpopular; and the more so because the good which it produces is much less evident to common perception than the evil which it inflicts. It bears the blame of all the mischief which is done, or supposed to be done, by its authority or by its connivance. It does not get the credit, on the other hand, of having prevented those innumerable abuses which do not exist solely because the House of Commons exists.

A large part of the nation is certainly desirous of a reform in the representative system. How large that part may be, and how strong its desires on the subject may be, it is difficult to say. It is only at intervals that the clamour on the subject is loud and vehement. But it seems to us that, during the remissions, the feeling gathers strength, and that every successive burst is more violent than that which preceded it. The public attention may be for a time diverted to the Catholic claims or the mercantile code; but it is probable that at no very distant period, perhaps in the lifetime of the present generation, all other questions will merge in that which is, in a certain degree, connected with them all.

Already we seem to ourselves to perceive the signs of unquiet times, the vague presentiment of something great and strange which pervades the community, the restless and turbid hopes of those who have everything to gain, the dimly hinted forebodings of those who have everything to lose. Many indications might be mentioned, in themselves, indeed, as insignificant as straws; but even the direction of a straw, to borrow the illustration of Bacon, will show from what quarter the storm is setting in.

A great statesman might, by judicious and timely reformations, by reconciling the two great branches of the natural aristocracy, the capitalists and the landowners, and by so widening the base of the government as to interest in its defence the whole of the middle class, that brave, honest, and sound-hearted class, which is as anxious for the maintenance of order and the security of property as it is hostile to corruption and oppression, succeed in averting a struggle to which no rational friend of liberty or of law can look forward without great apprehensions. There are those who will be contented with nothing but demolition; and there are those who shrink from all repair. There are innovators who long for a President and a National Convention; and there are bigots who, while cities larger and richer than the capitals of many great kingdoms are calling out for representatives to watch over their interests, select some hackneyed jobber in boroughs, some peer of the narrowest and smallest mind, as the fittest depositary of a forfeited franchise. Between these extremes there lies a more excellent way. Time is bringing round another crisis analogous to that which occurred in the seventeenth century. We stand in a situation similar to that in which our ancestors stood under the James I. It will soon again be necessary to reform that we may serve, to save the fundamental principles of the Constitution by alterations in the subordinate parts. It will then be possible, as it was possible a hundred years ago, to protect vested rights, to secure every useful institution,— every institution endeared by antiquity and noble associations, and, at the same time, to introduce into the system improvements harmonizing with the original plan. It remains to be seen whether two hundred years have made us wiser.

We know of no great revolution which might not have been prevented by compromise early and graciously made. Firmness is a great virtue in public affairs; but it has its proper sphere. Conspiracies and insurrections in which small minorities are engaged, the outbreakings of popular violence unconnected with any extensive project or any durable principle, are best repressed by vigour and decision. To shrink from them is to make them formidable. But no wise ruler will confound the pervading taint with the slight local irritation. No wise ruler will treat the deeply seated discontents of a great party, as he treats the fury of a mob which destroys, mills and power-looms. The neglect of this distinction has been fatal even to governments strong in the power of the sword. The present time is indeed a time of peace and order. But it is at such a time that fools are most thoughtless, and wise men most thoughtful. That the discontents which have agitated the country during the late and the present reign, and which, though not always noisy, are never wholly dormant, will again break forth with aggravated symptoms, is almost as certain as that the tides and seasons will follow their appointed course. But in all movements of the human mind which tend to great revolutions there is a crisis at which moderate concession may amend, conciliate and preserve. Happy will it be for England if, at that crisis, her interests be confided to men for whom history has not recorded the long series of human crimes and follies in vain.

SOUTHEY'S COLLOQUIES ON SOCIETY.

Sir Thomas More; or, Colloquies on the Progress and Prospects of Society. By ROBERT SOUTHEY, Esq., LL.D., Poet Laureate. 2 vols. 8vo. Lond. 1829.

IT would be scarcely possible for a man of Mr. Southey's talents and acquirements to write two volumes so large as those before us, which should be wholly destitute of information and amusement. Yet we do not remember to have read with so little satisfaction any equal quantity of matter, written by any man of real abilities. We have, for some time past, observed with great regret the strange infatuation which leads the Poet-laureate to abandon those departments of literature in which he might excel, and to lecture the public on sciences of which he has still the very alphabet to learn. He has now, we think, done his worst. The subject which he has at last undertaken to treat is one which demands all the highest intellectual and moral qualities of a philosophical statesman,—an understanding at once comprehensive and acute, —a heart at once upright and charitable. Mr. Southey brings to the task two faculties which were never, we believe, vouchsafed in measure so copious to any human being,—the faculty of believing without a reason, and the faculty of hating without a provocation.

It is, indeed, most extraordinary that a mind like Mr. Southey's,—a mind richly endowed in many respects by nature, and highly cultivated by study,— a mind which has exercised considerable influence on the most enlightened generation of the most enlightened people that ever existed—should be utterly destitute of the power of discerning truth from falsehood. Yet such is the fact. Government is to Mr. Southey one of the fine arts. He judges of a theory or a public measure, of a religion, a political party, a peace or a war, as men judge of a picture or a statue, by the effect produced on his imagination. A chain of associations is to him what a chain of reasoning is to other men; and what he calls his opinions, are in fact merely his tastes.

Part of this description might, perhaps, apply to a much greater man, Mr. Burke. But Mr. Burke, assuredly, possessed an understanding admirably fitted for the investigation of truth,—an understanding stronger than that of any statesman, active or speculative, of the eighteenth century,—stronger than everything, except his own fierce and ungovernable sensibility. Hence, he generally chose his side like a fanatic, and defended it like a philosopher. His conduct, in the most important events of his life,—at the time of the impeachment of Hastings, for example, and at the time of the French Revolution,—seems to have been prompted by those feelings and motives, which Mr. Coleridge has so happily described:

"Stormy pity, and the cherish'd lure
Of pomp, and proud precipitance of soul."

Hindostan, with its vast cities, its gorgeous pagodas, its infinite swarms of dusky population, its long-descended dynasties, its stately etiquette, excited in a mind so capacious, so imaginative, and so susceptible, the most intense interest. The peculiarities of the costume, of the manners, and of the laws, the very mystery which hung over the language and origin of the people, seized his imagination. To plead in Westminster Hall, in the name of the English people, at the bar of the English nobles, for great nations and kings separated from him by half the world, seemed to him the height of human glory. Again, it is not difficult to perceive, that his hostility to the French Revolution principally arose from the vexation which he felt, at having all his old political associations disturbed, at seeing the well-known boundary-marks of states obliterated, and the names and distinctions with which the history of Europe had been filled for ages, swept away. He felt like an antiquarian whose shield had been scoured, or a connoisseur, who found his Titian retouched. But however he came by an opinion, he had no sooner got it, than he did his best to make out a legitimate title to it. His reason, like a spirit in the service of an enchanter, though spell-bound, was still mighty. It did whatever work his passions and his imagination might impose. But it did that work, however arduous, with marvellous dexterity and vigour. His course was not determined by argument; but he could defend the wildest course by arguments more plausible, than those by which common men support opinions, which they have adopted, after the fullest deliberation. Reason has scarcely ever displayed, even in those well-constituted minds of which she occupies the throne, so much power and energy as in the lowest offices of that imperial servitude.

Now, in the mind of Mr. Southey, reason has no place at all, as either leader or follower, as either sovereign or slave. He does not seem to know what an argument is. He never uses arguments himself. He never troubles himself to answer the arguments of his opponents. It has never occurred to him, that a man ought to be able to give some better account of the way in which he has arrived at his opinions than merely that it is his will and pleasure to hold them,—that there is a difference between assertion and demonstration, —that a rumour does not always prove a fact,—that a fact does not always prove a theory,—that two contradictory propositions cannot be undeniable truths,—that to beg the question, is not the way to settle it,—or that when an objection is raised, it ought to be met with something more convincing, than "scoundrel" and "blockhead."

It would be absurd to read the works of such a writer for political instruction. The utmost that can be expected from any system promulgated by him is that it may be splendid and affecting,—that it may suggest sublime and pleasing images. His scheme of philosophy is a mere day-dream, a poetical creation, like the Domdaniel caverns, the Swerga, or Padalon; and indeed, it bears no inconsiderable resemblance to those gorgeous visions. Like them, it has something of invention, grandeur, and brilliancy. But like them, it is grotesque and extravagant, and perpetually violates that conventional probability which is essential to the effect even of works of art.

The warmest admirers of Mr. Southey will scarcely, we think, deny that his success has almost always borne an inverse proportion to the degree in which his undertakings have required a logical head. His poems, taken in the mass, stand far higher than his prose works. The Laureate Odes, indeed, among which the Vision of Judgment must be classed, are, for the most part, worse than Pye's, and as bad as Cibber's; nor do we think him generally happy in short pieces. But his longer poems, though full of faults, are nevertheless very extraordinary productions. We doubt greatly whether they will be read fifty years hence,—but that if they are read, they will be admired, we have no doubt whatever.

But though in general we prefer Mr. Southey's poetry to his prose, we must make one exception. The Life of Nelson is, beyond all doubt, the most perfect and the most delightful of his works. The fact is, as his poems most abundantly prove, that he is by no means so skilful in designing, as in filling up. It was therefore an advantage to him to be furnished with an outline of characters and events, and to have no other task to perform than that of touching the cold sketch into life. No writer, perhaps, ever lived, whose talents so precisely qualified him to write the history of the great naval warrior. There were no fine riddles of the human heart to read—no theories to found— no hidden causes to develope—no remote consequences to predict. The character of the hero lay on the surface. The exploits were brilliant and picturesque. The necessity of adhering to the real course of events saved Mr. Southey from those faults which deform the original plan of almost every one of his poems, and which even his innumerable beauties of detail scarcely redeem. The subject did not require the exercise of those reasoning powers the want of which is the blemish of his prose. It would not be easy to find in all literary history, an instance of a more exact hit between wind and water. John Wesley, and the Peninsular War, were subjects of a very different kind, —subjects which required all the qualities of a philosophic historian. In Mr. Southey's works on these subjects, he has, on the whole, failed. Yet there are charming specimens of the art of narration in both of them. The Life of Wesley will probably live. Defective as it is, it contains the only popular account of a most remarkable moral revolution, and of a man whose eloquence and logical acuteness might have rendered him eminent in literature, whose genius for government was not inferior to that of Richelieu, and who, whatever his errors may have been, devoted all his powers, in defiance of obloquy and derision, to what he sincerely considered as the highest good of his species. The History of the Peninsular War is already dead:—indeed, the second volume was dead-born. The glory of producing an imperishable record of that great conflict seems to be reserved for Colonel Napier.

The Book of the Church contains some stories very prettily told. The rest is mere rubbish. The adventure was manifestly one which could be achieved only by a profound thinker, and in which even a profound thinker might have failed, unless his passions had been kept under strict control. In all those works in which Mr. Southey has completely abandoned narration, and undertaken to argue moral and political questions, his failure has been complete and ignominious. On such occasions, his writings are rescued from utter contempt and derision solely by the beauty and purity of the English. We find, we confess, so great a charm in Mr. Southey's style, that, even when he writes nonsense, we generally read it with pleasure, except, indeed, when he tries to be droll. A more insufferable jester never existed. He very often attempts to be humorous, and yet we do not remember a single occasion on which he has succeeded farther than to be quaintly and flippantly dull. In one of his works, he tells us that Bishop Sprat was very properly so called, inasmuch as he was a very small poet. And in the book now before us, he cannot quote Francis Bugg without a remark on his unsavoury name. A man might talk folly like this by his own fireside; but that any human being, after having made such a joke, should write it down, and copy it out, and transmit it to the printer, and correct the proof-sheets, and send it forth into the world, is enough to make us ashamed of our species.

The extraordinary bitterness of spirit which Mr. Southey manifests towards his opponents is, no doubt, in a great measure to be attributed to the manner in which he forms his opinions. Differences of taste, it has often been remarked, produce greater exasperation than differences on points of science. But this is not all. A peculiar austerity marks almost all Mr. Southey's judgments of men and actions. We are far from blaming him for fixing on a high standard of morals, and for applying that standard to every case. But rigour ought to be accompanied by discernment, and of discernment Mr. Southey seems to be utterly destitute. His mode of judging is monkish; it is exactly what we should expect from a stern old Benedictine, who had been preserved from many ordinary frailties by the restraints of his situation. No man out of a cloister ever wrote about love, for example, so coldly and at the same time so grossly. His descriptions of it are just what we should hear from a recluse who knew the passion only from the details of the confessional. Almost all his heroes make love either like seraphim or like cattle. He seems to have no notion of anything between the Platonic passion of the Glendoveer, who gazes with rapture on his mistress's leprosy, and the brutal appetite of Arvalan and Roderick. In Roderick, indeed, the two characters are united. He is first all clay, and then all spirit; he goes forth a Tarquin, and comes back too ethereal to be married. The only love-scene, as far as we can recollect, in Madoc, consists of the delicate attentions which a savage, who has drunk too much of the prince's metheglin, offers to Goervyl. It would be the labour of a week to find in all the vast mass of Mr. Southey's poetry a single passage indicating any sympathy with those feelings which have consecrated the shades of Vaucluse and the rocks of Meillerie.

Indeed, if we except some very pleasing images of paternal tendernesss and filial duty, there is scarcely anything soft or humane in Mr. Southey's poetry. What theologians call the spiritual sins are his cardinal virtues—hatred, pride, and the insatiable thirst of vengeance. These passions he disguises under the name of duties; he purifies them from the alloy of vulgar interests; he ennobles them by uniting them with energy, fortitude, and a severe sanctity of manners, and then holds them up to the admiration of mankind. This is the spirit of Thalaba, of Ladurlad, of Adosinda, of Roderick after his regeneration. It is the spirit which, in all his writings, Mr. Southey appears to affect. "I do well to be angry," seems to be the predominant feeling of his mind. Almost the only mark of charity which he vouchsafes to his opponents is to pray for their conversion, and this he does in terms not unlike those in which we can imagine a Portuguese priest interceding with Heaven for a Jew delivered over to the secular arm after a relapse.

We have always heard, and fully believe, that Mr. Southey is a very amiable and humane man; nor do we intend to apply to him personally any of the remarks which we have made on the spirit of his writings. Such are the caprices of human nature. Even Uncle Toby troubled himself very little about the French grenadiers who fell on the glacis of Namur. And when Mr. Southey takes up his pen, he changes his nature as much as Captain Shandy when he girt on his sword. The only opponents to whom he gives quarter are those in whom he finds something of his own character reflected. He seems to have an instinctive antipathy for calm, moderate men—for men who shun extremes and who render reasons. He has treated Mr. Owen, of Lanark, for example, with infinitely more respect than he has shown to Mr. Hallam or to Dr. Lingard; and this for no reason that we can discover, except that Mr. Owen is more unreasonably and hopelessly in the wrong than any speculator of our time.

Mr. Southey's political system is just what we might expect from a man who regards politics not as a matter of science, but as a matter of taste and feeling. All his schemes of government have been inconsistent with themselves. In his youth he was a republican; yet, as he tells us in his preface to these Colloquies, he was even then opposed to the Catholic claims. He is now a violent Ultra-Tory. Yet while he maintains, with vehemence approaching to ferocity, all the sterner and harsher parts of the Ultra-Tory theory of government, the baser and dirtier part of that theory disgusts him. Exclusion, persecution, severe punishments for libellers and demagogues, proscriptions, massacres, civil war, if necessary, rather than any concession to a discontented people,—these are the measures which he seems inclined to recommend. A severe and gloomy tyranny—crushing opposition, silencing remonstrance, drilling the minds of the people into unreasoning obedience—has in it something of grandeur which delights his imagination. But there is nothing fine in the shabby tricks and jobs of office. And Mr. Southey, accordingly, has no toleration for them. When a democrat, he did not perceive that his system led logically, and would have led practically, to the removal of religious distinctions. He now commits a similar error. He renounces the abject and paltry part of the creed of his party, without perceiving that it is also an essential part of that creed. He would have tyranny and purity together; though the most superficial observation might have shown him that there can be no tyranny without corruption.

It is high time, however, that we should proceed to the consideration of the work, which is our more immediate subject, and which, indeed, illustrates in almost every page our general remarks on Mr. Southey's writings. In the preface, we are informed that the author, notwithstanding some statements to the contrary, was always opposed to the Catholic claims. We fully believe this; both because we are sure that Mr. Southey is incapable of publishing a deliberate falsehood, and because his averment is in itself probable. It is exactly what we should have expected that, even in his wildest paroxysms of democratic enthusiasm, Mr. Southey would have felt no wish to see a simple remedy applied to a great practical evil; that the only measure which all the great statesmen of two generations have agreed with each other in supporting would be the only measure which Mr. Southey would have agreed with himself in opposing. He has passed from one extreme of political opinion to another, as Satan, in Milton, went round the globe, contriving constantly to "ride with darkness." Wherever the thickest shadow of the night may at any moment chance to fall, there is Mr. Southey. It is not everybody who could have so dexterously avoided blundering on the daylight in the course of a journey to the Antipodes.

Mr. Southey has not been fortunate in the plan of any of his fictitious narratives. But he has never failed so conspicuously as in the work before us; except, indeed, in the wretched Vision of Judgment. In November 1817, it seems, the Laureate was sitting over his newspaper, and meditating about the death of the Princess Charlotte. An elderly person, of very dignified aspect, makes his appearance announces himself as a stranger from a distant country, and apologises very politely for not having provided himself with letters of introduction. Mr. Southey supposes his visitor to be some American gentleman, who has come to see the lakes and the lake-poets, and accordingly proceeds to perform, with that grace which only long experience can give, all the duties which authors owe to starers. He assures his guest that some of the most agreeable visits which he has received have been from Americans, and that he knows men among them whose talents and virtues would do honour to any country. In passing, we may observe, to the honour of Mr. Southey, that, though he evidently has no liking for the American institutions, he never speaks of the people of the United States with that pitiful affectation of contempt by which some members of his party have done more than wars or tariffs can do to excite mutual enmity between two communities formed for mutual friendship. Great as the faults of his mind are, paltry spite like this has no place in it. Indeed, it is scarcely conceivable that a man of his sensibility and his imagination should look without pleasure and national pride on the vigorous and splendid youth of a great people, whose veins are filled with our blood, whose minds are nourished with our literature, and on whom is entailed the rich inheritance of our civilisation, our freedom, and our glory.

But we must return to Mr. Southey's study at Keswick. The visitor informs the hospitable poet that he is not an American, but a spirit. Mr. Southey, with more frankness than civility, tells him that he is a very queer one. The stranger holds out his hand. It has neither weight nor substance. Mr. Southey upon this becomes more serious; his hair stands on end; and he adjures the spectre to tell him what he is, and why he comes. The ghost turns out to be Sir Thomas More. The traces of martyrdom, it seems, are worn in the other world, as stars and ribbauds are worn in this. Sir Thomas shows the poet a red streak round his neck, brighter than a ruby, and informs him that Cranmer wears a suit of flames in paradise,—the right hand glove, we suppose, of peculiar brilliancy.

Sir Thomas pays but a short visit on this occasion, but promises to cultivate the new acquaintance which he has formed, and, after begging that his visit may be kept secret from Mrs. Southey, vanishes into air.

The rest of the book consists of conversations between Mr. Southey and the spirit about trade, currency, Catholic emancipation, periodical literature, female nunneries, butchers, snuff, book-stalls, and a hundred other subjects. Mr. Southey very hospitably takes an opportunity to lionize the ghost round the lakes, and directs his attention to the most beautiful points of view. Why a spirit was to be evoked for the purpose of talking over such matters, and seeing such sights—why the vicar of the parish, a blue-stocking from London, or an American, such as Mr. Southey supposed his aerial visitor to be, might not have done as well—we are unable to perceive. Sir Thomas tells Mr. Southey nothing about future events, and indeed absolutely disclaims the gift of prescience. He has learned to talk modern English: he has read all the new publications, and loves a jest as well as when he jested with the executioner, though we cannot say that the quality of his wit has materially improved in paradise. His powers of reasoning, too, are by no means in as great vigour as when he sate on the woolsack; and though he boasts that he is "divested of all those passions which cloud the intellects and warp the understandings of men," we think him—we must confess—far less stoical than formerly. As to revelations, he tells Mr. Southey at the outset to expect none from him. The Laureate expresses some doubts, which assuredly will not raise him in the opinion of our modern millennarians, as to the divine authority of the Apocalypse. But the ghost preserves an impenetrable silence. As far as we remember, only one hint about the employments of disembodied spirits escapes him. He encourages Mr. Southey to hope that there is a Paradise Press, at which all the valuable publications of Mr. Murray and Mr. Colburn are reprinted as regularly as at Philadelphia; and delicately insinuates, that Thalaba and the Curse of Kehama are among the number. What a contrast does this absurd fiction present to those charming narratives which Plato and Cicero prefixed to their dialogues! What cost in machinery, yet what poverty of effect! A ghost brought in to say what any man might have said! The glorified spirit of a great statesman and philosopher dawdling, like a bilious old Nabob at a watering-place, over quarterly reviews and novels—dropping in to pay long calls—making excursions in search of the picturesque! The scene of St. George and St. Denys in the Pucelle is hardly more ridiculous. We know what Voltaire meant. Nobody, however, can suppose that Mr. Southey means to make game of the mysteries of a higher state of existence. The fact is, that in the work before us, in the Vision of Judgment, and in some of his other pieces, his mode of treating the most solemn subjects differs from that of open scoffers only as the extravagant representations of sacred persons and things in some grotesque Italian paintings differ from the caricatures which Carlile exposes in the front of his shop. We interpret the particular act by the general character. What in the window of a convicted blasphemer we call blasphemous, we call only absurd and ill-judged in an altar-piece.

We now come to the conversations which pass between Mr. Southey and Sir Thomas More, or rather between two Southeys, equally eloquent, equally angry, equally unreasonable, and equally given to talk about what they do not understand. Perhaps we could not select a better instance of the spirit which pervades the whole book than the discussion touching butchers. These persons are represented as castaways, as men whose employment hebetates the faculties and hardens the heart; not that the poet has any scruples about the use of animal food. He acknowledges that it is for the good of the animals themselves that men should feed upon them. "Nevertheless," says he, "I cannot but acknowledge, like good old John Fox, that the sight of a slaughter-house or shambles, if it does not disturb this clear conviction, excites in me uneasiness and pain, as well as loathing. And that they produce a worse effect upon the persons employed in them, is a fact acknowledged by that law or custom which excludes such persons from sitting on juries upon cases of life and death."

This is a fair specimen of Mr. Southey's mode of looking at all moral questions. Here is a body of men engaged in an employment, which, by his own account, is beneficial, not only to mankind, but to the very creatures on whom we feed. Yet he represents them as men who are necessarily reprobates—as men who must necessarily be reprobates, even in the most improved state of society—even, to use his own phrase, in a Christian Utopia. And what reasons are given for a judgment so directly opposed to every principle of sound and manly morality? Merely this, that he cannot abide the sight of their apparatus—that, from certain peculiar associations, he is affected with disgust when he passes by their shops. He gives, indeed, another reason; a certain law or custom, which never existed but in the imaginations of old women, and which, if it had existed, would have proved just as much against butchers as the ancient prejudice against the practice of taking interest for money, proves against the merchants of England. Is a surgeon a castaway? We believe that nurses, when they instruct children in that venerable law or custom which Mr. Southey so highly approves, generally join the surgeon to the butcher. A dissecting-room would, we should think, affect the nerves of most people as much as a butcher's shambles. But the most amusing circumstance is, that Mr. Southey, who detests a butcher, should look with special favour on a soldier. He seems highly to approve of the sentiment of General Meadows, who swore that a grenadier was the highest character in this world or in the next; and assures us, that a virtuous soldier is placed in the situation which most tends to his improvement, and will most promote his eternal interests. Human blood, indeed, is by no means an object of so much loathing to Mr. Southey, as the hides and paunches of cattle. In 1814, he poured forth poetical maledictions on all who talked of peace with Buonaparte. He went over the field of Waterloo,—a field, beneath which twenty thousand of the stoutest hearts that ever beat are mouldering,—and came back in an ecstasy, which he mistook for poetical inspiration. In most of his poems,— particularly in his best poem, Roderick,—and in most of his prose works, particularly in the history of the Peninsular War, he shows a delight in snuffing up carnage, which would not have misbecome a Scandinavian bard, but which sometimes seems to harmonize ill with the Christian morality. We do not, however, blame Mr. Southey for exulting, even a little ferociously, in the brave deeds of his countrymen, or for finding something "comely and reviving" in the bloody vengeance inflicted by an oppressed people on its oppressors. Now, surely, if we find that a man whose business is to kill Frenchmen may be humane, we may hope that means may be found to render a man humane whose business is to kill sheep. If the brutalizing effect of such scenes as the storm of St. Sebastian may be counteracted, we may hope that in a Christian Utopia, some minds might be proof against the kennels and dressers of Aldgate. Mr. Southey's feeling, however, is easily explained. A butcher's knife is by no means so elegant as a sabre, and a calf does not bleed with half the grace of a poor wounded hussar.

It is in the same manner that Mr. Southey appears to have formed his opinion of the manufacturing system. There is nothing which he hates so bitterly. It is, according to him, a system more tyrannical than that of the feudal ages,—a system of actual servitude,—a system which destroys the bodies and degrades the minds of those who are engaged in it. He expresses a hope that the competition of other nations may drive us out of the field; that our foreign trade may decline, and that we may thus enjoy a restoration of national sanity and strength. But he seems to think that the extermination of the whole manufacturing population would be a blessing, if the evil could be removed in no other way.

Mr. Southey does not bring forward a single fact in support of these views, and, as it seems to us, there are facts which lead to a very different conclusion. In the first place, the poor-rate is very decidedly lower in the manufacturing than in the agricultural districts. If Mr. Southey will look over the Parliamentary returns on this subject, he will find that the amount of parish relief required by the labourers in the different counties of England, is almost exactly in inverse proportion to the degree in which the manufacturing system has been introduced into those counties. The returns for the years ending in March 1825, and in March 1828, are now before us. In the former year, we find the poor-rate highest in Sussex,—about twenty shillings to every inhabitant. Then come Buckinghamshire, Essex, Suffolk, Bedfordshire, Huntingdonshire, Kent, and Norfolk. In all these the rate is above fifteen shillings a-head. We will not go through the whole. Even in Westmoreland, and the North Riding of Yorkshire, the rate is at more than eight shillings. In Cumberland and Monmouthshire, the most fortunate of all the agricultural districts, it is at six shillings. But in the West Riding of Yorkshire, it is as low as five shillings; and when we come to Lancashire, we find it at four shillings,—one-fifth of what it is in Sussex. The returns of the year ending in March, 1828, are a little, and but a little, more unfavourable to the manufacturing districts. Lancashire, even in that season of distress, required a smaller poor-rate than any other district, and little more than one-fourth of the poor-rate raised in Sussex. Cumberland alone, of the agricultural districts, was as well off as the West Riding of Yorkshire. These facts seem to indicate that the manufacturer is both in a more comfortable and in a less dependent situation than the agricultural labourer.

As to the effect of the manufacturing system on the bodily health, we must beg leave to estimate it by a standard far too low and vulgar for a mind so imaginative as that of Mr. Southey—the proportion of births and deaths. We know that, during the growth of this atrocious system—this new misery,—(we use the phrases of Mr. Southey,)—this new enormity—this birth of a portentous age—this pest, which no man can approve whose heart is not seared, or whose understanding has not been darkened—there has been a great diminution of mortality—and that this diminution has been greater in the manufacturing towns than anywhere else. The mortality still is, as it always was, greater in towns than in the country. But the difference has diminished in an extraordinary degree. There is the best reason to believe that the annual mortality of Manchester about the middle of the last century was one in twenty-eight; it is now reckoned at one in forty-five. In Glasgow and Leeds a similar improvement has taken place. Nay, the rate of mortality in those three great capitals of the manufacturing districts is now considerably less than it was fifty years ago over England and Wales taken together—open country and all. We might with some plausibility maintain that the people live longer because they are better fed, better lodged, better clothed, and better attended in sickness; and that these improvements are owing to that increase of national wealth which the manufacturing system has produced.

Much more might be said on this subject. But to what end? It is not from bills of mortality and statistical tables that Mr. Southey has learned his political creed. He cannot stoop to study the history of the system which he abuses—to strike the balance between the good and evil which it has produced —to compare district with district, or generation with generation. We will give his own reason for his opinion—the only reason which he gives for it—in his own words :—

"We remained awhile in silence, looking upon the assemblage of dwellings below. Here, and in the adjoining hamlet of Millbeck, the effects of manufactures and of agriculture may be seen and compared. The old cottages are such as the poet and the painter equally delight in beholding. Substantially built of the native stone without mortar, dirtied with no white lime, and their long, low roofs covered with slate, if they had been raised by the magic of some indigenous Amphion's music, the materials could not have adjusted themselves more beautifully in accord with the surrounding scene; and time has still further harmonized them with weather-stains, lichens, and moss, short grasses, and short fern, and stone-plants of various kinds. The ornamented chimneys, round or square, less adorned than those which, like little turrets, crest the houses of the Portuguese peasantry; and yet not less happily suited to their place, the hedge of clipt box beneath the windows, the rose-bushes beside the door, the little patch of flower-ground, with its tall hollyhocks in front; the garden beside, the bee-hives, and the orchard with its bank of daffodils and snow-drops, the earliest and the profusest in these parts, indicate in the owners some portion of ease and leisure, some regard to neatness and comfort, some sense of natural, and innocent, and healthful enjoyment. The new cottages of the manufacturers are upon the manufacturing pattern—naked, and in a row.

"How is it, said I, that everything which is connected with manufactures presents such features of unqualified deformity? From the largest of Mammon's temples down to the poorest hovel in which his helotry are stalled, these edifices have all one character. Time will not mellow them; nature will neither clothe nor conceal them; and they will remain always as offensive to the eye as to the mind."

Here is wisdom. Here are the principles on which nations are to be governed. Rose-bushes and poor-rates, rather than steam-engines and independence. Mortality and cottages with weather-stains, rather than health and long life with edifices which time cannot mellow. We are told that our age has invented atrocities beyond the imagination of our fathers; that society has been brought into a state compared with which extermination would be a blessing;—and all because the dwellings of cotton-spinners are naked and rectangular. Mr. Southey has found out a way, he tells us, in which the effects of manufactures and agriculture may be compared. And what is this way? To stand on a hill, to look at a cottage and a manufactory, and to see which is the prettier. Does Mr. Southey think that the body of the English peasantry live, or ever lived, in substantial and ornamented cottages, with box-edges, flower-gardens, bee-hives, and orchards? If not, what is his parallel worth? We despise those *filosofastri*, who think that they serve the cause of science by depreciating literature and the fine arts. But if anything could excuse their narrowness of mind, it would be such a book as this. It is not strange that when one enthusiast makes the picturesque the test of political good, another should feel inclined to proscribe altogether the pleasures of taste and imagination.

Thus it is that Mr. Southey reasons about matters with which he thinks himself perfectly conversant. We cannot, therefore, be surprised to find that he commits extraordinary blunders when he writes on points of which he acknowledges himself to be ignorant. He confesses that he is not versed in political economy—that he has neither liking nor aptitude for it; and he then proceeds to read the public a lecture concerning it which fully bears out his confession.

"All wealth," says Sir Thomas More, "in former times was tangible. It consisted in land, money, or chattels, which were either of real or conventional value."

Montesinos, as Mr. Southey somewhat affectedly calls himself, answers:—

"Jewels, for example, and pictures, as in Holland,—where indeed at one time tulip bulbs answered the same purpose."

"That bubble," says Sir Thomas, "was one of those contagious insanities to which communities are subject. All wealth was real, till the extent of commerce rendered a paper currency necessary; which differed from precious stones and pictures in this important point, that there was no limit to its production."

"We regard it," says Montesinos, "as the representative of real wealth; and, therefore, limited always to the amount of what it represents."

"Pursue that notion," answers the ghost, "and you will be in the dark presently. Your provincial bank-notes, which constitute almost wholly the circulating medium of certain districts, pass current to-day. To-morrow, tidings may come that the house which issued them has stopped payment, and what do they represent then? You will find them the shadow of a shade."

We scarcely know at which end to begin to disentangle this knot of absurdities. We might ask why it should be a greater proof of insanity in men to set a high value on rare tulips than on rare stones, which are neither more useful nor more beautiful? We might ask how it can be said that there is no limit to the production of paper money when a man is hanged if he issues any in the name of another, and is forced to cash what he issues in his own? But Mr. Southey's error lies deeper still. "All wealth," says he, "was tangible and real till paper currency was introduced." Now, was there ever, since men emerged from a state of utter barbarism, an age in which there were no debts? Is not a debt, while the solvency of the debtor is undoubted, always reckoned as part of the wealth of the creditor? Yet is it tangible and real wealth? Does it cease to be wealth, because there is the security of a written acknowledgment for it? And what else is paper currency? Did Mr. Southey ever read a bank-note? If he did, he would see that it is a written acknowledgment of a debt, and a promise to pay that debt. The promise may be violated—the debt may remain unpaid—those to whom it was due may suffer: but this is a risk not confined to cases of paper currency—it is a risk inseparable from the relation of debtor and creditor. Every man who sells goods for anything but ready money runs the risk of finding that what he considered as part of his wealth one day is nothing at all the next day. Mr. Southey refers to the picture galleries of Holland. The pictures were undoubtedly real and tangible possessions. But surely, it might happen that a burgomaster might owe a picture-dealer a thousand guilders for a Teniers. What in this case corresponds to our paper money is not the picture, which is tangible, but the claim of the picture-dealer on his customer for the price of the picture, which is not tangible. Now, would not the picture-dealer consider this claim as part of his wealth? Would not a tradesman who knew of it give credit to the picture dealer the more readily on account of it? The burgomaster might be ruined. If so, would not those consequences follow which, as Mr. Southey tells us, were never heard of till paper money came into use? Yesterday this claim was worth a thousand guilders. To-day what is it? The shadow of a shade.

It is true that the more readily claims of this sort are transferred from hand to hand, the more extensive will be the injury produced by a single failure. The laws of all nations sanction, in certain cases, the transfer of rights not yet reduced into possession. Mr. Southey would scarcely wish, we should think, that all endorsements of bills and notes should be declared invalid. Yet even if this were done the transfer of claims would imperceptibly take place to a very great extent. When the baker trusts the butcher, for example, he is in fact, though not in form, trusting the butcher's customers. A man who owes large bills to tradesmen and fails to pay them, almost always produces distress through a very wide circle of people whom he never dealt with.

In short, what Mr. Southey takes for a difference in kind, is only a difference of form and degree. In every society men have claims on the property of others. In every society there is a possibility that some debtors may not be able to fulfil their obligations. In every society, therefore, there is wealth which is not tangible, and which may become the shadow of a shade.

Mr. Southey then proceeds to a dissertation on the national debt, which he considers in a new and most consolatory light, as a clear addition to the income of the country.

"You can understand," says Sir Thomas, "that it constitutes a great part of the national wealth."

"So large a part," answers Montesinos, "that the interest amounted, during the prosperous time of agriculture, to as much as the rental of all the land in Great Britain; and at present to the rental of all lands, all houses, and all other fixed property put together."

The ghost and the Laureate agree that it is very desirable that there should be so secure and advantageous a deposit for wealth as the funds afford. Sir Thomas then proceeds:—

"Another and far more momentous benefit must not be overlooked; the expenditure of an annual interest, equalling, as you have stated, the present rental of all fixed property."

"That expenditure," quoth Montesinos, "gives employment to half the industry in the kingdom, and feeds half the mouths. Take, indeed, the weight of the national debt from this great and complicated social machine, and the wheels must stop."

From this passage we should have been inclined to think that Mr. Southey supposes the dividend to be a free-gift periodically sent down from heaven to the fundholders, as quails and manna were sent to the Israelites; were it not that he has vouchsafed, in the following question and answer, to give the public some information which, we believe, was very little needed.

"Whence comes the interest?" says Sir Thomas.

"It is raised," answers Montesinos, "by taxation."

Now, has Mr. Southey ever considered what would be done with this sum if it were not paid as interest to the national creditor? If he would think over this matter for a short time, we suspect that the "momentous benefit" of which he talks would appear to him to shrink strangely in amount. A fundholder, we will suppose, spends an income of five hundred pounds a-year, and his ten nearest neighbours pay fifty pounds each to the tax-gatherer, for the purpose of discharging the interest of the national debt. If the debt were wiped out—a measure, be it understood, which we by no means recommend— the fundholder would cease to spend his five hundred pounds a-year. He would no longer give employment to industry, or put food into the mouths of labourers. This Mr. Southey thinks a fearful evil. But is there no mitigating circumstance? Each of his ten neighbours has fifty pounds more than formerly. Each of them will, as it seems to our feeble understandings, employ more industry, and feed more mouths, than formerly. The sum is exactly the same. It is in different hands. But on what grounds does Mr. Southey call upon us to believe that it is in the hands of men who will spend less liberally or less judiciously? He seems to think that nobody but a fundholder can employ the poor; that if a tax is remitted, those who formerly used to pay it proceed immediately to dig holes in the earth, and bury the sum which the government had been accustomed to take; that no money can set industry in motion till it has been taken by the tax-gatherer out of one man's pocket and put into another man's. We really wish that Mr. Southey would try to prove this principle, which is, indeed, the foundation of his whole theory of finance; for we think it right to hint to him that our hard-hearted and unimaginative generation will expect some more satisfactory reason than the only one with which he has yet favoured it,—a similitude touching evaporation and dew.

Both the theory and the illustration, indeed, are old friends of ours. In every season of distress which we can remember, Mr. Southey has been proclaiming that it is not from economy, but from increased taxation, that the country must expect relief; and he still, we find, places the undoubting faith of a political Diafoirus, in his

"Resaignare, repurgare, et reclysterizare."

"A people," he tells us, "may be too rich, but a government cannot be so."

"A state," says he, "cannot have more wealth at its command than may be employed for the general good, a liberal expenditure in national works being one of the surest means for promoting national prosperity; and the benefit being still more obvious, of an expenditure directed to the purposes of national improvement. But a people may be too rich."

We fully admit that a state cannot have at its command more wealth than may be employed for the general good. But neither can individuals, or bodies of individuals, have at their command more wealth than may be employed for the general good. If there be no limit to the sum which may be usefully laid out in public works and national improvement, then wealth, whether in the hands of private men or of the government, may always, if the possessors choose to spend it usefully, be usefully spent. The only ground, therefore, on which Mr. Southey can possibly maintain that a government cannot be too rich, but that a people may be too rich, must be this: that governments are more likely to spend their money on good objects than private individuals.

But what is useful expenditure? "A liberal expenditure in national works," says Mr. Southey, "is one of the surest means for promoting national prosperity." Does he mean the wealth of the state? If so, his reasoning runs thus:—The more wealth a state has the better; for the more wealth a state has, the more wealth it will have. This is surely something like that fallacy which is ungallantly termed a lady's reason. If by national prosperity he means the wealth of the people, of how gross a contradiction is he guilty. A people, he tells us, may be too rich—a government cannot—for a government can employ its riches in making the people richer. The wealth of the people is to be taken from them, because they have too much, and laid out in works which will yield them more.

We are really at a loss to determine whether Mr. Southey's reason for recommending large taxation is that it will make the people rich, or that it will make them poor. But we are sure, that if his object is to make them rich, he takes the wrong course. There are two or three principles respecting public works which, as an experience of vast extent proves, may be trusted in almost every case.

It scarcely ever happens that any private man, or body of men, will invest property in a canal, a tunnel, or a bridge, but from an expectation that the outlay will be profitable to them. No work of this sort can be profitable to private speculators, unless the public be willing to pay for the use of it. The public will not pay of their own accord for what yields no profit or convenience to them. There is thus a direct and obvious connection between the motive which induces individuals to undertake such a work, and the utility of the work.

Can we find any such connection in the case of a public work executed by a government? If it is useful, are the individuals who rule the country richer? If it is useless, are they poorer? A public man may be solicitous for his credit; but is not he likely to gain more credit by an useless display of ostentatious architecture in a great town than by the best road or the best canal in some remote province? The fame of public works is a much less certain test of their utility than the amount of toll collected at them. In a corrupt age, there will be direct embezzlement. In the purest age, there will be abundance of jobbing. Never were the statesmen of any country more sensitive to public opinion, and more spotless in pecuniary transactions, than those who have of late governed England. Yet we have only to look at the buildings recently erected in London for a proof of our rule. In a bad age, the fate of the public is to be robbed. In a good age, it is much milder—merely to have the dearest and the worst of everything.

Buildings for state purposes the state must erect. And here we think that, in general, the state ought to stop. We firmly believe that five hundred thousand pounds subscribed by individuals for railroads or canals would produce more advantage to the public than five millions voted by Parliament for the same purpose. There are certain old saws about the master's eye and about everybody's business in which we place very great faith.

There is, we have said, no consistency in Mr. Southey's political system. But if there be in it any leading principle, if there be any one error which diverges more widely and variously than any other, it is that of which his theory about national works is a ramification. He conceives that the business of the magistrate is not merely to see that the persons and property of the people are secure from attack, but that he ought to be a perfect jack-of-all-trades,—architect, engineer, schoolmaster, merchant, theologian,—a Lady Bountiful in every parish,—a Paul Pry in every house, spying, eaves-dropping, relieving, admonishing, spending our money for us, and choosing our opinions for us. His principle is, if we understand it rightly, that no man can do anything so well for himself as his rulers, be they who they may, can do it for him; that a government approaches nearer and nearer to perfection in proportion as it interferes more and more with the habits and notions of individuals.

He seems to be fully convinced that it is in the power of government to relieve the distresses under which the lower orders labour. Nay, he considers doubt on this subject as impious. We cannot refrain from quoting his argument on this subject. It is a perfect jewel of logic.

"Many thousands in your metropolis," says Sir Thomas More, "rise every morning without knowing how they are to subsist during the day; as many of them, where they are to lay their heads at night. All men, even the vicious themselves, know that wickedness leads to misery; but many, even among the good and the wise, have yet to learn that misery is almost as often the cause of wickedness."

"There are many," says Montesinos, "who know this, but believe that it is not in the power of human institutions to prevent this misery. They see the effect, but regard the causes as inseparable from the condition of human nature."

"As surely as God is good," replies Sir Thomas, "so surely there is no such thing as necessary evil. For, by the religious mind, sickness, and pain, and death, are not to be accounted evils."

Now, if sickness, pain, and death are not evils, we cannot understand why it should be an evil that thousands should rise without knowing how they are to subsist. The only evil of hunger is that it produces first pain, then sickness, and finally death. If it did not produce these it would be no calamity. If these are not evils, it is no calamity. We cannot conceive why it should be a greater impeachment of the Divine goodness, that some men should not be able to find food to eat, than that others should have stomachs which derive no nourishment from food when they have eaten it. Whatever physical effects want produces may also be produced by disease. Whatever salutary effects disease may produce may also be produced by want. If poverty makes men thieves, disease and pain often sour the temper and contract the heart.

We will propose a very plain dilemma. Either physical pain is an evil, or it is not an evil. If it is evil, then there is necessary evil in the universe. If it is not, why should the poor be delivered from it?

Mr. Southey entertains as exaggerated a notion of the wisdom of governments as of their power. He speaks with the greatest disgust of the respect now paid to public opinion. That opinion is, according to him, to be distrusted and dreaded; its usurpation ought to be vigorously resisted, and the practice of yielding to it is likely to ruin the country. To maintain police is, according to him, only one of the ends of government. Its duties are patriarchal and paternal. It ought to consider the moral discipline of the people as its first object, to establish a religion, to train the whole community in that religion, and to consider all dissenters as its own enemies.

"Nothing," says Sir Thomas, "is more certain than that religion is the basis upon which civil government rests; that from religion power derives its authority, laws their efficacy, and both their zeal and sanction; and it is necessary that this religion be established as for the security of the state, and for the welfare of the people, who would otherwise be moved to and fro with every wind of doctrine. A state is secure in proportion as the people are attached to its institutions; it is, therefore, the first and plainest rule of sound policy, that the people be trained up in the way they should go. The state that neglects this prepares its own destruction; and they who train them in any other way are undermining it. Nothing in abstract science can be more certain than these positions are."

"All of which," answers Montesinos, "are nevertheless denied by our professors of the arts Babblative and Scribblative; some in the audacity of evil designs, and others in the glorious assurance of impenetrable ignorance."

The greater part of the two volumes before us is merely an amplification of these absurd paragraphs. What does Mr. Southey mean by saying that religion is demonstrably the basis of civil government? He cannot surely mean that men have no motives except those derived from religion for establishing and supporting civil government, that no temporal advantage is derived from civil government, that man would experience no temporal inconvenience from living in a state of anarchy? If he allows, as we think he must allow, that it is for the good of mankind in this world to have civil government, and that the great majority of mankind have always thought it for their good in this world to have civil government, we then have a basis for government quite distinct from religion. It is true that the Christian religion sanctions government as it sanctions everything which promotes the happiness and virtue of our species. But we are at a loss to conceive in what sense religion can be said to be the basis of government, in which it is not also the basis of the practices of eating, drinking, and lighting fires in cold weather. Nothing in history is more certain than that government has existed, has received some obedience and given some protection, in times in which it derived no support from religion,—in times in which there was no religion that influenced the hearts and lives of men. It was not from dread of Tartarus, or belief in the Elysian fields, that an Athenian wished to have some institutions which might keep Orestes from filching his cloak, or Midias from breaking his head. "It is from religion," says Mr. Southey, "that power derives its authority, and laws their efficacy." From what religion does our power over the Hindoos derive its authority, or the law in virtue of which we hang Brahmins its efficacy? For thousands of years civil government has existed in almost every corner of the world,—in ages of priestcraft,—in ages of fanaticism,—in ages of Epicurean indifference,—in ages of enlightened piety. However pure or impure the faith of the people might be; whether they adored a beneficent or a malignant power; whether they thought the soul mortal or immortal, they have, as soon as they ceased to be absolute savages, found out their need of civil government, and instituted it accordingly. It is as universal as the practice of cookery. Yet it is as certain, says Mr. Southey, as any thing in abstract science, that government is founded on religion. We should like to know what notion Mr. Southey has of the demonstrations of abstract science. But a vague one, we suspect.

The proof proceeds. As religion is the basis of government, and as the state is secure in proportion as the people are attached to its institutions, it is therefore, says Mr. Southey, the first rule of policy that the government should train the people in the way in which they should go; and it is plain that those who train them in any other way are undermining the state.

Now, it does not appear to us to be the first object that people should always believe in the established religion, and be attached to the established government. A religion may be false. A government may be oppressive. And whatever support government gives to false religions, or religion to oppressive governments, we consider as a clear evil.

The maxim that governments ought to train the people in the way in which they should go sounds well. But is there any reason for believing that a government is more likely to lead the people in the right way than the people to fall into the right way of themselves? Have there not been governments which were blind leaders of the blind? Are there not still such governments? Can it be laid down as a general rule that the movement of political and religious truth is rather downwards from the government to the people than upwards from the people to the government? These are questions which it is of importance to have clearly resolved. Mr. Southey declaims against public opinion, which is now, he tells us, usurping supreme power. Formerly, according to him, the laws governed; now public opinion governs. What are laws but expressions of the opinion of some class which has power over the rest of the community? By what was the world ever governed, but by the opinion of some person or persons? By what else can it ever be governed? What are all systems, religious, political, or scientific, but opinions resting on evidence more or less satisfactory? The question is not between human opinion, and some higher and more certain mode of arriving at truth, but between opinion and opinion,—between the opinion of one man and another, or of one class and another, or of one generation and another. Public opinion is not infallible; but can Mr. Southey construct any institutions which shall secure to us the guidance of an infallible opinion? Can Mr. Southey select any family,—any profession—any class, in short, distinguished by any plain badge from the rest of the community, whose opinion is more likely to be just than this much-abused public opinion? Would he choose the peers, for example? Or the two hundred tallest men in the country? Or the poor Knights of Windsor? Or children who are born with cawls, seventh sons of seventh sons? We cannot suppose that he would recommend popular election; for that is merely an appeal to public opinion. And to say that society ought to be governed by the opinion of the wisest and best, though true, is useless. Whose opinion is to decide who are the wisest and best?

Mr. Southey and many other respectable people seem to think that when they have once proved the moral and religious training of the people to be a most important object, it follows, of course, that it is an object which the government ought to pursue. They forget that we have to consider, not merely the goodness of the end, but also the fitness of the means. Neither in the natural nor in the political body have all members the same office. There is surely no contradiction in saying that a certain section of the community may be quite competent to protect the persons and property of the rest, yet quite unfit to direct our opinions, or to superintend our private habits.

So strong is the interest of a ruler to protect his subjects against all depredations and outrages except his own,—so clear and simple are the means by which this end is to be effected, that men are probably better off under the worst governments in the world than they would be in a state of anarchy. Even when the appointment of magistrates has been left to chance, as in the Italian Republics, things have gone on better than they would have done, if there had been no magistrates at all, and every man had done what seemed right in his own eyes. But we see no reason for thinking that the opinions of the magistrate are more likely to be right than those of any other man. None of the modes by which rulers are appointed,—popular election, the accident of the lot, or the accident of birth,—afford, as far as we can perceive, much security for their being wiser than any of their neighbours. The chance of their being wiser than all their neighbours together is still smaller. Now we cannot conceive how it can be laid down, that it is the duty and the right of one class to direct the opinions of another, unless it can be proved that the former class is more likely to form just opinions than the latter.

The duties of government would be, as Mr. Southey says that they are, paternal, if a government were necessarily as much superior in wisdom to a people, as the most foolish father, for a time, is to the most intelligent child, and if a government loved a people as fathers generally love their children. But there is no reason to believe that a government will either have the paternal warmth of affection or the paternal superiority of intellect. Mr. Southey might as well say that the duties of the shoemaker are paternal, and that it is an usurpation in any man not of the craft to say that his shoes are bad, and to insist on having better. The division of labour would be no blessing, if those by whom a thing is done were to pay no attention to the opinion of those for whom it is done. The shoemaker, in the Relapse, tells Lord Foppington that his lordship is mistaken in supposing that his shoe pinches. "It does not pinch—it cannot pinch—I know my business—and I never made a better shoe." This is the way in which Mr. Southey would have a government treat a people who usurp the privilege of thinking. Nay, the shoemaker of Vanburgh has the advantage in the comparison. He contented himself with regulating his customer's shoes, about which he knew something, and did not presume to dictate about the coat and hat. But Mr. Southey would have the rulers of a country prescribe opinions to the people, not only about politics, but about matters concerning which a government has no peculiar sources of information,—concerning which any man in the streets may know as much, and think as justly, as a king,—religion and morals.

Men are never so likely to settle a question rightly as when they discuss it freely. A government can interfere in discussion only by making it less free than it would otherwise be. Men are most likely to form just opinions when they have no other wish than to know the truth, and are exempt from all influence, either of hope or fear. Government, as government, can bring nothing but the influence of hopes and fears to support its doctrines. It carries on controversy, not with reasons, but with threats and bribes. If it employs reasons, it does so not in virtue of any powers which belong to it as a government. Thus, instead of a contest between argument and argument, we have a contest between argument and force. Instead of a contest in which truth, from the natural constitution of the human mind, has a decided advantage over falsehood, we have a contest in which truth can be victorious only by accident.

And what, after all, is the security which this training gives to governments? Mr. Southey would scarcely recommend that discussion should be more effectually shackled, that public opinion should be more strictly disciplined into conformity with established institutions, than in Spain and Italy. Yet we know that the restraints which exist in Spain and Italy have not prevented atheism from spreading among the educated classes, and especially among those whose office it is to minister at the altars of God. All our readers know how, at the time of the French Revolution, priest after priest came forward to declare that his doctrine, his ministry, his whole life, had been a lie—a mummery during which he could scarcely compose his countenance sufficiently to carry on the imposture. This was the case of a false, or at least a grossly corrupted religion. Let us take, then, the case of all others the most favourable to Mr. Southey's argument. Let us take that form of religion which he holds to be the purest—the system of the Arminian part of the Church of England. Let us take the form of government which he most admires and regrets—the government of England in the time of Charles I. Would he wish to see a closer connection between Church and State than then existed? Would he wish for more powerful ecclesiastical tribunals? for a more zealous king? for a more active primate? Would he wish to see a more complete monopoly of public instruction given to the Established Church? Could any government do more to train the people in the way in which he would have them go? And in what did all this training end? The report of the state of the province of Canterbury, delivered by Laud to his master at the close of 1639, represents the Church of England as in the highest and most palmy state. So effectually had the government pursued that policy which Mr. Southey wishes to see revived that there was scarcely the least appearance of dissent. Most of the bishops stated that all was well among their flocks. Seven or eight persons in the diocese of Peterborough had seemed ·efractory to the Church, but had made ample submission. In Norfolk and Suffolk all whom there had been reason to suspect had made profession of conformity, and appeared to observe it strictly. It is confessed that there was a little difficulty in bringing some of the vulgar in Suffolk to take the sacrament at the rails in the chancel. This was the only open instance of non-conformity which the vigilant eye of Laud could find in all the dioceses of his twenty-one suffragans, on the very eve of a revolution in which primate and Church, and monarch and monarchy, were to perish together.

At which time would Mr. Southey pronounce the Constitution more secure —in 1639, when Laud presented this report to Charles, or now, when thousands of meetings openly collect millions of dissenters, when designs against the tithes are openly avowed, when books attacking not only the establishment, but the first principles of Christianity, are openly sold in the streets? The signs of discontent, he tells us, are stronger in England now than in France when the States-General met; and hence he would have us infer that a revolution like that of France may be at hand. Does he not know that the danger of states is to be estimated, not by what breaks out of the public mind, but by what stays in it? Can he conceive anything more terrible than the situation of a government which rules without apprehension over a people of hypocrites,—which is flattered by the press and cursed in the inner chambers, —which exults in the attachment and obedience of its subjects, and knows not that those subjects are leagued against it in a free-masonry of hatred, the sign of which is every day conveyed in the glance of ten thousand eyes, the pressure of ten thousand hands, and the tone of ten thousand voices? Profound and ingenious policy ! Instead of curing the disease, to remove those symptoms by which alone its nature can be known! To leave the serpent his deadly sting, and deprive him only of his warning rattle !

When the people whom Charles had so assiduously trained in the good way had rewarded his paternal care by cutting off his head, a new kind of training came into fashion. Another government arose, which, like the former, considered religion as its surest basis, and the religious discipline of the people as its first duty. Sanguinary laws were enacted against libertinism; profane pictures were burned; drapery was put on indecorous statues; the theatres were shut up; fast-days were numerous; and the Parliament resolved that no person should be admitted into any public employment unless the House should be first satisfied of his vital godliness. We know what was the end of this training. We know that it ended in impiety, in filthy and heartless sensuality, in the dissolution of all ties of honour and morality. We know that at this very day scriptural phrases, scriptural names, perhaps some scriptural doctrines, excite disgust and ridicule, solely because they are associated with the austerity of that period.

Thus has the experiment of training the people in established forms of religion been twice tried in England on a large scale, once by Charles and Laud, and once by the Puritans. The High Tories of our time still entertain many of the feelings and opinions of Charles and Laud, though in a mitigated form; nor is it difficult to see that the heirs of the Puritans are still amongst us. It would be desirable that each of these parties should remember how little advantage or honour it formerly derived from the closest alliance with power,—that it fell by the support of rulers, and rose by their opposition,—that of the two systems, that in which the people were at any time being drilled, was always at that time the unpopular system,—that the training of the High Church ended in the reign of the Puritans, and the training of the Puritans in the reign of the harlots.

This was quite natural. Nothing is so galling and detestable to a people not broken in from the birth, as a paternal, or, in other words, a meddling government,—a government which tells them what to read, and say, and eat, and drink, and wear. Our fathers could not bear it two hundred years ago; and we are not more patient than they. Mr. Southey thinks that the yoke of the Church is dropping off, because it is loose. We feel convinced that it is borne only because it is easy, and that, in the instant in which an attempt is made to tighten it, it will be flung away. It will be neither the first nor the strongest yoke that has been broken asunder and trampled under foot in the day of the vengeance of England.

How far Mr. Southey would have the government carry its measures for training the people in the doctrines of the Church, we are unable to discover. In one passage Sir Thomas More asks with great vehemence,

"Is it possible that your laws should suffer the unbelievers to exist as a party?

"Vetitum est adeo sceleris nihil?"

Montesinos answers. "They avow themselves in defiance of the laws. The fashionable doctrine which the press at this time maintains is, that this is a matter in which the laws ought not to interfere, every man having a right, both to form what opinion he pleases upon religious subjects, and to promulgate that opinion."

It is clear, therefore, that Mr. Southey would not give full and perfect toleration to infidelity. In another passage, however, he observes with some truth, though too sweepingly, that "any degree of intolerance short of that full extent which the Papal Church exercises where it has power, acts upon the opinions which it is intended to suppress, like pruning upon vigorous plants; they grow the stronger for it." These two passages put together would lead us to the conclusion that, in Mr. Southey's opinion, the utmost severity ever employed by the Roman Catholic Church in the days of its greatest power, ought to be employed against unbelievers in England; in plain words, that Carlile and his shopmen ought to be burned in Smithfield, and that every person who, when called upon, should decline to make a solemn profession of Christianity, ought to suffer the same fate. We do not, however, believe that Mr. Southey would recommend such a course, though his language would, in the case of any other writer, justify us in supposing this to be his meaning. His opinions form no system at all. He never sees, at one glance, more of a question than will furnish matter for one flowing and well-turned sentence; so that it would be the height of unfairness to charge him personally with holding a doctrine, merely because that doctrine is deducible, though by the closest and most accurate reasoning, from the premises which he has laid down. We are, therefore, left completely in the dark as to Mr. Southey's opinions about toleration. Immediately after censuring the government for not punishing infidels, he proceeds to discuss the question of the Catholic disabilities—now, thank God, removed—and defends them on the ground that the Catholic doctrines tend to persecution, and that the Catholics persecuted when they had power.

"They must persecute," says he, "if they believe their own creed, for conscience-sake; and if they do not believe it, they must persecute for policy; because it is only by intolerance that so corrupt and injurious a system can be upheld."

That unbelievers should not be persecuted is an instance of national depravity at which the glorified spirits stand aghast. Yet a sect of Christians is to be excluded from power, because those who formerly held the same opinions were guilty of persecution. We have said that we do not very well know what Mr. Southey's opinion about toleration is. But, on the whole, we take it to be this, that everybody is to tolerate him, and that he is to tolerate nobody.

We will not be deterred by any fear of misrepresentation from expressing our hearty approbation of the mild, wise, and eminently Christian manner in which the Church and the Government have lately acted with respect to blasphemous publications. We praise them for not having thought it necessary to encircle a religion pure, merciful, and philosophical,—a religion to the evidences of which the highest intellects have yielded,—with the defences of a false and bloody superstition. The ark of God was never taken till it was surrounded by the arms of earthly defenders. In captivity, its sanctity was sufficient to vindicate it from insult, and to lay the hostile fiend prostrate on the threshold of his own temple. The real security of Christianity is to be found in its benevolent morality, in its exquisite adaptation to the human heart, in the facility with which its scheme accommodates itself to the capacity of every human intellect, in the consolation which it bears to the house of mourning, in the light with which it brightens the great mystery of the grave. To such a system it can bring no addition of dignity or of strength that it is part and parcel of the common law. It is not now for the first time left to rely on the force of its own evidences, and the attractions of its own beauty. Its sublime theology confounded the Grecian schools in the fair conflict of reason with reason. The bravest and wisest of the Cæsars found their arms and their policy unavailing when opposed to the weapons that were not carnal, and the kingdom that was not of this world. The victory which Porphyry and Diocletian failed to gain, is not, to all appearance, reserved for any of those who have in this age directed their attacks against the last restraint of the powerful, and the last hope of the wretched. The whole history of the Christian religion shows that she is in far greater danger of being corrupted by the alliance of power, than of being crushed by its opposition. Those who thrust temporal sovereignty upon her, treat her as their prototypes treated her author. They bow the knee, and spit upon her; they cry Hail! and smite her on the cheek; they put a sceptre into her hand, but it is a fragile reed; they crown her, but it is with thorns; they cover with purple the wounds which their own hands have inflicted on her; and inscribe magnificent titles over the cross on which they have fixed her to perish in ignominy and pain.

The general view which Mr. Southey takes of the prospects of society is very gloomy; but we comfort ourselves with the consideration that Mr. Southey is no prophet. He foretold, we remember, on the very eve of the abolition of the Test and Corporation Acts, that these hateful laws were immortal, and that pious minds would long be gratified by seeing the most solemn religious rite of the Church profaned, for the purpose of upholding her political supremacy. In the book before us, he says that Catholics cannot possibly be admitted into Parliament until those whom Johnson called "the bottomless Whigs" come into power. While the book was in the press, the prophecy was falsified, and a Tory of the Tories, Mr. Southey's own favourite hero, won and wore that noblest wreath, "*Ob cives servatos.*"

The signs of the times, Mr. Southey tells us, are very threatening. His fears for the country would decidedly preponderate over his hopes, but for his firm reliance on the mercy of God. Now, as we know that God has once suffered this civilized world to be overrun by savages, and the Christian religion to be corrupted by doctrines which made it, for some ages, almost as bad as Paganism, we cannot think it inconsistent with his attributes that similar calamities should again befall mankind.

We look, however, on the state of the world, and of this kingdom in particular, with much greater satisfaction and with better hopes. Mr. Southey speaks with contempt of those who think the savage state happier than the social. On this subject, he says, Rousseau never imposed on him even in his youth. But he conceives that a community which has advanced a little way in civilization is happier than one which has made greater progress. The Britons in the time of Cæsar were happier, he suspects, than the English of the nineteenth century. On the whole, he selects the generation which preceded the Reformation as that in which the people of this country were better off than at any time before or since.

This opinion rests on nothing, as far as we can see, except his own individual associations. He is a man of letters; and a life destitute of literary pleasures seems insipid to him. He abhors the spirit of the present generation, the severity of its studies, the boldness of its inquiries, and the disdain with which it regards some old prejudices by which his own mind is held in bondage. He dislikes an utterly unenlightened age. He dislikes an investigating and reforming age. The first twenty years of the sixteenth century would have exactly suited him. They furnished just the quantity of intellectual excitement which he requires. The learned few read and wrote largely. A scholar was held in high estimation; but the rabble did not presume to think; and even the most inquiring and independent of the educated classes paid more reverence to authority, and less to reason, than is usual in our time. This is a state of things in which Mr. Southey would have found himself quite comfortable; and, accordingly, he pronounces it the happiest state of things ever known in the world.

The savages were wretched, says Mr. Southey; but the people in the time of Sir Thomas More were happier than either they or we. Now, we think it quite certain that we have the advantage over the contemporaries of Sir Thomas More in every point in which they had any advantage over savages.

Mr. Southey does not even pretend to maintain that the people in the sixteenth century were better lodged or clothed than at present. He seems to admit that in these respects there has been some little improvement. It is indeed a matter about which scarcely any doubt can exist in the most perverse mind, that the improvements of machinery have lowered the price of manufactured articles, and have brought within the reach of the poorest some conveniences which Sir Thomas More or his master could not have obtained at any price.

The labouring classes, however, were, according to Mr. Southey, better fed three hundred years ago than at present. We believe that he is completely in error on this point. The condition of servants in noble and worthy families, and of scholars at the Universities, must surely have been better in those times than that of common day-labourers; and we are sure that it was not better than that of our workhouse paupers. From the household book of the Northumberland family, we find that in one of the greatest establishments of the kingdom the servants lived almost entirely on salt meat, without any bread at all. A more unwholesome diet can scarcely be conceived. In the reign of Edward VI. the state of the students at Cambridge is described to us, on the very best authority, as most wretched. Many of them dined on pottage made of a farthing's worth of beef with a little salt and oatmeal, and literally nothing else. This account we have from a contemporary master of St. John's. Our parish poor now eat wheaten bread. In the sixteenth century the labourer was glad to get barley, and was often forced to content himself with poorer fare. In Harrison's introduction to Holinshed we have an account of the state of our working population in the "golden days," as Mr. Southey calls them, of good Queen Bess. "The gentilitie," says he, "commonly provide themselves sufficiently of wheat for their own tables, whylest their household and poore neighbours in some shires are inforced to content themselves with rice or barleie; yea, and in time of dearth, many with bread made eyther of beanes, peason, or otes, or of altogether, and some acornes among. I will not say that this extremity is oft so well to be seen in time of plentie as of dearth, but if I should I could easily bring my trial: for albeit there be much more grounde eared nowe almost in everye place then hath beene of late yeares, yet such a price of corne continueth in eache towne and markete, without any just cause, that the artificer and poore labouring man is not able to reach unto it, but is driven to content himself with horse-corne; I mean beanes, peason, otes, tares, and lintelles." We should like to see what the effect would be of putting any parish in England now on allowance of "horse-corne." The helotry of Mammon are not, in our day, so easily enforced to content themselves as the peasantry of that happy period, as Mr. Southey considers it, which elapsed between the fall of the feudal and the rise of the commercial tyranny.

"The people," says Mr. Southey, "are worse fed than when they were fishers." And yet in another place he complains that they will not eat fish. "They have contracted," says he, "I know not how, some obstinate prejudice against a kind of food at once wholesome and delicate, and everywhere to be obtained cheaply and in abundance, were the demand for it as general as it ought to be." It is true that the lower orders have an obstinate prejudice against fish. But hunger has no such obstinate prejudices. If what was formerly a common diet is now eaten only in times of severe pressure, the inference is plain. The people must be fed with what they at least think better food than that of their ancestors.

The advice and medicine which the poorest labourer can now obtain, in disease or after an accident, is far superior to what Henry VIII. could have commanded. Scarcely any part of the country is out of the reach of practitioners, who are probably not so far inferior to Sir Henry Halford as they are superior to Sir Anthony Denny. That there has been a great improvement in this respect Mr. Southey allows. Indeed, he could not well have denied it. "But," says he, "the evils for which these sciences are the palliative have increased since the time of the Druids in a proportion that heavily overweighs the benefit of improved therapeutics." We know nothing either of the diseases or the remedies of the Druids. But we are quite sure that the improvement of medicine has far more than kept pace with the increase of disease during the last three centuries. This is proved by the best possible evidence. The term of human life is decidedly longer in England than in any former age respecting which we possess any information on which we can rely. All the rants in the world about picturesque cottages and temples of Mammon will not shake this argument. No test of the state of society can be named so decisive as that which is furnished by bills of mortality. That the lives of the people of this country have been gradually lengthening during the course of several generations, is as certain as any fact in statistics; and that the lives of men should [become longer and longer while their physical condition during life is becoming worse and worse is utterly incredible.

Let our readers think over these circumstances. Let them take into account the sweating sickness and the plague. Let them take into account that fearful disease which first made its appearance in the generation to which Mr. Southey assigns the palm of felicity, and raged through Europe with a fury at which the physician stood aghast, and before which the people were swept away by thousands. Let them consider the state of the northern counties, constantly the scene of robberies, rapes, massacres, and conflagrations. Let them add to all this the fact that seventy-two thousand persons suffered death by the hands of the executioner during the reign of Henry VIII., and judge between the nineteenth and the sixteenth century.

We do not say that the lower orders in England do not suffer severe hardships. But, in spite of Mr. Southey's assertions, and in spite of the assertions of a class of politicians who, differing from Mr. Southey in every point, agree with him in this, we are inclined to doubt whether they really suffer greater physical distress than the labouring classes of the most flourishing countries of the Continent.

It will scarcely be maintained that the lazzaroni who sleep under the porticos of Naples, or the beggars who besiege the convents of Spain, are in a happier situation than the English commonalty. The distress which has lately been experienced in the northern part of Germany, one of the best governed and most prosperous districts of Europe, surpasses, if we have been correctly informed, anything which has of late years been known among us. In Norway and Sweden the peasantry are compelled to constantly mix bark with their bread, and even this expedient has not always preserved whole families and neighbourheods from perishing together of famine. An experiment has lately been tried in the kingdom of the Netherlands, which has been cited to prove the possibility of establishing agricultural colonies on the waste lands of England; but which proves to our minds nothing so clearly as this, that the rate of subsistence to which the labouring classes are reduced in the Netherlands is miserably low, and very far inferior to that of the English paupers. No distress which the people here have endured for centuries approaches to that which has been felt by the French in our own time. The beginning of the year 1817 was a time of great distress in this island. But the state of the lowest classes here was luxury compared with that of the people of France. We find in Magendie's *Journal de Physiologie Experimentale*, a paper on a point of physiology connected with the distress of that season. It appears that the inhabitants of six departments—Aix, Jura, Doubs, Haute Saones, Vosges, and Saone et Loire—were reduced first to oatmeal and potatoes, and at last to nettles, bean stalks, and other kinds of herbage fit only for cattle; that when the next harvest enabled them to eat barley bread, many of them died from intemperate indulgence in what they thought an exquisite repast; and that a dropsy of a peculiar character was produced by the hard fare of the year. Dead bodies were found on the roads and in the fields. A single surgeon dissected six of these, and found the stomach shrunk, and filled with the unwholesome aliments which hunger had driven men to share with beasts. Such extremity of distress as this is never heard of in England, or even in Ireland. We are, on the whole, inclined to think, though we would speak with diffidence on a point on which it would be rash to pronounce a positive judgment without a much longer and closer investigation than we have bestowed upon it, that the labouring classes of this island, though they have their grievances and distresses, some produced by their own improvidence, some by the errors of their rulers, are, on the whole, better off as to physical comforts than the inhabitants of any equally extensive district of the old world. On this very account suffering is more acutely felt and more loudly bewailed here than elsewhere. We must take into the account the liberty of discussion, and the strong interest which the opponents of a ministry always have to exaggerate the extent of the public disasters. There are many parts of Europe in which the people quietly endure distress that here would shake the foundations of the state, in which the inhabitants of a whole province turn out to eat grass with less clamour than one Spitalfields weaver would make here, if the overseers were to put him on barley bread. In those new countries in which a civilized population has at its command a boundless extent of the richest soil the condition of the labourer is probably happier than in any society which has lasted for many centuries. But in the old world we must confess ourselves unable to find any satisfactory record of any great nation, past or present, in which the working classes have been in a more comfortable situation than in England during the last thirty years. When this island was thinly peopled, it was barbarous. There was little capital; and that little was insecure. It is now the richest and the most highly civilized spot in the world; but the population is dense. Thus we have never known that golden age which the lower orders in the United States are now enjoying. We have never known an age of liberty, of order, and of education, an age in which the mechanical sciences were carried to a great height, yet in which the people were not sufficiently numerous to cultivate even the most fertile valleys. But when we compare our own condition with that of our ancestors, we think it clear that the advantages arising from the progress of civilization have far more than counterbalanced the disadvantages arising from the progress of population. While our numbers have increased tenfold, our wealth has increased a hundredfold. Though there are so many more people to share the wealth now existing in the country than there were in the sixteenth century, it seems certain that a greater share falls to almost every individual than fell to the share of any of the corresponding class in the sixteenth century. The king keeps a more splendid court. The establishments of the nobles are more magnificent. The esquires are richer, the merchants are richer, the shopkeepers are richer. The serving-man, the artisan, and the husbandman, have a more copious and palatable supply of food, better clothing, and better furniture. This is no reason for tolerating abuses, or for neglecting any means of ameliorating the condition of our poorer countrymen. But it is a reason against telling them, as some of our philosophers are constantly telling them, that they are the most wretched people who ever existed on the face of the earth.

We have already adverted to Mr. Southey's amusing doctrine about national wealth. A state, says he, cannot be too rich; but a people may be too rich. His reason for thinking this is extremely curious.

"A people may be too rich, because it is the tendency of the commercial, and more especially of the manufacturing system, to collect wealth rather than to diffuse it. Where wealth is necessarily employed in any of the speculations of trade, its increase is in proportion to its amount. Great capitalists become like pikes in a fish-pond, who devour the weaker fish; and it is but too certain, that the poverty of one part of the people seems to increase in the same ratio as the riches of another. There are examples of this in history. In Portugal, when the high tide of wealth flowed in from the conquests in Africa and the East, the effect of that great influx was not more visible in the augmented splendour of the court, and the luxury of the higher ranks, than in the distress of the people."

Mr. Southey's instance is not a very fortunate one. The wealth which did so little for the Portuguese was not the fruit, either of manufactures or of commerce carried on by private individuals. It was the wealth, not of the people, but of the government and its creatures, of those who, as Mr. Southey thinks, can never be too rich. The fact is, that Mr. Southey's proposition is opposed to all history, and to the phenomena which surround us on every side. England is the richest country in Europe, the most commercial and the most manufacturing. Russia and Poland are the poorest countries in Europe. They have scarcely any trade, and none but the rudest manufactures. Is wealth more diffused in Russia and Poland than in England? There are individuals in Russia and Poland, whose incomes are probably equal to those of our richest countrymen. It may be doubted, whether there are not, in those countries, as many fortunes of eighty thousand a-year as here. But are there as many fortunes of five thousand a-year, or of one thousand a-year? There are parishes in England which contain more people of between five hundred and three thousand pounds a-year than could be found in all the dominions of the Emperor Nicholas. The neat and commodious houses which have been built in London and its vicinity, for people of this class, within the last thirty years, would of themselves form a city larger than the capitals of some European kingdoms. And this is the state of society in which the great proprietors have devoured the smaller!

The cure which Mr. Southey thinks that he has discovered is worthy of the sagacity which he has shown in detecting the evil. The calamities arising from the collection of wealth in the hands of a few capitalists are to be remedied by collecting it in the hands of one great capitalist, who has no conceivable motive to use it better than other capitalists—the all-devouring state.

It is not strange that, differing so widely from Mr. Southey as to the past progress of society, we should differ from him also as to its probable destiny. He thinks, that to all outward appearance, the country is hastening to destruction; but he relies firmly on the goodness of God. We do not see either the piety or the rationality of thus confidently expecting that the Supreme Being will interfere to disturb the common succession of causes and effects. We, too, rely on his goodness—on his goodness as manifested, not in extraordinary interpositions, but in those general laws which it has pleased him to establish in the Physical and in the moral world. We rely on the natural tendency of the human intellect to truth, and on the natural tendency of society to improvement. We know no well-authenticated instance of a people which has decidedly retrograded in civilisation and prosperity, except from the influence of violent and terrible calamities—such as those which laid the Roman Empire in ruins, or those which, about the beginning of the sixteenth century, desolated Italy. We know of no country which, at the end of fifty years of peace and tolerably good government, has been less prosperous than at the beginning of that period. The political importance of a state may decline, as the balance of power is disturbed by the introduction of new forces. Thus the influence of Holland and of Spain is much diminished. But are Holland and Spain poorer than formerly? We doubt it. Other countries have outrun them. But we suspect that they have been positively, though not relatively, advancing. We suspect that Holland is richer than when she sent her navies up the Thames,—that Spain is richer than when a French king was brought captive to the footstool of Charles V.

History is full of the signs of this natural progress of society. We see in almost every part of the annals of mankind how the industry of individuals, struggling up against wars, taxes, famines, conflagrations, mischievous prohibitions, and more mischievous protections, creates faster than governments can squander, and repairs whatever invaders can destroy. We see the capital of nations increasing, and all the arts of life approaching nearer and nearer to perfection, in spite of the grossest corruption and the wildest profusion on the part of rulers.

The present moment is one of great distress. But how small will that distress appear when we think over the history of the last forty years;—a war, compared with which all other wars now sink into insignificance;—taxation, such as the most heavily taxed people of former times could not have conceived; —a debt larger than all the public debts that ever existed in the world added together;—the food of the people studiously rendered dear;—the currency imprudently debased, and imprudently restored. Yet is the country poorer than in 1790? We fully believe that, in spite of all the misgovernment of her rulers, she has been almost constantly becoming richer and richer. Now and then there has been a stoppage, now and then a short retrogression; but as to the general tendency there can be no doubt. A single breaker may recede, but the tide is evidently coming in.

If we were to prophesy that in the year 1930 a population of fifty millions, better fed, clad, and lodged than the English of our time, will cover these islands,—that Sussex and Huntingdonshire will be wealthier than the wealthiest parts of the West-Riding of Yorkshire now are,—that cultivation, rich as that of a flower-garden, will be carried to the very tops of Ben Nevis and Helvellyn, —that machines, constructed on principles yet undiscovered, will be in every house,—that there will be no highways but railroads, no travelling but by steam,—that our debt, vast as it seems to us, will appear to our great grandchildren a trifling encumbrance, which might easily be paid off in a year or two,—many people would think us insane. We prophesy nothing; but this we say—If any person had told the Parliament which met in perplexity and terror after the crash in 1720, that in 1830 the wealth of England would surpass all their wildest dreams—that the annual revenue would equal the principal of that debt which they considered as an intolerable burden—that for one man of £10,000 then living, there would be five men of £50,000; that London would be twice as large and twice as populous, and that nevertheless the mortality would have diminished to one half what it then was,—that the post-office would bring more into the exchequer than the excise and customs had brought in together under Charles II.,—that stage-coaches would run from London to York in twenty-four hours—that men would sail without wind, and would be beginning to ride without horses—our ancestors would have given as much credit to the prediction as they gave to Gulliver's Travels. Yet the prediction would have been true; and they would have perceived that it was not altogether absurd, if they had considered that the country was then raising every year a sum which would have purchased the fee-simple of the revenue of the Plantagenets—ten times what supported the government of Elizabeth— three times what, in the time of Oliver Cromwell, had been thought intolerably oppressive. To almost all men the state of things under which they have been used to live seems to be the necessary state of things. We have heard it said that five per cent. is the natural interest of money, that twelve is the natural number of a jury, that forty shillings is the natural qualification of a county voter. Hence it is, that though, in every age, everybody knows that up to his own time progressive improvement has been taking place, nobody seems to reckon on any improvement during the next generation. We cannot absolutely prove that those are in error who tell us that society has reached a turning point,—that we have seen our best days. But so said all who came before us, and with just as much apparent reason. "A million a-year will beggar us," said the patriots of 1640. "Two millions a-year will grind the country to powder," was the cry in 1660. "Six millions a-year, and a debt of fifty millions!" exclaimed Swift—"the high allies have been the ruin of us.". "A hundred and forty millions of debt!" said Junius—"well may we say that we owe Lord Chatham more than we shall ever pay, if we owe him such a load as this." "Two hundred and forty millions of debt!" cried all the statesmen of

1783 in chorus—"what abilities, or what economy on the part of a minister can save a country so burdened?" We know that if, since 1783, no fresh debt had been incurred, the increased resources of the country would have enabled us to defray that burden at which Pitt, Fox, and Burke stood aghast—to defray it over and over again, and that with much lighter taxation than what we have actually borne. On what principle is it, that when we see nothing but improvement behind us, we are to expect nothing but deterioration before us?

It is not by the intermeddling of Mr. Southey's idol—the omniscient and omnipotent State—but by the prudence and energy of the people that England has hitherto been carried forward in civilisation; and it is to the same prudence and the same energy that we now look with comfort and good hope. Our rulers will best promote the improvement of the people by strictly confining themselves to their own legitimate duties—by leaving capital to find its most lucrative course, commodities their fair price, industry and intelligence their natural reward, idleness and folly their natural punishment—by maintaining peace, by defending property, by diminishing the price of law, and by observing strict economy in every department of the state. Let the government do this—the people will assuredly do the rest.

MR. ROBERT MONTGOMERY'S POEMS.

1, The Omnipresence of the Deity: A Poem. By ROBERT MONTGOMERY. Eleventh Edition. London. 1830.

2. Satan: A Poem. By ROBERT MONTGOMERY. Second Edition. London. 1830.

THE wise men of antiquity loved to convey instruction under the covering of apologue; and, though this practice of theirs is generally thought childish, we shall make no apology for adopting it on the present occasion. A generation which has bought eleven editions of a poem by Mr. Robert Montgomery may well condescend to listen to a fable of Pilpay.

A pious Brahmin, it is written, made a vow that on a certain day he would sacrifice a sheep, and on the appointed morning he went forth to buy one. There lived in his neighbourhood three rogues who knew of his vow, and laid a scheme for profiting by it. The first met him and said, "Oh, Brahmin, wilt thou buy a sheep? I have one fit for sacrifice." "It is for that very purpose," said the holy man, "that I came forth this day." Then the impostor opened a bag, and brought out of it an unclean beast, an ugly dog, lame and blind. Thereon the Brahmin cried out, "Wretch, who touchest things impure and utterest things untrue, callest thou that cur a sheep?" "Truly," answered the other, "it is a sheep of the finest fleece, and of the sweetest flesh. Oh, Brahmin, it will be an offering most acceptable to the gods." "Friend," said the Brahmin, "either thou or I must be blind."

Just then one of the accomplices came up. "Praised be the gods," said this second rogue, "that I have been saved the trouble of going to the market for a sheep! This is such a sheep as I wanted. For how much wilt thou sell it?" When the Brahmin heard this, his mind waved to and fro, like one swinging in the air at a holy festival. "Sir," said he to the new comer, "take heed what thou dost; this is no sheep, but an unclean cur." "Oh, Brahmin," said the new comer, "thou art drunk or mad!"

At this time the third confederate drew near. "Let us ask this man," said the Brahmin, "what the creature is, and I will stand by what he shall say." To this the others agreed; and the Brahmin called out, "Oh, stranger, what dost thou call this beast?" "Surely, oh, Brahmin," said the knave; "it is a fine sheep." Then the Brahmin said, "Surely the gods have taken away my senses,"—and he asked pardon of him who carried the dog, and bought it for a measure of rice and a pot of ghee, and offered it up to the gods, who, being wroth at this unclean sacrifice, smote him with a sore disease in all his joints.

Thus, or nearly thus, if we remember rightly, runs the story of the Sanscrit Æsop. The moral, like the moral of every fable that is worth the telling, lies on the surface. The writer evidently means to caution us against the practice of puffers,—a class of people who have more than once talked the public into most absurd errors, but who surely never played a more curious or a more difficult trick than when they passed Mr. Robert Montgomery off upon the world as a great poet.

In an age in which there are so few readers that a writer cannot subsist on the sum arising from the sale of his works, no man who has not an independent fortune can devote himself to literary pursuits, unless he is assisted by patronage. In such an age, accordingly, men of letters too often pass their lives in dangling at the heels of the wealthy and powerful; and all the faults which dependence tends to produce pass into their character. They become the parasites and slaves of the great. It is melancholy to think how many of the highest and most exquisitely formed of human intellects have been condemned to the ignominious labour of disposing the commonplaces of adulation in new forms, and brightening them into new splendour. Horace, invoking Augustus in the most enthusiastic language of religious veneration,—Statius flattering a tyrant, and the minion of a tyrant, for a morsel of bread,—Ariosto versifying the whole genealogy of a niggardly patron,—Tasso extolling the heroic virtues of the wretched creature who locked him up in a mad-house,— these are but a few of the instances which might easily be given of the degradation to which those must submit who, not possessing a competent fortune, are resolved to write when there are scarcely any who read.

This evil the progress of the human mind tends to remove. As a taste for books becomes more and more common, the patronage of individuals becomes less and less necessary. In the earlier part of the last century a marked change took place. The tone of literary men, both in this country and in France, became higher and more independent. Pope boasted that he was the "one poet" who had "pleased by manly ways;" he derided the soft dedications with which Halifax had been fed,—asserted his own superiority over the pensioned Boileau,—and gloried in being not the follower but the friend of nobles and princes. The explanation of all this is very simple. Pope was the first Englishman who, by the mere sale of his writings, realized a sum which enabled him to live in comfort and in perfect independence. Johnson extols him for the magnanimity which he showed in inscribing his Iliad, not to a minister or a peer, but to Congreve. In our time, this would scarcely be a subject for praise. Nobody is astonished when Mr. Moore pays a compliment of this kind to Sir Walter Scott, or Sir Walter Scott to Mr. Moore. The idea of either of those gentlemen looking out for some lord who would be likely to give him a few guineas in return for a fulsome dedication, seems laughably incongruous. Yet this is exactly what Dryden or Otway would have done; and it would be hard to blame them for it. Otway is said to have been choked with a piece of bread which he devoured in the rage of hunger; and, whether this story be true or false, he was beyond all question miserably poor. Dryden, at near seventy, when at the head of the literary men of England, without equal or second, received three hundred pounds for his fables,—a collection of ten thousand verses,—and such verses as no man then living, except himself, could have produced. Pope, at thirty, had laid up between six and seven thousand pounds,—the fruits of his poetry. It was not, we suspect, because he had a higher spirit, or a more scrupulous conscience, than his predecessors, but because he had a larger income, that he kept up the dignity of the literary character so much better than they had done.

From the time of Pope to the present day, the readers have been constantly becoming more and more numerous; and the writers, consequently, more and more independent. It is assuredly a great evil that men, fitted by their talents and acquirements to enlighten and charm the world, should be reduced to the necessity of flattering wicked and foolish patrons in return for the very sustenance of life. But though we heartily rejoice that this evil is removed, we cannot but see with concern that another evil has succeeded to it. The public is now the patron, and a most liberal patron. All that the rich and powerful bestowed on authors from the time of Mæcenas to that of Harley would not, we apprehend, make up a sum equal to that which has been paid by English booksellers to authors during the last thirty years. Men of letters have accordingly ceased to court individuals, and have begun to court the public. They formerly used flattery. They now use puffing.

Whether the old or the new vice be the worse,—whether those who formerly lavished insincere praise on others, or those who now contrive, by every art of beggary and bribery, to stun the public with praises of themselves, disgrace their vocation the more deeply,—we shall not attempt to decide. But of this we are sure,—that it is high time to make a stand against the new trickery. The puffing of books is now so shamefully and so successfully practised that it is the duty of all who are anxious for the purity of the national taste, or for the honour of the literary character, to join in discountenancing it. All the pens that ever were employed in magnifying Bish's lucky office, Romanis's fleecy hosiery, Packwood's razor straps, and Rowland's Kalydor,—all the placard-bearers of Dr. Eady,—all the wall-chalkers of Day and Martin,—seem to have taken service with the poets and novelists of this generation. Devices which, in the lowest trades, are considered as disreputable are adopted without scruple, and improved upon with a despicable ingenuity by people engaged in a pursuit which never was, and never will be, considered as a mere trade by any man of honour and virtue. A butcher of the highest class disdains to ticket his meat. A mercer of the highest class would be ashamed to hang up papers in his window inviting the passers-by to look at the stock of a bankrupt, all of the first quality, and going for half the value. We expect some reserve, some decent pride, in our hatter and our bootmaker. But no artifice by which notoriety can be obtained is thought too abject for a man of letters.

It is amusing to think over the history of most of the publications which have had a run during the last few years. The publisher is often the publisher of some periodical work. In this periodical work the first flourish of trumpets is sounded. The peal is then echoed and re-echoed by all the other periodical works over which the publisher or the author, or the author's coterie, may have any influence. The newspapers are for a fortnight filled with puffs of all the various kinds which Sheridan recounted,—direct, oblique, and collusive. Sometimes the praise is laid on thick for simple-minded people. "Pathetic," "sublime," "splendid," "graceful, brilliant wit," "exquisite humour," and other phrases equally flattering, fall in a shower as thick and as sweet as the sugar-plums at a Roman carnival. Sometimes greater art is used. A sinecure has been offered to the writer if he would suppress his work, or if he would even soften down a few of his incomparable portraits. A distinguished military and political character has challenged the inimitable satirist of the vices of the great; and the puffer is glad to learn that the parties have been bound over to keep the peace. Sometimes it is thought expedient that the puffer should put on a grave face, and utter his panegyric in the form of admonition! "Such attacks on private character cannot be too much condemned. Even the exuberant wit of our author and the irresistible power of his withering sarcasm, are no excuses for that utter disregard which he manifests for the feelings of others. We cannot but wonder that a writer of such transcendent talents,—a writer who is evidently no stranger to the kindly charities and sensibilities of our nature, should show so little tenderness to the foibles of noble and distinguished individuals, with whom it is clear, from every page of his work, that he must have been constantly mingling in society." These are but tame and feeble imitations of the paragraphs with which the daily papers are filled whenever an attorney's clerk or an apothecary's assistant undertakes to tell the public, in bad English and in worse French, how people tie their neckcloths and eat their dinners in Grosvenor Square. The editors of the higher and more respectable newspapers usually prefix the words "Advertisement," or "From a Correspondent," to such paragraphs. But this makes little difference. The panegyric is extracted, and the significant heading omitted. The fulsome eulogy makes its appearance on the covers of all the Reviews and Magazines, with "Times" or "Globe" affixed, though the editors of the Times and the Globe have no more to do with it than with Goss's way of making old rakes young again.

That people who live by personal slander should practise these arts is not surprising. Those who stoop to write calumnious books may well stoop to puff them;—and that the basest of all trades should be carried on in the basest of all manners is quite proper, and as it should be. But how any man who has the least self-respect, the least regard for his own personal dignity, can condescend to persecute the public with this Rag Fair importunity we do not understand. Extreme poverty may, indeed, in some degree, be an excuse for employing these shifts, as it may be an excuse for stealing a leg of mutton. But we really think that a man of spirit and delicacy would quite as soon satisfy his wants in one way as in the other.

It is no excuse for an author that the praises of journalists are procured by the money or influence of his publisher, and not by his own. It is his business to take such precautions as may prevent others from doing what must degrade him. It is for his honour as a gentleman, and if he is really a man of talents, it will eventually be for his honour and interest as a writer, that his works should come before the public, recommended by their own merits alone, and should be discussed with perfect freedom. If his objects be really such as he may own without shame, he will find that they will, in the long run, be better attained by suffering the voice of criticism to be fairly heard. At present, we too often see a writer attempting to obtain literary fame as Shakespeare's usurper obtains sovereignty. The publisher plays Buckingham to the author's Richard. Some few creatures of the conspiracy are dexterously disposed here and there in the crowd. It is the business of these hirelings to throw up their caps, and clap their hands, and utter their *vivas*. The rabble at first stare and wonder, and at last join in shouting for shouting's sake; and thus a crown is placed on a head which has no right to it, by the huzzas of a few servile dependents.

The opinion of the great body of the reading public is very materially influenced even by the unsupported assertions of those who assume a right to criticise. Nor is the public altogether to blame on this account. Most, even of those who have really a great enjoyment in reading, are in the same state, with respect to a book, in which a man, who has never given particular attention to the art of painting, is with respect to a picture. Every man who has the least sensibility or imagination, derives a certain pleasure from pictures. Yet a man of the highest and finest intellect might, unless he had formed his taste by contemplating the best pictures, be easily persuaded by a knot of connoisseurs that the worst daub in Somerset House was a miracle of art. If he deserves to be laughed at, it is not for his ignorance of pictures, but or his ignorance of men. He knows that there is a delicacy of taste in painting which he does not possess; that he cannot discriminate hands, as practised judges can; that he is not familiar with the finest models; that he has never looked at them with close attention; and that, when the general effect of a piece has pleased him or displeased him, he has never troubled himself to ascertain why. When, therefore, people whom he thinks more competent to judge than himself, and of whose sincerity he entertains no doubt, assure him that a particular work is exquisitely beautiful, he takes it for granted that they must be in the right. He returns to the examination, resolved to find or imagine beauties; and if he can work himself up into something like admiration, he exults in his own proficiency.

Just such is the manner in which nine readers out of ten judge of a book. They are ashamed to dislike what men, who speak as having authority, declare to be good. At present, however contemptible a poem or novel may be, there is not the least difficulty in procuring favourable notices of it from all sorts of publications, daily, weekly, and monthly. In the meantime, little or nothing is said on the other side. The author and the publisher are interested in crying up the book. Nobody has any very strong interest in crying it down. Those who are best fitted to guide the public opinion think it beneath them to expose mere nonsense, and comfort themselves by reflecting that such popularity cannot last. This contemptuous lenity has been carried too far. It is perfectly true that reputations which have been forced into an unnatural bloom fade almost as soon as they have expanded; nor have we any apprehensions that puffing will ever raise any scribbler to the rank of a classic. It is, indeed, amusing to turn over some late volumes of periodical works, and to see how many immortal productions have, within a few months, been gathered to the poems of Blackmore and the novels of Mrs. Behn; how many "profound views of human nature," and "exquisite delineations of fashionable manners," and "vernal, and sunny, and refreshing thoughts," and "high imaginings," and "young breathings," and "embodyings," and "pinings," and "minglings with the beauty of the universe," and "harmonies which dissolve the soul in a passionate sense of loveliness and divinity," the world has contrived to forget. The names of the books and the writers are buried in as deep an oblivion as the name of the builder of Stonehenge. Some of the well-puffed "fashionable novels" of the last, hold the pastry of the present year; and others of the class, which are now extolled in language almost too high flown for the merits of Don Quixote, will, we have no doubt, line the trunks of eighteen hundred and thirty-one. But, though we have no apprehensions that puffing will ever confer permanent reputation on the undeserving, we still think its influence most pernicious. Men of real merit will, if they persevere, at last reach the station to which they are entitled, and intruders will be ejected with contempt and derision. But it is no small evil that the avenues to fame should be blocked up by a swarm of noisy, pushing, elbowing pretenders, who, though they will not ultimately be able to make good their own entrance, hinder, in the meantime, those who have a right to enter. All who will not disgrace themselves by joining in the unseemly scuffle must expect to be at first hustled and shouldered back. Some men of talents accordingly turn away in dejection from pursuits in which success appears to bear no proportion to desert. Others employ in self-defence the means by which competitors, far inferior to themselves, appear for a time to obtain a decided advantage. There are few who have sufficient confidence in their own powers, and sufficient elevation of mind, to wait with secure and contemptuous patience while dunce after dunce presses before them. Those who will not stoop to the baseness of the modern fashion are too often discouraged. Those who stoop to it are always degraded.

We have of late observed with great pleasure some symptoms which lead us to hope that respectable literary men of all parties are beginning to be impatient of this insufferable nuisance. And we purpose to do what in us lies for the abating of it. We do not think that we can more usefully assist in this good work than by showing our honest countrymen what that sort of poetry is which puffing can drive through eleven editions; and how easily any bellman might, if a bellman would stoop to the necessary degree of meanness, become "a master-spirit of the age." We have no enmity to Mr. Robert Montgomery. We know nothing whatever about him, except what we have learned from his books, and from the portrait prefixed to one of them, in which he appears to be doing his very best to look like a man of genius and sensibility, though with less success than his strenuous exertions deserve. We select him because his works have received more enthusiastic praise and have deserved more unmixed contempt than any which, as far as our knowledge extends, have appeared within the last three or four years. His writing bears the same relation to poetry which a Turkey-carpet bears to a picture. There are colours in the Turkey-carpet out of which a picture might be made. There are words in Mr. Montgomery's verses which, when disposed in certain orders and combinations, have made, and will again make good poetry. But, as they now stand, they seem to be put together on principle, in such a manner as to give no image of anything in the "heavens above, or in the earth beneath, or in the waters under the earth."

The poem on the Omnipresence of the Deity commences with a description of the creation, in which we can find only one thought which has the least pretension to ingenuity, and that one thought is stolen from Dryden, and marred in the stealing—

"Last, softly beautiful as music's close,
Angelic woman into being rose."

The all-pervading influence of the Supreme Being is then described in a few tolerable lines borrowed from Pope, and a great many intolerable lines of Mr. Robert Montgomery's own. The following may stand as a specimen:—

"But who could trace Thine unrestricted course,
Though Fancy follow'd with immortal force?
There's not a blossom fondled by the breeze,
There's not a fruit that beautifies the trees,
There's not a particle in sea or air,
But nature owns thy plastic influence there!
With fearful gaze, still be it mine to see
How all is filled and vivified by Thee;
Upon thy mirror, earth's majestic view,
To paint Thy Presence, and to feel it too."

The last two lines contain an excellent specimen of Mr. Robert Montgomery's Turkey-carpet style of writing. The majestic view of earth is the mirror of God's presence, and on this mirror Mr. Robert Montgomery paints God's presence. The use of a mirror, we submit, is not to be painted upon.

A few more lines, as bad as those which we have quoted, bring us to one of the most amusing instances of literary pilfering which we remember. It might be of use to plagiarists to know, as a general rule, that what they steal is, to employ a phrase common in advertisements, of no use to any but the right owner. We never fell in, however, with any plunderer who so little understood how to turn his booty to good account as Mr. Montgomery. Lord Byron, in a passage which everybody knows by heart, has said, addressing the sea,

> 'Time writes no wrinkle on thine azure brow."

Mr. Robert Montgomery very coolly appropriates the image, and reproduces the stolen goods in the following form :

> "And Thou, vast Ocean, on whose awful face
> Time's iron feet can print no ruin-trace."

So may such ill-got gains ever prosper !
The effect which the ocean produces on atheists is then described in the following lofty lines :

> "Oh ! never did the dark-soul'd ATHEIST stand,
> And watch the breakers boiling on the strand,
> And, while Creation stagger'd at his nod,
> Mock the dread presence of the mighty God!
> We hear Him in the wind-heaved ocean's roar,
> Hurling her billowy crags upon the shore ;
> We hear Him in the riot of the blast,
> And shake, while rush the raving whirlwinds past !"

If Mr. Robert Montgomery's genius were not far too free and aspiring to be shackled by the rules of syntax, we should suppose that it is at the nod of the atheist that creation shudders, and that it is this same dark-souled atheist who hurls billowy crags upon the shore.

A few more lines bring us to another instance of unprofitable theft. Sir Walter Scott has these lines in the Lord of the Isles :

> "The dew that on the violet lies,
> Mocks the dark lustre of thine eyes."

This is pretty taken separately, and, as is almost always the case with good things of good writers, much prettier in its place than can even be conceived by those who use it only detached from the context. Now for Mr. Montgomery—

> "And the bright dew-bead on the bramble lies,
> Like liquid rapture upon beauty's eyes."

The comparison of a violet, bright with the dew, to a woman's eyes, is as perfect as a comparison can be. Sir Walter's lines are part of a song addressed to a woman, and the comparison is, therefore, peculiarly natural and graceful. Dew on the bramble is no more like a woman's eyes than dew anywhere else. There is a very pretty Eastern tale of which the fate of plagiarists often reminds us. The slave of a magician saw his master wave his wand, and heard him give orders to the spirits who arose at the summons. He accordingly stole the wand, and waved it himself in the air, but he had not observed that his master used the left hand for that purpose. The spirits thus irregularly summoned, tore him to pieces, instead of obeying his orders. There are very few who can safely venture to conjure with the rod of Sir Walter, and we are sure that Mr. Robert Montgomery is not one of them.

Mr. Campbell, in one of his most pleasant pieces, has this line—

> "The sentinel stars set their watch in the sky."

The thought is good—and has a very striking propriety where Mr. Campbell has placed it—in the mouth of a soldier telling his dream. But, though Shakespeare assures us that "every true man's apparel fits your thief," it is by no means the case, as we have already seen, that every true poet's similitude fits your plagiarist. Let us see how Mr. Robert Montgomery uses the image—

> "Ye quenchless stars! so eloquently bright,
> Untroubled sentries of the shadowy night,
> While half the world is lapp'd in downy dreams,
> And round the lattice creep your midnight beams,
> How sweet to gaze upon your placid eyes,
> In lambent beauty looking from the skies."

Certainly the ideas of eloquence—of untroubled repose—of placid eyes, on the lambent beauty of which it is sweet to gaze, harmonize admirably with the idea of a sentry!

We would not be understood, however, to say, that Mr. Robert Montgomery cannot make similitudes for himself. A very few lines farther on, we find one which has every mark of originality, and on which, we will be bound, none of the poets whom he has plundered will ever think of making reprisals:

> "The soul, aspiring, pants its source to mount,
> As streams meander level with their fount."

We take this to be, on the whole, the worst similitude in the world. In the first place, no stream meanders, or can possibly meander, level with its fount. In the next place, if streams did meander level with their founts, no two motions can be less like than that of meandering level and that of mounting upwards.

We have then an apostrophe to the Deity, couched in terms which, in any writer who dealt in meanings, we should call profane, but to which, we suppose, Mr. Robert Montgomery attaches no idea whatever.

> "Yes! pause and think, within one fleeting hour,
> How vast a universe obeys Thy power;
> Unseen, but felt, Thine interfused control
> Works in each atom, and pervades the whole;
> Expands the blossom, and erects the tree,
> Conducts each vapour, and commands each sea,
> Beams in each ray, bids whirlwinds be unfurl'd,
> Unrols the thunder, and upheaves a world!"

No field-preacher ever carried his irreverent familiarity so far as to bid the Supreme Being stop and meditate on the importance of the interests which are under his care. The grotesque indecency of such an address throws into shade the subordinate absurdities of the passage, the unfurling of whirlwinds, the unrolling of thunder, and the upheaving of worlds.

Then comes a curious specimen of our poet's English—

> "Yet not alone created realms engage
> Thy faultless wisdom, grand, primeval sage!
> For all the thronging woes to life allied
> Thy mercy tempers, and Thy cares provide."

We should be glad to know what the word 'For' means here. If it is a preposition, it makes nonsense of the words, "Thy mercy tempers." If it is an adverb, it makes nonsense of the words, "Thy cares provide."

These beauties we have taken, almost at random, from the first part of the poem. The second part is a series of descriptions of various events,—a battle —a murder—an execution—a marriage—a funeral—and so forth. Mr. Robert Montgomery terminates each of these descriptions by assuring us that the Deity was present at the battle, murder, execution, marriage, or funeral, in question. And this proposition, which might be safely predicated of every event that ever happened, or ever will happen, forms the only link which connects these descriptions with the subject, or with each other.

How the descriptions are executed, our readers are probably by this time able to conjecture. The battle is made up of the battles of all ages and nations; "red-mouth'd cannons, uproaring to the clouds," and "hands grasping firm the glittering shield." The only military operations of which this part of the poem reminds us are those which reduced the Abbey of Quedtinburgh to submission. The Templar with his cross—the Austrian and Prussian grenadiers in full uniform—and Curtius and Dentatus with their battering-ram. We ought not to pass by unnoticed the slain war-horse, who will no more

"Roll his red eye, and rally for the fight;"

or the slain warrior, who, while "lying on his bleeding breast," contrives to "stare ghastly and grimly on the skies." As to this last exploit, we can only say, as Dante did on a similar occasion,—

"Forse per forza gia di parlasia
Si stravolse cosi alcun del tutto;
Ma io nol vidi, nè credo che sia."

The tempest is thus described—

"But lo! around the marsh'lling clouds unite,
Like thick battalions halting for the fight;
The sun sinks back, the tempest-spirits sweep
Fierce through the air, and flutter on the deep.
Till from their caverns rush the maniac blasts,
Tear the loose sails, and split the creaking masts,
And the lash'd billows, rolling in a train,
Rear their white heads, and race along the main!"

What, we should like to know, is the difference between the two operations which Mr. Robert Montgomery so accurately distinguishes from each other,—the fierce sweeping of the tempest-spirits through the air and the rushing of the maniac blasts from their caverns? And why does the former operation end exactly when the latter commences?

We cannot stop over each of Mr. Robert Montgomery's descriptions. We have a shipwrecked sailor, who "visions a viewless temple in the air;"—a murderer, who stands on a heath, "with ashy lips, in cold convulsion spread;" —a pious man, to whom, as he lies in bed at night,

"The panorama of past life appears,
Warms his pure mind, and melts it into tears;"

a traveller, who loses his way owing to the thickness of the "cloud-battalion," and the want of "heaven-lamps, to beam their holy light." We have a description of a convicted felon, stolen from that incomparable passage in Crabbe's Borough, which has made many a rough and cynical reader cry like a child. We can, however, conscientiously declare that persons of the most excitable sensibility may safely venture upon it in Mr. Robert Montgomery's alteration. Then we have the "poor, mindless, pale-faced, maniac boy," who

"Rolls his vacant eye,
To greet the glowing fancies of the sky."

What are the glowing fancies of the sky? And what is the meaning of the two lines which almost immediately follow?

"A soulless thing, a spirit of the woods,
He loves to commune with the fields and floods."

How can a soulless thing be a spirit? Then comes a panegyric on the Sunday. A baptism follows;—after that a marriage;—and we then proceed, in due course, to the visitation of the sick and the burial of the dead.

Often as Death has been personified, Mr. Montgomery has found something new to say about him.

> "O Death ! thou dreadless vanquisher of earth,
> The elements shrank blasted at thy birth !
> Careering round the world like tempest wind,
> Martyrs before, and victims strew'd behind ;
> Ages on ages cannot grapple thee,
> Dragging the world into eternity !"

If there be any one line in this passage about which we are more in the dark than about the rest, it is the fourth. What the difference may be between the victims and the martyrs, and why the martyrs are to lie before Death, and the victims behind him, are to us great mysteries.

We now come to the third part, of which we may say with honest Cassio, "Why, this is a more excellent song than the other." Mr. Robert Montgomery is very severe on the infidels, and undertakes to prove that, as he elegantly expresses it,

> "One great Enchanter helm'd the harmonious whole."

What an enchanter has to do with helming, or what a helm has to do with harmony, we do not quite understand. He proceeds with his argument thus:

> "And dare men dream that dismal Chance has framed
> All that the eye perceives, or tongue has named ;
> The spacious world, and all its wonders, born
> Designless, self-created, and forlorn ;
> Like to the flashing bubbles on a stream,
> Fire from the cloud, or phantom in a dream ?"

We should be sorry to stake our faith in a higher Power on Mr. Robert Montgomery's logic. Does he believe that lightning, and bubbles, and the phenomena of dreams, are designless and self-created ? If he does, we cannot conceive why he may not believe that the whole universe is designless and self-created. A few lines before he tells us that it is the Deity who bids "thunder rattle from the skiey deep." His theory is therefore this, that God made the thunder, but that the lightning made itself.

But Mr. Robert Montgomery's metaphysics are not at present our game. He proceeds to set forth the fearful effects of atheism.

> "Then, blood-stain'd Murder, bare thy hideous arm,
> And thou, Rebellion, welter in thy storm :
> Awake ye spirits of avenging crime ;
> Burst from your bonds, and battle with the time !"

Mr. Robert Montgomery is fond of personification, and belongs, we need not say, to that school of poets who hold that nothing more is necessary to a personification in poetry than to begin a word with a capital letter. Murder may, without impropriety, bare her arm,—as she did long ago, in Mr. Campbell's Pleasures of Hope. But what possible motive Rebellion can have for weltering in her storm,—what avenging crime may be,—who its spirits may be,—why they should burst from their bonds,—what their bonds may be,—why they should battle with the time,—what the time may be,—and what a battle between the time and the spirits of avenging crime would resemble, we must confess ourselves quite unable to understand.

> "And here let Memory turn her tearful glance
> On the dark horrors of tumultuous France,
> When blood and blasphemy defiled her land,
> And fierce Rebellion shook her savage hand."

Whether Rebellion shakes her own hand, shakes the hand of Memory, or shakes the hand of France, or what any one of these metaphors would mean, we know no more than we know what is the sense of the following passage:

> "Let the foul orgies of infuriate crime
> Picture the raging havoc of that time,
> When leagued Rebellion march'd to kindle man,
> Fright in her rear, and Murder in her van,
> And thou, sweet flower of Austria, slaughter'd Queen,
> Who dropp'd no tear upon the dreadful scene,
> When gush'd the life-blood from thine angel form,
> And martyr'd beauty perish'd in the storm,
> Once worshipp'd paragon of all who saw,
> Thy look obedience, and thy smile a law," &c.

What is the distinction between the foul orgies and the raging havoc which the foul orgies are to picture? Why does Fright go behind Rebellion, and Murder before? Why should not Murder fall behind Fright? Or why should not all the three walk abreast? We have read of a hero who had

> "Amazement in his van, with Flight combined,
> And Sorrow's faded form, and Solitude behind."

Gray, we suspect, could have given a reason for disposing the allegorical attendants of Edward thus. But to proceed,—"Flower of Austria" is stolen from Byron. "Dropped" is false English. "Perish'd in the storm" means nothing at all; and "thy look obedience" means the very reverse of what Mr. Robert Montgomery intends to say.

Our poet then proceeds to demonstrate the immortality of the soul :—

> "And shall the soul, the fount of reason, die,
> When dust and darkness round its temple lie?
> Did God breathe in it no ethereal fire,
> Dimless and quenchless, though the breath expire."

The soul is a fountain; and therefore it is not to die, though dust and darkness lie round its temple, because an ethereal fire has been breathed into it, which cannot be quenched though its breath expire. Is it the fountain or the temple that breathes, and has fire breathed into it?

Mr. Montgomery apostrophizes the

> "Immortal beacons,—spirits of the just,"

and describes their employments in another world, which are to be, it seems, bathing in light, hearing fiery streams flow, and riding on living cars of lightning. The deathbed of the sceptic is described with what we suppose is meant for energy.

> "See how he shudders at the thought of death!
> What doubt and horror hang upon his breath,
> The gibbering teeth, glazed eye, and marble limb,
> Shades from the tomb stalk out and stare at him."

A man as stiff as marble shuddering and gibbering violently would certainly present so curious a spectacle that the shades, if they came in his way, might well stare.

We then have the deathbed of a Christian made as ridiculous as false imagery and false English can make it. But this is not enough :—The Day of Judgment is to be described,—and a roaring cataract of nonsense is poured forth upon this tremendous subject. Earth, we are told, is dashed into eternity. Furnace blazes wheel round the horizon, and burst into bright wizard phantoms. Racing hurricanes unroll and whirl quivering fire-clouds. The white waves gallop. Shadowy worlds career around. The red and raging eye of Imagination is then forbidden to pry further. But further Mr. Robert Montgomery persists in prying. The stars bound through the airy roar. The unbosomed deep yawns on the ruin. The billows of eternity then begin to advance. The world glares in fiery slumber. A car comes forward driven by living thunder.

"Creation shudders with sublime dismay,
And in a blazing tempest whirls away."

And this is fine poetry! This is what ranks its writer with the master-spirits of the age! This is what has been described over and over again, in terms which would require some qualification if used respecting Paradise Lost! It is too much that this patchwork, made by stitching together old odds and ends of what, when new, was, for the most part, but tawdry frippery, is to be picked off the dunghill on which it ought to rot, and to be held up to admiration as an inestimable specimen of art. And what must we think of a system, by means of which verses like those which we have quoted—verses fit only for the poet's corner of the *Morning Post*—can produce emolument and fame? The circulation of this writer's poetry has been greater than that of Southey's Roderic, and beyond all comparison greater than that of Cary's Dante, or of the best works of Coleridge. Thus encouraged, Mr. Robert Montgomery has favoured the public with volume after volume. We have given so much space to the examination of his first and most popular performance that we have none to spare for his Universal Prayer, and his smaller poems, which, as the puffing journals tell us, would alone constitute a sufficient title to literary immortality. We shall pass at once to his last publication, entitled Satan.

This poem was ushered into the world with the usual roar of acclamation. But the thing was now past a joke. Pretensions so unfounded, so impudent, and so successful, had aroused a spirit of resistance. In several magazines and reviews, accordingly, Satan has been handled somewhat roughly, and the arts of the puffers have been exposed with good sense and spirit. We shall, therefore, be very concise.

Of the two poems, we rather prefer that on the Omnipresence of the Deity, for the same reason which induced Sir Thomas More to rank one bad book above another. "Marry, this is somewhat. This is rhyme. But the other is neither rhyme nor reason." Satan is a long soliloquy, which the Devil pronounces in five or six thousand lines of blank verse conccerning geography, politics, newspapers, fashionable society, theatrical amusements, Sir Walter Scott's novels, Lord Byron's poetry, and Mr. Martin's pictures. The new designs for Milton have, as was natural, particularly attracted the attention of a personage who occupies so conspicuous a place in them. Mr. Martin must be pleased to learn that, whatever may be thought of those performances on earth, they give full satisfaction in Pandemonium, and that he is there thought to have hit off the likenesses of the various Thrones and Dominations very happily.

The motto to the poem of Satan is taken from the Book of Job:—"Whence comest thou?—From going to and fro in the earth, and walking up and down in it." And certainly Mr. Robert Montgomery has not failed to make his hero go to and fro, and walk up and down. With the exception, however, of this propensity to locomotion, Satan has not one Satanic quality. Mad Tom had told us that "the prince of darkness is a gentleman;" but we had yet to learn that he is a respectable and pious gentleman, whose principle fault is that he is something of a twaddle, and far too liberal of his good advice. That happy change in his character which Origen anticipated, and of which Tillotson did not despair, seems to be rapidly taking place. Bad habits are not eradicated in a moment. It is not strange, therefore, that so old an offender should now and then relapse for a short time into wrong dispositions. But to give him his due, as the proverb recommends, we must say that he always returns, after two or three lines of impiety, to his preaching tone. We would seriously advise Mr. Montgomery to omit, or alter, about a hundred lines in different parts of this large volume, and to republish it under the name of Gabriel. The reflections of which it consists would come less absurdly, as far as there is a more and a less in extreme absurdity, from a good than from a bad angel.

We can afford room only for a single quotation. We give one taken at random—neither worse nor better, as far as we can perceive, than any other equal number of lines in the book. The Devil goes to the play, and moralises thereon as follows:—

> "Music and Pomp their mingling spirit shed
> Around me; beauties in their cloud-like robes
> Shine forth,—a scenic paradise, it glares
> Intoxication through the reeling sense
> Of flush'd enjoyment. In the motly host
> Three prime gardations may be ranked : the first
> To mount upon the wings of Shakspeare's mind,
> And win a flash of his Promethean thought,—
> To smile and weep, to shudder, and achieve
> A round of passionate omnipotence
> Attend: the second, are a sensual tribe
> Convened to hear romantic harlots sing,
> On forms to banquet a lascivious gaze,
> While the bright perfidy of wanton eyes
> Through brain and spirit darts delicious fire:
> The last, a throng most pitiful! who seem,
> With their corroded figures, rayless glance
> And death-like struggle of decaying age,
> Like painted skeletons in charnel pomp
> Set forth to satirise the human kind !—
> How fine a prospect for demoniac view !
> 'Creatures whose souls outbalance worlds awake!'
> Methinks I hear a pitying angel cry."

Here we conclude. If our remarks give pain to Mr. Robert Montgomery, we are sorry for it. But, at whatever cost of pain to individuals, literature must be purified from this taint. And, to show that we are not actuated by any feelings of personal enmity towards him, we hereby give notice that, as soon as any book shall, by means of puffing, reach a second edition, our intention is to do unto the writer of it as we have done unto Mr. Robert Montgomery.

CIVIL DISABILITIES OF THE JEWS.

Statement of the Civil Disabilities and Privations affecting Jews in England. 8vo. London. 1829.

THE distinguished member of the House of Commons who, towards the close of the late Parliament, brought forward a proposition for the relief of the Jews, has given notice of his intention to renew it. The force of reason, in the last session carried it through one stage, in spite of the opposition of power. Reason and power are now on the same side; and we have little doubt that they will conjointly achieve a decisive victory. In order to contribute our share to the success of just principles, we propose to pass in review, as rapidly as possible, some of the arguments, or phrases claiming to be arguments, which have been employed to vindicate a system full of absurdity and injustice.

The Constitution—it is said—is essentially Christian; and, therefore, to admit Jews to office is to destroy the Constitution. Nor is the Jew injured by being excluded from political power. For no man has any right to power.

A man has a right to his property;—a man has a right to be protected from personal injury. These rights the law allows to the Jew; and with these rights it would be atrocious to interfere. But it is a mere matter of favour to admit any man to political power; and no man can justly complain that he is shut out from it.

We cannot but admire the ingenuity of this contrivance for shifting the burden of the proof from off those to whom it properly belongs, and who would, we suspect, find it rather cumbersome. Surely no Christian can deny that every human being has a right to be allowed every gratification which produces no harm to others, and to be spared every mortification which produces no good to others. Is it not a source of mortification to any class of men that they are excluded from political power? If it be, they have, on Christian principles, a right to be freed from that mortification, unless it can be shown that their exclusion is necessary for the averting of some greater evil. The presumption is evidently in favour of toleration. It is for the prosecutor to make out his case.

The strange argument which we are considering would prove too much even for those who advance it. If no man has a right to political power, then neither Jew nor Christian has such a right. The whole foundation of government is taken away. But if government be taken away, the property and the persons of men are insecure; and it is acknowledged that men have a right to their property and to personal security. If it be right that the property of men should be protected, and if this can only be done by means of government, then it must be right that government should exist. Now, there cannot be government unless some person or persons possess political power. Therefore, it is right that some person or persons should possess political power. That is to say, some person or persons must have a right to political power.

It will hardly be denied that government is a means for the attainment of an end. If men have a right to the end, they have a right to this—that the means shall be such as will accomplish the end. It is because men are not in the habit of considering what the end of government is that Catholic disabilities and Jewish disabilities have been suffered to exist so long. We hear of essentially Protestant governments and essentially Christian governments—words which mean just as much as essentially Protestant cookery, or essentially Christian horsemanship. Government exists for the purpose of keeping the peace—for the purpose of compelling us to settle our disputes by arbitration, instead of settling them by blows—for the purpose of compelling us to supply our wants by industry, instead of supplying them by rapine. This is the only operation for which the machinery of government is fit, the only operation which wise governments ever attempt to perform. If there is any class of people who are not interested, or do not think themselves interested, in the security of property and the maintenance of order, that class ought to have no share of the powers which exist for the purpose of securing property and maintaining order. But why a man should be less fit to exercise those powers because he wears a beard, because he does not eat ham, because he goes to the synagogue on Saturdays instead of going to the church on Sundays, we cannot conceive.

The points of difference between Christianity and Judaism have very much to do with a man's fitness to be a bishop or a rabbi. But they have no more to do with his fitness to be a magistrate, a legislator, or a minister of finance, than with his fitness to be a cobbler. Nobody has ever thought of compelling cobblers to make any declaration on the true faith of a Christian. Any man would rather have his shoes mended by a heretical cobbler than by a person who had subscribed all the thirty-nine articles, but had never handled an awl

Men act thus, not because they are indifferent to religion, but because they do not see what religion has to do with the mending of their shoes. Yet religion has as much to do with the mending of shoes as with the budget and the army estimates. We have surely had several signal proofs within the last twenty years that a very good Christian may be a very bad Chancellor of the Exchequer.

But it would be monstrous, say the persecutors, that Jews should legislate for a Christian community. This is a palpable misrepresentation. What is proposed is, not that the Jews should legislate for a Christian community, but that a legislature composed of Christians and Jews should legislate for a community composed of Christians and Jews. On nine hundred and ninety-nine questions out of a thousand,—on all questions of police, of finance, of civil and criminal law, of foreign policy,—the Jew, as a Jew, has no interest hostile to that of the Christian, or even to that of the Churchman. On questions relating to the ecclesiastical establishment, the Jew and the Churchman may differ. But they cannot differ more widely than the Catholic and the Churchman, or the Independent and the Churchman. The principle that Churchmen ought to monopolize the whole power of the state would at least have an intelligible meaning. The principle that Christians ought to monopolize it has no meaning at all. For no question connected with the ecclesiastical institutions of the country can possibly come before Parliament, with respect to which there will not be as wide a difference between Christians as there can be between any Christian and any Jew.

In fact, the Jews are not now excluded from political power. They possess it; and as long as they are allowed to accumulate large fortunes, they must possess it. The distinction which is sometimes made between civil privileges and political power is a distinction without a difference. Privileges are power. Civil and political are synonymous words—the one derived from the Latin, the other from the Greek. Nor is this mere verbal quibbling. If we look for a moment at the facts of the case, we shall see that the things are inseparable, or rather identical.

That a Jew should be a judge in a Christian country would be most shocking. But he may be a juryman. He may try issues of fact; and no harm is done. But if he should be suffered to try issues of law, there is an end of the Constitution. He may sit in a box plainly dressed, and return verdicts. But that he should sit on the bench in a black gown and white wig, and grant new trials, would be an abomination not to be thought of among baptized people. The distinction is certainly most philosophical.

What power in civilized society is so great as that of the creditor over the debtor? If we take this away from the Jew, we take away from him the security of his property. If we leave it to him, we leave to him a power more despotic by far than that of the king and all his cabinet.

It would be impious to let a Jew sit in Parliament. But a Jew may make money; and money may make members of Parliament. Gatton and Old Sarum may be the property of a Hebrew. An elector of Penryn will take ten pounds from Shylock rather than nine pounds nineteen shillings and elevenpence three-farthings from Antonio. To this no objection is made. That a Jew should possess the substance of legislative power, that he should command eight votes on every division, as if he were the great Duke of Newcastle himself, is exactly as it should be. But that he should pass the bar and sit down on those mysterious cushions of green leather, that he should cry "hear" and "order," and talk about being on his legs, and being, for one, free to say this and to say that, would be a profanation sufficient to bring ruin on the country.

That a Jew should be privy councillor to a Christian king would be an eternal disgrace to the nation. But the Jew may govern the money-market, and the money-market may govern the world. The minister may be in doubt as to his scheme of finance till he has been closeted with the Jew. A congress of sovereigns may be forced to summon the Jew to their assistance. The scrawl of the Jew on the back of a piece of paper may be worth more than the royal word of three kings, or the national faith of three new American republics. But that he should put Right Honourable before his name would be the most frightful of national calamities.

It was in this way that some of our politicians reasoned about the Irish Catholics. The Catholics ought to have no political power. The sun of England is set for ever if the Catholics exercise political power. Give them everything else; but keep political power from them. These wise men did not see that, when everything else had been given, political power had been given. They continued to repeat their cuckoo song, when it was no longer a question whether Catholics should have political power or not, when a Catholic association bearded the Parliament, when a Catholic agitator exercised infinitely more authority than the Lord Lieutenant.

If it is our duty as Christians to exclude the Jews from political power, it must be our duty to treat them as our ancestors treated them—to murder them, and banish them, and rob them. For in that way, and in that way alone, can we really deprive them of political power. If we do not adopt this course, we may take away the shadow, but we must leave them the substance. We may do enough to pain and irritate them; but we shall not do enough to secure ourselves from danger, if danger really exists. Where wealth is there power must inevitably be.

The English Jews, we are told, are not Englishmen. They are a separate people, living locally in this island, but living morally and politically in communion with their brethren who are scattered over all the world. An English Jew looks on a Dutch or a Portuguese Jew as his countryman, and on an English Christian as a stranger. This want of patriotic feeling, it is said, renders a Jew unfit to exercise political functions.

The argument has in it something plausible; but a close examination shows it to be quite unsound. Even if the alleged facts are admitted, still the Jews are not the only people who have preferred their sect to their country. The feeling of patriotism, when society is in a healthful state, springs up by a natural and inevitable association, in the minds of citizens who know that they owe all their comforts and pleasures to the bond which unites them in one community. But, under partial and oppressive governments these associations cannot acquire that strength which they have in a better state of things. Men are compelled to seek from their party that protection which they ought to receive from their country, and they, by a natural consequence, transfer to their party that affection which they would otherwise have felt for their country. The Huguenots of France called in the help of England against their Catholic kings. The Catholics of France called in the help of Spain against a Huguenot king. Would it be fair to infer, that at present the French Protestants would wish to see their religion made dominant by the help of a Prussian or English army? Surely not. And why is it that they are not willing, as they formerly were willing, to sacrifice the interests of their country to the interests of their religious persuasion? The reason is obvious:—because they were persecuted then, and are not persecuted now. The English Puritans, under Charles I., prevailed on the Scotch to invade England. Do the Protestant Dissenters of our time wish to see the Church put down by an invasion of foreign Calvinists? If not, to what cause are we to attribute the change? Surely to this, that the Protestant Dissenters are far better treated now than in the seventeenth century. Some of the most illustrious public men that England ever produced were inclined to take refuge from the tyranny of Laud in North America. Was this because Presbyterians are incapable of loving their country?—But it is idle to multiply instances. Nothing is so offensive to a man who knows anything of history or of human nature as to hear those who exercise the powers of government accuse any sect of foreign attachments. If there be any proposition universally true in politics, it is this, that foreign attachments are the fruit of domestic misrule. It has always been the trick of bigots to make their subjects miserable at home, and then to complain that they look for relief abroad;—to divide society, and to wonder that it is not united;—to govern as if a section of the state were the whole, and to censure the other sections of the state for their want of patriotic spirit. If the Jews have not felt towards England like children, it is because she has treated them like a stepmother. There is no feeling which more certainly develops itself in the minds of men living under tolerably good government than the feeling of patriotism. Since the beginning of the world there never was any nation, or any large portion of any nation, not cruelly oppressed, which was wholly destitute of that feeling. To make it, therefore, ground of accusation against a class of men that they are not patriotic is the most vulgar legerdemain of sophistry. It is the logic which the wolf employs against the lamb. It is to accuse the mouth of the stream of poisoning the source. It is to put the effect before the cause. It is to vindicate oppression by pointing at the depravation which oppression has produced.

If the English Jews really felt a deadly hatred to England,—if the weekly prayer of their synagogues were that all the curses denounced by Ezekiel on Tyre and Egypt might fall on London,—if, in their solemn feasts, they called down blessings on those who should dash their children to pieces on the stones, still, we say, their hatred to their countrymen would not be more intense than that which sects of Christians have often borne to each other. But, in fact, the feeling of the Jews is not such. It is precisely what, in the situation in which they are placed, we should expect it to be. They are treated far better than the French Protestants were treated in the sixteenth and seventeenth centuries, or than our Puritans were treated in the time of Laud. They, therefore, have no rancour against the government or against their countrymen. It will not be denied that they are far better affected to the state than the followers of Coligni or Vane. But they are not so well treated as the dissenting sects of Christians are now treated in England; and on this account, and, we firmly believe, on this account alone, they have a more exclusive spirit. Till we have carried the experiment farther, we are not entitled to conclude that they cannot be made Englishmen altogether. The tyrant who punished their fathers for not making bricks without straw, was not more unreasonable than the statesman who treats them as aliens and abuses them for not entertaining all the feelings of natives.

Rulers must not be suffered thus to absolve themselves of their solemn responsibility. It does not lie in their mouths to say that a sect is not patriotic —it is their business to make it patriotic. History and reason clearly indicate the means. The English Jews are, as far as we can see, precisely what our government has made them. They are precisely what any sect,—what any class of men, treated as they have been treated,—would have been. If all the red-haired people in Europe had, for centuries, been outraged and oppressed, banished from this place, imprisoned in that, deprived of their money, deprived of their teeth, convicted of the most improbable crimes on the feeblest evidence, dragged at horses' tails, hanged, tortured, burned alive,—if, when manners became milder, they had still been subject to debasing restrictions and exposed to vulgar insults, locked up in particular streets in some countries, pelted and ducked by the rabble in others, excluded everywhere from magistracies and honours,—what would be the patriotism of gentlemen with red hair? And if, under such circumstances, a proposition were made for admitting red-haired men to office, how striking a speech might an eloquent admirer of our old institutions deliver against so revolutionary a measure! "These men," he might say, "scarcely consider themselves as Englishmen. They think a red-haired Frenchman or a red-haired German more closely connected with them than a man with brown hair born in their own parish. If a foreign sovereign patronises red hair, they love him better than their own native king. They are not Englishmen:—they cannot be Englishmen:—nature has forbidden it :—experience proves it to be impossible. Right to political power they have none; for no man has a right to political power. Let them enjoy personal security; let their property be under the protection of the law. But if they ask for leave to exercise power over a community of which they are only half members—a community the constitution of which is essentially dark-haired—let us answer them in the words of our wise ancestors, *Nolumus leges Angliæ mutari.*"

But, it is said, the Scriptures declare that the Jews are to be restored to their own country; and the whole nation looks forward to that restoration. They are, therefore, not so deeply interested as others in the prosperity of England. It is not their home, but merely the place of their sojourn,—the house of their bondage. This argument first appeared in the Times newspaper, and has attracted a degree of attention proportioned rather to the general talent with which that journal is conducted than to its own intrinsic force. It belongs to a class of sophisms by which the most hateful persecutions may easily be justified. To charge men with practical consequences which they themselves deny is disingenuous in controversy ;—it is atrocious in government. The doctrine of predestination, in the opinion of many people, tends to make those who hold it utterly immoral. And certainly it would seem that a man who believes his eternal destiny to be already irrevocably fixed is likely to indulge his passions without restraint, and to neglect his religious duties. If he is an heir of wrath, his exertions must be unavailing. If he is preordained to life, they must be superfluous. But would it be wise to punish every man who holds the higher doctrines of Calvinism, as if he had actually committed all those crimes which we know some German Anabaptists to have committed? Assuredly not. The fact notoriously is that there are many Calvinists as moral in their conduct as any Arminian, and many Arminians as loose as any Calvinist.

It is altogether impossible to reason from the opinions which a man professes to his feelings and his actions; and, in fact, no person is ever such a fool as to reason thus, except when he wants a pretext for persecuting his neighbours. A Christian is commanded, under the strongest sanctions, to do as he would be done by. Yet to how many of the twenty-four millions of professing Christians in these islands would any man in his senses lend a thousand pounds without security? A man who should act, for one day, on the supposition that all the people about him were influenced by the religion which they professed, would find himself ruined before night; and no man ever does act on that supposition in any of the ordinary concerns of life, in borrowing, in lending, in buying, or in selling. But when any of our fellow-creatures are to be oppressed, the case is different. Then we represent those motives which we know to be so feeble for good as omnipotent for evil. Then we lay to the charge of our victims all the vices and follies to which their doctrines, however remotely, seem to tend. We forget that the same weakness, the same laxity, the same disposition to prefer the present to the future, which make men worse than a good religion, make them better than a bad one.

It was in this way that our ancestors reasoned, and that some people in our time still reason, about the Catholics. A Papist believes himself bound to obey the pope. The pope has issued a bull deposing Queen Elizabeth. Therefore every Papist will treat her grace as an usurper. Therefore every Papist is a traitor. Therefore every Papist ought to be hanged, drawn, and quartered. To this logic we owe some of the most hateful laws that ever disgraced our history. Surely the answer lies on the surface. The Church of Rome may have commanded these men to treat the queen as an usurper. But she has commanded them to do many other things which they have never done. She enjoins her priests to observe strict purity. You are always taunting them with their licentiousness. She commands all her followers to fast often, to be charitable to the poor, to take no interest for money, to fight no duels, to see no plays. Do they obey these injunctions? If it be the fact that very few of them strictly observe her precepts, when her precepts are opposed to their passions and interests, may not loyalty, may not humanity, may not the love of ease, may not the fear of death, be sufficient to prevent them from executing those wicked orders which she has issued against the sovereign of England? When we know that many of these people do not care enough for their religion to go without beef on a Friday for it, why should we think that they will run the risk of being racked and hanged for it?

People are now reasoning about the Jews as our fathers reasoned about the Papists. The law which is inscribed on the walls of the synagogues prohibits covetousness. But if we were to say that a Jew mortgagee would not foreclose because God had commanded him not to covet his neighbour's house, everybody would think us out of our wits. Yet it passes for an argument to say that a Jew will take no interest in the prosperity of the country in which he lives, that he will not care how bad its laws and police may be,—how heavily it may be taxed,—how often it may be conquered and given up to spoil,—because God has promised that, by some unknown means, and at some undetermined time, perhaps ten thousand years hence, the Jews shall migrate to Palestine. Is not this the most profound ignorance of human nature? Do we not know that what is remote and indefinite affects men far less than what is near and certain? Besides, the argument, too, applies to Christians as strongly as to Jews. The Christian believes, as well as the Jew, that at some future period the present order of things will come to an end. Nay, many Christians believe that the Messiah will shortly establish a kingdom on the earth, and reign visibly over all its inhabitants. Whether this doctrine be orthodox or not we shall not here inquire. The number of people who hold it is very much greater than the number of Jews residing in England. Many of those who hold it are distinguished by rank, wealth, and ability. It is preached from pulpits, both of the Scottish and of the English Church. Noblemen and members of Parliament have written in defence of it. Now wherein does this doctrine differ, as far as its political tendency is concerned, from the doctrine of the Jews? If a Jew is unfit to legislate for us because he believes that he or his remote descendants will be removed to Palestine, can we safely open the House of Commons to a fifth-monarchy man, who expects that before this generation shall pass away, all the kingdoms of the earth will be swallowed up in one divine empire?

Does a Jew engage less eagerly than a Christian in any competition which the law leaves open to him? Is he less active and regular in his business than his neighbours? Does he furnish his house meanly because he is a pilgrim and sojourner in the land? Does the expectation of being restored to the country of his fathers make him insensible to the fluctuations of the stock-exchange? Does he, in arranging his private affairs, ever take into the account the chance of his migrating to Palestine? If not, why are we to suppose that feelings which never influence his dealings as a merchant, or his dispositions as a testator, will acquire a boundless influence over him as soon as he becomes a magistrate or a legislator?

There is another argument which we would not willingly treat with levity, and yet which we scarcely know how to treat seriously. Scripture, it is said, is full of terrible denunciations against the Jews. It is foretold that they are to be wanderers. Is it then right to give them a home? It is foretold that they are to be oppressed. Can we with propriety suffer them to be rulers? To admit them to the rights of citizens is manifestly to insult the Divine oracles.

We allow that to falsify a prophecy inspired by Divine wisdom would be a most atrocious crime. It is, therefore, a happy circumstance for our frail species that it is a crime which no man can possibly commit. If we admit the Jews to a seat in Parliament we shall, by so doing, prove that the prophecies in question, whatever they may mean, do not mean that the Jews shall be excluded from Parliament.

In fact, it is already clear that the prophecies do not bear the meaning put upon them by the respectable persons whom we are now answering. In France and in the United States the Jews are already admitted to all the rights of citizens. A prophecy, therefore, which should mean that the Jews would never, during the course of their wanderings, be admitted to all the rights of citizens in the places of their sojourn would be a false prophecy. This, therefore, is not the meaning of the prophecies of Scripture.

But we protest altogether against the practice of confounding prophecy with precept—of setting up predictions which are often obscure against a morality which is always clear. If actions are to be considered as just and good merely because they have been predicted, what action was ever more laudable than that crime which our bigots are now, at the end of eighteen centuries, urging us to avenge on the Jews—that crime which made the earth shake and blotted out the sun from heaven? The same reasoning which is now employed to vindicate the disabilities imposed on our Hebrew countrymen will equally vindicate the kiss of Judas and the judgment of Pilate. "The Son of man goeth, as it is written of him; but woe to that man by whom the Son of man is betrayed." And woe to those who, in any age or in any country, disobey his benevolent commands under pretence of accomplishing his predictions. If this argument justifies the laws now existing against the Jews, it justifies equally all the cruelties which have ever been committed against them—the sweeping edicts of banishment and confiscation, the dungeon, the rack, and the slow fire. How can we excuse ourselves for leaving property to people who are to "serve their enemies in hunger, and in thirst, and in nakedness, and in want of all things;"—for giving protection to the persons of those who are to "fear day and night, and to have none assurance of their life;"—for not seizing on the children of a race whose "sons and daughters are to be given unto another people?"

We have not so learned the doctrines of Him who commanded us to love our neighbour as ourselves, and who, when He was called upon to explain what He meant by a neighbour, selected as an example a heretic and an alien. Last year, we remember, it was represented by a pious writer in the John Bull newspaper, and by some other equally fervid Christians, as a monstrous indecency, that the measure for the relief of the Jews should be brought forward in Passion week. One of these humorists ironically recommended that it should be read a second time on Good Friday. We should have had no objection; nor do we believe that the day could be commemorated in a more worthy manner. We know of no day fitter for terminating long hostilities and repairing cruel wrongs than the day on which the religion of mercy was founded. We know of no day fitter for blotting out from the statute-book the last traces of intolerance than the day on which the spirit of intolerance produced the foulest of all judicial murders, the day on which the list of the victims of intolerance, that noble list wherein Socrates and More are enrolled, was glorified by a yet greater and holier name.

MOORE'S LIFE OF LORD BYRON.

Letters and Journals of Lord Byron; with Notices of his Life. By THOMAS MOORE, Esq. 2 vols. 4to. London. 1830.

WE have read this book with the greatest pleasure. Considered merely as a composition, it deserves to be classed among the best specimens of English prose which our age has produced. It contains, indeed, no single passage equal to two or three which we could select from the Life of Sheridan. But, as a whole, it is immeasurably superior to that work. The style is agreeable, clear, and manly, and when it rises into eloquence, rises without effort or ostentation. Nor is the matter inferior to the manner.

It would be difficult to name a book which exhibits more kindness, fairness, and modesty. It has evidently been written, not for the purpose of showing, what, however, it often shows, how well its author can write, but for the purpose of vindicating, as far as truth will permit, the memory of a celebrated man who can no longer vindicate himself. Mr. Moore never thrusts himself between Lord Byron and the public. With the strongest temptations to egotism, he has said no more about himself than the subject absolutely required. A great part—indeed, the greater part, of these volumes, consists of extracts from the letters and journals of Lord Byron; and it is difficult to speak too highly of the skill which has been shown in the selection and arrangement. We will not say that we have not occasionally remarked in these two large quartos an anecdote which should have been omitted, a letter which should have been suppressed, a name which should have been concealed by asterisks, or asterisks which do not answer the purpose of concealing the name. But it is impossible, on a general survey, to deny that the task has been executed with great judgment and great humanity. When we consider the life which Lord Byron had led, his petulance, his irritability, and his communicativeness, we cannot but admire the dexterity with which Mr. Moore has contrived to exhibit so much of the character and opinions of his friend, with so little pain to the feelings of the living.

The extracts from the journals and correspondence of Lord Byron are in the highest degree valuable—not merely on account of the information which they contain respecting the distinguished man by whom they were written, but on account also of their rare merit as compositions. The letters, at least those which were sent from Italy,—are among the best in our language. They are less affected than those of Pope and Walpole;—they have more matter in them than those of Cowper. Knowing that many of them were not written merely for the person to whom they were directed, but were general epistles, meant to be read by a large circle, we expected to find them clever and spirited, but deficient in ease. We looked with vigilance for instances of stiffness in the language and awkwardness in the transitions. We have been agreeably disappointed; and we must confess that, if the epistolary style of Lord Byron was artificial, it was a rare and admirable instance of that highest art which cannot be distinguished from nature.

Of the deep and painful interest which this book excites no abstract can give a just notion. So sad and dark a story is scarcely to be found in any work of fiction; and we are little disposed to envy the moralist who can read it without being softened.

The pretty fable by which the Duchess of Orleans illustrates the character of her son the Regent might, with little change, be applied to Byron. All the fairies, save one, had been bidden to his cradle. All the gossips had been profuse of their gifts. One had bestowed nobility, another genius, a third beauty. The malignant elf who had been uninvited came last, and, unable to reverse what her sisters had done for their favourite, had mixed up a curse with every blessing. In the rank of Lord Byron, in his understanding, in his character, in his very person, there was a strange union of opposite extremes. He was born to all that men covet and admire. But in every one of those eminent advantages which he possessed over others was mingled something of misery and debasement. He was sprung from a house, ancient, indeed, and noble, but degraded and impoverished by a series of crimes and follies which had attained a scandalous publicity. The kinsman whom he succeeded had died poor, and, but for merciful judges, would have died upon the gallows. The young peer had great intellectual powers; yet there was an unsound part in his mind. He had naturally a generous and feeling heart; but his temper was wayward and irritable. He had a head which statuaries loved to copy, and a foot the deformity of which the beggars in the streets mimicked. Distinguished at once by the strength and by the weakness of his intellect, affectionate yet perverse, a poor lord, and a handsome cripple, he required, if ever man required, the firmest and the most judicious training. But capriciously as nature had dealt with him, the parent to whom the office of forming his character was intrusted was more capricious still. She passed from paroxysms of rage to paroxysms of tenderness. At one time she stifled him with her caresses;—at another time she insulted his deformity. He came into the world; and the world treated him as his mother had treated him,— sometimes with fondness, sometimes with cruelty, never with justice. It indulged him without discrimination, and punished him without discrimination. He was truely a spoiled child,—not merely the spoiled child of his parent, but the spoiled child of nature, the spoiled child of fortune, the spoiled child of fame, the spoiled child of society. His first poems were received with a contempt which, feeble as they were, they did not absolutely deserve. The poem which he published on his return from his travels was, on the other hand, extolled far above its merit. At twenty-four he found himself on the highest pinnacle of literary fame, with Scott, Wordsworth, Southey, and a crowd of other distinguished writers beneath his feet. There is scarcely an instance in history of so sudden a rise to so dizzy an eminence.

Everything that could stimulate, and everything that could gratify the strongest propensities of our nature—the gaze of a hundred drawing-rooms, the acclamations of the whole nation, the applause of applauded men, the love of the loveliest women,—all this world and all the glory of it were at once offered to a young man to whom nature had given violent passions, and whom education had never taught to control them. He lived as many men live who have no similar excuse to plead for their faults. But his countrymen and his countrywomen would love him and admire him. They were resolved to see in his excesses only the flash and outbreak of that same fiery mind which glowed in his poetry. He attacked religion; yet in religious circles his name was mentioned with fondness; and in many religious publications his works were censured with singular tenderness. He lampooned the Prince Regent; yet he could not alienate the Tories. Everything, it seemed, was to be forgiven to youth, rank, and genius.

Then came the reaction. Society, capricious in its indignation as it had been capricious in its fondness, flew into a rage with its froward and petted darling. He had been worshipped with an irrational idolatry. He was persecuted with an irrational fury. Much has been written about those unhappy domestic occurrences which decided the fate of his life. Yet nothing is, nothing ever was, positively known to the public but this, that he quarrelled with his lady, and that she refused to live with him. There have been hints in abundance, and shrugs and shakings of the head, and "Well, well, we know," and "We could an if we would," and "If we list to speak," and "There be that might an they list." But we are not aware that there is before the world, substantiated by credible, or even by tangible evidence, a single fact indicating that Lord Byron was more to blame than any other man who is on bad terms with his wife. The professional men whom Lady Byron consulted were undoubtedly of opinion that she ought not to live with her husband. But it is to be remembered that they formed that opinion without hearing both sides. We do not say, we do not mean to insinuate, that Lady Byron was in any respect to blame. We think that those who condemn her on the evidence which is now before the public are as rash as those who condemn her husband. We will not pronounce any judgment, we cannot, even in our own minds, form any judgment on a transaction which is so imperfectly known to us. It would have been well if, at the time of the separation, all those who knew as little about the matter then as we know about it now had shown that forbearance which, under such circumstances, is but common justice.

We know no spectacle so ridiculous as the British public in one of its periodical fits of morality. In general, elopements, divorces, and family quarrels, pass with little notice. We read the scandal, talk about it for a day, and forget it. But once in six or seven years our virtue becomes outrageous. We cannot suffer the laws of religion and decency to be violated. We must make a stand against vice. We must teach libertines that the English people appreciate the importance of domestic ties. Accordingly, some unfortunate man, in no respect more depraved than hundreds whose offences have been treated with lenity, is singled out as an expiatory sacrifice. If he has children, they are to be taken from him. If he has a profession, he has to be driven from it. He is cut by the higher orders, and hissed by the lower. He is, in truth, a sort of whipping-boy, by whose vicarious agonies all the other transgressors of the same class are, it is supposed, sufficiently chastised. We reflect very complacently on our own severity, and compare with great pride the high standard of morals established in England with the Parisian laxity. At length our anger is satiated. Our victim is ruined and heartbroken. And our virtue goes quietly to sleep for seven years more.

It is clear that those vices which destroy domestic happiness ought to be as much as possible repressed. It is equally clear that they cannot be repressed by penal legislation. It is, therefore, right and desirable that public opinion should be directed against them. But it should be directed against them uniformly, steadily, and temperately, not by sudden fits and starts. There should be one weight and one measure. Decimation is always an objectionable mode of punishment. It is the resource of judges too indolent and hasty to investigate facts and to discriminate nicely between shades of guilt. It is an irrational practice, even when adopted by military tribunals. When adopted by the tribunal of public opinion, it is infinitely more irrational. It is good that a certain portion of disgrace should constantly attend on certain bad actions. But it is not good that the offenders should merely have to stand the risks of a lottery of infamy, that ninety-nine out of every hundred should escape, and that the hundredth, perhaps the most innocent of the hundred, should pay for all. We remember to have seen a mob assembled in Lincoln's Inn to hoot a gentleman against whom the most oppressive proceeding known to the English law was then in progress. He was hooted because he had been an indifferent and unfaithful husband, as if some of the most popular men of the age,—Lord Nelson for example,—had not been unfaithful husbands. We remember a still stronger case. Will posterity believe that, in an age in which men whose gallantries were universally known, and had been legally proved, filled some of the highest offices in the state and in the army, presided at the meetings of religious and benevolent institutions,—were the delight of every society, and the favourites of the multitude,—a crowd of moralists went to the theatre, in order to pelt a poor actor for disturbing the conjugal felicity of an alderman? What there was in the circumstances either of the offender or of the sufferer to vindicate the zeal of the audience, we could never conceive. It has never been supposed that the situation of an actor is peculiarly favourable to the rigid virtues, or that an alderman enjoys any special immunity from injuries such as that which on this occasion roused the anger of the public. But such is the justice of mankind.

In these cases the punishment was excessive; but the offence was known and proved. The case of Lord Byron was harder. True Jedwood justice was dealt out to him. First came the execution, then the investigation, and last of all, or rather not at all, the accusation. The public, without knowing anything whatever about the transactions in his family, flew into a violent passion with him, and proceeded to invent stories which might justify its anger. Ten or twenty different accounts of the separation, inconsistent with each other, with themselves, and with common sense, circulated at the same time. What evidence there might be for anyone of these, the virtuous people who repeated them neither knew or cared. For, in fact, these stories were not the causes, but the effects of the public indignation. They resembled those loathsome slanders which Goldsmith and other abject libellers of the same class were in the habit of publishing about Bonaparte;—how he poisoned a girl with arsenic when he was at the military school,—that he hired a grenadier to shoot Dessaix at Marengo,—that he filled St. Cloud with all the pollutions of Capreæ. There was a time when anecdotes like these obtained some credence from persons who, hating the French emperor without knowing why, were eager to believe anything which might justify their hatred. Lord Byron fared in the same way. His countrymen were in a bad humour with him. His writings and his character had lost the charm of novelty. He had been guilty of the offence which, of all offences, is punished most severely; he had been over-praised; he had excited too warm an interest; and the public, with its usual justice, chastised him for its own folly. The attachments of the multitude bear no small resemblance to those of the wanton enchantress in the Arabian Tales, who, when the forty days of her fondness were over, was not content with dismissing her lovers, but condemned them to expiate, in loathsome shapes, and under severe punishments, the crime of having once pleased her too well.

The obloquy which Byron had to endure was such as might well have shaken a more constant mind. The newspapers were filled with lampoons. The theatres shook with execrations. He was excluded from circles where he had lately been the observed of all observers. All those creeping things that riot in the decay of nobler natures hastened to their repast; and they were right;—they did after their kind. It is not every day that the savage envy of aspiring dunces is gratified by the agonies of such a spirit, and the degradation of such a name.

The unhappy man left his country for ever. The howl of contumely followed, him across the sea, up the Rhine, over the Alps; it gradually waxed fainter; it died away. Those who had raised it began to ask each other what, after all, was the matter about which they had been so clamorous, and wished to invite back the criminal whom they had just chased from them. His poetry became more popular than it had ever been; and his complaints were read with tears by thousands and tens of thousands who had never seen his face.

He had fixed his home on the shores of the Adriatic, in the most picturesque and interesting of cities, beneath the brightest of skies, and by the brightest of seas. Censoriousness was not the vice of the neighbours whom he had chosen. They were a race corrupted by a bad government and a bad religion, long renowned for skill in the arts of voluptuousness, and tolerant of all the caprices of sensuality. From the public opinion of the country of his adoption, he had nothing to dread. With the public opinion of the country of his birth, he was at open war. He plunged into wild and desperate excesses, ennobled by no generous or tender sentiment. From his Venetian harem he sent forth volume after volume, full of eloquence, of wit, of pathos, of ribaldry, and of bitter disdain. His health sank under the effects of his intemperance. His hair turned grey. His food ceased to nourish him. A hectic fever withered him up. It seemed that his body and mind were about to perish together.

From this wretched degradation he was in some measure rescued by a connection, culpable indeed, yet such as, if it were judged by the standard of morality established in the country where he lived, might be called virtuous. But an imagination polluted by vice, a temper embittered by misfortune, and a frame habituated to the fatal excitement of intoxication, prevented him from fully enjoying the happiness which he might have derived from the purest and most tranquil of his many attachments. Midnight draughts of ardent spirits and Rhenish wines had begun to work the ruin of his fine intellect. His verse lost much of the energy and condensation which had distinguished it. But he would not resign, without a struggle, the empire which he had exercised over the men of his generation. A new dream of ambition rose before him;—to be the chief of a literary party; to be the great mover of an intellectual revolution;—to guide the public mind of England from his Italian retreat, as Voltaire had guided the public mind of France from the villa of Ferney. With this hope, as it should seem, he established The Liberal. But, powerfully as he had affected the imaginations of his contemporaries, he mistook his own powers if he hoped to direct their opinions; and he still more grossly mistook his own disposition, if he thought that he could long act in concert with other men of letters. The plan failed, and failed ignominiously. Angry with himself, angry with his coadjutors, he relinquished it, and turned to another project, the last and noblest of his life.

A nation, once the first among the nations, pre-eminent in knowledge, pre-eminent in military glory, the cradle of philosophy, of eloquence, and of the fine arts, had been for ages bowed down under a cruel yoke. All the vices which tyranny generates,—the abject vices which it generates in those who submit to it,—the ferocious vices which it generates in those who struggle against it,—had deformed the character of that miserable race. The valour which had won the great battle of human civilisation,—which had saved Europe, which had subjugated Asia, lingered only among pirates and robbers. The ingenuity, once so conspicuously displayed in every department of physical and moral science, had been depraved into a timid and servile cunning. On a sudden this degraded people had risen on their oppressors. Discountenanced or betrayed by the surrounding potentates, they had found in themselves something of that which might well supply the place of all foreign assistance,—something of the energy of their fathers.

As a man of letters, Lord Byron could not but be interested in the event of this contest. His political opinions, though, like all his opinions, unsettled, leaned strongly towards the side of liberty. He had assisted the Italian insurgents with his purse, and, if their struggle against the Austrian government had been prolonged, would probably have assisted them with his sword. But to Greece he was attached by peculiar ties. He had when young resided in that country. Much of his most splendid and popular poetry had been inspired by its scenery and by its history. Sick of inaction,—degraded in his own eyes by his private vices and by his literary failures,—pining for untried excitement and honourable distinction,—he carried his exhausted body and his wounded spirit to the Grecian camp.

His conduct in his new situation showed so much vigour and good sense as to justify us in believing that, if his life had been prolonged, he might have distinguished himself as a soldier and a politician. But pleasure and sorrow had done the work of seventy years upon his delicate frame. The hand of death was upon him: he knew it; and the only wish which he uttered was that he might die sword in hand.

This was denied to him. Anxiety, exertion, exposure, and those fatal stimulants which had become indispensable to him, soon stretched him on a sick bed, in a strange land, amidst strange faces, without one human being he loved near him. There, at thirty-six, the most celebrated Englishman of the nineteenth century closed his brilliant and miserable career.

We cannot even now retrace those events without feeling something of what was felt by the nation when it was first known that the grave had closed over so much sorrow and so much glory;—something of what was felt by those who saw the hearse, with its long train of coaches, turn slowly northward, leaving behind it that cemetery which had been consecrated by the dust of so many great poets, but of which the doors were closed against all that remained of Byron. We well remember that on that day rigid moralists could not refrain from weeping for one so young, so illustrious, so unhappy, gifted with such rare gifts, and tried by such strong temptations. It is unnecessary to make any reflections. The history carries its moral with it. Our age has indeed been fruitful of warnings to the eminent, and of consolations to the obscure. Two men have died within our recollection who, at the time of life at which many people have hardly completed their education, had raised themselves, each in his own department, to the height of glory. One of them died at Longwood; the other at Missolonghi.

It is always difficult to separate the literary character of a man who lives in our time from his personal character. It is peculiarly difficult to make this separation in the case of Lord Byron. For it is scarcely too much to say that Lord Byron never wrote without some reference, direct or indirect, to himself. The interest excited by the events of his life mingles itself in our minds, and probably in the minds of almost all our readers, with the interest which properly belongs to his works. A generation must pass away before it will be possible to form a fair judgment of his books, considered merely as books. At present they are not only books, but relics. We will, however, venture, though with unfeigned diffidence, to offer some desultory remarks on his poetry.

His lot was cast in the time of a great literary revolution. That poetical dynasty which has dethroned the successors of Shakespeare and Spenser was, in its turn, dethroned by a race who represented themselves as heirs of the ancient line, so long dispossessed by usurpers. The real nature of this revolution has not, we think, been comprehended by the great majority of those who concurred in it.

If this question were proposed,—wherein especially does the poetry of our times differ from that of the last century?—ninety-nine persons out of a hundred would answer that the poetry of the last century was correct, but cold and mechanical, and that the poetry of our time, though wild and irregular, presented far more vivid images, and excited the passions far more strongly than that of Parnell, or Addison, or Pope. In the same manner we constantly hear it said that the poets of the age of Elizabeth had far more genius, but far less correctness, than those of the age of Anne. It seems to be taken for granted that there is some necessary incompatibility, some antithesis between correctness and creative power. We rather suspect that this notion arises merely from an abuse of words, and that it has been the parent of many of the fallacies which perplex the science of criticism.

What is meant by correctness in poetry? If by correctness be meant the conforming to rules which have their foundation in truth and in the principles of human nature, then correctness is only another name for excellence. If by correctness be meant the conforming to rules purely arbitrary, correctness may be another name for dulness and absurdity.

A writer who describes visible objects falsely and violates the propriety of character,—a writer who makes the mountains "nod their drowsy heads" at night, or a dying man take leave of the world with a rant like that of Maximin, may be said, in the high and just sense of the phrase, to write incorrectly. He violates the first great law of his art. His imitation is altogether unlike the thing imitated. The four poets who are most eminently free from incorrectness of this description are Homer, Dante, Shakespeare, and Milton. They are, therefore, in one sense, and that the best sense, the most correct of poets.

When it is said that Virgil, though he had less genius than Homer, was a more correct writer, what sense is attached to the word correctness? Is it meant that the story of the Æneid is developed more skilfully than that of the Odyssey?—that the Roman describes the face of the external world, or the emotions of the mind, more accurately than the Greek?—that the characters of Achates and Mnestheus are more nicely discriminated, and more consistently supported, than those of Achilles, of Nestor, and of Ulysses? The fact incontestably is that, for every violation of the fundamental laws of poetry which can be found in Homer, it would be easy to find twenty in Virgil.

Troilus and Cressida is perhaps of all the plays of Shakespeare that which is commonly considered as the most incorrect. Yet it seems to us infinitely more correct, in the sound sense of the term, than what are called the most correct plays of the most correct dramatists. Compare it, for example, with the Iphigénie of Racine. We are sure that the Greeks of Shakspeare bear a far greater resemblance than the Greeks of Racine to the real Greeks who besieged Troy; and for this reason, that the Greeks of Shakespeare are human beings, and the Greeks of Racine mere names—mere words printed in capitals at the heads of paragraphs of declamation. Racine, it is true, would have shuddered at the thought of making Agamemnon quote Aristotle. But of what use is it to avoid a single anachronism, when the whole play is one anachronism,—the sentiments and phrases of Versailles in the camp of Aulis?

In the sense in which we are now using the word correctness, we think that Sir Walter Scott, Mr. Wordsworth, Mr. Coleridge, are far more correct writers than those who are commonly extolled as the models of correctness,—Pope, for example, and Addison. The single description of a moonlight night in Pope's Iliad contains more inaccuracies than can be found in all the Excursion. There is not a single scene in Cato in which everything that conduces to poetical illusion,—all the propriety of character, of language, of situation, is not more grossly violated than in any part of the Lay of the Last Minstrel. No man can possibly think that the Romans of Addison resemble the real

Romans so closely as the moss-troopers of Scott resemble the real moss-troopers. Wat Tinlinn and William of Deloraine are not, it is true, persons of so much dignity as Cato. But the dignity of the persons represented has as little to do with the correctness of poetry as with the correctness of painting. We prefer a gipsy by Reynolds to his Majesty's head on a sign-post, and a Borderer by Scott to a Senator by Addison.

In what sense, then, is the word correctness used by those who say, with the author of the Pursuits of Literature, that Pope was the most correct of English Poets, and that next to Pope came the late Mr. Gifford? What is the nature and value of that correctness the praise of which is denied to Macbeth, to Lear, and to Othello, and given to Hoole's translations and to all the Seatonian prize-poems? We can discover no eternal rule,—no rul· founded in reason and in the nature of things,—which Shakspeare does not observe much more strictly than Pope. But if by correctness be meant the conforming to a narrow legislation which, while lenient to the *mala in se*, multiplies, without a shadow of reason, the *mala prohibita*, if by correctness be meant a strict attention to certain ceremonious observances, which are no more essential to poetry than etiquette to good government, or than the washings of a Pharisee to devotion, then, assuredly, Pope may be a more correct poet than Shakspeare : and, if the code were a little altered, Colley Cibber might be a more correct poet than Pope. But it may well be doubted whether this kind of correctness be a merit,—nay, whether it be not an absolute fault.

It would be amusing to make a digest of the irrational laws which bad critics have framed for the government of poets. First in celebrity and in absurdity stand the dramatic unities of place and time. No human being has ever been able to find any thing that could, even by courtesy, be called an argument for these unities, except that they have been deduced from the general practice of the Greeks. It requires no very profound examination to discover that the Greek dramas, often admirable as compositions, are, as exhibitions of human character and human life, far inferior to the English plays of the age of Elizabeth. Every scholar knows that the dramatic part of the Athenian tragedies was at first subordinate to the lyrical part. It would, therefore, have been little less than a miracle if the laws of the Athenian stage had been found to suit plays in which there was no chorus. All the greatest masterpieces of the dramatic art have been composed in direct violation of the unities, and could never have been composed if the unities had not been violated. It is clear, for example, that such a character as that of Hamlet could never have been developed within the limits to which Alfieri confined himself. Yet such was the reverence of literary men during the last century for these unities that Johnson, who, much to his honour, took the opposite side, was, as he says, "frightened at his own temerity," and "afraid to stand against the authorities which might be produced against him."

There are other rules of the same kind without end. "Shakspeare," says Rymer, "ought not to have made Othello black; for the hero of a tragedy ought always to be white." "Milton," says another critic, "ought not to have taken Adam for his hero; for the hero of an epic poem ought always to be victorious." "Milton," says another, "ought not to have put so many similes into his first book; for the first book of an epic poem ought always to be the most unadorned. There are no similes in the first book of the Iliad." ,, Milton," says another, ought not to have placed in an epic poem such lines as these :—

"I also erred in overmuch admiring."

And why not? The critic is ready with a reason.—a lady's reason. "Such lines," says he, "are not, it must be allowed, unpleasing to the ear, but the redundant syllable ought to be confined to the drama, and not admitted into epic poetry." As to the redundant syllable in heroic rhyme on serious subjects, it has been, from the time of Pope downward, prescribed by the general consent of all the correct school. No magazine would have admitted so incorrect a couplet as that of Drayton:

"As when we lived untouch'd with these disgraces,
When as our kingdom was our dear embraces."

Another law of heroic rhyme, which, fifty years ago, was considered as fundamental, was, that there should be a pause,—a comma at least, at the end of every couplet. It was also provided that there should never be a full stop except at the end of a couplet. Well do we remember to have heard a most correct judge of poetry revile Mr. Rogers for the incorrectness of that most sweet and graceful passage,

" 'Twas thine, Maria, thine without a sigh
At midnight in a sister's arms to die.

. . . . .

Nursing the young to health."

Sir Roger Newdigate is fairly entitled, we think, to be ranked among the great critics of this school. He made a law that none of the poems written for the Prize which he established at Oxford should exceed fifty lines. This law seems to us to have at least as much foundation in reason as any of those which we have mentioned ;—nay, much more, for the world, we believe, is pretty well agreed in thinking that the shorter a prize-poem is, the better.

We do not see why we should not make a few more rules of the same kind ;— why we should not enact that the number of scenes in every act shall be three or some multiple of three,—that the number of lines in every scene shall be an exact square,—that the *dramatis personæ* shall never be more nor fewer than sixteen,—and that, in heroic rhymes, every thirty-sixth line shall have twelve syllables. If we were to lay down these canons, and to call Pope, Goldsmith, and Addison incorrect writers for not having complied with our whims, we should act precisely as those critics act who find incorrectness in the magnificent imagery and the varied music of Coleridge and Shelley.

The correctness which the last century prized so much resembles the correctness of those pictures of the garden of Eden which we see in old Bibles.— We have an exact square, enclosed by the rivers Pison, Gihon, Hiddekel, and Euphrates, each with a convenient bridge in the centre,—rectangular beds of flowers,—a long canal, neatly bricked and railed in,—the tree of knowledge, clipped like one of the limes behind the Tuileries, standing in the centre of the grand alley,—the snake twined round it,—the man on the right hand, the woman on the left, and the beasts drawn up in an exact circle round them. In one sense the picture is correct enough. That is to say, the squares are correct ; the circles are correct ; the man and the woman are in a most correct line with the tree ; and the snake forms a most correct spiral.

But if there were a painter so gifted that he could place on the canvas that glorious paradise, seen by the interior eye of him whose outward sight had failed with long watching and labouring for liberty and truth,—if there were a painter who could set before us the mazes of the sapphire brook, the lake with its fringe of myrtles, the flowery meadows, the grottoes overhung by vines, the forests shining with Hesperian fruit and with the plumage of gorgeous birds, the massy shade of that nuptial bower which showered down roses on the sleeping lovers,—what should we think of a connoisseur who should tell us that this painting, though finer than the absurd picture in the old Bible, was not so correct? Surely we should answer,—It is both finer and more correct; and it is finer because it is more correct. It is not made up of correctly drawn diagrams; but it is a correct painting,—a worthy representation of that which it is intended to represent.

It is not in the fine arts alone that this false correctness is prized by narrow-minded men,—by men who cannot distinguish means from ends, or what is accidental from what is essential. M. Jourdain admired correctness in fencing. "You had no business to hit me then. You must never thrust in *quart* till you have thrust in *tierce*." M. Tomès liked correctness in medical practice. "I stand up for Artemius. That he killed his patient is plain enough. But still he acted quite according to rule. A man dead is a man dead; and there is an end of the matter. But if rules are to be broken, there is no saying what consequences may follow." We have heard of an old German officer who was a great admirer of correctness in military operations. He used to revile Bonaparte for spoiling the science of war, which had been carried to such exquisite perfection by Marshal Daun. "In my youth we used to march and countermarch all the summer without gaining or losing a square league, and then we went into winter quarters. And now comes an ignorant, hot-headed young man, who flies about from Boulogne to Ulm, and from Ulm to the middle of Moravia, and fights battles in December. The whole system of his tactics is monstrously incorrect." The world is of opinion, in spite of critics like these, that the end of fencing is to hit, that the end of medicine is so cure, that the end of war is to conquer, and that those means are the most correct which best accomplish the ends.

And has poetry no end,—no eternal and immutable principles? Is poetry, like heraldry, mere matter of arbitrary regulation? The heralds tell us that certain scutcheons and bearings denote certain conditions, and that to put colours on colours, or metals on metals, is false blazonry. If all this were reversed,—if every coat of arms in Europe were new fashioned,—if it were decreed that *or* should never be placed but on *argent*, or *argent* but on *or*,—that illegitimacy should be denoted by a *lozenge*, and widowhood by a *bend*,—the new science would be just as good as the old science, because both the new and the old would be good for nothing. The mummery of Portcullis and Rouge Dragon, as it has no other value than that which caprice has assigned to it, may well submit to any laws which caprice may impose on it. But it is not so with that great imitative art, to the power of which all ages, the rudest and the most enlightened, bear witness. Since its first great masterpieces were produced, everything that is changeable in this world has been changed. Civilisation has been gained, lost, gained again. Religions, and languages, and forms of government, and usages of private life, and modes of thinking, all have undergone a succession of revolutions. Everything has passed away but the great features of nature, and the heart of man, and the miracles of that art of which it is the office to reflect back the heart of man and the features of nature. Those two strange old poems, the wonder of ninety generations, still retain all their freshness. They still command the veneration of minds enriched by the literature of many nations and ages. They are still, even in wretched translations, the delight of schoolboys. Having survived ten thousand capricious fashions, having seen successive codes of criticism become obsolete, they still remain immortal with the immortality of truth,—the same when perused in the study of an English scholar as when they were first chanted at the banquets of the Ionian princes.

Poetry is, as that most acute of human beings, Aristotle said more than two thousand years ago, imitation. It is an art analogous in many respects to the arts of painting, sculpture, and acting. The imitations of the painter, the sculptor, and the actor, are, indeed, within certain limits, more perfect than those of the poet. The machinery which the poet employs consists merely of words; and words cannot, even when employed by such an artist as Homer or Dante, present to the mind images of visible objects quite so lively and exact as those which we carry away from looking on the works of the brush and the chisel. But, on the other hand, the range of poetry is infinitely wider than that of any other imitative art, or than that of all the other imitative arts together. The sculptor can imitate only form; the painter only form and colour; the actor, until the poet supplies him with words, only form, colour, and motion. Poetry holds the outer world in common with the other arts. The heart of man is the province of poetry, and of poetry alone. The painter, the sculptor, and the actor, when the actor is unassisted by the poet, can exhibit no more of human passion and character than that small portion which overflows into the gesture and the face,—always an imperfect, often a deceitful sign—of that which is within. The deeper and more complex parts of human nature can be exhibited by means of words alone. Thus the objects of the imitation of poetry are the whole external and the whole internal universe, the face of nature, the vicissitudes of fortune, man as he is in himself, man as he appears in society, all things of which we can form an image in our minds by combining together parts of things which really exist. The domain of this imperial art is commensurate with the imaginative faculty.

An art essentially imitative ought not surely to be subjected to rules which tend to make its imitations less perfect than they otherwise would be; and those who obey such rules ought to be called, not correct, but incorrect artists. The true way to judge of the rules by which English poetry was governed during the last century is to look at the effects which they produced.

It was in 1780 that Johnson completed his Lives of the Poets. He tells us in that work that, since the time of Dryden, English poetry had shown no tendency to relapse into its general savageness, that its language had been refined, its numbers tuned, and its sentiments improved. It may, perhaps, be doubted whether the nation had any great reason to exult in the refinements and improvements which gave it Douglas for Othello, and the Triumphs of Temper for the Fairy Queen.

It was during the thirty years which preceded the appearance of Johnson's Lives that the diction and versification of English poetry were, in the sense in which the word is commonly used, most correct. Those thirty years form the most deplorable part of our literary history. They have bequeathed to us scarcely any poetry which deserves to be remembered. Two or three hundred lines of Gray, twice as many of Goldsmith, a few stanzas of Beattie and Collins, a few strophes of Mason, and a few clever prologues and satires, were the masterpieces of this age of consummate excellence. They may all be printed in one volume, and that volume would be by no means a volume of extraordinary merit. It would contain no poetry of the very highest class, and little which could be placed very high in the second class. The Paradise Regained or Comus would outweigh it all.

At last, when poetry had fallen into such utter decay that Mr. Hayley was thought a great poet, it began to appear that the excess of the evil was about to work the cure. Men became tired of an insipid conformity to a standard which derived no authority from nature or reason. A shallow criticism had taught them to ascribe a superstitious value to the spurious correctness of poetasters. A deeper criticism brought them back to the true correctness of the first great masters. The eternal laws of poetry regained their power, and the temporary fashions which had superseded those laws went after the wig of Lovelace and the hoop of Clarissa.

G

It was in a cold and barren season that the seeds of that rich harvest which we have reaped were first sown. While poetry was every year becoming more feeble and more mechanical,—while the monotonous versification which Pope had introduced, no longer redeemed by his brilliant wit and his compactness of expression, palled on the ear of the public,—the great works of the dead were every day attracting more and more of the admiration which they deserved. The plays of Shakespeare were better acted, better edited, and better known than they had ever been. Our noble old ballads were again read with pleasure, and it became a fashion to imitate them. Many of the imitations were altogether contemptible. But they showed that men had at least begun to admire the excellence which they could not rival. A literary revolution was evidently at hand. There was a ferment in the minds of men, —a vague craving for something new, a disposition to hail with delight anything which might at first sight wear the appearance of originality. A reforming age is always fertile of impostors. The same excited state of public feeling which produced the great separation from the see of Rome produced also the excesses of the Anabaptists. The same stir in the public mind of Europe which overthrew the abuses of the old French government, produced the Jacobins and Theophilanthropists. Macpherson and Della Crusca were to the true reformers of English poetry what Knipperdoling was to Luther, or Clootz to Turgot. The public was never more disposed to believe stories without evidence, and to admire books without merit. Anything which could break the dull monotony of the correct school was acceptable.

The forerunner of the great restoration of our literature was Cowper. His literary career began and ended at nearly the same time with that of Alfieri. A parallel between Alfieri and Cowper may, at first sight, seem as unpromising as that which a loyal Presbyterian minister is said to have drawn, in 1745, between George II. and Enoch. It may seem that the gentle, shy, melancholy Calvinist, whose spirit had been broken by fagging at school,—who had not courage to earn a livelihood by reading the titles of bills in the House of Lords,—and whose favourite associates were a blind old lady and an evangelical divine, could have nothing in common with the haughty, ardent, and voluptuous nobleman,—the horse jockey, the libertine, who fought Lord Ligonier in Hyde Park, and robbed the Pretender of his queen. But though the private lives of these remarkable men present scarcely any points of resemblance, their literary lives bear a close analogy to each other. They both found poetry in its lowest state of degradation,—feeble, artificial, and altogether nerveless. They both possess precisely the talents which fitted them for the task of raising it from that deep abasement. They cannot, in strictness, be called great poets. They had not in any very high degree the creative power,

"The vision and the faculty divine;"

but they had great vigour of thought, great warmth of feeling,—and what, in their circumstances, was above all things important, a manliness of taste which approached to roughness. They did not deal in mechanical versification and conventional phrases. They wrote concerning things the thought of which set their hearts on fire; and thus what they wrote, even when it wanted every other grace, had that inimitable grace which sincerity and strong passion impart to the rudest and most homely compositions. Each of them sought for inspiration in a noble and affecting subject, fertile of images which had not yet been hackneyed. Liberty was the muse of Alfieri, —Religion was the muse of Cowper. The same truth is found in their lighter pieces. They were not among those who deprecated the severity or deplored the absence of an unreal mistress in melodious commonplaces. Instead of raving about imaginary Chloes and Sylvias, Cowper wrote of Mrs. Unwin's knitting-needles. The only love-verses of Alfieri were addressed to one whom he truly and passionately loved. "Tutte le rime amorose che seguono," says he, "tutte sono per essa, e ben sue, e di ei solamente; poichè mai d'altra donna per certo non canterò."

These great men were not free from affectation. But their affectation was directly opposed to the affectation which generally prevailed. Each of them expressed, in strong and bitter language, the contempt which he felt for the effeminate poetasters who were in fashion both in England and in Italy. Cowper complains that

"Manner is all in all, whate'er is writ,
The substitute for genius, taste, and wit."

He praised Pope; yet he regretted that Pope had

"Made poetry a mere mechanic art,
And every warbler had his tune by heart."

Alfieri speaks with similar scorn of the tragedies of his predecessors. "Mi cadevano dalle mani per la languidezza, trivialità e prolissità dei modi e del verso, senza parlare poi della snervatezza dei pensieri. Or perchè mai questa nostra divina lingua, sì maschia anco, ed energica, e feroce, in bocca di Dante, dovrà ella farsi così sbiadata ed eunuca nel dialogo tragico?"

To men thus sick of the languid manner of their contemporaries ruggedness seemed a venial fault, or rather a positive merit. In their hatred of meretricious ornament, and of what Cowper calls "creamy smoothness," they erred on the opposite side. Their style was too austere, their versification too harsh. It is not easy, however, to overrate the service which they rendered to literature. Their merit is rather that of demolition than that of construction. The intrinsic value of their poems is considerable. But the example which they set of mutiny against an absurd system was invaluable. The part which they performed was rather that of Moses than that of Joshua. They opened the house of bondage;—but they did not enter the promised land.

During the twenty years which followed the death of Cowper, the revolution in English poetry was fully consummated. None of the writers of this period, not even Sir Walter Scott, contributed so much to the consummation as Lord Byron. Yet Lord Byron contributed to it unwillingly, and with constant self-reproach and shame. All his tastes and inclinations led him to take part with the school of poetry which was going out against the school which was coming in. Of Pope himself he spoke with extravagant admiration. He did not venture directly to say that the little man of Twickenham was a greater poet than Shakespeare or Milton; but he hinted pretty clearly that he thought so. Of his contemporaries, scarcely any had so much of his admiration as Mr. Gifford, who, considered as a poet, was merely Pope, without Pope's wit and fancy, and whose satires are decidedly inferior in vigour and poignancy to the very imperfect juvenile performance of Lord Byron himself. He now and then praised Mr. Wordsworth and Mr. Coleridge, but ungraciously and without cordiality. When he attacked them, he brought his whole soul to the work. Of the most elaborate of Mr. Wordsworth's poems he could find nothing to say, but that it was "clumsy, and frowsy, and his aversion." Peter Bell excited his spleen to such a degree that he apostrophized the shades of Pope and Dryden, and demanded of them whether it were possible that such trash could evade contempt? In his heart he thought his own Pilgrimage of Harold inferior to his Imitation of Horace's Art of Poetry,—a feeble echo of Pope and Johnson. This insipid performance he repeatedly designed to publish, and was withheld only by the solicitations of his friends. He has distinctly declared his approbation of the unities, the most absurd laws by which genius was ever held in servitude. In one of his works, we think in his letter to Mr. Bowles, he compares the poetry of the eighteenth century to the Parthenon, and that of the nineteenth to a Turkish mosque, and boasts that, though he had assisted his contemporaries in building their grotesque and barbarous edifice, he had never joined them in defacing the remains of a chaster and more graceful architecture. In another letter he compares the change which had recently passed on English poetry to the decay of Latin poetry after the Augustan age. In the time of Pope, he tells his friend, it was all Horace with us. It is all Claudian now.

For the great old masters of the art he had no very enthusiastic veneration. In his letter to Mr. Bowles he uses expressions which clearly indicate that he preferred Pope's Iliad to the original. Mr. Moore confesses that his friend was no very fervent admirer of Shakespeare. Of all the poets of the first class, Lord Byron seems to have admired Dante and Milton most. Yet in the fourth canto of Childe Harold he places Tasso,—a writer not merely inferior to them, but of quite a different order of mind,—on at least a footing of equality with them. Mr. Hunt is, we suspect, quite correct in saying that Lord Byron could see little or no merit in Spenser.

But Lord Byron the critic and Lord Byron the poet were two very different men. The effects of the noble writer's theory may indeed often be traced in his practice. But his disposition led him to accommodate himself to the literary taste of the age in which he lived; and his talents would have enabled him to accommodate himself to the taste of any age. Though he said much of his contempt for men, and though he boasted that amidst the inconstancy of fortune and of fame he was all-sufficient to himself, his literary career indicated nothing of that lonely and unsocial pride which he affected. We cannot conceive him, like Milton or Wordsworth, defying the criticism of his contemporaries, retorting their scorn, and labouring on a poem in the full assurance that it would be unpopular, and in the full assurance that it would be immortal. He has said, by the mouth of one of his heroes, in speaking of political greatness, that "he must serve who fain would sway;" and this he assigns as a reason for not entering into political life. He did not consider that the sway which he had exercised in literature had been purchased by servitude,—by the sacrifice of his own taste to the taste of the public.

He was the creature of his age; and whenever he had lived he would have been the creature of his age. Under Charles I. he would have been more quaint than Donne. Under Charles II. the rants of his rhyming plays would have pitted it, boxed it, and galleried it, with those of any Bayes or Bilboa. Under George I. the monotonous smoothness of his versification and the terseness of his expression would have made Pope himself envious.

As it was, he was the man of the last thirteen years of the eighteenth century, and of the first twenty-three years of the nineteenth century. He belonged half to the old, and half to the new school of poetry. His personal taste led him to the former; his thirst of praise to the latter;—his talents were equally suited to both. His fame was a common ground on which the zealots on both sides,—Gifford, for example, and Shelley,—might meet. He was the representative, not of either literary party, but of both at once, and of their conflict, and of the victory by which that conflict was terminated. His poetry fills and measures the whole of the vast interval through which our literature has moved since the time of Johnson. It touches the Essay on Man at the one extremity, and the Excursion at the other.

There are several parallel instances in literary history. Voltaire, for example, was the connecting link between the France of Louis XIV. and the France of Louis XVI.,—between Racine and Boileau on the one side, and Condorcet and Beaumarchais on the other. He, like Lord Byron, put himself at the head of an intellectual revolution,—dreading it all the time,—murmuring at it,—sneering at it,—yet choosing rather to move before his age in any direction than to be left behind and forgotten. Dryden was the connecting link between the literature of the age of James I., and the literature of the age of Anne. Oromasdes and Arimanes fought for him. Arimanes carried him off. But his heart was to the last with Oromasdes. Lord Byron was, in the same manner, the mediator between two generations—between two hostile poetical sects. Though always sneering at Mr. Wordsworth, he was yet, though perhaps unconsciously, the interpreter between Mr. Wordsworth and the multitude. In the Lyrical Ballads and the Excursion Mr. Wordsworth appeared as the high priest of a worship of which nature was the idol. No poems have ever indicated a more exquisite perception of the beauty of the outer world, or a more passionate love and reverence for that beauty. Yet they were not popular;—and it is not likely that they ever will be popular as the poetry of Sir Walter Scott is popular. The feeling which pervaded them was too deep for general sympathy. Their style was often too mysterious for general comprehension. They made a few esoteric disciples, and many scoffers. Lord Byron founded what may be called an exoteric Lake school of poetry; and all the readers of poetry in England, we might say in Europe, hastened to sit at his feet. What Mr. Wordsworth had said like a recluse, Lord Byron said like a man of the world—with less profound feeling, but with more perspicuity, energy, and conciseness. We would refer our readers to the last two cantos of Childe Harold and to Manfred, in proof of these observations.

Lord Byron, like Mr. Wordsworth, had nothing dramatic in his genius. He was indeed the reverse of a great dramatist, the very antithesis to a great dramatist. All his characters,—Harold looking back on the western sky, from which his country and the sun are disappearing together,—the Giaour, standing apart in the gloom of the side-aisle, and casting a haggard scowl from under his long hood at the crucifix and the censer,—Conrad leaning on his sword by the watchtower,—Lara smiling on the dancers,—Alp gazing steadily on the fatal cloud as it passes before the moon,—Manfred wandering among the precipices of Berne,—Azzo on the judgment-seat,—Ugo at the bar,—Lambro frowning on the siesta of his daughter and Juan,—Cain presenting his unacceptable offering—are essentially the same. The varieties are varieties merely of age, situation, and outward show. If ever Lord Byron attempted to exhibit men of a different kind, he always made them either insipid or unnatural. Selim is nothing. Bonnivart is nothing. Don Juan, in the first and best cantos, is a feeble copy of the Page in the Marriage of Figaro. Johnson, the man whom Juan meets in the slave-market, is a most striking failure. How differently would Sir Walter Scott have drawn a bluff, fearless Englishman, in such a situation! The portrait would have seemed to walk out of the canvas.

Sardanapalus is more coarsely drawn than any dramatic personage that we can remember. His heroism and his effeminacy,—his contempt of death and his dread of a weighty helmet,—his kingly resolution to be seen in the foremost ranks, and the anxiety with which he calls for a looking-glass, that he may be seen to advantage, are contrasted, it is true, with all the point of

Juvenal. Indeed, the hint of the character seems to have been taken from what Juvenal says of Otho:

> "Speculum civilis sarcina belli.
> Nimirum summi ducis est occidere Galbam,
> Et curare cutem summi constantia civis,
> Bedriaci in campo spolium affectare Palati,
> Et pressum in faciem digitis extendere panem."

These are excellent lines in a satire. But it is not the business of the dramatist to exhibit characters in this sharp, antithetical way. It is not thus that Shakespeare makes Prince Hal rise from the rake of Eastcheap into the hero of Shrewsbury, and sink again into the rake of Eastcheap. It is not thus that Shakespeare has exhibited the union of effeminacy and valour in Antony. A dramatist cannot commit a greater error than that of following those pointed descriptions of character in which satirists and historians indulge so much. It is by rejecting what is natural that satirists and historians produce these striking characters. Their great object generally is to ascribe to every man as many contradictory qualities as possible: and this is an object easily attained. By judicious selection and judicious exaggeration, the intellect and the disposition of any human being might be described as being made up of nothing but startling contrasts. If the dramatist attempts to create a being answering to one of these descriptions, he fails, because he reverses an imperfect analytical process. He produces, not a man, but a personified epigram. Very eminent writers have fallen into this snare. Ben Jonson has given us a Hermogenes, taken from the lively lines of Horace; but the inconsistency which is so amusing in the satire appears unnatural and disgusts us in the play. Sir Walter Scott has committed a far more glaring error of the same kind in the novel of Peveril. Admiring, as every judicious reader must admire, the keen and vigorous lines in which Dryden satirised the Duke of Buckingham, he attempted to make a Duke of Buckingham to suit them—a real living Zimri; and he made, not a man, but the most grotesque of all monsters. A writer who should attempt to introduce into a play or a novel such a Wharton as the Wharton of Pope, or a Lord Hervey answering to Sporus, would fail in the same manner.

But to return to Lord Byron; his women, like his men, are all of one breed. Haidee is a half-savage and girlish Julia; Julia is a civilized and matronly Haidee. Leila is a wedded Zuleika, Zuleika a virgin Leila. Gulnare and Medora appear to have been intentionally opposed to each other. Yet the difference is a difference of situation only. A slight change of circumstances would, it should seem, have sent Gulnare to the lute of Medora, and armed Medora with the dagger of Gulnare.

It is hardly too much to say, that Lord Byron could exhibit only one man and only one woman,—a man proud, moody, cynical,—with defiance on his brow, and misery in his heart, a scorner of his kind, implacable in revenge, yet capable of deep and strong affection:—a woman all softness and gentleness, loving to caress and to be caressed, but capable of being transformed by love into a tigress.

Even these two characters, his only two characters, he could not exhibit dramatically. He exhibited them in the manner, not of Shakespeare, but of Clarendon. He analysed them; he made them analyse themselves; but he did not make them show themselves. He tells us, for example, in many lines of great force and spirit, that the speech of Lara was bitterly sarcastic—that he talked little of his travels—that if he was much questioned about them, his answers became short, and his brow gloomy. But we have none of Lara's sarcastic speeches or short answers. It is not thus that the great masters of human nature have portrayed human beings. Homer never tells us that Nestor loved to relate long stories about his youth. Shakespeare never tells us that in the mind of Iago everything that is beautiful and endearing was associated with some filthy and debasing idea.

It is curious to observe the tendency which the dialogue of Lord Byron always has to lose its character of a dialogue, and to become soliloquy. The scenes between Manfred and the Chamois-hunter,—between Manfred and the Witch of the Alps,—between Manfred and the Abbot, are instances of this tendency. Manfred, after a few unimportant speeches, has all the talk to himself. The other interlocutors are nothing more than good listeners. They drop an occasional question of ejaculation which sets Manfred off again on the inexhaustible topic of his personal feelings. If we examine the fine passages in Lord Byron's dramas—the description of Rome, for example, in Manfred—the description of a Venetian revel in Marino Faliero—the invective which the old doge pronounces against Venice, we shall find that there is nothing dramatic in them, that they derive none of their effect from the character or situation of the speaker, and that they would have been as fine, or finer, if they had been published as fragments of blank verse by Lord Byron. There is scarcely a speech in Shakespeare of which the same could be said. No skilful reader of the plays of Shakespeare can endure to see what are called the fine things taken out, under the name of "Beauties," or of "Elegant Extracts," or to hear any single passage, "To be or not to be," for example, quoted as a sample of the great poet. "To be or not to be" has merit undoubtedly as a composition. It would have merit if put into the mouth of a chorus. But its merit as a composition vanishes when compared with its merit as belonging to Hamlet. It is not too much to say that the great plays of Shakespeare would lose less by being deprived of all the passages which are commonly called the fine passages than those passages lose by being read separately from the play. This is, perhaps, the highest praise which can be given to a dramatist.

On the other hand, it may be doubted whether there is, in all Lord Byron's plays, a single remarkable passage which owes any portion of its interest or effect to its connection with the characters or the action. He has written only one scene, as far as we can recollect, which is dramatic even in manner—the scene between Lucifer and Cain. The conference in that scene is animated, and each of the interlocutors has a fair share of it. But this scene, when examined, will be found to be a confirmation of our remarks. It is a dialogue only in form. It is a soliloquy in essence. It is in reality a debate carried on within one single unquiet and sceptical mind. The questions and the answers, the objections and the solutions, all belong to the same character.

A writer who showed so little dramatic skill in works professedly dramatic was not likely to write narrative with dramatic effect. Nothing could indeed be more rude and careless than the structure of his narrative poems. He seems to have thought, with the hero of the Rehearsal, that the plot was good for nothing but to bring in fine things. His two longest works, Childe Harold and Don Juan, have no plan whatever. Either of them might have been extended to any length, or cut short at any point. The state in which the Giaour appears illustrates the manner in which all his poems were constructed. They are all, like the Giaour, collections of fragments; and, though there may be no empty spaces marked by asterisks, it is still easy to perceive, by the clumsiness of the joining, where the parts for the sake of which the whole was composed end and begin.

It was in description and meditation that he excelled. "Description," as he said in Don Juan, "was his *forte*." His manner is indeed peculiar, and is almost unequalled;—rapid, sketchy, full of vigour; the selection happy; the strokes few and bold. In spite of the reverence which we feel for the genius of Mr. Wordsworth, we cannot but think that the minuteness of his descriptions often diminishes their effect. He has accustomed himself to gaze on nature with the eye of a lover,—to dwell on every feature,—and to mark every change of aspect. Those beauties which strike the most negligent observer, and those which only a close attention discovers, are equally familiar to him, and are equally prominent in his poetry. The proverb of old Hesiod, that half is often more than the whole, is eminently applicable to description. The policy of the Dutch, who cut down most of the precious trees in the Spice Islands, in order to raise the value of what remained, was a policy which poets would do well to imitate. It was a policy which no poet understood better than Lord Byron. Whatever his faults might be, he was never, while his mind retained its vigour, accused of prolixity.

His descriptions, great as was their intrinsic merit, derived their principal interest from the feeling which always mingled with them. He was himself the beginning, the middle, and the end, of all his own poetry,—the hero of every tale,—the chief object in every landscape. Harold, Lara, Manfred, and a crowd of other characters, were universally considered merely as loose incognitos of Byron; and there is every reason to believe that he meant them to be so considered. The wonders of the outer world,—the Tagus, with the mighty fleets of England riding on its bosom,—the towers of Cintra overhanging the shaggy forests of cork-trees and willows,—the glaring marble of Pentelicus,—the banks of the Rhine,—the glaciers of Clarens,—the sweet lake of Leman,—the dell of Egeria, with its summer-birds and rustling lizards,—the shapeless ruins of Rome overgrown with ivy and wall-flowers,—the stars, the sea, the mountains,—all were mere accessaries,—the background to one dark and melancholy figure.

Never had any writer so vast a command of the whole eloquence of scorn, misanthropy, and despair. That Marah was never dry. No art could sweeten, no draughts could exhaust, its perennial waters of bitterness. Never was there such variety in monotony as that of Byron. From maniac laughter to piercing lamentation, there was not a single note of human anguish of which he was not master. Year after year, and month after month, he continued to repeat that to be wretched is the destiny of all; that to be eminently wretched is the destiny of the eminent; that all the desires by which we are cursed lead alike to misery,—if they are not gratified, to the misery of disappointment,—if they are gratified, to the misery of satiety. His principal heroes are men who have arrived by different roads at the same goal of despair,—who are sick of life,—who are at war with society,—who are supported in their anguish only by an unconquerable pride resembling that of Prometheus on the rock, or of Satan in the burning marl; who can master their agonies by the force of their will, and who, to the last, defy the whole power of earth and heaven. He always described himself as a man of the same kind with his favourite creations, as a man whose heart had been withered,—whose capacity for happiness was gone and could not be restored, but whose invincible spirit dared the worst that could befall him here or hereafter.

How much of this morbid feeling sprang from an original disease of the mind,—how much from real misfortune,—how much from the nervousness of dissipation,—how much was fanciful,—how much of it was merely affected,—it is impossible for us, and would probably have been impossible for the most intimate friends of Lord Byron, to decide. Whether there ever existed, or can ever exist, a person answering to the description which he gave of himself, may be doubted: but that he was not such a person is beyond all doubt. It is ridiculous to imagine that a man who mind was really imbued with scorn of his fellow-creatures would have published three or four books every year in order to tell them so; or that a man who could say with truth that he neither sought sympathy nor needed it would have admitted all Europe to hear his farewell to his wife, and his blessings on his child. In the second canto of Childe Harold, he tells us that he is insensible to fame and obloquy:

> "Ill may such contest now the spirit move,
> Which heeds nor keen reproof nor partial praise."

Yet we know on the best evidence that, a day or two before he published these lines, he was greatly, indeed childishly, elated by the compliments paid to his maiden speech in the House of Lords.

We are far, however, from thinking that his sadness was altogether feigned. He was naturally a man of great sensibility;—he had been ill-educated;—his feelings had been early exposed to sharp trials;—he had been crossed in his boyish love;—he had been mortified by the failure of his first literary efforts;— he was straitened in pecuniary circumstances;—he was unfortunate in his domestic relations;—the public treated him with cruel injustice;—his health and spirits suffered from his dissipated habits of life;—he was, on the whole, an unhappy man. He early discovered that, by parading his unhappiness before the multitude, he excited an unrivalled interest. The world gave him every encouragement to talk about his mental sufferings. The effect which his first confessions produced induced him to affect much that he did not feel; and the affectation probably reacted on his feelings. How far the character in which he exhibited himself was genuine, and how far theatrical, it would probably have puzzled himself to say.

There can be no doubt that this remarkable man owed the vast influence which he exercised over his contemporaries at least as much to his gloomy egotism as to the real power of his poetry. We never could very clearly understand how it is that egotism, so unpopular in conversation, should be so popular in writing; or how it is that men who affect in their compositions qualities and feelings which they have not impose so much more easily on their contemporaries than on posterity. The interest which the loves of Petrarch excited in his own time, and the pitying fondness with which half Europe looked upon Rousseau, are well known. To readers of our age, the love of Petrarch seems to have been love of that kind which breaks no hearts, and the sufferings of Rousseau to have deserved laughter rather than pity,— to have been partly counterfeited, and partly the consequences of his own perverseness and vanity.

What our grandchildren may think of the character of Lord Byron, as exhibited in his poetry, we will not pretend to guess. It is certain that the interest which he excited during his life is without a parallel in literary history. The feeling with which young readers of poetry regarded him can be conceived only by those who have experienced it. To people who are unacquainted with real calamity, "nothing is so dainty sweet as lovely melancholy." This faint image of sorrow has in all ages been considered by young gentlemen as an agreeable excitement. Old gentlemen and middle-aged gentlemen have so many real causes of sadness that they are rarely inclined "to be as sad as night only for wantonness." Indeed, they want the power almost as much as the inclination. We know very few persons engaged in active life who, even if they were to procure stools to be melancholy upon, and were to sit down with all the premeditation of Master Stephen, would be able to enjoy much of what somebody calls the "ecstasy of woe."

Among that large class of young persons whose reading is almost entirely confined to works of imagination the popularity of Lord Byron was unbounded. They bought pictures of him; they treasured up the smallest relics of him; they learned his poems by heart, and did their best to write like him, and to look like him. Many of them practised at the glass in the hope of catching the curl of the upper lip, and the scowl of the brow, which appear in some of his portraits. A few discarded their neckcloths in imitation of their great leader. For some years the Minerva press sent forth no novel without a mysterious, unhappy, Lara-like peer. The number of hopeful undergraduates and medical students who became things of dark imaginings, —on whom the freshness of the heart ceased to fall like dew,—whose passions had consumed themselves to dust, and to whom the relief of tears was denied, passes all calculation. This was not the worst. There was created in the minds of many of these enthusiasts a pernicious and absurd association between intellectual power and moral depravity. From the poetry of Lord Byron they drew a system of ethics, compounded of misanthropy and voluptuousness, a system in which the two great commandments were, to hate your neighbour, and to love your neighbour's wife.

The affectation has passed away; and a few more years will destroy whatever yet remains of that magical potency which once belonged to the name of Byron. To us he is still a man, young, noble, and unhappy. To our children he will be merely a writer; and their impartial judgment will appoint his place among writers, without regard to his rank or to his private history. That his poetry will undergo a severe sifting, that much of what has been admired by his contemporaries will be rejected as worthless, we have little doubt. But we have as little doubt that, after the closest scrutiny, there will still remain much that can only perish with the English language.

SAMUEL JOHNSON.

The Life of Samuel Johnson, LL.D. Including a Journal of a Tour to the Hebrides, by JAMES BOSWELL, *Esq. A new Edition, with numerous Additions and Notes. By* JOHN WILSON CROKER, *LL.D., F.R.S.* 5 vols. 8vo. London. 1831.

THIS work has greatly disappointed us. Whatever faults we may have been prepared to find in it, we fully expected that it would be a valuable addition to English literature; that it would contain many curious facts, and many judicious remarks; that the style of the notes would be neat, clear, and precise; and that the typographical execution would be, as in new editions of classical works it ought to be, almost faultless. We are sorry to be obliged to say that the merits of Mr. Croker's performance are on a par with those of a certain leg of mutton on which Dr. Johnson dined, while travelling from London to Oxford, and which he, with characteristic energy, pronounced to be "as bad as bad could be; ill fed, ill killed, ill kept, and ill dressed." That part of the volumes before us for which the editor is responsible is ill compiled, ill arranged, ill written, and ill printed.

Nothing in the work has astonished us so much as the ignorance or carelessness of Mr. Croker with respect to facts and dates. Many of his blunders are such as we should be surprised to hear any well educated gentleman commit, even in conversation. The notes absolutely swarm with misstatements into which the editor never would have fallen if he had taken the slightest pains to investigate the truth of his assertions, or if he had even been well acquainted with the book on which he undertook to comment. We will give a few instances.

Mr. Croker tells us in a note that Derrick, who was master of the ceremonies at Bath, died very poor in 1760.* We read on; and, a few pages later, we find Dr. Johnson and Boswell talking of the same Derrick as still living and reigning,—as having retrieved his character,—as possessing so much power over his subjects at Bath, that his opposition might be fatal to Sheridan's lectures on oratory.† And all this is in 1763. The fact is that Derrick died in 1769.

In one note we read, that Sir Herbert Croft, the author of that pompous and foolish account of Young, which appears among the Lives of the Poets, died in 1805.‡ Another note in the same volume states that this same Sir Herbert Croft died at Paris, after residing abroad for fifteen years, on the 27th of April, 1816.§

Mr. Croker informs us that Sir William Forbes, of Pitsligo, the author of the life of Beattie, died in 1816.‖ A Sir William Forbes undoubtedly died in that year,—but not the Sir William Forbes in question, whose death took place in 1806. It is notorious, indeed, that the biographer of Beattie lived just long enough to complete the history of his friend. Eight or nine years before the date which Mr. Croker has assigned for Sir William's death, Sir Walter Scott lamented that event in the introduction to the fourth canto of Marmion. Every school-girl knows the lines:

> "Scarce had lamented Forbes paid
> The tribute to his Minstrel's shade:
> The tale of friendship scarce was told,
> Ere the narrator's heart was cold:
> Far may we search before we find
> A heart so manly and so kind!"

In one place we are told, that Allan Ramsay, the painter, was born in 1709, and died in 1784; ¶ in another, that he died in 1784, in the seventy-first year of his age.** If the latter statement be correct, he must have been born in or about 1713.

In one place Mr. Croker says, that at the commencement of the intimacy between Dr. Johnson and Mrs. Thrale, in 1765, the lady was twenty-five years old.†† In other places he says that Mrs. Thrale's thirty-fifth year coincided with Dr. Johnson's seventieth.‡‡ Johnson was born in 1709. If, therefore, Mrs. Thrale's thirty-fifth year coincided with Johnson's seventieth, she could have been only twenty-one year's old in 1765. This is not all. Mr. Croker, in another place, assigns the year 1777 as the date of the complimentary lines which Johnson made on Mrs. Thrale's thirty-fifth birthday.§§ If this date be correct, Mrs. Thrale must have been born in 1742, and could have been only twenty-three when her acquaintance with Johnson commenced. Two of Mr. Croker's three statements must be false. We will not decide between them; we will only say, that the reasons which he gives for thinking that Mrs. Thrale was exactly thirty-five years old when Johnson was seventy, appear to us utterly frivolous.

Again, Mr. Croker informs his readers that "Lord Mansfield survived Johnson *full* ten years." ‖‖ Lord Mansfield survived Dr. Johnson just eight years and a quarter.

Johnson found in the library of a French lady, whom he visited during his short visit to Paris, some works which he regarded with great disdain. "I looked," says he, "into the books in the lady's closet, and, in contempt, showed them to Mr. Thrale. Prince Titi,—Bibliothèque des Fées,—and other books." ¶¶ "The History of Prince Titi," observes Mr. Croker, "was

---

* I. 394.   † I. 404.   ‡ IV. 321.   § IV. 428.   ‖ II. 262.
¶ IV. 105.   ** V. 282.   †† I. 510.   ‡‡ IV. 271, 322.
§§ III. 463.   ‖‖ II. 151.   ¶¶ III. 271.

said to be the autobiography of Frederick Prince of Wales, but was probably written by Ralph his secretary." A more absurd note never was penned. The history of Prince Titi, to which Mr. Croker refers, whether written by Prince Frederick or by Ralph, was certainly never published. If Mr. Croker had taken the trouble to read with attention that very passage in Park's Royal and Noble Authors which he cites as his authority, he would have seen that the manuscript was given up to the government. Even if this memoir had been printed, it is not very likely to find its way into a French lady's bookcase. And would any man in his senses speak contemptuously of a French lady, for having in her possession an English work, so curious and interesting as a Life of Prince Frederick, whether written by himself or by a confidential secretary, must have been? The history at which Johnson laughed was a very proper companion to the Bibliothèque des Fées,—a fairy tale about good Prince Titi and naughty Prince Violent. Mr. Croker may find it in the Magasin des Enfans, the first French book which the little girls of England read to their governesses.

Mr. Croker states that Mr. Henry Bate, who afterwards assumed the name of Dudley, was proprietor of the Morning Herald, and fought a duel with George Robinson Stoney, in consequence of some attacks on Lady Strathmore which appeared in that paper.* Now, Mr. Bate was then connected, not with the Morning Herald, but with the Morning Post; and the dispute took place before the Morning Herald was in existence. The duel was fought in January, 1777. The Chronicle of the Annual Register for that year contains an account of the transaction, and distinctly states that Mr. Bate was editor of the Morning Post. The Morning Herald, as any person may see by looking at any number of it, was not established till some years after this affair. For this blunder there is, we must acknowledge, some excuse; for it certainly seems almost incredible to a person living in our time that any human being should ever have stooped to fight with a writer in the Morning Post.

"James de Duglas," says Mr. Croker, "was requested by King Robert Bruce, in his last hours, to repair with his heart to Jerusalem, and humbly to deposit it at the sepulchre of our Lord, which he did in 1329."† Now, it is well known that he did no such thing, and for a very sufficient reason,—because he was killed by the way. Nor was it in 1329 that he set out. Robert Bruce died in 1329, and the expedition of Douglas took place in the following year, "*Quand le printems vint et la saison,*" says Froissart,—in June, 1330, says, Lord Hailes, whom Mr. Croker cites as the authority for his statement.

Mr. Croker tells us that the great Marquis of Montrose was beheaded at Edinburgh in 1650.‡ There is not a forward boy at any school in England who does not know that the marquis was hanged. The account of the execution is one of the finest passages in Lord Clarendon's History. We can scarcely suppose that Mr. Croker has never read that passage; and yet we can scarcely suppose that any person who has ever perused so noble and pathetic a story can have utterly forgotten all its most striking circumstances.

"Lord Townshend," says Mr. Croker, "was not secretary of state till 1720."§ Can Mr. Croker possibly be ignorant that Lord Townshend was made secretary of state at the accession of George I. in 1714,—that he continued to be secretary of state till he was displaced by the intrigues of Sunderland and Stanhope at the close of 1716,—and that he returned to the office of secretary of state, not in 1720, but in 1721? Mr. Croker, indeed, is

---

* V. 196.   † IV. 29.   ‡ II. 526.   § III 32.

generally unfortunate in his statements respecting the Townshend family. He tells us that Charles Townshend, the chancellor of the exchequer, was "nephew of the prime minister, and son of a peer who was secretary of state, and leader of the House of Lords."* Charles Townshend was not nephew, but grand-nephew of the Duke of Newcastle,—not son, but grandson, of the Lord Townshend who was secretary of state, and leader of the House of Lords.

"General Burgoyne surrendered at Saratoga," says Mr. Croker, "in March, 1778."† General Burgoyne surrendered on the 17th of October, 1777.

"Nothing," says Mr. Croker, "can be more unfounded than the assertion that Byng fell a martyr *to political party*. By a strange coincidence of circumstances, it happened that there was a total change of administration between his condemnation and his death : so that one party presided at his trial, and another at his execution : there can be no stronger proof that he was *not* a political martyr."‡ Now, what will our readers think of this writer, when we assure them that this statement, so confidently made respecting events so notorious, is absolutely untrue? One and the same administration was in office when the court-martial on Byng commenced its sittings, through the whole trial, at the condemnation, and at the execution. In the month of November, 1756, the Duke of Newcastle and Lord Hardwicke resigned; the Duke of Devonshire became first lord of the treasury, and Mr. Pitt, secretary of state. This administration lasted till the month of April, 1757. Byng's court-martial began to sit on the 28th of December, 1756. He was shot on the 14th of March, 1757. There is something at once diverting and provoking in the cool and authoritative manner in which Mr. Croker makes these random assertions. We do not suspect him of intentionally falsifying history. But of this high literary misdemeanour we do without hesitation accuse him,— that he has no adequate sense of the obligation which a writer, who professes to relate facts, owes to the public. We accuse him of a negligence and an ignorance analogous to that *crassa negligentia* and that *crassa ignorantia* on which the law animadverts in magistrates and surgeons, even when malice and corruption are not imputed. We accuse him of having undertaken a work which, if not performed with strict accuracy, must be very much ¦worse than useless, and of having performed it as if the difference between an accurate and an inaccurate statement was not worth the trouble of looking into the most common book of reference.

But we must proceed. These volumes contain mistakes more gross, if possible, than any that we have yet mentioned. Boswell has recorded some observations made by Johnson on the changes which took place in Gibbon's religious opinions. That Gibbon when a lad at Oxford turned Catholic is well known. "It is said," cried the Doctor, laughing, "that he has been a Mahommedan." "This sarcasm," says the editor, "probably alludes to the tenderness with which Gibbon's malevolence to Christianity induced him to treat Mahommedanism in his history." Now the sarcasm was uttered in 1776, and that part of the History of the Decline and Fall of the Roman Empire which relates to Mahommedanism was not published till 1788, twelve years after the date of this conversation, and near four years after the death of Johnson.

"It was in the year 1761," says Mr. Croker, "that Goldsmith published his Vicar of Wakefield. This leads the editor to observe a more serious inaccuracy of Mrs. Piozzi than Mr. Boswell notices, when he says Johnson left her Iable to go and sell the Vicar of Wakefield for Goldsmith. Now, Dr. Johnson was not acquainted with the Thrales till 1765, four years after the book had

* III. 368. † IV. 222. ‡ I. 298.

been published."* Mr. Croker, in reprehending the fancied inaccuracy of Mrs. Thrale, has himself shown a degree of inaccuracy, or, to speak more properly, a degree of ignorance, hardly credible. The Traveller was not published till 1765; and it is a fact as notorious as any in literary history, that the Vicar of Wakefild, though written before the Traveller, was published after it. It is a fact which Mr. Croker may find in any common life of Goldsmith, —in that written by Mr. Chalmers, for example. It is a fact which, as Boswell tells us, was distinctly stated by Johnson in a conversation with Sir Joshua Reynolds. It is, therefore, quite possible and probable that the celebrated scene of the landlady, the sheriff's officer, and the bottle of Madeira may have taken place in 1765. Now, Mrs. Thrale expressly says that it was near the beginning of her acquaintance with Johnson, in 1765, or, at all events, not later than 1766, that he left her table to succour his friend. Her accuracy is, therefore, completely vindicated.

The very page which contains this monstrous blunder contains another blunder, if possible, more monstrous still. Sir Joseph Mawbey, a foolish member of Parliament, at whose speeches and whose pigstyes the wits of Brookes's were, fifty years ago, in the habit of laughing most unmercifully, stated, on the authority of Garrick, that Johnson, while sitting in a coffeehouse at Oxford, about the time of his doctor's degree, used some contemptuous expressions respecting Home's play and Macpherson's Ossian. "Many men," he said, "many women, and many children, might have written Douglas." Mr. Croker conceives that he has detected an inaccuracy, and glories over poor Sir Joseph in a most characteristic manner. " I have quoted this anecdote solely with the view of showing to how little credit hearsay anecdotes are in general entitled. Here is a story published by Sir Joseph Mawbey, a member of the House of Commons, and a person every way worthy of credit, who says he had it from Garrick. Now mark :—Johnson's visit to Oxford, about the time of his doctor's degree, was in 1754, the first time he had been there since he left the university. But Douglas was not acted till 1756, and Ossian not published till 1760. All, therefore, that is new in Sir Joseph Mawbey's story is false."† Assuredly, we need not go far to find ample proof that a member of the House of Commons may commit a very gross error. Now mark, say we, in the language of Mr. Croker. The fact is that Johnson took his Master's degree in 1754,‡ and his Doctor's degree in 1775.§ In the spring of 1776 ‖ he paid a visit to Oxford, and at this visit a conversation respecting the works of Home and Macpherson might have taken place, and, in all probability, did take place. The only real objection to the story Mr. Croker has missed. Boswell states, apparently on the best authority, that as early, at least, as the year 1763, Johnson, in conversation with Blair, used the same expressions respecting Ossian which Sir Joseph represents him as having used respecting Douglas.¶ Sir Joseph or Garrick confounded, we suspect, the two stories. But their error is venial compared with that of Mr. Croker.

We will not multiply instances of this scandalous inaccuracy. It is clear that a writer who, even when warned by the text on which he is commenting, falls into such mistakes as these, is entitled to no confidence whatever. Mr. Croker has committed an error of four years with respect to the publication of Goldsmith's novel,—an error of twelve years with respect to the publication of part of Gibbon's History,—an error of twenty-one years with respect to one of the most remarkable events in Johnson's life. Two of these three errors he has committed while ostentatiously displaying his own accuracy and correcting what he represents as the loose assertions of others. How can his

---

* V. 409.   † V. 409.   ‡ I. 262.   § III. 205.   ‖ III. 326.   ¶ I. 405.

readers take on trust his statements concerning the births, marriages, divorces, and deaths of a crowd of people whose names are scarcely known to this generation? It is not likely that a person who is ignorant of what almost everybody knows can know that of which almost everybody is ignorant. We did not open this book with any wish to find blemishes in it. We have made no curious researches. The work itself, and a very common knowledge of literary and political history, have enabled us to detect the mistakes which we have pointed out, and many other mistakes of the same kind. We must say, and we say it with regret, that we do not consider the authority of Mr. Croker, unsupported by other evidence, as sufficient to justify any writer who may follow him in relating a single anecdote or in assigning a date to a single event.

Mr. Croker shows almost as much ignorance and heedlessness in his criticisms as in his statements concerning facts. Dr. Johnson said, very reasonably, as it appears to us, that some of the satires of Juvenal are too gross for imitation. Mr. Croker, who, by the way, is angry with Johnson for defending Prior's tales against the charge of indecency, resents this aspersion on Juvenal, and indeed refuses to believe that the doctor can have said anything so absurd. "He probably said—some *passages* of them—for there are none of Juvenal's satires to which the same objection may be made as to one of Horace's, that it is *altogether* gross and licentious."* Surely Mr. Croker can never have read the second and ninth satires of Juvenal.

Indeed, the decisions of this editor on points of classical learning, though pronounced in a very authoritative tone, are generally such that, if a schoolboy under our care were to utter them, our soul assuredly should not spare for his crying. It is no disgrace to a gentleman who has been engaged during near thirty years in political life that he has forgotten his Greek and Latin. But he becomes justly ridiculous if, when no longer able to construe a plain sentence, he affects to sit in judgment on the most delicate questions of style and metre. From one blunder, a blunder which no good scholar would have made, Mr. Croker was saved, as he informs us, by Sir Robert Peel, who quoted a passage exactly in point from Horace. We heartily wish that Sir Robert, whose classical attainments are well known, had been more frequently consulted. Unhappily he was not always at his friend's elbow; and we have, therefore, a rich abundance of the strangest errors. Boswell has preserved a poor epigram by Johnson, inscribed "Ad Lauram parituram." Mr Croker censures the poet for applying the word puella to a lady in Laura's situation, and for talking of the beauty of Lucina. "Lucina," he says, "was never famed for her beauty."† If Sir Robert Peel had seen this note, he probably would have again refuted Mr. Croker's criticisms by an appeal to Horace. In the secular ode Lucina is used as one of the names of Diana, and the beauty of Diana is extolled by all the most orthodox doctors of the ancient mythology, from Homer in his Odyssey, to Claudian in his Rape of Proserpine, In another ode, Horace describes Diana as the goddess who assists the "laborantes utero puellas." But we are ashamed to detain our readers with this fourth-form learning.

Boswell found, in his tour to the Hebrides, an inscription written by a Scotch minister. It runs thus: "Joannes Macleod, &c., gentis suæ Philarchus, &c., Floræ Macdonald matrimoniali vinculo conjugatus turrem hanc Beganodunensem proævorum habitaculum longe vetustissimum, diu penitus labefactatam, anno æræ vulgaris MDCLXXXVL instauravit."—"The minister," says Mr. Croker, "seems to have been no contemptible Latinist. Is not Philarchus a very happy term to express the paternal and kindly authority of

---

* I. 167.   † I. 132.

t e t:ad of a clan?"* The composition of this eminent Latinist, short as it is, contains several words that are just as much Coptic as Latin, to say nothing of the incorrect structure of the sentence. The word Philarchus, even if it were a happy term expressing a paternal and kindly authority, would prove nothing for the minister's Latin, whatever it might prove for his Greek. But it is clear that the word Philarchus means, not a man who rules by love, but a man who loves rule. The Attic writers of the best age use the word φίλαρχος in the sense which we assign to it. Would Mr. Croker translate φιλόσοφος, a man who acquires wisdom by means of love, or φιλοκερδής, a man who makes money by means of love? In fact, it requires no Bentley or Casaubon to perceive that Philarchus is merely a false spelling for Phylarchus,—the chief of a tribe.

Mr. Croker has favoured us with some Greek of his own. "At the al'ar," says Dr. Johnson, "I recommended my θ φ." "These letters," says the editor, "(which Dr. Strahan seems not to have understood) probably mean θνητοὶ φίλοι, *departed friends*."† Johnson was not a first-rate Greek scholar; but he knew more Greek than most boys when they leave school? and no schoolboy could venture to use the word θνητοι in the sense which Mr. Croker ascribes to it without imminent danger of a flogging.

Mr. Croker has also given us a specimen of his skill in translating Latin. Johnson wrote a note in which he consulted his friend, Dr. Lawrence, on the propriety of losing some blood. The note contains these words:—"Si per te licet, imperatur nuncio Holderum ad me deducere." Johnson should rather have written "imperatum est." But the meaning of the words is perfectly clear. "If you say yes, the messenger has orders to bring Holder to me." Mr. Croker translates the words as follows: "If you consent, pray tell the messenger to bring Holder to me."‡ If Mr Croker is resolved to write on points of classical learning, we would advise him to begin by giving an hour every morning to our old friend Corderius.

Indeed, we cannot open any volume of this work in any place, and turn it over for two minutes in any direction, without lighting on a blunder. Johnson, in his life of Tickell, stated that a poem entitled the Royal Progress, which appears in the last volume of the Spectator, was written on the accession of Geo'g: I. The word "arrival" was afterwards substituted for "accession." "The reader will observe," says Mr. Croker, "that the Whig term *accession*, which might imply legality, was altered into a statement of the simple fact of King George's *arrival*."§ Now Johnson, though a bigoted Tory, was not quite such a fool as Mr. Croker here represents him to be. In the Life of Granville, Lord Lansdowne, which stands a very few pages from the Life of Tickell, mention is made of the accession of Anne, and the accession of George I. The word arrival was used in the Life of Tickell for the simplest of all reasons. It was used because the subject of the Royal Progress was the arrival of the king, and not his accession, which took place near two months before his arrival.

The editor's want of perspicacity is, indeed, very amusing. He is perpetually telling us that he cannot understand something in the text which is as plain as language can make it. "Mattaire," said Dr. Johnson, "wrote Latin verses from time to time, and published a set in his old age, which he called *Senilia*, in which he shows so little learning or taste in writing as to make Carteret a dactyl."|| Hereupon we have this note: "The editor does not understand this objection, nor the following observation." The following observation, which Mr. Croker cannot understand, is simply this: "In

* II. 452.   † IV. 232.   ‡ V. 47.   § IV. 425. || IV. 336.

matters of genealogy," says Johnson, "it is necessary to give the bare names as they are. But in poetry and in prose of any elegance in the writing, they require to have inflection given to them." If Mr. Croker had told Johnson that this was unintelligible, the doctor would probably have replied, as he replied on another occasion, "I have found you a reason, sir; I am not bound to find you an understanding." Everybody who knows anything of Latinity knows that, in genealogical tables, Joannes Baro de Carteret, or Vicecomes de Carteret, may be tolerated, but that in compositions which pretend to elegance, Carteretus, or some other form which admits of inflections, ought to be used.

All our readers have doubtless seen the two distichs of Sir William Jones, respecting the division of the time of a lawyer. One of the distichs is translated from some old Latin lines; the other is original. The former runs thus:

> "Six hours to sleep, to law's grave study six,
> Four spend in prayer, the rest on nature fix."

"Rather," says Sir William Jones,

> "Six hours to law, to soothing slumbers seven,
> Ten to the world 'lot, and all to heaven."

The second couplet puzzles Mr. Croker strangely. "Sir William," says he, "has shortened his day to twenty-three hours, and the general advice of 'all to heaven,' destroys the peculiar appropriation of a certain period to religious exercises."[*] Now, we did not think that it was in human dulness to miss the meaning of the lines so completely. Sir William distributes twenty-three hours among various employments. One hour is thus left for devotion. The reader expects that the verse will end with—"and one to heaven." The whole point of the lines consists in the unexpected substitution of "all" for 'one." The conceit is wretched enough; but it is perfectly intelligible, and never, we will venture to say, perplexed man, woman, or child before.

Poor Tom Davies, after failing in business, tried to live by his pen. Johnson called him "an author generated by the corruption of a bookseller." This is a very obvious and even a commonplace allusion to the famous dogma of the old physiologists. Dryden made a similar allusion to that dogma before Johnson was born. Mr. Croker, however, is unable to understand what the doctor meant. "The expression," he says, "seems not quite clear." And he proceeds to talk about the generation of insects, about bursting into gaudier life, and Heaven knows what.[†]

There is a still stranger instance of the editor's talent for finding out difficulty in what is perfectly plain. "No man," said Johnson, "can now be made a bishop for his learning and piety." "From this too just observation," says Boswell, "there are some eminent exceptions." Mr. Croker is puzzled by Boswell's very natural and simple language. "That a general observation should be pronounced *too just*, by the very person who admits that it is not universally just, is not a little odd."[‡]

A very large proportion of the two thousand five hundred notes which the editor boasts of having added to those of Boswell and Malone consists of the flattest and poorest reflections, reflections such as the least intelligent reader is quite competent to make for himself,—and such as no intelligent reader would think it worth while to utter aloud. They remind us of nothing so much as of those profound and interesting annotations which are pencilled by sempstresses and apothecaries' boys on the dog-eared margins of novels

---

[*] V. 634.   [†] IV. 272.   [‡] III. 398.

borrowed from circulating libraries;—"How beautiful!"—"Cursed prosy!" —"I don't like Sir Reginald Malcolm at all."—"I think Pelham is a sad dandy."—Mr. Croker is perpetually stopping us in our progress through the most delightful narrative in the language, to observe that really Dr. Johnson was very rude,—that he talked more for victory than for truth,—that his taste for port wine with capillaire in it was very odd,—that Boswell was impertinent,—that it was foolish in Mrs. Thrale to marry the music-master; and other "merderies" of the same kind, to borrow the energetic word of Rabelais.

We cannot speak more favourably of the manner in which the notes are written than of the matter of which they consist. We find in every page words used in wrong senses, and constructions which violate the plainest rules of grammar. We have the low vulgarism of "mutual friend," for "common friend." We have "fallacy" used as synonymous with "falsehood" or "misstatement." We have many such inextricable labyrinths of pronouns as that which follows: "Lord Erskine was fond of this anecdote; he told it to the editor the first time that he had the honour of being in his company." Lastly, we have a plentiful supply of sentences resembling those which we subjoin. "Markland, *who*, with Jortin and Thirlby, Johnson calls three contemporaries of great eminence."* "Warburton himself did not feel, as Mr. Boswell was disposed to think he did, kindly or gratefully *of* Johnson."† "It was *him* that Horace Walpole called a man who never made a bad figure but as an author."‡ We must add that the printer has done his best to fill both the text and the notes with all sorts of blunders. In truth, he and the editor have between them made the book so bad, that we do not well see how it could have been worse.

When we turn from the commentary of Mr. Croker to the work of our old friend Boswell, we find it not only worse printed than in any other edition with which we are acquainted, but mangled in the most wanton manner. Much that Boswell inserted in his narrative is, without the shadow of a reason, degraded to the appendix. The editor has also taken upon himself to alter or omit passages which he considers as indecorous. This prudery is quite unintelligible to us. There is nothing immoral in Boswell's book, nothing which tends to inflame the passions. He sometimes uses plain words. But if this be a taint which requires expurgation, it would be desirable to begin by expurgating the morning and evening lessons. Mr. Croker has performed the delicate office which he has undertaken in the most capricious manner. One strong, old-fashioned, English word, familiar to all who read their Bibles, is exchanged for a softer synonym in some passages, and suffered to stand unaltered in others. In one place a faint allusion made by Johnson to an indelicate subject,—an allusion so faint that, till Mr. Croker's note pointed it out to us, we had never noticed it, and of which we are quite sure that the meaning would never be discovered by any of those for whose sake books are expurgated,—is altogether omitted. In another place, a coarse and stupid jest of Dr. Taylor on the same subject, expressed in the broadest language,— almost the only passage, as far as we remember, in all Boswell's book, which we should have been inclined to leave out,—is suffered to remain.

We complain, however, much more of the additions than of the omissions. We have half of Mrs. Thrale's book, scraps of Mr. Tyers, scraps of Mr. Murphy, scraps of Mr. Cradock, long prosings of Sir John Hawkins, and connecting observations by Mr. Croker himself, inserted into the midst of Boswell's text. To this practice we most decidedly object. An editor might as well publish Thucydides with extracts from Diodorus interspersed, or in-

---

* IV. 377.   † IV. 415.   ‡ II. 461.

corporate the Lives of Suetonius with the History and Annals of Tacitus. Mr. Croker tells us, indeed, that he has done only what Boswell wished to do, and was prevented from doing by the law of copyright. We doubt this greatly. Boswell has studiously abstained from availing himself of the information given by his rivals, on many occasions on which he might have cited them without subjecting himself to the charge of piracy. Mr. Croker has himself, on one occasion, remarked very justly that Boswell was very reluctant to owe any obligation to Hawkins. But, be this as it may, if Boswell had quoted from Sir John and from Mrs. Thrale, he would have been guided by his own taste and judgment in selecting his quotations. On what he quoted he would have commented with perfect freedom; and the borrowed passages, so selected, and accompanied by such comments, would have become original. They would have dovetailed into the work.—No hitch, no crease, would have been discernible. The whole would appear one and indivisible,

"Ut per læve severos
Effundat junctura ungues."

This is not the case with Mr. Croker's insertions. They are not chosen as Boswell would have chosen them. They are not introduced as Boswell would have introduced them. They differ from the quotations scattered through the original Life of Johnson, as a withered bough stuck in the ground differs from a tree skilfully transplanted with all its life about it.

Not only do these anecdotes disfigure Boswell's book; they are themselves disfigured by being inserted in his book. The charm of Mrs. Thrale's little volume is utterly destroyed. The feminine quickness of observation,—the feminine softness of heart,—the colloquial incorrectness and vivacity of style, —the little amusing airs of a half-learned lady,—the delightful garrulity,— the "dear Doctor Johnson,"—the "it was so comical,"—all disappear in Mr. Croker's quotations.—The lady ceases to speak in the first person; and her anecdotes, in the process of transfusion, become as flat as champagne in decanters, or Herodotus in Beloe's version. Sir John Hawkins, it is true, loses nothing; and for the best of reasons. Sir John had nothing to lose.

The course which Mr. Croker ought to have taken is quite clear. He should have reprinted Boswell's narrative precisely as Boswell wrote it; and in the notes or the appendix he should have placed any anecdotes which he might have thought it advisable to quote from other writers. This would have been a much more convenient course for the reader, who has now constantly to keep his eye on the margin in order to see whether he is perusing Boswell, Mrs. Thrale, Murphy, Hawkins, Tyers, Cradock, or Mr. Croker. We greatly doubt whether even the Tour to the Hebrides ought to have been inserted in the midst of the Life. There is one marked distinction between the two works. Most of the Tour was seen by Johnson in manuscript. It does not appear that he ever saw any part of the Life.

We love, we own, to read the great productions of the human mind as they were written. We have this feeling even about scientific treatises; though we know that the sciences are always in a state of progression, and that the alterations made by a modern editor in an old book on any branch of natural or political philosophy are likely to be improvements. Many errors have been detected by writers of this generation in the speculations of Adam Smith. A short cut has been made to much knowledge at which Sir Isaac Newton arrived through arduous and circuitous paths. Yet we still look with peculiar veneration on the Wealth of Nations and on the Principia, and should regret to see either of those great works garbled even by the ablest hands. But in works which owe much of their interest to the character and situation of the writers the case is infinitely stronger. What man of taste and feeling can endure harmonies, *rifacimenti*, abridgments, expurgated editions? Who ever reads a stage-copy of a play when he can procure the original? Who ever cut open Mrs. Siddons's Milton? Who ever got through ten pages of Mr. Gilpin's translation of John Bunyan's Pilgrim into modern English? Who would lose, in the confusion of a Diatessaron, the peculiar charm which belongs to the narrative of the disciple whom Jesus loved? The feeling of a reader who has become intimate with any great original work is that which Adam expressed towards his bride:

"Should God create another Eve, and I
Another rib afford, yet loss of thee
Would never from my heart."

No substitute, however exquisitely formed, will fill the void left by the original. The second beauty may be equal or superior to the first; but still it is not she.

The reasons which Mr. Croker has given for incorporating passages from Sir John Hawkins and Mrs. Thrale with the narrative of Boswell would vindicate the adulteration of half the classical works in the language. If Pepys's Diary and Mrs. Hutchinson's Memoirs had been published a hundred years ago, no human being can doubt that Mr. Hume would have made great use of those books in his History of England. But would it, on that account, be judicious in a writer of our own times to publish an edition of Hume's History of England, in which large additions from Pepys and Mrs. Hutchinson should be incorporated with the original text? Surely not. Hume's history, be its faults what they may, is now one great entire work, the production of one vigorous mind, working on such materials as were within its reach. Additions made by another hand may supply a particular deficiency, but would grievously injure the general effect. With Boswell's book the case is stronger. There is scarcely, in the whole compass of literature, a book which bears interpolation so ill. We know no production of the human mind which has so much of what may be called the race, so much of the peculiar flavour of the soil from which it sprang. The work could never have been written if the writer had not been precisely what he was. His character is displayed in every page, and this display of character gives a delightful interest to many passages which have no other interest.

The Life of Johnson is assuredly a great—a very great work. Homer is not more decidedly the first of heroic poets,—Shakespeare is not more decidedly the first of dramatists,—Demosthenes is not more decidedly the first of orators, than Boswell is the first of biographers. He has no second. He has distanced all his competitors so decidedly that it is not worth while to place them. Eclipse is first, and the rest nowhere.

We are not sure that there is in the whole history of the human intellect so strange a phenomenon as this book. Many of the greatest men that ever lived have written biography. Boswell was one of the smallest men that ever lived, and he has beaten them all. He was, if we are to give any credit to his own account or to the united testimony of all who knew him, a man of the meanest and feeblest intellect. Johnson described him as a fellow who had missed his only chance of immortality by not having been alive when the Dunciad was written. Beauclerk used his name as a proverbial expression for a bore. He was the laughing-stock of the whole of that brilliant society which has owed to him the greater part of its fame. He was always laying himself at the feet of some eminent man, and begging to be spit upon and trampled upon. He was always earning some ridiculous nickname, and then "binding it as a crown unto him,"—not merely in metaphor, but literally. He exhibited himself, at the Shakespeare Jubilee, to all the crowd which filled Stratford-on-Avon, with a placard round his hat bearing the inscription of *Corsica Boswell.* In his Tour, he proclaimed to all the world that at Edinburgh he was known by the appellation of *Paoli Boswell.* Servile and impertinent,—shallow and pedantic,—a bigot and a sot,—bloated with family pride, and eternally blustering about the dignity of a born gentleman, yet stooping to be a tale-bearer, an eaves-dropper, a common butt in the taverns of London,—so curious to know everybody who was talked about, that, Tory and high Churchman as he was, he manœuvred, we have been told, for an introduction to Tom Paine,—so vain of the most childish distinctions, that when he had been to court, he drove to the office where his book was printing, without changing his clothes, and summoned all the printer's devils to admire his new ruffles and sword ;—such was this man, —and such he was content and proud to be. Everything which another man would have hidden,—everything the publication of which would have made another man hang himself, was matter of gay and clamorous exultation to his weak and diseased mind. What silly things he said,—what bitter retorts he provoked,—how at one place he was troubled with evil presentiments which came to nothing,—how at another place, on waking from a drunken doze, he read the Prayer-book and took a hair of the dog that had bitten him,—how he went to see men hanged, and came away maudlin,—how he added five hundred pounds to the fortune of one of his babies because she was not frightened at Johnson's ugly face,—how he was frightened out of his wits at sea,—and how the sailors quieted him as they would have quieted a child,—how tipsy he was at Lady Cork's one evening, and how much his merriment annoyed the ladies,—how impertinent he was to the Duchess of Argyle, and with what stately contempt she put down his impertinence,—how Colonel Macleod sneered to his face at his impudent obtrusiveness,—how his father and the very wife of his bosom laughed and fretted at his fooleries ;—all these things he proclaimed to all the world, as if they had been subjects for pride and ostentatious rejoicing. All the caprices of his temper, all the illusions of his vanity, all his hypochondriac whimsies, all his castles in the air, he displayed with a cool self-complacency, a perfect unconsciousness that he was making a fool of himself, to which it is impossible to find a parallel in the whole history of mankind. He has used many people ill ; but assuredly he has used nobody so ill as himself.

That such a man should have written one of the best books in the world is strange enough. But this is not all. Many persons who have conducted themselves foolishly in active life, and whose conversation has indicated no superior powers of mind, have left us valuable works. Goldsmith was very justly described by one of his contemporaries as an inspired idiot, and by another as a being

"Who wrote like an angel, and talked like poor Poll."

La Fontaine was in society a mere simpleton. His blunders would not come in amiss among the stories of Hierocles. But these men attained literary eminence in spite of their weaknesses. Boswell attained it by reason of his weaknesses. If he had not been a great fool, he would never have been a great writer. Without all the qualities which made him the jest and the torment of those among whom he lived,—without the officiousness, the inquisitiveness, the effrontery, the toad-eating, the insensibility to all reproof, he never could have produced so excellent a book. He was a slave proud of his servitude,—a Paul Pry, convinced that his own curiosity and garrulity were virtues, —an unsafe companion who never scrupled to repay the most liberal hospitality by the basest violation of confidence,—a man without delicacy, without shame, without sense enough to know when he was hurting the feelings of others, or when he was exposing himself to derision ; and because he was all this, he has, in an important department of literature, immeasurably surpassed such writers as Tacitus, Clarendon, Alfieri, and his own idol, Johnson.

Of the talents which ordinarily raise men to eminence as writers, Boswell had absolutely none. There is not in all his books a single remark of his own on literature, politics, religion, or society, which is not either commonplace or absurd. His dissertations on hereditary gentility, on the slave-trade, and on the entailing of landed estates, may serve as examples. To say that these passages are sophistical would be to pay them an extravagant compliment. They have no pretence to argument, or even to meaning. He has reported innumerable observations made by himself in the course of conversation. Of those observations we do not remember one which is above the intellectual capacity of a boy of fifteen. He has printed many of his own letters, and in these letters he is always ranting or twaddling. Logic, eloquence, wit, taste, all those things which are generally considered as making a book valuable, were utterly wanting to him. He had, indeed, a quick observation and a retentive memory. These qualities, if he had been a man of sense and virtue, would scarcely of themselves have sufficed to make him conspicuous; but as he was a dunce, a parasite, and a coxcomb, they have made him immortal.

Those parts of his book which, considered abstractedly, are most utterly worthless, are delightful when we read them as illustrations of the character of the writer. Bad in themselves, they are good dramatically, like the nonsense of Justice Shallow, the clipped English of Dr. Caius, or the misplaced consonants of Fluellen. Of all confessors, Boswell is the most candid. Other men who have pretended to lay open their own hearts,—Rousseau, for example, and Lord Byron,—have evidently written with a constant view to effect, and are to be then most distrusted when they seem to be most sincere. There is scarcely any man who would not rather accuse himself of great crimes and of dark and tempestuous passions than proclaim all his little vanities and wild fancies. It would be easier to find a person who would avow actions like those of Cæsar Borgia or Danton, than one who would publish a day-dream like those of Alnaschar and Malvolio. Those weaknesses which most men keep covered up in the most secret places of the mind, not to be disclosed to the eye of friendship or of love, were precisely the weaknesses which Boswell paraded before all the world. He was perfectly frank, because the weakness of his understanding and the tumult of his spirits prevented him from knowing when he made himself ridiculous. His book resembles nothing so much as the conversation of the inmates of the Palace of Truth.

His fame is great; and it will, we have no doubt, be lasting; but it is fame of a peculiar kind, and indeed marvellously resembles infamy. We remember no other case in which the world has made so great a distinction between a book and its author. In general, the book and the author are considered as one. To admire the book is to admire the author. The case of Boswell is an exception,—we think the only exception, to this rule. His work is universally allowed to be interesting, instructive, eminently original: yet it has brought him nothing but contempt. All the world reads it : all the world delights in it : yet we do not remember ever to have read or ever to have heard any expression of respect and admiration for the man to whom we owe so much instruction and amusement. While edition after edition of his book was coming forth, his son, as Mr. Croker tells us, was ashamed of it, and hated to hear it mentioned. This feeling was natural and reasonable. Sir Alexander saw that, in proportion to the celebrity of the work, was the degradation of the author. The very editors of this unfortunate gentleman's books have forgotten their allegiance, and, like those Puritan casuists who took arms by the authority of the king against his person, have attacked the writer while doing homage to the writings. Mr. Croker, for example, has published two thousand five hundred notes on the life of Johnson, and yet scarcely ever mentions the biographer whose performance he has taken such pains to illustrate without some expression of contempt.

An ill-natured man Boswell certainly was not. Yet the malignity of the most malignant satirist could scarcely cut deeper than his thoughtless loquacity. Having himself no sensibility to derision and contempt, he took it for granted that all others were equally callous. He was not ashamed to exhibit himself to the whole world as a common spy, a common tattler, a humble companion without the excuse of poverty,—and to tell a hundred stories of his own pertness and folly, and of the insults which his pertness and folly brought upon him. It was natural that he should show little discretion in cases in which the feelings or the honour of others might be concerned. No man, surely, ever published such stories respecting persons whom he professed to love and revere. He would infallibly have made his hero as contemptible as he has made himself, had not his hero really possessed some moral and intellectual qualities of a very high order. The best proof that Johnson was really an extraordinary man is that his character, instead of being degraded, has, on the whole, been decidedly raised by a work in which all his vices and weaknesses are exposed more unsparingly than they ever were exposed by Churchill or by Kenrick.

Johnson grown old, Johnson in the fulness of his fame and in the enjoyment of a competent fortune, is better known to us than any other man in history. Everything about him,—his coat, his wig, his figure, his face, his scrofula, his St. Vitus's dance, his rolling walk, his blinking eye, the outward signs which too clearly marked his approbation of his dinner, his insatiable appetite for fish-sauce and veal-pie with plums, his inextinguishable thirst for tea, his trick of touching the posts as he walked, his mysterious practice of treasuring up scraps of orange-peel, his morning slumbers, his midnight disputations, his contortions, his mutterings, his gruntings, his puffings, his vigorous, acute, and ready eloquence, his sarcastic wit, his vehemence, his insolence, his fits of tempestuous rage, his queer inmates,—old Mr. Levett and blind Mrs. Williams, the cat Hodge and the negro Frank,—all are as familiar to us as the objects by which we have been surrounded from childhood. But we have no minute information respecting those years of Johnson's life during which his character and his manners became immutably fixed. We know him, not as he was known to the men of his own generation, but as he was known to men whose father he might have been. That celebrated club of which he was the most distinguished member contained few persons who could remember a time when his fame was not fully established and his habits completely formed. He had made himself a name in literature while Reynolds and the Wartons were still boys. He was about twenty years older than Burke, Goldsmith, and Gerard Hamilton, about thirty years older than Gibbon, Beauclerk, and Langton, and about forty years older than Lord Stowell, Sir William Jones, and Windham. Boswell and Mrs. Thrale, the two writers from whom we derive most of our knowledge respecting him, never saw him till long after he was fifty years old, till most of his great works had become classical, and till the pension bestowed on him by the Crown had placed him above poverty. Of those eminent men who were his most intimate associates towards the close of his life, the only one, as far as we remember, who knew him during the first ten or twelve years of his residence in the capital, was David Garrick; and it does not appear that during tho.e years David Garrick saw much of his fellow-townsman.

Johnson came up to London precisely at the time when the condition of a man of letters was most miserable and degraded. It was a dark night between two sunny days. The age of the Mæcenases had passed away. The age of general curiosity and intelligence had not arrived. The number of readers is at present so great that a popular author may subsist in comfort and opulence on the profits of his works. In the reigns of William III., of Anne, and of George I., even such men as Congreve and Addison would scarcely have been able to live like gentlemen by the mere sale of their writings. But the deficiency of the natural demand for literature was, at the close of the seventeenth and at the beginning of the eighteenth century, more than made up by artificial encouragement,—by a vast system of bounties and premiums. There was, perhaps, never a time at which the rewards of literary merit were so splendid,—at which men who could write well found such easy admittance into the most distinguished society, and to the highest honours of the state. The chiefs of both the great parties into which the kingdom was divided patronised literature with emulous munificence. Congreve, when he had scarcely attained his majority, was rewarded for his first comedy with places which made him independent for life. Smith, though his Hippolytus and Phædra failed, would have been consoled with three hundred a-year but for his own folly. Rowe was not only poet laureate, but also land-surveyor of the Customs in the port of London, clerk of the council to the Prince of Wales, and secretary of the Presentations to the Lord Chancellor. Hughes was secretary to the Commissions of the Peace. Ambrose Philips was judge of the Prerogative Court in Ireland. Locke was Commissioner of Appeals and of the Board of Trade. Newton was Master of the Mint. Stepney and Prior were employed in embassies of high dignity and importance. Gay, who commenced life as apprentice to a silk mercer, became a secretary of Legation at five-and-twenty. It was to a poem on the Death of Charles II., and to the City and Country Mouse, that Montague owed his introduction into public life, his earldom, his garter, and his auditorship of the Exchequer. Swift, but for the unconquerable prejudice of the queen, would have been a bishop. Oxford, with his white staff in his hand, passed through the crowd of his suitors to welcome Parnell, when that ingenious writer deserted the Whigs. Steele was a commissioner of stamps and a member of Parliament. Arthur Mainwaring was a commissioner of the Customs and auditor of the imprest. Tickell was secretary to the Lords Justices of Ireland. Addison was secretary of state.

This liberal patronage was brought into fashion, as it seems, by the magnificent Dorset, who alone of all the noble versifiers in the court of Charles II. possessed talents for composition which would have made him eminent without the aid of a coronet. Montague owed his elevation to the favour of Dorset, and imitated through the whole course of his life the liberality to which he was himself so greatly indebted. The Tory leaders,—Harley and Bolingbroke in particular,—vied with the chiefs of the Whig party in zeal for the encouragement of letters. But soon after the accession of the house of Hanover a change took place. The supreme power passed to a man who cared little for poetry or eloquence. The importance of the House of Commons was constantly on the increase. The government was under the necessity of bartering for Parliamentary support much of that patronage which had been employed in fostering literary merit; and Walpole was by no means inclined to divert any part of the fund of corruption to purposes which he considered as idle. He had eminent talents for government and for debate. But he had paid little attention to books, and felt little respect for authors. One of the coarse jokes of his friend Sir Charles Hanbury Williams was far more pleasing to him than Thomson's Seasons or Richardson's Pamela. He had observed that some of the distinguished writers whom the favour of Halifax had turned into statesmen had been mere encumbrances to their party, dawdlers in office and mutes in Parliament. During the whole course of his administration, therefore, he scarcely befriended a single man of genius. The best writers of the age gave all their support to the opposition, and contributed to excite that discontent which, after plunging the nation into a foolish and unjust war, overthrew the minister to make room for men less able and equally unscrupulous. The opposition could reward its eulogists with little more than promises and caresses. St. James's would give nothing:—Leicester House had nothing to give.

Thus, at the time when Johnson commenced his literary career, a writer had little to hope from the patronage of powerful individuals. The patronage of the public did not yet furnish the means of comfortable subsistence. The prices paid by booksellers to authors were so low that a man of considerable talents and unremitting industry could do little more than provide for the day which was passing over him. The lean kine had eaten up the fat kine. The thin and withered ears had devoured the good ears. The season of rich harvests was over, and the period of famine had begun. All that is squalid and miserable might now be summed up in the word—Poet. That word denoted a creature dressed like a scarecrow, familiar with compters and sponging-houses, and perfectly qualified to decide on the comparative merits of the Common Side in the King's Bench prison and of Mount Scoundrel in the Fleet. Even the poorest pitied him; and they well might pity him. For if their condition was equally abject, their aspirings were not equally high, nor their sense of insult equally acute. To lodge in a garret up four pair of stairs, to dine in a cellar among footmen out of place,—to translate ten hours a day for the wages of a ditcher,—to be hunted by bailiffs from one haunt of beggary and pestilence to another, from Grub Street to St. George's Fields, and from St. George's Fields to the alleys behind St. Martin's Church,—to sleep on a bulk in June and amidst the ashes of a glass-house in December,—to die in a hospital, and to be buried in a parish vault, was the fate of more than one writer who, if he had lived thirty years earlier, would have been admitted to the sittings of the Kitcat or the Scriblerus club, would have sat in Parliament, and would have been entrusted with embassies to the High Allies; who, if he had lived in our time would have received from the booksellers several hundred pounds a year.

As every climate has its peculiar diseases, so every walk of life has its peculiar temptations. The literary character, assuredly, has always had its share of faults,—vanity, jealousy, morbid sensibility. To these faults were now superadded all the faults which are commonly found in men whose livelihood is precarious, and whose principles are exposed to the trial of severe distress. All the vices of the gambler and of the beggar were blended with those of the author. The prizes in the wretched lottery of book-making were scarcely less ruinous than the blanks. If good fortune came, it came in such a manner that it was almost certain to be abused. After months of starvation and despair, a full third night or a well-received dedication filled the pocket of the lean, ragged, unwashed poet with guineas. He hastened to enjoy those luxuries with the images of which his mind had been haunted while he was sleeping amidst the cinders and eating potatoes at the Irish ordinary in Shoe Lane. A week of taverns soon qualified him for another year of night-cellars. Such was the life of Savage, of Boyse, and of a crowd of others.

Sometimes blazing in gold-laced hats and waistcoats; sometimes lying in bed because their coats had gone to pieces, or wearing paper cravats because their linen was in pawn; sometimes drinking champagne and tokay with Betty Careless; sometimes standing at the window of an eating-house in Porridge Island, to snuff up the scent of what they could not afford to taste; they knew luxury;—they knew beggary;—but they never knew comfort. These men were irreclaimable. They looked on a regular and frugal life w.th the same aversion which an old gipsy or a Mohawk hunter feels for a stationary abode, and for the restraint and securities of civilized communities. They were as untameable, as much wedded to their desolate freedom, as the wild ass. They could no more be broken in to the offices of social man than the unicorn could be trained to serve and abide by the crib. It was well if they did not, like beasts of a still fiercer race, tear the hands which ministered to their necessities. To assist them was impossible; and the most benevolent of mankind at length became weary of giving relief which was dissipated with the wildest profusion as soon as it had been received. If a sum was bestowed on the wretched adventurer, such as, properly husbanded, might have supplied him for six months, it was instantly spent in strange freaks of sensuality, and before forty-eight hours had elapsed, the poet was again pestering all his acquaintance for twopence to get a plate of shin of beef at a subterraneous cookshop. If his friends gave him an asylum in their houses, those houses were forthwith turned into bagnios and taverns. All order was destroyed; all business was suspended. The most good-natured host began to repent of his eagerness to serve a man of genius in distress when he heard his guest roaring for fresh punch at five o'clock in the morning.

A few eminent writers were more fortunate. Pope had been raised above poverty by the active patronage which, in his youth, both the great political parties had extended to his Homer. Young had received the only pension ever bestowed, to the best of our recollection, by Sir Robert Walpole, as the reward of mere literary merit. One or two of the many poets who attached themselves to the opposition, Thomson, in particular, and Mallet, obtained, after much severe suffering, the means of subsistence from their political friends. Richardson, like a man of sense, kept his shop; and his shop kept him, which his novels, admirable as they are, would scarcely have done. But nothing could be more deplorable than the state even of the ablest men, who at that time depended for subsistence on their writings. Johnson, Collins, Fielding, and Thomson, were certainly four of the most distinguished persons that England produced during the eighteenth century. It is well known that they were all four arrested for debt.

Into calamities and difficulties such as these Johnson plunged in his twenty-eighth year. From that time till he was three or four and fifty, we have little information respecting him; little, we mean, compared with the full and accurate information which we possess respecting his proceedings and habits towards the close of his life. He emerged at length from cock-lofts and sixpenny ordinaries into the society of the polished and the opulent. His fame was established. A pension sufficient for his wants had been conferred on him: and he came forth to astonish a generation with which he had almost as little in common as with Frenchmen or Spaniards.

In his early years he had occasionally seen the great; but he had seen them as a beggar. He now came among them as a companion. The demand for amusement and instruction had, during the course of twenty years, been gradually increasing. The price of literary labour had risen; and those rising men of letters with whom Johnson was henceforth to associate were, for the most part, persons widely different from those who had walked about with him all night in the streets for want of a lodging. Burke, Robertson, the Wartons, Gray, Mason, Gibbon, Adam Smith, Beattie, Sir William Jones, Goldsmith, and Churchill were the most distinguished writers of what may be called the second generation of the Johnsonian age. Of these men Churchill was the only one in whom we can trace the stronger lineaments of that character which, when Johnson first came up to London, was common among authors. Of the rest, scarcely any had felt the pressure of severe poverty. All had been early admitted into the most respectable society on an equal footing. They were men of quite a different species from the dependents of Curll and Osborne.

Johnson came among them the solitary specimen of a past age, the last survivor of the genuine race of Grub Street hacks; the last of that generation of authors whose abject misery and whose dissolute manners had furnished inexhaustible matter to the satirical genius of Pope. From nature he had received an uncouth figure, a diseased constitution, and an irritable temper. The manner in which the earlier years of his manhood had been passed had given to his demeanour, and even to his moral character, some peculiarities appalling to the civilized beings who were the companions of his old age. The perverse irregularity of his hours, the slovenliness of his person, his fits of strenuous exertion, interrupted by long intervals of sluggishness, his strange abstinence, and his equally strange voracity, his active benevolence, contrasted with the constant rudeness and the occasional ferocity of his manners in society, made him, in the opinion of those with whom he lived during the last twenty years of his life, a complete original. An original he was, undoubtedly, in some respects. But if we possessed full information concerning those who shared his early hardships, we should probably find that what we call his singularities of manner were for the most part failings which he had in common with the class to which he belonged. He ate at Streatham Park as he had been used to eat behind the screen at St. John's Gate, when he was ashamed to show his ragged clothes. He ate as it was natural that a man should eat, who, during a great part of his life, had passed the morning in doubt whether he should have food for the afternoon. The habits of his early life had accustomed him to bear privation with fortitude, but not to taste pleasure with moderation. He could fast; but when he did not fast, he tore his dinner like a famished wolf, with the veins swelling on his forehead, and the perspiration running down his cheeks. He scarcely ever took wine. But when he drank it, he drank it greedily and in large tumblers. There were, in fact, mitigated symptoms of that same moral disease which raged with such deadly malignity in his friends Savage and Boyse. The roughness and violence which he showed in society were to be expected from a man whose temper, not naturally gentle, had been long tried by the bitterest calamities—by the want of meat, of fire, and of clothes, by the importunity of creditors, by the insolence of booksellers, by the derision of fools, by the insincerity of patrons, by that bread which is the bitterest of all food, by those stairs which are the most toilsome of all paths, by that deferred hope which makes the heart sick. Through all these things the ill-dressed, coarse, ungainly pedant had struggled manfully up to eminence and command. It was natural that, in the exercise of his power, he should be " eo immitior, qui toleraverat," that, though his heart was undoubtedly generous and humane, his demeanour in society should be harsh and despotic. For severe distress he had sympathy, and not only sympathy, but munificent relief. But for the suffering which a harsh word inflicts upon a delicate mind he had no pity; for it was a kind of suffering which he could scarcely conceive. He would carry home on his shoulders a sick and starving girl from the streets. He turned his house into a place of refuge for a crowd of wretched old creatures who could find no other asylum; nor could all their peevishness and ingratitude weary out his benevolence. But the pangs of wounded vanity seemed to him ridiculous; and he scarcely felt sufficient compassion even for the pangs of wounded affection. He had seen and felt so much of sharp misery that he was not affected by paltry vexations; and he seemed to think that everybody ought to be as much hardened to those vexations as himself. He was angry with Boswell for complaining of a headache,—with Mrs. Thrale for grumbling about the dust on the road, or the smell of the kitchen. These were, in his phrase, "foppish lamentations," which people ought to be ashamed to utter in a world so full of misery. Goldsmith crying because the Good-natured Man had failed inspired him with no pity. Though his own health was not good, he detested and despised valetudinarians. Even great pecuniary losses, unless they reduced the loser absolutely to beggary, moved him very little. People whose hearts had been softened by prosperity might cry, he said, for such events; but all that could be expected of a plain man was not to laugh.

A person who troubled himself so little about small or sentimental grievances of human life was not likely to be very attentive to the feelings of others in the ordinary intercourse of society. He could not understand how a sarcasm or a reprimand could make any man really unhappy. "My dear doctor," said he to Goldsmith, "what harm does it do a man to call him Holofernes?" "Pooh, ma'am," he exclaimed to Mrs. Carter, "who is the worse for being talked of uncharitably?" Politeness has been well defined as benevolence in small things. Johnson was impolite, not because he wanted benevolence, but because small things appeared smaller to him than to people who had never known what it was to live for fourpence-halfpenny a day.

The characteristic peculiarity of his intellect was the union of great powers with low prejudices. If we judged of him by the best parts of his mind, we should place him almost as high as he was placed by the idolatry of Boswell;—if by the worst parts of his mind, we should place him even below Boswell himself. Where he was not under the influence of some strange scruple, or some domineering passion, which prevented him from boldly and fairly investigating a subject, he was a wary and acute reasoner, a little too much inclined to scepticism, and a little too fond of paradox. No man was less likely to be imposed upon by fallacies in argument or by exaggerated statements of fact. But if, while he was beating down sophisms and exposing false testimony, some childish prejudices, such as would excite laughter in a well managed nursery, came across him, he was smitten as if by enchantment. His mind dwindled away under the spell from gigantic elevation to dwarfish littleness. Those who had lately been admiring its amplitude and its force were now as much astonished at its strange narrowness and feebleness as the fisherman in the Arabian tale, when he saw the Genie, whose stature had overshadowed the whole sea-coast, and whose might seemed equal to a contest with armies, contract himself to the dimensions of his small prison, and lie there the helpless slave of the charm of Solomon.

Johnson was in the habit of sifting with extreme severity the evidence for all stories which were merely odd. But when they were not only odd but miraculous, his severity relaxed. He began to be credulous precisely at the point where the most credulous people begin to be sceptical. It is curious to observe, both in his writings and in his conversation, the contrast between the disdainful manner in which he rejects unauthenticated anecdotes, even when they are consistent with the general laws of nature, and the respectful manner in which he mentions the wildest stories relating to the invisible world. A man who told him of a water-spout or a meteoric stone generally had the lie direct given him for his pains. A man who told him of a prediction or a dream wonderfully accomplished was sure of a courteous hearing. "Johnson," observed Hogarth, "like king David, says in his haste that all men are liars." "His incredulity," says Mrs. Thrale, "amounted almost to disease." She tells us how he browbeat a gentleman who gave him an account of a hurricane in the West Indies, and a poor Quaker who related some strange circumstance about the red-hot balls fired at the siege of Gibraltar. "It is not so. It cannot be true. Don't tell that story again. You cannot think how poor a figure you make in telling it." He once said, half-jestingly, we suppose, that for six months he refused to credit the fact of the earthquake at Lisbon, and that he still believed the extent of the calamity to be greatly exaggerated. Yet he related with a grave face how old Mr. Cave of St. John's Gate saw a ghost, and how this ghost was something of a shadowy being. He went himself on a ghost-hunt to Cock Lane, and was angry with John Wesley for not following up another scent of the same kind with proper spirit and perseverance. He rejects the Celtic genealogies and poems without the least hesitation; yet he declares himself willing to believe the stories of the second sight. If he had examined the claims of the Highland seers with half the severity with which he sifted the evidence for the genuineness of Fingal, he would, we suspect, have come away from Scotland with a mind fully made up. In his Lives of the Poets we find that he is unwilling to give credit to the accounts of Lord Roscommon's early proficiency in his studies; but he tells with great solemnity an absurd romance about some intelligence preternaturally impressed on the mind of that nobleman. He avows himself to be in great doubt about the truth of the story, and ends by warning his readers not wholly to slight such impressions.

Many of his sentiments on religious subjects are worthy of a liberal and enlarged mind. He could discern clearly enough the folly and meanness of all bigotry except his own. When he spoke of the scruples of the Puritans, he spoke like a person who had really obtained an insight into the divine philosophy of the New Testament, and who considered Christianity as a noble scheme of government, tending to promote the happiness and to elevate the moral nature of man. The horror which the sectaries felt for cards, Christmas ale, plum-porridge, mince-pies, and dancing bears, excited his contempt. To the arguments urged by some very worthy people against showy dress he replied with admirable sense and spirit, "Let us not be found, when our Master calls us, stripping the lace off our waistcoats, but the spirit of contention from our souls and tongues. Alas! sir, a man who cannot get to heaven in a green coat will not find his way thither the sooner in a grey one." Yet he was himself under the tyranny of scruples as unreasonable as those of Hudibras or Ralpho, and carried his zeal for ceremonies and for ecclesiastical dignities to lengths altogether inconsistent with reason or with Christian charity. He has gravely noted down in his diary that he once committed the sin of drinking coffee on Good Friday. In Scotland he thought it his duty to pass several months without joining in public worship solely because the ministers of the kirk had not been ordained by bishops. His mode of estimating the piety of his neighbours was somewhat singular. "Campbell," said he, "is a good man,—a pious man. I am afraid he has not been in the inside of a church for many years; but he never passes a church without pulling off his hat:—this shows he has good principles." Spain and Sicily must surely contain many pious robbers and well-principled assassins. Johnson could easily see that a Roundhead who named all his children after Solomon's singers, and talked in the House of Commons about seeking the Lord, might be an unprincipled villain, whose religious mummeries only aggravated his guilt. But a man who took off his hat when he passed a church episcopally consecrated must be a good man, a pious man, a man of good principles. Johnson could easily see that those persons who looked on a dance or a laced waistcoat as sinful deemed most ignobly of the attributes of God and of the ends of revelation. But with what a storm of invective he would have overwhelmed any man who had blamed him for celebrating the close of Lent with sugarless tea and butterless buns!

Nobody spoke more contemptuously of the cant of patriotism. Nobody saw more clearly the error of those who represented liberty not as a means, but as an end, and who proposed to themselves, as the object of their pursuit, the prosperity of the state as distinct from the prosperity of the individuals who compose the state. His calm and settled opinion seems to have been that forms of government have little or no influence on the happiness of society. This opinion, erroneous as it is, ought at least to have preserved him from all intemperance on political questions. It did not, however, preserve him from the lowest, fiercest, and most absurd extravagances of party spirit,— from rants which, in everything but the diction, resembled those of Squire Western. He was, as a politician, half ice and half fire. On the side of his intellect he was a mere pococurante,—far too apathetic about public affairs,— far too sceptical as to the good or evil tendency of any form of polity. His passions, on the contrary, were violent even to slaying against all who leaned to Whiggish principles. The well-known lines which he inserted in Goldsmith's Traveller express what seems to have been his deliberate judgment:

"How small, of all that human hearts endure,
That part which kings or laws can cause or cure!"

He had previously put expressions very similar into the mouth of Rasselas. It is amusing to contrast these passages with the torrents of raving abuse which he poured forth against the Long Parliament and the American Congress. In one of the conversations reported by Boswell this inconsistency displays itself in the most ludicrous manner.

"Sir Adam Ferguson," says Boswell, "suggested that luxury corrupts a people, and destroys the spirit of liberty. JOHNSON: 'Sir, that is all visionary. I would not give half a guinea to live under one form of government rather than another. It is of no moment to the happiness of an individual. Sir, the danger of the abuse of power is nothing to a private man. What Frenchman is prevented passing his life as he pleases?'—SIR ADAM: 'But, sir, in the British Constitution it is surely of importance to keep up a spirit in the people, so as to preserve a balance against the crown.'—JOHNSON: 'Sir, I perceive you are a vile Whig. Why all this childish jealousy of the power of the crown? The crown has not power enough.'"

One of the old philosophers, Lord Bacon tells us, used to say that life and death were just the same to him. "Why then," said an objector, "do you not kill yourself?" The philosopher answered, "Because it is just the same." If the difference between two forms of government be not worth half a guinea, it is not easy to see how Whiggism can be viler than Toryism, or how the crown can have too little power. If private men suffer nothing from political abuses, zeal for liberty is doubtless ridiculous. But zeal for monarchy must be equally so. No person could have been more quick sighted than Johnson to such a contradiction as this in the logic of an antagonist.

The judgments which Johnson passed on books were, in his own time, regarded with superstitious veneration, and, in our time, are generally treated with indiscriminate contempt. They are the judgments of a strong but enslaved understanding. The mind of the critic was hedged round by an uninterrupted fence of prejudices and superstitions. Within his narrow limits, he displayed a vigour and an activity which ought to have enabled him to clear the barrier that confined him.

How it chanced that a man who reasoned on his premises so ably should assume his premises so foolishly is one of the great mysteries of human nature. The same inconsistency may be observed in the schoolmen of the middle ages. Those writers show so much acuteness and force of mind in arguing on their wretched *data* that a modern reader is perpetually at a loss to comprehend how such minds came by such *data*. Not a flaw in the superstructure of the theory which they are rearing escapes their vigilance. Yet they are blind to the obvious unsoundness of the foundation. It is the same with some eminent lawyers. Their legal arguments are intellectual prodigies, abounding with the happiest analogies and the most refined distinctions. The principles of their arbitrary science being once admitted, the statute-book and the reports being once assumed as the foundations of jurisprudence, these men must be allowed to be perfect masters of logic. But if a question arises as to the postulates on which their whole system rests,—if they are called upon to vindicate the fundamental maxims of that system which they have passed their lives in studying, these very men often talk the language of savages or of children. Those who have listened to a man of this class in his own court, and who have witnessed the skill with which he analyses and digests a vast mass of evidence, or reconciles a crowd of precedents which at first sight seem contradictory, scarcely know him again when, a few hours later, they hear him speaking on the other side of Westminster Hall in his capacity of legislator. They can scarcely believe that the paltry quirks which are faintly heard through a storm of coughing, and which cannot impose on the plainest country gentleman, can proceed from the same sharp and vigorous intellect which had excited their admiration under the same roof, and on the same day.

Johnson decided literary questions like a lawyer, not like a legislator. He never examined foundations where a point was already ruled. His whole code of criticism rested on pure assumption, for which he sometimes quoted a precedent or an authority, but rarely troubled himself to give a reason drawn from the nature of things. He took it for granted that the kind of poetry which flourished in his own time, which he had been accustomed to hear praised from his childhood, and which he had himself written with success, was the best kind of poetry. In his biographical work he has repeatedly laid it down as an undeniable proposition that during the latter part of the seventeenth century, and the earlier part of the eighteenth, English poetry had been in a constant progress of improvement. Waller, Denham, Dryden, and Pope, had been, according to him, the great reformers. He judged of all works of the imagination by the standard established among his own contemporaries. Though he allowed Homer to have been a greater man than Virgil, he seems to have thought the Æneid a greater poem than the Iliad. Indeed, he well might have thought so; for he preferred Pope's Iliad to Homer's. He pronounced that, after Hoole's translation of Tasso, Fairfax's would hardly be reprinted. He could see no merit in our fine old English ballads, and always spoke with the most provoking contempt of Percy's fondness for them. Of all the great original works which appeared during his time, Richardson's novels alone excited his admiration. He could see little or no merit in Tom Jones, in Gulliver's Travels, or in Tristram Shandy. To Thomson's Castle of Indolence he vouchsafed only a line of cold commendation,—of commendation much colder than what he has bestowed on the creation of that portentous bore, Sir Richard Blackmore. Gray was, in his dialect, a barren rascal. Churchill was a blockhead. The contempt which he felt for the trash of Macpherson was, indeed, just; but it was, we suspect, just by chance. He despised the Fingal for the very reason which led many men of genius to admire it. He despised it, not because it was essentially commonplace, but because it had a superficial air of originality.

He was undoubtedly an excellent judge of compositions fashioned on his own principles. But when a deeper philosophy was required,—when he undertook to pronounce judgment on the works of those great minds which "yield homage only to eternal laws,"—his failure was ignominious. He criticised Pope's epitaphs excellently. But his observations on Shakespeare's plays and Milton's poems seem to us for the most part as wretched as if they had been written by Rymer himself, whom we take to have been the worst critic that ever lived.

Some of Johnson's whims on literary subjects can be compared only to that strange nervous feeling which made him uneasy if he had not touched every post between the Mitre tavern and his own lodgings. His preference of Latin epitaphs to English epitaphs is an instance. An English epitaph, he said, would disgrace Smollett. He declared that he would not pollute the walls of Westminster Abbey with an English epitaph on Goldsmith. What reason there can be for celebrating a British writer in Latin, which there was not for covering the Roman arches of triumph with Greek inscriptions, or for commemorating the deeds of the heroes of Thermopylæ in Egyptian hieroglyphics, we are utterly unable to imagine.

On men and manners,—at least on the men and manners of a particular place and a particular age,—Johnson had certainly looked with a most observant and discriminating eye. His remarks on the education of children, on marriage, on the economy of families, on the rules of society, are always striking, and generally sound. In his writings, indeed, the knowledge of life which he possessed in an eminent degree is very imperfectly exhibited. Like those unfortunate chiefs of the middle ages who were suffocated by their own chain-mail and cloth of gold, his maxims perish under that load of words which was designed for their ornament and their defence. But it is clear from the remains of his conversations, that he had more of that homely wisdom which nothing but experience and observation can give than any writer since the time of Swift. If he had been content to write as he talked, he might have left books on the practical art of living superior to the Directions to Servants.

Yet even his remarks on society, like his remarks on literature, indicate a mind at least as remarkable for narrowness as for strength. He was no master of the great science of human nature. He had studied, not the *genus* man, but the *species* Londoner. Nobody was ever so thoroughly conversant with all the forms of life and all the shades of moral and intellectual character which were to be seen from Islington to the Thames, and from Hyde-Park corner to Mile-end green. But his philosophy stopped at the first turnpike-gate. Of the rural life of England he knew nothing; and he took it for granted that every body who lived in the country was either stupid or miserable. "Country gentlemen," said he, "must be unhappy; for they have not enough to keep their lives in motion;"—as if all those peculiar habits and associations which made Fleet Street and Charing Cross the finest views in the world to himself had been essential parts of human nature. Of remote countries and past times he talked with wild and ignorant presumption. "The Athenians of the age of Demosthenes," he said to Mrs. Thrale, "were a people of brutes, a barbarous people." In conversation with Sir Adam Ferguson he used similar language. "The boasted Athenians," he said, "were barbarians. The mass of every people must be barbarous where there is no printing." The fact was this: he saw that a Londoner who could not read, was a very stupid and brutal fellow: he saw that great refinement of taste and activity of intellect were rarely found in a Londoner who had not read much; and, because it was by means of books that people acquired almost all their knowledge in the society with which he was acquainted, he concluded, in defiance of the strongest and clearest evidence, that the human mind can be cultivated by means of books alone. An Athenian citizen might possess very few volumes; and the largest library to which he had access might be much less valuable than Johnson's bookcase in Bolt Court. But the Athenian might pass every morning in conversation with Socrates, and might hear Pericles speak four or five times every month. He saw the plays of Sophocles and Aristophanes:—he walked amidst the friezes of Phidias and the paintings of Zeuxis:—he knew by heart the choruses of Æschylus:—he heard the rhapsodist at the corner of the street reciting the Shield of Achilles or the Death of Argus:—he was a legislator conversant with high questions of alliance, revenue, and war:—he was a soldier trained under a liberal and generous discipline:—he was a judge, compelled every day to weigh the effect of opposite arguments. These things were in themselves an education,—an education eminently fitted, not, indeed, to form exact or profound thinkers, but to give quickness to the perceptions, delicacy to the taste, fluency to the expression, and politeness to the manners. All this was overlooked. An Athenian who did not improve his mind by reading was, in Johnson's opinion, much such a person as a Cockney who made his mark,—much such a person as black Frank before he went to school, and far inferior to a parish clerk or a printer's devil.

Johnson's friends have allowed that he carried to a ridiculous extreme his unjust contempt for foreigners. He pronounced the French to be a very silly people,—much behind us,—stupid, ignorant creatures. And this judgment he formed after having been at Paris about a month, during which he would not talk French for fear of giving the natives an advantage over him in conversation. He pronounced them, also, to be an indelicate people, because a French footman touched the sugar with his fingers. That ingenious and amusing traveller, M. Simond, has defended his countrymen very successfully against Johnson's accusation, and has pointed out some English practices which, to an impartial spectator, would seem at least as inconsistent with physical cleanliness and social decorum as those which Johnson so bitterly reprehended. To the sage, as Boswell loves to call him, it never occurred to doubt that there must be something eternally and immutably good in the usages to which he had been accustomed. In fact, Johnson's remarks on society beyond the bills of mortality are generally of much the same kind with those of honest Tom Dawson, the English footman in Dr. Moore's Zeluco. "Suppose the king of France has no sons, but only a daughter, then, when the king dies, this here daughter, according to that there law, cannot be made queen, but the next near relative, provided he is a man, is made king, and not the last king's daughter, which, to be sure, is very unjust. The French footguards are dressed in blue, and all the marching regiments in white, which has a very foolish appearance for soldiers; and as for blue regimentals, it is only fit for the blue horse or the artillery."

Johnson's visit to the Hebrides introduced him to a state of society completely new to him; and a salutary suspicion of his own deficiencies seems on that occasion to have crossed his mind for the first time. He confessed,

H

in the last paragraph of his Journey, that his thoughts on national manners were the thoughts of one who had seen but little,—of one who had passed his time almost wholly in cities. This feeling, however, soon passed away. It is remarkable that to the last he entertained a fixed contempt for all those modes of life and those studies which lead to emancipate the mind from the prejudices of a particular age or a particular nation. Of foreign travel and of history he spoke with the fierce and boisterous contempt of ignorance. "What does a man learn by travelling? Is Beauclerk the better for travelling? What did Lord Charlemont learn in his travels, except that there was a snake in one of the pyramids of Egypt?" History was, in his opinion, to use the fine expression of Lord Plunkett, an old almanack: historians could, as he conceived, claim no higher dignity than that of almanack-makers; and his favourite historians were those who, like Lord Hailes, aspired to no higher dignity. He always spoke with contempt of Robertson. Hume he would not even read. He affronted one of his friends for talking to him about Catiline's conspiracy, and declared that he never desired to hear of the Punic war again as long as he lived.

Assuredly one fact which does not directly affect our own interests, considered in itself, is not better worth knowing than another fact. The fact that there is a snake in a pyramid, or the fact that Hannibal crossed the Alps by the great St. Bernard, are in themselves as unprofitable to us as the fact that there is a green blind in a particular house in Threadneedle Street, or the fact that a Mr. Smith comes into the city every morning on the top of one of the Blackwall stages. But it is certain that those who will not crack the shell of history will not get at the kernel. Johnson, with hasty arrogance, pronounced the kernel worthless, because he saw no value in the shell. The real use of travelling to distant countries and of studying the annals of past times is to preserve men from the contraction of mind which those can hardly escape whose whole communion is with one generation and one neighbourhood, who arrive at conclusions by means of an induction not sufficiently copious, and who, therefore, constantly confound exceptions with rules, and accidents with essential properties. In short, the real use of travelling and of studying history is to keep men from being what Tom Dawson was in fiction, and Samuel Johnson in reality.

Johnson, as Mr. Burke most justly observed, appears far greater in Boswell's books than in his own. His conversation appears to have been quite equal to his writings in matter, and far superior to them in manner. When he talked, he clothed his wit and his sense in forcible and natural expressions. As soon as he took his pen in his hand to write for the public, his style became systematically vicious. All his books are written in a learned language, in a language—which nobody hears from his mother or his nurse,—in a language in which nobody ever quarrels, or drives bargains, or makes love,—in a language in which nobody ever thinks. It is clear that Johnson himself did not think in the dialect in which he wrote. The expressions which came first to his tongue were simple, energetic, and picturesque. When he wrote for publication, he did his sentences out of English into Johnsonese. His letters from the Hebrides to Mrs. Thrale are the original of that work of which the Journey to the Hebrides is the translation; and it is amusing to compare the two versions. "When we were taken upstairs," says he in one of his letters, "a dirty fellow bounced out of the bed in which one of us was to lie." This incident is recorded in the Journey as follows: "Out of one of the beds on which we were to repose started up, at our entrance, a man black as a Cyclops from the forge." Sometimes Johnson translated aloud. "The Rehearsal," he said, very unjustly, "has not wit enough to keep it sweet;"

then, after a pause, "it has not vitality enough to preserve it from putrefaction."

Mannerism is pardonable, and is sometimes even agreeable, when the manner, though vicious, is natural. Few readers, for example, would be willing to part with the mannerism of Milton or of Burke. But a mannerism which does not sit easy on the mannerist, which has been adopted on principle, and which can be sustained only by constant effort, is always offensive. And such is the mannerism of Johnson.

The characteristic faults of his style are so familiar to all our readers, and have been so often burlesqued, that it is almost superfluous to point them out. It is well known that he made less use than any other eminent writer of those strong, plain words, Anglo-Saxon or Norman-French, of which the roots lie in the inmost depths of our language : and that he felt a vicious partiality for terms which, long after our own speech had been fixed, were borrowed from the Greek and Latin, and which, therefore, even when lawfully naturalised, must be considered as born aliens, not entitled to rank with the king's English. His constant practice of padding out a sentence with useless epithets, till it became as stiff as the bust of an exquisite,—his antithetical forms of expression, constantly employed even where there is no opposition in the ideas expressed,—his big words wasted on little things,—his harsh inversions, so widely different from those graceful and easy inversions which give variety, spirit, and sweetness to the expression of our great old writers,—all these peculiarities have been imitated by his admirers, and parodied by his assailants, till the public has become sick of the subject.

Goldsmith said to him, very wittily and very justly, "If you were to write a fable about little fishes, doctor, you would make the little fishes talk like whales." No man surely ever had so little talent for personation as Johnson. Whether he wrote in the character of a disappointed legacy-hunter or an empty town fop, of a crazy virtuoso or a flippant coquette, he wrote in the same pompous and unbending style. His speech, like Sir Piercy Shafton's euphuistic eloquence, betrayed him under every disguise. Euphelia and Rhodoclea talk as finely as Imlac the poet, or Seged, Emperor of Ethiopia. The gay Cornelia describes her reception at the country-house of her relations in such terms as these :—"I was surprised, after the civilities of my first reception, to find, instead of the leisure and tranquillity which a rural life always promises, and, if well-conducted, always affords, a confused wildness of care, and a tumultuous hurry of diligence, by which every face was clouded, and every motion agitated." The gentle Tranquilla informs us that she "had not passed the earlier part of life without the flattery of courtship, and the joys of triumph ; but had danced the round of gaiety amidst the murmurs of envy and the gratulations of applause,—had been attended from pleasure to pleasure by the great, the sprightly, and the vain, and had seen her regard solicited by the obsequiousness of gallantry, the gaiety of wit, and the timidity of love." Surely Sir John Falstaff himself did not wear his petticoats with a worse grace. The reader may well cry out, with honest Sir Hugh Evans, "I like not when a 'oman has a great peard ; I spy a great peard under her muffler."

We had something more to say. But our article is already too long ; and we must close it. We would fain part in good humour from the hero, from the biographer, and even from the editor, who, ill as he has performed his task, has at least this claim to our gratitude, that he has induced us to read Boswell's book again. As we close it the club-room is before us, and the table on which stand the omelet for Nugent, and the lemons for Johnson. There are assembled those heads which live for ever on the canvas of Reynolds. There are the spectacles of Burke and the tall, thin form of Langton, the courtly sneer of Beauclerk, and the beaming smile of Garrick, Gibbon tapping his snuff-box and Sir Joshua with his trumpet in his ear. In the foreground is that strange figure which is as familiar to us as the figures of those among whom we have been brought up,—the gigantic body, the huge, massy face, seamed with the scars of disease, the brown coat, the black worsted stockings, the grey wig with the scorched foretop, the dirty hands, the nails bitten and pared to the quick. We see the eyes and mouth moving with convulsive twitches; we see the heavy form rolling; we hear it puffing, and then comes the "Why, sir!" and the "What then, sir?" and the "No, sir!" and the "You don't see your way through the question, sir!"

What a singular destiny has been that of this remarkable man! To be regarded in his own age as a classic, and in ours as a companion!—To receive from his contemporaries that full homage which men of genius have in general received only from posterity!—To be more intimately known to posterity than other men are known to their contemporaries! That kind of fame which is commonly the most transient is, in his case, the most durable. The reputation of those writings, which he probably expected to be immortal, is every day fading; while those peculiarities of manner and that careless table-talk, the memory of which he probably thought would die with him, are likely to be remembered as long as the English language is spoken in any quarter of the globe.

JOHN BUNYAN.

The Pilgrim's Progress, with a Life of John Bunyan. By ROBERT SOUTHEY, Esq., LL.D. Poet-Laureate. Illustrated with Engravings. 8vo. London. 1830.

THIS is an eminently beautiful and splendid edition of a book which well deserves all that the printer and the engraver can do for it. The Life of Bunyan is, of course, not a performance which can add much to the literary reputation of such a writer as Mr. Southey. But it is written in excellent English, and, for the most part, in an excellent spirit. Mr. Southey propounds, we need not say, many opinions from which we altogether dissent; and his attempts to excuse the odious persecution to which Bunyan was subjected have sometimes moved our indignation. But we will avoid this topic. We are at present much more inclined to join in paying homage to the genius of a great man than to engage in a controversy concerning Church government and toleration.

We must not pass without notice the engravings with which this volume is decorated. Some of Mr. Heath's woodcuts are admirably designed and executed. Mr. Martin's illustrations do not please us quite so well. His Valley of the Shadow of Death is not that Valley of the Shadow of Death which Bunyan imagined. At all events, it is not that dark and horrible glen which has from childhood been in our mind's eye. The valley is a cavern: the quagmire is a lake: the straight path runs zigzag: and Christian appears like a speck in the darkness of the immense vault. We miss, too, those hideous forms which make so striking a part of the description of Bunyan, and which Salvator Rosa would have loved to draw. It is with unfeigned diffidence that we pronounce judgment on any question relating to the art of painting. But it appears to us that Mr. Martin has not of late been fortunate in his choice of subjects. He should never have attempted to illustrate the Paradise Lost. There can be no two manners more directly opposed to each other than the manner of his painting and the manner of Milton's poetry. Those things which are mere accessaries in the descriptions become the principal objects in the pictures; and those figures which are most prominent in the descriptions can be detected in the pictures only by a very close scrutiny. Mr. Martin has succeeded perfectly in representing the pillars and candelabras of Pandemonium. But he has forgotten that Milton's Pandemonium is merely the background to Satan. In the picture, the Archangel is scarcely visible amidst the endless colonnades of his infernal palace. Milton's Paradise, again, is merely the background to his Adam and Eve. But in Mr. Martin's picture the landscape is everything. Adam, Eve, and Raphael, attract much less notice than the lake and the mountains, the gigantic flowers, and the giraffes which feed upon them. We read that James II. sat to Verelst, the great flower-painter. When the performance was finished, his majesty appeared in the midst of a bower of sunflowers and tulips, which completely drew away all attention from the central figure. All who looked at the portrait took it for a flower-piece. Mr. Martin, we think, introduces his immeasurable spaces, his innumerable multitudes, his gorgeous prodigies of architecture and landscape, almost as unseasonably as Verelst introduced his flower-pots and nosegays. If Mr. Martin were to paint Lear in the storm, we suspect that the blazing sky, the sheets of rain, the swollen torrents, and the tossing forest would draw away all attention from the agonies of the insulted king and father. If he were to paint the death of Lear, the old man asking the by-standers to undo his button, would be thrown into the shade by a vast blaze of pavilions, standards, armour, and heralds' coats. Mr. Martin would illustrate the Orlando Furioso well,—the Orlando Innamorato still better,—the Arabian Nights best of all. Fairy palaces and gardens, porticos of agate, and groves flowering with emeralds and rubies,—inhabited by people for whom nobody cares,—these are his proper domain. He would succeed admirably in the enchanted ground of Alcina, or the mansion of Aladdin. But he should avoid Milton and Bunyan.

The characteristic peculiarity of the Pilgrim's Progress is that it is the only work of its kind which possesses a strong human interest. Other allegories only amuse the fancy. The allegory of Bunyan has been read by many thousands with tears. There are some good allegories in Johnson's works, and some of still higher merit by Addison. In these performances there is, perhaps, as much wit and ingenuity as in the Pilgrim's Progress. But the pleasure which is produced by the Vision of Mirza, the Vision of Theodore, the genealogy of Wit, or the contest between Rest and Labour, is exactly similar to the pleasure which we derive from one of Cowley's odes or from a canto of Hudibras. It is a pleasure which belongs wholly to the understanding, and in which the feelings have no part whatever. Nay, even Spenser himself, though assuredly one of the greatest poets that ever lived, could not succeed in the attempt to make allegory interesting. It was in vain that he lavished the riches of his mind on the House of Pride and the House of Temperance. One unpardonable fault, the fault of tediousness, pervades the whole of the Fairy Queen. We become sick of Cardinal Virtues and Deadly Sins, and long for the society of plain men and women. Of the persons who read the first canto, not one in ten reaches the end of the first book, and not one in a hundred perseveres to the end of the poem. Very few and very weary are those who are in at the death of the Blatant Beast. If the last six books, which are said to have been destroyed in Ireland, had been preserved, we doubt whether any heart less stout than that of a commentator would have held out to the end.

It is not so with the Pilgrim's Progress. That wonderful book, while it obtains admiration from the most fastidious critics, is loved by those who are too simple to admire it. Dr. Johnson, all whose studies were desultory, and who hated, as he said, to read books through, made an exception in favour of the Pilgrim's Progress. That work, he said, was one of the two or three works which he wished longer. It was by no common merit that the illiterate sectary extracted praise like this from the most pedantic of critics and the most bigoted of Tories. In the wildest parts of Scotland the Pilgrim's Progress is the delight of the peasantry. In every nursery the Pilgrim's Progress is a greater favourite than Jack the Giant-killer. Every reader knows the straight and narrow path as well as he knows a road in which he has gone backward and forward a hundred times. This is the highest miracle of genius,—that things which are not should be as though they were,—that the imaginations of one mind should become the personal recollections of another. And this miracle the tinker has wrought. There is no ascent, no declivity, no resting-place, no turn-stile, with which we are not perfectly acquainted. The wicket gate, and the desolate swamp which separates it from the City of Destruction, —the long line of road, as straight as a rule can make it,—the Interpreter's house, and all its fair shows,—the prisoner in the iron cage,—the palace, at the doors of which armed men kept guard, and on the battlements of which walked persons clothed all in gold,—the cross and the sepulchre,—the steep hill and the pleasant arbour,—the stately front of the House Beautiful by the wayside,—the low, green valley of Humiliation, rich with grass and covered with flocks,—all are as well known to us as the sights of our own street. Then we come to the narrow place where Apollyon strode right across the whole breadth of the way, to stop the journey of Christian, and where afterwards the pillar was set up to testify how bravely the pilgrim had fought the good fight. As we advance, the valley becomes deeper and deeper. The shade of the precipices on both sides falls blacker and blacker. The clouds gather overhead. Doleful voices, the clanking of chains, and the rushing of many feet to and fro, are heard through the darkness. The way, hardly discernible in gloom, runs close by the mouth of the burning pit, which sends forth its flames, its noisome smoke, and its hideous shapes, to terrify the adventurer. Thence he goes on, amidst the snares and pitfalls, with the mangled bodies of those who have perished lying in the ditch by his side. At the end of the long, dark valley he passes the dens in which the old giants dwelt, amidst the bones of those whom they had slain.

Then the road passes straight on through a waste moor, till at length the towers of a distant city appear before the traveller; and soon he is in the midst of the innumerable multitudes of Vanity Fair. There are the jugglers and the apes, the shops and the puppet-shows. There are Italian Row, and French Row, and Spanish Row, and British Row, with their crowds of buyers, sellers, and loungers, jabbering all the languages of the earth.

Thence we go on by the little hill of the silver mine, and through the meadow of lilies, along the bank of that pleasant river which is bordered on both sides by fruit-trees. On the left side branches off the path leading to the Horrible Castle, the court-yard of which is paved with the skulls of pilgrims; and right onward are the sheepfolds and orchards of the Delectable Mountains.

From the Delectable Mountains, the way lies through the fogs and briers of the Enchanted Ground, with here and there a bed of soft cushions spread under a green arbour. And beyond is the land of Beulah, where the flowers, the grapes, and the songs of birds never cease; and where the sun shines night and day. Thence are plainly seen the golden pavements and streets of pearl, on the other side of that black and cold river over which there is no bridge.

All the stages of the journey,—all the forms which cross or overtake the pilgrims,—giants, and hobgoblins, ill-favoured ones and shining ones,—the tall, comely, swarthy Madam Bubble, with her great purse by her side, and her fingers playing with the money,—the black man in the bright vesture, Mr. Worldly Wiseman and my Lord Hategood,—Mr. Talkative and Mrs. Timorous,—all are actually existing beings to us. We follow the travellers through their allegorical progress with interest not inferior to that with which we follow Elizabeth from Siberia to Moscow, or Jeanie Deans from Edinburgh to London. Bunyan is almost the only writer who ever gave to the abstract the interest of the concrete. In the works of many celebrated authors, men are mere personifications. We have not an Othello, but jealousy, not an Iago, but perfidy, not a Brutus, but patriotism. The mind of Bunyan, on the contrary, was so imaginative that personifications, when he dealt with them, became men. A dialogue between two qualities, in his dream, has more dramatic effect than a dialogue between two human beings in most plays. In this respect the genius of Bunyan bore a great resemblance to that of a man who had very little else in common with him, Percy Bysshe Shelley. The strong imagination of Shelley made him an idolator in his own despite. Out of the most indefinite terms of a hard, cold, dark metaphysical system, he made a gorgeous Pantheon, full of beautiful, majestic, and life-like forms. He turned atheism itself into a mythology, rich with visions as glorious as the gods that live in the marble of Phidias, or the virgin saints that smile on us from the canvas of Murillo. The Spirit of Beauty, the Principle of Good, the Principle of Evil, when he treated of them, ceased to be abstractions. They took shape and colour. They were no longer mere words; but "intelligible forms," "fair humanities," objects of love, of adoration, or of fear. As there can be no stronger sign of a mind destitute of the poetical faculty than that tendency which was so common among the writers of the French school to turn images into abstractions—Venus, for example, into Love, Minerva into Wisdom, Mars into War, and Bacchus into Festivity,—so there can be no stronger sign of a mind truly poetical than a disposition to reverse this abstracting process, and to make individuals out of generalities. Some of the metaphysical and ethical theories of Shelley were certainly most absurd and pernicious. But we doubt whether any modern poet has possessed in an equal degree some of the highest qualities of the great ancient masters. The words bard and inspiration, which seem so cold and affected when applied to other modern writers, have a perfect propriety when applied to him. He was not an author, but a bard. His poetry seems not to have been an art, but an inspiration. Had he lived to the full age of man, he might not improbably have given to the world some great work of the very highest rank in design and execution. But, alas!

ἀλάμπετι ᾔδε ἥδου (ἔκλυσέ θινί)
τὸν Μοισαῖς φίλον ἄνδρα, τὸν οὐ Νημοσύνην ἀπεχθῆ.

But we must return to Bunyan. The Pilgrim's Progress undoubtedly is not a perfect allegory. The types are often inconsistent with each other; and sometimes the allegorical disguise is altogether thrown off. The river, for example, is emblematic of death; and we are told that every human being must pass through the river. But Faithful does not pass through it. He is martyred, not in shadow, but in reality, at Vanity Fair. Hopeful talks to Christian about Esau's birthright and about his own convictions of sin as Bunyan might have talked with one of his own congregation. The damsels at the House Beautiful catechize Christiana's boys, as any good ladies might catechize any boys at a Sunday School. But we do not believe that any man, whatever might be his genius, and whatever his good luck, could long continue a figurative history without falling into many inconsistencies. We are sure that inconsistencies, scarcely less gross than the worst into which Bunyan has fallen, may be found in the shortest and most elaborate allegories of the Spectator and the Rambler. The Tale of a Tub and the History of John Bull swarm with similar errors,—if the name of error can be properly applied to that which is unavoidable. It is not easy to make a simile go on all-fours. But we believe that no human ingenuity could produce such a centipede as a long allegory in which the correspondence between the outward sign and the thing signified should be exactly preserved. Certainly no writer, ancient or modern, has yet achieved the adventure. The best thing, on the whole, that an allegorist can do, is to present to his readers a succession of analogies, each of which may separately be striking and happy, without looking very nicely to see whether they harmonize with each other. This Bunyan has done; and, though a minute scrutiny may detect inconsistencies in every page of his tale, the general effect which the tale produces on all persons, learned and unlearned, proves that he has done well. The passages which it is most difficult to defend are those in which he altogether drops the allegory, and puts in the mouth of his pilgrims religious ejaculations and disquisitions better suited to his own pulpit at Bedford or Reading than to the Enchanted Ground or to the Interpreter's Garden. Yet even these passages, though we will not undertake to defend them against the objections of critics, we feel that we could ill spare. We feel that the story owes much of its charm to these occasional glimpses of solemn and affecting subjects, which will not be hidden, which force themselves through the veil, and appear before us in their native aspect. The effect is not unlike that which is said to have been produced on the ancient stage, when the eyes of the actor were seen flaming through his mask, and giving life and expression to what would else have been an inanimate and uninteresting disguise.

It is very amusing and very instructive to compare the Pilgrim's Progress with the Grace Abounding. The latter work is, indeed, one of the most remarkable pieces of autobiography in the world. It is a full and open confession of the fancies which passed through the mind of an illiterate man, whose affections were warm, whose nerves were irritable, whose imagination was ungovernable, and who was under the influence of the strongest religious excitement. In whatever age Bunyan had lived the history of his feelings would, in all probability, have been very curious. But the time in which his lot was cast was the time of a great stirring of the human mind. A tremendous burst of public feeling, produced by the tyranny of the hierarchy, menaced the old ecclesiastical institutions with destruction. To the gloomy regularity of one intolerant Church had succeeded the licence of innumerable sects, drunk with the sweet and heady must of their new liberty. Fanaticism, engendered by persecution, and destined to engender fresh persecution in turn, spread rapidly through society. Even the strongest and most commanding minds were not proof against this strange taint. Any time might have produced George Fox and James Naylor. But to one time alone belong the frantic delusions of such a statesman as Vane, and the hysterical tears of such a soldier as Cromwell.

The history of Bunyan is the history of a most excitable mind in an age of excitement. By most of his biographers he has been treated with gross injustice. They have understood in a popular sense all those strong terms of self-condemnation which he employed in a theological sense. They have, therefore, represented him as an abandoned wretch, reclaimed by means almost miraculous;—or, to use their favourite metaphor, "as a brand plucked from the burning." Mr. Ivimey calls him the depraved Bunyan and the wicked tinker of Elstow. Surely Mr. Ivimey ought to have been too familiar with the bitter accusations which the most pious people are in the habit of bringing against themselves, to understand literally all the strong expressions which are to be found in the Grace Abounding. It is quite clear, as Mr. Southey most justly remarks, that Bunyan never was a vicious man. He married very early; and he solemnly declares that he was strictly faithful to his wife. He does not appear to have been a drunkard. He owns, indeed, that when a boy he never spoke without an oath. But a single admonition cured him of this bad habit for life; and the cure must have been wrought early; for at eighteen he was in the army of the Parliament; and, if he had carried the vice of profaneness into that service, he would doubtless have received something more than an admonition from Serjeant Bind-their-kings-in-chains, or Captain Hew-Agag-in-pieces-before-the-Lord. Bell-ringing and playing at hockey on Sundays seem to have been the worst vices of this depraved tinker. They would have passed for virtues with Archbishop Laud. It is quite clear that, from a very early age, Bunyan was a man of a strict life and of a tender conscience. "He had been," says Mr. Southey, "a blackguard." Even this, we think, too hard a censure. Bunyan was not, we admit, so fine a gentleman as Lord Digby; but he was a blackguard no otherwise than as every labouring man that ever lived has been a blackguard. Indeed, Mr. Southey acknowledges this. "Such he might have been expected to be by his birth, breeding, and vocation. Scarcely, indeed, by possibility, could he have been otherwise." A man whose manners and sentiments are decidedly below those of his class deserves to be called a blackguard. But it is surely unfair to apply so strong a word of reproach to one who is only what the great mass of every community must inevitably be.

Those horrible internal conflicts which Bunyan has described with so much power of language prove, not that he was a worse man than his neighbours, but that his mind was constantly occupied by religious considerations,—that his fervour exceeded his knowledge,—and that his imagination exercised despotic power over his body and mind. He heard voices from heaven; he saw strange visions of distant hills, pleasant and sunny as his own Delectable Mountains: from those abodes he was shut out, and placed in a dark and horrible wilderness, where he wandered through ice and snow, striving to make his way into the happy region of light. At one time he was seized with an inclination to work miracles. At another time he thought himself actually possessed by the devil. He could distinguish the blasphemous whispers. He felt his infernal enemy pulling at his clothes behind him. He spurned with his feet and struck with his hands at the destroyer. Sometimes he was tempted to sell his part in the salvation of mankind. Sometimes a violent impulse urged him to start up from his food, to fall on his knees, and to break forth into prayer. At length he fancied that he had committed the unpardonable sin. His agony convulsed his robust frame. He was, he says, as if his breast bone would split; and this he took for a sign that he was destined to burst asunder like Judas. The agitation of his nerves made all his movements tremulous; and this trembling, he supposed, was a visible mark of his reprobation, like that which had been set on Cain. At one time, indeed, an encouraging voice seemed to rush in at the window, like the noise of wind, but very pleasant, and commanded, as he says, a great calm in his soul. At another time, a word of comfort "was spoke loud unto him;"—it showed "a great word;—it seemed to be writ in great letters." But these intervals of ease were short. His state, during two years and a half, was generally the most horrible that the human mind can imagine. "I walked," says he, with his own peculiar eloquence, "to a neighbouring town, and sat down upon a settle in the street, and fell into a very deep pause about the most fearful state my sin had brought me to; and, after long musing, I lifted up my head; but methought I saw as if the sun that shineth in the heavens did grudge to give me light; and as if the very stones in the street, and tiles upon the houses, did band themselves against me. Methought that they all combined together to banish me out of the world. I was abhorred of them, and unfit to dwell among them, because I had sinned against the Saviour. Oh, how happy now was every creature over I! for they stood fast, and kept their station. But I was gone and lost." Scarcely any madhouse could produce an instance of delusion so strong, or of misery so acute.

It was through this Valley of the Shadow of Death, overhung by darkness, peopled with devils, resounding with blasphemy and lamentation, and passing amidst quagmires, snares, and pitfalls, close by the very mouth of hell, that Bunyan journeyed to that bright and fruitful land of Beulah, in which he sojourned during the latter period of his pilgrimage. The only trace which his cruel sufferings and temptations seem to have left behind them was an affectionate compassion for those who were still in the state in which he had once been. Religion has scarcely ever worn a form so calm and soothing as in his allegory. The feeling which predominates through the whole book is a feeling of tenderness for weak, timid, and harassed minds. The character of Mr. Fearing, of Mr. Feeblemind, of Mr. Despondency and his daughter Miss Muchafraid, the account of poor Littlefaith who was robbed by the three thieves of his spending money, the description of Christian's terror in the dungeons of Giant Despair and in his passage through the river, all clearly show how strong a sympathy Bunyan felt, after his own mind had become clear and cheerful, for persons afflicted with religious melancholy.

Mr. Southey, who has no love for the Calvinists, admits that, if Calvinism had never worn a blacker appearance than in Bunyan's works, it would never have become a term of reproach. In fact, those works of Bunyan with which we are acquainted are by no means more Calvinistic than the articles and homilies of the Church of England. The moderation of his opinions on the subject of predestination gave offence to some zealous persons. We have seen an absurd allegory, the heroine of which is named Hephzibah, written by some raving supralapsarian preacher who was dissatisfied with the mild theology of the Pilgrim's Progress. In this foolish book, if we recollect rightly, the Interpreter is called the Enlightener, and the House Beautiful is Castle Strength. Mr. Southey tells us that the Catholics had also their Pilgrim's Progress, without a Giant Pope, in which the Interpreter is the Director, and the House Beautiful, Grace's Hall. It is surely a remarkable proof of the power of Bunyan's genius, that two religious parties, both of which regarded his opinions as heterodox, should have had recourse to him for assistance.

There are, we think, some characters and scenes in the Pilgrim's Progress which can be fully comprehended and enjoyed only by persons familiar with the history of the times through which Bunyan lived. The character of Mr. Greatheart, the guide, is an example. His fighting is, of course, allegorical; but the allegory is not strictly preserved. He delivers a sermon on imputed righteousness to his companions; and, soon after, he gives battle to Giant Grim, who had taken upon him to back the lions. He expounds the fifty-third chapter of Isaiah to the household and guests of Gaius; and then he sallies out to attack Slaygood, who was of the nature of flesh-eaters, in his ten. These are inconsistencies; but they are inconsistencies which add, we think, to the interest of the narrative. We have not the least doubt that Bunyan had in view some stout old Greatheart of Naseby and Worcester, who prayed with his men before he drilled them, who knew the spiritual state of every dragoon in his troop, and who, with the praises of God in his mouth, and a two-edged sword in his hand, had turned to flight, on many fields of battle, the swearing, drunken bravoes of Rupert and Lunsford.

Every age produces such men as By-ends. But the middle of the seventeenth century was eminently prolific of such men. Mr. Southey thinks that the satire was aimed at some particular individual; and this seems by no means improbable. At all events, Bunyan must have known many of those hypocrites who followed religion only when religion walked in silver slippers, when the sun shone, and when the people applauded. Indeed, he might have easily found all the kindred of By-ends among the public men of his time. He might have found among the peers my Lord Turn-about, my Lord Timeserver, and my Lord Fair-speech; in the House of Commons, Mr. Smoothman, Mr. Anything, and Mr. Facing-both-ways; nor would "the parson of the parish, Mr. Two-tongues," have been wanting. The town of Bedford probably contained more than one politician who, after contriving to raise an estate by seeking the Lord during the reign of the saints, contrived to keep what he had got by persecuting the saints during the reign of the strumpets—and more than one priest who, during repeated changes in the discipline and doctrines of the Church, had remained constant to nothing but his benefice.

One of the most remarkable passages in the Pilgrim's Progress is that in which the proceedings against Faithful are described. It is impossible to doubt that Bunyan intended to satirise the mode in which state trials were conducted under Charles II. The licence given to the witnesses for the prosecution, the shameless partiality and ferocious insolence of the judge, the precipitancy and the blind rancour of the jury, remind us of those odious mummeries which, from the Restoration to the Revolution, were merely forms preliminary to hanging, drawing, and quartering. Lord Hategood performs the office of counsel for the prisoners as well as Scroggs himself could have performed it.

"JUDGE. Thou runagate, heretic, and traitor, hast thou heard what these honest gentlemen have witnessed against thee?

"FAITHFUL. May I speak a few words in my own defence?

"JUDGE. Sirrah, sirrah! thou deservest to live no longer; but to be slain immediately upon the place; yet, that all men may see our gentleness to thee, let us hear what thou, vile runagate, hast to say."

No person who knows the state trials can be at a loss for parallel cases. Indeed, write what Bunyan would, the baseness and cruelty of the lawyers of those times "sinned up to it still," and even went beyond it. The imaginary trial of Faithful, before a jury composed of personified vices, was just and merciful, when compared with the real trial of Lady Alice Lisle before that tribunal where all the vices sat in the person of Jefferies.

The style of Bunyan is delightful to every reader, and invaluable as a study to every person who wishes to obtain a wide command over the English language. The vocabulary is the vocabulary of the common people. There is not an expression, if we except a few technical terms of theology, which would puzzle the rudest peasant. We have observed several pages which do not contain a single word of more than two syllables. Yet no writer has said more exactly what he meant to say. For magnificence, for pathos, for vehement exhortation, for subtle disquisition, for every purpose of the poet, the orator, and the divine, this homely dialect,—the dialect of plain working men,

—was perfectly sufficient. There is no book in our literature on which we would so readily stake the fame of the old unpolluted English language,—no book which shows so well how rich that language is in its own proper wealth, and how little it has been improved by all that it has borrowed.

Cowper said, forty or fifty years ago, that he dared not name John Bunyan in his verse, for fear of moving a sneer. To our refined forefathers, we suppose, Lord Roscommon's Essay on Translated Verse, and the Duke of Buckinghamshire's Essay on Poetry, appeared to be compositions infinitely superior to the allegory of the preaching tinker. We live in better times; and we are not afraid to say that, though there were many clever men in England during the latter half of the seventeenth century, there were only two great creative minds. One of those minds produced the Paradise Lost, the other the Pilgrim's Progress.

JOHN HAMPDEN.

Some Memorials of John Hampden, his Party, and his Times. By LORD NUGENT. 2 vols. 8vo. London. 1831

WE have read this book with great pleasure, though not exactly with the kind of pleasure which we had expected. We had hoped that Lord Nugent would have been able to collect, from family papers and local traditions, much new and interesting information respecting the life and character of the renowned leader of the Long Parliament,—the first of those great English commoners whose plain addition of Mister has, to our ears, a more majestic sound than the proudest of the feudal titles. In this hope we have been disappointed; but assuredly not from any want of zeal or diligence on the part of the noble biographer. Even at Hampden, there are, it seems, no important papers relating to the most illustrious proprietor of that ancient domain. The most valuable memorials of him which still exist, belong to the family of his friend, Sir John Eliot. Lord Eliot has furnished the portrait which is engraved for this work, together with some very interesting letters. The portrait is undoubtedly an original, and probably the only original now in existence. The intellectual forehead, the mild penetration of the eye, and the inflexible resolution expressed by the lines of the mouth, sufficiently guarantee the likeness. We shall probably make some extracts from the letters. They contain almost all the new information that Lord Nugent has been able to procure respecting the private pursuits of the great man whose memory he worships with an enthusiastic, but not extravagant, veneration.

The public life of Hampden is surrounded by no obscurity. His history, more particulary from the year 1640 to his death, is the history of England. These memoirs must be considered as memoirs of the history of England; and, as such, they well deserve to be attentively perused. They contain some curious facts which, to us at least, are new,—much spirited narrative, many judicious remarks, and much eloquent declamation.

We are not sure that even the want of information respecting the private character of Hampden is not in itself a circumstance as strikingly characteristic as any which the most minute chronicler,—O'Meara, Mrs. Thrale, or Boswell himself,—ever recorded concerning their heroes. The celebrated Puritan leader is an almost solitary instance of a great man who neither sought nor shunned greatness,—who found glory only because glory lay in the plain path of duty. During more than forty years he was known to his country neighbours as a gentleman of cultivated mind, of high principles, of polished address, happy in his family, and active in the discharge of local duties;—and to political men, as an honest, industrious, and sensible member of Parliament, not eager to display his talents, stanch to his party, and attentive to the interests of his constituents. A great and terrible crisis came. A direct attack was made by an arbitrary government on a sacred right of Englishmen, —on a right which was the chief security for all their other rights. The nation looked round for a defender. Calmly and unostentatiously the plain Buckinghamshire esquire placed himself at the head of his countrymen, and right before the face and across the path of tyranny. The times grew darker and more troubled. Public service, perilous, arduous, delicate, was required; and to every service the intellect and the courage of this wonderful man were found fully equal. He became a debater of the first order, a most dexterous manager of the House of Commons, a negotiator, a soldier. He governed a fierce and turbulent assembly, abounding in able men, as easily as he had governed his family. He showed himself as competent to direct a campaign as to conduct the business of the petty sessions. We can scarcely express the admiration which we feel for a mind so great, and, at the same time, so healthful and so well proportioned,—so willingly contracting itself to the humblest duties,—so easily expanding itself to the highest,—so contented in repose,—so powerful in action. Almost every part of this virtuous and blameless life which is not hidden from us in modest privacy is a precious and splendid portion of our national history. Had the private conduct of Hampden afforded the slightest pretence for censure, he would have been assailed by the same blind malevolence which, in defiance of the clearest proofs, still continues to call Sir John Eliot an assassin. Had there been even any weak part in the character of Hampden, had his manners been in any respect open to ridicule, we may be sure that no mercy would have been shown to him by the writers of Charles's faction. Those writers have carefully preserved every little circumstance which could tend to make their opponents odious or contemptible. They have told us that Pym broke down in a speech, that Ireton had his nose pulled by Hollis, that the Earl of Northumberland cudgeled Henry Marten, that St. John's manners were sullen, that Vane had an ugly face, that Cromwell had a red nose. They have made themselves merry with the cant of injudicious zealots. But neither the artful Clarendon nor the scurrilous Denham could venture to throw the slightest imputation on the morals or the manners of Hampden. What was the opinion entertained respecting him by the best men of his time, we learn from Baxter. That eminent person,—eminent not only for his piety and his fervid devotional eloquence, but for his moderation, his knowledge of political affairs, and his skill in judging of characters,—declared in the Saint's Rest that one of the pleasures which he hoped to enjoy in heaven was the society of Hampden. In the editions printed after the Restoration, the name of Hampden was omitted. "But I must tell the reader," says Baxter, "that I did blot it out, not as changing my opinion of the person. . . . Mr. John Hampden was one that friends and enemies acknowledged to be most eminent for prudence, piety, and peaceable counsels, having the most universal praise of any gentleman that I remember of that age. I remember a moderate, prudent, aged gentleman, far from him, but acquainted with him, whom I have heard saying, that if he might choose what person he would be then in the world, he would be John Hampden." We cannot but regret that we have not fuller memorials of a man who, after passing through the most severe temptations by which human virtue can be tried,—after acting a most conspicuous part in a revolution and a civil war, could yet deserve such praise as this from such authority. Yet the want of memorials is surely the best proof that hatred itself could find no blemish on his memory.

The story of his early life is soon told. He was the head of a family which had been settled in Buckinghamshire before the Conquest. Part of the estate which he inherited had been bestowed by Edward the Confessor on Baldwyn de Hampden, whose name seems to indicate that he was one of the Norman favourites of the last Saxon king. During the contest between the houses of York and Lancaster, the Hampdens adhered to the party of the Red Rose, and were, consequently, persecuted by Edward IV., and favoured by Henry VII. Under the Tudors, the family was great and flourishing. Griffith Hampden, high sheriff of Buckinghamshire, entertained Elizabeth with great magnificence at his seat. His son, William Hampden, sate in the Parliament which that queen summoned in the year 1593. William married Elizabeth Cromwell, aunt of the celebrated man who afterwards governed the British islands with more than regal power; and from this marriage sprang John Hampden.

He was born in 1594. In 1597 his father died, and left him heir to a very large estate. After passing some years at the grammar-school of Thame, young Hampden was sent, at fifteen, to Magdalene College, in the University of Oxford. At nineteen, he was admitted a student of the Inner Temple, where he made himself master of the principles of the English law. In 1619 he married Elizabeth Symeon, a lady to whom he appears to have been fondly attached. In the following year he was returned to Parliament by a borough which has in our time obtained a miserable celebrity, the borough of Grampound.

Of his private life during his early years little is known beyond what Clarendon has told us. "In his entrance into the world," says that great historian, "he indulged himself in all the licence in sports, and exercises, and company, which were used by men of the most jolly conversation." A remarkable change, however, passed on his character. "On a sudden," says Clarendon, "from a life of great pleasure and licence, he retired to extraordinary sobriety and strictness,—to a more reserved and melancholy society." It is probable that this change took place when Hampden was about twenty-five years old. At that age he was united to a woman whom he loved and esteemed. At that age he entered into political life. A mind so happily constituted as his would naturally, under such circumstances, relinquish the pleasures of dissipation for domestic enjoyments and public duties.

His enemies have allowed that he was a man in whom virtue showed itself in its mildest and least austere form. With the morals of a Puritan, he had the manners of an accomplished courtier. Even after the change in his habits, "he preserved," says Clarendon, "his own natural cheerfulness and vivacity, and, above all, a flowing courtesy to all men." These qualities distinguished him from most of the members of his sect and his party, and, in the great crisis in which he afterwards took a principal part, were of scarcely less service to the country than his keen sagacity and his dauntless courage.

In January, 1621, Hampden took his seat in the House of Commons. His mother was exceedingly desirous that her son should obtain a peerage. His family, his possessions, and his personal accomplishments were such as would, in any age, have justified him in pretending to that honour. But in the reign of James I. there was one short cut to the House of Lords. It was but to ask, to pay, and to have. The sale of titles was carried on as openly as the sale of boroughs in our times. Hampden turned away with contempt from the degrading honours with which his family desired to see him invested, and attached himself to the party which was in opposition to the court.

It was about this time, as Lord Nugent has justly remarked, that parliamentary opposition began to take a regular form. From a very early age, the English had enjoyed a far larger share of liberty than had fallen to the lot of any neighbouring people. How it chanced that a country conquered and enslaved by invaders—a country of which the soil had been portioned out among foreign adventurers, and of which the laws were written in a foreign tongue—a country given over to that worst tyranny, the tyranny of caste over caste,—should have become the seat of civil liberty, the object of the admiration and envy of surrounding states, is one of the most obscure problems in the philosophy of history. But the fact is certain. Within a century and a half after the Norman conquest, the Great Charter was conceded. Within two centuries after the Conquest, the first House of Commons met. Froissart tells us, what, indeed, his whole narrative sufficiently proves, that, of all the nations of the fourteenth century, the English were the least disposed to endure oppression. "C'est le plus périlleux peuple qui soit au monde, et plus outrageux et orgueilleux." The good canon probably did not perceive that all the prosperity and internal peace which this dangerous people enjoyed were the fruits of the spirit which he designates as proud and outrageous. He has, however, borne ample testimony to the effect, though he was not sagacious enough to trace it to its cause. "En le royaume d'Angleterre," says he, "toutes gens, laboureurs et marchands, ont appris de vivre en paix, et à mener leurs marchandises paisiblement, et les laboureurs labourer." In the fifteenth century, though England was convulsed by the struggle between the two branches of the royal family, the physical and moral condition of the people continued to improve. Villenage almost wholly disappeared. The calamities of war were little felt, except by those who bore arms. The oppressions of the government were little felt, except by the aristocracy. The institutions of the country, when compared with the institutions of the neighbouring kingdoms, seem to have been not undeserving of the praises of Fortescue. The government of Edward IV., though we call it cruel and arbitrary, was humane and liberal when compared with that of Louis XI., or that of Charles the Bold. Comines, who had lived amidst the wealthy cities of Flanders, and who had visited Florence and Venice, had never seen a people so well governed as the English. "Or selon mon advis," says he, "entre toutes les seigneuries du monde, dont j'ay connoissance, ou la chose publique est mieulx traitée, et ou regne moins de violence sur le peuple, et ou il n'y a nuls édifices abbatus ny demolis pour guerre, c'est Angleterre ; et tombe le sort et le malheur sur ceulx qui font la guerre.

About the close of the fifteenth and the commencement of the sixteenth century, a great portion of the influence which the aristocracy had possessed passed to the Crown. No English king has ever enjoyed such absolute power as Henry VIII. But while the royal prerogatives were acquiring strength at the expense of the nobility, two great revolutions took place, destined to be the parents of many revolutions, the invention of printing and the reformation of the Church.

The immediate effect of the Reformation in England was by no means favourable to political liberty. The authority which had been exercised by the popes was transferred almost entire to the king. Two formidable powers which had often served to check each other were united in a single despot. If the system on which the founders of the Church of England acted could have been permanent, the Reformation would have been, in a political sense, the greatest curse that ever fell on our country. But that system carried within it the seeds of its own death. It was possible to transfer the name of Head of the Church from Clement to Henry ; but it was impossible to transfer to the new establishment the veneration which the old establishment had inspired. Mankind had not broken one yoke in pieces only in order to put on another. The supremacy of the Bishop of Rome had been for ages considered as a fundamental principle of Christianity. It had for it everything that could make a prejudice deep and strong,—venerable antiquity, high authority, general consent. It had been taught in the first lessons of the nurse. It was taken for granted in all the exhortations of the priest. To remove it was to break innumerable associations, and to give a great and perilous shock to the principles. Yet this prejudice, strong as it was, could not stand in the great day of the deliverance of the human reason. And it was not to be expected that the public mind, just after freeing itself by an unexampled effort, from a bondage which it had endured for ages, would patiently submit to a tyranny which could plead no ancient title. Rome had at least prescription on its side. But Protestant intolerance,—despotism in an upstart sect,—infallibility claimed by guides who acknowledged that they had passed the greater part of their lives in error,—restraints imposed on the liberty of private judgment, at the pleasure of rulers who could vindicate their own proceedings only by asserting the liberty of private judgment,—these things could not long be borne. Those who had pulled down the crucifix could not long continue to persecute for the surplice. It required no great sagacity to perceive the inconsistency and dishonesty of men who, dissenting from almost all Christendom, would suffer none to dissent from themselves, who demanded freedom of conscience, yet refused to grant it,—who execrated persecution, yet persecuted,—who urged reason against the authority of one opponent, and authority against the reasons of another. Bonner acted at least in accordance with his own principles. Cranmer could vindicate himself from the charge of being a heretic only by arguments which made him out to be a murderer.

Thus the system on which the English princes acted with respect to ecclesiastical affairs for some time after the Reformation was a system too obviously unreasonable to be lasting. The public mind moved while the government moved, but would not stop where the government stopped. The same impulse which had carried millions away from the Church of Rome continued to carry them forward in the same direction. As Catholics had become Protestants, Protestants became Puritans; and the Tudors and Stuarts were as unable to avert the latter change as the popes had been to avert the former. The dissenting party increased and became strong under every kind of discouragement and oppresssion. They were a sect. The government persecuted them, and they became an opposition. The old constitution of England furnished to them the means of resisting the sovereign without breaking the law. They were the majority of the House of Commons. They had the power of giving or withholding supplies; and, by a judicious exercise of this power, they might hope to take from the Church its usurped authority over the consciences of men, and from the Crown some part of the vast prerogative which it had recently acquired at the expense of the nobles and of the pope.

The faint beginnings of this memorable contest may be discerned early in the reign of Elizabeth. The conduct of her last Parliament made it clear that one of those great revolutions which policy may guide but cannot stop was in progress. It was on the question of monopolies that the House of Commons gained its first great victory over the throne. The conduct of the extraordinary woman who then governed England is an admirable study for politicians who live in unquiet times. It shows how thoroughly she understood the people whom she ruled, and the crisis in which she was called to act. What she held she held firmly. What she gave she gave graciously. She saw that it was necessary to make a concession to the nation; and she made it, not grudgingly, not tardily, not as a matter of bargain and sale, not, in a word, as Charles I. would have made it, but promptly and cordially. Before a bill could be framed or an address presented, she applied a remedy to the evil of which the nation complained. She expressed in the warmest terms her gratitude to her faithful Commons for detecting abuses which interested persons had concealed from her. If her successors had inherited her wisdom with her crown, Charles I. might have died of old age, and James II. would never have seen St. Germain's.

She died; and the kingdom passed to one who was, in his own opinion, the greatest master of kingcraft that ever lived,—but who was, in truth, one of those kings whom God seems to send for the express purpose of hastening revolutions. Of all the enemies of liberty whom Britain has produced, he was at once the most harmless and the most provoking. His office resembled that of the man who, in a Spanish bull-fight, goads the torpid savage to fury, by shaking a red rag in the air, and by now and then throwing a dart, sharp enough to sting, but too small to injure. The policy of wise tyrants has always been to cover their violent acts with popular forms. James was always obtruding his despotic theories on his subjects without the slightest necessity. His foolish talk exasperated them infinitely more than forced loans or benevolences would have done. Yet, in practice, no king ever held his prerogatives less tenaciously. He neither gave way gracefully to the advancing spirit of liberty nor took vigorous measures to stop it, but retreated before it with ludicrous haste, blustering and insulting as he retreated. The English people had been governed during nearly a hundred and fifty years by princes who, whatever might be their frailties or their vices, had all possessed great force of character, and who, whether beloved or hated, had always been feared. Now, at length, for the first time since the day when the sceptre of Henry IV. dropped from the hand of his lethargic grandson, England had a king whom she despised.

The follies and vices of the man increased the contempt which was produced by the feeble policy of the sovereign. The indecorous gallantries of the court, —the habits of gross intoxication in which even the ladies indulged,—were alone sufficient to disgust a people whose manners were beginning to be strongly tinctured with austerity. But these were trifles. Crimes of the most frightful kind had been discovered; others were suspected. The strange story of the Gowries was not forgotten. The ignominious fondness of the king for his minions,—the perjuries, the sorceries, the poisonings, which his chief favourites had planned within the walls of his palace,—the pardon which, in direct violation of his duty and of his word, he had granted to the mysterious threats of a murderer, made him an object of loathing to many of his subjects. What opinion grave and moral persons residing at a distance from the court entertained respecting him we learn from Mrs. Hutchinson's Memoirs. England was no place,—the seventeenth century no time,—for Sporus and Locusta.

This was not all. The most ridiculous weaknesses seemed to meet in the wretched Solomon of Whitehall,—pedantry, buffoonery, garrulity, low curiosity, the most contemptible personal cowardice. Nature and education had done their best to produce a finished specimen of all that a king ought not to be. His awkward figure, his rolling eye, his rickety walk, his nervous tremblings, his slobbering mouth, his broad Scotch accent, were imperfections which might have been found in the best and greatest man. Their effect, however, was to make James and his office objects of contempt, and to dissolve those associations which had been created by the noble bearing of preceding monarchs, and which were in themselves no inconsiderable fence to royalty.

The sovereign whom James most resembled was, we think, Claudius Cæsar. Both had the same feeble and vacillating temper, the same childishness, the same coarseness, the same poltroonery. Both were men of learning; both wrote and spoke,—not indeed well,—but still in a manner in which it seems almost incredible that men so foolish should have written or spoken. The follies and indecencies of James are well described in the words which Suetonius uses respecting Claudius: "Multa talia, etiam privatis deformia, necdum principi, neque infacundo, neque indocto, immo etiam, pertinaciter liberalibus studiis dedito." The description given by Suetonius of the manner in which the Roman prince transacted business exactly suits the Briton. "In cognoscendo ac decernendo mira varietate animi fuit, modo circumspectus et sagax, modo inconsultus ac præceps, nonnumquam frivolus amentique similis." Claudius was ruled successively by two bad women: James successively by two bad men. Even the description of the person of Claudius, which we find in the ancient memoirs, might, in many points, serve for that of James: "Ceterum et ingredientem destituebant poplites minus firmi, et remisse quid vel serio agentem multa dehonestabant, risus indecens, ira turpior, spumante rictu,—præterea linguæ titubantia."

The Parliament which James had called soon after his accession had been refractory. His second Parliament, called in the spring of 1614, had been more refractory still. It had been dissolved after a session of two months; and during six years the king had governed without having recourse to the legislature. During those six years, melancholy and disgraceful events, at home and abroad, had followed one another in rapid succession;—the divorce of Lady Essex, the murder of Overbury, the elevation of Villiers, the pardon of Somerset, the disgrace of Coke, the execution of Raleigh, the battle of Prague, the invasion of the Palatinate by Spinola, the ignominious flight of the son-in-law of the English king, the depression of the Protestant interest all over the Continent. All the extraordinary modes by which James could venture to raise money had been tried. His necessities were greater than ever; and he was compelled to summon the Parliament in which Hampden made his first appearance as a public man.

This Parliament lasted about twelve months. During that time it visited with deserved punishment several of those who during the preceding six years had enriched themselves by peculation and monopoly. Michell, one of the grasping patentees who had purchased of the favourite the power of robbing the nation, was fined and imprisoned for life. Mompesson, the original, it is said, of Massinger's Overreach, was outlawed and deprived of his ill-gotten wealth. Even Sir Edward Villiers, the brother of Buckingham, found it convenient to leave England. A greater name is to be added to the ignominious list. By this Parliament was brought to justice that illustrious philosopher whose memory genius has half redeemed from the infamy due to servility, to ingratitude, and to corruption.

After redressing internal grievances the Commons proceeded to take into consideration the state of Europe. The king flew into a rage with them for meddling with such matters, and, with characteristic judgment, drew them into a controversy about the origin of their House and of its privileges. When he found that he could not convince them, he dissolved them in a passion, and sent some of the leaders of the Opposition to ruminate on his logic in prison.

During the time which elapsed between this dissolution and the meeting of the next Parliament, took place the celebrated negotiation respecting the Infanta. The would-be despot was unmercifully browbeaten. The would-be Solomon was ridiculously overreached. "Steenie," in spite of the begging and sobbing of his dear "dad and gossip," carried off baby Charles in triumph to Madrid. The sweet lads, as James called them, came back safe, but without their errand. The great master of kingcraft, in looking for a Spanish match, had found a Spanish war. In February, 1624, a Parliament met, during the whole sitting of which James was a mere puppet in the hands of his "baby," and of his "poor slave and dog." The Commons were disposed to support the king in the vigorous policy which his son and his favourite urged him to adopt. But they were not disposed to place any confidence in their feeble sovereign and his dissolute courtiers, or to relax in their efforts to remove public grievances. They, therefore, lodged the money which they voted for the war in the hands of Parliamentary Commissioners. They impeached the treasurer, Lord Middlesex, for corruption, and they passed a bill by which patents of monopoly were declared illegal.

Hampden did not, during the reign of James, take any prominent part in public affairs. It is certain, however, that he paid great attention to the details of Parliamentary business, and to the local interests of his own county. It was in a great measure owing to his exertions that Wendover and some other boroughs on which the popular party could depend recovered the elective franchise, in spite of the opposition of the court.

The health of the king had for some time been declining. On the twenty-seventh of March, 1625, he expired. Under his weak rule the spirit of liberty had grown strong, and had become equal to a great contest. The contest was brought on by the policy of his successor. Charles bore no resemblance to his father. He was not a driveller, or a pedant, or a buffoon, or a coward. It would be absurd to deny that he was a scholar and a gentleman, a man of exquisite taste in the fine arts, a man of strict morals in private life. His talents for business were respectable; his demeanour was kingly. But he was false, imperious, obstinate, narrow-minded, ignorant of the temper of his people, unobservant of the signs of his times. The whole principle of his government was resistance to public opinion; nor did he make any real concession to that opinion till it mattered not whether he resisted or conceded,—till the nation, which had long ceased to love him or to trust him, had at last ceased to fear him.

His first Parliament met in June, 1625. Hampden sat in it as burgess for Wendover. The king wished for money. The Commons wished for the redress of grievances. The war, however, could not be carried on without funds. The plan of the Opposition was, it should seem, to dole out supplies by small sums, in order to prevent a speedy dissolution. They gave the king two subsidies only, and proceeded to complain that his ships had been employed against the Huguenots in France, and to petition in behalf of the Puritans who were persecuted in England. The king dissolved them, and raised money by letters under his Privy Seal. The supply fell far short of what he needed; and, in the spring of 1626, he called together another Parliament. In this Parliament Hampden again sat for Wendover.

The Commons resolved to grant a very liberal supply, but to defer the final passing of the act for that purpose till the grievances of the nation should be redressed. The struggle which followed far exceeded in violence any that had yet taken place. The Commons impeached Buckingham. The king threw the managers of the impeachment into prison. The Commons denied the right of the king to levy tonnage and poundage without their consent. The king dissolved them. They put forth a remonstrance. The king circulated a declaration vindicating his measures, and committed some of the most distinguished members of the Opposition to close custody. Money was raised by a forced loan, which was apportioned among the people according to the rate at which they had been respectively assessed to the last subsidy. On this occasion it was that Hampden made his first stand for the fundamental principle of the English Constitution. He positively refused to lend a farthing. He was required to give his reasons. He answered "that he could be content to lend as well as others, but feared to draw upon himself that curse in Magna Charta, which should be read twice a year, against those who infringe it." For this spirited answer the Privy Council committed him close prisoner to the Gate House.

After some time he was again brought up; but he persisted in his refusal, and was sent to a place of confinement in Hampshire.

The government went on, oppressing at home, and blundering in all its measures abroad. A war was foolishly undertaken against France, and more foolishly conducted. Buckingham led an expedition against Rhé, and failed ignominiously. In the meantime soldiers were billeted on the people. Crimes of which ordinary justice should have taken cognisance were punished by martial law. Near eighty gentlemen were imprisoned for refusing to contribute to the forced loan. The lower people who showed any signs of insubordination were pressed into the fleet, or compelled to serve in the army. Money, however, came in slowly; and the king was compelled to summon another Parliament. In the hope of conciliating his subjects, he set at liberty the persons who had been imprisoned for refusing to comply with his unlawful demands. Hampden regained his freedom, and was immediately re-elected burgess for Wendover.

Early in 1628 the Parliament met. During its first session the Commons prevailed on the king, after many delays and much equivocation, to give, in return for five subsidies, his full and solemn assent to that celebrated instrument—the second great charter of the liberties of England,—known by the name of the Petition of Right. By agreeing to this act the king bound himself to raise no taxes without the consent of Parliament, to imprison no man except by legal process, to billet no more soldiers on the people, and to leave the cognisance of offences to the ordinary tribunals.

In the summer this memorable Parliament was prorogued. It met again in January, 1629. Buckingham was no more. That weak, violent, and dissolute adventurer, who, with no talents or acquirements but those of a mere courtier, had, in a great crisis of foreign and domestic politics, ventured on the part of prime minister, had fallen, during the recess of Parliament, by the hand of an assassin. Both before and after his death the war had been feebly and unsuccessfully conducted. The king had continued, in direct violation of the Petition of Right, to raise tonnage and poundage without the consent of Parliament. The troops had again been billeted on the people; and it was clear to the Commons that the five subsidies which they had given as the price of the national liberties had been given in vain.

They met accordingly in no complying humour. They took into their most serious consideration the measures of the government concerning tonnage and poundage. They summoned the officers of the custom-house to their bar. They interrogated the barons of the exchequer. They committed one of the sheriffs of London. Sir John Eliot, a distinguished member of the Opposition, and an intimate friend of Hampden, proposed a resolution condemning the unconstitutional imposition. The Speaker said that the king had commanded him to put no such question to the vote. This decision produced the most violent burst of feeling ever seen within the walls of Parliament. Hayman remonstrated vehemently against the disgraceful language which had been heard from the chair. Eliot dashed the paper which contained his resolution on the floor of the House. Valentine and Hollis held the Speaker down in his seat by main force, and read the motion amidst the loudest shouts. The door was locked—the key was laid on the table. Black Rod knocked for admittance in vain. After passing several strong resolutions, the House adjourned. On the day appointed for its meeting it was dissolved by the king, and several of its most eminent members, among whom were Hollis and Sir John Eliot, were committed to prison.

Though Hampden had as yet taken little part in the debates of the House, he had been a member of many very important committees, and had read and written much concerning the law of Parliament. A manuscript volume of Parliamentary cases, which is still in existence, contains many extracts from his notes.

He now retired to the duties and pleasures of a rural life. During the eleven years which followed the dissolution of the Parliament of 1628, he resided at his seat in one of the most beautiful parts of the county of Buckingham. The house, which has since his time been greatly altered, and which is now, we believe, almost entirely neglected, was then an old English mansion built in the days of the Plantagenets and the Tudors. It stood on the brow of a hill which overlooks a narrow valley. The extensive woods which surround it were pierced by long avenues. One of those avenues the grandfather of the great statesman had cut for the approach of Elizabeth; and the opening, which is still visible for many miles, retains the name of the Queen's Gap. In this delightful retreat Hampden passed several years, performing with great activity all the duties of a landed gentleman and a magistrate, and amusing himself with books and with field sports.

He was not in his retirement unmindful of his persecuted friends. In particular, he kept up a close correspondence with Sir John Eliot, who was confined in the Tower. Lord Nugent has published several of the letters. We may perhaps be fanciful;—but it seems to us that every one of them is an admirable illustration of some part of the character of Hampden which Clarendon has drawn.

Part of the correspondence relates to the two sons of Sir John Eliot. These young men were wild and unsteady; and their father, who was now separated from them, was naturally anxious about their conduct. He at length resolved to send one of them to France, and the other to serve a campaign in the Low Countries. The letter which we subjoin shows that Hampden, though rigorous towards himself, was not uncharitable towards others, and that his puritanism was perfectly compatible with the sentiments and the tastes of an accomplished gentleman. It also illustrates admirably what has been said of him by Clarendon:—"He was of that rare affability and temper in debate, and of that seeming humility and submission of judgment, as if he brought no opinion of his own with him, but a desire of information and instruction. Yet he had so subtle a way of interrogating, and, under cover of doubts, insinuating his objections, that he infused his own opinions into those from whom he pretended to learn and receive them."

The letter runs thus:—"I am so perfectly acquainted with your clear insight into the dispositions of men, and ability to fit them with courses suitable, that, had you bestowed sons of mine as you have done your own, my judgment durst hardly have called it into question, especially when, in laying the design, you have prevented the objections to be made against it. For if Mr. Richard Eliot will, in the intermissions of action, add study to practice and adorn that lively spirit with flowers of contemplation, he will raise our expectations of another Sir Edward Vere, that had this character —all summer in the field, all winter in his study—in whose fall fame makes this kingdom a great loser; and, having taken this resolution from counsel with the highest wisdom, as I doubt not you have, I hope and pray that the same power will crown it with a blessing answerable to your wish. The way you take with my other friend shows you to be none of the Bishop of Exeter's converts;* of whose mind neither am I superstitiously. But had my opinion

* Lord Nugent, we think, has misunderstood this passage. Hampden seems to allude to Bishop Hall's sixth satire, in which the custom of sending young men abroad is censured, and an academic life recommended. We have a general recollection that there is something to the same effect in Hall's prose-work; but have not time to search them.

been asked, I should, as vulgar conceits use me to do, have showed my power rather to raise objections than to answer them. A temper* between France and Oxford, might have taken away his scruples, with more advantage to his years. .... For although he be one of those that, if his age were looked for in no other book but that of the mind, would be found no ward if he should die to-morrow, yet it is a great hazard, methinks, to see so sweet a disposition guarded with no more, amongst a people whereof many make it their religion to be superstitious in impiety, and their behaviour to be affected in ill manners. But God, who only knoweth the periods of life and opportunities to come, hath designed him, I hope, for his own service betime, and stirred up your providence to husband him so early for great affairs. Then shall he be sure to find Him in France that Abraham did in Sechem and Joseph in Egypt, under whose wing alone is perfect safety."

Sir John Eliot employed himself, during his imprisonment, in writing a treatise on government, which he transmitted to his friend. Hampden's criticisms are strikingly characteristic. They are written with all that "flowing courtesy" which is ascribed to him by Clarendon. The objections are insinuated with so much delicacy that they could scarcely gall the most irritable author. We see too how highly Hampden valued in the writings of others that conciseness which was one of the most striking peculiarities of his own eloquence. Sir John Eliot's style was, it seems, too diffuse, and it is impossible not to admire the skill with which this is suggested. "The piece," says Hampden; "is as complete an image of the pattern as can be drawn by lines,—a lively character of a large mind,—the subject, method, and expression, excellent and homogeneal; and, to say the truth, sweetheart, somewhat exceeding my commendations. My words cannot render them to the life. Yet,—to show my ingenuity rather than wit,—would not a less model have given a full representation of that subject,—not by diminution but by contraction of parts? I desire to learn. I dare not say.—The variations upon each particular seem many;—all, I confess, excellent. The fountain was full, the channel narrow; that may be the cause; or that the author resembled Virgil, who made more verses by many than he intended to write. To extract a just number, had I seen all his, I could easily have bid him make fewer; but if he had bade me tell him which he should have spared, I had been posed."

This is evidently the writing not only of a man of good sense and natural good taste, but of a man of literary habits. Of the studies of Hampden little is known. But, as it was at one time in contemplation to give him the charge of the education of the Prince of Wales, it cannot be doubted that his acquirements were considerable. Davila, it is said, was one of his favourite writers. The moderation of Davila's opinions and the perspicuity and manliness of his style could not but recommend him to so judicious a reader. It is not improbable that the parallel between France and England, the Huguenots and the Puritans, had struck the mind of Hampden, and that he already felt within himself powers not unequal to the lofty part of Coligni.

While he was engaged in these pursuits, a heavy domestic calamity fell on him. His wife, who had borne him nine children, died in the summer of 1634. She lies in the parish church of Hampden, close to the manor-house. The tender and energetic language of her epitaph still attests the bitterness of her husband's sorrow, and the consolation which he found in a hope full of immortality.

In the meantime, the aspect of public affairs grew darker and darker. The

---

* A middle course—a compromise.

health of Eliot had sunk under an unlawful imprisonment of several years. The brave sufferer refused to purchase liberty, though liberty would to him have been life, by recognizing the authority which had confined him. In consequence of the representations of his physicians, the severity of restraint was somewhat relaxed. But it was in vain. He languished and expired, a martyr to that good cause for which his friend Hampden was destined to meet a more brilliant, but not a more honourable death.

All the promises of the king were violated without scruple or shame. The Petition of Right, to which he had, in consideration of moneys duly numbered, given a solemn assent, was set at naught. Taxes were raised by the royal authority. Patents of monopoly were granted. The old usages of feudal times were made pretexts for harassing the people with exactions unknown during many years. The Puritans were persecuted with cruelty worthy of the Holy Office. They were forced to fly from the country. They were imprisoned. They were whipped. Their ears were cut off. Their noses were slit. Their cheeks were branded with red-hot iron. But the cruelty of the oppressor could not tire out the fortitude of the victims. The mutilated defenders of liberty again defied the vengeance of the Star Chamber, —came back with undiminished resolution to the place of their glorious infamy, and manfully presented the stumps of their ears to be grubbed out by the hangman's knife. The hardy sect grew up and flourished in spite of everything that seemed likely to stunt it—struck its roots deep into a barren soil, and spread its branches wide to an inclement sky. The multitude thronged round Prynne in the pillory with more respect than they paid to Mainwaring in the pulpit, and treasured up the rags which the blood of Burton had soaked, with a veneration such as mitres and surplices had ceased to inspire.

For the misgovernment of this disastrous period Charles himself is principally responsible. After the death of Buckingham, he seems to have been his own prime minister. He had, however, two counsellors who seconded him, or went beyond him, in intolerance and lawless violence; the one a superstitious driveller, as honest as a vile temper would suffer him to be, the other a man of great valour and capacity, but licentious, faithless, corrupt, and cruel.

Never were faces more strikingly characteristic of the individuals to whom they belonged, than those of Laud and Strafford, as they still remain portrayed by the most skilful hand of that age. The mean forehead, the pinched features, the peering eyes, of the prelate, suit admirably with his disposition. They mark him out as a lower kind of Saint Dominic,—differing from the fierce and gloomy enthusiast who founded the Inquisition, as we might imagine the familiar imp of a spiteful witch to differ from an archangel of darkness. When we read his judgments,—when we read the report which he drew up, setting forth that he had sent some separatists to prison, and imploring the royal aid against others,—we feel a movement of indignation. We turn to his Diary, and we are at once as cool as contempt can make us. There we learn how his picture fell down, and how fearful he was lest the fall should be an omen: how he dreamed that the Duke of Buckingham came to bed to him,—that King James walked past him,—that he saw Thomas Flaxage in green garments, and the Bishop of Worcester with his shoulders wrapped in linen. In the early part of 1627, the sleep of this great ornament of the Church seems to have been much disturbed. On the fifth of January, he saw a merry old man with a wrinkled countenance, named Grove, lying on the ground. On the fourteenth of the same memorable month he saw the Bishop of Lincoln jump on a horse and ride away. A day or two after this he dreamed that he gave the king drink in a silver cup, and that the king refused it, and called for a glass. Then he dreamed that he had turned Papist;—of all his dreams the only one, we suspect, which came through the gate of horn. But of these visions, our favourite is that which, as he has recorded, he enjoyed on the night of Friday, the ninth of February, 1627. "I dreamed," says he, "that I had the scurvy; and that forthwith all my teeth became loose. There was one in especial in my lower jaw, which I could scarcely keep in with my finger till I had called for help." Here was a man to have the superintendence of the opinions of a great nation!

But Wentworth,—who ever names him without thinking of those harsh, dark features, ennobled by their expression into more than the majesty of an antique Jupiter;—of that brow, that eye, that cheek, that lip, wherein, as in a chronicle, are written the events of many stormy and disastrous years,—high enterprise accomplished, frightful dangers braved, power unsparingly exercised, suffering unshrinkingly borne;—of that fixed look, so full of severity, of mournful anxiety, of deep thought, of dauntless resolution, which seems at once to forbode and to defy a terrible fate, as it lowers on us from the living canvas of Vandyke? Even at this day the haughty earl overawes posterity as he overawed his contemporaries, and excites the same interest when arraigned before the tribunal of history which he excited at the bar of the House of Lords. In spite of ourselves, we sometimes feel towards his memory a certain relenting similar to that relenting which his defence, as Sir John Denham tells us, produced in Westminster Hall.

This great, brave, bad man entered the House of Commons at the same time with Hampden and took the same side with Hampden. Both were among the richest and most powerful commoners in the kingdom. Both were equally distinguished by force of character, and by personal courage. Hampden had more judgment and sagacity than Wentworth. But no orator of that time equalled Wentworth in force and brilliancy of expression. In 1626 both these eminent men were committed to prison by the king; Wentworth, who was among the leaders of the Opposition, on account of his parliamentary conduct; Hampden, who had not as yet taken a prominent part in debate, for refusing to pay taxes illegally imposed.

Here their path separated. After the death of Buckingham, the king attempted to seduce some of the chiefs of the Opposition from their party; and Wentworth was among those who yielded to the seduction. He abandoned his associates, and hated them ever after with the deadly hatred of a renegade. High titles and great employments were heaped upon him. He became Earl of Strafford, Lord Lieutenant of Ireland, President of the Council of the North; and he employed all his power for the purpose of crushing those liberties of which he had been the most distinguished champion. His counsels respecting public affairs were fierce and arbitrary. His correspondence with Laud abundantly proves that government without parliaments, government by the sword, was his favourite scheme. He was unwilling even that the course of justice between man and man should be unrestrained by the royal prerogative. He grudged to the Court of King's Bench and Common Pleas even that measure of liberty which the most absolute of the Bourbons allowed to the Parliaments of France.

In Ireland, where he stood in the place of the king, his practice was in strict accordance with his theory. He set up the authority of the executive government over that of the courts of law. He permitted no person to leave the island without his licence. He established vast monopolies for his own private benefit. He imposed taxes arbitrarily. He levied them by military force. Some of his acts are described even by the partial Clarendon as powerful acts,—acts which marked a nature excessively imperious,—acts which caused dislike and terror in sober and dispassionate persons,—high acts of oppression. Upon a most frivolous charge, he obtained a capital sentence from a court-martial against a man of high rank who had given him offence. He debauched the daughter-in-law of the Lord Chancellor of Ireland, and then commanded that nobleman to settle his estate according to the wishes of the lady. The Chancellor refused. The Lord Lieutenant turned him out of office, and threw him into prison. When the violent acts of the Long Parliament are blamed, let it not be forgotten from what a tyranny they rescued the nation.

Among the humbler tools of Charles were Chief Justice Finch and Noy the Attorney-General. Noy had, like Wentworth, supported the cause of liberty in Parliament, and had, like Wentworth, abandoned that cause for the sake of office. He devised, in conjunction with Finch, a scheme of exaction which made the alienation of the people from the throne complete. A writ was issued by the king, commanding the city of London to equip and man ships of war for his service. Similar writs were sent to the towns along the coast. These measures, though they were direct violations of the Petition of Right, had at least some show of precedent in their favour. But, after a time, the government took a step for which no precedent could be pleaded, and sent writs of Ship-money to the inland counties. This was a stretch of power on which Elizabeth herself had not ventured, even at a time when all laws might with propriety have been made to bend to that highest law, the safety of the state. The inland counties had not been required to furnish ships, or money in the room of ships, even when the Armada was approaching our shores. It seemed intolerable that a prince who, by assenting to the Petition of Right, had relinquished the power of levying Ship-money even in the out-ports, should be the first to levy it on parts of the kingdom where it had been unknown under the most absolute of his predecessors.

Clarendon distinctly admits that this tax was intended, not only for the support of the navy, but "for a spring and magazine that should have no bottom, and for an everlasting supply of all occasions." The nation well understood this; and from one end of England to the other the public mind was strongly excited.

Buckinghamshire was assessed at a ship of four hundred and fifty tons, or a sum of four thousand five hundred pounds. The share of the tax which fell to Hampden was very small; so small, indeed, that the sheriff was blamed for setting so wealthy a man at so low a rate. But, though the sum demanded was a trifle, the principle of demand was despotism. Hampden, after consulting the most eminent constitutional lawyers of the time, refused to pay the few shillings at which he was assessed, and determined to incur all the certain expense, and the probable danger, of bringing to a solemn hearing this great controversy between the people and the crown. "Till this time," says Clarendon, "he was rather of reputation in his own country than of public discourse or fame in the kingdom; but then he grew the argument of all tongues, every man inquiring who and what he was that durst, at his own charge, support the liberty and prosperity of the kingdom."

Towards the close of the year 1636, this great cause came on in the Exchequer Chamber before all the judges of England. The leading counsel against the writ was the celebrated Oliver St. John, a man whose temper was melancholy, whose manners were reserved, and who was as yet little known in Westminster Hall, but whose great talents had not escaped the penetrating eye of Hampden. The Attorney-General and Solicitor-General appeared for the Crown.

The arguments of the counsel occupied many days; and the Exchequer Chamber took a considerable time for deliberation. The opinion of the bench was divided. So clear was the law in favour of Hampden that, though the judges held their situations only during the royal pleasure, the majority against him was the least possible. Four of the twelve pronounced in his favour; a fifth took a middle course. The remaining seven gave their voices or the writ.

The only effect of this decision was to make the public indignation stronger and deeper. "The judgment," says Clarendon, "proved of more advantage and credit to the gentleman condemned than to the king's service." The courage which Hampden had shown on this occasion, as the same historian tells us, "raised his reputation to a great height generally throughout the kingdom." Even courtiers and crown-lawyers spoke respectfully of him. "His carriage," says Clarendon, "throughout that agitation, was with that rare temper and modesty, that they who watched him narrowly to find some advantage against his person to make him less resolute in his cause, were compelled to give him a just testimony." But his demeanour, though it impressed Lord Falkland with the deepest respect,—though it drew forth the praises of Solicitor-General Herbert,—only kindled into a fiercer flame the ever-burning hatred of Strafford. That minister, in his letters to Laud, murmured against the lenity with which Hampden was treated. "In good faith," he wrote, "were such men rightly served, they should be whipped into their right wits." Again, he says, "I still wish Mr. Hampden, and others to his likeness, were well whipped into their right senses. And if the rod be so used that it smart not, I am the more sorry."

The person of Hampden was now scarcely safe. His prudence and moderation had hitherto disappointed those who would gladly have had a pretence for sending him to the prison of Eliot. But he knew that the eye of a tyrant was on him. In the year 1637 misgovernment had reached its height. Eight years had passed without a Parliament. The decision of the Exchequer Chamber had placed at the disposal of the Crown the whole property of the English people. About the time at which that decision was pronounced, Prynne, Bastwick, and Burton were mutilated by the sentence of the Star Chamber, and sent to rot in remote dungeons. The estate and the person of every man who had opposed the Court were at its mercy.

Hampden determined to leave England. Beyond the Atlantic Ocean, a few of the persecuted Puritans had formed, in the wilderness of Connecticut, a settlement which has since become a prosperous commonwealth, and which, in spite of the lapse of time, and of the change of government, still retains something of the character given to it by its first founders. Lord Saye and Lord Brooke were the original projectors of this scheme of emigration. Hampden had been early consulted respecting it. He was now, it appears, desirous to withdraw himself beyond the reach of oppressors who, as he probably suspected, and as we know, were bent on punishing his manful resistance to their tyranny. He was accompanied by his kinsman Oliver Cromwell, over whom he possessed great influence, and in whom alone he had discovered, under an exterior appearance of coarseness and extravagance, those great and commanding talents which were afterwards the admiration and the dread of Europe.

The cousins took their passage in a vessel which lay in the Thames, and which was bound for North America. They were actually on board when an order of council appeared, by which the ship was prohibited from sailing. Seven other ships, filled with emigrants, were stopped at the same time.

Hampden and Cromwell remained; and with them remained the Evil Genius of the House of Stuart. The tide of public affairs was even now on the turn. The king had resolved to change the ecclesiastical constitution of Scotland, and to introduce into the public worship of that kingdom ceremonies which the great body of the Scots regarded as popish. This absurd attempt produced first discontents, then riots, and at length open rebellion. A provisional government was established at Edinburgh, and its authority was obeyed throughout the kingdom. This government raised an army, appointed a general, and called a general assembly of the Kirk. The famous instrument called the Covenant was put forth at this time, and was eagerly subscribed by the people.

The beginnings of this formidable insurrection were strangely neglected by the king and his advisers. But towards the close of the year 1638 the danger became pressing. An army was raised, and early in the following spring Charles marched northward at the head of a force sufficient, as it seemed, to reduce the Covenanters to submission.

But Charles acted at this conjuncture as he acted at every important conjuncture throughout his life. After oppressing, threatening, and blustering, he hesitated and failed. He was bold in the wrong place, and timid in the wrong place. He would have shown his wisdom by being afraid before the liturgy was read in St. Giles's church. He put off his fear till he had reached the Scottish border with his troops. Then, after a feeble campaign, he concluded a treaty with the insurgents, and withdrew his army. But the terms of the pacification were not observed. Each party charged the other with foul play. The Scots refused to disarm. The king found great difficulty in re-assembling his forces. His late expedition had drained his treasury. The revenues of the next year had been anticipated. At another time he might have attempted to make up the deficiency by illegal expedients; but such a course would clearly have been dangerous when part of the island was in rebellion. It was necessary to call a Parliament. After eleven years of suffering, the voice of the nation was to be heard once more.

In April, 1640, the Parliament met; and the king had another chance of conciliating his people. The new House of Commons was, beyond all comparison, the least refractory House of Commons that had been known for many years. Indeed, we have never been able to understand how, after so long a period of misgovernment, the representatives of the nation should have shown so moderate and so loyal a disposition. Clarendon speaks with admiration of their dutiful temper. "The house, generally," says he, "was exceedingly disposed to please the king, and to do him service." "It could never be hoped," he observes elsewhere, "that more sober or dispassionate men would ever meet together in that place, or fewer who brought ill purposes with them."

In this Parliament Hampden took his seat as member for Buckinghamshire, and thenceforward, till the day of his death, gave himself up, with scarcely any intermission, to public affairs. He took lodgings in Gray's Inn Lane, near the house occupied by Pym, with whom he lived in habits of the closest intimacy. He was now decidedly the most popular man in England. The Opposition looked to him as their leader, and the servants of the king treated him with marked respect. Charles requested the Parliament to vote an immediate supply, and pledged his word that if they would gratify him in this request, he would afterwards give them time to represent their grievances to him. The grievances under which the nation suffered were so serious, and the royal word had been so shamefully violated, that the Commons could hardly be expected to comply with this request. During the first week of the session, the minutes of the proceedings against Hampden were laid on the table by Oliver St. John, and a committee reported that the case was matter of grievance. The king sent a message to the Commons, offering, if they would vote him twelve subsidies, to give up the prerogative of Ship-money. Many years before, he had received five subsidies in consideration of his assent to the Petition of Right. By assenting to that petition, he had given up the right of levying Ship-money, if he ever possessed it. How he had observed the promises made to his third Parliament, all England knew; and it was not strange that the Commons should be somewhat unwilling to buy from him, over and over again, their own ancient and undoubted inheritance.

His message, however, was not unfavourably received. The Commons were ready to give a large supply; but they were not disposed to give it in exchange for a prerogative of which they altogether denied the existence. If they acceded to the proposal of the king, they recognized the legality of the writs of Ship-money.

Hampden, who was a greater master of parliamentary tactics than any man of his time, saw that this was the prevailing feeling, and availed himself of it with great dexterity. He moved that the question should be put, "Whether the House would consent to the proposition made by the king, as contained in the message." Hyde interfered, and proposed that the question should be divided;—that the sense of the House should be taken merely on the point, "Supply or no supply;" and that the manner and the amount should be left for subsequent consideration.

The majority of the House was for granting a supply, but against granting it in the manner proposed by the king. If the House had divided on Hampden's question, the Court would have sustained a defeat; if on Hyde's, the Court would have gained an apparent victory. Some members called for Hyde's motion,—others for Hampden's. In the midst of the uproar, the secretary of state, Sir Harry Vane, rose and stated that the supply would not be accepted unless it were voted according to the tenor of the message. Vane was supported by Herbert, the solicitor-general. Hyde's motion was, therefore, no further pressed, and the debate on the general question was adjourned till the next day.

On the next day the king came down to the House of Lords, and dissolved the Parliament with an angry speech. His conduct on this occasion has never been defended by any of his apologists. Clarendon condemns it severely. "No man," says he, "could imagine what offence the Commons had given." The offence which they had given is plain. They had, indeed, behaved most temperately and most respectfully. But they had shown a disposition to redress wrongs and to vindicate the laws; and this was enough to make them hateful to a king whom no law could bind, and whose whole government was one system of wrong.

The nation received the intelligence of the dissolution with sorrow and indignation. The only persons to whom this event gave pleasure were those few discerning men who thought that the maladies of the state were beyond the reach of gentle remedies. Oliver St. John's joy was too great for concealment. It lighted up his dark and melancholy features, and made him, for the first time, indiscreetly communicative. He told Hyde that things must be worse before they could be better, and that the dissolved Parliament would never have done all that was necessary. St. John, we think, was in the right. No good could then have been done by any Parliament which did not adopt as its great principle, that no confidence could safely be placed in the king, and that, while he enjoyed more than the shadow of power, the nation would never enjoy more than the shadow of liberty.

As soon as Charles had dismissed the Parliament, he threw several members of the House of Commons into prison. Ship-money was exacted more rigor-

easily than ever; and the mayor and sheriffs of London were prosecuted before the Star Chamber for slackness in levying it. Wentworth, it is said, observed with characteristic insolence and cruelty, that things would never go right till the aldermen were hanged. Large sums were raised by force on those counties in which the troops were quartered. All the wretched shifts of a beggared exchequer were tried. Forced loans were raised. Great quantities of goods were bought on long credit and sold for ready money. A scheme for debasing the currency was under consideration. At length, in August, the king again marched northward.

The Scots advanced into England to meet him. It is by no means improbable that this bold step was taken by the advice of Hampden, and of those with whom he acted; and this has been made matter of grave accusation against the English Opposition. To call in the aid of foreigners in a domestic quarrel is the worst of treasons, it is said, and that the Puritan leaders, by taking this course, showed that they were regardless of the honour and independence of the nation, and anxious only for the success of their own faction. We are utterly unable to see any distinction between the case of the Scotch invasion in 1640 and the case of the Dutch invasion in 1688;—or, rather, we see distinctions which are to the advantage of Hampden and his friends. We believe Charles to have been, beyond all comparison, a worse and more dangerous king than his son. The Dutch were strangers to us,— the Scots a kindred people, speaking the same language, subjects of the same crown, not aliens in the eye of the law. If, indeed, it had been possible that a Scotch army or a Dutch army could have enslaved England, those who persuaded Leslie to cross the Tweed, and those who signed the invitation to the Prince of Orange, would have been traitors to their country. But such a result was out of the question. All that either a Scotch or a Dutch invasion could do was to give the public feeling of England an opportunity to show itself. Both expeditions would have ended in complete and ludicrous discomfiture, had Charles and James been supported by their soldiers and their people. In neither case, therefore, was the independence of England endangered; in both cases her liberties were preserved.

The second campaign of Charles against the Scots was short and ignominious. His soldiers, as soon as they saw the enemy, ran away as English soldiers have never run either before or since. It can scarcely be doubted that their flight was the effect, not of cowardice, but of disaffection. The four northern counties of England were occupied by the Scotch army, and the king retired to York.

The game of tyranny was now up. Charles had risked and lost his last stake. It is impossible to retrace the mortifications and humiliations which this bad man now had to endure, without a feeling of vindictive pleasure. His army was mutinous;—his treasury was empty;—his people clamoured for a Parliament; addresses and petitions against the government were presented. Strafford was for shooting those who presented them by martial law: but the king could not trust the soldiers. A great council of Peers was called at York; but the king could not trust even the Peers. He struggled, he evaded, he hesitated, he tried every shift, rather than again face the representatives of his injured people. At length no shift was left. He made a truce with the Scots, and summoned a Parliament.

The leaders of the popular party had, after the late dissolution, remained in London for the purpose of organizing a scheme of opposition to the Court. They now exerted themselves to the utmost. Hampden, in particular, rode from county to county, exhorting the electors to give their votes to men worthy of their confidence. The great majority of the returns was on the side of the Opposition. Hampden was himself chosen member both for Wendover and Buckinghamshire. He made his election to serve for the county.

On the third of November, 1640,—a day to be long remembered,—met that great Parliament, destined to every extreme of fortune,—to empire and to servitude,—to glory and to contempt;—at one time the sovereign of its sovereign,—at another time the servant of its servants, and the tool of its tools. From the first day of meeting the attendance was great; and the aspect of the members was that of men not disposed to do the work negligently. The dissolution of the late Parliament had convinced most of them that half measures would no longer suffice. Clarendon tells us, that "the same men who, six months before, were observed to be of very moderate tempers, and to wish that gentle remedies might be applied, talked now in another dialect both of kings and persons; and said that they must now be of another temper than they were the last Parliament." The debt of vengeance was swollen by all the usury which had been accumulating during many years; and payment was made to the full.

This memorable crisis called forth parliamentary abilities such as England had never before seen. Among the most distinguished members of the House of Commons were Falkland, Hyde, Digby, young Harry Vane, Oliver St. John, Denzil Hollis, Nathaniel Fiennes. But two men exercised a paramount influence over the legislature and the country,—Pym and Hampden; and by the universal consent of friends and enemies, the first place belonged to Hampden.

On occasions which required set speeches Pym generally took the lead. Hampden very seldom rose till late in a debate. His speaking was of that kind which has, in every age, been held in the highest estimation by English Parliaments,—ready, weighty, perspicuous, condensed. His perception of the feelings of the House was exquisite,—his temper unalterably placid—his manner eminently courteous and gentlemanlike. "Even with those," says Clarendon, "who were able to preserve themselves from his infusions, and who discerned those opinions to be fixed in him with which they could not comply, he always left the character of an ingenious and conscientious person." His talents for business were as remarkable as his talents for debate. "He was," says Clarendon, "of an industry and vigilance not to be tired out or wearied by the most laborious, and of parts not to be imposed upon by the most subtle and sharp." Yet it was rather to his moral than to his intellectual qualities that he was indebted for the vast influence which he possessed. "When this parliament began,"—we again quote Clarendon,—"the eyes of all men were fixed upon him, as their *patriæ pater*, and the pilot that must steer the vessel through the tempests and rocks which threatened it. And I am persuaded his power and interest at that time were greater to do good or hurt than any man's in the kingdom, or than any man of his rank hath had in any time; for his reputation of honesty was universal, and his affections seemed so publicly guided, that no corrupt or private ends could bias them. . . . He was, indeed a very wise man, and of great parts, and possessed with the most absolute spirit of popularity, and the most absolute faculties to govern the people, of any man I ever knew."

It is sufficient to recapitulate shortly the acts of the Long Parliament during its first session. Strafford and Laud were impeached and imprisoned. Strafford was afterwards attainted by bill, and executed. Lord Keeper Finch fled to Holland, Secretary Windebank to France. All those whom the king had, during the last twelve years, employed for the oppression of his people,—from the servile judges who had pronounced in favour of the crown against Hampden, down to the sheriffs who had distrained for Ship-money, and the custom house officers who had levied tonnage and poundage,—were summoned to answer for their conduct. The Star Chamber, the High Commission Court, the Council of York, were abolished. Those unfortunate victims of Laud who, after undergoing ignominious exposure and cruel manglings, had been sent to languish in distant prisons, were set at liberty, and conducted through London in triumphant procession. The king was compelled to give the judges patents for life or during good behaviour. He was deprived of those oppressive powers which were the last relics of the old feudal tenures. The Forest Courts and the Stannary Courts were reformed. It was provided that the Parliament then sitting should not be prorogued or dissolved without its own consent, and that a Parliament should be held at least once every three years.

Many of these measures Lord Clarendon allows to have been most salutary; and few persons will, in our times, deny that, in the laws passed during this session, the good greatly preponderated over the evil. The abolition of those three hateful courts,—the Northern Council, the Star Chamber, and the High Commission, would alone entitle the Long Parliament to the lasting gratitude of Englishmen.

The proceeding against Strafford undoubtedly seems hard to people living in our days. It would probably have seemed merciful and moderate to people living in the sixteenth century. It is curious to compare the trial of Charles's minister with the trial, if it can be so called, of Lord Sudley, in the blessed reign of Edward VI. None of the great reformers of our Church doubted the propriety of passing an act of Parliament for cutting off Lord Sudley's head without a legal conviction. The pious Cranmer voted for that act; the pious Latimer preached for it; the pious Edward returned thanks for it; and all the pious Lords of the council together exhorted their victim to what they were pleased facetiously to call "the quiet and patient suffering of justice."

But it is not necessary to defend the proceedings against Strafford by any such comparison. They are justified, in our opinion, by that which alone justifies capital punishment or any punishment,—by that which alone justifies war,— by the public danger. That there is a certain amount of public danger which will justify a legislature in sentencing a man to death by an *ex post facto* law, few people, we suppose, will deny. Few people, for example, will deny that the French Convention was perfectly justified in placing Robespierre, St. Just, and Couthon *hors la loi* without a trial. This proceeding differed from the proceeding against Strafford only in being much more rapid and violent. Strafford was fully heard. Robespierre was not suffered to defend himself. Was there, then, in the case of Strafford, a danger sufficient to justify an act of attainder? We believe that there was. We believe that the contest in which the Parliament was engaged against the king was a contest for the security of our property,—for the liberty of our persons,—for every thing which makes us to differ from the subjects of Don Miguel. We believe that the cause of the Commons was such as justified them in resisting the king, in raising an army, in sending thousands of brave men to kill and to be killed. An act of attainder is surely not more a departure from the ordinary course of law than a civil war. An act of attainder produces much less suffering than a civil war. We are, therefore, unable to discover on what principle it can be maintained that a cause which justifies a civil war will not justify an act of attainder.

Many specious arguments have been urged against the *ex post facto* law by which Strafford was condemned to death. But all these arguments proceed on the supposition that the crisis was an ordinary crisis. The attainder was, in truth, a revolutionary measure. It was part of a system of resistance which oppression had rendered necessary. It is as unjust to judge of the conduct pursued by the Long Parliament towards Strafford on ordinary principles, as it would have been to indict Fairfax for murder because he cut down a cornet at Naseby. From the day on which the houses met there was a war waged by them against the king,—a war for all that they held dear,—a war carried on at first by means of parliamentary forms,—at last by physical force; and, as in the second stage of that war, so in the first, they were entitled to do many things which, in quiet times, would have been culpable.

We must not omit to mention that those men who were afterwards the most distinguished ornaments of the king's party supported the bill of attainder. It is almost certain that Hyde voted for it. It is quite certain that Falkland both voted and spoke for it. The opinion of Hampden, as far as it can be collected from a very obscure note of one of his speeches, seems to have been that the proceeding by bill was unnecessary, and that it would be a better course to obtain judgment on the impeachment.

During this year the court opened a negotiation with the leaders of the Opposition. The Earl of Bedford was invited to form an administration on popular principles. St. John was made solicitor-general. Hollis was to have been secretary of state, and Pym chancellor of the exchequer. The post of tutor to the Prince of Wales was designed for Hampden. The death of the Earl of Bedford prevented this arrangement from being carried into effect; and it may be doubted whether, even if that nobleman's life had been prolonged, Charles would ever have consented to surround himself with counsellors whom he could not but hate and fear.

Lord Clarendon admits that the conduct of Hampden during this year was mild and temperate,—that he seemed disposed rather to soothe than to excite the public mind, and that, when violent and unreasonable motions were made by his followers, he generally left the House before the division, lest he should seem to give countenance to their extravagance. His temper was moderate. He sincerely loved peace. He felt also great fear lest too precipitate a movement should produce a reaction. The events which took place early in the next session clearly showed that this fear was not unfounded.

During the autumn the Parliament adjourned for a few weeks. Before the recess, Hampden was despatched to Scotland by the House of Commons, nominally as a commissioner, to obtain security for a debt which the Scots had contracted during the late invasion; but in truth that he might keep watch over the king, who had now repaired to Edinburgh, for the purpose of finally adjusting the points of difference which remained between him and his northern subjects. It was the business of Hampden to dissuade the Covenanters from making their peace with the Court, at the expense of the popular party in England.

While the king was in Scotland the Irish rebellion broke out. The suddenness and violence of this terrible explosion excited a strange suspicion in the public mind. The queen was a professed Papist. The king and the Archbishop of Canterbury had not indeed been reconciled to the see of Rome; but they had, while acting towards the Puritan party with the utmost rigour, and speaking of that party with the utmost contempt, shown great tenderness and respect towards the Catholic religion and its professors. In spite of the wishes of successive Parliaments, the Protestant separatists had been cruelly persecuted. And at the same time, in spite of the wishes of those very Parliaments, the laws—the unjust and wicked laws—which were in force against the Papists had not been carried into execution. The Protestant nonconformists had not yet learned toleration in the school of suffering. They reprobated the partial lenity which the government showed towards idolaters, and, with some show of reason, ascribed to bad motives conduct which, in such a king as Charles, and such a prelate as Laud, could not possibly be ascribed to humanity or to liberality of sentiment. The violent Arminianism of the archbishop,—his childish attachment to ceremonies, his superstitious veneration for altars, vestments, and painted windows, his bigoted zeal for the Constitution and the privileges of his order, his known opinions respecting the celibacy of the clergy,—had excited great disgust throughout that large party which was every day becoming more and more hostile to Rome, and more and more inclined to the doctrines and the discipline of Geneva. It was believed by many that the Irish rebellion had been secretly encouraged by the court; and, when the Parliament met again in November, after a short recess, the Puritans were more intractable than ever.

But that which Hampden had feared had come to pass. A reaction had taken place. A large body of moderate and well-meaning men, who had heartily concurred in the strong measures adopted during the preceding year, were inclined to pause. Their opinion was that, during many years, the country had been grievously misgoverned, and that a great reform had been necessary;—but that a great reform had been made,—that the grievances of the nation had been fully redressed,—that sufficient vengeance had been exacted for the past, that sufficient security had been provided for the future,—and that it would, therefore, be both ungrateful and unwise to make any further attacks on the royal prerogative. In support of this opinion many plausible arguments have been used. But to all these arguments there is one short answer.—The king could not be trusted.

At the head of those who may be called the Constitutional Royalists were Falkland, Hyde, and Culpeper. All these eminent men had, during the former year, been in very decided opposition to the court. In some of those very proceedings with which their admirers reproach Hampden, they had taken at least as great a part as Hampden. They had all been concerned in the impeachment of Strafford. They had all, there is reason to believe, voted for the Bill of Attainder. Certainly none of them voted against it. They had all agreed to the act which made the consent of the Parliament necessary to its own dissolution or prorogation. Hyde had been among the most active of those who attacked the Council of York. Falkland had voted for the exclusion of the bishops from the Upper House. They were now inclined to halt in the path of reform, perhaps to retrace a few of their steps.

A direct collision soon took place between the two parties into which the House of Commons, lately at almost perfect unity with itself, was now divided. The opponents of the government moved that celebrated address to the king which is known by the name of the Grand Remonstrance. In this address all the oppressive acts of the preceding fifteen years were set forth with great energy of language; and, in conclusion, the king was entreated to employ no ministers in whom the Parliament could not confide.

The debate on the Remonstrance was long and stormy. It commenced at nine in the morning of the 21st of November, and lasted till after midnight. The division showed that a great change had taken place in the temper of the House. Though many members had retired from exhaustion, three hundred voted; and the Remonstrance was carried by a majority of only nine. A violent debate followed, on the question whether the minority should be allowed to protest against this decision. The excitement was so great that several members were on the point of proceeding to personal violence. "We had sheathed our swords in each other's bowels," says an eyewitness, "had not the sagacity and great calmness of Mr. Hampden, by a short speech, prevented it." The House did not rise till two in the morning.

The situation of the Puritan leaders was now difficult and full of peril. The small majority which they still had might soon become a minority. Out of doors, their supporters in the higher and middle classes were beginning to fall off. There was a growing opinion that the king had been hardly used. The English are always inclined to side with a weak party which is in the wrong, rather than with a strong party which is in the right. Even the idlers in the street will not suffer a man to be struck down. And as it is with a boxing-match, so it is with a political contest. Thus it was that a violent reaction took place in favour of Charles II. against the Whigs in 1681. Thus it was that an equally violent reaction took place in favour of George III. against the coalition in 1784. A similar reaction was beginning to take place during the second year of the Long Parliament. Some members of the Opposition "had resumed," says Clarendon, "their old resolution of leaving the kingdom." Oliver Cromwell openly declared that he and many others would have emigrated if they had been left in a minority on the question of the Remonstrance.

Charles had now a last chance of regaining the affection of his people. If he could have resolved to give his confidence to the leaders of the moderate party in the House of Commons, and to regulate his proceedings by their advice, he might have been, not, indeed, as he had been, a despot, but the powerful and respected king of a free people. The nation might have enjoyed liberty and repose under a government with Falkland at its head, checked by a constitutional Opposition under the conduct of Hampden. It was not necessary that, in order to accomplish this happy end, the king should sacrifice any part of his lawful prerogative, or submit to any conditions inconsistent with his dignity. It was necessary only that he should abstain from treachery, from violence, from gross breaches of the law. This was all that the nation was then disposed to require of him. And even this was too much.

For a short time he seemed inclined to take a wise and temperate course. He resolved to make Falkland secretary of state, and Culpeper chancellor of the exchequer. He declared his intention of conferring in a short time some important office on Hyde. He assured these three persons that he would do nothing relating to the House of Commons without their joint advice, and that he would communicate all his designs to them in the most unreserved manner. This resolution, had he adhered to it, would have averted many years of blood and mourning. But "in very few days," says Clarendon, "he did fatally swerve from it."

On the 3rd of January, 1642, without giving the slightest hint of his intention to those advisers whom he had solemnly promised to consult, he sent down the attorney-general to impeach Lord Kimbolton, Hampden, Pym, Hollis, and two other members of the House of Commons, at the bar of the Lords, on a charge of high treason. It is difficult to find in the whole history of England such an instance of tyranny, perfidy, and folly. The most precious and ancient rights of the subject were violated by this act. The only way in which Hampden and Pym could legally be tried for treason at the suit of the king, was by a petty jury on a bill found by a grand jury. The attorney-general had no right to impeach them. The House of Lords had no right to try them.

The Commons refused to surrender their members. The Peers showed no inclination to usurp the unconstitutional jurisdiction which the king attempted to force on them. A contest began, in which violence and weakness were on the one side, law and resolution on the other. Charles sent an officer to seal up the lodgings and trunks of the accused members. The

Commons sent their sergeant to break the seals. The tyrant resolved to follow up one outrage by another. In making the charge, he had struck at the institution of juries. In executing the arrest, he struck at the privileges of Parliament. He resolved to go to the House in person, with an armed force, and there to seize the leaders of the Opposition, while engaged in the discharge of their parliamentary duties.

What was his purpose? Is it possible to believe that he had no definite purpose,—that he took the most important step of his whole reign without having for one moment considered what might be its effects? Is it possible to believe that he went merely for the purpose of making himself a laughing-stock,—that he intended, if he had found the accused members, and if they had refused, as it was their right and duty to refuse, the submission which he illegally demanded, to leave the House without bringing them away? If we reject both these suppositions, we must believe,—and we certainly do believe,—that he went fully determined to carry his unlawful design into effect by violence; and, if necessary, to shed the blood of the chiefs of the Opposition on the very floor of the Parliament House.

Lady Carlisle conveyed intelligence of the design to Pym. The five members had time to withdraw before the arrival of Charles. They left the House as he was entering New Palace Yard. He was accompanied by about two hundred halberdiers of his guard, and by many gentlemen of the court armed with swords. He walked up Westminster Hall. At the southern door of that vast building his attendants divided to the right and left, and formed a lane to the door of the House of Commons. He knocked,—entered,—darted a look towards the place which Pym usually occupied, and, seeing it empty, walked up to the table. The Speaker fell on his knee. The members rose and uncovered their heads in profound silence, and the king took his seat in the chair. He looked round the House. But the five members were nowhere to be seen. He interrogated the Speaker. The Speaker answered, that he was merely the organ of the House, and had neither eyes to see, nor tongue to speak, but according to their direction. The baffled tyrant muttered a few feeble sentences about his respect for the laws of the realm, [and the privileges of Parliament, and retired. As he passed along the benches, several resolute voices called out audibly—" Privilege ! " He returned to Whitehall with his company of bravoes, who, while he was in the House, had been impatiently waiting in the lobby for the word, cocking their pistols, and crying " Fall on." That night he put forth a proclamation, directing that the posts should be stopped, and that no person should, at his peril, venture to harbour the accused members.

Hampden and his friends had taken refuge in Coleman Street. The city of London was indeed the fastness of public liberty, and was, in those times, a place of at least as much importance as Paris during the French Revolution. The city, properly so called, now consists in a great measure of immense warehouses and counting-houses, which are frequented by traders and their clerks during the day, and left in almost total solitude during the night. It was then closely inhabited by three hundred thousand persons, to whom it was not merely a place of business, but a place of constant residence. This great body had as complete a civil and military organization as if it had been an independent republic. Each citizen had his company; and the companies, which now seem to exist only for the delectation of epicures and of antiquaries, were then formidable brotherhoods, the members of which were almost as closely bound together as the members of a Highland clan. How strong these artificial ties were, the numerous and valuable legacies anciently bequeathed by citizens to their corporations abundantly prove. The municipal offices were filled by the most opulent and respectable merchants of the kingdom. The pomp of the magistracy of the capital was inferior only to that which surrounded the person of the sovereign. The Londoners loved their city with that patriotic love which is found only in small communities, like those of ancient Greece, or like those which arose in Italy during the middle ages. The numbers, the intelligence, the wealth of the citizens, the democratical form of their local government, and their vicinity to the court and to the Parliament, made them one of the most formidable bodies in the kingdom. Even as soldiers they were not to be despised. In an age in which war is a profession, there is something ludicrous in the idea of battalions composed of apprentices and shopkeepers, and officered by aldermen. But, in the early part of the seventeenth century, there was no standing army in the island; and the militia of the metropolis was not inferior in training to the militia of other places. A city which could furnish many thousands of armed men, abounding in natural courage, and not absolutely untinctured with military discipline, was a formidable auxiliary in times of internal dissension. On several occasions during the civil war, the trainbands of London distinguished themselves highly; and at the battle of Newbury, in particular, they repelled the fiery onset of Rupert, and saved the army of the Parliament from destruction.

The people of this great city had long been thoroughly devoted to the national cause. Great numbers of them had signed a protestation in which they declared their resolution to defend the privileges of Parliament. Their enthusiasm had of late begun to cool. But the impeachment of the five members, and the insult offered to the House of Commons, inflamed them to fury. Their houses, their purses, their pikes, were at the command of the Commons. London was in arms all night. The next day the shops were closed; the streets were filled with immense crowds. The multitude pressed round the king's coach, and insulted him with opprobrious cries. The House of Commons, in the meantime, appointed a committee to sit in the city, for the purpose of inquiring into the circumstances of the late outrage. The members of the committee were welcomed by a deputation of the common council. Merchant Tailors' Hall, Goldsmiths' Hall, and Grocers' Hall, were fitted up for their sittings. A guard of respectable citizens, duly relieved twice a day, was posted at their doors. The sheriffs were charged to watch over the safety of the accused members, and to escort them to and from the committee with every mark of honour.

A violent and sudden revulsion of feeling, both in the House and out of it, was the effect of the late proceedings of the king. The Opposition regained in a few hours all the ascendency which it had lost. The Constitutional Royalists were filled with shame and sorrow. They felt that they had been cruelly deceived by Charles. They saw that they were unjustly, but not unreasonably, suspected by the nation. Clarendon distinctly says that they perfectly detested the counsels by which the king had been guided, and were so much displeased and dejected at the unfair manner in which he had treated them that they were inclined to retire from his service. During the debates on the subject they preserved a melancholy silence. To this day the advocate of Charles take care to say as little as they can about his visit to the House of Commons, and, when they cannot avoid mention of it, attribute to infatuation an act which, on any other supposition, they must admit to have been a frightful crime.

The Commons, in a few days, openly defied the king, and ordered the accused members to attend in their places at Westminster and to resume their parliamentary duties. The citizens resolved to bring back the champions of liberty in triumph before the windows of Whitehall. Vast preparations were made by land and water for this great festival.

The king had remained in his palace, humbled, dismayed, and bewildered, "feeling," says Clarendon, "the trouble and agony which usually attend generous and magnanimous minds upon their having committed errors;" feeling, we should say, the despicable repentance which attends the bungling villain who, having attempted to commit a crime, finds that he has only committed a folly. The populace hooted and shouted all day before the gates of the royal residence. The wretched man could not bear to see the triumph of those whom he had destined to the gallows and the quartering-block. On the day preceding that which was fixed for their return, he fled, with a few attendants, from that palace which he was never to see again till he was led through it to the scaffold.

On the 11th of January the Thames was covered with boats, and its shores with the gazing multitude. Armed vessels, decorated with streamers, were ranged in two lines from London Bridge to Westminster Hall. The members returned by water in a ship manned by sailors who had volunteered their services. The trainbands of the city, under the command of the sheriffs, marched along the Strand, attended by a vast crowd of spectators, to guard the avenues to the House of Commons; and thus, with shouts and loud discharges of ordnance, the accused patriots were brought back by the people whom they had served and for whom they had suffered. The restored members, as soon as they had entered the House, expressed, in the warmest terms, their gratitude to the citizens of London. The sheriffs were warmly thanked by the Speaker in the name of the Commons; and orders were given that a guard selected from the trainbands of the city should attend daily to watch over the safety of the Parliament.

The excitement had not been confined to London. When intelligence of the danger to which Hampden was exposed reached Buckinghamshire, it excited the alarm and indignation of the people. Four thousand freeholders of that county, each of them wearing in his hat a copy of the protestation in favour of the privileges of Parliament, rode up to London to defend the person of their beloved representative. They came in a body to assure Parliament of their full resolution to defend its privileges. Their petition was couched in the strongest terms. "In respect," said they, "of that latter attempt upon the honourable House of Commons, we are now come to offer our service to that end, and resolved, in their just defence, to live and die."

A great struggle was clearly at hand. Hampden had returned to Westminster much changed. His influence had hitherto been exerted rather to restrain than to excite the zeal of his party. But the treachery, the contempt of law, the thirst for blood, which the king had now shown, left no hope of a peaceable adjustment. It was clear that Charles must be either a puppet or a tyrant,—that no obligation of love or of honour could bind him,—and that the only way to make him harmless was to make him powerless.

The attack which the king had made on the five members was not merely irregular in manner. Even if the charges had been preferred legally, if the Grand Jury of Middlesex had found a true bill, if the accused persons had been arrested under a proper warrant and at a proper time and place, there would still have been in the proceeding enough of perfidy and injustice to vindicate the strongest measures which the Opposition could take. To impeach Pym and Hampden was to impeach the House of Commons. It was notoriously on account of what they had done as members of that House that they were selected as objects of vengeance; and in what they had done as members of that House the majority had concurred. Most of the charges brought against them were common between them and the Parliament. They were accused, indeed, and it may be with reason, of encouraging the Scotch army to invade England. In doing this they had committed what was, in strictness of law, a high offence,—the same offence which Devonshire and Shrewsbury committed in 1688. But the king had promised pardon and oblivion to those who had been the principals in the Scotch insurrection. Did it then consist with his honour to punish the accessories? He had bestowed marks of his favour on the leading Covenanters. He had given the great seal of Scotland to Lord Louden, the chief of the rebels, a marquisate to the Earl of Argyle, an earldom to Leslie, who had brought the Presbyterian army across the Tweed. On what principle was Hampden to be attainted for advising what Leslie was ennobled for doing? In a court of law, of course, no Englishman could plead an amnesty granted to the Scots. But, though not an illegal, it was surely an inconsistent and a most unkingly course, after pardoning the heads of the rebellion in one kingdom, to hang, draw, and quarter their accomplices in another.

The proceedings of the king against the five members, or rather against that Parliament which had concurred in almost all the acts of the five members, was the cause of the civil war. It was plain that either Charles or the House of Commons must be stripped of all real power in the state. The best course which the Commons could have taken would perhaps have been to depose the king, as their ancestors had deposed Edward II. and Richard II., and as their children afterwards deposed James. Had they done this,—had they placed on the throne a prince whose character and whose situation would have been a pledge for his good conduct, they might safely have left to that prince all the constitutional prerogatives of the Crown, the command of the armies of the state, the power of making peers, the power of appointing ministers, a veto on bills passed by the two Houses. Such a prince, reigning by their choice, would have been under the necessity of acting in conformity with their wishes. But the public mind was not ripe for such a measure. There was no Duke of Lancaster,—no Prince of Orange, —no great and eminent person, near in blood to the throne, yet attached to the cause of the people. Charles was then to remain king; and it was therefore necessary that he should be king only in name. A William III., or a George I., whose title to the crown was identical with the title of the people to their liberty, might safely be trusted with extensive powers. But new freedom could not exist in safety under the old tyrant. Since he was not to be deprived of the name of king, the only course which was left was to make him a mere trustee, nominally seised of prerogatives of which others had the use,—a Grand Lama,—a Roi Fainéant,—a phantom resembling those Dagoberts and Childeberts who wore the badges of royalty, while Ebroin and Charles Martel held the real sovereignty of the state.

The conditions which the Parliament propounded were hard, but, we are sure, not harder than those which even the Tories, in the Convention of 1689, would have imposed on James, if it had been resolved that James should continue to be king. The chief condition was that the command of the militia and the conduct of the war in Ireland should be left to the Parliament. On this point was that great issue joined, whereof the two parties put themselves on God and on the sword.

We think, not only that the Commons were justified in demanding for themselves the power to dispose of the military force, but that it would have been absolute insanity in them to leave that force at the disposal of the king. From the very beginning of his reign it had evidently been his object to govern by an army. His third Parliament had complained, in the Petition of

Right, of his fondness for martial law, and of the vexatious manner in which he billeted his soldiers on the people. The wish nearest the heart of Strafford, was, as his letters prove, that the revenue might be brought into such a state as would enable the king to keep a standing military establishment. In 1640 Charles had supported an army in the northern counties by lawless exactions. In 1641 he had engaged in an intrigue the object of which was to bring that army to London for the purpose of overawing the Parliament. His late conduct had proved that, if he were suffered to retain even a small body-guard of his own creatures near his person, the Commons would be in danger of outrage, perhaps of massacre. The Houses were still deliberating under the protection of the militia of London. Could the command of the whole armed force of the realm have been, under these circumstances, safely confided to the king? Would it not have been frenzy in the Parliament to raise and pay an army of fifteen or twenty thousand men for the Irish war, and to give to Charles the absolute control of this army, and the power of selecting, promoting, and dismissing officers at his pleasure? Was it not probable that this army might become, what it is the nature of armies to become, what so many armies formed under much more favourable circumstances have become, what the army of the English Commonwealth became, what the army of the French Republic became,—an instrument of despotism? Was it not possible that the soldiers might forget that they were also citizens, and might be ready to serve their general against their country? Was it not certain that, on the first day on which Charles could venture to revoke his concessions, and to punish his opponents, he would establish an arbitrary government, and exact a bloody revenge?

Our own times furnish a parallel case. Suppose that a revolution should take place in Spain,—that the constitution of Cadiz should be re-established,—that the Cortes should meet again,—that the Spanish Prynnes and Burtons, who are now wandering in rags round Leicester Square, should be restored to their country,—Ferdinand VII. would, in that case, of course repeat all the oaths and promises which he had made in 1820, and broke in 1823. But would it not be madness in the Cortes, even if they were to leave him the name of king, to leave him more than the name? Would not all Europe scoff at them, if they were to permit him to assemble a large army for an expedition to America, to model that army at his pleasure, to put it under the command of officers chosen by himself? Should we not say that every member of the constitutional party who might concur in such a measure would most richly deserve the fate which he would probably meet,—the fate of Riego and of the Empecinado? We are not disposed to pay compliments to Ferdinand; nor do we perceive that we pay him any compliment when we say that of all sovereigns in history, he seems to us most to resemble, in some very important points, King Charles I. Like Charles, he is pious after a certain fashion; like Charles, he has made large concessions to his people, after a certain fashion. It is well for him that he has had to deal with men who bore very little resemblance to the English Puritans.

The Commons would have the power of the sword; the king would not part with it; and nothing remained but to try the chances of war. Charles still had a strong party in the country. His august office,—his dignified manners,—his solemn protestations that he would for the time to come respect the liberties of his subjects,—pity for fallen greatness,—fear of violent innovation, secured for him many adherents. He had with him the Church, the Universities, a majority of the nobles and of the old landed gentry. The austerity of the Puritan manners drove most of the gay and dissolute youth of that age to the royal standard. Many good, brave, and moderate men, who disliked his former conduct, and who entertained doubts touching his present sincerity, espoused his cause unwillingly, and with many painful misgivings, because, though they dreaded his tyranny much, they dreaded democratic violence more.

On the other side was the great body of the middle orders of England,—the merchants, the shopkeepers, the yeomanry, headed by a very large and formidable minority of the peerage and of the landed gentry. The Earl of Essex, a man of respectable abilities and of some military experience, was appointed to the command of the Parliamentary army.

Hampden spared neither his fortune nor his person in the cause. He subscribed two thousand pounds to the public service. He took a colonel's commission in the army, and went into Buckinghamshire to raise a regiment of infantry. His neighbours eagerly enlisted under his command. His men were known by their green uniform and by their standard, which bore on one side the watchword of the Parliament, "God with us," and on the other the device of Hampden, "Vestigia nulla retrorsum." This motto well described the line of conduct which he pursued. No member of his party had been so temperate, while there remained a hope that legal and peaceable measures might save the country. No member of his party showed so much energy and vigour when it became necessary to appeal to arms. He made himself thoroughly master of his military duty, and "performed it," to use the words of Clarendon, "upon all occasions most punctually." The regiment which he had raised and trained was considered as one of the best in the service of the Parliament. He exposed his person in every action with an intrepidity which made him conspicuous even amongst thousands of brave men. "He was," says Clarendon, "of a personal courage equal to his best parts; so that he was an enemy not to be wished wherever he might have been made a friend, and as much to be apprehended where he was so as any man could deserve to be." Though his military career was short, and his military situation subordinate, he fully proved that he possessed the talents of a great general, as well as those of a great statesman.

We shall not attempt to give a history of the war. Lord Nugent's account of the military operations is very animated and striking. Our abstract would be dull, and probably unintelligible. There was, in fact, for some time no great and connected system of operations on either side. The war of the two parties was like the war of the Arimanes and Oromasdes, neither of whom, according to the Eastern theologians, has any exclusive domain,—who are equally omnipresent,—who equally pervade all space,—who carry on their eternal strife within every particle of matter. There was a petty war in almost every county. A town furnished troops to the Parliament while the manor-house of the neighbouring peer was garrisoned for the king. The combatants were rarely disposed to march far from their own homes. It was reserved for Fairfax and Cromwell to terminate this desultory warfare, by moving one overwhelming force successively against all the scattered fragments of the royal party.

It is a remarkable circumstance that the officers who had studied tactics in what were considered as the best schools,—under Vere in the Netherlands,—and under Gustavus Adolphus in Germany,—displayed far less skill than those commanders who had been bred to peaceful employments, and who never saw even a skirmish till the civil war broke out. An unlearned person might hence be inclined to suspect that the military art is no very profound mystery, that its principles are the principles of plain good sense, and that a quick eye, a cool head, and a stout heart will do more to make a general than all the diagrams of Jomini. This, however, is certain, that

Hampden showed himself a far better officer than Essex, and Cromwell than Leslie.

The military errors of Essex were probably in some degree produced by political timidity. He was honestly, but not warmly, attached to the cause of the Parliament; and next to a great defeat he dreaded a great victory. Hampden, on the other hand, was for vigorous and decisive measures. When he drew the sword, as Clarendon has well said, he threw away the scabbard. He had shown that he knew better than any public man of his time how to value and how to practise moderation. But he knew that the essence of war is violence, and that moderation in war is imbecility. On several occasions, particularly during the operations in the neighbourhood of Brentford, he remonstrated earnestly with Essex. Wherever he commanded separately, the boldness and rapidity of his movements presented a striking contrast to the sluggishness of his superior.

In the Parliament he possessed boundless influence. His employments towards the close of 1642 have been described by Denham in some lines which, though intended to be sarcastic, convey in truth the highest eulogy. Hampden is described in this satire as perpetually passing and repassing between the military station at Windsor and the House of Commons at Westminster,—as overawing the general, and as giving law to that Parliament which knew no other law. It was at this time that he organised that celebrated association of counties, to which his party was principally indebted for its victory over the king.

In the early part of 1643, the shires lying in the neighbourhood of London, which were devoted to the cause of the Parliament, were incessantly annoyed by Rupert and his cavalry. Essex had extended his lines so far that almost every point was vulnerable. The young prince, though not a great general, was an active and enterprising partisan, frequently surprised posts, burnt villages, swept away cattle, and was again at Oxford before a force sufficient to encounter him could be assembled.

The languid proceedings of Essex were loudly condemned by the troops. All the ardent and daring spirits in the parliamentary party were eager to have Hampden at their head. Had his life been prolonged, there is every reason to believe that the supreme command would have been intrusted to him. But it was decreed that, at this conjuncture, England should lose the only man who united perfect disinterestedness to eminent talents,—the only man who, being capable of gaining the victory for her, was incapable of abusing that victory when gained.

In the evening of the seventeenth of June, Rupert darted out of Oxford with his cavalry on a predatory expedition. At three in the morning of the following day, he attacked and dispersed a few parliamentary soldiers who lay at Postcombe. He then flew to Chinnor, burned the village, killed or took all the troops who were posted there, and prepared to hurry back with his booty and his prisoners to Oxford.

Hampden had, on the preceding day, strongly represented to Essex the danger to which this part of the line was exposed. As soon as he received intelligence of Rupert's incursion, he sent off a horseman with a message to the general. The cavaliers, he said, could only return by Chiselhampton Bridge. A force ought to be instantly despatched in that direction for the purpose of intercepting them. In the meantime, he resolved to set out with all the cavalry that he could muster, for the purpose of impeding the march of the enemy till Essex could take measures for cutting off their retreat. A considerable body of horse and dragoons volunteered to follow him. He was not their commander. He did not even belong to their branch of the service,

But "he was," says Clarendon, "second to none but the general himself in the observance and application of all men." On the field of Chalgrove he came up with Rupert. A fierce skirmish ensued. In the first charge, Hampden was struck in the shoulder by two bullets, which broke the bone, and lodged in the body. The troops of the Parliament lost heart and gave way. Rupert, after pursuing them for a short time, hastened to cross the bridge, and made his retreat unmolested to Oxford.

Hampden, with his head drooping, and his hands leaning on his horse's neck, moved feebly out of the battle. The mansion which had been inhabited by his father-in-law, and from which in his youth he had carried home his bride Elizabeth, was in sight. There still remains an affecting tradition that he looked for a moment towards that beloved house, and made an effort to go thither to die. But the enemy lay in that direction. He turned his horse towards Thame, where he arrived almost fainting with agony. The surgeons dressed his wounds. But there was no hope. The pain which he suffered was most excruciating. But he endured it with admirable firmness and resignation. His first care was for his country. He wrote from his bed several letters to London concerning public affairs, and sent a last pressing message to the head-quarters, recommending that the dispersed forces should be concentrated. When his public duties were performed, he calmly prepared himself to die. He was attended by a clergyman of the Church of England, with whom he had lived in habits of intimacy, and by the chaplain of the Buckinghamshire Green-coats, Dr. Spurton, whom Baxter describes as a famous and excellent divine.

A short time before his death the sacrament was administered to him. He declared that, though he disliked the government of the Church of England, he yet agreed with that Church in all essential matters of doctrine. His intellect remained unclouded. When all was nearly over, he lay murmuring faint prayers for himself and for the cause for which he died. "Lord Jesus," he exclaimed, in the moment of his last agony, "receive my soul—O Lord, save my country.—O Lord, be merciful to ——" In that broken ejaculation passed away his noble and fearless spirit.

He was buried in the parish church of Hampden. His soldiers, bareheaded, with reversed arms and muffled drums and colours, escorted his body to the grave, singing, as they marched, that lofty and melancholy psalm in which the fragility of human life is contrasted with the immutability of Him in whose sight a thousand years are but as yesterday when it is passed, and as a watch in the night.

The news of Hampden's death produced as great a consternation in his party, according to Clarendon, as if their whole army had been cut off. The journals of the time amply prove that the Parliament and all its friends were filled with grief and dismay. Lord Nugent has quoted a remarkable passage from the next Weekly Intelligencer. "The loss of Colonel Hampden goeth near the heart of every man that loves the good of the king and country, and makes some conceive little content to be at the army now that he is gone. The memory of this deceased colonel is such, that in no age to come but it will more and more be had in honour and esteem;—a man so religious, and of that prudence, judgment, temper, valour, and integrity, that he hath left few his like behind."

He had indeed left none his like behind him. There still remained, indeed, in his party many acute intellects, many eloquent tongues, many brave and honest hearts. There still remained a rugged and clownish soldier,—half fanatic, half buffoon,—whose talents, discerned as yet only by one penetrating eye, were equal to all the highest duties of the soldier and the prince. But in Hampden, and in Hampden alone, were united all the qualities which, in such a crisis, were necessary to save the State,—the valour and energy of Cromwell, the discernment and eloquence of Vane, the humanity and moderation of Manchester, the stern integrity of Hale, the ardent public spirit of Sydney. Others might possess the qualities which were necessary to save the popular party in the crisis of danger; he alone had both the power and the inclination to restrain its excesses in the hour of triumph. Others could conquer; he alone could reconcile. A heart as bold as his brought up the cuirassiers who turned the tide of battle on Marston Moor. As skilful an eye as his watched the Scotch army descending from the heights over Dunbar. But it was when to the sullen tyranny of Laud and Charles had succeeded the fierce conflict of sects and factions, ambitious of ascendency and burning for revenge, —it was when the vices and ignorance which the old tyranny had generated threatened the new freedom with destruction, that England missed the sobriety, the self-command the perfect soundness of judgment, the perfect rectitude of intention, to which the history of revolutions furnishes no parallel, or furnishes a parallel in Washington alone.

BURGHLEY AND HIS TIMES.

Memoirs of the Life and Administration of the Right Honourable William Cecil Lord Burghley, Secretary of State in the Reign of King Edward VI., and Lord High Treasurer of England in the Reign of Queen Elizabeth. Containing an Historical View of the Times in which he lived, and of the many eminent and illustrious Persons with whom he was connected; with Extracts from his Private and Official Correspondence and other Papers, now first published from the Originals. By the Reverend EDWARD NARES, D.D., *Regius Professor of Modern History in the University of Oxford.* 3 vols. 4to. London: 1828, 1832.

THE work of Dr. Nares has filled us with astonishment similar to that which Captain Lemuel Gulliver felt when first he landed in Brobdingnag, and saw corn as high as the oaks in the New Forest, thimbles as large as buckets, and wrens of the bulk of turkeys. The whole book, and every component part of it, is on a gigantic scale. The title is as long as an ordinary preface. The prefatory matter would furnish out an ordinary book; and the book contains as much reading as an ordinary library. We cannot sum up the merits of the stupendous mass of paper which lies before us better than by saying that it consists of about two thousand closely printed pages, that it occupies fifteen hundred inches cubic measure; and that it weighs sixty pounds avoirdupois. Such a book might, before the deluge, have been considered as light reading by Hilpa and Shalum. But unhappily the life of man is now threescore years and ten; and we cannot but think it somewhat unfair in Doctor Nares to demand from us so large a portion of so short an existence.

Compared with the labour of reading through these volumes, all other labours—the labour of thieves on the treadmill, of children in factories, of negroes in sugar plantations—are an agreeable recreation. There was, it is said, a criminal in Italy, who was suffered to make his choice between Guicciardini and the galleys. He chose the history. But the war of Pisa was too much for him. He changed his mind, and went to the oar. Guicciardini, though certainly not the most amusing of writers, is a Herodotus or a Froissart, when compared with Doctor Nares. It is not merely in bulk, but in specific gravity also, that these memoirs exceed all other human compositions. On every subject which the Professor discusses, he produces three times as many pages as another man; and one of his pages is as tedious as another man's three. His book is swelled to its vast dimensions by endless repetitions, by episodes which have nothing to do with the main action, by quotations from books which are in every circulating library, and by reflections which, when they happen to be just, are so obvious that they must necessarily occur to the mind of every reader. He employs more words in expounding and defending a truism than any other writer would employ in supporting a paradox. Of the rules of historical perspective, he has not the faintest notion. There is neither foreground nor background in his delineation. The wars of Charles V. in Germany are detailed at almost as much length as in Robertson's life of that prince. The troubles of Scotland are related as fully as in M'Crie's Life of John Knox. It would be most unjust to deny that Doctor Nares is a man of great industry and research; but he is so utterly incompetent to arrange the materials which he has collected that he might as well have left them in their original repositories.

Neither the facts which Doctor Nares has discovered, nor the arguments which he urges, will, we apprehend, materially alter the opinion generally entertained by judicious readers of history concerning his hero. Lord Burghley can hardly be called a great man. He was not one of those whose genius and energy change the fate of empires. He was by nature and habit one of those who follow—not one of those who lead. Nothing that is recorded, either of his words or of his actions, indicates intellectual or moral elevation. But his talents, though not brilliant, were of an eminently useful kind; and his principles, though not inflexible, were not more relaxed than those of his associates and competitors. He had a cool temper, a sound judgment, great powers of application, and a constant eye to the main chance. In his youth he was, it seems, fond of practical jokes. Yet even out of these he contrived to extract some pecuniary profit. When he was studying the law at Gray's Inn, he lost all his furniture and books to his companion at the gaming table. He accordingly bored a hole in the wall which separated his chambers from those of his associate, and at midnight bellowed through this passage threats of damnation and calls to repentance in the ears of the victorious gambler, who lay sweating with fear all night, and refunded his winnings on his knees next day. "Many other like merry jests," says his old biographer, "I have heard him tell, too long to be here noted." To the last, Burghley was somewhat jocose; and some of his sportive sayings have been recorded by Bacon. They show much more shrewdness than generosity, and are, indeed, neatly expressed reasons for exacting money rigorously, and for keeping it carefully. It must, however, be acknowledged that he was rigorous and careful for the public advantage as well as for his own. To extol his moral character as Doctor Nares has extolled it is absurd. It would be equally absurd to represent him as a corrupt, rapacious, and bad-hearted man. He paid great attention to the interests of the state, and great attention also to the interest of his own family. He never deserted his friends till it was very inconvenient to stand by them, was an excellent Protestant when it was not very advantageous to be a Papist—recommended a tolerant policy to his mistress as strongly as he could recommend it without hazarding her favour—never put to the rack any person from whom it did not seem probable that useful information might be derived—and was so moderate in his desires that he left only three hundred distinct landed estates, though he might, as his honest servant assures us, have left much more, "if he would have taken money out of the Exchequer for his own use, as many Treasurers have done."

Burghley, like the old Marquis of Winchester, who preceded him in the custody of the White Staff, was of the willow, and not of the oak. He first rose into notice by defending the supremacy of Henry VIII. He was subsequently favoured and promoted by the Duke of Somerset. He not only contrived to escape unhurt when his patron fell, but became an important member of the administration of Northumberland. Doctor Nares assures us over and over again that there could have been nothing base in Cecil's conduct on this occasion; for, says he, Cecil continued to stand well with Cranmer. This, we confess, hardly satisfies us. We are much of the mind of Falstaff's tailor. We must have better assurance for Sir John than Bardolph's. We like not the security.

Through the whole course of that miserable intrigue which was carried on round the dying bed of Edward VI., Cecil so demeaned himself as to avoid, first, the displeasure of Northumberland, and afterwards the displeasure of Mary. He was prudently unwilling to put his hand to the instrument which changed the course of the succession. But the furious Dudley was master of the palace. Cecil, therefore, according to his own account, excused himself from signing as a party, but consented to sign as a witness. It is not easy to describe his dexterous conduct at this most perplexing crisis, in language more appropriate than that which is employed by old Fuller:—"His hand wrote it as secretary of state," says that quaint writer; "but his heart consented not thereto. Yea, he openly opposed it; though at last yielding to the greatness of Northumberland, in an age when it was present drowning not to swim with the stream. But as the philosopher tell us, that though the planets be whirled about daily from east to west, by the motion of the *primum mobile*, yet have they also a contrary proper motion of their own from west to east, which they slowly, though surely, move at their leisure; so Cecil had secret counter-endeavours against the strain of the court herein, and privately advanced his rightful intentions against the foresaid duke's ambition."

This was undoubtedly the most perilous conjuncture of Cecil's life. Wherever there was a safe course, he was safe. But here every course was full of danger. His situation rendered it impossible for him to be neutral. If he acted on either side—if he refused to act at all—he ran a fearful risk. He saw all the difficulties of his position. He sent his money and plate out of London, made over his estates to his son, and carried arms about his person. His best arms, however, were his sagacity and his self-command. The plot in which he had been an unwilling accomplice ended, as it was natural that so odious and absurd a plot should end, in the ruin of its contrivers. In the meantime, Cecil quietly extricated himself, and, having been successively patronised by Henry, by Somerset, and by Northumberland, continued to flourish under the protection of Mary.

He had no aspirations after the crown of martyrdom. He confessed himself, therefore, with great decorum, heard mass in Wimbledon Church at Easter, and, for the better ordering of his spiritual concerns, took a priest into his house. Doctor Nares, whose simplicity passes that of any casuist with whom we are acquainted, vindicates his hero by assuring us that this was not, superstition, but pure unmixed hypocrisy. "That he did in some manner conform, we shall not be able, in the face of existing documents, to deny; while we feel in our own minds abundantly satisfied that, during this very trying reign, he never abandoned the prospect of another revolution in favour of Protestantism." In another place, the Doctor tells us that Cecil went to mass "with no idolatrous intention." Nobody, we believe, ever accused him of idolatrous intentions. The very ground of the charge against him is that he had no idolatrous intentions. Nobody would have blamed him if he had really gone to Wimbledon Church, with the feelings of a good Catholic, to worship the host. Doctor Nares speaks in several places with just severity of the sophistry of the Jesuits, and with just admiration of the incomparable letters of Pascal. It is somewhat strange, therefore, that he should adopt, to the full extent, the jesuitical doctrine of the direction of intentions.

We do not blame Cecil for not choosing to be burnt. The deep stain upon his memory is that, for differences of opinion for which he would risk nothing himself, he, in the day of his power, took away without scruple the lives of others. One of the excuses suggested in these Memoirs for his conforming, during the reign of Mary, to the Church of Rome, is that he may have been of the same mind with those German Protestants who were called Adiaphorists, and who considered the popish rites as matters indifferent. Melancthon was one of those moderate persons, and "appears," says Doctor Nares, "to have gone greater lengths than any imputed to Lord Burghley." We should have thought this not only an excuse, but a complete vindication, if Burghley had been an Adiaphorist for the benefit of others as well as for his own. If the popish rites were matters of so little moment that a good Protestant might lawfully practice them for safety, how could it be just or humane that a Papist should be hanged, drawn, and quartered, for practising them from a sense of duty? Unhappily these non-essentials soon became matters of life and death. Just at the very time at which Burghley attained the highest point of power and favour, an Act of Parliament was passed by which the penalties of high treason were denounced against persons who should do in sincerity what he had done from cowardice.

Early in the reign of Mary, Cecil was employed in a mission scarcely consistent with the character of a zealous Protestant. He was sent to escort the Papal Legate, Cardinal Pole, from Brussels to London. The great body of moderate persons, who cared more for the quiet of the realm than for the controverted points which were in issue between the Churches, seem to have placed their chief hope in the wisdom and humanity of the gentle Cardinal. Cecil, it is clear, cultivated the friendship of Pole with great assiduity, and received great advantage from the Legate's protection.

But the best protection of Cecil, during the gloomy and disastrous reign of Mary, was that which he derived from his own prudence and from his own temper,—a prudence which could never be lulled into carelessness,—a temper which could never be irritated into rashness. The Papists could find no occasion against him. Yet he did not lose the esteem even of those sterner Protestants who had preferred exile to recantation. He attached himself to the persecuted heiress of the throne, and entitled himself to her gratitude and confidence. Yet he continued to receive marks of favour from the Queen. In the House of Commons, he put himself at the head of the party opposed to the Court. Yet, so guarded was his language that, even when some of those who acted with him were imprisoned by the Privy Council, he escaped with impunity.

At length Mary died: Elizabeth succeeded; and Cecil rose at once to greatness. He was sworn in Privy Councillor and Secretary of State to the new sovereign before he left her prison of Hatfield; and he continued to serve her during forty years, without intermission, in the highest employments. His abilities were precisely those which keep men long in power. He belonged to the class of the Walpoles, the Pelhams, and the Liverpools,—not to that of the St. Johns, the Carterets, the Chathams, and the Cannings. If he had been a man of original genius and of a commanding mind, it would have been scarcely possible for him to keep his power or even his head. There was not room in one government for an Elizabeth and a Richelieu. What the haughty daughter of Henry needed, was a moderate, cautious, flexible minister, skilled in the details of business,—competent to advise, but not aspiring to command. And such a minister she found in Burghley. No arts could shake the confidence which she reposed in her old and trusty servant. The courtly graces of Leicester, the brilliant talents and accomplishments of Essex, touched the fancy, perhaps the heart of the woman; but no rival could deprive the Treasurer of the place which he possessed in the favour of the Queen. She sometimes chid him sharply; but he was the man whom she delighted to honour. For Burghley, she forgot her usual parsimony both of wealth and of dignities. For Burghley, she relaxed that severe etiquette to which she was unreasonably attached. Every other person to whom she addressed her speech, or on whom the glance of her eagle eye fell, instantly sank on his knee. For Burghley alone, a chair was set in her presence; and there the old minister, by birth only a plain Lincolnshire esquire, took his ease, while the haughty heirs of the Fitzalans and the De Veres humbled themselves to the dust around him. At length, having survived all his early coadjutors and rivals, he died full of years and honours. His royal mistress visited him on his deathbed, and cheered him with assurances of her affection and esteem; and his power passed, with little diminution, to a son who inherited his abilities, and whose mind had been formed by his counsels.

The life of Burghley was commensurate with one of the most important periods in the history of the world. It exactly measures the time during which the House of Austria held unrivalled superiority and aspired to universal dominion. In the year in which Burghley was born, Charles V. obtained the imperial crown. In the year in which Burghley died, the vast designs which had, during near a century, kept Europe in constant agitation, were buried in the same grave with the proud and sullen Philip.

The life of Burghley was commensurate also with the period during which a great moral revolution was effected,—a revolution the consequences of which were felt, not only in the cabinets of princes, but at half the firesides in Christendom. He was born when the great religious schism was just commencing. He lived to see that schism complete,—and to see a line of demarcation, which, since his death, has been very little altered, strongly drawn between Protestant and Catholic Europe.

The only event of modern times which can be properly compared with the Reformation is the French Revolution, or, to speak more accurately, that great revolution of political feeling which took place in almost every part of the civilised world during the eighteenth century, and which obtained in France its most terrible and signal triumph. Each of these memorable events may be described as a rising up of the human reason against a Caste. The one was a struggle of the laity against the clergy for intellectual liberty; the other was a struggle of the people against the privileged orders for political liberty. In both cases the spirit of innovation was at first encouraged by the class to which it was likely to be most prejudicial. It was under the patronage of Frederic, of Catherine, of Joseph, and of the French nobles, that the philosophy which afterwards threatened all the thrones and aristocracies of Europe with destruction first became formidable. The ardour with which men betook themselves to liberal studies, at the close of the fifteenth and the beginning of the sixteenth century, was zealously encouraged by the heads of that very Church to which liberal studies were destined to be fatal. In both cases, when the explosion came, it came with a violence which appalled and disgusted many of those who had previously been distinguished by the freedom of their opinions. The violence of the democratic party in France made Burke a Tory and Alfieri a courtier. The violence of the chiefs of the German schism made Erasmus a defender of abuses, and turned the author of Utopia into a persecutor. In both cases, the convulsion which had overthrown deeply-seated errors, shook all the principles on which society rests to their very foundations. The minds of men were unsettled. It seemed for a time that all order and morality were about to perish with the prejudices with which they had been long and intimately associated. Frightful cruelties were committed. Immense masses of property were confiscated. Every part of Europe swarmed with exiles. In moody and turbulent spirits zeal soured into malignity, or foamed into madness. From the political agitation of the eighteenth century sprang the Jacobins. From the religious agitation of the sixteenth century sprang the Anabaptists. The partisans of Robespierre robbed and murdered in the name of fraternity and equality. The followers of Kniperdoling robbed and murdered in the name of Christian liberty. The feeling of patriotism was, in many parts of Europe, almost wholly extinguished. All the old maxims of foreign policy were changed. Physical boundaries were superseded by moral boundaries. Nations made war on each other with new arms,—with arms which no fortifications, however strong by nature or by art, could resist,—with arms before which rivers parted like the Jordan, and ramparts fell down like the walls of Jericho. Those arms were opinions, reasons, prejudices. The great masters of fleets and armies were often reduced to confess, like Milton's warlike angel, how hard they found it

"To exclude
Spiritual substance with corporeal bar."

Europe was divided, as Greece had been divided during the period concerning which Thucydides wrote. The conflict was not, as it is in ordinary times, between state and state, but between two omnipresent factions, each of which was in some places dominant and in other places oppressed, but which, openly or covertly, carried on their strife in the bosom of every society. No man asked whether another belonged to the same country with himself, but whether he belonged to the same sect. Party spirit seemed to justify and consecrate acts which, in any other times, would have been considered as the foulest of treasons. The French emigrant saw nothing disgraceful in bringing Austrian and Prussian hussars to Paris. The Irish or Italian democrat saw no impropriety in serving the French Directory against his own native government. So, in the sixteenth century, the fury of theological factions often suspended all national animosities and jealousies. The Spaniards were invited into France by the League; the English were invited into France by the Huguenots.

We by no means intend to underrate or to palliate the crimes and excesses which, during the last generation, were produced by the spirit of democracy. But, when we hear men zealous for the Protestant religion constantly represent the French Revolution as radically and essentially evil on account of those crimes and excesses, we cannot but remember that the deliverance of our ancestors from the house of their spiritual bondage was effected "by plagues and by signs, by wonders and by war." We cannot but remember that, as in the case of the French Revolution, so also in the case of the Reformation, those who rose up against tyranny were themselves deeply tainted with the vices which tyranny engenders. We cannot but remember that libels scarcely less scandalous than those of Hebert, mummeries scarcely less absurd than those of Clootz, and crimes scarcely less atrocious than those of Marat, disgrace the early history of Protestantism. The Reformation is an event long past. That volcano has spent its rage. The wide waste produced by its outbreak is forgotten. The landmarks which were swept away have been replaced. The ruined edifices have been repaired. The lava has covered with a rich incrustation the fields which it once devastated, and, after having turned a garden into a desert, has again turned the desert into a still more beautiful and fruitful garden. The second great eruption is not yet over. The marks of its ravages are still all around us. The ashes are still hot beneath our feet. In some directions, the deluge of fire continues to spread. Yet experience surely entitles us to believe that this explosion, like that which preceded it, will fertilise the soil which it has devastated. Already, in those parts which have suffered most severely, rich cultivation and secure dwellings have begun to appear amidst the waste. The more we read of the history of past ages,—the more we observe the signs of our own times,—the more do we feel our hearts filled and swelled up by a good hope for the future destinies of the human race.

The history of the Reformation in England is full of strange problems. The most prominent and extraordinary phenomenon which it presents to us is the gigantic strength of the government contrasted with the feebleness of the religious parties. During the twelve or thirteen years which followed the death of Henry VIII., the religion of the state was thrice changed. Protestantism was established by Edward; the Catholic Church was restored by Mary; Protestantism was again established by Elizabeth. The faith of the nation seemed to depend on the personal inclinations of the sovereign. Nor was this all. An established church was then, as a matter of course, a persecuting church. Edward persecuted Catholics. Mary persecuted Protestants. Elizabeth persecuted Catholics again. The father of those three sovereigns had enjoyed the pleasure of persecuting both sects at once, and had sent to death, on the same hurdle, the heretic who denied the real presence, and the traitor who denied the royal supremacy. There was nothing in England like that fierce and bloody opposition which, in France, each of the religious factions in its turn offered to the government. We had neither a Coligny nor a Mayenne,—neither a Moncontour nor an Ivry. No English city braved sword and famine for the reformed doctrines with the spirit of Rochelle, or for the Catholic doctrines with the spirit of Paris. Neither sect in England formed a League. Neither sect extorted a recantation from the sovereign. Neither sect could obtain from an adverse sovereign even a toleration. The English Protestants, after several years of domination, sank down with scarcely a struggle under the tyranny of Mary. The Catholics, after having regained and abused their old ascendancy, submitted patiently to the severe rule of Elizabeth. Neither Protestants nor Catholics engaged in any great and well-organized scheme of resistance. A few wild and tumultuous risings,—suppressed as soon as they appeared,—a few dark conspiracies, in which only a small number of desperate men engaged,—such were the utmost efforts made by these two parties to assert the most sacred of human rights, attacked by the most odious tyranny.

The explanation of these circumstances which has generally been given is very simple, but by no means satisfactory. The power of the crown, it is said, was then at its height, and was, in fact, despotic. This solution, we own, seems to us to be no solution at all.

It has long been the fashion,—a fashion introduced by Mr. Hume,—to describe the English monarchy in the sixteenth century as an absolute monarchy. And such undoubtedly it appears to a superficial observer. Elizabeth, it is true, often spoke to her parliaments in language as haughty and imperious as that which the Great Turk would use to his divan. She punished with great severity members of the House of Commons who, in her opinion, carried the freedom of debate too far. She assumed the power of legislating by means of proclamations. She imprisoned her subjects without bringing them to a legal trial. Torture was often employed, in defiance of the laws of England, for the purpose of extorting confessions from those who were shut up in her dungeons. The authority of the Star Chamber and of the Ecclesiastical Commission was at its highest point. Severe restraints were imposed on political and religious discussion. The number of presses were at one time limited. No man could print without a license; and every work had to undergo the scrutiny of the Primate, or the Bishop of London. Persons whose writings were displeasing to the Court were cruelly mutilated, like Stubbs, or put to death, like Penry. Nonconformity was severely punished. The Queen prescribed the exact rule of religious faith and discipline; and whoever departed from that rule, either to the right or to the left, was in danger of severe penalties.

Such was this government. Yet we know that it was loved by the great body of those who lived under it. We know that, during the fierce contests of the sixteenth century, both the hostile parties spoke of the time of Elizabeth as of a golden age. That great queen has now been lying two hundred and thirty years in Henry VII.'s chapel. Yet her memory is still dear to the hearts of a free people.

The truth seems to be that the government of the Tudors was, with a few occasional deviations, a popular government, under the forms of despotism. At first sight, it may seem that the prerogatives of Elizabeth were not less ample than those of Louis XIV., —and her parliaments were as obsequious as his parliaments,—that her warrant had as much authority as his *lettre-de-cachet*. The extravagance with which her courtiers eulogized her personal and mental charms went beyond the adulation of Boileau and Moliere. Louis would have blushed to receive from those who composed the gorgeous circles of Marli and Versailles such outward marks of servitude as the haughty Britoness exacted of all who approached her. But the power of Louis rested on the support of his army. The power of Elizabeth rested solely on the support of her people. Those who say that her power was absolute do not sufficiently consider in what her power consisted. Her power consisted in the willing obedience of her subjects, in their attachment to her person and to her office, in their respect for the old line from which she sprang, in their sense of the general security which they enjoyed under her government. These were the means, and the only means, which she had at her command for carrying her decrees into execution, for resisting foreign enemies, and for crushing domestic treason. There was not a ward in the city,—there was not a hundred in any shire in England, which could not have overpowered the handful of armed men who composed her household. If a hostile sovereign threatened invasion,—if an ambitious noble raised the standard of revolt,— she could have recourse only to the trainbands of her capital and the array of her counties,—to the citizens and yeomen of England, commanded by the merchants and esquires of England.

Thus, when intelligence arrived of the vast preparations which Philip was making for the subjugation of the realm, the first person to whom the government thought of applying for assistance was the Lord Mayor of London. They sent to ask him what force the city would engage to furnish for the defence of the kingdom against the Spaniards. The Mayor and Common Council, in return, desired to know what force the Queen's Highness wished them to furnish. The answer was,—fifteen ships and five thousand men. The Londoners deliberated on the matter, and, two days after, "humbly intreated the council, in sign of their perfect love and loyalty to prince and country, to accept ten thousand men, and thirty ships amply furnished."

People who could give such signs as these of their loyalty were by no means to be misgoverned with impunity. The English in the sixteenth century were, beyond all doubt, a free people. They had not, indeed, the outward show of freedom; but they had the reality. They had not as good a constitution as we have; but they had that without which the best constitution is as useless as the king's proclamation against vice and immorality,—that which, without any constitution, keeps rulers in awe,—force, and the spirit to use it. Parliaments, it is true, were rarely held, and were not very respectfully treated. The great charter was often violated. But the people had a security against gross and systematic misgovernment, far stronger than all the parchment that was ever marked with the sign manual, and than all the wax that was ever pressed by the great seal.

It is a common error in politics to confound means with ends. Constitutions, charters, petitions of right, declarations of right, representative assemblies, electoral colleges, are not good government; nor do they, even when most elaborately constructed, necessarily produce good government. Laws exist in vain for those who have not the courage and the means to defend them. Electors meet in vain where want makes them the slaves of the landlord, or where superstition makes them the slaves of the priest. Representative assemblies sit in vain unless they have at their command, in the last resort, the physical power which is necessary to make their deliberations free, and their votes effectual.

The Irish are better represented in parliament than the Scotch, who indeed are not represented at all. But are the Irish better governed than the Scotch? Surely not. This circumstance has of late been used as an argument against reform. It proves nothing against reform. It proves only this,—that laws have no magical, no supernatural virtue; that laws do not act like Aladdin's lamp or Prince Ahmed's apple; that priestcraft, that ignorance, that the rage of contending factions, may make good institutions useless; that intelligence, sobriety, industry, moral freedom, firm union, may supply in a great measure the defects of the worst representative system. A people whose education and habits are such, that, in every quarter of the world, they rise above the mass of those with whom they mix, as surely as oil rises to the top of water,—a people of such temper and self-government that the wildest popular excesses recorded in their history partake of the gravity of judicial proceedings, and of the solemnity of religious rites,—a people whose national pride and mutual attachment have passed into a proverb,—a people whose high and fierce spirit, so forcibly described in the haughty motto which encircles their thistle, preserved their independence, during a struggle of centuries, from the encroachments of wealthier and more powerful neighbours,—such a people cannot be long oppressed. Any government, however constituted, must respect their wishes and tremble at their discontents. It is indeed most desirable that such a people should exercise a direct influence on the conduct of affairs, and should make their wishes known through constitutional organs. But some influence, direct or indirect, they will assuredly possess. Some organ, constitutional or unconstitutional, they will assuredly find. They will be better governed under a good constitution than under a bad constitution. But they will be better governed under the worst constitutions than some other nations under the best. In any general classification of constitutions, the constitution of Scotland must be reckoned as one of the worst, perhaps as the worst, in Christian Europe. Yet the Scotch are not ill-governed. And the reason is simply that they will not bear to be ill-governed.

In some of the Oriental monarchies, in Afghanistan for example, though there exists nothing which a European publicist would call a Constitution, the sovereign generally governs in conformity with certain rules established for the public benefit; and the sanction of those rules is, that every Afghan approves them, and that every Afghan is a soldier.

The monarchy of England in the sixteenth century was a monarchy of this kind. It is called an absolute monarchy, because little respect was paid by the Tudors to those institutions which we have been accustomed to consider as the sole checks on the power of the sovereign. A modern Englishman can hardly understand how the people can have had any real security for good government under kings who levied benevolences, and chid the House of Commons as they would have chid a pack of dogs. People do not sufficiently consider that, though the legal checks were feeble, the natural checks were strong. There was one great and effectual limitation on the royal authority,—the knowledge that, if the patience of the nation were severely tried, the nation would put forth its strength, and that its strength would be found irresistible. If a large body of Englishmen became thoroughly discontented, instead of presenting requisitions, holding large meetings, passing resolutions, signing petitions, forming associations, and unions, they rose up; they took their halberds and their bows; and, if the sovereign was not sufficiently popular to find among his subjects other halberds and other bows to oppose to the rebels, nothing remained for him but a repetition of the horrible scenes of Berkeley and Pomfret. He had no regular army which could, by its superior arms and its superior skill, overawe or vanquish the sturdy Commons of his realm, abounding in the native hardihood of Englishmen, and trained in the simple discipline of the militia.

It has been said that the Tudors were as absolute as the Cæsars. Never was parallel so unfortunate. The government of the Tudors was the direct opposite to the government of Augustus and his successors. The Cæsars ruled despotically, by means of a great standing army, under the decent forms of a republican constitution. They called themselves citizens. They mixed unceremoniously with other citizens. In theory they were only the elective magistrates of a free commonwealth. Instead of arrogating to themselves despotic power, they acknowledged allegiance to the senate. They were merely the lieutenants to that venerable body. They mixed in debate. They even appeared as advocates before the courts of law. Yet they could safely indulge in the wildest freaks of cruelty and rapacity, while their legions remained faithful. Our Tudors, on the other hand, under the titles and forms of monarchical supremacy, were essentially popular magistrates. They had no means of protecting themselves against the public hatred; and they were, therefore, compelled to court the public favour. To enjoy all the state and all the personal indulgences of absolute power,—to be adored with Oriental prostrations,—to dispose at will of the liberty and even of the life of ministers and courtiers,—this the nation granted to the Tudors. But the condition on which they were suffered to be the tyrants of Whitehall was that they should be the mild and paternal sovereigns of England. They were under the same restraints with regard to their people under which a military despot is placed with regard to his army. They would have found it as dangerous to grind their subjects with cruel taxation as Nero would have found it to leave his prætorians unpaid. Those who immediately surrounded the royal person, and engaged in the hazardous game of ambition, were exposed to the most fearful dangers. Buckingham, Cromwell, Surrey, Sudley, Somerset, Suffolk, Norfolk, Percy, Essex, perished on the scaffold. But in general the country gentlemen hunted and the merchant traded in peace. Even Henry, as cruel as Domitian, but far more politic, contrived, while reeking with the blood of the Lamiæ, to be a favourite with the cobblers.

The Tudors committed very tyrannical acts. But in their ordinary dealings with the people they were not, and could not safely be, tyrants. Some excesses were easily pardoned. For the nation was proud of the high and fiery blood of its magnificent princes, and saw, in many proceedings which a lawyer would even then have condemned, the outbreak of the same noble spirit which so manfully hurled foul scorn at Parma and at Spain. But to this endurance there was a limit. If the government ventured to adopt measures which the people really felt to be oppressive, it was soon compelled to change its course. When Henry VIII. attempted to raise a forced loan of unusual amount by proceedings of unusual rigour, the opposition which he encountered was such as appalled even his stubborn and imperious spirit. The people, we are told, said that, if they were treated thus, "then were it worse than the taxes of France; and England should be bond, and not free." The county of Suffolk rose in arms. The king prudently yielded to an opposition which, if he had persisted, would, in all probability, have taken the form of a general rebellion. Towards the close of the reign of Elizabeth, the people felt themselves aggrieved by the monopolies. The queen, proud and courageous as she was, shrank from a contest with the nation, and, with admirable sagacity, conceded all that her subjects had demanded, while it was yet in her power to concede with dignity and grace.

It cannot be imagined that a people who had in their own hands the means of checking their princes would suffer any prince to impose upon them a religion generally detested. It is absurd to suppose that, if the nation had been decidedly attached to the Protestant faith, Mary could have re-established the Papal supremacy. It is equally absurd to suppose that, if the nation had been zealous for the ancient religion, Elizabeth could have restored the Protestant Church. The truth is, that the people were not disposed to engage in a struggle either for the new or for the old doctrines. Abundance of spirit was shown when it seemed likely that Mary would resume her father's grants of church property, or that she would sacrifice the interests of England to the husband whom she regarded with unmerited tenderness. That queen found that it would be madness to attempt the restoration of the abbey lands. She found that her subjects would never suffer her to make her hereditary kingdom a fief of Castile. On these points she encountered a steady resistance, and was compelled to give way. If she was able to establish the Catholic worship and to persecute those who would not conform to it, it was evidently because the people cared far less for the Protestant religion than for the rights of property and for the independence of the English crown. In plain words, they did not think the difference between the hostile sects worth a struggle. There was undoubtedly a zealous Protestant party and a zealous Catholic party. But both these parties were, we believe, very small. We doubt whether both together made up, at the time of Mary's death, the twentieth part of the nation. The remaining nineteen twentieths halted between the two opinions, and were not disposed to risk a revolution in the government, for the purpose of giving to either of the extreme factions an advantage over the other.

We possess no data which will enable us to compare with exactness the force of the two sects. Mr. Butler asserts that, even at the accession of James I., a majority of the population of England were Catholics. This is pure assertion; and is not only unsupported by evidence, but, we think, completely disproved by the strongest evidence. Dr. Lingard is of opinion that the Catholics were one half of the nation in the middle of the reign of Elizabeth. Richton says that, when Elizabeth came to the throne, the Catholics were two thirds of the nation, and the Protestants only one third. The most judicious and impartial of English historians, Mr. Hallam, is, on the contrary, of opinion that two thirds were Protestants, and only one third Catholics. To us, we must confess, it seems incredible that, if the Protestants were really two to one, they should have borne the government of Mary, or that, if the Catholics were really two to one, they should have borne the government of Elizabeth.

It is absolutely incredible that a sovereign who has no standing army, and whose power rests solely on the loyalty of his subjects, can continue for years to persecute a religion to which the majority of his subjects are sincerely attached. In fact, the Protestants did rise up against one sister, and the Catholics against the other. Those risings clearly showed how small and feeble both the parties were. Both in the one case and in the other the nation ranged itself on the side of the government, and the insurgents were speedily put down and punished. The Kentish gentlemen who took up arms for the reformed doctrines against Mary, and the great Northern Earls who displayed the banner of the Five Wounds against Elizabeth, were alike considered by the great body of their countrymen as wicked disturbers of the public peace.

The account which Cardinal Bentivoglio gave of the state of religion in England well deserves consideration. The zealous Catholics he reckoned at one thirtieth part of the nation. The people who would without the least scruple become Catholics, if the Catholic religion were established, he estimated at four fifths of the nation. We believe this account to have been very near the truth. We believe that the people, whose minds were made up on either side, who were inclined to make any sacrifice or run any risk for either side, were very few. Each side had a few enterprising champions, and a few stout-hearted martyrs; but the nation, undetermined in its opinions and feelings, resigned itself implicitly to the guidance of the government, and lent to the sovereign for the time being an equally ready aid against either of the extreme parties.

We are very far from saying that the English of that generation were irreligious. They held firmly those doctrines which are common to the Catholic and to the Protestant theology. But they had no fixed opinion as to the matters in dispute between the churches. They were in a situation resembling that of those Borderers whom Sir Walter Scott has described with so much spirit,

"Who sought the beeves that made their broth
In England and in Scotland both."

And who

"Nine times outlawed had been
By England's king and Scotland's queen."

They were sometimes Protestants, sometimes Catholics; sometimes half Protestants, half Catholics.

The English had not, for ages, been bigoted papists. In the fourteenth century the first and perhaps the greatest of the reformers, John Wickliffe, had stirred the public mind to its inmost depths. During the same century a scandalous schism in the Catholic Church had diminished in many parts of Europe the reverence in which the Roman Pontiffs were held. It is clear that a hundred years before the time of Luther a great party in this kingdom was eager for a change at least as extensive as that which was subsequently effected by Henry VIII. The House of Commons, in the reign of Henry IV., proposed a confiscation of ecclesiastical property, more sweeping and violent even than that which took place under the administration of Thomas Cromwell; and though defeated in this attempt they succeeded in depriving the clerical order of some of its most oppressive privileges. The splendid conquests of Henry V. turned the attention of the nation from domestic reform. The Council of Constance removed some of the grossest of those scandals which had deprived the Church of the public respect. The authority of that venerable synod propped up the sinking authority of the Popedom. A considerable reaction took place. It cannot, however, be doubted, that there was still some concealed Lollardism in England; or that many who did not absolutely dissent from any doctrine held by the Church of Rome were jealous of the wealth and power enjoyed by her ministers. At the very beginning of the reign of Henry VIII., a struggle took place between the clergy and the courts of law, in which the courts of law remained victorious. One of the bishops, on that occasion, declared that the common people entertained the strongest prejudices against his order, and that a clergyman had no chance of fair play before a lay tribunal. The London juries, he said, entertained such a spite to the Church that they would find Abel guilty of the murder of Cain. This was said a few months before the time when Martin Luther began to preach at Wittenburg against indulgences.

As the Reformation did not find the English bigoted Papists, so neither was it conducted in such a manner as to make them zealous Protestants. It was not under the direction of men like that fiery Saxon who swore that he would go to Worms, though he had to face as many devils as there were tiles on the houses, or like that brave Switzer who was struck down while praying in front of the ranks of Zurich. No preacher of religion had the same power here which Calvin had at Geneva and Knox in Scotland. The government put itself early at the head of the movement, and thus acquired power to regulate, and occasionally to arrest, the movement.

To many persons it appears extraordinary that Henry VIII. should have been able to maintain himself so long in an intermediate position between the Catholic and Protestant parties. Most extraordinary it would indeed be, if we were to suppose that the nation consisted of none but decided Catholics and decided Protestants. The fact is that the great mass of the people was neither Catholic nor Protestant, but was, like its sovereign, midway between the two sects. Henry, in that very part of his conduct which has been represented as most capricious and inconsistent, was probably following a policy far more pleasing to the majority of his subjects than a policy like that of Edward, or a policy like that of Mary, would have been. Down even to the very close of the reign of Elizabeth, the people were in a state somewhat resembling that in which, as Machiavelli says, the inhabitants of the Roman empire were, during the transition from heathenism to Christianity: "sendo la maggior parte di loro incerti a quale Dio dovessero ricorrere." They were generally, we think, favourable to the royal supremacy. They disliked the policy of the Court of Rome. Their spirit rose against the interference of a foreign priest with their national concerns. The bull which pronounced sentence of deposition against Elizabeth, the plots which were formed against her life, the usurpation of her titles by the Queen of Scotland, the hostility of Philip, excited their strongest indignation. The cruelties of Bonner were remembered with disgust. Some parts of the new system,—the use of the English language,—in public worship, and the communion in both kinds, were undoubtedly popular. On the other hand, the early lessons of the nurse and the priest were not forgotten. The ancient ceremonies were long remembered with affectionate reverence. A large portion of the ancient theology lingered to the last in the minds which had been imbued with it in childhood.

The best proof that the religion of the people was of this mixed kind is furnished by the Drama of that age. No man would bring unpopular opinions prominently forward in a play intended for representation. And we may safely conclude, that feelings and opinions which pervade the whole Dramatic Literature of the age, are feelings and opinions of which the men of that generation generally partook.

The greatest and most popular dramatists of the Elizabethan age treat religious subjects in a very remarkable manner. They speak respectfully of the fundamental doctrines of Christianity. But they speak neither like Catholics nor like Protestants, but like persons who are wavering between the two systems, or who have made a system for themselves out of parts selected from both. They seem to hold some of the Romish rites and doctrines in high respect. They treat the vow of celibacy, for example, so tempting,—and, in later times, so common a subject for ribaldry,—with mysterious reverence. The members of a religious order whom they introduce are holy and venerable men. We remember in their plays nothing resembling the coarse ridicule with which the Catholic religion and its ministers were assailed, two generations later, by dramatists who wished to please the multitude. We remember no Friar Dominic,—no Father Foigard,—among the characters drawn by those great poets. The scene at the close of the Knight of Malta might have been written by a fervent Catholic. Massinger shows a great fondness for ecclesiastics of the Romish Church, and has even gone so far as to bring a virtuous and interesting Jesuit on the stage. Ford, in that fine play which it is painful to read and scarcely decent to name, assigns a highly creditable part to the Friar. The partiality of Shakspeare for Friars is well known. In Hamlet, the Ghost complains that he died without extreme unction, and, in defiance of the article which condemns the doctrine of purgatory, declares that he is

"Confined to fast in fires
Till the foul crimes, done in his days of nature,
Are burnt and purged away."

These lines, we suspect, would have raised a tremendous storm in the theatre at any time during the reign of Charles II. They were clearly not written by a zealous Protestant, or for zealous Protestants. Yet the author of King John and Henry VIII. was surely no friend to papal supremacy.

There is, we think, only one solution of the phenomena which we find in the history and in the drama of that age. The religion of the English was a mixed religion, like that of the Samaritan settlers, described in the second book of Kings, who "feared the Lord, and served their graven images;"—like that of the Judaizing Christians who blended the ceremonies and doctrines of the synagogue with those of the church;—like that of the Mexican Indians, who, during many generations after the subjugation of their race, continued to unite with the rites learned from their conquerors the worship of the grotesque idols which had been adored by Montezuma and Guatemozin.

These feelings were not confined to the populace. Elizabeth herself was by no means exempt from them. A crucifix, with wax lights burning round it, stood in her private chapel. She always spoke with disgust and anger of the marriage of priests. "I was in horror," says Archbishop Parker, "to hear such words to come from her mild nature and Christian learned conscience, as she spake concerning God's holy ordinance and institution of matrimony." Burghley prevailed on her to connive at the marriages of churchmen. But she would only connive; and the children sprung from such marriages were illegitimate till the accession of James I.

That which is, as we have said, the great stain on the character of Burghley is also the great stain on the character of Elizabeth. Being herself an Adiaphorist,—having no scruple about conforming to the Romish Church when conformity was necessary to her own safety,—retaining to the last moment of her life a fondness for much of the doctrine and much of the ceremonial of that church,—she yet subjected that church to a persecution even more odious than the persecution with which her sister had harassed the Protestants. We say more odious. For Mary had at least the plea of fanaticism. She did nothing for her religion which she was not prepared to suffer for it. She had held it firmly under persecution. She fully believed it to be essential to salvation. If she burned the bodies of her subjects, it was in order to rescue their souls. Elizabeth had no such pretext. In opinion, she was little more than half a Protestant. She had professed, when it suited her, to be wholly a Catholic. There is an excuse,—a wretched excuse,—for the massacres of Piedmont and the *Autos-da-fe* of Spain. But what can be said in defence of a ruler who is at once indifferent and intolerant?

If the great Queen, whose memory is still held in just veneration by Englishmen, had possessed sufficient virtue and sufficient enlargement of mind to adopt those principles which More, wiser in speculation than in action, had avowed in the preceding generation, and by which the excellent L'Hospital regulated his conduct in her own time, how different would be the colour of the whole history of the last two hundred and fifty years! She had the happiest opportunity ever vouchsafed to any sovereign of establishing perfect freedom of conscience throughout her dominions, without danger to her government, without scandal to any large party among her subjects. The nation, as it was clearly ready to profess either religion, would, beyond all doubt, have been ready to tolerate both. Unhappily for her own glory and for the public peace, she adopted a policy from the effects of which the empire is still suffering. The yoke of the Established Church was pressed down on the people till they could bear it no longer. Then a reaction came. Another reaction followed. To the tyranny of the Establishment succeeded the tumultuous conflict of sects, infuriated by manifold wrongs, and drunk with unwonted freedom. To the conflict of sects succeeded again the cruel domination of one persecuting church. At length oppression put off its most horrible form, and took a milder aspect. The penal laws against dissenters were abolished. But exclusions and disabilities still remained. These exclusions and disabilities, after having generated the most fearful discontents,—after having rendered all government in one part of the kingdom impossible,—after having brought the state to the very brink of ruin, have, in our times, been removed, but, though removed, have left behind them a rankling which may last for many years. It is melancholy to think with what ease Elizabeth might have united all conflicting sects under the shelter of the same impartial laws and the same paternal throne, and thus have placed the nation in the same situation, as far as the rights of conscience are concerned, in which we at last stand, after all the heart-burnings, the persecutions, the conspiracies, the seditions, the revolutions, the judicial murders, the civil wars, of ten generations.

This is the dark side of her character. Yet she surely was a great woman. Of all the sovereigns who exercised a power which was seemingly absolute, but which in fact depended for support on the love and confidence of their subjects, she was by far the most illustrious. It has often been alleged as an excuse for the misgovernment of her successors that they only followed her example,—that precedents might be found in the transactions of her reign for persecuting the Puritans, for levying money without the sanction of the House of Commons, for confining men without bringing them to trial, for interfering with the liberty of parliamentary debate. All this may be true. But it is no good plea for her successors: and for this plain reason, that they were her successors. She governed one generation, they governed another; and between the two generations there was almost as little in common as between the people of two different countries. It was not by looking at the particular measures which Elizabeth had adopted, but by looking at the great general principles of her government, that those who followed her were likely to learn the art of managing untractable subjects. If, instead of searching the records of her reign for precedents which might seem to vindicate the mutilation of Prynne and the imprisonment of Eliot, the Stuarts had attempted to discover the fundamental rules which guided her conduct in all her dealings with her people, they would have perceived that their policy was then most unlike to hers, when to a superficial observer it would have seemed most to resemble hers. Firm, haughty,—sometimes unjust and cruel, in her proceedings towards individuals or towards small parties, —she avoided with care, or retracted with speed, every measure which seemed likely to alienate the great mass of the people. She gained more honour and more love by the manner in which she repaired her errors than she would have gained by never committing errors. If such a man as Charles I. had been in her place when the whole nation was crying out against the monopolies, he would have refused all redress; he would have dissolved the Parliament, and imprisoned the most popular members. He would have called another Parliament. He would have given some vague and delusive promises of relief in return for subsidies. When entreated to fulfil his promises, he would have again dissolved the Parliament, and again imprisoned his leading opponents. The country would have become more agitated than before. The next House of Commons would have been more unmanageable than that which preceded it. The tyrant would have agreed to all that the nation demanded. He would have solemnly ratified an act abolishing monopolies for ever. He would have received a large supply in return for this concession; and within half a year new patents, more oppressive than those which had been cancelled, would have been issued by scores. Such was the policy which brought the heir of a long line of kings, in early youth the darling of his countrymen, to a prison and a scaffold.

Elizabeth, before the House of Commons could address her, took out of their mouths the words which they were about to utter in the name of the nation. Her promises went beyond their desires. Her performance followed close upon her promise. She did not treat the nation as an adverse party— as a party which had an interest opposed to hers—as a party to which she was to grant as few advantages as possible, and from which she was to extort as much money as possible. Her benefits were given, not sold; and when once given, they were never withdrawn. She gave them too with a frankness, an effusion of heart, a princely dignity, a motherly tenderness, which enhanced their value. They were received by the sturdy country gentlemen who had come up to Westminster full of resentment, with tears of joy, and shouts of "God save the Queen." Charles I. gave up half the prerogatives of his crown to the Commons; and the Commons sent him in return the Grand Remonstrance.

We had intended to say something concerning that illustrious group of which Elizabeth is the central figure—that group which the last of the bards saw in vision from the top of Snowdon, encircling the Virgin Queen,

"Many a baron bold,
And gorgeous dames, and statesmen old
In bearded majesty."

We had intended to say something concerning the dexterous Walsingham, the impetuous Oxford, the graceful Sackville, the all-accomplished Sydney;— concerning Essex, the ornament of the court and of the camp, the model of chivalry, the munificent patron of genius, whom great virtues, great courage, great talents, the favour of his sovereign, the love of his countrymen—all that seemed to ensure a happy and glorious life, led to an early and an ignominious death;—concerning Raleigh, the soldier, the sail the orator, the poet, the historian, the philos ourselves sometimes reviewing the Queen's guar a Spanish galleon—then answering the chiefs House of Commons—then again murmuring of near the ears of her Highness's maids of honou the Talmud, or collating Polybius with Livy. something concerning the literature of that s concerning those two incomparable men, the of Philosophers, who have made the Elizabe important era in the history of the human m... Augustus, or of Leo. But subjects so vast require a sp.... we can at present afford. We therefore stop here, fearing that, if we pr...., our article may swell to a bulk exceeding that of all other reviews, as much as Doctor Nares's book exceeds the bulk of all other histories.

WAR OF THE SUCCESSION IN SPAIN.

History of the War of the Succession in Spain. By LORD MAHON. 8vo. London. 1832.

THE days when Miscellanies in Prose and Verse by a Person of Honour, and Romances of M. Scuderi, done into English by a Person of Quality, were attractive to readers and profitable to booksellers, have long gone by. The literary privileges once enjoyed by lords are as obsolete as their right to kill the king's deer on their way to Parliament, or as their old remedy of *scandalum magnatum*. Yet we must acknowledge that, though our political opinions are by no means aristocratical, we always feel kindly disposed toward noble authors. Industry and a taste for intellectual pleasures are peculiarly respectable in those who can afford to be idle, and who have every temptation to be dissipated. It is impossible not to wish success to a man who, finding himself placed, without any exertion or any merit on his part, above the mass of society, voluntarily descends from his eminence in search of distinctions which he may justly call his own.

This is, we think, the second appearance of Lord Mahon in the character of an author. His first book was creditable to him, but was in every respect inferior to the work which now lies before us. He has undoubtedly some of the most valuable qualities of an historian—great diligence in examining authorities—great judgment in weighing testimony—and great impartiality in estimating characters. We are not aware that he has in any instance forgotten the duties belonging to his literary functions in the feelings of a kinsman. He does no more than justice to his ancestor Stanhope; he does full justice to Stanhope's enemies and rivals. His narrative is very perspicuous, and is also entitled to the praise, seldom, we grieve to say, deserved by modern writers, of being very concise. It must be admitted, however, that, with many of the best qualities of a literary veteran, he has some of the faults of a literary novice. He has not yet acquired a great command of words. His style is seldom easy, and is sometimes unpleasantly stiff. He is so bigoted a purist that he transforms the Abbé d'Estrées into an Abbot. We do not like to see French words introduced into English composition; but, after all, the first law of writing, that law to which all other laws are subordinate, is this—that the words employed shall be such as convey to the reader the meaning of the writer. Now an Abbot is the head of a religious house;

principles quite a different sort of person. It is better undoubtedly to use an English word than a French word; but it is better to use a French word than to use an English word.

Lord Mahon is also a little too fond of uttering moral reflections in a style d sententious and oracular. We will give one instance: "Strange as it seems, experience shows that we usually feel far more animosity against those whom we have injured than against those who injure us: and this remark holds good with every degree of intellect, with every class of fortune, with a prince or a peasant, a stripling or an elder, a hero or a prince." This remark might have seemed strange at the court of Nimrod or Chedorlaomer; but it has now been for many generations considered as a truism rather than a paradox. Every boy has written on the thesis "*Odisse quem laseris.*" Scarcely any lines in English Poetry are better known than that vigorous couplet:—

"Forgiveness to the injured does belong:—
But they ne'er pardon who have done the wrong."

The historians and philosophers have quite done with this maxim, and have abandoned it, like other maxims which have lost their gloss, to bad novelists, by whom it will very soon be worn to rags.

It is no more than justice to say that the faults of Lord Mahon's book are precisely the faults which time seldom fails to cure, and that the book, in spite of faults, is a valuable addition to our historical literature.

Whoever wishes to be well acquainted with the morbid anatomy of governments, whoever wishes to know how great states may be made feeble and wretched, should study the history of Spain. The empire of Philip II. was undoubtedly one of the most powerful and splendid that ever existed in the world. In Europe, he ruled Spain, Portugal, the Netherlands on both sides of the Rhine, Franche Comté, Roussillon, the Milanese, and the Two Sicilies. Tuscany, Parma, and the other small states of Italy, were as completely dependent on him as the Nizam and the Rajah of Berar now are on the East India Company. In Asia, the King of Spain was master of the Philippines and of all those rich settlements which the Portuguese had made on the coasts of Malabar and Coromandel, in the Peninsula of Malacca, and in the Spice-islands of the Eastern Archipelago. In America, his dominions extended on each side of the equator into the temperate zone. There is reason to believe that his annual revenue amounted, in the season of his greatest power, to four millions sterling—a sum nearly eight times as large as that which England yielded to Elizabeth. He had a standing army of fifty thousand excellent troops, at a time when England had not a single battalion in constant pay. His ordinary naval force consisted of a hundred and forty galleys. He held, what no other prince in modern times has held, the dominion both of the land and of the sea. During the greater part of his reign, he was supreme on both elements. His soldiers marched up to the capital of France; his ships menaced the shores of England.

It is no exaggeration to say that during several years his power over Europe was greater than even that of Napoleon. The influence of the French conqueror never extended beyond low-water mark. The narrowest strait was to his power what it was of old believed that a running stream was to the sorceries of a witch. While his army entered every metropolis from Moscow to Lisbon, the English fleets blockaded every port from Dantzic to Trieste. Sicily, Sardinia, Majorca, Guernsey, enjoyed security through the whole course of a war which endangered every throne on the Continent. The victorious and imperial nation which had filled its museums with the spoils of Antwerp, of Florence, and of Rome, was suffering painfully from the want of luxuries which use had made necessaries. While pillars and arches were rising to commemorate the French conquests, the conquerors were trying to manufacture coffee out of succory, and sugar out of beetroot. The influence of Philip on the Continent was as great as that of Napoleon. The Emperor of Germany was his kinsman. France, torn by religious dissensions, was never a formidable opponent, and was sometimes a dependent ally. At the same time Spain had what Napoleon desired in vain—ships, colonies, and commerce. She long monopolised the trade of America and of the Indian Ocean. All the gold of the West, and all the spices of the East, were received and distributed by her. During many years of war, her commerce was interrupted only by the predatory enterprises of a few roving privateers. Even after the defeat of the Armada, English statesmen continued to look with great dread on the maritime power of Philip. "The King of Spain," said the Lord Keeper to the two Houses in 1593, "since he hath usurped upon the kingdom of Portugal, hath thereby grown mighty by gaining the East Indies: so as, how great soever he was before, he is now thereby manifestly more great : . . . He keepeth a navy armed to impeach all trade of merchandise from England to Gascoigne and Guienne, which he attempted to do this last vintage ; so as he is now become as a frontier enemy to all the west of England, as well as all the south parts, as Sussex, Hampshire, and the Isle of Wight. Yea, by means of his interest in St. Maloes, a port full of shipping for the war, he is a dangerous neighbour to the Queen's isles of Jersey and Guernsey, ancient possessions of this crown, and never conquered in the greatest wars with France."

The ascendancy which Spain then had in Europe was, in one sense, well deserved. It was an ascendancy which had been gained by unquestioned superiority in all the arts of policy and of war. In the sixteenth century, Italy was not more decidedly the land of the fine arts, Germany was not more decidedly the land of bold theological speculation, than Spain was the land of statesmen and of soldiers. The character which Virgil has ascribed to his countrymen might have been claimed by the grave and haughty chiefs who surrounded the throne of Ferdinand the Catholic and of his immediate successors. That majestic art,—"*premere imperio populos*,"—was not better understood by the Romans in the proudest days of their republic, than by Gonsalvo and Ximenes, Cortes and Alva. The skill of the Spanish diplomatists was renowned throughout Europe. In England the name of Gondomar is still remembered. The sovereign nation was unrivalled both in regular and irregular warfare. The impetuous chivalry of France, the serried phalanx of Switzerland, were alike found wanting when brought face to face with the Spanish infantry. In the wars of the New World, where something different from ordinary strategy was required in the general, and something different from ordinary discipline in the soldier,—where it was every day necessary to meet by some new expedient the varying tactics of a barbarous enemy,—the Spanish adventurers, sprung from the common people, displayed a fertility of resource, and a talent for negotiation and command, to which history scarcely affords a parallel.

The Castilian of those times was to the Italian what the Roman, in the days of the greatness of Rome, was to the Greek. The conqueror had less ingenuity, less taste, less delicacy of perception than the conquered ; but far more pride, firmness, and courage,—a more solemn demeanour, a stronger sense of honour. The one had more subtlety in speculation, the other more energy in action. The vices of the one were those of a coward ;—the vices of the other were those of a tyrant. It may be added that the Spaniard, like the Roman, did not disdain to study the arts and the language of those whom he oppressed. A revolution took place in the literature of Spain, not unlike that revolution which, as Horace tells us, took place in the poetry of Latium : "*Capta ferum victorem cepit.*" The slave took prisoner the enslaver. The old Castilian ballads gave place to sonnets in the style of Petrarch, and to heroic poems in the stanza of Ariosto, as the national songs of Rome were driven out by imitations of Theocritus, and translations from Menander.

In no modern society,—not even in England during the reign of Elizabeth,—has there been so great a number of men eminent at once in literature and in the pursuits of active life, as Spain produced during the sixteenth century. Almost every distinguished writer was also distinguished as a soldier or a politician. Boscan bore arms with high reputation. Garcilaso de Vega, the author of the sweetest and most graceful pastoral poem of modern times, after a short but splendid military career, fell sword in hand at the head of a storming party. Alonzo de Ercilla bore a conspicuous part in that war of Arauco, which he afterwards celebrated in one of the best heroic poems that Spain has produced. Hurtado de Mendoza, whose poems have been compared to those of Horace, and whose charming little novel is evidently the model of Gil Blas, has been handed down to us by history as one of the sternest of those iron proconsuls who were employed by the House of Austria to crush the lingering public spirit of Italy. Lope sailed in the Armada; Cervantes was wounded at Lepanto.

It is curious to consider with how much awe our ancestors in those times regarded a Spaniard. He was, in their apprehension, a kind of demon, horribly malevolent, but withal most sagacious and powerful. "They be verye wyse and politicke," says an honest Englishman, in a memorial addressed to Mary, "and can, thorowe ther wysdome, reform and brydell ther owne natures for a tyme, and applye ther conditions to the maners of those men with whom they meddell gladlye by friendshippe; whose mischievous maners a man shall never knowe untyll he come under ther subjection : but then shall he parfectlye parceyve and fele them : which thynge I praye God England never do; for in dissimulations untyll they have ther purposes, and afterwards in oppression and tyrannye, when they can obtayne them, they do exceed all other nations upon the earthe." This is just such language as Arminius would have used about the Romans, or as an Indian statesman of our times might use about the English. It is the language of a man burning with hatred, but cowed by those whom he hates; and painfully sensible of their superiority, not only in power, but in intelligence.

But how art thou fallen from heaven, O Lucifer, son of the morning! How art thou cut down to the ground, that didst weaken the nations! If we overleap a hundred years, and look at Spain towards the close of the seventeenth century, what a change do we find! The contrast is as great as that which the Rome of Gallienus and Honorius presents to the Rome of Marius and Cæsar. Foreign conquest had begun to eat into every part of that gigantic monarchy on which the sun never set. Holland was gone, and Portugal, and Artois, and Roussillon, and Franche Comté. In the East, the empire founded by the Dutch far surpassed in wealth and splendour that which the old tyrants still retained. In the West, England had seized, and still held, settlements in the midst of the Mexican sea. The mere loss of territory was, however, of little moment. The reluctant obedience of distant provinces generally costs more than it is worth.

Empires which branch out widely are often more flourishing for a little timely pruning. Adrian acted judiciously when he abandoned the conquests of Trajan, and England was never so rich, so great, so formidable to foreign princes, so absolutely mistress of the sea, as since the loss of her American colonies. The Spanish empire was still, in outward appearance, great and magnificent. The European dominions subject to the last feeble Prince of the House of Austria were far more extensive than those of Louis XIV. The American dependencies of the Castilian crown still extended to the north of Cancer and to the south of Capricorn. But within this immense body there was an incurable decay, an utter want of tone, an utter prostration of strength. An ingenious and diligent population, eminently skilled in arts and manufactures, had been driven into exile by stupid and remorseless bigots. The glory of the Spanish pencil had departed with Velasquez and Murillo. The splendid age of Spanish literature had closed with Solis and Calderon. During the seventeenth century many states had formed great military establishments. But the Spanish army, so formidable under the command of Alva and Farnese, had dwindled away to a few thousand men, ill paid and ill disciplined. England, Holland, and France had great navies. But the Spanish navy was scarcely equal to the tenth part of that mighty force which, in the time of Philip II., had been the terror of the Atlantic and the Mediterranean. The arsenals were deserted. The magazines were unprovided. The frontier fortresses were ungarrisoned. The police were utterly inefficient for the protection of the people. Murders were committed in the face of day with perfect impunity. Bravoes and discarded serving-men, with swords at their sides, swaggered every day through the most public streets and squares of the capital, disturbing the public peace, and setting at defiance the ministers of justice. The finances were in frightful disorder. The people paid much. The Government received little. The American viceroys and the farmers of the revenue became rich, while the merchants broke—while the peasantry starved—while the body-servants of the sovereign remained unpaid—while the soldiers of the royal guard repaired daily to the doors of convents, and battled there with the crowd of beggars for a porringer of broth and a morsel of bread. Every remedy which was tried aggravated the disease. The currency was altered; and this frantic measure produced its never-failing effects. It destroyed all credit, and increased the misery which it was intended to relieve. The American gold, to use the words of Ortiz, was to the necessities of the state but as a drop of water to the lips of a man raging with thirst. Heaps of unopened despatches accumulated in the offices, while the ministers were concerting with bedchamber-women and Jesuits the means of tripping up each other. Every foreign power could plunder and insult with impunity the heir of Charles the Fifth. Into such a state had the mighty kingdom of Spain fallen, while one of its smallest dependencies—a country not so large as the province of Estremadura or Andalusia, situated under an inclement sky, and preserved only by artificial means from the inroads of the ocean—had become a power of the first class, and treated on terms of equality with the courts of London and Versailles.

The manner in which Lord Mahon explains the financial situation of Spain by no means satisfies us. "It will be found," says he, "that those individuals deriving their chief income from mines, whose yearly produce is uncertain and varying, and seems rather to spring from fortune than to follow industry, are usually careless, unthrifty, and irregular in their expenditure. The example of Spain might tempt us to apply the same remark to states." Lord Mahon would find it difficult, we suspect, to make out his analogy. Nothing could be more uncertain and varying than the gains and losses of those who were in the habit of putting into the state lotteries. But no part of the public income was more certain than that which was derived from the lotteries. We believe that this case is very similar to that of the American mines. Some veins of ore exceeded expectation; some fell below it. Some of the private speculators drew blanks, and others gained prizes. But the revenue of the state depended, not on any particular vein, but on the whole annual produce of two great continents. This annual produce seems to have been almost constantly on the increase during the seventeenth century. The Mexican mines were, through the reigns of Philip IV. and Charles II., in a steady course of improvement; and in South America, though the district of Potosi was not so productive as formerly, other places more than made up for the deficiency. We very much doubt whether Lord Mahon can prove that the income which the Spanish government derived from the mines of America fluctuated more than the income derived from the internal taxes of Spain itself.

All the causes of the decay of Spain resolve themselves into one cause, bad government. The valour, the intelligence, the energy which, at the close of the fifteenth and the beginning of the sixteenth century, had made the Spaniards the first nation in the world, were the fruits of the old institutions of Castile and Arragon, institutions eminently favourable to public liberty. These institutions the first Princes of the House of Austria attacked and almost wholly destroyed. Their successors expiated the crime. The effect of a change from good government to bad government is not fully felt for some time after the change has taken place. The talents and the virtues which a good constitution generates may for a time survive that constitution. Thus the reigns of princes who have established absolute monarchy on the ruins of popular forms of government often shine in history with a peculiar brilliancy. But when a generation or two has passed away, then comes signally to pass that which was written by Montesquieu,—that despotic governments resemble those savages who cut down the tree in order to get at the fruit. During the first years of tyranny, is reaped the harvest sown during the last years of liberty. Thus the Augustan age was rich in great minds formed in the generation of Cicero and Cæsar. The fruits of the policy of Augustus were reserved for posterity. Philip II. was the heir of the Cortes and of the Justiza Mayor; and they left him a nation which seemed able to conquer all the world. What Philip left to his successors is well known.

The shock which the great religious schism of the sixteenth century gave to Europe, was scarcely felt in Spain. In England, Germany, Holland, France, Denmark, Switzerland, Sweden, that shock had produced, with some temporary evil, much durable good. The principles of the Reformation had triumphed in some of those countries. The Catholic Church had maintained its ascendency in others. But though the event had not been the same in all, all had been agitated by the conflict. Even in France, in Southern Germany, and in the Catholic cantons of Switzerland, the public mind had been stirred to its inmost depths. The hold of ancient prejudice had been somewhat loosened. The Church of Rome, warned by the danger which she had narrowly escaped, had, in those parts of her dominion, assumed a milder and more liberal character. She sometimes condescended to submit her high pretensions to the scrutiny of reason, and availed herself more sparingly than in former times of the aid of the secular arm. Even when persecution was employed, it was not persecution in the worst and most frightful shape. The severities of Louis XIV., odious as they were, cannot be compared with those which, at the first dawn of the Reformation, had been inflicted on the heretics in many parts of Europe.

The only effect which the Reformation had produced in Spain had been to make the Inquisition more vigilant and the commonalty more bigoted. The times of refreshing came to all neighbouring countries. One people alone remained, like the fleece of the Hebrew warrior, dry in the midst of that benignant and fertilising dew. While other nations were putting away childish things, the Spaniard still thought as a child and understood as a child. Among the men of the seventeenth century, he was the man of the fifteenth century or of a still darker period,—delighted to behold an Auto-da-fe, and ready to volunteer on a Crusade.

The evils produced by a bad government and a bad religion seemed to have attained their greatest height during the last years of the seventeenth century While the kingdom was in this deplorable state, the King was hastening to an early grave. His days had been few and evil. He had been unfortunate in all his wars, in every part of his internal administration, and in all his domestic relations. His first wife, whom he tenderly loved, died very young. His second wife exercised great influence over him, but seems to have been regarded by him rather with fear than with love. He was childish; and his constitution was so completely shattered that, at little more than thirty years of age, he had given up all hopes of posterity. His mind was even more distempered than his body. He was sometimes sunk in listless melancholy, and sometimes harassed by the wildest and most extravagant fancies. He was not, however, wholly destitute of the feelings which became his station. His sufferings were aggravated by the thought that his own dissolution might not improbably be followed by the dissolution of his empire.

Several princes laid claim to the succession. The King's eldest sister had married Louis XIV. The Dauphin would, therefore, in the common course of inheritance, have succeeded to the crown. But the Infanta had, at the time of her espousals, solemnly renounced, in her own name, and in that of her posterity, all claim to the succession. This renunciation had been confirmed in due form by the Cortes. A younger sister of the King had been the first wife of Leopold, Emperor of Germany. She too had at her marriage renounced her claims to the Spanish crown; but the Cortes had not sanctioned the renunciation, and it was therefore considered as invalid by the Spanish jurists. The fruit of this marriage was a daughter, who had espoused the Elector of Bavaria. The Electoral Prince of Bavaria inherited her claim to the throne of Spain. The Emperor Leopold was son of a daughter of Philip III., and was therefore first cousin to Charles. No renunciation whatever had been exacted from his mother at the time of her marriage.

The question was certainly very complicated. That claim which, according to the ordinary rules of inheritance, was the strongest, had been barred by a contract executed in the most binding form. The claim of the Electoral Prince of Bavaria was weaker. But so also was the contract which bound him not to prosecute his claim. The only party against whom no instrument of renunciation could be produced was the party who, in respect of blood, had the weakest claim of all.

As it was clear that great alarm would be excited throughout Europe if either the Emperor or the Dauphin should become King of Spain, each of those Princes offered to waive his pretensions in favour of his second son;— the Emperor, in favour of the Archduke Charles; the Dauphin, in favour of Philip Duke of Anjou.

Soon after the peace of Ryswick, William III. and Louis XIV. determined to settle the question of the succession without consulting either Charles or the Emperor. France, England, and Holland, became parties to a treaty by which it was stipulated that the Electoral Prince of Bavaria should succeed to Spain, the Indies, and the Netherlands. The imperial family was to be bought off with the Milanese; and the Dauphin was to have the Two Sicilies.

The great object of the King of Spain and of all his counsellors was to avert the dismemberment of the monarchy. In the hope of attaining this end, Charles determined to name a successor. A will was accordingly framed by

K

which the crown was bequeathed to the Bavarian Prince. Unhappily, this will had scarcely been signed when the Prince died. The question was again unsettled, and presented greater difficulties than before.

A new Treaty of Partition was concluded between France, England, and Holland. It was agreed that Spain, the Indies, and the Netherlands, should descend to the Archduke Charles. In return for this great concession made by the Bourbons to a rival house, it was agreed that France should have the Milanese, or an equivalent in a more commodious situation,—if possible, the Province of Lorraine.

Arbuthnot, some years later, ridiculed the Partition Treaty with exquisite humour and ingenuity. Everybody must remember his description of the paroxysm of rage into which poor old Lord Strutt fell, on hearing that his runaway servant Nick Frog, his clothier John Bull, and his old enemy Louis Baboon, had come with quadrants, poles, and inkhorns, to survey his estate, and to draw his will for him. Lord Mahon speaks of this arrangement with grave severity. He calls it, "an iniquitous compact, concluded without the slightest reference to the welfare of the states so readily parcelled and allotted; insulting to the pride of Spain, and tending to strip that country of its hard-won conquests." The most serious part of this charge would apply to half the treaties which have been concluded in Europe, quite as strongly as to the Partition Treaty. What regard was shown in the treaty of the Pyrenees to the welfare of the people of Dunkirk and Roussillon,—in the treaty of Nimeguen to the welfare of the people of Franche Comté,—in the treaty of Utrecht to the welfare of the people of Flanders,—in the treaty of 1735 to the welfare of the people of Tuscany? All Europe remembers, and our latest posterity will, we fear, have reason to remember how coolly, at the last great pacification of Christendom, the people of Poland, of Norway, of Belgium, and of Lombardy, were allotted to masters whom they abhorred. The statesmen who negotiated the Partition Treaty were not so far beyond their age and ours in wisdom and virtue as to trouble themselves much about the happiness of the people whom they were apportioning among foreign masters. But it will be difficult to prove that the stipulations which Lord Mahon condemns were in any respect unfavourable to the happiness of those who were to be transferred to new rulers. The Neapolitans would certainly have lost nothing by being given to the Dauphin, or to the Great Turk. Addison, who visited Naples about the time at which the Partition Treaty was signed, has left us a frightful description of the misgovernment under which that part of the Spanish Empire groaned. As to the people of Lorraine, a union with France would have been the happiest event which could have befallen them. Louis was already their sovereign for all purposes of cruelty and exaction. He had kept their country during many years in his own hands. At the peace of Ryswick, indeed, their Duke had been allowed to return. But the conditions which had been imposed on him made him a mere vassal of France.

We cannot admit that the Treaty of Partition was objectionable because it "tended to strip Spain of hard-won conquests." The inheritance was so vast, and the claimants so mighty, that without some dismemberment it was scarcely possible to make a peaceable arrangement. If any dismemberment was to take place, the best way of effecting it surely was to separate from the monarchy those nations which were at a great distance from Spain,—which were not Spanish in manners, in language, or in feelings,—which were both worse governed and less valuable than the old provinces of Castile and Arragon, and which, having always been governed by foreigners, would not be likely to feel acutely the humiliation of being turned over from one master to another.

That England and Holland had a right to interfere is plain. The question of the Spanish succession was not an internal question, but a European question. And this Lord Mahon admits. He thinks that, when the evil had been done, and a French Prince was reigning at the Escurial, England and Holland were justified in attempting, not merely to strip Spain of its remote dependencies, but to conquer Spain itself:—that they were justified in attempting to put, not merely the passive Flemings and Italians, but the reluctant Castilians and Asturians, under the dominion of a stranger. The danger against which the Partition Treaty was intended to guard was precisely the same danger which afterwards was made the ground of war. It will be difficult to prove that a danger which was sufficient to justify the war was insufficient to justify the provisions of the treaty. If, as Lord Mahon contends, it was better that Spain should be subjugated by main force than that she should be governed by a Bourbon, it was surely better that she should be deprived of Lombardy and the Milanese than that she should be governed by a Bourbon.

Whether the treaty was judiciously framed is quite another question. We disapprove of the stipulations. But we disapprove of them, not because we think them bad, but because we think that there was no chance of their being executed. Louis was the most faithless of politicians. He hated the Dutch. He hated the Government which the Revolution had established in England. He had every disposition to quarrel with his new allies. It was quite certain that he would not observe his engagements, if it should be for his interest to violate them. Even if it should be for his interest to observe them, it might well be doubted whether the strongest and clearest interest would induce a man so haughty and self-willed to co-operate heartily with two governments which had always been the objects of his scorn and aversion.

When intelligence of the second Partition Treaty arrived at Madrid it roused to momentary energy the languishing ruler of a languishing state. The Spanish ambassador at the court of London was directed to remonstrate with the government of William; and his remonstrances were so insolent that he was commanded to leave England. Charles retaliated by dismissing the English and Dutch ambassadors. The French King, though the chief author of the Partition Treaty, succeeded in turning the whole wrath of Charles and of the Spanish people from himself, and in directing it against the two maritime powers. Those powers had now no agent at Madrid. Their perfidious ally was at liberty to carry on his intrigues unchecked; and he fully availed himself of this advantage.

A long contest was maintained with varying success by the factions which surrounded the miserable King. On the side of the Imperial family was the Queen, herself a Princess of that family; with her were allied the confessor of the King, and most of the ministers. On the other side were two of the most dexterous politicians of that age, Cardinal Porto Carrero, Archbishop of Toledo, and Harcourt, the ambassador of Louis.

Harcourt was a noble specimen of the French aristocracy in the days of its highest splendour,—a finished gentleman, a brave soldier, and a skilful diplomatist. His courteous and insinuating manners,—his Parisian vivacity, tempered with Castilian gravity,—made him the favourite of the whole court. He became intimate with the grandees. He caressed the clergy. He dazzled the multitude by his magnificent style of living. The prejudices which the people of Madrid had conceived against the French character,—the vindictive feelings generated during centuries of national rivalry,—gradually yielded to his arts; while the Austrian ambassador, a surly, pompous, niggardly German, made himself and his country more and more unpopular every day.

Harcourt won over the court and the city; Porto Carrero managed the King. Never were knave and dupe better suited to each other. Charles was sick, nervous, and extravagantly superstitious. Porto Carrero had learned in the exercise of his profession the art of exciting and soothing such minds; and he employed that art with the calm and demure cruelty which is the characteristic of wicked and ambitious priests.

He first supplanted the confessor. The state of the poor King during the conflict between his two spiritual advisers was horrible. At one time he was induced to believe that his malady was the same with that of the wretches described in the New Testament, who dwelt among the tombs, whom no chains could bind and whom no man dared to approach. At another time a sorceress who lived in the mountains of the Asturias was consulted about his malady. Several persons were accused of having bewitched him. Porto Carrero recommended the appalling rite of exorcism, which was actually performed. The ceremony made the poor King more nervous and miserable than ever. But it served the turn of the Cardinal, who, after much secret trickery, succeeded in casting out, not the devil, but the confessor.

The next object was to get rid of the ministers. Madrid was supplied with provisions by a monopoly. The government looked after this most delicate concern as it looked after everything else. The partisans of the House of Bourbon took advantage of the negligence of the administration. On a sudden the supply of food failed. Exorbitant prices were demanded. The people rose. The royal residence was surrounded by an immense multitude. The Queen harangued them. The priests exhibited the Host. All was in vain. It was necessary to awaken the King from his uneasy sleep, and to carry him to the balcony. There a solemn promise was given that the unpopular advisers of the crown should be forthwith dismissed. The mob left the palace and proceeded to pull down the houses of the ministers. The adherents of the Austrian line were thus driven from power, and the government was intrusted to the creatures of Porto Carrero. The King left the city in which he had suffered so cruel an insult for the magnificent retreat of the Escurial. Here his hypochondriac fancy took a new turn. Like his ancestor, Charles V., he was haunted by a strange curiosity to pry into the secrets of that grave to which he was hastening. In the cemetery which Philip II. had formed beneath the pavement of the church of St. Lawrence reposed three generations of Castilian princes. Into these vaults the unhappy monarch descended by torchlight, and penetrated to that superb and gloomy chamber where, round the great black crucifix, were ranged the coffins of the kings and queens of Spain. There he commanded his attendants to open the massy chests of bronze in which the relics of his predecessors decayed. He looked on the ghastly spectacle with little emotion till the coffin of his first wife was unclosed, and she appeared before him—such was the skill of the embalmer—in all her well-remembered beauty. He cast one glance on those beloved features, unseen for eighteen years, those features over which corruption seemed to have no power, and rushed from the vault, exclaiming, "She is with God ; and I shall soon be with her." The awful sight completed the ruin of his body and mind. The Escurial became hateful to him; and he hastened to Aranjuez. But the shades and waters of that delicious island-garden, so fondly celebrated in the sparkling verse of Calderon, brought no solace to their unfortunate master. Having tried medicine, exercise, and amusement in vain, he returned to Madrid to die.

He was now beset on every side by the bold and skilful agents of the House of Bourbon. The leading politicians of his court assured him that Louis, and Louis alone, was sufficiently powerful to preserve the Spanish monarchy undivided, and that Austria would be utterly unable to prevent the Treaty of Partition from being carried into effect. Some celebrated lawyers gave it as their opinion that the act of renunciation executed by the late Queen of France ought to be construed according to the spirit, and not according to the letter. The letter undoubtedly excluded the French princes. The spirit was merely this,—that ample security should be taken against the union of the French and Spanish crowns on one head.

In all probability, neither political nor legal reasonings would have sufficed to overcome the partiality which Charles felt for the House of Austria. There had always been a close connection between the two great royal lines which sprang from the marriage of Philip and Juana. Both had always regarded the French as their natural enemies. It was necessary to have recourse to religious terrors; and Porto Carrero employed those terrors with true professional skill. The King's life was drawing to a close. Would the most Catholic prince commit a great sin on the brink of the grave? And what could be a greater sin than, from an unreasonable attachment to a family name, from an unchristian antipathy to a rival house, to set aside the rightful heir of an immense heritage? The tender conscience and the feeble intellect of Charles were strongly wrought upon by these appeals. At length Porto Carrero ventured on a master-stroke. He advised Charles to apply for counsel to the Pope. The King, who, in the simplicity of his heart, considered the successor of St. Peter as an infallible guide in spiritual matters, adopted the suggestion; and Porto Carrero, who knew that his holiness was a mere tool of France, awaited with perfect confidence the result of the application. In the answer which arrived from Rome the King was solemnly reminded of the great account which he was soon to render, and cautioned against the flagrant injustice which he was tempted to commit. He was assured that the right was with the house of Bourbon, and reminded that his own salvation ought to be dearer to him than the house of Austria. Yet he still continued irresolute. His attachment to his family, his aversion to France, were not to be overcome even by Papal authority. At length he thought himself actually dying, when the Cardinal redoubled his efforts. Divine after divine, well tutored for the occasion, was brought to the bed of the trembling penitent. He was dying in the commission of known sin. He was defrauding his relatives. He was bequeathing civil war to his people. He yielded, and signed that memorable testament, the cause of many calamities to Europe. As he affixed his name to the instrument, he burst into tears. "God," he said, "gives kingdoms and takes them away. I am already one of the dead."

The will was kept secret during the short remainder of his life. On the 3rd of November, 1700, he expired. All Madrid crowded to the Palace. The gates were thronged. The antechamber was filled with ambassadors and grandees, eager to learn what dispositions the deceased sovereign had made. At length the folding-doors were flung open. The Duke of Abrantes came forth, and announced that the whole Spanish monarchy was bequeathed to Philip, Duke of Anjou. Charles had directed that, during the interval which might elapse between his death and the arrival of his successor, the government should be administered by a council, of which Porto Carrero was the chief member.

Louis acted as the English ministers might have guessed that he would act. With scarcely the show of hesitation, he broke through all the obligations of the Partition Treaty, and accepted for his grandson the splendid legacy of Charles. The new sovereign hastened to take possession of his dominions. The whole court of France accompanied him to Sceaux. His brothers escorted him to that frontier which, as they weakly imagined, was to be a frontier no longer. "The Pyrenees," said Louis, "have ceased to exist." Those very Pyrenees, a few years later, were the theatre of a war between the heir of Louis and the prince whom France was now sending to govern Spain.

If Charles had ransacked Europe to find a successor whose moral and intellectual character resembled his own, he could not have chosen better. Philip was not so sickly as his predecessor, but he was quite as weak, as indolent, and as superstitious; he very soon became quite as hypochondriacal and eccentric, and he was even more uxorious. He was, indeed, a husband of ten thousand. His first object when he became King of Spain was to procure a wife. From the day of his marriage to the day of her death his first object was to have her near him, and to do what she wished. As soon as his wife died his first object was to procure another. Another was found, as unlike the former as possible. But she was a wife;—and Philip was content. Neither by day nor by night, neither in sickness nor in health, neither in time of business nor in time of relaxation, did he ever suffer her to be absent from him for half an hour. His mind was naturally feeble; and he had received an enfeebling education. He had been brought up amidst the dull magnificence of Versailles. His grandfather was as imperious and as ostentatious in his intercourse with the royal family as in public acts. All those who grew up immediately under the eye of Louis had the manners of persons who had never known what it was to be at ease. They were all taciturn, shy, and awkward. In all of them, except the Duke of Burgundy, the evil went further than the manners. The Dauphin, the Duke of Berri, Philip of Anjou were men of insignificant characters. They had no energy, no force of will. They had been so little accustomed to judge or to act for themselves that implicit dependence had become necessary to their comfort. The new King of Spain, emancipated from control, resembled that wretched German captive who, when the irons which he had worn for years were knocked off, fell prostrate on the floor of his prison. The restraints which had enfeebled the mind of the young Prince were required to support it. Till he had a wife he could do nothing; and when he had a wife he did whatever she chose.

While this lounging, moping boy was on his way to Madrid, his grandfather was all activity. Louis had no reason to fear a contest with the Empire single-handed. He made vigorous preparations to encounter Leopold. He overawed the States-General by means of a great army. He attempted to soothe the English government by fair professions. William was not deceived. He fully returned the hatred of Louis; and, if he had been free to act according to his own inclinations, he would have declared war as soon as the contents of the will were known. But he was bound by constitutional restraints. Both his person and his measures were unpopular in England. His secluded life and his cold manners disgusted a people accustomed to the graceful affability of Charles II. His foreign accent and his foreign attachments were offensive to the national prejudices. His reign had been a season of distress, following a season of rapidly increasing prosperity. The burdens of the late war and the expense of restoring the currency had been severely felt. Nine clergymen out of ten were Jacobites at heart, and had sworn allegiance to the new dynasty only in order to save their benefices. A large proportion of the country gentlemen belonged to the same party. The whole body of agricultural proprietors was hostile to that interest which the creation of the national debt had brought into notice, and which was believed to be peculiarly favoured by the court—the moneyed interest. The middle classes were fully determined to keep out James and his family. But they regarded William only as the less of two evils; and, as long as there was no imminent danger of a counter-revolution, were disposed to thwart and mortify the sovereign, by whom they were, nevertheless, ready to stand, in case of necessity, with their lives and fortunes. They were sullen and dissatisfied. "There was," as Somers expressed it in a remarkable letter to William, "a deadness and want of spirit in the nation universally."

Everything in England was going on as Louis could have wished. The leaders of the Whig party had retired from power, and were extremely unpopular, on account of the unfortunate issue of the Partition Treaty. The Tories, some of whom still cast a lingering look towards St. Germain's, were in office, and had a decided majority in the House of Commons. William was so much embarrassed by the state of parties in England that he could not venture to make war on the House of Bourbon. He was suffering under a complication of severe and incurable diseases. There was every reason to believe that a few months would dissolve the fragile tie which bound up that feeble body with that ardent and unconquerable soul. If Louis could succeed in preserving peace for a short time, it was probable that all his vast designs would be securely accomplished. Just at this crisis, the most important crisis of his life, his pride and his passions hurried him into an error which undid all that forty years of victory and intrigue had done,—which produced the dismemberment of the kingdom of his grandson, and brought invasion, bankruptcy, and famine on his own.

James II. died at St. Germain's. Louis paid him a farewell visit, and was so much moved by the solemn parting, and by the grief of the exiled Queen, that, losing sight of all considerations of policy, and actuated, as it should seem, merely by compassion and a not ungenerous vanity, he acknowledged the Prince of Wales as King of England.

The indignation which the Castilians had felt when they heard that three foreign powers had undertaken to regulate the Spanish succession was nothing to the rage with which the English learned that their good neighbour had taken the trouble to provide them with a king. Whigs and Tories joined in condemning the proceedings of the French court. The cry for war was raised by the city of London, and echoed and re-echoed from every corner of the realm. William saw that his time was come. Though his wasted and suffering body could hardly move without support, his spirit was as energetic and resolute as when, at twenty-three, he bade defiance to the combined forces of England and France. He left the Hague, where he had been engaged in negotiating with the States and the Emperor a defensive treaty against the ambitious designs of the Bourbons. He flew to London. He remodelled the Ministry. He dissolved the Parliament. The majority of the new House of Commons was with the King; and the most vigorous preparations were made for war.

Before the commencement of active hostilities William was no more. But the Grand Alliance of the European princes against the Bourbons was already constructed. "The master workman died," says Mr. Burke; "but the work was formed on true mechanical principles, and it was as truly wrought." On the 15th of May, 1702, war was proclaimed by concert at Vienna, at London, and at the Hague.

Thus commenced that great struggle by which Europe, from the Vistula to the Atlantic Ocean, was agitated during twelve years. The two hostile coalitions were, in respect of territory, wealth, and population, not unequally matched. On the one side were France, Spain, and Bavaria; on the other, England, Holland, the Empire, and a crowd of inferior Powers.

That part of the war which Lord Mahon has undertaken to relate, though not the least important, is certainly the least attractive. In Italy, in Germany, and in the Netherlands, great means were at the disposal of great generals. Mighty battles were fought. Fortress after fortress was subdued. The iron chain of the Belgian strongholds was broken. By a regular and connected series of operations extending through several years, the French were driven back from the Danube and the Po into their own provinces. The war in Spain, on the contrary, is made up of events which seem to have no dependence on each other. The turns of fortune resemble those which take place in a dream. Victory and defeat are not followed by their usual consequences. Armies spring out of nothing, and melt into nothing. Yet, to judicious readers of history, the Spanish conflict is perhaps more interesting than the campaigns of Marlborough and Eugene. The fate of the Milanese and of the Low Countries was decided by military skill. The fate of Spain was decided by the peculiarities of the national character.

When the war commenced, the young king was in a most deplorable situation. On his arrival at Madrid he found Porto Carrero at the head of affairs, and he did not think fit to displace the man to whom he owed his crown. The Cardinal was a mere intriguer, and in no sense a statesman. He had acquired, in the court and in the confessional, a rare degree of skill in all the tricks by which weak minds are managed.—But of the noble science of government,—of the sources of national prosperity,—of the causes of national decay,—he knew no more than his master. It is curious to observe the contrast between the dexterity with which he ruled the conscience of a foolish valetudinarian, and the imbecility which he showed when placed at the head of an empire. On what grounds Lord Mahon represents the Cardinal as a man "of splendid genius,"—"of vast abilities," we are unable to discover. Louis was of a very different opinion, and Louis was very seldom mistaken in his judgment of character. "Everybody," says he, in a letter to his ambassador, "knows how incapable the Cardinal is. He is an object of contempt to his countrymen."

A few miserable savings were made, which ruined individuals without producing any perceptible benefit to the state. The police became more and more inefficient. The disorders of the capital were increased by the arrival of French adventurers,—the refuse of Parisian brothels and gaming-houses. These wretches considered the Spaniards as a subjugated race, whom the countrymen of the new sovereign might cheat and insult with impunity. The King sate eating and drinking all night, lay in bed all day,—yawned at the council table, and suffered the most important papers to lie unopened for weeks. At length he was roused by the only excitement of which his sluggish nature was susceptible. His grandfather consented to let him have a wife. The choice was fortunate. Maria Louisa, Princess of Savoy, a beautiful and graceful girl of thirteen, already a woman in person and mind at an age when the females of colder climates are still children, was the person selected. The King resolved to give her the meeting in Catalonia. He left his capital, of which he was already thoroughly tired. At setting out he was mobbed by a gang of beggars. He, however, made his way through them, and repaired to Barcelona.

Louis was perfectly aware that the Queen would govern Philip. He, accordingly, looked about for somebody to govern the Queen. He selected the Princess Orsini to be first lady of the bedchamber,—no insignificant post in the household of a very young wife and a very uxorious husband. The lady was the daughter of a French peer, and the widow of a Spanish grandee. She was, therefore, admirably fitted by her position to be the instrument of the court of Versailles at the court of Madrid. The Duke of Orleans called her, in words too coarse for translation, the Lieutenant of Captain Maintenon;

and the appellation was well deserved. She aspired to play in Spain the part which Madame de Maintenon had played in France. But, though at least equal to her model in wit, information, and talents for intrigue, she had not that self-command, that patience, that imperturbable evenness of temper, which had raised the widow of a buffoon to be the consort of the proudest of kings. The Princess was more than fifty years old, but was still vain of her fine eyes, and her fine shape; she still dressed in the style of a girl; and she still carried her flirtations so far as to give occasion for scandal. She was, however, polite, eloquent, and not deficient in strength of mind. The bitter Saint Simon owns that no person whom she wished to attach could long resist the graces of her manners and of her conversation.

We have not time to relate how she obtained, and how she preserved her empire over the young couple in whose household she was placed,—how she became so powerful that neither minister of Spain nor ambassador from France could stand against her,—how Louis himself was compelled to court her—how she received orders from Versailles to retire—how the Queen took part with her favourite attendant—how the King took part with the Queen—and how, after much squabbling, lying, shuffling, bullying, and coaxing, the dispute was adjusted. We turn to the events of the war.

When hostilities were proclaimed at London, Vienna, and the Hague, Philip was at Naples. He had been with great difficulty prevailed upon, by the most urgent representations from Versailles, to separate himself from his wife, and to repair without her to his Italian dominions, which were then menaced by the Emperor. The Queen acted as Regent, and, child as she was, seems to have been quite as competent to govern the kingdom as her husband or any of his ministers.

In August, 1702, an armament, under the command of the Duke of Ormond, appeared off Cadiz. The Spanish authorities had no funds and no regular troops. The national spirit, however, supplied in some degree what was wanting. The nobles and peasantry advanced money. The peasantry were formed into what the Spanish writers call bands of heroic patriots, and what General Stanhope calls a "rascally foot militia." If the invaders had acted with vigour and judgment, Cadiz would probably have fallen. But the chiefs of the expedition were divided by national and professional feelings—Dutch against English, and land against sea. Sparre, the Dutch general, was sulky and perverse—according to Lord Mahon, because he was a citizen of a republic. Bellasys, the English general, embezzled the stores—we suppose, because he was the subject of a monarchy. The Duke of Ormond, who had the command of the whole expedition, proved on this occasion, as on every other, destitute of the qualities which great emergencies require. No discipline was kept; the soldiers were suffered to rob and insult those whom it was most desirable to conciliate. Churches were robbed; images were pulled down; nuns were violated. The officers shared the spoil, instead of punishing the spoilers; and at last the armament, loaded, to use the words of Stanhope, "with a great deal of plunder and infamy," quitted the scene of Essex's glory, leaving the only Spaniard of note who had declared for them to be hanged by his countrymen.

The fleet was off the coast of Portugal, on the way back to England, when the Duke of Ormond received intelligence that the treasure-ships from America had just arrived in Europe, and had, in order to avoid his armament, repaired to the harbour of Vigo. The cargo consisted, it was said, of more than three millions sterling in gold and silver, besides much valuable merchandise. The prospect of plunder reconciled all disputes. Dutch and English, admirals and generals, were equally eager for action. The Spaniards might with the greatest ease have secured the treasure by simply landing it; but it was a fundamental law of Spanish trade that the galleons should unload at Cadiz, and at Cadiz only. The Chamber of Commerce at Cadiz, in the true spirit of monopoly, refused, even at this conjuncture, to bate one jot of its privilege. The matter was referred to the Council of the Indies: that body deliberated and hesitated just a day too long. Some feeble preparations for defence were made. Two ruined towers at the mouth of the bay of Vigo were garrisoned by a few ill-armed and untrained rustics; a boom was thrown across the entrance of the basin; and a few French ships of war, which had convoyed the galleons from America, were moored within. But all was to no purpose. The English ships broke the boom: Ormond and his soldiers scaled the forts; the French burned their ships, and escaped to the shore. The conquerors shared some millions of dollars;—some millions more were sunk. When all the galleons had been captured or destroyed came an order in due form allowing them to unload.

When Philip returned to Madrid,—in the beginning of 1703, he found the finances more embarrassed, the people more discontented, and the hostile coalition more formidable than ever. The loss of the galleons had occasioned a great deficiency in the revenue. The Admiral of Castile, one of the greatest subjects in Europe, had fled to Lisbon and sworn allegiance to the Archduke. The King of Portugal soon after acknowledged Charles as King of Spain, and prepared to support the title of the house of Austria by arms.

On the other side, Louis sent to the assistance of his grandson an army of 12,000 men, commanded by the Duke of Berwick. Berwick was the son of James the Second and Arabella Churchill. He had been brought up to expect the highest honours which an English subject could enjoy; but the whole course of his life was changed by the revolution which overthrew his infatuated father. Berwick became an exile, a man without a country; and from that time forward his camp was to him in the place of a country, and professional honour was his patriotism. He ennobled his wretched calling. There was a stern, cold, Brutus-like virtue in the manner in which he discharged the duties of a soldier of fortune. His military fidelity was tried by the strongest temptations and was found invincible. At one time he fought against his uncle; at another he fought against the cause of his brother; yet he was never suspected of treachery, or even of slackness.

Early in 1704 an army, composed of English, Dutch, and Portuguese, was assembled on the western frontier of Spain. The Archduke Charles had arrived at Lisbon, and appeared in person at the head of his troops. The military skill of Berwick held the Allies in check through the whole campaign. On the south, however, a great blow was struck. An English fleet, under Sir George Rooke, having on board several regiments commanded by the Prince of Hesse Darmstadt, appeared before the rock of Gibraltar. That celebrated stronghold which nature has made all but impregnable, and against which all the resources of the military art have been employed in vain, was taken as easily as if it had been an open village in a plain. The garrison went to say their prayers instead of standing on their guard. A few English sailors climbed the rock. The Spaniards capitulated; and the British flag was placed on those ramparts from which the combined armies and navies of France and Spain have never been able to pull it down. Rooke proceeded to Malaga, gave battle in the neighbourhood of that port to a French squadron, and after a doubtful action returned to England.

But greater events were at hand. The English government had determined to send an expedition to Spain, under the command of Charles Mordaunt Earl of Peterborough. This man was, if not the greatest, yet assuredly the

excepted. Indeed, Peterborough may be described as a polite, learned, and amorous Charles XII. His courage had all the French impetuosity, and all the English steadiness. His fertility and activity of mind were almost beyond belief. They appeared in every thing that he did,—in his campaigns, in his negoitations, in his familiar correspondence, in his lightest and most unstudied conversation. He was a kind friend, a generous enemy, and in deportment a thorough gentleman. But his splendid talents and virtues were rendered almost useless to his country, by his levity, his restlessness, his irritability, his morbid craving for novelty and for excitement. He loved to fly round Europe faster than a travelling courier. He was at the Hague one week, at Vienna the next. Then he took a fancy to see Madrid ; and he had scarcely reached Madrid, when he ordered horses and set off for Copenhagen. No attendants could keep up with his speed. No bodily infirmities could confine him. Old age, disease, imminent death, produced scarcely any effect on his intrepid spirit. Just before he underwent the most horrible of surgical operations, his conversation was as sprightly as that of a young man in the full vigour of health. On the day after the operation, in spite of the entreaties of his medical advisers, he would set out on a journey. His figure was that of a skeleton. But his elastic mind supported him under fatigues and sufferings which seemed sufficient to bring the most robust man to the grave. Change of employment was as necessary to him as change of place. He loved to dictate six or seven letters at once. Those who had to transact business with him complained that though he talked with great ability on every subject, he could never be kept to the point. " Lord Peterborough," said Pope, " would say very pretty and lively things in his letters, but they would be rather too gay and wandering ; whereas, were Lord Bolingbroke to write to an emperor, or to a statesman, he would fix on that point which was the most material, would set it in the strongest and finest light, and manage it so as to make it the most serviceable to his purpose." What Peterborough was to Bolingbroke as a writer, he was to Marlborough as a general. He was, in truth, the last of the knights-errant,—brave to temerity,—liberal to profusion,—courteous in his dealings with enemies,—the protector of the oppressed,—the adorer of women. His virtues and vices were those of the *Round Table*. Indeed, his character can hardly be better summed up than in the lines in which the author of that clever little poem, *Monks and Giants*, has described Sir Tristram.

" His birth, it seems, by Merlin's calculation,
Was under Venus, Mercury, and Mars :
His mind with all their attributes was mix'd,
And, like those planets, wandering and unfix'd.

" From realm to realm he ran, and never staid :
Kingdoms and crowns he won, and gave away :
It seem'd as if his labours were repaid
By the mere noise and movement of the fray :
No conquests nor acquirements had he made :
His chief delight was, on some festive day,
To ride triumphant, prodigal, and proud,
And shower his wealth amidst the shouting crowd.

" His schemes of war were sudden, unforeseen,
Inexplicable both to friend and foe ;
It seem'd as if some momentary spleen
Inspired the project, and impelled the blow ;
And most his fortune and success were seen
With means the most inadequate and low ;
Most master of himself, and least encumber'd,
When overmatch'd, entangled, and outnumber'd."

In June, 1705, this remarkable man arrived in Lisbon with five thousand Dutch and English soldiers. There the Archduke embarked with a large train of attendants, whom Peterborough entertained magnificently during the voyage at his own expense. From Lisbon the armament proceeded to Gibraltar, and, having taken the Prince of Hesse Darmstadt on board, steered towards the north-east along the coast of Spain.

The first place at which the expedition touched, after leaving Gibraltar, was Altea in Valencia. The wretched misgovernment of Philip had excited great discontent throughout this province. The invaders were eagerly welcomed. The peasantry flocked to the shore, bearing provisions, and shouting, —"Long live Charles III." The neighbouring fortress of Denia surrendered without a blow.

The imagination of Peterborough took fire. He conceived the hope of finishing the war at one blow. Madrid was but a hundred and fifty miles distant. There was scarcely one fortified place on the road. The troops of Philip were either on the frontiers of Portugal or on the coast of Catalonia. At the capital there was no military force, except a few horse who formed a guard of honour round the person of Philip. But the scheme of pushing into the heart of a great kingdom with an army of only seven thousand men, was too daring to please the Archduke. The Prince of Hesse Darmstadt, who, in the reign of the late King of Spain, had been Governor of Catalonia, and who overrated his own influence in that province, was of opinion that they ought instantly to proceed thither, and to attack Barcelona. Peterborough was hampered by his instructions, and found it necessary to submit.

On the sixteenth of August the fleet arrived before Barcelona; and Peterborough found that the task assigned to him by the Archduke and the Prince was one of almost insuperable difficulty. One side of the city was protected by the sea; the other by the strong fortifications of Monjuich. The walls were so extensive, that thirty thousand men would scarcely have been sufficient to invest them. The garrison was as numerous as the besieging army. The best officers in the Spanish service were in the town. The hopes which the Prince of Darmstadt had formed of a general rising in Catalonia were grievously disappointed. The invaders were joined only by about fifteen hundred armed peasants, whose services cost more than they were worth.

No general was ever in a more deplorable situation than that in which Peterborough was now placed. He had always objected to the scheme of besieging Barcelona. His objections had been overruled. He had to execute a project which he had constantly represented as impracticable. His camp was divided into hostile factions, and he was censured by all. The Archduke and the Prince blamed him for not proceeding instantly to take the town; but suggested no plan by which seven thousand men could be enabled to do the work of thirty thousand. Others blamed their general for giving up his own opinion to the childish whims of Charles, and for sacrificing his men in an attempt to perform what was impossible. The Dutch commander positively declared that his soldiers should not stir: Lord Peterborough might give what orders he chose; but to engage in such a siege was madness; and the men should not be sent to certain death when there was no chance of obtaining any advantage.

At length, after three weeks of inaction, Peterborough announced his fixed determination to raise the siege. The heavy cannon were sent on board. Preparations were made for re-embarking the troops. Charles and the Prince of Hesse were furious; but most of the officers blamed their general for having delayed so long the measure which he had at last found it necessary to take. On the 12th of September there were rejoicings and public entertainments in

Barcelona for this great deliverance. On the following morning the English flag was flying on the ramparts of Monjuich. The genius and energy of one man had supplied the place of fory battalions.

At midnight Peterborough had called on the Prince of Hesse, with whom he had not for some time been on speaking terms. "I have resolved, sir," said the Earl, "to attempt an assault; you may accompany us, if you think fit, and see whether I and my men deserve what you have been pleased to say of us." The Prince was startled. The attempt, he said, was hopeless; but he was ready to take his share; and, without further discussion, he called for his horse.

Fifteen hundred English soldiers were assembled under the Earl. A thousand more had been posted as a body of reserve, at a neighbouring convent, under the command of Stanhope. After a winding march along the foot of the hills, Peterborough and his little army reached the walls of Monjuich. There they halted till daybreak. As soon as they were descried, the enemy advanced into the outer ditch to meet them. This was the event on which Peterborough had reckoned, and for which his men were prepared. The English received the fire, rushed forward, leaped into the ditch, put the Spaniards to flight, and entered the works together with the fugitives. Before the garrison had recovered from their first surprise, the Earl was master of the outworks, had taken several pieces of cannon, and had thrown up a breastwork to defend his men. He then sent off for Stanhope's reserve. While he was waiting for this reinforcement, news arrived that three thousand men were marching from Barcelona towards Monjuich. He instantly rode out to take a view of them; but no sooner had he left his troops than they were seized with a panic. Their situation was indeed full of danger; they had been brought into Monjuich, they scarcely knew how; their numbers were small; their general was gone; their hearts failed them, and they were proceeding to evacuate the fort. Peterborough received information of these occurrences in time to stop the retreat. He galloped up to the fugitives, addressed a few words to them, and put himself at their head. The sound of his voice and the sight of his face restored all their courage, and they marched back to their former position.

The Prince of Hesse had fallen in the confusion of the assault; but everything else went well. Stanhope arrived; the detachment which had marched out of Barcelona retreated; the heavy cannon were disembarked, and brought to bear on the inner fortifications of Monjuich, which speedily fell. Peterborough, with his usual generosity, rescued the Spanish soldiers from the ferocity of his victorious army, and paid the last honours with great pomp to his rival the Prince of Hesse.

The reduction of Monjuich was the first of a series of brilliant exploits. Barcelona fell; and Peterborough had the glory of taking, with a handfull of men, one of the largest and strongest towns of Europe. He had also the glory, not less dear to his chivalrous temper, of saving the life and honour of the beautiful Duchess of Popoli, whom he met flying with dishevelled hair, from the fury of the soldiers. He availed himself dexterously of the jealousy with which the Catalonians regarded the inhabitants of Castile. He guaranteed to the province in the capital of which he was now quartered all its ancient rights and liberties, and thus succeeded in attaching the population to the Austrian cause.

The open country declared in favour of Charles. Tarragona, Tortosa, Gerona, Lerida, San Mateo, threw open their gates. The Spanish Government sent the Count of Las Torres with seven thousand men to reduce San Mateo. The Earl of Peterborough, with only twelve hundred men, raised the siege. His officers advised him to be content with this extraordinary success.

Charles urged him to return to Barcelona; but no remonstrances could stop such a spirit in the midst of such a career. It was the depth of winter. The country was mountainous. The roads were almost impassable. The men were ill-clothed. The horses were knocked up. The retreating army was far more numerous than the pursuing army. But difficulties and dangers vanished before the energy of Peterborough. He pushed on, driving Las Torres before him. Nules surrendered to the mere terror of his name; and, on the 4th of February, 1706, he arrived in triumph at Valencia. There he learned that a body of four thousand men was on the march to join Las Torres. He set out at dead of night from Valencia—passed the Xucar—came unexpectedly on the encampment of the enemy, and slaughtered, dispersed, or took the whole reinforcement. The Valencians, as we are told by a person who was present, could scarcely believe their eyes when they saw the prisoners brought in.

In the meantime, the Courts of Madrid and Versailles, exasperated and alarmed by the fall of Barcelona and by the revolt of the surrounding country, determined to make a great effort. A large army, nominally commanded by Philip, but really under the orders of Marshal Tessé, entered Catalonia. A fleet under the Count of Toulouse, one of the natural children of Louis XIV., appeared before the port of Barcelona. The city was attacked at once by sea and land. The person of the Archduke was in considerable danger. Peterborough, at the head of about three thousand men, marched with great rapidity from Valencia. To give battle, with so small a force, to a great regular army under the conduct of a Marshal of France, would have been madness. The Earl therefore took his post on the neighbouring mountains, harassed the enemy with incessant alarms, cut off their stragglers, intercepted their communications with the interior, and introduced supplies, both of men and provisions, into the town. He saw, however, that the only hope of the besieged was on the side of the sea. His commission from the British government gave him supreme power not only over the army, but, whenever he should be actually on board, over the navy also. He put out to sea at night in an open boat, without communicating his design to any person. He was picked up, several leagues from the shore, by one of the ships of the English squadron. As soon as he was on board, he announced himself as first in command, and sent a pinnace with his orders to the Admiral. Had these orders been given a few hours earlier, it is probable that the whole French fleet would have been taken. As it was, the Count of Toulouse put out to sea. The port was open. The town was relieved. On the following night the enemy raised the siege and retreated to Rouisillon. Peterborough returned to Valencia; and Philip, who had been some weeks absent from his wife, could endure the misery of separation no longer, and flew to rejoin her at Madrid.

At Madrid, however, it was impossible for him or for her to remain. The splendid success which Peterborough had obtained on the eastern coast of the Peninsula had inspired the sluggish Galway with emulation. He advanced into the heart of Spain. Berwick retreated. Alcantara, Ciudad Rodrigo, and Salamanca fell, and the conquerors marched towards the capital.

Philip was earnestly pressed by his advisers to remove the seat of government to Burgos. The advanced guard of the allied army was already seen on the heights above Madrid. It was known that the main body was at hand. The unfortunate Prince fled with his Queen and his household. The royal wanderers, after travelling eight days on bad roads, under a burning sun, and sleeping eight nights in miserable hovels, one of which fell down and nearly crushed them both to death, reached the metropolis of Old Castile. In the meantime, the invaders had entered Madrid in triumph, and had proclaimed the Archduke in the streets of the imperial city. Arragon, ever jealous of the

Castilian ascendency, followed the example of Catalonia. Saragossa revolted without seeing an enemy. The governor whom Philip had set over Carthagena betrayed his trust, and surrendered to the Allies the best arsenal and the last ships which Spain possessed.

Toledo had been for some time the retreat of two ambitious, turbulent, and vindictive intriguers, the Queen Dowager and Cardinal Porto Carrero. They had long been deadly enemies. They had led the adverse factions of Austria and France. Each had in turn domineered over the weak and disordered mind of the late King. At length the impostures of the priest had triumphed over the blandishments of the woman; Porto Carrero had remained victorious; and the Queen had fled in shame and mortification from the court where she had once been supreme. In her retirement she was soon joined by him whose arts had destroyed her influence. The Cardinal, having held power just long enough to convince all parties of his incompetency, had been dismissed to his See, cursing his own folly and the ingratitude of the House which he had served too well. Common interests and common enmities reconciled the fallen rivals. The Austrian troops were admitted into Toledo without opposition. The Queen Dowager flung off that mournful garb which the widow of a King of Spain wears through her whole life, and blazed forth in jewels. The Cardinal blessed the standards of the invaders in his magnificent cathedral, and lighted up his palace in honour of the great deliverance. It seemed that the struggle had terminated in favour of the Archduke, and that nothing remained for Philip but a prompt flight into the dominions of his grandfather.

So judged those who were ignorant of the character and habits of the Spanish people. There is no country in Europe which it is so easy to overrun as Spain:—there is no country in Europe which it is more difficult to conquer. Nothing can be more contemptible than the regular military resistance which it offers to an invader:—nothing more formidable than the energy which it puts forth when its regular military resistance has been beaten down. Its armies have long borne too much resemblance to mobs; but its mobs have had, in an unusual degree, the spirit of armies. The soldier, as compared with other soldiers, is deficient in military qualities; but the peasant has as much of those qualities as the soldier. In no country have such strong fortresses been taken by a mere *coup-de-main:* in no country have unfortified towns made so furious and obstinate a resistance to great armies. War in Spain has, from the days of the Romans, had a character of its own; it is a fire which cannot be raked out; it burns fiercely under the embers; and long after it has, to all seeming, been extinguished, bursts forth more violently than ever. This was seen in the last war. Spain had no army which could have looked in the face an equal number of French or Prussian soldiers; but one day laid the Prussian monarchy in the dust; one day put the crown of France at the disposal of invaders. No Jena, no Waterloo, would have enabled Joseph to reign in quiet at Madrid.

The conduct of the Castilians throughout the War of the Succession was most characteristic. With all the odds of number and situation on their side, they had been ignominiously beaten. All the European dependencies of the Spanish crown were lost. Catalonia, Arragon, and Valencia had acknowledged the Austrian Prince. Gibraltar had been taken by a few sailors; Barcelona stormed by a few dismounted dragoons. The invaders had penetrated into the centre of the Peninsula, and were quartered at Madrid and Toledo. While these events had been in progress, the nation had scarcely given a sign of life. The rich could hardly be prevailed on to give or to lend for the support of war; the troops had shown neither discipline nor courage; and now, at last, when it seemed that all was lost—when it seemed that the most sanguine must relinquish all hope—the national spirit awoke, fierce, proud, and unconquerable. The people had been sluggish when the circumstances might well have inspired hope; they reserved all their energy for what appeared to be a season of despair. Castile, Leon, Andalusia, Estremadura, rose at once; every peasant procured a firelock or a pike; the Allies were masters only of the ground on which they trod. No soldier could wander a hundred yards from the main body of the invading army without imminent risk of being poniarded; the country through which the conquerors had passed to Madrid, and which, as they thought, they had subdued, was all in arms behind them; their communications with Portugal were cut off. In the meantime, money began, for the first time, to flow rapidly into the treasury of the fugitive king. "The day before yesterday," says the Princess Orsini, in a letter written at this time, "the priest of a village which contains only a hundred and twenty houses brought a hundred and twenty pistoles to the Queen. 'My flock,' said he, 'are ashamed to send you so little; but they beg you to believe that in this purse there are a hundred and twenty hearts faithful even to the death.' The good man wept as he spoke; and indeed we wept too. Yesterday another small village, in which there are only twenty houses, sent us fifty pistoles."

While the Castilians were everywhere arming in the cause of Philip, the Allies were serving that cause as effectually by their mismanagement Galway stayed at Madrid, where his soldiers indulged in such boundless licentiousness that one half of them were in the hospitals. Charles remained dawdling in Catalonia. Peterborough had taken Requena, and wished to march towards Madrid, and to effect a junction with Galway; but the Archduke refused his consent to the plan. The indignant general remained accordingly in his favourite city, on the beautiful shores of the Mediterranean, reading Don Quixote, giving balls and suppers, trying in vain to get some good sport out of the Valencia bulls, and making love, not in vain, to the Valencian women.

At length the Archduke advanced into Castile, and ordered Peterborough to join him. But it was too late. Berwick had already compelled Galway to evacuate Madrid; and, when the whole force of the Allies was collected at Guadalaxara, it was found to be decidedly inferior in numbers to that of the enemy.

Peterborough formed a plan for regaining possession of the capital. His plan was rejected by Charles. The patience of the sensitive and vainglorious hero was worn out. He had none of that serenity of temper which enabled Marlborough to act in perfect harmony with Eugene, and to endure the vexatious interference of the Dutch deputies. He demanded permission to leave the army. Permission was readily granted; and he set out for Italy. That there might be some pretext for his departure, he was commissioned by the Archduke to raise a loan in Genoa on the credit of the revenues of Spain.

From that moment to the end of the campaign the tide of fortune ran strong against the Austrian cause. Berwick had placed his army between the Allies and the frontiers of Portugal. They retreated on Valencia, and arrived in that province, leaving about ten thousand prisoners in the hands of the enemy.

In January, 1707, Peterborough arrived at Valencia from Italy, no longer bearing a public character, but merely as a volunteer. His advice was asked, and it seems to have been most judicious. He gave it as his decided opinion that no offensive operations against Castile ought to be undertaken. It would be easy, he said, to defend Arragon, Catalonia, and Valencia, against Philip. The inhabitants of those parts of Spain were attached to the cause of the Archduke; and the armies of the House of Bourbon would be resisted by the whole population. In a short time the enthusiasm of the Castilians might abate. The government of Philip might commit unpopular acts. Defeats in the

Netherlands might compel Louis to withdraw the succours which he had furnished to his grandson. Then would be the time to strike a decisive blow. This excellent advice was rejected. Peterborough, who had now received formal letters of recall from England, departed before the opening of the campaign; and with him departed the good fortune of the Allies. Scarcely any general had ever done so much with means so small. Scarcely any general had ever displayed equal originality and boldness. He possessed, in the highest degree, the art of conciliating those whom he had subdued. But he was not equally successful in winning the attachment of those with whom he acted. He was adored by the Catalonians and Valencians; but he was hated by the prince whom he had all but made a great king, and by the generals whose fortune and reputation were staked on the same venture with his own. The English government could not understand him. He was so eccentric that they gave him no credit for the judgment which he really possessed. One day he took towns with horse-soldiers; then again he turned some hundreds of infantry into cavalry at a minute's notice. He obtained his political intelligence chiefly by means of love affairs, and filled his despatches with epigrams. The ministers thought that it would be highly impolitic to intrust the conduct of the Spanish war to so volatile and romantic a person. They therefore gave the command to Lord Galway, an experienced veteran—a man who was in war what Molière's doctors were in medicine, who thought it much more honourable to fail according to rule than to succeed by innovation, and who would have been very much ashamed of himself if he had taken Monjuich by means so strange as those which Peterborough employed. This great commander conducted the campaign of 1707 in the most scientific manner. On the plain of Almanza he encountered the army of the Bourbons. He drew up his troops according to the methods prescribed by the best writers, and in a few hours lost eighteen thousand men, a hundred and twenty standards, all his baggage, and all his artillery. Valencia and Arragon were instantly conquered by the French, and, at the close of the year, the mountainous province of Catalonia was the only part of Spain which still adhered to Charles.

"Do you remember, child," says the foolish woman in the Spectator to her husband, "that the pigeon-house fell the very afternoon that our careless wench spilt the salt upon the table?"—"Yes, my dear," replies the gentleman, "and the next post brought us an account of the battle of Almanza." The approach of disaster in Spain had been for some time indicated by omens much clearer than the mishap of the salt-cellar;—an ungrateful prince, an undisciplined army, a divided council, envy triumphant over merit, a man of genius recalled, a pedant and a sluggard intrusted with supreme command. The battle of Almanza decided the fate of Spain. The loss was such as Marlborough or Eugene could scarcely have retrieved, and was certainly not to be retrieved by Stanhope and Staremberg.

Stanhope, who took the command of the English army in Catalonia, was a man of respectable abilities, both in military and civil affairs, but fitter, we conceive, for a second than for a first place. Lord Mahon, with his usual candour, tells us, what we believe, was not known before, that his ancestor's most distinguished exploit, the conquest of Minorca, was suggested by Marlborough. Staremberg, a cold, methodical tactician of the German school, was sent by the emperor to command in Catalonia. Two languid campaigns followed, during which neither of the hostile armies did anything memorable, but during which both were nearly starved.

At length, in 1710, the chiefs of the Allied forces resolved to venture on bolder measures. They began the campaign with a daring move—pushed into Arragon, defeated the troops of Philip at Almenara, defeated them again at Saragossa, and advanced to Madrid. The king was again a fugitive. The Castilians sprang to arms with the same enthusiasm which they had displayed in 1706. The conquerors found the capital a desert. The people shut themselves up in their houses, and refused to pay any mark of respect to the Austrian prince. It was necessary to hire a few children to shout before him in the streets. Meanwhile, the court of Philip at Valladolid was thronged by nobles and prelates. Thirty thousand people followed their king from Madrid to his new residence. Women of rank, rather than remain behind, performed the journey on foot. The peasants enlisted by thousands. Money, arms, and provisions were supplied in abundance by the zeal of the people. The country round Madrid was infested by small parties of irregular horse. The Allies could not send off a despatch to Arragon, or introduce a supply of provisions into the capital. It was unsafe for the archduke to hunt in the immediate vicinity of the palace which he occupied.

The wish of Stanhope was to winter in Castile. But he stood alone in the council of war; and, indeed, it is not easy to understand how the Allies could have maintained themselves, through so unpropitious a season, in the midst of so hostile a population. Charles, whose personal safety was the first object of the generals, was sent with an escort of cavalry to Catalonia in November; and in December the army commenced its retreat towards Arragon.

But the Allies had to do with a master-spirit. The King of France had lately sent the Duke of Vendome to command in Spain. This man was distinguished by the filthiness of his person, by the brutality of his demeanour, by the gross buffoonery of his conversation, and by the impudence with which he abandoned himself to the most nauseous of all vices. His sluggishness was almost incredible. Even when engaged in a campaign, he often passed whole days in his bed. His strange torpidity had been the cause of some of the most severe defeats which the French had sustained in Italy and Flanders. But when he was roused by any great emergency, his resources, his energy, and his presence of mind were such as had been found in no French general since the death of Luxembourg.

At this crisis, Vendome was all himself. He set out from Talavera with his troops, and pursued the retreating army of the Allies with a speed perhaps never equalled in such a season and in such a country. He marched night and day. He swam, at the head of his cavalry, the flooded stream of Henares, and, in a few days, overtook Stanhope, who was at Brihuega with the left wing of the Allied army. "Nobody with me," says the English general, "imagined that they had any foot within some days' march of us; and our misfortune is owing to the incredible diligence which their army made." Stanhope had but just time to send off a messenger to the centre of the army, which was some leagues from Brihuega, before Vendome was upon him. The town was invested on every side. The walls were battered with cannon. A mine was sprung under one of the gates. The English kept up a terrible fire till their powder was spent. They then fought desperately with the bayonet against overwhelming odds. They burned the houses which the assailants had taken. But all was to no purpose. The British general saw that resistance could produce only a useless carnage. He concluded a capitulation; and his gallant little army became prisoners of war on honourable terms.

Scarcely had Vendome signed the capitulation, when he learned that Staremberg was marching to the relief of Stanhope. Preparations were instantly made for a general action. On the day following that on which the English had delivered up their arms, was fought the obstinate and bloody fight of Villa-Viciosa. Staremberg remained master of the field. Vendome reaped all the fruits of the engagement. The Allies spiked their cannon, and retired towards

Arragon. But even in Arragon they found no place to rest. Vendome was behind them. The guerilla parties were around them. They fled to Catalonia; but Catalonia was invaded by a French army from Rouissillon. At length, the Austrian general, with six thousand harassed and dispirited men, the remains of a great and victorious army, took refuge in Barcelona, almost the only place in Spain which still recognised the authority of Charles.

Philip was now much safer at Madrid than his grandfather at Paris. All hope of conquering Spain in Spain was at an end. But in other quarters the House of Bourbon was reduced to the last extremity. The French armies had undergone a series of defeats in Germany, in Italy, and in the Netherlands. An immense force, flushed with victory, and commanded by the greatest generals of the age, was on the borders of France. Louis had been forced to humble himself before the conquerors. He had even offered to abandon the cause of his grandson; and his offer had been rejected. But a great turn in affairs was approaching.

The English administration which had commenced the war against the House of Bourbon was an administration composed of Tories. But the war was a Whig war. It was the favourite scheme of William, the Whig king. Louis had provoked it by recognising, as sovereign of England, a prince peculiarly hateful to the Whigs. It had placed England in a position of marked hostility to that power from which alone the Pretender could expect efficient succour. It had joined England in the closest union to a Protestant and republican state—to a state which had assisted in bringing about the Revolution, and which was willing to guarantee the execution of the Act of Settlement. Marlborough and Godolphin found that they were more zealously supported by their old opponents than by their old associates. Those ministers who were zealous for the war were gradually converted to Whiggism. The rest dropped off, and were succeeded by Whigs. Cowper became Chancellor. Sunderland, in spite of the very just antipathy of Anne, was made Secretary of State. On the death of the Prince of Denmark a more extensive change took place. Wharton became Lord Lieutenant of Ireland, and Somers President of the Council. At length the administration was wholly in the hands of the Low Church party.

In the year 1710 a violent change took place. The Queen had always been a Tory at heart. Her religious feelings were all on the side of the Established Church. Her family feelings pleaded in favour of her exiled brother. Her interest disposed her to favour the zealots of prerogative. The affection which she felt for the Duchess of Marlborough was the great security of the Whigs. That affection had at length turned to deadly aversion. While the great party which had long swayed the destinies of Europe was undermined by bedchamber women at St. James's, a violent storm gathered in the country. A foolish parson had preached a foolish sermon against the principles of the Revolution. The wisest members of the government were for letting the man alone. But Godolphin, inflamed with all the zeal of a new-made Whig, and exasperated by a nickname which was applied to him in this unfortunate discourse, insisted that the preacher should be impeached. The exhortations of the mild and sagacious Somers were disregarded. The impeachment was brought; the doctor was convicted; and the accusers were ruined. The clergy came to the rescue of the persecuted clergyman. The country gentry came to the rescue of the clergy. A display of Tory feelings, such as England had not witnessed since the closing years of Charles II.'s reign, appalled the Ministers and gave boldness to the Queen. She turned out the Whigs, called Harley and St. John to power, and dissolved the Parliament. The elections went strongly against the late government. Stanhope, who had in his absence been put in nomination for Westminster, was defeated by a Tory candidate. The new Ministers, finding themselves masters of the new Parliament, were induced by the strongest motives to conclude a peace with France. The whole system of alliance in which the country was engaged was a Whig system. The general by whom the English armies had constantly been led to victory, and for whom it was impossible to find a substitute, was now, whatever he might formerly have been, a Whig general. If Marlborough were discarded, it was probable that some great disaster would follow. Yet, if he were to retain his command, every great action which he might perform would raise the credit of the party in opposition.

A peace was therefore concluded between England and the Princes of the House of Bourbon. Of that peace Lord Mahon speaks in terms of the severest reprehension. He is indeed an excellent Whig of the time of the first Lord Stanhope. "I cannot but pause for a moment," says he, "to observe how much the course of a century has inverted the meaning of our party nicknames—how much a modern Tory resembles a Whig of Queen Anne's reign, and a Tory of Queen Anne's reign a modern Whig."

We grant one half of Lord Mahon's proposition: from the other half we altogether dissent. We allow that a modern Tory resembles, in many things, a Whig of Queen Anne's reign. It is natural that such should be the case. The worst things of one age often resemble the best things of another. The livery of an English footman outshines the royal robes of King Pomarre. A modern shopkeeper's house is as well furnished as the house of a considerable merchant in Anne's reign. Very plain people now wear finer cloth than Beau Fielding or Beau Edgeworth could have procured in Queen Anne's reign. We would rather trust to the apothecary of a modern village than to the physician of a large town in Anne's reign. A modern boarding-school miss could tell the most learned Professor of Anne's reign some things in geography, astronomy, and chemistry, which would surprise him.

The science of government is an experimental science; and therefore it is, like all other experimental sciences, a progressive science. Lord Mahon would have been a very good Whig in the days of Harley. But Harley, whom Lord Mahon censures so severely, was very Whiggish when compared even with Clarendon; and Clarendon was quite a democrat when compared with Lord Burleigh. If Lord Mahon lives, as we hope he will, fifty years longer, we have no doubt that, as he now boasts of the resemblance which the Tories of our time bear to the Whigs of the Revolution, he will then boast of the resemblance borne by the Tories of 1882 to those immortal patriots, the Whigs of the Reform Bill.

Society, we believe, is constantly advancing in knowledge. The tail is now where the head was some generations ago. But the head and the tail still keep their distance. A nurse of this century is as wise as a justice of the quorum and custalorum in Shallow's time. The wooden spoon of this year would puzzle a senior wrangler of the reign of George the Second. A boy from the National School reads and spells better than half the knights of the shire in the October Club. But there is still as wide a difference as ever between justices and nurses, senior wranglers and wooden spoons, members of Parliament and children at charity schools. In the same way, though a Tory may now be very like what a Whig was 120 years ago, the Whig is as much in advance of the Tory as ever. The stag, in the Treatise on the Bathos, who "feared his hind feet would o'ertake the fore," was not more mistaken than Lord Mahon, if he thinks that he has really come up with the Whigs. The absolute position of the parties has been altered; the relative position remains unchanged. Through the whole of that great movement, which began before these party-names existed, and which will continue after they have become obsolete—through the whole of that great movement of which the Charter of John, the institution of the House of Commons, the extinction of Villanage, the separation from the See of Rome, the expulsion of the Stuarts, the reform of the Representative System, are successive stages—there have been, und·r some name or other, two sets of men—those who were before their age, and those who were behind it—those who were the wisest among their contemporaries, and those who gloried in being no wiser than their great-grandfathers. It is delightful to think that, in due time, the last of those who struggle in the rear of the great march will occupy the place now occupied by the advanced guard. The Tory Parliament of 1710 would have passed for a most liberal Parliament in the days of Elizabeth; and there are at present few members of the Conservative Club who would not have been fully qualified to sit with Halifax and Somers at the Kit-cat.

Though, therefore, we admit that a modern Tory bears some resemblance to a Whig of Queen Anne's reign, we can by no means admit that a Tory of Anne's reign resembled a modern Whig. Have the modern Whigs passed laws for the purpose of closing the entrance of the House of Commons against the new interests created by trade? Do the modern Whigs hold the doctrine of divine right? Have the modern Whigs laboured to exclude all dissenters from office and power? The modern Whigs are, indeed, at the present moment, like the Tories of 1712, desirous of peace, and of close union with France. But is there no difference between the France of 1712 and the France of 1832? Is France now the stronghold of the "Popish tyranny" and the "arbitrary power" against which our ancestors fought and prayed? Lord Mahon will find, we think, that his parallel is, in all essential circumstances, as incorrect as that which Fluellen drew between Macedon and Monmouth, or as that which an ingenious Tory lately discovered between Archbishop Williams and Archbishop Vernon.

We agree with Lord Mahon in thinking highly of the Whigs of Queen Anne's reign. But that part of their conduct which he selects for especial praise is precisely the part which we think most objectionable. We reveie them as the great champions of political and of intellectual liberty. It is true that, when raised to power, they were not exempt from the faults which power naturally engenders. It is true that they were men born in the seventeenth century, and that they were therefore ignorant of many truths which are familiar to the men of the nineteenth century. But they were what the reformers of the Church were before them, and what the reformers of the House of Commons have been since—the leaders of their species in a right direction. It is true that they did not allow to political discussion that latitude which appears to us reasonable and safe; but to them we owe the removal of the Censorship. It is true that they did not carry the principle of religious liberty to its full extent; but to them we owe the Toleration Act.

Though, however, we think that the Whigs of Anne's reign were, as a body, far superior in wisdom and public virtue to their contemporaries, the Tories, we by no means hold ourselves bound to defend all the measures of our favourite party. A life of action, if it is to be useful, must be a life of compromise. But speculation admits of no compromise. A public man is often under the necessity of consenting to measures which he dislikes, lest he should endanger the success of measures which he thinks of vital importance. But the historian lies under no such necessity. On the contrary, it is one of his most sacred duties to point out clearly the errors of those whose general conduct he admires.

It seems to us, then, that, on the great question which divided England during the last four years of Anne's reign, the Tories were in the right and the Whigs in the wrong. That question was, whether England ought to conclude peace without exacting from Philip a resignation of the Spanish crown?

No Parliamentary struggle, from the time of the Exclusion Bill to the time of the Reform Bill, has been so violent as that which took place between the authors of the Treaty of Utrecht and the War Party. The Commons were for peace ; the Lords were for vigorous hostilities. The Queen was compelled to choose which of her two highest prerogatives she would exercise—whether she would create Peers, or dissolve the Parliament. The ties of party superseded the ties of neighbourhood and of blood; the members of the hostile factions would scarcely speak to each other, or bow to each other ; the women appeared at the theatres bearing the badges of their political sect. The schism extended to the most remote counties of England. Talents, such as had never before been displayed in political controversy, were enlisted in the service of the hostile parties. On one side was Steele, gay, lively, drunk with animal spirits and with factious animosity, and Addison, with his polished satire, his inexhaustible fertility of fancy, and his graceful simplicity of style. In the front of the opposite ranks appeared a darker and fiercer spirit—the apostate politician, the ribald priest, the perjured lover—a heart burning with hatred against the whole human race—a mind richly stored with images from the dunghill and the lazar-house. The Ministers triumphed, and the peace was concluded Then came the reaction. A new sovereign ascended the throne. The Whigs enjoyed the confidence of the King and of the Parliament. The unjust severity with which the Tories had treated Marlborough and Walpole was more than retaliated. Harley and Prior were thrown into prison ; Bolingbroke and Ormond were compelled to take refuge in a foreign land. The wounds inflicted in this desperate conflict continued to rankle for many years. It was long before the members of either party could discuss the question of the Peace of Utrecht with calmness and impartiality. That the Whig Ministers had sold us to the Dutch ; that the Tory Ministers had sold us to the French ; that the war had been carried on only to fill the pockets of Marlborough ; that the peace had been concluded only to facilitate the return of the Pretender ;—these imputations and many others, utterly unfounded, or grossly exaggerated, were hurled backward and forward by the political disputants of the last century. In our time the question may be discussed without irritation. We will state, as concisely as possible, the reasons which have led us to the conclusion at which we have arrived.

The dangers which were to be apprehended from the Peace were two: First, the danger that Philip might be induced, by feelings of private affection, to act in strict concert with the elder branch of his house—to favour the French trade at the expense of England—and to side with the French Government in future wars ; secondly, the danger that the posterity of the Duke of Burgundy might become extinct—that Philip might become heir by blood to the French crown—and that thus two great monarchies might be united under one sovereign.

The first danger appears to us altogether chimerical. Family affection has seldom produced much effect on the policy of princes. The state of Europe at the time of the Peace of Utrecht proved that in politics the ties of interest are much stronger than those of consanguinity. The Elector of Bavaria had been driven from his dominions by his father-in-law ; Victor Amadeus was in arms against his sons-in-law ; Anne was seated on a throne from which she had assisted to push a most indulgent father. It is true that Philip had been accustomed from childhood to regard his grandfather with profound veneration. It was probable, therefore, that the influence of Louis at Madrid would be very great. But Louis was more than seventy years old ; he could not live long; his heir was an infant in the cradle. There was surely no reason to think that the policy of the King of Spain would be swayed by his regard for a nephew whom he had never seen.

In fact, soon after the peace, the two branches of the House of Bourbon began to quarrel. A close alliance was formed between Philip and Charles, lately competitors for the Castilian crown. A Spanish princess, bethrothed to the King of France, was sent back in the most insulting manner to her native country; and a decree was put forth by the Court of Madrid commanding every Frenchman to leave Spain. It is true that, fifty years after the Peace of Utrecht, an alliance of peculiar strictness was formed between the French and Spanish governments. But it is certain that both governments were actuated on that occasion, not by domestic affection, but by common interests and common enmities. Their compact, though called the Family Compact, was as purely a political compact as the league of Cambrai, or the league of Pilnitz.

The second danger was that Philip might have succeeded to the crown of his native country. This did not happen. But it might have happened; and at one time it seemed very likely to happen. A sickly child alone stood between the King of Spain and the heritage of Louis the Fourteenth. Philip, it is true, solemnly renounced his claim to the French crown. But the manner in which he had obtained possession of the Spanish crown had proved the inefficacy of such renunciations. The French lawyers declared Philip's renunciation null, as being inconsistent with the fundamental law of the monarchy. The French people would probably have sided with him whom they would have considered as the rightful heir. Saint Simon, though much less the slave of prejudice than most of his countrymen, and though strongly attached to the regent, declared, in the presence of that prince, that he never would support the claims of the House of Orleans, against those of the King of Spain. "If such," he said, "be my feelings, what must be the feelings of others?" Bolingbroke, it is certain, was fully convinced that the renunciation was worth no more than the paper on which it was written, and demanded it only for the purpose of blinding the English Parliament and people.

Yet, though it was at one time probable that the posterity of the Duke of Burgundy would become extinct, and though it is almost certain that, if the posterity of the Duke of Burgundy had become extinct, Philip would have successfully preferred his claim to the crown of France, we still defend the principle of the Treaty of Utrecht. In the first place, Charles had, soon after the battle of Villa-Viciosa, inherited, by the death of his elder brother, all the dominions of the House of Austria. It might be argued that if to these dominions he had added the whole monarchy of Spain, the Balance of Power would have been seriously endangered. The union of the Austrian dominions and Spain would not, it is true, have been so alarming an event as the union of France and Spain. But Charles was actually emperor. Philip was not, and never might be, King of France. The certainty of the less evil might well be set against the chance of the greater evil.

But, in fact, we do not believe that Spain would long have remained under the government either of an Emperor or of a King of France. The character of the Spanish people was a better security to the nations of Europe than any will, any instrument of renunciation, or any treaty. The same energy which the people of Castile had put forth when Madrid was occupied by the Allied armies, they would have again put forth as soon as it appeared that their country was about to become a province of France. Though they were no longer masters abroad, they were by no means disposed to see foreigners set over them at home. If Philip had become King of France, and had attempted to govern Spain by mandates from Versailles, a second Grand Alliance would easily have effected what the first had failed to accomplish. The Spanish nation would have rallied against him as zealously as it had before rallied round him. And of this he seems to have been fully aware. For many years the favourite hope of his heart was that he might ascend the throne of his grandfather; but he seems never to have thought it possible that he could reign at once in the country of his adoption and in the country of his birth.

These were the dangers of the peace; and they seem to us to be of no very formidable kind. Against these dangers are to be set off the evils of war and the risk of failure. The evils of the war,—the waste of life, the suspension of trade, the expenditure of wealth, the accumulation of debt,—require no illustration. The chances of failure it is difficult at this distance of time to calculate with accuracy. But we think that an estimate approximating to the truth may, without much difficulty, be formed. The Allies had been victorious in Germany, Italy, and Flanders. It was by no means improbable that they might fight their way into the very heart of France. But at no time since the commencement of the war had their prospects been so dark in that country which was the very object of the struggle. In Spain they held only a few square leagues. The temper of the great majority of the nation was decidedly hostile to them. If they had persisted,—if they had obtained success equal to their highest expectations,—if they had gained a series of victories as splendid as those of Blenheim and Ramilies,—if Paris had fallen,—if Lewis had been a prisoner—we still doubt whether they would have accomplished their object. They would still have had to carry on interminable hostilities against the whole population of a country which affords peculiar facilities to irregular warfare, and in which invading armies suffer more from famine than from the sword.

We are, therefore, for the peace of Utrecht. It is true that we by no means admire the statesmen who concluded that peace. Harley, we believe, was a solemn trifler,—St. John a brilliant knave. The great body of their followers consisted of the country clergy and the country gentry—two classes of men who were then immeasurably inferior in respectability and intelligence to decent shopkeepers or farmers of our time. Parson Barnabas, Parson Trulliber, Sir Wilful Witwould, Sir Francis Wronghead, Squire Western, Squire Sullen, such were the people who composed the main strength of the Tory party during the sixty years which followed the Revolution. It is true that the means by which the Tories came into power in 1710 were most disreputable. It is true that the manner in which they used their power was often unjust and cruel. It is true that, in order to bring about their favourite project of peace, they resorted to slander and deception, without the slightest scruple. It is true that they passed off on the British nation a renunciation which they knew to be invalid. It is true that they gave up the Catalans to the vengeance of Philip, in a manner inconsistent with humanity and national honour. But on the great question of Peace or War, we cannot but think that, though their motives may have been selfish and malevolent, their decision was beneficial to the state.

But we have already exceeded our limits. It remains only for us to bid Lord Mahon heartily farewell, and to assure him that, whatever dislike we may feel for his political opinions, we shall always meet him with pleasure on the neutral ground of literature.

HORACE WALPOLE. (OCTOBER, 1833.)

Letters of Horace Walpole, Earl of Orford, to Sir Horace Mann, British Envoy at the Court of Tuscany. Now first published from the Originals in the Possession of the Earl of WALDEGRAVE. Edited by Lord DOVER. 3 vols. 8vo. London: 1833.

WE cannot transcribe this title-page without strong feelings of regret. The editing of these volumes was the last of the useful and modest services rendered to literature by a nobleman of amiable manners, of untarnished public and private character, and of cultivated mind. On this, as on other occasions, Lord Dover performed his part diligently, judiciously, and without the slightest ostentation. He had two merits which are rarely found together in a commentator. He was content to be merely a commentator—to keep in the background, and to leave the foreground to the author whom he had undertaken to illustrate. Yet, though willing to be an attendant, he was by no means a slave; nor did he consider it as part of his editorial duty to see no faults in the writer, to whom he faithfully and assiduously rendered the humblest literary offices.

The faults of Horace Walpole's head and heart are indeed sufficiently glaring. His writings, it is true, rank as high among the delicacies of intellectual epicures as the Strasburg pies among the dishes described in the *Almanach des Gourmands*. But, as the *paté-de foie-gras* owes its excellence to the diseases of the wretched animal which furnishes it, and would be good for nothing if it were not made of livers preternaturally swollen, so none but an unhealthy and disorganised mind could have produced such literary luxuries as the work of Walpole.

He was, unless we have formed a very erroneous judgment of his character, the most eccentric, the most artificial, the most fastidious, the most capricious of men. His mind was a bundle of inconsistent whims and affectations. His features were covered by mask within mask. When the outer disguise of obvious affectation was removed, you were still as far as ever from seeing the real man. He played innumerable parts, and over-acted them all. When he talked misanthropy, he out-Timoned Timon. When he talked philanthropy, he left Howard at an immeasurable distance. He scoffed at Courts, and kept a chronicle of their most trifling scandal—at Society, and was blown about by its slightest veerings of opinion—at Literary fame, and left fair copies of his private letters, with copious notes, to be published after his decease—at Rank, and never for a moment forgot that he was an Honourable—at the practice of Entail, and tasked the ingenuity of conveyancers to tie up his villa in the strictest settlement.

The conformation of his mind was such that whatever was little seemed to him great, and whatever was great seemed to him little. Serious business was a trifle to him, and trifles were his serious business. To chat with blue stockings—to write little copies of complimentary verses on little occasions—to superintend a private press—to preserve from natural decay the perishable topics of Ranelagh and White's—to record divorces and bets, Miss Chudleigh's absurdities and George Selwyn's good sayings—to decorate a grotesque house with pie-crust battlements—to procure rare engravings and antique chimney-boards—to match old gauntlets—to lay out a maze of walks within five acres of ground—these were the grave employments of his long life. From these he turned to politics as to an amusement. After the labours of the print-shop and the auction room, he unbent his mind in the House of Commons. And having indulged in the recreation of making laws, and voting millions, he returned to more important pursuits—to researches after Queen Mary's comb,

Wolsey's red hat, the pipe which Van Tromp smoked during his last sea-fight, and the spur which King William struck into the flank of Sorrel.

In everything in which he busied himself—in the fine arts, in literature, in public affairs—he was drawn by some strange attraction from the great to the little, and from the useful to the odd. The politics in which he took the keenest interests, were politics scarcely deserving of the name. The growlings of George the Second—the flirtations of Princess Emily with the Duke of Grafton—the amours of Prince Frederic and Lady Middlesex—the squabbles between Gold Stick and the Master of the Buckhounds—the disagreements between the tutors of Prince George—these matters engaged almost all the attention which Walpole could spare from matters more important still—from bidding for Zinckes and Petitots—from cheapening fragments of tapestry and handles of old lances—from joining bits of painted glass, and from setting up memorials of departed cats and dogs. While he was fetching and carrying the gossip of Kensington Palace and Carlton House, he fancied that he was engaged in politics, and when he recorded that gossip, he fancied that he was writing history.

He was, as he himself has told us, fond of faction as an amusement. He loved mischief: but he loved quiet; and he was constantly on the watch for opportunities of gratifying both his tastes at once. He sometimes contrived, without showing himself, to disturb the course of ministerial negotiations and to spread confusion through the political circles. He does not himself pretend that, on these occasions, he was actuated by public spirit; nor does he appear to have had any private advantage in view. He thought it a good practical joke to set public men together by the ears; and he enjoyed their perplexities, their accusations, and their recriminations, as a malicious boy enjoys the embarrassment of a misdirected traveller.

About politics, in the high sense of the word, he knew nothing, and cared nothing. He called himself a Whig. His father's son could scarcely assume any other name. It pleased him also to affect a foolish dislike of kings as kings, and a foolish love and admiration of rebels as rebels: and perhaps, while kings were not in danger, and while rebels were not in being, he really believed that he held the doctrines which he professed. To go no further than the letters now before us, he is perpetually boasting to his friend Mann of his aversion to royalty and to royal persons. He calls the crime of Damien—that least bad of murders—the murder "of a king." He hung up in his villa a facsimile of the death-warrant of Charles, with the inscription, "*Major Charta*." Yet the most superficial knowledge of history might have taught him that the Restoration, and the crimes and follies of the twenty-eight years which followed the Restoration, were the effects of this Greater Charter. Nor was there much in the means by which that instrument was obtained that could gratify a judicious lover of liberty. A man must hate kings very bitterly before he can think it desirable that the representatives of the people should be turned out of doors by dragoons, in order to get at a king's head. Walpole's Whiggism, however, was of a very harmless kind. He kept it, as he kept the old spears and helmets at Strawberry Hill, merely for show. He would just as soon have thought of taking down the arms of the ancient Templars and Hospitallers from the walls of his hall, and setting off on a crusade to the Holy Land, as of acting in the spirit of those daring warriors and statesmen, great even in their errors, whose names and seals were affixed to the warrant which he prized so highly. He liked revolution and regicide only when they were a hundred years old. His republicanism, like the courage of a bully, or the love of a fribble, was strong and ardent when there was no occasion for it, and subsided when he had an opportunity of bringing it to the proof. As soon as the revolutionary spirit really began to stir in Europe—as soon as the hatred of kings became something more than a sonorous phrase—he was frightened into a fanatical royalist, and became one of the most extravagant alarmists of those wretched times. In truth, his talk about liberty, whether he knew it or not, was from the beginning a mere cant—the remains of a phraseology which had meant something in the mouths of those from whom he had learned it, but which, in his mouth, meant about as much as the oath by which the Knights of the Bath bind themselves to redress the wrongs of all injured ladies. He had been fed in his boyhood with Whig speculations on government. He must have often seen, at Houghton or in Downing Street, men who had been Whigs when it was as dangerous to be a Whig as to be a highwayman—men who had voted for the exclusion bill, who had been concealed in garrets and cellars after the battle of Sedgmoor, and who had set their names to the declaration that they would live and die with the Prince of Orange. He had acquired the language of these men, and he repeated it by rote, though it was at variance with all his tastes and feelings—just as some old Jacobite families persisted in praying for the Pretender and in passing their glasses over the water-decanter when they drank the King's health, long after they had become loyal supporters of the government of George the Third. He was a Whig by the accident of hereditary connexion; but he was essentially a courtier; and not the less a courtier because he pretended to sneer at the objects which excited his admiration and envy. His real tastes perpetually show themselves through the thin disguise. While professing all the contempt of Bradshaw or Ludlow for crowned heads, he took the trouble to write a book concerning Royal Authors. He pryed with the utmost anxiety into the most minute particulars relating to the Royal Family. When he was a child, he was haunted with a longing to see George the First, and gave his mother no peace till she had found a way of gratifying his curiosity. The same feeling, covered with a thousand disguises, attended him to the grave. No observation that dropped from the lips of Majesty seemed to him too trifling to be recorded. The French songs of Prince Frederic—compositions certainly not deserving of preservation on account of their intrinsic merit—have been carefully preserved for us by this contemner of royalty. In truth, every page of Walpole's works bewrays him. This Diogenes, who would be thought to prefer his tub to a palace, and who has nothing to ask of the masters of Windsor and Versailles but that they will stand out of his light, is a gentleman-usher at heart.

He had, it is plain, an uneasy consciousness of the frivolity of his favourite pursuits; and this consciousness produced one of the most diverting of his ten thousand affectations. His busy idleness,—his indifference to matters which the world generally regards as important,—his passion for trifles,—he thought fit to dignify with the name of philosophy. He spoke of himself as of a man whose equanimity was proof to ambitious hopes and fears, who had learned to rate power, wealth, and fame at their true value, and whom the conflict of parties, the rise and fall of statesmen, the ebb and flow of public opinion, moved only to a smile of mingled compassion and disdain. It was owing to the peculiar elevation of his character that he cared about a pinnacle of lath and plaster more than about the Middlesex election, and about a miniature of Grammont more than about the American Revolution. Pitt and Murray might talk themselves hoarse about trifles. But questions of government and war were too insignificant to detain a mind which was occupied in recording the scandal of club-rooms and the whispers of the back-stairs, and which was even capable of selecting and disposing chairs of ebony and shields of rhinoceros-skin.

One of his innumerable whims was an extreme dislike to be considered man of letters. Not that he was indifferent to literary fame. Far from it. Scarcely any writer has ever troubled himself so much about the appearance which his works were to make before posterity. But he had set his heart on incompatible objects. He wished to be a celebrated author, and yet to be a mere idle gentleman—one of those epicurean gods of the earth who do nothing at all, and who pass their existence in the contemplation of their own perfections. He did not like to have anything in common with the wretches who lodged in the little courts behind St. Martin's Church, and stole out on Sundays to dine with their bookseller. He avoided the society of authors. He spoke with lordly contempt of the most distinguished among them. He tried to find out some way of writing books, as M. Jourdain's father sold cloth, without derogating from his character of *Gentilhomme*. "Lui, marchand? C'est pure médisance: il ne l'a jamais été. Tout ce qu'il faisait, c'est qu'il était fort obligeant, fort officieux; et comme il se connaissait fort bien en étoffes, il en allait choisir de tous les côtés, les faisait apporter chez lui, et en donnait à ses amis pour de l'argent." There are several amusing instances of his feeling on this subject in the letters now before us. Mann had complimented him on the learning which appeared in the "Catalogue of Royal and Noble Authors;" and it is curious to see how impatiently Walpole bore the imputation of having attended to anything so unfashionable as the improvement of his mind. "I know nothing. How should I? I who have always lived in the big busy world; who lie a-bed all the morning, call it morning as long as you please; who sup in company; who have played at faro half my life, and now at loo till two and three in the morning; who have always loved pleasure; haunted auctions. . . . . How I have laughed when some of the Magazines have called me the learned gentleman. Pray don't be like the Magazines." This folly might be pardoned in a boy. But a man of forty-three, as Walpole then was, ought to be quite as much ashamed of playing at loo till three every morning as of being so vulgar a thing as a learned gentleman.

The literary character has undoubtedly its full share of faults, and of very serious and offensive faults. If Walpole had avoided those faults, we could have pardoned the fastidiousness with which he declined all fellowship with men of learning. But from those faults Walpole was not one jot more free than the garreteers from whose contact he shrunk. Of literary meannesses and literary vices, his life and his works contain as many instances as the life and the works of any member of Johnson's club. The fact is, that Walpole had the faults of Grub Street, with a large addition from St. James's Street— the vanity, the jealousy, the irritability of a man of letters—the affected superciliousness and apathy of a man of *ton*.

His judgment of literature—of contemporary literature especially—was altogether perverted by his aristocratical feelings. No writer surely was ever guilty of so much false and absurd criticism. He almost invariably speaks with contempt of those books which are now universally allowed to be the best that appeared in his time; and, on the other hand, he speaks of writers of rank and fashion as if they were entitled to the same precedence in literature which would have been allowed to them in a drawing-room. In these letters, for example, he says that he would rather have written the most absurd lines in Lee than Thomson's Seasons. The periodical paper called "The World," on the other hand, was by "our first writers." Who, then, were the first writers of England in the year 1753? Walpole has told us in a note. Our readers will probably guess that Hume, Fielding, Smollett, Richardson, Johnson, Warburton, Collins, Akenside Gray, Dyer, Young, Warton, Mason, or some of those distinguished men, were in the list. Not one of them. Our first writers, it seems, were Lord Chesterfield, Lord Bath, Mr. W. Whithed,

Sir Charles Williams, Mr. Soame Jenyns, Mr. Cambridge, Mr. Coventry. Of these seven personages, Whithed was the lowest in station, but was the most accomplished tuft-hunter of his time. Coventry was of a noble family. The other five had among them two Peerages, two seats in the House of Commons, three seats in the Privy Council, a baronetcy, a blue riband, a red riband, about a hundred thousand pounds a year, and not ten pages that are worth reading. The writings of Whithed, Cambridge, Coventry, and Lord Bath are forgotten. Soame Jenyns is remembered chiefly by Johnson's review of the foolish Essay on the Origin of Evil. Lord Chesterfield stands much lower in the estimation of posterity than he would have done, if his letters had never been published. The lampoons of Sir Charles Williams are now read only by the curious, and, though not without occasional flashes of wit, have always seemed to us, we must own, very poor performances.

Walpole judged of French literature after the same fashion. He understood and loved the French language. Indeed, he loved it too well. His style is more deeply tainted with Gallisms than that of any other English writer with whom we are acquainted. His composition often reads, for a page together, like a rude translation from the French. We meet every minute with such sentences as these, "One knows what temperaments Annibal Carracci painted." "The impertinent personage!" "She is dead rich." "Lord Dalkeith is dead of the small-pox in three days." "What was ridiculous, the man who seconded the motion happened to be shut out." "It will now be seen whether he or they are most patriot."

His love for the French language was of a peculiar kind. He loved it as having been for a century the vehicle of all the polite nothings of Europe, as the sign by which the freemasons of fashion recognised each other in every capital from Petersburg to Naples, as the language of raillery, as the language of anecdote, as the language of memoirs, as the language of correspondence. Its higher uses he altogether disregarded. The literature of France has been to ours what Aaron was to Moses—the expositor of great truths which would else have perished for want of a voice to utter them with distinctness. The relation which existed between Mr. Bentham and M. Dumont is an exact illustration of the intellectual relation in which the two countries stand to each other. The great discoveries in physics, in metaphysics, in political science, are ours. But no foreign nation except France has received them from us by direct communication. Isolated by our situation—isolated by our manners, we found truth, but we did not impart it. France has been the interpreter between England and mankind.

In the time of Walpole, this process of interpretation was in full activity. The great French writers were busy in proclaiming through Europe the names of Bacon, of Newton, and of Locke. The English principles of toleration, the English respect for personal liberty, the English doctrine that all power is a trust for the public good, were making rapid progress. There is scarcely anything in history so interesting as that great stirring up of the mind of France—that shaking of the foundations of all established opinions—that uprooting of old truth and old error. It was plain that mighty principles were at work, whether for evil or for good. It was plain that a great change in the whole social system was at hand. Fanatics of one kind might anticipate a golden age, in which men should live under the simple dominion of reason, in perfect equality and perfect amity, without property, or marriage, or king, or God. A fanatic of another kind might see nothing in the doctrines of the philosophers but anarchy and atheism, might cling more closely to every old abuse, and might regret the good old days when St. Dominic and Simon de Montfort put down the growing heresies of Provence. A wise man would have seen with regret the excesses into which the reformers were running; but he would have done justice to their genius and to their philanthropy. He would have censured their errors; but he would have remembered that, as Milton has said, error is but opinion in the making. While he condemned their hostility to religion, he would have acknowledged that it was the natural effect of a system under which religion had been constantly exhibited to them in forms which common sense rejected and at which humanity shuddered. While he condemned some of their political doctrines as incompatible with all law, all property, and all civilisation, he would have acknowledged that the subjects of Louis XV. had every excuse which men could have for being eager to pull down, and for being ignorant of the far higher art of setting up. While anticipating a fierce conflict—a great and wide-wasting destruction—he would yet have looked forward to the final close with a good hope for France and for mankind.

Walpole had neither hopes nor fears. Though the most Frenchified English writer of the eighteenth century, he troubled himself little about the portents which were daily to be discerned in the French literature of his time. While the most eminent Frenchmen were studying with enthusiastic delight English politics and English philosophy, he was studying as intently the gossip of the old court of France. The fashions and scandal of Versailles and Marli—fashions and scandal a hundred years old—occupied him infinitely more than a great moral revolution which was taking place in his sight. He took a prodigious interest in every noble sharper whose vast volume of wig, and infinite length of riband, had figured at the dressing or at the tucking up of Louis XIV., and of every profligate woman of quality who had carried her train of lovers backward and forward from king to parliament, and from parliament to king, during the wars of the *Fronde*. These were the people of whom he treasured up the smallest memorial, of whom he loved to hear the most trifling anecdote, and for whose likenesses he would have given any price. Of the great French writers of his own time, Montesquieu is the only one of whom he speaks with enthusiasm. And even of Montesquieu he speaks with less enthusiasm than of that abject thing, Crébillon the younger, a scribbler as licentious as Louvet and as dull as Rapin. A man must be strangely constituted who can take interest in pedantic journals of the blockades laid by the Duke of A. to the hearts of the Marquise de B. and the Comtesse de C. This trash Walpole extols in language sufficiently high for the merits of "Don Quixote." He wished to possess a likeness of Crébillon; and Liotard, the first painter of miniatures then living, was employed to preserve the features of the profligate twaddler. The admirer of the *Sopha* and of the *Lettres Athéniennes* had little respect to spare for the men who were then at the head of French literature. He kept carefully out of their way. He tried to keep other people from paying them any attention. He could not deny that Voltaire and Rousseau were clever men; but he took every opportunity of depreciating them. Of D'Alembert he spoke with a contempt which, when the intellectual powers of the two men are compared, seems exquisitely ridiculous. D'Alembert complained that he was accused of having written Walpole's squib against Rousseau. "I hope," says Walpole, "that nobody will attribute D'Alembert's works to me." He was in little danger.

It is impossible to deny, however, that Walpole's writings have real merit, and merit of a very rare, though not of a very high kind. Sir Joshua Reynolds used to say that, though nobody would for a moment compare Claude to Raphael, there would be another Raphael before there was another Claude. And we own that we expect to see fresh Humes and fresh Burkes before we again fall in with that peculiar combination of moral and intellectual qualities to which the writings of Walpole owe their extraordinary popularity.

It is easy to describe him by negatives. He had not a creative imagination. He had not a pure taste. He was not a great reasoner. There is indeed scarcely any writer in whose works it would be possible to find so many contradictory judgments, so many sentences of extravagant nonsense. Nor was it only in his familiar correspondence that he wrote in this flighty and inconsistent manner, but in long and elaborate books—in books repeatedly transcribed and intended for the public eye. We will give an instance or two ; for, without instances, readers not very familiar with his works, will scarcely understand our meaning. In the "Anecdotes of Painting," he states, very truly, that the art declined after the commencement of the civil wars. He proceeds to inquire why this happened. The explanation, we should have thought, would have been easily found. The loss of the most munificent and judicious patron that the fine arts ever had in England—for such undoubtedly was Charles—the troubled state of the country—the distressed condition of many of the aristocracy—perhaps also the austerity of the victorious party. These circumstances, we conceive, fully account for the phenomenon. But this solution was not odd enough to satisfy Walpole. He discovers another cause for the decline of the art—the want of models. Nothing worth painting, it seems, was left to paint. "How picturesque," he exclaims, "was the figure of an Anabaptist !" —As if puritanism had put out the sun and withered the trees ;—as if the civil wars had blotted out the expression of character and passion from the human lip and brow ;—as if many of the men whom Vandyke painted had not been living in the time of the Commonwealth, with faces a little the worse for wear ;—as if many of the beauties afterwards portrayed by Lely were not in their prime before the Restoration ;—as if the costume or the features of Cromwell and Milton were less picturesque than those of the round-faced peers, as like each other as eggs to eggs, who look out from the middle of the periwigs of Kneller. In the Memoirs, again, Walpole sneers at the Prince of Wales, afterwards George the Third, for presenting a collection of books to one of the American colleges during the Seven Years' War, and says that, instead of books, his Royal Highness ought to have sent arms and ammunition—as if a war ought to suspend all study and all education—or as if it were the business of the Prince of Wales to supply the colonies with military stores out of his own pocket. We have perhaps dwelt too long on these passages ; but we have done so because they are specimens of Walpole's manner. Everybody who reads his works with attention will find that they swarm with loose and foolish observations like those which we have cited ;—observations which might pass in conversation or in a hasty letter, but which are unpardonable in books deliberately written and repeatedly corrected.

He appears to have thought that he saw very far into men ; but we are under the necessity of altogether dissenting from his opinion. We do not conceive that he had any power of discerning the finer shades of character. He practised an art, however, which, though easy, and even vulgar, obtains for those who practise it the reputation of discernment with ninety-nine people out of a hundred. He sneered at everybody, put on every action the worst construction it would bear, "spelt every man backward," to borrow the Lady Hero's phrase,

> "Turned every man the wrong side out,
> And never gave to truth and virtue that
> Which simpleness and merit purchaseth."

In this way any man may, with little sagacity and little trouble, be considered by those whose good opinion is not worth having as a great judge of character.

It is said that the hasty and rapacious Kneller used to send away the ladies who sat to him as soon as he had sketched their faces, and to paint the figure and hands from his housemaid. It was in much the same way that Walpole portrayed the minds of others. He copied from the life only those glaring and obvious peculiarities which could not escape the most superficial observation. The rest of the canvass he filled up, in a careless dashing way, with knave and fool, mixed in such proportions as pleased Heaven. What a difference between these daubs and the masterly portraits of Clarendon!

There are contradictions without end in the sketches of character which abound in Walpole's works. But if we were to form our opinion of his eminent contemporaries from a general survey of what he has written concerning them, we should say that Pitt was a strutting, ranting, mouthing actor, — Charles Townsend an impudent and voluble jack-pudding,—Murray a demure, cold-blooded, cowardly hypocrite,—Hardwick an insolent upstart, with the understanding of a pettifogger and the heart of a hangman,—Temple an impertinent poltroon,—Egmont a solemn coxcomb,—Lyttelton a poor creature whose only wish was to go to heaven in a coronet,—Onslow a pompous proser, —Washington a braggart,—Lord Camden sullen,—Lord Townsend malevolent, —Secker an atheist who had shammed Christian for a mitre,—Whitefield an impostor who swindled his converts out of their watches. The Walpoles fare little better than their neighbours. Old Horace is constantly represented as a coarse, brutal, niggardly buffoon, and his son as worthy of such a father. In short, if we are to trust this discerning judge of human nature, England in his time contained little sense and no virtue, except what was distributed between himself, Lord Waldgrave, and Marshal Conway.

Of such a writer it is scarcely necessary to say that his works are destitute of every charm which is derived from elevation or from tenderness of sentiment. When he chose to be humane and magnanimous,—for he sometimes, by way of variety, tried this affectation,—he overdid his part most ludicrously. None of his many disguises sat so awkwardly upon him. For example, he tells us that he did not choose to be intimate with Mr. Pitt.—And why? Because Mr. Pitt had been among the persecutors of his father? Or because, as he repeatedly assures us, Mr. Pitt was a disagreeable man in private life? Not at all; but because Mr. Pitt was too fond of war, and was great with too little reluctance. Strange that a habitual scoffer like Walpole should imagine that this cant could impose on the dullest reader! If Molière had put such a speech into the mouth of Tartuffe, we should have said that the fiction was unskilful, and that Orgon could not have been such a fool as to be taken in by it. Of the twenty-six years during which Walpole sat in Parliament, thirteen were years of war. Yet he did not, during all those thirteen years, utter a single word or give a single vote tending to peace. His most intimate friend,—the only friend, indeed, to whom he appears to have been sincerely attached,—Conway—was a soldier, was fond of his profession, and was perpetually entreating Mr. Pitt to give him employment. In this Walpole saw nothing but what was admirable. Conway was a hero for soliciting the command of expeditions which Mr. Pitt was a monster for sending out.

What then is the charm, the irresistible charm, of Walpole's writings? It consists, we think, in the art of amusing without exciting. He never convinces the reason, or fills the imagination, or touches the heart; but he keeps the mind of the reader constantly attentive, and constantly entertained. He had a strange ingenuity peculiarly his own,—an ingenuity which appeared in all that he did,—in his building, in his gardening, in his upholstery, in the matter and in the manner of his writings. If we were to adopt the classification,— not a very accurate classification,—which Akenside has given of the pleasures of the imagination, we should say that with the Sublime and the Beautiful Walpole had nothing to do, but that the third province, the Odd, was his peculiar domain. The motto which he prefixed to his "Catalogue of Royal and Noble Authors" might have been inscribed with perfect propriety over the door of every room in his house, and on the title-page of every one of his books ; " Dove diavolo, Messer Ludovico, avete pigliate tante coglionerie?" In his villa, every apartment is a museum ; every piece of furniture is a curiosity ; there is something strange in the form of the shovel ; there is a long story belonging to the bell-rope. We wander among a profusion of rarities, of trifling intrinsic value, but so quaint in fashion, or connected with such remarkable names and events, that they may well detain our attention for a moment. A moment is enough. Some new relic, some new unique, some new carved work, some new enamel, is forthcoming in an instant. One cabinet of trinkets is no sooner closed than another is opened. It is the same with Walpole's writings. It is not in their utility, it is not in their beauty, that their attraction lies. They are to the works of great historians and poets what Strawberry Hill is to the Museum of Sir Hans Sloane or to the Gallery of Florence. Walpole is constantly showing us things,—not of very great value indeed,—yet things which we are pleased to see, and which we can see nowhere else. They are baubles ; but they are made curiosities either by his grotesque workmanship or by some association belonging to them. His style is one of those peculiar styles by which everybody is attracted, and which nobody can safely venture to imitate. He is a mannerist whose manner has become perfectly easy to him. His affectation is so habitual and so universal that it can hardly be called affectation. The affectation is the essence of the man. It pervades all his thoughts and all his expressions. If it were taken away, nothing would be left. He coins new words, distorts the senses of old words, and twists sentences into forms which make grammarians stare. But all this he does, not only with an air of ease, but as if he could not help doing it. His wit was, in its essential properties, of the same kind with that of Cowley and Donne. Like theirs, it consisted in an exquisite perception of points of analogy and points of contrast too subtile for common observation. Like them, Walpole perpetually startles us by the ease with which he yokes together ideas between which there would seem, at first sight, to be no connection. But he did not, like them, affect the gravity of a lecture, and draw his illustrations from the laboratory and from the schools. His tone was light and fleering ; his topics were the topics of the club and the ball-room ; and therefore his strange combinations and far-fetched illusions, though very closely resembling those which tire us to death in the poems of the time of Charles the First, are read with pleasure constantly new.

No man who has written so much is so seldom tiresome. In his books there are scarcely any of those passages which, in our school days, we used to call *skip*. Yet he often wrote on subjects which are generally considered as dull,—on subjects which men of great talents have in vain endeavoured to render popular. When we compare the Historic Doubts about Richard the Third with Whitaker's and Chalmers's books on a far more interesting question,—the character of Mary Queen of Scots ;—when we compare the Anecdotes of Painting with Nichols's Anecdotes, or even with Mr. D'Israeli's Quarrels of Authors and Calamities of Authors, we at once see Walpole's superiority, not in industry, not in learning, not in accuracy, not in logical power, but in the art of writing what people will like to read. He rejects all but the attractive parts of his subject. He keeps only what is in itself amusing, or what can be made so by the artifice of his diction. The coarser morsels of antiquarian learning he abandons to others, and sets out an entertainment worthy of a Roman epicure,—an entertainment consisting of nothing but delicacies,—the brains of singing-birds, the roe of mullets, the sunny halves of

L

peaches. This, we think, is the great merit of his romance. There is little skill in the delineation of the characters. Manfred is as commonplace a tyrant, Jerome as commonplace a confessor, Theodore as commonplace a young gentleman, Isabella and Matilda as commonplace a pair of young ladies, as are to be found in any of the thousand Italian castles in which condottieri have revelled or in which imprisoned duchesses have pined. We cannot say that we much admire the big man whose sword is dug up in one quarter of the globe, whose helmet drops from the clouds in another, and who, after clattering and rustling for some days, ends by kicking the house down. But the story, whatever its value may be, never flags for a single moment. There are no digressions, or unseasonable descriptions, or long speeches. Every sentence carries the action forward. The excitement is constantly renewed. Absurd as is the machinery, insipid as are the human actors, no reader probably ever thought the book dull.

Walpole's Letters are generally considered as his best performances, and, we think, with reason. His faults are far less offensive to us in his correspondence than in his books. His wild, absurd, and ever-changing opinions about men and things are easily pardoned in familiar letters. His bitter, scoffing, depreciating disposition does not show itself in so unmitigated a manner as in his "Memoirs." A writer of letters must in general be civil and friendly to his correspondent at least, if to no other person.

He loved letter-writing, and had evidently studied it as an art. It was, in truth, the very kind of writing for such a man,—for a man very ambitious to rank among wits, yet nervously afraid that, while obtaining the reputation of a wit, he might loose caste as a gentleman. There was nothing vulgar in writing a letter. Not even Ensign Northerton, not even the Captain described in Hamilton's Baron,—and Walpole, though the author of many quartos, had some feelings in common with those gallant officers,—would have denied that a gentleman might sometimes correspond with a friend. Whether Walpole bestowed much labour on the composition of his letters, it is impossible to judge from internal evidence. There are passages which seem perfectly unstudied. But the appearance of ease may be the effect of labour. There are passages which have a very artificial air. But they may have been produced without effort by a mind of which the natural ingenuity had been improved into morbid quickness by constant exercise. We are never sure that we see him as he was. We are never sure that what appears to be nature is not an effect of art. We are never sure that what appears to be art is not merely habit which has become second nature.

In wit and animation the present collection is not superior to those which have preceded it. But it has one great advantage over them all. It forms a connected whole,—a regular journal of what appeared to Walpole the most important transactions of the last twenty years of George the Second's reign. It contains much new information concerning the history of that time,—the portion of English history of which common readers know the least.

The earlier letters contain the most lively and interesting account which we possess of that "great Walpolean battle," to use the words of Junius, which terminated in the retirement of Sir Robert. Horace entered the House of Commons just in time to witness the last desperate struggle which his father, surrounded by enemies and traitors, maintained, with a spirit as brave as that of the column of Fontenoy, first for victory, and then for honourable retreat. Horace was, of course, on the side of his family. Lord Dover seems to have been enthusiastic on the same side, and goes so far as to call Sir Robert "the glory of the Whigs."

Sir Robert deserved this high eulogium, we think, as little as he deserved the abusive epithets which have often been coupled with his name. A fair character of him still remains to be drawn: and, whenever it shall be drawn, it will be equally unlike the portrait by Coxe and the portrait by Smollett.

He had, undoubtedly, great talents and great virtues. He was not, indeed, like the leaders of the party which opposed his Government,—a brilliant orator. He was not a profound scholar, like Carteret, or a wit and a fine gentleman, like Chesterfield. In all these respects his deficiencies were remarkable. His literature consisted of a scrap or two of Horace and an anecdote or two from the end of the Dictionary. His knowledge of history was so limited that, in the great debate on the Excise Bill, he was forced to ask Attorney-General Yorke who Empson and Dudley were. His manners were a little too coarse and boisterous even for that age of Westerns and Topehalls. When he ceased to talk of politics, he could talk of nothing but women; and he dilated on his favourite theme with a freedom which shocked even that plain-spoken generation, and which was quite unsuited to his age and station. The noisy revelry of his summer festivities at Houghton gave much scandal to grave people, and annually drove his kinsman and colleague, Lord Townshend, from the neighbouring mansion of Rainham.

But, however ignorant Walpole might be of general history and of general literature, he was better acquainted than any man of his day with what it concerned him most to know, mankind, the English nation, the Court, the House of Commons, and his own office. Of foreign affairs he knew little; but his judgment was so good that his little knowledge went very far. He was an excellent parliamentary debater, an excellent parliamentary tactician, and an excellent man of business. No man ever brought more industry or more method to the transacting of affairs. No minister in his time did so much; yet no minister had so much leisure.

He was a good-natured man who had during thirty years seen nothing but the worst parts of human nature in other men. He was familiar with the malice of kind people, and the perfidy of honourable people. Proud men had licked the dust before him. Patriots had begged him to come up to the price of their puffed and advertised integrity. He said after his fall that it was a dangerous thing to be a minister,—that there were few minds which would not be injured by the constant spectacle of meanness and depravity. To his honour it must be confessed that few minds have come out of such a trial so little damaged in the most important parts. He retired, after more than twenty years of power, with a temper not soured, with a heart not hardened, with simple tastes, with frank manners, and with a capacity for friendship. No stain of treachery, of ingratitude, or of cruelty rests on his memory. Factious hatred, while flinging on his name every other foul aspersion, was compelled to own that he was not a man of blood. This would scarcely seem a high eulogium on a statesman of our times. It was then a rare and honourable distinction. The contests of parties in England had long been carried on with a ferocity unworthy of a civilised people. Sir Robert Walpole was the minister who gave to our Government that character of lenity which it has since generally preserved. It was perfectly known to him that many of his opponents had dealings with the Pretender. The lives of some were at his mercy. He wanted neither Whig nor Tory precedents for using his advantage unsparingly. But with a clemency to which posterity has never done justice, he suffered himself to be thwarted, vilified, and at last overthrown, by a party which included many men whose necks were in his power.

That he practised corruption on a large scale is, we think, indisputable. But whether he deserves all the invectives which have been uttered against him on that account may be questioned. No man ought to be severely censured for not being beyond his age in virtue. To buy the votes of constituents is as immoral as to buy the votes of representatives. The candidate who gives five guineas to the freeman is as culpable as the man who gives three hundred guineas to the member. Yet we know that, in our own time, no man is thought wicked or dishonourable,—no man is cut,—no man is black-balled, because, under the old system of election, he was returned, in the only way in which he could be returned, for East Retford, for Liverpool, or for Stafford. Walpole governed by corruption because, in his time, it was impossible to govern otherwise. Corruption was unnecessary to the Tudors; for their Parliaments were feeble. The publicity which has of late years been given to parliamentary proceedings has raised the standard of morality among public men. The power of public opinion is so great that, even before the reform of the representation, a faint suspicion that a minister had given pecuniary gratifications to Members of Parliament in return for their votes would have been enough to ruin him. But, during the century which followed the Restoration, the House of Commons was in that situation in which assemblies must be managed by corruption or cannot be managed at all. It was not held in awe, as in the sixteenth century, by the throne. It was not held in awe, as in the nineteenth century, by the opinion of the people. Its constitution was oligarchical. Its deliberations were secret. Its power in the State was immense. The Government had every conceivable motive to offer bribes. Many of the members, if they were not men of strict honour and probity, had no conceivable motive to refuse what the Government offered. In the reign of Charles the Second, accordingly, the practice of buying votes in the House of Commons was commenced by the daring Clifford, and carried to a great extent by the crafty and shameless Danby. The Revolution, great and manifold as were the blessings of which it was directly or remotely the cause, at first aggravated this evil. The importance of the House of Commons was now greater than ever. The prerogatives of the Crown were more strictly limited than ever; and those associations in which, more than in its legal prerogatives, its power had consisted, were completely broken. No prince was ever in so helpless and distressing a situation as William the Third. The party which defended his title was, on general grounds, disposed to curtail his prerogative. The party, which was, on general grounds, friendly to prerogative, was adverse to his title. There was no quarter in which both his office and his person could find favour. But while the influence of the House of Commons in the Government was becoming paramount, the influence of the people over the House of Commons was declining. It mattered little in the time of Charles the First whether that House were or were not chosen by the people:—it was certain to act for the people, because it would have been at the mercy of the Court but for the support of the people. Now that the Court was at the mercy of the House of Commons,—that large body of members who were not returned by popular election had nobody to please but themselves. Even those who were returned by popular election did not live, as now, under a constant sense of responsibility. The constituents were not, as now, daily apprised of the votes and speeches of their representatives. The privileges which had in old times been indispensably necessary to the security and efficiency of Parliaments were now superfluous. But they were still carefully maintained,—by honest legislators from superstitious veneration,— by dishonest legislators for their own selfish ends. They had been a useful defence to the Commons during a long and doubtful conflict with powerful sovereigns. They were now no longer necessary for that purpose; and they became a defence to the members against their constituents. That secrecy which had been absolutely necessary in times when the Privy Council was in the habit of sending the leaders of Opposition to the Tower was preserved in times when a vote of the House of Commons was sufficient to hurl the most powerful minister from his post.

The Government could not go on unless the Parliament could be kept in order. And how was the Parliament to be kept in order? Three hundred years ago it would have been enough for a statesman to have the support of the Crown. It would now, we hope and believe, be enough for him to enjoy the confidence and approbation of the great body of the middle class. A hundred years ago it would not have been enough to have both Crown and people on his side. The Parliament had shaken off the control of the Royal prerogative. It had not yet fallen under the control of public opinion. A large proportion of the members had absolutely no motive to support any administration except their own interest, in the lowest sense of the word. Under these circumstances, the country could be governed only by corruption. Bolingbroke, who was the ablest and the most vehement of those who raised the cry against corruption, had no better remedy to propose than that the Royal prerogative should be strengthened. The remedy would no doubt have been efficient. The only question is, whether it would not have been worse than the disease. The fault was in the constitution of the Legislature; and to blame those ministers who managed the Legislature in the only way in which it could be managed is gross injustice. They submitted to extortion because they could not help themselves. We might as well accuse the poor Lowland farmers who paid "black mail" to "Rob Roy" of corrupting the virtue of the Highlanders, as accuse Sir Robert Walpole of corrupting the virtue of Parliament. His crime was merely this,—that he employed his money more dexterously, and got more support in return for it, than any of those who preceded or followed him.

He was himself incorruptible by money. His dominant passion was the love of power: and the heaviest charge which can be brought against him is that to this passion he never scrupled to sacrifice the interests of his country.

One of the maxims which, as his son tells us, he was most in the habit of repeating was, *quieta non movere*. It was indeed the maxim by which he generally regulated his public conduct. It is the maxim of a man more solicitous to hold power long than to use it well. It is remarkable that, though he was at the head of affairs during more than twenty years, not one great measure, not one important change for the better or for the worse in any part of our institutions, marks the period of his supremacy. Nor was this because he did not clearly see that many changes were very desirable. He had been brought up in the school of toleration, at the feet of Somers and of Burnet. He disliked the shameful laws against Dissenters. But he never could be induced to bring forward a proposition for repealing them. The sufferers represented to him the injustice with which they were treated, boasted of their firm attachment to the House of Brunswick and to the Whig party, and reminded him of his own repeated declarations of good will to their cause. He listened, assented, promised, and did nothing. At length, the question was brought forward by others, and the Minister, after a hesitating and evasive speech, voted against it. The truth was that he remembered to the latest day of his life that terrible explosion of high church feeling which the foolish prosecution of a foolish parson had occasioned in the days of Queen Anne. If the Dissenters had been turbulent he would probably have relieved them: but while he apprehended no danger from them, he would not run the slightest risk for their sake. He acted in the same manner with respect to other questions. He knew the state of the Scotch Highlands. He was constantly predicting another insurrection in that part of the empire,

Yet, during his long tenure of power, he never attempted to perform what was then the most obvious and pressing duty of a British Statesman,—to break the power of the Chiefs, and to establish the authority of law through the furthest corners of the Island. Nobody knew better than he that, if this were not done, great mischiefs would follow. But the Highlands were tolerably quiet in his time. He was content to meet daily emergencies by daily expedients; and he left the rest to his successors. They had to conquer the Highlands in the midst of a war with France and Spain, because he had not regulated the Highlands in a time of profound peace.

Sometimes, in spite of all his caution, he found that measures which he had hoped to carry through quietly had caused great agitation. When this was the case he generally modified or withdrew them. It was thus that he cancelled Wood's patent in compliance with the absurd outcry of the Irish. It was thus that he frittered away the Porteous Bill to nothing, for fear of exasperating the Scotch. It was thus that he abandoned the Excise Bill, as soon as he found that it was offensive to all the great towns of England. The language which he held about that measure in a subsequent session is strikingly characteristic. Pulteney had insinuated that the scheme would be again brought forward. "As to the wicked scheme," said Walpole, "as the gentleman is pleased to call it, which he would persuade gentlemen is not yet laid aside, I for my part assure this House I am not so mad as ever again to engage in anything that looks like an Excise; though, in my private opinion, I still think it was a scheme that would have tended very much to the interest of the nation."

The conduct of Walpole with regard to the Spanish war is the great blemish of his public life. Archdeacon Coxe imagined that he had discovered one grand principle of action to which the whole public conduct of his hero ought to be referred. "Did the administraton of Walpole," says the biographer, "present any uniform principle which may be traced in every part, and which gave combination and consistency to the whole? Yes, and that principle was THE LOVE OF PEACE." It would be difficult, we think, to bestow a higher eulogium on any statesman. But the eulogium is far too high for the merits of Walpole. The great ruling principle of his public conduct was indeed a love of peace, but not in the sense in which Archdeacon Coxe uses the phrase. The peace which Walpole sought was not the peace of the country, but the peace of his own administration. During the greater part of his public life, indeed, the two objects were inseparably connected. At length he was reduced to the necessity of choosing between them—of plunging the State into hostilities for which there was no just ground, and by which nothing was to be got, or of facing a violent opposition in the country, in Parliament, and even in the royal closet. No person was more thoroughly convinced than he of the absurdity of the cry against Spain. But his darling power was at stake, and his choice was soon made. He preferred an unjust war to a stormy session. It is imposible to say of a Minister who acted thus that the love of peace was the one grand principle to which all his conduct is to be referred. The governing principle of his conduct was neither love of peace nor love of war, but love of power.

The praise to which he is fairly entitled is this, that he understood the true interest of his country better than any of his contemporaries, and that he pursued that interest whenever it was not incompatible with the interest of his own intense and grasping ambition. It was only in matters of public moment that he shrank from agitation and had recourse to compromise. In his contests for personal influence there was no timidity, no flinching. He would have all or none. Every member of the Government who would not submit to his ascendency was turned out or forced to resign. Liberal of everything else, he was avaricious of nothing but power. Cautious everywhere else, when power was at stake he had all the boldness of Wolsey or Chatham. He might easily have secured his authority if he could have been induced to divide it with others. But he would not part with one fragment of it to purchase defenders for all the rest. The effect of this policy was that he had able enemies and feeble allies. His most distinguished coadjutors left him one by one, and joined the ranks of the Opposition. He faced the increasing array of his enemies with unbroken spirit, and thought it far better that they should inveigh against his power than that they should share it.

The Opposition was in every sense formidable. At its head were two royal personages,—the exiled head of the House of Stuart, the disgraced heir of the House of Brunswick. One set of members received directions from Avignon. Another set held their consultations and banquets at Norfolk House. The majority of the landed gentry,—the majority of the parochial clergy,—one of the universities,—and a strong party in the City of London and in the other great towns were decidedly adverse to the Government. Of the men of letters, some were exasperated by the neglect with which the Minister treated them,—a neglect which was the more remarkable, because his predecessors, both Whig and Tory, had paid court with emulous munificence to the wits and the poets ;—others were honestly inflamed by party zeal ; almost all lent their aid to the Opposition. In truth, all that was alluring to ardent and imaginative minds was on that side ;—old associations—new visions of political improvement—high-flown theories of loyalty—high-flown theories of liberty—the enthusiasm of the Cavalier—the enthusiasm of the Roundhead. The Tory gentleman, fed in the common-rooms of Oxford with the doctrines of Filmer and Sacheverell, and proud of the exploits of his great-grandfather, who had charged with Rupert Marston—who had held out the old manor-house against Fairfax, and who, after the king's return, had been set down for a Knight of the Royal Oak—flew to that section of the opposition which, under pretence of assailing the existing administration, was in truth assailing the reigning dynasty. The young republican, fresh from his Livy and his Lucan, and flowing with admiration of Hampden, of Russell, and of Sydney, hastened with equal eagerness to those benches from which eloquent voices thundered nightly against the tyranny and perfidy of courts. So many young politicians were caught by these declamations that Sir Robert, in one of his best speeches, observed that the Opposition consisted of three bodies—the Tories, the discontented Whigs, who were known by the name of the Patriots, and the Boys. In fact almost every young man of warm temper and lively imagination, whatever his political bias might be, was drawn into the party adverse to the Government ; and some of the most distinguished among them—Pitt, for example, among public men, and Johnson among men of letters—afterwards openly acknowledged their mistake.

The aspect of the opposition, even while it was still a minority in the House of Commons, was very imposing. Among those who, in Parliament or out of Parliament, assailed the administration of Walpole were Bolingbroke, Carteret, Chesterfield, Argyle, Pulteney, Wyndham, Doddington, Pitt, Lyttleton, Barnard, Pope, Swift, Gay, Arbuthnot, Fielding, Johnson, Thomson, Akenside, Glover.

The circumstance that the opposition was divided into two parties diametrically opposed to each other in political opinions was long the safety of Walpole. It was at last his ruin. The leaders of the minority knew that it would be difficult for them to bring forward any important measure without producing an immediate schism in their party. It was with very great difficulty that the Whigs in opposition had been induced to give a sullen and silent vote for the repeal of the Septennial Act. The Tories, on the other hand, could not be induced to support Pulteney's motion for an addition to the income of Prince Frederic. The two parties had cordially joined in calling out for a war with Spain; but they now had their war. Hatred of Walpole was almost the only feeling which was common to them. On this one point, therefore, they concentrated their whole strength. With gross ignorance, or gross dishonesty, they represented the minister as the main grievance of the state. His dismissal,—his punishment,—would prove the certain cure for all the evils which the nation suffered. What was to be done after his fall,—how misgovernment was to be prevented in future,—were questions to which there were as many answers as there were noisy and ill-informed members of the Opposition. The only cry in which all could join was, "Down with Walpole!" So much did they narrow the disputed ground,—so purely personal did they make the question,—that they threw out friendly hints to the other members of the Administration, and declared that they refused quarter to the Prime Minister alone. His tools might keep their heads, their fortunes, 'even their places, if only the great father of corruption were given up to the just vengeance of the nation.

If the fate of Walpole's colleagues had been inseparably bound up with his, he probably would, even after the unfavourable elections of 1741, have been able to weather the storm. But as soon as it was understood that the attack was directed against him alone, and that if he were sacrificed, his associates might expect advantages and honourable terms, the ministerial ranks began to waver, and the murmur of *sauve qui peut* was heard. That Walpole had foul play is almost certain, but to what extent it is difficult to say. Lord Islay was suspected; the Duke of Newcastle something more than suspected. It would have been strange, indeed, if his Grace had been idle when treason was hatching.

"Che Gan fu traditor prima che nato." "His name," said Sir Robert, "is perfidy."

Never was a battle more manfully fought out than the last struggle of the old statesman. His clear judgment, his long experience, and his fearless spirit, enabled him to maintain a defensive war through half the session. To the last his heart never failed him; and when at last he yielded, he yielded not to the threats of his enemies, but to the entreaties of his dispirited and refractory followers. When he could no longer retain his power, he compounded for honour and security, and retired to his garden and his paintings, leaving to those who had overthrown him—shame, discord, and ruin.

Everything was in confusion. It had been said that the confusion was produced by the dexterous policy of Walpole; and, undoubtedly, he did his best to sow dissension amongst his triumphant enemies. But there was little for him to do. Victory had completely dissolved the hollow truce, which the two sections of the opposition had but imperfectly observed, even while the event of the contest was still doubtful. A thousand questions were opened in a moment. A thousand conflicting claims were preferred. It was impossible to follow any line of policy which would not have been offensive to a large portion of the successful party. It was impossible to find places for a tenth part of those who thought that they had a right to be considered. While the parliamentary leaders were preaching patience and confidence,—while their followers were clamouring for reward, a still louder voice was heard from without,—the terrible cry of a people angry, they hardly knew with whom,—

and impatient, they hardly knew for what. The day of retribution had arrived. The opposition reaped that which they had sown. Inflamed with hatred and cupidity, despairing of success by any ordinary mode of political warfare, and blind to consequences which, though remote, were certain, they had conjured up a devil whom they could not lay. They had made the public mind drunk with calumny and declamation. They had raised expectations which it was impossible to satisfy. The downfall of Walpole was to be the beginning of a political millennium; and every enthusiast had figured to himself that millennium according to the fashion of his own wishes. The republican expected that the power of the Crown would be reduced to a mere shadow,—the high Tory that the Stuarts would be restored,—the moderate Tory that the golden days which the Church and the landed interest had enjoyed during the last years of Queen Anne, would immediately return. It would have been impossible to satisfy everybody. The conquerors satisfied nobody.

We have no reverence for the memory of those who were then called the patriots. We are for the principles of good government against Walpole, and for Walpole against the opposition. It was most desirable that a purer system should be introduced; but, if the old system was to be retained, no man was so fit as Walpole to be at the head of affairs. There were frightful abuses in the government—abuses more than sufficient to justify a strong opposition. But the party opposed to Walpole, while they stimulated the popular fury to the highest point, were at no pains to direct it aright. Indeed they studiously misdirected it. They misrepresented the evil. They prescribed inefficient and pernicious remedies. They held up a single man as the sole cause of all the vices of a bad system which had been in full operation before his entrance into public life, and which continued to be in full operation when some of these very brawlers had succeeded to his power. They thwarted his best measures. They drove him into an unjustifiable war against his will. Constantly talking in magnificent language about tyranny, corruption, wicked ministers, servile courtiers, the liberty of Englishmen, the Great Charter, the rights for which our fathers bled—Timoleon, Brutus, Hampden, Sydney—they had absolutely nothing to propose which would have been an improvement on our institutions. Instead of directing the public mind to definite reforms which might have completed the work of the revolution,—which might have brought the legislature into harmony with the nation, and which might have prevented the Crown from doing by influence what it could no longer do by prerogative,—they excited a vague craving for change, by which they profited for a single moment, and of which, as they well deserved, they were soon the victims.

Among the reforms which the state then required, there were two of paramount importance,—two which would alone have remedied almost every abuse, and without which all other remedies would have been unavailing,—the publicity of parliamentary proceedings, and the abolition of the rotten boroughs. Neither of these was thought of. It seems to us clear that, if these were not adopted, all other measures would have been illusory. Some of the patriots suggested changes which would, beyond all doubt, have increased the existing evils a hundredfold. These men wished to transfer the disposal of employments and the command of the army from the Crown to the Parliament; and this on the very ground that the Parliament had long been a grossly corrupt body. The security against corruption was to be that the members, instead of having a portion of the public plunder doled out to them by a minister, were to help themselves.

The other schemes of which the public mind was full were less dangerous than this. Some of them were in themselves harmless. But none of them would have done much good, and most of them were extravagantly absurd. What they were we may learn from the instructions which many constituent bodies, immediately after the change of administration, sent up to their representatives. A more deplorable collection of follies can hardly be imagined. There is, in the first place, a general cry for Walpole's head. Then there are bitter complaints of the decay of trade—a decay which, in the judgment of these enlightened politicians, was brought about by Walpole and corruption. They would have been nearer to the truth if they had attributed their sufferings to the war into which they had driven Walpole against his better judgment. He had foretold the effects of his unwilling concession. On the day when hostilities against Spain were proclaimed, when the heralds were attended into the city by the chiefs of the opposition, when the Prince of Wales himself stopped at Temple Bar to drink success to the English arms, the Minister heard all the steeples of the city jingling with a merry peal, and muttered, "They may ring the bells now: they will be ringing their hands before long."

Another grievance, for which of course Walpole and corruption were answerable, was the great exportation of English wool. In the judgment of the sagacious electors of several large towns, the remedying of this evil was a matter second only in importance to the hanging of Sir Robert. There were also earnest injunctions that the members should vote against standing armies in time of peace,—injunctions which were, to say the least, ridiculously unseasonable in the midst of a war which was likely to last, and which did actually last, as long as the Parliament. The repeal of the Septennial Act, as was to be expected, was strongly pressed. Nothing was more natural than that the voters should wish for a triennial recurrence of their bribes and their ale. We feel firmly convinced that the repeal of the Septennial Act, unaccompanied by a complete reform of the constitution of the elective body, would have been an unmixed curse to the country. The only rational recommendation which we can find in all these instructions is, that the number of Placemen in Parliament should be limited, and that pensioners should not be allowed to sit there. It is plain, however, that this cure was far from going to the root of the evil, and that, if it had been adopted the consequence would probably have been that secret bribery would have been more practised than ever.

We will give one more instance of the absurd expectations which the declamations of the opposition had raised in the country. Akenside was one of the fiercest and most uncompromising of the young patriots out of Parliament. When he found that the change of administration had produced no change of system, he gave vent to his indignation in the "Epistle to Curio," the best poem that he ever wrote,—a poem, indeed, which seems to indicate that, if he had left lyric composition to Gray and Collins, and had employed his powers in grave and elevated satire, he might have disputed the pre-eminence of Dryden. But, whatever be the literary merits of the epistle, we can say nothing in praise of the political doctrines which it inculcates. The poet, in a rapturous apostrophe to the Spirits of the Great Men of Antiquity, tells us what he expected from Pulteney, at the moment of the fall of the tyrant.

> "See private life by wisest arts reclaimed,
> See ardent youth to noblest manners framed,
> See us achieve whate'er was sought by you,
> If Curio—only Curio—will be true."

It was Pulteney's business, it seems, to abolish faro and masquerades, to stint the young Duke of Marlborough to a bottle of brandy a day, and to prevail on Lady Vane to be content with three lovers at a time.

Whatever the people wanted, they certainly got nothing. Walpole retired in safety; and the multitude were defrauded of the expected show on Tower Hill. The Septennial Act was not repealed. The Placemen were not turned out of the House of Commons. Wool, we believe, was still exported. "Private life" afforded as much scandal as if the reign of Walpole and corruption had continued; and "ardent youth" fought with watchmen and betted with blacklegs as much as ever.

The colleagues of Walpole had, after his retreat, admitted some of the chiefs of the opposition into the Government. They soon found themselves compelled to submit to the ascendency of one of their new allies. This was Lord Carteret, afterwards Earl Granville. No public man of that age had greater courage, greater ambition, greater activity, greater talents for debate, or for declamation. No public man had such profound and extensive learning. He was familiar with the ancient writers. His knowledge of modern languages was prodigious. The privy council, when he was present, needed no interpreter. He spoke and wrote French, Italian, Spanish, Portuguese, German, even Swedish. He had pushed his researches into the most obscure nooks of literature. He was as familiar with Canonists and Schoolmen as with orators and poets. He had read all that the universities of Saxony and Holland had produced on the most intricate questions of public law. Harte, in the preface to the second edition of his History of Gustavus Adolphus, bears a remarkable testimony to the extent and accuracy of Lord Carteret's knowledge. "It was my good fortune or prudence to keep the main body of my army (or in other words my matters of fact) safe and entire. The late Earl of Granville was pleased to declare himself of this opinion; especially when he found that I had made Chemnitius one of my principal guides; for his Lordship was apprehensive I might not have seen that valuable and authentic book, which is extremely scarce. I thought myself happy to have contented his Lordship even in the lowest degree: for he understood the German and Swedish histories to the highest perfection."

With all this learning, Carteret was far from being a pedant. His was not one of those cold spirits of which the fire is put out by the fuel. In council, in debate, in society, he was all life and energy. His measures were strong, prompt, and daring, his oratory animated and glowing. His spirits were constantly high. No misfortune, public or private, could depress him. He was at once the most unlucky and the happiest public man of his time.

He had been Secretary of State in Walpole's administration, and had acquired considerable influence over the mind of George the First. The other Ministers could speak no German. The King could speak no English. All the communication that Walpole held with his master was in very bad Latin. Carteret dismayed his colleagues by the volubility with which he addressed his Majesty in German. They listened with envy and terror to the mysterious gutterals which might possibly convey suggestions very little in unison with their wishes.

Walpole was not a man to endure such a colleague as Carteret. The King was induced to give up his favourite. Carteret joined the opposition, and signalised himself at the head of that party till, after the retirement of his old rival, he again became Secretary of State.

During some months he was chief Minister,—indeed sole Minister. He gained the confidence and regard of George the Second. He was at the same time in high favour with the Prince of Wales. As a debater in the House of Lords, he had no equal among his colleagues. Among his opponents, Chesterfield alone could be considered as his match. Confident in his talents, and in the royal favour, he neglected all those means by which the power of

Walpole had been created and maintained. His head was full of treaties and expeditions, of schemes for supporting the Queen of Hungary and for humbling the House of Bourbon. He contemptuously abandoned to others all the drudgery, and, with the drudgery, all the fruits of corruption. The patronage of the Church and of the Bar he left to the Pelhams as a trifle unworthy of his care. One of the judges,—Chief Justice Willes, if we remember rightly,— went to him to beg some ecclesiastical preferment for a friend. Carteret said, that he was too much occupied with continental politics to think about the disposal of places and benefices. "You may rely on it, then," said the Chief Justice, "that people who want places and benefices will go to those who have more leisure." The prediction was accomplished. It would have been a busy time indeed in which the Pelhams had wanted leisure for jobbing; and to the Pelhams the whole cry of place-hunters and pension-hunters resorted. The parliamentary influence of the two brothers became stronger every day, till at length they were at the head of a decided majority in the House of Commons. Their rival, meanwhile, conscious of his powers, sanguine in his hopes, and proud of the storm which he had conjured upon the Continent, would brook neither superior nor equal. "His rants," says Horace Walpole, "are amazing; so are his parts and his spirits." He encountered the opposition of his colleagues, not with the fierce haughtiness of the first Pitt, or the cold unbending arrogance of the second, but with a gay vehemence, a good-humoured imperiousness, that bore everything down before it. The period of his ascendency was known by the name of the "Drunken Administration;" and the expression was not altogether figurative. His habits were extremely convivial; and champagne probably lent its aid to keep him in that state of joyous excitement in which his life was passed.

That a rash and impetuous man of genius like Carteret should not have been able to maintain his ground in Parliament against the crafty and selfish Pelhams is not strange. But it is less easy to understand why he should have been generally unpopular throughout the country. His brilliant talents, his bold and open temper, ought, it should seem, to have made him a favourite with the public. But the people had been bitterly disappointed; and he had to face the first burst of their rage. His close connection with Pulteney, now the most detested man in the nation, was an unfortunate circumstance. He had, indeed, only three partisans,—Pulteney, the King, and the Prince of Wales,—a most singular assemblage.

He was driven from his office. He shortly after made a bold, indeed a desperate, attempt to recover power. The attempt failed. From that time he relinquished all ambitious hopes, and retired laughing to his books and his bottle. No statesman ever enjoyed success with so exquisite a relish, or submitted to defeat with so genuine and unforced a cheerfulness. Ill as he had been used, he did not seem, says Horace Walpole, to have any resentment, or indeed any feeling except thirst.

These letters contain many good stories,—some of them no doubt grossly exaggerated, about Lord Carteret;—how, in the height of his greatness he fell in love at first sight on a birthday with Lady Sophia Fermor, the handsome daughter of Lord Pomfret;—how he plagued the Cabinet every day with reading to them her ladyship's letters;—how strangely he brought home his bride;—what fine jewels he gave her;—how he fondled her at Ranelagh;— and what queen-like state she kept in Arlington Street. Horace Walpole has spoken less bitterly of Carteret than of any public man of that time, Fox, perhaps, excepted; and this is the more remarkable, because Carteret was one of the most inveterate enemies of Sir Robert. In the Memoirs, Horace Walpole, after passing in review all the great men whom England had produced within his memory, concludes by saying, that in genius none of them equalled Lord Granville. Smollett, in Humphrey Clinker, pronounces a similar judgment in coarser language. "Since Granville was turned out, there has been no minister in this nation worth the meal that whitened his periwig."

Carteret fell; and the reign of the Pelhams commenced. It was Carteret's misfortune to be raised to power when the public mind was still smarting from recent disappointment. The nation had been duped, and was eager for revenge. A victim was necessary,—and on such occasions the victims of popular rage are selected like the victim of Jephthah. The first person who comes in the way is made the sacrifice. The wrath of the people had now spent itself; and the unnatural excitement was succeeded by an unnatural calm. To an irrational eagerness for something new, succeeded an equally irrational disposition to acquiesce in everything established. A few months back the people had been disposed to impute every crime to men in power, and to lend a ready ear to the high professions of men in opposition. They were now disposed to surrender themselves implicitly to the management of Ministers, and to look with suspicion and contempt on all who pretended to public spirit. The name of patriot had become a by-word of derision. Horace Walpole scarcely exaggerated when he said that, in those times, the most popular declaration which a candidate could make on the hustings was that he had never been and never would be a patriot. At this conjuncture took place the rebellion of the Highland clans. The alarm produced by that event quieted the strife of internal factions. The suppression of the insurrection crushed for ever the spirit of the Jacobite party. Room was made in the Government for a few Tories. Peace was patched up with France and Spain. Death removed the Prince of Wales, who had contrived to keep together a small portion of that formidable opposition of which he had been the leader in the time of Sir Robert Walpole. Almost every man of weight in the House of Commons was officially connected with the Government. The even tenor of the session of Parliament was ruffled only by an occasional harangue from Lord Egmont on the army estimates. For the first time since the accession of the Stuarts there was no opposition. This singular good fortune, denied to the ablest statesmen,—to Salisbury, to Stafford, to Clarendon, to Walpole,—had been reserved for the Pelhams.

Henry Pelham, it is true, was by no means a contemptible person. His understanding was that of Walpole on a somewhat smaller scale. Though not a brilliant orator, he was, like his master, a good debater, a good parliamentary tactician, a good man of business. Like his master, he distinguished himself by the neatness and clearness of his financial expositions. Here the resemblance ceased. Their characters were altogether dissimilar. Walpole was good-humoured, but would have his way: his spirits were high, and his manners frank even to coarseness. The temper of Pelham was yielding, but peevish: his habits were regular, and his deportment strictly decorous. Walpole was constitutionally fearless, Pelham constitutionally timid. Walpole had to face a strong opposition; but no man in the Government durst wag a finger against him. Almost all the opposition which Pelham had to encounter was from members of the Government of which he was the head. His own paymaster spoke against his estimates. His own secretary-at-war spoke against his Regency Bill. In one day Walpole turned Lord Chesterfield, Lord Burlington, and Lord Clinton out of the royal household—dismissed the highest dignitaries of Scotland from their posts—and took away the regiments of the Duke of Bolton and Lord Cobham, because he suspected them of having encouraged the resistance to the Excise Bill. He would far rather have contended with the strongest minority, under the ablest leaders, than have tolerated mutiny in his own party. It would have gone hard with any of his colleagues who had ventured to divide the House of Commons against him. Pelham, on the other hand, was disposed to bear anything rather than drive from office any man round whom a new opposition could form. He therefore endured with fretful patience the insubordination of Pitt and Fox. He thought it far better to connive at their occasional infractions of discipline than to hear them, night after night, thundering against corruption and wicked ministers from the other side of the house.

We wonder that Sir Walter Scott never tried his hand on the Duke of Newcastle. An interview between his Grace and Jeannie Deans would have been delightful, and by no means unnatural. There is scarcely any public man in our history of whose manners and conversation so many particulars have been preserved. Single stories may be unfounded or exaggerated, but all the stories about him, whether told by people who were perpetually seeing him in Parliament and attending his levee in Lincoln's Inn Fields, or by Grub Street writers who never had more than a glimpse of his star through the windows of his gilded coach, are of the same character. Horace Walpole and Smollet differed in their tastes and opinions as much as two human beings could differ. They kept quite different society. The one played at cards with countesses, and corresponded with ambassadors. The other passed his life surrounded by printers' devils and famished scribblers. Yet Walpole's Duke and Smollett's Duke are as like as if they were both from one hand. Smollett's Newcastle runs out of his dressing-room, with his face covered with soap-suds, to embrace the Moorish envoy. Walpole's Newcastle pushes his way into the Duke of Grafton's sick room to kiss the old nobleman's plasters. No man was ever so unmercifully satirised. But in truth he was himself a satire ready made. Al lthat the art of the satirist does for other ridiculous men, nature had done for him. Whatever was absurd about him stood out with grotesque prominence from the rest of his character. He was a living, moving, talking, caricature. His gait was a shuffling trot; his utterance a rapid stutter; he was always in a hurry; he was never in time; he abounded in fulsome caresses and in hysterical tears. His oratory resembled that of Justice Shallow. It was nonsense effervescent with animal spirits and impertinence. Of his ignorance many anecdotes remain, some well authenticated, some probably invented at coffee-houses, but all exquisitely characteristic. "Oh—yes—yes—to be sure—Annapolis must be defended—troops must be sent to Annapolis—Pray where is Annapolis?"—"Cape Breton an island! wonderful!—show it me in the map. So it is, sure enough. My dear sir,—you always bring us good news. I must go and tell the King that Cape Breton is an island."

And this man was, during near thirty years, Secretary of State,—and, during near ten years, first Lord of the Treasury! His large fortune, his strong hereditary connection, his great parliamentary interest, will not alone explain this extraordinary fact. His success is a signal instance of what may be effected by a man who devotes his whole heart and soul without reserve to one object. He was eaten up by ambition. His love of influence and authority resembled the avarice of the old usurer in the Fortunes of Nigel. It was so intense a passion that it supplied the place of talents, that it inspired even fatuity with cunning. "Have no money dealings with my father," says Martha to Lord Glenvarloch," for dotard as he is, he will make an ass of you." It was as dangerous to have any political connection with Newcastle as to buy and sell with old Trapbois. He was greedy after power with a greediness all his own. He was jealous of all his colleagues, and even of his own brother. Under the disguise of levity he was false beyond all example of political falsehood. All the able men of his time ridiculed him as a dunce, a driveller, a child who never knew his own mind for an hour together; and he overreached them all round.

If the country had remained at peace, it is not impossible that this man would have continued at the head of affairs without admitting any other person to a share of his authority until the throne was filled by a new Prince, who brought with him new maxims of government, new favourites, and a strong will. But the inauspicious commencement of the Seven Years' War brought on a crisis to which Newcastle was altogether unequal. After a calm of fifteen years the spirit of the nation was again stirred to its inmost depths. In a few days the whole aspect of the political world was changed.

But that change is too remarkable an event to be discussed at the end of an article already too long. It is probable that we may, at no remote time, resume the subject.

THACKERAY'S HISTORY OF THE EARL OF CHATHAM.
(JANUARY, 1834.)

A History of the Right Honourable William Pitt, Earl of Chatham, containing his Speeches in Parliament, a considerable portion of his Correspondence when Secretary of State, upon French, Spanish, and American Affairs, never before published; and an Account of the principal Events and Persons of his Times connected with his Life, Sentiments, and Administration. By the Rev. FRANCIS THACKERAY, A.M. 2 vols. 4to. London, 1827.

THOUGH several years have elapsed since the publication of this work, it is still, we believe, a new publication to most of our readers. Nor are we surprised at this. The book is large, and the style heavy. The information which Mr. Thackeray has obtained from the State Paper Office is new; but much of it is very uninteresting. The rest of his narrative is very little better than Gifford's or Tomline's Life of the second Pitt, and tells us little or nothing that may not be found quite as well told in the Parliamentary History, the Annual Register, and other works equally common.

Almost every mechanical employment, it is said, has a tendency to injure some one or other of the bodily organs of the artisan. Grinders of cutlery die of consumption; weavers are stunted in their growth; smiths become blear-eyed. In the same manner almost every intellectual employment has a tendency to produce some intellectual malady. Biographers, translators, editors, all, in short, who employ themselves in illustrating the lives or the writings of others, are peculiarly exposed to the *Lues Boswelliana*, or disease of admiration. But we scarcely remember ever to have seen a patient so far gone in this distemper as Mr. Thackeray. He is not satisfied with forcing us to confess that Pitt was a great orator, a vigorous minister, an honourable and high-spirited gentleman. He will have it, that all virtues and all accomplishments met in his hero. In spite of Gods, men, and columns, Pitt must be a poet,—a poet capable of producing a heroic poem of the first order;—and we are assured that we ought to find many charms in such lines as these :—

> "Midst all the tumults of the warring sphere,
> My light-charged bark may haply *glide* :
> Some gale may waft, some conscious thought shall cheer,
> And the small freight unanxious *glide*."

Pitt was in the army for a few months in time of peace. Mr. Thackeray accordingly insists on our confessing that, if the young cornet had remained in the service, he would have been one of the ablest commanders that ever lived. But this is not all. Pitt, it seems, was not merely a great poet *in esse*, and a great general *in posse*, but a finished example in moral excellence,— the just man made perfect. He was in the right when he attempted to establish an inquisition, and to give bounties for perjury, in order to get Walpole's head. He was in the right when he declared Walpole to have been an excellent minister. He was in the right when, being in Opposition, he maintained that no peace ought to be made with Spain, till she should formally renounce the right of search. He was in the right when, being in office, he silently acquiesced in a treaty by which Spain did not renounce the right of search. When he left the Duke of Newcastle,—when he coalesced with the Duke of Newcastle,—when he thundered against subsidies,—when he lavished subsidies with unexampled profusion,—when he execrated the Hanoverian connection,—when he declared that Hanover ought to be as dear to us as Hampshire, he was still invariably speaking the language of a virtuous and enlightened statesman.

The truth is, that there scarcely ever lived a person who had so little claim to this sort of praise as Pitt. He was undoubtedly a great man. But his was not a complete and well-proportioned greatness. The public life of Hampden or of Somers resembles a regular drama, which can be criticized as a whole, and every scene of which is to be viewed in connection with the main action. The public life of Pitt, on the other hand, is a rude though striking piece,—a piece abounding in incongruities,—a piece without any unity of plan, but redeemed by some noble passages, the effect of which is increased by the tameness or extravagance of what precedes and of what follows. His opinions were unfixed. His conduct at some of the most important conjunctures of his life was evidently determined by pride and resentment. He had one fault, which of all human faults is most rarely found in company with true greatness. He was extremely affected. He was an almost solitary instance of a man of real genius, and of a brave, lofty, and commanding spirit, without simplicity of character. He was an actor in the Closet, an actor at Council, an actor in Parliament; and even in private society he could not lay aside his theatrical tones and attitudes. We know that one of the most distinguished of his partisans often complained that he could never obtain admittance to Lord Chatham's room till everything was ready for the representation,—till the dresses and properties were all correctly disposed,—till the light was thrown with Rembrandt-like effect on the head of the illustrious performer,—till the flannels had been arranged with the air of a Grecian drapery, and the crutch placed as gracefully as that of Belisarius or Lear.

Yet, with all his faults and affectations, Pitt had, in a very extraordinary degree, many of the elements of greatness. He had splendid talents, strong passions, quick sensibility, and vehement enthusiasm for the grand and the beautiful. There was something about him which ennobled tergiversation itself. He often went wrong,—very wrong. But, to quote the language of Wordsworth,

"He still retained,
'Mid such abasement, what he had received
From nature, an intense and glowing mind."

In an age of low and dirty prostitution,—in the age of Doddington and Sandys, —it was something to have a man who might perhaps, under some strong excitement, have been tempted to ruin his country, but who never would have stooped to pilfer from her,—a man whose errors arose, not from a sordid desire of gain, but from a fierce thirst for power, for glory, and for vengeance. His tory owes to him this attestation,—that, at a time when anything short of direct embezzlement of the public money was considered as quite fair in public men, he showed the most scrupulous disinterestedness,—that, at a time when it seemed to be generally taken for granted that Government could be upheld only by the basest and most immoral arts, he appealed to the better and nobler parts of human nature,—that he made a brave and splendid attempt to do, by means of public opinion, what no other statesman of his day thought it possible to do, except by means of corruption,—that he looked for support, not, like the Pelhams, to a strong Aristocratical connection, not, like Bute, to the personal favour of the sovereign, but to the middle class of Englishmen,—that he inspired that class with a firm confidence in his integrity and ability,—that, backed by them, he forced an unwilling court and an unwilling oligarchy to admit him to an ample share of power,—and that he used his power in such a manner as clearly proved him to have sought it, not for the sake of profit or patronage, but from a wish to establish for himself a great and durable reputation by means of eminent services rendered to the state.

The family of Pitt was wealthy and respectable. His grandfather was Governor of Madras; and brought back from India that celebrated diamond which the Regent Orleans, by the advice of Saint-Simon, purchased for upwards of three millions of livres, and which is still considered as the most precious of the crown jewels of France. Governor Pitt bought estates and rotten boroughs, and sat in the House of Commons for Old Sarum. His son Robert was at one time member for Old Sarum, and at another for Oakhampton. Robert had two sons. Thomas, the elder, inherited the estates and the Parliamentary interest of his father. The second was the celebrated William Pitt.

He was born in November, 1708. About the early part of his life little more is known than that he was educated at Eton, and that at seventeen he was entered at Trinity College, Oxford. During the second year of his residence at the University, George the First died; and the event was, after the fashion of that generation, celebrated by the Oxonians in many very middling copies of verses. On this occasion Pitt published some Latin lines, which Mr. Thackeray has preserved. They prove that the young student had but a very limited knowledge even of the mechanical part of his art. All true Etonians will hear with concern that their illustrious schoolfellow is guilty of making the first syllable in *labenti* short. The matter of the poem is as worthless as that of any college exercise that was ever written before or since. There is, of course, much about Mars, Themis, Neptune, and Cocytus. The Muses are earnestly entreated to weep for Cæsar, for Cæsar, says the Poet, loved the Muses;—Cæsar, who could not read a line of Pope, and who loved nothing but punch and fat women.

Pitt had been, from his school-days, cruelly tormented by the gout, and was at last advised to travel for his health. He accordingly left Oxford without taking a degree, and visited France and Italy. He returned, however, without having received much benefit from his excursion, and continued, till the close of his life, to suffer most severely from his constitutional malady.

His father was now dead, and had left very little to the younger children. It was necessary that William should choose a profession. He decided for the army, and a cornet's commission was procured for him in the Blues.

But, small as his fortune was, his family had both the power and the inclination to serve him. At the general election of 1734, his elder brother, Thomas, was chosen both for Old Sarum and for Oakhampton. When Parliament met in 1735, Thomas made his election to serve for Oakhampton, and William was returned for Old Sarum.

Walpole had now been, during fourteen years, at the head of affairs. He had risen to power under the most favourable circumstances. The whole of the Whig party,—of that party which professed peculiar attachment to the principles of the Revolution, and which exclusively enjoyed the confidence of the reigning house,—had been united in support of his administration. Happily for him, he had been out of office when the South-Sea Act was passed; and, though he does not appear to have foreseen all the consequences of that measure, he had strenuously opposed it, as he opposed all the measures, good and bad, of Sunderland's administration. When the South-Sea Company were voting dividends of fifty per cent,—when a hundred pounds of their stock were selling for eleven hundred pounds,—when Threadneedle Street was daily crowded with the coaches of dukes and prelates,—when divines and philosophers turned gamblers,—when a thousand kindred bubbles were daily blown into existence,—the periwig company, and the Spanish-jackass company, and the quicksilver-fixation company,—Walpole's calm good sense preserved him from the general infatuation. He condemned the prevailing madness in public, and turned a considerable sum by taking advantage of it in private. When the crash came,—when ten thousand families were reduced to beggary in a day,—when the people in the frenzy of their rage and despair, clamoured, not only against the lower agents in the juggle, but against the Hanoverian favourites, against the English ministers, against the King himself,—when Parliament met, eager for confiscation and blood,—when members of the House of Commons proposed that the directors should be treated like parricides in ancient Rome, tied up in sacks, and thrown into the Thames, Walpole was the man on whom all parties turned their eyes. Four years before he had been driven from power by the intrigues of Sunderland and Stanhope, and the lead in the House of Commons had been intrusted to Craggs and Aislabie. Stanhope was no more. Aislabie was expelled from Parliament on account of his disgraceful conduct regarding the South-Sea scheme. Craggs was saved by a timely death from a similar mark of infamy. A large minority in the House of Commons voted for a severe censure on Sunderland, who, finding it impossible to withstand the force of the prevailing sentiment, retired from office, and outlived his retirement but a very short time. The schism which had divided the Whig party was now completely healed. Walpole had no opposition to encounter except that of the Tories; and the Tories were naturally regarded by the King with the strongest suspicion and dislike.

For a time business went on with a smoothness and despatch such as had not been known since the days of the Tudors. During the session of 1724, for example, there was hardly a single division. It is not impossible that, by taking the course which Pelham afterwards took,—by admitting into the Government all the rising talents and ambition of the Whig party, and by making room here and there for a Tory not unfriendly to the House of Brunswick,—Walpole might have averted the tremendous conflict in which he passed the later years of his administration, and in which he was at length vanquished. The Opposition which overthrew him was an Opposition created by his own policy,—by his own insatiable love of power.

In the very act of forming his ministry he turned one of the ablest and most attached of his supporters into a deadly enemy. Pulteney had strong public and private claims to a high situation in the new arrangement. His fortune was immense. His private character was respectable. He was already a distinguished speaker. He had acquired official experience in an important post. He had been, through all changes of fortune, a consistent Whig. When the Whig party was split into two sections, Pulteney had resigned a valuable place, and had followed the fortunes of Walpole. Yet, when Walpole returned to power, Pulteney was not invited to take office. An angry discussion took place between the friends. The minister offered a peerage. It was impossible for Pulteney not to discern the motive of such an offer. He indignantly refused to accept it. For some time he continued to brood over his wrongs, and to watch for an opportunity of revenge. As soon as a favourable conjuncture arrived he joined the minority, and became the greatest leader of Opposition that the House of Commons had ever seen.

Of all the members of the Cabinet, Carteret was the most eloquent and accomplished. His talents for debate were of the first order; his knowledge of foreign affairs superior to that of any living statesman; his attachment to the Protestant succession was undoubted. But there was not room in one Government for him and Walpole. Carteret retired, and was, from that time forward, one of the most persevering and formidable enemies of his old colleague.

If there was any man with whom Walpole could have consented to make a partition of power, that man was Lord Townshend. They were distant kinsmen by birth, near kinsmen by marriage. They had been friends from childhood. They had been school-fellows at Eton. They were country neighbours in Norfolk. They had been in office together under Godolphin. They had gone into Opposition together when Harley rose to power. They had been persecuted by the same House of Commons. They had, after the death of Anne, been recalled together to office. They had again been driven out together by Sunderland, and had again come back together when the influence of Sunderland had declined. Their opinions on public affairs almost always coincided. They were both men of frank, generous, and compassionate natures; their intercourse had been for many years affectionate and cordial. But the ties of blood, of marriage, and of friendship, the memory of mutual services, the memory of common persecutions, were insufficient to restrain that ambition which domineered over all the virtues and vices of Walpole. He was resolved, to use his own metaphor, that the firm of the house should be, not Townshend and Walpole, but Walpole and Townshend. At length the rivals proceeded to personal abuse before witnesses, seized each other by the collar, and grasped their swords. The women squalled. The men parted the combatants.* By friendly intervention the scandal of a duel between cousins, brothers-in-law, old friends, and old colleagues, was prevented. But the disputants could not long continue to act together. Townshend retired, and, with rare moderation and public spirit, refused to take any part in politics. He could not, he said, trust his temper. He feared that the recollection of his private wrongs might impel him to follow the example of Pulteney, and to oppose measures which he thought generally beneficial to the country. He therefore never visited London after his resignation, but passed the closing years of his life in dignity and repose among his trees and pictures at Rainham.

Next went Chesterfield. He too was a Whig and a friend of the Protestant succession. He was an orator, a courtier, a wit, and a man of letters. He was at the head of *ton* in days when, in order to be at the head of *ton*, it was not sufficient to be dull and supercilious. It was evident that he submitted impatiently to the ascendency of Walpole. He murmured against the Excise Bill. His brothers voted against it in the House of Commons. The Minister acted with characteristic caution and characteristic energy;—caution in the conduct of public affairs; energy where his own administration was

---

* The scene of this extraordinary quarrel was, we believe, a house in Cleveland Square, now occupied by Mr. Ellice, the Secretary at War. It was then the residence of Colonel Selwyn.

concerned. He withdrew his Bill, and turned out all his hostile or wavering colleagues. Chesterfield was stopped on the great staircase of St. James's, and summoned to deliver up the staff which he bore as Lord Steward of the Household. A crowd of noble and powerful functionaries,—the Dukes of Montrose and Bolton, Lord Burlington, Lord Stair, Lord Cobham, Lord Marchmont, Lord Clifton,—were at the same time dismissed from the service of the Crown.

Not long after these events the Opposition was reinforced by the Duke of Argyle, a man vainglorious indeed and fickle, but brave, eloquent and popular. It was in a great measure owing to his exertions that the Act of Settlement had been peaceably carried into effect in England immediately after the death of Anne, and that the Jacobite rebellion which, during the following year, broke out in Scotland, was suppressed. He too carried over to the minority the aid of his great name, his talents, and his paramount influence in his native country.

In each of these cases taken separately, a skilful defender of Walpole might perhaps make out a case for him. But when we see that during a long course of years all the footsteps are turned the same way,—that all the most eminent of those public men who agreed with the Minister in their general views of policy left him, one after another, with sore and irritated minds, we find it impossible not to believe that the real explanation of the phenomenon is to be found in the words of his son, "Sir Robert Walpole loved power so much that he would not endure a rival."* Hume has described this famous minister with great felicity in one short sentence—"moderate in exercising power, not equitable in engrossing it." Kind-hearted, jovial, and placable as Walpole was, he was yet a man with whom no persons of high pretensions and high spirit could long continue to act. He had, therefore, to stand against an Opposition containing all the most accomplished statesmen of the age, with no better support than that which he received from persons like his brother Horace or Henry Pelham, whose industrious mediocrity gave him no cause for jealousy, or from clever adventurers, whose situation and character diminished the dread which their talents might have inspired. To this last class belonged Fox, who was too poor to live without office; Sir William Yonge, of whom Walpole himself said, that nothing but such parts could buoy up such a character, and that nothing but such a character could drag down such parts; and Winnington, whose private morals lay, justly or unjustly, under imputations of the worst kind.

The discontented Whigs were, not perhaps in number, but certainly in ability, experience, and weight, by far the most important part of the Opposition. The Tories furnished little more than rows of ponderous foxhunters, fat with Staffordshire or Devonshire ale,—men who drank to the King over the water, and believed that all the fundholders were Jews,—men whose religion consisted in hating the Dissenters, and whose political researches had led them to fear, like Squire Western, that their land might be sent over to Hanover to be put in the sinking-fund. The eloquence of these patriotic squires, the remnant of the once formidable October Club, seldom went beyond a hearty Ay or No. Very few members of this party had distinguished themselves much in Parliament, or could, under any circumstances, have been called to fill any high office; and those few had generally, like Sir William Wyndham, learned in the company of their new associates the doctrines of toleration and political liberty, and might indeed with strict propriety be called Whigs.

---

* Memoirs, Vol. I, p. 201.

It was to the Whigs in Opposition, the patriots as they were called, that the most distinguished of the English youth who at this season entered into public life, attached themselves. These inexperienced politicians felt all the enthusiasm which the name of liberty naturally excites in young and ardent minds. They conceived that the theory of the Tory Opposition and the practice of Walpole's Government were alike inconsistent with the principles of liberty. They accordingly repaired to the standard which Pulteney had set up. While opposing the Whig minister, they professed a firm adherence to the purest doctrines of Whiggism. He was the schismatic; they were the true Catholics, the peculiar people, the depositaries of the orthodox faith of Hampden and Russell, the one sect which, amidst the corruptions generated by time and by the long possession of power, had preserved inviolate the principles of the Revolution. Of the young men who attached themselves to this portion of the Opposition the most distinguished were Lyttelton and Pitt.

When Pitt entered Parliament, the whole political world was attentively watching the progress of an event which soon added great strength to the Opposition, and particularly to that section of the Opposition in which the young statesman enrolled himself. The Prince of Wales was gradually becoming more and more estranged from his father and his father's ministers, and more and more friendly to the patriots.

Nothing is more natural than that, in a monarchy where a constitutional Opposition exists, the heir-apparent of the throne should put himself at the head of that Opposition. He is impelled to such a course by every feeling of ambition and of vanity. He cannot be more than second in the estimation of the party which is in. He is sure to be the first member of the party which is out. The highest favour which the existing administration can expect from him is that he will not discard them. But, if he joins the Opposition, all his associates expect that he will promote them; and the feelings which men entertain towards one from whom they hope to obtain great advantages which they have not are far warmer than the feelings with which they regard one who, at the very utmost, can only leave them in possession of what they already had. An heir-apparent, therefore, who wishes to enjoy, in the highest perfection, all the pleasure that can be derived from eloquent flattery and profound respect will always join those who are struggling to force themselves into power. This is, we believe, the true explanation of a fact which Lord Granville attributed to some natural peculiarity in the illustrious House of Brunswick. "This family," said he at Council, we suppose after his daily half-gallon of Burgundy, "always has quarrelled, and always will quarrel, from generation to generation." He should have known something of the matter; for he had been a favourite with three successive generations of the royal house. We cannot quite admit his explanation; but the fact is indisputable. Since the accession of George the First, there have been four Princes of Wales, and they have all been almost constantly in Opposition.

Whatever might have been the motives which induced Prince Frederick to join the party opposed to Sir Robert Walpole, his support infused into many members of that party a courage and an energy of which they stood greatly in need. Hitherto it had been impossible for the discontented Whigs not to feel some misgivings when they found themselves dividing, night after night, with uncompromising Jacobites who were known to be in constant communication with the exiled family, or with Tories who had impeached Somers, who had murmured against Harley and St. John as too remiss in the cause of the Church and the landed interest, and who, if they were not inclined to attack the reigning family, yet considered the introduction of that family as, at best, only the less of two great evils,—as a necessary but painful and humiliating preservative against Popery. The Minister might plausibly say that Pulteney and Carteret, in the hope of gratifying their own appetite for office and for revenge, did not scruple to serve the purposes of a faction hostile to the Protestant succession. The appearance of Frederick at the head of the patriots silenced this reproach. The leaders of the Opposition might now boast that their proceedings were sanctioned by a person as deeply interested as the King himself in maintaining the Act of Settlement, and that, instead of serving the purposes of the Tory party, they had brought that party over to the side of Whiggism. It must indeed be admitted that, though both the King and the Prince behaved in a manner little to their honour,—though the father acted harshly, the son disrespectfully, and both childishly,—the royal family was rather strengthened than weakened by the disagreement of its two most distinguished members. A large class of politicians, who had considered themselves as placed under sentence of perpetual exclusion from office, and who, in their despair, had been almost ready to join in a counter-revolution as the only mode of removing the proscription under which they lay, now saw with pleasure an easier and safer road to power opening before them, and thought it far better to wait till, in the natural course of things, the Crown should descend to the heir of the House of Brunswick, than to risk their lands and their necks in a rising for the House of Stewart. The situation of the royal family resembled the situation of those Scotch families in which father and son took opposite sides during the rebellion, in order that, come what might, the estate might not be forfeited.

In April, 1736, Frederick was married to the Princess of Saxe Gotha, with whom he afterwards lived on terms very similar to those on which his father had lived with Queen Caroline. The Prince adored his wife, and thought her in mind and person the most attractive of her sex. But he thought that conjugal fidelity was an unprincely virtue; and, in order to be like Henry the Fourth and the Regent Orleans, he affected a libertinism for which he had no taste, and frequently quitted the only woman whom he loved for ugly and disagreeable mistresses.

The address which the House of Commons presented to the King on the occasion of the Prince's marriage was moved, not by the Minister, but by Pulteney, the leader of the Whigs in Opposition. It was on this motion that Pitt, who had not broken silence during the session in which he took his seat, addressed the House for the first time. "A contemporary historian," says Mr. Thackeray, "describes Mr. Pitt's first speech as superior even to the models of ancient eloquence. According to Tindal, it was more ornamented than the speeches of Demosthenes and less diffuse than those of Cicero." This unmeaning phrase has been a hundred times quoted. That it should ever have been quoted, except to be laughed at, is strange. The vogue which it has obtained may serve to show in how slovenly a way most people are content to think. Did Tindal, who first used it, or Archdeacon Coxe and Mr. Thackeray, who have borrowed it, ever in their lives hear any speaking which did not deserve the same compliment? Did they ever hear speaking less ornamented than that of Demosthenes, or more diffuse than that of Cicero? We know no living orator, from Lord Brougham down to Mr. Hunt, who is not entitled to the same magnificent eulogy. It would be no very flattering compliment to a man's figure to say,—that he was taller than the Polish Count, and shorter than G'ant O'Brien,—fatter than the *Anatomie Vivante*, and more slender than Daniel Lambert.

Pitt's speech, as it is reported in the Gentleman's Magazine, certainly deserves Tindal's compliment, and deserves no other. It is just as empty and wordy as a maiden speech on such an occasion might be expected to be. But the fluency and the personal advantages of the young orator instantly caught the ear and eye of his audience. He was, from the day of his first appearance, always heard with attention; and exercise soon developed the great powers which he possessed.

In our time, the audience of a member of Parliament is the nation. The three or four hundred persons who may be present while a speech is delivered may be pleased or disgusted by the voice and action of the orator; but, in the reports which are read the next day by hundreds of thousands, the difference between the noblest and the meanest figure, between the richest and the shrillest tones, between the most graceful and the most uncouth gesture, altogether vanishes. A hundred years ago, scarcely any report of what passed within the walls of the House of Commons was suffered to get abroad. In those times, therefore, the impression which a speaker might make on the persons who actually heard him was every thing. The impression out of doors was hardly worth a thought. In the Parliaments of that time, therefore, as in the ancient commonwealths, those qualifications which enhance the immediate effect of a speech, were far more important ingredients in the composition of an orator than they would appear to be in our time. All those qualifications Pitt possessed in the highest degree. On the stage, he would have been the finest Brutus or Coriolanus ever seen. Those who saw him in his decay, when his health was broken, when his mind was jangled, when he had been removed from that stormy assembly of which he thoroughly knew the temper, and over which he possessed unbounded influence, to a small, a torpid, and an unfriendly audience, say that his speaking was then, for the most part, a low, monotonous muttering, audible only to those who sat lose to him,— that when violently excited, he sometimes raised his voice for a few minutes, but that it soon sank again into an unintelligible murmur. Such was the Earl of Chatham; but such was not William Pitt. His figure, when he first appeared in Parliament, was strikingly graceful and commanding, his features high and noble, his eye full of fire. His voice, even when it sank to a whisper, was heard to the remotest benches; and when he strained it to its full extent, the sound rose like the swell of the organ of a great cathedral, shook the house with its peal, and was heard through lobbies and down staircases, to the Court of Requests and the precincts of Westminster Hall. He cultivated all these eminent advantages with the most assiduous care. His action is described by a very malignant observer as equal to that of Garrick. His play of countenance was wonderful: he frequently disconcerted a hostile orator by a single glance of indignation or scorn. Every tone, from the impassioned cry to the thrilling aside was perfectly at his command. It is by no means improbable that the pains which he took to improve his great personal advantages had, in some respects, a prejudicial operation, and tended to nourish in him that passion for theatrical effect which, as we have already remarked, was one of the most conspicuous blemishes in his character.

But it was not solely or principally to outward accomplishments that Pitt owed the vast influence which, during nearly thirty years, he exercised over the House of Commons. He was undoubtedly a great orator; and from the descriptions of his contemporaries, and the fragments of his speeches which still remain, it is not difficult to discover the nature and extent of his oratorical powers.

He was no speaker of set speeches. His few prepared discourses were complete failures. The elaborate panegyric which he pronounced on General Wolfe was considered as the very worst of all his performances. "No man," says a critic who had often heard him, "ever knew so little what he was going to say." Indeed his facility amounted to a vice. He was not the master, but the slave of his own speech. So little self-command had he when once he felt the impulse, that he did not like to take part in a debate when his mind was full of an important secret of state. "I must sit still," he once said to Lord Shelburne on such an occasion; "for, when once I am up, every thing that is in my mind comes out."

Yet he was not a great debater. That he should not have been so when first he entered the House of Commons is not strange. Scarcely any person has ever become so without long practice, and many failures. It was by slow degrees, as Burke said, that the late Mr. Fox became the most brilliant and powerful debater that ever Parliament saw. Mr. Fox himself attributed his own success to the resolution which he formed when very young, of speaking, well or ill, at least once every night. "During five whole sessions," he used to say, "I spoke every night but one; and I regret only that I did not speak on that night too." Indeed, it would be difficult to name any great debater, with the exception of Mr. Stanley, whose knowledge of the science of parliamentary defence resembles an instinct, who has not made himself a master of his art at the expense of his audience.

But as this art is one which even the ablest men have seldom acquired without long practice, so it is one which men of respectable abilities, with assiduous and intrepid practice, seldom fail to acquire. It is singular that in such an art, Pitt, a man of splendid talents, of great fluency, of great boldness,—a man whose whole life was passed in parliamentary conflict,—a man who, during several years, was the leading minister of the Crown in the House of Commons,—should never have attained to high excellence. He spoke without premeditation; but his speech followed the course of his own thoughts and not the course of the previous discussion. He could, indeed, treasure up in his memory some detached expression of a hostile orator, and make it the text for sparkling ridicule or burning invective. Some of the most celebrated bursts of his eloquence were called forth by an unguarded word, a laugh, or a cheer. But this was the only sort of reply in which he appears to have excelled. He was perhaps the only great English orator who did not think it any advantage to have the last word, and who generally spoke by choice before his most formidable opponents. His merit was almost entirely rhetorical. He did not succeed either in exposition or in refutation; but his speeches abounded with lively illustrations, striking apophthegms, well told anecdotes, happy allusions, passionate appeals. His invective and sarcasm were terrific. Perhaps no English orator was ever so much feared.

But that which gave most effect to his declamation was the air of sincerity, of vehement feeling, of moral elevation, which belonged to all that he said. His style was not always in the purest taste. Several contemporary judges pronounced it too florid. Walpole, in the midst of the rapturous eulogy which he pronounces on one of Pitt's greatest orations, owns that some of the metaphors were too forced. The quotations and classical stories are sometimes too trite for a clever schoolboy. But these were niceties for which the audience cared little. The enthusiasm of the orator infected all who heard him; his ardour and his noble bearing put fire into the most frigid conceit, and gave dignity to the most puerile allusion.

His powers soon began to give annoyance to the Government; and Walpole determined to make an example of the patriotic cornet. Pitt was accordingly dismissed from the service. Mr. Thackeray absurdly says that the Minister took this step, because he plainly saw that it would have been vain to think of buying over so honourable and disinterested an opponent. We do not dispute Pitt's integrity; but we do not know what proof he had given of it when he was turned out of the army; and we are sure that Walpole was not likely to give credit for inflexible honesty to a young adventurer who had never had an opportunity of refusing anything. The truth is, that it was not Walpole's practice to buy off enemies. Mr. Burke truly says, in the Appeal to the Old Whigs, "Walpole gained very few over from the Opposition." He knew his business far too well. He knew that for one mouth, which is stopped with a place, fifty other mouths will be instantly opened. He knew that it would have been very bad policy in him to give the world to understand that more was to be got by thwarting his measures than by supporting them. These maxims are as old as the origin of parliamentary corruption in England. Pepys learned them, as he tells us, from the counsellors of Charles the Second.

Pitt was no loser. He was made Groom of the Bedchamber to the Prince of Wales, and continued to declaim against the ministers with unabated violence and with increasing ability. The question of maritime right, then agitated between Spain and England, called forth all his powers. He clamoured for war with a vehemence which it is not easy to reconcile with reason or humanity, but which appears to Mr. Thackeray worthy of the highest admiration. We will not stop to argue a point on which we had long thought that all well informed people were agreed. We could easily show, we think, that, if any respect be due to international law,—if right, where societies of men are concerned, be anything but another name for might,—if we do not adopt the doctrine of the Bucaniers, which seems to be also the doctrine of Mr. Thackeray, that treaties mean nothing within thirty degrees of the line,—the war with Spain was altogether unjustifiable. But the truth is, that the promoters of that war have saved the historian the trouble of trying them: they have pleaded guilty. "I have seen," says Burke, "and with some care examined, the original documents concerning certain important transactions of those times. They perfectly satisfied me of the extreme injustice of that war, and of the falsehood of the colours which Walpole, to his ruin, and guided by a mistaken policy, suffered to be daubed over that measure. Some years after, it was my fortune to converse with many of the principal actors against that minister, and with those who principally excited that clamour. None of them, no not one, did in the least defend the measure, or attempt to justify their conduct. They condemned it as freely as they would have done in commenting upon any proceeding in history in which they were totally unconcerned."* Pitt, on subsequent occasions, gave ample proof that he was one of those tardy penitents.

The elections of 1741 were unfavourable to Walpole; and after a long and obstinate struggle he found it necessary to resign. The Duke of Newcastle and Lord Hardwicke opened a negotiation with the leading patriots, in the hope of forming an administration on a Whig basis. At this conjuncture, Pitt, Lyttleton, and those persons who were most nearly connected with them acted in a manner very little to their honour. They attempted to come to an understanding with Walpole, and offered, if he would use his influence with the King in their favour, to screen him from prosecution. They even went so far as to engage for the concurrence of the Prince of Wales. But Walpole knew that the assistance of the Boys, as he called the young patriots, would avail him nothing if Pulteney and Carteret should prove intractable, and would be superfluous if the great leaders of the Opposition could be gained.

* Letters on a Regicide Peace.

He, therefore, declined the proposal. It is remarkable that Mr. Thackeray, who has thought it worth while to preserve Pitt's bad college verses, has not even alluded to this story,—a story which is supported by strong testimony, and which may be found in so common a book as Coxe's Life of Walpole.

The new arrangements disappointed almost every member of the Opposition, and none more than Pitt. He was not invited to become a placeman; and he therefore stuck firmly to his old trade of patriot. Fortunate it was for him that he did so. Had he taken office at this time, he would in all probability have shared largely in the unpopularity of Pulteney, Sandys, and Carteret. He was now the fiercest and most implacable of those who called for vengeance on Walpole. He spoke with great energy and ability in favour of the most unjust and violent propositions which the enemies of the fallen minister could invent. He urged the House of Commons to appoint a secret tribunal for the purpose of investigating the conduct of the late First Lord of the Treasury. This was done. The great majority of the inquisitors were notoriously hostile to the accused statesman. Yet they were compelled to own that they could find no fault in him. They therefore called for new powers, for a bill of indemnity to witnesses,—or, in plain words, for a bill to reward all who who might give evidence, true or false, against the Earl of Orford. This bill Pitt supported,—Pitt, who had himself offered to be a screen between Lord Orford and public justice. These are melancholy facts. Mr. Thackeray omits them, or hurries over them as fast as he can; and, as eulogy is his business, he is in the right to do so. But, though there are many parts of the life of Pitt which it is more agreeable to contemplate, we know none more instructive. What must have been the general state of political morality, when a young man, considered, and justly considered, as the most public-spirited and spotless statesman of his time, could attempt to force his way into office by means so disgraceful!

The Bill of Indemnity was rejected by the Lords. Walpole withdrew himself quietly from the public eye; and the ample space which he had left vacant was soon occupied by Carteret. Against Carteret Pitt began to thunder with as much zeal as he had ever manifested against Sir Robert. To Carteret he transferred most of the hard names which were familiar to his eloquence, sole minister, wicked minister, odious minister, execrable minister. The great topic of his invective was the favour shown to the German dominions of King George. He attacked with great violence, and with an ability which raised him to the very first rank among the parliamentary speakers, the practice of paying Hanoverian troops with English money. The House of Commons had lately lost some of its most distinguished ornaments. Walpole and Pulteney had accepted peerages; Sir William Wyndham was dead; and among the rising men none could be considered as, on the whole, a match for Pitt.

During the recess of 1744, the old Duchess of Marlborough died. She carried to her grave the reputation of being decidedly the best hater of her time. In the time of Queen Anne, her temper had ruined the party to which she belonged and the husband whom she adored. Time had made her neither wiser nor kinder. Whoever was at any moment great and prosperous was the object of her fiercest detestation. She had hated Walpole; she now hated Carteret.

Pope, long before her death, predicted the fate of her vast property:

"To heirs unknown descends the unguarded store,
Or wanders, heaven-directed, to the poor."

Pitt was poor enough; and to him heaven directed a portion of the wealth of the haughty dowager. She left him a legacy of ten thousand pounds, in consideration of "the noble defence he had made for the support of the laws of England, and to prevent the ruin of his country."

The will was made in August. The Duchess died in October. In November Pitt was a courtier. The Pelhams had forced the King, much against his will, to part with Lord Carteret, now Earl Granville. They proceeded, after this victory, to form the Government on that basis called by the name of "the broad bottom." Lyttelton had a seat at the Treasury, and several other friends of Pitt were provided for. But Pitt himself was, for the present, forced to be content with promises. The King resented most highly some expressions which the ardent orator had used in the debate on the Hanoverian troops. But Newcastle and Pelham expressed the strongest confidence that time and their exertions would soften the royal displeasure.

Pitt, on his part, omitted nothing that might facilitate his admission to office. He resigned his place in the household of Prince Frederick, and, when Parliament met, exerted his eloquence in support of the Government. The Pelhams were really sincere in their endeavours to remove the strong prejudices which had taken root in the King's mind. They knew that Pitt was not a man to be deceived with ease or offended with impunity. They were afraid that they should not be long able to put him off with promises. Nor was it their interest so to put him off. There was a strong tie between him and them. He was the enemy of their enemy. The brothers hated and dreaded the eloquent, aspiring, and imperious Granville. They had traced his intrigues in many quarters. They knew his influence over the royal mind. They knew that, as soon as a favourable opportunity should arrive, he would be recalled to the head of affairs. They resolved to bring things to a crisis; and the question on which they took issue with their master was, whether Pitt should or should not be admitted to office. They chose their time with more skill than generosity. It was when rebellion was actually raging in Britain, when the Pretender was master of the northern extremity of the island, that they tendered their resignations. The King found himself deserted, in one day, by the whole strength of that party which had placed his family on the throne. Lord Granville tried to form a government; but it soon appeared that the parliamentary interest of the Pelhams was irresistible, and that the King's favourite statesman could count only on about thirty Lords and eighty members of the House of Commons. The scheme was given up. Granville went away laughing. The ministers came back stronger than ever; and the King was now no longer able to refuse anything that they might be pleased to demand. All that he could do was to mutter that it was very hard that Newcastle, who was not fit to be Chamberlain to the most insignificant prince in Germany, should dictate to the King of England.

One concession the ministers graciously made. They agreed that Pitt should not be placed in a situation in which it would be necessary for him to have frequent interviews with the King. Instead, therefore, of making their new ally Secretary-at-War, as they had intended, they appointed him Vice-Treasurer of Ireland, and in a few months promoted him to the office of Paymaster of the Forces.

This was, at that time, one of the most lucrative offices in the Government. The salary was but a small part of the emolument which the Paymaster derived from his place. He was allowed to keep a large sum,—seldom less than one hundred thousand pounds, constantly in his hands;—and the interest on this sum,—probably about four thousand pounds a year,—he might appropriate to his own use. This practice was not secret, nor was it considered as disreputable. It was the practice of men of undoubted honour, both before and after the time of Pitt. He, however, refused to accept one farthing beyond the salary which the law had annexed to his office. It had been usual for foreign princes who received the pay of England to give to the Paymaster of the Forces a small per centage on the subsidies. These ignominious vails Pitt resolutely declined.

Disinterestedness of this kind was, in his days, very rare. His conduct surprised and amused politicians. It excited the warmest admiration throughout the body of the people. In spite of the inconsistencies of which Pitt had been guilty,—in spite of the strange contrast between his violence in Opposition and his tameness in office,—he still possessed a large share of the public confidence. The motives which may lead a politician to change his connections or his general line of conduct are often obscure; but disinterestedness in money matters everybody can understand. Pitt was thenceforth considered as a man who was proof to all sordid temptations. If he acted ill, it might be from an error in judgment; it might be from resentment; it might be from ambition. But poor as he was, he had vindicated himself from all suspicion of covetousness.

Eight quiet years followed,—eight years during which the minority, feeble from the time of Lord Granville's defeat, continued to dwindle till it became almost invisible. Peace was made with France and Spain in 1748. Prince Frederick died in 1751; and with him died the very semblance of opposition. All the most distinguished survivors of the party which had supported Walpole and of the party which had opposed him were united under his successor. The fiery and vehement spirit of Pitt had for a time been laid to rest. He silently acquiesced in that very system of Continental measures which he had lately condemned. He ceased to talk disrespectfully about Hanover. He did not object to the treaty with Spain, though that treaty left us exactly where we had been when he uttered his spirit-stirring harangues against the pacific policy of Walpole. Now and then glimpses of his former self appeared; but they were few and transient. Pelham knew with whom he had to deal, and felt that an ally, so little used to control, and so capable of inflicting injury, might well be indulged in an occasional fit of waywardness.

Two men, little, if at all, inferior to Pitt in powers of mind, held, like him, subordinate offices in the government. One of these, Murray, was successively Solicitor-General and Attorney-General. This distinguished person far surpassed Pitt in correctness of taste, in power of reasoning, in depth and variety of knowledge. His parliamentary eloquence never blazed into sudden flashes of dazzling brilliancy; but its clear, placid, and mellow splendour was never for an instant overclouded. Intellectually he was, we believe, fully equal to Pitt; but he was deficient in the moral qualities to which Pitt owed most of his success. Murray wanted the energy, the courage, the all-grasping and all-risking ambition, which make men great in stirring times. His heart was a little cold, his temper cautious even to timidity, his manner decorous even to formality. He never exposed his fortunes or his fame to any risk which he could avoid. At one time he might, in all probability, have been Prime Minister. But the object of all his wishes was the judicial bench. The situation of Chief Justice might not be so splendid as that of First Lord of the Treasury; but it was dignified; it was quiet; it was secure; and therefore it was the favourite situation of Murray.

Fox, the father of the great man whose mighty efforts in the cause of peace, of truth, and of liberty, have made that name immortal, was Secretary-at-War. He was a favourite with the King, with the Duke of Cumberland, and with some of the most powerful individuals of the great Whig connection. His parliamentary talents were of the highest order. As a speaker he was in almost all respects the very opposite to Pitt. His figure was ungraceful; his face, as Reynolds and Roubiliac have preserved it to us, indicated a strong understanding; but the features were coarse, and the general aspect dark and lowering. His manner was awkward; his delivery was hesitating; he was often at a stand for want of a word; but as a debater,—as a master of that keen, weighty, manly logic, which is suited to the discussion of political questions,—he has perhaps never been surpassed except by his son. In reply he was as decidedly superior to Pitt as in declamation he was his inferior. Intellectually the balance was nearly even between the rivals. But here, again, the moral qualities of Pitt turned the scale. Fox had undoubtedly many virtues. In natural disposition as well as in talents, he bore a great resemblance to his more celebrated son. He had the same sweetness of temper, the same strong passions, the same openness, boldness, and impetuosity, the same cordiality towards friends, the same placability towards enemies. No man was more warmly or justly beloved by his family or by his associates. But unhappily he had been trained in a bad political school,—in a school the doctrines of which were, that political virtue is the mere coquetry of political prostitution,—that every patriot has his price,—that Government can be carried on only by means of corruption,—and that the state is given as a prey to statesmen. These maxims were too much in vogue throughout the lower ranks of Walpole's party, and were too much encouraged by Walpole himself, who, from contempt of what is in our day called *humbug*, often ran extravagantly and offensively into the opposite extreme. The loose political morality of Fox presented a remarkable contrast to the ostentatious purity of Pitt. The nation distrusted the former, and placed implicit confidence in the latter. But almost all the statesmen of the age had still to learn that the confidence of the nation was worth having. While things went on quietly, while there was no opposition, while everything was given by the favour of a small ruling junto, Fox had a decided advantage over Pitt; but when dangerous times came, when Europe was convulsed with war, when Parliament was broken up into factions, when the public mind was violently excited, the favourite of the people rose to supreme power, while his rival sank into insignificance.

Early in the year 1754 Henry Pelham died unexpectedly. "Now I shall have no more peace," exclaimed the old King, when he heard the news. He was in the right. Pelham had succeeded in bringing together and keeping together all the talents of the kingdom. By his death the highest post to which an English subject can aspire was left vacant; and at the same moment, the influence which had yoked together and reined in so many turbulent and ambitious spirits was withdrawn.

Within a week after Pelham's death, it was determined that the Duke of Newcastle should be placed at the head of the Treasury; but the arrangement was still far from complete. Who was to be the leading Minister of the Crown in the House of Commons? Was the office to be intrusted to a man of eminent talents? And would not such a man in such a place demand and obtain a larger share of power and patronage than Newcastle would be disposed to concede? Was a mere drudge to be employed? And what probability was there that a mere drudge would be able to manage a large and stormy assembly, abounding with able and experienced men?

Pope has said of that wretched miser Sir John Cutler,

"Cutler saw tenants break and houses fall For very want;—he could not build a wall."

Newcastle's love of power resembled Cutler's love of money. It was an avarice which thwarted itself,—a penny-wise and pound-foolish cupidity. An immediate outlay was so painful to him that he would not venture to make the most desirable improvement. If he could have found it in his heart to cede at once a portion of his authority, he might probably have ensured the continuance of what remained; but he thought it better to construct a weak and rotten government, which tottered at the smallest breath, and fell in the first storm, than to pay the necessary price for sound and durable materials. He wished to find some person who would be willing to accept the lead of the House of Commons on terms similar to those on which Secretary Craggs had acted under Sunderland, five-and-thirty years before. Craggs could hardly be called a minister. He was a mere agent for the Minister. He was not trusted with the higher secrets of state, but obeyed implicitly the directions of his superior, and was, to use Doddington's expression, merely Lord Sunderland's man. But times were changed. Since the days of Sunderland, the importance of the House of Commons had been constantly on the increase. During many years the person who conducted the business of the Government in that House had almost always been Prime Minister. Under these circumstances it was not to be supposed that any person who possessed the talents necessary for the situation, would stoop to accept it on such terms as Newcastle was disposed to offer.

Pitt was ill at Bath; and, had he been well and in London, neither the King nor Newcastle would have been disposed to make any overtures to him. The cool and wary Murray had set his heart on professional objects. Negotiations were opened with Fox. Newcastle behaved like himself,—that is to say, childishly and basely. The proposition which he made was, that Fox should be Secretary of State, with the lead of the House of Commons; that the disposal of the secret-service-money, or, in plain words, the business of buying members of Parliament, should be left to the First Lord of the Treasury; but that Fox should be exactly informed of the way in which this fund was employed.

To these conditions Fox assented. But the next day every thing was in confusion. Newcastle had changed his mind. The conversation which took place between Fox and the Duke is one of the most curious in English history. "My brother," said Newcastle, "when he was at the Treasury, never told anybody what he did with the secret-service-money. No more will I." The answer was obvious. Pelham had been, not only First Lord of the Treasury, but also manager of the House of Commons; and it was therefore unnecessary for him to confide to any other person his dealings with the members of that House. "But how," said Fox, "can I lead in the Commons without information on this head? How can I talk to gentlemen when I do not know which of them have received gratifications and which have not? And who," he continued, "is to have the disposal of places?"—"I myself," said the Duke.—"How then am I to manage the House of Commons?"—"Oh, let the members of the House of Commons come to me." Fox then mentioned the general election which was approaching, and asked how the ministerial burghs were to be filled up. "Do not trouble yourself," said Newcastle, "that is all settled." This was too much for human nature to bear Fox refused to accept the Secretaryship of State on such terms; and the Duke confided the management of the House of Commons to a dull, harmless man, whose name is almost forgotten in our time,—Sir Thomas Robinson.

When Pitt returned from Bath he affected great moderation, though his haughty soul was boiling with resentment. He did not complain of the manner in which he had been passed by, but said openly that, in his opinion, Fox was the fittest man to lead the House of Commons. The rivals, reconciled by their common interest and their common enmities, concerted a plan of operations for the next session. "Sir Thomas Robinson lead us!" said Pitt to Fox. "The Duke might as well send his jack-boot to lead us."

The elections of 1754 were favourable to the administration. But the aspect of foreign affairs was threatening. In India the English and the French had been employed, ever since the peace of Aix-la-Chapelle, in cutting each other's throats. They had lately taken to the same practice in America. It might have been foreseen that stirring times were at hand,—times which would call for abilities very different from those of Newcastle and Robinson.

In November the Parliament met; and before the end of that month the new Secretary of State had been so unmercifully baited by the Paymaster of the Forces and the Secretary at War that he was thoroughly sick of his situation. Fox attacked him with great force and acrimony. Pitt affected a kind of contemptuous tenderness for Sir Thomas, and directed his attacks principally against Newcastle. On one occasion, he asked in tones of thunder whether Parliament sat only to register the edicts of one too-powerful subject? The Duke was scared out of his wits. He was afraid to dismiss the mutineers; he was afraid to promote them; but it was absolutely necessary to do something. Fox, as the less proud and intractable of the refractory pair, was preferred. A seat in the Cabinet was offered to him on condition that he would give efficient support to the ministry in Parliament. In an evil hour for his fame and his fortunes he accepted the offer, and abandoned his connection with Pitt, who never forgave this desertion.

Sir Thomas, assisted by Fox, contrived to get through the business of the year without much trouble. Pitt was waiting his time. The negotiations pending between France and England took every day a more unfavourable aspect. Towards the close of the session the King sent a message to inform the House of Commons that he had found it necessary to make preparations for war. The House returned an address of thanks, and passed a vote of credit. During the recess, the old animosity of both nations was inflamed by a series of disastrous events. An English force was cut off in America; and several French merchantmen were taken in the West Indian Seas. It was plain that an appeal to arms was at hand.

The first object of the King was to secure Hanover; and Newcastle was disposed to gratify his master. Treaties were concluded, after the fashion of those times, with several petty German princes, who bound themselves to find soldiers if England would find money; and, as it was suspected that Frederick the Second had set his heart on the electoral dominions of his uncle, Russia was hired to keep Prussia in awe.

When the stipulations of these treaties were made known, there arose throughout the kingdom a murmur from which a judicious observer might easily prognosticate the approach of a tempest. Newcastle encountered strong opposition, even from those whom he had always considered as his tools. Legge, the Chancellor of the Exchequer, refused to sign the Treasury warrants which were necessary to give effect to the treaties. Those persons who were supposed to possess the confidence of the young Prince of Wales and of his mother, held very menacing language. In this perplexity Newcastle sent for Pitt, hugged him, patted him, smirked at him, wept over him, and lisped out the highest compliments, and the most splendid promises. The King, who had hitherto been as sulky as possible, would be civil to him at the levée,—he should be brought into the Cabinet,—he should be consulted about every thing,—if he would only be so good as to support the Hessian subsidy in the House of Commons. Pitt coldly declined the proffered seat in the Cabinet,—expressed the highest love and reverence for the King,—and said that, if his Majesty felt a strong personal interest in the Hessian treaty he would so far deviate from the line which he had traced out for himself as to give that treaty his support. "Well, and the Russian subsidy," said Newcastle. "No," said Pitt, "not a system of subsidies." The Duke summoned Lord Hardwicke to his aid; but Pitt was inflexible. Murray would do nothing,—Robinson could do nothing. It was necessary to have recourse to Fox. He became Secretary of State, with the full authority of a leader in the House of Commons; and Sir Thomas was pensioned off on the Irish establishment.

In November, 1755, the Houses met. Public expectation was wound up to the height. After ten quiet years there was to be an Opposition, countenanced by the heir-apparent of the throne, and headed by the most brilliant orator of the age, and backed by a strong party throughout the country. The debate on the address was long remembered as one of the greatest parliamentary conflicts of that generation. It began at three in the afternoon, and lasted till five the next morning. It was on this night that Gerard Hamilton delivered that *single speech* from which his nickname was derived. His eloquence threw into the shade every orator except Pitt, who declaimed against the subsidies for an hour and a half with extraordinary energy and effect. Those powers which had formerly spread terror through the majorities of Walpole and Carteret were now displayed in their highest perfection before an audience long unaccustomed to such exhibitions. One fragment of this celebrated oration remains in a state of tolerable preservation. It is the comparison between the coalition of Fox and Newcastle, and the junction of the Rhone and the Saone. "At Lyons," said Pitt, "I was taken to see the place where the two rivers meet,—the one gentle, feeble, languid, and, though languid, yet of no depth, the other a boisterous and impetuous torrent; but different as they are, they meet at last." The amendment moved by the Opposition was rejected by a great majority; and Pitt and Legge were immediately dismissed from their offices. Lyttleton, whose friendship for Pitt had, during some time, been cooling, succeeded Legge as Chancellor of the Exchequer.

During several months the contest in the House of Commons was extremely sharp. Warm debates took place on the estimates,—debates still warmer on the subsidiary treaties. The Government succeeded in every division; but the fame of Pitt's eloquence, and the influence of his lofty and determined character, continued to increase through the Session; and the events which followed the prorogation made it utterly impossible for any other person to manage the Parliament or the country.

The war began in every part of the world with events disastrous to England, and even more shameful than disastrous. But the most humiliating of these events was the loss of Minorca, The Duke of Richelieu, an old fop who had passed his life from sixteen to sixty in seducing women for whom he cared not one straw, landed on that island with a French army, and succeeded in reducing it. Admiral Byng was sent from Gibraltar to throw succours into Port-Mahon; but he did not think fit to engage the French squadron, and sailed back without having effected his purpose. The people were inflamed to madness. A storm broke forth, which appalled even those who remembered the days of "Excise" and of "South-Sea." The shops were filled with labels and caricatures. The walls were covered with placards. The City of London called for vengeance, and the cry was echoed from every corner of the kingdom. Dorsetshire, Huntingdonshire, Bedfordshire, Buckinghamshire, Somersetshire, Lancashire, Suffolk, Shropshire, Surrey, sent up strong addresses to the throne, and instructed their representatives to vote for a strict inquiry into the causes of the late disasters. In the great towns the feeling was as strong as in the counties. In some of the instructions it was even recommended that the supplies should be stopped.

The nation was in a state of angry and sullen despondency, almost unparalleled in history. People have, in all ages, been in the habit of talking about the good old times of their ancestors, and the degeneracy of their contemporaries. This is in general merely a cant. But in 1756 it was something more. At this time appeared Brown's "Estimate," a book now remembered only by the allusions in Cowper's "Table Talk," and in Burke's "Letters on a Regicide Peace." It was universally read, admired, and believed. The author fully convinced his readers that they were a race of cowards and scoundrels; that nothing could save them; that they were on the point of being enslaved by their enemies, and that they richly deserved their fate. Such were the speculations to which ready credence was given at the outset of the most glorious war in which England had ever been engaged.

Newcastle now began to tremble for his place, and for the only thing which was dearer to him than his place,—his neck. The people were not in a mood to be trifled with. Their cry was for blood. For this once they might be contented with the sacrifice of Byng. But what if fresh disasters should take place? What if an unfriendly sovereign should ascend the throne? What if a hostile House of Commons should be chosen?

At length, in October, the decisive crisis came. Fox had been long sick of the perfidy and levity of Newcastle, and now began to fear that he might be made a scapegoat to save the old intriguer who, imbecile as he seemed, never wanted dexterity where danger was to be avoided. Fox threw up his office. Newcastle had recourse to Murray; but Murray had now within his reach the favourite object of his ambition. The situation of Chief Justice of the King's Bench was vacant; and the Attorney-General was fully resolved to obtain it, or to go into Opposition. Newcastle offered him any terms,—the Duchy of Lancaster for life,—a tellership of the Exchequer,—any pension that he chose to ask,—two thousand a year,—six thousand a year. When the Ministers found that Murray's mind was made up, they pressed for delay,—the delay of a session, a month, a week, a day. Would he only make his appearance once more in the House of Commons? Would he only speak in favour of the address? He was inexorable, and peremptorily said that they might give or withhold the Chief-Justiceship, but that he would be Attorney-General no longer.

Newcastle now contrived to overcome the prejudices of the King, and overtures were made to Pitt, through Lord Hardwicke. Pitt knew his power, and showed that he knew it. He demanded as an indispensable condition that Newcastle should be altogether excluded from the new arrangement.

The Duke was now in a state of ludicrous distress. He ran about chattering and crying, asking advice and listening to none. In the mean time, the Session drew near. The public excitement was unabated. Nobody could be found to face Pitt and Fox in the House of Commons. Newcastle's heart failed him, and he tendered his resignation.

The King sent for Fox, and directed him to form the plan of an administration in concert with Pitt. But Pitt had not forgotten old injuries, and positively refused to act with Fox.

The King now applied to the Duke of Devonshire, and this mediator succeeded in making an arrangement. He consented to take the Treasury. Pitt became Secretary of State, with the lead of the House of Commons. The Great Seal was put into commission; Legge returned to the Exchequer; and Lord Temple, whose sister Pitt had lately married, was placed at the head of the Admiralty.

It was clear from the first that this administration would last but a very short time. It lasted not quite five months; and, during those five months, Pitt and Lord Temple were treated with rudeness by the King, and found but feeble support in the House of Commons. It is a remarkable fact that the Opposition prevented the re-election of some of the new Ministers. Pitt, who sat for one of the boroughs which were in the Pelham interest, found some difficulty in obtaining a seat after his acceptance of the seals. So destitute was the new Government of that sort of influence without which no Government could then be durable. One of the arguments most frequently urged against the Reform Bill was that, under a system of popular representation, men whose presence in the House of Commons was necessary to the conducting of public business might often find it impossible to find seats. Should this inconvenience ever be felt there cannot be the slightest difficulty in devising and applying a remedy. But those who threatened us with this evil ought to have remembered that, under the old system, a great man called to power at a great crisis by the voice of the whole nation was in danger of being excluded by an aristocratic coterie from that House of which he was the most distinguished ornament.

The most important event of this short administration was the trial of Byng. On that subject public opinion is still divided. We think the punishment of the Admiral altogether unjust and absurd. Treachery, cowardice, ignorance amounting to what lawyers have called *crassa ignorantia*, are fit objects of severe penal inflictions. But Byng was not found guilty of treachery, of cowardice, or of gross ignorance of his profession. He died for doing what the most loyal subject, the most intrepid warrior, the most experienced seaman, might have done. He died for an error in judgment,—an error such as the greatest commanders,—Frederic, Napoleon, Wellington,—have often committed, and have often acknowledged. Such errors are not proper objects of punishment, for this reason,—that the punishing of them tends not to prevent them, but to produce them. The dread of an ignominious death may stimulate sluggishness to exertion, may keep a traitor to his standard, may prevent a coward from running away, but it has no tendency to bring out those qualities which enable men to form prompt and judicious decisions in great emergencies. The best marksman may be expected to fail when the apple which is to be his mark is set on his child's head. We cannot conceive anything more likely to deprive an officer of his self-possession at the time when he most needs it than the knowledge that, if the judgment of his superiors should not agree with his, he will be executed with every circumstance of shame. Queens, it has often been said, run far greater risk in childbed than private women, merely because their medical attendants are more anxious. The surgeon who attended Marie Louise was altogether unnerved by his emotions. "Compose yourself," said Bonaparte; "imagine that you are assisting a poor girl in the Faubourg St. Antoine." This was surely a far wiser course than that of the Eastern king in the Arabian Nights' Entertainments, who proclaimed that the physicians who failed to cure his daughter should have their heads chopped off. Bonaparte knew mankind well; and, as he acted towards this surgeon, he acted towards his officers. No sovereign was ever so indulgent to mere errors of judgment; and it is certain that no sovereign ever had in his service so many military men fit for the highest commands.

Pitt certainly acted a brave and honest part on this occasion. He ventured to put both his power and his popularity to hazard, and spoke manfully for Byng, both in Parliament and in the royal presence. But the King was inexorable. "The House of Commons, Sir," said Pitt, "seems inclined to mercy." "Sir," answered the King, "you have taught me to look for the sense of my people in other places than the House of Commons." The saying has more point than most of those which are recorded of George the Second, and, though sarcastically meant, contains a high and just compliment to Pitt.

The King disliked Pitt, but absolutely hated Temple. The new Secretary of State, his Majesty said, had never read Vatel, and was tedious and pompous, but respectful. The First Lord of the Admiralty was grossly impertinent. Walpole tells one story, which, we fear, is much too good to be true. He assures us that Temple entertained his royal master with an elaborate parallel between Byng's behaviour at Minorca, and his Majesty's behaviour at Oudenarde. The advantage was all on the side of the Admiral; and the obvious inference was, that if Byng ought to be shot, the King must richly deserve to be hanged.

This state of things could not last. Early in April, Pitt and all his friends were turned out, and Newcastle was summoned to St. James's. But the public discontent was not extinguished. It had subsided when Pitt was called to power. But it still glowed under the embers; and it now burst at once into a flame. The stocks fell. The Common Council met. The freedom of the city was voted to Pitt. All the greatest corporate towns followed the example. "For some weeks," says Walpole, "it rained gold boxes."

This was the turning point of Pitt's life. It might have been expected that a man of so haughty and vehement a nature, treated so ungraciously by the Court, and supported so enthusiastically by the people, would have eagerly taken the first opportunity of showing his power and gratifying his resentment; and an opportunity was not wanting. The members for many counties and large towns had been instructed to vote for an enquiry into the circumstances which had produced the miscarriage of the preceding year. A motion for enquiry had been carried in the House of Commons, without opposition; and, a few days after Pitt's dismissal, the investigation commenced. Newcastle and his colleagues obtained a vote of acquittal; but the minority were so strong that they could not venture to ask for a vote of approbation, as they had at first intended; and it was thought by some shrewd observers that, if Pitt had exerted himself to the utmost of his power, the enquiry might have ended in a censure, if not in an impeachment.

Pitt showed on this occasion a moderation and self-government which was not habitual to him. He had found by experience that he could not stand alone. His eloquence and his popularity had done much,—very much for him. Without rank, without fortune, without borough interest,—hated by the King, hated by the aristocracy,—he was a person of the first importance in the state. He had been suffered to form a ministry, and to pronounce sentence of exclusion on all his rivals,—on the most powerful nobleman of the Whig party,—on the ablest debater in the House of Commons. And he now found that he had gone too far. The English Constitution was not, indeed, without a popular element. But other elements generally predominated. The confidence and admiration of the nation might make a statesman formidable at the head of an Opposition,—might load him with framed and glazed parchments and gold boxes,—might possibly, under very peculiar circumstances, such as those of the preceding year, raise him for a time to power. But, constituted as Parliament then was, the favourite of the people could not depend on a majority in the people's own House. The Duke of Newcastle, however contemptible in morals, manners, and understanding, was a dangerous enemy. His rank, his wealth, his unrivalled parliamentary interest, would alone have made him important. But this was not all. The Whig aristocracy regarded him as their leader. His long possession of power had given him a kind of prescriptive right to possess it still. The House of Commons had been elected when he was at the head of affairs. The members for the ministerial boroughs had all been nominated by him. The public offices swarmed with his creatures.

Pitt desired power,—and he desired it, we really believe, from high and generous motives. He was, in the strict sense of the word, a patriot. He had no general liberality, none of that philanthropy which the great French writers of his time preached to all the nations of Europe. He loved England as an Athenian loved the City of the Violet Crown—as a Roman loved the "maxima rerum Roma." He saw his country insulted and defeated. He saw the national spirit sinking. Yet he knew what the resources of the empire, vigorously employed, could effect; and he felt that he was the man to employ them vigorously. "My Lord," he said to the Duke of Devonshire, "I am sure that I can save this country, and that nobody else can."

Desiring, then, to be in power, and feeling that his abilities and the public confidence were not alone sufficient to keep him in power against the wishes of the Court and of the aristocracy, he began to think of a coalition with Newcastle.

Newcastle was equally disposed to a reconciliation. He, too, had profited by his recent experience. He had found that the Court and the aristocracy, though powerful, were not everything in the state. A strong oligarchical connection, a great borough interest, ample patronage, and secret-service-money, might, in quiet times, be all that a Minister needed; but it was unsafe to trust wholly to such support in time of war, of discontent, and of agitation. The composition of the House of Commons was not wholly aristocratical; and, whatever be the composition of large deliberative assemblies, their spirit is always in some degree popular. Where there are free debates, eloquence must have admirers, and reason must make converts. Where there is a free press, the governors must live in constant awe of the opinions of the governed.

Thus these two men, so unlike in character, so lately mortal enemies, were necessary to each other. Newcastle had fallen in November, for want of that public confidence which Pitt possessed, and of that parliamentary support which Pitt was better qualified than any man of his time to give. Pitt had fallen in April, for want of that species of influence which Newcastle had passed his whole life in acquiring and hoarding. Neither of them had power enough to support himself. Each of them had power enough to overturn the other. Their union would be irresistible. Neither the King nor any party in the state would be able to stand against them.

Under these circumstances, Pitt was not disposed to proceed to extremities against his predecessors in office. Something, however, was due to consistency; and something was necessary for the preservation of his popularity. He did little; but that little he did in such a manner as to produce great effect. He came down to the House in all the pomp of gout, his legs swathed in flannels, his arm dangling in a sling. He kept his seat through several fatiguing days, in spite of pain and languor. He uttered a few sharp and vehement sentences; but, during the greater part of the discussion, his language was unusually gentle.

When the inquiry had terminated without a vote either of approbation or of censure, the great obstacle to a coalition was removed. Many obstacles, however, remained. The King was still rejoicing in his deliverance from the proud and aspiring Minister who had been forced on him by the cry of the nation. His Majesty's indignation was excited to the highest point when it appeared that Newcastle, who had, during thirty years, been loaded with marks of royal favour, and who had bound himself, by a solemn promise, never to coalesce with Pitt, was meditating a new perfidy. Of all the statesmen of that age, Fox had the largest share of royal favour. A coalition between Fox and Newcastle was the arrangement which the King wished to bring about. But the Duke was too cunning to fall into such a snare. As a speaker in Parliament, Fox might perhaps be, on the whole, as useful to an administration as his great rival; but he was one of the most unpopular men in England. Then, again, Newcastle felt all that jealousy of Fox which, according to the proverb, generally exists between two of a trade. Fox would certainly intermeddle with that department which the Duke was most desirous to reserve entire to himself,—the jobbing department. Pitt, on the other hand, was quite willing to leave the drudgery of corruption to any who might be inclined to undertake it.

During eleven weeks England remained without a ministry; and in the meantime Parliament was sitting, and a war was raging. The prejudices of the King, the haughtiness of Pitt, the jealousy, levity, and treachery of Newcastle, delayed the settlement. Pitt knew the Duke too well to trust him without security. The Duke loved power too much to be inclined to give security. While they were haggling, the King was in vain attempting to produce a final rupture between them, or to form a Government without them. At one time he applied to Lord Waldegrave, an honest and sensible man, but unpractised in affairs. Lord Waldegrave had the courage to accept the Treasury, but soon found that no administration formed by him had the smallest chance of standing a single week.

At length the King's pertinacity yielded to the necessity of the case. After exclaiming with great bitterness, and with some justice, against the Whigs, who ought, he said, to be ashamed to talk about liberty while they submitted to be the footmen of the Duke of Newcastle, he notified submission. The influence of the Prince of Wales prevailed on Pitt to abate a little, and but a little, of his high demands; and all at once, out of the chaos in which parties had for some time been rising, falling, meeting, separating, arose a government as strong at home as that of Pelham, as successful abroad as that of Godophin.

Newcastle took the Treasury. Pitt was Secretary of State, with the lead in the House of Commons, and with the supreme direction of the war and of foreign affairs. Fox, the only man who could have given much annoyance to the new government, was silenced with the office of Paymaster, which, during the continuance of that war, was probably the most lucrative place in the whole Government. He was poor, and the situation was tempting; yet it cannot but seem extraordinary that a man who had played a first part in politics, and whose abilities had been found not unequal to that part,—who had sat in the Cabinet, who had led the House of Commons, who had been twice intrusted by the King with the office of forming a ministry, who was regarded as the rival of Pitt, and who at one time seemed likely to be a successful rival,—should have consented, for the sake of emolument, to take a subordinate place and to give silent votes for all the measures of a government to the deliberations of which he was not summoned.

The first measures of the new administration were characterised rather by vigour than by judgment. Expeditions were sent against different parts of the French coast with little success. The small island of Aix was taken, Rochefort threatened, a few ships burned in the harbour of St. Maloes, and a few guns and mortars brought home as trophies from the fortifications of Cherbourg. But before long conquests of a very different kind filled the kingdom with pride and rejoicing. A succession of victories undoubtedly brilliant, and, as it was thought, not barren, raised to the highest point the fame of the minister to whom the conduct of the war had been intrusted. In July, 1758, Louisbourg fell. The whole island of Cape Breton was reduced; the fleet to which the Court of Versailles had confided the defence of French America was destroyed. The captured standards were borne in triumph from Kensington Palace to the city, and were suspended in St. Paul's Church, amidst the roar of guns and kettle-drums, and the shouts of an immense multitude. Addresses of congratulation came in from all the great towns of England. Parliament met only to decree thanks and monuments, and to bestow, without one murmur, supplies more than double of those which had been given during the war of the Grand Alliance.

The year 1759 opened with the conquest of Goree. Next fell Guadaloupe; then Ticonderoga; then Niagara. The Toulon squadron was completely defeated by Boscawen off Cape Lagos. But the greatest exploit of the year was the achievement of Wolfe on the heights of Abraham. The news of his glorious death and of the fall of Quebec reached London in the very week in which the Houses met. All was joy and triumph; envy and faction were forced to join in the general applause. Whigs and Tories vied with each other in extolling the genius and energy of Pitt. His colleagues were never talked of or thought of. The House of Commons, the nation, the colonies, our allies, our enemies, had their eyes fixed on him alone.

Scarcely had Parliament voted a monument to Wolfe when another great event called for fresh rejoicings. The Brest fleet, under the command of Conflans, had put out to sea. It was overtaken by an English squadron under Hawke. Conflans attempted to take shelter close under the French coast. The shore was rocky,—the night was black,—the wind was furious,—the Bay of Biscay ran high. But Pitt had infused into every branch of the service a spirit which had long been unknown. No British seaman was disposed to err on the same side with Byng. The pilot told Hawke that the attack could not be made without the greatest danger. "You have done your duty in remonstrating," answered Hawke; "I will answer for every thing. I command you to lay me alongside the French admiral." The result was a complete victory.

The year 1760 came; and still triumph followed triumph. Montreal was taken; the whole province of Canada was subjugated; the French fleets underwent a succession of disasters in the seas of Europe and America.

In the mean time conquests equalling in rapidity, and far surpassing in magnitude, those of Cortes and Pizarro, had been achieved in the east. In the space of three years the English had founded a mighty empire. The French had been defeated in every part of India. Chandernagore had surrendered to Clive, Pondicherry to Coote. Throughout Bengal, Bahar, Orissa, and the Carnatic, the authority of the East India Company was more absolute than that of Acbar or Aurungzebe had ever been.

On the continent of Europe the odds were against England. We had but one important ally, the King of Prussia; and he was attacked, not only by France, but also by Russia and Austria. Yet even on the Continent the energy of Pitt triumphed over all difficulties. Vehemently as he had condemned the practice of subsidising foreign princes, he now carried that practice farther than Carteret himself would have ventured to do. The active and able Sovereign of Prussia received such pecuniary assistance as enabled him to maintain the conflict on equal terms against his powerful enemies. On no subject had Pitt ever spoken with so much eloquence and ardour as on the mischiefs of the Hanoverian connection. He now declared, not without much show of reason, that it would be unworthy of the English people to suffer their King to be deprived of his electoral dominions in an English quarrel. He assured his countrymen that they should be no losers, and that he would conquer America for them in Germany. By taking this line he conciliated the King, and lost no part of his influence with the nation. In Parliament, such was the ascendancy which his eloquence, his success, his high situation, his pride, and his intrepidity had obtained for him, that he took liberties with the House of which there had been no example, and which have never since been imitated. No orator could there venture to reproach him with inconsistency. One unfortunate man made the attempt, and was so much disconcerted by the scornful demeanour of the Minister, that he stammered, stopped, and sat down. Even the old Tory country gentlemen, to whom the very name of Hanover had been odious, gave their hearty *ayes* to subsidy after subsidy. In a lively contemporary satire,—much more lively indeed than delicate,—this remarkable conversion is not unhappily described :

"No more they make a fiddle-faddle
About a Hessian horse or saddle.
No more of continental measures ;
No more of wasting British treasures.
Ten millions and a vote of credit,—
'Tis right. He can't be wrong who did it."

The success of Pitt's continental measures was such as might have been expected from their vigour. When he came into power, Hanover was in imminent danger ; and before he had been in office three months, the whole electorate was in the hands of France. But the face of affairs was speedily changed. The invaders were driven out. An army, partly English, partly Hanoverian, partly composed of soldiers furnished by the petty princes of Germany, was placed under the command of Prince Ferdinand of Brunswick. The French were beaten in 1758 at Crevelt. In 1759 they received a still more complete and humiliating defeat at Minden.

In the meantime, the nation exhibited all the signs of wealth and prosperity. The merchants of London had never been more thriving. The importance of several great commercial and manufacturing towns,—of Glasgow in particular,—dates from this period. The fine inscription on the monument of Lord Chatham in Guildhall records the general opinion of the citizens of London, that under his administration commerce had been "united with and made to flourish by war."

It must be owned that these signs of prosperity were in some degree delusive. It must be owned that some of our conquests were rather splendid than useful. It must be owned that the expense of the war never entered into Pitt's consideration. Perhaps it would be more correct to say that the cost of his victories increased the pleasure with which he contemplated them. Unlike other men in his situation, he loved to exaggerate the sums which the nation was laying out under his direction. He was proud of the sacrifices and efforts which his eloquence and his success had induced his countrymen to make. The price at which he purchased faithful service and complete victory, though far smaller than that which his son, the most profuse and incapable of war ministers, paid for treachery, defeat, and shame, was long and severely felt by the nation.

Even as a war minister, Pitt is scarcely entitled to all the praise which his contemporaries lavished on him. We, perhaps, from ignorance, cannot discern in his arrangements any appearance of profound or dexterous combination. Several of his expeditions, particularly those which were sent to the coast of France, were at once costly and absurd. Our Indian conquests, though they add to the splendour of the period during which he was at the head of affairs, were not planned by him. He had undoubtedly great energy, great determination, great means at his command. His temper was enterprising; and, situated as he was, he had only to follow his temper. The wealth of a rich nation, the valour of a brave nation, were ready to support him in every attempt.

In one respect, however, he deserved all the praise that he has ever received. The success of our arms was perhaps owing less to the skill of his dispositions than to the national resources and the national spirit. But that the national spirit rose to the emergency,—that the national resources were contributed with unexampled cheerfulness,—this was undoubtedly his work. The ardour of his spirit had set the whole kingdom on fire. It inflamed every soldier who dragged the cannon up the heights of Quebec, and every sailor who boarded the French ships among the rocks of Brittany. The Minister, before he had been long in office, had imparted to the commanders whom he employed his own impetuous, adventurous, and defying character. They, like him, were disposed to risk everything,—to play double or quits to the last,—to think nothing done while anything remained,—to fail rather than not to attempt. For the errors of rashness there might be indulgence. For over-caution, for faults like those of Lord George Sackville, there was no mercy. In other times, and against other enemies, this mode of warfare might have failed. But the state of the French government and of the French nation gave every advantage to Pitt. The fops and intriguers of Versailles were appalled and bewildered by his vigour. A panic spread through all ranks of society. Our enemies soon considered it as a settled thing that they were always to be beaten. Thus victory begot victory; till, at last, wherever the forces of the two nations met, they met with disdainful confidence on the one side, and with a craven fear on the other.

The situation which Pitt occupied at the close of the reign of George the Second was the most enviable ever occupied by any public man in English history. He had conciliated the King; he domineered over the House of Commons; he was adored by the people; he was admired by all Europe. He was the first Englishman of his time, and he had made England the first country in the world. The "Great Commoner,"—the name by which he was often designated,—might look down with scorn on coronets and garters. The nation was drunk with joy and pride. The Parliament was as quiet as it had been under Pelham. The old party distinctions were almost effaced; nor was their place yet supplied by distinctions of a still more important kind. A new generation of country squires and rectors had arisen, who knew not the Stuarts. The Dissenters were tolerated; the Catholics not cruelly persecuted. The Church was drowsy and indulgent. The great civil and religious conflict which began at the Reformation seemed to have terminated in universal repose. Whigs and Tories, Churchmen and Puritans, spoke with equal reverence of the constitution, and with equal enthusiasm of the talents, virtues, and services of the Minister.

A few years sufficed to change the whole aspect of affairs. A nation convulsed by faction, a throne assailed by the fiercest invective, a House of Commons hated and despised by the nation, England set against Scotland, Britain set against America, a rival legislature sitting beyond the Atlantic, English blood shed by English bayonets, our armies capitulating, our conquests wrested from us, our enemies hastening to take vengeance for past humiliation, our flag scarcely able to maintain itself in our own seas,—such was the spectacle which Pitt lived to see. But the history of this great revolution requires far more space than we can at present bestow. We leave the "Great Commoner" in the zenith of his glory. It is not impossible that we may take some other opportunity of tracing his life to its melancholy, yet not inglorious close.

SIR JAMES MACKINTOSH. HISTORY OF THE REVOLUTION.
(JULY, 1835.)

History of the Revolution in England, in 1688. Comprising a View of the Reign of James the Second, from his Accession to the Enterprise of the Prince of Orange, by late Right Honourable Sir JAMES MACKINTOSH, and completed to the Settlement of the Crown, by the Editor. To which is prefixed a Notice of the Life, Writings, and Speeches of Sir James Mackintosh. 4to. London: 1834.

IT is with unfeigned diffidence that we venture to give our opinion of the last work of Sir James Mackintosh. We have in vain tried to perform what ought to be to a critic an easy and habitual act. We have in vain tried to separate the book from the writer, and to judge of it as if it bore some unknown name. But it is to no purpose. All the lines of that venerable countenance are before us. All the little peculiar cadences of that voice from which scholars and statesmen loved to receive the lessons of a serene and benevolent wisdom are in our ears. We will attempt to preserve strict impartiality. But we are not ashamed to own that we approach this relic of a virtuous and most accomplished man with feelings of respect and gratitude which may possibly pervert our judgment.

It is hardly possible to avoid instituting a comparison between this work and another celebrated Fragment. Our readers will easily guess that we allude to Mr. Fox's History of James the Second. The two books relate to the same subject. Both were posthumously published. Neither had received the last corrections. The authors belonged to the same political party, and held the same opinions concerning the merits and defects of the English constitution, and concerning most of the prominent characters and events in English history. They had thought much on the principles of government; yet they were not mere speculators. They had ransacked the archives of rival kingdoms, and pored on folios which had mouldered for ages in deserted libraries; but they were not mere antiquaries. They had one eminent qualification for writing history:—they had spoken history, acted history, lived history. The turns of political fortune, the ebb and flow of popular feeling, the hidden mechanism by which parties are moved, all these things were the subjects of their constant thought and of their most familiar conversation. Gibbon has remarked that his history is much the better for his having been an officer in the militia and a member of the House of Commons. The remark is most just. We have not the smallest doubt that his campaign, though he never saw an enemy, and his parliamentary attendance, though he never made a speech, were of far more use to him than years of retirement and study would have been. If the time that he spent on parade and at mess in Hampshire, or on the Treasury Bench and at Brookes's during the storms which overthrew Lord North and Lord Shelburne, had been passed in the Bodleian Library, he might have avoided some inaccuracies;—he might have enriched his notes with a greater number of references; but he would never have produced so lively a picture of the court, the camp, and the senate·

house. In this respect Mr. Fox and Sir James Mackintosh had great advantages over almost every English historian who has written since the time of Burnet. Lord Lyttelton had indeed the same advantages, but he was incapable of using them. Pedantry was so deeply fixed in his nature that the Hustings, the Treasury, the Exchequer, the House of Commons, the House of Lords, left him the same dreaming schoolboy that they found him.

When we compare the two interesting works of which we have been speaking, we have little difficulty in awarding the superiority to that of Sir James Mackintosh. Indeed, the superiority of Mr. Fox to Sir James as an orator is hardly more clear than the superiority of Sir James to Mr. Fox as a historian. Mr. Fox with a pen in his hand, and Sir James on his legs in the House of Commons, were, we think, each out of his proper element. They were men, it is true, of far too much judgment and ability to fail scandalously in any undertaking to which they brought the whole power of their minds. The History of James the Second will always keep its place in our libraries as a valuable book; and Sir James Mackintosh succeeded in winning and maintaining a high place among the parliamentary speakers of his time. Yet we could never read a page of Mr. Fox's writing, we could never listen for a quarter of an hour to the speaking of Sir James, without feeling that there was a constant effort, a tug up hill. Nature, or habit which had become nature, asserted its rights. Mr. Fox wrote debates. Sir James Mackintosh spoke essays.

As far as mere diction was concerned, indeed, Mr. Fox did his best to avoid those faults which the habit of public speaking is likely to generate. He was so nervously apprehensive of sliding into some colloquial incorrectness of debasing his style by a mixture of Parliamentary slang, that he ran into the opposite error, and purified his vocabulary with a scrupulosity unknown to any purist. "Ciceronem Allobroga dixit." He would not allow Addison, Bolingbroke, or Middleton to be a sufficient authority for an expression. He declared he would use no word which was not to be found in Dryden. In any other person we should have called this solicitude mere foppery; and, in spite of all our admiration for Mr. Fox, we cannot but think that his extreme attention to the petty niceties of language was hardly worthy of so manly and so capacious an understanding. There were purists of this kind at Rome; and their fastidiousness was censured by Horace, with that perfect good sense and good taste which characterise all his writings. There were purists of this kind at the time of the revival of letters; and the two greatest scholars of that time raised their voices, the one from within, the other from without the Alps, against a scrupulosity so unreasonable. "Carent," said Politian, "quæ scribunt isti viribus et vita, carent actu, carent effectu, carent indole. . . . Nisi liber ille præsto sit ex quo quid excerpant, colligere tria verba non possunt. . . . Horum semper igitur oratio tremula, vacillans, infirma. . . . Quæso ne ista superstitione te alliges. . . . Ut bene currere non potest qui pedem ponere studet in alienis tantum vestigiis, ita nec bene scribere qui tanquam de præscripto non audet egredi."—"Posthac," exclaims Erasmus, "non licebit episcopos appellare patres reverendos, nec in calce literarum scribere annum a Christo nato, quod id nusquam faciat Cicero. Quid autem ineptius quam, toto seculo novato, religione, imperiis, magistratibus, locorum vocabulis, ædificiis, cultu, moribus, non aliter audere loqui quam locutus est Cicero? Si revivisceret ipse Cicero, rideret hoc Ciceronianorum genus."

While Mr. Fox winnowed and sifted his phraseology with a care which seems hardly consistent with the simplicity and elevation of his mind, and of which the effect really was to debase and enfeeble his style, he was little on his guard against those more serious improprieties of manner into which a great orator who undertakes to write history is in danger of falling. There is about the whole book a vehement, contentious, replying manner. Almost every argument is put in the form of an interrogation, an ejaculation, or a sarcasm. The writer seems to be addressing himself to some imaginary audience:—to be tearing in pieces a defence of the Stuarts which has just been pronounced by an imaginary Tory. Take, for example, his answer to Hume's remarks on the execution of Sydney; and substitute "the honourable gentleman," or "the noble Lord" for the name of Hume. The whole passage sounds like a powerful reply, thundered at three in the morning from the Opposition Bench. While we read it, we can almost fancy that we see and hear the great English debater, such as he has been described to us by the few who can still remember the Westminster Scrutiny and the Oczakow Negotiations, in the full paroxysm of inspiration, foaming, screaming, choked by the rushing multitude of his words.

It is true that the passage to which we have referred, and several other passages which we could point out, are admirable, when considered merely as exhibitions of mental power. We at once recognise in them that consummate master of the whole art of intellectual gladiatorship, whose Speeches, imperfectly as they have been transmitted to us, should be studied day and night by every man who wishes to learn the science of logical defence. We find in several parts of the History of James the Second fine specimens of that which we conceive to have been the great characteristic of Demosthenes among the Greeks, and of Fox among the orators of England,—reason penetrated, and, if we may venture on the expression, made red hot by passion. But this is not the kind of excellence proper to history; and it is hardly too much to say that whatever is strikingly good in Mr. Fox's Fragment is out of place.

With Sir James Mackintosh the case was reversed. His proper place was his library, a circle of men of letters, or a chair of moral and political philosophy. He distinguished himself highly in Parliament. But nevertheless Parliament was not exactly the sphere for him. The effect of his most successful speeches was small when compared with the quantity of ability and learning which was expended on them. We could easily name men who, not possessing a tenth part of his intellectual powers, hardly ever address the House of Commons without producing a greater impression than was produced by his most splendid and elaborate orations. His luminous and philosophical disquisition on the Reform Bill was spoken to empty benches. Those, indeed, who had the wit to keep their seats, picked up hints which, skilfully used, made the fortune of more than one speech. But "it was caviare to the general." And even those who listened to Sir James with pleasure and admiration could not but acknowledge that he rather lectured than debated. An artist who should waste on a panorama, on a scene, or on a transparency, the exquisite finishing which we admire in some of the small Dutch interiors, would not squander his powers more than this eminent man too often did. His audience resembled the boy in the Heart of Mid-Lothian, who pushes away the lady's guineas with contempt, and insists on having the white money. They preferred the silver with which they were familiar, and which they were constantly passing about from hand to hand, to the gold which they had never before seen, and with the value of which they were unacquainted.

It is much to be regretted, we think, that Sir James Mackintosh did not wholly devote his later years to philosophy and literature. His talents were not those which enable a speaker to produce with rapidity a series of striking but transitory impressions,—and to excite the minds of five hundred gentlemen at midnight, without saying anything that any one of them will be able to remember in the morning. His arguments were of a very different texture from those which are produced in Parliament at a moment's notice,—which puzzle a plain man, who, if he had them before him in writing, would soon detect their fallacy, and which the great debater who employs them forgets within half an hour, and never thinks of again. Whatever was valuable in the compositions of Sir James Mackintosh was the ripe fruit of study and of meditation. It was the same with his conversation. In his most familiar talk there was no wildness, no inconsistency, no amusing nonsense, no exaggeration for the sake of momentary effect. His mind was a vast magazine, admirably arranged; everything was there; and everything was in its place. His judgments on men, on sects, on books, had been often and carefully tested and weighed, and had then been committed, each to its proper receptacle, in the most capacious and accurately constructed memory that any human being ever possessed. It would have been strange indeed if you had asked for anything that was not to be found in that immense storehouse. The article which you required was not only there. It was ready. It was in its own proper compartment. In a moment it was brought down, unpacked, and displayed. If those who enjoyed the privilege,—for a privilege indeed it was,—of listening to Sir James Mackintosh, had been disposed to find some fault in his conversation, they might perhaps have observed that he yielded too little to the impulse of the moment. He seemed to be recollecting, not creating. He never appeared to catch a sudden glimpse of a subject in a new light. You never saw his opinions in the making,—still rude, still inconsistent, and requiring to be fashioned by thought and discussion. They came forth, like the pillars of that temple in which no sound of axes or hammers was heard, finished, rounded, and exactly suited to their places. What Mr. Charles Lamb has said, with much humour and some truth, of the conversation of Scotchmen in general, was certainly true of this eminent Scotchman. He did not find, but bring. You could not cry halves to anything that turned up while you were in his company.

The intellectual and moral qualities which are most important in a historian, he possessed in a very high degree. He was singularly mild, calm, and impartial in his judgments of men, and of parties. Almost all the distinguished writers who have treated of English history are advocates. Mr. Hallam and Sir James Mackintosh alone are entitled to be called judges. But the extreme austerity of Mr. Hallam takes away something from the pleasure of reading his learned, eloquent, and judicious writings. He is a judge, but a hanging judge, the Page or Buller of the High Court of Literary Justice. His black cap is in constant requisition. In the long calendar of those whom he has tried, there is hardly one who has not, in spite of evidence to character and recommendations to mercy, been sentenced and left for execution. Sir James, perhaps, erred a little on the other side. He liked a maiden assize, and came away with white gloves, after sitting in judgment on batches of the most notorious offenders. He had a quick eye for the redeeming parts of a character, and a large toleration for the infirmities of men exposed to strong temptations. But this lenity did not arise from ignorance or neglect of moral distinctions. Though he allowed perhaps too much weight to every extenuating circumstance that could be urged in favour of the transgressor, he never disputed the authority of the law, or showed his ingenuity by refining away its enactments. On every occasion he showed himself firm where principles were in question, but full of charity towards individuals.

We have no hesitation in pronouncing this Fragment decidedly the best history now extant of the reign of James the Second. It contains much new and curious information, of which excellent use has been made. The accuracy of the narrative is deserving of high admiration. We have noticed only one mistake of the smallest importance, and that, we believe, is to be laid to the charge of the editor, who has far more serious blunders to answer for. The pension of 60,000 livres, which Lord Sunderland received from France, is said to have been equivalent to £2,500 sterling. Sir James had perhaps for a moment forgotten,—his editor had certainly never heard,—that a great depreciation of French coin took place after 1688. When Sunderland was in power the livre was worth about eighteen-pence, and his pension consequently amounted to £4,500. This is really the only inaccuracy of the slightest moment that we have been able to discover in several attentive perusals.

We are not sure that the book is not in some degree open to the charge which the idle citizen in the Spectator brought against his pudding ; "Mem. too many plums, and no suet." There is perhaps too much disquisition and too little narrative ; and indeed this is the fault into which, judging from the habits of Sir James's mind, we should have thought him most likely to fall. What we assuredly did not anticipate was, that the narrative would be better executed than the disquisitions. We expected to find, and we have found, many just delineations of character, and many digressions full of interest,—such as the account of the order of Jesuits, and of the state of prison discipline in England a hundred and fifty years ago. We expected to find, and we have found, many reflections breathing the spirit of a calm and benignant philosophy. But we did not, we own, expect to find that Sir James could tell a story as well as Voltaire or Hume. Yet such is the fact ; and if any person doubts it, we would advise him to read the account of the events which followed the issuing of King James's declaration,—the meeting of the clergy, the violent scene at the privy council, the commitment, trial, and acquittal of the bishops. The most superficial reader must be charmed, we think, by the liveliness of the narrative. But no person who is not acquainted with that vast mass of intractable materials of which the valuable and interesting part has been extracted and condensed can fully appreciate the skill of the writer. Here, and indeed throughout the book, we find many harsh and careless expressions which the author would probably have removed if he had lived to complete his work. But, in spite of these blemishes, we must say that we should find it difficult to point out, in any modern history, any passage of equal merit. We find in it the diligence, the accuracy, and the judgment of Hallam, united to the vivacity and the colouring of Southey. A history of England, written throughout in this manner, would be the most fascinating book in the language. It would be more in request at the circulating libraries than the last novel.

Sir James was not, we think, gifted with poetical imagination. But that lower kind of imagination which is necessary to the historian he had in large measure. It is not the business of the historian to create new worlds, and to people them with new races of beings. He is to Homer and Shakspeare, to Dante and Milton, what Nollekins was to Canova, or Lawrence to Michael Angelo. The object of the historian's imitation is not within him ; it is furnished from without. It is not a vision of beauty and grandeur discernible only by the eye of his own mind, but a real model which he did not make, and which he cannot alter. Yet his is not a mere mechanical imitation. The triumph of his skill is to select such parts as may produce the effect of the whole, to bring out strongly all the characteristic features, and to throw the light and shade in such a manner as may heighten the effect. This skill, as far as we can judge from the unfinished work now before us, Sir James Mackintosh possessed in an eminent degree.

The style of this Fragment is weighty, manly, and unaffected. There are, as we have said, some expressions which seem to us harsh, and some which we think inaccurate. These would probably have been corrected, if Sir James had lived to superintend the publication. We ought to add that the printer has by no means done his duty. One misprint in particular is so serious as to require notice. Sir James Mackintosh has paid a high and just tribute to the genius, the integrity, and the courage of a good and great man, a distinguished ornament of English literature, a fearless champion of English liberty, Thomas Burnet, Master of the Charter House, and author of that most eloquent and imaginative work, the *Telluris Theoria Sacra*. Wherever the name of this celebrated man occurs, it is printed "Bennet," both in the text and in the index. This cannot be mere negligence. It is plain that Thomas Burnet and his writings were never heard of by the gentleman who has been employed to edit this volume, and who, not content with deforming Sir James Mackintosh's text by such blunders, has prefixed to it a bad Memoir, has appended to it a bad Continuation, and has thus succeeded in expanding the volume into one of the thickest, and debasing it into one of the worst that we ever saw. Never did we fall in with so admirable an illustration of the old Greek proverb, which tells us that half is sometimes more than the whole. Never did we see a case in which the increase of the bulk was so evidently a diminution of the value.

Why such an artist was selected to preface so fine a Torso, we cannot pretend to conjecture. We read that, when the Consul Mummius, after the taking of Corinth, was preparing to send to Rome some works of the greatest Grecian sculptors, he told the packers that if they broke his Venus or his Apollo, he would force them to restore the limbs which should be wanting. A head by a hewer of mile-stones joined to a bosom by Praxiteles would not surprise or shock us more than this supplement. The Memoir contains much that is worth reading; for it contains many extracts from the compositions of Sir James Mackintosh. But when we pass from what the biographer has done with his scissors to what he has done with his pen, we can find nothing worthy of approbation. Instead of confining himself to the only work which he is competent to perform,—that of relating facts in plain words,—he favours us with his opinions about Lord Bacon, and about the French literature of the age of Louis XIV.; and with opinions, more absurd still, about the poetry of Homer, whom it is evident, from his criticisms, that he cannot read in the original. He affects, and for aught we know, feels something like contempt for the celebrated man whose life he has undertaken to write, and whom he was incompetent to serve in the capacity even of a corrector of the press. Our readers may form a notion of the spirit in which the whole narrative is composed, from expressions which occur at the beginning. This biographer tells us that Mackintosh, on occasion of taking his medical degree at Edinburgh, "not only put off the writing of his Thesis to the last moment, but was an hour behind his time on the day of examination, and kept the Academic Senate waiting for him in full conclave." This irregularity, which no sensible professor would have thought deserving of more than a slight reprimand, is described by the biographer, after a lapse of nearly half a century, as an incredible instance "not so much of indolence as of gross negligence and bad taste." But this is not all. Our biographer has contrived to procure a copy of the Thesis, and has sate down with his *As in præsenti* and his *Propria quæ maribus* at his side, to pick out blunders in a composition written by a youth of twenty-one, on the occasion alluded to. He finds one mistake,—such a mistake as the greatest scholar might commit when in haste, and as the veriest schoolboy would detect when at leisure. He glories over this precious discovery with all the exultation of a pedagogue. "Deceived by the passive termination of the deponent verb *defungor*, Mackintosh misuses it in a passive sense." He is not equally fortunate in his other discovery. "*Laudis conspurcare*" whatever he may think, is not an improper phrase. Mackintosh meant to say that there are men whose praise is a disgrace. No person, we are sure, who has read this Memoir, will doubt that there are men whose abuse is an honour.

But we must proceed to more important matters. This writer evidently wishes to impress his readers with a belief that Sir James Mackintosh, from interested motives, abandoned the doctrines of the Vindiciæ Gallicæ. Had his statements appeared in their natural place, we should leave them to their natural fate. We would not stoop to defend Sir James Mackintosh from the attacks of fourth-rate magazines and pothouse newspapers. But here his own fame is turned against him. A book of which not one copy would ever have been bought but for his name in the titlepage is made the vehicle of the slander. Under such circumstances we cannot help exclaiming, in the words of one of the most amiable of Homer's heroes,—

" Νῦν τις ἐυηείης Πατροκλῆος δειλοῖο
Μνησάσθω· πᾶσιν γὰρ ἐπίστατο μείλιχος εἶναι
Ζωὸς ἐών· νῦν δ᾽ αὖ θάνατος καὶ μοῖρα κιχάνει."

We have no difficulty in admitting, that, during the ten or twelve years which followed the appearance of the Vindiciæ Gallicæ, the opinions of Sir James Mackintosh underwent some change. But did this change pass on him alone? Was it not common? Was it not almost universal? Was there one honest friend of liberty in Europe or in America whose ardour had not been damped, whose faith in the high destinies of mankind had not been shaken? Was there one observer to whom the French Revolution, or revolutions in general, appeared in exactly the same light on the day when the Bastile fell, and on the day when the Girondists were dragged to the scaffold,— the day when the Directory shipped off their principal opponents for Guiana, or the day when the Legislative Body was driven from its hall at the point of the bayonet? We do not speak of enthusiastic and light-minded people, —of wits like Sheridan, of poets like Alfieri; but of the most virtuous and intelligent practical statesmen, and of the deepest, the calmest, the most impartial political speculators of that time. What was the language and conduct of Lord Spencer, of Lord Fitzwilliam, of Mr. Grattan? What is the tone of M. Dumont's Memoirs, written just at the close of the eighteenth century? What Tory could have spoken with greater disgust and contempt of the French Revolution and its authors? Nay, this writer, a republican, and the most upright and zealous of republicans, has gone so far as to say that Mr. Burke's work on the Revolution had saved Europe. The name of M. Dumont naturally suggests that of Mr. Bentham. He, we presume, was not ratting for a place; and what language did he hold at that time? Look at his little treatise entitled *Sophismes Anarchiques*. In that treatise he says, that the atrocities of the Revolution were the natural consequences of the absurd principles on which it was commenced;—that, while the chiefs of the constituent assembly gloried in the thought that they were pulling down aristocracy, they never saw that their doctrines tended to produce an evil a hundred times more formidable,—anarchy;—that the theory laid down in the "Declaration of the Rights of Man" had, in a great measure, produced the crimes of the Reign of Terror;—that none but an eyewitness could imagine the horrors of a state of society in which comments on that Declaration were put forth by men with no food in their bellies, with rags on their backs, and with arms in their hands. He praises the English Parliament for the dislike which it has always shown to abstract reasonings, and to the affirming of general principles. In M. Dumont's preface to the "Treatise on the Principles of Legislation,"—a preface written under the eye of Mr. Bentham, and published with his sanction,—are the following still more remarkable expressions:—"M. Bentham est bien loin d'attacher une préférence exclusive à aucune forme de gouvernement. Il pense que la meilleure constitution pour un peuple est celle à laquelle il est accoutumé. . . . Le vice fondamental des théories sur les constitution politiques, c'est de commencer par attaquer celles qui existent, et d'exciter tout au moins des inquiétudes et des jallousies de pouvoir. Une telle disposition n'est point favorable au perfectionnement des lois. La seule époque où l'on puisse entreprendre avec succès de grandes réforme de législation, est celle où les passions publiques sont calmes, et où le gouvernement jouit de la stabilité la plus grande. L'objet de M. Bentham, en cherchant dans le vice des lois la cause de la plupart des maux, a été constamment d'éloigner le plus grand de tous, le bouleversement de l'autorité, les revolution de propriété et de pouvoir."

To so conservative a frame of mind had the excesses of the French Revolution brought the most uncompromising reformers of that time. And why is one person to be singled out from among millions, and arraigned before posterity as a traitor to his opinions, only because events produced on him the effect which they produced on a whole generation? This biographer may, for aught we know, have revelations from heaven like Mr. Percival, or pure anticipated cognitions like the disciples of Kant. But such poor creatures as Mackintosh, Dumont, and Bentham, had nothing but observation and reason to guide them; and they obeyed the guidance of observation and reason. How is it in physics? A traveller falls in with a fruit which he has never before seen. He tastes it, and finds it sweet and refreshing. He praises it, and resolves to introduce it into his own country. But in a few minutes he is taken violently sick; he is convulsed; he is at the point of death; no medicine gives him relief. He of course pronounces this delicious food a poison, blames his own folly in tasting it, and cautions his friends against it. After a long and violent struggle he recovers, and finds himself much exhausted by his sufferings, but free from some chronic complaints which had been the torment of his life. He then changes his opinion again, and pronounces this fruit a very powerful remedy, which ought to be employed only in extreme cases and with great caution, but which ought not to be absolutely excluded from the "Pharmacopœia." And would it not be the height of absurdity to call such a man fickle and inconsistent, because he had repeatedly altered his judgment? If he had not altered his judgment, would he have been a rational being? It was exactly the same with the French Revolution. That event was a new phenomenon in politics. Nothing that had gone before enabled any person to judge with certainty of the course events might take. At first the effect was the reform of great abuses; and honest men rejoiced. Then came commotion, proscription, confiscation, the bankruptcy, the assignats, the maximum, civil war, foreign war, revolutionary tribunals, guillotinades, noyades, fusillades. Yet a little while, and a military despotism rose out of the confusion, and threatened the independence of every state in Europe. And yet again a little while, and the old dynasty returned, followed by a train of emigrants eager to restore the old abuses. We have now, we think, the whole before us. We should therefore be justly accused of levity or insincerity if our language concerning these events were constantly changing. It is our deliberate opinion that the French Revolution, in spite of all its crimes and follies, was a great blessing to mankind. But it was not only natural, but inevitable, that those who had only seen the first act should be ignorant of the catastrophe, and should be alternately elated and depressed as the plot went on disclosing itself to them. A man who had held exactly the same opinion about the Revolution in 1789, in 1794, in 1804, in 1814, and in 1834, would have been either a divinely inspired prophet, or an obstinate fool. Mackintosh was neither. He was simply a wise and good man; and the change which passed on his mind was a change which passed on the mind of almost every wise and good man in Europe. In fact, few of his contemporaries changed so little. The rare moderation and calmness of his temper preserved him alike from extravagant elation and extravagant despondency. He was never a Jacobin. He was never an Antijacobin. His mind oscillated undoubtedly; but the extreme points of the oscillation were not very remote. Herein he differed greatly from some persons of distinguished talents who entered into life at nearly the same time with him. Such persons we have seen rushing from one wild extreme to another,—out-Paining Paine,—out-Castlereaghing Castlereagh,—Pantisocratists,—Ultra-Tories,—heretics,—persecutors,—breaking the old laws against sedition,—calling for new and sharper laws against sedition,—writing democratic dramas,—writing Laureate odes,—panegyrising Marten,—panegyrising Laud,—consistent in nothing but in an intolerance which in any person would be offensive, but which is altogether unpardonable in men who, by their own confession, have had such ample experience of their own fallibility. We readily concede to some of these persons the praise of eloquence and poetical invention; nor are we by any means disposed, even where they have been gainers by their conversions, to question their sincerity. It would be most uncandid to attribute to sordid motives actions which admit of a less discreditable explanation. We think that the conduct of these persons has been precisely what was to be expected from men who were gifted with strong imagination and quick sensibility, but who were neither accurate observers nor logical reasoners. It was natural that such men should see in the victory of the third estate of France the dawn of a new Saturnian age. It was natural that the rage of their disappointment should be proportioned to the extravagance of their hopes. Though the direction of their passions was altered, the violence of those passions was the same. The force of the rebound was proportioned to the force of the original impulse. The pendulum swung furiously to the left, because it had been drawn too far to the right.

We own that nothing gives us so high an idea of the judgment and temper of Sir James Mackintosh as the manner in which he shaped his course through those times. Exposed successively to two opposite infections, he took both in their very mildest form. The constitution of his mind was such that neither of the diseases which committed such havoc all round him could in any serious degree, or for any great length of time, derange his intellectual health. He, like every honest and enlightened man in Europe, saw with delight the great awakening of the French nation. Yet he never, in the season of his warmest enthusiasm, proclaimed doctrines inconsistent with the safety of property, and the just authority of governments. He, like almost every other honest and enlightened man, was discouraged and perplexed by the terrible events which followed. Yet he never in the most gloomy times abandoned the cause of peace, of liberty, and of toleration. In that great convulsion which overset almost every other understanding, he was indeed so much shaken that he leaned sometimes in one direction and sometimes in the other; but he never lost his balance. The opinions in which he at last reposed, and to which, in spite of strong temptations, he adhered with a firm, a disinterested, an ill-requited fidelity, were a just mean between those which he had defended with youthful ardour and with more than manly prowess against Mr. Burke, and those to which he had inclined during the darkest and saddest years in the history of modern Europe. We are much mistaken if this be the picture either of a weak or of a dishonest mind.

What the political opinions of Sir James Mackintosh were in his later years is written in the annals of his country. Those annals will sufficiently refute what his biographer has ventured to assert in the very advertisement to this work. "Sir James Mackintosh," says he, "was avowedly and emphatically a Whig of the Revolution : and since the agitation of religious liberty and parliamentary reform became a national movement, the great transaction of 1688 has been more dispassionately, more correctly, and less highly estimated." While we transcribe the words our anger cools down into scorn. If they mean anything, they must mean that the opinions of Sir James Mackintosh concerning religious liberty and parliamentary reform went no further than those of the authors of the revolution ;—in other words, that Sir James Mackintosh opposed Catholic emancipation, and quite approved of the old constitution of the House of Commons. The allegation is confuted by twenty volumes of parliamentary debates, nay, by innumerable passages in the very fragment which this writer has done his little utmost to deface. We tell him that Sir James Mackintosh has often done more for religious liberty and for parliamentary reform in a quarter of an hour than the feeble abilities of his biographer will ever effect in the whole course of a long life.

We shall not, we hope, be suspected of a bigoted attachment to the doctrines and practices of past generations. Our creed is that the science of government is an experimental science, and that, like all other experimental sciences, it is generally in a state of progression. No man is so obstinate an admirer of the old times as to deny that medicine, surgery, botany, chemistry, engineering, navigation, are better understood now than in any former age. We conceive that it is the same with political science. Like those physical sciences which we have mentioned, it has always been working itself clearer and clearer, and depositing impurity after impurity. There was a time when the most powerful of human intellects were deluded by the gibberish of the astrologer and the alchemist ; and just so there was a time when the most enlightened and virtuous statesmen thought it the first duty of a government to persecute heretics, to found monasteries, to make war on Saracens. But time advances: facts accumulate ; doubts arise. Faint glimpses of truth begin to appear, and shine more and more unto the perfect day. The highest intellects, like the tops of mountains, are the first to catch and to reflect the dawn. They are bright, while the level below is still in darkness. But soon the light, which at first illuminated only the loftiest eminences, descends on the plain, and penetrates to the deepest valley. First come hints, then fragments of systems, then defective systems, then complete and harmonious systems. The sound opinion, held for a time by one bold speculator, becomes the opinion of a small minority, of a strong minority, of a majority,— of mankind. Thus, the great progress goes on, till schoolboys laugh at the jargon which imposed on Bacon,—till country rectors condemn the illiberality and intolerance of Sir Thomas More.

Seeing these things,—seeing that, by the confession of the most obstinate enemies of innovation, our race has hitherto been almost constantly advancing in knowledge, and not seeing any reason to believe that, precisely at the point of time at which we came into the world, a change took place in the faculties of the human mind, or in the mode of discovering truth, we are reformers : we are on the side of progress. From the great advances which European society has made, during the last four centuries, in every species of knowledge, we infer, not that there is no more room for improvement, but that, in every science which deserves the name, immense improvements may be confidently expected.

But the very considerations which lead us to look forward with sanguine hope to the future prevent us from looking back with contempt on the past. We do not flatter ourselves with the notion that we have attained perfection, and that no more truth remains to be found. We believe that we are wiser than our ancestors. We believe, also, that our posterity will be wiser than we. It would be gross injustice in our grandchildren to talk of us with contempt, merely because they may have surpassed us;—to call Watt a fool, because mechanical powers may be discovered which may supersede the use of steam;—to deride the efforts which have been made in our time to improve the discipline of prisons, and to enlighten the minds of the poor, because future philanthropists may devise better places of confinement than Mr. Bentham's Panopticon, and better places of education than Mr. Lancaster's Schools. As we would have our descendants judge us, so ought we to judge our fathers. In order to form a correct estimate of their merits, we ought to place ourselves in their situation,—to put out of our minds, for a time, all that knowledge which they, however eager in the pursuit of truth, could not have, and which we, however negligent we may have been, could not help having. It was not merely difficult, but absolutely impossible, for the best and greatest of men, two hundred years ago, to be what a very commonplace person in our days may easily be, and indeed must necessarily be. But it is too much that the benefactors of mankind, after having been reviled by the dunces of their own generation for going too far, should be reviled by the dunces of the next generation for not going far enough.

The truth lies between two absurd extremes. On one side is the bigot who pleads the wisdom of our ancestors as a reason for not doing what they in our place would be the first to do,—who opposes the Reform Bill because Lord Somers did not see the necessity of Parliamentary Reform,—who would have opposed the Revolution because Ridley and Cranmer professed boundless submission to the royal prerogative,—and who would have opposed the Reformation because the Fitzwalters and Mareschals, whose seals are set to the Great Charter, were devoted adherents to the Church of Rome. On the other side is the conceited sciolist who speaks with scorn of the Great Charter, because it did not reform the Church; of the Reformation, because it did not limit the prerogative; and of the Revolution, because it did not purify the House of Commons. The former of these errors we have often combated, and shall always be ready to combat: the latter, though rapidly spreading, has not, we think, yet come under our notice. The former error bears directly on practical questions, and obstructs useful reforms. It may, therefore, seem to be, and probably is, the more mischievous of the two. But the latter is equally absurd; it is at least equally symptomatic of a shallow understanding and an unamiable temper; and, if it should ever become general, it will, we are satisfied, produce very prejudicial effects. Its tendency is to deprive the benefactors of mankind of their honest fame, and to put the best and the worst men of past times on the same level. The author of a great reformation is almost always unpopular in his own age. He generally passes his life in disquiet and danger. It is therefore for the interest of the human race that the memory of such men should be had in reverence, and that they should be supported against the scorn and hatred of their contemporaries by the hope of leaving a great and imperishable name. To go on the forlorn hope of truth is a service of peril. Who will undertake it, if it be not also a service of honour? It is easy enough, after the ramparts are carried, to find men to plant the flag on the highest tower. The difficulty is to find men who are ready to go first into the breach; and it would be bad policy indeed to insult their remains because they fell in the breach, and did not live to penetrate to the citadel.

Now here we have a book written by a man, who is a very bad specimen of the English of the nineteenth century,—a man who knows nothing but what it is a scandal to know. And, if we were to judge by the self-complacent pity with which the writer speaks of the great statesmen and philosophers of a former age, we should guess that he was the author of the most original and important inventions in political science. Yet not so :—for men who are able to make discoveries are generally disposed to make allowances. Men who are eagerly pressing forward in pursuit of truth are grateful to everyone who has cleared an inch of the way for them. It is, for the most part, the man below mediocrity, the man who has just capacity enough to pick up and repeat the commonplaces which are fashionable in his own time,—it is he, we say, who looks with disdain on the very intellects to which it is owing that those commonplaces are not still considered as startling paradoxes or damnable heresies. This writer is just the man who, if he had lived in the seventeenth century, would have devoutly believed that the Papists burned London,—who would have swallowed the whole of Oates' story about the forty thousand soldiers, disguised as pilgrims, who were to meet in Gallicia, and sail thence to invade England,—who would have carried a Protestant flail under his coat, —and who would have been furious if the story of the warming-pan had been questioned. It is quite natural that such a man should speak with contempt of the great reformers of that time, because they did not know some things which he never would have known but for the salutary effects of their exertions. The men to whom we owe it that we have a House of Commons are sneered at because they did not suffer the debates of the House to be published. The authors of the Toleration Act are treated as bigots, because they did not go the whole length of Catholic Emancipation. Just so we have heard a baby, mounted on the shoulders of its father, cry out, "how much taller I am than Papa!"

This gentleman can never want matter for pride, if he finds it so easily. He may boast of an indisputable superiority to all the greatest men of all past ages. He can read and write : Homer probably did not know a letter. He has been taught that the earth goes round the sun : Archimedes held that the sun went round the earth. He is aware that there is a place called New Holland : Columbus and Gama went to their graves in ignorance of the fact. He has heard of the Georgium Sidus : Newton was ignorant of the existence of such a planet. He is acquainted with the use of gunpowder : Hannibal and Cæsar won their victories with sword and spear. We submit, however, that this is not the way in which men are to be estimated. We submit that a wooden spoon of our day would not be justified in calling Galileo and Napier blockheads, because they never heard of the differential calculus. We submit that Caxton's press in Westminster Abbey, rude as it is, ought to be looked at with quite as much respect as the best constructed machinery that ever, in our time, impressed the clearest type on the finest paper. Sydenham first discovered that the cool regimen succeeded best in cases of small-pox. By this discovery he saved the lives of hundreds of thousands : and we venerate his memory for it, though he never heard of inoculation. Lady Mary Montague brought inoculation into use; and we respect her for it, though she never heard of vaccination. Jenner introduced vaccination : we admire him for it, and we shall continue to admire him for it, although some still safer and more agreeable preservative should be discovered. It is thus that we ought to judge of the events and the men of other times. They were behind us. It could not be otherwise. But the question with respect to them is not where they were, but which way they were going. Were their faces set in the right or in the wrong direction? Were they in the front or in the rear of their generation? Did they exert themselves to help onward the great movement of the human race, or to stop it? This is not charity, but simple justice and common sense. It is the fundamental law of the world in which we live that truth shall grow,—first the blade, then the ear, after that the full corn in the ear. A person who complains of the men of 1688 for not having been men of 1835 might just as well complain of a projectile for describing a parabola, or of quicksilver for being heavier than water.

Undoubtedly we ought to look at ancient transactions by the light of modern knowledge. Undoubtedly it is among the first duties of a historian to point out the faults of the eminent men of former generations. There are no errors which are so likely to be drawn into precedent, and therefore none which it is so necessary to expose, as the errors of persons who have a just title to the gratitude and admiration of posterity. In politics, as in religion, there are devotees who show their reverence for a departed saint by converting his tomb into a sanctuary for crime. Receptacles of wickedness are suffered to remain undisturbed in the neighbourhood of the church which glories in the relics of some martyred apostle. Because he was merciful, his bones give security to assassins. Because he was chaste, the precinct of his temple is filled with licensed stews. Privileges of an equally absurd kind have been set up against the jurisdiction of political philosophy. Vile abuses cluster thick round every glorious event,—round every venerable name; and this evil assuredly calls for vigorous measures of literary police. But the proper course is to abate the nuisance without defacing the shrine,—to drive out the gangs of thieves and prostitutes without doing foul and cowardly wrong to the ashes of the illustrious dead.

In this respect, two historians of our own time may be proposed as models, Sir James Mackintosh and Mr. Mill. Differing in most things, in this they closely resemble each other. Sir James is lenient—Mr. Mill is severe. But neither of them ever omits, in the apportioning of praise and of censure, to make ample allowance for the state of political science and political morality in former ages. In the work before us, Sir James Mackintosh speaks with just respect of the Whigs of the Revolution, while he never fails to condemn the conduct of that party towards the members of the Church of Rome. His doctrines are the liberal and benevolent doctrines of the nineteenth century. But he never forgets that the men whom he is describing were men of the seventeenth century.

From Mr. Mill this indulgence, or, to speak more properly, this justice, was less to be expected. That gentleman, in some of his works, appears to consider politics not as an experimental, and therefore a progressive science, but as a science of which all the difficulties may be resolved by short synthetical arguments drawn from truths of the most vulgar notoriety. Were this opinion well founded, the people of one generation would have little or no advantage over those of another generation. But though Mr. Mill, in some of his Essays, has been thus misled, as we conceive, by a fondness for neat and precise forms of demonstration, it would be gross injustice not to admit that, in his history, he has employed a very different method of investigation with eminent ability and success. We know no writer who takes so much pleasure in the truly useful, noble, and philosophical employment of tracing the progress of sound opinions from their embryo state to their full maturity. He eagerly culls from old Despatches and Minutes every expression in which he can discern the imperfect germ of any great truth which has since been fully developed. He never fails to bestow praise on those who, though far from coming up to his standard of perfection, yet rose in a small degree above the common level of their contemporaries. It is thus that the annals of past times ought to be written. It is thus, especially, that the annals of our own country ought to be written.

The history of England is emphatically the history of progress. It is the history of a constant movement of the public mind, of a constant change in the institutions of a great society. We see that society, at the beginning of the twelfth century, in a state more miserable than the state in which the most degraded nations of the East now are. We see it subjected to the tyranny of a handful of armed foreigners. We see a strong distinction of caste separating the victorious Norman from the vanquished Saxon. We see the great body of the population in a state of personal slavery. We see the most debasing and cruel superstition exercising boundless dominion over the most elevated and benevolent minds. We see the multitude sunk in brutal ignorance, and the studious few engaged in acquiring what did not deserve the name of knowledge. In the course of seven centuries the wretched and degraded race have become the greatest and most highly civilized people that ever the world saw,—have spread their dominion over every quarter of the globe,—have scattered the seeds of mighty empires and republics over vast continents of which no dim intimation had ever reached Ptolemy or Strabo,—have created a maritime power which would annihilate in a quarter of an hour the navies of Tyre, Athens, Carthage, Venice, and Genoa together,—have carried the science of healing, the means of locomotion and correspondence, every mechanical art, every manufacture, every thing that promotes the convenience of life, to a perfection which our ancestors would have thought magical,—have produced a literature abounding with works not inferior to the noblest which Greece has bequeathed to us,—have discovered the laws which regulate the motions of the heavenly bodies,—have speculated with exquisite subtilty on the operations of the human mind,—have been the acknowledged leaders of the human race in the career of political improvement. The history of England is the history of this great change in the moral, intellectual, and physical state of the inhabitants of our own island. There is much amusing and instructive episodical matter; but this is the main action. To us, we will own, nothing is so interesting and delightful as to contemplate the steps by which the England of Domesday Book,—the England of the Curfew and the Forest Laws,—the England of crusaders, monks, schoolmen, astrologers, serfs, outlaws,—became the England which we know and love,—the classic ground of liberty and philosophy, the school of all knowledge, the mart of all trade. The Charter of Henry Beauclerk,—the great Charter,—the first assembling of the House of Commons,—the extinction of personal slavery,—the separation from the see of Rome,—the Petition of Right,—the Habeas Corpus Act,—the Revolution,—the establishment of the liberty of unlicensed printing,—the abolition of religious disabilities,—the reform of the representative system,—all these seem to us to be the successive stages of one great revolution; nor can we fully comprehend any one of these memorable events unless we look at it in connection with those which preceded and with those which followed it. Each of those great and ever-memorable struggles,—Saxon against Norman,—Villein against Lord,—Protestant against Papist,—Roundhead against Cavalier,—Dissenter against Churchman,—Manchester against Old Sarum, was, in its own order and season, a struggle on the result of which were staked the dearest interests of the human race; and every man who, in the contest which, in his time, divided our country, distinguished himself on the right side, is entitled to our gratitude and respect.

Whatever the conceited editor of this book may think, those persons who estimate most correctly the value of the improvements which have recently been made in our institutions are precisely the persons who are least disposed to speak slightingly of what was done in 1688. Such men consider the Revolution as a reform, imperfect, indeed, but still most beneficial to the English people and to the human race,—as a reform which has been the fruitful parent of reforms,—as a reform, the happy effects of which are at this moment felt, not only throughout our own country, but in the cities of France and in the depth of the forests of Ohio. We shall be pardoned, we hope, if we call the attention of our readers to the causes and to the consequences of that great event.

We said that the history of England is the history of progress; and, when we take a comprehensive view of it, it is so. But when examined in small separate portions, it may with more propriety be called a history of actions and re-actions. We have often thought that the motion of the public mind in our country resembles that of the sea when the tide is rising. Each successive wave rushes forward, breaks, and rolls back; but the great flood is steadily coming in. A person who looked on the waters only for a moment might fancy that they were retiring, or that they obeyed no fixed law, but were rushing capriciously to and fro. But when he keeps his eye on them for a quarter of an hour, and sees one sea-mark disappear after another, it is impossible for him to doubt of the general direction in which the ocean is moved. Just such has been the course of events in England. In the history of the national mind, which is, in truth, the history of the nation, we must carefully distinguish between that recoil which regularly follows every advance from a great general ebb. If we take short intervals,—if we compare 1640 and 1660, 1680 and 1685, 1708 and 1712, 1782 and 1794, we find a retrogression. But if we take centuries,—if, for example, we compare 1794 with 1660 or with 1685,—we cannot doubt in which direction society is proceeding.

The interval which elapsed between the Restoration and the Revolution naturally divides itself into three periods. The first extends from 1660 to 1679, the second from 1679 to 1681, the third from 1681 to 1688.

In 1660 the whole nation was mad with loyal excitement. If we had to choose a lot from among all the multitude of those which men have drawn since the beginning of the world, we would select that of Charles the Second on the day of his return. He was in a situation in which the dictates of ambition coincided with those of benevolence, in which it was easier to be virtuous than to be wicked, to be loved than to be hated, to earn pure and imperishable glory than to become infamous. For once the road of goodness was a smooth descent. He had done nothing to merit the affection of his people. But they had paid him in advance without measure. Elizabeth, after the rout of the Armada, or after the abolition of Monopolies, had not excited a thousandth part of the enthusiasm with which the young exile was welcomed home. He was not, like Louis the Eighteenth, imposed on his subjects by foreign conquerors; nor did he, like Louis the Eighteenth, come back to a country which had undergone a complete change. The house of Bourbon was placed in Paris as a trophy of the victory of the European confederation. Their return was inseparably associated in the public mind with the cession of extensive provinces, with the payment of an immense tribute, with the devastation of flourishing departments, with the occupation of the kingdom by hostile armies, with the emptiness of those niches in which the Gods of Athens and

Rome had been the objects of a new idolatry, with the nakedness of those walls on which the Transfiguration had shown with light as glorious as that which overhung Mount Tabor. They came back to a land in which they could recognize nothing. The seven sleepers of the legend, who closed their eyes when the Pagans were persecuting the Christians, and woke when the Christians were persecuting each other, did not find themselves in a world more completely new to them. Twenty years had done the work of twenty generations. Events had come thick. Men had lived fast. The old institutions and the old feelings had been torn up by the roots. There was a new Church founded and endowed by the usurper; a new nobility whose titles were taken from fields of battle, disastrous to the ancient line; a new chivalry whose crosses had been won by exploits which had seemed likely to make the banishment of the emigrants perpetual. A new code was administered by a new magistracy. A new body of proprietors held the soil by a new tenure. The most ancient local distinctions had been effaced. The most familiar names had become obsolete. There was no longer a Normandy or a Burgundy, a Brittany or a Guienne. The France of Louis the Sixteenth had passed away as completely as one of the Preadamite worlds. Its fossil remains might now and then excite curiosity. But it was as impossible to put life into the old institutions as to animate the skeletons which are embedded in the depths of primeval strata. It was as absurd to think that France could again be placed under the Feudal system, as that our globe could be overrun by mammoths. The revolution in the laws and in the form of government was but an outward sign of that mightier revolution which had taken place in the heart and brain of the people, and which affected every transaction of life,—trading, farming, studying, marrying, and giving in marriage. The French whom the emigrant Prince had to govern were no more like the French of his youth, than the French of his youth were like the French of the Jaquerie. He came back to a people who knew not him nor his house,—to a people to whom a Bourbon was no more than a Carlovingian or a Merovingian. He might substitute the white flag for the tricolor; he might put lilies in the place of bees; he might order the initials of the Emperor to be carefully effaced. But he could turn his eyes nowhere without meeting some object which reminded him that he was a stranger in the palace of his fathers. He returned to a country in which even the passing traveller is every moment reminded that there has lately been a great dissolution and reconstruction of the social system. To win the hearts of a people under such circumstances would have been no easy task even for Henry the Fourth.

In the English Revolution the case was altogether different. Charles was not imposed on his countrymen, but sought by them. His restoration was not attended by any circumstance which could inflict a wound on their national pride. Insulated by our geographical position, insulated by our character, we had fought out our quarrels and effected our reconciliation among ourselves. Our great internal questions had never been mixed up with the still greater question of national independence. The political doctrines of the Roundheads were not, like those of the French philosophers, doctrines of universal application. Our ancestors, for the most part, took their stand, not on a general theory, but on the particular constitution of the realm. They asserted the rights, not of men, but of Englishmen. Their doctrines therefore were not contagious; and, had it been otherwise, no neighbouring country was then susceptible of the contagion. The language in which our discussions were generally conducted was scarcely known even to a single man of letters out of the islands. Our local situation made it almost impossible that we should effect great conquests on the Continent. The kings of Europe had, therefore, no reason to fear that their subjects would follow the example of the English Puritans. They looked with indifference, perhaps with complacency, on the death of the monarch and the abolition of the monarchy. Clarendon complains bitterly of their apathy. But we believe that this apathy was of the greatest service to the royal cause. If a French or Spanish army had invaded England, and if that army had been cut to pieces, as we have no doubt that it would have been, on the first day on which it came face to face with the soldiers of Preston and Dunbar,—with Colonel Fight-the-good-Fight, and Captain Smite-them-hip-and-thigh,—the House of Cromwell would probably now have been reigning in England. The nation would have forgotten all the misdeeds of the man who had cleared the soil of foreign invaders.

Happily for Charles, no European state, even when at war with the Commonwealth, chose to bind up its cause with that of the wanderers who were playing in the garrets of Paris and Cologne at being Princes and Chancellors. Under the administration of Cromwell, England was more respected and dreaded than any power in Christendom; and, even under the ephemeral governments which followed his death, no foreign state ventured to treat her with contempt. Thus Charles came back, not as a mediator between his people and a victorious enemy, but as a mediator between internal factions. He was heir to the conquests and to the influence of the able usurper who had excluded him.

The old government of England, as it had been far milder than the old government of France, had been far less violently and completely subverted. The old institutions had been spared, or imperfectly eradicated. The laws had undergone little alteration. The tenures of the soil were still to be learned from Littleton and Coke. The great charter was mentioned with as much reverence in the parliaments of the Commonwealth as in those of any earlier or of any later age. A new Confession of Faith and a new Ritual had been introduced into the church. But the bulk of the ecclesiastical property still remained. The colleges still held their estates. The parson still received his tithes. The Lords had, at a crisis of great excitement, been excluded by military violence from their House; but they retained their titles and an ample share of the public veneration. When a nobleman made his appearance in the House of Commons he was received with ceremonious respect. Those few Peers who consented to assist at the inauguration of the Protector were placed next to himself, and the most honourable offices of the day were assigned to them. We learn from the debates of Richard's Parliament how strong a hold the old aristocracy had on the affections of the people. One member of the House of Commons went so far as to say that, unless their Lordships were peaceably restored, the country might soon be convulsed by a war of the Barons. There was indeed at that time no great party hostile to the Upper House. There was nothing exclusive in the constitution of that body. It was regularly recruited from among the most distinguished of the country gentlemen, the lawyers, and the clergy. The most powerful nobles of the century which preceded the civil war, the Duke of Somerset, the Duke of Northumberland, Lord Sudley, the Earl of Leicester, Lord Burleigh, the Earl of Salisbury, the Duke of Buckingham, the Earl of Strafford, had all been commoners, and had all raised themselves, by courtly arts, or by parliamentary talents, not merely to seats in the House of Lords, but to the first influence in that assembly. Nor had the general conduct of the Peers been such as to make them unpopular. They had not, indeed, in opposing arbitrary measures shown so much eagerness and pertinacity as the Commons. But still they had opposed those measures. They had, at the beginning of the discontents, a common interest with the people. If Charles had succeeded in his scheme of governing without parliaments, the consequence of the Peers would have been grievously diminished. If he had been able to raise taxes by his own authority, the estates of the Peers would have been as much at his mercy as those of the merchants or the farmers. If he had obtained the power of imprisoning his subjects at his pleasure, a Peer ran far greater risk of incurring the royal displeasure, and of being accommodated with apartments in the Tower, than any city trader or country squire. Accordingly Charles found that the Great Council of Peers which he convoked at York would do nothing for him. In the most useful reforms which were made during the first session of the Long Parliament, the Peers concurred heartily with the Lower House; and a large minority of the English nobles stood by the popular side through the first years of the war. At Edgehill, Newbury, Marston, and Naseby, the army of the houses was commanded by members of the aristocracy. It was not forgotten that a Peer had imitated the example of Hampden in refusing the payment of the ship-money, or that a Peer had been among the six members of the legislature whom Charles illegally impeached.

Thus the old constitution of England was without difficulty re-established; and of all the parts of the old constitution the monarchical part was, at the time, dearest to the body of the people. It had been injudiciously depressed, and it was in consequence unduly exalted. From the day when Charles the First became a prisoner had commenced a reaction in favour of his person and of his office. From the day when the axe fell on his neck before the windows of his palace, that reaction became rapid and violent. At the Restoration it had attained such a point that it could go no further. The people were ready to place at the mercy of their Sovereign all their most ancient and precious rights. The most servile doctrines were publicly avowed. The most moderate and constitutional opposition was condemned. Resistance was spoken of with more horror than any crime which a human being can commit. The Commons were more eager than the King himself to avenge the wrongs of the royal house; more desirous than the bishops themselves to restore the church; more ready to give money than the ministers to ask for it. They abrogated some of the best laws passed in the first session of the Long Parliament,—laws which Falkland had supported, and which Hyde had not opposed. They might probably have been induced to go further, and to restore the High Commission and the Star Chamber. All the contemporary accounts represent the nation as in a state of hysterical excitement, of drunken joy. In the immense multitude which crowded the beach at Dover, and bordered the road along which the King travelled to London, there was not one who was not weeping. Bonfires blazed. Bells jingled. The streets were thronged at night by boon-companions, who forced all the passers-by to swallow on bended knees brimming glasses to the health of his Most Sacred Majesty, and the damnation of Red-nosed Noll. That tenderness to the fallen which has, through many generations, been a marked feature of the national character, was for a time hardly discernible. All London crowded to shout and laugh round the gibbet where hung the rotting remains of a Prince who had made England the dread of the world,—who had been the chief founder of her maritime greatness and of her colonial empire,—who had conquered Scotland and Ireland,—who had humbled Holland and Spain,—the terror of whose name had been as a guard round every English traveller in remote countries, and round every Protestant congregation in the heart of Catholic empires. When some of those brave and honest though misguided men who had sate in judgment on their King were dragged on hurdles to a death of prolonged torture, their last prayers were interrupted by the hisses and execrations of thousands.

Such was England in 1660. In 1679 the whole face of things had changed. At the former of those epochs twenty years of commotion had made the majority of the people ready to buy repose at any price. At the latter epo.h twenty years of misgovernment had made the same majority desirous to obtain security for their liberties at any risk. The fury of their returning loyalty had spent itself in its first outbreak. In a very few months they had hanged and half-hanged, quartered and embowelled enough to satisfy them. The Roundhead party seemed to be not merely overcome, but too much broken and scattered ever to rally again. Then commenced the reflux of public opinion. The nation began to find out to what a man it had intrusted, without conditions, all its dearest interests,—on what a man it had lavished all its fondest affection. On the ignoble nature of the restored exile, adversity had exhausted all her discipline in vain. He had one immense advantage over most other princes. Though born in the purple, he was far better acquainted with the vicissitudes of life and the diversities of character than most of his subjects. He had known restraint, danger, penury, and dependence. He had often suffered from ingratitude, insolence, and treachery. He had received many signal proofs of faithful and heroic attachment. He had seen, if ever man saw, both sides of human nature. But only one side remained in his memory. He had learned only to despise and to distrust his species,—to consider integrity in men, and modesty in women, as mere acting;—nor did he think it worth while to keep his opinion to himself. He was incapable of friendship; yet he was perpetually led by favourites without being in the smallest degree duped by them. He knew that their regard to his interests was all simulated; but, from a certain easiness which had no connection with humanity, he submitted, half-laughing at himself, to be made the tool of any woman whose person attracted him, or of any man whose tattle diverted him. He thought little and cared less about religion. He seems to have passed his life in dawdling suspense between Hobbism and Popery. He was crowned in his youth with the Covenant in his hand; he died at last with the Host sticking in his throat; and, during most of the intermediate years, was occupied in persecuting both Covenanters and Catholics. He was not a tyrant from the ordinary motives. He valued power for its own sake little, and fame still less. He does not appear to have been vindictive, or to have found any pleasing excitement in cruelty. What he wanted was to be amused,—to get through the twenty-four hours pleasantly without sitting down to dry business. Sauntering was, as Sheffield expresses it, the true Sultana Queen of his Majesty's affections. A sitting in council would have been insupportable to him if the Duke of Buckingham had not been there to make mouths at the Chancellor. It has been said, and is highly probable, that in his exile, he was quite disposed to sell his rights to Cromwell for a good round sum. To the last, his only quarrel with his Parliaments was that they often gave him trouble and would not always give him money. If there was a person for whom he felt a real regard, that person was his brother. If there was a point about which he really entertained a scruple of conscience or of honour, it was the descent of the crown. Yet he was willing to consent to the Exclusion Bill for £600,000; and the negotiation was broken off only because he insisted on being paid beforehand. To do him justice, his temper was good; his manners agreeable; his natural talents above mediocrity. But he was sensual, frivolous, false, and cold-hearted, beyond almost any Prince of whom history makes mention.

Under the government of such a man, the English people could not be long in recovering from the intoxication of loyalty. They were then, as they are still, a brave, proud, and high-spirited race, unaccustomed to defeat, to shame, or to servitude. The splendid administration of Oliver had taught them to consider their country as a match for the greatest empires of the earth, as the first of maritime powers, as the head of the Protestant interest. Though, in the day of their affectionate enthusiasm, they might sometimes extol the royal prerogative in terms which would have better become the courtiers of Aurungzebe, they were not men whom it was quite safe to take at their word. They were much more perfect in the theory than in the practice of passive obedience. Though they might deride the austere manners and scriptural phrases of the Puritans, they were still at heart a religious people. The majority saw no great sin in field-sports, stage-plays, promiscuous dancing, cards, fairs, starch, or false hair. But gross profaneness and licentiousness were regarded with general horror; and the Catholic religion was held in utter detestation by nine-tenths of the middle class.

Such was the nation which, awaking from its rapturous trance, found itself sold to a foreign, a despotic, a Popish court,—defeated on its own seas and rivers by a state of far inferior resources,—and placed under the rule of pandars and buffoons. Our ancestors saw the best and ablest divines of the age turned out of their benefices by hundreds. They saw the prisons filled with men guilty of no other crime than that of worshipping God according to the fashion generally prevailing throughout Protestant Europe. They saw a Popish Queen on the throne, and a Popish heir on the steps of the throne. They saw unjust aggression followed by feeble war, and feeble war ending in disgraceful peace. They saw a Dutch fleet riding triumphant in the Thames. They saw the triple alliance broken, the Exchequer shut up, the public credit shaken, the arms of England employed, in shameful subordination to France, against a country which seemed to be the last asylum of civil and religious liberty. They saw Ireland discontented, and Scotland in rebellion. They saw, meantime, Whitehall swarming with sharpers and courtesans. They saw harlot after harlot, and bastard after bastard, not only raised to the highest honours of the peerage, but supplied out of the spoils of the honest, industrious, and ruined public creditor, with ample means of supporting the new dignity. The government became more odious every day. Even in the bosom of that very House of Commons which had been elected by the nation in the ecstasy of its penitence, of its joy, and of its hope, an opposition sprang up and became powerful. Loyalty which had been proof against all the disasters of the civil war, which had survived the routs of Naseby and Worcester, which had never flinched from sequestration and exile, which the Protector could never intimidate or seduce, began to fail in this last and hardest trial. The storm had long been gathering. At length it burst with a fury which threatened the whole frame of society with dissolution.

When the general election of January, 1679, took place, the nation had retraced the path which it had been describing from 1640 to 1660. It was again in the same mood in which it had been when, after twelve years of misgovernment, the Long Parliament assembled. In every part of the country, the name of courtier had become a by-word of reproach. The old warriors of the Covenant again ventured out of those retreats in which they had, at the time of the Restoration, hidden themselves from the insults of the triumphant malignants, and in which, during twenty years, they had preserved in full vigour

> "The unconquerable will
> And study of revenge, immortal hate,
> With courage never to submit or yield,
> And what is else not to be overcome."

Then were again seen in the streets faces which called up strange and terrible recollections of the days when the saints, with the high praises of God in their mouths, and a two-edged sword in their hands, had bound kings with chains, and nobles with links of iron. Then were again heard voices which had shouted "Privilege" by the coach of Charles I. in the time of his tyranny, and had called for "Justice" in Westminster Hall on the day of his trial. It has been the fashion to represent the excitement of this period as the effect of the Popish plot. To us it seems clear that the Popish plot was rather the effect than the cause of the general agitation. It was not the disease, but a symptom, though, like many other symptoms, it aggravated the severity of the disease. In 1660 or 1661 it would have been utterly out of the power of such men as Oates or Bedloe to give any serious disturbance to the Government. They would have been laughed at, pilloried, well pelted, soundly whipped, and speedily forgotten. In 1678 or 1679 there would have been an outbreak, if those men had never been born. For years things had been steadily tending to such a consummation. Society was one vast mass of combustible matter. No mass so vast and so combustible ever waited long for a spark.

Rational men, we suppose, are now fully agreed that by far the greater part, if not the whole, of Oates' story was a pure fabrication. It is indeed highly probable that, during his intercourse with the Jesuits, he may have heard much wild talk about the best means of re-establishing the Catholic religion in England, and that from some of the absurd daydreams of the zealots with whom he then associated he may have taken hints for his narrative. But we do not believe that he was privy to anything which deserved the name of conspiracy. And it is quite certain that, if there be any small portion of truth in his evidence, that portion is so deeply buried in falsehood that no human skill can now effect a separation. We must not, however, forget, that we see his story by the light of much information which his contemporaries did not at first possess. We have nothing to say for the witnesses, but something in mitigation to offer on behalf of the public. We own that the credulity which the nation showed on that occasion seems to us, though censurable indeed, yet not wholly inexcusable.

Our ancestors knew, from the experience of several generations at home and abroad, how restless and encroaching was the disposition of the Church of Rome. The heir-apparent of the crown was a bigoted member of that church. The reigning King seemed far more inclined to show favour to that church than to the Presbyterians. He was the intimate ally, or rather the hired servant, of a powerful King, who had already given proofs of his determination to tolerate within his dominions no other religion than that of Rome. The Catholics had begun to talk a bolder language than formerly, and to anticipate the restoration of their worship in all its ancient dignity and splendour. At this juncture, it is rumoured that a Popish plot has been discovered. A distinguished Catholic is arrested on suspicion. It appears that he has destroyed almost all his papers. A few letters, however, have escaped the flames; and these letters are found to contain much alarming matter, strange expressions about subsidies from France, allusions to a vast scheme which would "give the greatest blow to the Protestant religion that it had ever received," and which "would utterly subdue a pestilent heresy." It was natural that those who saw these expressions, in letters which had been overlooked, should suspect that there was some horrible villany in those which had been carefully destroyed. Such was the feeling of the House of Commons: "Question, question, Coleman's letters!" was the cry which drowned the voices of the minority.

Just after the discovery of these papers, a magistrate who had been distinguished by his independent spirit, and who had taken the deposition of the informer, is found murdered, under circumstances which make it almost incredible that he should have fallen either by robbers or by his own hands. Many of our readers can remember the state of London just after the murders of Mar and Williamson,—the terror which was on every face,—the careful barring of doors,—the providing of blunderbusses and watchmen's rattles. We know of a shopkeeper who on that occasion sold three hundred rattles in about ten hours. Those who remember that panic may be able to form some notion of the state of England after the death of Godfrey. Indeed, we must say that, after having read and weighed all the evidence now extant on that mysterious subject, we incline to the opinion that he was assassinated, and assassinated by Catholics,—not assuredly by Catholics of the least weight or note, but by some of those crazy and vindictive fanatics who may be found in every large sect, and who are peculiarly likely to be found in a persecuted sect. Some of the violent Cameronians had recently, under similar exasperation, committed similar crimes.

It was natural that there should be a panic; and it was natural that the people should, in a panic, be unreasonable and credulous. It must be remembered also that they had not at first, as we have, the means of comparing the evidence which was given on different trials. They were not aware of one tenth part of the contradictions and absurdities which Oates had committed. The blunders, for example, into which he fell before the Council, his mistake about the person of Don John of Austria, and about the situation of the Jesuits' College at Paris, were not publicly known. He was a bad man; but the spies and deserters by whom governments are informed of conspiracies are generally bad men. His story was strange and frightful; but it was not more strange and frightful than a well-authenticated Popish plot, which some few people then living might remember,—the Gunpowder treason. Oates' account of the burning of London was in itself by no means so improbable as the project of blowing up King, Lords, and Commons,—a project which had not only been entertained by very distinguished Catholics, but which had very narrowly missed of success. As to the design on the King's person, all the world knew that, within a century, two kings of France and a prince of Orange had been murdered by the Catholics, purely from religious enthusiasm,—that Elizabeth had been in constant danger of a similar fate,—and that such attempts, to say the least, had not been discouraged by the highest authority of the Church of Rome. The characters of some of the accused persons stood high; but so did that of Anthony Babington, and that of Everard Digby. Those who suffered denied their guilt to the last; but no persons versed in criminal proceedings would attach any importance to this circumstance. It was well known also that the most distinguished Catholic casuists had written largely in defence of regicide, of mental reservation, and of equivocation. It was not quite impossible that men whose minds had been nourished with the writings of such casuists might think themselves justified in denying a charge which, if acknowledged, would bring great scandal on the Church. The trials of the accused Catholics were exactly like all the state trials of those days; that is to say, as infamous as they could be. They were neither fairer nor less fair than those of Algernon Sydney, of Rosewell, of Cornish,—of all the unhappy men, in short, whom a predominant party brought to what was then facetiously called justice. Till the Revolution purified our institutions and our manners, a state trial was a murder preceded by the uttering of certain gibberish and the performance of certain mummeries.

When the Houses met in the autumn of 1678, the Opposition had now the great body of the nation with them. Thrice the King dissolved the Parliament; and thrice the constituent body sent him back representatives fully determined to keep strict watch on all his measures, and to exclude his brother from the throne. Had the character of Charles resembled that of his father, this intestine discord would infallibly have ended in a civil war. Obstinacy and passion would have been his ruin. His levity and apathy were his security. He resembled one of those light Indian boats which are safe because they are pliant, which yield to the impact of every wave, and which therefore bound without danger through a serf in which a vessel ribbed with heart of oak would inevitably perish. The only thing about which his mind was unalterably made up was that, to use his own phrase, he would not go on his travels again for anybody, or for anything. His easy, indolent behaviour produced all the effects of the most artful policy. He suffered things to take their course; and if Achitophel had been at one of his ears, and Machiavel at the other, they could have given him no better advice than to let things take their course. He gave way to the violence of the movement, and waited for the corresponding violence of the rebound. He exhibited himself to his subjects in the interesting character of an oppressed king, who was ready to do anything to please them, and who asked of them, in return, only some consideration for his conscientious scruples and for his feelings of natural affection,—who was ready to accept any ministers,—to grant any guarantees for public liberty, but who could not find it in his heart to take away his brother's birthright. Nothing more was necessary. He had to deal with a people whose noble weakness it has always been not to press too hardly on the vanquished,—with a people the lowest and most brutal of whom cry "Shame!" if they see a man struck when he is on the ground. The resentment which the nation had felt towards the Court began to abate as soon as the Court was manifestly unable to offer any resistance. The panic which Godfrey's death had excited gradually subsided. Every day brought to light some new falsehood or contradiction in the stories of Oates and Bedloe. The people were glutted with the blood of Papists, as they had, twenty years before, been glutted with the blood of regicides. When the first sufferers in the plot were brought to the bar, the witnesses for the defence were in danger of being torn in pieces by the mob. Judges, jurors, and spectators seemed equally indifferent to justice, and equally eager for revenge. Lord Stafford, the last sufferer, was pronounced not guilty by a large minority of his peers; and when he protested his innocence on the scaffold, the people cried out, "God bless you, my lord; we believe you, my lord." The extreme folly of the Opposition in setting up the feeble and pusillanimous Monmouth as a claimant to the throne did them great harm. The story about the box and the marriage contract was an absurd romance; and the attempt to make a son of Lucy Waters King of England was alike offensive to the pride of the nobles and to the moral feeling of the middle class. The old Cavalier party, the great majority of the landed gentry, the clergy and the universities almost to a man, began to draw together, and to form in close array round the throne.

A similar reaction had begun to take place in favour of Charles the First during the second session of the Long Parliament; and, if that prince had been honest or sagacious enough to keep himself strictly within the limits of the law, we have not the smallest doubt that he would in a few months have found himself at least as powerful as his best friends, Lord Falkland, Culpeper, or Hyde, would have wished to see him. By illegally impeaching the leaders of the Opposition, and by making in person a wicked attempt on the House of Commons, he stopped and turned back that tide of loyal feeling which was just beginning to run strongly. The son, quite as little restrained by law or by honour as the father, was, luckily for himself, a man of a lounging, careless temper, and from temper, we believe, rather than from policy, escaped that great error which cost the father so dear. Instead of trying to pluck the fruit before it was ripe, he lay still till it fell mellow into his very mouth. If he had arrested Lord Shaftesbury and Lord Russell in a manner not warranted by law, it is not improbable that he would have ended his life in exile. He took the sure course. He employed only his legal prerogatives, and he found them amply sufficient for his purpose.

During the first eighteen or nineteen years of his reign, he had been playing the game of his enemies. From 1678 to 1681, his enemies had played his game. They owed their power to his misgovernment. He owed the recovery of his power to their violence. The great body of the people came back to him after their estrangement with impetuous affection. He had scarcely been more popular when he landed on the coast of Kent than when, after several years of restraint and humiliation, he dissolved his last Parliament.

Nevertheless, while this flux and reflux of opinion went on, the cause of public liberty was steadily gaining. There had been a great reaction in favour of the throne at the Restoration. But the Star Chamber, the High Commission, the Ship-money, had for ever disappeared. There was now another similar reaction. But the Habeas-Corpus Act had been passed during the short predominance of the Opposition, and it was not repealed.

The King, however, supported as he was by the nation, was quite strong enough to inflict a terrible revenge on the party which had lately held him in bondage. In 1681 commenced the third of those periods into which we have divided the history of England from the Restoration to the Revolution. During this period a third great reaction took place. The excesses of tyranny restored to the cause of liberty the hearts which had been alienated from that cause by the excesses of faction. In 1681, the King had almost all his enemies at his feet. In 1688, the King was an exile in a strange land.

The whole of that machinery which had lately been in motion against the Papists was now put in motion against the Whigs,—browbeating judges, packed juries, lying witnesses, clamorous spectators. The ablest chief of the party fled to a foreign country and died there. The most virtuous man of the party was beheaded. Another of its most distinguished members preferred a voluntary death to the shame of a public execution. The boroughs on which the government could not depend were, by means of legal quibbles, deprived of their charters; and their constitution was remodelled in such a manner as almost to insure the return of representatives devoted to the Court. All parts of the kingdom emulously sent up the most extravagant assurances of the love which they bore to their sovereign, and of the abhorrence with which they regarded those who questioned the divine origin of the boundless extent of his power. It is scarcely necessary to say that, in this hot competition of bigots and slaves, the University of Oxford had the unquestioned preeminence. The glory of being farther behind the age than any other portion of the British people, is one which that learned body acquired early, and has never lost.

Charles died, and his brother came to the throne; but, though the person of the sovereign was changed, the love and awe with which the office was regarded were undiminished. Indeed, it seems that, of the two princes, James was, in spite of his religion, rather the favourite of the High Church party. He had been specially singled out as the mark of the Whigs; and this circumstance sufficed to make him the idol of the Tories. He called a parliament. The loyal gentry of the counties and the packed voters of the remodelled boroughs gave him a parliament such as England had not seen for a century,—a parliament beyond all comparison the most obsequious that ever sat under a prince of the House of Stuart. One insurrectionary movement, indeed, took place in England, and another in Scotland. Both were put down with ease, and punished with tremendous severity. Even after that bloody circuit, which will never be forgotten while the English race exists in any part of the globe, no member of the House of Commons ventured to whisper even the mildest censure on Jeffries. Edmund Waller, emboldened by his great age and his high reputation, attacked the cruelty of the military chiefs; and this is the brightest part of his long and checkered public life. But even Waller did not venture to arraign the still more odious cruelty of the Chief Justice. It is hardly too much to say that James, at that time, had little reason to envy the extent of authority possessed by Louis XIV.

By what means this vast power was in three years broken down,—by what perverse and frantic misgovernment the tyrant revived the spirit of the vanquished Whigs, turned to fixed hostility the neutrality of the trimmers, and drove from him the landed gentry, the Church, the army, his own creatures, his own children,—is well known to our readers. But we wish to say something about one part of the question, which in our own time has a little puzzled some very worthy men, and about which the author of the "Continuation" before us pours forth, as might be expected, much nonsense.

James, it is said, declared himself a supporter of toleration. If he violated the constitution, he at least violated it for one of the noblest ends that any statesman ever had in view. His object was to free millions of his countrymen from penal laws and disabilities which hardly any person now considers as just. He ought, therefore, to be regarded as blameless, or, at worst, as guilty only of employing irregular means to effect a most praiseworthy purpose. A very ingenious man, whom we believe to be a Catholic, Mr. Banim, has written an historical novel, of the literary merit of which we cannot speak very highly, for the purpose of inculcating this opinion. The editor of Sir James Mackintosh's Fragment assures us that the standard of James bore the nobler inscription, and so forth;—the meaning of which is, that William and the other authors of the Revolution were vile Whigs, who drove out James for being a Radical;—that the crime of the King was his going farther in liberality than his subjects;—that he was the real champion of freedom; and that Somers, Locke, Newton, and other narrow-minded people of the same sort, were the real bigots and oppressors.

Now, we admit that if the premises can be made out, the conclusion follows. If it can be shown that James did sincerely wish to establish perfect freedom of conscience, we shall think his conduct deserving not only of indulgence but of praise. We shall applaud even his illegal acts. We conceive that so noble and salutary an object would have justified resistance on the part of subjects. We can, therefore, scarcely deny that it would at least justify encroachment on the part of a king. But it can be proved, we think, by the strongest evidence, that James had no such object in view; and that, under the pretence of establishing perfect religious liberty, he was trying to establish the ascendency and the exclusive dominion of the Church of Rome.

It is true that he professed himself a supporter of toleration. Every sect clamours for toleration when it is down. We have not the smallest doubt that, when Bonner was in the Marshalsea, he thought it a very hard thing that a man should be locked up in a gaol for not being able to understand the words, "This is my body," in the same way with the lords of the council. It would not be very wise to conclude that a beggar is full of Christian charity, because he assures you that God will reward you if you give him a penny; or that a soldier is humane, because he cries out lustily for quarter when a bayonet is at his throat. The doctrine which, from the very first origin of religious dissensions, has been held by all bigots of all sects, when condensed into a few words, and stripped of rhetorical disguise, is simply this:—I am in the right, and you are in the wrong. When you are the stronger, you ought to tolerate me; for it is your duty to tolerate truth. But when I am the stronger, I shall persecute you; for it is my duty to persecute error.

The Catholics lay under severe restraints in England. James wished to remove those restraints; and therefore he held a language favourable to liberty of conscience. But the whole history of his life proves that this was a mere pretence. In 1679 he held similar language, in a conversation with the magistrates of Amsterdam; and the author of the "Continuation" refers to this circumstance as a proof that the King had long entertained a strong feeling on the subject. Unhappily it proves only the utter insincerity of all the King's later professions. If he had pretended to be converted to the doctrines of toleration after his accession to the throne, some credit might have been due to his professions. But we know most certainly that, in 1679, and long after that year, James was a most bloody and remorseless persecutor. After 1679, he was placed at the head of the government of Scotland. And what had been his conduct in that country? He had hunted down the scattered remnant of the Covenanters with a barbarity of which no other prince of modern times, Philip the Second excepted, had ever shown himself capable. He had indulged himself in the amusement of seeing the torture of the "Boot" inflicted on the wretched enthusiasts whom persecution had driven to resistance. After his accession, almost his first act was to obtain from the servile parliament of Scotland a law for inflicting death on preachers at conventicles held within houses, and on both preachers and hearers at conventicles held in the open air. All this he had done for a religion which was not his own. All this he had done, not in defence of truth against error, but in defence of one damnable error against another,—in defence of the Episcopalian against the Presbyterian apostacy. Louis XIV. is justly censured for trying to dragoon his subjects to heaven. But it was reserved for James to torture and murder for the difference between two reads to hell. And this man, so deeply imbued with the poison of intolerance that, rather than not persecute at all, he would persecute people out of one heresy into another,—this man is held up as the champion of religious liberty! This man, who persecuted in the cause of the unclean panther, would not, we are told, have persecuted for the sake of the milk-white and immortal hind.

And what was the conduct of James at the very time when he was professing zeal for the rights of conscience? Was he not even then persecuting to the very best of his power? Was he not employing all his legal prerogatives, and many prerogatives which were not legal, for the purpose of forcing his subjects to conform to his creed? While he pretended to abhor the laws which excluded Dissenters from office, was he not himself dismissing from office his ablest, his most experienced, his most faithful servants, on account of their religious opinions? For what offence was Lord Rochester driven from the Treasury? He was closely connected with the Royal House. He was at the head of the Tory party. He had stood firmly by James in the most trying emergencies. But he would not change his religion, and he was dismissed. That we may not be suspected of overstating the case, Dr. Lingard, a very competent, and assuredly not a very willing witness, shall speak for us. "The King," says that able but partial writer, "was disappointed; he complained to Barillon of the obstinacy and insincerity of the treasurer; and the latter received from the French envoy a very intelligible hint that the loss of office would result from his adhesion to his religious creed. He was, however, inflexible; and James, after a long delay, communicated to him, but with considerable embarrassment and many tears, his final determination. He had hoped, he said, that Rochester, by conforming to the Church of Rome, would have spared him the unpleasant task; but kings must sacrifice their feelings to their duty." And this was the King who wished to have all men of all sects rendered alike capable of holding office. These proceedings were alone sufficient to take away all credit from his liberal professions; and such, as we learn from the despatches of the Papal Nuncio, was really the effect. "Pare," says D'Adda, writing a few days after the retirement of Rochester, "pare che gli animi sono inaspriti della voce che corre trà il popolo, d' esser cacciato il detto ministro per non essere Cattolico, perciò tirarsi al esterminio de Protestanti." Was it ever denied that the favours of the Crown were constantly bestowed and withhold purely on account of the religious opinions of the claimants? And if these things were done in the green tree, what would have been done in the dry? If James acted thus when he had the strongest motives to court his Protestant subjects, what course was he likely to follow when he had obtained from them all that he asked?

Who again was his closest ally? And what was the policy of that ally? The subjects of James, it is true, did not know half the infamy of their sovereign. They did not know, as we know, that, while he was lecturing them on the blessings of equal toleration, he was constantly congratulating his good brother Louis on the success of that intolerant policy which had turned the fairest tracts of France into deserts, and driven into exile myriads of the most peaceful, industrious, and skilful artizans in the world. But the English did know that the two princes were bound together in the closest union. They saw their sovereign with toleration on his lips separating himself from those states which had first set the example of toleration, and connecting himself by the strongest ties with the most faithless and merciless persecutor who could then be found on any continental throne.

By what advice, again, was James guided? Who were the persons in whom he placed the greatest confidence, and who took the warmest interest in his schemes? The ambassador of France,—the Nuncio of Rome,—and Father Petre, the Jesuit. These were the people who showed the greatest anxiety that the King's plan might succeed. And is this not enough to prove that the establishment of equal toleration was not his plan? Was Louis for toleration? Was the Vatican for toleration? Was the order of Jesuits for toleration? We know that the liberal professions of James were highly approved by those very governments, by those very societies, whose theory and practice it notoriously was to keep no faith with heretics, and to give no quarter to heretics. And are we, in order to save James's reputation for sincerity, to believe that all at once those governments and those societies had changed their nature,— had discovered the criminality of all their former conduct,—had adopted principles far more liberal than those of Locke, of Leighton, or of Tillotson? Which is the more probable supposition,—that the King who had revoked the edict of Nantes, the Pope under whose sanction the Inquisition was then imprisoning and burning, the religious order which, in every controversy in which it had ever been engaged, had called in the aid either of the magistrate or of the assassin, should have become as thorough-going friends to religious liberty as Dr. Franklin and Mr. Jefferson afterwards were,—or that a Jesuit-ridden bigot should be induced to dissemble for the good of the Church?

The game which the Jesuits were playing was no new game. A hundred years before they had preached up political freedom, just as they were now preaching up religious freedom. They had tried to raise the republicans against Henry the Fourth and Elizabeth, just as they were now trying to raise the Protestant Dissenters against the Church establishment. In the sixteenth century, the tools of Philip the Second were constantly teaching doctrines that bordered on Jacobinism,—constantly insisting on the right of the people to cashier kings, and of every private citizen to plunge his dagger into the heart of a wicked ruler. In the seventeenth century the persecutors of the Huguenots were crying out against the tyranny of the Established Church of England, and vindicating with the utmost fervour the right of all men to adore God after his own fashion. In both cases they were alike insincere. In both cases the fool who had trusted them would have found himself miserably duped. A good and wise man would doubtless disapprove of the arbitrary measures of Elizabeth. But would he have really served the interests of political liberty if he had put faith in the professions of the Romish casuists, joined their party, and taken a share in Northumberland's revolt, or in Babington's conspiracy? Would he not have been assisting to establish a far worse tyranny than that which he was trying to put down? In the same manner, a good and wise man would doubtless see very much to condemn in the conduct of the Church of England under the Stuarts. But was he therefore to join the King and the Catholics against that Church? And was it not plain that, by so doing, he would assist in setting up a spiritual despotism, compared with which the despotism of the establishment was as a little finger to the loins,—as a chastisement of whips to a chastisement of scorpions?

Louis had a far stronger mind than James. He had at least an equally high sense of honour. He was in a much less degree the slave of his priests. He had promised to respect the edict of Nantes as solemnly as James had promised to respect the religious liberty of the English people. Had Louis kept his word? And was not one such instance of treachery enough for one generation?

The plan of James seems to us perfectly intelligible. The toleration which, with the concurrence and applause of all the most cruel persecutors in Europe, he was offering to his people, was meant simply to divide them. This is the most obvious and vulgar of political artifices. We have seen it employed a hundred times within our own memory. At this moment we see the Carlists in France hallooing on the "extreme left" against the "centre left." Four years ago the same trick was practised in England. We heard old buyers and sellers of boroughs,—men who had been seated in the House of Commons by the unsparing use of ejectments, and who had, through their whole lives, opposed every measure which tended to increase the power of the democracy,—abusing the Reform Bill as not democratic enough, appealing to the labouring classes, execrating the tyranny of the ten-pound householders, and exchanging compliments and caresses with the most noted incendiaries of our time. The cry of universal toleration was employed by James, just as the cry of universal suffrage was lately employed by some veteran Tories. The object of the mock democrats of our time was to produce a conflict between the middle classes and the multitude, and thus to prevent all reform. The object of James was to produce a conflict between the Church and the Protestant dissenters, and thus to facilitate the victory of the Catholics over both.

We do not believe that he could have succeeded. But we do not think his plan so utterly frantic and hopeless as it has generally been thought; and we are sure that, if he had been allowed to gain his first point, the people would have had no remedy left but an appeal to physical force,—which would have been made under most unfavourable circumstances. He conceived that the Tories, hampered by their professions of passive obedience, would have submitted to his pleasure, and that the Dissenters, seduced by his delusive promises of relief, would have given him strenuous support. In this way he hoped to obtain a law, nominally for the removal of all re'igious disabilities, but really for the excluding of all Protestants from all offices. It is never to be forgotten that a prince who has all the patronage of the state in his hands can, without violating the letter of the law, establish whatever test he chooses. And, from the whole conduct of James, we have not the smallest doubt that he would have availed himself of his power to the utmost. The statute-book might declare all Englishmen equally capable of holding office; but to what end, if all offices were in the gift of a sovereign resolved not to employ a single heretic? We firmly believe that not one post in the government, in the army, in the navy, on the bench, or at the bar,—not one peerage, nay not one ecclesiastical benefice in the royal gift, would have been bestowed on any Protestant of any persuasion. Even while the King had still strong motives to dissemble, he had made a Catholic Dean of Christ Church and a Catholic President of Magdalen College. There seems to be no doubt that the See of York was kept vacant for another Catholic. If James had been suffered to follow this course for twenty years, every military man from a general to a drummer, every officer of a ship, every judge, every King's counsel, every lord-lieutenant of a county, every justice of the peace, every ambassador, every minister of state, every person employed in the royal household, in the custom-house, in the post-office, in the excise, would have been a Catholic. The Catholics would have had a majority in the House of Lords, even if that majority had been made, to use Sunderland's threat, by calling up a whole troop of the guards to that house. Catholics would have had, we believe, the chief weight even in the Convocation. Every bishop, every dean, every holder of a crown living, every head of every college which was subject to the royal power, would have belonged to the Church of Rome. Almost all the places of liberal education would have been under the direction of Catholics. The whole power of licensing books would have been in the hands of Catholics. All this immense mass of power would have been steadily supported by the arms and by the gold of France, and would have descended to an heir whose whole education would have been conducted with a view to one single end,—the complete re-establishment of the Catholic religion. The House of Commons would have been the only legal obstacle. But the rights of a great portion of the electors were at the mercy of the courts of law; and the courts of law were absolutely dependent on the Crown. We cannot, therefore, think it altogether impossible that a house might have been packed which would have restored the days of Mary.

We certainly do not believe that this would have been tamely borne. But we do believe that, if the nation had been deluded by the King's professions of toleration, all this would have been attempted, and could have been averted only by a most bloody and destructive contest, in which the whole Protestant population would have been opposed to the Catholics. On the one side would have been a vast numerical superiority. But on the other side would have been the whole organization of government, and two great disciplined armies, that of James and that of Louis. We do not doubt that the nation would have achieved its deliverance. But we believe that the struggle would have shaken the whole fabric of society, and that the vengeance of the conquerors would have been terrible and unsparing.

But James was stopped at the outset. He thought himself secure of the

Tories, because they professed to consider all resistance as sinful,—and of the Protestant Dissenters, because he offered them relief. He was in the wrong as to both. The error into which he fell about the Dissenters was very natural. But the confidence which he placed in the loyal assurances of the High Church party was the most exquisitely ludicrous proof of folly that a politician ever gave.

Only imagine a man acting for one single day on the supposition that all his neighbours believe all that they profess, and act up to all that they believe. Imagine a man acting on the supposition that he may safely offer the deadliest injuries and insults to everybody who says that revenge is sinful; or that he may safely intrust all his property without security to any person who says that it is wrong to steal. Such a character would be too absurd for the wildest farce. Yet the folly of James did not stop short of this incredible extent. Because the clergy had declared that resistance to oppression was in no case lawful, he conceived that he might oppress them exactly as much as he chose, without the smallest danger of resistance. He quite forgot that, when they magnified the royal prerogative, the prerogative was exerted on their side,—that, when they preached endurance, they had nothing to endure,—that, when they declared it unlawful to resist evil, none but Whigs and Dissenters suffered any evil. It had never occurred to him that a man feels the calamities of his enemies with one sort of sensibility, and his own with quite a different sort. It had never occurred to him as possible that a reverend divine might think it the duty of Baxter and Bunyan to bear insults and to lie in dungeons without murmuring, and yet, when he saw the smallest chance that his own prebend might be transferred to some sly Father from Italy or Flanders, might begin to discover much matter for useful meditation in the texts touching Ehud's knife and Jael's hammer. His Majesty was not aware, it should seem, that people do sometimes reconsider their opinions; and that nothing more disposes a man to reconsider his opinions than a suspicion, that, if he adheres to them, he is very likely to be a beggar or a martyr. Yet it seems strange that these truths should have escaped the royal mind. Those Churchmen who had signed the Oxford declaration in favour of passive obedience had also signed the thirty-nine articles. And yet the very man who confidently expected that, by a little coaxing and bullying, he should induce them to renounce the articles, was thunderstruck when he found that they were disposed to soften down the doctrines of the declaration. Nor did it necessarily follow that even if the theory of the Tories had undergone no modification, their practice would coincide with their theory. It might, one should think, have crossed the mind of a man of fifty, who had seen a great deal of the world, that people sometimes do what they think wrong. Though a prelate might hold that Paul directs us to obey even a Nero, it might not on that account be perfectly safe to treat the Right Reverend Father in God after the fashion of Nero, in the hope that he would continue to obey on the principles of Paul. The King indeed had only to look at home. He was at least as much attached to the Catholic Church as any Tory gentleman or clergyman could be to the Church of England. Adultery was at least as clearly and as strongly condemned by his Church as resistance by the Church of England. Yet his priests could not keep him from Arabella Sedley. While he was risking his crown for the sake of his soul, he was risking his soul for the sake of an ugly, dirty mistress. There is something delightfully grotesque in the spectacle of a man who, while living in the habitual violation of his own known duties, is unable to believe that any temptation can draw any other person aside from the path of virtue.

James was disappointed in all his calculations. His hope was that the Tories would follow their principles, and that the Non-conformists would follow their interests. Exactly the reverse took place. The Tories sacrificed the principle of non-resistance to their interests; the Non-conformists rejected the delusive offers of the King, and stood firmly by their principles. The two parties whose strife had convulsed the empire during half a century were united for a moment; and all that vast royal power which three years before had seemed immovably fixed vanished at once like chaff in a hurricane.

The very great length to which this article has already been extended renders it impossible for us to discuss, as we had meant to do, the characters and conduct of the leading English statesmen at this crisis. But we must offer a few remarks on the spirit and tendency of the Revolution of 1688.

The editor of this volume quotes the Déclaration of Right, and tells us that, by looking at it, we may "judge at a glance whether the authors of the Revolution achieved all they might and ought, in their position, to have achieved;—whether the Commons of England did their duty to their constituents, their country, posterity, and universal freedom." We are at a loss to imagine how this writer can have read and transcribed the Declaration of Right, and yet have so utterly misconceived its nature. That famous document is, as its very name imports, declaratory, and not remedial. It was never meant to be a measure of reform. It neither contained, nor was designed to contain, any allusion to those innovations which the authors of the Revolution considered as desirable, and which they speedily proceeded to make. The Declaration was merely a recital of certain old and wholesome laws which had been violated by the Stuarts, and a solemn protest against the validity of any precedent which might be set up in opposition to those laws. The words as quoted by this writer himself run thus: "They do claim, demand, and insist upon all and singular the premises as their undoubted rights and liberties." Before a man begins to make improvements on his estate, he must know its boundaries. Before a legislature sits down to reform a constitution, it is fit to ascertain what that constitution really is. This is all that the Declaration was intended to do; and to quarrel with it because it did not directly introduce any beneficial changes is to quarrel with meat for not being clothing.

The principle on which the authors of the Revolution acted cannot be mistaken. They were perfectly aware that the English institutions stood in need of reform. But they also knew that an important point was gained if they could settle once for all, by a solemn compact, the matters which had, during several generations, been in controversy between the parliament and the crown. They therefore most judiciously abstained from mixing up the irritating and perplexing question of what *ought* to be the law with the plain question of what *was* the law. As to the claims set forth in the Declaration of Right, there was little room for debate. Whigs and Tories were generally agreed as to the illegality of the dispensing power and of taxation imposed by the royal prerogative. The articles were therefore adjusted in a very few days. But if the Parliament had determined to revise the whole constitution, and to provide new securities against misgovernment, before proclaiming the new sovereign, months would have been lost in disputes. The coalition which had delivered the country would have been instantly dissolved. The Whigs would have quarrelled with the Tories; the Lords with the Commons, the Church with the Dissenters; and all this storm of conflicting interests and conflicting theories would have been raging round a vacant throne. In the meantime, the greatest power on the Continent was attacking our allies, and meditating a descent on our own territories.

Dundee was raising the Highlands. The authority of James was still owned by the Irish. If the authors of the Revolution had been fools enough to take this course, we have little doubt that Luxembourg would have been upon them in the midst of their constitution-making. They might probably have been interrupted in a debate on Filmer's and Sydney's theories of government by the entrance of the musqueteers of Louis's household, and have been marched off, two and two, to frame imaginary monarchies and commonwealths in the Tower. We have had in our own time abundant experience of the effects of such folly. We have seen nation after nation enslaved, because the friends of liberty wasted in discussions upon abstract questions the time which ought to have been employed in preparing for vigorous national defence. This editor, apparently, would have had the English Revolution of 1688 end as the Revolutions of Spain and Naples ended in our days. Thank God, our deliverers were men of a very different order from the Spanish and Neapolitan legislators. They might, on many subjects, hold opinions which, in the nineteenth century, would not be considered as liberal. But they were not dreaming pedants. They were statesmen accustomed to the management of great affairs. Their plans of reform, were not so extensive as those of the lawgivers of Cadiz; but what they planned, that they effected; and what they effected, that they maintained against the fiercest hostility at home and abroad.

Their first object was to seat William on the throne; and they were right. We say this without any reference to the eminent personal qualities of William, or to the follies and crimes of James. If the two princes had interchanged characters, our opinion would still have been the same. It was even more necessary to England at that time that her king should be a usurper than that he should be a hero. There could be no security for good government without a change of dynasty. The reverence for hereditary right and the doctrine of passive obedience had taken such a hold on the minds of the Tories, that, if James had been restored to power on any conditions, their attachment to him would in all probability have revived, as the indignation which recent oppression had produced faded from their minds. It had become indispensable to have a sovereign whose title to his throne was strictly bound up with the title of the nation to its liberties. In the compact between the Prince of Orange and the Convention, there was one most important article which, though not expressed, was perfectly understood by both parties, and for the performance of which the country had securities far better than all the vows that Charles I. or Ferdinand VII. ever took in the day of their weakness, and broke in the day of their power. The article was this,—that William would in all things conform himself to what should appear to be the fixed and deliberate sense of his Parliament. The security for the performance was this,—that he had no claim to the throne except the choice of Parliament, and no means of maintaining himself on the throne but the support of Parliament. All the great and inestimable reforms which speedily followed the Revolution were implied in those simple words:—"The Lords Spiritual and Temporal, and Commons, assembled at Westminster, do resolve that William and Mary, Prince and Princess of Orange, be, and be declared King and Queen of England."

And what were the reforms of which we speak? We will shortly recount some which we think the most important; and we will then leave our readers to judge whether those who consider the Revolution as a mere change of dynasty, beneficial to a few aristocrats, but useless to the body of the people, or those who consider it as a happy era in the history of the British nation, and of the human species, have judged more correctly of its nature.

Foremost in the list of the benefits which our country owes to the Revolution we place the Toleration Act. It is true that this measure fell short of the wishes of the leading Whigs. It is true also that, where Catholics were concerned, even the most enlightened of the leading Whigs held opinions by no means so liberal as those which are happily common at the present day. Those distinguished statesmen did however make a noble, and, in some respects, a successful struggle for the rights of conscience. Their wish was to bring the great body of the Protestant Dissenters within the pale of the Church by judicious alterations in the Liturgy and the Articles, and to grant to those who still remained without that pale the most ample toleration. They framed a plan of comprehension which would have satisfied a great majority of the seceders; and they proposed the complete abolition of that absurd and odious test which, after having been, during a century and a half, a scandal to the pious and a laughing-stock to the profane, was at length removed in our own time. The immense power of the Clergy and of the Tory gentry frustrated these excellent designs. The Whigs, however, did much. They succeeded in obtaining a law in the provisions of which a philosopher will doubtless find much to condemn, but which had the practical effect of enabling almost every Protestant Non-conformist to follow the dictates of his own conscience without molestation. Scarcely a law in the statute-book is theoretically more objectionable than the Toleration Act. But we question whether in the whole of that vast mass of legislation, from the Great Charter downwards, there be a single law which has so much diminished the sum of human suffering,—which has done so much to allay bad passions,—which has put an end to so much petty tyranny and vexation,—which has brought gladness, peace, and a sense of security to so many private dwellings.

The second of those great reforms which the Revolution produced was the final establishment of the Presbyterian Kirk in Scotland. We shall not now inquire whether the Episcopal or the Calvinistic form of Church government be more agreeable to primitive practice. Far be it from us to disturb with our doubts the repose of any Oxonian Bachelor of Divinity who conceive that the English prelates, with their baronies and palaces, their purple and their fine linen, their mitred carriages and their sumptuous tables, are the true successors and exact resemblances of those ancient bishops who lived by catching fish and mending tents. We say only that the Scotch, doubtless from their own inveterate stupidity and malice, were not Episcopalians; that they could not be made Episcopalians; that the whole power of government had been in vain employed for the purpose of converting them; that the fullest instruction on the mysterious questions of the Apostolical succession and the imposition of hands had been imparted by the very logical process of putting the legs of the students into wooden boots, and driving two or more wedges between their knees; that a course of divinity lectures, of the most edifying kind, had been given in the Grass-market of Edinburgh; yet that, in spite of all the exertions of those great theological professors, Lauderdale and Dundee, the Covenanters were as obstinate as ever. The contest between the Scotch nation and the Anglican Church had produced nearly thirty years of the most frightful misgovernment ever seen in any part of Great Britain. If the Revolution had produced no other effect than that of freeing the Scotch from the yoke of an establishment which they detested, and giving them one to which they were attached, it would have been one of the happiest events in our history.

The third great benefit which the country derived from the Revolution was the alteration in the mode of granting the supplies. It had been the practice to settle on every prince, at the commencement of his reign, the produce of certain taxes which, it was supposed, would yield a sum sufficient to defray the ordinary expenses of government. The distribution of the revenue was left wholly to the sovereign. He might be forced by a war, or by his own profusion, to ask for an extraordinary grant. But, if his policy were economical and pacific, he might reign many years without once being under the necessity of summoning his Parliament, or of taking their advice when he had summoned them. This was not all. The natural tendency of every society in which property enjoys tolerable security is to increase in wealth. With the national wealth, the produce of the customs, of the excise, and of the post-office, would of course increase; and thus it might well happen that taxes which, at the beginning of a long reign, were barely sufficient to support a frugal government in time of peace, might, before the end of that reign, enable the sovereign to imitate the extravagance of Nero or Heliogabalus,—to raise great armies,—to carry on expensive wars. Something of this sort had actually happened under Charles the Second, though his reign, reckoned from the Restoration, lasted only twenty-five years. His first Parliament settled on him taxes estimated to produce £1,200,000 a year. This they thought sufficient, as they allowed nothing for a standing army in time of peace. At the time of Charles's death, the annual produce of these taxes considerably exceeded a million and a half; and the King who, during the years which immediately followed his accession, was perpetually in distress, and perpetually asking his Parliaments for money, was at last able to keep a body of regular troops without any assistance from the House of Commons. If his reign had been as long as that of George the Third, he would probably, before the close of it, have been in the annual receipt of several millions over and above what the ordinary expenses of the state required; and of those millions he would have been as absolutely master as the King now is of the sum allotted for his privy-purse. He might have spent them in luxury, in corruption, in paying troops to overawe his people, or in carrying into effect wild schemes of foreign conquest. The authors of the Revolution applied a remedy to this great abuse. They settled on the King, not the fluctuating produce of certain fixed taxes, but a fixed sum sufficient for the support of his own royal state. They established it as a rule that all the expenses of the army, the navy, and the ordnance should be brought annually under the review of the House of Commons, and that every sum voted should be applied to the service specified in the vote. The direct effect of this change was important. The indirect effect has been more important still. From that time the House of Commons has been really the paramount power in the state. It has, in truth, appointed and removed ministers, declared war, and concluded peace. No combination of the King and the Lords has ever been able to effect anything against the Lower House, backed by its constituents. Three or four times, indeed, the sovereign has been able to break the force of an opposition by dissolving the Parliament. But if that experiment should fail, if the people should be of the same mind with their representatives,—he would clearly have no course left but to yield, to abdicate, or to fight.

The next great blessing which we owe to the Revolution is the purification of the administration of justice in political cases. Of the importance of this change no person can judge who is not well acquainted with the earlier volumes of the State Trials. Those volumes are, we do not hesitate to say, the most frightful record of baseness and depravity that is extant in the world. Our hatred is altogether turned away from the crimes and the criminals, and directed against the law and its ministers. We see villanies as black as ever were imputed to any prisoner at any bar daily committed on the bench and in the jury box. The worst of the bad acts which brought discredit on the old parliaments of France,—the condemnation of Lally, for example, or even that of Calas,—may seem praiseworthy when compared with those which follow each other in endless succession as we turn over that huge chronicle of the shame of England. The magistrates of Paris and Toulouse were blinded by prejudice, passion, or bigotry. But the abandoned judges of our own country committed murder with their eyes open. The cause of this is plain. In France there was no constitutional opposition. If a man held language offensive to the government, he was at once sent to the Bastile or to Vincennes. But in England, at least after the days of the Long Parliament, the King could not, by a mere act of his prerogative, rid himself of a troublesome politician. He was forced to remove those who thwarted him by means of perjured witnesses, packed juries, and corrupt, hard-hearted, brow-beating judges. The Opposition naturally retaliated whenever they had the upper hand. Every time that the power passed from one party to the other, took place a proscription and a massacre, thinly disguised under the forms of judicial procedure. The tribunals ought to be sacred places of refuge, where, in all the vicissitudes of public affairs, the innocent of all parties may find shelter. They were, before the Revolution, an unclean public shambles, to which each party in its turn dragged its opponents, and where each found the same venal ferocious butchers waiting for its custom. Papist or Protestant, Tory or Whig, Priest or Alderman, all was one to those greedy and savage natures, provided only there was money to earn and blood to shed.

Of course, these worthless judges soon created around them, as was natural, a breed of informers more wicked, if possible, than themselves. The trial by jury afforded little or no protection to the innocent. The juries were nominated by the sheriffs. The sheriffs were in most parts of England nominated by the Crown. In London, the great scene of political contention, those officers were chosen by the people. The fiercest parliamentary election of our time will give but a faint notion of the storm which raged in the city on the day when two infuriated parties, each bearing its badge, met to select the men in whose hands were to be the issues of life and death for the coming year. On that day, nobles of the highest descent did not think it beneath them to canvass and marshal the livery, to head the procession, and to watch the poll. On that day, the great chiefs of parties waited in an agony of suspense for the messenger who was to bring from Guildhall the news whether their lives and estates were, for the next twelve months, to be at the mercy of a friend or a foe. In 1681, Whig sheriffs were chosen; and Shaftesbury defied the whole power of the government. In 1682 the sheriffs were Tories. Shaftesbury fled to Holland. The other chiefs of the party broke up their councils, and retired in haste to their country-seats. Sidney on the scaffold told those sheriffs that his blood was on their heads. Neither of them could deny the charge; and one of them wept with shame and remorse.

Thus every man who then meddled with public affairs took his life in his hand. The consequence was that men of gentle natures stood aloof from contests in which they could not engage without hazarding their own necks and the fortunes of their children. This was the course adopted by Sir William Temple, by Evelyn, and by many other men who were, in every respect, admirably qualified to serve the State. On the other hand, those resolute and enterprising spirits who put their heads and lands to hazard in the game of politics naturally acquired, from the habit of playing for so deep a stake, a reckless and desperate turn of mind. It was, we seriously believe, as safe to be a highwayman as to be a distinguished leader of Opposition. This may serve to explain, and in some degree to excuse, the violence with which the factions of that age are justly reproached. They were fighting, not for office, but for life. If they reposed for a moment from the work of agitation, if they suffered the public excitement to flag, they were lost men. Hume, in describing this state of things, has employed an image which seems hardly to suit the general simplicity of his style, but which is by no means too strong for the occasion. "Thus," says he, "the two parties actuated by mutual rage, but cooped up within the narrow limits of the law, levelled with poisoned daggers the most deadly blows against each other's breast, and buried in their factions divisions all regard to truth, honour, and humanity."

From this terrible evil the Revolution set us free. The law which secured to the judges their seats during life or good behaviour did something. The law subsequently passed for regulating trials in cases of treason did much more. The provisions of that law show, indeed, very little legislative skill. It is not framed on the principle of securing the innocent, but on the principle of giving a great chance of escape to the accused, whether innocent or guilty. This, however, is decidedly a fault on the right side. The evil produced by the occasional escape of a bad citizen is not to be compared with the evils of the Reign of Terror, for such it was, which preceded the Revolution. Since the passing of this law scarcely one single person has suffered death in England, as a traitor, who had not been convicted on overwhelming evidence, to the satisfaction of all parties, of a really great crime against the State. Attempts have been made in times of great excitement, to bring in persons guilty of high treason for acts which, though sometimes highly blamable, did not necessarily imply a design of altering the government by physical force. All those attempts have failed. For a hundred and forty years no statesman, while engaged in constitutional opposition to a government, has had the axe before his eyes. The smallest minorities, struggling against the most powerful majorities, in the most agitated times, have felt themselves perfectly secure. Pulteney and Fox were the two most distinguished leaders of Opposition since the Revolution. Both were personally obnoxious to the Court. But the utmost harm that the utmost anger of the Court could do to them was to strike off the "Right Honourable" from before their names.

But of all the reforms produced by the Revolution, perhaps the most important was the full establishment of the liberty of unlicensed printing. The Censorship which, under some form or other, had existed, with rare and short intermissions, under every government, monarchical or republican, from the time of Henry the Eighth downwards, expired, and has never since been renewed.

We are aware that the great improvements which we have recapitulated were, in many respects, imperfectly and unskilfully executed. The authors of those improvements sometimes, while they removed or mitigated a great practical evil, continued to recognise the erroneous principle from which that evil had sprung. Sometimes, when they had adopted a sound principle, they shrank from following it to all the conclusions to which it would have led them. Sometimes they failed to perceive that the remedies which they applied to one disease of the State were certain to generate another disease, and to render another remedy necessary. Their knowledge was inferior to ours; nor were they always able to act up to their knowledge. The pressure of circumstances, the necessity of compromising differences of opinion, the power and violence of the party which was altogether hostile to the new settlement, must be taken into the account. When these things are fairly weighed, there will, we think, be little difference of opinion among liberal and right-minded men as to the real value of what the great events of 1688 did for this country.

We have recounted what appear to us the most important of those changes which the Revolution produced on our laws. The changes which it produced in our laws, however, were not more important than the change which it indirectly produced in the public mind. The Whig party had, during seventy years, an almost uninterrupted possession of power. It had always been the fundamental doctrine of that party, that power is a trust for the people; that it is given to magistrates, not for their own, but for the public advantage; that, where it is abused by magistrates, even by the highest of all, it may lawfully be withdrawn. It is perfectly true that the Whigs were not more exempt than other men from the vices and infirmities of our nature, and that, when they had power, they sometimes abused it. But still they stood firm to their theory. That theory was the badge of their party. It was something more. It was the foundation on which rested the power of the houses of Nassau and Brunswick. Thus, there was a government interested in propagating a class of opinions which most governments are interested in discouraging,—a government which looked with complacency on all speculations tending to democracy, and with extreme aversion on all speculations favourable to arbitrary power. There was a King who decidedly preferred a republican to a believer in the divine right of Kings; who considered every attempt to exalt his prerogative as an attack on his title; and who reserved all his favours for those who declaimed on the natural equality of men, and the popular origin of government. This was the state of things from the Revolution till the death of George the Second. The effect was what might have been expected. Even in that profession which has generally been most disposed to magnify the prerogative, a great change took place. Bishopric after bishopric and deanery after deanery were bestowed on Whigs and Latitudinarians. The consequence was that Whiggism and Latitudinarianism were professed by the ablest and most aspiring churchmen.

Hume complained bitterly of this at the close of his history. "The Whig party," says he, "for a course of near seventy years, has almost without interruption enjoyed the whole authority of government, and no honours or offices could be obtained but by their countenance and protection. But this event, which in some particulars has been advantageous to the state, has proved destructive to the truth of history, and has established many gross falsehoods, which it is unaccountable how any civilized nation could have embraced with regard to its domestic occurrences. Compositions the most despicable, both for style and matter,"—in a note he instances the writings of Locke, Sydney, Hoadley, and Rapin,—"have been extolled and propagated and read as if they had equalled the most celebrated remains of antiquity. And forgetting that a regard to liberty, though a laudable passion, ought commonly to be subservient to a reverence for established government, the prevailing faction has celebrated only the partisans of the former." We will not here enter into an argument about the merit of Rapin's History, or Locke's political speculations. We call Hume merely as evidence to a fact well known to all reading men, that the literature patronised by the English Court and the English ministry, during the first half of the eighteenth century was of that kind which courtiers and ministers generally do all in their power to discountenance, and tended to inspire zeal for the liberties of the people rather that respect for the authority of the government.

There was still a very strong Tory party in England. But that party was in opposition. Many of its members still held the doctrine of passive obedience. But they did not admit that the existing dynasty had any claim to such obedience. They condemned resistance. But by resistance they meant the keeping out of James the Third, and not the turning out of George the Second. No Radical of our times could grumble more at the expenses of the royal household, could exert himself more strenuously to reduce the military establishment, could oppose with more earnestness every proposition for arming the executive with extraordinary powers, or could pour more unmitigated abuse on placemen and courtiers. If a writer were now, in a massive Dictionary, to define a Pensioner as a traitor and a slave, the Excise as a hateful tax, the Commissioners of the Excise as wretches,—if he were to write a satire full of reflections on men who receive "the price of boroughs and of souls," who "explain their country's dear-bought rights away," or

"Whom pensions can incite
To vote a patriot black, a courtier white,"

we should set him down for something more democratic than a Whig. Yet this was the language which Johnson, the most bigoted of Tories and High Churchmen, held under the administration of Walpole and Pelham.

Thus doctrines favourable to public liberty were inculcated alike by those who were in power and by those who were in opposition. It was by means of these doctrines alone that the former could prove that they had a King *de jure*. The servile theories of the latter did not prevent them from offering every molestation to one whom they considered as merely a King *de facto*. The attachment of one party to the House of Hanover, of the other to that of Stuart, induced both to talk a language much more favourable to popular rights than to monarchical power. What took place at the first representation of "Cato" is no bad illustration of the way in which the two great sections of the community almost invariably acted. A play, the whole merit of which consists in its stately rhetoric,—a rhetoric sometimes not unworthy of Lucan,—about hating tyrants and dying for freedom, is brought on the stage in a time of great political excitement. Both parties crowd to the theatre. Each affects to consider every line as a compliment to itself, and an attack on its opponents. The curtain falls amidst an unanimous roar of applause. The Whigs of the "Kit Cat" embrace the author, and assure him that he has rendered an inestimable service to liberty. The Tory secretary of state presents a purse to the chief actor for defending the cause of liberty so well. The history of that night was, in miniature, the history of two generations.

We well know how much sophistry there was in the reasonings, and how much exaggeration in the declamations of both parties. But when we compare the state in which political science was at the close of the reign of George the Second with the state in which it had been when James the Second came to the throne, it is impossible not to admit that a prodigious improvement had taken place. We are no admirers of the political doctrines laid down in Blackstone's Commentaries. But if we consider that those Commentaries were read with great applause in the very schools where, within the memory of some persons then living, books had been publicly burned by order of the University of Oxford for containing the "damnable doctrine," that the English monarchy is limited and mixed, we cannot deny that a salutary change had taken place. "The Jesuits," says Pascal, in the last of his incomparable letters, "have obtained a Papal decree, condemning Galileo's doctrine about the motion of the earth. It is all in vain. If the world is really turning round, all mankind together will not be able to keep it from turning, or to keep themselves from turning with it." The decrees of Oxford were as ineffectual to stay the great moral and political revolution as those of the Vatican to stay the motion of our globe. That learned University found itself not only unable to keep the mass from moving, but unable to keep itself from moving along with the mass. Nor was the effect of the discussions and speculations of that period confined to our own country. While the Jacobite party was in the last dotage and weakness of its paralytic old age, the political philosophy of England began to produce a mighty effect on France, and, through France, on Europe.

Here another vast field opens itself before us. But we must resolutely turn away from it. We will conclude by earnestly advising all our readers to study Sir James Mackintosh's valuable Fragment, and by expressing the satisfaction we have received from learning, since this article was written, that the intelligent publishers of the volume before us have resolved to reprint the Fragment in a separate form, without those accompaniments which have hitherto impeded its circulation. The resolution is as creditable to them as the publication is sure to be acceptable to the lovers of English History.

LORD BACON. (JULY, 1837.)

The Works of Francis Bacon, Lord Chancellor of England. A New Edition. By BASIL MONTAGU, Esq. 16 vols., 8vo. London, 1825-1834.

WE return our hearty thanks to Mr. Montagu, as well for his very valuable edition of Lord Bacon's works, as for the instructive life of the immortal author contained in the last volume. We have much to say on the subject of this life, and will often find ourselves obliged to dissent from the opinions of the biographer. But about his merit as a collector of the materials out of which opinions are formed, there can be no dispute; and we readily acknowledge that we are in a great measure indebted to his minute and accurate researches for the means of refuting what we cannot but consider as his errors.

The labour which has been bestowed on this volume has been a labour of love. The writer is evidently enamoured of the subject. It fills his heart. It constantly overflows from his lips and his pen. Those who are acquainted with the Courts in which Mr. Montagu practices with so much ability and success well know how often he enlivens the discussion of a point of law by citing some weighty aphorism, or some brilliant illustration, from the "De Augmentis" or the "Novum Organum." The Life before us doubtless owes much of its value to the honest and generous enthusiasm of the writer. This feeling has stimulated his activity, has sustained his perseverance, has called forth all his ingenuity and eloquence; but, on the other hand, we must frankly say that it has, to a great extent, perverted his judgment.

We are by no means without sympathy for Mr. Montagu, even in what we consider as his weakness. There is scarcely any delusion which has a better claim to be indulgently treated than that under the influence of which a man ascribes every moral excellence to those who have left imperishable monuments of their genius. The causes of this error lie deep in the inmost recesses of human nature. We are all inclined to judge of others as we find them. Our estimate of a character always depends much on the manner in which that character affects our own interests and passions. We find it difficult to think well of those by whom we are thwarted or depressed; and we are ready to admit every excuse for the vices of those who are useful or agreeable to us. This is, we believe, one of those illusions to which the whole human race is subject, and which experience and reflection can only partially remove. It is, in the phraseology of Bacon, one of the *idola tribus*. Hence it is that the moral character of a man eminent in letters or in the fine arts is treated, often by contemporaries—almost always by posterity—with extraordinary tenderness. The world derives pleasure and advantage from the performances of such a man. The number of those who suffer by his personal vices is small, even in his own time, when compared with the number of those to whom his talents are a source of gratification. In a few years all those whom he has injured disappear. But his works remain, and are a source of delight to millions. The genius of Sallust is still with us. But the Numidians whom he plundered, and the unfortunate husbands who caught him in their houses at unseasonable hours, are forgotten. We suffer ourselves to be delighted by the keenness of Clarendon's observation, and by the sober majesty of his style, till we forget the oppressor and the bigot in the historian. Falstaff and Tom Jones have survived the gamekeepers whom Shakspeare cudgelled and the landladies whom Fielding bilked. A great writer is the friend and benefactor of his readers, and they cannot but judge of him under the deluding influence of friendship and gratitude. We all know how unwilling we are to admit the truth of any disgraceful story about a person whose society we like, and from whom we have received favours: how long we struggle against evidence; how fondly, when the facts cannot be disputed, we cling to the hope that that there may be some explanation or some extenuating circumstance with which we are unacquainted. Just such is the feeling which a man of liberal education naturally entertains towards the great minds of former ages. The debt which he owes to them is incalculable. They have guided him to truth. They have filled his mind with noble and graceful images. They have stood by him in all vicissitudes—comforters in sorrow, nurses in sickness, companions in solitude. These friendships are exposed to no danger from the occurrences by which other attachments are weakened or dissolved. Time glides by; fortune is inconstant; tempers are soured; bonds which seem indissoluble are daily sundered by interest, by emulation, or by caprice. But no such cause can affect the silent converse which we hold with the highest of human intellects. That placid intercourse is disturbed by no jealousies or resentments. These are the old friends who are never seen with new faces, who are the same in wealth and in poverty, in glory and in obscurity. With the dead there is no rivalry. In the dead there is no change. Plato is never sullen. Cervantes is never petulent. Demosthenes never comes unseasonably. Dante never stays too long. No difference of political opinion can alienate Cicero. No heresy can excite the horror of Bossuet.

Nothing, then, can be more natural than that a person endowed with sensibility and imagination should entertain a respectful and affectionate feeling towards those great men with whose minds he holds daily communion. Yet nothing can be more certain than that such men have not always deserved in their own persons to be regarded with respect or affection. Some writers, whose works will continue to instruct and delight mankind to the remotest ages, have been placed in such situations that their actions and motives are as well known to us as the actions and motives of one human being can be known to another; and unhappily their conduct has not always been such as an impartial judge can contemplate with approbation. But the fanaticism of the devout worshipper of genius is proof against all evidence and all argument. The character of his idol is matter of faith; and the province of faith is not to be invaded by reason. He maintains his superstition with a credulity as boundless, and a zeal as unscrupulous, as can be found in the most ardent partisans of religious or political factions. The most overwhelming proofs are rejected; the plainest rules of morality are explained away; extensive and important portions of history are completely distorted. The enthusiast misrepresents facts with all the effrontery of an advocate, and confounds right and wrong with all the dexterity of a Jesuit—and all this only in order that some man who has been in his grave for ages may have a fairer character than he deserves.

Middleton's "Life of Cicero" is a striking instance of the influence of this sort of partiality. Never was there a character which it was easier to read than that of Cicero. Never was there a mind keener or more critical than that of Middleton. Had the Doctor brought to the examination of his favourite statesman's conduct but a very small part of the acuteness and severity which he displayed when he was engaged in investigating the high pretensions of Epiphanius and Justin Martyr, he could not have failed to produce a most valuable history of a most interesting portion of time. But this most ingenious and learned man, though

"So wary held and wise
That, as 'twas said, he scarce received
For gospel what the church believed,"

had a superstition of his own. The great iconoclast was himself an idolator. The great *Avvocato del Diavolo*, while he disputed, with no small ability, the claims of Cyprian and Athanasius to a place in the Calendar, was himself composing a lying legend in honour of St. Tully! He was holding up as a model of every virtue a man whose talents and acquirements, indeed, can never be too highly extolled, and who was by no means destitute of amiable qualities, but whose whole soul was under the dominion of a girlish vanity and a craven fear. Actions for which Cicero himself, the most eloquent and skilful of advocates, could contrive no excuse, actions which in his confidential correspondence he mentioned with remorse and shame, are represented by his biographer as wise, virtuous, heroic. The whole history of that great revolution which overthrew the Roman aristocracy, the whole state of parties, the character of every public man, is elaborately misrepresented, in order to make out something which may look like a defence of one most eloquent and accomplished trimmer.

The volume before us reminds us now and then of the "Life of Cicero." But there is this marked difference. Dr. Middleton evidently had an uneasy consciousness of the weakness of his cause, and, therefore, resorted to the most disengenuous shifts, to unpardonable distortions and suppressions of facts. Mr. Montagu's faith is sincere and implicit. He practices no trickery. He conceals nothing. He puts the facts before us in the full confidence that they will produce on our minds the effect which they have produced on his own. It is not till he comes to reason from facts to motives that his partiality shows itself; and then he leaves Middleton himself far behind. His work proceeds on the assumption that Bacon was an eminently virtuous man. From the tree Mr. Montagu judges of the fruit. He is forced to relate many actions which, if any man but Bacon had committed them, nobody but Bacon would have dreamed of defending—actions which are readily and completely explained by supposing Bacon to have been a man whose principles were not strict, and whose spirit was not high, actions which can be explained in no other way without resorting to some grotesque hypothesis for which there is not a tittle of evidence. But any hypothesis is, in Mr. Montagu's opinion, more probable than that his hero should ever have done anything very wrong.

This mode of defending Bacon seems to us by no means *Baconian*. To take a man's character for granted, and then from his character to infer the moral quality of all his actions, is surely a process the very reverse of that which is recommended in the "Novum Organum." Nothing, we are sure, could have led Mr. Montagu to depart so far from his master's precepts, except zeal for his master's honour. We shall follow a different course. We shall attempt, with the valuable assistance which Mr. Montagu has afforded us, to frame such an account of Bacon's life as may enable our readers correctly to estimate his character.

It is hardly necessary to say that Francis Bacon was the son of Sir Nicholas Bacon, who held the great seal of England during the first twenty years of the reign of Elizabeth. The fame of the father has been thrown into shade by that of the son. But Sir Nicholas was no ordinary man. He belonged to a set of men whom it is easier to describe collectively than separately, whose minds were formed by one system of discipline, who belonged to one rank in society, to one university, to one party, to one sect, to one administration, and who resembled each other so much in talents, in opinions, in habits, in fortunes, that one character, we had almost said one life, may, to a considerable extent, serve for them all.

They were the first generation of statesmen by profession that England produced. Before their time the division of labour had, in this respect, been very imperfect. Those who had directed public affairs had been, with few exceptions, warriors or priests; warriors whose rude courage was neither guided by science nor softened by humanity,—priests whose learning and abilities were habitually devoted to the defence of tyranny and imposture. The Hotspurs, the Nevilles, the Cliffords—rough, illiterate and unreflecting—brought to the council-board the fierce and imperious disposition which they had acquired amidst the tumult of predatory war, or in the gloomy repose of the garrisoned and moated castle. On the other side was the calm and subtle prelate—versed in all that was then considered as learning—trained in the Schools to manage words and, in the Confessional to manage hearts—seldom superstitious, but skilful in practising on the superstition of others—false, as it was natural that a man should be whose profession imposed on all who were not saints the necessity of being hypocrites—selfish, as it was natural that a man should be who could form no domestic ties and cherish no hope of legitimate posterity—more attached to his order than to his country, and guiding the politics of England with a constant side glance at Rome. But the increase of wealth, the progress of knowledge, and the reformation of religion produced a great change. The nobles ceased to be military chieftains; the priests ceased to possess a monopoly of learning; and a new and remarkable species of politicians appeared.

These men came from neither of the classes which had, till then, almost exclusively furnished ministers of state. They were all laymen; yet they were all men of learning; and they were all men of peace. They were not members of the aristocracy. They inherited no titles, no large domains, no armies of retainers, no fortified castles. Yet they were not low men, such as those whom princes, jealous of the power of a nobility, have sometimes raised from forges and cobblers' stalls to the highest situations. They were all gentlemen by birth. They had all received a liberal education. It is a remarkable fact that they were all members of the same university. The two great national seats of learning had even then acquired the characters which they still retain. In intellectual activity and in readiness to admit improvements, the superiority was then, as it has ever since been, on the side of the less ancient and splendid institution. Cambridge had the honour of educating those celebrated Protestant Bishops whom Oxford had the honour of burning; and at Cambridge were formed the minds of all those statesmen to whom chiefly is to be attributed the secure establishment of the reformed religion in the north of Europe.

The statesmen of whom we speak passed their youth surrounded by the incessant din of theological controversy. Opinions were still in a state of chaotic anarchy, intermingling, separating, advancing, receding. Sometimes the stubborn bigotry of the Conservatives seemed likely to prevail. Then the impetuous onset of the Reformers for a moment carried all before it. Then again the resisting mass made a desperate stand; arrested the movement, and forced it slowly back. The vacillation which at that time appeared in English legislation, and which it has been the fashion to attribute to the caprice and to the power of one or two individuals, was truly a national vacillation. It was not only in the mind of Henry that the new theology obtained the ascendant one day, and that the lessons of the nurse and of the priest regained their influence at another. It was not only in the House of Tudor that the husband was exasperated by the opposition of the wife—that the son dissented from the opinions of the father—that the brother persecuted the sister—that one sister persecuted another. The principles of Conservation and Reform carried on their warfare in every part of society, in every congregation, in every school of learning, round the hearth of every private family, in the recesses of every reflecting mind.

It was in the midst of this ferment that the minds of the persons whom we are describing were developed. They were born Reformers. They belonged by nature to that order of men who always form the front ranks in the great intellectual progress. They were, therefore, one and all, Protestants. In religious matters, however, though there is no reason to doubt that they were sincere, they were by no means zealous. None of them chose to run the smallest personal risk during the reign of Mary. None of them favoured the unhappy attempt of Northumberland in favour of his daughter-in-law. None of them shared in the desperate councils of Wyatt. They contrived to have business on the continent; or, if they stayed in England, they heard Mass and kept Lent with great decorum. When those dark and perilous years had gone by, and when the crown had descended to a new sovereign, they took the lead in the reformation of the Church. But they proceeded, not with the impetuosity of theologians, but with the calm determination of statesmen. They acted, not like men who considered the Romish worship as a system too offensive to God and too destructive of souls to be tolerated for an hour, but like men who regarded the points in dispute among Christians as in themselves unimportant, and who were not restrained by any scruple of conscience from professing, as they had before professed, the Catholic faith of Mary, the Protestant faith of Edward, or any of the numerous intermediate combinations which the caprice of Henry and the temporising policy of Cranmer had formed out of the doctrines of both the hostile parties. They took a deliberate view of the state of their own country and of the continent. They satisfied themselves as to the learning of the public mind; and they chose their side. They placed themselves at the head of the Protestants of Europe, and staked all their fame and fortunes on the success of their party.

It is needless to relate how dexterously, how resolutely, how gloriously they directed the politics of England during the eventful years which followed—how they succeeded in uniting their friends and separating their enemies—how they humbled the pride of Philip—how they backed the unconquerable spirit of Coligni—how they rescued Holland from tryanny—how they founded the maritime greatness of their country—how they outwitted the artful politicians of Italy, and tamed the ferocious chieftains of Scotland. It is impossible to deny that they committed many acts which would justly bring on a statesman of our time censures of the most serious kind. But, when we consider the state of morality in their age and the unscrupulous character of the adversaries against whom they had to contend, we are forced to admit that it is not without reason that their names are still held in veneration by their countrymen.

There were, doubtless, many diversities in their intellectual and moral character. But there was a strong family likeness. The constitution of their minds was remarkably sound. No particular faculty was pre-eminently developed; but manly health and vigour were equally diffused through the whole. They were men of letters. Their minds were by nature and by exercise well fashioned for speculative pursuits. It was by circumstances, rather than by any strong bias of inclination, that they were led to take a prominent part in active life. In active life, however, no men could be more perfectly free from the faults of mere theorists and pedants. No men observed more accurately the signs of the times. No men had a greater practical acquaintance with human nature. Their policy was generally characterised rather by vigilance, by moderation, and by firmness, than by invention, or by the spirit of enterprise.

They spoke and wrote in a manner worthy of their excellent sense. Their eloquence was less copious and less ingenious, but far purer and more manly than that of the succeeding generation. It was the eloquence of men who had lived with the first translators of the Bible, and with the authors of the Book of Common Prayer. It was luminous, dignified, solid, and very slightly tainted with that affectation which deformed the style of the ablest men of the next age. If, as sometimes chanced, they were under the necessity of taking a part in the theological controversies on which the dearest interests of kingdoms were then staked, they acquited themselves as if their whole lives had been passed in the Schools and the Convocation.

There was something in the temper of these celebrated men which secured them against the proverbial inconstancy both of the court and of the multitude. No intrigue, no combination of rivals could deprive them of the confidence of their Sovereign. No parliament attacked their influence. No mob coupled their names with any odious grievance. Their power ended only with their lives. In this respect, their fate presents a most remarkable contrast to that of the enterprising and brilliant politicians of the preceding and of the succeeding generation. Burleigh was minister during forty years. Sir Nicholas Bacon held the great seal more than twenty years. Sir Thomas Smith was Secretary of State eighteen years. Sir Francis Walsingham about as long. They all died in office, and in the enjoyment of public respect and royal favour. Far different had been the fate of Wolsey, Cromwell, Norfolk, Somerset and Northumberland. Far different also was the fate of Essex, of Raleigh, and of the still more illustrious man whose life we propose to consider.

The explanation of this circumstance is perhaps contained in the motto which Sir Nicholas Bacon inscribed over the entrance of his hall at Gorhambury, *Mediocria firma*. This maxim was constantly borne in mind by himself and his colleagues. They were more solicitous to lay the foundations of their power deep, than to raise the structure to a conspicuous but insecure height. None of them aspired to be sole Minister. None of them provoked envy by an ostentatious display of wealth and influence. None of them affected to outshine the ancient aristocracy of the kingdom. They were free from that childish love of titles which characterised the successful courtiers of the generation which preceded them and of that which followed them. As to money, none of them could, in that age, justly be considered as rapacious. Some of them would, even in our time, deserve the praise of eminent disinterestedness. Their fidelity to the State was incorruptible. Their private morals were without stain. Their households were sober and well-governed.

Among these statesmen, Sir Nicholas Bacon was generally considered as ranking next to Burleigh. He was called by Camden "Sacris conciliis alterum columen;" and by George Buchanan,

"Diu Britannici
Regni secundum columen."

The second wife of Sir Nicholas and mother of Francis Bacon was Anne, one of the daughters of Sir Anthony Cooke, a man of distinguished learning, who had been tutor to Edward the Sixth. Sir Anthony had paid considerable attention to the education of his daughters, and lived to see them all splendidly and happily married. Their classical acquirements made them conspicuous even among the women of fashion of that age. Katherine, who became Lady Killigrew, wrote Latin hexameters and pentameters which would appear with credit in the *Musæ Etonenses*. Mildred, the wife of Lord Burleigh, was described by Roger Ascham as the best Greek scholar among the young women of England, Lady Jane Grey always excepted. Anne, the mother of Francis Bacon, was distinguished both as a linguist and as a theologian. She corresponded in Greek with Bishop Jewel, and translated his "Apologia" from the

Latin so correctly that neither he nor Archbishop Parker could suggest a single alteration.* She also translated a series of sermons on fate and free-will from the Tuscan of Bernardo Ochino. This fact is the more curious, as Ochino was one of that small and audacious band of Italian reformers—anathematised alike by Wittenberg, by Geneva, by Zurich and by Rome—from which the Socinian sect deduces its origin.

Lady Bacon was doubtless a lady of highly cultivated mind, after the fashion of her age. But we must not suffer ourselves to be deluded into the belief that she and her sisters were more accomplished women than many who are now living. On this subject there is, we think, much misapprehension. We have often heard men who wish, as almost all men of sense wish, that women should be highly educated, speak with rapture of the English ladies of the sixteenth century, and lament that they can find no modern damsel resembling those fair pupils of Ascham and Aylmer who compared, over their embroidery, the styles of Isocrates and Lysias, and who, while the horns were sounding and the dogs in full cry, sat in the lonely oriel, with eyes rivetted to that immortal page which tells how meekly and bravely the first great martyr of intellectual liberty took the cup from his weeping goaler. But surely these complaints have very little foundation. We would by no means disparage the ladies of the sixteenth century or their pursuits. But we conceive that those who extol them at the expense of the women of our time forget one very obvious and very important circumstance. In the time of Henry the Eighth and Edward the Sixth, a person who did not read Greek and Latin could read nothing, or next to nothing. The Italian was the only modern language which possessed anything that could be called a literature. All the valuable books then extant in all the vernacular dialects of Europe would hardly have filled a single shelf. England did not yet possess Shakspeare's "Plays" and the "Fairy Queen;" nor France Montaigne's "Essays;" nor Spain "Don Quixote." In looking round a well-furnished library, how few English or French books can we find which were extant when Lady Jane Grey and Queen Elizabeth received their education. Chaucer, Gower, Froissart, Comines, Rabelais, nearly complete the list. It was therefore absolutely necessary that a woman should be uneducated or classically educated. Indeed, without a knowledge of one of the ancient languages, no person could then have any clear notion of what was passing in the political, the literary, or the religious world. The Latin was in the sixteenth century all, and more than all, that the French was in the eighteenth. It was the language of courts as well as of the schools. It was the language of diplomacy; it was the language of theological and political controversy. Being a fixed language, while the living languages were in a state of fluctuation, being universally known to the learned and the polite, it was employed by almost every writer who aspired to a wide and durable reputation. A person who was ignorant of it was shut out from all acquaintance—not merely with Cicero and Virgil, not merely with heavy treatises on canon-law and school divinity; but with the most interesting memoirs, state papers and pamphlets of his own time; nay, even with the most admired poetry and the most popular squibs which appeared on the fleeting topics of the day—with Buchanan's complimentary verses, with Erasmus's dialogues, with Hutten's epistles.

"This is no longer the case. All political and religious controversy is now conducted in the modern languages. The ancient tongues are used only in comments on the ancient writers. The great productions of Athenian and Roman genius are indeed still what they were. But though their positive value

---

* Strype's Life of Parker.

is unchanged, their relative value, when compared with the whole mass of mental wealth possessed by mankind, has been constantly falling. They were the intellectual all of our ancestors. They are but a part of our treasures. Over what tragedy could Lady Jane Grey have wept, over what comedy could she have smiled, if the ancient dramatists had not been in her library? A modern reader can make shift without "Œdipus" and "Medea" while he possesses "Othello" and "Hamlet." If he knows nothing of Pyrgopolynices and Thraso, he is familiar with Bobadil, and Bessus, and Pistol, and Parolles. If he cannot enjoy the delicious irony of Plato, he may find some compensation in that of Pascal. If he is shut out from "Nephelococcygia," he may take refuge in "Lilliput." We are guilty, we hope, of no irreverence towards those great nations to which the human race owes art, science, taste, civil and intellectual freedom, when we say that the stock bequeathed by them to us has been so carefully improved that the accumulated interest now exceeds the principal. We believe that the books which have been written in the languages of Western Europe during the last two hundred and fifty years are of greater value than all the books which at the beginning of that period were extant in the world. With the modern languages of Europe, English women are at least as well acquainted as English men. When, therefore, we compare the acquirements of Lady Jane Grey with those of an accomplished young woman of our own time, we have no hesitation in awarding the superiority to the latter. We hope that our readers will pardon this digression. It is long; but it can hardly be called unseasonable, if it tends to convince them that they are mistaken in thinking that their great-great-grandmothers were superior women to their sisters and their wives.

Francis Bacon, the youngest son of Sir Nicholas, was born at York House, his father's residence in the Strand, on the 22nd of January, 1561. His health was very delicate,* and to this circumstance may be partly attributed that gravity of carriage and that love of sedentary pursuits which distinguished him from other boys. Everybody knows how much his premature readiness of wit and sobriety of deportment amused the Queen, and how she used to call him her young Lord Keeper. We are told that, while still a mere child, he stole away from his playfellows to a vault in St. James's Fields, for the purpose of investigating the cause of a singular echo which he had observed there. It is certain that, at only twelve, he busied himself with very ingenious speculations on the art of legerdemain—a subject which, as Professor Dugald Stewart has most justly observed, merits much more attention from philosophers than it has ever received. These are trifles. But the eminence which Bacon afterwards attained makes them interesting.

In the thirteenth year of his age he was entered at Trinity College, Cambridge. That celebrated school of learning enjoyed the peculiar favour of the Lord Treasurer and the Lord Keeper, and acknowledged the advantages which it derived from their patronage in a public letter which bears date just a month after the admission of Francis Bacon.* The master was Whitgift, afterwards Archbishop of Canterbury, a narrow-minded, mean and tyrannical priest, who gained power by servility and adulation, and employed it in persecuting with impartial cruelty those who agreed with Calvin about Church Government and those who differed from Calvin touching the doctrine of Reprobation. He was now in a chrysalis state—putting off the worm and putting on the dragon-fly— a kind of intermediate grub between sycophant and oppressor. He was indemnifying himself for the court which he found it expedient to pay to the Ministers by exercising much petty tyranny within his own college. It would be unjust, however, to deny him the praise of having rendered about this time

† Strype's Life of Whitgift.

one important service to letters. He stood up manfully against those who wished to make Trinity College a mere appendage to Westminster school, and by this act—the only good act, as far as we remember, of his long public life— he saved the noblest place of education in England from the degrading fate of King's College and New College.

It has often been said that Bacon, while still at College, planned that great intellectual revolution with which his name is inseparably connected. The evidence on this subject, however, is hardly sufficient to prove what is in itself so improbable as that any definite scheme of that kind should have been so early formed, even by so powerful and active a mind. But it is certain that, after a residence of three years at Cambridge, Bacon departed, carrying with him a profound contempt for the course of study pursued there, a fixed conviction that the system of academic education in England was radically vicious, a just scorn for the trifles on which the followers of Aristotle had wasted their powers, and no great reverence for Aristotle himself.

In his sixteenth year he visited Paris, and resided there for some time under the care of Sir Amias Paulet, Elizabeth's minister at the French court, and one of the ablest and most upright of the many valuable servants whom she employed. France was at that time in a deplorable state of agitation. The Huguenots and the Catholics were mustering all their force for the fiercest and most protracted of their many struggles; while the prince, whose duty it was to protect and to restrain both, had by his vices and follies degraded himself so deeply that he had no authority over either. Bacon, however, made a tour through several provinces, and appears to have passed some time at Poitiers. We have abundant proof that during his stay on the Continent he did not neglect literary and scientific pursuits. But his attention seems to have been chiefly directed to statistics and diplomacy. It was at this time that he wrote those "Notes on the State of Europe" which are printed in his works. He studied the principles of the art of deciphering with great interest, and invented one cipher so ingenious that, many years later, he thought it deserving of a place in the "De Augmentis." In February, 1580, while engaged in these pursuits, he received intelligence of the almost sudden death of his father, and instantly returned to England.

His prospects were greatly overcast by this event. He was most desirous to obtain a provision which might enable him to devote himself to literature and politics. He applied to the government, and it seems strange that he should have applied in vain. His wishes were moderate. His hereditary claims on the administration were great. He had himself been favourably noticed by the Queen. His uncle was Prime Minister. His own talents were such as any minister might have been eager to enlist in the public service. But his solicitations were unsuccessful. The truth is that the Cecils disliked him, and did all that they could decently do to keep him down. It has never been alleged that Bacon had done anything to merit this dislike; nor is it at all probable that a man whose temper was naturally mild, whose manners were courteous, who, through life, nursed his fortunes with the utmost care, and who was fearful even to a fault of offending the powerful, would have given any just cause of displeasure to a kinsman who had the means of rendering him essential service and of doing him irreparable injury. The real explanation, we have no doubt, is this: Robert Cecil, the Treasurer's second son, was younger by a few months than Bacon. He had been educated with the utmost care, had been initiated, while still a boy, in the mysteries of diplomacy and court-intrigue, and was just at this time about to be produced on the stage of public life. The wish nearest to Burleigh's heart was that his own greatness might descend to this favourite child. But even Burleigh's fatherly partiality could hardly prevent him from perceiving that Robert, with all his abilities and acquirements, was no match for his cousin Francis. This seems to us the only rational explanation of the Treasurer's conduct. Mr. Montagu is more charitable. He supposes that Burleigh was influenced merely by affection for his nephew, and was "little disposed to encourage him to rely on others rather than on himself, and to venture on the quicksands of politics instead of the certain profession of the law." If such were Burleigh's feelings, it seems strange that he should have suffered his son to venture on those quicksands from which he so carefully preserved his nephew. But the truth is, that if Burleigh had been so disposed, he might easily have secured to Bacon a comfortable provision which should have been exposed to no risk. And it is equally certain that he showed as little disposition to enable his nephew to live by a profession as to enable him to live without a profession. That Bacon himself attributed the conduct of his relatives to jealousy of his superior talents, we have not the smallest doubt. In a letter written many years after to Villiers, he expresses himself thus: "Countenance, encourage and advance able men in all kinds, degrees and professions. For in the time of *the Cecils, the father and the son*, able men were by design and of purpose suppressed."*

Whatever Burleigh's motives might be, his purpose was unalterable. The supplications which Francis addressed to his uncle and aunt were earnest, humble, and almost servile. He was the most promising and accomplished young man of his time. His father had been the brother-in-law, the most useful colleague, the nearest friend of the Minister. But all this availed poor Francis nothing. He was forced, much against his will, to betake himself to the study of the law. He was admitted at Gray's Inn; and, during some years, he laboured there in obscurity.

What the extent of his legal attainments may have been, it is difficult to say. It was not hard for a man of his powers to acquire that very moderate portion of technical knowledge which, when joined to quickness, tact, wit, ingenuity, eloquence and knowledge of the world, is sufficient to raise an advocate to the highest professional eminence. The general opinion appears to have been that which was on one occasion expressed by Elizabeth. "Bacon," said she, "hath a great wit and much learning; but in law showeth to the utmost of his knowledge, and is not deep." The Cecils, we suspect, did their best to spread this opinion by whispers and insinuations. Coke openly proclaimed it, with that rancorous insolence which was habitual to him. No reports are more readily believed than those which disparage genius and soothe the envy of conscious mediocrity. It must have been inexpressibly consoling to a stupid sergeant, the forerunner of him who, a hundred and fifty years later, "shook his head at Murray as a wit," to know that the most profound thinker and the most accomplished orator of the age was very imperfectly acquainted with the law touching *bastard eigné* and *mulier puisné*, and confounded the right of free fishery with that of common piscary.

It is certain that no man in that age, or indeed during the century and a half which followed, was better acquainted with the philosophy of law. His technical knowledge was quite sufficient, with the help of his admirable talents and of his insinuating address, to procure clients. He rose very rapidly into business, and soon entertained hopes of being called within the bar. He applied to Lord Burleigh for that purpose, but received a testy refusal. Of the grounds of that refusal we can, in some measure, judge by Bacon's answer, which is still extant. It seems that the old Lord, whose temper, age and gout, had by no means altered for the better, and who omitted no opportunity of

---

* See page 61, Vol. XII. of the present edition.

marking his dislike of the showy, quick-witted young men of the rising generation, took this opportunity to read Francis a very sharp lecture on his vanity and want of respect for his betters. Francis returned a most submissive reply, thanked the Treasurer for the admonition, and promised to profit by it. Strangers meanwhile were less unjust to the young barrister than his nearest kinsman had been. In his twenty-sixth year he became a bencher of his Inn; and two years later he was appointed Lent reader. At length, in 1590, he obtained for the first time some show of favour from the Court. He was sworn in Queen's Counsel extraordinary. But this mark of honour was not accompanied by any pecuniary emolument. He continued, therefore, to solicit his powerful relatives for some provision which might enable him to live without drudging at his profession. He bore, with a patience and serenity which, we fear, bordered on meanness, the morose humours of his uncle and the sneering reflections which his cousin cast on speculative men lost in philosophical dreams and too wise to be capable of transacting public business. At length the Cecils were generous enough to procure for him the reversion of the Registrarship of the Star Chamber. This was a lucrative place; but, as many years elapsed before it fell in, he was still under the necessity of labouring for his daily bread.

In the Parliament which was called in 1593, he sat as member for the county of Middlesex, and soon attained eminence as a debater. It is easy to perceive from the scanty remains of his oratory that the same compactness of expression and richness of fancy which appear in his writings characterised his speeches; and that his extensive acquaintance with literature and history enabled him to entertain his audience with a vast variety of illustrations and allusions which were generally happy and apposite, but which were probably not least pleasing to the taste of that age when they were such as would now be thought childish or pedantic. It is evident also that he was, as indeed might have been expected, perfectly free from those faults which are generally found in an advocate who, after having risen to eminence at the bar, enters the House of Commons; that it was his habit to deal with every great question, not in small detached portions, but as a whole; that he refined little, and that his reasonings were those of a capacious rather than a subtle mind. Ben Jonson, a most unexceptionable judge, has described his eloquence in words, which, though often quoted, will bear to be quoted again. "There happened in my time one noble speaker who was full of gravity in his speaking. His language, where he could spare or pass by a jest, was nobly censorious. No man ever spoke more neatly, more pressly, more weightily, or suffered less emptiness, less idleness, in what he uttered. No member of his speech but consisted of his own graces. His hearers could not cough or look aside from him without loss. He commanded where he spoke, and had his judges angry and pleased at his devotion. No man had their affections more in his power. The fear of every man that heard him, was lest he should make an end." From the mention which is made of judges, it would seem that Jonson had heard Bacon only at the bar. Indeed, we imagine that the House of Commons was then almost inaccessible to strangers. It is not probable that a man of Bacon's nice observation would speak in Parliament exactly as he spoke in the Court of Queen's Bench. But the graces of manner and language must, to a great extent, have been common between the Queen's Counsel and the Knight of the Shire.

Bacon tried to play a very difficult game in politics. He wished to be at once a favourite at Court and popular with the multitude. If any man could have succeeded in this attempt, a man of talents so rare, of judgment so prematurely ripe, of temper so calm and of manners so plausible, might have been expected to succeed. Nor indeed did he wholly fail. Once, however, he indulged in a burst of patriotism which cost him a long and bitter remorse, and which he never ventured to repeat. The Court asked for large subsidies and for speedy payment. The remains of Bacon's speech breathe all the spirit of the Long Parliament. "The gentlemen," said he, "must sell their plate, and the farmers their brass pots, ere this will be paid; and for us, we are here to search the wounds of the realm, and not to skim them over. The dangers are these. First, we shall breed discontent and endanger her Majesty's safety, which must consist more in the love of the people than their wealth. Secondly, this being granted in this sort, other princes hereafter will look for the like; so that we shall put an evil precedent on ourselves and our posterity; and in histories, it is to be observed, of all nations the English are not to be subject, base, or taxable." The Queen and her ministers resented this outbreak of public spirit in the highest manner. Indeed, many an honest member of the House of Commons had, for a much smaller matter, been sent to the Tower by the proud and hot-blooded Tudors. The young patriot condescended to make the most abject apologies. He adjured the Lord Treasurer to show some favour to his poor servant and ally. He bemoaned himself to the Lord Keeper in a letter which may keep in countenance the most unmanly of the epistles which Cicero wrote during his banishment. The lesson was not thrown away. Bacon never offended in the same manner again.

He was now satisfied that he had little to hope from the patronage of these powerful kinsmen whom he had solicited during twelve years with such meek pertinacity, and he began to look towards a different quarter. Among the courtiers of Elizabeth had lately appeared a new favourite—young, noble, wealthy, accomplished, eloquent, brave, generous, aspiring—a favourite who had obtained from the grey-headed Queen such marks of regard as she had scarce vouchsafed to Leicester in the season of the passions; who was at once the ornament of the palace and the idol of the city; who was the common patron of men of letters and of men of the sword; who was the common refuge of the persecuted Catholic and of the persecuted Puritan. The calm prudence which had enabled Burleigh to shape his course through so many dangers, and the vast experience which he had acquired in dealing with two generations of colleagues and rivals, seemed scarcely sufficient to support him in this new competition; and Robert Cecil sickened with fear and envy as he contemplated the rising fame and influence of Essex.

The history of the factions which, towards the close of the reign of Elizabeth, divided her court and her council, though pregnant with instruction, is by no means interesting or pleasing. Both parties employed the means which are familiar to unscrupulous statesmen; and neither had, or even pretended to have, any important end in view. The public mind was then reposing from one great effort, and collecting strength for another. That impetuous and appalling rush with which the human intellect had moved forward in the career of truth and liberty, during the fifty years which followed the separation of Luther from the communion of the Church of Rome, was now over. The boundary between Protestantism and Popery had been fixed very nearly where it still remains. England, Scotland, the Northern kingdoms were on one side; Ireland, Spain, Portugal, Italy, on the other. The line of demarcation ran, as it still runs, through the midst of the Netherlands, of Germany and of Switzerland, dividing province from province, electorate from electorate, and canton from canton. France might be considered as a debatable land, in which the contest was still undecided. Since that time, the two religions have done little more than maintain their ground. A few occasional incursions have been made. But the general frontier remains the same. During two hundred and fifty years no great society has risen up like one man and emancipated itself by one mighty effort from the enthralling superstition of ages. This spectacle was common in the middle of the sixteenth century. Why has it ceased to be so? Why has so violent a movement been followed by so long a repose? The doctrines of the reformers are not less agreeable to reason or to revelation now than formerly. The public mind is assuredly not less enlightened now than formerly. Why is it that Protestantism, after carrying every thing before it in a time of comparatively little knowledge and little freedom, should make no perceptible progress in a reasoning and tolerant age—that the Luthers, the Calvins, the Knoxes, the Zwingles, should had left no successors—that during two centuries and a half fewer converts should have been brought over from the Church of Rome than at the time of the Reformation were sometimes gained in a year? This has always appeared to us one of the most curious and interesting problems in history. On some other occasion we may perhaps attempt to solve it. At present it is enough to say that, at the close of Elizabeth's reign, the Protestant party, to borrow the language of the Apocalypse, had left its first love and had ceased to do it first works.

The great struggle of the sixteenth century was over. The great struggle of the seventeenth century had not commenced. The confessors of Mary's reign were dead. The members of the Long Parliament were still in their cradles. The Papists had been deprived of all power in the state. The Puritans had not yet attained any formidable extent of power. True it is that a student, well acquainted with the history of the next generation, can easily discern in the proceedings of the last Parliaments of Elizabeth the germ of great and ever memorable events. But to the eye of a contemporary nothing of this appeared. The two sections of ambitious men who were struggling for power differed from each other on no important public question. Both belonged to the Established Church. Both professed boundless loyalty to the Queen. Both approved the war with Spain. There is not, as far as we are aware, any reason to believe that they entertained different views concerning the succession to the Crown. Certainly neither faction had any great measure of reform in view. Neither attempted to redress any public grievance. The most odious and pernicious grievance under which the nation then suffered was a source of profit to both, and was defended by both with equal zeal. Raleigh held a monopoly of cards, Essex a monopoly of sweet wines. In fact, the only ground of quarrel between the parties was that they could not agree as to their respective shares of power and patronage.

Nothing in the political conduct of Essex entitles him to esteem ; and the pity with which we regard his early and terrible end is diminished by the consideration that he put to hazard the lives and fortunes of his most attached friends, and endeavoured to throw the whole country into confusion, for objects purely personal. Still, it is impossible not to be deeply interested for a man so brave, high-spirited and generous ; for a man who, while he conducted himself towards his sovereign with a boldness such as was then found in no other subject, conducted himself towards his dependents with a delicacy such as has rarely been found in any other patron. Unlike the vulgar herd of benefactors, he desired to inspire, not gratitude, but affection. He tried to make those whom he befriended feel towards him as towards an equal. His mind, ardent, susceptible, naturally disposed to admiration of all that is great and beautiful, was fascinated by the genius and the accomplishments of Bacon. A close friendship was soon formed between them—a friendship destined to have a dark, a mournful, a shameful end.

In 1594 the office of Attorney-General became vacant, and Bacon hoped to obtain it. Essex made his friend's cause his own—sued, expostulated, promised, threatened—but all in vain. It is probable that the dislike felt by the Cecils for Bacon had been increased by the connection which he had lately formed with the Earl. Robert was then on the point of being made Secretary of State. He happened one day to be in the same coach with Essex, and a remarkable conversation took place between them. "My Lord," said Sir Robert, "the Queen has determined to appoint an Attorney-General without more delay. I pray your Lordship to let me know whom you will favour." "I wonder at your question," replied the Earl. "You cannot but know that resolutely, against all the world, I stand for your cousin, Francis Bacon." "Good Lord!" cried Cecil, unable to bridle his temper, "I wonder your Lordship should spend your strength on so unlikely a matter. Can you name one precedent of so raw a youth promoted to so great a place?" This objection came with a singularly bad grace from a man who, though younger than Bacon, was in daily expectation of being made Secretary of State. The blot was too obvious to be missed by Essex, who seldom forbore to speak his mind. "I have made no search," said he, "for precedents of young men who have filled the office of Attorney-General. But I could name to you, Sir Robert, a man younger than Francis, less learned and equally inexperienced, who is suing and striving with all his might for an office of far greater weight." Sir Robert had nothing to say but that he thought his own abilities equal to the place which he hoped to obtain, and that his father's long services deserved such a mark of gratitude from the Queen—as if his abilities were comparable to his cousin's, or as if Sir Nicholas Bacon had done no service to the State. Cecil then hinted that, if Bacon would be satisfied with the Solicitorship, that might be of easier digestion to the Queen. "Digest me no digestions," said the generous and ardent Earl. "The Attorneyship for Francis is that I must have; and in that I will spend all my power, might, authority and amity; and with tooth and nail procure the same for him against whomsoever; and whosoever getteth this office out of my hands for any other, before he have it, it shall cost him the coming by. And this be you assured of, Sir Robert, for now I fully declare myself; and for my own part, Sir Robert, I think strange both of my Lord Treasurer and you, that can have the mind to seek the preference of a stranger before so near a kinsman; for if you weigh in a balance the parts every way of his competitor and him, only excepting five poor years of admitting to a house of court before Francis, you shall find in all other respects whatsoever no comparison between them."

When the office of Attorney-General was filled up, the Earl pressed the Queen to make Bacon Solicitor-General, and, on this occasion, the old Lord Treasurer professed himself not unfavourable to his nephew's pretensions. But after a contest which lasted more than a year and a half, and in which Essex, to use his own words, "spent all his power, might, authority and amity," the place was given to another. Essex felt this disappointment keenly, but found consolation in the most munificent and delicate liberality. He presented Bacon with an estate worth near two thousand pounds, situated at Twickenham; and this, as Bacon owned many years after, "with so kind and noble circumstances as the manner was worth more than the matter."

It was soon after these events that Bacon first appeared before the public as a writer. Early in 1597 he published a small volume of "Essays," which was afterwards enlarged by successive additions to many times its original bulk. This little work was, as it well deserved to be, exceedingly popular. It was reprinted in a few months; it was translated into Latin, French and Italian; and it seems to have at once established the literary reputation of its author. But though Bacon's reputation rose, his fortunes were still depressed. He was in great pecuniary difficulties; and, on one occasion, was arrested in the street at the suit of a goldsmith for a debt of £300, and was carried to a sponging-house in Coleman Street.

The kindness of Essex was in the meantime indefatigable. In 1596 he sailed on his memorable expedition to the coast of Spain. At the very moment of his embarkation, he wrote to several of his friends, commending to them, during his own absence, the interests of Bacon. He returned, after performing the most brilliant military exploit that was achieved on the Continent by English arms during the long interval which elapsed between the battle of Agincourt and that of Blenheim. His valour, his talents, his humane and generous disposition had made him the idol of his countrymen, and had extorted praise from the enemies whom he had conquered.* He had always been proud and headstrong; and his splendid success seems to have rendered his faults more offensive than ever. But to his friend Francis he was still the same. Bacon had some thoughts of making his fortune by marriage, and had begun to pay court to a widow of the name of Hatton. The eccentric manners and violent temper of this woman made her a disgrace and a torment to her connections. But Bacon was not aware of her faults, or was disposed to overlook them for the sake of her ample fortune. Essex pleaded his friend's cause with his usual ardour. The letters which the Earl addressed to Lady Hatton and to her mother are still extant, and are highly honourable to him. "If," he wrote, "she were my sister or my daughter, I protest I would as confidently resolve to further it as I now persuade you;" and again, "If my faith be anything, I protest, if I had one as near me as she is to you, I had rather match her with him than with men of far greater titles." The suit, happily for Bacon, was unsuccessful. The lady indeed was kind to him in more ways than one. She rejected him; and she accepted his enemy. She married that narrow-minded, bad-hearted pedant, Sir Edward Coke, and did her best to make him as miserable as he deserved to be.

The fortunes of Essex had now reached their height, and began to decline. He possessed indeed all the qualities which raise men to greatness rapidly. But he had neither the virtues nor the vices which enable men to retain greatness long. His frankness, his keen sensibility to insult and injustice, were by no means agreeable to a sovereign naturally impatient of opposition, and accustomed, during forty years, to the most extravagant flattery and the most abject submission. The daring and contemptuous manner in which he bade defiance to his enemies excited their deadly hatred. His administration in Ireland was unfortunate, and in many respects highly blamable. Though his brilliant courage and his impetuous activity fitted him admirably for such enterprises as that of Cadiz, he did not possess the caution, patience and resolution necessary for the conduct of a protracted war in which difficulties were to be gradually surmounted, in which much discomfort was to be endured, and in which few splendid exploits could be achieved. For the civil duties of his high place he was still less qualified. Though eloquent and accomplished, he was in no sense a statesman. The multitude indeed still continued to regard even his faults with fondness. But the Court had ceased to give him credit, even for the merit which he really possessed. The person on whom, during the decline of his influence, he chiefly depended—to whom he confided his perplexities, whose advice he solicited, whose intercession he employed—was his friend Bacon. The lamentable truth must be told. This friend, so loved, so trusted, bore a principal part in ruining the Earl's fortunes, in shedding his blood, and in blackening his memory.

But let us be just to Bacon. We believe that, to the last, he had no wish

* See Cervantes's Novela de la Espanola Inglesa.

to injure Essex. Nay, we believe that he sincerely exerted himself to serve Essex, as long as he thought that he could serve Essex without injuring himself. The advice which he gave to his noble benefactor was generally most judicious. He did all in his power to dissuade the Earl from accepting the Government of Ireland. "For," says he, "I did as plainly see his overthrow chained as it were by destiny to that journey, as it is possible for a man to ground a judgment upon future contingents." The prediction was accomplished. Essex returned in disgrace. Bacon attempted to mediate between his friend and the Queen; and, we believe, honestly employed all his address for that purpose. But the task which he had undertaken was too difficult, delicate and perilous even for so wary and dexterous an agent. He had to manage two spirits equally proud, resentful and ungovernable. At Essex House, he had to calm the rage of a young hero incensed by multiplied wrongs and humiliations, and then to pass to Whitehall for the purpose of soothing the peevishness of a sovereign, whose temper, never very gentle, had been rendered morbidly irritable by age, by declining health, and by the long habit of listening to flattery and exacting implicit obedience. It is hard to serve two masters. Situated as Bacon was, it was scarcely possible for him to shape his course so as not to give one or both of his employers reason to complain. For a time he acted as fairly as, in circumstances so embarrassing, could reasonably be expected. At length he found that, while he was trying to prop the fortunes of another, he was in danger of shaking his own. He had disobliged both the parties whom he wished to reconcile. Essex thought him wanting in zeal as a friend—Elizabeth thought him wanting in duty as a subject. The Earl looked on him as a spy of the Queen—the Queen as a creature of the Earl. The reconciliation which he had laboured to effect appeared utterly hopeless. A thousand signs, legible to eyes far less keen than his, announced that the fall of his patron was at hand. He shaped his course accordingly. When Essex was brought before the council to answer for his conduct in Ireland, Bacon, after a faint attempt to excuse himself from taking part against his friend, submitted himself to the Queen's pleasure, and appeared at the bar in support of the charges. But a darker scene was behind. The unhappy young nobleman, made reckless by despair, ventured on a rash and criminal enterprise which rendered him liable to the highest penalties of the law. What course was Bacon to take? This was one of those conjunctures which show what men are. To a high-minded man, wealth, power, court-favour, even personal safety, would have appeared of no account when opposed to friendship, gratitude and honour. Such a man would have stood by the side of Essex at the trial—would have "spent all his power, might, authority and amity" in soliciting a mitigation of the sentence—would have been a daily visitor at the cell—would have received the last injunctions and the last embrace on the scaffold—would have employed all the powers of his intellect to guard from insult the fame of his generous, though erring, friend. An ordinary man would neither have incurred the danger of succouring Essex, nor the disgrace of assailing him. Bacon did not even preserve neutrality. He appeared as counsel for the prosecution. In that situation, he did not confine himself to what would have been amply sufficient to procure a verdict. He employed all his wit, his rhetoric and his learning—not to insure a conviction—for the circumstances were such that a conviction was inevitable—but to deprive the unhappy prisoner of all those excuses which, though legally of no value, yet tended to diminish the moral guilt of the crime, and which, therefore, though they could not justify the peers in pronouncing an acquittal, might incline the Queen to grant a pardon. The Earl urged as a palliation of his frantic acts that he was surrounded by powerful and inveterate enemies, that they had ruined his fortunes; that they sought his life, and that their persecutions had driven him to despair. This was true, and Bacon well knew it to be true. But he affected to treat it as an idle pretence. He compared Essex to Pisistratus, who, by pretending to be in imminent danger of assassination, and by exhibiting self-inflicted wounds, succeeded in establishing tyranny at Athens. This was too much for the prisoner to bear. He interrupted his ungrateful friend by calling on him to quit the part of an advocate, to come forward as a witness, and to tell the Lords whether, in old times, he, Francis Bacon, had not, under his own hand, repeatedly asserted the truth of what he now represented as idle pretexts. It is painful to go on with this lamentable story. Bacon returned a shuffling answer to the Earl's question, and, as if the allusion to Pisistratus were not sufficiently offensive, made another allusion still more unjustifiable. He compared Essex to Henry, Duke of Guise, and the rash attempt in the city to the day of the barricades at Paris. Why Bacon had recourse to such a topic it is difficult to say. It was quite unnecessary for the purpose of obtaining a verdict. It was certain to produce a strong impression on the mind of the haughty and jealous princess on whose pleasure the Earl's fate depended. The faintest allusion to the degrading tutelage in which the last Valois had been held by the House of Lorraine was sufficient to harden her heart against a man who in rank, in military reputation, in popularity among the citizens of the capital, bore some resemblance to the Captain of the League. Essex was convicted. Bacon made no effort to save him, though the Queen's feelings were such that he might have pleaded his benefactor's cause, possibly with success, certainly without any serious danger to himself. The unhappy nobleman was executed. His fate excited strong, perhaps unreasonable, feelings of compassion and indignation. The Queen was received by the citizens of London with gloomy looks and faint acclamations. She thought it expedient to publish a vindication of her late proceedings. The faithless friend who had assisted in taking the Earl's life was now employed to murder the Earl's fame. The Queen had seen some of Bacon's writings, and had been pleased with them. He was accordingly selected to write "A Declaration of the Practices and Treasons attempted and committed by Robert, Earl of Essex," which was printed by authority. In the succeeding reign, Bacon had not a word to say in defence of this performance, a performance abounding in expressions which no generous enemy would have employed respecting a man who had so dearly expiated his offences. His only excuse was, that he wrote it by command—that he considered himself as a mere secretary—that he had particular instructions as to the way in which he was to treat every part of the subject—and that, in fact, he had furnished only the arrangement and the style.

We regret to say that the whole conduct of Bacon through the course of these transactions appears to Mr. Montagu not merely excusable, but deserving of high admiration. The integrity and benevolence of this gentlemen are so well known that our readers will probably be at a loss to conceive by what steps he can have arrived at so extraordinary a conclusion: and we are half afraid that they will suspect us of practising some artifice upon them when we report the principal arguments which he employs.

In order to get rid of the charge of ingratitude, Mr. Montagu attempts to show that Bacon lay under greater obligations to the Queen than to Essex. What these obligations were it is not easy to discover. The situation of Queen's Counsel and a remote reversion were surely favours very far below Bacon's personal and hereditary claims. They were favours which had not cost the Queen a groat, nor had they put a groat into Bacon's purse. It was necessary to rest Elizabeth's claims to gratitude on some other ground; and this Mr. Montagu felt. "What perhaps was her greatest kindness," says he, "instead of having hastily advanced Bacon, she had, with a continuance of her friendship, made him bear the yoke in his youth. Such were his obligations to Elizabeth." Such indeed they were. Being the son of one of her oldest and most faithful ministers—being himself the ablest and most accomplished young man of his time—he had been condemned by her to drudgery, to obscurity, to poverty. She had depreciated his acquirements. She had checked him in the most imperious manner, when in Parliament he ventured to act an independent part. She had refused to him the professional advancement to which he had a just claim. To her it was owing that, while younger men—not superior to him in extraction, and far inferior to him in every kind of personal merit—were filling the highest offices of the state, adding manor to manor, rearing palace after palace, he was lying at a sponging-house for a debt of three hundred pounds. Assuredly if Bacon owed gratitude to Elizabeth, he owed none to Essex. If the Queen really was his best friend, the Earl was his worst enemy. We wonder that Mr. Montagu did not press this argument a little further. He might have maintained that Bacon was excusable in revenging himself on a man who had attempted to rescue his youth from the salutary yoke imposed on it by the Queen—who had wished to advance him hastily—who, not content with attempting to inflict the Attorney-Generalship upon him, had been so cruel as to present him with a landed estate.

Again, we can hardly think Mr. Montagu serious when he tells us that Bacon was bound for the sake of the public not to destroy his own hopes of advancement; and that he took part against Essex from a wish to obtain power which might enable him to be useful to his country. We really do not know how to refute such arguments except by stating them. Nothing is impossible which does not involve a contradiction. It is barely possible that Bacon's motives for acting as he did on this occasion may have been gratitude to the Queen for keeping him poor and a desire to benefit his fellow-creatures in some high situation. And there is a possibility that Bonner may have been a good Protestant who, being convinced that the blood of martyrs is the seed of the Church, heroically went through all the drudgery and infamy of persecution that he might inspire the English people with an intense and lasting hatred of popery. There is a possibility that Jeffreys may have been an ardent lover of liberty, and that he may have beheaded Algernon Sydney and burned Elizabeth Gaunt only in order to produce a reaction which might lead to the limitation of the prerogative. There is a possibility that Thurtell may have killed Weare only in order to give the youth of England an impressive warning against gaming and bad company. There is a possibility that Fauntleroy may have forged powers of attorney only in order that his fate might turn the attention of the public to the defects of the penal law. These things, we say, are possible. But they are so extravagantly improbable that a man who should act on such suppositions would be fit only for Saint Luke's. And we do not see why suppositions on which no rational man would act in ordinary life should be admitted into history.

Mr. Montagu's notion that Bacon desired power only in order to do good to mankind appears somewhat strange to us, when we consider how Bacon afterwards used power, and how he lost it. Surely the service which he rendered to mankind by taking Lady Wharton's broad pieces and Sir John Kennedy's cabinet was not of such vast importance as to sanctify all the means which might conduce to that end. If the case were fairly stated, it would, we much fear, stand thus: Bacon was a servile advocate that he might be a corrupt judge.

Mr. Montagu conceives that none but the ignorant and unreflecting can think Bacon censurable for anything that he did as counsel for the Crown; and that no advocate can justifiably use any discretion as to the party for whom he appears. We will not at present inquire whether the doctrine which is held on this subject by English lawyers be or be not agreeable to reason and morality—whether it be right that a man should, with a wig on his head and a band round his neck, do for a guinea what, without those appendages, he would think it wicked and infamous to do for an empire—whether it be right that, not merely believing but knowing a statement to be true, he should do all that can be done by sophistry, by rhetoric, by solemn asseveration, by indignant exclamation, by gesture, by play of features, by terrifying one honest witness, by perplexing another, to cause a jury to think that statement false. It is not necessary on the present occasion to decide these questions. The professional rules, be they good or bad, are rules to which many wise and virtuous men have conformed, and are daily conforming. If, therefore, Bacon did no more than these rules required of him, we shall readily admit that he was blameless. But we conceive that his conduct was not justifiable according to any professional rules that now exist, or that ever existed in England. It has always been held that in criminal cases, in which the prisoner was denied the help of counsel, and, above all, in capital cases, advocates were both entitled and bound to exercise a discretion. It is true that after the Revolution, when the Parliament began to make inquisition for the innocent blood which had been shed by the last Stuarts, a feeble attempt was made to defend the lawyers who had been accomplices in the murder of Sir Thomas Armstrong, on the ground that they had only acted professionally. The wretched sophism was silenced by the execrations of the House of Commons. "Things will never be well done," said Mr. Foley, "till some of that profession be made examples." "We have a new sort of monsters in the world," said the younger Hampden, "haranguing a man to death. These I call bloodhounds. Sawyer is very criminal and guilty of this murder." "I speak to discharge my conscience," said Mr. Garroway. "I will not have the blood of this man at my door. Sawyer demanded judgment against him and execution. I believe him guilty of the death of this man. Do what you will with him." "If the profession of the law," said the elder Hampden, "gives a man authority to murder at this rate, it is the interest of all men to rise and exterminate that profession." Nor was this language held only by unlearned country gentlemen. Sir William Williams, one of the ablest and most unscrupulous lawyers of the age, took the same view of the case. He had not hesitated, he said, to take part in the prosecution of the Bishops, because they were allowed counsel. But he maintained that, where the prisoner was not allowed counsel, the Counsel for the Crown was bound to exercise a discretion; and that every lawyer who neglected this distinction was a betrayer of the law. But it is unnecessary to cite authority. It is known to everybody who has ever looked into a court of quarter-sessions that lawyers do exercise a discretion in criminal cases; and it is plain to every man of common sense that, if they did not exercise such a discretion, they would be a more hateful body of men than those bravoes who used to hire out their stilettoes in Italy.

Bacon appeared against a man who was indeed guilty of a great offence, but who had been his benefactor and friend. He did more than this. Nay, he did more than a person who had never seen Essex would have been justified in doing. He employed all the art of an advocate in order to make the prisoner's conduct appear more inexcusable and more dangerous to the state than it really had been. All that professional duty could, in any case, have required of him would have been to conduct the cause so as to insure a conviction. But from the nature of the circumstances there could not be the smallest doubt that the Earl would be found guilty. The character of the crime was unequivocal. It had been committed recently—in broad daylight—in the streets of the capital—in the presence of thousands. If ever there was an occasion on which an advocate had no temptation to resort to extraneous topics for the purpose of blinding the judgment and inflaming the passions of a tribunal, this was that occasion. Why then resort to arguments which, while they could add nothing to the strength of the case, considered in a legal point of view, tended to aggravate the moral guilt of the fatal enterprise, and to excite fear and resentment in that quarter from which alone the Earl could now expect mercy? Why remind the audience of the arts of the ancient tyrants? Why deny, what everybody knew to be the truth, that a powerful faction at court had long sought to effect the ruin of the prisoner? Why, above all, institute a parallel between the unhappy culprit and the most wicked and most successful rebel of the age? Was it absolutely impossible to do all that professional duty required without reminding a jealous sovereign of the League, of the barricades, and of all the humiliations which a too powerful subject had heaped on Henry the Third?

But if we admit the plea which Mr. Montagu urges in defence of what Bacon did as an advocate, what shall we say of the "Declaration of the Treasons of Robert, Earl of Essex?" Here at least there was no pretence of professional obligation. Even those who may think it the duty of a lawyer to hang, draw and quarter his benefactors for a proper consideration, will hardly say that it is his duty to write abusive pamphlets against them after they are in their graves. Bacon excused himself by saying that he was not answerable for the matter of the book, and that he furnished only the language. But why did he endow such purposes with words? Could no hack writer, without virtue or shame, be found to exaggerate the errors, already so dearly expiated, of a gentle and noble spirit? Every age produces those links between the man and the baboon. Every age is fertile of Concanens, of Gildons and of Antony Pasquins. But was it for Bacon so to prostitute his intellect? Could he not feel that, while he rounded and pointed some period dictated by the envy of Cecil, or gave a plausible form to some slander invented by the dastardly malignity of Cobham, he was not sinning merely against his friend's honour and his own? Could he not feel that letters, eloquence, philosophy, were all degraded in his degradation?

The real explanation of all this is perfectly obvious; and nothing but a partiality amounting to a ruling passion could cause anybody to miss it. The moral qualities of Bacon were not of a high order. We do not say that he was a bad man. He was not inhuman or tyrannical. He bore with meekness his high civil honours, and the far higher honours gained by his intellect. He was very seldom, if ever, provoked into treating any person with malignity and insolence. No man more readily held up the left cheek to those who had smitten the right. No man was more expert at the soft answer which turneth away wrath. He was never accused of intemperance in his pleasures. His even temper, his flowing courtesy, the general respectability of his demeanour made a favourable impression on those who saw him in situations which do not severely try the principles. His faults were—we write it with pain—coldness of heart and meanness of spirit. He seems to have been incapable of feeling strong affection, of facing great dangers, of making great sacrifices. His desires were set on things below. Wealth, precedence, titles, patronage—the mace, the seals, the coronet—large houses, fair gardens, rich manors, massy services of plate, gay hangings, curious cabinets—had as great attractions for him as for any of the courtiers who dropped on their knees in the dirt when Elizabeth passed by and then hastened home to write to the King of Scots that her Grace seemed to be breaking fast. For these objects he had stooped to everything and endured everything. For these he had sued in the humblest manner, and, when unjustly and ungraciously repulsed, had thanked those who had repulsed him, and had began to sue again. For these objects, as soon as he found that the smallest show of independence in parliament was offensive to the Queen, he had abased himself to the dust before her, and implored forgiveness in terms better suited to a convicted thief than to a knight of the shire. For these he joined, and far these he forsook, Lord Essex. He continued to plead his patron's cause with the queen as long as he thought that by pleading that cause he might serve himself. Nay, he went further, for his feelings, though not warm, were kind; he pleaded that cause as long as he thought that he could plead it without injury to himself. But when it became evident that Essex was going headlong to his ruin, Bacon began to tremble for his own fortunes. What he had to fear would not indeed have been very alarming to a man of lofty character. It was not death. It was not imprisonment. It was the loss of court favour. It was the being left behind by others in the career of ambition. It was the having leisure to finish the "Instauratio Magna." The Queen looked coldly on him. The courtiers began to consider him as a marked man. He determined to change his line of conduct, and to proceed in a new course with so much vigour as to make up for lost time. When once he had determined to act against his friend, knowing himself to be suspected, he acted with more zeal than would have been necessary or justifiable if he had been employed against a stranger. He exerted his professional talents to shed the Earl's blood, and his literary talents to blacken the Earl's memory. It is certain that his conduct excited at the time great and general disapprobation. While Elizabeth lived, indeed, this disapprobation, though deeply felt, was not loudly expressed. But a great change was at hand.

The health of the Queen had long been decaying; and the operation of age and disease was now assisted by acute mental suffering. The pitiable melancholy of her last days has generally been ascribed to her fond regret for Essex. But we are disposed to attribute her dejection partly to physical causes and partly to the conduct of her courtiers and ministers. They did all in their power to conceal from her the intrigues which they were carrying on at the Court of Scotland. But her keen sagacity was not to be so deceived. She did not know the whole. But she knew that she was surrounded by men who were impatient for that new world which was to begin at her death, who had never been attached to her by affection, and who were now but very slightly attached to her by interest. Prostration and flattery could not conceal from her the cruel truth, that those whom she had trusted and promoted had never loved her and were fast ceasing to fear her. Unable to avenge herself, and too proud to complain, she suffered sorrow and resentment to prey on her heart, till, after a long career of power, prosperity and glory, she died, sick and weary of the world.

James mounted the throne: and Bacon employed all his address to obtain for himself a share of the favour of his new master. This was no difficult task. The faults of James, both as a man and as a prince, were numerous; but insensibility to the claims of genius and learning was not among them. He was indeed made up of two men, a witty, well-read scholar, who wrote, disputed and harangued, and a nervous, drivelling idiot, who acted. If he had been a Canon of Christ Church, or a Prebendary of Westminster, it is not improbable that he would have left a highly respectable name to posterity, that he would have distinguished himself among the translators of the Bible, and among the Divines who attended the Synod of Dort ; and that he would have been regarded by the literary world as no contemptible rival of Vossius and Casaubon. But fortune placed him in a situation in which his weakness covered him with disgrace, and in which his accomplishments brought him no honour. In a college, much eccentricity and childishness would have been readily pardoned in so learned a man. But all that learning could do for him on the throne was to make people think him a pedant as well as a fool.

Bacon was favourably received at Court ; and soon found that his chance of promotion was not diminished by the death of the Queen. He was solicitous to be knighted, for two reasons which are somewhat amusing. The King had already dubbed half London, and Bacon found himself the only untitled person in his mess at Gray's Inn. This was not very agreeable to him. He had also, to quote his own words, "found an Alderman's daughter a handsome maiden, to his liking." On both these grounds, he begged his cousin, Robert Cecil, "if it might please his good Lordship," to use his interest in his behalf. The application was successful. Bacon was one of three hundred gentlemen who, on the coronation-day, received the honour, if it is to be so called, of knighthood. The handsome maiden, a daughter of Alderman Barnham, soon after consented to become Sir Francis's lady.

The death of Elizabeth, though on the whole it improved Bacon's prospects, was in one respect an unfortunate event for him. The new King had always felt kindly towards Lord Essex, who had been zealous for the Scotch Succession ; and, as soon as he came to the throne, began to show favour to the House of Devereux, and to those who had stood by that house in its adversity. Everybody was now at liberty to speak out respecting those lamentable events in which Bacon had borne so large a share. Elizabeth was scarcely cold when the public feeling began to manifest itself by marks of respect towards Lord Southampton. That accomplished nobleman, who will be remembered to the latest ages as the generous and discerning patron of Shakspeare, was held in honour by his contemporaries chiefly on account of the devoted affection which he had borne to Essex. He had been tried and convicted together with his friend ; but the Queen had spared his life, and, at the time of her death, he was still a prisoner. A crowd of visitors hastened to the Tower to congratulate him on his approaching deliverance. With that crowd Bacon could not venture to mingle. The multitude loudly condemned him ; and his conscience told him that the multitude had but too much reason. He excused himself to Southampton by letter, in terms which, if he had, as Mr. Montagu conceives, done only what as a subject and an advocate he was bound to do, must be considered as shamefully servile. He owns his fear that his attendance would give offence, and that his professions of regard would obtain no credit. "Yet," says he, "it is as true as a thing that God knoweth, that this great change hath wrought in me no other change towards your Lordship than this, that I may safely be that to you now which I was truly before."

How Southampton received these apologies we are not informed. But it is certain that the general opinion was pronounced again Bacon in a manner not to be misunderstood. Soon after his marriage he put forth a defence of his conduct in the form of a "Letter to the Earl of Devon." This tract seems to us to prove only the exceeding badness of a cause for which such talents could do so little.

It is not probable that Bacon's defence had much effect on his contemporaries. But the unfavourable impression which his conduct had made appears to have been gradually effaced. Indeed it must be some very peculiar cause that can make a man like him long unpopular. His talents secured him from contempt, his temper and his manners from hatred. There is scarcely any story so black that it may not be got over by a man of great abilities, whose abilities are united with caution, good humour, patience and affability—who pays daily sacrifice to Nemesis—who is a delightful companion, a serviceable, though not an ardent, friend, and a dangerous, yet a placable, enemy. Waller, in the next generation, was an eminent instance of this. Indeed Waller had much more than may at first sight appear in common with Bacon. To the higher intellectual qualities of the great English philosopher—to the genius which has made an immortal epoch in the history of science—Waller had indeed no pretensions. But the mind of Waller, as far as it extended, coincided with that of Bacon, and might, so to speak, have been cut out of that of Bacon. In the qualities which make a man an object of interest and veneration to posterity, there was no comparison between them. But in the qualities by which chiefly a man is known to his contemporaries there was a striking similarity. Considered as men of the world, as courtiers, as politicians, as associates, as allies, as enemies, they had nearly the same merits and the same defects. They were not malignant. They were not tyrannical. But they wanted warmth of affection and elevation of sentiment. There were many things which they loved better than virtue and which they feared more than guilt. Yet, even after they had stooped to acts of which it is impossible to read the account in the most partial narratives without strong disapprobation and contempt, the public still continued to regard them with a feeling not easily to be distinguished from esteem. The hyperbole of Juliet seemed to be verified with respect to them. "Upon their brows shame was ashamed to sit." Everybody seemed as desirous to throw a veil over their misconduct as if it had been his own. Clarendon, who felt, and who had reason to feel, strong personal dislike towards Waller, speaks of him thus: "There needs no more to be said to extol the excellence and power of his wit and pleasantness of his conversation, than that it was of magnitude enough to cover a world of very great faults—that is, so to cover them that they were not taken notice of to his reproach—viz., a narrowness in his nature to the lowest degree, an abjectness and want of courage to support him in any virtuous undertaking— an insinuation and servile flattery to the height the vainest and most imperious nature could be contented with. . . . It had power to reconcile him to those whom he had most offended and provoked, and continued to his age with that rare felicity, that his company was acceptable where his spirit was odious, and he was at least pitied where he was most detested." Much of this, with some softening, might, we fear, be applied to Bacon. The influence of Waller's talents, manners and accomplishments died with him; and the world has pronounced an unbiassed sentence on his character. A few flowing lines are not bribe sufficient to pervert the judgment of posterity. But the influence of Bacon is felt, and will long be felt, over the whole civilised world. Leniently as he was treated by his contemporaries, posterity has treated him more leniently still. Turn where we may, the trophies of that mighty intellect are full in view. We are judging Manlius in sight of the Capitol.

Under the reign of James, Bacon grew rapidly in fortune and favour. In 1604 he was appointed King's Counsel with a fee of forty pounds a year, and a pension of sixty pounds a year was settled upon him. In 1607 he became Solicitor-General, in 1612 Attorney-General. He continued to distinguish himself in Parliament, particularly by his exertions in favour of one excellent measure on which the King's heart was set, the union of England and Scotland. It was not difficult for such an intellect to discover many irresistible arguments in favour of such a scheme. He conducted the great case of the *Post Nati* in the Exchequer Chamber; and the decision of the judges—a decision the legality of which may be questioned, but the beneficial effect of which must be acknowledged—was in a great measure attributed to his dexterous management. While actively engaged in the House of Commons and in the courts of law, he still found leisure for letters and philosophy. The noble treatise on the "Advancement of Learning," which at a later period was expanded into the "De Augmentis," appeared in 1605. The "Wisdom of the Ancients," a work which, if it had proceeded from any other writer would have been considered as a masterpiece of wit and learning, but which adds little to the fame of Bacon, was printed in 1609. In the meantime the "Novum Organum" was slowly proceeding. Several distinguished men of learning had been permitted to see sketches or detached portions of that extraordinary book; and, though they were not generally disposed to admit the soundness of the author's views, they spoke with the greatest admiration of his genius. Sir Thomas Bodley, the founder of one of the most magnificent of English libraries, was among those stubborn Conservatives who considered the hopes with which Bacon looked forward to the future destinies of the human race as utterly chimerical, and who regarded with distrust and aversion the innovating spirit of the new schismatics in philosophy. Yet even Bodley, after perusing the "Cogitata et Visa," one of the most precious of those scattered leaves out of which the great oracular volume was afterwards made up, acknowledged that in "those very points, and in all proposals and plots in that book, Bacon showed himself a master-workman;" and that "it could not be gainsaid but all the treatise over did abound with choice conceits of the present state of learning, and with worthy contemplations of the means to procure it." In 1612 a new edition of the "Essays" appeared, with additions surpassing the original collection both in bulk and quality. Nor did these pursuits distract Bacon's attention from a work, the most arduous, the most glorious and the most useful that even his mighty powers could have achieved, "the reducing and recompiling," to use his own phrase, "of the laws of England."

Unhappily he was at that very time employed in perverting those laws to the vilest purposes of tyranny. When Oliver St. John was brought before the Star Chamber for maintaining that the King had no right to levy benevolences, and was for his manly and constitutional conduct sentenced to imprisonment during the royal pleasure and to a fine of five thousand pounds, Bacon appeared as counsel for the prosecution. About the same time he was deeply engaged in a still more disgraceful transaction. An aged clergyman, of the name of Peacham, was accused of treason on account of some passages of a sermon which was found in his study. The sermon, whether written by him or not, had never been preached. It did not appear that he had any intention of preaching it. The most servile lawyers of those servile times were forced to admit that there were great difficulties both as to the facts and as to the law. Bacon was employed to remove those difficulties. He was employed to settle the question of law by tampering with the Judges and the question of fact by torturing the prisoner. Three judges of the Court of King's Bench were tractable. But Coke was made of different stuff. Pedant, bigot and brute as he was, he had qualities which bore a strong, though a very disagreeable, resemblance to some of the highest virtues which a public man can possess. He was an exception to a maxim which we believe to be generally true—that those who trample on the helpless are disposed to cringe to the powerful. He behaved with gross rudeness to his juniors at the bar, and with execrable cruelty to prisoners on trial for their lives. But he stood up manfully against the King and the King's favourites. No man of that age appeared to so little advantage when he was opposed to an inferior and was in the wrong. But, on the other hand, it is but fair to admit that no man of that age made so creditable a figure when he was opposed to a superior and happened to be in the right. On such occasions, his half-suppressed insolence and his impracticable obstinacy had a respectable and interesting appearance, when compared with the abject servility of the bar and of the bench. On the present occasion he was stubborn and surly. He declared that it was a new and highly improper practice in the Judges to confer with a law-officer of the Crown about capital cases which they were afterwards to try, and for some time he resolutely kept aloof. But Bacon was equally artful and persevering. "I am not wholly out of hope," said he in a letter to the King, "that my Lord Coke himself, when I have in some dark manner put him in doubt that he shall be left alone, will not be singular." After some time Bacon's dexterity was successful, and Coke, sullenly and reluctantly, followed the example of his brethren. But in order to convict Peacham it was necessary to find facts as well as law. Accordingly, this wretched old man was put to the rack, and, while undergoing the horrible infliction, was examined by Bacon, but in vain. No confession could be wrung out of him, and Bacon wrote to the King, complaining that Peacham had a dumb devil. At length the trial came on. A conviction was obtained; but the charges were so obviously futile that the government could not, for very shame, carry the sentence into execution, and Peacham was suffered to languish away the short remainder of his life in a prison.

All this frightful story Mr. Montagu relates fairly. He neither conceals nor distorts any material fact. But he can see nothing deserving of condemnation in Bacon's conduct. He tells us most truly that we ought not to try the men of one age by the standard of another; that Sir Matthew Hale is not to be pronounced a bad man because he left a woman to be executed for witchcraft; that posterity will not be justified in censuring judges of our time for selling offices in their courts, according to the established practice, bad as that practice was—and that Bacon is entitled to similar indulgence. "To persecute the lover of truth," says Mr. Montagu, "for opposing established customs, and to censure him in after ages for not having been more strenuous in opposition, are errors which will never cease until the pleasure of self-elevation from the depression of superiority is no more."

We have no dispute with Mr. Montagu about the general proposition. We assent to every word of it. But does it apply to the present case? Is it true that in the time of James I. it was the established practice for the law-officers of the Crown to hold private consultations with the judges touching capital cases which those judges were afterwards to try? Certainly not. In the very page in which Mr. Montagu asserts that "the influencing a judge out of court seems at that period scarcely to have been considered as improper," he gives the very words of Sir Edward Coke on the subject. "I will not thus declare what may be my judgment by these auricular confessions of *new* and pernicious tendency, and *not according to the customs of the realm.*" Is it possible to imagine that Coke—who had himself been Attorney-General during thirteen years, who had conducted a far greater number of important state-prosecutions than any other lawyer named in English history, and who had passed with scarcely any interval from the Attorney-Generalship to the first seat in the first criminal court in the realm—could have been startled at an invitation to confer with the crown-lawyers, and could have pronounced the practice new, if it had really been an established usage? We well know that, where property only was at stake, it was then a common, though a most culpable, practice in the judges to listen to private solicitation. But the practice of tampering with judges in order to procure capital convictions we believe to have been new, first, because Coke, who understood those matters better than any man of his time, asserted it to be new; and secondly, because neither Bacon nor Mr. Montagu has shown a single precedent.

How then stands the case? Even thus: Bacon was not conforming to an usage then generally admitted to be proper. He was not even the last lingering adherent of an old abuse. It would have been sufficiently disgraceful to such a man to be in this last situation. Yet this last situation would have been honourable compared with that in which he stood. He was guilty of attempting to introduce into the courts of law an odious abuse for which no precedent could be found. Intellectually, he was better fitted than any man that England has ever produced for the work of improving her institutions. But, unhappily, we see that he did not scruple to exert his great powers for the purpose of introducing into those institutions new corruptions of the foulest kind.

The same, or nearly the same, may be said of the torturing of Peacham. If it be true that in the time of James I. the propriety of torturing prisoners was generally allowed, we should admit this as an excuse, though we should admit it less readily in the case of such a man as Bacon than in the case of an ordinary lawyer or politician. But the fact is that the practice of torturing prisoners was then generally acknowledged by lawyers to be illegal and was execrated by the public as barbarous. More than thirty years before Peacham's trial that practice was so loudly condemned by the voice of the nation that Lord Burleigh found it necessary to publish an apology for having occasionally resorted to it.* But, though the dangers which then threatened the government were of a very different kind from those which were to be apprehended from anything that Peacham could write—though the life of the Queen and the dearest interests of the state were in jeopardy—though the circumstances were such that all ordinary laws might seem to be superseded by that highest law, the public safety—the apology did not satisfy the country: and the queen found it expedient to issue an order positively forbidding the torturing of state-prisoners on any pretence whatever. From that time, the practice of torturing, which had always been unpopular, which had always been illegal, had also been unusual. It is well known that in 1628, only fourteen years after the time when Bacon went to the Tower to listen to the yells of Peacham, the judges decided that Felton, a criminal who neither deserved nor was likely to obtain any extraordinary indulgence, could not lawfully be put to the question. We, therefore, say that Bacon stands in a very different situation from that in which Mr. Montagu tries to place him. Bacon was here distinctly behind his age. He was one of the last of the tools of power who persisted in a practice the most barbarous and the most absurd that has ever disgraced jurisprudence—in a practice of which, in the preceding generation, Elizabeth and her ministers had been ashamed—in a practice which, a few years later, no sycophant in all the Inns of Court had the heart or the forehead to defend.

Bacon far behind his age! Bacon far behind Sir Edward Coke! Bacon clinging to exploded abuses! Bacon withstanding the progress of improvement! Bacon struggling to push back the human mind! The words seem strange. They sound like a contradiction in terms. Yet the fact is even so: and the explanation may be readily found by any person who is not blinded by prejudice. Mr. Montagu cannot believe that so extraordinary a man as Bacon could be guilty of a bad action; as if history were not made up of the bad actions of extraordinary men—as if all the most noted destroyers and deceivers of our species, all the founders of arbitrary governments and false religions had not been extraordinary men—as if nine-tenths of the calamities which have befallen the human race had any other origin than the union of high intelligence with low desires.

Bacon knew this well. He has told us that there are persons "scientia

---

* This paper is contained in the Harleian Miscellany. It is dated 1583.

tanquam angeli alati, cupiditatibus vero tanquam serpentes qui humi reptant";* and it did not require his admirable sagacity and his extensive converse with mankind to make the discovery. Indeed, he had only to look within. The difference between the soaring angel and the creeping snake was but a type of the difference between Bacon the philosopher and Bacon the Attorney-General —Bacon seeking for truth and Bacon seeking for the Seals. Those who survey only one-half of his character may speak of him with unmixed admiration or with unmixed contempt. But those only judge of him correctly who take in at one view Bacon in speculation and Bacon in action. They will have no difficulty in comprehending how one and the same man should have been far before his age and far behind it—in one line the boldest and most useful of innovators—in another one the most obstinate champion of the foulest abuses. In his library, all his rare powers were under the guidance of an honest ambition—of an enlarged philanthrophy—of a sincere love of truth. There, no temptation drew him away from the right course. Thomas Aquinas could pay no fees—Duns Scotus could confer no peerages. The Master of the Sentences had no rich reversions in his gift. Far different was the situation of the great philosopher when he came forth from his study and his laboratory to mingle with the crowd which filled the galleries of Whitehall. In all that crowd there was no man equally qualified to render great and lasting services to mankind. But in all that crowd there was not a heart more set on things which no man ought to suffer to be necessary to his happiness— on things which can often be obtained only by the sacrifice of integrity and honour. To be the leader of the human race in the career of improvement— to found on the ruins of ancient intellectual dynasties a more prosperous and a more enduring empire—to be revered by the latest generations as the most illustrious among the benefactors of mankind—all this was within his reach. But all this availed him nothing while some quibbling special pleader was promoted before him to the bench—while some heavy country gentleman took precedence of him by virtue of a purchased coronet—while some pander, happy in a fair wife, could obtain a more cordial salute from Buckingham— while some buffoon, versed in all the latest scandal of the court, could draw a louder laugh from James.

During a long course of years, Bacon's unworthy ambition was crowned with success. His sagacity early enabled him to perceive who was likely to become the most powerful man in the kingdom. He probably knew the King's mind before it was known to the King himself, and attached himself to Villiers while the less discerning crowd of courtiers still continued to fawn on Somerset. The influence of the younger favourite became greater daily. The contest between the rivals might, however, have lasted long, but for that frightful crime which, in spite of all that could be effected by the research and ingenuity of historians, is still covered with so mysterious an obscurity. The descent of Somerset had been a gradual and almost imperceptible lapse. It now became a headlong fall; and Villiers, left without a competitor, rapidly rose to a height of power such as no subject since Wolsey had attained.

There were many points of resemblance between the two celebrated courtiers who, at different times, extended their patronage to Bacon. It is difficult to say whether Essex or Villiers was more eminently distinguished by those graces of person and manner which have always been rated in courts at much more than their real value. Both were constitutionally brave; and both, like most men who are constitutionally brave, were open and unreserved. Both were rash and headstrong. Both were destitute of the abilities and of

---

* De Augmentis, Lib. v. Cap. 1.

the information which are necessary to statesmen. Yet both, trusting to the accomplishments which had made them conspicuous in tilt-yards and ballrooms, aspired to rule the state. Both owed their elevation to the personal attachment of the sovereign; and in both cases this attachment was of so eccentric a kind that it perplexed observers—that it still continues to perplex historians—and that it gave rise to much scandal which we are inclined to think unfounded. Each of them treated the sovereign whose favour he enjoyed with a rudeness which approached to insolence. This petulance ruined Essex, who had to deal with a spirit naturally as proud as his own and accustomed, during nearly half a century, to the most respectful observance. But there was a wide difference between the haughty daughter of Henry and her successor. James was timid from the cradle. His nerves, naturally weak, had not been fortified by reflection or by habit. His life, till he came to England, had been a series of mortifications and humiliations. With all his high notions of the origin and extent of his prerogatives, he was never his own master for a day. In spite of his kingly title, in spite of his despotic theories, he was to the last a slave at heart. Villiers treated him like one; and this course, though adopted, we believe, merely from temper, succeeded as well as if it had been a system of policy formed after mature deliberation.

In generosity, in sensibility, in capacity for friendship, Essex far surpassed Buckingham. Indeed, Buckingham can scarcely be said to have had any friend with the exception of the two princes over whom successively he exercised so wonderful an influence. Essex was to the last adored by the people. Buckingham was always a most unpopular man, except perhaps for a very short time after his return from the childish visit to Spain. Essex fell a victim to the rigour of the government amidst the lamentations of the people. Buckingham, execrated by the people, and solemnly declared a public enemy by the representatives of the people, fell by the hand of one of the people, and was lamented by none but his master.

The way in which the two favourites acted towards Bacon was highly characteristic, and may serve to illustrate the old and true saying—that a man is generally more inclined to feel kindly towards one on whom he has conferred favours than towards one from whom he has received them. Essex loaded Bacon with benefits, and never thought that he had done enough. It seems never to have crossed the mind of the powerful and wealthy noble that the poor barrister whom he treated with such munificent kindness was not his equal. It was, we have no doubt, with perfect sincerity that he declared that he would willingly give his sister or daughter in marriage to his friend. He was in general more than sufficiently sensible of his own merits; but he did not seem to know that he had ever deserved well of Bacon. On that cruel day when they saw each other for the last time at the bar of the Lords, Essex taxed his perfidious friend with unkindness and insincerity, but never with ingratitude. Even in such a moment, more bitter than the bitterness of death, that noble heart was too great to vent itself in such a reproach.

Villiers, on the other hand, owed much to Bacon. When their acquaintance began, Sir Francis was a man of mature age, of high station and of established fame as a politician, an advocate and a writer. Villiers was little more than a boy, a younger son of a house then of no great note. He was but just entering on the career of court favour; and none but the most discerning observers could as yet perceive that he was likely to distance all his competitors. The countenance and advice of a man so highly distinguished as the Attorney-General must have been an object of the highest importance to the young adventurer. But though Villiers was the obliged party, he was less warmly attached to Bacon, and far less delicate in his conduct towards Bacon, than Essex had been.

To do the new favourite justice, he early exerted his influence in behalf of his illustrious friend. In 1616 Sir Francis was sworn of the Privy Council, and in March, 1617, on the retirement of Lord Brackley, was appointed keeper of the Great Seal.

On the 7th of May, the first day of term, he rode in state to Westminster Hall, with the Lord Treasurer on his right hand, the Lord Privy Seal on his left, a long procession of students and ushers before him, and a crowd of peers, privy-councillors and judges following in his train. Having entered his court, he addressed the splendid auditory in a grave and dignified speech, which proves how well he understood those judicial duties which he afterwards performed so ill. Even at that moment—the proudest moment of his life in the estimation of the vulgar, and, it may be, even in his own—he cast back a look of lingering affection towards those noble pursuits from which, as it seemed, he was about to be estranged. "The depth of the three long vacations," said he, "I would reserve in some measure free from business of estate, and for studies, arts and sciences, to which of my own nature I am most inclined."

The years during which Bacon held the Great Seal were among the darkest and most shameful in English history. Everything at home and abroad was mismanaged. First came the execution of Raleigh; an act which, if done in a proper manner, might have been defensible, but which, under all the circumstances, must be considered as a dastardly murder. Worse was behind—the war of Bohemia—the successes of Tilly and Spinola—the Palatinate conquered—the King's son-in-law an exile—the house of Austria dominant on the Continent—the Protestant religion and the liberties of the Germanic body trodden under foot. In the meantime the wavering and cowardly policy of England furnished matter of ridicule to all the nations of Europe. The love of peace which James professed would, even when indulged to an impolitic excess, have been respectable if it had proceeded from tenderness for his people. But the truth is that, while he had nothing to spare for the defence of the natural allies of England, he resorted without scruple to the most illegal and oppressive devices for the purpose of enabling Buckingham and Buckingham's relations to outshine the ancient aristocracy of the realm. Benevolences were exacted. Patents of monopoly were multiplied. All the resources which could have been employed to replenish a beggared exchequer at the close of a ruinous war were put in motion during this season of ignominious peace.

The vices of the administration must be chiefly ascribed to the weakness of the King and to the levity and violence of the favourite. But it is impossible to acquit the Lord Keeper. For those odious patents, in particular, which passed the Great Seal while it was in his charge, he must be held answerable. In the speech which he made on first taking his seat in his court, he had pledged himself to discharge this important part of his functions with the greatest caution and impartiality. He had declared that he "would walk in the light," "that men should see that no particular turn or end led him, but a general rule." Mr. Montagu would have us believe that Bacon acted up to these professions. He says that "the power of the favourite did not deter the Lord Keeper from staying grants and patents when his public duty demanded this interposition." Does Mr. Montagu consider patents of monopoly as good things? or does he mean to say that Bacon stayed every patent of monopoly that came before him? Of all patents in our history, the most disgraceful was that which was granted to Sir Giles Mompesson—supposed to be the original of Massinger's Overreach—and to Sir Francis Michell—from whom Justice Greedy is supposed to have been drawn—for the exclusive manufacturing of gold and silver lace. The effect of this monopoly was of course that the metal employed in the manufacture was adulterated, to the great loss of the public. But this was a trifle. The patentees were armed with powers as great as have ever been given to farmers of the revenue in the worst governed countries. They were authorised to search houses and to arrest interlopers; and these formidable powers were used for purposes viler than even those for which they were given—for the wreaking of old grudges, and for the corrupting of female chastity. Was not this a case in which public duty demanded the interposition of the Lord Keeper? And did the Lord Keeper interpose? He did. He wrote to inform the King that he "had considered of the fitness and conveniency of the gold and silver thread business"—"that it was convenient that it should be settled"—that he "did conceive apparent likelihood that it would redound much to his Majesty's profit"—that, therefore, "it were good it were settled with all convenient speed." The meaning of all this was, that certain of the house of Villiers were to go shares with Overreach and Greedy in the plunder of the public. This was the way in which, when the favourite pressed for patents—lucrative to his relations and to his creatures, ruinous and vexatious to the body of the people—the chief guardian of the laws interposed. Having assisted the patentees to obtain this monopoly, Bacon assisted them also in the steps which they took for the purpose of guarding it. He committed several people to close confinement for disobeying his tyrannical edict. It is needless to say more. Our readers are now able to judge whether, in the matter of patents, Bacon acted conformably to his professions, or deserved the praise which his biographer has bestowed on him.

In his judicial capacity his conduct was not less reprehensible. He suffered Buckingham to dictate many of his decisions. Bacon knew as well as any man that a judge who listens to private solicitations is a disgrace to his post. He had himself, before he was raised to the woolsack, represented this strongly to Villiers, then just entering on his career. "By no means," said Sir Francis, in a letter of advice addressed to the young courtier—"by no means be you persuaded to interpose yourself, either by word or letter, in any cause depending in any court of justice, nor suffer any great man to do it where you can hinder it. If it should prevail, it perverts justice; but if the judge be so just, and of such courage as he ought to be, as not to be inclined thereby, yet it always leaves a taint of suspicion behind it." Yet he had not been Lord Keeper a month when Buckingham began to interfere in chancery suits, and his interference was, as might have been expected, successful.

Mr. Montagu's reflections on the excellent passage which we have quoted above are exceedingly amusing. "No man," says he, "more deeply felt the evils which then existed of the interference of the Crown and of statesmen to influence judges. How beautifully did he admonish Buckingham, regardless as he proved of all admonition!" We should be glad to know how it can be expected that admonition will be regarded by him who receives it when it is altogether neglected by him who gives it. We do not defend Buckingham; but what was his guilt to Bacon's? Buckingham was young, ignorant, thoughtless—dizzy with the rapidity of his ascent and the height of his position. That he should be eager to serve his relations, his flatterers, his mistresses—that he should not fully apprehend the immense importance of a pure administration of justice—that he should think more about those who were bound to him by private ties than about the public interest—all this was perfectly natural and not altogether unpardonable. Those who intrust a petulant, hot-blooded, ill-informed lad with power, are more to blame than he for the mischief which he may do with it. How could it be expected of a lively page, raised by a wild freak of fortune to the first influence in the empire, that he should have bestowed any serious thought on the principles which ought to guide judicial decisions? Bacon was the ablest public man then living in Europe. He was nearly sixty years old. He had though much, and to good purpose, on the general principles of law. He had for many years borne a part daily in the administration of justice. It was impossible that a man with a tithe of his sagacity and experience should not have known that a judge who suffers friends or patrons to dictate his decrees violates the plainest rules of duty. In fact, as we have seen, he knew this well: he expressed it admirably. Neither on this occasion, nor on any other, could his bad actions be attributed to any defect of the head. They sprang from quite a different cause.

A man who stooped to render such services to others was not likely to be scrupulous as to the means by which he enriched himself. He and his dependents accepted large presents from persons who were engaged in Chancery suits. The amount of the plunder which he collected in this way it is impossible to estimate. There can be no doubt that he received very much more than was proved on his trial, though, it may be, less than was suspected by the public. His enemies stated his illicit gains at a hundred thousand pounds. But this was probably an exaggeration.

It was long before the day of reckoning arrived. During the interval between the second and third Parliaments of James, the nation was absolutely governed by the Crown. The prospects of the Lord Keeper were bright and serene. His great place rendered the splendour of his talents even more conspicuous, and gave an additional charm to the serenity of his temper, the courtesy of his manners and the eloquence of his conversation. The pillaged suitor might mutter. The austere Puritan patriot might, in his retreat, grieve that one on whom God had bestowed without measure all the abilities which qualify men to take the lead in great reforms should be found among the adherents of the worst abuses. But the murmurs of the suitor and the lamentations of the patriot had scarcely any avenue to the ears of the powerful. The king, and the minister who was the King's master, smiled on their illustrious flatterer. The whole crowd of courtiers and nobles sought his favour with emulous eagerness. Men of wit and learning hailed with delight the elevation of one who had so signally shown that a man of profound learning and of brilliant wit might understand, far better than any plodding dunce, the art of thriving in the world.

Once, and but once, this course of prosperity was for a moment interrupted. It would seem that even Bacon's brain was not strong enough to bear, without some discomposure the inebriating effect of so much good fortune. For some time after his elevation, he showed himself a little wanting in that wariness and self-command to which, more than even to his transcendent talents, his elevation was to be ascribed. He was by no means a good hater. The temperature of his revenge, like that of his gratitude, was scarcely ever more than lukewarm. But there was one person whom he had long regarded with an animosity which, though studiously suppressed, was perhaps the stronger for the suppression. The insults and injuries which, when a young man struggling into note and professional practice, he had received from Sir Edward Coke, were such as might move the most placable nature to resentment. About the time at which Bacon received the Seals, Coke had, on account of his contumacious resistance to the royal pleasure, been deprived of his seat in the Court of King's Bench, and had ever since languished in retirement. But Coke's opposition to the Court, we fear, was the effect not of good principles, but of a bad temper. Perverse and testy as he was, he wanted true fortitude and dignity of character. His obstinacy, unsupported by virtuous motives, was not proof against disgrace. He solicited a reconciliation with the favourite, and his solicitations were successful. Sir John Villiers, the brother of Buckingham, was looking out for a rich wife. Coke had a large fortune and an unmarried daughter. A bargain was struck. But Lady Coke—the lady whom twenty years before Essex had wooed on behalf of Bacon—would not hear of the match. A violent and scandalous family quarrel followed. The mother carried the girl away by stealth. The father pursued them, and regained possession of his daughter by force. The King was then in Scotland, and Buckingham had attended him thither. Bacon was, during their absence, at the head of affairs in England. He felt towards Coke as much malevolence as it was in his nature to feel towards anybody. His wisdom had been laid to sleep by prosperity. In an evil hour he determined to interfere in the disputes which agitated his enemy's household. He declared for the wife, countenanced the Attorney-General in filing an information in the Star Chamber against the husband, and wrote strongly to the King and the favourite against the proposed marriage. The language which he used in those letters shows that, sagacious as he was, he did not quite know his place, that he was not fully acquainted with the extent either of Buckingham's power, or of the change which the possession of that power had produced in Buckingham's character. He soon had a lesson which he never forgot. The favourite received the news of the Lord Keeper's interference with feelings of the most violent resentment, and made the King even more angry than himself. Bacon's eyes were at once opened to his error, and to all its possible consequences. He had been elated, if not intoxicated, by greatness. The shock sobered him in an instant. He was all himself again. He apologised submissively for his interference. He directed the Attorney-General to stop the proceedings against Coke. He sent to tell Lady Coke that he could do nothing for her. He announced to both the families that he was desirous to promote the connection. Having given these proofs of contrition, he ventured to present himself before Buckingham. But the young upstart did not think that he had yet sufficiently humbled an old man who had been his friend and his benefactor, who was the highest civil functionary in the realm, and the most eminent man of letters of the world. It is said that on two successive days Bacon repaired to Buckingham's house—that on two successive days he was suffered to remain in an antechamber among footboys, seated on an old wooden box, with the Great Seal of England at his side; and that when at length he was admitted, he flung himself on the floor, kissed the favourite's feet, and vowed never to rise till he was forgiven. Sir Anthony Weldon, on whose authority this story rests, is likely enough to have exaggerated the meanness of Bacon and the insolence of Buckingham. But it is difficult to imagine that so circumstantial a narrative, written by a person who avers that he was present on the occasion, can be wholly without foundation; and, unhappily, there is little in the character either of the favourite or of the Lord Keeper to make the narrative improbable. It is certain that are conciliation took place on terms humiliating to Bacon, who never more ventured to cross any purpose of anybody who bore the name of Villiers. He put a strong curb on those angry passions which had for the first time in his life mastered his prudence. He went through the forms of a reconciliation with Coke, and did his best, by seeking opportunities of paying little civilities, and by avoiding all that could produce collision, to tame the untamable ferocity of his old enemy.

In the main, however, his life, while he held the Great Seal, was, in outward appearance, most enviable. In London he lived with great dignity at York House, the venerable mansion of his father. Here it was that, in January, 1620, he celebrated his entrance into his sixtieth year amidst a splendid circle of friends. He had then exchanged the appellation of Keeper for the higher title of Chancellor. Ben Jonson was one of the party, and wrote on the occasion some of the happiest of his rugged rhymes. "All things," he tells us, " seemed to smile about the whole house, ' the fire, the wine, the men.' " The spectacle of the accomplished host, after a life marked by no great disaster, entered on a green old age, in the enjoyment of riches, power, high honours, undiminished mental activity and vast literary reputation, made a strong impression on the poet, if we may judge from those well-known lines :

> "England's high Chancellor, the destined heir,
> In his soft cradle, to his father's chair,
> Whose even thread the fates spin round and full
> Out of their choicest and their whitest wool."

In the intervals of rest which Bacon's political and judicial functions afforded, he was in the habit of retiring to Gorhambury. At that place, his business was literature and his favourite amusement gardening, which, in one of his most pleasing essays, he calls "the purest of human pleasures." In his magnificent grounds he erected, at a cost of ten thousand pounds, a retreat to which he repaired when he wished to avoid all visitors and to devote himself wholly to study. On such occasions, a few young men of distinguished talents were sometimes the companions of his retirement. And among them his quick eye soon discerned the superior abilities of Thomas Hobbes. It is not probable, however, that he fully appreciated the powers of his disciple, or foresaw the vast influence, both for good and for evil, which that most vigorous and acute of human intellects was destined to exercise on the two succeeding generations.

In January, 1621, Bacon had reached the zenith of his fortunes. He had just published the " Novum Organum "; and that extraordinary book had drawn forth the warmest expressions of admiration from the ablest men in Europe. He had obtained honours of a widely different kind, but perhaps not less valued by him. He had been created Baron Verulam. He had subsequently been raised to the higher dignity of Viscount St. Albans. His patent was drawn in the most flattering terms, and the Prince of Wales signed it as a witness. The ceremony of investiture was performed with great state at Theobalds, and Buckingham condescended to be one of its chief actors. Posterity has felt that the greatest of English philosophers could derive no accession of dignity from any title which James could bestow, and, in defiance of the royal letters patent, has obstinately refused to degrade Francis Bacon into Viscount St. Albans.

In a few weeks was signally brought to the test the value of those objects for which Bacon had sullied his integrity, had resigned his independence, had violated the most sacred obligations of friendship and gratitude, had flattered the worthless, had persecuted the innocent, had tampered with judges, had tortured prisoners, had plundered suitors, had wasted on paltry intrigues all the powers of the most exquisitely constructed intellect that has ever been bestowed on any of the children of men. A sudden and terrible reverse was at hand. A Parliament had been summoned. After six years of silence, the voice of the nation was again to be heard. Only three days after the pageant which was performed at Theobalds in honour of Bacon, the Houses met.

Want of money had, as usual, induced the King to convoke his Parliament. But it may be doubted whether, if he or his ministers had been at all aware of the state of public feeling, they would not have tried any expedient, or borne with any inconvenience, rather than have ventured to face the deputies of a justly exasperated nation. But they did not discern those times. Indeed, almost all the political blunders of James, and of his more unfortunate son, arose from one great error. During the fifty years which preceded the long Parliament, a great and progressive change was taking place in the public mind. [The nature and extent of this change was not in the least understood by either of the first two Kings of the House of Stuart, or by any of their advisers. That the nation became more and more discontented every year, that every House of Commons was more unmanageable than that which had preceded it, were facts which it was impossible not to perceive. But the Court could not understand why these things were so. The Court could not see that the English people and the English Government, though they might once have been well suited to each other, were suited to each other no longer, that the nation had outgrown its old institutions, was every day more uneasy under them, was pressing against them, and would soon burst through them. The alarming phenomena, the existence to which no sycophant could deny, were ascribed to every cause except the true. "In my first parliament," said James, "I was a novice. In my next, there was a kind of beasts called *undertakers*," and so forth. In the third Parliament he could hardly be called a novice, and those beasts, the *undertakers*, did not exist. Yet his third Parliament gave him more trouble than either the first or second.

The Parliament had no sooner met than the House of Commons proceeded, in a temperate and respectful, but most determined manner, to discuss the public grievances. Their first attacks were directed against those odious patents, under cover of which Buckingham and his creatures had pillaged and oppressed the nation. The vigour with which these proceedings were conducted spread dismay through the Court. Buckingham thought himself in danger, and, in his alarm, had recourse to an adviser who had lately acquired considerable influence over him, Williams, Dean of Westminster. This person had already been of great use to the favourite in a very delicate matter. Buckingham had set his heart on marrying Lady Catherine Manners, daughter and heiress of the Earl of Rutland. But the difficulties were great. The Earl was haughty and impracticable, and the young lady was a Catholic. Williams soothed the pride of the father, and found arguments which, for a time at least, quieted the conscience of the daughter. For these services he had been rewarded with considerable preferment in the Church; and he was now rapidly rising to the same place in the regard of Buckingham which had formerly been occupied by Bacon.

Williams was one of those who are wiser for others than for themselves. His own public life was unfortunate, and was made unfortunate by his strange want of judgment and self-command at several important conjunctures. But the counsel which he gave on this occasion showed no want of worldly wisdom. He advised the favourite to abandon all thoughts of defending the monopolies, to find some foreign embassy for his brother, Sir Edward, who was deeply implicated in the villainies of Mompesson, and to leave the other offenders to the justice of Parliament. Buckingham received this advice with the warmest expressions of gratitude, and declared that a load had been lifted from his heart. He then repaired with Williams to the royal presence. They found the King engaged in earnest consultation with Prince Charles. The plan of operations proposed by the Dean was fully discussed, and approved in all its parts.

The first victims whom the Court abandoned to the vengeance of the Commons were Sir Giles Mompesson and Sir Francis Michell. It was some time before Bacon began to entertain any apprehensions. His talents and his address gave him great influence in the house, of which he had lately become a member, as indeed they must have done in any assembly. In the House of Commons he had many personal friends and many warm admirers. But at length, about six weeks after the meeting of Parliament, the storm burst.

A committee of the lower House had been appointed to inquire into the state of the Courts of Justice. On the 15th of March the chairman of that committee, Sir Robert Philips, member for Bath, reported that great abuses had been discovered. "The person," said he, "against whom these things are alleged is no less than the Lord Chancellor, a man so endued with all parts, both of nature and art, as that I will say no more of him, being not able to say enough." Sir Robert then proceeded to state, in the most temperate manner, the nature of the charges. A person of the name of Aubrey had a case depending in Chancery. He had been almost ruined by law expenses, and his patience had been exhausted by the delays of the court. He received a hint from some of the hangers-on of the Chancellor, that a present of one hundred pounds would expedite matters. The poor man had not the sum required. However, having found out an usurer who accommodated him with it at a high interest, he carried it to York House. The Chancellor took the money, and his dependents assured the suitor that all would go right. Aubrey was, however, disappointed, for, after considerable delay, "a killing decree" was pronounced against him. Another suitor of the name of Egerton complained that he had been induced by two of the Chancellor's jackals to make his Lordship a present of four hundred pounds, and that, nevertheless, he had not been able to obtain a decree in his favour. The evidence to these facts was overwhelming. Bacon's friends could only entreat the House to suspend its judgment, and to send up the case to the Lords, in a form less offensive than an impeachment.

On the nineteenth of March, the King sent a message to the Commons, expressing his deep regret that so eminent a person as the Chancellor should be suspected of misconduct. His Majesty declared that he had no wish to screen the guilty from justice, and proposed to appoint a new kind of tribunal, consisting of eighteen commissioners, who might be chosen from among the members of the two Houses, to investigate the matter. The Commons were not disposed to depart from their regular course of proceeding. On the same day they held a conference with the Lords, and delivered in the heads of the accusation against the Chancellor. At this conference, Bacon was not present. Overwhelmed with shame and remorse, and abandoned by all those in whom he had weakly put his trust, he shut himself up in his chamber from the eyes of men. The dejection of his mind soon disordered his body. Buckingham, who visited him by the King's order, "found his Lordship very sick and heavy." It appears, from a pathetic letter which the unhappy man addressed to the Peers on the day of the conference, that he neither expected nor wished to survive his disgrace. During several days he remained in his bed, refusing to see any human being. He passionately told his attendants to leave him—to forget him—never again to name his name, never to remember that there had been such a man in the world. In the meantime, fresh instances of corruption were every day brought to the knowledge of his accusers. The number of charges rapidly increased from two to twenty-three. The Lords entered on the investigation of the case with laudable alacrity. Some witnesses were examined at the bar of the House. A select committee was appointed to take the despositions of others; and the inquiry was rapidly proceeding, when, on the twenty-sixth of March, the King adjourned the Parliament for three weeks.

This measure revived Bacon's hopes. He made the most of his short respite. He attempted to work on the feeble mind of the King. He appealed to all the strongest feelings of James, to his fears, to his vanity, to his high notions of prerogative. Would the Solomon of the age commit so gross an error as to encourage the encroaching spirit of Parliaments? Would God's anointed, accountable to God alone, pay homage to the clamorous multitude? "Those," exclaimed he, "who now strike at the Chancellor will soon strike at the Crown. I am the first sacrifice. I wish I may be the last." But all his eloquence and address were employed in vain. Indeed, whatever Mr. Montagu may say, we are firmly convinced that it was not in the King's power to save Bacon without having recourse to measures which would have convulsed the realm. The Crown had not sufficient influence in Parliament to procure an acquittal in so clear a case of guilt. And to dissolve a Parliament which is universally allowed to have been one of the best Parliaments that ever sat, which had acted liberally and respectfully towards the Sovereign, and which enjoyed in the highest degree the favour of the people, only in order to stop a grave, temperate and constitutional inquiry into the personal integrity of the first judge in the kingdom, would have been a measure more scandalous and absurd than any of those which were the ruin of the House of Stuart. Such a measure, while it would have been as fatal to the Chancellor's honour as a conviction, would have endangered the very existence of the monarchy. The King, acting by the advice of Williams, very properly refused to engage in a dangerous struggle with his people for the purpose of saving from legal condemnation a minister whom it was impossible to save from dishonour. He advised Bacon to plead guilty, and promised to do all in his power to mitigate the punishment. Mr. Montagu is exceedingly angry with James on this account. But though we are, in general, very little inclined to admire that Prince's conduct, we really think that his advice was, under all the circumstances, the best advice that could have been given.

On the seventeenth of April the Houses reassembled, and the Lords resumed their inquiries into the abuses of the Court of Chancery. On the 22nd, Bacon addressed to the Peers a letter, which Prince Charles condescended to deliver. In this artful and pathetic composition, the Chancellor acknowledged his guilt in guarded and general terms, and, while acknowledging, endeavoured to palliate it. This, however, was not thought sufficient by his judges. They required a more particular confession, and sent him a copy of the charges. On the 30th he delivered a paper in which he admitted, with few and unimportant reservations, the truth of the accusations brought against him, and threw himself entirely on the mercy of his peers. "Upon advised consideration of the charges," said he, "descending into my own conscience, and calling my memory to account, so far as I am able, I do plainly and ingenuously confess that I am guilty of corruption, and do renounce all defence."

The Lords came to a resolution that the Chancellor's confession appeared to be full and ingenuous, and sent a committee to inquire of him whether it was really subscribed by himself. The deputies, among whom was Southampton, the common friend, many years before, of Bacon and Essex, performed their duty with great delicacy. Indeed, the agonies of such a mind and the degradation of such a name might well have softened the most obdurate natures. "My Lords," said Bacon, "it is my act, my hand, my heart. I beseech your Lordships to be merciful to a broken reed." They withdrew; and he again retired to his chamber in the deepest dejection. The next day, the sergeant-at-arms and the usher of the House of Lords came to conduct him to Westminster Hall, where sentence was to be pronounced. But they found him so unwell that he could not leave his bed; and this excuse for his absence was readily accepted. In no quarter does there appear to have been the smallest desire to add to his humiliation. The sentence was, however, severe

—the more severe, no doubt, because the Lords knew that it would not be executed, and that they had an excellent opportunity of exhibiting, at small cost, the inflexibility of their justice, and their abhorrence of corruption. Bacon was condemned to pay a fine of forty thousand pounds and to be imprisoned in the Tower during the King's pleasure. He was declared incapable of holding any office in the State or of sitting in Parliament, and he was banished for life from the verge of the court. In such misery and shame ended that long career of worldly wisdom and worldly prosperity.

Even at this pass Mr. Montagu does not desert his hero. He seems indeed to think that the attachment of an editor ought to be as devoted as that of Mr. Moore's lovers; and cannot conceive what biography was made for,

"if 'tis not the same
Through grief and through danger, through sin and through shame."

He assures us that Bacon was innocent—that he had the means of making a perfectly satisfactory defence—that when "he plainly and ingenuously confessed that he was guilty of corruption," and when he afterwards solemnly affirmed that his confession was "his act, his hand, his heart," he was telling a great lie, and that he refrained from bringing forward proofs of his innocence, because he durst not disobey the King and the favourite, who, for their own selfish objects, pressed him to plead guilty.

Now, in the first place, there is not the smallest reason to believe that, if James and Buckingham thought Bacon had a good defence, they would have prevented him from making it. What conceivable motive had they for doing so? Mr. Montagu perpetually repeats that it was their interest to sacrifice Bacon. But he overlooks an obvious distinction. It was their interest to sacrifice Bacon on the supposition of his guilt, but not on the supposition of his innocence. James was very properly unwilling to run the risk of protecting his Chancellor against the Parliament. But if the Chancellor had been able, by force of argument, to obtain an acquittal from the Parliament, we have no doubt that both the King and Villiers would have heartily rejoiced. They would have rejoiced, not merely on account of their friendship for Bacon, which seems, however, to have been as sincere as most friendships of that sort, but on selfish grounds. Nothing could have strengthened the government more than such a victory. The King and the favourite abandoned the Chancellor because they were unable to avert his disgrace and unwilling to share it. Mr. Montagu mistakes effect for cause. He thinks that Bacon did not prove his innocence because he was not supported by the Court. The truth evidently is that the Court did not venture to support Bacon because he could not prove his innocence.

Again, it seems strange that Mr. Montagu should not perceive that, while attempting to vindicate Bacon's reputation, he is really casting on it the foulest of all aspersions. He imputes to his idol a degree of meanness and depravity more loathsome than judical corruption itself. A corrupt judge may have many good qualities. But a man who, to please a powerful patron, solemnly declares himself guilty of corruption, when he knows himself to be innocent, must be a monster of servility and impudence. Bacon was—to say nothing of his highest claims to respect—a gentleman, a nobleman, a scholar, a statesman, a man of the first consideration in society, a man far advanced in years. Is it possible to believe that such a man would, to gratify any human being, irreparably ruin his own character by his own act? Imagine a grey-headed judge, full of years and honours, owning with tears, with pathetic assurances of his penitence and of his sincerity, that he has been guilty of shameful malpractices, repeatedly asseverating the truth of his confession, subscribing it with his own hand, submitting to conviction, receiving a humilating sentence and acknowledging its justice, and all this when he has it in his power to show that his conduct has been irreproachable! The thing is incredible. But if we admit it to be true, what must we think of such a man, if, indeed, he deserves the name of man, who thinks anything that kings and minions can bestow more precious than honour, or anything that they can inflict more terrible than infamy?

Of this most disgraceful imputation we fully acquit Bacon. He had no defence; and Mr. Montagu's affectionate attempt to make a defence for him has altogether failed.

The grounds on which Mr. Montagu rests the case are two; the first, that the taking of presents was usual and—what he seems to consider as the same thing—not discreditable; the second, that these presents were not taken as bribes.

Mr. Montagu brings forward many facts in support of his first proposition. He is not content with showing that many English judges formerly received gifts from suitors, but collects similar instances from foreign nations and ancient times. He goes back to the commonwealths of Greece, and attempts to press into his service a line of Homer and a sentence of Plutarch, which, we fear, will hardly serve his turn. The gold of which Homer speaks was not intended to fee the judges, but was paid into court for the benefit of the successful litigant; and the gratuities which Pericles, as Plutarch states, distributed among the members of the Athenian tribunals, were legal wages paid out of the public revenue. We can supply Mr. Montagu with passages much more in point. Hesiod, who, like poor Aubrey, had "a killing decree" made against him in the Chancery of Ascra, was so uncivil as to designate the learned persons who presided in that court as $\beta\alpha\sigma\iota\lambda\tilde{\eta}\alpha\varsigma$ $\delta\omega\rho\sigma\phi\acute{\alpha}\gamma\sigma\upsilon\varsigma$. Plutarch and Diodorus have handed down to the latest ages the respectable name of Anytus, the son of Anthemius, the first defendant who, eluding all the safeguards which the ingenuity of Solon could devise, succeeded in corrupting a bench of Athenian judges. We are, indeed, so far from grudging Mr. Montagu the aid of Greece, that we will give him Rome into the bargain. We acknowledge that the honourable senators who tried Verres received presents which were worth more than the fee-simple of York House and Gorhambury together, and that the no less honourable senators and knights who professed to believe in the *alibi* of Clodius, obtained marks still more extraordinary of the esteem and gratitude of the defendant. In short, we are ready to admit that, before Bacon's time and in Bacon's time, judges were in the habit of receiving gifts from suitors.

But is this a defence? We think not. The robberies of Cacus and Barabbas are no justification for those of Turpin. The conduct of the two men of Belial, who swore away the life of Naboth, has never been cited as an excuse for the perjuries of Oates and Dangerfield. Mr. Montagu has confounded two things which it is necessary carefully to distinguish from each other if we wish to form a correct judgment of the characters of men of other countries and other times. That an immoral action is, in a particular society, generally considered as innocent is a good plea for an individual who, being one of that society and having adopted the notions which prevail among his neighbours, commits that action. But the circumstance that a great many people are in the habit of committing immoral actions is no plea at all. We should think it unjust to call St. Louis a wicked man because, in an age in which toleration was generally regarded as a sin, he persecuted heretics. We should think it unjust to call Cowper's friend, John Newton, a hypocrite and monster because, at a time when the slave-trade was commonly considered by the most respectable people as an innocent and beneficial traffic, he went, largely provided with hymn-books and handcuffs, on a Guinea voyage. But the circumstance that there are fifty thousand thieves in London is no excuse for a fellow who is caught breaking into a shop. No man is to be blamed for not making discoveries in morality, for not finding out that something which everybody else thinks to be good is really bad. But, if a man does that which he and all around him know to be bad, it is no excuse for him that others have done the same. We should be ashamed of spending so much time in pointing out so clear a distinction, but that Mr. Montagu seems altogether to overlook it.

Now, to apply these principles to the case before us; let Mr. Montagu prove that, in Bacon's age, the practices for which Bacon was punished were generally considered as innocent, and we admit that he has made out his point. But this we defy him to do. That these practices were common we admit; but they were common just as all wickedness to which there is strong temptation always was and always will be common. They were common just as theft, cheating, perjury, adultery have always been common. They were common, not because people did not know what was right, but because people liked to do what was wrong. They were common, though prohibited by law. They were common, though condemned by public opinion. They were common, because in that age law and public opinion united had not sufficient force to restrain the greediness of powerful and unprincipled magistrates. They were common, as every crime will be common when the gain to which it leads is great and the chance of punishment small. But, though common, they were universally allowed to be altogether unjustifiable; they were in the highest degree odious; and, though many were guilty of them, none had the audacity publicly to avow and defend them.

We could give a thousand proofs that the opinion then entertained concerning these practices was such as we have described. But we will content ourselves with calling a single witness—honest Hugh Latimer. His sermons—preached more than seventy years before the inquiry into Bacon's conduct—abound with the sharpest invectives against those very practices of which Bacon was guilty, and which, as Mr. Montagu seems to think, nobody ever considered as blamable till Bacon was punished for them. We could easily fill twenty pages with the homely, but just and forcible, rhetoric of the brave old bishop. We shall select a few passages as fair specimens, and no more than fair specimens, of the rest. "*Omnes diligunt munera.* They all love bribes. Bribery is a princely kind of thieving. They will be waged by the rich, either to give sentence against the poor, or to put off the poor man's cause. This is the noble theft of princes and magistrates. They are bribe-takers. *Nowadays they call them gentle rewards. Let them leave their colouring and call them by their Christian name—bribes.*" And again: "Cambyses was a great emperor, such another as our master is. He had many lord-deputies, lord-presidents and lieutenants under him. It is a great while ago since I read the history. It chanced he had under him, in one of his dominions, a briber, a gift-taker, a gratifier of rich men; he followed gifts as fast as he that followed the pudding; a handmaker in his office to make his son a great man: as the old saying is, 'Happy is the child whose father goeth to the devil.' The cry of the poor widow came to the emperor's ear and caused him to flay the judge quick, and he laid his skin in the chair of judgment that all judges that should give judgment afterwards should sit in the same skin. Surely it was a goodly sign, a goodly monument, the sign of the judge's skin. *I pray God we may once see the skin in England.*" "I am sure," says he, in another sermon, "this is *scala inferni*, the right way to hell, to be covetous, to take bribes and pervert justice. If a judge should ask me the way to hell, I would show him this way."

First, let him be a covetous man; let his heart be poisoned with covetousness. Then let him go a little further and take bribes; and, lastly, pervert judgment. Lo, here is the mother, and the daughter, and the daughter's daughter. Avarice is the mother: she brings forth bribe-taking, and bribe-taking perverting of judgment. There lacks a fourth thing to make up the mess, which, so help me God, if I were judge, should be *hangum tuum*, a Tyburn tippet to take with him; an it were the judge of the King's Bench, my Lord Chief Judge of England, *yea, an it were my Lord Chancellor himself, to Tyburn with him.*" We will quote but one more passage. "He that took the silver basin and ewer for a bribe, thinketh that it will never come out. But he may now know that I know it, and I know it not alone; there be more beside me that know it. Oh, briber and bribery! He was never a good man that will so take bribes. Nor can I believe that he that is a briber will be a good justice. It will never be merry in England till we have the skins of such. *For what needeth bribery where men do their things uprightly?*"

This was not the language of a great philosopher who had made new discoveries in moral and political science. It was the plain talk of a plain man, who sprang from the body of the people, who sympathised strongly with their wants and their feelings, and who boldly uttered their opinions. It was on account of the fearless way in which stout-hearted old Hugh exposes the misdeeds of men in ermine tippets and gold collars that the Londoners cheered him as he walked down the Strand to preach at Whitehall—struggled for a touch of his gown, and bawled "Have at them, Father Latimer." It is plain, from the passages which we have quoted, and from fifty others which we might quote, that, long before Bacon was born, the accepting of presents by a judge was known to be a wicked and shameful act—that the fine words under which it was the fashion to veil such corrupt practices were even then seen through by the common people—that the distinction on which Mr. Montagu insists between compliments and bribes was even then laughed at as a mere "colouring." There may be some oratorical exaggeration in what Latimer says about the Tyburn tippet and the sign of the judge's skin; but the fact that he ventured to use such expressions is amply sufficient to prove that the gift-taking judges, the receivers of silver basins and ewers, were regarded as such pests of the commonwealth that a venerable divine might, without any breach of Christian charity, publicly pray to God for their detection and their condign punishment.

Mr. Montagu tells us, most justly, that we ought not to transfer the opinions of our age to a former age. But he has himself committed a greater error than that against which he has cautioned his readers. Without any evidence, nay, in the face of the strongest evidence, he ascribes to the people of a former age a set of opinions which no people ever held. But any hypothesis is in his view more probable than that Bacon should have been a dishonest man. We firmly believe that, if papers were to be discovered which should irresistibly prove that Bacon was concerned in the poisoning of Sir Thomas Overbury, Mr. Montagu would tell us that, at the beginning of the seventeenth century, it was not thought improper in a man to put arsenic into the broth of his friends, and that we ought to blame, not Bacon, but the age in which he lived.

But why should we have recourse to any other evidence, when the proceeding against Lord Bacon is itself the best evidence on the subject? When Mr. Montagu tells us that we ought not to transfer the opinions of our age to Bacon's age, he appears altogether to forget that it was by men of Bacon's own age that Bacon was prosecuted, tried, convicted and sentenced. Did not they know what their own opinions were? Did not they know whether they thought the taking of gifts by a judge a crime or not? Mr. Montague complains bitterly that Bacon was induced to abstain from making a defence. But, if Bacon's defence resembled that which is made for him in the volume before us, it would have been unnecessary to trouble the Houses with it. The Lords and Commons did not want Bacon to tell them the thoughts of their own hearts— to inform them that they did not consider such practices as those in which they had detected him as at all culpable. Mr. Montagu's proposition may indeed be fairly stated thus:—It was very hard that Bacon's contemporaries should think it wrong in him to do what they did not think it wrong in him to do. Hard indeed; and withal somewhat improbable. Will any person say that the Commons, who impeached Bacon for taking presents, and the Lords, who sentenced him to fine, imprisonment and degradation for taking presents, did not know that the taking of presents was a crime? Or, will any person say that Bacon did not know what the whole House of Commons and the whole House of Lords knew? Nobody who is not prepared to maintain one of these absurd propositions can deny that Bacon committed what he knew to be a crime.

It cannot be pretended that the Houses were seeking occasion to ruin Bacon, and that they therefore brought him to punishment on charges which they themselves knew to be frivilous. In no quarter was there the faintest indication of a disposition to treat him harshly. Through the whole proceeding there was no symptom of personal animosity or of factious violence in either House. Indeed, we will venture to say that no State Trial in our History is more creditable to all who took part in it, either as prosecutors or judges. The decency, the gravity, the public spirit; the justice moderated, but not unnerved, by compassion—which appeared in every part of the transaction—would do honour to the most respectable public men of our own times. The accusers, while they discharged their duty to their constituents by bringing the misdeeds of the Chancellor to light, spoke with admiration of his many eminent qualities. The Lords, while condemning him, complimented him on the ingenuousness of his confession, and spared him the humiliation of a public appearance at their bar. So strong was the contagion of good feeling that even Sir Edward Coke, for the first time in his life, behaved like a gentleman. No criminal ever had more temperate prosecutors than Bacon. No criminal ever had more favourable judges. If he was convicted, it was because it was impossible to acquit him without offering the grossest outrage to justice and common sense.

Mr. Montagu's other argument, namely, that Bacon, *though he took gifts, did not take bribes*, seems to us as futile as that which we have considered. Indeed, we might be content to leave it to be answered by the plainest man among our readers. Demosthenes noticed it with contempt more than two thousand years ago. Latimer, we have seen, treated this sophistry with similar disdain. "Leave colouring," said he, "and call these things by their Christian name, bribes." Mr. Montagu attempts—somewhat unfairly, we must say—to represent the presents which Bacon received, as similar to the perquisites which suitors paid to the members of the Parliaments of France. The French magistrate had a legal right to his fee; and the amount of the fee was regulated by law. Whether this be a good mode of remunerating judges is not the question. But what analogy is there between payments of this sort and the presents which Bacon received—presents which were not sanctioned by the law, which were not made under the public eye, and of which the amount was regulated only by private bargain between the magistrate and the suitor? Again, it is mere trifling to say that Bacon could not have meant to act corruptly because he employed the agency of men of rank, of bishops, privy councillors and members of parliament—as if the whole history of that generation was not full of the low actions of high people; as if it was not notorious that men, as exalted in rank as any of the decoys that Bacon employed, had pimped for Somerset and poisoned Overbury.

"But," says Mr. Montagu, "these presents were made openly and with the greatest publicity." This would indeed be a strong argument in favour of Bacon. But we deny the fact. In one, and one only, of the cases in which Bacon was accused of corruptly receiving gifts, does he appear to have received a gift publicly. This was in a matter depending between the Company of Apothecaries and the Company of Grocers. Bacon, in his Confession, insisted strongly on the circumstance that he had on this occasion taken presents publicly, as a proof that he had not taken them corruptly. Is it not clear that, if he had taken the presents mentioned in the other charges in the same public manner, he would have dwelt on this point in his answer to those charges? The fact that he insists so strongly on the publicity of one particular present is of itself sufficient to prove that the other presents were not publicly taken. Why he took this present publicly and the rest secretly is evident. He on that occasion acted openly because he was acting honestly. He was not on that occasion sitting judicially. He was called in to effect an amicable arrangement between two parties. Both were satisfied with his decision. Both joined in making him a present in return for his trouble. Whether it was quite delicate in a man of his rank to accept a present under such circumstances may be questioned. But there is no ground in this case for accusing him of corruption.

Unhappily, the very circumstances which prove him to have been innocent in this case prove him to have been guilty on the other charges. Once, and once only, he alleges hat he received a present publicly. The inference is, that in all the other cases mentioned in the articles against him he received presents secretly. When we examine the single case in which he alleges that he received a present publicly, we find that it is also the single case in which there was no gross impropriety in his receiving a present. Is it then possible to doubt that his reason for not receiving other presents in as public a manner was, that he knew that it was wrong to receive them?

One argument still remains, plausible in appearance, but admitting of easy and complete refutation. The two chief complainants, Aubrey and Egerton, had both made presents to the Chancellor. But he had decided against them both. Therefore, he had not received those presents as bribes. "The complaints of his accusers were," says Mr. Montagu, "not that the gratuities had, but that they had not, influenced Bacon's judgment, as he had decided against them."

The truth is, that it is precisely in this way that an extensive system of corruption is generally detected. A person who, by a bribe, has procured a decree in his favour, is by no means likely to come forward of his own accord as an accuser. He is content. He has his *quid pro quo*. He is not impelled either by interested or by vindictive motives to bring the transaction before the public. On the contrary, he has almost as strong motives for holding his tongue as the judge himself can have. But when a judge practises corruption, as we fear that Bacon practised it, on a large scale, and has many agents looking out in different quarters for prey, it will sometimes happen that he will be bribed on both sides. It will sometimes happen that he will receive money from suitors who are so obviously in the wrong that he cannot with decency do anything to serve them. Thus, he will now and then be forced to pronounce against a person from whom he has received a present; and he makes that person a deadly enemy. The hundreds who have got what they paid for remain quiet. It is the two or three who have paid, and have nothing to show for their money, who are noisy.

The memorable case of the Goëzmans is an example of this. Beaumarchais had an important suit depending before the Parliament of Paris. M. Goëzman was the judge on whom chiefly the decision depended. It was hinted to Beaumarchais that Madame Goëzman might be propitiated by a present. He accordingly offered certain rouleaus of Louis d'or to the lady, who received them graciously. There can be no doubt that, if the decision of the court had been favourable to him, these things would never have been known to the world. But he lost his cause. Almost the whole sum which he had expended in bribery was immediately refunded; and those who had disappointed him probably thought that he would not, for the mere gratification of his malevolence, make public a transaction which was discreditable to himself as well as to them. They knew little of him. He soon taught them to curse the day in which they had dared to trifle with a man of so revengeful and turbulent a spirit—of such dauntless effrontery, and of such eminent talents for controversy and satire. He compelled the Parliament to put a degrading stigma on M. Goëzman. He drove Madame Goëzman to a convent. Till it was too late to pause, his excited passions did not suffer him to remember that he could effect their ruin only by disclosures ruinous to himself. We could give other instances. But it is needless. No person well acquainted with human nature can fail to perceive that, if the doctrine for which Mr. Montagu contends were admitted, society would be deprived of almost the only chance which it has of detecting the corrupt practices of judges.

We return to our narrative. The sentence of Bacon had scarcely been pronounced when it was mitigated. He was indeed sent to the Tower. But this was merely a form. In two days he was set at liberty, and soon after he retired to Gorhambury. His fine was speedily released by the Crown. He was next suffered to present himself at Court; and at length, in 1624, the rest of his punishment was remitted. He was now at liberty to resume his seat in the House of Lords, and he was actually summoned to the next Parliament. But age, infirmity and, perhaps, shame prevented him from attending. The Government allowed a pension of one thousand two hundred pounds a year; and his whole annual income is estimated by Mr. Montagu at two thousand five hundred pounds—a sum which was probably above the average income of a nobleman of that generation, and which was certainly sufficient for comfort and even for splendour. Unhappily, Bacon was fond of display, and unused to pay minute attention to domestic affairs. He was not easily persuaded to give up any part of the magnificence to which he had been accustomed in the time of his power and prosperity. No pressure of distress could induce him to part with the woods of Gorhambury. "I will not," he said, "be stripped of my feathers." He travelled with so splendid an equipage and so large a retinue, that Prince Charles, who once fell in with him on the road, exclaimed with surprise— "Well; do what we can, this man scorns to go out in snuff." This carelessness and ostentation reduced him to frequent distress. He was under the necessity of parting with York House, and of taking up his residence, during his visits to London, at his old chambers in Gray's Inn. He had other vexations, the exact nature of which is unknown. It is evident from his will that some part of his wife's conduct had greatly disturbed and irritated him.

But, whatever might be his pecuniary difficulties, or his conjugal discomforts, the powers of his intellect still remained undiminished. Those noble studies, for which he had found leisure in the midst of professional drudgery and of courtly intrigues, gave to this last sad stage of his life a dignity beyond what power or titles could bestow. Impeached, convicted, sentenced, driven with ignominy from the presence of his Sovereign, shut out from the deliberations of his fellow nobles, loaded with debt, branded with dishonour, sinking under the weight of years, sorrows and diseases—Bacon was Bacon still. "My conceit of his person," says Ben Jonson, very finely, "was never increased towards him by his place or honours; but I have, and do, reverence him for the greatness that was only proper to himself, in that he seemed to me ever, by his work, one of the greatest men and most worthy of admiration that had been in many ages. In his adversity I ever prayed that God would give him strength; for greatness he could not want."

The services which he rendered to letters during the last five years of his life, amidst ten thousand distractions and vexations, increase the regret with which we think on the many years which he had wasted—to use the words of Sir Thomas Bodley—"on such study as was not worthy of such a student." He commenced a "Digest of the Laws of England," a "History of England under the Princes of the House of Tudor," a "Body of Natural History," a "Philosophical Romance." He made extensive and valuable additions to his "Essays." He published the inestimable treatise, "De Augmentis Scientiarum." The very trifles with which he amused himself in hours of pain and languor bore the mark of his mind. The best jest book in the world is that which he dictated from memory, without referring to any book, on a day on which illness had rendered him incapable of serious study.

The great apostle of experimental philosophy was destined to be its martyr. It had occurred to him that snow might be used with advantage for the purpose of preventing animal substances from putrefying. On a very cold day, early in the spring of the year 1626, he alighted from his coach near Highgate, in order to try the experiment. He went into a cottage, bought a fowl, and with his own hands stuffed it with snow. While thus engaged he felt a sudden chill, and was soon so much indisposed that it was impossible for him to return to Gray's Inn. The Earl of Arundel, with whom he was well acquainted, had a house at Highgate. To that house Bacon was carried. The Earl was absent; but the servants who were in charge of the place showed great respect and attention to the illustrious guest. Here, after an illness of about a week, he expired early on the morning of Easterday, 1626. His mind appears to have retained its strength and liveliness to the end. He did not forget the fowl which had caused his death. In the last letter that he ever wrote, with fingers which, as he said, could not steadily hold a pen, he did not omit to mention that the experiment of the snow had succeeded "excellently well."

Our opinion of the moral character of this great man has already been sufficiently explained. Had his life been passed in literary retirement, he would, in all probability, have deserved to be considered, not only as a great philosopher, but as a worthy and good-natured member of society. But neither his principles nor his spirit were such as could be trusted when strong temptations were to be resisted and serious dangers to be braved.

In his will he expressed, with singular brevity, energy, dignity and pathos, a mournful consciousness that his actions had not been such as to entitle him to the esteem of those under whose observation his life had been passed; and, at the same time, a proud confidence that his writings had secured for him a high and permanent place among the benefactors of mankind. So, at least, we understand those striking words which have been often quoted, but which we must quote once more—"For my name and memory, I leave it to men's charitable speeches, and to foreign nations, and to the next age."

His confidence was just. From the day of his death his fame has been constantly and steadily progressive; and we have no doubt that his name will be named with reverence, to the latest ages and to the remotest ends of the civilised world.

The chief peculiarity of Bacon's philosophy seems to us to have been this, that it aimed at things altogether different from those which his predecessors had proposed to themselves. This was his own opinion. "Finis scientiarum," says he, "a nemine adhuc bene positus est."* And again, "Omnium gravissimus error in deviatione ab ultimo doctrinarum fine consistit."† "Nec ipsa meta," says he, elsewhere, "adhuc ulli, quod sciam, mortalium posita est et defixa."‡ The more carefully his works are examined, the more clearly, we think, it will appear that this is the real clue to his whole system, and that he used means different from those used by other philosophers, because he wished to arrive at an end altogether different from theirs.

What then was the end which Bacon proposed to himself? It was, to use his own emphatic expression, "fruit." It was the multiplying of human enjoyments and the mitigating of human sufferings. It was "the relief of man's estate."§ It was "commodis humanis inservire."|| It was "efficaciter operari ad sublevanda vitæ humanæ incommoda."¶ It was "dotare vitam humanam novis inventis et copiis."** It was "genus humanum novis operibus et potestatibus continuo dotare."†† This was the object of all his speculations in every department of science, in natural philosophy, in legislation, in politics, in morals.

Two words form the key of the Baconian doctrine—Utility and Progress. The ancient philosophy disdained to be useful and was content to be stationary. It dealt largely in theories of moral perfection, which were so sublime that they never could be more than theories; in attempts to solve insoluble enigmas; in exhortations to the attainment of unattainable frames of mind. It could not condescend to the humble office of ministering to the comfort of human beings. All the schools regarded that offices as degrading; some censured it as immoral. Once indeed Posidonius, a distinguished writer of the age of Cicero and Cæsar, so far forgot himself as to enumerate, among the humbler blessings which mankind owed to philosophy, the discovery of the principle of the arch and the introduction of the use of metals. This eulogy was considered as an affront, and was taken up with proper spirit. Seneca vehemently disclaims these insulting compliments.‡‡ Philosophy, according to him, has nothing to do with teaching men to rear arched roofs over their heads. The true philosopher does not care whether he has an arched roof or any roof. Philosophy has nothing to do with teaching men the uses of metals. She teaches us to be independent of all material substances, of all mechanical contrivances. The wise man lives according to nature. Instead of attempting to add to the physical comforts of his species, he regrets that his lot was not cast in that golden age when the human race had no protection against the cold but the skins of wild beasts—no screen from the sun but a cavern. To impute to such a man any share in the invention or improvement of a plough, a ship, or a mill, is an insult. "In my own time," says Seneca, "there have been inventions of this sort—transparent windows—tubes for diffusing warmth equally through all parts of a building—shorthand, which has been carried to such a perfection that a writer can keep pace with the most rapid speaker. But the inventing of such things is drudgery for the lowest slaves: philosophy lies deeper. It is not her office to teach men how to use their hands. The object of her lessons is to form the soul. *Non est inquam, instrumentorum ad usus necessarios opifex.*" If the *non* were left out, this last sentence would be no bad description of the Baconian philosophy, and would, indeed, very

---

* Novum Organum, Lib. 1, Aph. 81. † De Augmentis, Lib. 1.
‡ Cogitata et Visa. § Advancement of Learning, Book 1.
|| De Augmentis, Lib. 7, Cap. 1. ¶ Ib., Lib. 2, Cap. 2.
** Novum Organum, Lib. 1, Aph. 81. †† Cogitata et Visa.
‡‡ Seneca, Epist. 90.

much resemble several expressions in the "Novum Organum." "We shall next be told," exclaims Seneca, "that the first shoemaker was a philosopher." For our own part, if we are forced to make our choice between the first shoemaker and the author of the three books "On Anger," we pronounce for the shoemaker. It may be worse to be angry than to be wet. But shoes have kept millions from being wet; and we doubt whether Seneca ever kept any body from being angry.

It is very reluctantly that Seneca can be brought to confess that any philosopher had ever paid the smallest attention to anything that could possibly promote what vulgar people would consider as the well-being of mankind. He labours to clear Democritus from the disgraceful imputation of having made the first arch, and Anacharsis from the charge of having contrived the potter's wheel. He is forced to own that such a thing might happen; and it may also happen, he tells us, that a philosopher may be swift of foot. But it is not in his character of philosopher that he either wins a race or invents a machine. No, to be sure. The business of a philosopher was to declaim in praise of poverty with two millions sterling out at usury—to meditate epigrammatic conceits about the evils of luxury in gardens which moved the envy of sovereigns—to rant about liberty while fawning on the insolent and pampered freedmen of a tyrant—to celebrate the divine beauty of virtues with the same pen which had just before written a defence of the murder of a mother by a son.

From the cant of this philosophy—a philosophy meanly proud of its own unprofitableness—it is delightful to turn to the lessons of the great English teacher. We can almost forgive all the faults of Bacon's life when we read that singularly graceful and dignified passage :—"Ego certe, ut de me ipso, quod res est, loquar, et in iis quæ nunc edo, et in iis quæ in posterum meditor, dignitatem ingenii et nominis mei, si qua sit, sæpius sciens et volens projicio, *dum commodis humanis inserviam;* quique architectus fortasse in philosophia et scientiis esse debeam, etiam operarius, et bajulus, et quidvis demum fio, cum haud pauca quæ omnino fieri necesse sit, alii autem ob innatam superbiam subterfugiant, ipse sustineam et exsequar."* This *philanthropia,* which, as he said in one of the most remarkable of his early letters, "was so fixed in his mind as it could not be removed"—this majestic humility—this persuasion that nothing can be too insignificant for the attention of the wisest which is not too insignificant to give pleasure or pain to the meanest—is the great characteristic distinction, the essential spirit of the Baconian philosophy. We trace it in all that Bacon has written on Physics, on Laws, on Morals. And we conceive that from this peculiarity all the other peculiarities of his system directly and almost necessarily sprang.

The spirit which appears in the passage of Seneca, to which we have referred, tainted the whole body of the ancient philosophy from the time of Socrates downwards, and took possession of intellects with which that of Seneca cannot for a moment be compared. It pervades the dialogues of Plato. It may be distinctly traced in many parts of the works of Aristotle. Bacon has dropped hints from which it may be inferred that, in his opinion, the prevalence of this feeling was in a great measure to be attributed to the influence of Socrates. Our great countryman evidently did not consider the revolution which Socrates effected in philosophy as a happy event, and he constantly maintained that the earlier Greek speculators, Democritus in particular, were, on the whole, superior to their more celebrated successors.†

---

* De Augmentis, Lib. 7, Cap. 1.
† Novum Organum, Lib. 1, Aph. 71, 79. De Augmentis, Lib. 3, Cap. 4. De Principiis atque Originibus. Cogitata et Visa. Redargutio Philosophiarum.

Assuredly, if the tree which Socrates planted and Plato watered is to be judged of by its flowers and leaves, it is the noblest of trees. But if we take the homely test of Bacon—if we judge of the tree by its *fruits*—our opinion of it may perhaps be less favourable. When we sum up all the useful truths which we owe to that philosophy, to what do they amount? We find, indeed, abundant proofs that some of those who cultivated it were men of the first order of intellect. We find among their writings incomparable specimens both of dialectical and rhetorical art. We have no doubt that the ancient controversies were of use, in so far as they served to exercise the faculties of the disputants; for there is no controversy so idle that it may not be of use in this way. But when we look for something more—for something which adds to the comforts or alleviates the calamities of the human race—we are forced to own ourselves disappointed. We are forced to say with Bacon, that this celebrated philosophy ended in nothing but disputation, that it was neither a vineyard nor an olive-ground, but an intricate wood of briars and thistles from which those who lost themselves in it brought back many scratches and no food.*

We readily acknowledge that some of the teachers of this unfruitful wisdom were among the greatest men that the world has ever seen. If we admit the justice of Bacon's censure, we admit it with regret similar to that which Dante felt when he learned the fate of those illustrious heathens who were doomed to the first circle of Hell.

"Gran duol mi prese al cuor quando lo "ntesi,
Perocchè gente di molto valore
Conobbi che 'n quel limbo eran sospesi."

But in truth the very admiration which we feel for the eminent philosophers of antiquity forces us to adopt the opinion that their powers were systematically misdirected. For how else could it be that such powers should effect so little for mankind? A pedestrian may show as much muscular vigour on a treadmill as on the highway road. But on the road his vigour will assuredly carry him forward; and on the treadmill he will not advance an inch. The ancient philosophy was a treadmill, not a path. It was made up of revolving questions—of controversies which were always beginning again. It was a contrivance for having much exertion and no progress. We must acknowledge that more than once, while contemplating the doctrines of the Academy and the Portico, even as they appear in the transparent splendour of Cicero's incomparable diction, we have been tempted to mutter with the surly centurion in Persius—"Cur quis non prandeat hoc est?" What is the highest good—whether pain be an evil—whether all things be fated—whether we can be certain of anything—whether we can be certain that we are certain of nothing—whether a wise man can be unhappy—whether all departures from right be equally reprehensible—these, and other questions of the same sort, occupied the brains, the tongues and the pens of the ablest men in the civilised world during several centuries. This sort of philosophy, it is evident, could not be progressive. It might indeed sharpen and invigorate the minds of those who devoted themselves to it; and so might the disputes of the orthodox Lilliputians and the heretical Blefuscudians about the big ends and the little ends of eggs. But such disputes could add nothing to the stock of knowledge. The human mind, accordingly, insteading of marching, merely marked time. It took as much trouble as would have sufficed to carry it forward; and yet remained on the same spot. There was no accumulation of truth—no heritage of truth acquired by the labour of one generation and bequeathed to another,

* Novum Organum, Lib I, Aph. 73.

to be again transmitted with large additions to a third. Where this philosophy was in the time of Cicero, there it continued to be in the time of Seneca, and there it continued to be in the time of Favorinus. The same sects were still battling, with the same unsatisfactory arguments, about the same interminable questions. There had been no want of ingenuity, of zeal, of industry. Every trace of intellectual cultivation was there, except a harvest. There had been plenty of ploughing, harrowing, reaping, threshing. But the garners contained only smut and stubble.

The ancient philosophers did not neglect natural science; but they did not cultivate it for the purpose of increasing the power and ameliorating the condition of man. The taint of barrenness had spread from ethical to physical speculations. Seneca wrote largely on natural philosophy, and magnified the importance of that study. But why? Not because it tended to assuage suffering, to multiply the conveniences of life, to extend the empire of man over the material word; but solely because it tended to raise the mind above low cares, to separate it from the body, to exercise its subtilty in the solution of very obscure questions.* Thus natural philosophy was considered in the light merely of a mental exercise. It was made subsidiary to the art of disputation; and it consequently proved altogether barren of useful discoveries.

There was one sect, which, however absurd and pernicious some of its doctrines may have been, ought, it should seem, to have merited an exception from the general censure which Bacon has pronounced on the ancient schools of wisdom. The Epicurean, who referred all happiness to bodily pleasure and all evil to bodily pain, might have been expected to exert himself for the purpose of bettering his own physical condition and that of his neighbours. But the thought seems never to have occurred to any member of that school. Indeed, their notion, as reported by their great poet, was, that no more improvements were to be expected in the arts which conduce to the comfort of life,

"Ad victum quæ flagitat usus
Omnia jam ferme mortalibus esse parata."

This contented despondency—this disposition to admire what has been done, and to expect that nothing more will be done—is strongly characteristic of all the schools which preceded the school of Fruit and Progress. Widely as the Epicurean and the Stoic differed on most points, they seem to have quite agreed in their contempt for pursuits so vulgar as to be useful. The philosophy of both was a garrulous, declaiming, canting, wrangling philosophy. Century after century they continued to repeat their hostile war-cries— Virtue and Pleasure; and in the end it appeared that the Epicurean had added as little to the quantity of pleasure as the Stoic to the quantity of virtue. It is on the pedestal of Bacon, not on that of Epicurus, that those noble lines ought to be inscribed:

"O tenebris tantis tam clarum extollere lumen
Qui primus potuisti, ILLUSTRANS COMMODA VITÆ."

In the fifth century, Christianity had conquered Paganism, and Paganism had infected Christianity. The Church was now victorious and corrupt. The rites of the Pantheon had passed into her worship—the subtilties of the Academy into her creed. In an evil day, says Bacon, though with great pomp and solemnity, was the ill-starred alliance stricken between the old philosophy and the new faith.† Questions widely different from those which

---

* Seneca, Nat. Quæst. prof. Lib. 3. † Cogitata et Visa.

had employed the ingenuity of Pyrrho and Carneades, but just as subtle, just as interminable and just as unprofitable, exercised the minds of the lively and voluble Greeks. When learning began to arrive in the West, similar trifles occupied the sharp and vigorous intellects of the Schoolmen. There was another sowing of the wind and another reaping of the whirlwind. The great work of improving the condition of the human race was still considered as unworthy of a man of learning. Those who undertook that task, if what they effected could be readily comprehended, were despised as mechanics; if not, they were in danger of being burned as conjurers.

There cannot be a stronger proof of the degree in which the human mind had been misdirected than the history of the two greatest events which took place during the middle ages. We speak of the invention of Gunpowder and of the invention of Printing. The dates of both are unknown. The authors of both are unknown. Nor was this because men were too rude and ignorant to value intellectual superiority. The inventor of gunpowder appears to have been contemporary with Petrarch and Boccaccio. The inventor of printing was contemporary with Nicholas the Fifth, with Cosmo de' Medici, and with a crowd of distinguished scholars. But the human mind still retained that fatal bent which it had received two thousand years earlier. George of Trebisond and Marsilio Ficino would not easily have been brought to believe that the inventor of the printing press had done more for mankind than themselves, or than those ancient writers of whom they were the enthusiastic votaries.

At length the time arrived when the barren philosophy, which had, during so many ages, employed the faculties of the ablest of men, was destined to fall. It had worn many shapes. It had mingled itself with many creeds. It had survived revolutions in which empires, religions, languages, races had perished. Driven from its ancient haunts, it had taken sanctuary in that Church which it had persecuted; and had, like the daring fiends of the poet, placed its seat

"next the seat of God,
And with its darkness dared affront his light."

Words and more words and nothing but words had been all the fruit of all the toil of all the most renowned sages of sixty generations. But the days of this sterile exuberance were numbered.

Many causes predisposed the public mind to a change. The study of a great variety of ancient writers, though it did not give a right direction to philosophical research, did much towards destroying that blind reverence for authority which had prevailed when Aristotle ruled alone. The rise of the Florentine sect of Platonists, a sect to which belonged some of the finest minds of the fifteenth century, was not an unimportant event. The mere substitution of the Academic for the Peripatetic philosophy would indeed have done little good. But anything was better than the old habit of unreasoning servility. It was something to have a choice of tyrants. "A spark of freedom," as Gibbon has justly remarked, "was produced by this collision of adverse servitude."

Other causes might be mentioned. But it is chiefly to the great reformation of religion that we owe the great reformation of philosophy. The alliance between the Schools and the Vatican had for ages been so close that those who threw off the dominion of the Vatican could not continue to recognise the authority of the Schools. Most of the great reformers treated the Peripatetic philosophy with contempt, and spoke of Aristotle as if Aristotle had been answerable for all the dogmas of Thomas Aquinas. "Nullo apud Lutheranos philosophiam esse in pretio"* was a reproach which the defenders of the Church of Rome loudly repeated, and which many of the Protestant leaders considered as a compliment. Scarcely any text was more frequently cited by them than that in which St. Paul cautions the Colossians not to let any man spoil them by philosophy. Luther, almost at the outset of his career, went so far as to declare that no man could be at once a proficient in the school of Aristotle and in that of Christ; Zwingle, Bucer, Peter Martyr, Calvin held similar language. In some of the Scotch universities, the Aristotelian system was discarded for that of Ramus. Thus, before the birth of Bacon, the empire of the scholastic philosophy had been shaken to its foundations. There was in the intellectual world an anarchy resembling that which in the political world often follows the overthrow of an old and deeply rooted government. Antiquity, prescription, the sound of great names had ceased to awe mankind. The dynasty which had reigned for ages was at an end; and the vacant throne was left to be struggled for by pretenders.

The first effect of this great revolution was, as Bacon most justly observed,† to give for a time an undue importance to the mere graces of style. The new breed of scholars, the Aschams and Buchanans, nourished with the finest compositions of the Augustan age, regarded with loathing the dry, crabbed and barbarous diction of respondents and opponents. They were far less studious about the matter of their works than about the manner. They succeeded in reforming Latinity; but they never even aspired to effect a reform in philosophy.

At this time Bacon appeared. It is altogether incorrect to say, as has often been said, that he was the first man who rose up against the Aristotelian philosophy when in the height of its power. The authority of that philosophy had, as we have shown, received a fatal blow long before he was born. Several speculators, among whom Ramus was the best known, had recently attempted to form new sects. Bacon's own expressions about the state of public opinion in the time of Luther are clear and strong: "Accedebat," says he, "odium et contemptus, illis ipsis temporibus ortus erga Scholasticos." And again, "Scholasticorum doctrina despectui prorsus haberi coepit tanquam aspera et barbara."‡ The part which Bacon played in this great change was the part, not of Robespierre, but of Bonaparte. When he came forward the ancient order of things had been subverted. Some bigots still cherished with devoted loyalty the remembrance of the fallen monarchy and exerted themselves to effect a restoration. But the majority had no such feeling. Freed, yet not knowing how to use their freedom, they pursued no determinate course, and had found no leader capable of conducting them.

That leader at length arose. The philosophy which he taught was essentially new. It differed from that of the celebrated ancient teachers, not merely in method, but in object. Its object was the good of mankind, in the sense in which the mass of mankind always have understood, and always will understand, the word good. "Meditor," said Bacon, "instaurationem philosophiæ ejusmodi quæ nihil inanis aut abstracti habeat, quæque vitæ humanæ conditiones in melius provehat."§

The difference between the philosophy of Bacon and that of his predecessors cannot, we think, be better illustrated than by comparing his views on some

---

* We quote, on the authority of Bayle, from Melchior Cano. a schol.atic divine of great reputation.
† De Augmentis, Lib. 1.
‡ Both these passages are in the first book of the De Augme..tis.
§ Redargutio Philosophiarum.

important subjects with those of Plato. We select Plato, because we conceive that he did more than any other person towards giving to the minds of speculative men that bent which they retained till they received from Bacon a new impulse in a diametrically opposite direction.

It is curious to observe how differently these great men estimated the value of every kind of knowledge. Take Arithmetic for example. Plato, after speaking slightly of the convenience of being able to reckon and compute in the ordinary transactions of life, passes to what he considers as a far more important advantage. The study of the properties of numbers, he tells us, habituates the mind to the contemplation of pure truth and raises it above the material universe. He would have his disciples apply themselves to this study, not that they may be able to buy or sell, not that they may qualify themselves to be shop-keepers or travelling merchants, but that they may learn to withdraw their minds from the ever-shifting spectacle of this visible and tangible world and to fix them on the immutable essences of things.*

Bacon, on the other hand, valued this branch of knowledge only on account of its uses with reference to that visible and tangible world which Plato so much despised. He speaks with scorn of the mystical arithmetic of the later Platonists, and laments the propensity of mankind to employ, on mere matters of curiosity, powers, the whole exertion of which is required for purposes of solid advantage. He advises arithmeticians to leave these trifles and to employ themselves in framing convenient expressions which may be of use in physical researches.†

The same reasons which led Plato to recommend the study of arithmetic, led him to recommend also the study of mathematics. The vulgar crowd of geometricians, he says, will not understand him. They have practice always in view. They do not know that the real use of the science is to lead man to the knowledge of abstract, essential, eternal truth.‡ Indeed, if we are to believe Plutarch, Plato carried this feeling so far that he considered geometry as degraded by being applied to any purpose of vulgar utility. Archytas, it seems, had framed machines of extraordinary power on mathematical principles.§ Plato remonstrated with his friend, and declared that this was to degrade a noble, intellectual exercise into a low craft, fit only for carpenters and wheelwrights. The office of geometry, he said, was to discipline the mind, not to minister to the base wants of the body. His interference was successful; and from that time, according to Plutarch, the science of mechanics was considered as unworthy of the attention of a philosopher.

Archimedes, in a later age, imitated and surpassed Archytas. But even Archimedes was not free from the prevailing notion that geometry was degraded by being employed to produce anything useful. It was with difficulty that he was induced to stoop from speculation to practice. He was half ashamed of those inventions which were the wonder of hostile nations; and always spoke of them slightingly as mere amusements—as trifles in which a mathematician might be suffered to relax his mind after intense application to the higher parts of his science.

The opinion of Bacon on this subject was diametrically opposed to that of the ancient philosophers. He valued geometry chiefly, if not solely, on account of those uses which to Plato appeared so base. And it is remarkable that the longer he lived the stronger this feeling became. When, in 1605, he

---

* Plato's Republic, Book 7. † De Augmentis, Lib. 3. Cap 6.
‡ Plato's Republic, Book 7.
§ Plutarch, Sympos. viii. and Life of Marcellus. The machines of Archytas are also mentioned by Aulus Gellius and Diogenes Laertius.

wrote the two books on the "Advancement of Learning," he dwelt on the advantages which mankind derived from mixed mathematics; but he at the same time admitted, that the beneficial effect produced by mathematical study on the intellect, though a collateral advantage, was "no less worthy than that which was principal and intended." But it is evident that his views underwent a change. When, nearly twenty years later, he published the "De Augmentis," which is the Treatise on the "Advancement of Learning" greatly expanded and carefully corrected, he made important alterations in the part which related to mathematics. He condemned with severity the high pretensions of the mathematicians—"delicias et fastum mathematicorum." Assuming the well-being of the human race to the end of knowledge,* he pronounced that mathematical science could claim no higher rank than that of an appendage, or an auxiliary, to other sciences. Mathematical science, he says, is the handmaid of natural philosophy—she ought to demean herself as such; and he declares that he cannot conceive by what ill chance it has happened that she presumes to claim precedence over her mistress. He predicts—a prediction which would have made Plato shudder—that as more and more discoveries are made in physics, there will be more and more branches of mixed mathematics. Of that collateral advantage, the value of which, twenty years before, he rated so highly, he says not one word. This omission cannot have been the effect of mere inadvertance. His own treatise was before him. From that treatise he deliberately expunged whatever was favourable to the study of pure mathematics, and inserted several keen reflections on the ardent votaries of that study. This fact, in our opinion, admits of only one explanation. Bacon's love of those pursuits which directly tend to improve the condition of mankind, and his jealousy of all pursuits merely curious, had grown upon him, and had, it may be, become immoderate. He was afraid of using any expression which might have the effect of inducing any man of talents to employ in speculations, useful only to the mind of the speculator, a single hour which might be employed in extending the empire of man over matter.†
If Bacon erred here, we must acknowledge that we greatly prefer his error to the opposite error of Plato. We have no patience with a philosophy which, like those Roman matrons who swallowed abortives in order to preserve their shapes, takes pains to be barren for fear of being homely.

Let us pass to astronomy. This was one of the sciences which Plato exhorted his disciples to learn, but for reasons far removed from common habits of thinking. "Shall we set down astronomy," says Socrates, "among the subjects of study?" ‡ "I think so," answers his young friend Glaucon: "to know something about the seasons, about the months and the years is of use for military purposes as well as for agriculture and navigation." "It amuses me," says Socrates, "to see how afraid you are lest the common herd of people should accuse you of recommending useless studies." He then proceeds in that pure and magnificent diction, which, as Cicero said, Jupiter would use if Jupiter spoke Greek, to explain that the use of astronomy is not to add to the vulgar comforts of life, but to assist in raising the mind to the contemplation of things which are to be perceived by the pure intellect alone. The knowledge of the actual motions of the heavenly bodies he considers as of little value. The appearances which make the sky beautiful at night are, he tells us, like the figures which a geometrician draws on the sand, mere examples, mere helps to feeble minds. We must get beyond them; we must

---

* Usui et commodis hominum consulimus.
† Compare the passage relating to mathematics in the Second Book of the Advancement of Learning with the De Augmentis, Lib. 3, Cap. 6.
‡ Plato's Republic, Book 7.

neglect them; we must attain to an astronomy which is as independent of the actual stars as geometrical truth is independent of the lines of an ill-drawn diagram. This is, we imagine, very nearly, if not exactly, the astronomy which Bacon compared to the ox of Prometheus*—a sleek, well-shaped hide, stuffed with rubbish, goodly to look at, but containing nothing to eat. He complained that astronomy had, to its great injury, been separated from natural philosophy, of which it was one of the noblest provinces, and annexed to the domain of mathematics. The world stood in need, he said, of a very different astronomy—of a *living astronomy*,† of an astronony which should set‡ forth the nature, the motion and the influences of the heavenly bodies as they really are.

On the greatest and most useful of all inventions—the invention of alphabetical writing—Plato did not look with much complacency. He seems to have thought that the use of letters had operated on the human mind as the use of the go-cart in learning to walk, or of corks in learning to swim is said to operate on the human body. It was a support which soon became indispensable to those who used it—which made vigorous exertion first unnecessary and then impossible. The powers of the intellect would, he conceived, have been more fully developed without this delusive aid. Men would have been compelled to exercise the understanding and the memory, and, by deep and assiduous meditation, to make truth thoroughly their own. Now, on the contrary, much knowledge is traced on paper, but little is engraved in the soul. A man is certain that he can find information at a moment's notice when he wants it. He therefore suffers it to fade from his mind. Such a man cannot in strictness be said to know anything. He has the show without the reality of wisdom. These opinions Plato has put into the mouth of an ancient king of Egypt.§ But it is evident from the context that they were his own; and so they were understood to be by Quinctilian.∥ Indeed they are in perfect accordance with the whole Platonic system.

Bacon's views, as may easily be supposed, were widely different.¶ The powers of the memory, he observes, without the help of writing, can do little towards the advancement of any useful science. He acknowledges that the memory may be disciplined to such a point as to be able to perform very extraordinary feats. But on such feats he sets little value. The habits of his mind, he tells us, are such that he is not disposed to rate highly any accomplishment, however rare, which is of no practical use to mankind. As to these prodigious achievements of the memory, he ranks them with the exhibitions of rope-dancers and tumblers. "The two performances," he says, "are much of the same sort. The one is an abuse of the powers of the body, the other is an abuse of the powers of the mind. Both may perhaps excite our wonder, but neither is entitled to our respect."

To Plato, the science of medicine appeared one of very disputable advantage.** He did not indeed object to quick cures for acute disorders, or for injuries produced by accidents. But the art which resists the slow sap of a chronic disease—which repairs frames enervated by lust, swollen by gluttony, or inflamed by wine—which encourages sensuality by mitigating the natural punishment of the sensualist, and prolongs existence when the intellect has ceased to retain its entire energy—had no share of his esteem. A life protracted by medical skill he pronounced to be a long death. The exercise

---

* De Augmentis, Lib. 3, Cap. 4.   † Astronomia viva.
‡ "Quæ substantiam et motum et influxum cœlestium, prout re vera sunt proponat." Compare this language with Plato's "τὰ δ' ἐν τῷ οὐρανῷ ἐάσωμεν."
§ Plato's Phædrus.   ∥ Quinctilian, XI.
¶ De Augmentis, Lib. 5, Cap. 5.   ** Plato's Republic, Book 3.

of the art of medicine ought, he said, to be tolerated so far as that art may serve to cure the occasional distempers of men whose constitutions are good. As to those who have bad constitutions, let them die—and the sooner the better. Such men are unfit for war, for magistracy, for the management of their domestic affairs. That, however, is comparatively of little consequence. But they are incapable of study and speculation. If they engage in any vigorous mental exercise, they are troubled with giddiness and fulness of the head, all which they lay to the account of philosopy. The best thing that can happen to such wretches is to have done with life at once. He quotes mythical authority in support of this doctrine; and reminds his disciples that the practice of the sons of Æsculapius, as described by Homer, extended only to the cure of external injuries.

Far different was the philosophy of Bacon. Of all the sciences, that which he seems to have regarded with the greatest interest was the science which, in Plato's opinion, would not be tolerated in a well regulated community. To make men perfect was no part of Bacon's plan. His humble aim was to make imperfect men comfortable. The beneficence of his philosophy resembled the beneficence of the Common Father, whose sun rises on the evil and the good—whose rain descends for the just and the unjust. In Plato's opinion man was made for philosophy; in Bacon's opinion philosophy was made for man; it was a means to an end—and that end was to increase the pleasures and to mitigate the pains of millions who are not, and cannot be, philosophers. That a valetudinarian, who took great pleasure in being wheeled along his terrace, who relished his boiled chicken and his weak wine and water, and who enjoyed a hearty laugh over the Queen of Navarre's tales, should be treated as a *caput lupinum* because he could not read the Timæus without a headache was a notion which the humane spirit of the English school of wisdom altogether rejected. Bacon would not have thought it beneath the dignity of a philosopher to contrive an improved garden chair for such a valetudinarian—to devise some way of rendering his medicines more palatable—to invent repasts which he might enjoy, and pillows on which he might sleep soundly; and this though there might not be the smallest hope that the mind of the poor invalid would ever rise to the contemplation of the ideal beautiful and the ideal good. As Plato had cited the religious legends of Greece to justify his contempt for the more recondite parts of the art of healing, Eacon vindicated the dignity of that art by appealing to the example of Christ; and reminded his readers that the great Physician of the soul did not disdain to be also the physician of the body.*

When we pass from the science of medicine to that of legislation, we find the same difference between the systems of these two great men. Plato, at the commencement of the fine Dialogue on Laws, lays it down as a fundamental principle, that the end of legislation is to make men virtuous. It is unnecessary to point out the extravagant conclusions to which such a proposition leads. Bacon well knew to how great an extent the happiness of every society must depend on the virtue of its members; and he also knew what legislators can, and what they cannot, do for the purpose of promoting virtue. The view which he has given of the end of legislation, and of the principal means for the attainment of that end, has always seemed to us eminently happy, even among the many happy passages of the same kind with which his works abound. "Finis et scopus quem leges intueri atque ad quem jussiones et sanctiones suas dirigere debent, non alius est quam ut cives feliciter degant. Id fiet si pietate et religione recte instituti, moribus honesti, armis adversus hostes externos tuti,

---

* De Augmen's, Lib. 4, Cap. 2.

legum auxilio adversus seditiones et privatas injurias muniti, imperio et magistratibus obsequentes, copiis et opibus locupletes et florentes fuerint."*
The end is the well-being of the people. The means are the imparting of moral and religious education; the providing of everything necessary for defence against foreign enemies; the maintaining of internal order; the establishing of a judicial, financial and commercial system under which wealth may be rapidly accumulated and securely enjoyed.

Even with respect to the form in which laws ought to be drawn, there is a remarkable difference of opinion between the Greek and the Englishman. Plato thought a preamble essential; Bacon thought it mischievous. Each was consistent with himself. Plato, considering the moral improvement of the people as the end of legislation, justly inferred that a law which commanded and threatened, but which neither convinced the reason nor touched the heart, must be a most imperfect law. He was not content with deterring from theft a man who still continued to be a thief at heart—with restraining a son who hated his mother from beating his mother. The only obedience on which he set much value, was the obedience which an enlightened understanding yields to reason, and which a virtuous disposition yields to precepts of virtue. He really seems to have believed that, by prefixing to every law an eloquent and pathetic exhortation, he should, to a great extent, render penal enactments superfluous. Bacon entertained no such romantic hopes; and he well knew the practical inconveniences of the course which Plato recommended. " Neque nobis," says he, " prologi legum qui inepti olim habiti sunt, et leges introducunt disputantes non jubentes, utique placerent, si priscos mores ferre possemus . . . . Quantum fieri potest prologi evitentur, et lex incipiat a jussione."†

Had Plato lived to finish the "Critias," a comparison between that noble fiction and the "New Atlantis" would probably have furnished us with still more striking instances. It is amusing to think with what horror he would have seen such an institution as Solomon's House rising in his republic; with what vehemence he would have ordered the brewhouses, the perfume-houses and the dispensatories to be pulled down; and with what inexorable rigour he would have driven beyond the frontier all the Fellows of the College, Merchants of Light and Depredators, Lamps and Pioneers.

To sum up the whole, we should say that the aim of the Platonic philosophy was to exalt man into a god. The aim of the Baconian philosophy was to provide man with what he requires while he continues to be man. The aim of the Platonic Philosophy was to raise us far above vulgar wants. The aim of the Baconian philosophy was to supply our vulgar wants. The former aim was noble; but the latter was attainable. Plato drew a good bow; but, like Acestes in Virgil, he aimed at the stars, and, therefore, though there was no want of strength or skill, the shot was thrown away. His arrow was indeed followed by a track of dazzling radiance, but it struck nothing.

> " Volans liquidis in nubibus arsit arundo
> Signavitque viam flammis, tenuisque recessit
> Consumta in ventos."

Bacon fixed his eye on a mark which was placed on the earth and within bow-shot, and hit it in the white. The philosophy of Plato began in words and ended in words—noble words indeed—words such as were to be expected from the finest of human intellects exercising boundless dominion over the finest of human languages. The philosophy of Bacon began in observations and ended in arts.

The boast of the ancient philosophers was, that their doctrine formed the

---

* Ib., Lib. 8, Cap. 3. Aph. 5. † De Augmentis, Lib. 8, Cap. 3, Aph. 69.

minds of men to a high degree of wisdom and virtue. This was indeed the only practical good which the most celebrated of those teachers even pretended to effect; and undoubtedly if they had effected this, they would have deserved the greatest praise. But the truth is, that in those very matters in which alone they professed to do any good to mankind, in those very matters for the sake of which they neglected all the vulgar interests of mankind, they did nothing, or worse than nothing. They promised what was impracticable; they despised what was practicable; they filled the world with long words and long beards; and they left it as wicked and as ignorant as they found it.

An acre in Middlesex is better than a principality in Utopia. The smallest actual good is better than the most magnificent promises of impossibilities. The wise man of the Stoics would, no doubt, be a grander object than a steam-engine. But there are steam-engines. And the wise man of the Stoics is yet to be born. A philosophy which should enable a man to feel perfectly happy while in agonies of pain would be better than a philosophy which assuages pain. But we know that there are remedies which will assuage pain; and we know that the ancient sages liked the toothache just as little as their neighbours. A philosophy which should extinguish cupidity would be better than a philosophy which should devise laws for the security of property. But it is possible to make laws which shall, to a very great extent, secure property. And we do not understand how any motives which the ancient philosophy furnished could extinguish cupidity. We know, indeed, that the philosophers were no better than other men. From the testimony of friends as well as of foes, from the confessions of Epictetus and Seneca, as well as from the sneers of Lucian and the fierce invectives of Juvenal, it is plain that these teachers of virtue had all the vices of their neighbours, with the additional vice of hypocrisy. Some people may think the object of the Baconian philosophy a low object, but they cannot deny that, high or low, it has been attained. They cannot deny that every year makes an addition to what Bacon called "fruit." They cannot deny that mankind have made, and are making, great and constant progress in the road which he pointed out to them. Was there any such progressive movement among the ancient philosophers? After they had been declaiming eight hundred years, had they made the world better than when they began?

Our belief is that, among the philosophers themselves, instead of a progressive improvement there was a progressive degeneracy. An abject superstition, which Democritus or Anaxagoras would ha' e rejected with scorn, added the last disgrace to the long dotage of the Stoic and Platonic schools. Those unsuccessful attempts to articulate, which are so delightful and interesting in a child, shock and disgust in an aged paralytic; and, in the same way, those wild and mythological fictions which charm us when we hear them lisped by Greek poetry in its infancy, excite a mixed sensation of pity and loathing when mumbled by Greek philosophy in its old age. We know that guns, cutlery, spy-glasses, clocks are better in our time than they were in the time of our fathers, and were better in the time of our fathers than they were in the time of our grandfathers. We might, therefore, be inclined to think that, when a philosophy which boasted that its object was the elevation and purification of the mind, and which for this object neglected the sordid office of ministering to the comforts of the body, had flourished in the highest honour for many hundreds of years, a vast moral amelioration must have taken place. Was it so?. Look at the schools of this wisdom four centuries before the Christian era and four centuries after that era. Compare the men whom those schools formed at those two periods. Compare Plato and Libanius. Compare Pericles and Julian. This philosophy confessed, nay boasted, that for every end but one it was useless. Had it attained that one end?

Suppose that Justinian, when he closed the schools of Athens, had called on the last few sages who still haunted the Portico and lingered round the ancient plane-trees to show their title to public veneration—suppose that he had said: "A thousand years have elapsed since, in this famous city, Socrates posed Protagoras and Hippias; during those thousand years a large proportion of the ablest men of every generation has been employed in constant efforts to bring to perfection the philosophy which you teach; that philosophy has been munificently patronised by the powerful; its professors have been held in the highest esteem by the public; it has drawn to itself almost all the sap and vigour of the human intellect: and what has it effected? What profitable truth has it taught us which we should not equally have known without it? What has it enabled us to do which we should not have been equally able to do without it?" Such questions, we suspect, would have puzzled Simplicius and Isidore. Ask a follower of Bacon what the new philosophy, as it was called in the time of Charles the Second, has effected for mankind, and his answer is ready: "It has lengthened life; it has mitigated pain; it has extinguished diseases; it has increased the fertility of the soil; it has given new securities to the mariner; it has furnished new arms to the warrior; it has spanned great rivers and estuaries with bridges of form unknown to our fathers; it has guided the thunderbolt innocuously from heaven to earth; it has lighted up the night with the splendour of the day; it has extended the range of the human vision; it has multiplied the power of the human muscles; it has accelerated motion; it has annihilated distance; it has facilitated intercourse, correspondence, all friendly offices, all despatch of business; it has enabled man to descend to the depths of the sea, to soar into the air, to penetrate securely into the noxious recesses of the earth, to traverse the land in cars which whirl along without horses, and the ocean in ships which sail against the wind. These are but a part of its fruits, and of its first fruits. For it is a philosophy which never rests, which has never attained, which is never perfect. Its law is progress. A point which yesterday was invisible is its goal to-day and will be its starting-post to-morrow."

Great and various as the powers of Bacon were, he owes his wide and durable fame chiefly to this, that all those powers received their direction from common sense. His love of the vulgar useful, his strong sympathy with the popular notions of good and evil, and the openness with which he avowed that sympathy, are the secret of his influence. There was in his system no cant, no illusion. He had no annointing for broken bones, no fine theories *de finibus*, no arguments to persuade men out of their senses. He knew that men, and philosophers as well as other men, do actually love life, health, comfort, honour, security, the society of friends; and do actually dislike death, sickness, pain, poverty, disgrace, danger, separation from those to whom they are attached. He knew that religion, though it often regulates and moderates these feelings, seldom eradicates them; nor did he think it desirable for mankind that they should be eradicated. The plan of eradicating them by conceits like those of Seneca, or syllogisms like those of Chrysippus, was too preposterous to be for a moment entertained by a mind like his. He did not understand what wisdom there could be in changing names where it was impossible to change things—in denying that blindness, hunger, the gout, the rack were evils, and calling them ἀποπροήγμενα—in refusing to acknowledge that health, safety, plenty were good things, and dubbing them by the name of ἀδιάφορα. In his opinions on all these subjects, he was not a Stoic, nor an Epicurean, nor an Academic, but what would have been called by Stoics, Epicureans and Academics a mere Ιδιώτης—a mere common man. And it was precisely because he was so that his name makes so great an era in the history of the world. It was because he dug deep that he was able to pile high. It was because, in order to lay his foundations, he went down into those parts of human nature which lie low, but which are not liable to change, that the fabric which he reared has risen to so stately an elevation and stands with such immovable strength.

We have sometimes thought that an amusing fiction might be written, in which a disciple of Epictetus and a disciple of Bacon should be introduced as fellow-travellers. They come to a village where the small-pox has just begun to rage, and find houses shut up, intercourse suspended, the sick abandoned, mothers weeping in terror over their children. The Stoic assures the dismayed population that there is nothing bad in the small-pox, and that to a wise man disease, deformity, death, the loss of friends are not evils. The Baconian takes out a lancet and begins to vaccinate. They find a body of miners in great dismay. An explosion of noisome vapours has just killed many of those who were at work and the survivors are afraid to venture into the cavern. The Stoic assures them that such an accident is nothing but a mere ἀποτραγγμενον. The Baconian, who has no such fine word at his command, contents himself with devising a safety-lamp. They find a shipwrecked merchant wringing his hands on the shore. His vessel, with an inestimable cargo, has just gone down, and he is reduced in a moment from opulence to beggary. The Stoic exhorts him not to seek happiness in things which lie without himself, and repeats the whole chapter of Epictetus πρὸς τοὺς τὴν ἀπορίαν δεδοικότας. The Baconian constructs a diving-bell, goes down in it, and returns with the most precious effects from the wreck. It would be easy to multiply illustrations of the difference between the philosophy of thorns and the philosophy of fruit—the philosophy of words and the philosophy of works.

Bacon had been accused of overrating the importance of those sciences which minister to the physical well-being of man, and of underrating the importance of moral philosophy; and it cannot be denied that persons who read the "Novum Organum" and the "De Augmentis," without adverting to the circumstances under which those works were written, will find much that may seem to countenance the accusation. It is certain, however, that, though in practice he often went very wrong, and though, as his historical work and his essays prove, he did not hold, even in theory, very strict opinions on points of political morality, he was far too wise a man not to know how much our well-being depends on the regulation of our minds. The world for which he wished was not, as some people seem to imagine, a world of water-wheels, power-looms, steam-carriages, sensualists and knaves. He would have been as ready as Zeno himself to maintain that no bodily comforts which could be devised by the skill and labour of a hundred generations would give happiness to a man whose mind was under the tyranny of licentious appetite, of envy, of hatred, or of fear. If he sometimes appeared to ascribe importance too exclusively to the arts which increase the outward comforts of our species, the reason is plain. Those arts had been most unduly depreciated. They had been represented as unworthy of the attention of a man of liberal education. "Cogitavit," says Bacon of himself, "eam esse opinionem sive æstimationem humidam et damnosam, minui nempe majestatem mentis humanæ, si in experimentis et rebus particularibus, sensui subjectis, et in materia terminatis, diu ac multum versetur: præsertim cum hujusmodi res ad inquirendum laboriosæ, ad meditandum ignobiles, ad discendum asperæ, ad practicam illiberales, numero infinitæ, et subtilitate pusillæ videri soleant, et ob hujusmodi conditiones, gloriæ artium minus sint accommodatæ."* This opinion seemed to him "omnia in familia

---

* Cogitata et Visa. The expression *opinio humida* may surprise a reader not accustomed to Bacon's style. The allusion is to the maxim of Heraclitus the obscure: "Dry

humana turbasse." It had undoubtedly caused many arts which were of the greatest utility, and which were susceptible of the greatest improvements, to be neglected by speculators and abandoned to joiners, masons, smiths, weavers, apothecaries. It was necessary to assert the dignity of those arts, to bring them prominently forward, to proclaim that, as they have a most serious effect on human happiness, they are not unworthy of the attention of the highest human intellects. Again, it was by illustrations drawn from these arts that Bacon could most easily illustrate his principles. It was by improvements effected in these arts that the soundness of his principles could be most speedily and decisively brought to the test and made manifest to common understandings. He acted like a wise commander who thins every other part of his line to strengthen a point where the enemy is attacking with peculiar fury, and on the fate of which the event of the battle seems likely to depend. In the "Novum Organum," however, he distinctly and most truly declares that his philosophy is no less a Moral than a Natural Philosophy—that, though his illustrations are drawn from physical science, the principles which those illustrations are intended to explain are just as applicable to Ethical and Political enquiries as to enquiries into the nature of Heat and Vegetation.*

He frequently treated of moral subjects; and he almost always brought to those subjects that spirit which was the essence of his whole system. He has left us many admirable practicable observations on what he somewhat quaintly called the *Georgics* of the mind—on the mental culture which tends to produce good dispositions. Some persons, he said, might accuse him of spending labour on a matter so simple that his predecessors had passed it by with contempt. He desired such persons to remember that he had from the first announced the objects of his search to be, not the splendid and the surprising, but the useful and the true—not the deluding dreams which go forth through the shining portal of ivory, but the humbler realities of the gate of horn.†

True to this principal, he indulged in no rants about the fitness of things, the all-sufficiency of virtue and the dignity of human nature. He dealt not at all in resounding nothings, such as those with which Bolingbroke pretended to comfort himself in exile, and in which Cicero sought consolation after the loss of Tullia. The casuistical subtilties which occupied the attention of the keenest spirits of his age had, it should seem, no attractions for him. The treatises of the doctors, whom Escobar afterwards compared to the four beasts and the four-and-twenty elders in the Apocalypse, Bacon dismissed with most contemptuous brevity. "Inanes plerumque evadunt et futiles."‡ Nor did he ever meddle with those enigmas which have puzzled hundreds of generations and will puzzle hundreds more. He said nothing about the grounds of moral obligation, or the freedom of the human will. He had no inclination to employ himself in labours resembling those of the damned in the Grecian Tartarus—to spin for ever on the same wheel round the same pivot—to gape for ever after the same deluding clusters—to pour water for ever into the same bottomless buckets—to pace for ever to and fro on the same wearisome path after the same recoiling stone. He exhorted his disciples to prosecute researches of a very different description; to consider moral science as a practical science—a science of which the object was to cure the diseases and perturbations of the mind—and which could be improved only by a method analogous to that which has improved medicine and surgery. Moral philosophers ought, he said, to set themselves vigorously to work for the purpose of

---

light is the best." By dry light, Bacon understood the light of the intellect not obscured by the mists of passion, interest or prejudice.
* Novum Organum, Lib. 1, Aph. 127. † De Augmentis, Lib. 7, Cap. 3.
‡ De Augmentis, Lib. 7, Cap. 2.

discovering what are the actual effects produced on the human character by particular modes of education, by the indulgence of particular habits, by the study of particular books, by society, by emulation, by imitation. Then we might hope to find out what mode of training was most likely to preserve and restore moral health.*

What he was as a natural philosopher and a moral philosopher, that he was also as a theologian. He was, we are convinced, a sincere believer in the divine authority of the Christian revelation. Nothing can be found in his writings, or in any other writings, more eloquent and pathetic than some passages which were apparently written under the influence of strong devotional feeling. He loved to dwell on the power of the Christian religion to effect much that the ancient philosophers could only promise. He loved to consider that religion as the bond of charity, the curb of evil passions, the consolation of the wretched, the support of the timid, the hope of the dying. But controversies on speculative points of theology seemed to have engaged scarcely any portion of his attention. In what he wrote on Church Government he showed, as far as he dared, a tolerant and charitable spirit. He troubled himself not at all about Homoousians and Homoiousians, Monothelites and Nestorians. He lived in an age in which disputes on the most subtle points of divinity excited an intense interest throughout Europe; and nowhere more than in England. He was placed in the very thick of the conflict. He was in power at the time of the Synod of Dort, and must for months have been daily deafened with talk about election, reprobation and final perseverance. Yet we do not remember a line in his works from which it can be inferred that he was either a Calvinist or an Arminian. While the world was resounding with the noise of a disputatious philosophy and a disputatious theology, the Baconian school, like Alworthy seated between Square and Thwackum, preserved a calm neutrality—half scornful, half benevolent, and content with adding to the sum of practical good, left the war of words to those who liked it.

We have dwelt long on the end of the Baconian philosophy, because from this peculiarity all the other peculiarities of that philosophy necessarily arose. Indeed, scarcely any person who proposed to himself the same end with Bacon could fail to hit upon the same means.

The vulgar notion about Bacon we take to be this—that he invented a new method of arriving at truth, which method is called Induction; and that he exposed the fallacy of the syllogistic reasoning which had been in vogue before his time. This notion is about as well founded as that of the people who, in the middle ages, imagined that Virgil was a great conjurer. Many, who are far too well informed to talk such extravagant nonsense, entertain what we think incorrect notions as to what Bacon really effected in this matter.

The inductive method has been practised ever since the beginning of the world by every human being. It is constantly practised by the most ignorant clown, by the most thoughtless schoolboy, by the very child at the breast. That method leads the clown to the conclusion that if he sows barley he shall not reap wheat. By that method the schoolboy learns that a cloudy day is the best for catching trout. The very infant, we imagine, is led by induction to expect milk from his mother, or nurse, and none from his father.

Not only is it not true that Bacon invented the inductive method, but it is not true that he was the first person who correctly analysed that method and explained its uses. Aristotle had long before pointed out the absurdity of supposing that syllogistic reasoning could ever conduct men to the discovery of any new principle; had shown that such discoveries must be made by

---

* Ib., Lib. 7, Cap. 3.

induction and by induction alone; and had given the history of the inductive process, concisely indeed, but with great perspicuity and precision.*

Again, we are not inclined to ascribe much practical value to the analysis of the inductive method which Bacon has given in the second book of the "Novum Organum." It is indeed an elaborate and correct analysis. But it is an analysis of that which we are all doing from morning to night, and which we continue to do even in our dreams. A plain man finds his stomach out of order. He never heard Lord Bacon's name. But he proceeds in the strictest conformity with the rules laid down in the second book of the "Novum Organum," and satisfies himself that minced pies have done the mischief. "I ate mince pies on Monday and Wednesday, and I was kept awake by indigestion all night." This is the *comparentia ad intellectum instantiarum convenientium*. "I did not eat any on Tuesday and Friday, and I was quite well." This is the *comparentia instantiarum in proximo quæ natura data privantur*. "I ate very sparingly of them on Sunday, and was very slightly indisposed in the evening. But on Christmas-day I almost dined on them, and was so ill that I was in great danger." This is the *comparentia instantiarum secundum magis et minus*. "It cannot have been the brandy which I took with them. For I have drunk brandy daily for years without being the worse for it." This is the *rejectio naturarum*. Our invalid then proceeds to what is termed by Bacon the *Vindemiatio*, and pronounces that minced pies do not agree with him.

We might go on to what are called by Bacon *prærogativæ instantiarum*. For example: "It must be something peculiar to minced pies, for I can eat any other pastry without the least bad effect." This is the *instantia solitaria*. We might easily proceed, but we have already sufficiently explained our meaning. We repeat that we dispute neither the ingenuity nor the accuracy of the theory contained in the second book of the "Novum Organum," but we think that Bacon greatly overrated its utility. We conceive that the inductive process, like many other processes, is not likely to be better performed merely because men know how they perform it. William Tell would not have been one whit more likely to cleave the apple if he had known that his arrow would describe a parabola under the influence of the attraction of the earth. Captain Barclay would not have been more likely to walk a thousand miles in a thousand hours if he had known the place and name of every muscle in his legs. Monsieur Jourdain probably did not pronounce D and F more correctly after he had been apprised that D is pronounced by touching the teeth with the end of the tongue and F by putting the upper teeth on the lower lip. We cannot perceive that the study of grammar makes the smallest difference in the speech of people who have always lived in good society. Not one Londoner in ten thousand can lay down the rules for the proper use of *will* and *shall*. Yet not one Londoner in a million ever misplaces his *will* and *shall*. No man uses figures of speech with more propriety because he knows that one figure is called a metonymy and another a synecdoche. A drayman, in a passion, calls out, "You are a pretty fellow," without suspecting that he is uttering irony, and that irony is one of the four primary tropes. The old systems of rhetoric were never regarded by the most experienced and discerning judges as of any use for the purpose of forming an orator. "Ego hanc vim intelligo," said Cicero, "esse in præceptis omnibus, non ut ea secuti oratores eloquentiæ laudem sint adepti, sed quæ sua sponte homines eloquentes facerent, ea quosdam observasse, atque id egisse; sic esse non eloquentiam ex artificio, sed artificium ex eloquentia natum."† We must own that we entertain the

---

* See the last chapter of the Posterior Analytics and the first of the Metaphysics.
† De Oratore, Lib. 1.

same opinion concerning the study of Logic which Cicero entertained concerning the study of Rhetoric. A man of sense syllogises in *celarent* and *cesare* all day long without suspecting it; and, though he may not know what an *ignoratio elenchi* is, has no difficulty in exposing it whenever he falls in with it; which is likely to be as often as he falls in with a reverend Master of Arts nourished on mode and figure in the cloisters of Oxford. Considered merely as an intellectual feat, the "Organum" of Aristotle can scarcely be admired too highly. But the more we compare individual with individual, school with school, nation with nation, generation with generation, the more do we lean to the opinion that the knowledge of the theory of logic has no tendency whatever to make men good reasoners.

What Aristotle did for the syllogistic process, Bacon has, in the second book of the "Novum Organum," done for the inductive process; that is to say he has analysed it well. His rules are quite proper, but we do not need them, because they are drawn from our own constant practice.

But though everybody is constantly performing the process described in the second book of the "Novum Organum," some men perform it well and some perform it ill. Some are led by it to truth and some to error. It led Franklin to discover the nature of lightning. It led thousands, who had less brains than Franklin, to believe in animal magnetism. But this was not because Franklin went through the process described by Bacon and the dupes of Mesmer through a different process. The *comparentiæ* and *rejectiones* of which we have given examples will be found in the most unsound inductions. We have heard that an eminent judge of the last generation was in the habit of jocosely propounding after dinner a theory, that the cause of the prevalence of Jacobinism was the practice of bearing three names. He quoted on the one side Charles James Fox, Richard Brinsley Sheridan, John Horne Tooke, John Philpot Curran, Samuel Taylor Coleridge, Theobald Wolfe Tone. These were *instantiæ convenientes*. He then proceeded to cite instances *absentia in proximo*, William Pitt, John Scott, William Windham, Samuel Horsley, Henry Dundas, Edmund Burke. He might have gone on to instances *secundum magis et minus*. The practice of giving children three names has been for some time a growing practice, and Jacobinism has also been growing. The practice of giving children three names is more common in America than in England. In England we still have a king and a House of Lords; but the Americans are republicans. The *rejectiones* are obvious. Burke and Theobald Wolfe Tone were both Irishmen; therefore the being an Irishman is not the cause of Jacobinism. Horsley and Horn Tooke are both clergymen; therefore the being a clergyman is not the cause of Jacobinism. Fox and Windham were both educated at Oxford; therefore the being educated at Oxford is not the cause of Jacobinism. Pitt and Horne Tooke were both educated at Cambridge; therefore the being educated at Cambridge is not the cause of Jacobinism. In this way, our Inductive philosopher arrives at what Bacon calls the *Vintage*, and pronounces that the having three names is the cause of Jacobinism.

Here is an induction corresponding with Bacon's analysis and ending in a monstrous absurdity. In what, then, does this induction differ from the induction which leads us to the conclusion that the presence of the sun is the cause of our having more light by day than by night? The difference evidently is not in the kind of instances, but in the number of instances; that is to say, the difference is not in that part of the process for which Bacon has given precise rules, but in a circumstance for which no precise rule can possibly be given. If the learned author of the theory about Jacobinism had enlarged either of his tables a little, his system would have been destroyed. The names of Tom Payne and William Wyndham Grenville would have been sufficient to do the work.

It appears to us, then, that the difference between a sound and an unsound induction, or, to use the Baconian phraseology, between the interpretation of nature and the anticipation of nature, does not lie in this—that the interpreter of nature goes through the process analysed in the second book of the "Novum Organum" and the anticipator through a different process. Now, precepts can do little towards making men patient and attentive and still less towards making them sagacious and judicious. It is very well to tell men to be on their guard against prejudices, not to believe facts on slight evidence, not to be content with a scanty collection of facts, to put out of their minds the *idola* which Bacon has so finely decribed. But these rules are too general to be of much practical use. The question is What is a prejudice? How long does the incredulity with which I hear a new theory propounded continue to be a wise and salutary incredulity? When does it become an *idolum specus*, the unreasonable pertinacity of a too sceptical mind? What is slight evidence? What collection of facts is scanty? Will ten instances do, or fifty, or a hundred? In how many months would the first human beings who settled on the shores of the ocean have been justified in believing that the moon had an influence on the tides? After how many experiments would Jenner have been justified in believing that he had discovered a safeguard against the small pox? These are questions to which it would be most desirable to have a precise answer; but, unhappily, they are questions to which no precise answer can be returned.

We think, then, that it is possible to lay down accurate rules, as Bacon has done, for the performance of that part of the inductive process which all men perform alike; but that these rules, though accurate, are not wanted because in truth they only tell us to do what we are all doing. We think that it is impossible to lay down any precise rule for the performing of that part of the inductive process which a great experimental philosopher performs in one way and a superstitious old woman in another.

On this subject, we think, Bacon was in an error. He certainly attributed to his rules a value which did not belong to them. He went so far as to say that, if his method of making discoveries were adopted, little would depend on the degree of force or acuteness of any intellect; that all minds would be reduced to one level; that his philosophy resembled a compass or a rule which equalises all hands, and enables the most unpractised person to draw a more correct circle or line than the best draftsmen can produce without such aid.* This really seems to us as extravagant as it would have been in Lindley Murray to announce that everybody who should learn his Grammar would write as good English as Dryden; or in that very able writer, Dr. Whately, to promise that all the readers of his "Logic" would reason like Chillingworth, and that all the readers of his "Rhetoric" would speak like Burke. That Bacon was altogether mistaken as to this point will now hardly be disputed. His philosophy has flourished during two hundred years, and has produced none of this levelling. The interval between a man of talents and a dunce is as wide as ever; and is never more clearly discernible than when they engage in researches which require the constant use of induction.

It will be seen that we do not consider Bacon's ingenious analysis of the inductive method as a very useful performance. Bacon was not, as we have already said, the inventor of the inductive method. He was not even the person who first analysed the inductive method correctly, though he undoubtedly analysed it more minutely than any who preceded him. He was not the

---

* Novum Organum, Præf. and Lib. 1, Aph. 122.

person who first showed that by the inductive method alone new truth could be discovered. But he was the person who first turned the minds of speculative men, long occupied in verbal disputes, to the discovery of new truth; and, by doing so, he at once gave to the inductive method an importance and dignity which had never before belonged to it. He was not the maker of that road; he was not the discoverer of that road; he was not the person who first surveyed and mapped that road. But he was the person who first called the public attention to an inexhaustible mine of wealth, which had been utterly neglected, and which was accessible by that road alone. By doing so he caused that road, which had previously been trodden only by peasants and higglers, to be frequented by a higher class of travellers.

That which was eminently his own in his system was the end which he proposed to himself. The end being given, the means, as it appears to us, could not well be mistaken. If others had aimed at the same object with Bacon, we hold it to be certain that they would have employed the same method with Bacon. It would have been hard to convince Seneca that the inventing of a safety-lamp was an employment worthy of a philosopher. It would have been hard to persuade Thomas Aquinas to descend from the making of syllogisms to the making of gunpowder. But Seneca would never have doubted for a moment that it was only by means of a series of experiments that a safety-lamp could be invented. Thomas Aquinas would never have thought that his *barbara* and *baralipton* would enable him to ascertain the proportion which charcoal ought to bear to saltpetre in a pound of gunpowder. Neither common sense nor Aristotle would have suffered him to fall into such an absurdity.

By stimulating men to the discovery of *new* truth, Bacon stimulated them to employ the inductive method, the only method—even the ancient philosophers and the schoolmen themselves being judges—by which new truth can be discovered. By stimulating men to the discovery of *useful* truth, he furnished them with a motive to perform the inductive process well and carefully. His predecessors had been anticipators of nature. They had been content with first principles, at which they had arrived by the most scanty and slovenly induction. And why was this? It was, we conceive, because their philosophy proposed to itself no practical end, because it was merely an exercise of the mind. A man who wants to contrive a new machine or a new medicine has a strong motive to observe accurately and patiently, and to try experiment after experiment. But a man who merely wants a theme for disputation or declamation has no such motive. He is therefore content with premises grounded on assumption, or on the most scanty and hasty induction. Thus, we conceive, the schoolmen acted. On their foolish premises they often argued with great ability; and as their object was "*ascensum subjugare, non res,*"* to be victorious in controversy, not to be victorious over nature, they were consistent. For just as much logical skill could be shown in reasoning on false as on true premises. But the followers of the new philosophy, proposing to themselves the discovery of useful truth as their object, must have altogether failed of attaining that object if they had been content to build theories on superficial induction.

Bacon has remarked† that in all ages, when philosophy was stationary, the mechanical arts went on improving. Why was this? Evidently because the mechanic was not content with so careless a mode of induction as served the purpose of the philosopher. And why was the philosopher more easily satisfied than the mechanic? Evidently because the object of the mechanic was to mould things, whilst the object of the philosopher was only to mould words.

---

* Novum Organum, Lib. 1, Aph. 29. † De Augmentis, Lib. 1.

Careful induction is not at all necessary to the making of a good syllogism. But it is indispensable to the making of a good shoe. Mechanics, therefore, have always been, as far as the range of their humble but useful callings extended, not anticipators, but interpreters of nature. And when a philosophy arose, the object of which was to do on a large scale what the mechanic does on a small scale—to extend the power and to supply the wants of man—the truth of the premises, which logically is a matter altogether unimportant, became a matter of the highest importance; and the careless induction with which men of learning had previously been satisfied gave place, of necessity, to an induction far more accurate and satisfactory.

What Bacon did for inductive philosophy may, we think, be fairly stated thus. The objects of preceding speculators were objects which could be attained without careful induction. Those speculators, therefore, did not perform the inductive process carefully. Bacon stirred up men to pursue an object which could be attained only by induction, and by induction carefully performed; and consequently induction was more carefully performed. We do not think that the importance of what Bacon did for inductive philosophy has ever been overrated. But we think that the nature of his services is often mistaken, and was not fully understood even by himself. It was not by furnishing philosophers with rules, nor performing the inductive process well, but by furnishing them with a motive for performing it well, that he conferred so vast a benefit on society.

To give to the human mind a direction which it shall retain for ages is the rare prerogative of a few imperial spirits. It cannot, therefore, be uninteresting to inquire what was the moral and intellectual constitution which enabled Bacon to exercise so vast an influence on the world.

In the temper of Bacon—we speak of Bacon the philosopher, not of Bacon the lawyer and politician—there was a singular union of audacity and sobriety. The promises which he made to mankind might, to a superficial reader, seem to resemble the rants which a great dramatist has put into the mouth of an Oriental conqueror half-crazed by good fortune and by violent passions.

> "He shall have chariots easier than air,
> Which I will have invented; and thyself,
> That art the messenger, shall ride before him
> On a horse cut out of an entire diamond,
> That shall be made to go with golden wheels,
> I know not how yet."

But Bacon performed what he promised. In truth, Fletcher would not have dared to make Arbaces promise, in his wildest fits of excitement, the tithe of what the Baconian philosophy has performed.

The true philosophical temperament may, we think, be described in four words—much hope, little faith; a disposition to believe that anything, however extraordinary, may be done; an indisposition to believe that anything extraordinary has been done. In these points the constitution of Bacon's mind seems to us to have been absolutely perfect. He was at once the Mammon and the Surly of his friend Ben. Sir Epicure did not indulge in visions more magnificent and gigantic. Surly did not sift evidence with keener and more sagacious incredulity.

Closely connected with this peculiarity of Bacon's temper was a striking peculiarity of his understanding. With great minuteness of observation, he had an amplitude of comprehension such as has never yet been vouchsafed to any other human being. The small, fine mind of Labruyère had not a more delicate tact than the large intellect of Bacon. The "Essays" contain abundant proofs that no nice feature of character, no peculiarity in the ordering of a house, a garden, or a court-masque could escape the notice of one whose mind was capable of taking in the whole world of knowledge. His understanding resembled the tent which the fairy Paribanou gave to Prince Ahmed. Fold it; and it seemed a toy for the hand of a lady. Spread it; and the armies of powerful Sultans might repose beneath its shade.

In keenness of observation he has been equalled, though, perhaps, never surpassed. But the largeness of his mind was all his own. The glance with which he surveyed the intellectual universe resembled that which the Archangel, from the golden threshold of heaven, darted down into the new creation.

> "Round he surveyed—and well might, where he stood
> So high above the circling canopy
> Of night's extended shade—from eastern point
> Of Libra, to the fleecy star which bears
> Andromeda far off Atlantic seas
> Beyond the horizon."

His knowledge differed from that of other men as a terrestrial globe differs from an Atlas which contains a different country on every leaf. The towns and roads of England, France and Germany are better laid down in the Atlas than on the globe. But while we are looking at England we see nothing of France; and while we are looking at France we see nothing of Germany. We may go to the Atlas to learn the bearings and distances of York and Bristol, or of Dresden and Prague. But it is useless if we want to know the bearings and distances of France and Martinique, or of England and Canada. On the globe we shall not find all the market towns in our own neighbourhood; but we shall learn from it the comparative extent and the relative position of all the kingdoms of the earth. "I have taken," said Bacon, in a letter written when he was only thirty-one to his uncle Lord Burleigh, "I have taken all knowledge to be my province." In any other young man, indeed in any other man, this would have been a ridiculous flight of presumption. There have been thousands of better mathematicians, astronomers, chemists, physicians, botanists, mineralogists than Bacon. No man would go to Bacon's works to learn any particular science or art, any more than he would go to a twelve-inch globe in order to find his way from Kennington turnpike to Clapham Common. The art which Bacon taught was the art of inventing arts. The knowledge in which Bacon excelled all men was a knowledge of the mutual relations of all departments of knowledge.

The mode in which he communicated his thoughts was exceedingly peculiar. He had no touch of that disputatious temper which he often censured in his predecessors. He effected a vast intellectual revolution in opposition to a vast mass of prejudices; yet he never engaged in any controversy; nay, we cannot at present recollect, in all his philosophical works, a single passage of a controversial character. All those works might with propriety have been put into the form which he adopted in the work entitled "Cogitata et Visa," "Franciscus Baconus sic cogitavit." These are thoughts which have occured to me; weigh them well, and take them or leave them.

Borgia said of the famous expedition of Charles the Eighth, that the French had conquered Italy, not with steel, but with chalk; for that the only exploit which they had found necessary for the purpose of taking military occupation of any place had been to mark the doors of the houses where they meant to quarter. Bacon often quoted this saying, and loved to apply it to the victories of his own intellect.* His philosophy, he said, came as a guest, not as an

---

* Novum Organum, Lib. 1, Aph. 35, and elsewhere.

enemy. She found no difficulty in gaining admittance, without a contest, into every understanding fitted, by its structure and by its capacity, to receive her. In all this we think that he acted most judiciously; first, because, as he himself remarked, the difference between his school and other schools was a difference so fundamental that there was hardly any common ground on which a controversial battle could be fought; and, secondly, because his mind, eminently observant, pre-eminently discursive and capacious, was, we conceive, neither formed by nature nor disciplined by habit for dialectical combat.

Though Bacon did not arm his philosophy with the weapons of logic, he adorned her profusely with all the richest decorations of rhetoric. His eloquence, though not untainted with the vicious taste of his age, would alone have entitled him to a high rank in literature. He had a wonderful talent for packing thought close and rendering it portable. In wit, if by wit be meant the power of perceiving analogies between things which appear to have nothing in common, he never had an equal, not even Cowley, not even the author of "Hudibras." Indeed, he possessed this faculty, or rather this faculty possessed him, to a morbid degree. When he abandoned himself to it without reserve, as he did in the "Sapienta Veterum" and at the end of the second book of the "De Augmentis," the feats which he performed were not merely admirable, but portentious, and almost shocking. On those occasions we marvel at him as clowns on a fair-day marvel at a juggler, and can hardly help thinking that the devil must be in him.

These, however, were freaks in which his ingenuity now and then wantoned with scarcely any other object than to astonish and amuse. But it occasionally happened that, when he was engaged in grave and profound investigations, his wit obtained the mastery over all his other faculties and led him into absurdities into which no dull man could possibly have fallen. We will give the most striking instance which at present occurs to us. In the third book of the "De Augmentis" he tells us that there are some principles which are not peculiar to one science, but are common to several. That part of philosophy which concerns itself with these principles is, in his nomenclature, designated as *philosophia prima*. He then proceeds to mention some of the principles with which this *philosophia prima* is conversant. One of them is this. An infectious disease is more likely to be communicated while it is in progress than when it has reached its height. This, says he, is true in medicine. It is also true in morals; for we see that the example of very abandoned men injures public morality less than the example of men in whom vice has not yet extinguished all good qualities. Again, he tells us that in music a discord ending in a concord is agreeable, and that the same thing may be noted in the affections. Once more, he tells us, that in physics the energy with which a principle acts is often increased by the antiperistasis of its opposite, and that it is the same in the contests of factions. If this be indeed the *philosophia prima*, we are quite sure that the greatest philosophical work of the nineteenth century is Mr. Moore's "Lalla Rookh." The similitudes which we have cited are very happy similitudes. But that a man like Bacon should have taken them for more, that he should have thought the discovery of such resemblances as these an important part of philosophy, has always appeared to us one of the most singular facts in the history of letters.

The truth is, that his mind was wonderfully quick in perceiving analogies of all sorts. But, like several eminent men whom we could name, both living and dead, he sometimes appeared strangely deficient in the power of distinguishing rational from fanciful analogies; analogies which are arguments from analogies which are mere illustrations; analogies like that which Bishop Butler so ably pointed out between natural and revealed religion from analogies like that which Addison discovered between the series of Grecian Gods carved by Phidias and the series of English kings painted by Kneller. This want of discrimination has led to many strange political speculations. Sir William Temple deduced a theory of government from the properties of the pyramid. Mr. Southey's whole system of finance is grounded on the phenomena of evaporation and rain. In theology, this perverted ingenuity has made still wilder work. From the time of Irenæus and Origen down to the present day, there has not been a single generation in which great divines have not been led into the most absurd expositions of Scripture by mere incapacity to distinguish analogies proper, to use the scholastic phrase, from analogies metaphorical.* It is curious that Bacon has himself mentioned this very kind of delusion among the *idola specus*, and has mentioned it in language which, we are inclined to think, indicates that he knew himself to be subject to it. It is the vice, he tells us, of subtle minds to attach too much importance to slight distinctions; it is the vice, on the other hand, of high and discursive intellects to attach too much importance to slight resemblances; and, he adds, that when this last propensity is indulged to excess, it leads men to catch at shadows instead of substances.†

Yet we cannot wish that Bacon's wit had been less luxuriant. For—to say nothing of the pleasure which it affords—it was in the vast majority of cases employed for the purpose of making obscure truth plain—of making repulsive truth attractive—of fixing in the mind for ever truth which might otherwise have left but a transient impression.

The poetical faculty was powerful in Bacon's mind, but not, like his wit, so powerful as occasionally to usurp the place of his reason and to tyrannise over the whole man. No imagination was ever at once so strong and so thoroughly subjugated. It never stirred but at a signal from good sense. It stopped at the first check from good sense. Yet, though disciplined to such obedience, it gave noble proofs of its vigour. In truth, much of Bacon's life was passed in a visionary world—amidst things as strange as any that are described in the "Arabian Tales," or in those romances on which the curate and barber of Don Quixote's village performed so cruel an *auto-de-fé*—amidst buildings more sumptuous than the palace of Aladdin—fountains more wonderful than the golden water of Parizade,—conveyances more rapid than the hippogryph of Ruggiero—arms more formidable than the lance of Astolfo—remedies more efficacious than the balsam of Fierabras. Yet in his magnificent day-dreams there was nothing wild—nothing but what sober reason sanctioned. He knew that all the secrets, feigned by poets to have been written in the books of enchanters, are worthless when compared with the mighty secrets which are really written in the book of nature, and which, with time and patience, will be read there. He knew that all the wonders wrought by all the talismans in fable were trifles when compared to the wonders which might reasonably be expected from the philosophy of *fruit*; and that, if his words sank deep into the minds of men, they would produce effects such as superstition had never ascribed to the incantations of Merlin and Michael Scott. It was here that he loved to let his imagination loose. He loved to picture to himself the world as it would be when his philosophy should, in his own noble phrase, "have enlarged the bounds of human empire.'‡ We might refer to many instances. But we will content ourselves with the strongest, the description of the House of Solomon in the "New Atlantis." By most of Bacon's contemporaries, and by some people of our time, this remarkable passage

---

* See some interesting remarks on this subject in Bishop Berkeley's Minute Philosopher, Dialogue IV.
† Novum Organum, Lib. 1. Aph. 55. ‡ New Atlantis.

would, we doubt not, be considered as an ingenious rodomontade, a counterpart to the adventures of Sindbad or Baron Munchausen. The truth is, that there is not to be found in any human composition a passage more eminently distinguished by profound and serene wisdom. The boldness and originality of the fiction is far less wonderful than the nice discernment which carefully excluded from that long list of prodigies everything that can be pronounced impossible, everything that can be proved to lie beyond the mighty magic of induction and time. Already some parts, and not the least startling parts, of this glorious prophecy have been accomplished, even according to the letter; and the whole, construed according to the spirit, is daily accomplishing all around us.

One of the most remarkable circumstances in the history of Bacon's mind is the order in which its powers expanded themselves. With him the fruit came first and remained till the last; the blossoms did not appear till late. In general, the development of the fancy is to the development of the judgment what the growth of a girl is to the growth of a boy. The fancy attains at an earlier period to the perfection of its beauty, its power and its fruitfulness; and, as it is first to ripen, it is also first to fade. It has generally lost something of its bloom and freshness before the sterner faculties have reached maturity, and is commonly withered and barren while those faculties still retain all their energy. It rarely happens that the fancy and judgment grow together. It happens still more rarely that the judgment grows faster than the fancy. This seems, however, to have been the case with Bacon. His boyhood and youth appear to have been singularly sedate. His gigantic scheme of philosophical reform is said by some writers to have been planned before he was fifteen, and was undoubtedly planned while he was still young. He observed as vigilantly, meditated as deeply and judged as temperately when he gave his first work to the world as at the close of his long career. But in eloquence, in sweetness and variety of expression, and in richness of illustration, his later writings are far superior to those of his youth. In this respect the history of his mind bears some resemblance to the history of the mind of Burke. The treatise on the "Sublime and Beautiful," though written on a subject which the coldest metaphysician could hardly treat without being occasionally betrayed into florid writing, is the most unadorned of all Burke's works. It appeared when he was twenty-five or twenty-six. When, at forty, he wrote the "Thoughts on the Causes of the existing Discontents," his reason and his judgment had reached their full maturity, but his eloquence was still in its splendid dawn. At fifty, his rhetoric was quite as rich as good taste would permit; and when he died, at almost seventy, it had become ungracefully gorgeous. In his youth he wrote on the emotions produced by mountains and cascades, by the masterpieces of painting and sculpture, by the faces and necks of beautiful women, in the style of a Parliamentary report. In his old age he discussed treaties and tariffs in the most fervid and brilliant language of romance. It is strange that the essay on the "Sublime and Beautiful" and the "Letter to a Noble Lord" should be the production of one man. But it is far more strange that the essay should have been a production of his youth and the letter of his old age.

We will give very short specimens of Bacon's two styles. In 1597, he wrote thus:—"Crafty men contemn studies, simple men admire them, and wise men use them; for they teach not their own use; that is a wisdom without them, and won by observation. Read not to contradict, nor to believe, but to weigh and consider. Some books are to be tasted, others to be swallowed, and some few to be chewed and digested. Reading maketh a full man, conference a ready man, and writing an exact man. And, therefore, if a man write little, he had need have a great memory; if he confer little, have a present wit; and if he read little, have much cunning to seem to know that he doth not. Histories make men wise, poets witty, the mathematics subtle, natural philosophy deep, morals grave, logic and rhetoric able to contend." It will hardly be disputed that this is a passage to be "chewed and digested." We do not believe that Thucydides himself has anywhere compressed so much thought into so small a space.

In the additions which Bacon afterwards made to the "Essays," there is nothing superior in truth or weight to what we have quoted. But his style was constantly becoming richer and softer. The following passage, first published in 1625, will show the extent of the change:—"Prosperity is the blessing of the Old Testament; adversity is the blessing of the New, which carrieth the greater benediction and the clearer evidence of God's favour. Yet, even in the Old Testament, if you listen to David's harp, you shall hear as many hearse-like airs as carols; and the pencil of the Holy Ghost hath laboured more in describing the afflictions of Job than the felicities of Solomon. Prosperity is not without many fears and distastes; and adversity is not without comforts and hopes. We see in needleworks and embroideries it is more pleasing to have a lively work upon a sad and solemn ground, than to have a dark and melancholy work upon a lightsome ground. Judge therefore of the pleasure of the heart by the pleasure of the eye. Certainly virtue is like precious odours, most fragrant when they are incensed or crushed; for prosperity doth best discover vice, but adversity doth best discover virtue.

It is by the "Essays" that Bacon is best known to the multitude. The "Novum Organum" and the "De Augmentis" are much talked of, but little read. They have produced indeed a vast effect on the opinions of mankind; but they have produced it through the operation of intermediate agents. They have moved the intellects which have moved the world. It is in the "Essays" alone that the mind of Bacon is brought into immediate contact with the minds of ordinary readers. There he opens an exoteric school, and talks to plain men, in language which everybody understands, about things in which everybody is interested. He has thus enabled those who must otherwise have taken his merits on trust to judge for themselves; and the great body of readers have, during several generations, acknowledged that the man who has treated with such consummate ability questions with which they are familiar, may well be supposed to deserve all the praise bestowed on him by those who have sat in his inner school.

Without any disparagement to the admirable treatise, "De Augmentis," we must say that, in our judgment, Bacon's greatest performance is the first book of the "Novum Organum." All the peculiarities of his extraordinary mind are found there in the highest perfection. Many of the aphorisms, but particularly those in which he gives examples of the influence of the *idola*, show a nicety of observation that has never been surpassed. Every part of the book blazes with wit, but with wit which is employed only to illustrate and decorate truth. No book ever made so great a revolution in the mode of thinking—overthrew so many prejudices—introduced so many new opinions. Yet no book was ever written in a less contentious spirit. It truly conquers with chalk and not with steel. Proposition after proposition enters into the mind—is received not as an invader, but as a welcome friend—and, though previously unknown, becomes at once domesticated. But what we most admire is the vast capacity of that intellect which, without effort, takes in at once all the domains of science—all the past, the present and the future—all the errors of two thousand years—all the encouraging signs of the passing times—all the bright hopes of the coming age. Cowley, who was among the most ardent, and not among the least discerning followers of the new philosophy, has, in one of his finest poems, compared Bacon to Moses standing on Mount Pisgah. It is to Bacon, we think, as he appears in the first book of the "Novum Organum," that the comparison applies with peculiar felicity. There we see the great Lawgiver looking round from his lonely elevation on an infinite expanse; behind him a wilderness of dreary sands and bitter waters in which successive generations have sojourned, always moving, yet never advancing, reaping no harvest and building no abiding city; before him a goodly land, a land of promise, a land flowing with milk and honey. While the multitude below saw only the flat, sterile desert in which they had so long wandered, bounded on every side by a near horizon, or diversified only by some deceitful mirage, he was gazing from a far higher stand on a far lovelier country—following with his eye the long course of fertilising rivers through ample pastures and under the bridges of great capitals—measuring the distances of marts and havens—and portioning out all those wealthy regions from Dan to Beersheba.

It is painful to turn back from contemplating Bacon's philosophy to contemplate his life. Yet, without so turning back, it is impossible fairly to estimate his powers. He left the University at an earlier age than that at which most people repair thither. While yet a boy he was plunged into the midst of diplomatic business. Thence he passed to the study of a vast technical system of law, and worked his way up through a succession of laborious offices to the highest post in his profession. In the meantime he took an active part in every Parliament; he was an adviser of the crown; he paid court with the greatest assiduity and address to all whose favour was likely to be of use to him; he lived much in society; he noticed the slightest peculiarities of character and the slightest changes of fashion. Scarcely any man has led a more stirring life than that which Bacon led from sixteen to sixty. Scarcely any man has been better entitled to be called a thorough man of the world. The founding of a new philosophy, the imparting of a new direction to the minds of speculators—this was the amusement of his leisure, the work of hours occasionally stolen from the Woolsack and the Council Board. This consideration, while it increases the admiration with which we regard his intellect, increases also our regret that such an intellect should so often have been unworthily employed. He well knew the better course, and had, at one time, resolved to pursue it. "I confess," said he, in a letter written when he was still young, "that I have as vast contemplative ends as I have moderate civil ends." Had his civil ends continued to be moderate, he would have been, not only the Moses, but the Joshua of philosophy. He would have fulfilled a large part of his own magnificent predictions. He would have led his followers, not only to the verge, but into the heart of the promised land. He would not merely have pointed out, but would have divided the spoil. Above all, he would have left, not only a great, but a spotless name. Mankind would then have been able to esteem their illustrious benefactor. We should not then be compelled to regard his character with mingled contempt and admiration—with mingled aversion and gratitude. We should not then regret that there should be so many proofs of the narrowness and selfishness of a heart, the benevolence of which was yet large enough to take in all races and all ages. We should not then have to blush for the disingenuousness of the most devoted worshipper of speculative truth—for the servility of the boldest champion of intellectual freedom. We should not then have seen the same man at one time far in the van and at another time far in the rear of his generation. We should not then be forced to own that he who first treated legislation as a science was among the last Englishmen who used the rack—that he who first summoned philosophers to the great work of interpreting nature was among the last Englishmen who sold justice. And we should conclude our survey of a life, placidly, honourably, beneficiently passed "in industrious observations, grounded conclusions, and profitable inventions and discoveries,"[*] with feelings very different from those with which we now turn away from the chequered spectacle of so much glory and so much shame.

SIR WILLIAM TEMPLE. (OCTOBER, 1838.)

Memoirs of the Life, Works and Correspondence of Sir William Temple. By the Right Hon. THOMAS PEREGRINE COURTENAY. 2 vols., 8vo. London, 1836.

MR. COURTENAY has long been well known to politicians as an industrious and useful official man, and as an upright and consistent member of Parliament. He has been one of the most moderate, and, at the same time, one of the least pliant, members of the Conservative party. His conduct has, on some questions, been so Whiggish, that both those who applauded and those who condemned it have questioned his claim to be considered as a Tory. But his Toryism, such as it is, he has held fast through all changes of fortune and fashion; and he has at last retired from public life, leaving behind him, to the best of our belief, no personal enemy, and carrying with him the respect and goodwill of many who strongly dissent from his opinions.

This book, the fruit of Mr. Courtenay's leisure, is introduced by a preface in which he informs us that the assistance furnished to him from various quarters "has taught him the superiority of literature to politics for developing the kindlier feelings and conducing to an agreeable life." We are truly glad that Mr. Courtenay is so well satisfied with his new employment, and we heartily congratulate him on having been driven by events to make an exchange which, advantageous as it is, few people make while they can avoid it. He has little reason, in our opinion, to envy any of those who are still engaged in a pursuit from which, at most, they can only expect that, by relinquishing liberal studies and social pleasures—by passing nights without sleep and summers without one glimpse of the beauty of nature—they may attain that laborious, that invidious, that closely watched slavery which is mocked by the name of power.

The volumes before us are fairly entitled to the praise of diligence, care, good sense and impartiality; and these qualities are sufficient to make a book valuable, but not quite sufficient to make it readable. Mr. Courtenay has not sufficiently studied the arts of selection and compression. The information with which he furnishes us must still, we apprehend, be considered as so much raw material. To manufacturers it will be highly useful; but it is not yet in such a form that it can be enjoyed by the idle consumer. To drop metaphor, we are afraid that this work will be less acceptable to those who read for the sake of reading than those who read in order to write.

We cannot help adding, though we are extremely unwilling to quarrel with Mr. Courtenay about politics, that the book would not be at all the worse if it contained fewer snarls against the Whigs of the present day. Not only are these passages out of place, but some of them are intrinsically such that they would become the editor of a third-rate party newspaper better than a gentleman of Mr. Courtenay's talents and knowledge. For example, we are

---

[*] From a Letter of Bacon to Lord Burleigh.

told that "it is a remarkable circumstance, familiar to those who are acquainted with history, but suppressed by the new Whigs, that the liberal politicians of the seventeenth century and the greater part of the eighteenth never extended their liberality to the native Irish, or the professors of the ancient religion." What schoolboy of fourteen is ignorant of this remarkable circumstance? What Whig, new or old, was ever such an idiot as to think that it could be suppressed? Really, we might as well say that it is a remarkable circumstance, familiar to people well read in history, but carefully suppressed by the Clergy of the Established Church, that in the fifteenth century England was Catholic. We are tempted to make some remarks on another passage, which seems to be the peroration of a speech intended to have been spoken against the Reform Bill, but we forbear.

We doubt whether it will be found that the memory of Sir William Temple owes much to Mr. Courtenay's researches. Temple is one of those men whom the world has agreed to praise highly without knowing much about them, and who are therefore more likely to lose than to gain by a close examination. Yet he is not without fair pretensions to the most honourable place among the statesmen of his time. A few of them equalled or surpassed him in talents; but they were men of no good repute for honesty. A few may be named whose patriotism was purer, nobler and more disinterested than his; but they were men of no eminent ability. Morally, he was above Shaftesbury; intellectually, he was above Russell.

To say of a man that he occupied a high position in times of misgovernment, of corruption, of civil and religious faction, and that, nevertheless, he contracted no great stain, and bore no part in any great crime; that he won the esteem of a profligate Court and of a turbulent people, without being guilty of any disgraceful subserviency to either—seems to be very high praise; and all this may with truth be said of Temple.

Yet Temple is not a man to our taste. A temper not naturally good, but under strict command—a constant regard to decorum—a rare caution in playing that mixed game of skill and hazard, human life—a disposition to be content with small and certain winnings rather than to go on doubling the stake—these seem to us to be the most remarkable features of his character. This sort of moderation when united, as in him it was, with very considerable abilities, is, under ordinary circumstances, scarcely to be distinguished from the highest and purest integrity, and yet may be perfectly compatible with laxity of principle, with coldness of heart, and with the most intense selfishness. Temple, we fear, had not sufficient warmth and elevation of sentiment to deserve the name of a virtuous man. He did not betray or oppress his country: nay, he rendered considerable services to her; but he risked nothing for her. No temptation which either the King or the Opposition could hold out ever induced him to come forward as the supporter either of arbitrary or of factious measures. But he was most careful not to give offence by strenuously opposing such measures. He never put himself prominently before the public eye, except at conjunctures when he was almost certain to gain and could not possibly lose—at conjunctures when the interest of the State, the views of the Court and the passions of the multitude all appeared for an instant to coincide. By judiciously availing himself of several of these rare moments, he succeeded in establishing a high character for wisdom and patriotism. When the favourable crisis was passed, he never risked the reputation which he had won. He avoided the great offices of State with a caution almost pusillanimous, and confined himself to quiet and secluded departments of public business, in which he could enjoy moderate but certain advantages without incurring envy. If the circumstances of the country became such that it was impossible to take any part in politics without some danger, he retired to his Library and his Orchard; and, while the nation groaned under oppression, or resounded with tumult and with the din of civil arms, amused himself by writing Memoirs and tying up Apricots. His political career bore some resemblance to the military career of Louis XIV. Louis, lest his royal dignity should be compromised by failure, never repaired to a siege till it had been reported to him by the most skilful officers in his service that nothing could prevent the fall of the place. When this was ascertained, the monarch, in his helmet and cuirass, appeared among the tents, held councils of war, dictated the capitulation, received the keys, and then returned to Versailles to hear his flatterers repeat that Turenne had been beaten at Mariendal, that Condé had been forced to raise the siege of Arras, and that the only warrior whose glory had never been obscured by a single check was Louis the Great! Yet Condé and Turenne will always be considered as captains of a very different order from the invincible Louis; and we must own that many statesmen, who have committed very great faults, appear to us to be deserving of more esteem that the faultless Temple. For in truth his faultlessness is chiefly to be ascribed to his extreme dread of all responsibility; to his determination rather to leave his country in a scrape than to run any chance of being in a scrape himself. He seems to have been averse from danger; and it must be admitted that the dangers to which a public man was exposed, in those days of conflicting tyranny and sedition, were of the most serious kind. He could not bear discomfort, bodily or mental. His lamentations when, in the course of his diplomatic journeys, he was put a little out of his way, and forced, in the vulgar phrase, to rough it, are quite amusing. He talks of riding a day or two on a bad Westphalian road, of sleeping on straw for one night, of travelling in winter when the snow lay on the ground, as if he had gone on an expedition to the North Pole or to the source of the Nile. This kind of valetudinarian effeminacy, this habit of coddling himself, appears in all parts of his conduct. He loved fame, but not with the love of an exalted and generous mind. He loved it as an end, not at all as a means; as a personal luxury, not at all as an instrument of advantage to others. He scraped it together and treasured it up with a timid and niggardly thrift, and never employed the hoard in any enterprise, however virtuous and honourable, in which there was hazard of losing one particle. No wonder if such a person did little or nothing which deserves positive blame. But much more than this may justly be demanded of a man possessed of such abilities and placed in such a situation. Had Temple been brought before Dante's infernal tribunal, he would not have been condemned to the deeper recesses of the abyss. He would not have been boiled with Dundee in the crimson pool of Bulicame, or hurled with Danby into the seething pitch of Malebolge, or congealed with Churchill in the eternal ice of Giudecca; but he would perhaps have been placed in the dark vestibule next to the shade of that inglorious pontiff—

"Che fece per viltate il gran rifiuto."

Of course a man is not bound to be a politician any more than he is bound to be a soldier; and there are perfectly honourable ways of quitting both politics and the military profession. But neither in the one way of life, nor in the other, is any man entitled to take all the sweet and leave all the sour. A man who belongs to the army only in time of peace—who appears at reviews in Hyde Park, escorts the Sovereign with the utmost valour and fidelity to and from the House of Lords, and retires as soon as he thinks it likely that he may be ordered on an expedition—is justly thought to have disgraced himself. Some portion of the censure due to such a holiday soldier may justly fall on the mere holiday-politician, who flinches from his duties as soon as those duties become difficult and disagreeable—that is to say, as soon as it becomes peculiarly important that he should resolutely peform them.

But though we are far indeed from considering Temple as a perfect statesman, though we place him below many statesmen who have committed very great errors, we cannot deny that, when compared with his contemporaries, he makes a highly respectable appearance. The reaction which followed the victory of the popular party over Charles the First had produced a hurtful effect on the national character; and this effect was most discernible in the classes and in the places which had been most strongly excited by the recent revolution. The deterioration was greater in London than in the country, and was greatest of all in the courtly and official circles. Almost all that remained of what had been good and noble in the Cavaliers and Roundheads of 1642 was now to be found in the middling orders. The principles and feelings which prompted the Grand Remonstrance were still strong among the sturdy yeomen and the decent, God-fearing merchants. The spirit of Derby and Capel still glowed in many sequestered manor-houses; but among those political leaders who, at the time of the Restoration were still young, or in the vigour of manhood, there was neither a Southampton nor a Vane, neither a Falkland nor a Hampden. That pure, fervent and constant loyalty which, in the preceding reign, had remained unshaken on fields of disastrous battle, in foreign garrets and cellars, and at the bar of the High Court of Justice, was scarcely to be found among the rising courtiers. As little, or still less, could the new chiefs of parties lay claim to the great qualties of the statesmen who had stood at the head of the Long Parliament. Hampden, Pym, Vane, Cromwell are discriminated from the ablest politicians of the succeeding generation by all the strong lineaments which distinguish the men who produce revolutions from the men whom revolutions produce. The leader in a great change, the man who stirs up a reposing community and overthrows a deeply rooted system may be a very depraved man, but he can scarcely be destitute of some moral qualities which extort even from enemies a reluctant admiration; fixedness of purpose, intensity of will, enthusiasm, which is not the less fierce or persevering because it is sometimes disguised under the semblance of composure, and which bears down before it the force of circumstances and the opposition of reluctant minds. These qualities, variously combined with all sorts of virtues and vices, may be found, we think, in most of the authors of great Civil and Religious movements: in Cæsar, in Mahomet, in Hildebrand, in Dominic, in Luther, in Robespierre; and these qualities were found, in no scanty measure, among the chiefs of the party which opposed Charles the First. The character of the men whose minds are formed in the midst of the confusion which follows a great revolution is generally very different. Heat, the natural philosophers tell us, produces rarefaction of the air, and rarefaction of the air produces cold. So zeal makes revolutions, and revolutions make men zealous for nothing. The politicians of whom we speak, whatever may be their natural capacity or courage, are almost always characterised by a peculiar levity, a peculiar inconstancy, an easy, apathetic way of looking at the most solemn questions, a willingness to leave the direction of their course to fortune and popular opinion, a notion that one public cause is pretty nearly as good as another, and a firm conviction that it is much better to be the hireling of the worst cause than to be a martyr to the best.

This was most strikingly the case with the English statesmen of the generation which followed the Restoration. They had neither the enthusiasm of the Cavalier, nor the enthusiasm of the Republican. They had been early emancipated from the dominion of old usages and feelings; yet they had not acquired a strong passion for innovation. Accustomed to see old establishments shaking, falling, lying in ruins all around them; to live under a succession of constitutions, of which the average duration was about a twelvemonth, they had no religious reverence for prescription, nothing of that frame of mind which naturally springs from the habitual contemplation of immemorial antiquity and immovable stability. Accustomed, on the other hand, to see change after change welcomed with eager hope and ending in disappointment—to see shame and confusion of face follow the extravagant hopes and predictions of rash and fanatical innovators—they had learned to look on professions of public spirit and on schemes of reform with distrust and contempt. They sometimes talked the language of devoted subjects—sometimes that of ardent lovers of their country. But their secret creed seems to have been, that loyalty was one great delusion and patriotism another. If they really entertained any predilection for the monarchical or for the popular part of the constitution—for episcopacy or for presbyterianism—that predilection was feeble and languid, and instead of overcoming, as in the times of their fathers, the dread of exile, confiscation and death, was rarely of proof to resist the slightest impulse of selfish ambition or of selfish fear. Such was the texture of the presbyterianism of Lauderdale and of the speculative republicanism of Halifax. The sense of political honour seemed to be extinct. With the great mass of mankind, the test of integrity in a public man is consistency. This test, though very defective, is perhaps the best that any, except very acute, or very near observers, are capable of applying, and does undoubtedly enable the people to form an estimate of the characters of the great, which, on the whole, approximates to correctness. But during the latter part of the seventeenth century, inconsistency had necessarily ceased to be a disgrace, and a man was no more taunted with it, than he is taunted with being black at Timbuctoo. Nobody was ashamed of avowing what was common between him and the whole nation. In the short space of about seven years, the supreme power had been held by the Long Parliament, by a Council of Officers, by Barebones' Parliament, by a Council of Officers again, by a Protector according to the Instrument of Government, by a Protector according to the Humble Petition and Advice, by the Long Parliament again, by a third Council of Officers, by the Long Parliament a third time, by the Convention, and by the King. In such times, consistency is so inconvenient to a man who affects it, and to all who are connected with him, that it ceases to be regarded as a virtue and is considered as impracticable obstinacy and idle scrupulosity. Indeed, in such times, a good citizen may be bound in duty to serve a succession of Governments. Blake did so in one profession and Hale in another, and the conduct of both has been approved by posterity. But it is clear that when inconsistency with respect to the most important public questions has ceased to be a reproach, inconsistency with respect to questions of minor importance is not likely to be regarded as dishonourable. In a country in which many very honest people had, within the space of a few months, supported the government of the Protector, that of the Rump, and that of the King, a man was not likely to be ashamed of abandoning his party for a place, or of voting for a bill which he had opposed.

The public men of the times which followed the Restoration were by no means deficient in courage or ability; and some kinds of talent appear to have been developed amongst them to a remarkable—we might almost say, to a morbid and unnatural—degree. Neither Theramenes in ancient, nor Talleyrand in modern times, had a finer perception of all the peculiarities of character and of all the indications of coming change than some of our countrymen of those days. Their power of reading things of high import, in signs which to others were invisible or unintelligible, resembled magic. But the curse of Reuben was upon them all: "Unstable as water, thou shalt not excel."

This character is susceptible of innumerable modifications, according to the innumerable varieties of intellect and temper in which it may be found. Men of unquiet minds and violent ambition followed a fearfully eccentric course—darted wildly from one extreme to another—served and betrayed all parties in turn—showed their unblushing foreheads alternately in the van of the most corrupt administrations and of the most factious oppositions—were privy to the most guilty mysteries, first of the Cabal and then of the Rye House Plot—abjured their religion to win their sovereign's favour while they were secretly planning his overthrow—shrived themselves to Jesuits with letters in cypher from the Prince of Orange in their pockets—corresponded with the Hague whilst in office under James—and began to correspond with St. Germain's as soon as they had kissed hands for office under William. But Temple was not one of these. He was not destitute of ambition. But his was not one of those souls within which unsatisfied ambition anticipates the tortures of hell, gnaws like the worm which dieth not, and burns like the fire which is not quenched. His principle was to make sure of safety and comfort and to let greatness come if it would. It came; he enjoyed it; and, in the very first moment in which it could no longer be enjoyed without danger and vexation, he contentedly let it go. He was not exempt, we think, from the prevailing political immorality. His mind took the contagion, but took it *ad modum recipientis*—in a form so mild that an undiscerning judge might doubt whether it were indeed the same fierce pestilence that was raging all around. The malady partook of the constitutional languor of the patient. The general corruption, mitigated by his calm and unadventurous temperament, showed itself in omissions and desertions, not in positive crimes; and his inactivity, though sometimes timorous and selfish, becomes respectable when compared with the malevolent and perfidious restlessness of Shaftesbury and Sunderland.

Temple sprang from a family which, though ancient and honourable, had, before his time, been scarcely mentioned in our history; but which, long after his death, produced so many eminent men and formed such distinguished alliances, that it exercised, in a regular and constitutional manner, an influence in the state scarcely inferior to that which, in widely different times and by widely different arts, the house of Neville attained in England and that of Douglas in Scotland. During the latter years of George II. and through the whole reign of George III., members of that widely spread and powerful connection were almost constantly at the head either of the Government or of the Opposition. There were times when the "cousinhood," as it was once nicknamed, would of itself have furnished almost all the materials necessary for the construction of an efficient Cabinet. Within the space of fifty years, three First Lords of the Treasury, three Secretaries of State, two Keepers of the Privy Seal and four First Lords of the Admiralty were appointed from among the sons and grandsons of the Countess Temple.

So splendid have been the fortunes of the main stock of the Temple family, continued by female succession. William Temple, the first of the line who attained to any great historical eminence, was of a younger branch. His father, Sir John Temple, was Master of the Rolls in Ireland, and distinguished himself among the Privy Councillors of that kingdom by the zeal with which, at the commencement of the struggle between the Crown and the Long Parliament, he supported the popular cause. He was arrested by order of the Duke of Ormond, but regained his liberty by an exchange, repaired to England, and there sat in the House of Commons as burgess for Chichester. He attached himself to the Presbyterian party; and was one of those moderate members who, at the close of the year 1648, voted for treating with Charles on the basis to which that Prince had himself agreed, and who were, in consequence, turned out of the House, with small ceremony, by Colonel Pride. Sir John seems, however, to have made his peace with the victorious Independents, for, in 1653, he resumed his office in Ireland.

Sir John Temple was married to a sister of the celebrated Henry Hammond, a learned and pious divine who took the side of the King with very conspicuous zeal during the civil war, and was deprived of his preferment in the church after the victory of the Parliament. On account of the loss which Hammond sustained on this occasion, he has the honour of being designated, in the cant of that new brood of Oxonian secretaries who unite the worst parts of the Jesuit to the worst parts of the Orangeman, as Hammond, Presbyter, Doctor and Confessor.

William Temple, Sir John's eldest son, was born in London in the year 1628. He received his early education under his maternal uncle; was subsequently sent to school at Bishop-Stortford; and, at seventeen, began to reside at Emmanuel College, Cambridge, where the celebrated Cudworth was his tutor. The times were not favourable to study. The Civil War disturbed even the quiet cloisters and bowling-greens of Cambridge, produced violent revolutions in the government and discipline of the colleges, and unsettled the minds of the students. Temple forgot at Emmanuel all the little Greek which he had brought from Bishop-Stortford, and never retrieved the loss—a circumstance which would hardly be worth noticing but for the almost incredible fact that, fifty years later, he was so absurd as to set up his own authority against that of Bentley on questions of Greek history and philology. He made no proficiency either in the old philosophy which still lingered in the schools of Cambridge, or in the new philosophy of which Lord Bacon was the founder. But to the end of his life he continued to speak of the former with ignorant admiration and of the latter with equally ignorant contempt.

After residing at Cambridge two years, he departed without taking a degree, and set out upon his travels. He seems then to have been a lively, agreeable young man of fashion, not by any means deeply read, but versed in all the superficial accomplishments of a gentleman, and acceptable in all polite societies. In politics he professed himself a Royalist. His opinions on religious subjects seem to have been such as might be expected from a young man of quick parts, who had received a rambling education, who had not thought deeply, who had been disgusted by the morose austerity of the Puritans, and who, surrounded from childhood by the hubbub of conflicting sects, might easily learn to feel an impartial contempt for them all.

On his road to France he fell in with the son and daughter of Sir Peter Osborne. Sir Peter was governor of Guernsey for the King, and the young people were, like their father, warm for the royal cause. At an inn where they stopped in the Isle of Wight, the brother amused himself with inscribing on the windows his opinion of the ruling powers. For this instance of malignancy the whole party were arrested and brought before the governor. The sister, trusting to the tenderness which, even in those troubled times, scarcely any gentleman of any party ever failed to show where a woman was concerned, took the crime on herself, and was immediately set at liberty with her fellow-travellers.

This incident, as was natural, made a deep impression on Temple. He was only twenty. Dorothy Osborne was twenty-one. She is said to have been handsome; and there remains abundant proof that she possessed an ample share of the dexterity, the vivacity and the tenderness of her sex. Temple soon became, in the phrase of that time, her servant, and she returned his regard. But difficulties as great as ever expanded a novel to the fifth volume opposed their wishes. When the courtship commenced, the father of the hero was sitting in the Long Parliament; the father of the heroine was holding Guernsey for King Charles. Even when the war ended, and Sir Peter Osborne returned to his seat at Chicksands, the prospects of the lovers were scarcely less gloomy. Sir John Temple had a more advantageous alliance in view for his son. Dorothy Osborne was in the meantime besieged by as many suitors as were drawn to Belmont by the fame of Portia. The most distinguished on the list was Henry Cromwell. Destitute of the capacity, the energy, the magnanimity of his illustrious father, destitute also of the meek and placid virtues of his elder brother, this young man was perhaps a more formidable rival in love than either of them would have been. Mrs. Hutchinson, speaking the sentiments of the grave and aged, describes him as an "insolent foole," and a "debauched, ungodly cavalier." These expressions probably mean that he was one who, among young and dissipated people, would pass for a fine gentleman. Dorothy was fond of dogs of larger and more formidable breed than those which lie on modern hearth-rugs; and Henry Cromwell promised that the highest functionaries at Dublin should be set to work to procure her a fine Irish greyhound. She seems to have felt his attentions as very flattering, though his father was then only Lord-General, and not yet Protector. Love, however, triumphed over ambition, and the young lady appears never to have regretted her decision; though, in a letter written just at the time when all England was ringing with the news of the violent dissolution of the Long Parliament, she could not refrain from reminding Temple, with pardonable vanity, "how great she might have been, if she had been so wise as to have taken hold of the offer of H. C."

Nor was it only the influence of rivals that Temple had to dread. The relations of his mistress regarded him with personal dislike, and spoke of him as an unprincipled adventurer, without honour or religion, ready to render service to any party for the sake of preferment. This is, indeed, a very distorted view of Temple's character. Yet a character, even in the most distorted view taken of it by the most angry and prejudiced minds, generally retains something of its outline. No caricaturist ever represented Mr. Pitt as a Falstaff, or Mr. Fox as a skeleton; nor did any libeller ever impute parsimony to Sheridan, or profusion to Marlborough. It must be allowed that the turn of mind which the eulogists of Temple have dignified with the appellation of philosophical indifference, and which, however becoming it may be in an old and experienced statesman, has a somewhat ungraceful appearance in youth, might easily appear shocking to a family who were ready to fight or suffer martyrdom for their exiled King and their persecuted church. The poor girl was exceedingly hurt and irritated by these imputations on her lover, defended him warmly behind his back, and addressed to himself some very tender and anxious admonitions, mingled with assurances of her confidence in his honour and virtue. On one occasion she was most highly provoked by the way in which one of her brothers spoke of Temple. "We talked ourselves weary," she says; "he renounced me, and I defied him."

Nearly seven years did this arduous wooing continue. We are not accurately informed respecting Temple's movements during that time. But he seems to have led a rambling life, sometimes on the Continent, sometimes in Ireland, sometimes in London. He made himself master of the French and Spanish languages, and amused himself by writing essays and romances—an employment which at least served the purpose of forming his style. The specimen which Mr. Courtenay has preserved of these early compositions is by no means contemptible. Indeed, there is one passage on *Like and Dislike* which could have been produced only by a mind habituated carefully to reflect on its own operations, and which reminds us of the best things in Montaigne.

He appears to have kept up a very active correspondence with his mistress. His letters are lost, but hers have been preserved; and many of them appear in these volumes. Mr. Courtenay expresses some doubt whether his readers will think him justified in inserting so large a number of these epistles. We only wish that there were twice as many. Very little indeed of the diplomatic correspondence of that generation is so well worth reading. There is a vile phrase of which bad historians are exceeding fond—"the dignity of history." One writer is in possession of some anecdotes which would illustrate most strikingly the operation of the Mississippi scheme on the manners and morals of the Parisians. But he suppresses those anecdotes because they are too low for the dignity of history. Another is strongly tempted to mention some facts indicating the horrible state of the prisons of England two hundred years ago. But he hardly thinks that the sufferings of a dozen felons pigging together on bare bricks in a hole fifteen feet square would form a subject suited to the dignity of history. Another, from respect for the dignity of history, publishes an account of the reign of George the Second without ever mentioning Whitefield's preaching in Moorfields. How should a writer, who can talk about senates, and congresses of sovereigns, and pragmatic sanctions, and ravelins, and counterscarps, and battles where ten thousand men are killed and six thousand men, with fifty stand of colours and eighty guns taken, stoop to the Stock Exchange, to Newgate, to the theatre, to the tabernacle?

Tragedy has its dignity as well as history; and how much the tragic art has owed to that dignity any man may judge who will compare the majestic Alexandrines in which the Seigneur Oreste and Madame Andromaque utter their complaints, with the chattering of the fool in "Lear" and of the nurse in "Romeo and Juliet."

That a historian should not record trifles, that he should confine himself to what is important is perfectly true. But many writers seem never to have considered on what the historical importance of an event depends. They seem not to be aware that the importance of a fact, when that fact is considered with reference to its immediate effects, and the importance of the same fact, when that fact is considered as part of the materials for the construction of a science, are two very different things. The quantity of good or evil which a transaction produces is by no means necessarily proportioned to the quantity of light which that transaction affords as to the way in which good or evil may hereafter be produced. The poisoning of an emperor is in one sense a far more serious matter than the poisoning of a rat. But the poisoning of a rat may be an era in chemistry; and an emperor may be poisoned by such ordinary means, and with such ordinary symptoms, that no scientific journal would notice the occurrence. An action for an hundred thousand pounds is in one sense a more momentous affair than an action for fifty pounds. But it by no means follows that the learned gentlemen who report the proceedings of the courts of law ought to give a fuller account of an action for a hundred thousand pounds than of an action for fifty pounds. For a cause in which a large sum is at stake may be important only to the particular plaintiff and the particular defendant. A cause, on the other hand, in which a small sum is at stake, may establish some great principle interesting to half the families in the kingdom. The case is exactly the same with that class of subjects of which historians treat. To an Athenian, in the time of the Peloponnesian war, the result of the battle of Delium was far more important than the fate of the comedy of the "Knights." But to us the fact that the comedy of the "Knights" was brought on the Athenian stage with success is far more important than the fact that the

Athenian phalanx gave way at Delium. Neither the one event nor the other has now any intrinsic importance. We are in no danger of being speared by the Thebans. We are not quizzed in the "Knights." To us the importance of both events consists in the value of the general truth which is to be learned from them. What general truth do we learn from the accounts which have come down to us of the battle of Delium? Very little more than this, that when two armies fight, it is not improbable that one of them will be very soundly beaten—a truth which it would not, we apprehend, be difficult to establish, even if all memory of the battle of Delium were lost among men. But a man who becomes acquainted with the comedy of the "Knights," and with the history of that comedy, at once feels his mind enlarged. Society is presented to him under a new aspect. He may have read and travelled much. He may have visited all the countries of Europe and the civilised nations of the East. He may have observed the manners of many barbarous races. But here is something altogether different from everything which he has seen either among polished men, or among savages. Here is a community politically, intellectually and morally unlike any other community of which he has the means of forming an opinion. This is the really precious part of history—the corn which some threshers carefully sever from the chaff for the purpose of gathering the chaff into the garner and flinging the corn into the fire.

Thinking thus, we are glad to learn so much, and would willingly learn more, about the loves of Sir William and his mistress. In the seventeenth century, to be sure, Louis XIV. was a much more important person than Temple's sweetheart. But death and time equalise all things. Neither the great King nor the beauty of Bedfordshire—neither the gorgeous paradise of Marli nor Mistress Osborne's favourite walk "in the common that lay hard by the house, where a great many young wenches used to keep sheep and cows and sit in the shade singing of ballads," is anything to us. Louis and Dorothy are alike dust. A cotton-mill stands on the ruins of Marli, and the Osbornes have ceased to dwell under the ancient roof of Chicksands. But of that information for the sake of which alone it is worth while to study remote events, we find so much in the love letters which Mr. Courtenay has published, that we would gladly purchase equally interesting billets with ten times their weight in state-papers taken at random. To us surely it is as useful to know how the young ladies of England employed themselves a hundred and eighty years ago —how far their minds were cultivated, what were their favourite studies, what degree of liberty was allowed to them, what use they made of that liberty, what accomplishments they most valued in men, and what proofs of tenderness delicacy permitted them to give to favoured suitors—as to know all about the seizure of Franche Comté and the treaty of Nimeguen. The mutual relations of the two sexes seem to us to be at least as important as the mutual relations of any two governments in the world; and a series of letters written by a virtuous, amiable and sensible girl, and intended for the eye of her lover alone, can scarcely fail to throw some light on the relations of the sexes; whereas it is perfectly possible, as all who have made any historical researches can attest, to read bale after bale of despatches and protocols without catching one glimpse of light about the relations of governments.

Mr. Courtenay proclaims that he is one of Dorothy Osborne's devoted servants, and expresses a hope that the publication of her letters will add to the number. We must declare ourselves his rivals. She really seems to have been a very charming young woman—modest, generous, affectionate, intelligent and sprightly—a royalist, as was to be expected from her connections, without any of that political asperity which is as unwomanly as a long beard—religious, and occasionally gliding into a very pretty and endearing sort of preaching, yet not too good to partake of such diversions as London afforded under the melancholy rule of the Puritans, or to giggle a little at a ridiculous sermon from a divine who was thought to be one of the great lights of the Assembly at Westminster—with a little turn for coquetry, which was yet perfectly compatible with warm and disinterested attachment—and a little turn for satire, which yet seldom passed the bounds of good-nature. She loved reading; but her studies were not those of Queen Elizabeth and Lady Jane Grey. She read the verses of Cowley and Lord Broghill, French memoirs recommended by her lover, and the Travels of Fernando Mendez Pinto. But her favourite books were those ponderous French romances which modern readers know chiefly from the pleasant satire of Charlotte Lennox. She could not, however, help laughing at the vile English into which they were translated. Her own style is very agreeable; nor are her letters at all the worse for some passages in which raillery and tenderness are mixed in a very engaging namby-pamby.

When at last the constancy of the lovers had triumphed over all the obstacles which kinsmen and rivals could oppose to their union, a yet more serious calamity befell them. Poor Mistress Osborne fell ill of the small-pox and, though she escaped with life, lost all her beauty. To this most severe trial the affection and honour of the lovers of that age was not unfrequently subjected. Our readers probably remember what Mrs. Hutchinson tells us of herself. The lofty Cornelia-like spirit of the aged matron seems to melt into a long-forgotten softness when she relates how her beloved Colonel "married her as soon as she was able to quit the chamber, when the priest and all that saw her were affrighted to look on her. But God," she adds, with a not ungraceful vanity, "recompensed his justice and constancy by restoring her as well as before." Temple showed on this occasion the same "justice and constancy," which did so much honour to Colonel Hutchinson. The date of the marriage is not exactly known. But Mr. Courtenay supposes it to have taken place about the end of the year 1654. From this time we lose sight of Dorothy, and are reduced to form our opinion of the terms on which she and her husband were from very slight indications which may easily mislead us.

Temple soon went to Ireland, and resided with his father, partly at Dublin, partly in the county of Carlow. Ireland was probably then a more agreeable residence for the higher classes, as compared with England, than it has ever been before or since. In no part of the empire were the superiority of Cromwell's abilities and the force of his character so signally displayed. He had not the power, and probably had not the inclination, to govern that island in the best way. The rebellion of the aboriginal race had excited in England a strong religious and national aversion to them; nor is there any reason to believe that the Protector was so far beyond his age as to be free from the prevailing sentiment. He had vanquished them; he knew that they were in his power: and he regarded them as a band of malefactors and idolators who were mercifully treated if they were not smitten with the edge of the sword. On those who resisted he had made war as the Hebrews made war on the Canaanites. Drogheda was as Jericho and Wexford as Ai. To the remains of the old population, the conqueror granted a peace such as that which Joshua granted to the Gibeonites. He made them hewers of wood and drawers of water. But, good or bad, he could not be otherwise than great. Under favourable circumstances, Ireland would have found in him a most just and beneficent ruler. She found in him a tyrant—not a small teasing tyrant, such as those who have so long been her curse and her shame—but one of those awful tyrants who at long intervals seem to be sent on earth, like avenging angels, with some high commission of destruction and renovation. He was no man of half measures, of mean affronts and ungracious concessions. His

Protestant ascendency was not an ascendency of ribands, and fiddles, and statues, and processions. He would never have dreamed of abolishing penal laws against the Irish catholics and withholding from them the elective franchise—of giving them the elective franchise and excluding them from Parliament—of admitting them to Parliament and refusing to them a full and equal participation in all the blessings of society and government. The thing most alien from his clear intellect and his commanding spirit was petty persecution. He knew how to tolerate and he knew how to destroy. His administration in Ireland was an administration on what are now called Orange principles—followed out most ably, most steadily, most undauntedly, most unrelentingly, to every extreme consequence to which those principles lead; and it would, if continued, inevitably have produced the effect which he contemplated—an entire decomposition and reconstruction of society. He had a great and definite object in view—to make Ireland thoroughly English, to make it another Yorkshire or Norfolk. Thinly peopled as Ireland then was, this end was not unattainable; and there is every reason to believe that, if his policy had been followed during fifty years, this end would have been attained. Instead of an emigration, such as we now see from Ireland to England, there was, under his government, a constant and large emigration from England to Ireland. This tide of population ran almost as strongly as that which now runs from Massachusetts and Connecticut to the states behind the Ohio. The native race was driven back before the advancing van of the Anglo-Saxon population as the American Indians or the tribes of Southern Africa are now driven back before the white settlers. Those fearful phenomena which have almost invariably attended the planting of civilised colonies in uncivilised countries, and which had been known to the nations of Europe only by distant and questionable rumour, were now publicly exhibited in their sight. The words "extirpation," "eradication," were often in the mouths of the English back-settlers of Leinster and Munster—cruel words—yet, in their cruelty, containing more mercy than much softer expressions which have since been sanctioned by universities and cheered by Parliaments. For it is in truth more merciful to extirpate a hundred thousand people at once, and to fill the void with a well governed population, than to misgovern millions through a long succession of generations. We can much more easily pardon tremendous severities inflicted for a great object than an endless series of paltry vexations and oppressions inflicted for no rational object at all.

Ireland was fast becoming English. Civilisation and wealth were making rapid progress in almost every part of the island. The effects of that iron despotism are described to us by a hostile witness in very remarkable language. "Which is more wonderful," says Lord Clarendon, "all this was done and settled within little more than two years, to that degree of perfection that there were many buildings raised for beauty as well as use, orderly and regular plantations of trees, and fences and inclosures raised throughout the kingdom, purchases made by one from another at very valuable rates, and jointures made upon marriages, and all other conveyances and settlements executed, as in a kingdom at peace within itself, and where no doubt could be made of the validity of titles."

All Temple's feelings about Irish questions were those of a colonist and a member of the dominant caste. He troubled himself as little about the welfare of the remains of the old Celtic population as an English farmer on the Swan river troubles himself about the New Hollanders, or a Dutch Boer at the Cape about the Caffres. The years which he passed in Ireland, while the Cromwellian system was in full operation, he always described as "years of great satisfaction." Farming, gardening, county business, and studies, rather entertaining than profound, occupied his time. In politics he took no part, and, many years after, he attributed this inaction to his love of the ancient constitution, which, he said, "would not suffer him to enter into public affairs till the way was plain for the King's happy restoration." It does not appear, indeed, that any offer of employment was made to him. If he really did refuse any preferment, we may, without much breach of charity, attribute the refusal rather to the caution which, during his whole life, prevented him from running any risk than to the fervour of his loyalty.

In 1660 he made his first appearance in public life. He sat in the convention which, in the midst of the general confusion that preceded the Restoration, was summoned by the chiefs of the army of Ireland to meet in Dublin. After the King's return, an Irish parliament was regularly convoked, in which Temple represented the county of Carlow. The details of his conduct in this situation are not known to us. But we are told in general terms, and can easily believe, that he showed great moderation and great aptitude for business. It is probable that he also distinguished himself in debate; for, many years afterwards, he remarked that "his friends in Ireland used to think that, if he had any talent at all, it lay in that way."

In May, 1663, the Irish parliament was prorogued, and Temple repaired to England with his wife. His income amounted to about five hundred pounds a-year, a sum which was then sufficient for the wants of a family mixing in fashionable circles. He passed two years in London, where he seems to have led that easy, lounging life which was best suited to his temper.

He was not, however, unmindful of his interest. He had brought with him letters of introduction from the Duke of Ormond, then Lord-Lieutenant of Ireland, to Clarendon, and to Henry Bennet, Lord Arlington, who was Secretary of State. Clarendon was at the head of affairs. But his power was visibly declining, and was certain to decline more and more every day. An observer much less discerning than Temple might easily perceive that the Chancellor was a man who belonged to a by-gone world; a representative of a past age, of obsolete modes of thinking, of unfashionable vices, and of more unfashionable virtues. His long exile had made him a stranger in the country of his birth. His mind, heated by conflict and by personal suffering, was far more set against popular and tolerant courses than it had been at the time of the breaking out of the Civil War. He pined for the decorous tyranny of the old Whitehall; for the days of that sainted king who deprived his people of their money and their ears, but let their wives and daughters alone; and could scarcely reconcile himself to a court with a mistress and without a Star Chamber. By taking this course he made himself every day more odious, both to the sovereign, who loved pleasure much more than prerogative, and to the people, who dreaded royal prerogatives much more than royal pleasures; and was, at last, more detested by the Court than any chief of the Opposition, and more detested by the Parliament than any pandar of the Court.

Temple, whose great maxim was to offend no party, was not likely to cling to the falling fortunes of a minister the study of whose life was to offend all parties. Arlington, whose influence was gradually rising as that of Clarendon diminished, was the most useful patron to whom a young adventurer could attach himself. This statesman, without virtue, wisdom, or strength of mind, had raised himself to greatness by superficial qualities, and was the mere creature of the time, the circumstances and the company. The dignified reserve of manners, which he had acquired during a residence in Spain, provoked the ridicule of those who considered the usages of the French court as the only standard of good breeding, but served to impress the crowd with a favourable opinion of his sagacity and gravity. In situations where the solemnity of the Escurial would have been out of place, he threw it aside without difficulty, and conversed with great humour and vivacity. While the multitude were talking of "Bennet's grave looks,"* his mirth made his presence always welcome in the royal closet. While in the antechamber Buckingham was mimicking the pompous Castilian strut of the Secretary, for the diversion of Mistress Stuart, this stately Don was ridiculing Clarendon's sober counsels to the King within, till his Majesty cried with laughter and the Chancellor with vexation. There perhaps never was a man whose outward demeanour made such different impressions on different people. Count Hamilton, for example, describes him as a stupid formalist, who had been made secretary solely on account of his mysterious and important looks. Clarendon, on the other hand, represents him as man whose "best faculty was raillery," and who was "for his pleasant and agreeable humour acceptable unto the King." The truth seems to be that, destitute as he was of all the higher qualifications of a minister, he had a wonderful talent for becoming, in outward semblance, all things to all men. He had two aspects, a busy and serious one for the public, whom he wished to awe into respect, and a gay one for Charles, who thought that the greatest service which could be rendered to a prince was to amuse him. Yet both these were masks which he laid aside when they had served their turn. Long after, when he had retired to his deer-park and fish-ponds in Suffolk, and had no motive to act the part either of the hidalgo or of the buffoon, Evelyn, who was neither an unpractised nor an undiscerning judge, conversed much with him, and pronounced him to be a man of singularly polished manners and of great colloquial powers.

Clarendon, proud and imperious by nature, soured by age and disease, and relying on his great talents and services, sought out no new allies. He seems to have taken a sort of morose pleasure in slighting and provoking all the rising talent of the kingdom. His connections were almost entirely confined to the small circle, every day becoming smaller, of old cavaliers who had been friends of his youth or companions of his exile. Arlington, on the other hand, beat up everywhere for recruits. No man had a greater personal following, and no man exerted himself more to serve his adherents. It was a kind of habit with him to push up his dependents to his own level, and then to complain bitterly of their ingratitude because they did not choose to be his dependents any longer. It was thus that he quarrelled with two successive Treasurers, Gifford and Danby. To Arlington, Temple attached himself, and was not sparing of warm professions of affection, or even, we grieve to say, of gross and almost profane adulation. In no long time he obtained his reward.

England was in a very different situation with respect to foreign powers from that which she had occupied during the splendid administration of the Protector. She was engaged in war with the United Provinces, then governed with almost regal power by the Grand Pensionary, John de Witt; and though no war had ever cost the kingdom so much, none had ever been more feebly and meanly conducted. France had espoused the interests of the States-General. Denmark seemed likely to take the same side. Spain, indignant at the close political and matrimonial alliance which Charles had formed with the House of Braganza, was not disposed to lend him any assistance. The great plague of London had suspended trade, had scattered the ministers and nobles, had paralysed every department of the public service, and had increased the gloomy discontent which misgovernment had begun to excite

---

* "Bennet's grave looks were a pretence" is a line in one of the best political poems of that age.

throughout the nation. One Continental ally England possessed—the Bishop of Munster, a restless and ambitious prelate, bred a soldier, and still a soldier in all his tastes and passions. He hated the Dutch, who had interfered in the affairs of his see, and declared himself willing to risk his little dominions for the chance of revenge. He sent, accordingly, a strange kind of ambassador to London, a Benedictine monk, who spoke bad English and looked, says Lord Clarendon, "like a carter." This person brought a letter from the Bishop, offering to make an attack by land on the Dutch territory. The English ministers eagerly caught at the proposal, and promised a subsidy of 500,000 rix-dollars to their new ally. It was determined to send an English agent to Munster; and Arlington, to whose department the business belonged, fixed on Temple for this post.

Temple accepted the commission, and acquitted himself to the satisfaction of his employers, though the whole plan ended in nothing; and the Bishop, after pocketing an instalment of his subsidy, made haste to conclude a separate peace. Temple, at a later period, looked back with no great satisfaction to this part of his life, and excused himself for undertaking a negotiation from which little good could result, by saying that he was then young and very new to business. In truth, he could hardly have been placed in a situation where the eminent diplomatic talents which he possessed could have appeared to less advantage. He was ignorant of the German language, and did not easily accommodate himself to the manners of the people. He could not bear much wine; and none but a hard drinker had any chance of success in Westphalian society. Under all these disadvantages, however, he gave so much satisfaction that he was created a baronet and appointed resident at the viceregal court of Brussels.

Brussels suited Temple far better than the palaces of the boar-hunting and wine-bibbing princes of Germany. He now occupied the most important posts of observation in which a diplomatist could be stationed. He was placed in the territory of a great neutral power, between the territories of the two great powers which were at war with England. From this excellent school he soon came forth the most accomplished negotiator of his age.

In the meantime, the government of Charles had suffered a succession of humiliating disasters. The extravagance of the court had dissipated all the means which Parliament had supplied for the purpose of carrying on offensive hostilities. It was determined to wage only a defensive war; and even for defensive war the vast resources of England, managed by triflers and public robbers, were found insufficient. The Dutch insulted the British coasts, sailed up the Thames, took Sheerness, and carried their ravages to Chatham. The blaze of the ships burning in the river was seen at London; it was rumoured that a foreign army had landed at Gravesend; and military men seriously proposed to abandon the Tower. To such a depth of infamy had a bad administration reduced that proud and victorious nation, which a few years before had dictated its pleasure to Mazarine, to the States-General and to the Vatican. Humbled by the events of the war, and dreading the just anger of Parliament, the English Ministry hastened to huddle up a peace with France and Holland at Breda.

But a new scene was about to open. It had already been for sometime apparent to discerning observers that England and Holland were threatened by a common danger, much more formidable than any which they had reason to apprehend from each other. The old enemy of their independence and of their religion was no longer to be dreaded. The sceptre had passed away from Spain. That mighty empire, on which the sun never set, which had crushed the liberties of Italy and Germany, which had occupied Paris with its armies and covered the British seas with its sails, was at the mercy of every spoiler; and Europe saw with dismay the rapid growth of a new and more formidable power. Men looked to Spain and saw only weakness disguised and increased by pride—dominions of vast bulk and little strength, tempting, unwieldy and defenceless—an empty treasury—a haughty, sullen and torpid nation—a child on the throne—factions in the council—ministers who served only themselves, and soldiers who were terrible only to their countrymen. Men looked to France and saw a large and compact territory—a rich soil—a central situation—a bold, alert and ingenious people—large revenues—numerous and disciplined troops—an active and ambitious prince, in the flower of his age, surrounded by generals of unrivalled skill. The projects of Louis could be counteracted only by ability, vigour and union on the part of his neighbours. Ability and vigour had hitherto been found in the councils of Holland alone, and of union there was no appearance in Europe. The question of Portuguese independence separated England from Spain. Old grudges, recent hostilities, maritime pretensions, commercial competition separated England as widely from the United Provinces.

The great object of Louis, from the beginning to the end of his reign, was the acquisition of those large and valuable provinces of the Spanish monarchy which lay contiguous to the eastern frontier of France. Already, before the conclusion of the treaty of Breda, he had invaded those provinces. He now pushed on his conquests with scarcely any resistance. Fortress after fortress was taken. Brussels itself was in danger; and Temple thought it wise to send his wife and children to England. But his sister, Lady Giffard, who had been sometime his inmate, and who seems to have been a more important personage in his family than his wife, still remained with him.

De Witt saw the progress of the French arms with painful anxiety. But it was not in the power of Holland alone to save Flanders; and the difficulty of forming an extensive coalition for that purpose appeared almost insuperable. Louis, indeed, affected moderation. He declared himself willing to agree to a compromise with Spain. But these offers were undoubtedly mere professions, intended to quiet the apprehensions of the neighbouring powers; and, as his position became every day more and more advantageous, it was to be expected that he would rise in his demands.

Such was the state of affairs when Temple obtained from the English Ministry permission to make a tour in Holland incognito. In company with Lady Giffard he arrived at the Hague. He was not charged with any public commission, but he availed himself of this opportunity of introducing himself to De Witt. "My only business, sir," he said, "is to see the things which are most considerable in your country, and I should execute my design very imperfectly if I went away without seeing you." De Witt, who from report had formed a high opinion of Temple, was pleased by the compliment, and replied with a frankness and cordiality which at once led to intimacy. The two statesmen talked calmly over the causes which had estranged England from Holland, congratulated each other on the peace, and then began to discuss the new dangers which menaced Europe. Temple, who had no authority to say anything on behalf of the English Government, expressed himself very guardedly. De Witt, who was himself the Dutch Government, had no reason to be reserved. He openly declared that his wish was to see a general coalition formed for the preservation of Flanders. His simplicity and openness amazed Temple, who had been accustomed to the affected solemnity of his patron, the Secretary, and to the eternal doublings and evasions which passed for great feats of statesmanship among the Spanish politicians at Brussels. "Whoever," he wrote to Arlington, "deals with M. de Witt must go the same plain way that he pretends to in his negotiations, without refining, or colouring, or offering shadow for substance." He was scarcely less struck by the modest dwelling and frugal table of the first citizen of the richest state in the world. While Clarendon was amazing London with a dwelling more sumptuous than the palace of his master, while Arlington was lavishing his ill-gotten wealth on the decoys and orange-gardens and interminable conservatories of Euston— the great statesman who had frustrated all their plans of conquest, and the roar of whose guns they had heard with terror even in the galleries of Whitehall, kept only a single servant, walked about the streets in the plainest garb, and never used a coach except for visits of ceremony.

Temple sent a full account of his interview with De Witt to Arlington, who, in consequence of the fall of the Chancellor, now shared with the Duke of Buckingham the principal direction of affairs. Arlington showed no disposition to meet the advances of the Dutch minister. Indeed, as was amply proved a few years later, both he and his master were perfectly willing to purchase the means of misgoverning England by giving up, not only Flanders, but the whole Continent to France. Temple, who distinctly saw that a moment had arrived at which it was possible to reconcile his country with Holland—to reconcile Charles with the Parliament—to bridle the power of Louis—to efface the shame of the late ignominious war—to restore England to the same place in Europe which she had occupied under Cromwell, became more and more urgent in his representations. Arlington's replies were for some time couched in cold and ambiguous terms. But the events which followed the meeting of Parliament, in the autumn of 1667, appear to have produced an entire change in his views. The discontent of the nation was deep and general. The administration was attacked in all its parts. The King and the ministers laboured, not unsuccessfully, to throw on Clarendon the blame of past miscarriages; but though the Commons were resolved that the late Chancellor should be the first victim, it was by no means clear that he would be the last. The Secretary was personally attacked with great bitterness in the course of the debates. One of the resolutions of the Lower House against Clarendon could be understood only as a censure of the foreign policy of the Government as too favourable to France. To these events chiefly we are inclined to attribute the change which at this crisis took place in the measures of England. The Ministry seem to have felt that, if they wished to derive any advantage from Clarendon's downfall, it was necessary for them to abandon what was supposed to be Clarendon's system, and by some splendid and popular measure to win the confidence of the nation. Accordingly, in December, 1667, Temple received a despatch containing instructions of the highest importance. The plan which he had so strongly recommended was approved; and he was directed to visit De Witt as speedily as possible, and to ascertain whether the States were willing to enter into an offensive and defensive league with England against the projects of France. Temple, accompanied by his sister, instantly set out for the Hague, and laid the propositions of the English Government before the Grand Pensionary. The Dutch statesman answered, with characteristic straightforwardness, that he was fully ready to agree to a defensive alliance, but that it was the fundamental principle of the foreign policy of the States to make no offensive league under any circumstances whatever. With this answer, Temple hastened from the Hague to London had an audience of the King, related what had passed between himself and De Witt, exerted himself to remove the unfavourable opinion which had been conceived of the Grand Pensionary at the English court, and had the satisfaction of succeeding in all his objects. On the evening of the first of January, 1668, a council was held, at which Charles declared his resolution to unite with the Dutch on their own terms. Temple and his indefatigable sister immediately sailed again for the Hague, and, after weathering a violent storm in which they were very nearly lost, arrived in safety at the place of their destination.

On this occasion, as on every other, the dealings between Temple and De Witt were singularly fair and open. When they met, Temple began by recapitulating what had passed at their last interview. De Witt, who was as little given to lying with his face as with his tongue, marked his assent by his looks while the recapitulation proceeded, and, when it was concluded, answered that Temple's memory was perfectly correct, and thanked him for proceeding in so exact and sincere a manner. Temple then informed the Grand Pensionary that the King of England had determined to close with the proposal of a defensive alliance. De Witt had not expected so speedy a resolution; and his countenance indicated surprise as well as pleasure. But he did not retract; and it was speedily arranged that England and Holland should unite for the purpose of compelling Louis to abide by the compromise which he had formerly offered. The next object of the two statesmen was to induce another government to become a party to their league. The victories of Gustavus and Torstenson, and the political talents of Oxenstiern, had obtained for Sweden a consideration in Europe disproportioned to her real power; the princes of Northern Germany stood in great awe of her; and De Witt and Temple agreed that if she could be induced to accede to the league, "it would be too strong a bar for France to venture on." Temple went that same evening to Count Dona, the Swedish Minister at the Hague, took a seat in the most unceremonious manner; and, with that air of frankness and good-will by which he often succeeded in rendering his diplomatic overtures acceptable, explained the scheme which was in agitation. Dona was greatly pleased and flattered. He had not powers which would authorise him to conclude a treaty of such importance. But he strongly advised Temple and De Witt to do their part without delay, and seemed confident that Sweden would accede. The ordinary course of public business in Holland was too slow for the present emergency; and De Witt appeared to have some scruples about breaking through the established forms. But the urgency and dexterity of Temple prevailed. The States-General took the responsibility of executing the treaty with a celerity unprecedented in the annals of the federation, and indeed inconsistent with its fundamental laws. The state of public feeling was, however, such in all the provinces, that this irregularity was not merely pardoned, but applauded. When the instrument had been formerly signed, the Dutch Commissioners embraced the English Plenipotentiary with the warmest expressions of kindness and confidence. "At Breda," exclaimed Temple, "we embraced as friends, here as brothers."

This memorable negotiation occupied only five days. De Witt complimented Temple in high terms on having effected in so short a time what must, under other management, have been the work of months: and Temple, in his despatches, spoke in equally high terms of De Witt. "I must add these words, to do M. de Witt right, that I found him as plain, as direct and square in the course of this business as any man could be, though often stiff in points where he thought any advantage could accrue to his country; and have all the reason in the world to be satisfied with him; and for his industry, no man had ever more, I am sure. For these five days, at least, neither of us spent any idle hours, neither day nor night."

Sweden willingly acceded to the league, which is known in history by the name of the Triple Alliance; and, after some signs of ill-humour on the part of France, a general pacification was the result.

The Triple Alliance may be viewed in two lights; as a measure of foreign policy and as a measure of domestic policy; and under both aspects it seems to us deserving of all the praise which has been bestowed upon it.

Dr. Lingard, who is undoubtedly a very able and well informed writer, but whose great fundamental rule of judging seems to be that the popular opinion on a historical question cannot possibly be correct, speaks very slightingly of this celebrated treaty; and Mr. Courtenay, who by no means regards Temple with that profound veneration which is generally found in biographers, has conceded, in our opinion, far too much to Dr. Lingard.

The reasoning of Dr. Lingard is simply this. The Triple Alliance only compelled Louis to make peace on the terms on which, before the alliance was formed, he had offered to make peace. How can it then be said that this alliance arrested his career and preserved Europe from his ambition? Now, this reasoning is evidently of no force at all, except on the supposition that Louis would have held himself bound by his former offers if the alliance had not been formed; and, if Dr. Lingard thinks this a reasonable supposition, we should be disposed to say to him, in the words of that great politician, Mrs. Western: "Indeed, brother, you would make a fine plenipo to negotiate with the French. They would soon persuade you that they take towns out of mere defensive principles." Our own impression is that Louis made his offer only in order to avert some such measure as the Triple Alliance, and adhered to his offer only in consequence of that alliance. He had refused to consent to an armistice. He had made all his arrangements for a winter campaign. In the very week in which Temple and the States concluded their agreement at the Hague, Franche Comté was attacked by the French armies, and in three weeks the whole province was conquered. This prey Louis was compelled to disgorge. And what compelled him? Did the object seem to him small or contemptible? On the contrary, the annexation of Franche Comté to his kingdom was one of the favourite projects of his life. Was he withheld by regard for his word! Did he—who never in any other transaction of his reign showed the smallest respect for the most solemn obligations of public faith, who violated the Treaty of the Pyrenees, who violated the Treaty of Aix, who violated the Treaty of Nimeguen, who violated the Partition Treaty, who violated the Treaty of Utrecht—feel himself restrained by his word on this single occasion? Can any person who is acquainted with his character and with his whole policy doubt that, if the neighbouring powers would have looked quietly on, he would instantly have risen in his demands? How then stands the case? He wished to keep Franche Comté. It was not from regard to his word that he ceded Franche Comté. Why then did he cede Franche Comté? We answer, as all Europe answered at the time, from fear of the Triple Alliance.

But grant that Louis was not really stopped in his progress by this famous league; still it is certain that the world then, and long after, believed that he was so stopped, and that this was the prevailing impression in France as well as in other countries. Temple, therefore, at the very least, succeeded in raising the credit of his country and in lowering the credit of a rival power. Here there is no room for controversy. No grubbing among old state-papers will ever bring to light any document which will shake these facts—that Europe believed the ambition of France to have been curbed by the three powers—that England, a few months before the least among the nations, forced to abandon her own seas, unable to defend the mouths of her own rivers, regained almost as high a place in the estimation of her neighbours as she had held in the times of Elizabeth and Oliver; and that all this change of opinion was produced in five days by wise and resolute councils, without the firing of a single gun. That the Triple Alliance effected this will hardly be disputed; and, if it effected nothing else, it must still be regarded as a master-piece of diplomacy.

Considered as a measure of domestic policy, this treaty seems to be equally deserving of approbation. It did much to allay discontents, to reconcile the sovereign with a people who had, under his wretched administration, become ashamed of him and of themselves. It was a kind of pledge for internal good government. The foreign relations of the kingdom had at that time the closest connection with our domestic policy. From the Restoration to the accession of the House of Hanover, Holland and France were to England what the right-hand horseman and the left-hand horseman in Bürger's fine ballad were to the Wildgraf—the good and the evil counsellor—the angel of light and the angel of darkness. The ascendency of France was inseparably connected with the prevalence of tyranny in domestic affairs. The ascendency of Holland was as inseparably connected with the prevalence of political liberty and of mutual toleration among Protestant sects. How fatal and degrading an influence Louis was destined to exercise on the British counsels, how great a deliverance our country was destined to owe to the States, could not be foreseen when the Triple Alliance was concluded. Yet even then all discerning men considered it as a good omen for the English constitution and the reformed religion, that the Government had attached itself to Holland and had assumed a firm and somewhat hostile attitude towards France. The fame of this measure was the greater because it stood so entirely alone. It was the single eminently good act performed by the Government during the interval between the Restoration and the Revolution.* Every person who had the smallest part in it, and some who had no part in it at all, battled for a share of the credit. The most close-fisted republicans were ready to grant money for the purpose of carrying into effect the provisions of this popular alliance; and the great Tory poet of that age, in his finest satires, repeatedly spoke with reverence of the "triple bond."

This negotiation raised the fame of Temple both at home and abroad to a great height, to such a height, indeed, as seems to have excited the jealousy of his friend Arlington. While London and Amsterdam resounded with acclamations of joy, the Secretary, in very cold official language, communicated to his friend the approbation of the King; and, lavish as the Government was of titles and money, its ablest servant was neither ennobled nor enriched.

Temple's next mission was to Aix-la-Chapelle, where a general congress met for the purpose of perfecting the work of the Triple Alliance. On his road he received abundant proofs of the estimation in which he was held. Salutes were fired from the walls of the towns through which he passed; the population poured forth into the streets to see him; and the magistrates entertained him with speeches and banquets. After the close of the negotiations at Aix, he was appointed Ambassador at the Hague. But in both these missions he experienced much vexation from the rigid and, indeed, unjust parsimony of the Government. Profuse to many unworthy applicants, the Ministers were niggardly to him alone. They secretly disliked his politics; and they seem to have indemnified themselves for the humiliation of adopting his measures by cutting down his salary and delaying the settlement of his outfit.

At the Hague he was received with cordiality by De Witt, and with the most signal marks of respect by the States-General. His situation was in one point extremely delicate. The Prince of Orange, the hereditary chief of the faction opposed to the administration of De Witt, was the nephew of Charles.

* "The only good public thing that hath been done since the king came into England."—Pepys's Diary, February 14, 1867-68.

To preserve the confidence of the ruling party, without showing any want of respect to so near a relation of his own master, was no easy task. But Temple acquitted himself so well that he appears to have been in great favour both with the Grand Pensionary and with the Prince.

In the main, the years which he spent at the Hague seem, in spite of some pecuniary difficulties occasioned by the ill-will of the English Ministers, to have passed very agreeably. He enjoyed the highest personal consideration. He was surrounded by objects interesting in the highest degree to a man of his observant turn of mind. He had no wearing labour, no heavy responsibility; and, if he had no opportunity of adding to his high reputation, he ran no risk of impairing it.

But evil times were at hand. Though Charles had for a moment deviated into a wise and dignified policy, his heart had always been with France; and France employed every means of seduction to lure him back. His impatience of control, his greediness for money, his passion for beauty, his family affections, all his tastes, all his feelings were practised on with the utmost dexterity. His interior Cabinet was now composed of men such as that generation, and that generation alone, produced; of men at whose audacious profligacy the rats of our own time look with the same sort of admiring despair with which our sculptors contemplate the Theseus and our painters the Cartoons. To be a real, hearty, deadly enemy of the liberties and religion of the nation was in that dark conclave an honourable distinction—a distinction which belonged only to the daring and impetuous Clifford. His associates were men to whom all creeds and all constitutions were alike; who were equally ready to profess and to persecute the faith of Geneva, of Lambeth and of Rome; who were equally ready to be tools of power without any sense of loyalty, and stirrers of sedition without any zeal for freedom.

It was hardly possible even for a man so penetrating as De Witt to foresee to what depths of wickedness and infamy this execrable administration would descend. Yet many signs of the great woe which was coming on Europe— the visit of the Duchess of Orleans to her brother—the unexplained mission of Buckingham to Paris—the sudden occupation of Lorraine by the French—made the Grand Pensionary uneasy; and his alarm increased when he learned that Temple had received orders to repair instantly to London. De Witt earnestly pressed for an explanation. Temple very sincerely replied that he hoped that the English Ministers would adhere to the principles of the Triple Alliance. "I can answer," he said, "only for myself. But that I can do. If a new system is to be adopted, I will never have any part in it. I have told the King so; and I will make my words good. If I return you will know more: and if I do not return you will guess more." De Witt smiled, and answered that he would hope the best, and would do all in his power to prevent others from forming unfavourable surmises.

In October, 1670, Temple reached London; and all his worst suspicions were immediately more than confirmed. He repaired to the Secretary's house, and was kept an hour and a half waiting in the ante-chamber whilst Lord Ashley was closeted with Arlington. When at length the doors were thrown open, Arlington was dry and cold, asking trifling questions about the voyage, and then, in order to escape from the necessity of discussing business, called in his daughter, an engaging little girl of three years old, who was long after described by poets as "dressed in all the bloom of smiling nature," and whom Evelyn, one of the witnesses of her inauspicious marriage, mournfully designated as "the sweetest, hopefullest, most beautiful child, and most virtuous too." Any particular conversation was impossible; and Temple, who with all his constitutional or philosophical indifference, was sufficiently sensitive on the side of vanity, felt this treatment keenly. The next day he offered himself to the notice of the King, who was snuffing up the morning air and feeding his ducks in the Mall. Charles was civil, but, like Arlington, carefully avoided all conversation on politics. Temple found that all his most respectable friends were entirely excluded from the secrets of the inner council, and were awaiting in anxiety and dread for what those mysterious deliberations might produce. At length he obtained a glimpse of light. The bold spirit and fierce passions of Clifford made him the most unfit of all men to be the keeper of a momentous secret. He told Temple, with great vehemence, that the States had behaved basely, that De Witt was a rogue and a rascal, that it was below the King of England, or any other king, to have anything to do with such wretches; that this ought to be made known to all the world, and that it was the duty of the Minister at the Hague to declare it publicly. Temple commanded his temper as well as he could, and replied calmly and firmly, that he should make no such declaration, and that if he were called upon to give his opinion of the States and their Ministers, he would say exactly what he thought.

He now saw clearly that the tempest was gathering fast—that the great alliance which he had formed and over which he had watched with parental care was about to be dissolved—that times were at hand when it would be necessary for him, if he continued in public life, either to take part decidedly against the Court or to forfeit the high reputation which he enjoyed at home and abroad. He began to make preparations for retiring altogether from business. He enlarged a little garden which he had purchased at Sheen, and laid out some money in ornamenting his house there. He was still nominally ambassador to Holland; and the English Ministers continued during some months to flatter the States with the hope that he would speedily return. At length, in June, 1671, the designs of the Cabal were ripe. The infamous treaty with France had been ratified. The season of deception was past and that of insolence and violence had arrived. Temple received his formal dismission, kissed the King's hand, was repaid for his services with some of those vague compliments and promises which cost so little to the cold heart, the easy temper and the ready tongue of Charles, and quietly withdrew to his little nest, as he called it, at Sheen.

There he amused himself with gardening, which he practised so successfully that the fame of his fruit soon spread far and wide. But letters were his chief solace. He had, as we have mentioned, been from his youth in the habit of diverting himself with composition. The clear and agreeable language of his despatches had early attracted the notice of his employers; and, before the peace of Breda, he had, at the request of Arlington, published a pamplet on the war, of which nothing is now known, except that it had some vogue at the time, and that Charles, not a contemptible judge, pronounced it to be very well written. Temple had also, a short time before he began to reside at the Hague, written a treatise on the state of Ireland, in which he showed all the feelings of a Cromwellian. He had gradually formed a style singularly lucid and melodious—superficially deformed, indeed, by Gallicisms and Hispanicisms, picked up in travel or in negotiation—but at the bottom pure English—generally flowing with careless simplicity, but occasionally rising even into Ciceronian magnificence. The length of his sentences has often been remarked. But in truth this length is only apparent. A critic who considers as one sentence everything that lies between two full stops will undoubtedly call Temple's sentences long. But a critic who examines them carefully will find that they are not swollen by parenthetical matter; that their structure is scarcely ever intricate; that they are formed merely by accumulation; and that, by the simple process of leaving out conjunctions, and substituting full stops for colons and semicolons, they might, without any alteration in the order of the words, be broken up into very short periods with no sacrifice except that of euphony. The long sentences of Hooker and Clarendon, on the contrary, are really long sentences, and cannot be turned into short ones without being entirely taken to pieces.

The best known of the works which Temple composed during his first retreat from official business are an "Essay on Government," which seems to us exceedingly childish, and an "Account of the United Provinces," which we think a master-piece of its kind. Whoever compares these two treatises will probably agree with us in thinking that Temple was not a very deep or accurate reasoner, but was an excellent observer—that he had no call to philosophical speculation, but that he was qualified to excel as a writer of Memoirs and Travels.

While Temple was engaged in these pursuits, the great storm which had long been brooding over Europe burst with such fury as for a moment seemed to threaten ruin to all free governments and all Protestant churches. France and England, without seeking for any decent pretext, declared war against Holland. The immense armies of Louis poured across the Rhine and invaded the territory of the United Provinces. The Dutch seemed to be paralysed by terror. Great towns opened their gates to straggling parties. Regiments flung down their arms without seeing an enemy. Guelderland, Overyssel, Utrecht were overrun by the conquerors. The fires of the French camp were seen from the walls of Amsterdam. In the first madness of despair, the devoted people turned their rage against the most illustrious of their fellow-citizens. De Ruyter was saved with difficulty from assassins. De Witt was torn to pieces by an infuriated rabble. No hope was left to the Commonwealth, save in the dauntless, the ardent, the indefatigable, the unconquerable spirit which glowed under the frigid demeanour of the young Prince of Orange.

That great man rose at once to the full dignity of his part and approved himself a worthy descendant of the line of heroes who had vindicated the liberties of Europe against the house of Austria. Nothing could shake his fidelity to his country—not his close connection with the royal family of England—not the most earnest solicitations—not the most tempting offers. The spirit of the nation—that spirit which had maintained the great conflict against the gigantic power of Philip—revived in all its strength. Counsels, such as are inspired by a generous despair, and are almost always followed by a speedy dawn of hope, were gravely concerted by the statesmen of Holland. To open their dykes—to man their ships—to leave their country, with all its miracles of art and industry—its cities, its canals, its villas, its pastures and its tulip gardens—buried under the waves of the German Ocean—to bear to a distant climate their Calvinistic faith and their old Batavian liberties—to fix, perhaps with happier auspices, the new Stadthouse of their Commonwealth under other stars and amidst a strange vegetation in the Spice Islands of the Eastern seas—such were the plans which they had the spirit to form; and it is seldom that men who have the spirit to form such plans are reduced to the necessity of executing them.

The allies had, during a short period, obtained success beyond their hopes. This was their auspicious moment. They neglected to improve it. It passed away; and it returned no more. The Prince of Orange arrested the progress of the French armies. Louis returned to be amused and flattered at Versailles. The country was under water. The winter approached. The weather became stormy. The fleets of the combined kings could no longer keep the sea. The Republic had obtained a respite; and the circumstances were such that a respite was, in a military view, important; in a political view, almost decisive.

The alliance against Holland, formidable as it was, was yet of such a nature that it could not succeed at all unless it succeeded at once. The English Ministers could not carry on the war without money. They could legally obtain money only from the Parliament; and they were most unwilling to call the Parliament together. The measures which Charles had adopted at home were even more unpopular than his foreign policy. He had bound himself by a treaty with Louis to re-establish the Catholic religion in England; and, in pursuance of this design, he had entered on the same path which his brother afterwards trod with greater obstinacy to a more fatal end. He had annulled by his own sole authority the laws against Catholics and other dissenters. The matter of the Declaration of Indulgence exasperated one half of his subjects and the manner the other half. Liberal men would have rejoiced to see toleration granted, at least to all Protestant sects. Many high churchmen had no objection to the King's dispensing power. But a tolerant act done in an unconstitutional way excited the opposition of all who were zealous either for the Church or for the privileges of the pople, that is to say, of ninety-nine Englishmen out of a hundred. The ministers were, therefore, most unwilling to meet the Houses. Lawless and desperate as their counsels were, the boldest of them had too much value for his neck to think of resorting to benevolences, privy-seals, ship-money, or any of the other unlawful modes of extortion which former kings had employed. The audacious fraud of shutting up the Exchequer furnished them with about twelve hundred thousand pounds, a sum which, even in better hands than theirs, would hardly have sufficed for the war-charges of a single year. And this was a step which could never be repeated; a step which, like most breaches of public faith, was speedily found to have caused pecuniary difficulties greater than those which it removed. All the money that could be raised was gone; Holland was not conquered; and the King had no resource but in a Parliament.

Had a general election taken place at this crisis, it is probable that the country would have sent up representatives as resolutely hostile to the Court as those who met in November, 1640; that the whole domestic and foreign policy of the Government would have been instantly changed; and that the members of the Cabal would have expiated their crimes on Tower Hill. But the House of Commons was still the same which had been elected twelve years before in the midst of the transports of joys, repentance and loyalty which followed the Restoration; and no pains had been spared to attach it to the Court by places, pensions and bribes. To the great mass of the people it was scarcely less odious than the Cabinet itself. Yet, though it did not immediately proceed to those strong measures which a new House would in all probability have adopted, it was sullen and unmanageable, and undid, slowly indeed, and by degrees, but most effectually, all that the Ministers had done. In one session it annihilated their system of internal government. In a second session it gave a death-blow to their foreign policy.

The dispensing power was the first object of attack. The Commons would not expressly approve the war; but neither did they as yet expressly condemn it; and they were even willing to grant the King a supply for the purpose of continuing hostilities on condition that he would redress internal grievances, among which the Declaration of Indulgence held the foremost place.

Shaftesbury, who was Chancellor, saw that the game was up—that he had got all that was to be got by siding with despotism and Popery, and that it was high time to think of being a demagogue and a good Protestant. The Lord Treasurer, Clifford, was marked out by his boldness, by his openness, by his zeal for the Catholic religion, by something which, compared with the villany of his colleagues, might almost be called honesty, to be the scapegoat of the whole conspiracy. The King came in person to the House of Peers for the purpose of requesting their Lordships to meditate between him and the Commons touching the Declaration of Indulgence. He remained in the House while his speech was taken into consideration—a common practice with him; for the debates amused his sated mind, and were sometimes, he used to say, as good as a comedy. A more sudden turn his Majesty had certainly never seen in any comedy of intrigue, either at his own play-house, or at the Duke's, than that which this memorable debate produced. The Lord Treasurer spoke with characteristic ardour and intrepedity in defence of the Declaration. When he sat down, the Lord Chancellor rose from the woolsack, and, to the amazement of the King and of the House, attacked Clifford—attacked the Declaration for which he had himself spoken in Council—gave up the whole policy of the Cabinet—and declared himself on the side of the House of Commons. Even that age had not witnessed so portentous a display of impudence.

The King, by the advice of the French Court, which cared much more about the war on the Continent than about the conversion of the English heretics, determined to save his foreign policy at the expense of his plans in favour of the Catholic church. He obtain a supply; and in return for this concession he cancelled the Declaration of Indulgence—and made a formal renunciation of the dispensing power before he prorogued the Houses.

But it was no more in his power to go on with the war than to maintain his arbitary system at home. His Ministry, betrayed within and fiercely assailed from without, went rapidly to pieces. Clifford threw down the white staff and retired to the woods of Ugbrook, vowing, with bitter tears, that he would never again see that turbulent city and that perfidious Court. Shaftesbury was ordered to deliver up the Great Seal, and instantly carried over his front of brass and his tongue of poison to the ranks of the Opposition. The remaining members of the Cabal had neither the capacity of the late Chancellor, nor the courage and enthusiasm of the late Treasurer. They were not only unable to carry on their former projects, but began to tremble for their own lands and heads. The Parliament, as soon as it again met, began to murmur against the alliance with France and the war with Holland; and the murmur gradually swelled into a fierce and terrible clamour. Strong resolutions were adopted against Lauderdale and Buckingham. Articles of impeachment were exhibited against Arlington. The Triple Alliance was mentioned with reverence in every debate; and the eyes of all men were turned towards the quiet orchard where the author of that great league was amusing himself with reading and gardening.

Temple was ordered to attend the King, and was charged with the office of negotiating a separate peace with Holland. The Spanish Ambassador to the Court of London had been empowered by the States-General to treat in their name. With him Temple came to a speedy agreement, and in three days a treaty was concluded.

The highest honours of the State were now within Temple's reach. After the retirement of Clifford, the white staff had been delivered to Thomas Osborne, soon after created Earl of Danby, who was related to Lady Temple, and had, many years earlier, travelled and played tennis with Sir William. Danby was an interested and unscrupulous man, but by no means destitute of abilities or of judgment. He was, indeed, a far better adviser than any in whom Charles had hitherto reposed confidence. Clarendon was a man of another generation, and did not in the least understand the society which he had to govern. The members of the Cabal were ministers of a foreign power and enemies of the Established Church, and had, in consequence, raised against themselves and their master an irresistible storm of national and religious hatred. Danby wished to strengthen and extend the prerogative; but he had the sense to see that this could be done only by a complete change of system. He knew the English people and the House of Commons; and he knew that the course which Charles had recently taken, if obstinately pursued, might well end before the windows of the Banqueting-House. He saw that the true policy of the Crown was to ally itself, not with the feeble, the hated, the down-trodden Catholics, but with the powerful, the wealthy, the popular, the dominant Church of England; to trust for aid, not to a foreign Prince whose name was hateful to the British Nation and whose succours could be obtained only on terms of vassalage, but to the old Cavalier party, to the landed gentry, the clergy and the universities. By rallying round the throne the whole strength of the Royalists and High Churchmen, and by using without stint all the resources of corruption, he flattered himself that he could manage the Parliament. That he failed is to be attributed less to himself than to his master. Of the disgraceful dealings which were still kept up with the French Court, Danby deserved little or none of the blame, though he suffered the whole punishment.

Danby, with great parliamentary talents, had paid little attention to European politics, and wished for the help of some person on whom he could rely in this department. A plan was accordingly arranged for making Temple Secretary of State. Arlington was the only member of the Cabal who still held office in England. The temper of the House of Commons made it necessary to remove him, or rather, to require him to sell out; for at that time the great offices of State were bought and sold as commissions in the army now are. Temple was informed that he should have the Seals if he would pay Arlington six thousand pounds. The transaction had nothing in it discreditable, according to the notions of that age, and the investment would have been a good one; for we imagine that at that time the gains which a Secretary of State might make, without doing anything considered as improper, were very considerable. Temple's friends offered to lend him the money; but he was fully determined not to take a post of so much responsibility in times so agitated and under a prince on whom so little reliance could be placed, and accepted the embassy to the Hague, leaving Arlington to find another purchaser.

Before Temple left England, he had a long audience of the King, to whom he spoke with great severity of the measures adopted by the late Ministry. The King owned that things had turned out ill. "But," said he; "if I had been well served, I might have made a good business of it." Temple was alarmed at this language, and inferred from it that the system of the Cabal had not been abandoned, but only suspended. He therefore thought it his duty to go, as he expresses it, "to the bottom of the matter." He strongly represented to the King the impossibility of establishing either absolute government or the Catholic religion in England; and concluded by repeating an observation which he had heard at Brussels from M. Gourville, a very intelligent Frenchman, well known to Charles: "A king of England," said Gourville, "who is willing to be the man of his people, is the greatest king in the world; but if he wishes to be more, by Heaven he is nothing at all!" The King betrayed some symptons of impatience during this lecture; but at last he laid his hand kindly on Temple's shoulder and said, "You are right and so is Gourville, and I will be the man of my people."

With this assurance, Temple repaired to the Hague in July, 1674. Holland was now secure, and France was surrounded on every side by enemies.

Spain and the Empire were in arms for the purpose of compelling Louis to abandon all that he had acquired since the treaty of the Pyrenees. A congress for the purpose of putting an end to the war was opened at Nimeguen under the mediation of England in 1675; and to that congress Temple was deputed. The work of conciliation, however, went on very slowly. The belligerent powers were still sanguine, and the mediating power was unsteady and insincere.

In the meantime, the Opposition in England became more and more formidable, and seemed fully determined to force the King into a war with France. Charles was desirous of making some appointments which might strengthen the administration and conciliate the confidence of the public. No man was more esteemed by the nation than Temple; yet he had never been concerned in any opposition to any government. In July, 1677, he was sent for from Nimeguen. Charles received him with caresses, earnestly pressed him to accept the seals of Secretary of State, and promised to bear half the charge of buying out the present holder. Temple was charmed by the kindness and politeness of the King's manner and by the liveliness of his Majesty's conversation, but his prudence was not to be so laid asleep. He calmly and steadily excused himself. The King affected to treat his excuses as mere jests, and gaily said, "Go, get you gone to Sheen. We shall have no good of you till you have been there; and when you have rested yourself, come up again." Temple withdrew and stayed two days at his villa, but returned to town in the same mind, and the King was forced to consent at least to a delay.

But while Temple thus carefully shunned the responsibility of bearing a part in the general direction of affairs, he gave a signal proof of that never-failing sagacity which enabled him to find out ways of distinguishing himself without risk. He had a principal share in bringing about an event which was at the time hailed with general satisfaction, and which subsequently produced consequences of the highest importance. This was the marriage of the Prince of Orange and the Lady Mary.

In the following year, Temple returned to the Hague; and thence he was ordered, in the close of 1678, to repair to Nimeguen, for the purpose of signing the hollow and unsatisfactory treaty by which the distractions of Europe were for a short time suspended. He grumbled much at being required to sign bad articles which he had not framed, and still more at having to travel in very cold weather. After all, a difficulty of etiquette prevented him from signing, and he returned to the Hague. Scarcely had he arrived there when he received intelligence that the King, whose embarrassments were now far greater than ever, was fully resolved immediately to appoint him Secretary of State. He a third time declined that high post, and began to make preparations for a journey to Italy; thinking, doubtless, that he should spend his time much more pleasantly among pictures and ruins than in such a whirlpool of political and religious frenzy as was then raging in London.

But the King was in extreme necessity and was no longer to be so easily put off. Temple received positive orders to repair instantly to England. He obeyed, and found the country in a state even more fearful than that which he had pictured to himself.

Those are terrible conjunctures, when the discontents of a nation—not light and capricious discontents, but discontents which have been steadily increasing during a long series of years—have attained their full maturity. The discerning few predict the approach of these conjunctures, but predict in vain. To the many, the evil season comes as a total eclipse of the sun at noon comes to a people of savages. Society, which but a short time before was in a state of perfect repose, is on a sudden agitated with the most fearful convulsions and seems to be on the verge of dissolution ; and the rulers who, till the mischief was beyond the reach of all ordinary remedies, had never bestowed one thought on its existence, stand bewildered and panic-stricken, without hope or resource, in the midst of the confusion. One such conjuncture this generation has seen. God grant that we may never see another ! At such a conjuncture it was that Temple landed on English ground in the beginning of 1679.

The Parliament had obtained a glimpse of the King's dealings with France, and their anger had been unjustly directed against Danby, whose conduct as to that matter had been, on the whole, deserving rather of praise than of censure. The Popish plot, the murder of Godfrey, the infamous inventions of Oates, the discovery of Colman's letters had excited the nation to madness. All the disaffection which had been generated by eighteen years of misgovernment had come to the birth together. At this moment the King had been advised to dissolve that Parliament which had been elected just after his restoration, and which, though its composition had since that time been greatly altered, was still far more deeply imbued with the old cavalier spirit than any that had preceded, or that was likely to follow it. The general election had commenced, and was proceeding with a degree of excitement never before known. The tide ran furiously against the Court. It was clear that a majority of the new House of Commons would be—to use a word which came into fashion a few months later—decided Whigs. Charles had found it necessary to yield to the violence of the public feeling. The Duke of York was on the point of retiring to Holland. "I never," says Temple, who had seen the abolition of monarchy, the dissolution of the Long Parliament, the fall of the Protectorate, the declaration of Monk against the Rump, "I never saw greater disturbance in men's minds."

The King now with the utmost emergency besought Temple to take the seals. The pecuniary part of the arrangement no longer presented any difficulty, and Sir William was not quite so decided in his refusal as he had formerly been. He took three days to consider the posture of affairs and to examine his own feelings, and he came to the conclusion that "the scene was unfit for such an actor as he knew himself to be." Yet he felt that, by refusing help to the King at such a crisis, he might give much offence and incur much censure. He shaped his course with his usual dexterity. He affected to be very desirous of a seat in Parliament ; yet he contrived to be an unsuccessful candidate ; and, when all the writs were returned, he represented that it would be useless for him to take the seals till he could procure admittance to the House of Commons ; and in this manner he succeeded in avoiding the greatness which others desired to thrust upon him.

The Parliament met ; and the violence of its proceedings surpassed all expectation. The Long Parliament itself, with much greater provocation, had at its commencement been less violent. The Treasurer was instantly driven from office, impeached, sent to the Tower. Sharp and vehement votes were passed on the subject of the Popish Plot. The Commons were prepared to go much further, to wrest from the King his prerogative of mercy in cases of high political crimes and to alter the succession to the Crown. Charles was thoroughly perplexed and dismayed. Temple saw him almost daily, and thought him impressed with a deep sense of his errors and of the miserable state into which they have brought him. Their conferences became longer and more confidential ; and Temple began to flatter himself with the hope that he might be able to reconcile parties at home as he had reconciled hostile States abroad ; that he might be able to suggest a plan which should allay all heats, efface the memory of all past grievances, secure the nation from misgovernment and protect the Crown against the encroachments of Parliament.

Temple's plan was that the existing Privy Council, which consisted of fifty members, should be dissolved; that there should no longer be a small interior council, like that which is now designated as the Cabinet; that a new Privy Council of thirty members should be appointed; and that the King should pledge himself to govern by the constant advice of this body, to suffer all his affairs of every kind to be freely debated there, and not to reserve any part of the public business for a secret committee.

Fifteen of the members of this new council were to be great officers of State. The other fifteen were to be independent noblemen and gentlemen of the greatest weight in the country. In appointing them, particular regard was to be had to the amount of their property. The whole annual income of the counsellors was estimated at £300,000. The annual income of all the members of the House of Commons was not supposed to exceed £400,000. The appointment of wealthy counsellors Temple describes as "a chief regard, necessary to this Constitution."

This plan was the subject of frequent conversation between the King and Temple. After a month passed in discussions to which no third person appears to have been privy, Charles declared himself satisfied of the expediency of the proposed measure and resolved to carry it into effect.

It is much to be regretted that Temple has left us no account of these conferences. Historians have, therefore, been left to form their own conjectures as to the object of this very extraordinary plan, "this Constitution," as Temple himself calls it. And we cannot say that any explanation which has yet been given seems to us quite satisfactory. Indeed, almost all the writers whom we have consulted appear to consider the change as merely a change of administration, and so considering it, they generally applaud it. Mr. Courtenay, who has evidently examined this subject with more attention than has often been bestowed upon it, seems to think Temple's scheme very strange, unintelligible and absurd. It is with very great diffidence that we offer our own solution of what we have always thought one of the great riddles of English history. We are strongly inclined to suspect that the appointment of the new Privy Council was really a much more remarkable event than has generally been supposed, and that what Temple had in view was to effect, under colour of a change of administration, a permanent change in the Constitution.

The plan, considered merely as a plan for the formation of a Cabinet, is so obviously inconvenient, that we cannot easily believe this to have been Temple's chief object. The number of the new Council alone would be a most serious objection. The largest cabinets of modern times have not, we believe, consisted of more than fifteen members. Even this number has generally been thought too large. The Marquess Wellesley, whose judgment on a question of executive administration is entitled to as much respect as that of any statesman that England ever produced, expressed, on a very important occasion,* his conviction that even thirteen was an inconveniently large number. But in a Cabinet of thirty members what chance could there be of finding unity, secrecy, expedition, any of the qualities which such a body ought to possess? If, indeed, the members of such a Cabinet were closely bound together by interest, if they all had a deep stake in the permanence of the Administration, if the majority were dependent on a small number of leading men, the thirty might perhaps act as a smaller number would act, though more slowly, more awkwardly, and with more risk of improper disclosures. But the council which Temple proposed was so framed that if, instead of thirty members, it had contained only

---

* In the negotiations of 1812.

ten, it would still have been the most unwieldly and discordant Cabinet that ever sat. One half of the members were to be persons holding no office— persons who had no motive to compromise their opinions, or to take any share of the responsibility of an unpopular measure—persons, therefore, who might be expected, as often as there might be a crisis requiring the most cordial co-operation, to draw off from the rest and to throw every difficulty in the way of the public business. The circumstance that they were men of enormous private wealth only made the matter worse. The House of Commons is a checking body; and therefore it is desirable that it should, to a great extent, consist of men of independent fortune, who receive nothing and expect nothing from the Government. But with executive boards the case is quite different. Their business is not to check, but to act. The very same things, therefore, which are the virtues of Parliaments may be vices in Cabinets. We can hardly conceive a greater curse to the country than an Administration, the members of which should be as perfectly independent of each other, and as little under the necessity of making mutual concessions, as the representatives of London and Devonshire in the House of Commons are and ought to be. Now Temple's new Council was to contain fifteen members who were to hold no offices, and the average amount of whose private estates was ten thousand pounds a year—an income which, in proportion to the wants of a man of rank of that period, was at least equal to thirty thousand a year in our time. Was it to be expected that such men would gratuitously take on themselves the labour and responsibility of Ministers, and the unpopularity which the best Ministers must sometimes be prepared to brave? Could there be any doubt that an Opposition would soon be formed within the Cabinet itself, and that the consequence would be disunion, altercation, tardiness in operations, the divulging of secrets, everything most alien from the nature of an executive council?

Is it possible to imagine that considerations so grave and so obvious should have altogether escaped the notice of a man of Temple's sagacity and experience? One of two things appears to us to be certain—either that his project has been misunderstood, or that his talents for public affairs have been overrated.

We lean to the opinion that his project has been misunderstood. His new Council, as we have shown, would have been an exceedingly bad Cabinet. The inference which we are inclined to draw is this—that he meant his Council to serve some other purpose than that of a mere Cabinet. Barillon used four or five words which contain, we think, the key of the whole mystery. Mr. Courtenay calls them pithy words; but he does not, if we are right, apprehend their whole force. " Ce sont," said Barillon, " des états, non des conseils."

In order clearly to understand what we imagine to have been Temple's views, we must remember that the Government of England was at that moment, and had been during nearly eighty years, in a state of transition. A change, not the less real nor the less extensive because disguised under ancient names and forms, was in constant progress. The theory of the Constitution— the fundamental laws which fix the powers of the three branches of the legislature—underwent no material change between the time of Elizabeth and the time of William III. The most celebrated laws of the seventeenth century on those subjects—the Petition of Right—the Declaration of Right—are purely declaratory. They purport to be merely recitals of the old polity of England. They do not establish free government as a salutary improvement, but claim it as an undoubted and immemorial inheritance. Nevertheless, there can be no doubt that, during the period of which we speak, all the mutual relations of all the orders of the State did practically undergo an entire change. The letter of the law might be unaltered; but, at the beginning of the seventeenth century, the power of the Crown was, in fact, decidedly predominant in the State; and, at the end of that century, the power of Parliament, and especially of the Lower House, had become, in fact, decidedly predominant. At the beginning of the century, the sovereign perpetually violated, with little or no opposition, the clear privileges of Parliament. At the close of the century, the Parliament had virtually drawn to itself just as much as it chose of the prerogative of the Crown. The sovereign retained the shadow of that authority of which the Tudors had held the substance. He had a legislative veto which he never ventured to exercise—a power of appointing Ministers, whom an address of the Commons could at any moment force him to discard—a power of declaring war, which, without Parliamentary support, could not be carried on for a single day. The Houses of Parliament were now not merely legislative assemblies—not merely checking assemblies. They were great Councils of State, whose voice, when loudly and firmly raised, was decisive on all questions of foreign and domestic policy. There was no part of the whole system of Government with which they had not power to interfere by advice equivalent to command; and, if they abstained from intermeddling with some departments of the executive administration, they were withheld from doing so only by their own moderation and by the confidence which they reposed in the ministers of the Crown. There is perhaps no other instance in history of a change so complete in the real constitution of an empire unaccompanied by any corresponding change in the theoretical constitution. The disguised transformation of the Roman commonwealth into a despotic monarchy, under the long administration of Augustus, is perhaps the nearest parallel.

This great alteration did not take place without strong and constant resistance on the part of the Kings of the house of Stuart. Till 1642, that resistance was generally of an open, violent and lawless nature. If the Commons refused supplies, the sovereign levied a "benevolence." If the Commons impeached a favourite minister, the sovereign threw the chiefs of the Opposition into prison. Of these efforts to keep down the Parliament by despotic force, without the pretext of law, the last, the most celebrated and the most wicked was the attempt to seize the five members. That attempt was the signal for civil war, and was followed by eighteen years of blood and confusion.

The days of trouble passed by; the exiles returned; the throne was again set up in its high place; the peerage and the hierarchy recovered their ancient splendour. The fundamental laws, which had been recited in the Petition of Right, were again solemnly recognised. The theory of the English constitution was the same on the day when the hand of Charles the Second was kissed by the kneeling Houses at Whitehall as on the day when his father set up the royal standard at Nottingham. There was a short period of doting fondness, a *hysterica passio* of loyal repentance and love. But emotions of this sort are transitory; and the interests on which depends the progress of great societies are permanent. The transport of reconciliation was soon over; and the old struggle recommenced.

The old struggle recommenced—but not precisely after the old fashion. The sovereign was not indeed a man whom any common warning would have restrained from the grossest violations of law. But it was no common warning that he had received. All around him were the recent signs of the vengeance of an oppressed nation—the fields on which the noblest blood of the island had been poured forth—the castles shattered by the cannon of the Parliamentary armies—the hall where sat the stern tribunal to whose bar had been led, through lowering ranks of pikemen, the captive heir of a hundred kings—the stately pilasters, before which the great execution had been so fearlessly done in the face of heaven and earth. The restored Prince, admonished by the fate of his father, never ventured to attack his Parliaments with open and arbitrary violence. It was at one time by means of the Parliament itself, at another time by means of the courts of law, that he attempted to regain for the Crown its old predominance. He began with great advantages. The Parliament of 1661 was called while the nation was still full of joy and tenderness. The great majority of the House of Commons were zealous royalists. All the means of influence which the patronage of the Crown afforded were used without limit. Bribery was reduced to a system. The King, when he could spare money from his pleasures for nothing else, could spare it for purposes of corruption. While the defence of the coasts was neglected, while ships rotted, while arsenals lay empty, while turbulent crowds of unpaid seamen swarmed in the streets of the seaports, something could still be scraped together in the Treasury for the members of the House of Commons. The gold of France was largely employed for the same purpose. Yet it was found, as indeed might have been foreseen, that there is a natural limit to the effect which can be produced by means like these. There is one thing which the most corrupt senates are unwilling to sell; and that is the power which makes them worth buying. The same selfish motives which induce them to take a price for a particular vote, will induce them to oppose every measure of which the effect would be to lower the importance, and consequently the price, of their votes. About the income of their power, so to speak, they are quite ready to make bargains. But they are not easily persuaded to part with any fragment of the principal. It is curious to observe how, during the long continuance of this Parliament—the Pensionary Parliament, as it was nicknamed by contemporaries—though every circumstance seemed to be favourable to the Crown, the power of the Crown was constantly sinking and that of the Commons constantly rising. The meetings of the Houses were more frequent than in former reigns; their interference was more harassing to the Government than in former reigns; they had begun to make peace, to make war, to pull down, if they did not set up, Administrations. Already a new class of statesmen had appeared, unheard of before that time, but common ever since. Under the Tudors and the earlier Stuarts, it was generally by courtly arts, or by official skill and knowledge, that a politician raised himself to power. From the time of Charles II. down to our own days a different species of talent, Parliamentary talent, has been the most valuable of all the qualifications of an English statesman. It has stood in the place of all other acquirements. It has covered ignorance, weakness, rashness, the most fatal maladministration. A great negotiator is nothing when compared with a great debater; and a Minister who can make a successful speech need trouble himself little about an unsuccessful expedition. This is the talent which has made judges without law and diplomatists without French—which has sent to the Admiralty men who did not know the stern of a ship from her bowsprit and to the India Board men who did not know the difference between a rupee and a pagoda—which made a foreign secretary of Mr. Pitt, who, as George II. said, had never opened Vattel—and which was very near making a Chancellor of the Exchequer of Mr. Sheridan, who could not work a sum in long division. This was the sort of talent which raised Clifford from obscurity to the head of affairs. To this talent Danby—by birth a simple country gentleman—owed his white staff, his garter and his dukedom. The encroachment of the power of the Parliament on the power of the Crown resembled a fatality, or the operation of some great law of nature. The will of the individual on the throne, or of the individuals in the two Houses, seemed to go for nothing. The King might be eager to encroach; yet something constantly drove him back. The Parliament might be loyal, even servile; yet something constantly urged them forward.

These things were done in the green tree. What then was likely to be done in the dry? The Popish Plot and the general election came together, and found a people predisposed to the most violent excitation. The composition of the House of Commons was changed. The Legislature was filled with men who leaned to Republicanism in politics and to Presbyterianism in religion. They no sooner met than they commenced an attack on the Government, which, if successful, must have made them supreme in the State.

Where was this to end? To us, who have seen the solution, the question presents few difficulties. But to a statesman of the age of Charles II.—to a statesman who wished, without depriving the Parliament of its privileges, to maintain the monarch in his old supremacy—it must have appeared very perplexing.

Clarendon had, when Minister, struggled honestly, perhaps, but, as was his wont, obstinately, proudly and offensively against the growing power of the Commons. He was for allowing them their old authority and not one atom more. He would never have claimed for the Crown a right to levy taxes from the people without the consent of Parliament. But when the Parliament, in the first Dutch war, most properly insisted on knowing how it was that the money which they had voted had produced so little effect, and began to inquire through what hands it had passed and on what services it had been expended, Clarendon considered this as a monstrous innovation. He told the King, as he himself says, "that he could not be too indulgent in the defence of the privileges of Parliament, and that he hoped he would never violate any of them; but he desired him to be equally solicitous to prevent the excesses in Parliament, and not to suffer them to extend their jurisdiction to cases they have nothing to do with; and that to restrain them within their proper bounds and limits is as necessary as it is to preserve them from being invaded; and that this was such a new encroachment as had no bottom." This is a single instance. Others might easily be given.

The bigotry, the strong passions, the haughty and disdainful temper, which made Clarendon's great abilities a source of almost unmixed evil to himself and to the public, had no place in the character of Temple. To Temple, however, as well as to Clarendon, the rapid change which was taking place in the real working of the Constitution gave great disquiet; particularly as he had never sat in the English Parliament, and therefore regarded it with none of the predilection which men naturally feel for a body to which they belong, and for a theatre on which their own talents have been advantageously displayed.

To wrest by force from the House of Commons its newly acquired powers was impossible; nor was Temple a man to recommend such a stroke, even if it had been possible. But was it possible that the House of Commons might be induced to let those powers drop—that, as a great revolution had been effected without any change in the outward form of the Government, so a great counter-revolution might be effected in the same manner—that the Crown and the Parliament might be placed in nearly the same relative position in which they had stood in the reign of Elizabeth, and that this might be done without one sword drawn, without one execution, and with the general acquiescence of the nation?

The English people—it was probably thus that Temple argued—will not bear to be governed by the unchecked power of the sovereign, nor ought they to be so governed. At present there is no check but the Parliament. The limits which separate the power of checking those who govern from the power of governing are not easily to be defined. The Parliament, therefore, supported by the nation, is rapidly drawing to itself all the powers of Government. If it were possible to frame some other check on the power of the Crown, some check which might be less galling to the Sovereign than that by which he is now constantly tormented, and yet which might appear to the people to be a tolerable security against maladministration, Parliaments would probably meddle less, and they would be less supported by public opinion in their meddling. That the King's hands may not be rudely tied by others, he must consent to tie them lightly himself. That the executive administration may not be usurped by the checking body, something of the character of a checking body must be given to the body which conduct the executive administration. The Parliament is now arrogating to itself every day a larger share of the functions of the Privy Council. We must stop the evil by giving to the Privy Council something of the constitution of a Parliament. Let the nation see that all the King's measures are directed by a Cabinet composed of representatives of every order in the State, by a Cabinet which contains, not placemen alone, but independent and popular noblemen and gentlemen who have large estates and no salaries, and who are not likely to sacrifice the public welfare, in which they have a deep stake, and the credit which they have obtained with the country, to the pleasure of a Court from which they receive nothing. When the ordinary administration is in such hands as these, the people will be quite content to see the Parliament become, what it formerly was, an extraordinary check. They will be quite willing that the House of Commons should meet only once in three years for a short session, and should take as little part in matters of state as it did a hundred years ago.

Thus we believe that Temple reasoned : for on this hypothesis his scheme is intelligible, and on any other hypothesis appears to us, as it does to Mr. Courtenay, exceedingly absurd and unmeaning. This Council was strictly what Barillon called it, an assembly of States. There are the representatives of all the great sections of the community, of the Church, of the law, of the Peerage, of the Commons. The exclusion of one half of the counsellors from office under the Crown, an exclusion which is quite absurd when we consider the Council merely as an executive board, becomes at once perfectly reasonable when we consider the Council as a body intended to restrain the Crown as well as to exercise the powers of the crown, to perform some of the functions of a Parliament as well as the functions of a Cabinet. We see, too, why Temple dwelt so much on the private wealth of the members, why he instituted a comparison between their united incomes and the united incomes of the members of the House of Commons. Such a parallel would have been idle in the case of a mere Cabinet. It is extremely significant in the case of a body intended to supersede the House of Commons in some very important functions.

We can hardly help thinking that the notion of this Parliament on a small scale was suggested to Temple by what he had himself seen in the United Provinces. The original assembly of the States-General consisted, as he tells us, of above eight hundred persons. But this great body was represented by a smaller Council of about thirty, which bore the name and exercised the powers of the States-General. At last the real states altogether ceased to meet ; and their power, though still a part of the theory of the Constitution, became obsolete in practice. We do not, of course, imagine that Temple either expected or wished that Parliaments should be thus disused ; but he did expect, we think, that something like what had happened in Holland would happen in England, and that a large portion of the functions lately assumed by

Parliament would be quietly transferred to the miniature Parliament which he proposed to create.

Had this plan, with some modifications, been tried at an earlier period, in a more composed state of the public mind and by a better sovereign, we are by no means certain that it might not have effected the purpose for which it was designed. The restraint imposed on the King by the Council of Thirty, whom he had himself chosen, would have been feeble indeed when compared with the restraint imposed by Parliament. But it would have been more constant. It would have acted every year and all the year round; and before the Revolution the sessions of Parliament were short and the recesses long. The advice of the Council would probably have prevented any very monstrous and scandalous measures; and would consequently have prevented the discontents which follow such measures, and the salutary laws which are the fruit of such discontents. We believe for example, that the second Dutch war would never have been approved by such a Council as that which Temple proposed. We are quite certain that the shutting up of the Exchequer would never even have been mentioned in such a Council. The people, pleased to think that Lord Russell, Lord Cavendish and Mr. Powle, unplaced and unpensioned, were daily representing their grievances and defending their rights in the Royal presence, would not have pined quite so much for the meeting of Parliaments. The Parliament, when it met, would have found fewer and less glaring abuses to attack. There would have been less misgovernment and less reform. We should not have been cursed with the Cabal, or blessed with the Habeas Corpus Act. In the meantime, the Council, considered as an executive Council, would, unless some at least of its powers had been delegated to a smaller body, have been feeble, dilatory, divided, unfit for everything which requires secrecy and despatch, and peculiarly unfit for the administration of war.

The Revolution put an end, in a very different way, to the long contest between the King and the Parliament. From that time, the House of Commons has been predominant in the State. The Cabinet has really been from that time a committee nominated by the Crown out of the prevailing party in Parliament. Though the minority in the Commons are constantly proposing to condemn executive measures, or to call for papers which may enable the House to sit in judgment on such measures, these propositions are scarcely ever carried; and, if a proposition of this kind is carried against the Government, a change of Ministry almost necessarily follows. Growing and struggling power always gives more annoyance and is more unmanageable than established power. The House of Commons gave infinitely more trouble to the Ministers of Charles II. than to any Ministers of later times ; for in the time of Charles II., the House was checking Ministers in whom it did not confide. Now that its ascendancy is fully established, it either confides in Ministers or turns them out. This is undoubtedly a far better state of things than that which Temple wished to introduce. The modern Cabinet is a far better Executive Council than his. The worst House of Commons that has sate since the Revolution was a far more efficient check on misgovernment than his fifteen independent counsellors would have been. Yet, everything considered, it seems to us that his plan was the work of an observant, ingenious and fertile mind.

On this occasion, as on every occasion on which he came prominently forward, Temple had the rare good fortune to please the public as well as the Sovereign. The general exultation was great when it was known that the old Council, made up of the most odious tools of power, was dismissed ; that small interior committees, rendered odious by the recent memory of the Cabal, were to be disused; and that the King would adopt no measure till it had been discussed and approved by a body, of which one half consisted of independent gentlemen and noblemen, and in which such persons as Russell, Cavendish, and Temple himself, had seats. Town and country were in a ferment of joy, The bells were rung, bonfires were lighted; and the acclamations of England were re-echoed by the Dutch, who considered the influence obtained by Temple as a certain omen of good for Europe. It is, indeed, much to the honour of his sagacity that every one of his great measures should, in such times, have pleased every party which he had any interest in pleasing. This was the case with the Triple Alliance, with the Treaty which concluded the second Dutch war, with the marriage of the Prince of Orange, and finally, with the institution of this new Council.

The only people who grumbled were those popular leaders of the House of Commons who were not among the Thirty; and, if our view of the measure be correct, they were precisely the people who had good reason to grumble. They were precisely the people whose activity and whose influence the new Council was intended to destroy.

But there was very soon an end of the bright hopes and loud applauses with which the publication of this scheme had been hailed. The perfidious levity of the King and the ambition of the chiefs of parties produced the instant, entire and irremediable failure of a plan which nothing but firmness, public spirit and self-denial on the part of all concerned in it could conduct to a happy issue. Even before the project was divulged, its author had already found reason to apprehend that it would fail. Considerable difficulty was experienced in framing the list of counsellors. There were two men in particular about whom the King and Temple could not agree—two men deeply tainted with the vices common to the English statesmen of that age, but unrivalled in talents, address and influence. These were the Earl of Shaftesbury and George Savile, Viscount Halifax.

It was a favourite exercise among the Greek sophists to write panegyrics on characters proverbial for depravity. One professor of rhetoric sent to Socrates a panegyric on Busiris; and Socrates himself wrote another which has come down to us. It is, we presume, from an ambition of the same kind that some writers have lately shown a disposition to eulogise Shaftesbury. But the attempt is vain. The charges against him rest on evidence not to be invalidated by any arguments which human wit can devise, or by any information which may be found in old trunks and escrutoires.

It is certain that, just before the Restoration, he declared to the Regicides that he would be damned, body and soul, rather than suffer a hair of their heads to be hurt, and that, just after the Restoration, he was one of the judges who sentenced them to death. It is certain that he was a principal member of the most profligate Administration ever known, and that he was afterwards a principal member of the most profligate Opposition ever known. It is certain that, in power, he did not scruple to violate the great fundamental principle of the Constitution in order to exalt the Catholics, and that, out of power, he did not scruple to violate every principle of justice in order to destroy them. There were in that age honest men, William Penn is an instance, who valued toleration so highly that they would willingly have seen it established, even by an illegal exertion of the prerogative. There were many honest men who dreaded arbitrary power so much, that, on account of the alliance between Popery and arbitrary power, they were disposed to grant no toleration to Papists. On both those classes we look with indulgence, though we think both in the wrong. But Shaftesbury belonged to neither class. He united all that was worst in both. From the friends of toleration he borrowed their contempt for the Constitution and from the friends of liberty their contempt for the rights of conscience. We never can admit that his conduct as a member of the Cabal was redeemed by his conduct as a leader of Opposition. On the contrary, his life was such that every part of it, as if by a skilful contrivance, reflects infamy on every other. We should never have known how abandoned a prostitute he was in place, if we had not known how desperate an incendiary he was out of it. To judge of him fairly, we must bear in mind that the Shaftesbury who, in office, was the chief author of the Declaration of Indulgence, was the same Shaftesbury who, out of office, excited and kept up the savage hatred of the rabble of London against the very class to whom that Declaration of Indulgence was intended to give illegal relief.

It is amusing to see the excuses that are made for him. We will give two specimens. It is acknowledged that he was one of the Ministry which made the alliance with France against Holland, and that this alliance was most pernicious. What, then, is the defence? Even this—that he betrayed his master's counsels to the Electors of Saxony and Brandenburg and tried to rouse all the Protestant powers of Germany to defend the States. Again, it is acknowledged that he was deeply concerned in the Declaration of Indulgence, and that his conduct on this occasion was not only unconstitutional, but quite inconsistent with the course which he afterwards took respecting the professors of the Catholic faith. What, then, is the defence? Even this—that he meant only to allure concealed Papists to avow themselves and thus to become open marks for the vengeance of the public. As often as he is charged with one treason, his advocates vindicate him by confessing two. They had better leave him where they find him. For him there is no escape upwards. Every outlet by which he can creep out of his present position, is one which lets him down into a still lower and fouler depth of infamy. To whitewash an Ethiopian is a proverbially hopeless attempt; but to whitewash an Ethiopian by giving him a new coat of blacking is an enterprise more extraordinary still. That in the course of Shaftesbury's unscrupulous and revengeful opposition to the Court he rendered one or two most useful services to his country, we admit. And he is, we think, fairly entitled, if that be any glory, to have his name eternally associated with the Habeas Corpus Act in the same way in which the name of Henry VIII. is associated with the reformation of the Church and that of Jack Wilkes with the freedom of the press.

While Shaftesbury was still living, his character was elaborately drawn by two of the greatest writers of the age—by Butler, with characteric brilliancy of wit—by Dryden, with even more than characteristic energy and loftiness—by both with all the inspiration of hatred. The sparkling illustrations of Butler have been thrown into the shade by the brighter glory of that gorgeous satiric Muse, who comes sweeping by in sceptred pall, borrowed from her most august sisters. But the descriptions well deserve to be compared. The reader will at once perceive a considerable difference between Butler's

"politician,
With more heads than a beast in vision,"

and the Ahithophel of Dryden. Butler dwells on Shaftesbury's unprincipled versatility; on his wonderful and almost instinctive skill in discerning the approach of a change of fortune; and on the dexterity with which he extricated himself from the snares in which he left his associates to perish.

"Our state-artificer foresaw
Which way the world began to draw.
For as old sinners have all points
O' th' compass in their bones and joints,

> Can by their pangs and aches find
> All turns and changes of the wind,
> And better than by Napier's bones
> Feel in their own the age of moons
> So guilty sinners in a state
> Can by their crimes prognosticate,
> And in their consciences feel pain
> Some days before a shower of rain.
> He, therefore, wisely cast about
> All ways he could to insure his throat."

In Dryden's great portrait, on the contrary, violent passion, implacable revenge, boldness amounting to temerity, are the most striking features. Ahithophel is one of the "great wits to madness near allied." And again—

> "A daring pilot in extremity,
> Pleased with the danger when the waves went high,
> He sought the storms; but, for a calm unfit,
> Would steer too nigh the sands to boast his wit."*

The dates of the two poems will, we think, explain this discrepancy. The third part of "Hudibras" appeared in 1678, when the character of Shaftesbury had as yet but imperfectly developed itself. He had, indeed, been a traitor to every party in the State, but his treasons had hitherto prospered. Whether it were accident or sagacity, he had timed his desertions in such a manner that fortune seemed to go to and fro with him from side to side. The extent of his perfidy was known; but it was not till the Popish Plot furnished him with a machinery which seemed sufficiently powerful for all his purposes, that the audacity of his spirit and the fierceness of his malevolent passions became fully manifest. His subsequent conduct showed undoubtedly great ability, but not ability of the sort for which he had formerly been so eminent. He was now headstrong, sanguine, full of impetuous confidence in his own wisdom and his own good luck. He, whose fame as a political tactician had hitherto rested chiefly on his skilful retreats, now set himself to break down all the bridges behind him. His plans were castles in the air: his talk was rodomontade. He took no thought for the morrow: he treated the Court as if the King were already a prisoner in his hands: he built on the favour of the multitude, as if that favour were not proverbially inconstant. The signs of the coming reaction were discerned by men of far less sagacity than his, and scared from his side men more consistent than he had ever pretended to be. But on him they were lost. The counsel of Ahithophel—that counsel which was as if a man had inquired of the oracle of God—was turned into foolishness. He who had become a by-word, for the certainty with which he foresaw and the suppleness with which he evaded danger, now, when beset on

---

* It has never, we believe, been remarked, that two of the most striking lines in the description of Ahithophel are borrowed from a most obscure quarter. In Knolles's History of the Turks, printed more than sixty years before the appearance of Absalom and Ahithophel, are the following verses, under a portrait of the Sultan Mustapha the First.—

> "Greatnesse on goodnesse loves to slide, not stand,
> And leaves for Fortune's ice Vertue's firme land."

Dryden's words are—

> "But wild Ambition loves to slide, not stand,
> And Fortune's ice prefers to Virtue's land."

The circumstance is the more remarkable, because Dryden has really no couplet more intensely Drydenian, both in thought and expression, than this, of which the whole thought, and almost the whole expression, are stolen.

As we are on this subject, we cannot refrain from observing that Mr. Courtenay has done Dryden injustice, by inadvertently attributing to him some feeble lines which are in Tate's part of Absalom and Ahithophel.

every side with snares and death, seemed to be smitten with a blindness as strange as his former clear-sightedness, and, turning neither to the right nor to the left, strode straight on with desperate hardihood to his doom. There fore, after having early acquired and long preserved the reputation of infallible wisdom and invariable success, he lived to see a mighty ruin wrought by his own ungovernable passions—to see the great party which he had led vanquished, and scattered, and trampled down—to see all his own devilish enginery, of lying witnesses, partial sheriffs, packed juries, unjust judges, bloodthirsty mobs, ready to be employed against himself and his most devoted followers—to fly from that proud city whose favour had almost raised him to be Mayor of the Palace—to hide himself in squalid retreats—to cover his grey head with ignominious disguises—and he died in hopeless exile, sheltered by a State, which he had cruelly injured and insulted, from the vengeance of a master whose favour he had purchased by one series of crimes and forfeited by another.

Halifax had, in common with Shaftesbury, and with almost all the politicians of that age, a very loose morality where the public was concerned; but in his case the prevailing infection was modified by a very peculiar constitution both of heart and head—by a temper singularly free from gall, and by a refining and sceptical understanding. He changed his course as often as Shaftesbury; but he did not change it to the same extent or in the same direction. Shaftesbury was the very reverse of a trimmer. His disposition led him generally to do his utmost to exalt the side which was up and to depress the side which was down. His transitions were from extreme to extreme. While he stayed with a party he went all lengths for it—when he quitted it he went all lengths against it. Halifax was emphatically a trimmer—a trimmer both by intellect and by constitution. The name was fixed on him by his contemporaries; and he was so far from being ashamed of it that he assumed it as a badge of honour. He passed from faction to faction. But instead of adopting and inflaming the passions of those whom he joined, he tried to diffuse among them something of the spirit of those whom he had just left. While he acted with the Opposition, he was suspected of being a spy of the Court; and when he had joined the Court, all the Tories were dismayed by his Republican doctrines.

He wanted neither arguments nor eloquence to exhibit what was commonly regarded as his wavering policy in the fairest light. He trimmed, he said, as the temperate zone trims between intolerable heat and intolerable cold, as a good government trims between despotism and anarchy, as a pure church trims between the errors of the Papist and those of the Anabaptist. Nor was this defence by any means without weight; for, though there is abundant proof that his integrity was not of strength to withstand the temptations by which his cupidity and vanity were sometimes assailed, yet his dislike of extremes, and a forgiving and compassionate temper which seems to have been natural to him, preserved him from all participation in the worst crimes of his time. If both parties accused him of deserting them, both were compelled to admit that they had great obligations to his humanity, and that, though an uncertain friend, he was a placable enemy. He voted in favour of Lord Stafford, the victim of the Whigs; he did his utmost to save Lord Russell, the victim of the Tories; and, on the whole, we are inclined to think that his public life, though far indeed from faultless, has as few great stains as that of any politician who took an active part in affairs during the troubled and disastrous period of ten years which elapsed between the fall of Lord Danby and the Revolution.

His mind was much less turned to particular observations and much more to general speculations than that of Shaftesbury. Shaftesbury knew the King, the Council, the Parliament, the city better than Halifax; but Halifax would have written a far better treatise on political science than Shaftesbury. Shaftesbury shone more in consultation and Halifax in controversy: Shaftesbury was more fertile in expedients and Halifax in arguments. Nothing that remains from the pen of Shaftesbury will bear a comparison with the political tracts of Halifax. Indeed, very little of the prose of that age is so well worth reading as the "Character of a Trimmer" and the "Anatomy of an Equivalent." What particularly strikes us in those works, is the writer's passion for generalisation. He was treating of the most exciting subjects in the most agitated times—he was himself placed in the very thick of the civil conflict—yet there is no acrimony, nothing inflammatory, nothing personal. He preserves an air of cold superiority—a certain philosophical serenity—which is perfectly marvellous; he treats every question as an abstract question—begins with the wildest propositions—argues those propositions on general grounds—and often, when he has brought out his theorem, leaves the reader to make the application, without adding an allusion to particular men or to passing events. This speculative turn of mind rendered him a bad adviser in cases which required celerity. He brought forward, with wonderful readiness and copiousness, arguments, replies to those arguments, rejoinders to those replies, general maxims of policy, and analogous cases from history. But Shaftesbury was the man for a prompt decision. Of the parliamentary eloquence of these celebrated rivals, we can judge only by report; and, so judging, we should be inclined to think that, though Shaftesbury was a distinguished speaker, the superiority belonged to Halifax. Indeed the readiness of Halifax in debate, the extent of his knowledge, the ingenuity of his reasoning, the liveliness of his expression, and the silver clearness and sweetness of his voice seem to have made the strongest impression on his contemporaries. By Dryden he is described as

"of piercing wit and pregnant thought,
Endued by nature and by learning taught
To move assemblies."

His oratory is utterly and irretrievably lost to us, like that of Somers, of Bolingbroke, of Charles Townshend—of many others who were accustomed to rise amidst the breathless expectation of senates and to sit down amidst reiterated bursts of applause. But old men, who lived to admire the eloquence of Pulteney in its meridian and that of Pitt in its splendid dawn, still murmured that they had heard nothing like the great speeches of Lord Halifax on the Exclusion Bill. The power of Shaftesbury over large masses was unrivalled. Halifax was disqualified by his whole character, moral and intellectual, for the part of a demagogue. It was in small circles, and, above all, in the House of Lords, that his ascendency was felt.

Shaftesbury seems to have troubled himself very little about theories of government. Halifax was, in speculation, a strong republican, and did not conceal it. He often made hereditary monarchy and aristocracy the subjects of his keen pleasantry, while he was fighting the battles of the Court, and obtaining for himself step after step in the peerage. In this way, he attempted to gratify at once his intellectual vanity and his more vulgar ambition. He shaped his life according to the opinion of the multitude, and indemnified himself by talking according to his own. His colloquial powers were great; his perception of the ridiculous exquisitely fine; and he seems to have had the rare art of preserving the reputation of good breeding and good nature while habitually indulging a strong propensity to mockery.

Temple wished to put Halifax into the new council and to leave out

Shaftesbury. The King objected strongly to Halifax, to whom he had taken a great dislike, which is not accounted for and which did not last long. Temple replied that Halifax was a man eminent both by his station and by his abilities, and would, if excluded, do everything against the new arrangement that could be done by eloquence, sarcasm and intrigue. All who were consulted were of the same mind; and the King yielded, but not till Temple had almost gone on his knees. This point was no sooner settled than his Majesty declared that he would have Shaftesbury too. Temple again had recourse to entreaties and expostulations. Charles told him that the enmity of Shaftesbury would be at least as formidable as that of Halifax; and this was true; but Temple might have replied that by giving power to Halifax they gained a friend and that by giving power to Shaftesbury they only strengthened an enemy. It was vain to argue and protest. The King only laughed and jested at Temple's anger; and Shaftesbury was not only sworn of the Council, but appointed Lord President.

Temple was so bitterly mortified by this step that he had at one time resolved to have nothing to do with the new Administration, and seriously thought of disqualifying himself from sitting in council by omitting to take the Sacrament. But the urgency of Lady Temple and Lady Giffard induced him to abandon that intention.

The Council was organised on the twenty-first of April, 1679; and, on the very next day, one of the fundamental principles on which it had been constructed was violated. A secret committee, or, in the modern phrase, a cabinet, of nine members was formed. But as this committee included Shaftesbury and Monmouth, it contained within itself the elements of as much faction as would have sufficed to impede all business. Accordingly there soon arose a small interior cabinet, consisting of Essex, Sunderland, Halifax and Temple. For a time perfect harmony and confidence subsisted between the four. But the meetings of the thirty were stormy. Sharp retorts passed between Shaftesbury and Halifax, who led the opposite parties. In the Council, Halifax generally had the advantage. But it soon became apparent that Shaftesbury still had at his back the majority of the House of Commons. The discontents, which the change of Ministry had for a moment quieted, broke forth again with redoubled violence; and the only effect which the late measures appeared to have produced was that the Lord President, with all the dignity and authority belonging to his high place, stood at the head of the Opposition. The impeachment of Lord Danby was eagerly prosecuted. The Commons were determined to exclude the Duke of York from the throne. All offers of compromise were rejected. It must not be forgotten, however, that, in the midst of the confusion, one inestimable law, the only benefit which England has derived from the troubles of that period, but a benefit which may well be set off against a great mass of evil, the Habeas Corpus Act, was pushed through the Houses and received the royal assent.

The King, finding the parliament as troublesome as ever, determined to prorogue it; and he did so without even mentioning his intention to the Council by whose advice he had pledged himself, only a month before, to conduct the Government. The counsellors were generally dissatisfied; and Shaftesbury swore, with great vehemence, that if he could find out who the secret advisers were, he would have their heads.

The Parliament rose; London was deserted; and Temple retired to his villa, whence, on council days, he went to Hampton Court. The post of Secretary was again and again pressed on him by his master and by his three colleagues of the inner Cabinet. Halifax in particular, threatened laughingly to burn down the house at Sheen. But Temple was immovable. His short experience of English politics had disgusted him; and he felt himself so much oppressed by the responsibility under which he at present lay that he had no inclination to add to the load.

When the term fixed for the prorogation had nearly expired, it became necessary to consider what course should be taken. The King and his four confidential advisers thought that a new Parliament might possibly be more manageable, and could not possibly be more refractory, than that which they now had, and they therefore determined on a dissolution. But, when the question was proposed at council, the majority, jealous, it should seem, of the small directing knot, and unwilling to bear the unpopularity of the measures of Government while excluded from all power, joined Shaftesbury; and the members of the Cabinet were left alone in the minority. The King, however, had made up his mind, and ordered the Parliament to be instantly dissolved. Temple's council was now nothing more than an ordinary privy council, if indeed it were not something less; and though Temple threw the blame of this on the King, on Lord Shaftesbury, on everybody but himself, it is evident that the failure of his plan is to be traced to its own inherent defects. His council was too large to transact business which required expedition, secrecy and cordial co-operation. A Cabinet was therefore formed within the Council. The Cabinet and the majority of the Council differed: and, as was to be expected, the Cabinet carried their point. Four votes outweighed six-and-twenty. This being the case, the meetings of the thirty were not only useless, but positively noxious.

At the ensuing election, Temple was chosen for the university of Cambridge. The only objection that was made to him by the members of that learned body was that, in his little work on Holland, he had expressed great approbation of the tolerant policy of the States; and this blemish, however serious, was overlooked in consideration of his high reputation and of the strong recommendations with which he was furnished by the Court.

During the summer he remained at Sheen, and amused himself with rearing melons; leaving to the three other members of the inner Cabinet the whole direction of public affairs. Som unexplained cause began, about this time, to alienate them from him. They do not appear to have been made angry by any part of his conduct, or to have disliked him personally. But they had, we suspect, taken the measure of his mind, and satisfied themselves that he was not a man for that troubled time, and that he would be a mere incumbrance to them. Living themselves for ambition, they despised his love of ease. Accustomed to deep stakes in the game of political hazard, they despised his piddling play. They looked on his cautious measures with the sort of scorn with which the gamblers at the ordinary, in Sir Walter Scott's novel, regarded Nigel's practice of never touching a card but when he was certain to win. He soon found that he was left out of their secrets. The King had about this time a dangerous illness. The Duke of York, on receiving the news, returned from Holland; the sudden appearance of the detested Popish successor excited anxiety throughout the country. Temple was greatly amazed and disturbed. He hastened up to London and visited Essex, who professed to be astonished and mortified, but could not disguise a sneering smile. Temple then saw Halifax, who talked to him much about the pleasures of the country, the anxieties of office, and the vanity of all human things, but carefully avoided politics, and when the Duke's return was mentioned, only sighed, shook his head, shrugged his shoulders, and lifted up his eyes and hands. In a short time Temple found that his two friends had been quizzing him, and that they themselves had sent for the Duke in order that his Royal Highness might, if the King should die, be on the spot to frustrate the designs of Monmouth.

He was soon convinced, by a still stronger proof, that, though he had not exactly offended his master or his colleagues in the Cabinet, he had ceased to enjoy their confidence. The result of the general election had been decidedly unfavourable to the Government; and Shaftesbury impatiently expected the day when the Houses were to meet. The King, guided by the advice of the inner Cabinet, determined on a step of the highest importance. He told the Council that he had resolved to prorogue the new Parliament for a year, and requested them not to object; for he had, he said, considered the subject fully, and had made up his mind. All who were not in the secret were thunderstruck—Temple as much as any. Several members rose, and entreated to be heard against the prorogation. But the King silenced them, and declared that his resolution was unalterable. Temple, greatly hurt at the manner in which both himself and the Council had been treated, spoke with great spirit. He would not, he said, disobey the King by objecting to a measure on which his Majesty was determined to hear no argument, but he would most earnestly entreat his Majesty, if the present Council was incompetent to give advice, to dissolve it and select another, for it was absurd to have counsellors who did not counsel, and who were summoned only to be silent witnesses of the acts of others. The King listened courteously. But the members of the Cabinet resented this reproof highly; and from that day Temple was almost as much estranged from them as from Shaftesbury.

He wished to retire altogether from business. But just at this time Lord Russell, Lord Cavendish, and some other counsellors of the popular party, waited on the King in a body, declared their strong disapprobation of his measures, and requested to be excused from attending any more at council. Temple feared that if, at this moment, he also were to withdraw, he might be supposed to act in concert with those decided opponents of the Court, and to have determined on taking a course hostile to the Government. He, therefore, continued to go occasionally to the board; but he had no longer any real share in the direction of public affairs.

At length the long term of the prorogation expired. In October, 1680, the Houses met; and the great question of the Exclusion was revived. Few parliamentary contests in our history appear to have called forth a greater display of talent—none certainly ever called forth more violent passions. The whole nation was convulsed by party spirit. The gentlemen of every county, the traders of every town, the boys of every public school were divided into exclusionists and abhorrers. The book-stalls were covered with tracts on the sacredness of hereditary right, on the omnipotence of Parliament, on the dangers of a disputed succession, on the dangers of a Popish reign. It was in the midst of this ferment that Temple took his seat, for the first time, in the House of Commons.

The occasion was a very great one. His talents, his long experience of affairs, his unspotted public character, the high posts which he had.filled seemed to mark him out as a man on whom much would depend. He acted like himself. He saw that if he supported the Exclusion, he made the King and the heir presumptive his enemies, and that, if he opposed it, he made himself an object of hatred to the unscrupulous and turbulent Shaftesbury. He neither supported nor opposed it. He quietly absented himself from the House. Nay, he took care, he tells us, never to discuss the question in any society whatever. Lawrence Hyde, afterwards Earl of Rochester, asked him why he did not attend in his place. Temple replied that he acted according to Solomon's advice, neither to oppose the mighty, nor to go about to stop the current of a river. The advice, whatever its value may be, is not to be found either in the canonical or apocryphal writings ascribed to Solomon.

But Temple was much in the habit of talking about books which he had never read; and one of those books, we are afraid, was his Bible. Hyde answered: "You are a wise and quiet man." And this might be true. But surely such wise and quiet men have no call to be members of Parliament in critical times.

A single session was quite enough for Temple. When the Parliament was dissolved, and another summoned at Oxford, he obtained an audience of the King, and begged to know whether his Majesty wished him to continue in Parliament. Charles, who had a singularly quick eye for the weaknesses of all who came near him, had no doubt seen through and through Temple, and rated the Parliamentary support of so cool and guarded a friend at its proper value. He answered good-naturedly, but we suspect a little contemptuously, "I doubt, as things stand, your coming into the House will not do much good. I think you may as well let it alone." Sir William accordingly informed his constituents that he should not again apply for their suffrages; and set off for Sheen, resolving never again to meddle with public affairs. He soon found that the King was displeased with him. Charles, indeed, in his usual easy way, protested that he was not angry—not at all. But in a few days he struck Temple's name out of the list of Privy Counsellors. Why this was done, Temple declares himself unable to comprehend. But surely it hardly required his long and extensive converse with the world to teach him that there are conjunctures when men think that all who are not with them are against them—that there are conjunctures when a lukewarm friend, who will not put himself the least out of his way, who will make no exertion, who will run no risk, is more distasteful than an enemy. Charles had hoped that the fair character of Temple would add credit to an unpopular and suspected Government. But his Majesty soon found that this fair character resembled pieces of furniture which we have seen in the drawing-rooms of very precise old ladies, and which are a great deal too white to be used. This exceeding niceness was altogether out of season. Neither party wanted a man who was afraid of taking a part, of incurring abuse, of making enemies. There were probably many good and moderate men who would have hailed the appearance of a respectable mediator. But Temple was not a mediator. He was merely a neutral.

At last, however, he had escaped from public life, and found himself at liberty to follow his favourite pursuits. His fortune was easy. He had about fifteen hundred a year, besides the Mastership of the Rolls in Ireland, an office in which he had succeeded his father, and which was then a mere sinecure for life, requiring no residence. His reputation, both as a negotiator and a writer, stood high. He resolved to be safe, to enjoy himself, and to let the world take its course; and he kept his resolution.

Darker times followed. The Oxford Parliament was dissolved. The Tories were triumphant. A terrible vengeance was inflicted on the chiefs of the Opposition. Temple learned in his retreat the disastrous fate of several of his old colleagues in council. Shaftesbury fled to Holland. Russell died on the scaffold. Essex added a yet sadder and more fearful story to the bloody chronicles of the Tower. Monmouth clung in agonies of supplication round the knees of the stern uncle whom he had wronged, and tasted a bitterness worse than that of death—the bitterness of knowing that he had humbled himself in vain. A tyrant trampled on the liberties and religion of the realm. The national spirit swelled high under the oppression. Disaffection spread even to the strongholds of loyalty—to the cloisters of Westminster, to the schools of Oxford, to the guard-room of the household troops, to the very hearth and bed-chamber of the Sovereign. But the troubles which agitated the whole society did not reach the quiet orangery in which Temple loitered away several years without once seeing the smoke of London. He now and then appeared in the circle at Richmond or Windsor. But the only expressions which he is recorded to have used during these perilous times were, that he would be a good subject, but that he had done with politics.

The Revolution came. Temple remained strictly neutral during the short struggle; and then transferred to the new settlement the same languid sort of loyalty which he had felt for his former masters. He paid court to William at Windsor, and William dined with him at Sheen. But, in spite of the most pressing solicitations, he refused to become Secretary of State. The refusal evidently proceeded only from his dislike of trouble and danger; and not, as some of his admirers would have us believe, from any scruple of conscience or honour. For he consented that his son should take the office of Secretary at War under the new Sovereign. This unfortunate young man destroyed himself within a week after his appointment, from vexation at finding that his advice had led the King into some improper steps with regard to Ireland. He seems to have inherited his father's extreme sensibility to failure without that singular prudence which kept his father out of all situations in which any serious failure was to be apprehended. The blow fell heavily on the family. They retired in deep dejection to Moor Park, which they now preferred to Sheen, on account of the greater distance from London. In that spot,* then very secluded, Temple passed the remainder of his life. The air agreed with him. The soil was fruitful and well suited to an experimental farmer and gardener. The grounds were laid out with the angular regularity which Sir William had admired in the flower-beds of Haarlem and the Hague. A beautiful rivulet, flowing from the hills of Surrey, bounded the domain. But a straight canal which, bordered by a terrace, intersected the garden, was probably more admired by the lovers of the picturesque in that age. The house was small, but neat and well-furnished; the neighbourhood very thinly peopled. Temple had no visitors, except a few friends who were willing to travel twenty or thirty miles in order to see him, and now and then a foreigner whom curiosity brought to have a look at the author of the Triple Alliance.

Here, in May, 1694, died Lady Temple. From the time of her marriage we know little of her, except that her letters were always greatly admired, and that she had the honour to correspond constantly with Queen Mary. Lady Giffard, who, as far as appears, had always been on the best terms with her sister-in-law, still continued to live with Sir William.

But there were other inmates of Moor Park to whom a far higher interest belongs. An eccentric, uncouth, disagreeable young Irishman, who had narrowly escaped plucking at Dublin, attended Sir William as an amanuensis, for twenty pounds a-year and his board—dined at the second table, wrote bad verses in praise of his employer, and made love to a very pretty, dark-eyed young girl who waited on Lady Giffard. Little did Temple imagine that the coarse exterior of his dependent concealed a genius equally suited to politics and to letters; a genius destined to shake great kingdoms, to stir the laughter and the rage of millions, and to leave to posterity memorials which can perish only with the English language. Little did he think that the flirtation in his servants' hall, which he perhaps scarcely deigned to make the subject of a jest, was the beginning of a long unprosperous love which was to be as widely famed as the passion of Petrarch or of Abelard. Sir William's secretary was Jonathan Swift. Lady Giffard's waiting-maid was poor Stella.

---

* Mr. Courtenay (vol. ii., p. 160), confounds Moor Park in Surrey, where Temple resided, with the Moor Park in Hertfordshire, which he praises in the Essay on Gardening.

Swift retained no pleasing recollection of Moor Park. And we may easily suppose a situation like his to have been intolerably painful to a mind haughty, irascible, and conscious of pre-eminent ability. Long after, when he stood in the Court of Requests with a circle of gartered peers round him, or punned and rhymed with Cabinet Ministers over Secretary St. John's "Monte-Pulciano," he remembered, with deep and sore feeling, how miserable he used to be for days together when he suspected that Sir William had taken something ill. He could hardly believe that he, the same Swift who chid the Lord Treasurer, rallied the Captain General and confronted the pride of the Duke of Buckingham with pride still more inflexible, could be the same being who had passed nights of sleepless anxiety in musing over a cross look or a testy word of a patron. "Faith," he wrote to Stella, with bitter levity, "Sir William spoiled a fine gentlemen." Yet, in justice to Temple, we must say that there is no reason to think that Swift was more unhappy at Moor Park than he would have been in a similar situation under any roof in England. We think also that the obligations which the mind of Swift owed to that of Temple were not inconsiderable. Every judicious reader must be struck by the peculiarities which distinguish Swift's political tracts from all similar works produced by mere men of letters. Let any person compare, for example, the "Conduct of the Allies," or the "Letter to the October Club," with Johnson's "False Alarm," or "Taxation no Tyranny," and he will be at once struck by the difference of which we speak. He may possibly think Johnson a greater man than Swift. He may possibly prefer Johnson's style to Swift's. But he will at once acknowledge that Johnson writes like a man who has never been out of his study. Swift writes like a man who has passed his whole life in the midst of public business, and to whom the most important affairs of state are as familiar as his weekly bills.

> "Turn him to any cause of policy,
> The Gordian knot of it he will unloose,
> Familiar as his garter."

The difference, in short, between a political pamphlet by Johnson and a political pamphlet by Swift, is as great as the difference between an account of a battle by Doctor Southey and the account of the same battle by Colonel Napier. It is impossible to doubt that the superiority of Swift is to be, in a great measure, attributed to his long and close connection with Temple.

Indeed, remote as the alleys and flower-pots of Moor Park were from the haunts of the busy and the ambitious, Swift had ample opportunities of becoming acquainted with the hidden causes of many great events. William was in the habit of consulting Temple, and occasionally visited him. Of what passed between them very little is known. It is certain, however, that when the Triennial Bill had been carried through the two Houses, his Majesty, who was exceedingly unwilling to pass it, sent the Earl of Portland to learn Temple's opinion. Whether Temple thought the bill in itself a good one does not appear; but he clearly saw how imprudent it must be in a prince, situated as William was, to engage in an altercation with his Parliament; and directed Swift to draw up a paper on the subject, which, however, did not convince the King.

The chief amusement of Temple's declining years was literature. After his final retreat from business, he wrote his very agreeable "Memoirs," corrected and transcribed many of his letters, and published several miscellaneous treatises, the best of which, we think, is that on "Gardening." The style of his essays is, on the whole, excellent—almost always pleasing, and now and then lately and splendid. The matter is generally of much less value; as our readers will readily believe when we inform them that Mr. Courtenay—a biographer—that is to say, a literary vassal bound by the immemorial law of his tenure to render, homage, aids, reliefs, and all other customary services to his lord—avows that he cannot give an opinion about the essay on "Heroic Virtue," because he cannot read it without skipping—a circumstance which strikes us as peculiarly strange, when we consider how long Mr. Courtenay was at the India Board, and how many thousand paragraphs of the copious official eloquence of the East he must have perused.

One of Sir William's pieces, however, deserve notice : not, indeed, on account of its intrinsic merit, but on account of the light which it throws on some curious weaknesses of his character, and on account of the extraordinary effects which it produced in the republic of letters. A most idle and contemptible controversy had arisen in France touching the comparative merit of the ancient and modern writers. It was certainly not to be expected that, in that age, the question would be tried according to those large and philosophical principles of criticism which guided the judgments of Lessing and Herder. But it might have been expected that those who undertook to decide the point would at least take the trouble to read and understand the authors on whose merits they were to pronounce. Now, it is no exaggeration to say that, among the disputants who clamoured, some for the ancients and some for the moderns, very few were decently acquainted with either ancient or modern literature, and not a single one was well acquainted with both. In Racine's amusing preface to the "Iphigénie," the reader may find noticed a most ridiculous mistake, into which one of the champions of the moderns fell about a passage in the "Alcestis" of Euripides. Another writer blames Homer for mixing the four Greek dialects —Doric, Ionic, Æolic and Attic—just, says he, as if a French poet were to put Gascon phrases and Picard phrases into the midst of his pure Parisian writing. On the other hand, it is no exaggeration to say that the defenders of the ancients were entirely unacquainted with the greatest productions of later times ; nor, indeed, were the defenders of the moderns better informed. The parallels which were instituted in the course of this dispute are inexpressibly ridiculous. Balzac was selected by the rival of Cicero. Corneille was declared to unite the merits of Æschylus, Sophocles and Euripides. We should like to see a "Prometheus" after Corneille's fashion. The "Provincial Letters"—masterpieces undoubtedly of reasoning, wit and eloquence—were pronounced to be superior to all the writings of Plato, Cicero and Lucian together—particularly in the art of dialogue—an art in which, as it happens, Plato far excelled all men, and in which Pascal, great and admirable in other respects, is notoriously very deficient.

This childish controversy spread to England ; and some mischievous dæmon suggested to Temple the thought of undertaking the defence of the ancients. As to his qualifications for the task, it is sufficient to say that he knew not a word of Greek. But his vanity, which, when he was engaged in the conflicts of active life and surrounded by rivals, had been kept in tolerable order by his discretion, now, when he had long lived in seclusion and had become accustomed to regard himself as by far the first man of his circle, rendered him blind by his own deficiencies. In an evil hour he published an "Essay on Ancient and Modern Learning." The style of this treatise is very good—the matter ludicrous and contemptible to the last degree. There we read how Lycurgus travelled into India and brought the Spartan laws from that country—how Orpheus and Musæus made voyages in search of knowledge, and how Orpheus attained to a depth of learning which has made him renowned in all succeeding ages—how Pythagoras passed twenty-two years in Egypt, and, after graduating there, spent twelve years more at Babylon, where the Magi admitted him as *eundem*—how the ancient Brahmins lived two hundred years—how the earliest Greek philosophers foretold earthquakes and plagues and put down riots by magic—and how much Ninus surpassed in abilities any of his successors on the throne of Assyria. The moderns, he owns, have found out the circulation of the blood; but, on the other hand, they have quite lost the art of magic; nor can any modern fiddler enchant fishes, fowls and serpents by his performance. He tells us that "Thales, Pythagoras, Democritus, Hippocrates, Plato, Aristotle and Epicurus made greater progresses in the several empires of science than any of their successors have since been able to reach"; which is as much as if he had said that the greatest names in British science are Merlin, Michael Scott, Dr. Sydenham and Lord Bacon. Indeed, the manner in which he mixes the historical and the fabulous reminds us of those classical dictionaries, intended for the use of schools, in which Narcissus, the lover of himself, and Narcissus, the freedman of Claudius—Pollux, the son of Jupiter and Leda, and Pollux, the author of the "Onomasticon"—are ranged under the same headings, and treated as personages equally real. The effect of this arrangement resembles that which would be produced by a dictionary of modern names, consisting of such articles as the following:—"Jones, William, an eminent Orientalist, and one of the Judges of the Supreme Court of Judicature in Bengal—Davy, a fiend, who destroys ships—Thomas, a foundling, brought up by Mr. Allworthy." It is from such sources as these that Temple seems to have learned all that he knew about the ancients. He puts the story of Orpheus between the Olympic games and the battle of Arbela; as if we had exactly as much reason for believing that Orpheus led beasts with his lyre as we have for believing that there were races at Pisa, or that Alexander conquered Darius.

He manages little better when he comes to the moderns. He gives us a catalogue of those whom he regards as the greatest wits of later times. It is sufficient to say that in his list of Italians he has omitted Dante, Petrarch, Ariosto and Tasso; in his list of Spaniards, Lope and Calderon; in his list of French, Pascal, Bossuet, Molière, Corneille, Racine and Boileau; and in his list of English, Chaucer, Spenser, Shakespeare and Milton.

In the midst of all this vast mass of absurdity one paragraph stands out preeminent. The doctrine of Temple—not a very comfortable doctrine—is that the human race is constantly degenerating and that the oldest books in every kind are the best. In confirmation of this doctrine, he remarks that the "Fables" of Æsop are the best Fables, and the "Letters" of Phalaris the best Letters in the world. On the merit of the "Letters" of Phalaris he dwells with great warmth and with extraordinary felicity of language. Indeed, we could hardly select a more favourable specimen of the graceful and easy majesty to which his style sometimes rises than this unlucky passage. He knows, he says, that some learned men, or men who pass for learned—such as Politian—have doubted the genuineness of these letters. But of these doubts he speaks with the greatest contempt. Now it is perfectly certain, first, that the letters are very bad; secondly, that they are spurious; and thirdly, that, whether they be bad or good, spurious or genuine, Temple could know nothing of the matter, inasmuch as he was no more able to construe a line of them than to decipher an Egyptian obelisk.

This essay, silly as it is, was exceedingly well received both in England and on the Continent. And the reason is evident. The classical scholars, who saw its absurdity, were generally on the side of the ancients, and were inclined rather to veil than to expose the blunders of an ally; the champions of the moderns were generally as ignorant as Temple himself; and the multitude was charmed by his flowing and melodious diction. He was doomed, however, to smart, as he well deserved, for his vanity and folly.

Christchurch at Oxford was then widely and justly celebrated as a place where the lighter parts of classical learning were cultivated with success. With the deeper mysteries of philology neither the instructors nor the pupils had the smallest acquaintance. They fancied themselves Scaligers, as Bentley scornfully said, as soon as they could write a copy of Latin verses with only two or three small faults. From this College proceeded a new edition of the "Letters" of Phalaris, which were rare, and had been in request since the appearance of Temple's essay. The nominal editor was Charles Boyle, a young man of noble family and promising parts; but some older members of the society lent their assistance. While this work was in preparation, an idle quarrel, occasioned, it should seem, by the negligence and misrepresentations of a bookseller, arose between Boyle and the King's Librarian, Richard Bentley. Boyle, in the preface to his edition, inserted a bitter reflection on Bentley. Bentley revenged himself by proving that the "Epistles" of Phalaris were forgeries; and, in his remarks on this subject, treated Temple, not indecently, but with no great reverence.

Temple, who was quite unaccustomed to any but the most respectful usage; who, even while engaged in politics, had always shrunk from all rude collision, and had generally succeeded in avoiding it; and whose sensitiveness had been increased by many years of seclusion and flattery, was moved to most violent resentment, complained, very unjustly, of Bentley's foul-mouthed raillery, and declared that he had commenced an answer, but had laid it aside, "having no mind to enter the lists with such a mean, dull, unmannerly pedant." Whatever may be thought of the temper which Sir William showed on this occasion, we cannot too highly applaud his discretion in not finishing and publishing his answer, which would certainly have been a most extraordinary performance.

He was not, however, without defenders. Like Hector, when struck down prostrate by Ajax, he was in an instant covered with a thick crowd of shields.

> Οὔτις ἐδυνήσατο ποιμένα λαῶν
> Οὐτάσαι, οὐδὲ βαλεῖν· πρὶν γὰρ περίβησαν ἄριστοι,
> Πουλυδάμας τε, καὶ Αἰνείας, καὶδιος Ἀγήνωρ,
> Σαρπηδών τ' ἀρχὸς Λυκίων, καὶ Γλαῦκος ἀμύμων.

Christchurch was up in arms; and though that College seems then to have been almost destitute of severe and accurate learning, no academical society could show a greater array of orators, wits, politicians—bustling adventurers who united the superficial accomplishments of the scholar with the manners and arts of the man of the world; and this formidable body resolved to try how far smart repartees, well-turned sentences, confidence, puffing and intrigue could—on the question whether a Greek book were or were not genuine —supply the place of a little knowledge of Greek.

Out came the "Reply to Bentley," bearing the name of Boyle, but in truth written by Atterbury, with the assistance of Smalridge and others. A most remarkable book it is, and often reminds us of Goldsmith's observation, that "the French would be the best cooks in the world if they had any butcher's meat; for that they can make ten dishes out of a nettle-top." It really deserves the praise, whatever that praise may be worth, of being the best book ever written by any man on the wrong side of a question of which he was profoundly ignorant. The learning of the confederacy is that of a schoolboy, and not of an extraordinary schoolboy; but it is used with the skill and address of most able, artful and experienced men: it is beaten out to the very thinnest leaf, and is disposed in such a way as to seem ten times larger than it is. The dexterity with which they avoid grappling with those parts of the subject with which they know themselves to be incompetent to deal with is quite wonderful.

Now and then, indeed, they commit disgraceful blunders, for which old Busby, under whom they had studied, would have whipped them all round. But this circumstance only raises our opinion of the talents which made such a fight with such scanty means. Let our readers, who are not acquainted with the controversy, imagine a Frenchman, who has acquired just English enough to read the Spectator with a dictionary, coming forward to defend the genuineness of Rowley's "Poems" against Percy and Farmer, and they will have some notion of the feat which Atterbury had the audacity to undertake, and which, for a time, it was really thought that he had performed.

The illusion was soon dispelled. Bentley's answer for ever settled the question, and established his claim to the first place among classical scholars. Nor do those do him justice who represent the controversy as a battle between wit and learning. For though there is a lamentable deficiency of learning on the side of Boyle, there is no want of wit on the side of Bentley. Other qualities, too, as valuable as either wit or learning, appear conspicuously in Bentley's book—a rare sagacity, an unrivalled power of combination, a perfect mastery of all the weapons of logic. He was greatly indebted to the furious outcry which the misrepresentations, sarcasms and intrigues of his opponents had raised against him; an outcry in which fashionable and political circles joined, and which was echoed by thousands who did not know whether Phalaris ruled in Sicily or in Siam. His spirit—daring even to rashness—self-confident even to negligence—and proud even to insolent ferocity—was awed for the first and for the last time—awed, not into meanness or cowardice, but into wariness and sobriety. For once he ran no risks; he left no crevice unguarded; he wantoned in no paradoxes; above all, he returned no railing for the railing of his enemies. In almost everything that he has written, we can discover proofs of genius and learning. But it is only here that his genius and learning appear to have been constantly under the guidance of good sense and good temper. Here, we find none of that besotted reliance on his own powers and on his own luck, which he showed when he undertook to edit Milton; none of that perverted ingenuity which deforms so many of his notes on Horace; none of that disdainful carelessness by which he laid himself open to the keen and dexterous thrust of Middleton; none of that extravagant vaunting and savage scurrility by which he afterwards dishonoured his studies and his profession, and degraded himself almost to the level of De Pauw.

Temple did not live to witness the utter and irreparable defeat of his champions. He died, indeed, at a fortunate moment, just after the appearance of Boyle's book, and while all England was laughing at the way in which the Christchurch men had handled the pedant. In Boyle's book, Temple was praised in the highest terms and compared to Memmius—not a very happy comparison, for the only particular information which we have about Memmius is, that in agitated times he thought it his duty to attend exclusively to politics; and that his friends could not venture, except when the Republic was quiet and prosperous, to intrude on him with their philosophical and poetical productions. It is on this account that Lucretius puts up the exquisitely beautiful prayer for peace with which his poem opens:

"Nam neque nos agere hoc patriaï tempore iniquo
Possumus æquo animo, nec Memmi clara propago
Talibus in rebus communi deesse saluti."

This description is surely by no means applicable to a statesman who had, through the whole course of his life, carefully avoided exposing himself in seasons of trouble; who had repeatedly refused, in most critical conjunctures, to be Secretary of State; and who now, in the midst of revolutions, plots, foreign and domestic wars, was quietly writing nonsense about the visits of Lycurgus to the Brahmins, and the tunes which Arion played to the Dolphin.

We must not omit to mention that, while the controversy about Phalaris was raging, Swift, in order to show his zeal and attachment, wrote the "Battle of the Books"—the earliest piece in which his peculiar talents are discernible. We may observe that the bitter dislike of Bentley, bequeathed by Temple to Swift, seems to have been communicated by Swift to Pope, to Arbuthnot, and to others, who continued to tease the great critic long after he had shaken hands very cordially both with Boyle and with Atterbury.

Sir William Temple died at Moor Park in January, 1699. He appears to have suffered no intellectual decay. His heart was buried under a sun-dial, which still stands in his favourite garden. His body was laid in Westminster Abbey by the side of his wife; and a place hard by was set apart for Lady Giffard, who long survived him. Swift was his literary executor, and superintended the publication of his "Letters" and "Memoirs," not without some acrimonious contests with the family.

Of Temple's character little more remains to be said. Burnet accuses him of holding irreligious opinions and corrupting everybody who came near him. But the vague assertion of so rash and partial a writer as Burnet, about a man with whom, as far as we know, he never exchanged a word, is of very little weight. It is, indeed, by no means improbable that Temple may have been a freethinker. The Osbornes thought him so when he was a very young man. And it is certain that a large proportion of the gentleman of rank and fashion who made their entrance into society while the Puritan party was at the height of power, and while the memory of the reign of that party was still recent, conceived a strong disgust for all religion. The imputation was common between Temple and all the most distinguished courtiers of the age. Rochester and Buckingham were open scoffers, and Mulgrave very little better. Shaftesbury, though more guarded, was supposed to agree with them in opinion. All the three noblemen who were Temple's colleagues during the short time of his continuance in the Cabinet were of very indifferent repute as to orthodoxy. Halifax, indeed, was generally considered as an atheist, but he solemnly denied the charge, and, indeed, the truth seems to be that he was more religiously disposed than most of the statemen of that age; though two impulses which were unusually strong in him, a passion for ludicrous images and a passion for subtle speculations, sometimes prompted him to talk on serious subjects in a manner which gave great and just offence. It is not unlikely that Temple, who seldom went below the surface of any question, may have been infected with the prevailing scepticism. All that we can say on the subject is, that there is no trace of impiety in his works, and that the ease with which he carried his election for an university, where the majority of the voters were clergymen, though it proves nothing as to his opinions, must, we think, be considered as proving that he was not, as Burnet seems to insinuate, in the habit of talking atheism to all who came near him.

Temple, however, will scarcely carry with him any great accession of authority to the side either of religion or of infidelity. He was no profound thinker. He was merely a man of lively parts and quick observation, a man of the world among men of letters, a man of letters among men of the world. Mere scholars were dazzled by the Ambassador and Cabinet counsellor, mere politicians by the Essayist and Historian. But neither as a writer nor as a statesman can we allot to him any very high place. As a man, he seems to us to have been excessively selfish, but very sober, wary and farsighted in his selfishness; to have known better than most people know what he really wanted in life; and to have pursued what he wanted with much more than ordinary steadiness and sagacity, never suffering himself to be drawn aside either by bad or by good feelings. It was his constitution to dread failure more than he desired success, to prefer security, comfort, repose, leisure, to the turmoil and anxiety which are inseparable from greatness; and this natural langour of mind, when contrasted with the malignant energy of the keen and restless spirits among whom his lot was cast, sometimes appears to resemble the moderation of virtue. But we must own that he seems to us to sink into littleness and meanness when we compare him, we do not say with any high ideal standard of morality, but with many of those frail men who, aiming at noble ends, but often drawn from the right path by strong passions and strong temptations, have left to posterity a doubtful and checkered fame.

GLADSTONE ON CHURCH AND STATE. (APRIL, 1839.)

The State in its Relations with the Church. Second Edition. By W. E. GLADSTONE, Esq., Student of Christ Church and M.P. for Newark. 8vo. London, 1839.

THE author of this volume is a young man of unblemished character and of distinguished parliamentary talents, the rising hope of those stern and unbending Tories who follow reluctantly and mutinously a leader whose experience and eloquence are indispensable to them, but whose cautious temper and moderate opinions they abhor. It would not be at all strange if Mr. Gladstone were one of the most unpopular men in England. But we believe that we do him no more than justice when we say that his abilities and his demeanour have obtained for him the respect and goodwill of all parties. His first appearance in the character of an author is therefore an interesting event; and it is natural that the gentle wishes of the public should go with him to his trial.

We are much pleased, without any reference to the soundness or unsoundness of Mr. Gladstone's theories, to see a grave and elaborate treatise on an important part of the philosophy of Government proceed from the pen of a young man who is rising to eminence in the House of Commons. There is little danger that people engaged in the conflicts of active life will be too much addicted to general speculation. The opposite vice is that which most easily besets them. The times and tides of business and debate tarry for no man. A politician must often talk and act before he has thought and read. He may be very ill-informed respecting a question; all his notions about it may be vague and inaccurate; but speak he must, and if he is a man of talents, of tact and of intrepidity, he soon finds that, even under such circumstances, it is possible to speak successfully. He finds that there is a great difference between the effect of written words, which are perused and reperused in the stillness of the closet, and the effect of spoken words which, set off by the graces of utterance and gesture, vibrate for a single moment on the ear. He finds that he may blunder without much chance of being detected, that he may reason sophistically and escape unrefuted. He finds that, even on knotty questions of trade and legislation, he can without reading ten pages or thinking ten minutes, draw forth loud plaudits, and sit down with the credit of having made an excellent speech. Lysias, says Plutarch, wrote a defence for a man who was to be tried before one of the Athenian tribunals. Long before the defendant had learned the speech by heart, he became so much dissatisfied with it that he went in great distress to the author. "I was delighted with your speech the first time I read it; but I liked it less the second time, and still less the third time, and now it seems to me to be no defence nt all." "My good friend," says Lysias, "you quite forget that the judges are to hear it only once. The case is the same in the English Parliament. It would be as idle in an orator to waste deep meditation and long research on his speeches, as it would be in the manager of a theatre to adorn all the crowd of courtiers and ladies, who cross over the stage in a procession with real pearls and diamonds. It is not by accuracy or profundity that men become the masters of great assemblies. And why be at the charge of providing logic of the best quality when a very inferior article will be equally acceptable? Why go as deep into a question as Burke, only in order to be, like Burke, coughed down, or left speaking to green benches and red boxes? This has long appeared to us to be the most serious of the evils which are to be set off against the many blessings of popular government. It is a fine and true saying of Bacon, that "reading makes a full man, talking a ready man, and writing an exact man." The tendency of institutions like those of England is to encourage readiness in public men at the expense both of fulness and of exactness. The keenest and most vigorous minds of every generation, minds often admirably fitted for the investigation of truth, are habitually employed in producing arguments, such as no man of sense would ever put in a treatise intended for publication, arguments which are just good enough to be used once, when aided by fluent delivery and pointed language. The habit of discussing questions in this way necessarily reacts on the intellects of our ablest men, particularly of those who are introduced into parliament at a very early age, before their minds have expanded to full maturity. The talent for debate is devoloped in such men to a degree which, to the multitude, seems as marvellous as the performance of an Italian *improvisatore*. But they are fortunate indeed if they retain unimpaired the faculties which are required for close reasoning or for enlarged speculation. Indeed, we should sooner expect a great original work on political science, such a work for example as the "Wealth of Nations," from an apothecary in a country town, or from a Minister in the Hebrides than from a statesman who ever since he was one-and-twenty had been a distinguished debater in the House of Commons.

We, therefore, hail with pleasure, though assuredly not with unmixed pleasure, the appearance of this work. That a young politician should, in the intervals afforded by his parliamentary avocations, have constructed and propounded, with much study and mental toil, an original theory on a great problem in politics, is a circumstance which, abstracted from all consideration of the soundness or unsoundness of his opinions, must be considered as highly creditable to him. We certainly cannot wish that Mr. Gladstone's doctrines may become fashionable among public men. But we heartily wish that his laudable desire to penetrate beneath the surface of questions, and to arrive, by long and intent meditation, at the knowledge of great general laws, were much more fashionable than we at all expect it to become.

Mr. Gladstone seems to us to be, in many respects, exceedingly well qualified for philosophical investigation. His mind is of large grasp; nor is he deficient in dialectical skill. But he does not give his intellect fair play. There is no want of light, but a great want of what Bacon would have called dry light. Whatever Mr. Gladstone sees is refracted and distorted by a false medium of passions and prejudices. His style bears a remarkable analogy to his mode of thinking, and indeed exercises great influence on his mode of thinking. His rhetoric, though often good of its kind, darkens and perplexes the logic which it should illustrate. Half his acuteness and diligence, with a barren imagination and a scanty vocabulary, would have saved him from almost all his mistakes. He has one gift most dangerous to a speculator—a vast command of a kind of language, grave and majestic, but of vague and uncertain import—of a kind of language which affects us much in the same way in which the lofty diction of the Chorus cf Clouds affected the simple-hearted Athenian.

ὦ γῆ τοῦ φθέγματος, ὡς ἱερὸν, καὶ σεμνὸν, καὶ τερατῶδες.

When propositions have been established, and nothing remains but to amplify and decorate them, this dim magnificence may be in place. But if it is admitted into a demonstration, it is very much worse than absolute nonsense—just as that transparent haze, through which the sailor sees capes and mountains of false sizes and in false bearings, is more dangerous than utter darkness. Now, Mr. Gladstone is fond of employing the phraseology of which we speak in those parts of his works which require the utmost perspicuity and precision of which human language is capable; and in this way he deludes first himself and then his readers. The foundations of his theory, which ought to be buttresses of adamant, are made out of the flimsy materials which are fit only for perorations. This fault is one which no subsequent care or industry can correct. The more strictly Mr. Gladstone reasons on his premises, the more absurd are the conclusions which he brings out; and, when at last his good sense and good nature recoil from the horrible practical inferences to which this theory leads, he is reduced sometimes to take refuge in arguments inconsistent with his fundamental doctrines, and sometimes to escape from the legitimate consequences of his false principles under cover of equally false history.

It would be unjust not to say that this book, though not a good book, shows more talent than many good books. It abounds with eloquent and ingenious passages. It bears the signs of much patient thought. It is written throughout with excellent taste and excellent temper; nor does it, so far as we have observed, contain one expression unworthy of a gentleman, a scholar, or a Christian. But the doctrines which are put forth in it appear to us, after full and calm consideration, to be false; to be in the highest degree pernicious; and to be such as, if followed out in practice to their legitimate consequences, would inevitably produce the dissolution of society: and for this opinion we shall proceed to give our reasons with that freedom which the importance of the subject requires, and which Mr. Gladstone, both by precept and by example, invites us to use, but, we hope, without rudeness, and, we are sure, without malevolence.

Before we enter on an examination of this theory, we wish to guard ourselves against one misconception. It is possible that some persons who have read Mr. Gladstone's book carelessly, and others who have merely heard in conversation, or seen in a newspaper, that the member for Newark has written in defence of the Church of England against the supporters of the voluntary system, may imagine that we are writing in defence of the voluntary system, and that we desire the abolition of the Established Church. This is not the case. It would be as unjust to accuse us of attacking the Church because we attack Mr. Gladstone's doctrines as it would be to accuse Locke of wishing for anarchy because he refuted Filmer's patriarchal theory of government; or to accuse Blackstone of recommending the confiscation of ecclesiastical property because he denied that the right of the rector to tithe was derived from the Levitical law. It is to be observed that Mr. Gladstone rests his case on entirely new grounds, and does not differ more widely from us than from some of those who have hitherto been considered as the most illustrious champions of the Church. He is not content with the "Ecclesiastical Polity," and rejoices that the latter part of that celebrated work "does not carry with it the weight of Hooker's plenary authority." He is not content with Bishop Warburton's

"Alliance of Church and State." "The propositions of that work generally," he says, "are to be received with qualification;" and he agrees with Bolingbroke in thinking that Warburton's whole theory rests on a fiction. He is still less satisfied with Paley's defence of the Church, which he pronounces to be "tainted by the original vice of false ethical principles" and "full of the seeds of evil." He conceives that Dr. Chalmers has taken a partial view of the subject and "put forth much questionable matter." In truth, on almost every point on which we are opposed to Mr. Gladstone, we have on our side the authority of some divine, eminent as a defender of existing establishments.

Mr. Gladstone's whole theory rests on this great fundamental proposition— that the propagation of Religious Truth is one of the principal ends of Government, as government. If Mr. Gladstone has not proved this proposition, his system vanishes at once.

We are desirous, before we enter on the discussion of this important question, to point out clearly a distinction which, though very obvious, seems to be overlooked by many excellent people. In their opinion, to say that the ends of government are temporal and not spiritual, is tantamount to saying that the temporal welfare of man is of more importance than his spiritual welfare. But this is an entire mistake. The question is not whether spiritual interests be or be not superior in importance to temporal interests, but whether the machinery which happens at any moment to be employed for the purpose of protecting certain temporal interests of a society be necessarily such a machinery as is fitted to promote the spiritual interests of that society. It is certain that without a division of duties the world could not go on. It is of very much more importance that men should have food than that they should have pianofortes. Yet it by no means follows that every pianoforte-maker ought to add the business of a baker to his own; for, if he did so, we should have both much worse music and much worse bread. It is of much more importance that the knowledge of religious truth should be widely diffused than that the art of sculpture should flourish among us. Yet it by no means follows that the Royal Academy ought to unite with its present functions those of the Society for Promoting Christian Knowledge, to distribute theological tracts, to send forth missionaries, to turn out Nollekens for being a Catholic, Bacon for being a methodist and Flaxman for being a Swedenborgian. For the effect of such folly would be that we should have the worst possible Academy of Arts and the worst possible Society for the Promotion of Christian Knowledge. The community, it is plain, would be thrown into universal confusion if it were supposed to be the duty of every association which is formed, for one good object, to promote every other good object.

As to some of the ends of civil government, all people are agreed. That it is designed to protect our persons and our property—that it is designed to compel us to satisfy our wants, not by rapine, but by industry—that it is designed to compel us to decide our differences, not by the strong hand, but by arbitration—that it is designed to direct our whole force as that of one man against any other society which may offer us injury—these are propositions which will hardly be disputed.

Now these are matters in which man, without any reference to any higher being, or to any future state, is very deeply interested. Every man, be he idolater, Mahometan, Jew, Papist, Socinian, Deist or Atheist, naturally loves life, shrinks from pain, desires comforts which can be enjoyed only in communities where property is secure. To be murdered, to be tortured, to be robbed, to be sold into slavery, to be exposed to the outrages of gangs of foreign banditti calling themselves patriots, these are evidently evils from which men of every religion, and men of no religion, wish to be protected; and, therefore,

It will hardly be disputed that men of every religion, and of no religion, have thus far a common interest in being well governed.

But the hopes and fears of man are not limited to this short life and to this visible world. He finds himself surrounded by the signs of a power and wisdom higher than his own; and, in all ages and nations, men of all orders of intellects, from Bacon and Newton down to the rudest tribes of cannibals, have believed in the existence of some superior mind. Thus far the voice of mankind is almost unanimous. But whether there be one God, or many—what may be God's natural and what His moral attributes—in what relation His creatures stand to Him—whether He have ever disclosed Himself to us by any other revelation than that which is written in all the parts of the glorious and well-ordered world which He has made—whether His revelation be contained in any permanent record—how that record should be interpreted, and whether it have pleased Him to appoint any unerring interpreter on earth—these are questions respecting which there exists the widest diversity of opinion, and respecting some of which a large part of our race has, ever since the dawn of regular history, been deplorably in error.

Now here are two great objects: one is the protection of the persons and estates of citizens from injury; the other is the propagation of religious truth. No two objects more entirely distinct can well be imagined. The former belongs wholly to the visible and tangible world in which we live; the latter belongs to that higher world which is beyond the reach of our senses. The former belongs to this life; the latter to that which is to come. Men who are perfectly agreed as to the importance of the former object, and as to the way of obtaining it, differ as widely as possible respecting the latter object. We must, therefore, pause before we admit that the persons, be they who they may, who are intrusted with power for the promotion of the former object ought always to use that power for the promotion of the latter object.

Mr. Gladstone conceives that the duties of governments are paternal—a doctrine which we shall not believe till he can show us some government which loves its subjects as a father loves a child, and which is as superior in intelligence to its subjects as a father is to a child. He tells us in lofty, though somewhat indistinct language, that "Government occupies in moral the place of τὸ πᾶν in physical science." If government be indeed τὸ πᾶν in moral science, we do not understand why rulers should not assume all the functions which Plato assigned to them. Why should they not take away the child from the mother, select the nurse, regulate the school, overlook the playground, fix the hours of labour and of recreation, prescribe what ballads shall be sung, what tunes shall be played, what books shall be read, what physic shall be swallowed? Why should not they choose our wives, limit our expenses, and stint us to a certain number of dishes, of glasses of wine, and of cups of tea? Plato, whose hardihood in speculation was perhaps more wonderful than any other peculiarity of his extraordinary mind, and who shrank from nothing to which his principles led, went this whole length. Mr. Gladstone is not so intrepid. He contents himself with laying down this proposition—that whatever be the body which in any community is employed to protect the persons and property of men, that body ought also, in its corporate capacity, to profess a religion, to employ its power for the propagation of that religion, and to require conformity to that religion as an indispensable qualification for all civil office. He distinctly declares that he does not in this proposition confine his view to orthodox governments, or even to Christian governments. The circumstance that a religion is false does not, he tells us, diminish the obligation of governors, as such, to uphold it. If they neglect to do so, "We cannot," he says, "but regard the fact as aggravating the case the holders of such creed." "I do not scruple to affirm," he adds, " that, if a Mahometan conscientiously believes his religion to come from God and to teach divine truth, he must believe that truth to be beneficial, and beneficial beyond all other things, to the soul of man ; and he must, therefore, and ought to desire its extension, and to use for its extension all proper and legitimate means ; and that, if such Mahometan be a prince, he ought to count among those means the application of whatever influence or funds he may lawfully have at his disposal for such purposes."

Surely this is a hard saying. Before we admit that the Emperor Julian, in employing the influence and the funds at his disposal for the extinction of Christianity, was doing no more than his duty—before we admit that the Arian Theodoric would have committed a crime if he had suffered a single believer in the divinity of Christ to hold any civil employment in Italy— before we admit that the Dutch Government is bound to exclude from office all members of the Church of England ; the King of Bavaria to exclude from office all Protestants ; the Great Turk to exclude from office all Christians ; the King of Ava to exclude from office all who hold the unity of God—we think ourselves entitled to demand very full and accurate demonstration. When the consequences of a doctrine are so startling, we may well require that its foundations shall be very solid.

The following paragraph is a specimen of the arguments by which Mr. Gladstone has, as he conceives, established his great fundamental proposition :—

' "We may state the same proposition in a more general form, in which it surely must command universal assent. Wherever there is power in the universe, that power is the property of God, the King of that universe—his property of right, however for a time withholden or abused. Now this property is, as it were, realised, is used according to the will of the owner, when it is used for the purposes he has ordained, and in the temper of mercy, justice, truth and faith which he has taught us. But those principles never can be truly, never can be permanently entertained in the human breast, except by a continual reference to their source, and the supply of the Divine grace. The powers, therefore, that dwell in individuals acting as a government, as well as those that dwell in individuals acting for themselves, can only be secured for right uses by applying to them a religion."

Here are propositions of vast and indefinite extent, conveyed in language which has a certain obscure dignity and sanctity, attractive, we doubt not, to many minds. But the moment that we examine these propositions closely, the moment that we bring them to the test by running over but a very few of the particulars which are included in them, we find them to be false and extravagant. The doctrine which "must surely command universal assent" is, that every association of human beings which exercises any power whatever —that is to say, every association of human beings—is bound, as such association, to profess a religion. Imagine the effect which would follow if this principle were really in force during four-and-twenty hours. Take one instance out of a million. A stage-coach company has power over its horses. This power is the property of God. It is used according to the will of God when it is used with mercy. But the principle of mercy can never be truly or permantly entertained in the human breast without continual reference to God. The powers, therefore, that dwell in individuals acting as a stage-coach company, can only be secured for right uses by applying to them a religion. Every stage-coach company ought, therefore, in its collective capacity to profess some one faith—to have its articles, and its public worship, and its tests. That this conclusion, and an infinite number of other conclusions equally strange, follows of necessity from Mr. Gladstone's principle, is as certain as it is that two and two make four. And, if the legitimate conclusions be so absurd, there must be something unsound in the principle.

We will quote another passage of the same sort:—

"Why, then, we now come to ask, should the governing body in a state profess a religion? First, because it is composed of individual *men;* and they, being appointed to act in a definite moral capacity, must sanctify their acts done in that capacity by the offices of religion; inasmuch as the acts cannot otherwise be acceptable to God, or anything but sinful and punishable in themselves. And whenever we turn our face away from God in our conduct, we are living atheistically. . . . . . . In fulfilment, then, of his obligations as an individual, the statesman must be a worshipping man. But his acts are public—the powers and instruments with which he works are public—acting under and by the authority of the law, he moves at his word ten thousand subject arms; and because such energies are thus essentially public, and wholly out of the range of mere individual agency, they must be sanctified not only by the private personal prayers and piety of those who fill public situations, but also by public acts of the men composing the public body. They must offer prayer and praise in their public and collective character—in that character wherein they constitute the organ of the nation and wield its collective force. Wherever there is a reasoning agency there is a moral duty and responsibility involved in it. The governors are reasoning agents for the nation, in their conjoint acts as such. And therefore there must be attached to this agency, as that without which none of our responsibilities can be met, a religion. And this religion must be that of the conscience of the governor, or none."

Here again we find propositions of vast sweep, and of sound so orthodox and solemn that many good people, we doubt not, have been greatly edified by it. But let us examine the words closely and it will immediately become plain that, if these principles be once admitted, there is an end of all society. No combination can be formed for any purpose of mutual help—for trade, for public works, for the relief of the sick or the poor, for the promotion of art or science—unless the members of the combination agree in their theological opinions. Take any such combination at random—the London and Birmingham Railway Company for example—and observe to what consequences Mr. Gladstone's arguments inevitably lead. "Why should the Directors of the Railway Company, in their collective capacity, profess a religion? First, because the direction is composed of individual men appointed to act in a definite moral capacity, bound to look carefully to the property, the limbs and the lives of their fellow-creatures—bound to act diligently for their constituents—bound to govern their servants with humanity and justice—bound to fulfil with fidelity many important contracts. They must, therefore, sanctify their acts by the offices of religion, or these acts will be sinful and punishable in themselves. In fulfilment, then, of his obligations as an individual, the Director of the London and Birmingham Railway Company must be a worshipping man. But his acts are public. He acts for a body. He moves at his word ten thousand subject arms. And because these energies are out of the range of his mere individual agency, they must be sanctified by public acts of devotion. The Railway Directors must offer prayer and praise in their public and collective character, in that character wherewith they constitute the organ of the Company and wield its collected power. Wherever there is reasoning agency, there is moral responsibility. The Directors are reasoning agents for the Company. And therefore there must be attached to this agency, as that without which none of our responsibilities can be met—a religion. And this religion must be that of the conscience of the Director himself, or none. There must be public worship and a test. No Jew, no Socinian, no Presbyterian, no Catholic, no Quaker must be permitted to be the organ of the Company and to wield its collected force?" Would Mr. Gladstone really defend this proposition? We are sure that he would not: but we are sure that to this proposition, and to innumerable similar propositions, his reasoning inevitably leads,

Again;—

"National will and agency are indisputably one, binding either a dissentient minority, or the subject body, in a manner that nothing but the recognition of the doctrine of national personality can justify. National honour and good faith are words in every one's mouth. How do they less imply a personality in nations than the duty towards God, for which we now contend? They are strictly and essentially distinct from the honour and good faith of the individuals composing the nation. France is a person to us, and we to her. A wilful injury done to her is a moral act, and a moral act quite distinct from the acts of all the individuals composing the nation. Upon broad facts like these we may rest, without resorting to the more technical proof which the laws afford in their manner of dealing with corporations. If, then, a nation have unity of will, have pervading sympathies, have capability of reward and suffering contingent upon its acts, shall we deny its responsibility; its need of a religion to meet that responsibility? . . . . A nation then, having a personality, lies under the obligation, like the individuals composing its governing body, of sanctifying the acts of that personality by the offices of religion, and thus we have a new and imperative ground for the existence of a state religion."

A new ground we have here, certainly, but whether very imperative may be doubted. Is it not perfectly clear that this argument applies with exactly as much force to every combination of human beings for a common purpose as to governments? Is there any such combination in the world, whether technically a corporation or not, which has not this collective personality from which Mr. Gladstone deduces such extraordinary consequences? Look at banks, insurance offices, dock companies, canal companies, gas companies, hospitals, dispensaries, associations for the relief of the poor, associations for apprehending malefactors, associations of medical pupils for procuring subjects, associations of country gentlemen for keeping fox-hounds, book societies, benefit societies, clubs of all ranks, from those which have lined Pall-Mall and St. James's Street with their palaces down to the Free-and-easy which meets in the shabby parlour of a village inn. Is there a single one of these combinations to which Mr. Gladstone's arguments will not apply as well as to the State? In all these combinations—in the Bank of England, for example, or in the Athenæum club—the will and agency of the society are one, and bind the dissentient minority. The Bank and the Athenæum have a good faith and a justice different from the good faith and justice of the individual members. The Bank is a person to those who deposit bullion with it. The Athenæum is a person to the butcher and the wine-merchant. If the Athenæum keeps money at the Bank, the two societies are as much persons to each other as England and France. Either society may increase in prosperity; either may fall into difficulties. If, then, they have this unity of will; if they are capable of doing and suffering good and evil; can we, to use Mr. Gladstone's words, "deny their responsibility, or their need of a religion to meet that responsibility?" Joint-stock banks, therefore, and clubs, "having a personality, lie under the necessity of sanctifying that personality by the offices of religion;" and thus we have "a new and imperative ground" for requiring all the directors and clerks of joint-stock banks, and all the members of clubs, to qualify by taking the sacrament.

The truth is, that Mr. Gladstone has fallen into an error very common among men of less talents than his own. It is not unusual for a person who is eager to prove a particular proposition to assume a *major* of huge extent, which includes that particular proposition, without ever reflecting that it includes a great deal more. The fatal facility with which Mr. Gladstone multiplies expressions stately and sonorous, but of indeterminate meaning, eminently qualifies him to practise this sleight on himself and on his readers. He lays down broad general doctrines about power, when the only power of which he is thinking is the power of governments, about conjoint action, when the only conjoint action of which he is thinking is the conjoint action of citizens in a state. He first resolves on his conclusion. He then makes a *major* of most comprehensive dimensions and, having satisfied himself that it contains his conclusion, never troubles himself about what else it may contain. And as soon as we examine it, we find that it contains an infinite number of conclusions, every one of which is a monstrous absurdity.

It is perfectly true that it would be a very good thing if all the members of all the associations in the world were men of sound religious views. We have no doubt that a good Christian will be under the guidance of Christian principles in his conduct as director of a canal company or steward of a charity dinner. If he were—to recur to a case which we have before put—a member of a stage-coach company, he would, in that capacity, remember that "a righteous man regardeth the life of his beast." But it does not follow that ever association of men must, therefore, as such association, profess a religion. It is evident that many great and useful objects can be attained in this world only by co-operation. It is equally evident that there cannot be efficient co-operation if men proceed on the principle that they must not co-operate for one object unless they agree about other objects. Nothing seems to us more beautiful or admirable in our social system than the facility with which thousands of people, who perhaps agree only on a single point, combine their energies for the purpose of carrying that single point. We see daily instances of this. Two men, one of them obstinately prejudiced against missions, the other president of a missionary society, sit together at the board of a hospital and heartily concur in measures for the health and comfort of the patients. Two men, one of whom is a zealous supporter and the other a zealous opponent of the system pursued in Lancaster's schools, meet at the Mendicity Society and act together with the utmost cordiality. The general rule we take to be undoubtedly this, that it is lawful and expedient for men to unite in an association for the promotion of a good object, though they may differ with respect to other objects of still higher importance.

It will hardly be denied that the security of the persons and property of men is a good object, and that the best way, indeed the only way, of promoting that object, is to combine men together in certain great corporations which are called States. These corporations are very variously and, for the most part, very imperfectly organised. Many of them abound with frightful abuses. But it seems reasonable to believe that the worst that ever existed was, on the whole, preferable to complete anarchy.

Now, reasoning from analogy, we should say that these great corporations would, like all other associations, be likely to attain their end most perfectly if that end were kept singly in view; and that to refuse the services of those who are admirably qualified to promote that end, because they are not also qualified to promote some other end, however excellent, seems at first sight as unreasonable as it would be to provide that nobody who was not a fellow of the Antiquarian Society should be a governor of the Eye Infirmary; or that nobody who was not a member of the Society for promoting Christianity among the Jews should be a trustee of the Theatrical Fund.

It is impossible to name any collection of human beings to which Mr. Gladstone's reasonings would apply more strongly than to an army? Where shall we find more complete unity of action than in an army? Where else do so many human beings implicitly obey one ruling mind? What other mass is there which moves so much like one man? Where is such tremendous power intrusted to those who command? Where is so awful a responsibility laid upon them? If Mr. Gladstone has made out, as he conceives, an imperative necessity for a State Religion, much more has he made it out to be imperatively necessary that every army should, in its collective capacity, profess a religion. Is he prepared to adopt this consequence?

On the morning of the thirteenth of August, in the year 1704, two great captains, equal in authority, united by close private and public ties, but of different creeds, prepared for a battle, on the event of which were staked the liberties of Europe. Marlborough had passed a part of the night in prayer, and before daybreak received the sacrament according to the rites of the Church of England. He then hastened to join Eugene, who had probably just confessed himself to a Popish priest. The generals consulted together, formed their plan in concert, and repaired each to his own post. Marlborough gave orders for public prayers. The English chaplains read the service at the head of the English regiments. The Calvinistic chaplains of the Dutch army, with heads on which hand of Bishop had never been laid, poured forth their supplications in front of their countrymen. In the meantime the Danes might listen to their Lutheran ministers, and Capauchins might encourage the Austrian squadrons, and pray to the Virgin for a blessing on the arms of the Holy Roman Empire. The battle commences, and these men of various religions all act like members of one body. The Catholic and the Protestant general exert themselves to assist and to surpass each other. Before sunset the empire is saved: France has lost in a day the fruits of eighty years of intrigue and of victory, and the allies, after conquering together, return thanks to God separately, each after his own form of worship. Now, is this practical atheism? Would any man in his senses say, that because the allied army had unity of action and a common interest, and because a heavy responsibility lay on its Chiefs, it was therefore imperatively necessary that the army should, as an army, have one established religion—that Eugene should be deprived of his command for being a Catholic—that all the Dutch and Austrian colonels should be broken for not subscribing the Thirty-nine Articles? Certainly not. The most ignorant grenadier on the field of battle would have seen the absurdity of such a proposition. "I know," he would have said, "that the Prince of Savoy goes to mass and that our Corporal John cannot abide it, but what has the mass to do with the taking of the village of Blenheim? The Prince wants to beat the French, and so does Corporal John. If we stand by each other we shall most likely beat them. If we send all the Papists and Dutch away, Tallard will have every man of us." Mr. Gladstone himself, we imagine, would admit that our honest grenadier would have the best of the argument, and if so, what follows? Even this, that all Mr. Gladstone's general principles, about power, and responsibility, and personality, and conjoint action, must be given up, and that, if his theory is to stand at all, it must stand on some other foundation.

We have now, we conceive, shown that it may be proper to form men into combinations for important purposes, which combinations shall have unity and common interests, and shall be under the direction of rulers entrusted with great power and lying under solemn responsibility, and yet that it may be highly improper that these combinations should, as such, profess any one system of religious belief, or perform any joint act of religious worship. How, then, is it proved that this may not be the case with some of those great combinations which we call States? We firmly believe that it is the case with some states. We firmly believe that there are communities in which it would be as absurd to mix up theology with government as it would have been in the right wing of the allied army at Blenheim to commence a controversy with the left wing, in the middle of the battle, about purgatory, and the worship of images.

It is the duty, Mr. Gladstone tells us, of the persons, be they who they may, who hold supreme power in the state, to employ that power in order to promote whatever they may deem to be theological truth. Now, surely, before he can call on us to admit this proposition, he is bound to prove that these persons are likely to do more good than harm by so employing their power. The first question is, whether a government, proposing to itself the propagation of religious truth as one of its principal ends, is more likely to lead the people right than to lead them wrong? Mr. Gladstone evades this question; and perhaps it was his wisest course to do so.

"If," says he, "the government be good, let it have its natural duties and powers at its command; but, if not good, let it be made so..... We follow, therefore, the true course in looking first for the true idea, or abstract conception of a government, of course with allowance for the evil and frailty that are in man, and then in examining whether there be comprised in that idea a capacity and consequent duty on the part of a government to lay down any laws or devote any means for the purposes of religion—in short, to exercise a choice upon religion."

Of course, Mr. Gladstone has a perfect right to argue any abstract question, provided that he will constantly bear in mind that it is only an abstract question that he is arguing. Whether a perfect government would or would not be a good machinery for the propagation of religious truth, is certainly a harmless, and may, for aught we know, be an edifying subject of inquiry. But it is very important that we should remember that there is not, and never has been, any such government in the world. There is no harm at all in inquiring what course a stone thrown into the air would take if the law of gravitation did not operate. But the consequences would be unpleasant if the inquirer, as soon as he had finished his calculation, were to begin to throw stones about in all directions, without considering that his conclusion rests on a false hypothesis, and that his projectiles, instead of flying away through infinite space, will speedily return in parabolas and break the windows and heads of his neighbours.

It is very easy to say that governments are good, or if not good, ought to be made so. But what is meant by good government? And how are all the bad governments in the world to be made good? And of what value is a theory which is true only on a supposition in the highest degree extravagant?

We do not admit that, if a government were, for all its temporal ends, as perfect as human frailty allows, such a government would, therefore, be necessarily qualified to propogate true religion. For we see that the fitness of governments to propogate true religion is by no means proportioned to their fitness for the temporal end of their institution. Looking at individuals, we see that the princes under whose rule nations have been most ably protected from foreign and domestic disturbance, and have made the most rapid advances in civilisation, have been by no means good teachers of divinity. Take, for example, the best French sovereign, Henry the Fourth, a king who restored order, terminated a terrible civil war, brought the finances into an excellent condition, made his country respected throughout Europe, and endeared himself to the great body of the people whom he ruled. Yet this man was twice a Huguenot and twice a Papist. He was, as Davila hints, strongly suspected of having no religion at all in theory, and was certainly not much under religious restraints in his practice. Take the Czar Peter, the Empress Catharine, Frederic the Great. It will surely not be disputed that these sovereigns, with all their faults, were, if we consider them with reference merely to the temporal ends of government, far above the average of merit. Considered as theological guides, Mr. Gladstone would probably put them below the most abject drivellers of the Spanish branch of the house of Bourbon. Again, when we pass from individuals to systems, we by no means find that the aptitude of governments for propagating religious truth is proportioned to their aptitude for secular functions. Without being blind admirers either of the French or of the American institutions, we think it clear that the persons and property of citizens are better protected in France and in New England than in almost any society that now exists or that has ever existed ; very much better, certainly, than in the Roman empire under the orthodox rule of Constantine and Theodosius. But neither the government of France, nor that of New England is so organised as to be fit for the propogation of theological doctrines. Nor do we think it improbable that the most serious religious errors might prevail in a state which, considered merely with reference to temporal objects, might approach far nearer than any that has ever been known to the *idea* of what a state should be.

But we shall leave this abstract question and look at the world as we find it. Does, then, the way in which governments generally obtain their power make it at all probable that they will be more favourable to orthodoxy than to hetorodoxy? A nation of barbarians pours down on a rich and unwarlike empire, enslaves the people, portions out the land and blends the institutions which it finds in the cities with those which it has brought from the woods. A handful of daring adventurers from a civilised nation wander to some savage country and reduce the aboriginal race to bondage. A successful general turns his arms against the state which he serves. A society, made brutal by oppression, rises madly on its masters, sweeps away all old laws and usages, and, when its first paroxysm of rage is over, sinks down passively under any form of polity which may spring out of the chaos. A chief of a party, as at Florence, becomes imperceptibly a sovereign and the founder of a dynasty. A captain of mercenaries, as at Milan, seizes on a city, and by the sword makes himself its ruler. An elective senate, as at Venice, usurps permanent and hereditary power. It is in events such as these that governments have generally originated ; and we can see nothing in such events to warrant us in believing that the governments thus called into existence will be peculiarly well fitted to distinguish between religious truth and heresy.

When, again, we look at the constitutions of governments which have become settled, we find no great security for the orthodoxy of rulers. One magistrate holds power because his name was drawn out of a purse ; another, because his father held it before him. There are representative systems of all sorts, large constituent bodies, small constituent bodies, universal suffrage, high pecuniary qualifications. We see that, for the temporal ends of government, some of these constitutions are very skilfully constructed, and that the very worst of them is preferable to anarchy. But it passes our understanding to comprehend what connection any one of them has with theological truth.

And how stands the fact? Have not almost all the governments in the world always been in the wrong on religious subjects ? Mr. Gladstone, we imagine, would say that, except in the time of Constantine, of Jovian and of a very few of their successors, and occasionally in England since the Reformation, no government has ever been sincerely friendly to the pure and apostolical Church of Christ. If, therefore, it be true that every ruler is bound in conscience to use his power for the propogation of his own religion, it will follow that, for one ruler who has been bound in conscience to use his power for the propogation of truth, a thousand have been bound in conscience to use their power for the propagation of falsehoods. Surely this is a conclusion from which common sense recoils. Surely, if experience shows that a certain machine when used to produce a certain effect does not produce that effect once in a thousand times, but produces, in the vast majority of cases, an effect directly contrary, we cannot be wrong in saying that it is not a machine of which the principal end is to be so used.

If, indeed, the magistrate would content himself with laying his opinions and reasons before the people, and would leave the people, uncorrupted by hope or fear, to judge for themselves, we should see little reason to apprehend that his interference in favour of error would be seriously prejudicial to the interests of truth. Nor do we, as will hereafter be seen, object to his taking this course when it is compatible with the efficient discharge of his more especial duties. But this will not satisfy Mr. Gladstone. He would have the magistrate resort to means which have a great tendency to make malcontents, to make hypocrites, to make careless nominal conformists, but no tendency whatever to produce honest and rational conviction. It seems to us quite clear that an inquirer who has no wish except to know the truth is more likely to arrive at the truth than an inquirer who knows that, if he decides one way, he shall be rewarded, and that, if he decides the other way, he shall be punished. Now, Mr. Gladstone would have governments propagate their opinions by excluding all dissenters from all civil offices. That is to say, he would have governments propagate their opinions by a process which has no reference whatever to the truth or falsehood of those opinions, by arbitrarily uniting certain worldly advantages with one set of doctrines and certain worldly inconveniences with another set. It is of the very nature of argument to serve the interests of truth; but if rewards and punishments serve the interests of truth, it is by mere accident. It is very much easier to find arguments for the divine authority of the Gospel than for the divine authority of the Koran. But it is just as easy to bribe or rack a Jew into Mahometanism as into Christianity.

From racks, indeed, and from all penalties directed against the persons, the property and the liberty of heretics, the humane spirit of Mr. Gladstone shrinks with horror. He only maintains that conformity to the religion of the state ought to be an indispensable qualification for office; and he would think it his duty, if he had the power, to revise the Test Act, to enforce it rigorously, and to extend it to important classes who were formerly exempt from its operation.

This is indeed a legitimate consequence of his principles. But why stop here? Why not roast dissenters at slow fires? All the general reasonings, on which this theory rests evidently lead to sanguinary persecution. If the propagation of religious truth be a principal end of government, as government; if it be the duty of a government to employ for that end its constitutional power; if the constitutional power of governments extends, as it most unquestionably does, to the making of laws for the burning of heretics; if burning be, as it most assuredly is in many cases, a most effectual mode of suppressing opinions—why should we not burn? If the relation in which government ought to stand to the people be, as Mr. Gladstone tells us, *a paternal relation*, we are irresistibly led to the conclusion that persecution is justifiable. For the right of propagating opinions by punishment is one which belongs to parents as clearly as the right to give instruction. A boy is compelled to attend family worship: he is forbidden to read irreligious books: if he will not learn his catechism, he is sent to bed without his supper: if he plays truant at church-time, a task is set him. If he should display the precocity of his talents by expressing impious opinions before his brothers and sisters, we should not much blame his father for cutting short the controversy with a horse-whip. All the reasons which lead us to think that parents are peculiarly fitted to conduct the education of their children, and that education is the principal end of a parental relation, lead us also to think that parents ought to be allowed to use punishment, if necessary, for the purpose of forcing children, who are incapable of judging for themselves, to receive religious instruction and to attend religious worship. Why, then, is this prerogative of punishment, so eminently paternal, to be withheld from a paternal government? It seems to us, also, to be the height of absurdity to employ civil disabilities for the propagation of an opinion and then to shrink from employing other punishments for the same purpose. For nothing can be clearer than that, if you punish at all, you ought to punish enough. The pain caused by punishment is pure unmixed evil, and never ought to be inflicted except for the sake of some good. It is mere foolish cruelty to provide penalties which torment the criminal without preventing the crime. Now it is possible, by sanguinary persecution, unrelentingly inflicted, to suppress opinions. In this way the Albigenses were put down. In this way the Lollards were put down. In this way the fair promise of the Reformation was blighted in Italy and Spain. But we may safely defy Mr. Gladstone to point out a single instance in which the system which he recommends has succeeded.

And why should he be so tender-hearted? What reason can he give for hanging a murderer and suffering an heresiarch to escape without even a pecuniary mulct? Is the heresiarch a less pernicious member of society than the murderer? Is not the loss of one soul a greater evil than the extinction of many lives? And the number of murders committed by the most profligate bravo that ever let out his poniard to hire in Italy, or by the most savage buccaneer that ever prowled on the Windward Station, is small indeed when compared with the number of souls which have been caught in the snares of one dexterous heresiarch. If, then, the heresiarch causes infinitely greater evils than the murderer, why is he not as proper an object of penal legislation as the murderer? We can give a reason—a reason, short, simple, decisive and consistent. We do not extenuate the evil which the heresiarch produces, but we say that it is not evil of that sort against which it is the end of government to guard. But how Mr. Gladstone, who considers the evil which the heresiarch produces as evil of the sort against which it is the end of government to guard, can escape from the obvious consequence of his doctrine, we do not understand. The world is full of parallel cases. An orange-woman stops up the pavement with her wheelbarrow and a policeman takes her into custody. A miser who has amassed a million suffers an old friend and benefactor to die in the workhouse, and cannot be questioned before any tribunal for his baseness and ingratitude. Is this because legislators think the orange-woman's conduct worse than the miser's? Not at all. It is because the stopping-up of the pathway is one of the evils against which it is the business of the public authorities to protect society and heartlessness is not one of those evils. It would be the height of folly to say that the miser ought, indeed, to be punished, but that he ought to be punished less severely than the orange-woman.

The heretical Constantius persecutes Athanasius; and why not? Shall Cæsar punish the robber, who has taken one purse and spare the wretch who has taught millions to rob the Creator of His honour and to bestow it on the creature? The orthodox Theodosius persecutes the Arians; and with equal reason. Shall an insult offered to the Cæsarean majesty be expiated by death; and shall there be no penalty for him who degrades to the rank of a creature the Almighty, the infinite Creator? We have a short answer for both: "To Cæsar the things which are Cæsar's." Cæsar is appointed for the punishment of robbers and rebels. He is not appointed for the purpose of either propagating or exterminating the doctrine of the consubstantiality of the Father and the Son. "Not so," says Mr. Gladstone. "Cæsar is bound in conscience to propagate whatever he thinks to be the truth as to this question. Constantius is bound to establish the Arian worship throughout the empire, and to displace the bravest captains of his legions and the ablest ministers of his treasury if they hold the Nicene faith. Theodosius is equally bound to turn out every public servant whom his Arian predecessors have put in. But if Constantius lays on Athanasius a fine of a single *aureus*, if Theodosius imprisons an Arian presbyter for a week, this is most unjustifiable oppression." Our readers will be curious to know how this distinction is made out.

The reasons which Mr. Gladstone gives against persecution affecting life, limb and property may be divided into two classes; first, reasons which can be called reasons only by extreme courtesy, and which nothing but the most deplorable necessity would ever have induced a man of his abilities to use; and secondly, reasons which are really reasons, and which have so much force that they not only completely prove his exception, but completely upset his general rule. His artillery on this occasion is composed of two sorts of pieces, pieces which will not go off at all and pieces which go off with a vengeance and recoil with most crushing effect upon himself.

"We, as fallible creatures," says Mr. Gladstone, "have no right, from any bare speculations of our own, to administer pains and penalties to our fellow-creatures, whether on social or religious grounds. We have the right to enforce the laws of the land by such pains and penalties, because it is expressly given by Him who has declared that the civil rulers are to bear the sword for the punishment of evil-doers and for the encouragement of them that do well. And so, in things spiritual, had it pleased God to give to the Church or the State this power, to be permanently exercised over their members, or mankind at large, we should have the right to use it; but it does not appear to have been so received and, consequently, it should not be exercised."

We should be sorry to think that the security of our lives and property from persecution rested on no better ground than this. Is not a teacher of heresy an evil-doer? Has not heresy been condemned in many countries, and in our own among them, by the laws of the land, which, as Mr. Gladstone says, it is justifiable to enforce by penal sanctions? If a heretic is not specially mentioned in the text to which Mr. Gladstone refers, neither is an assassin, a kidnapper or a highwayman. And, if the silence of the New Testament as to all interference of governments to stop the progress of heresy be a reason for not fining or imprisoning heretics, it is surely just as good a reason for not excluding them from office.

"God," says Mr. Gladstone, "has seen fit to authorise the employment of force in the one case and not in the other; for it was with regard to chastisement inflicted by the sword for an insult offered to himself that the Redeemer declared his kingdom not to be of this world; meaning, apparently in an especial manner, that it should be otherwise than after this world's fashion in respect to the sanctions by which its laws should be maintained."

Now here Mr. Gladstone, quoting from memory, has fallen into an error. The very remarkable words which he cites do not appear to have had any reference to the wound inflicted by Peter on Malchus. They were addressed to Pilate, in answer to the question, "Art thou the King of the Jews?" We cannot help saying that we are surprised that Mr. Gladstone should not have more accurately verified a quotation on which, according to him, principally depends the right of a hundred millions of his fellow-subjects—idolaters, Mussulmans, Catholics and dissenters—to their property, their liberty and their lives.

Mr. Gladstone's interpretations of Scripture are lamentably destitute of one recommendation which he considers as of the highest value: they are by no means in accordance with the general precepts or practice of the Church from the time when the Christians became strong enough to persecute down to a very recent period. A dogma favourable to toleration is certainly not a dogma *quod semper, quod ubique, quod omnibus*. Bossuet was able to say, we fear with too much truth, that on one point all Christians had long been unanimous, the right of the civil magistrate to propagate truth by the sword; that even heretics had been orthodox as to this right, and that the Anabaptists and Socinians were the first who called it in question. We will not pretend to say what is the best explanation of the text under consideration, but we are sure that Mr. Gladstone's is the worst. According to him, government ought to exclude dissenters from office, but not to fine them, because Christ's kingdom is not of this world. We do not see why the line may not be drawn at a hundred other places as well as that which he has chosen. We do not see why Lord Clarendon, in recommending the act of 1664 against conventicles, might not have said, "It hath been thought by some that this *classis* of men might with advantage be not only imprisoned but pilloried. But, methinks, my Lords, we are inhibited from the punishment of the pillory by that Scripture, 'My kingdom is not of this world.'" Archbishop Laud, when he sate on Burton in the Star-Chamber, might have said, "I pronounce for the pillory; and indeed, I could wish that all such wretches were delivered to the fire, but that our Lord hath said that his kingdom is not of this world." And Gardiner might have written to the Sheriff of Oxfordshire: "See that execution be done without fail on Master Ridley and Master Latimer, as you will answer the same to the Queen's grace at your peril. But if they shall desire to have some gunpowder for the shortening of their torment, I see not but you may grant it, as it is written, *Regnum meum non est de hoc mundo;* that is to say, My kingdom is not of this world."

But Mr. Gladstone has other arguments against persecution, arguments which are of so much weight that they are decisive not only against persecution but against his whole theory. "The government," he says, "is incompetent to exercise minute and constant supervision over religious opinion." And hence he infers, that "a government exceeds its province when it comes to adapt a scale of punishments to variations in religious opinion according to their respective degrees of variation from the established creed. To decline affording countenance to sects is a single and simple rule. To punish their professors according to their several errors, even were there no other objection, is one for which the state must assume functions wholly ecclesiastical and for which it is not intrinsically fitted."

This is, in our opinion, quite true. But how does it agree with Mr. Gladstone's theory? What! the government incompetent to exercise even such a degree of supervision over religious opinion as is implied by the punishment of the most deadly heresy! The government incompetent to measure even the grossest deviations from the standard of truth! The government not intrinsically qualified to judge of the comparative enormity of any theological errors! The government so ignorant on these subjects that it is compelled to leave, not merely subtle heresies—discernible only by the eye of a Cyril or a Bucer—but Socinianism, Deism, Mahometanism, Idolatry, Atheism, unpunished! To whom does Mr. Gladstone assign the office of selecting a religion for the state from among hundreds of religions, every one of which lays claim to truth? Even to this same government, which is now pronounced to be so unfit for theological investigations that it cannot venture to punish a man for worshipping a lump of stone with a score of heads and hands. We do not remember ever to have fallen in with a more extraordinary instance of inconsistency. When Mr. Gladstone wishes to prove that the government ought to establish and endow a religion, and to fence it with a Test Act, government is τὸ τᾶν in the moral world. Those who would confine it to secular ends take a low view of its nature. A religion must be attached to its agency, and this religion must be that of the conscience of the governor, or none. It is for the governor to decide between Papists and Protestants, Jansenists and Molinists, Arminians and Calvinists, Episcopalians and Presbyterians, Sabellians and Tritheists, Homoousians and Homoiousians, Nestorians and Eutychians, Monothelites and

Monophysites, Pædobaptists and Anabaptists. It is for him to rejudge the Acts of Nice and Rimini, of Ephesus and Chalcedon, of Constantinople and St. John Lateran, of Trent and Dort. It is for him to arbitrate between the Greek and the Latin procession, and to determine whether that mysterious *filioque* shall or shall not have a place in the national creed. When he has made up his mind, he is to tax the whole community in order to pay people to teach his opinion, whatever it may be. He is to rely on his own judgment, though it may be opposed to that of nine-tenths of the society. He is to act on his own judgment, at the risk of exciting the most formidable discontents. He is to inflict, perhaps on a great majority of the population, what, whether Mr. Gladstone may choose to call it persecution or not, will always be felt as persecution by those who suffer it. He is, on account of differences often too slight for vulgar comprehension, to deprive the state of the services of the ablest men. He is to debase and enfeeble the community which he governs from a Empire into a sect. In our own country, for example, millions of Catholics, millions of Protestant Dissenters, are to be excluded from all power and honours. A great hostile fleet is on the sea, but Nelson is not to command in the Channel if in the mystery of the Trinity he confounds the persons. An invading army has landed in Kent, but the Duke of Wellington is not to be at the head of our forces if he divides the substance. And after all this, Mr. Gladstone tells us that it would be wrong to imprison a Jew, a Mussulman or a Buddhist for a day, because really a government cannot understand these matters, and ought not to meddle with questions which belong to the Church. A singular theologian, indeed, this government! So learned that it is competent to exclude Grotius from office for being a Semi-Pelagian, so unlearned that it is incompetent to fine a Hindoo peasant a rupee for going on a pilgrimage to Juggernaut.

"To solicit and persuade one another," says Mr. Gladstone, "are privileges which belong to us all; and the wiser and better man is bound to advise the less wise and good; but he is not only not bound, he is not allowed, speaking generally, to coerce him. It is untrue, then, that the same considerations which bind a government to submit a religion to the free choice of the people would therefore justify their enforcing its adoption."

Granted. But it is true that all the same considerations which would justify a government in propagating a religion by means of civil disabilities would justify the propagating of that religion by penal laws. To solicit! Is it solicitation to tell a Catholic duke that he must abjure his religion, or walk out of the House of Lords? To persuade! Is it persuasion to tell a barrister of distinguished eloquence and learning that he shall grow old in his stuff gown, while his pupils are seated above him, in ermine, because he cannot digest the damnatory clauses of the Athanasian creed? Would Mr. Gladstone think that a religious system which he considers as false—Socinianism for example—was submitted to his free choice if it were submitted in these terms? "If you obstinately adhere to the faith of the Nicene fathers, you shall not be burnt in Smithfield; you shall not be sent to Dorchester gaol; you shall not even pay double land-tax. But you shall be shut out from all situations in which you might exercise your talents with honour to yourself and advantage to the country. The House of Commons, the bench of magistracy, are not for such as you. You shall see younger men, your inferiors in station and talents, rise to the highest dignities and attract the gaze of nations, while you are doomed to neglect and obscurity. If you have a son of the highest promise—a son such as other fathers would contemplate with delight—the development of his fine talents and of his generous ambition shall be a torture to you. You shall look on him as a being doomed to lead, as you have led, the abject life of a Roman or a Neapolitan in the midst of the great English people. All those high honours, so much more precious than the most costly gifts of despots, with which a free country decorates its illustrious citizens, shall be to him, as they have been to you, objects not of hope and virtuous emulation, but of hopeless, envious pining. Educate him, if you wish him to feel his degradation. Educate him, if you wish to stimulate his craving for what he never must enjoy. Educate him, if you would imitate the barbarity of that Celtic tyrant who fed his prisoners on salted food till they called eagerly for drink, and then let down an empty cup into the dungeon and left them to die of thirst." Is this to solicit, to persuade, to submit religion to the free choice of man? Would a fine of a thousand pounds—would imprisonment in Newgate for six months, under circumstances not disgraceful—give Mr. Gladstone the pain which he would feel if he were to be told that he was to be dealt with in the way in which he would himself deal with more than one half of his countrymen?

We are not at all surprised to find such inconsistency even in a man of Mr. Gladstone's talents. The truth is, that every man is, to a great extent, the creature of the age. It is to no purpose that he resists the influence which the vast mass, in which he is but an atom, must exercise on him. He may try to be a man of the tenth century: but he cannot. Whether he will or not, he must be a man of the nineteenth century. He shares in the motion of the moral as well as in that of the physical world. He can no more be as intolerant as he would have been in the days of the Tudors than he can stand in the evening exactly where he stood in the morning. The globe goes round from west to east; and he must go round with it. When he says that he is where he was, he means only that he has moved at the same rate with all around him. When he says that he has gone a good way to the westward, he means only that he has not gone to the eastward quite so rapidly as his neighbours. Mr. Gladstone's book is, in this respect, a very gratifying performance. It is the measure of what a man can do to be left behind by the world. It is the strenuous effort of a very vigorous mind to keep as far in the rear of the general progress as possible. And yet, with the most intense exertion, Mr. Gladstone cannot help being, on some important points, greatly in advance of Locke himself; and, with whatever admiration he may regard Laud; it is well for him, we can tell him, that he did not write in the days of that zealous primate, who would certainly have refuted the expositions of Scripture which we have quoted by one of the keenest arguments that can be addressed to human ears.

This is not the only instance in which Mr. Gladstone has shrunk in a very remarkable manner from the consequences of his own theory. If there be in the whole world a state to which this theory is applicable, that state is the British Empire in India. Even we, who detest paternal governments in general, shall admit that the duties of the government of India are, to a considerable extent, paternal. There, the superiority of the governors to the governed in moral science is unquestionable. The conversion of the whole people to the worst form that Christianity ever wore in the darkest ages would be a most happy event. It is not necessary that a man should be a Christian to wish for the propagation of Christianity in India. It is sufficient that he should be an European not much below the ordinary European level of good sense and humanity. Compare with the importance of the interests at stake, all those Scotch and Irish questions which occupy so large a portion of Mr. Gladstone's book, sink into insignificance. In no part of the world since the days of Theodosius has so large a heathen population been subject to a Christian government. In no part of the world is heathenism more cruel, more licentious, more fruitful of absurd rites and pernicious laws. Surely, if it be the duty of government to use its power and its revenue in order to bring seven millions of Irish Catholics over to the Protestant Church, it is *a fortiori* the duty of the government to use its power and its revenue in order to make seventy millions of idolaters Christians. If it be a sin to suffer John Howard or William Penn to hold any office in England because they are not in communion with the Established Church, surely it must be a crying sin indeed to admit to high situations men who bow down, in temples covered with emblems of vice, to the hideous images of sensual or malevolent gods.

But no. Orthodoxy, it seems, is more shocked by the priests of Rome than by the priests of Kalee. The plain red brick building, Adullam's Cave or Ebenezer Chapel—where uneducated men hear a half-educated man talk of the Christian law of love and the Christian hope of glory—is unworthy of the indulgence which is reserved for the shrine where the Thug suspends a portion of the spoils of murdered travellers and for the car which grinds its way through the bones of self-immolated pilgrims. "It would be," says Mr. Gladstone, "an absurd exaggeration to maintain it as the part of such a government as that of the British in India to bring home to the door of every subject at once the ministrations of a new and totally unknown religion." The government ought indeed to desire to propagate Christianity. But the extent to which they must do so must be "limited by the degree in which the people are found willing to receive it." He proposes no such limitation in the case of Ireland. He would give the Irish a Protestant Church whether they like it or not. "We believe," says he, "that that which we place before them is, whether they know it or not, calculated to be beneficial to them ; and that, if they know it not now, they will know it when it is presented to them fairly. Shall we, then, purchase their applause at the expense of their substantial, nay, their spiritual, interests?"

And why does Mr. Gladstone allow to the Hindoo a privilege which he denies to the Irishman ? Why does he reserve his greatest liberality for the most monstrous errors ? Why does he pay most respect to the opinion of the least enlightened people ? Why does he withhold the right to exercise paternal authority from that one government which is fitter to exercise paternal authority than any government that ever existed in the world ? We will give the reason in his own words.

"In British India," he says, "a small number of persons advanced to a higher grade of civilisation exercise the powers of government over an immensely greater number of less cultivated persons, not by coercion, but under free stipulation with the governed. Now, the rights of a government, in circumstances thus peculiar, obviously depend neither upon the unrestricted theory of paternal principles, nor upon any primordial or fictitious contract of indefinite powers, but upon an express and known treaty ; matter of positive agreement, not of natural ordinance."

Where Mr. Gladstone has seen this treaty we cannot guess ; for, though he calls it a "known treaty," we will stake our credit that it is quite unknown both at Calcutta and Madras, both in Leadenhall Street and Cannon Row— that it is not be found in any of the enormous folios of papers relating to India which fill the bookcases of members of Parliament—that it has utterly escaped the researches of all the historians of our Eastern empire—that in the long and interesting debates of 1813 on the admission of missionaries to India, debates of which the most valuable part has been excellently preserved by the care of the speakers, no allusion to this important instrument is to be found. The truth is that this treaty is a nonentity. It is by coercion, it is by the sword, and not by free stipulation with the governed, that England rules India ; nor is England bound by any contract whatever not to deal with Bengal as she deals with Ireland. She may set up a Bishop of Patna and a Dean of Hoogley; she may grant away the public revenue for the maintenance of prebendaries of Benares and canons of Moorshedabad; she may divide the country into parishes and place a rector with a stipend in every one of them; and all this without infringing any positive agreement. If there be such a treaty, Mr. Gladstone can have no difficulty in making known its date, its terms and, above all, the precise extent of the territory within which we have sinfully bound ourselves to be guilty of practical atheism. The last point is of great importance. For, as the provinces of our Indian empire were acquired at different times and in very different ways, no single treaty, indeed no ten treaties, will justify the system pursued by our government there.

The plain state of the case is this: No man in his senses would dream of applying Mr. Gladstone's theory to India; because, if so applied, it would inevitably destroy our empire, and, with our empire, the best chance of spreading Christianity among the natives. This Mr. Gladstone felt. In some way or other his theory was to be saved and the monstrous consequences avoided. Of intentional misrepresentation we are quite sure that he is incapable. But we cannot acquit him of that unconscious disingenuousness from which the most upright man, when strongly attached to an opinion, is seldom wholly free. We believe that he recoiled from the ruinous consequences which his system would produce if tried in India, but that he did not like to say so lest he should lay himself open to the charge of sacrificing principle to expediency, a word which is held in the utmost abhorrence by all his school. Accordingly, he caught at the notion of a treaty—a notion which must, we think, have originated in some rhetorical expression which he has imperfectly understood. There is one excellent way of avoiding the drawing of a false conclusion from a false *major*, and that is by having a false *minor*. Inaccurate history is an admirable corrective of unreasonable theory. And thus it is in the present case. A bad general rule is laid down and obstinately maintained wherever the consequences are not too monstrous for human bigotry. But when they become so horrible that even Christ Church shrinks—that even Oriel stands aghast—the rule is evaded by means of a fictitious contract. One imaginary obligation is set up against another. Mr. Gladstone first preaches to governments the duty of undertaking an enterprise just as rational as the Crusades and then dispenses them from it on the ground of a treaty which is just as authentic as the donation of Constantine to Pope Sylvester. His system resembles nothing so much as a forged bond with a forged release indorsed on the back of it.

With more show of reason he rests the claims of the Scotch Church on a contract. He considers that contract, however, as most unjustifiable, and speaks of the setting up of the Kirk as a disgraceful blot on the reign of William the Third. Surely it would be amusing, if it were not melancholy, to see a man of virtue and abilities unsatisfied with the calamities which one Church, constituted on false principles, has brought upon the empire, and repining that Scotland is not in the same state with Ireland—that no Scottish agitator is raising rent and putting county members in and out—that no Presbyterian association is dividing supreme power with the government—that no meetings of precursors and repealers are covering the side of the Calton Hill —that twenty-five thousand troops are not required to maintain order on the north of the Tweed—that the anniversary of the Battle of Bothwell Bridge is not regularly celebrated by insult, riot and murder. We could hardly find a stronger argument against Mr. Gladstone's system than that which Scotland furnishes. The policy which has been followed in that country has been directly opposed to the policy which he recommends. And the consequence is that Scotland, having been one of the rudest, one of the poorest, one of the most turbulent countries in Europe, has become one of the most highly civilised, one of the most flourishing, one of the most tranquil. The atrocities which were of common occurrence while an unpopular church was dominant are unknown. In spite of a mutual aversion, as bitter as ever separated one people from another, the two kingdoms which compose our island have been indissolubly joined together. Of the ancient national feeling there remains just enough to be ornamental and useful; just enough to inspire the poet and to kindle a generous and friendly emulation in the bosom of the soldier. But for all the ends of government the nations are one. And why are they so? The answer is simple. The nations are one for all the ends of government because in their union the true ends of government alone were kept in sight. The nations are one because the Churches are two.

Such is the union of England with Scotland; a union which resembles the union of the limbs of one healthful and vigorous body, all moved by one will, all co-operating for common ends. The system of Mr. Gladstone would have produced a union which can be compared only to that which is the subject of a wild Persian fable. King Zohak—we tell the story as Mr. Southey tells it to us—gave the devil leave to kiss his shoulders. Instantly two serpents sprang out who, in the fury of hunger, attacked his head and attempted to get at his brain. Zohak pulled them away and tore them with his nails. But he found that they were inseparable parts of himself and that what he was lacerating was his own flesh. Perhaps we might be able to find, if we looked round the world, some political union like this—some hideous monster of a state, cursed with one principle of sensation and two principles of volition—self-loathing and self-torturing—made up of parts which are driven by a frantic impulse to inflict mutual pain, yet are doomed to feel whatever they inflict; which are divided by an irreconcileable hatred, yet are blended in an indissoluble identity. Mr. Gladstone, from his tender concern for Zohak, is unsatisfied because the devil has as yet kissed only one shoulder—because there is not a snake mangling and mangled on the left to keep in countenance his brother on the right.

But we must proceed in our examination of his theory. Having, as he conceives, proved that it is the duty of every government to profess some religion or other, right or wrong, and to establish that religion, he then comes to the question, what religion a government ought to prefer; and he decides this question in favour of the form of Christianity established in England. The Church of England is, according to him, the pure Catholic Church of Christ, which possesses the apostolical succession of ministers, and within whose pale is to be found that unity which is essential to truth. For her decisions he claims a degree of reverence far beyond what she has ever, in any of her formularies, claimed for herself; far beyond what the moderate school of Bossuet demands for the Pope: and scarcely short of what the most bigoted Catholic would ascribe to Pope and General Council together. To separate from her communion is schism. To reject her traditions or interpretations of Scripture is sinful presumption.

Mr. Gladstone pronounces the right of private judgment, as it is generally understood throughout Protestant Europe, to be a monstrous abuse. He declares himself favourable, indeed, to the exercise of private judgment after a fashion of his own. We have, according to him, a right to judge all the doctrines of the Church of England to be sound, but not to judge any of them to be unsound. He has no objection, he assures us, to active inquiry into religious questions; on the contrary, he thinks such inquiry highly desirable as long as it does not lead to diversity of opinion—which is much the same thing as if he were to recommend the use of fire that will not burn down houses, or of brandy that will not make men drunk. He conceives it to be perfectly possible for mankind to exercise their intellects vigorously and freely on theological subjects, and yet to come to exactly the same conclusions with each other and with the Church of England. And for this opinion he gives, as far as we have been able to discover, no reason whatever, except that everybody who vigorously and freely exercises his understanding on Euclid's Theorems assents to them. "The activity of private judgment," he truly observes, "and the unity and strength of conviction in mathematics vary directly as each other." On this unquestionable fact he constructs a somewhat questionable argument. Everybody who freely inquires agrees, he says, with Euclid. But the Church is as much in the right as Euclid. Why, then, should not every free inquirer agree with the Church? We could put many similar questions. Either the affirmative or the negative of the proposition that King Charles wrote the "Icon Basilike" is as true as that two sides of a triangle are greater than the third side. Why, then, do Dr. Wordsworth and Mr. Hallam agree in thinking two sides of a triangle greater than the third side and yet differ about the genuineness of the "Icon Basilike"? The state of the exact sciences proves, says Mr. Gladstone, that, as respects religion, "the association of these two ideas, activity of inquiry and variety of conclusion, is a fallacious one." We might just as well turn the argument the other way, and infer from the variety of religious opinions that there must necessarily be hostile mathematical sects; some affirming and some denying that the square of the hypothenuse is equal to the squares of the sides. But we no not think either the one analogy or the other of the smallest value. Our way of ascertaining the tendency of free inquiry is simply to open our eyes and look at the world in which we live; and there we see that free inquiry on mathematical subjects produces unity, and that free inquiry on moral subjects produces discrepancy. There would undoubtedly be less discrepancy if inquirers were more diligent and candid. But discrepancy there will be among the most diligent and candid as long as the constitution of the human mind and the nature of moral evidence continue unchanged. That we have not freedom and unity together is a very sad thing; and so it is that we have not wings. But we are just as likely to see the one defect removed as the other. It is not only in religion that this discrepancy is found. It is the same with all matters which depend on moral evidence—with judicial questions, for example, and with political questions. All the judges may work a sum in the rule of three on the same principle and bring out the same conclusion. But it does not follow that, however honest and laborious they may be, they will all be of one mind on the Douglas case. So it is vain to hope that there may be a free constitution under which every representative will be unanimously elected and every law unanimously passed; and it would be ridiculous for a statesman to stand wondering and bemoaning himself because people, who agree in thinking that two and two make four, cannot agree about the new poor law, or the administration of Canada.

There are two intelligible and consistent courses which may be followed with respect to the exercise of private judgment; that of the Romanist, who interdicts it because of its inevitable inconveniences; and the course of the Protestant, who permits it in spite of its inevitable inconveniences. Both are more reasonable than Mr. Gladstone, who would have free private judgment without its inevitable inconveniences. The Romanist produces repose by means of stupefaction. The Protestant encourages activity, though he knows that where there is much activity there will be some aberration. Mr. Gladstone wishes for the unity of the fifteenth century with the active and searching spirit of the sixteenth. He might as well wish to be in two places at once.

When Mr. Gladstone says that we "actually require discrepancy of opinion—require and demand error, falsehood, blindness—and plume ourselves on such discrepancy as attesting a freedom which is only valuable when used for unity in the truth," he expresses himself with more energy than precision. Nobody loves discrepancy for the sake of discrepancy. But a person who conscientiously believes that free inquiry is, on the whole, beneficial to the interests of truth—and that, from the imperfections of the human faculties, wherever there is much free inquiry there will be some discrepancy—may, without impropriety, consider such discrepancy, though in itself an evil, as a sign of good. That there are fifty thousand thieves in London is a very melancholy fact. But, looked at in one point of view, it is a reason for exultation. For what other city could maintain fifty thousand thieves? What must be the mass of wealth, where the fragments gleaned by lawless pilfering rise to so large an amount? St. Kilda would not support a single pickpocket. The quantity of theft is, to a certain extent, an index of the quantity of useful industry and judicious speculation. And just as we may, from the great number of rogues in a town, infer that much honest gain is made there, so may we often, from the quantity of error in a community, draw a cheering inference as to the degree in which the public mind is turned to those inquiries which alone can lead to rational convictions of truth.

Mr. Gladstone seems to imagine that most Protestants think it possible for the same doctrine to be at once true and false; or that they think it immaterial whether, on a religious question, a man comes to a true or a false conclusion. If there be any Protestants who hold notions so absurd, we abandon them to his censure.

The Protestant doctrine touching the right of private judgment—that doctrine which is the common foundation of the Anglican, the Lutheran and the Calvinistic Churches—that doctrine by which every sect of dissenters vindicates its separation—we conceive not to be this, that opposite opinions may both be true; nor this, that truth and falsehood are both equally good; nor yet this, that all speculative error is necessarily innocent—but this, that there is on the face of the earth no visible body to whose decrees men are bound to submit their private judgment on points of faith.

Is there always such a visible body? Was there such a visible body in the year 1500? If not, why are we to believe that there is such a body in the year 1839? If there was such a body in 1500, what was it? Was it the Church of Rome? And how can the Church of England be orthodox now if the Church of Rome was orthodox then?

"In England," says Mr. Gladstone, "the case was widely different from that of the Continent. Her reformation did not destroy, but successfully maintained, the unity and succession of the Church in her apostolical ministry. We have, therefore, still among us the ordained hereditary witnesses of the truth, conveying it to us through an unbroken series from our Lord Jesus Christ and his Apostles. This is to us the ordinary voice of authority; of authority equally reasonable and equally true, whether we will hear, or whether we will forbear."

Mr. Gladstone's reasoning is not so clear as might be desired. We have among us, he says, ordained hereditary witnesses of the truth, and their voice is to us the voice of authority. Undoubtedly, if they are witnesses of the truth, their voice is the voice of authority. But this is little more than saying that the truth is the truth. Nor is truth more true because it comes in an unbroken series from the Apostles. The Nicene faith is not more true in the mouth of the Archbishop of Canterbury than in that of a Moderator of the General Assembly. If our respect for the authority of the Church is to be only consequent upon our conviction of the truth of her doctrines, we come at once to that monstrous abuse—the Protestant exercise of private judgment. But, if Mr. Gladstone means that we ought to believe that the Church of England speaks the truth because she has the apostolical succession, we greatly doubt whether such a doctrine can be maintained. In the first place, what proof have we of the fact? We have, indeed, heard it said that Providence would certainly have interfered to preserve the apostolical succession in the true Church. But this is an argument fitted for understandings of a different kind from Mr. Gladstone's. He will hardly tell us that the Church of England is the true Church because she has the succession, and that she has the succession because she is the true Church.

What evidence, then, have we for the fact of the apostolical succession? And here we may easily defend the truth against Oxford with the same arguments with which, in old times, the truth was defended by Oxford against Rome. In this stage of our combat with Mr. Gladstone, we need few weapons except those which we find in the well-furnished and well-ordered armoury of Chillingworth.

The transmission of orders from the Apostles to an English clergyman of the present day must have been through a very great number of intermediate persons. Now, it is probable that no Clergyman in the Church of England can trace up his spiritual genealogy from bishop to bishop even so far back as the time of the Reformation. There remains fifteen or sixteen hundred years during which the history of the transmission of his orders is buried in utter darkness. And whether he be a priest by succession from the Apostles depends on the question whether, during that long period, some thousands of events took place, any one of which may, without any gross improbability, be supposed not to have taken place. We have not a tittle of evidence for any one of these events. We do not even know the names or countries of the men to whom it is taken for granted that these events happened. We do not know whether the spiritual ancestors of any one of our contemporaries were Spanish or Armenian, Arian or Orthodox. In the utter absence of all particular evidence, we are surely entitled to require that there should be very strong evidence indeed that the strictest regularity was observed in every generation and that episcopal functions were exercised by none who were not bishops by succession from the Apostles. But we have no such evidence. In the first place, we have not full and accurate information touching the polity of the Church during the century which followed the persecution of Nero. That during this period the overseers of all the little Christian societies scattered through the Roman empire held their spiritual authority by virtue of holy orders derived from the Apostles, cannot be proved by contemporary testimony, or by any testimony which can be regarded as decisive. The question, whether the primitive ecclesiastical constitution bore a greater resemblance to the Anglican or to the Calvinistic model, has been fiercely disputed. It is a question on which men of eminent parts, learning and piety have differed, and do to this day differ very widely. It is a question on which at least a full half of the ability and erudition of Protestant Europe has, ever since the Reformation, been opposed to the Anglican pretensions. Mr. Gladstone himself, we are persuaded, would have the candour to allow that, if no evidence were admitted but that which is furnished by the genuine Christian literature of the first two centuries, judgment would not go in favour of prelacy. And, if he looked at the subject as calmly as he would look at a controversy respecting the Roman *Comitia* or the Anglo-Saxon Wittenagemote, he would probably think that the absence of contemporary evidence during so long a period was a defect which later attestations, however numerous, could but very imperfectly supply. It is surely impolitic to rest the doctrines of the English Church on a historical theory which, to ninety-nine Protestants out of a hundred, would seem much more questionable than any of those doctrines. Nor is this all. Extreme obscurity overhangs the history of the middle ages; and the facts which are discernible through that obscurity prove that the Church was exceedingly ill regulated. We read of sees of the highest dignity openly sold—transferred backwards and forwards by popular tumult—bestowed sometimes by a profligate woman on her paramour—sometimes by a warlike baron on a kinsman, still a stripling. We read of bishops of ten years old—of bishops of five years old—of many popes who were mere boys, and who rivalled the frantic dissoluteness of Caligula—nay, of a female pope. And though this last story, once believed throughout all Europe, has been disproved by the strict researches of modern criticism, the most discerning of those who reject it have admitted that it is not intrinsically improbable. In our own island, it was the complaint of Alfred that not a single priest south of the Thames, and very few on the north, could read either Latin or English. And this illiterate clergy exercised their ministry amidst a rude and half-heathen population, in which Danish pirates, unchristened, or christened by the hundred on a field of battle, were mingled with a Saxon peasantry scarcely better instructed in religion. The state of Ireland was still worse. "Tota illa per universam Hiberniam dissolutio ecclesiasticæ disciplinæ, illa ubique pro consuetudine Christiana sæva subintroducta barbaries"—are the expressions of St. Bernard. We are, therefore, at a loss to conceive how any clergyman can feel confident that his orders have come down correctly. Whether he be really a successor of the Apostles depends on an immense number of such contingencies as these—whether, under King Ethelwolf, a stupid priest might not, while baptising several scores of Danish prisoners who had just made their option between the font and the gallows, inadvertently omit to perform the rite on one of these graceless proselytes? whether, in the seventh century, an impostor, who had never received consecration, might not have passed himself off as a bishop on a rude tribe of Scots? whether a lad of twelve did really, by a ceremony huddled over when he was too drunk to know what he was about, convey the episcopal character to a lad of ten?

Since the first century, not less, in all probability, than a hundred thousand persons have exercised the functions of bishops. That many of these have not been bishops by apostolical succession is quite certain. Hooker admits that deviations from the general rule have been frequent; and, with a boldness worthy of his high and statesman-like intellect, pronounces them to have been often justifiable. "There may be," says he, "sometimes very just and sufficient reason to allow ordination made without a bishop. Where the Church must needs have some ordained, and neither hath nor can have possibly a bishop to ordain, in case of such necessity the ordinary institution of God hath given *oftentimes*, and may give place. And therefore we are not simply without exception to urge a lineal descent of power from the Apostles by continued succession of bishops in every effectual ordination." There can be little doubt, we think, that the succession, if it ever existed, has often been interrupted in ways much less respectable. For example, let us suppose—and we are sure that no well-informed person will think the supposition by any means improbable—that, in the third century, a man of no principle and some parts, who has, in the course of a roving and discreditable life, been a catechumen at Antioch and has there become familiar with Christian usages and doctrines, afterwards rambles to Marseilles, where he finds a Christian society, rich, liberal and simple-hearted. He pretends to be a Christian, attracts notice by his abilities and affected zeal, and is raised to the episcopal dignity without having ever been baptised. That such an event might happen, nay, was very likely to happen, cannot well be disputed by anyone who has read the "Life of Peregrinus." The very virtues, indeed, which distinguished the early Christians, seem to have laid them open to those arts which deceived

> "Uriel, though Regent of the Sun, and held
> The sharpest-sighted spirit of all in Heaven."

Now, this unbaptised impostor is evidently no successor of the Apostles. He is not even a Christian; and all orders derived through such a pretended bishop are altogether invalid. Do we know enough of the state of the world and of the Church in the third century to be able to say with confidence that there were not at that time twenty such pretended bishops? Every such case makes a break in the apostolical succession.

Now, suppose that a break, such as Hooker admits to have been both common and justifiable, or such as we have supposed to be produced by hypocrisy and cupidity, were found in the chain which connected the Apostles with any of the missionaries who first spread Christianity in the wilder parts of Europe—who can say how extensive the effect of this single break may be? Suppose that St. Patrick, for example, if ever there was such a man, or Theodore of Tarsus, who is said to have consecrated in the seventh century the first bishops of many English sees, had not the true apostolical orders, is it not conceivable that such a circumstance may affect the orders of many clergymen now living? Even if it were possible, which it assuredly is not, to prove that the Church had the apostolical orders in the third century, it would be impossible to prove that those orders were not in the twelfth century so far lost that no ecclesiastic could be certain of the legitimate descent of his own spiritual character. And if this were so, no subsequent precautions could repair the evil.

Chillingworth states the conclusion at which he had arrived on this subject in these very remarkable words: "That of ten thousand probables no one should be false; that of ten thousand requisites, whereof anyone may fail, not one should be wanting, this to me is extremely improbable and even cousin-german to impossible. So that the assurance hereof is like a machine composed of an innumerable multitude of pieces, of which it is strangely unlikely but some will be out of order, and yet, if anyone be so, the whole fabric falls of necessity to the ground: and he that shall put them together, and maturely consider all the possible ways of lapsing and nullifying a priesthood in the Church of Rome, will be very inclinable to think that it is a hundred to one that, among a hundred seeming priests, there is not one true one; nay, that is not a thing very improbable that, amongst those many millions which make up the Romish hierarchy, there are not twenty true." We do not pretend to know to what precise extent the canonists of Oxford agree with those of Rome as to the circumstances which nullify orders. We will not, therefore, go so far as Chillingworth. We only say that we see no satisfactory proof of the fact that the Church of England possesses the apostolical succession. And, after all, if Mr. Gladstone could prove the apostolical succession, what would the apostolical succession prove? He says that "we have among us the ordained heriditary witnesses of the truth, conveying it to us through an *unbroken* series from our Lord Jesus Christ and his Apostles." Is this the fact? Is there any doubt that the orders of the Church of England are generally derived from the Church of Rome? Does not the Church of England declare, does not Mr. Gladstone himself admit, that the Church of Rome teaches much error and condemns much truth? And is it not quite clear that, as far as the doctrines of the Church of England differ from those of the Church of Rome, so far the Church of England conveys the truth through a *broken* series?

That the Reformers, lay and clerical, of the Church of England, corrected all that required correction in the doctrines of the Church of Rome, and nothing more, may be quite true. But we never can admit the circumstance that the Church of England possesses the apostolical succession as a proof that she is thus perfect. No stream can rise higher than its fountain. The succession of ministers in the Church of England, derived as it is through the Church of Rome, can never prove more for the Church of England than it proves for the Church of Rome. But this is not all. The Arian Churches, which once predominated in the kingdoms of the Ostrogoths, the Visigoths, the Burgundians, the Vandals and the Lombards, were all episcopal churches, and all had a fairer claim than that of England to the apostolical succession, as being much nearer to the apostolical times. In the East, the Greek Church, which is at variance on points of faith with all the Western Churches, has an equal claim to this succession. The Nestorian, the Eutychian, the Jacobite Churches; all heretical, all condemned by councils of which even Protestant divines have generally spoken with respect; had an equal claim to the apostolical succession. Now if, of teachers having apostolical orders, a vast majority have taught much error—if a large proportion have taught deadly heresy—if, on the other hand, as Mr. Gladstone himself admits, churches not having apostolical orders—that of Scotland for example—have been nearer to the standard of orthodoxy than the majority of teachers who have had apostolical orders—how can he possibly call upon us to submit our private judgment to the authority of a Church on the ground that she has these orders?

Mr. Gladstone dwells much on the importance of unity in doctrine. Unity, he tells us, is essential to truth. And this is most unquestionable. But when he goes on to tell us that this unity is the characteristic of the Church of England, that she is one in body and in spirit, we are compelled to differ from him widely. The apostolical succession she may or may not have. But unity she most certainly has not, and never has had. It is matter of perfect notoriety that her formularies are framed in such a manner as to admit to her highest offices men who differ from each other more widely than a very high Churchman differs from a Catholic, or a very low Churchman from a Presbyterian; and that the general leaning of the Church, with respect to some important questions, has been sometimes one way and sometimes another. Take, for example, the questions agitated between the Calvinists and the Arminians. Do we find in the Church of England, with respect to those questions, that unity which is essential to truth? Was it ever found in the Church? Is it not certain that at the end of the sixteenth century the rulers of the Church held doctrines as Calvinistic as ever were held by any Cameronian, and not only held them, but persecuted everybody who did not hold them? And is it not equally certain that the rulers of the Church have, in very recent times, considered Calvinism as a disqualification for high preferment, if not for holy orders? Look at Archbishop Whitgift's Lambeth Articles—Articles in which the doctrine of reprobation is affirmed in terms strong enough for William Huntington, S. S. And then look at the eighty-seven questions which Bishop Marsh, within our own memory, propounded to candidates for ordination. We should be loth to say that either of these celebrated prelates had intruded into a Church whose doctrines he abhorred, and deserved to be stripped of his gown. Yet it is quite certain that one or other of them must have been very greatly in error. John Wesley again, and Cowper's friend, John Newton, were both Presbyters of this Church. Both were men of talent. Both we believe to have been men of rigid integrity—

men who would not have subscribed a Confession of Faith which they disbelieved for the richest bishopric in the empire. Yet, on the subject of predestination, Newton was strongly attached to doctrines which Wesley designated as "blasphemy which might make the ears of a Christian to tingle." Indeed, it will not be disputed that the clergy of the Established Church are divided as to these questions, and that her formularies are not found practically to exclude even scrupulously honest men of both sides from her altars. It is notorious that some of her most distinguished rulers think this latitude a good thing and would be sorry to see it restricted in favour of either opinion. And herein we most cordially agree with them. But what becomes of the unity of the Church and of that truth to which unity is essential? Mr. Gladstone tells us that the *Regium Donum* was given originally to orthodox Presbyterian ministers, but that part of it is now received by their heterodox successors. "This," he says, "serves to illustrate the difficulty in which governments entangle themselves when they covenant with arbitrary systems of opinion and not with the Church alone. The opinion passes away, but the gift remains." But is it not clear that if a strong Supralapsan had, under Whitgift's primacy, left a large estate at the disposal of the bishops for ecclesiastical purposes, in the hope that the rulers of the Church would abide by the Lambeth Articles, he would really have been giving his substance for the support of doctrines which he detested? The opinion would have passed away and the gift would have remained.

This is only a single instance. What wide differences of opinion respecting the operation of the sacraments are held by bishops and presbyters of the Church of England—all men who have conscientiously declared their assent to her articles—all men who are, according to Mr. Gladstone, ordained hereditary witnesses of the truth—all men whose voices make up what, he tells us, is the voice of true and reasonable authority! Here, again, the Church has not unity; and as unity is the essential condition of truth, the Church has not the truth.

Nay, take the very question which we are discussing with Mr. Gladstone. To what extent does the Church of England allow of the right of private judgment? What degree of authority does she claim for herself in virtue of the apostolical succession of her ministers? Mr. Gladstone, a very able and a very honest man, takes a view of this matter widely differing from the view taken by others whom he will admit to be as able and as honest as himself. People who altogether dissent from him on this subject eat the bread of the Church, preach in her pulpits, dispense her sacraments, confer her orders and carry on that apostolical succession, the nature and importance of which, according to him, they do not comprehend. Is this unity? Is this truth?

It will be observed that we are not putting cases of dishonest men, who, for the sake of lucre, falsely pretend to believe in the doctrines of an establishment. We are putting cases of men as upright as ever lived, who, differing on theological questions of the highest importance and avowing that difference, are yet priests and prelates of the same Church. We therefore say that, on some points which Mr. Gladstone himself thinks of vital importance, the Church has either not spoken at all, or, what is for all practical purposes the same thing, has not spoken in language to be understood even by honest and sagacious divines. The religion of the Church of England is so far from exhibiting that unity of doctrine which Mr. Gladstone represents as her distinguishing glory, that it is, in fact, a bundle of religious systems without number. It comprises the religious system of Bishop Tomline and the religious system of John Newton, and all the religious systems which lie between them. It comprises the religious system of Mr. Newman and the religious system of the Archbishop of Dublin, and all the religious systems which lie between them. All these different opinions are held, avowed, preached, printed within the pale of the Church by men of unquestioned integrity and understanding.

Do we make this diversity a topic of reproach to the Church of England? Far from it. We would oppose with all our power every attempt to narrow her basis. Would to God that a hundred and fifty years ago a good king and a good primate had possessed the power as well as the will to widen it! It was a noble enterprise, worthy of William and of Tillotson. But what becomes of all Mr. Gladstone's eloquent exhortations to unity? Is it not mere mockery to attach so much importance to unity in form and name, where there is so little in substance—to shudder at the thought of two churches in alliance with one state and to endure with patience the spectacle of a hundred sects battling within one church? And is it not clear that Mr. Gladstone is bound, on all his own principles, to abandon the defence of a church in which unity is not found? Is it not clear that he is bound to divide the House of Commons against every grant of money which may be proposed for the clergy of the Established Church in the Colonies? He objects to the vote for Maynooth because it is monstrous to pay one man to teach truth and another to denounce that truth as falsehood. But it is a mere chance whether any sum which he votes for the English Church in any dependency will go to the maintenance of an Arminian or a Calvinist, of a man like Mr. Froude or of a man like Dr. Arnold. It is a mere chance, therefore, whether it will go to support a teacher of truth or one who will denounce that truth as falsehood.

This argument seems to us at once to dispose of all that part of Mr. Gladstone's book which respects grants of public money to dissenting bodies. All such grants he condemns. But, surely, if it be wrong to give the money of the public for the support of those who teach any false doctrine, it is wrong to give that money for the support of the ministers of the Established Church. For it is quite certain that, whether Calvin or Arminius be in the right, whether Laud or Burnet be in the right, a great deal of false doctrine is taught by the ministers of the Established Church. If it be said that the points on which the clergy of the Church of England differ ought to be passed over for the sake of the many important points on which they agree, why may not the same argument be maintained with respect to other sects which hold, in common with the Church of England, the fundamental doctrines of Christianity? The principle that a ruler is bound in conscience to propagate religious truth, and to propagate no religious doctrine which is untrue, is abandoned as soon as it is admitted that a gentleman of Mr. Gladstone's opinions may lawfully vote the public money to a chaplain whose opinions are those of Paley or of Simeon. The whole question then becomes one of degree. Of course no individual and no government can justifiably propagate error for the sake of propagating error. But both individuals and governments must work with such machinery as they have ; and no human machinery is to be found which will impart truth without some alloy of error. We have shown irrefragably, as we think, that the Church of England does not afford such a machinery. The question then is, with what degree of imperfection in our machinery must we put up? And to this question we do not see how any general answer can be given. We must be guided by circumstances. It would, for example, be very criminal in a Protestant to contribute to the sending of Jesuit missionaries among a Protestant population. But we do not conceive that a Protestant would be to blame for giving assistance to Jesuit missionaries who might be engaged in converting the Siamese to Christianity. That tares are mixed with the wheat is matter of regret ; but it is better that wheat and tares should grow together than that the promise of the year should be blighted.

Mr. Gladstone, we see with deep regret, censures the British government in India for distributing a small sum among the Catholic priests who minister to the spiritual wants of our Irish soldiers. Now let us put a case to him. A Protestant gentleman is attended by a Catholic servant in a part of the country where there is no Catholic congregation within many miles. The servant is taken ill and is given over. He desires, in great trouble of mind, to receive the last sacraments of his church. His master sends off a messenger in a chaise and four with orders to bring a confessor from a town at a considerable distance. Here a Protestant lays out money for the purpose of causing religious instruction and consolation to be given by a Catholic priest. Has he committed a sin? Has he not acted like a good master and a good Christian? Would Mr. Gladstone accuse him of "laxity of religious principle," of "confounding truth with falsehood," of "considering the support of religion as a boon to an individual, not as a homage to truth?" But how if this servant had, for the sake of his master, undertaken a journey which removed him from the place where he might easily have obtained religious attendance? How if his death were occasioned by a wound received in defending his master? Should we not then say that the master had only fulfilled a sacred obligation of duty? Now, Mr. Gladstone himself owns that "nobody can think that the personality of the state is more stringent, or entails stronger obligations, than that of the individual." How then stands the case of the Indian government? Here is a poor fellow, enlisted in Clare or Kerry, sent over fifteen thousand miles of sea, quartered in a depressing and pestilential climate. He fights for the government; he conquers for it; he is wounded; he is laid on his pallet, withering away with fever, under that terrible sun, without a friend near him. He pines for the consolations of that religion which, neglected perhaps in the season of health and vigour, now comes back to his mind associated with all the overpowering recollections of his earlier days and of the home which he is never to see again. And because the state for which he dies sends a priest of his own faith to stand at his bedside and to tell him, in language which at once commands his love and confidence, of the common Father, of the common Redeemer, of the common hope of immortality; because the state for which he dies does not abandon him in his last moments to the care of heathen attendants, or employ a chaplain of a different creed to vex his departing spirit with a controversy about the Council of Trent; Mr. Gladstone finds that India presents "a melancholy picture," and that there is "a large allowance of false principle" in the system pursued there. Most earnestly do we hope that our remarks may induce Mr. Gladstone to reconsider this part of his work, and may prevent him from expressing in that high assembly, in which he must always be heard with attention, opinions so unworthy of his character.

We have now said almost all that we think it necessary to say respecting Mr. Gladstone's theory. And perhaps it would be safest for us to stop here. It is much easier to pull down than to build up. Yet, that we may give Mr. Gladstone his revenge, we will state concisely our own views respecting the alliance of Church and State.

We set out in company with Warburton, and remain with him pretty sociably till we come to his contract; a contract which Mr. Gladstone very properly designates as a fiction. We consider the primary end of government as a purely temporal end, the protection of the persons and property of men.

We think that government, like every other contrivance of human wisdom from the highest to the lowest, is likely to answer its main end best when it is constructed with a single view to that end. Mr. Gladstone, who loves Plato, will not quarrel with us for illustrating our proposition, after Plato's fashion, from the most familiar objects. Take cutlery, for example. A blade which is designed both to shave and to carve will certainly not shave so well as a razor, or carve so well as a carving knife. An academy of painting, which should also be a bank, would, in all probability exhibit very bad pictures and discount very bad bills. A gas company, which should also be an infant school society, would, we apprehend, light the streets ill and teach the children ill. On this principle, we think that government should be organised solely with a view to its main end; and that no part of its efficiency for that end should be sacrificed in order to promote any other end however excellent.

But does it follow from hence that governments ought never to promote any end other than their main end? In no wise. Though it is desirable that every institution should have a main end, and should be so formed as to be in the highest degree efficient for that main end, yet if, without any sacrifice of its efficiency for that end, it can promote any other good end, it ought to do so. Thus, the end for which a hospital is built is the relief of the sick, not the beautifying of the street. To sacrifice the health of the sick to splendour of architectural effect, to place the building in a bad air only that it may present a more commanding front to a great public place, to make the wards hotter or cooler than they ought to be in order that the columns and windows of the exterior may please the passers-by, would be monstrous. But if, without any sacrifice of the chief object, the hospital can be made an ornament to the metropolis, it would be absurd not to make it so.

In the same manner, if a government can, without any sacrifice of its main end, promote any other good end, it ought to do so. The encouragement of the fine arts, for example, is by no means the main end of government; and it would be absurd, in constituting a government, to bestow a thought on the question whether it would be a government likely to train Raphaels and Domenichinos. But it by no means follows that it is improper for a government to form a national gallery of pictures. The same may be said of patronage bestowed on learned men—of the publication of archives—of the collecting of libraries, menageries, plants, fossils, antiques—of journeys and voyages for purposes of geographical discovery or astronomical observation. It is not for these ends that government is constituted. But it may well happen that a government may have at its command resources which will enable it, without any injury to its main end, to serve these colateral ends far more effectually than any individual or any voluntary association could do. If so, government ought to serve these collateral ends.

It is still more evidently the duty of government to promote—always in subordination to its main end—everything which is useful as a means for the attaining of that main end. The improvement of steam navigation, for example, is by no means a primary object of government. But as steam vessels are useful for the purpose of national defence and for the purpose of facilitating intercourse between distant provinces, and thereby consolidating the force of the empire, it may be the bounden duty of government to encourage ingenious men to perfect an invention which so directly tends to make the state more efficient for its great primary end.

Now, on both these grounds, the instruction of the people may with propriety engage the care of the government. That the people should be well educated is in itself a good thing; and the state ought therefore to promote this object, if it can do so without any sacrifice of its primary object. The education of the people, conducted on those principles of morality which are common to all the forms of Christianity, is highly valuable as a means of promoting the main object for which government exists, and is on this ground well deserving the attention of rulers. We will not at present go into the general question of education, but will confine our remarks to the subject which is more immediately before us—namely, the religious instruction of the people.

We may illustrate our view of the policy which governments ought to pursue, with respect to religious instruction, by recurring to the analogy of a hospital. Religious instruction is not the main end for which a hospital is built; and to introduce into a hospital any regulations prejudicial to the health of the patients on the plea of promoting their spiritual improvement—to send a ranting preacher to a man who has just been ordered by the physician to lie quiet and try to get a little sleep—to impose a strict observance of Lent on a convalescent who has been advised to eat heartily of nourishing food—to direct, as the bigoted Pius the Fifth actually did, that no medical assistance should be given to any person who declined spiritual attendance—would be the most extravagant folly. Yet it by no means follows that it would not be right to have a chaplain to attend the sick, and to pay such a chaplain out of the hospital funds. Whether it will be proper to have such a chaplain at all, and of what religious persuasion such a chaplain ought to be, must depend on circumstances. There may be a town in which it would be impossible to set up a good hospital without the help of people of different opinions. And religious parties may run so high that, though people of different opinions are willing to contribute for the relief of the sick, they will not concur in the choice of any one chaplain. The high Churchmen insist that, if there is a paid chaplain, he shall be a high Churchman. The Evangelicals stickle for an Evangelical. Here it would evidently be absurd and cruel to let an useful and humane design, about which all are agreed, fall to the ground because all cannot agree about something else. The governors must either appoint two chaplains and pay them both, or they must appoint none; and every one of them must, in his individual capacity, do what he can for the purpose of providing the sick with such religious instruction and consolation as will, in his opinion, be most useful to them.

We should say the same of government. Government is not an institution for the propagation of religion, any more than St. George's Hospital is an institution for the propagation of religion: and the most absurd and pernicious consequences would follow if Government should pursue, as its primary end, that which can never be more than its secondary end, though intrinsically more important than its primary end. But a government which considers the religious instruction of the people as a secondary end, and follows out that principle faithfully, will, we think, be likely to do much good and little harm.

We will rapidly run over some of the consequences to which this principle leads, and point out how it solves some problems which, on Mr. Gladstone's hypothesis, admit of no satisfactory solution.

All persecutions directed against the persons or property of men is, on our principle, obviously indefensible. For the protection of the persons and property of men being the primary end of government, and religious instruction only a secondary end, to secure the people from heresy by making their lives, their limbs or their estates insecure, would be to sacrifice the primary end to the secondary end. It would be as absurd as it would be in the governors of a hospital to direct that the wounds of all Arian and Socinian patients should be dressed in such a way as to make them fester.

Again, on our principles, all civil disabilities on account of religious opinions are indefensible. For all such disabilities make government less efficient for its main end: they limit its choice of able men for the administration and defence of the state; they alienate from it the hearts of the sufferers; they deprive it of a part of its effective strength in all contests with foreign nations.

Such a course is as absurd as it would be in the governors of a hospital to reject an able surgeon because he is an Universal Restitutionist and to send a bungler to operate because he is perfectly orthodox.

Again, on our principles, no government ought to press on the people religious instruction, however sound, in such a manner as to excite among them discontents dangerous to public order. For here again government would sacrifice its primary end to an end intrinsically indeed of the highest importance, but still only a secondary end of government, as government. This rule at once disposes of the difficulty about India, a difficulty of which Mr. Gladstone can get rid only by putting in an imaginary discharge in order to set aside an imaginary obligation. There is assuredly no country where it is more desirable that Christianity should be propagated. But there is no country in which the government is so completely disqualified for the task. By using our power in order to make proselytes, we should produce the dissolution of society and bring utter ruin on all those interests for the protection of which government exists. Here the secondary end is, at present, inconsistent with the primary end, and must therefore be abandoned. Christian instruction given by individuals and voluntary societies may do much good. Given by the government it would do unmixed harm. At the same time, we quite agree with Mr. Gladstone in thinking that the English authorities in India ought not to participate in any idolatrous rite; and, indeed, we are fully satisfied that all such participation is not only unchristian, but also unwise and most undignified.

Supposing the circumstances of a country be such that the government may with propriety, on our principles, give religious instruction to a people. The next question is, what religion shall be taught? Bishop Warburton answers, the religion of the majority. And we so far agree with him that we can scarcely conceive any circumstances in which it would be proper to establish, as the one exclusive religion of the state, the religion of the minority. Such a preference could hardly be given without exciting most serious discontent and endangering those interests, the protection of which is the first object of government. But we never can admit that a ruler can be justified in assisting to spread a system of opinions solely because that system is pleasing to the majority. On the other hand, we cannot agree with Mr. Gladstone, who would of course answer that the only religion which a ruler ought to propagate is the religion of his own conscience. In truth, this is an impossibility. And, as we have shown, Mr. Gladstone himself, whenever he supports a grant of money to the Church of England, is really assisting to propagate, not the precise religion of his own conscience, but some one or more, he knows not how many or which, of the innumerable religions which lie between the confines of Pelagianism and those of Antinomianism, and between the confines of Popery and those of Presbyterianism. In our opinion, that religious instruction which the ruler ought, in his public capacity, to patronise, is the instruction from which he, in his conscience, believes that the people will learn most good with the smallest mixture of evil. And thus it is not necessarily his own religion that he will select. He will, of course, believe that his own religion is unmixedly good. But the question which he has to consider is, not how much good his religion contains, but how much good the people will learn if instruction is given them in that religion. He may prefer the doctrine and government of the Church of England to those of the Church of Scotland. But if he knows that a Scotch congregation will listen with deep attention and respect while an Erskine or a Chalmers sets before them the fundamental doctrines of Christianity; and that a glimpse of a cassock or a single line of a liturgy would be the signal for hooting and riot, and would probably bring stools and brickbats about the ears of the minister; he acts wisely if he conveys religious knowledge to the Scotch rather by means of that imperfect Church, as he may think it, from which they will learn much, than by means of that perfect Church from which they will learn nothing. The only end of teaching is, that men may learn; and it is idle to talk of the duty of teaching truth in ways which only cause men to cling more firmly to falsehood.

On these principles, we conceive that a statesman, who might be far indeed from regarding the Church of England with the reverence which Mr. Gladstone feels for her, might yet firmly oppose all attempts to destroy her. Such a statesman may be too well acquainted with her origin to look upon her with superstitious awe. He may know that she sprang from a compromise huddled up between the eager zeal of reformers and the selfishness of greedy, ambitious and time-serving politicians. He may find in every page of her annals ample cause for censure. He may feel that he could not, with ease to his conscience subscribe all her articles. He may regret that all the attempts which have been made to open her gates to large classes of nonconformists should have failed. Her episcopal polity he may consider as of purely human institution. He cannot defend her on the ground that she possesses the apostolical succession; for he does not know whether that succession may not be altogether a fable. He cannot defend her on the ground of her unity; for he knows that her frontier sects are much more remote from each other than one frontier is from the Church of Rome or the other from the Church of Geneva. But he may think that she teaches more truth with less alloy of error than would be taught by those who, if she were swept away, would occupy the vacant space. He may think that the effect produced by her beautiful services and by her pulpits on the national mind is, on the whole, highly beneficial. He may think that her civilising influence is usefully felt in remote districts. He may think that, if she were destroyed, a large portion of those who now compose her congregations would neglect all religious duties; and that a still larger part would fall under the influence of spiritual mountebanks, hungry for gain or drunk with fanaticism. While he would with pleasure admit that all the qualities of Christian pastors are to be found in large measure within the existing body of Dissenting ministers, he would perhaps be inclined to think that the standard of intellectual and moral character among that exemplary class of men may have been raised to its present high point and maintained there by the indirect influence of the Establishment. And he may be by no means satisfied that, if the Church were at once swept away, the place of our Sumners and Whateleys would be supplied by Doddridges and Halls. He may think that the advantages which we have described are obtained, or might, if the existing system were slightly modified, be obtained, without any sacrifice of the paramount objects which all governments ought to have chiefly in view. Nay, he may be of opinion that an institution, so deeply fixed in the hearts and minds of millions, could not be subverted without loosening and shaking all the foundations of civil society. With at least equal ease he would find reasons for supporting the Church of Scotland. Nor would he be under the necessity of resorting to any contract to justify the connection of two religious establishments with one government. He would think scruples on that head frivolous in any person who is zealous for a Church of which both Dr. Herbert Marsh and Dr. Daniel Wilson are bishops. Indeed, he would gladly follow out his principles much further. He would have been willing to vote in 1825 for Lord Francis Egerton's resolution, that it is expedient to give a public maintenance to the Catholic clergy of Ireland; and he would deeply regret that no such measure was adopted in 1829.

In this way, we conceive, a statesman might, on our principles, satisfy himself that it would be in the highest degree inexpedient to abolish the Church, either of England or of Scotland.

But if there were, in any part of the world, a national church regarded as heretical by four-fifths of the nation committed to its care—a church established and maintained by the sword—a church producing twice as many riots as conversions—a church which, though possessing great wealth and power, and though long backed by persecuting laws, had, in the course of many generations, been found unable to propagate its doctrines and barely able to maintain its ground—a church so odious, that fraud and violence, when used against its clear rights of property, were generally regarded as fair play—a church, whose ministers were preaching to desolate walls, and with difficulty obtaining their lawful subsistence by the help of bayonets—such a church, on our principles, could not, we must own, be defended. We should say that the state which allied itself with such a church postponed the primary end of government to the secondary; and that the consequences had been such as any sagacious observer would have predicted. Neither the primary nor the secondary end is attained. The temporal and spiritual interests of the people suffer alike. The minds of men, instead of being drawn to the church, are alienated from the state. The magistrate, after sacrificing order, peace, union, all the interests which it is his first duty to protect for the purpose of promoting pure religion, is forced, after the experience of centuries, to admit that he has really been promoting error. The sounder the doctrines of such a church—the more absurd and noxious the superstition by which those doctrines are opposed—the stronger are the arguments against the policy which has deprived a good cause of its natural advantages. Those who preach to rulers the duty of employing power to propagate truth would do well to remember that falsehood, though no match for truth alone, has often been found more than a match for truth and power together.

A statesman, judging on our principles, would pronounce without hesitation that a church, such as we have last described, never ought to have been set up. Further than this we will not venture to speak for him. He would doubtless remember that the world is full of institutions which, though they never ought to have been set up, yet, having been set up, ought not to be rudely pulled down; and that it is often wise in practice to be content with the mitigation of an abuse which, looking at it in the abstract, we might feel impatient to destroy.

We have done; and nothing remains but that we part from Mr. Gladstone with the courtesy of antagonists who bear no malice. We dissent from his opinions, but we admire his talents; we respect his integrity and benevolence; and we hope that he will not suffer political avocations so entirely to engross him as to leave him no leisure for literature and philosophy.

LORD CLIVE. (JANUARY, 1840.)

The Life of Robert, Lord Clive: collected from the Family Papers communicated by the Earl of Powis. By MAJOR-GENERAL SIR JOHN MALCOLM, KCB. 3 vols., 8vo. London, 1836.

WE have always thought it strange that, while the history of the Spanish empire in America is familiarly known to all the nations of Europe, the great actions of our countrymen in the East should, even among ourselves, excite little interest. Every schoolboy knows who imprisoned Montezuma and who strangled Atabalipa. But we doubt whether one in ten, even among English gentlemen of highly cultivated minds, can tell who won the battle of Buxar, who perpetrated the massacre of Patna, whether Sujah Dowlah ruled in Oude or in Travancore, or whether Holkar was a Hindoo or a Mussulman. Yet the victories of Cortes were gained over savages who had no letters, who were ignorant of the use of metals, who had not broken in a single animal to labour, who wielded no better weapons than those which could be made out of sticks, flints and fish-bones, who regarded a horse-soldier as a monster, half man and half beast, who took a harquebusier for a sorcerer able to scatter the thunder and lightning of the skies. The people of India, when we subdued them, were ten times as numerous as the vanquished Americans and were at the same time quite as highly civilised as the victorious Spaniards. They had reared cities larger and fairer than Saragossa or Toledo, and buildings more beautiful and costly than the cathedral of Seville. They could show bankers richer than the richest firms of Barcelona or Cadiz, viceroys whose splendour far surpassed that of Ferdinand the Catholic, myriads of cavalry and long trains of artillery which would have astonished the great Captain. It might have been expected that every Englishman who takes any interest in any part of history would be curious to know how a handful of his countrymen, separated from their home by an immense ocean, subjugated, in the course of a few years, one of the greatest empires in the world. Yet, unless we greatly err, this subject is, to most readers, not only insipid, but positively distasteful.

Perhaps the fault lies partly with the historians. Mr. Mill's book, though it has undoubtedly great and rare merit, is not sufficiently animated and picturesque to attract those who read for amusement. Orme, inferior to no English historian in style and power of painting, is minute even to tediousness. In one volume he allots, on an average, a closely printed quarto page to the events of every forty-eight hours. The consequence is, that his narrative, though one of the most authentic and one of the most finely written in our language, has never been very popular, and is now scarcely ever read.

We fear that Sir John Malcolm's volumes will not much attract those readers whom Orme and Mill have repelled. The materials placed at his disposal by the late Lord Powis were indeed of great value. But we cannot say that they have been very skilfully worked up. It would, however, be unjust to criticise with severity a work which, if the author had lived to complete and revise it, would probably have been improved by condensation and by a better arrangement. We are more disposed to perform the pleasing duty of expressing our gratitude to the noble family to which the public owes so much useful and curious information.

The effect of the book, even when we make the largest allowance for the partiality of those who have furnished and of those who have digested the materials, is, on the whole, greatly to raise the character of Lord Clive. We are far indeed from sympathising with Sir John Malcolm, whose love passes the love of biographers, and who can see nothing but wisdom and justice in the actions of his idol. But we are at least equally far from concurring in the severe judgment of Mr. Mill, who seems to us to show less discrimination in his account of Clive than in any other part of his valuable work. Clive, like most men who are born with strong passions, and tried by strong temptations, committed great faults. But every person who takes a fair and enlightened view of his whole career must admit that our island, so fertile in heroes and statesmen, has scarcely ever produced a man more truly great either in arms or in council.

The Clives had been settled, ever since the twelfth century, on an estate of no great value near Market-Drayton, in Shropshire. In the reign of George the First, this moderate but ancient inheritance was possessed by Mr. Richard

Clive, who seems to have been a plain man of no great tact or capacity. He had been bred to the law, and divided his time between professional business and the avocations of a small proprietor. He married a lady from Manchester of the name of Gaskill, and became the father of a very numerous family. His eldest son, Robert, the founder of the British empire in India, was born at the old seat of his ancestors on the twenty-ninth of September, 1725.

Some lineaments of the character of the man were early discerned in the child. There remain letters written by his relations when he was in his seventh year; and from these it appears that, even at that early age, his strong will and his fiery passions, sustained by a constitutional intrepidity which sometimes seemed hardly compatible with soundness of mind, had begun to cause great uneasiness to his family. "Fighting," says one of his uncles, "to which he is out of measure addicted, gives his temper such a fierceness and imperiousness that he flies out on every trifling occasion." The old people of the neighbourhood still remember to have heard from their parents how Bob Clive climbed to the top of the lofty steeple of Market-Drayton, and with what terror the inhabitants saw him seated on a stone spout near the summit. They also relate how he formed all the good-for-nothing lads of the town into a kind of predatory army, and compelled the shopkeepers to submit to a tribute of apples and halfpence, in consideration of which he guaranteed the security of their windows. He was sent from school to school, making very little progress in his learning, and gaining for himself everywhere the character of an exceedingly naughty boy. One of his masters, it is said, was sagacious enough to prophesy that the idle lad would make a great figure in the world. But the general opinion seems to have been that poor Robert was a dunce, if not a reprobate. His family expected nothing good from such slender parts and such a headstrong temper. It is not strange, therefore, that they gladly accepted for him, when he was in his eighteenth year, a writership in the service of the East India Company, and shipped him off to make a fortune or to die of a fever at Madras.

Far different were the prospects of Clive from those of the youths whom the East India College now annually sends to the Presidencies of our Asiatic empire. The Company was then purely a trading corporation. Its territory consisted of a few square miles, for which rent was paid to the native governments. Its troops were scarcely numerous enough to man the batteries of three or four ill-constructed forts which had been erected for the protection of the warehouses. The natives, who composed a considerable part of these little garrisons, had not yet been trained in the discipline of Europe, and were armed, some with swords and shields, some with bows and arrows. The business of the servant of the Company was not, as now, to conduct the judicial, financial and diplomatic business of a great country, but to take stock, to make advances to weavers, to ship cargoes, and to keep a sharp look-out on private traders who dared to infringe the monopoly. The younger clerks were so miserably paid that they could scarcely subsist without incurring debt; the elder enriched themselves by trading on their own account; and those who lived to rise to the top of the service often accumulated considerable fortunes.

Madras, to which Clive had been appointed, was, at this time, perhaps, the first in importance of the Company's settlements. In the preceding century, Fort St. George had arisen on a barren spot beaten by a raging surf; and in the neighbourhood a town, inhabited by many thousands of natives, had sprung up, as towns spring up in the East, with the rapidity of the prophet's gourd. There were already in the suburbs many white villas, each surrounded by its garden, whither the wealthy agents of the Company retired, after the labours of the desk and the warehouse, to enjoy the cool breeze which springs up at sunset from the Bay of Bengal. The habits of these mercantile grandees appear to have been more profuse, luxurious and ostentatious than those of the high judicial and political functionaries who have succeeded them. But comfort was far less understood. Many devices which now mitigate the heat of the climate, preserve health and prolong life were unknown. There was far less intercourse with Europe than at present. The voyage by the Cape, which in our time has often been performed within three months, was then very seldom accomplished in six, and was sometimes protracted to more than a year. Consequently, the Anglo-Indian was then much more estranged from his country, much more an Oriental in his tastes and habits, and much less fitted to mix in society after his return to Europe than the Anglo-Indian of the present day.

Within the fort and its precinct, the English governors exercised, by permission of the native rulers, an extensive authority. But they had never dreamed of claiming independent power. The surrounding country was ruled by the Nabob of the Carnatic, a deputy of the Viceroy of the Deccan, commonly called the Nizam, who was himself only a deputy of the mighty prince designated by our ancestors as the Great Mogul. Those names, once so august and formidable, still remain. There is still a Nabob of the Carnatic, who lives on a pension allowed to him by the Company out of the revenues of the province which his ancestors ruled. There is still a Nizam, whose capital is overawed by a British cantonment, and to whom a British resident gives, under the name of advice, commands which are not to be disputed. There is still a Mogul, who is permitted to play at holding courts and receiving petitions, but who has less power to help or hurt than the youngest civil servant of the Company.

Clive's voyage was unusually tedious even for that age. The ship remained some months at the Brazils, where the young adventurer picked up some knowledge of Portuguese and spent all his pocket-money. He did not arrive in India till more than a year after he had left England. His situation at Madras was most painful. His funds were exhausted. His pay was small. He had contracted debts.—He was wretchedly lodged—no small calamity in a climate which can be made tolerable to an European only by spacious and well-placed apartments. He had been furnished with letters of recommendation to a gentleman who might have assisted him; but when he landed at Fort St. George he found that this gentleman had sailed for England. His shy and haughty disposition withheld him from introducing himself. He was several months in India before he became acquainted with a single family. The climate affected his health and spirits. His duties were of a kind ill suited to his ardent and daring character. He pined for his home, and in his letters to his relations expressed his feelings in language softer and more pensive than we should have expected from the waywardness of his boyhood or from the inflexible sternness of his later years. "I have not enjoyed," says he, "one happy day since I left my native country;" and again, "I must confess, at intervals, when I think of my dear native England, it affects me in a very particular manner. . . . . If I should be so far blest as to revisit again my own country, but more especially Manchester, the centre of all my wishes, all that I could hope or desire for would be presented before me in one view."

One solace he found of the most respectable kind. The Governor possessed a good library, and permitted Clive to have access to it. The young man devoted much of his leisure to reading, and acquired at this time almost all the knowledge of books that he ever possessed. As a boy he had been too idle, as a man he soon became too busy, for literary pursuits.

But neither climate nor poverty, neither study nor the sorrows of a home-sick exile, could tame the desperate audacity of his spirit. He behaved to his official superiors as he had behaved to his schoolmasters, and was several times in danger of losing his situation. Twice, while residing in the Writer's Buildings, he attempted to destroy himself; and twice the pistol which he snapped at his own head failed to go off. This circumstance, it is said, affected him as a similar escape affected Wallenstein. After satisfying himself that the pistol was really well loaded, he burst forth into an exclamation that surely he was reserved for something great.

About this time an event which at first seemed likely to destroy all his hopes in life suddenly opened before him a new path to eminence. Europe had been during some years distracted by the war of the Austrian succession. George II. was the steady ally of Maria Theresa. The house of Bourbon took the opposite side. Though England was even then the first of maritime powers, she was not, as she has since become, more than a match on the sea for all the nations of the world together; and she found it difficult to maintain a contest against the united navies of France and Spain. In the eastern seas, France obtained the ascendency. Labourdonnais, governor of Mauritius, a man of eminent talents and virtues, conducted an expedition to the continent of India in spite of the opposition of the British fleet—landed, assembled an army, appeared before Madras, and compelled the town and fort to capitulate. The keys were delivered up; the French colours were displayed on Fort St. George; and the contents of the Company's warehouses were seized as prize of war by the conquerors. It was stipulated by the capitulation that the English inhabitants should be prisoners of war on parole, and that the town should remain in the hands of the French till it should be ransomed. Labourdonnais pledged his honour that only a moderate ransom should be required.

But the success of Labourdonnais had awakened the jealousy of his countryman, Dupleix, governor of Pondicherry. Dupleix, moreover, had already begun to revolve gigantic schemes, with which the restoration of Madras to the English was by no means compatible. He declared that Labourdonnais had gone beyond his powers; that conquests made by the French arms on the continent of India were at the disposal of the governor of Pondicherry alone; and that Madras should be rased to the ground. Labourdonnais was compelled to yield. The anger which the breach of the capitulation excited among the English was increased by the ungenerous manner in which Dupleix treated the principal servants of the Company. The Governor and several of the first gentlemen of Fort St. George were carried under a guard to Pondicherry and conducted through the town in a triumphal procession under the eyes of fifty thousand spectators. It was with reason thought that this gross violation of public faith absolved the inhabitants of Madras from the engagements into which they had entered with Labourdonnais. Clive fled from the town by night in the disguise of a Mussulman and took refuge at Fort St. David, one of the small English settlements subordinate to Madras.

The circumstances in which he was now placed naturally led him to adopt a profession better suited to his restless and intrepid spirit than the business of examining packages and casting accounts. He solicited and obtained an ensign's commission in the service of the Company, and at twenty-one entered on his military career. His personal courage, of which he had, while still a writer, given signal proof by a desperate duel with a military bully who was the terror of Fort St. David, speedily made him conspicuous even among hundreds of brave men. He soon began to show in his new calling other qualities which had not before been discerned in him—judgment, sagacity, deference to legitimate authority. He distinguished himself highly in several operations against the French, and was particularly noticed by Major Lawrence, who was then considered as the ablest British officer in India.

Clive had been only a few months in the army when intelligence arrived that peace had been concluded between Great Britain and France. Dupleix was in consequence compelled to restore Madras to the English Company, and the young ensign was at liberty to resume his former business. He did indeed return for a short time to his desk. He again quitted it in order to assist Major Lawrence in some petty hostilities with the natives, and then again returned to it. While he was thus wavering between a military and a commercial life, events took place which decided his choice. The politics of India assumed a new aspect. There was peace between the English and French Crowns; but there arose between the English and French Companies trading to the East a war most eventful and important—a war in which the prize was nothing less than the magnificent inheritance of the house of Tamerlane.

The empire which Baber and his Moguls reared in the sixteenth century was long one of the most extensive and splendid in the world. In no European kingdom was so large a population subject to a single prince, or so large a revenue poured into the treasury. The beauty and magnificence of the buildings erected by the sovereigns of Hindostan amazed even travellers who had seen St. Peter's. The innumerable retinues and gorgeous decorations, which surrounded the throne of Delhi, dazzled even eyes which were accustomed to the pomp of Versailles. Some of the great viceroys, who held their posts by virtue of commissions from the Mogul, ruled as many subjects and enjoyed as large an income as the King of France or the Emperor of Germany. Even the deputies of these deputies might well rank, as to extent of territory and amount of revenue, with the Grand Duke of Tuscany or the Elector of Saxony.

There can be little doubt that this great empire, powerful and prosperous as it appears on a superficial view, was yet, even in its best days, far worse governed than the worst governed parts of Europe now are. The administration was tainted with all the vices of Oriental despotism, and with all the vices inseparable from the domination of race over race. The conflicting pretensions of the princes of the royal house produced a long series of crimes and public disasters. Ambitious lieutenants of the sovereign sometimes aspired to independence. Fierce tribes of Hindoos, impatient of a foreign yoke, frequently withheld tribute, repelled the armies of the government from the mountain fastnesses, and poured down in arms on the cultivated plains. In spite, however, of much constant maladministration, in spite of occasional convulsions which shook the whole frame of society, this great monarchy, on the whole, retained, during some generations, an outward appearance of unity, majesty and energy. But, throughout the long reign of Aurungzebe, the state, notwithstanding all that the vigour and policy of the prince could effect, was hastening to dissolution. After his death, which took place in the year 1707, the ruin was fearfully rapid. Violent shocks from without co-operated with an incurable decay which was fast proceeding within; and in a few years the empire had undergone utter decomposition.

The history of the successors of Theodosius bears no small analogy to that of the successors of Aurungzebe. But perhaps the fall of the Carlovingians furnishes the nearest parallel to the falls of the Moguls. Charlemagne was scarcely interred when the imbecility and disputes of his descendants began to bring contempt on themselves and destruction on their subjects. The wide dominion of the Franks was severed into a thousand pieces. Nothing more than a nominal dignity was left to the abject heirs of an illustrious name, Charles the Bald, and Charles the Fat, and Charles the Simple. Fierce invaders, differing from each other in race, language and religion, flocked, as if by concert, from the farthest corners of the earth to plunder provinces which the government could no longer defend. The pirates of the Baltic extended their ravages from the Elbe to the Pyrenees, and at length fixed their seat in the rich valley of the Seine. The Hungarian, in whom the trembling monks fancied that they recognised the Gog or Magog of prophecy, carried back the plunder of the cities of Lombardy to the depths of the Pannonian forests. The Saracen ruled in Sicily, desolated the fertile plains of Campania, and spread terror even to the walls of Rome. In the midst of these sufferings, a great internal change passed upon the empire. The corruption of death, began to ferment into new forms of life. While the great body, as a whole, was torpid and passive, every separate member began to feel with a sense and to move with an energy all its own. Just here, in the most barren and dreary tract of European history, all feudal privileges, all modern nobility, take their source. To this point we trace the power of those princes who, nominally vassals, but really independent, long governed, with the titles of dukes, marquesses and counts, almost every part of the dominions which had obeyed Charlemagne.

Such, or nearly such, was the change which passed on the Mogul empire during the forty years which followed the death of Aurungzebe. A series of nominal sovereigns, sunk in indolence and debauchery, sauntered away life in secluded palaces, chewing bang, fondling concubines and listening to buffoons. A series of ferocious invaders had descended through the western passes to prey on the defenceless wealth of Hindostan. A Persian conqueror crossed the Indus, marched through the gates of Delhi, and bore away in triumph those treasures of which the magnificence had astounded Roe and Bernier—the Peacock Throne, on which the richest jewels of Golconda had been disposed by the most skilful hands of Europe, and the inestimable Mountain of Light, which, after many strange vicissitudes, lately shone in the bracelet of Runjeet Sing, and is now destined to adorn the hideous idol of Orissa. The Afghan soon followed to complete the work of devastation which the Persian had begun. The warlike tribes of Rajpoos threw off the Mussulman yoke. A band of mercenary soldiers occupied Rohilcund. The Seiks ruled on the Indus. The Jauts spread terror along the Jumna. The highlands which border on the western sea-coast of India poured forth a yet more formidable race—a race which was long the terror of every native power, and which yielded only after many desperate and doubtful struggles to the fortune and genius of England. It was under the reign of Aurungzebe that this wild clan of plunderers first descended from the mountains; and soon after his death, every corner of his wide empire learned to tremble at the mighty name of the Mahrattas. Many fertile viceroyalties were entirely subdued by them. Their dominions stretched across the peninsula from sea to sea. Their captains reigned at Poonah, at Gualior, in Guzerat, in Berar and in Tanjore. Nor did they, though they had become great sovereigns, therefore cease to be freebooters. They still retained the predatory habits of their forefathers. Every region which was not subject to their rule was wasted by their incursions. Wherever their kettle-drums were heard, the peasant threw his bag of rice on his shoulder, hid his small savings in his girdle, and fled with his wife and children to the mountains or the jungles—to the milder neighbourhood of the hyæna and the tiger. Many provinces redeemed their harvests by the payment of an annual ransom. Even the wretched phantom who still bore the imperial title stooped to pay this ignominious "black-mail." The camp-fires of one rapacious leader were seen from the walls of the palace of Delhi. Another, at the head of his innumerable cavalry, descended year after year on the ricefields of Bengal. Even the European factors trembled for their magazines. Less than a hundred years ago, it was thought necessary to fortify Calcutta against the horsemen of Berar; and the name of the Mahratta ditch still preserves the memory of the danger.

Wherever the viceroys of the Mogul retained authority they became sovereigns. They might still acknowledge in words the superiority of the house of Tamerlane; as a Count of Flanders or a Duke of Burgundy would have acknowledged the superiority of the most helpless driveller among the later Carlovingians. They might occasionally send to their titular sovereign a complimentary present, or solicit from him a title of honour. But they were, in truth, no longer lieutenants removable at pleasure, but independent hereditary princes. In this way originated those great Mussulman houses which formerly ruled Bengal and the Carnatic, and those which still, though in a state of vassalage, exercise some of the powers of royalty at Lucknow and Hyderabad.

In what was this confusion to end? Was the strife to continue during centuries? Was it to terminate in the rise of another great monarchy? Was the Mussulman or the Mahratta to be the Lord of India? Was another Baber to descend from the mountains and to lend the hardy tribes of Cabul and Chorasan against a wealthier and less warlike race? None of these events seemed improbable. But scarcely any man, however sagacious, would have thought it possible that a trading company, separated from India by fifteen thousand miles of sea, and possessing in India only a few acres for purposes of commerce, would, in less than a hundred years, spread its empire from Cape Comorin to the eternal snow of the Himalayas—would compel Mahratta and Mahommedan to forget their mutual feuds in common subjection—would tame down even those wild races which had resisted the most powerful of the Moguls—and having established a government far stronger than any ever known in those countries, would carry its victorious arms far to the east of the Burrampooter and far to the west of the Hydaspes—dictate terms of peace at the gates of Ava and seat its vassal on the throne of Candahar.

The man who first saw that it was possible to found an European empire on the ruins of the Mogul monarchy was Dupleix. His restless, capacious and inventive mind had formed this scheme at a time when the ablest servants of the English Company were busied only about invoices and bills of lading. Nor had he only proposed to himself the end. He had also a just and distinct view of the means by which it was to be attained. He clearly saw that the greatest force which the princes of India could bring into the field would be no match for a small body of men trained in the discipline and guided by the tactics of the West. He saw also that the natives of India might, under European commanders, be formed into armies such as Saxe or Frederic would be proud to command. He was perfectly aware that the most easy and convenient way in which an European adventurer could exercise sovereignty in India was to govern through the motions and to speak through the mouth of some glittering puppet dignified by the title of Nabob or Nizam. The arts both of war and policy, which a few years later were employed successfully by the English, were first understood and practised by this ingenious and aspiring Frenchman.

The state of India was such that scarcely any aggression could be without a decent pretext, either in old laws or in recent practice. All rights were in a state of utter uncertainty; and the Europeans who took part in the disputes of the natives confounded the confusion by applying to Asiatic politics the public law of the West and analogies drawn from the feudal system. If it was convenient to treat a Nabob as an independent prince, there was an excellent plea for doing so. He was independent, in fact. If it was convenient to treat him as a mere deputy of the Court of Delhi, there was no difficulty, for he was so in theory. If it was convenient to consider his office as an hereditary dignity, or as a dignity held during life only, or as a dignity held only during the good pleasure of the Mogul, arguments and precedents might be found for every one of those views. The party who had the heir of Baber in their hands represented him as the undoubted, the legitimate, the absolute sovereign, whom all subordinate authorities were bound to obey. The party against whom his name was used did not want plausible pretexts for maintaining that the empire was *de facto* dissolved; and that, though it might be proper to treat the Mogul with respect, as a venerable relique of an order of things which had passed away, it was absurd to regard him as the real master of Hindostan.

In the year 1748 died one of the most powerful of the new masters of India —the great Nizam al Mulk, Viceroy of the Deccan. His authority descended to his son, Nazir Jung. Of the provinces subject to this high functionary, the Carnatic was the wealthiest and the most extensive. It was governed by an ancient Nabob, whose name the English corrupted into Anaverdy Khan.

But there were pretenders to the government both of the viceroyalty and of the subordinate province. Mirzapha Jung, a grandson of Nizam al Mulk, appeared as the competitor of Nazir Jung. Chunda Sahib, son-in-law of a former Nabob of the Carnatic, disputed the title of Anaverdy Khan. In the unsettled state of Indian law, it was easy for both Mirzapha Jung and Chunda Sahib to make out something like a claim of right. In a society altogether disorganised, they had no difficulty in finding greedy adventurers to follow their standards. They united their interests, invaded the Carnatic and applied for assistance to the French, whose fame had been raised by their success against the English in the recent war on the coast of Coromandel.

Nothing could have happened more pleasing to the subtle and ambitious Dupleix. To make a Nabob of the Carnatic, to make a Viceroy of the Deccan, to rule under their names the whole of Southern India; this was indeed an attractive prospect. He allied himself with the pretenders, and sent four hundred French soldiers and two thousand Sepoys, disciplined after the European fashion, to the assistance of his confederates. A battle was fought. The French distinguished themselves greatly. Anaverdy Khan was defeated and slain. His son, Mahommed Ali, who was afterwards well known in England as the Nabob of Arcot, and who owes to the eloquence of Burke a most unenviable immortality, fled with a scanty remnant of his army to Trichinopoly; and the conquerors became at once masters of almost every part of the Carnatic.

This was but the beginning of the greatness of Dupleix. After some months of fighting, negotiation and intrigue, his ability and good fortune seemed to have prevailed everywhere. Nazir Jung perished by the hands of his own followers; Mirzapha Jung was master of the Deccan; and the triumph of French arms and French policy was complete. At Pondicherry all was exultation and festivity. Salutes were fired from the batteries and Te Deum sung in the churches. The new Nizam came thither to visit his allies, and the ceremony of his installation was performed there with great pomp. Dupleix, dressed in the garb worn by Mahommedans of the highest rank, entered the town in the same palanquin with the Nizam, and, in the pageant which followed, took precedence of all the court. He was declared Governor of India from the river Kristna to Cape Comorin, with authority superior even to that of Chunda Sahib. He was entrusted with the command of seven thousand cavalry. It was announced that no mint would be suffered to exist in the Carnatic except that at Pondicherry. A large portion of the treasures which former Viceroys of the Deccan had accumulated found its way into the coffers of the French governor. It was rumoured that he had received two hundred thousand pounds sterling in money, besides many valuable jewels. In fact, there could scarcely be any limit to his gains. He now ruled thirty millions of people with almost absolute power. No honour or emolument could be obtained from the government but by his intervention. No petition, unless signed by him, was even perused by the Nizam.

Mirzapha Jung survived his elevation only a few months. But another prince of the same house was raised to the throne by French influence, and ratified all the promises of his predecessor. Dupleix was now the greatest potentate in India. His countrymen boasted that his name was mentioned with awe even in the chambers of the palace of Delhi. The native population looked with amazement on the progress which, in the short space of four years, an European adventurer had made towards dominion in Asia. Nor was the vainglorious Frenchman content with the reality of power. He loved to display it with arrogant ostentation before the eyes of his subjects and of his rivals. Near the spot where his policy had obtained its chief triumph, by the fall of Nazir Jung and the elevation of Mirzapha, he determined to erect a column, on the four sides of which four pompous inscriptions, in four languages, should proclaim his victory to all the nations of the East. Medals stamped with emblems of his successes were buried beneath the foundations of this stately pillar, and round it arose a town bearing the haughty name of Dupleix Fatihabad, which is, being interpreted, the City of the Victory of Dupleix.

The English had made some feeble and irresolute attempts to stop the rapid and brilliant career of the rival Company, and continued to recognise Mahommed Ali as Nabob of the Carnatic. But the dominions of Mahommed Ali consisted of Trichinopoly alone, and Trichinopoly was now infested by Chunda Sahib and his French auxiliaries. To raise the siege seemed impossible. The small force which was then at Madras had no commander. Major Lawrence had returned to England, and not a single officer of established character remained in the settlement. The natives had learned to look with contempt on the mighty nation which was soon to conquer and to rule them. They had seen the French colours flying on Fort St. George, they had seen the chiefs of the English factory led in triumph through the streets of Pondicherry, they had seen the arms and counsels of Dupleix everywhere successful, while the opposition which the authorities of Madras had made to his progress had served only to expose their own weakness and to heighten his glory. At this moment, the valour and genius of an obscure English youth suddenly turned the tide of fortune.

Clive was now twenty-five years old. After hesitating for some time between a military and a commercial life, he had at length been placed in a post which partook of both characters, that of commissary to the troops with the rank of captain. The present emergency called forth all his powers. He represented to his superiors that unless some vigorous effort were made, Trichinopoly would fall, the house of Anaverdy Khan would perish, and the French would become the real masters of the whole peninsula of India. It was absolutely necessary to strike some daring blow. If an attack were made on Arcot, the capital of the Carnatic and the favourite residence of the Nabobs, it was not impossible that the siege of Trichinopoly would be raised. The heads of the English settlement, now thoroughly alarmed by the success of Dupleix, and apprehensive that, in the event of a new war between France and Great Britain, Madras would be instantly taken and destroyed, approved of Clive's plan, and intrusted the execution of it to himself. The young captain was put at the head of two hundred English soldiers and three hundred sepoys, armed and disciplined after the European fashion. Of the eight officers who commanded this little force under him, not a single one had ever been in action, and four of the eight were factors of the Company whom Clive's example had induced to offer their services. The weather was stormy; but Clive pushed on, through thunder, lightning and rain, to the gates of Arcot. The garrison, in a panic, evacuated the fort, and the English entered it without a blow.

But Clive well knew that he should not be suffered to retain undisturbed possession of his conquest. He instantly began to collect provisions, to throw up works, and to make preparations for sustaining a siege. The garrison, which had fled at his approach, had now recovered from its dismay, and, having been swollen by large reinforcements from the neighbourhood to a force of three thousand men, encamped close to the town. At dead of night, Clive marched out of the fort, attacked the camp by surprise, slew great numbers, dispersed the rest, and returned to his quarters without having lost a single man.

The intelligence of these events was soon carried to Chunda Sahib, who with his French allies was besieging Trichinopoly. He immediately detached four thousand men from his camp and sent them to Arcot. They were speedily joined by the remains of the force which Clive had lately scattered. They were further strengthened by two thousand men from Vellore; and by a still more important reinforcement of a hundred and fifty French soldiers whom Dupleix despatched from Pondicherry. The whole of this army, amounting to about ten thousand men, was under the command of Rajah Sahib, son of Chunda Sahib.

Rajah Sahib proceeded to invest the fort of Arcot, which seemed quite incapable of sustaining a siege. The walls were ruinous, the ditches dry, the ramparts too narrow to admit the guns, the battlements too low to protect the soldiers. The little garrison had been greatly reduced by casualties. It now consisted of a hundred and twenty Europeans and two hundred sepoys. Only four officers were left, the stock of provisions was scanty, and the commander, who had to conduct the defence under circumstances so discouraging, was a young man of five-and-twenty who had been bred a bookkeeper.

During fifty days the siege went on. During fifty days the young captain maintained the defence with a firmness, vigilance and ability which would have done honour to the oldest marshall in Europe. The breach, however, increased day by day. The garrison began to feel the pressure of hunger. Under such circumstances, any troops so scantily provided with officers might have been expected to show signs of insubordination; and the danger was peculiarly great in a force composed of men differing widely from each other in extraction, colour, language, manners and religion. But the devotion of the little band to its chief surpassed anything that is related of the Tenth Legion of Cæsar or of the Old Guard of Napoleon. The sepoys came to Clive, not to complain of their scanty fare, but to propose that all the grain should be given to the Europeans, who required more nourishment than the natives of Asia. The thin gruel, they said, which was strained away from the rice, would suffice for themselves. History contains no more touching instance of military fidelity, or of the influence of a commanding mind.

An attempt made by the government of Madras to relieve the place had failed. But there was hope from another quarter. A body of six thousand Mahrattas, half soldiers, half robbers, under the command of a chief named Morari Row, had been hired to assist Mahommed Ali, but thinking the French power irresistible and the triumph of Chunda Sahib certain, they had hitherto remained inactive on the frontiers of the Carnatic. The fame of the defence of Arcot roused them from their torpor. Morari Row declared that he had never before believed that Englishmen could fight, but that he would willingly help them since he saw that they had spirit to help themselves. Rajah Sahib learned that the Mahrattas were in motion. It was necessary for him to be expeditious. He first tried negotiation. He offered large bribes to Clive, which were rejected with scorn. He vowed that, if his proposals were not accepted, he would instantly storm the fort and put every man in it to the sword. Clive told him in reply, with characteristic haughtiness, that his father was an usurper, that his army was a rabble, and that he would do well to think twice before he sent such poltroons into a breach defended by English soldiers.

Rajah Sahib determined to storm the fort. The day was well suited to a bold military enterprise. It was the great Mahommedan festival which is sacred to the memory of Hosein, the son of Ali. The history of Islam contains nothing more touching than that mournful legend: How the chief of the Fatimites, when all his brave followers had perished round him, drank his latest draught of water and uttered his latest prayer—how the assassins carried his head in triumph—how the tyrant smote the lifeless lips with his staff—and how a few old men recollected with tears that they had seen those lips pressed to the lips of the Prophet of God. After the lapse of near twelve centuries, the recurrence of this solemn season excites the fiercest and saddest emotions in the bosoms of the devout Moslem of India. They work themselves up to such agonies of rage and lamentation that some, it is said, have given up the ghost from the mere effect of mental excitement. They believe that whoever, during this festival, falls in arms against the infidels, atones by his death for all the sins of his life, and passes at once to the garden of the Houris. It was at this time that Rajah Sahib determined to assault Arcot. Stimulating drugs were employed to aid the effect of religious zeal, and the besiegers, drunk with enthusiasm, drunk with bang, rushed furiously to the attack.

Clive had received secret intelligence of the design, had made his arrangements, and, exhausted by fatigue, had thrown himself on his bed. He was awakened by the alarm, and was instantly at his post. The enemy advanced, driving before them elephants whose foreheads were armed with iron plates. It was expected that the gates would yield to the shock of these living battering-rams. But the huge beasts no sooner felt the English musket-balls than they turned round and rushed furiously away, trampling on the multitude which had urged them forward. A raft was launched on the water which filled one part of the ditch. Clive, perceiving that his gunners at that post did not understand their business, took the management of a piece of artillery himself and cleared the raft in a few minutes. Where the moat was dry, the assailants mounted with great boldness; but they were received with a fire so heavy and so well directed, that it soon quelled the courage even of fanaticism and of intoxication. The rear ranks of the English kept the front ranks supplied with a constant succession of loaded muskets, and every shot told on the living mass below. After three desperate onsets, the besiegers retired behind the ditch.

The struggle lasted about an hour. Four hundred of the assailants fell. The garrison lost only five or six men. The besieged passed an anxious night, looking for a renewal of the attack. But when day broke the enemy were no more to be seen. They had retired, leaving to the English several guns and a large quantity of ammunition.

The news was received at Fort St. George with transports of joy and pride. Clive was justly regarded as a man equal to any command. Two hundred English soldiers and seven hundred sepoys were sent to him, and with this force he instantly commenced offensive operations. He took the fort of Timery, effected a junction with a division of Morari Row's army, and hastened, by forced marches, to attack Rajah Sahib, who was at the head of about five thousand men, of whom three hundred were French. The action was sharp; but Clive gained a complete victory. The military chest of Rajah Sahib fell into the hands of the conquerors. Six hundred sepoys, who had served in the enemy's army, came over to Clive's quarters, and were taken into the British service. Conjeveram surrendered without a blow. The governor of Arnee deserted Chunda Sahib and recognised the title of Mahommed Ali.

Had the entire direction of the war been entrusted to Clive, it would probably have been brought to a speedy close. But the timidity and incapacity which appeared in all the movements of the English, except where he was personally present, protracted the struggle. The Mahrattas muttered that his soldiers were of a different race from the British whom they found elsewhere. The effect of this languor was that in no long time Rajah Sahib, at the head of a considerable army, in which were four hundred French troops, appeared almost under the guns of Fort St. George, and laid waste the villas and gardens of the gentlemen of the English settlement. But he was again encountered and defeated by Clive. More than a hundred of the French were killed or taken, a loss more serious than that of thousands of natives. The victorious army marched from the field of battle to Fort St. David. On the road lay the City of the Victory of Dupleix and the stately monument which was designed to commemorate the triumphs of France in the East. Clive ordered both the city and the monument to be rased to the ground. He was induced, we believe, to take this step, not by personal or national malevolence, but by a just and profound policy. The town and its pompous name, the pillar and its vaunting inscriptions, were among the devices by which Dupleix had laid the public mind of India under a spell. This spell it was Clive's business to break. The natives had been taught that France was confessedly the first power in Europe, and that the English did not presume to dispute her supremacy. No measure could be more effectual for the removing of this delusion than the public and solemn demolition of the French trophies.

The government of Madras, encouraged by these events, determined to send a strong detachment, under Clive, to reinforce the garrison of Trichinopoly. But just at this conjuncture, Major Lawrence arrived from England and assumed the chief command. From the waywardness and impatience of control which had characterised Clive, both at school and in the counting-house, it might have been expected that he would not, after such achievements, act with zeal and good humour in a subordinate capacity. But Lawrence had early treated him with kindness; and it is bare justice to Clive to say that, proud and overbearing as he was, kindness was never thrown away upon him. He cheerfully placed himself under the orders of his old friend, and exerted himself as strenuously in the second post as he could have done in the first. Lawrence well knew the value of such assistance. Though himself gifted with no intellectual faculty higher than plain good sense, he fully appreciated the powers of his brilliant coadjutor. Though he had made a methodical study of military tactics, and, like all men regularly bred to a profession, was disposed to look with disdain on interlopers, he had yet liberality enough to acknowledge that Clive was an exception to common rules. "Some people," he wrote, "are pleased to term Captain Clive fortunate and lucky; but, in my opinion, from the knowledge I have of the gentleman, he deserved and might expect from his conduct everything as it fell out; a man of an undaunted resolution, of a cool temper, and of a presence of mind which never left him in the greatest danger—born a soldier; for, without a military education of any sort, or much conversing with any of the profession, from his judgment and good sense, he led on an army like an experienced officer and a brave soldier, with a prudence that certainly warranted success."

The French had no commander to oppose to the two friends. Dupleix, not inferior in talents for negotiation and intrigue to any European who has borne a part in the revolutions of India, was ill qualified to direct in person military operations. He had not been bred a soldier, and had no inclination to become one. His enemies accused him of personal cowardice; and he defended himself in a strain worthy of Captain Bobadil. He kept away from shot, he said, because silence and tranquility were propitious to his genius, and he found it difficult to pursue his meditations amidst the noise of fire-arms. He was thus under the necessity of intrusting to others the execution of his great warlike designs; and he bitterly complained that he was ill served. He had indeed been assisted by one officer of eminent merit, the celebrated Bussy. But Bussy had marched northward with the Nizam, and was fully employed in looking after his own interests and those of France at the court of that prince. Among the officers who remained with Dupleix, there was not a single man of talent; and many of them were boys, at whose ignorance and folly the common soldiers laughed.

The English triumphed everywhere. The besiegers of Trichinopoly were themselves besieged and compelled to capitulate. Chunda Sahib fell into the hands of the Mahrattas, and was put to death at the instigation probably of his competitor, Mahommed Ali. The spirit of Dupleix, however, was unconquerable, and his resources inexhaustible. From his employers in Europe he no longer received help or countenance. They condemned his policy. They allowed him no pecuniary assistance. They sent him for troops only the sweepings of the galleys. Yet still he persisted, intrigued, bribed, promised—lavished his private fortune, strained his credit, procured new diplomas from Delhi, raised up new enemies to the government of Madras on every side, and even among the allies of the English Company. But all was in vain. Slowly, but steadily, the power of Britain continued to increase and that of France to decline.

The health of Clive had never been good during his residence in India; and his constitution was now so much impaired that he determined to return to England. Before his departure he undertook a service of considerable difficulty, and performed it with his usual vigour and dexterity. The forts of Covelong and Chingleput were occupied by French garrisons. It was determined to send a force against them. But the only force available for this purpose was of such a description that no officer but Clive would risk his reputation by commanding it. It consisted of five hundred newly-levied sepoys and two hundred recruits who had just landed from England, and who were the worst and lowest wretches that the Company's crimps could pick up in the flash-houses of London. Clive, ill and exhausted as he was, undertook to make an army of this undisciplined rabble, and marched with them to Covelong. A shot from the fort killed one of these extraordinary soldiers; on which all the rest faced about and ran away, and it was with the greatest difficulty that Clive rallied them. On another occasion the noise of a gun terrified the sentinels so much that one of them was found, some hours later, at the bottom of a well. Clive gradually accustomed them to danger, and, by exposing himself constantly in the most perilous situations, shamed them into courage. He at length succeeded in forming a respectable force out of his unpromising materials. Covelong fell. Clive learned that a strong detachment was marching to relieve it from Chingleput. He took measures to prevent the enemy from learning that they were too late, laid an ambuscade for them on the road, killed a hundred of them with one fire, took three hundred prisoners, pursued the fugitives to the gates of Chingleput, laid siege instantly to that fastness, reputed one of the strongest in India, made a breach, and was on the point of storming, when the French commandant capitulated and retired with his men.

Clive returned to Madras victorious, but in a state of health which rendered it impossible for him to remain there long. He married at this time a young lady of the name of Maskelyne, sister of the eminent mathematician, who long held the post of Astronomer Royal. She is described as handsome and accomplished; and her husband's letters, it is said, contain proofs that he was devotedly attached to her.

Almost immediately after the marriage, Clive embarked with his bride for England. He returned a very different person from the poor slighted boy who had been sent out ten years before to seek his fortune. He was only twenty-seven; yet his country already respected him as one of her first soldiers. There was then general peace in Europe. The Carnatic was the only part of the world where the English and French were in arms against each other. The vast schemes of Dupleix had excited no small uneasiness in the city of London; and the rapid turn of fortune, which was chiefly owing to the courage and talents of Clive, had been hailed with great delight. The young captain was known at the India House by the honourable nickname of General Clive, and was toasted by that appellation at the feasts of the Directors. On his arrival in England he found himself an object of general interest and admiration. The East India Company thanked him for his services in the warmest terms, and presented him with a sword set with diamonds. With rare delicacy, he refused to receive this token of gratitude unless a similar compliment was paid to his friend and commander, Lawrence.

It may easily be supposed that Clive was most cordially welcomed home by his family, who were delighted by his success, though they seem to have been hardly able to comprehend how their naughty idle Bobby had become so great a man. His father had been singularly hard of belief. Not until the news of the defence of Arcot arrived in England was the old gentleman heard to growl out that after all the booby had something in him. His expressions of approbation became stronger and stronger as news arrived of one brilliant exploit after another; and he was at length immoderately fond and proud of his son.

Clive's relations had very substantial reasons for rejoicing at his return. Considerable sums of prize money had fallen to his share; and he had brought home a moderate fortune, part of which he expended in extricating his father from pecuniary difficulties and in redeeming the family estate. The remainder he appears to have dissipated in the course of about two years. He lived splendidly, dressed gaily even for those times, kept a carriage and saddle horses, and, not content with these ways of getting rid of his money, resorted to the most speedy and effectual of all modes of evacuation, a contested election followed by a petition.

At the time of the general election of 1754, the government was in a very singular state. There was scarcely any formal Opposition. The Jacobites had been cowed by the issue of the last rebellion. The Tory party had fallen into utter contempt. It had been deserted by all the men of talents who had belonged to it, and had scarcely given a sympton of life during some years. The small faction which had been held together by the influence and promises of Prince Frederic had been dispersed by his death. Almost every public man of distinguished talents in the kingdom, whatever his early connections might have been, was in office, and called himself a Whig. But this extraordinary appearance of concord was quite delusive. The administration itself was distracted by bitter enmities and conflicting pretensions. The chief object of its members was to depress and supplant each other. The prime minister, Newcastle, weak, timid, jealous and perfidious, was at once detested and despised by some of the most important members of his government, and by none more than by Henry Fox, the Secretary at War. This able, daring and ambitious man seized every opportunity of crossing the First Lord of the Treasury, from whom he well knew that he had little to dread and little to hope ; for Newcastle was through life equally afraid of breaking with men of parts and of promoting them.

Newcastle had set his heart on returning two members for St. Michael, one of those wretched Cornish boroughs which were swept away by the Reform Act in 1832. He was opposed by Lord Sandwich, whose influence had long been paramount there : and Fox exerted himself strenuously in Sandwich's behalf. Clive, who had been introduced to Fox and very kindly received by him, was brought forward on the Sandwich interest, and was returned. But a petition was presented against the return, and was backed by the whole influence of the Duke of Newcastle.

The case was heard, according to the usage of that time, before a committee of the whole House. Questions respecting elections were then considered merely as party questions. Judicial impartiality was not even affected. Sir Robert Walpole was in the habit of saying openly that, in election battles, there ought to be no quarter. On the present occasion the excitement was great. The matter really at issue was, not whether Clive had been properly or improperly returned, but whether Newcastle or Fox was to be master of the new House of Commons, and consequently first minister. The contest was long and obstinate, and success seemed to lean sometimes to one side and sometimes to the other. Fox put forth all his rare powers of debate, beat half the lawyers in the House at their own weapons, and carried division after division against the whole influence of the Treasury. The committee decided in Clive's favour. But when the resolution was reported to the House, things took a different course. The remnant of the Tory Opposition, contemptible as it was, had yet sufficient weight to turn the scale between the nicely balanced parties of Newcastle and Fox. Newcastle the Tories could only despise. Fox they hated, as the boldest and most subtle politician and the ablest debater among the Whigs—as the steady friend of Walpole—as the devoted adherent of the Duke of Cumberland. After wavering till the last moment, they determined to vote in a body with the Prime Minister's friends. The consequence was that the House, by a small majority, rescinded the decision of the committee, and Clive was unseated.

Ejected from Paliament and straitened in his means, he naturally began to look again towards India. The Company and the Government were eager to avail themselves of his services. A treaty favourable to England had indeed been concluded in the Carnatic. Dupleix had been superseded, and had returned with the wreck of his immense fortune to Europe, where calumny and chicanery soon hunted him to his grave. But many signs indicated that a war between France and Great Britian was at hand ; and it was therefore thought desirable to send an able commander to the Company's settlements in India. The Directors appointed Clive governor of Fort St. David. The King gave him the commission of a lieutenant-colonel in the British army, and in 1755 he again sailed for Asia.

The first service on which he was employed after he returned to the East was the reduction of the stronghold of Gheriah. This fortress, built on a craggy promontory and almost surrounded by the ocean, was the den of a pirate named Angria, whose barks had long been the terror of the Arabian

Gulf. Admiral Watson, who commanded the English squadron in the Eastern seas, burned Angria's fleet, while Clive attacked the fastness by land. The place soon fell, and a booty of a hundred and fifty thousand pounds sterling was divided among the conquerors.

After this exploit, Clive proceeded to his government of Fort St. David. Before he had been their two months, he received intelligence which called forth all the energy of his bold and active mind.

Of the provinces which had been subject to the house of Tamerlane, the wealthiest was Bengal. No part of India possessed such natural advantages both for agriculture and for commerce. The Ganges, rushing through a hundred channels to the sea, has formed a vast plain of rich mould which, even under the tropical sky, rivals the verdure of an English April. The rice fields yield an increase such as is elsewhere unknown. Spices, sugar, vegetable oils are produced with marvellous exuberance. The rivers afford an inexhaustible supply of fish. The desolate islands along the sea-coast, overgrown by noxious vegetation and swarming with deer and tigers, supply the cultivated districts with abundance of salt. The great stream which fertilises the soil is, at the same time, the chief highway of Eastern commerce. On its banks, and on those of its tributary waters, are the wealthiest marts, the most splendid capitals and the most sacred shrines of India. The tyranny of man had for ages struggled in vain against the overflowing bounty of nature. In spite of the Mussulman despot and of the Mahratta freebooter, Bengal was known through the East as the garden of Eden, as the rich kingdom. Its population multiplied exceedingly. Other provinces were nourished from the overflowing of its granaries; and the ladies of London and Paris were clothed in the delicate produce of its looms. The race by whom this rich tract was peopled, enervated by a soft climate and accustomed to peaceful employments, bore the same relation to other Asiatics which the Asiatics generally bear to the bold and energetic children of Europe. The Castilians have a proverb, that in Valencia the earth is water and the men women; and the description is at least equally applicable to the vast plain of the Lower Ganges. Whatever the Bengalee does he does languidly. His favourite pursuits are sedentary. He shrinks from bodily exertion; and, though voluble in dispute and singularly pertinacious in the war of chicane, he seldom engages in a personal conflict and scarcely ever enlists as a soldier. We doubt whether there be a hundred genuine Bengalees in the whole army of the East India Company. There never, perhaps, existed a people so thoroughly fitted by nature and by habit for a foreign yoke.

The great commercial companies of Europe had long possessed factories in Bengal. The French were settled, as they still are, at Chandernagore on the Hoogley. Lower down the stream, the English had built Fort William. A church and ample warehouses rose in the vicinity. A row of spacious houses, belonging to the chief factors of the East India Company, lined the banks of the river; and in the neighbourhood had sprung up a large and busy native town where some Hindoo merchants of great opulence had fixed their abode. But the tract now covered by the palaces of Chowringhee contained only a few miserable huts thatched with straw. A jungle, abandoned to water-fowl and alligators, covered the site of the present Citadel and the Course, which is now daily crowded at sunset with the gayest equipages of Calcutta. For the ground on which the settlement stood, the English, like other great landholders, paid rent to the government; and they were, like other great landholders, permitted to exercise a certain jurisdiction within their domain.

The great province of Bengal, together with Orissa and Bahar, had long been governed by a viceroy whom the English called Aliverdy Khan, and who, like the other viceroys of the Mogul, had become virtually independent. He died in 1756, and the sovereignty descended to his grandson, a youth under twenty years of age, who bore the name of Surajah Dowlah. Oriental despots are perhaps the worst class of human beings; and this unhappy boy was one of the worst specimens of his class. His understanding was naturally feeble and his temper naturally unamiable. His education had been such as would have enervated even a vigorous intellect and perverted even a generous disposition. He was unreasonable, because nobody ever dared to reason with him, and selfish, because he had never been made to feel himself dependent on the good will of others. Early debauchery had unnerved his body and his mind. He indulged immoderately in the use of ardent spirits, which inflamed his weak brain almost to madness. His chosen companions were flatterers sprung from the dregs of the people and recommended by nothing but buffoonery and servility. It is said that he had arrived at the last stage of human depravity, when cruelty becomes pleasing for its own sake—when the sight of pain as pain, where no advantage is to be gained, no offence punished, no danger averted, is an agreeable excitement. It had early been his amusement to torture beasts and birds; and, when he grew up, he enjoyed with still keener relish the misery of his fellow-creatures.

From a child Surajah Dowlah had hated the English. It was his whim to do so; and his whims was never opposed. He had also formed a very exaggerated notion of the wealth which might be obtained by plundering them; and his feeble and uncultivated mind was incapable of perceiving that the riches of Calcutta, had they been even greater than he imagined, would not compensate him for what he must lose if the European trade, of which Bengal was a chief seat, should be driven by his violence to some other quarter. Pretexts for a quarrel were readily found. The English, in expectation of a war with France, had begun to fortify their settlement without special permission from the Nabob. A rich native, whom he longed to plunder, had taken refuge at Calcutta and had not been delivered up. On such grounds as these, Surajah Dowlah marched with a great army against Fort William.

The servants of the Company at Madras had been forced by Dupleix to become statesmen and soldiers. Those in Bengal were still mere traders, and were terrified and bewildered by the approaching danger. The governor, who had heard much of Surajah Dowlah's cruelty, was frightened out of his wits, jumped into a boat and took refuge in the nearest ship. The military commandant thought that he could not do better than follow so good an example. The fort was taken after a feeble resistance; and great numbers of the English fell into the hands of the conquerors. The Nabob seated himself with regal pomp in the principal hall of the factory and ordered Mr. Holwell, the first in rank among the prisoners, to be brought before him. He abused the insolence of the English and grumbled at the smallness of the treasure which he had found, but promised to spare their lives, and retired to rest.

Then was committed that great crime, memorable for its singular atrocity, memorable for the tremendous retribution by which it was followed. The English captives were left to the mercy of the guards; and the guards determined to secure them for the night in the prison of the garrison, a chamber known by the fearful name of the Black Hole. Even for a single European malefactor, that dungeon would, in such a climate, have been too close and narrow. The space was only twenty feet square. The air-holes were small and obstructed. It was the summer solstice, the season when the fierce heat of Bengal can scarcely be rendered tolerable to natives of England by lofty halls and by the constant waving of fans. The number of the prisoners was one hundred and forty-six. When they were ordered to enter the cell, they imagined that the soldiers were joking; and being in high spirits on account of the promise of the Nabob to spare their lives, they laughed and jested at the absurdity of the notion. They soon discovered their mistake. They expostulated; they entreated; but in vain. The guards threatened to cut down all who hesitated. The captives were driven into the cell at the point of the sword, and the door was instantly shut and locked upon them.

Nothing in history or fiction—not even the story which Ugolino told in the sea of everlasting ice after he had wiped his bloody lips on the scalp of his murderer—approaches the horrors which were recounted by the few survivors of that night. They cried for mercy. They strove to burst the door. Holwell, who even in that extremity retained some presence of mind, offered large bribes to the jaolers. But the answer was that nothing could be done without the Nabob's orders, that the Nabob was asleep, and that he would be angry if anybody woke him. Then the prisoners went mad with despair. They trampled each other down, fought for the places at the windows, fought for the pittance of water with which the cruel mercy of the murderers mocked their agonies—raved, prayed, blasphemed—implored the guards to fire among them. The jaolers in the meantime held lights to the bars and shouted with laughter at the frantic struggles of their victims. At length the tumult died away in low gaspings and moanings. The day broke. The Nabob had slept off his debauch and permitted the door to be opened. But it was some time before the soldiers could make a lane for the survivors, by piling up on each side the heaps of corpses on which the burning climate had already begun to do its loathsome work. When at length a passage was made, twenty-three ghastly figures, such as their own mothers would not have known, staggered one by one out of the charnel-house. A pit was instantly dug. The dead bodies, a hundred and twenty-three in number, were flung into it promiscuously and covered up.

But these things, which, after the lapse of more than eighty years, cannot be told or read without horror, awakened neither remorse nor pity in the bosom of the savage Nabob. He inflicted no punishment on the murderers. He showed no tenderness to the survivors. Some of them, indeed, from whom nothing was to be got, were suffered to depart; but those from whom it was thought that anything could be extorted were treated with execrable cruelty. Holwell, unable to walk, was carried before the tyrant, who reproached him, threatened him, and sent him up the country in irons, together with some other gentlemen who were suspected of knowing more than they chose to tell about the treasures of the Company. These persons, still bowed down by the sufferings of that great agony, were lodged in miserable sheds and fed only with grain and water, till at length the intercessions of the female relations of the Nabob procured their release. One Englishwoman had survived that night. She was placed in the harem of the Prince at Moorshedabad.

Surajah Dowlah, in the meantime, sent letters to his nominal sovereign at Delhi, describing the late conquest in the most pompous language. He placed a garrison in Fort William, forbade Englishmen to dwell in the neighbourhood, and directed that in memory of his great actions, Calcutta should thenceforward be called Alinagore, that is to say, the Port of God.

In August the news of the fall of Calcutta reached Madras, and excited the fiercest and bitterest resentment. The cry of the whole settlement was for vengeance. Within forty-eight hours after the arrival of the intelligence, it was determined that an expedition should be sent to the Hoogley and that Clive should be at the head of the land forces. The naval armament was under the command of Admiral Watson. Nine hundred English infantry— fine troops and full of spirit—and fifteen hundred sepoys composed the army which sailed to punish a Prince who had more subjects and larger revenues than the King of Prussia or the Empress Maria Theresa. In October the expedition sailed, but it had to make its way against adverse winds and did not reach Bengal till December.

The Nabob was revelling in fancied security at Moorshedabad. He was so profoundly ignorant of the state of foreign countries that he often used to say that there were not ten thousand men in all Europe; and it had never occurred to him as possible that the English would dare to invade his dominions. But though undisturbed by any fear of their military power, he began to miss them greatly. His revenues fell off; and his ministers succeeded in making him understand that a ruler may sometimes find it more profitable to protect traders in the open enjoyment of their gains than to put them to the torture for the purpose of discovering hidden chests of gold and jewels. He was already disposed to permit the Company to resume its mercantile operations in his country when he received the news that an English armament was in the Hoogley. He instantly ordered all his troops to assemble at Moorshedabad and marched towards Calcutta.

Clive had commenced operations with his usual vigour. He took Budgebudge, routed the garrison of Fort William, recovered Calcutta, stormed and sacked Hoogley. The Nabob, already disposed to make some concessions to the English, was confirmed in his pacific disposition by these proofs of their power and spirit. He accordingly made overtures to the chiefs of the invading armament, and offered to restore the factory and to give compensation to those whom he had despoiled.

Clive's profession was war; and he felt that there was something discreditable in an accommodation with Surajah Dowlah. But his power was limited. A committee, chiefly composed of servants of the Company who had fled from Calcutta, had the principal direction of affairs; and these persons were eager to be restored to their posts and compensated for their losses. The government of Madras, apprised that war had commenced in Europe and apprehensive of an attack from the French, became impatient for the return of the armament. The promises of the Nabob were large, the chances of a contest doubtful; and Clive consented to treat, though he expressed his regret that things should not be concluded in so glorious a manner as he could have wished.

With this negotiation commences a new chapter in the life of Clive. Hitherto he had been merely a soldier carrying into effect, with eminent ability and valour, the plans of others. Henceforth he is to be chiefly regarded as a statesman; and his military movements are to be considered as subordinate to his political designs. That in his new capacity he displayed great talents and obtained great success, is undeniable. But it is also undeniable that the transactions in which he now began to take a part have left a stain on his moral character.

We can by no means agree with Sir John Malcolm, who is obstinately resolved to see nothing but honour and integrity in the conduct of his hero. But we can as little agree with Mr. Mill, who has gone so far as to say that Clive was a man ." to whom deception, when it suited his purpose, never cost a pang." Clive seems to us to have been constitutionally the very opposite of a knave—bold even to temerity—sincere even to indiscretion—hearty in friendship—open in enmity. Neither in his private life, nor in those parts of his public life in which he had to do with his countrymen, do we find any signs of a propensity to cunning. On the contrary, in all the disputes in which he was engaged as an Englishman against Englishmen—from his boxing-matches at school to those stormy altercations at the India House and in Parliament amidst which his later years were passed—his very faults were those of a high and magnanimous spirit. The truth seems to have been that he considered Oriental politics as a game in which nothing was unfair. He knew that the standard of morality among the natives of India differed widely from that established in England. He knew that he had to deal with men destitute of what in Europe is called honour—with men who would give any promise without hesitation and break any promise without shame—with men who would unscrupulously employ corruption, perjury, forgery to compass their ends. His letters show that the great difference between Asiatic and European morality was constantly in his thoughts. He seems to have imagined, most erroneously in our opinion, that he could effect nothing against such adversaries if he was content to be bound by ties from which they were free—if he went on telling truth and hearing none—if he fulfilled, to his own hurt, all his engagements with confederates who never kept an engagement that was not to their advantage. Accordingly, this man, in the other parts of his life an honourable English gentleman and a soldier, was no sooner matched against an Indian intriguer than he became himself an Indian intriguer, and descended, without scruple, to falsehood, to hypocritical caresses, to the substitution of documents and to the counterfeiting of hands.

The negotiations between the English and the Nabob were carried on chiefly by two agents—Mr. Watts, a servant of the Company, and a Bengalee of the name of Omichund. This Omichund had been one of the wealthiest native merchants resident at Calcutta and had sustained great losses in consequence of the Nabob's expedition against that place. In the course of his commercial transactions he had seen much of the English, and was peculiarly qualified to serve as a medium of communication between them and a native court. He possessed great influence with his own race, and had in large measure the Hindoo talents—quick observation, tact, dexterity, perseverance—and the Hindoo vices, servility, greediness and treachery.

The Nabob behaved with all the faithlessness of an Indian statesman and with all the levity of a boy whose mind had been enfeebled by power and self-indulgence. He promised, retracted, hesitated, evaded. At one time he advanced with his army in a threatening manner towards Calcutta; but when he saw the resolute front which the English presented, he fell back in alarm and consented to make peace with them on their own terms. The treaty was no sooner concluded than he formed new designs against them. He intrigued with the French authorities at Chandernagore. He invited Bussy to march from the Deccan to the Hoogley and to drive the English out of Bengal. All this was well known to Clive and Watson. They determined accordingly to strike a decisive blow and to attack Chandernagore before the force there could be strengthened by new arrivals, either from the south of India or from Europe. Watson directed the expedition by water, Clive by land. The success of the combined movements was rapid and complete. The fort, the garrison, the artillery, the military stores, all fell into the hands of the English. Nearly five hundred European troops were among the prisoners.

The Nabob had feared and hated the English, even while he was still able to oppose to them their French rivals. The French were now vanquished; and he began to regard the English with still greater fear and still greater hatred. His weak and unprincipled mind oscillated between servility and insolence. One day he sent a large sum to Calcutta, as part of the compensation due for the wrongs which he had committed. The next day he sent a present of jewels to Bussy, exhorting that distinguished officer to hasten to protect Bengal against "Clive, the daring in war, on whom," says his highness, "may all bad fortune attend." He ordered his army to march against the English. He countermanded his orders. He tore Clive's letters. He then sent answers in the most florid language of compliment. He ordered Watts out of his presence and threatened to impale him. He again sent for him and begged pardon for the insult. In the meantime, his wretched maladministration, his folly, his dissolute manners and his love of the lowest company had disgusted all classes of his subjects—soldiers, traders, civil functionaries, the proud and ostentatious Mahommedans, the timid, supple and parsimonious Hindoos. A formidable confederacy was formed against him, in which were included Roydullub, the minister of finance, Meer Jaffier, the principal commander of the troops, and Jugget Seit, the richest banker in India. The plot was confided to the English agents; and a communication was opened between the malcontents at Moorshedabad and the committee at Calcutta.

In the committee there was much hesitation; but Clive's voice was given in favour of the conspirators, and his vigour and firmness bore down all opposition. It was determined that the English should lend their powerful assistance to depose Surajah Dowlah and to place Meer Jaffier on the throne of Bengal. In return, Meer Jaffier promised ample compensation to the Company and its servants and a liberal donative to the army, the navy and the committee. The odious vices of Surajah Dowlah, the wrongs which the English had suffered at his hands, the dangers to which our trade must have been exposed, had he continued to reign, appear to us fully to justify the resolution of deposing him. But nothing can justify the dissimulation which Clive stooped to practise. He wrote to Surajah Dowlah in terms so affectionate that they for a time lulled that weak prince into perfect security. The same courier who carried this "soothing letter," as Clive calls it, to the Nabob, carried to Mr. Watts a letter in the following terms: "Tell Meer Jaffier to fear nothing. I will join him with five thousand men who never turned their backs. Assure him I will march night and day to his assistance and stand by him as long as I have a man left."

It was impossible that a plot which had so many ramifications should long remain entirely concealed. Enough reached the ears of the Nabob to arouse his suspicions. But he was soon quieted by the fictions and artifices which the inventive genius of Omichund produced with miraculous readiness. All was going well; the plot was nearly ripe; when Clive learned that Omichund was likely to play false. The artful Bengalee had been promised a liberal compensation for all that he had lost at Calcutta. But this would not satisfy him. His services had been great. He held the thread of the whole intrigue. By one word breathed in the ear of Surajah Dowlah, he could undo all that he had done. The lives of Watts, of Meer Jaffier, of all the conspirators, were at his mercy; and he determined to take advantage of his situation and to make his own terms. He demanded three hundred thousand pounds sterling as a price of his secrecy and of his assistance. The committee, incensed by the treachery and appalled by the danger, knew not what course to take. But Clive was more than Omichund's match in Omichund's own arts. The man, he said, was a villian. Any artifice which would defeat such knavery was justifiable. The best course would be to promise what was asked. Omichund would soon be at their mercy; and then they might punish him by witholding from him, not only the bribe which he now demanded, but all the compensation which all the other sufferers of Calcutta were to receive.

His advice was taken. But how was the wary and sagacious Hindoo to be deceived? He had demanded that an article touching his claims should be inserted in the treaty between Meer Jaffier and the English, and he would not be satisfied unless he saw it with his own eyes. Clive had an expedient ready. Two treaties were drawn up, one on white paper, the other on red, the former real, the latter fictitious. In the former, Omichund's name was not mentioned; the latter, which was to be shown to him, contained a stipulation in his favour.

But another difficulty arose. Admiral Watson had scruples about signing the red treaty. Omichund's vigilance and acuteness were such that the absence of so important a name would probably awaken his suspicions. But Clive was not a man to do anything by halves. We almost blush to write it. He forged Admiral Watson's name.

All was now ready for action. Mr. Watts fled secretly from Moorshedabad. Clive put his troops in motion, and wrote to the Nabob in a tone very different from that of his previous letters. He set forth all the wrongs which the British had suffered, offered to submit the points in dispute to the arbitration of Meer Jaffier, and concluded by announcing that, as the rains were about to set in, he and his men would do themselves the honour of waiting on his Highness for an answer.

Surajah Dowlah instantly assembled his whole force and marched to encounter the English. It had been agreed that Meer Jaffier should separate himself from the Nabob and carry over his division to Clive. But, as the decisive moment approached, the fears of the conspirator overpowered his ambition. Clive had advanced to Cossimbuzar; the Nabob lay with a mighty power a few miles off at Plassey; and still Meer Jaffier delayed to fulfil his engagements and returned evasive answers to the earnest remonstrances of the English general.

Clive was in a painfully anxious situation. He could place no confidence in the sincerity or in the courage of his confederate: and, whatever confidence he might place in his own military talents and in the valour and discipline of his troops, it was no light thing to engage an army twenty times as numerous as his own. Before him lay a river over which it was easy to advance, but over which, if things went ill, not one of his little band would ever return. On this occasion, for the first and for the last time, his dauntless spirit, during a few hours, shrank from the fearful responsibility of making a decision. He called a council of war. The majority pronounced against fighting; and Clive declared his concurrence with the majority. Long afterward, he said that he had never called but one council of war and that, if he had taken the advice of that council, the British would never have been masters of Bengal. But scarcely had the meeting broken up when he was himself again. He retired alone under the shade of some trees and passed near an hour there in thought. He came back determined to put everything to the hazard, and gave orders that all should be in readiness for passing the river on the morrow.

The river was passed; and, at the close of a toilsome day's march, the army, long after sunset, took up its quarters in a grove of mango-trees near Plassey, within a mile of the enemy. Clive was unable to sleep: he heard through the whole night the sound of drums and cymbals from the vast camp of the Nabob. It is not strange that even his stout heart should now and then have sunk when he reflected against what odds and for what a prize he was in a few hours to contend.

Nor was the rest of Surajah Dowlah more peaceful. His mind, at once weak and stormy, was distracted by wild and horrible apprehensions. Appalled by the greatness and nearness of the crisis, distrusting his captains, dreading everyone who approached him, dreading to be left alone, he sat gloomily in his tent, haunted, a Greek poet would have said, by the furies of those who had cursed him with their last breath in the Black Hole.

The day broke, the day which was to decide the fate of India. At sunrise the army of the Nabob, pouring through many openings of the camp, began to move towards the grove where the English lay. Forty thousand infantry, armed with firelocks, pikes, swords, bows and arrows, covered the plain. They were accompanied by fifty pieces of ordnance of the largest size, each tugged by a long team of white oxen, and each pushed on from behind by an elephant. Some smaller guns, under the direction of a few French auxiliaries, were perhaps more formidable. The cavalry were fifteen thousand, drawn, not from the effeminate population of Bengal, but from the bolder race which inhabits the northern provinces; and the practiced eye of Clive could perceive that both the men and the horses were more powerful than those of the Carnatic. The force which he had to oppose to this great multitude consisted of only three thousand men. But of these nearly a thousand were English; and all were led by English officers and trained in the English discipline. Conspicuous in the ranks of the little army were the men of the Thirty-Ninth Regiment, which still bears on its colours, amidst many honourable additions won under Wellington in Spain and Gascony, the name of Plassey and the proud motto *Primus in Indis.*

The battle commenced with a canonade, in which the artillery of the Nabob did scarcely any execution while the few field-pieces of the English produced great effect. Several of the most distinguished officers in Surajah Dowlah's service fell. Disorder began to spread through his ranks. His own terror increased every moment. One of the conspirators urged on him the expediency of retreating. The insidious advice, agreeing as it did with what his own terrors suggested, was readily received. He ordered his army to fall back, and this order decided his fate. Clive snatched the moment, and ordered his troops to advance. The confused and dispirited multitude gave way before the onset of disciplined valour. No mob attacked by regular soldiers was, ever more completely routed. The little band of Frenchmen, who alone ventured to confront the English, were swept down the stream of fugitives. In an hour the forces of Surajah Dowlah were dispersed, never to reassemble. Only five hundred of the vanquished were slain. But their camp, their guns, their baggage, innumerable wagons, innumerable cattle, remained in the power of the conquerors. With the loss of twenty-two soldiers killed and fifty wounded, Clive had scattered an army of near sixty thousand men and subdued an empire larger and more populous than Great Britain.

Meer Jaffier had given no assistance to the English during the action. But, as soon as he saw that the fate of the day was decided, he drew off his division of the army, and, when the battle was over, sent his congratulations to his ally. The next day he repaired to the English quarters, not a little uneasy as to the reception which awaited him there. He gave evident signs of alarm when a guard was drawn out to receive him with the honours due to his rank. But his apprehensions were speedily removed. Clive came forward to meet him, embraced him, saluted him as Nabob of the three great provinces of Bengal, Bahar and Orissa, listened graciously to his apologies, and advised him to march without delay to Moorshedabad.

Surajah Dowlah had fled from the field of battle with all the speed with which a fleet camel could carry him, and arrived at Moorshedabad in little more than twenty-four hours. There he called his counsellors round him. The wisest advised him to put himself into the hands of the English, from whom he had nothing worse to fear than deposition and confinement. But he attributed this suggestion to treachery. Others urged him to try the chance of war again. He approved the advice, and issued orders accordingly. But he wanted spirit to adhere even during one day to a manly resolution. He learned that Meer

Jaffier had arrived; and his terrors became insupportable. Disguised in a mean dress, with a casket of jewels in his hand, he let himself down at night from a window of his palace and, accompanied by only two attendants, embarked on the river for Patna.

In a few days Clive arrived at Moorshedabad, escorted by two hundred English soldiers and three hundred sepoys. For his residence had been assigned a palace, which was surrounded by a garden so spacious that all the troops who accompanied him could conveniently encamp within it. The ceremony of the installation of Meer Jaffier was instantly performed. Clive led the new Nabob to the seat of honour, placed him on it, presented to him, after the immemorial fashion of the East, an offering of gold, and then, turning to the natives who filled the hall, congratulated them on the good fortune which had freed them from a tyrant. He was compelled on this occasion to use the services of an interpreter; for it is remarkable that, long as he resided in India, intimately acquainted as he was with Indian politics and with the Indian character, and adored as he was by his Indian soldiery, he never learned to express himself with facility in any Indian language; and is said to have been sometimes under the necessity of employing the smattering of Portuguese which he had acquired, when a lad, in Brazil.

The new sovereign was now called upon to fulfil the engagements into which he had entered with his allies. A conference was held at the house of Jugget Seit, the great banker, for the purpose of making the necessary arrangements. Omichund came thither, fully believing himself to stand high in the favour of Clive, who, with dissimulation surpassing even the dissimulation of Bengal, had up to that day treated him with undiminished kindness. The white treaty was produced and read. Clive then turned to Mr. Scrafton, one of the servants of the Company, and said in English, "It is now time to undeceive Omichund." "Omichund," said Mr. Scrafton in Hindostanee, "the red treaty is a taken-in. You are to have nothing." Omichund fell back insensible into the arms of his attendants. He revived; but his mind was irreparably ruined. Clive, who though inscrupulous in his dealings with Indian politicians, was not inhuman, seems to have been touched. He saw Omichund a few days later, spoke to him kindly, advised him to make a pilgrimage to one of the great temples of India in the hope that change of scene might restore his health, and was even disposed, notwithstanding all that had passed, again to employ his talents in the public service. But from the moment of that sudden shock, the unhappy man sank gradually into idiocy. He who had formerly been distinguished by the strength of his understanding and the simplicity of his habits, now squandered the remains of his fortune on childish trinkets, and loved to exhibit himself dressed in rich garments and hung with precious stones. In this abject state he languished a few months and then died.

We should not think it necessary to offer any remarks for the purpose of directing the judgment of our readers with respect to this transaction, had not Sir John Malcolm undertaken to defend it in all its parts. He regrets, indeed, that it was necessary to employ means so liable to abuse as forgery; but he will not admit that any blame attaches to those who deceived the deceiver. He thinks that the English were not bound to keep faith with one who kept no faith with them.; and that if they had fulfilled their engagements with the wily Bengalee, so signal an example of successful treason would have produced a crowd of imitators. Now, we will not discuss this point on any rigid principles of morality. Indeed, it is quite unnecessary to do so; for, looking at the question as a question of expediency in the lowest sense of the word, and using no arguments but such as Machiavelli might have employed in his conferences with Borgia, we are convinced that Clive was altogether in the wrong, and that he committed, not merely a crime, but a blunder. That honesty is the best policy is a maxim which we firmly believe to be generally correct, even with respect to the temporal interest of individuals; but, with respect to societies, the rule is subject to still fewer exceptions, and that for this reason, that the life of societies is longer than the life of individuals. It is possible to mention men who have owed great worldly prosperity to breaches of private faith; but we doubt whether it be possible to mention a state which has on the whole been a gainer by a breach of public faith. The entire history of British India is an illustration of this great truth, that it is not prudent to oppose perfidy to perfidy—that the most efficient weapon with which men can encounter falsehood is truth. During a long course of years, the English rulers of India, surrounded by allies and enemies whom no engagement could bind, have generally acted with sincerity and uprightness, and the event has proved that sincerity and uprightness are wisdom. English valour and English intelligence have done less to extend and to preserve our Oriental empire than English veracity. All that we could have gained by imitating the doublings, the evasions, the fictions, the perjuries which have been employed against us, is as nothing when compared with what we have gained by being the one power in India on whose word reliance can be placed. No oath which superstition can devise, no hostage however precious, inspires a hundredth part of the confidence which is produced by the "yea, yea," and "nay, nay," of a British envoy. No fastness, however strong by art or nature, gives to its inmates a security like that enjoyed by the chief who, passing through the territories of powerful and deadly enemies, is armed with the British guarantee. The mightiest princes of the East can scarcely, by the offer of enormous usury, draw forth any portion of the wealth which is concealed under the hearths of their subjects. The British Government offers little more than four per cent.; and avarice hastens to bring forth tens of millions of rupees from its most secret repositories. A hostile monarch may promise mountains of gold to our sepoys, on condition that they will desert the standard of the Company. The Company promises only a moderate pension after a long service. But every sepoy knows that the promise of the Company will be kept; he knows that if he lives a hundred years his rice and salt are as secure as the salary of the Governor-General; and he knows that there is not another state in India which would not, in spite of the most solemn vows, leave him to die of hunger in a ditch as soon as he had ceased to be useful. The greatest advantage which a government can possess is to be the one trustworthy government in the midst of governments which nobody can trust. This advantage we enjoy in Asia. Had we acted during the last two generations on the principles which Sir John Malcolm appears to have considered as sound—had we, as often as we had to deal with people like Omichund, retaliated by lying and forging and breaking faith, after their fashion—it is our firm belief that no courage or capacity could have upheld our empire.

Sir John Malcolm admits that Clive's breach of faith could be justified only by the strongest necessity. As we think that breach of faith not only unnecessary, but most inexpedient, we need hardly say that we condemn it most severely.

Omichund was not the only victim of the revolution. Surajah Dowlah was taken a few days after his flight and was brought before Meer Jaffier. There he flung himself on the ground in convulsions of fear, and with tears and loud cries implored the mercy which he had never shown. Meer Jaffier hesitated; but his son Meeran, a youth of seventeen, who in feebleness of brain and savageness of nature greatly resembled the wretched captive, was implacable. Surajah Dowlah was led into a secret chamber, to which in a short time the ministers of death were sent. In this act the English bore no part; and Meer Jaffier understood so much of their feelings, that he thought it necessary to apologise to them for having avenged them on their most malignant enemy.

The shower of wealth now fell copiously on the Company and its servants. A sum of eight hundred thousand pounds sterling, in coined silver, was sent down the river from Moorshedabad to Fort William. The fleet which conveyed this treasure consisted of more than a hundred boats, and performed its triumphal voyage with flags flying and music playing. Calcutta, which but a few months ago had been desolate, was now more prosperous than ever. Trade revived, and the signs of affluence appeared in every English house. As to Clive, there was no limit to his acquisitions but his own moderation. The treasury of Bengal was thrown open to him. There were piled up, after the usage of Indian princes, immense masses of coin, among which might not seldom be detected the florins and byzants with which, before any European ship had turned the Cape of Good Hope, the Venetians purchased the stuffs and spices of the East. Clive walked between heaps of gold and silver, crowned with rubies and diamonds, and was at liberty to help himself. He accepted between two and three hundred thousand pounds.

The pecuniary transactions between Meer Jaffier and Clive were, sixteen years later, condemned by the public voice and severely criticised in Parliament. They are vehemently defended by Sir John Malcolm. The accusers of the victorious general represented his gains as the wages of corruption, or as plunder extorted at the point of the sword from a helpless ally. The biographer, on the other hand, considers these great acquisitions as free gifts, honourable alike to the donor and to the receiver, and compares them to the rewards bestowed by foreign powers on Marlborough, on Nelson and on Wellington. It had always, he says, been customary in the East to give and receive presents; and there was, as yet, no Act of Parliament positively prohibiting English functionaries in India from profiting by this Asiatic usage. This reasoning, we own, does not quite satisfy us. We fully acquit Clive of selling the interests of his employers or his country; but we cannot acquit him of having done what, if not in itself evil, was yet of evil example. Nothing is more clear than that a general ought to be the servant of his own government, and of no other. It follows, that whatever rewards he receives for his services ought to be given either by his own government, or with the full knowledge and approbation of his own government. This rule ought to be strictly maintained, even with respect to the merest bauble—with respect to a cross, a medal, or a yard of coloured riband. But how can any government be well served if those who command its forces are at liberty, without its permission, without its privity, to accept princely fortunes from its allies? Is it idle to say that there was then no Act of Parliament prohibiting the practice of taking presents from Asiatic sovereigns. It is not on the Act which was passed at a later period for the purpose of preventing any such taking of presents, but on grounds which were valid before that Act was passed—on grounds of common law and common sense—that we arraign the conduct of Clive. There is no Act that we know of prohibiting the Secretary of State for Foreign Affairs from being in the pay of continental powers, but it is not the less true that a Secretary who should receive a secret pension from France would grossly violate his duty and would deserve severe punishment. Sir John Malcolm compares the conduct of Clive with that of the Duke of Wellington. Suppose—and we beg pardon for putting such a supposition even for the sake of argument—that the Duke of Wellington had, after the campaign of 1815, and while he commanded the army of occupation in France, privately accepted two hundred thousand pounds from Louis the Eighteenth as a mark of gratitude for the great services which his Grace had rendered to the House of Bourbon; what would be thought of such a transaction? Yet the statute-book no more forbids the taking of presents in Europe now than it forbade the taking of presents in Asia then.

At the same time, it must be admitted that, in Clive's case, there were many extenuating circumstances. He considered himself as the general, not of the Crown, but of the Company. The Company had, by implication at least, authorised its agents to enrich themselves by means of the liberality of the native princes, and by other means still more objectionable. It was hardly to be expected that the servant should entertain stricter notions of his duty than were entertained by his masters. Though Clive did not distinctly acquaint his employers with what had taken place and request their sanction, he did not, on the other hand, by studied concealment, show that he was conscious of having done wrong. On the contrary, he avowed with the greatest openness that the Nabob's bounty had raised him to affluence. Lastly, though we think that he ought not in such a way to have taken anything, we must admit that he deserves praise for having taken so little. He accepted twenty lacs of rupees.; It would have cost him only a word to make the twenty forty. It was a very easy exercise of virtue to declaim in England against Clive's rapacity; but not one in a hundred of his accusers would have shown so much self-command in the treasury of Moorshedabad.

Meer Jaffier could be upheld on the throne only by the hand which had placed him on it. He was not, indeed, a mere boy, nor had he been so unfortunate as to be born in the purple. He was not, therefore, quite so imbecile or quite as depraved as his predecessor had been. But he had none of the talents or virtues which his post required; and his son and heir, Meeran, was another Surajah Dowlah. The recent revolution had unsettled the minds of men. Many chiefs were in open insurrection against the new Nabob. The viceroy of the rich and powerful province of Oude, who, like the other viceroys of the Mogul, was now in truth an independent sovereign, menaced Bengal with invasion. Nothing but the talents and authority of Clive could support the tottering government. While things were in this state, a ship arrived with despatches which had been written at the India House before the news of the Battle of Plassey had reached London. The Directors had determined to place the English settlements in Bengal under a government constituted in the most cumbrous and absurd manner; and, to make the matter worse, no place in the arrangement was assigned to Clive. The persons who were selected to form this new government, greatly to their honour, took on themselves the responsibility of disobeying these preposterous orders, and invited Clive to exercise the supreme authority. He consented; and it soon appeared that the servants of the Company had only anticipated the wishes of their employers. The Director's, on receiving news of Clive's brilliant success, instantly appointed him governor of their possessions in Bengal, with the highest marks of gratitude and esteem. His power was now boundless, and far surpassed even that which Dupleix had attained in the south of India. Meer Jaffier regarded him with slavish awe. On one occasion, the Nabob spoke with severity to a native chief of high rank whose followers had been engaged in a brawl with some of the Company's sepoys. "Are you yet to learn," he said, "who that Colonel Clive is, and in what station God has placed him?" The chief, who, as a famous jester and an old friend of Meer Jaffier, could venture to take liberties, answered, "I affront the Colonel! I, who never get up in the morning without making three low bows to his jackass!" This was hardly an exaggeration. Europeans and natives were alike at Clive's feet. The English regarded him as the only man who could force Meer Jaffier to keep his engagements with them. Meer Jaffier regarded him as the only man who could protect the new dynasty against turbulent subjects and encroaching neighbours.

It is but justice to say that Clive used his power ably and vigorously for the advantage of his country. He sent forth an expedition against the tract lying to the north of the Carnatic. In this tract the French still had the ascendancy; and it was important to dislodge them. The conduct of the enterprise was intrusted to an officer of the name of Forde, who was then little known, but in whom the keen eye of the governor had detected military talents of a high order. The success of the expedition was rapid and splendid.

While a considerable part of the army of Bengal was thus engaged at a distance, a new and formidable danger menaced the western frontier. The Great Mogul was a prisoner at Delhi in the hands of a subject. His eldest son, named Shah Alum, destined to be the sport during many years of adverse fortune, and to be the tool in the hands, first of the Mahrattas and then of the English, had fled from the palace of his father. His birth was still revered in India. Some powerful princes, the Nabob of Oude in particular, were inclined to favour him. Shah Alum found it easy to draw to his standard great numbers of the military adventurers with whom every part of the country swarmed. An army of forty thousand men, of various races and religions, Mahrattas, Rohillas, Jauts and Afghans, were speedily assembled round him; and he formed the design of overthrowing the upstart whom the English had elevated to a throne and of establishing his own authority throughout Bengal, Orissa and Bahar.

Jaffier's terror was extreme; and the only expedient which occurred to him was to purchase, by the payment of a large sum of money, an accomodation with Shah Alum. This expedient had been repeatedly employed by those who, before him, had ruled the rich and unwarlike provinces near the mouth of the Ganges. But Clive treated the suggestion with a scorn worthy of his strong sense and dauntless courage. "If you do this," he wrote, "you will have the Nabob of Oude, the Mahrattas, and many more, come from all parts of the confines of your country, who will bully you out of money till you have none left in your treasury. I beg your Excellency will rely on the fidelity of the English, and of those troops which are attached to you. He wrote in a similar strain to the governor of Patna, a brave native soldier whom he highly esteemed. "Come to no terms; defend your city to the last. Rest assured that the English are staunch and firm friends, and that they never desert a cause in which they have once taken a part."

He kept his word. Shah Alum had invested Patna, and was on the point of proceeding to storm, when he learned that the Colonel was advancing by forced marches. The whole army which was approaching consisted of only four hundred and fifty Europeans and two thousand five hundred sepoys. But Clive and his Englishmen were now objects of dread over all the East. As soon as his advanced guard appeared, the besiegers fled before him. A few French adventurers, who were about the person of the prince, advised him to try the chance of battle; but in vain. In a few days this great army, which had been regarded with so much uneasiness by the court of Moorshedabad, melted away before the mere terror of the British name.

The conqueror returned in triumph to Fort William. The joy of Meer Jaffier was as unbounded as his fears had been, and led him to bestow on his preserver a princely token of gratitude. The quit-rent, which the East India Company was bound to pay to the Nabob for the extensive lands held by them to the south of Calcutta, amounted to near thirty thousand pounds sterling a year. The whole of this splendid estate, sufficient to support with dignity the highest rank of the British peerage, was now conferred on Clive for life.

This present we think Clive justified in accepting. It was a present which, from its very nature, could be no secret. In fact, the Company itself was his tenant, and, by its acquiescence, signified its approbation of Meer Jaffier's grant.

But the gratitude of Meer Jaffier did not last long. He had for some time felt that the powerful ally who had set him up might pull him down, and had been looking round for support against the formidable strength by which he had himself been hitherto supported. He knew that it would be impossible to find among the natives of India any force which would look the Colonel's little army in the face. The French power in Bengal was extinct. But the fame of the Dutch had anciently been great in the Eastern seas, and it was not yet distinctly known in Asia how much the power of Holland had declined in Europe. Secret communications passed between the court of Moorshedabad and the Dutch factory at Chinsurah, and urgent letters were sent from Chinsurah, exhorting the goverment of Batavia to fit out an expedition which might balance the power of the English in Bengal. The authorities of Batavia, eager to extend the influence of their country, and still more eager to obtain for themselves a share of the wealth which had recently raised so many English adventurers to opulence, equipped a powerful armament. Seven large ships from Java arrived unexpectedly in the Hoogley. The military force on board amounted to fifteen hundred men, of whom about one half were Europeans. The enterprise was well timed. Clive had sent such large detachments to oppose the French in the Carnatic that his army was now inferior in number to that of the Dutch. He knew that Meer Jaffier secretly favoured the invaders. He knew that he took on himself a serious responsibility if he attacked the forces of a friendly power, that the English ministers could not wish to see a war with Holland added to that in which they were already engaged with France; that they might disavow his acts, that they might punish him. He had recently remitted a great part of his fortune to Europe through the Dutch East India Company, and he had therefore a strong interest in avoiding any quarrel. But he was satisfied that, if he suffered the Batavian armament to pass up the river and to join the garrison of Chinsurah, Meer Jaffier would throw himself into the arms of these new allies, and that the English ascendancy in Bengal would be exposed to most serious danger. He took his resolution with characteristic boldness, and was most ably seconded by his officers, particularly by Colonel Forde, to whom the most important part of the operations was intrusted. The Dutch attempted to force a passage. The English encountered them both by land and water. On both elements the enemy had a great superiority of force. On both they were signally defeated. Their ships were taken. Their troops were put to a total route. Almost all the European soldiers, who constituted the main strength of the invading army, were killed or taken. The conquerors sat down before Chinsurah, and the chiefs of that settlement, now thoroughly humbled, consented to the terms which Clive dictated. They engaged to build no fortifications and to raise no troops beyond a small force necessary for the police of their factories; and it was distinctly provided that any violation of these covenants should be punished with instant expulsion from Bengal.

Three months after this great victory, Clive sailed for England. At home, honours and rewards awaited him—not indeed equal to his claims or to his ambition; but still such as, when his age, his rank in the army and his original place in society are considered, must be pronounced rare and splendid. He was raised to the Irish peerage, and encouraged to expect an English title. George the Third, who had just ascended the throne, received him with great distinction. The ministers paid him marked attention; and Pitt, whose influence in the House of Commons and in the country was unbounded, was eager to mark his regard for one whose exploits had contributed so much to the lustre of that memorable period. The great orator had already in Parliament described Clive as a heaven-born general—as a man who, bred to the labour of the desk, had displayed a military genius which might excite the admiration of the King of Prussia. There were then no reporters in the gallery; but these words, emphatically spoken by the first statesman of the age, had passed from mouth to mouth, had been transmitted to Clive in Bengal, and had greatly delighted and flattered him. Indeed, since the death of Wolfe, Clive was the only English general of whom his countrymen had much reason to be proud. The Duke of Cumberland had been generally unfortunate; and his single victory, having been gained over his countrymen and used with merciless severity, had been more fatal to his popularity than his many defeats. Conway, versed in the learning of his profession, and personally courageous, wanted vigour and capacity. Granby, honest, generous and as brave as a lion, had neither science nor genius. Sackville, inferior in knowledge and abilities to none of his contemporaries, had incurred, unjustly as we believe, the imputation most fatal to the character of a soldier. It was under the command of a foreign general that the British had triumphed at Minden and Warburg. The people, therefore, as was natural, greeted with pride and delight a captain of their own, whose native courage and self-taught skill had placed him on a level with the great tacticians of Germany.

The wealth of Clive was such as enabled him to vie with the first grandees of England. There remains proof that he had remitted more than a hundred and eighty thousand pounds through the Dutch East India Company and more than forty thousand pounds through the English Company. The amount which he had sent home through private houses was also considerable. He had invested great sums in jewels, then a very common mode of remittance from India. His purchases of diamonds, at Madras alone, amounted to twenty-five thousand pounds. Besides a great mass of ready money, he had his Indian estate, valued by himself at twenty-seven thousand a year. His whole annual income, in the opinion of Sir John Malcolm, who is desirous to state it as low as possible, exceeded forty thousand pounds; and incomes of forty thousand pounds at the time of the accession of George the Third were at least as rare as incomes of a hundred thousand pounds now. We may safely affirm that no Englishman, who started with nothing, has ever, in any line of life, created such a fortune at the early age of thirty-four.

It would be unjust not to add that he made a creditable use of his riches. As soon as the battle of Plassey had laid the foundation of his fortune, he sent ten thousand pounds to his sisters, bestowed as much more on other poor friends and relations, ordered his agent to pay eight hundred a year to his parents and to insist that they should keep a carriage, and settled five hundred a year on his old commander Lawrence, whose means were very slender. The whole sum which he expended in this manner may be calculated at fifty thousand pounds.

He now set himself to cultivate Parliamentary interest. His purchases of land seem to have been made in a great measure with that view; and, after the general election of 1761, he found himself in the House of Commons at the head of a body of dependents whose support must have been important to any administration. In English politics, however, he did not take a prominent part. His first attachments, as we have seen, were to Mr. Fox; at a later period he was attracted by the genius and success of Mr. Pitt; but finally he connected himself in the closest manner with George Grenville. Early in the session of 1764, when the illegal and impolitic persecution of that worthless demagogue Wilkes had strongly excited the public mind, the town was amused by an anecdote, which we have seen in some unpublished memoirs of Horace Walpole. Old Mr. Richard Clive, who since his son's elevation had been introduced into society for which his former habits had not well fitted him, presented himself at the levee. The King asked him where Lord Clive was. "He will be in town very soon," said the old gentleman, loud enough to be heard by the whole circle, "and then your Majesty will have another vote."

But, in truth, all Clive's views were directed towards the country in which he had so eminently distinguished himself as a soldier and a statesman; and it was by considerations relating to India that his conduct as a public man in England was regulated. The power of the Company, though an anomaly, is in our time, we are firmly persuaded, a beneficial anomaly. In the time of Clive it was not merely an anomaly but a nuisance. There was no Board of Control. The Directors were for the most part mere traders, ignorant of general politics, ignorant of the peculiarities of the empire which had strangely become subject to them. The Court of Proprietors, wherever it chose to interfere, was able to have its way. That Court was more numerous as well as more powerful than at present; for then every share of five hundred pounds conferred a vote. The meetings were large, stormy, even riotous—the debates indecently virulent. All the turbulence of a Westminster election, all the trickery and corruption of a Grampound election, disgraced the proceedings of this assembly on questions of the most solemn importance. Fictitious votes were manufactured on a gigantic scale. Clive himself laid out a hundred thousand pounds in the purchase of stock, which he then divided among nominal proprietors on whom he could depend, and whom he brought down in his train to every discussion and every ballot. Others did the same, though not to quite so enormous an extent.

The interest taken by the public of England in Indian questions was then far greater than at present, and the reason is obvious. At present a writer enters the service young; he climbs slowly; he is fortunate if, at forty-five, he can return to his country with an annuity of a thousand a year, and with savings amounting to thirty thousand pounds. A great quantity of wealth is made by English functionaries in India; but no single functionary makes a very large fortune, and what is made is slowly, hardly and honestly earned. Only four or five high political offices are reserved for public men from England. The residencies, the secretaryships, the seats in the boards of revenue and in the Sudder courts are all filled by men who have given the best years of life to the service of the Company: nor can any talents, however splendid, or any connections, however powerful, obtain those lucrative posts for any person who has not entered by the regular door and mounted by the regular gradations. Seventy years ago, much less money was brought home from the East than in our time. But it was divided among a very much smaller number of persons, and immense sums were often accumulated in a few months. Any Englishman, whatever his age might be, might hope to be one of the lucky emigrants. If he made a good speech in Leadenhall Street, or published a clever pamphlet in defence of the chairman, he might be sent out in the Company's service, and might return in three or four years as rich as Pigot or as Clive. Thus the India House was a lottery-office, which invited everybody to take a chance and held out ducal fortunes as the prizes destined for the lucky few. As soon as it was known that there was a part of the world where a lieutenant-colonel had one morning received as a present an estate as large as that of the Earl of Bath or the Marquess of Rockingham, and where it seemed that such a trifle as ten or twenty thousand pounds was to be had by any British functionary for the asking, society began to exhibit all the symptoms of the South Sea year, a feverish excitement, an ungovernable impatience to be rich, a contempt for slow, sure and moderate gains.

At the head of the preponderating party in the India House, had long stood a powerful, able and ambitious director of the name of Sulivan. He had conceived a strong jealousy of Clive, and remembered with bitterness the audacity with which the late governor of Bengal had repeatedly set at nought the authority of the distant Directors of the Company. An apparent reconciliation took place after Clive's arrival; but enmity remained deeply rooted in the hearts of both. The whole body of Directors was then chosen annually. At the election of 1763, Clive attempted to break down the power of the dominant faction. The contest was carried on with a violence which he describes as tremendous. Sulivan was victorious, and hastened to take his revenge. The grant of rent which Clive had received from Meer Jaffier was, in the opinion of the best English lawyers, valid. It had been made by exactly the same authority from which the Company had received their chief possessions in Bengal, and the Company had long acquiesced in it. The Directors, however, most unjustly determined to confiscate it; and Clive was forced to file a bill in chancery against them.

But a great and sudden turn in affairs was at hand. Every ship from Bengal had for some time brought alarming tidings. The internal misgovernment of the province had reached such a point that it could go no further. What, indeed, was to be expected from a body of public servants exposed to temptation such that, as Clive once said, flesh and blood could not bear it—armed with irresistible power, and responsible only to the corrupt, turbulent, distracted, ill-informed Company, situated at such a distance that the average interval between the sending of a despatch and the receipt of an answer was above a year and a half? Accordingly, during the five years which followed the departure of Clive from Bengal, the misgovernment of the English was carried to a point such as seems hardly compatible with the very existence of society. The Roman proconsul, who, in a year or two, squeezed out of a province the means of rearing marble palaces and baths on the shores of Campania, of drinking from amber, of feasting on singing birds, of exhibiting armies of gladiators and flocks of camelopards—the Spanish viceroy, who, leaving behind him the curses of Mexico or Lima, entered Madrid with a long train of gilded coaches, and of sumpter-horses trapped and shod with silver, were now outdone. Cruelty, indeed, properly so called, was not among the vices of the servants of the Company. But cruelty itself could hardly have produced greater evils than were the effect of their unprincipled eagerness to be rich. They pulled down their creature, Meer Jaffier. They set up in his place another Nabob named Meer Cossim. But Meer Cossim had talents and a will; and, though sufficiently inclined to oppress his subjects himself, he could not bear to see them ground to the dust by oppressions which yielded him no profit—nay, which destroyed his revenue in the very source. The English accordingly pulled down Meer Cossim and set up Meer Jaffier again; and Meer Cossim, after revenging himself by a massacre surpassing in atrocity that of the Black Hole, fled to the dominions of the Nabob of Oude. At every one of these revolutions, the new prince divided among his foreign masters whatever could be scraped together in the treasury of his fallen predecessor. The immense population of his dominions was given up as a prey to those who had made him a sovereign and who could unmake him. The servants of the Company obtained—not for their employers, but for themselves—a monopoly of almost the whole internal trade. They forced the natives to buy dear and to sell cheap. They insulted with perfect impunity the tribunals, the police and the fiscal authorities of the country. They covered with their protection a set of native dependents who ranged through the provinces, spreading desolation and terror wherever they appeared. Every servant of a British factor was armed with all the power of his master; and his master was armed with all the power of the Company. Enormous fortunes were thus rapidly accumulated at Calcutta, while thirty millions of human beings were reduced to the last extremity of wretchedness. They had been accustomed to live under tyranny, but never under tyranny like this. They found the little finger of the Company thicker than the loins of Surajah Dowlah. Under their old masters, they had at least one resource : when the evil became insupportable, they rose and pulled down the government. But the English government was not to be so shaken off. That government, oppressive as the most oppressive form of barbarian despotism, was strong with all the strength of civilisation It resembled the government of evil Genii rather than the government of human tyrants. Even despair could not inspire the soft Bengalee with courage to confront men of English breed—the hereditary nobility of mankind, whose skill and valour had so often triumphed in spite of tenfold odds. The unhappy race never attempted resistance. Sometimes they submitted in patient misery. Sometimes they fled from the white man, as their fathers had been used to fly from the Mahratta ; and the palanquin of the English traveller was often carried through silent villages and towns, which the report of his approach had made desolate.

The foreign lords of Bengal were naturally objects of hatred to all the neighbouring powers ; and to all the haughty race presented a dauntless front. The English armies, everywhere outnumbered, were everywhere victorious. A succession of commanders, formed in the school of Clive, still maintained the fame of their country. " It must be acknowledged," says the Mussulman historian of those times, "that this nation's presence of mind, firmness of temper and undaunted bravery are past all question. They joined the most resolute courage to the most cautious prudence ; nor have they their equals in the art of ranging themselves in battle array and fighting in order. If to so many military qualifications they knew how to join the arts of government—if they exerted as much ingenuity and solicitude in relieving the people of God as they do in whatever concerns their military affairs—no nation in the world would be preferable to them or worthier of command. But the people under their dominion groan everywhere, and are reduced to poverty and distress. O God ! come to the assistance of thine afflicted servants and deliver them from the oppressions which they suffer."

It was impossible, however, that even the military establishment should long continue exempt from the vices which pervaded every other part of the government. Rapacity, luxury and the spirit of insubordination spread from the civil service to the officers of the army and from the officers to the soldiers. The evil continued to grow till every mess-room became the seat of conspiracy and cabal, and till the sepoys could be kept in order only by wholesale executions.

At length the state of things in Bengal began to excite uneasiness at home. A succession of revolutions ; a disorganised administration ; the natives pillaged, yet the Company not enriched; every fleet bringing back individuals able to purchase manors and to build stately dwellings, yet bringing back also alarming accounts of the financial prospects of the government; war on the frontiers; disaffection in the army; the national character disgraced by excesses resembling those of Verres and Pizarro; such was the spectacle which dismayed those who were conversant with Indian affairs. The general cry was that Clive, and Clive alone, could save the empire which he had founded.

' This feeling manifested itself in the strongest manner at a very full General Court of Proprietors. Men of all parties, forgetting their feuds and trembling for their dividends, exclaimed that Clive was the man whom the crisis required, that the oppressive proceedings which had been adopted respecting his estate ought to be dropped, and that he ought to be entreated to return to India.

Clive rose. As to his estate, he said, he would make such propositions to the Directors as would, he trusted, lead to an amicable settlement. But there was a still greater difficulty. It was proper to tell them that he never would undertake the government of Bengal while his enemy Sulivan was chairman of the Company. The tumult was violent. Sulivan could scarcely obtain a hearing. An overwhelming majority of the assembly was on Clive's side. Sulivan wished to try the result of a ballot. But, according to the by-laws of the Company, there can be no ballot except on a requisition signed by nine proprietors; and though hundreds were present, nine persons could not be found to set their hands to such a requisition.

Clive was in consequence nominated Governor and Commander-in-chief of the British possessions in Bengal. But he adhered to his declaration, and refused to enter on his office till the event of the next election of Directors should be known. The contest was obstinate; but Clive triumphed. Sulivan, lately absolute master of the India House, was within a vote of losing his own seat; and both the chairman and the deputy-chairman were friends of the new governor.

Such were the circumstances under which Lord Clive sailed for the third and last time to India. In May, 1765, he reached Calcutta; and he found the whole machine of government even more fearfully disorganised than he had anticipated. Meer Jaffier, who had some time before lost his eldest son Meeran, had died while Clive was on his voyage out. The English functionaries at Calcutta had already received from home strict orders not to accept presents from the native princes. But, eager for gain and unaccustomed to respect the commands of their distant, ignorant and negligent masters, they again set up the throne of Bengal for sale. About one hundred and forty thousand pounds sterling was distributed among nine of the most powerful servants of the Company; and, in consideration of this bribe, an infant son of the deceased Nabob was placed on the seat of his father. The news of the ignominious bargain met Clive on his arrival. In a private letter, written immediately after his landing to an intimate friend, he poured out his feelings in language which, proceeding from a man so daring, so resolute and so little given to theatrical display of sentiment, seems to us singularly touching. "Alas!" he says, "how is the English name sunk! I could not avoid paying the tribute of a few tears to the departed and lost fame of the British nation— irrecoverably so, I fear. However, I do declare, by that great Being who is the searcher of all hearts, and to whom we must be accountable if there be a hereafter, that I am come out with a mind superior to all corruption, and that I am determined to destroy these great and growing evils or perish in the attempt."

The Council met; and Clive stated to them his full determination to make a thorough reform, and to use for that purpose the whole of the ample authority, civil and military, which had been confided to him. Johnstone, one of the boldest and worst men in the assembly, made some show of opposition. Clive interrupted him, and haughtily demanded whether he meant to question the power of the new government. Johnstone was cowed, and disclaimed any such intention. All the faces round the board grew long and pale; and not another syllable of dissent was uttered.

Clive redeemed his pledge. He remained in India about a year and a half; and in that short time effected one of the most extensive, difficult and salutary reforms that ever was accomplished by any statesman. This was the part of his life on which he afterwards looked back with most pride. He had it in his power to triple his already splendid fortune; to connive at abuses while pretending to remove them; to conciliate the goodwill of all the English in Bengal by giving up to their rapacity a helpless and timid race who knew not where lay the island which sent forth their oppressors, and whose complaints had little chance of being heard across fifteen thousand miles of ocean. He knew that if he applied himself in earnest to the work of reformation, he should raise every bad passion in arms against him. He knew how unscrupulous, how implacable, would be the hatred of those ravenous adventurers who, having counted on accumulating in a few months' fortunes sufficient to support peerages, should find all their hopes frustrated. But he had chosen the good part; and he called up all the force of his mind for a battle far harder than that of Plassey. At first success seemed hopeless; but very soon all obstacles began to bend before that iron courage and that vehement will. The receiving of presents from the natives was rigidly prohibited. The private trade of the servants of the Company was put down. The whole settlement seemed to be set, as one man, against these measures. But the inexorable governor declared that, if he could not find support at Fort William, he would procure it elsewhere, and sent for some civil servants from Madras to assist him in carrying on the administration. The most factious of his opponents he turned out of their offices. The rest submitted to what was inevitable; and in a very short time all resistance was quelled.

But Clive was far too wise a man not to see that the recent abuses were partly to be ascribed to a cause which could not fail to produce similar abuses as soon as the pressure of his strong hand was withdrawn. The Company had followed a mistaken policy with respect to the remuneration of its servants. The salaries were too low to afford even those indulgences which are necessary to the health and comfort of Europeans in a tropical climate. To lay by a rupee from such scanty pay was impossible. It could not be supposed that men of even average abilities would consent to pass the best years of life in exile, under a burning sun, for no other consideration than these stinted wages. It had accordingly been understood, from a very early period, that the Company's agents were at liberty to enrich themselves by their private trade. This practice had been seriously injurious to the commercial interests of the corporation. That very intelligent observer, Sir Thomas Roe, in the reign of James the First, strongly urged the Directors to apply a remedy to the abuse. "Absolutely prohibit the private trade," said he; "for your business will be better done. I know this is harsh. Men profess they come not for bare wages. But you will take away this plea if you give great wages to their content; and then you know what you part from."

In spite of this excellent advice, the Company adhered to the old system, paid low salaries and connived at the by-gains of its servants. The pay of a member of Council was only three hundred pounds a year. Yet it was notorious that such a functionary could hardly live in India for less than ten times that sum; and it could not be expected that he would be content to live even handsomely in India without laying up something against the time of his return to England. This system, before the conquest of Bengal, might affect the amount of the dividends payable to the proprietors, but could do little harm in any other way. But the Company was now a ruling body. Its servants might still be called factors, junior merchants, senior merchants. But they were in truth proconsuls, propraetors, procurators of extensive regions. They had immense power. Their regular pay was universally admitted to be insufficient. They were, by the ancient usage of the service and by the implied permission of their employers, warranted in enriching themselves by indirect means; and this had been the origin of the frightful oppression and corruption which had desolated Bengal. Clive saw clearly that it was absurd to give men power and to expect that they would be content to live in penury. He justly concluded that no reform could be effectual which should not be coupled with a plan for liberally remunerating the civil servants of the Company. The Directors, he knew, were not disposed to sanction any increase of the salaries out of their own treasury. The only course which remained open to the governor was one which exposed him to much misrepresentation, but which we think him fully justified in adopting. He appropriated to the support of the service the monopoly of salt, which has formed, down to our own time, a principal head of Indian revenue; and he divided the proceeds according to a scale which seems to have been not unreasonably fixed. He was in consequence accused by his enemies, and has been accused by historians, of disobeying his instructions—of violating his promises—of authorising that very abuse which it was his special mission to destroy—namely, the trade of the Company's servants. But every discerning and impartial judge will admit that there was really nothing in common between the system which he set up and that which he was sent to destroy. The monopoly of salt had been a source of revenue to the governments of India before Clive was born. It continued to be so long after his death. The civil servants were clearly entitled to a maintenance out of the revenue; and all that Clive did was to charge a particular portion of the revenue with their maintenance. He thus, while he put an end to the practices by which gigantic fortunes had been rapidly accumulated, gave to every British functionary employed in the East the means of slowly, but surely, acquiring a competence. Yet, such is the injustice of mankind, that none of those acts which are the real stains of his life has drawn on him so much obloquy as this measure, which was in truth a reform necessary to the success of all his other reforms.

He had quelled the opposition of the civil service: that of the army was more formidable. Some of the retrenchments which had been ordered by the Directors affected the interests of the military service; and a storm arose, such as even Caesar would not willingly have faced. It was no light thing to encounter the resistance of those who held the power of the sword in a country governed only by the sword. Two hundred English officers engaged in a conspiracy against the government and determined to resign their commissions on the same day, not doubting that Clive would grant any terms rather than see the army, on which alone the British empire in the East rested, left without commanders. They little knew the unconquerable spirit with which they had to deal. Clive had still a few officers round his person on whom he could rely. He sent to Fort St. George for a fresh supply. He gave commissions even to mercantile agents who were disposed to support him at this crisis; and he sent orders that every officer who resigned should be instantly brought up to Calcutta. The conspirators found that they had miscalculated. The governor was inexorable. The troops were steady. The sepoys, over whom Clive had always possessed extraordinary influence, stood by him with unshaken fidelity. The leaders in the plot were arrested, tried and cashiered. The rest, humbled and dispirited, begged to be permitted to withdraw their resignations. Many of them declared their repentance even with tears. The younger offenders Clive treated with lenity. To the ringleaders he was inflexibly severe; but his severity was pure from all taint of private malevolence. While he sternly upheld the just authority of his office, he passed by personal insults and injuries with magnanimous disdain. One of the conspirators was accused of having planned the assassination of the governor; but Clive would not listen to the charge. "The officers," he said, "are Englishmen, not assassins."

While he reformed the civil service and established his authority over the army, he was equally successful in his foreign policy. His landing on Indian ground was the signal for immediate peace. The Nabob of Oude, with a large army, lay at that time on the frontier of Bahar. He had been joined by many Afghans and Mahrattas, and there was no small reason to expect a general coalition of all the native powers against the English. But the name of Clive quelled in an instant all opposition. The enemy implored peace in the humblest language, and submitted to such terms as the new governor choose to dictate.

At the same time, the Government of Bengal was placed on a new footing. The power of the English in that province had hitherto been altogether undefined. It was unknown to the ancient constitution of the empire and it had been ascertained by no compact. It resembled the power which, in the last decrepitude of the Western Empire, was exercised over Italy by the great chiefs of foreign mercenaries, the Ricimers and the Odoacers, who put up and pulled down at their pleasure a succession of insignificant princes dignified with the names of Cæsar and Augustus. But, as in the one case so in the other, the warlike strangers at length found it expedient to give to a domination which had been established by arms at once the sanction of law and ancient prescription. Theodoric thought it politic to obtain from the distant court of Byzantium a commission appointing him ruler of Italy; and Clive, in the same manner, applied to the Court of Delhi for a formal grant of the powers of which he already possessed the reality. The Mogul was absolutely helpless; and, though he murmured, had reason to be well pleased that the English were disposed to give solid rupees, which he never could have extorted from them, in exchange for a few Persian characters which cost him nothing. A bargain was speedily struck; and the titular sovereign of Hindostan issued a warrant, empowering the Company to collect and administer the revenues of Bengal, Orissa and Bahar.

There was still a Nabob, who stood to the British authorities in the same relation in which the last driveling Chilperics and Childerics of the Merovingian line stood to their able and vigorous Mayors of the Palace—to Charles Martel and to Pepin. At one time Clive had almost made up his mind to discard this phantom altogether; but he afterwards thought that it might be convenient still to use the name of the Nabob, particularly in dealings with other European Nations. The French, the Dutch and the Danes would, he conceived, submit far more readily to the authority of the native Prince, whom they had always been accustomed to respect, than to that of a rival trading corporation. This policy may, at that time, have been judicious. But the pretence was soon found to be too flimsy to impose on anybody, and it was altogether laid aside. The heir of Meer Jaffier still resides at Moorshedabad, the ancient capital of his house, still bears the title of Nabob, is still accosted by the English as "Your Highness," and is still suffered to retain a portion of the regal state which surrounded his ancestors. A pension of a hundred and sixty thousand pounds a year is annually paid to him by the government. His carriage is surrounded by guards and preceded by attendants with silver maces. His person and his dwelling are exempted from the ordinary authority of the ministers of justice. But he has not the smallest share of political power, and is, in fact, only a noble and wealthy subject of the Company.

It would have been easy for Clive, during his second administration in Bengal, to accumulate riches such as no subject in Europe possessed. He might, indeed, without subjecting the rich inhabitants of the province to any pressure beyond that to which their mildest rulers had accustomed them, have received presents to the amount of three hundred thousand pounds a-year. The neighbouring Princes would gladly have paid any price for his favour. But he appears to have strictly adhered to the rules which he had laid down for the guidance of others. The Prince of Benares offered him diamonds of great value. The Nabob of Oude pressed him to accept a large sum of money and a casket of costly jewels. Clive courteously, but peremptorily, refused; and it should be observed that he made no merit of his refusal, and that the fact did not come to light till after his death. He kept an exact account of his salary, of his share of the profits accruing from the trade in salt, and of those presents which, according to the fashion of the East, it would be churlish to refuse. Out of the sum arising from these resources, he defrayed the expenses of his situation. The surplus he divided among a few attached friends who had accompanied him to India. He always boasted, and as far as we can judge, he boasted with truth, that his last administration diminished instead of increasing his fortune.

One large sum indeed he accepted. Meer Jaffier had left him by will above sixty thousand pounds sterling in specie and jewels: and the rules which had been recently laid down extended only to presents from the living and did not affect legacies from the dead. Clive took the money, but not for himself. He made the whole over to the Company in trust for officers and soldiers invalided in their service. The fund which still bears his name owes its origin to this princely donation.

After a stay of eighteen months, the state of his health rendered it necessary for him to return to Europe. At the close of January, 1767, he quitted for the last time the country on whose destinies he had exercised so mighty an influence.

His second return from Bengal was not, like his first, greeted by the acclamations of his countrymen. Numerous causes were already at work which embittered the remaining years of his life and hurried him to an untimely grave. His old enemies at the India House were still powerful and active; and they had been reinforced by a large band of allies whose violence far exceeded their own. The whole crew of pilferers and oppressors from whom he had rescued Bengal persecuted him with the implacable rancour which belongs to such abject natures. Many of them even invested their property in India stock merely that they might be better able to annoy the man whose firmness had set bounds to their rapacity. Lying newspapers were set up for no purpose but to abuse him; and the temper of the public mind was then such, that these arts, which under ordinary circumstances would have been ineffectual against truth and merit, produced an extraordinary impression.

The great events which had taken place in India had called into existence a new class of Englishmen to whom their countrymen gave the name of Nabobs. These persons had generally sprung from families neither ancient nor opulent; they had generally been sent at an early age to the East; and they had there acquired large fortunes, which they had brought back to their native land. It was natural that, not having had much opportunity of mixing with the best society, they should exhibit some of the awkwardness and some of the pomposity of upstarts. It was natural that, during their sojourn in Asia, they should have acquired some tastes and habits surprising, if not disgusting, to persons who never had quitted Europe. It was natural that, having enjoyed great consideration in the East, they should not be disposed to sink into obscurity at home; and as they had money and had not birth or high connection, it was natural that they should display a little obtrusively the single advantage which they possessed. Wherever they settled there was a kind of feud between them and the old nobility and gentry similar to that which raged in France between the farmer-general and the marquess. This enmity to the aristocracy long continued to distinguish the servants of the Company. More than twenty years after the time of which we are now speaking, Burke pronounced that among the Jacobins might be reckoned "the East Indians almost to a man, who cannot bear to find that their present importance does not bear a proportion to there wealth.

The Nabobs soon became a most unpopular class of men. Some of them had in the East displayed eminent talents and rendered great services to the state; but at home their talents were not shown to advantage and their services were little known. That they had sprung from obscurity, that they had acquired great wealth, that they exhibited it insolently, that they spent it extravagantly, that they raised the price of everything in their neighbourhood from fresh eggs to rotten boroughs, that their liveries outshone those of dukes, that their coaches were finer than that of the Lord Mayor, that the examples of their large and ill-governed households corrupted half the servants in the country, that some of them, with all their magnificence, could not catch the tone of good society, but, in spite of the stud and the crowd of menials, of the plate and the Dresden china, of the venison and the Burgundy, were still low men; these were things which excited, both in the class from which they had sprung and in that into which they attempted to force themselves, the bitter aversion which is the effect of mingled envy and contempt. But when it was also rumoured that the fortune, which had enabled its possessor to eclipse the Lord Lieutenant on the race-ground, or to carry the county against the head of a house as old as "Domes-Day Book," had been accumulated by violating public faith—by deposing legitimate princes—by reducing whole provinces to beggary, all the higher and better as well as all the low and evil parts of human nature were stirred against the wretch who had obtained by guilt and dishonour, the riches which he now lavished with arrogant and inelegant profusion. The unfortunate Nabob seemed to be made up of those foibles against which comedy has pointed the most merciless ridicule, and of those crimes which have thrown the deepest gloom over tradegy—of Turcaret and Nero, of Monsieur Jourdain and Richard the Third. A tempest of execration and derision, such as can be compared only to that outbreak of public feeling against the Puritans which took place at the time of the Restoration, burst on the servants of the Company. The humane man was horror-struck at the way in which they had got their money, the thrifty man at the way in which they spent it. The Dilettante sneered at their want of taste. The Maccaroni black-balled them as vulgar fellows. Writers the most unlike in sentiment and style—Methodists and libertines, philosophers and buffoons—were for once on the same side. It is hardly too much to say that, during a space of about thirty years, the whole lighter literature of England was coloured by the feelings which we have described. Foote brought on the stage an Anglo-Indian chief, dissolute, ungenerous and tyrannical, ashamed of the humble friends of his youth, hating the aristocracy, yet childishly eager to be numbered among them, squandering his wealth on pandars and flatterers, tricking out his chairmen with the most costly hot-house flowers, and astounding the ignorant with jargon about rupees, lacs and jaghires. Mackenzie, with more delicate humour, depicted a plain country family raised by the Indian acquisitions of one of its members to sudden opulence and exciting derision by an awkward mimicry of the manners of the great. Cowper, in that lofty expostulation which glows with the very spirit of the Hebrew poets, placed the oppression of India foremost in the list of those national crimes for which God had punished England with years of disastrous war, with discomfiture in her own seas, and with the loss of her transatlantic empire. If any of our readers will take the trouble to search in the dusty recesses of circulating libraries for some novel published sixty years ago, the chance is that the villain or sub-villian of the story will prove to be a savage old Nabob, with an immense fortune, a tawny complexion, a bad liver and a worse heart.

Such, as far as we can now judge, was the feeling of the country respecting Nabobs in general. And Clive was eminently the Nabob—the ablest, the most celebrated, the highest in rank, the highest in fortune, of all the fraternity. His wealth was exhibited in a manner which could not fail to excite odium. He lived with great magnificence in Berkeley Square. He reared one palace in Shropshire and another at Claremont. His parliamentary influence might vie with that of the greatest families. But in all this splendour and power envy found something to sneer at. On some of his relations wealth and dignity seem to have sat as awkwardly as on Mackenzie's Margery Mushroom. Nor was he himself, with all his great qualities, free from those weaknesses which the satirists of that age represented as characteristic of his whole class. In the field, indeed, his habits were remarkably simple. He was constantly on horseback, was never seen but in his uniform, never wore silk, never entered a palanquin, and was content with the plainest fare. But when he was no longer at the head of an army, he laid aside this Spartan temperance for the ostentatious luxury of a Sybarite. Though his person was ungraceful, and though his harsh features were redeemed from vulgar ugliness only by their stern, dauntless and commanding expression, he was fond of rich and gay clothing, and replenished his wardrobe with absurd profusion. Sir John Malcolm gives us a letter worthy of Sir Matthew Mite, in which Clive orders "two hundred shirts, the best and finest that can be got for love or money." A few follies of this description, grossly exaggerated by report, produced an unfavourable impression on the public mind. But this was not the worst. Black stories, of which the greater part were pure inventions, were circulated respecting his conduct in the East. He had to bear the whole odium, not only of those bad acts to which he had once or twice stooped, but of all the bad acts of all the English in India—of bad acts committed when he was absent— nay, of bad acts which he had manfully opposed and severely punished. The very abuses against which he had waged an honest, resolute and successful war were laid to his account. He was, in fact, regarded as the personification of all the vices and weaknesses which the public, with or without reason, ascribed to the English adventurers in Asia. We have ourselves heard old men, who knew nothing of his history, but who still retained the prejudices conceived in their youth, talk of him as an incarnate fiend. Johnson always held this language. Brown, whom Clive employed to lay out his pleasure grounds, was amazed to see in the house of his noble employer a chest which had once been filled with gold from the treasury of Moorshedabad, and could not understand how the conscience of the criminal could suffer him to sleep with such an object so near to his bedchamber. The peasantry of Surrey looked with mysterious horror on the stately house which was rising at Claremont, and whispered that the great wicked lord had ordered the walls to be made so thick in order to keep out the devil, who would one day carry him away bodily. Among the gaping clowns who drank in this frightful story was a worthless ugly lad of the name of Hunter, since widely known as William Huntingdon, S.S. ; and the superstition, which was strangely mingled with the knavery of that remarkable impostor, seems to have derived no small nutriment from the tales which he heard of the life and character of Clive.*

In the meantime, the impulse which Clive had given to the administration of Bengal was constantly becoming fainter and fainter. His policy was to a great extent abandoned ; the abuses which he had suppressed began to revive ; and, at length, the evils which a bad government had engendered were aggravated by one of those fearful visitations which the best government cannot avert. In the summer of 1770, the rains failed ; the earth was parched up ; the tanks were empty ; the rivers shrank within their beds ; and a famine, such as is known only in countries where every household depends for support on its own little patch of cultivation, filled the whole valley of the Ganges with misery and death. Tender and delicate women, whose veils had never been lifted before the public gaze, came forth from the inner chambers in which Eastern jealousy had kept watch over their beauty, threw themselves on the earth before the passers-by, and, with loud wailings, implored a handful of rice for their children. The Hoogley every day rolled down thousands of corpses close to the porticoes and gardens of the English conquerors. The very streets of Calcutta were blocked up by the dying and the dead. The lean and feeble survivors had not energy enough to bear the bodies of their kindred to the funeral pile or to the holy river, or even to scare away the jackals and vultures, who fed on human remains in the face of day. The extent of the mortality was never ascertained, but it was popularly reckoned by millions. This melancholy intelligence added to the excitement which already prevailed in England on Indian subjects. The proprietors of East India stock were uneasy about their dividends. All men of common humanity were touched by the calamities of our unhappy subjects ; and indignation soon began to mingle itself with pity. It was rumoured that the Company's servants had created the famine by engrossing all the rice of the country ; that they had sold grain for eight, ten, twelve times the price at which they had bought it ; that one English functionary who, the year before, was not worth a hundred guineas, had, during that season of misery, remitted sixty thousand pounds to London. These charges we believe to have been unfounded. That servants of the Company had ventured, since Clive's departure, to deal in rice, is probable. That, if they dealt in rice, they must have gained by the scarcity, is certain. But there is no reason for thinking that they either produced or aggravated an evil which physical causes sufficiently explain. The outcry which was raised against them on this occasion was, we suspect, as absurd as the imputations which, in times of dearth at home, were once thrown by statesmen and judges, and are still thrown by two or three old women, on the corn factors. It was, however, so loud and so general that it appears to have imposed even on an intellect raised so high above vulgar prejudices as that of Adam Smith.† What was still more extraordinary, these unhappy events greatly increased the unpopularity of Lord Clive. He had been some years in England when the famine took place. None of his acts had the smallest tendency to produce such a calamity. If the servants of the Company had traded in rice, they had done so in direct contravention of the rule which he had laid down and, while in power, had resolutely enforced. But, in the eyes of his countrymen,

---

* See Huntingdon's Kingdom of Heaven taken by Prayer, and his Letters.
† Wealth of Nations, Book iv., chap. 5—Digression.

he was, as we have said, the Nabob, the Anglo-Indian character personified; and, while he was building and planting in Surrey, he was held responsible for all the effects of a dry season in Bengal.

Parliament had hitherto bestowed very little attention on our Eastern possessions. Since the death of George the Second, a rapid succession of weak administrations, each of which was in turn flattered and betrayed by the Court, had held the semblance of power. Intrigues in the palace, riots in the capital and insurrectionary movements in the American colonies had left the advisers of the Crown little leisure to study Indian politics. When they did interfere, their interference was feeble and irresolute. Lord Chatham, indeed, during the short period of his ascendancy in the councils of George the Third, had meditated a bold attack on the Company. But his plans were rendered abortive by the strange malady which about that time began to overcloud his splendid genius.

At length, in 1772, it was generally felt that Parliament could no longer neglect the affairs of India. The Government was stronger than any which had held power since the breach between Mr. Pitt and the great Whig connection in 1761. No pressing question of domestic or European policy required the attention of public men. There was a short and delusive lull between two tempests. The excitement produced by the Middlesex election was over; the discontents of America did not yet threaten civil war; the financial difficulties of the Company brought on a crisis; the Ministers were forced to take up the subject; and the whole storm, which had long been gathering, now broke at once on the head of Clive.

His situation was indeed singularly unfortunate. He was hated throughout the country, hated at the India House, hated, above all, by those wealthy and powerful servants of the Company whose rapacity and tyranny he had withstood. He had to bear the double odium of his bad and of his good actions, of every Indian abuse and of every Indian reform. The state of the political world was such that he could count on the support of no powerful connection. The party to which he had belonged, that of George Grenville, had been hostile to the Government, and yet had never cordially united with the other sections of the Opposition—with the little band which still followed the fortunes of Lord Chatham, or with the large and respectable body of which Lord Rockingham was the acknowledged leader. George Grenville was now dead: his followers were scattered; and Clive, unconnected with any of the powerful factions which divided the Parliament, could reckon only on the votes of those members who were returned by himself. His enemies, particularly those who were the enemies of his virtues, were unscrupulous, ferocious, implacable. Their malevolence aimed at nothing less than the utter ruin of his fame and fortune. They wished to see him expelled from Parliament, to see his spurs chopped off, to see his estate confiscated; and it may be doubted whether even such a result as this would have quenched their thirst for revenge.

Clive's parliamentary tactics resembled his military tactics. Deserted, surrounded, outnumbered, and with everything at stake, he did not even deign to stand on the defensive, but pushed boldly forward to the attack. At an early stage of the discussions on Indian affairs, he rose and, in a long and elaborate speech, vindicated himself from a large part of the accusations which had been brought against him. He is said to have produced a great impression on his audience. Lord Chatham, who, now the ghost of his former self, loved to haunt the scene of his glory, was that night under the gallery of the House of Commons, and declared that he had never heard a finer speech. It was subsequently printed under Clive's direction, and must be allowed to exhibit, not merely strong sense and a manly spirit, but talents both for disquisition and declamation which assiduous culture might have improved into the highest excellence. He confined his defence on this occasion to the measures of his last administration, and succeeded so far that his enemies thenceforth thought it expedient to direct their attacks chiefly against the earlier part of his life.

The earlier part of his life unfortunately presented some assailable points to their hostility. A committee was chosen by ballot to inquire into the affairs of India; and by this committee the whole history of that great revolution which threw down Surajah Dowlah and raised Meer Jaffier was sifted with malignant care. Clive was subjected to the most unsparing examination and cross-examination, and afterwards bitterly complained that he, the Baron of Plassey, had been treated like a sheep-stealer. The boldness and ingenuousness of his replies would alone suffice to show how alien from his nature were the frauds to which, in the course of his eastern negotiations, he had sometimes descended. He avowed the arts which he had employed to deceive Omichund, and resolutely said that he was not ashamed of them, and that, in the same circumstances, he would again act in the same manner. He admitted that he had received immense sums from Meer Jaffier; but he denied that, in doing so, he had violated any obligation of morality or honour. He laid claim, on the contrary, and not without some reason, to the praise of eminent disinterestedness. He described in vivid language the situation in which his victory had placed him—a great prince dependent on his pleasure; an opulent city afraid of being given up to plunder; wealthy bankers bidding against each other for his smiles; vaults piled with gold and jewels thrown open to him alone. "By God, Mr. Chairman," he exclaimed, "at this moment I stand astonished at my own moderation."

The inquiry was so extensive that the Houses rose before it had been completed. It was continued in the following session. When at length the committee had concluded its labours, enlightened and impartial men had little difficulty in making up their minds as to the result. It was clear that Clive had been guilty of some acts which it is impossible to vindicate without attacking the authority of all the most sacred laws which regulate the intercourse of individuals and of states. But it was equally clear that he had displayed great talents and even great virtues; that he had rendered eminent services both to his country and to the people of India; and that it was in truth not for his dealings with Meer Jaffier, nor for the fraud which he had practised on Omichund, but for his determined resistance to avarice and tyranny that he was now called in question.

Ordinary criminal justice knows nothing of set-off. The greatest desert cannot be pleaded in answer to a charge of the slightest transgression. If a man has sold beer on a Sunday morning, it is no defence that he has saved the life of a fellow-creature at the risk of his own. If he has harnessed a Newfoundland dog to his little child's carriage, it is no defence that he was wounded at Waterloo. But it is not in this way that we ought to deal with men who, raised far above ordinary restraints and tried by far more than ordinary temptations, are entitled to a more than ordinary measure of indulgence. Such men should be judged by their contemporaries as they will be judged by posterity. Their bad actions ought not indeed to be called good; but their good and bad actions ought to be fairly weighed—and if on the whole the good preponderate, the sentence ought to be one, not merely of acquittal, but of approbation. Not a single great ruler in history can be absolved by a judge who fixes his eye inexorably on one or two unjustifiable acts. Bruce the deliverer of Scotland, Maurice the deliverer of Germany, William the deliverer of Holland, his great descendant the deliverer of England, Murray the good regent, Cosmo the father of his country, Henry the

Fourth of France, Peter the Great of Russia—how would the best of them pass such a scrutiny? History takes wider views; and the best tribunal for great political cases is the tribunal which anticipates the verdict of history.

Reasonable and moderate men of all parties felt this in Clive's case. They could not pronounce him blameless; but they were not disposed to abandon him to that low-minded and rancorous pack who had run him down and were eager to worry him to death. Lord North, though not very friendly to him, was not disposed to go to extremities against him. While the inquiry was still in progress, Clive, who had some years before been created a Knight of the Bath, was installed with great pomp in Henry the Seventh's Chapel. He was soon after appointed Lord Lieutenant of Shropshire. When he kissed hands, George the Third, who had always been partial to him, admitted him to a private audience, talked to him half an hour on Indian politics, and was visibly affected when the persecuted general spoke of his services and of the way in which they had been requited.

At length the charges came in a definite form before the House of Commons. Burgoyne, chairman of the committee, a man of wit, fashion and honour, an agreeable dramatic writer, an officer whose courage was never questioned and whose skill was at that time highly esteemed, appeared as the accuser. The members of the administration took different sides; for in that age all questions were open questions, except such as were brought forward by the Government, or such as implied censure on the Government. Thurlow, the Attorney-General, was among the assailants. Wedderburne, the Solicitor-General, strongly attached to Clive, defended his friend with extraordinary force of argument and language. It is a curious circumstance that, some years later, Thurlow was the most conspicuous champion of Warren Hastings, while Wedderburne was among the most unrelenting persecutors of that great though not faultless statesman. Clive spoke in his own defence at less length and with less art than in the preceding year, but with much energy and pathos. He recounted his great actions and his wrongs; and, after bidding his hearers remember that they were about to decide not only on his honour but on their own, he retired from the House.

The Commons resolved that acquisitions made by the arms of the State belong to the State alone, and that it is illegal in the servants of the State to appropriate such acquisitions to themselves. They resolved that this wholesome rule appeared to have been systematically violated by the English functionaries in Bengal. On a subsequent day they went a step further, and resolved that Clive had, by means of the power which he possessed as commander of the British forces in India, obtained large sums from Meer Jaffier. Here the Commons stopped. They had voted the major and minor of Burgoyne's syllogism; but they shrank from drawing the logical conclusion. When it was moved that Lord Clive had abused his powers and set an evil example to the servants of the public, the previous question was put and carried. At length, long after the sun had risen on an animated debate, Wedderburne moved that Lord Clive had at the same time rendered great and meritorious services to his country; and this motion passed without a division.

The result of this memorable inquiry appears to us, on the whole, honourable to the justice, moderation and discernment of the Commons. They had indeed no great temptation to do wrong. They would have been very bad judges of an accusation brought against Jenkinson or against Wilkes. But the question respecting Clive was not a party question; and the House accordingly acted with the good sense and good feeling which may always be expected from an assembly of English gentlemen not blinded by faction.

The equitable and temperate proceedings of the British Parliament were set off to the greatest advantage by a foil. The wretched government of Louis the Fifteenth had murdered, directly or indirectly, almost every Frenchman who had served his country with distinction in the East. Labourdonnais was flung into the Bastile, and, after years of suffering, left it only to die. Dupleix, stripped of his immense fortune and broken-hearted by humiliating attendance in ante-chambers, sank into an obscure grave. Lally was dragged to the common place of execution with a gag between his lips. The Commons of England, on the other hand, treated their living captain with that discriminating justice which is seldom shown except to the dead. They laid down sound general principles; they delicately pointed out where he had deviated from those principles; and they tempered the gentle censure with liberal eulogy. The contrast struck Voltaire, always partial to England and always eager to expose the abuses of the Parliaments of France. Indeed, he seems, at this time, to have meditated a history of the conquest of Bengal. He mentioned his design to Dr. Moore, when that amusing writer visited him at Ferney. Wedderburne took great interest in the matter, and pressed Clive to furnish materials. Had the plan been carried into execution, we have no doubt that Voltaire would have produced a book containing much lively and picturesque narrative, many just and humane sentiments poignantly expressed, many grotesque blunders, many sneers at the Mosaic chronology, much scandal about the Catholic missionaries, and much sublime *theo-philanthropy*, stolen from the New Testament and put into the mouths of virtuous and philosophical Brahmins.

Clive was now secure in the enjoyment of his fortune and his honours. He was surrounded by attached friends and relations; and he had not yet passed the season of vigorous bodily and mental exertion. But clouds had long been gathering over his mind, and now settled on it in thick darkness. From early youth he had been subject to fits of that strange melancholy "which rejoiceth exceedingly and is glad when it can find the grave." While still a writer at Madras, he had twice attempted to destroy himself. Business and prosperity had produced a salutary effect on his spirits. In India, while he was occupied by great affairs, in England, while wealth and rank had still the charm of novelty, he had borne up against his constitutional misery. But he had now nothing to do and nothing to wish for. His active spirit in an inactive situation drooped and withered like a plant in an uncongenial air. The malignity with which his enemies had pursued him, the indignity with which he had been treated by the committee, the censure, lenient as it was, which the House of Commons had pronounced, the knowledge that he was regarded by a large portion of his countrymen as a cruel and perfidious tyrant, all concurred to irritate and depress him. In the meantime his temper was tried by acute physical suffering. During his long residence in tropical climates he had contracted several painful distempers. In order to obtain ease he called in the help of opium; and he was gradually enslaved by this treacherous ally. To the last, however, his genius occasionally flashed through the gloom. It was said that he would sometimes, after sitting silent and torpid for hours, rouse himself to the discussion of some great question, would display in full vigour all the talents of the soldier and the statesman, and would then sink back into his melancholy repose.

The disputes with America had now become so serious that an appeal to the sword seemed inevitable; and the Ministers were desirous to avail themselves of the services of Clive. Had he still been what he was when he raised the siege of Patna and annihilated the Dutch army and navy at the mouth of the Ganges, it is not improbable that the resistance of the colonists would have been put down and that the inevitable separation would have been deferred for a few years. But it was too late. His strong mind was fast sinking under many kinds of suffering. On the 22nd of November, 1774, he died by his own hand. He had just completed his forty-ninth year.

In the awful close of so much prosperity and glory, the vulgar saw only a confirmation of all their prejudices; and some men of real piety and genius so far forgot the maxims both of religion and of philosophy as confidently to ascribe the mournful event to the just vengeance of God and to the horrors of an evil conscience. It is with very different feelings that we contemplate the spectacle of a great mind ruined by the weariness of satiety, by the pangs of wounded honour, by fatal diseases and more fatal remedies.

Clive committed great faults; and we have not attempted to disguise them. But his faults, when weighed against his merits and viewed in connection with his temptations, do not appear to us to deprive him of his right to an honourable place in the estimation of posterity.

From his first visit to India dates the renown of the English arms in the East. Till he appeared, his countrymen were despised as mere pedlars, while the French were revered as a people formed for victory and command. His courage and capacity dissolved the charm. With the defence of Arcot commences that long series of Oriental triumphs which closes with the fall of Ghizni. Nor must we forget that he was only twenty-five years old when he approved himself ripe for military command. This is a rare if not a singular distinction. It is true that Alexander, Condé and Charles XII. won great battles at a still earlier age; but those princes were surrounded by veteran generals of distinguished skill, to those suggestions must be attributed the victories of the Granicus, of Rocroi and of Narva. Clive, an inexperienced youth, had yet more experience than any of those who served under him. He had to form himself, to form his officers and to form his army. The only man, as far as we recollect, who at an equally early age ever gave equal proofs of talents for war was Napoleon Bonaparte.

From Clive's second visit to India dates the political ascendancy of the English in that country. His dexterity and resolution realised, in the course of a few months, more than all the gorgeous visions which had floated before the imagination of Dupleix. Such an extent of cultivated territory, such an amount of revenue, such a multitude of subjects, was never added to the dominion of Rome by the most successful proconsul. Nor were such wealthy spoils ever borne under the arches of triumph, down the Sacred Way and through the crowded Forum to the threshold of Tarpeian Jove. The fame of those who subdued Antiochus and Tigranes grows dim when compared with the splendour of the exploits which the young English adventurer achieved at the head of an army not equal in numbers to one half of a Roman legion.

From Clive's third visit to India dates the purity of the administration of our Eastern empire. When he landed in Calcutta in 1765, Bengal was regarded as a place to which Englishmen were sent only to get rich, by any means, in the shortest possible time. He first made dauntless and unsparing war on that gigantic system of oppression, extortion and corruption. In that war he manfully put to hazard his ease, his fame and his splendid fortune. The same sense of justice which forbids us to conceal or extenuate the faults of his earlier days compels us to admit that those faults were nobly repaired. If the reproach of the Company and of its servants has been taken away—if in India the yoke of foreign masters, elsewhere the heaviest of all yokes, has been found lighter than that of any native dynasty—if to that gang of public robbers, which formerly spread terror through the whole plain of Bengal, has succeeded a body of functionaries not more highly distinguished by ability and diligence than by integrity, disinterestedness and public spirit—if we now see such men as Munro, Elphinstone and Metcalfe, after leading victorious armies, after making and deposing kings, return, proud of their honourable poverty, from a land which once held out to every greedy factor the hope of boundless wealth —the praise is in no small measure due to Clive. His name stands high on the roll of conquerors. But it is found in a better list, in the list of those who have done and suffered much for the happiness of mankind. To the warrior, history will assign a place in the same rank with Lucullus and Trajan. Nor will she deny to the reformer a share of that veneration with which France cherishes the memory of Turgot, and with which the latest generations of Hindoos will contemplate the statue of Lord William Bentinck.

VON RANKE. (October, 1840.)

The Ecclesiastical and Political History of the Popes of Rome during the Sixteenth and Seventeenth Centuries. By LEOPOLD RANKE, Professor in the University of Berlin. Translated from the German by SARAH AUSTIN. 3 vols., 8vo. London, 1840.

IT is hardly necessary for us to say that this is an excellent book excellently translated. The original work of Professor Ranke is known and esteemed wherever German literature is studied, and has been found interesting even in a most inaccurate and dishonest French version. It is, indeed, the work of a mind fitted both for minute researches and for large speculations. It is written also in an admirable spirit, equally remote from levity and bigotry, serious and earnest, yet tolerant and impartial. It is, therefore, with the greatest pleasure that we now see it take its place among the English classics. Of the translation we need only say that it is such as might be expected from the skill, the taste and the scrupulous integrity of the accomplished lady who, as an interpreter between the mind of Germany and the mind of Britain, has already deserved so well of both countries.

The subject of this book has always appeared to us singularly interesting. How it was that Protestantism did so much, yet did no more, how it was that the Church of Rome, having lost a large part of Europe, not only ceased to lose, but actually regained nearly half of what she had lost, is certainly a curious and most important question: and on this question Professor Ranke has thrown far more light than any other person who has written on it.

There is not, and there never was on this earth, a work of human policy so well deserving of examination as the Roman Catholic Church. The history of that Church joins together the two great ages of human civilisation. No other institution is left standing which carries the mind back to the times when the smoke of sacrifice rose from the Pantheon, and when camelopards and tigers bounded in the Flavian amphitheatre. The proudest royal houses are but of yesterday when compared with the line of the Supreme Pontiffs. That line we trace back in an unbroken series from the Pope who crowned Napoleon in the nineteenth century to the Pope who crowned Pepin in the eighth; and far beyond the time of Pepin the august dynasty extends till it is lost in the twilight of fable. The republic of Venice came next in antiquity. But the republic of Venice was modern when compared with the Papacy; and the republic of Venice is gone and the Papacy remains. The Papacy remains, not in decay, not a mere antique, but full of life and youthful vigour. The Catholic Church is still sending forth to the farthest ends of the world missionaries as zealous as those who landed in Kent with Augustin, and still confronting hostile kings with the same spirit with which she confronted Atilla. The number of her children is greater than in any former age. Her acquisitions in the New World have more than compensated her for what she has lost in the Old. Her spiritual ascendancy extends over the vast countries which lie between the plains of the Missouri and Cape Horn, countries which, a century hence, may not improbably contain a population as large as that which now inhabits Europe. The members of her communion are certainly not fewer than a hundred and fifty millions; and it will be difficult to show that all the other Christian sects united amount to a hundred and twenty millions. Nor do we see any sign which indicates that the term of her long dominion is approaching. She saw the commencement of all the governments and of all the ecclesiastical establishments that now exist in the world; and we feel no assurance that she is not destined to see the end of them all. She was great and respected before the Saxon had set foot on Britain, before the Frank had passed the Rhine, when Grecian eloquence still flourished at Antioch, when idols were still worshipped in the temple of Mecca. And she may still exist in undiminished vigour when some traveller from New Zealand shall, in the midst of a vast solitude, take his stand on a broken arch of London Bridge to sketch the ruins of St. Paul's.

We often hear it said that the world is constantly becoming more and more enlightened, and that this enlightening must be favourable to Protestantism and unfavourable to Catholicism. We wish that we could think so. But we see great reason to doubt whether this be a well-founded expectation. We see that during the last two hundred and fifty years the human mind has been in the highest degree active, that it has made great advances in every branch of natural philosophy—that it has produced innumerable inventions tending to promote the convenience of life—that medicine, surgery, chemistry, engineering have been very greatly improved—that government, police and law have been improved, though not to so great an extent as the physical sciences. Yet we see that, during these two hundred and fifty years, Protestantism has made no conquests worth speaking of. Nay, we believe that, as far as there has been a change, that change has been in favour of the Church of Rome. We cannot, therefore, feel confident that the progress of knowledge will necessarily be fatal to a system which has, to say the least, stood its ground in spite of the immense progress which knowledge has made since the days of Queen Elizabeth.

Indeed, the argument which we are considering seems to us to be founded on an entire mistake. There are branches of knowledge with respect to which the law of the human mind is progress. In mathematics, when once a proposition has been demonstrated, it is never afterwards contested. Every fresh story is as solid a basis for a new superstructure as the original foundation was. Here, therefore, there is a constant addition to the stock of truth. In the inductive sciences again, the law is progress. Every day furnishes new facts, and thus brings theory nearer and nearer to perfection. There is no chance that, either in the purely demonstrative or in the purely experimental sciences, the world will ever go back or even remain stationary. Nobody ever heard of a reaction against Taylor's theorem, or of a reaction against Harvey's doctrine of the circulation of the blood.

But with theology the case is very different. As respects natural religion—revelation being for the present altogether left out of the question—it is not easy to see that a philosopher of the present day is more favourably situated than Thales or Simonides. He has before him just the same evidences of design in the structure of the universe which the early Greeks had. We say just the same; for the discoveries of modern astronomers and anatomists have really added nothing to the force of that argument which a reflecting mind finds in every beast, bird, insect, fish, leaf, flower and shell. The reasoning by which Socrates, in Xenophon's hearing, confuted the little atheist Aristodemus, is exactly the reasoning of Paley's "Natural Theology." Socrates makes precisely the same use of the statues of Polycletus and the pictures of Zeuxis which Paley makes of the watch. As to the other great question—the question, what becomes of man after death—we do not see that a highly educated European, left to his unassisted reason, is more likely to be in the right than a Blackfoot Indian. Not a single one of the many sciences in which we surpass the Blackfoot Indians throws the smallest light on the state of the soul after the animal life is extinct. In truth, all the philosophers, ancient and modern, who have attempted, without the help of revelation, to prove the immortality of man, from Plato down to Franklin, appear to us to have failed deplorably.

Then, again, all the great enigmas which perplex the natural theologian are the same in all ages. The ingenuity of a people just emerging from barbarism is quite sufficient to propound those enigmas. The wisdom of Locke or Clarke is quite unable to solve them. It is a mistake to imagine that subtle speculations touching the Divine attributes, the origin of evil, the necessity of human actions, the foundation of moral obligation, imply any high degree of intellectual culture. Such speculations, on the contrary, are in a peculiar manner the delight of intelligent children and of half-civilised men. The number of boys is not small who, at fourteen, have thought enough on these questions to be fully entitled to the praise which Voltaire gives to Zadig. "Il en savait ce qu'on en a su dans tous les âges; c'est-à-dire, fort peu de chose." The book of Job shows that, long before letters and arts were known to Ionia, these vexing questions were debated with no common skill and eloquence under the tents of the Idumean Emirs; nor has human reason, in the course of three thousand years, discovered any satisfactory solution of the riddles which perplexed Eliphaz and Zophar.

Natural theology, then, is not a progressive science. That knowledge of our origin and of our destiny which we derive from revelation is indeed of very different clearness and of very different importance. But neither is revealed religion of the nature of a progressive science. All Divine truth is, according to the doctrine of the Protestant Churches, recorded in certain books. It is equally open to all who, in any age, can read those books; nor can all the discoveries of all the philosophers in the world add a single verse to any of those books. It is plain, therefore, that in divinity there cannot be a progress analogous to that which is constantly taking place in pharmacy, geology and navigation. A Christian of the fifth century with a Bible is on a par with a Christian of the nineteenth century with a Bible, candour and natural acuteness being, of course, supposed equal. It matters not at all that the compass, printing, gunpowder, steam, gas, vaccination and a thousand other discoveries and inventions, which were unknown in the fifth century, are familiar to the nineteenth. None of these discoveries and inventions has the smallest bearing on the question whether man is justified by faith alone, or whether the invocation of saints is an orthodox practice. It seems to us, therefore, that we have no security for the future against the prevalence of any theological error that ever has prevailed in time past among Christian men. We are confident that the world will never go back to the solar system of Ptolemy; nor is our confidence in the least shaken by the circumstance that even so great a man as Bacon rejected the theory of Galileo with scorn, for Bacon had not all the means of arriving at a sound conclusion which are within our reach and which secure people who would not have been worthy to mend his pens from falling into his mistakes. But we are very differently affected when we reflect that Sir Thomas More was ready to die for the doctrine of transubstantiation. He was a man of eminent talents. He had all the information on the subject that we have, or that, while the world lasts, any human being will have. The text, "This is my body," was in his New Testament as it is in ours. The absurdity of the literal interpretation was as great and as obvious in the sixteenth century as it is now. No progress that science has made, or will make, can add to what seems to us the overwhelmning force of the argument against the real presence. We are, therefore, unable to understand why what Sir Thomas More believed respecting transubstantiation may not be believed to the end of time by men equal in abilities and honesty to Sir Thomas More. But Sir Thomas More is one of the choice specimens of human wisdom and virtue; and the doctrine of transubstantiation is a kind of proof charge. A faith which stands that test will stand any test. The prophecies of Brothers and the miracles of Prince Hohenlohe sink to trifles in the comparison. One reservation, indeed, must be made. The books and traditions of a sect may contain, mingled with propositions strictly theological, other propositions, purporting to rest on the same authority, which relate to physics. If new discoveries should throw discredit on the physical propositions, the theological propositions, unless they can be separated from the physical propositions, will share in that discredit. In this way, undoubtedly, the progress of science may indirectly serve the cause of religious truth. The Hindoo mythology, for example, is bound up with a most absurd geography. Every young Brahmin, therefore, who learns geography in our colleges, learns to smile at the Hindoo mythology. If Catholicism has not suffered to an equal degree from the Papal decision that the sun goes round the earth, this is because all intelligent Catholics now hold, with Pascal, that, in deciding the point at all, the Church exceeded her powers, and was, therefore, justly left destitute of that supernatural assistance which, in the exercise of her legitimate functions, the promise of her Founder authorised her to expect.

This reservation affects not at all the truth of our proposition, that divinity, properly so called, is not a progressive science. A very common knowledge of history, a very little observation of life, will suffice to prove that no learning, no sagacity, affords a security against the greatest errors on subjects relating to the invisible world. Bayle and Chillingworth, two of the most sceptical of mankind, turned Catholics from sincere conviction. Johnson, incredulous on all other points, was a ready believer in miracles and apparitions. He would not believe in Ossian; but he believed in the second sight. He would not believe in the earthquake of Lisbon; but he was willing to believe in the Cock Lane Ghost.

For these reasons we have ceased to wonder at any vagaries of superstition. We have seen men, not of mean intellect or neglected education, but qualified by their talents and acquirements to attain eminence either in active or speculative pursuits—well read scholars, expert logicians, keen observers of life and manners—prophesying, interpreting, talking unknown tongues, working miraculous cures, coming down with messages from God to the House of Commons. We have seen an old woman, with no talents beyond the cunning of a fortuneteller and with the education of a scullion, exalted into a prophetess and surrounded by tens of thousands of devoted followers, many of whom were in station and knowledge immeasurably her superiors, and all this in the nineteenth century, and all this in London. Yet why not? For of the dealings of God with man no more has been revealed to the nineteenth century than to the first, or to London than to the wildest parish in the Hebrides. It is true that, in those things which concern this life and this world, man constantly becomes wiser and wiser. But it is no less true that, as respects a higher power and a future state, man, in the language of Goethe's scoffing fiend,

"bleibt stets von gleichem Schlag,
Und ist so wunderlich als wie am ersten Tag."

The history of Catholicism strikingly illustrates these observations. During the last seven centuries the public mind of Europe has made constant progress in every department of secular knowledge. But in religion we can trace no constant progress. The ecclesiastical history of that long period is a history of movement to and fro. Four times since the authority of the Church of Rome was established in Western Christendom has the human intellect risen up against her yoke. Twice she remained completely victorious. Twice she came forth from the conflict bearing the marks of cruel wounds, but with the principle of life still strong within her. When we reflect on the tremendous assaults which she has survived, we find it difficult to conceive in what way she is to perish.

The first of these insurrections broke out in the region where the beautiful language of *Oc* was spoken. That country, singularly favoured by nature, was, in the twelfth century, the most flourishing and civilised portion of Western Europe. It is in nowise a part of France. It had a distinct political existence, a distinct national character, distinct usages and a distinct speech. The soil was fruitful and well cultivated; and amidst the cornfields and vineyards arose many rich cities, each of which was a little republic, and many stately castles, each of which contained a miniature of an imperial court. It was there that the spirit of chivalry first laid aside its terrors, first took a humane and graceful form, first appeared as the inseparable associate of art and literature, of courtesy and love. The other vernacular dialects, which, since the fifth century, had sprung up in the ancient provinces of the Roman empire, were still rude and imperfect. The sweet Tuscan, the rich and energetic English were abandoned to artisans and shepherds. No clerk had ever condescended to use such barbarous jargon for the teaching of science, for the recording of great events, or for the painting of life and manners. But the language of Provence was already the language of the learned and polite, and was employed by numerous writers, studious of all the arts of composition and versification. A literature rich in ballads, in war-songs, in satire and, above all, in amatory poetry, amused the leisure of the knights and ladies whose fortified mansions adorned the banks of of the Rhone and Garonne. With civilisation had come freedom of thought. Use had taken away the horror with which misbelievers were elsewhere regarded. No Norman or Breton ever saw a mussulman except to give and receive blows on some Syrian field of battle. But the people of the rich countries which lay under the Pyrenees lived in habits of courteous and profitable intercourse with the Moorish kingdoms of Spain, and gave an hospitable welcome to skilful leeches and mathematicians who, in the schools of Cordova and Granada, had become versed in all the learning of the Arabians. The Greek, still preserving in the midst of political degradation, the ready wit and the inquiring spirit of his fathers, still able to read the most perfect of human compositions, still speaking the most powerful and flexible of human languages, brought to the marts of Narbonne and Toulouse, together with the drugs and silks of remote climates, bold and subtle theories long unknown to the ignorant and credulous West. The Paulician theology—a theology in which, as it should seem, many of the doctrines of the modern Calvinists were mingled with some doctrines derived from the ancient Manichees—spread rapidly through Provence and Languedoc. The clergy of the Catholic Church were regarded with loathing and contempt. "Viler than a priest"—"I would as soon be a priest"—became proverbial expressions. The papacy had lost all authority with all classes, from the great feudal princes down to the cultivators of the soil.

The danger to the hierarchy was indeed formidable. Only one transalpine nation had emerged from barbarism; and that nation had thrown off all respect for Rome. Only one of the vernacular languages of Europe had yet been extensively employed for literary purposes; and that language was a machine in the hand of heretics. The geographical position of the sectaries made the danger peculiarly formidable. They occupied a central region communicating directly with France, with Italy and with Spain. The provinces which were still untainted were separated from each other by this infected district. Under these circumstances it seemed probable that a single generation would suffice to spread the reformed doctrine to Lisbon, to London and to Naples. But this was not to be. Rome cried for help to the warriors of northern France. She appealed at once to their superstition and to their cupidity. To the devout believer she promised pardons as ample as those with which she had rewarded the deliverers of the Holy Sepulchre. To the rapacious and profligate she offered the plunder of fertile plains and wealthy cities. Unhappily, the ingenious and polished inhabitants of the Languedocian provinces were far better qualified to enrich and embellish their country than to defend it. Eminent in the arts of peace, unrivalled in the "gay science," elevated above many vulgar superstitions, they wanted that iron courage and that skill in martial exercises which distinguished the chivalry of the region beyond the Loire, and and were ill fitted to face enemies who, in every country, from Ireland to Palestine, had been victorious against tenfold odds. A war, distinguished even among wars of religion by merciless atrocity, destroyed the Albigensian heresy, and with that heresy the prosperity, the civilisation, the literature, the national existence of what was once the most opulent and enlightened part of the great European family. Rome, in the meantime, warned by that fearful danger from which the exterminating swords of her crusaders had narrowly saved her, proceeded to revise and to strengthen her whole system of polity. At this period were instituted the Order of Francis, the Order of Dominic, the Tribunal of the Inquisition. The new spiritual police was everywhere. No alley in a great city, no hamlet on a remote mountain, was unvisited by the begging friar. The simple Catholic, who was content to be no wiser than his fathers, found, wherever he turned, a friendly voice to encourage him. The path of the heretic was beset by innumerable spies; and the Church, lately in danger of utter subversion, now appeared to be impregnably fortified by the love, the reverence and the terror of mankind.

A century and a half passed away, and then came the second great rising up of the human intellect against the spiritual domination of Rome. During the two generations which followed the Albigensian crusade, the power of the Papacy had been at the height. Frederic II.—the ablest and most accomplished of the long line of German Cæsars—had in vain exhausted all the resources of military and political skill in the attempt to defend the rights of the civil power against the encroachments of the Church. The vengeance of the priesthood had pursued his house to the third generation. Manfred had perished on the field of battle, Conradin on the scaffold. Then a turn took place. The secular authority, long unduly depressed, regained the ascendant with startling rapidity. The change is doubtless to be ascribed chiefly to the general disgust excited by the way in which the Church had abused its power and its success. But something must be attributed to the character and situation of individuals. The man who bore the chief part in effecting this revolution was Philip the Fourth of France, surnamed the Beautiful, a despot by position, a despot by temperament, stern, implacable and unscrupulous, equally prepared for violence and for chicanery, and surrounded by a devoted band of men of the sword and of men of law. The fiercest and most highminded of the Roman Pontiffs, while bestowing kingdoms and citing great princes to his judgment-seat, was seized in his palace by armed men, and so foully outraged that he died mad with rage and terror. "Thus," sang the great Florentine poet, "was Christ, in the person of his vicar, a second time seized by ruffians, a second time mocked, a second time drenched with the vinegar and the gall."* The seat of the Papal court was carried beyond the Alps, and the Bishops of Rome became dependants of France. Then came the great schism of the West. Two Popes, each with a doubtful title, made all Europe ring with their mutual invectives and anathemas. Rome cried out against the corruptions of Avignon ; and Avignon, with equal justice, recriminated on Rome. The plain Christian people, brought up in the belief that it was a sacred duty to be in communion with the Head of the Church, were unable to discover, amidst conflicting testimonies and conflicting arguments, to which of the two worthless priests, who were cursing and reviling each other, the headship of the Church rightfully belonged. It was nearly at this juncture that the voice of John Wickliffe began to make itself heard. The public mind of England was soon stirred to its inmost depths : and the influence of the new doctrines was soon felt, even in the distant kingdom of Bohemia. In Bohemia, indeed, there had long been a predisposition to heresy. Merchants from the Lower Danube were often seen in the fairs of Prague ; and the Lower Danube was peculiarly the seat of the Paulician theology. The Church, torn by schism, and fiercely assailed at once in England and in the German empire, was in a situation scarcely less perilous than at the crisis which preceded the Albigensian crusade.

But this danger also passed by. The civil power gave its strenuous support to the Church ; and the Church made some show of reforming itself. The Council of Constance put an end to the schism. The whole Catholic world was again united under a single chief ; and rules were laid down which seemed to make it improbable that the power of that chief would be grossly abused. The most distinguished teachers of the new doctrine were put to death. The English government put down the Lollards with merciless rigour ; and, in the next generation, no trace of the second great revolt against the Papacy could be found except among the rude population of the mountains of Bohemia.

Another century went by ; and then began the third and the most memorable struggle for spiritual freedom. The times were changed. The great remains of Athenian and Roman genius were studied by thousands. The Church had no longer a monopoly of learning. The powers of the modern languages had at length been developed. The invention of printing had given new facilities to the intercourse of mind with mind. With such auspices commenced the great Reformation.

We will attempt to lay before our readers, in a short compass, what appears to us to be the real history of the contest which began with the preaching of Luther against the Indulgences, and which may, in one sense, be said to have been terminated a hundred and thirty years later by the treaty of Westphalia.

In the northern parts of Europe, the victory of Protestantism was rapid and decisive. The dominion of the Papacy was felt by the nations of Teutonic blood as the dominion of Italians, of foreigners, of men who were aliens in language, manners and intellectual constitution. The large jurisdiction exercised by the spiritual tribunals of Rome seemed to be a degrading badge of servitude. The sums, which, under a thousand pretexts, were exacted by a distant court, were regarded both as a humiliating and as a ruinous tribute. The character of that court excited the scorn and disgust of a grave, earnest, sincere and devout

---

* Purgatorio, xx. 87.

people. The new theology spread with a rapidity never known before. All ranks, all varieties of character joined the ranks of the innovators. Sovereigns impatient to appropriate to themselves the prerogatives of the Pope—nobles desirous to share the plunder of abbeys—suitors exasperated by the extortions of the Roman Camera—patriots impatient of a foreign rule—good men scandalised by the corruptions of the Church—bad men desirous of the license inseparable from great moral revolutions—wise men eager in the pursuit of truth—weak men allured by the glitter of novelty—all were found on one side. Alone among the northern nations, the Irish adhered to the ancient faith : and the cause of this seems to have been that the national feeling which, in happier countries, was directed against Rome, was in Ireland directed against England. In fifty years from the day on which Luther publicly renounced communion with the Church of Rome and burned the bull of Leo before the gates of Wittenberg, Protestantism attained its highest ascendency—an ascendency which it soon lost and which it has never regained. Hundreds, who could well remember Brother Martin, a devout Catholic, lived to see the revolution, of which he was the chief author, victorious in half the states of Europe. In England, Scotland, Denmark, Sweden, Livonia, Prussia, Saxony, Hesse, Wurtemburg, the Palatinate, in several cantons of Switzerland, in the Northern Netherlands, the Reformation had completely triumphed ; and in all the other countries on this side of the Alps and the Pyrenees, it seemed on the point of triumphing.

But while this mighty work was proceeding in the north of Europe, a revolution of a very different kind had taken place in the south. The temper of Italy and Spain was widely different from that of Germany and England. As the national feeling of the Teutonic nations impelled them to throw off the Italian supremacy, so the national feeling of the Italians impelled them to resist any change which might deprive their country of the honours and advantage of being the seat of the government of the Universal Church. It was in Italy that the tributes were spent of which foreign nations so bitterly complained. It was to adorn Italy that the traffic in Indulgencies had been carried to that scandalous excess which had roused the indignation of Luther. There was among the Italians both much piety and much impiety ; but, with very few exceptions, neither the piety nor the impiety took the turn of Protestantism. The religious Italians desired a reform of morals and discipline, but not a reform of doctrine, and least of all a schism. The irreligious Italians simply disbelieved Christianity without hating it. They looked at it as artists or as statesmen ; and, so looking at it, they liked it better in the established form than in any other. It was to them what the old Pagan worship was to Trajan and Pliny. Neither the spirit of Savonarola nor the spirit of Machiavelli had anything in common with that of the religious or political Protestants of the North.

Spain again was, with respect to the Catholic Church, in a situation very different from that of the Teutonic nations. Italy was, in fact, a part of the empire of Charles V. ; and the court of Rome was, on many important occasions, his tool. He had not, therefore, like the distant princes of the North, a strong selfish motive for attacking the Papacy. In fact, the very measures which provoked the Soverein of England to renounce all connection with Rome were dictated by the Sovereign of Spain. The feelings of the Spanish people concurred with the interest of the Spanish government. The attachment of the Castilian to the faith of his ancestors was peculiarly strong and ardent. With that faith were inseparably bound up the institutions, the independence and the glory of his country. Between the day when the last Gothic king was vanquished on the Xeres and the day when

Ferdinand and Isabella entered Granada in triumph, nearly eight hundred years had elapsed; and during those years the Spanish nation had been engaged in a desperate struggle against misbelievers. The Crusades had been merely an episode in the history of other nations. The existence of Spain had been one long Crusade. After fighting Mussulmans in the Old World, she began to fight heathens in the New. It was under the authority of a Papal bull that her children steered into unknown seas. It was under the standard of the cross that they marched fearlessly into the heart of great kingdoms. It was with the cry of "St. James for Spain" that they charged armies which outnumbered them a hundred fold. And men said that the Saint had heard the call, and had himself, in arms, on a grey war-horse, led the onset before which the worshippers of false gods had given way. After the battle, every excess of rapacity or cruelty was sufficiently vindicated by the plea that the sufferers were unbaptized. Avarice stimulated zeal. Zeal consecrated avarice. Proselytes and gold mines were sought with equal ardour. In the very year in which the Saxons, maddened by the exactions of Rome, broke loose from her yoke, the Spaniards, under the authority of Rome, made themselves masters of the empire and of the treasures of Montezuma. Thus Catholicism, which, in the public mind of Northern Europe, was associated with spoliation and oppression, was, in the public mind of Spain, associated with liberty, victory, dominion, wealth and glory.

It is not, therefore, strange that the effect of the great outbreak of Protestantism in one part of Christendom should have been to produce an equally violent outbreak of Catholic zeal in another. Two reformations were pushed on at once with equal energy and effect—a reformation of doctrine in the North—a reformation of manners and discipline in the South. In the course of a single generation, the whole spirit of the Church of Rome underwent a change. From the halls of the Vatican to the most secluded hermitage of the Apennines, the great revival was everywhere felt and seen. All the institutions anciently devised for the propagation and defence of the faith were furbished up and made efficient. Fresh engines of still more formidable power were constructed. Everywhere old religious communities were remodelled and new religious communities called into existence. Within a year after the death of Leo, the order of Camaldoli was purified. The Capuchins restored the old Franciscan discipline—the midnight prayer and the life of silence. The Barnabites and the society of Somasca devoted themselves to the relief and education of the poor. To the Theatine order a still higher interest belongs. Its great object was the same with that of our early Methodists—to supply the deficiencies of the parochial clergy. The Church of Rome, wiser than the Church of England, gave every countenance to the good work. The members of the new brotherhood preached to great multitudes in the streets and in the fields, prayed by the beds of the sick, and administered the last sacraments to the dying. Foremost among them in zeal and devotion was Gian Pietro Caraffa, afterwards Pope Paul IV. In the convent of the Theatines at Venice, under the eye of Caraffa, a Spanish gentleman took up his abode, tended the poor in the hospitals, went about in rags, starved himself almost to death, and often sallied into the streets, mounted on stones, and, waving his hat to invite the passers-by, began to preach in a strange jargon of mingled Castillian and Tuscan. The Theatines were among the most zealous and rigid of men; but to this enthusiastic neophyte their discipline seemed lax and their movements sluggish, for his own mind, naturally passionate and imaginative, had passed through a training which had given to all its peculiarities a morbid intensity and energy. In his early life he had been the very prototype of the hero of Cervantes. The single study of the young Hidalgo had been chivalrous romance; and his existence had been one gorgeous day-dream of princesses rescued and infidels subdued. He had chosen a Dulcinea, "no countess, no duchess"—these are his own words—"but one of far higher station;" and he flattered himself with the hope of laying at her feet the keys of Moorish castles and the jewelled turbans of Asiatic kings. In the midst of these visions of martial glory and prosperous love, a severe wound stretched him on a bed of sickness. His constitution was shattered and he was doomed to be a cripple for life. The palm of strength, grace and skill in knightly exercises was no longer for him. He could no longer hope to strike down gigantic soldans, or to find favour in the sight of beautiful women. A new vision then arose in his mind and mingled itself with his old delusions in a manner which to most Englishman must seem singular, but which those who know how close was the union between religion and chivalry in Spain will be at no loss to understand. He would still be a soldier; he would still be a knight errant; but the soldier and knight errant of the spouse of Christ. He would smite the Great Red Dragon. He would be the champion of the Woman clothed with the Sun. He would break the charm under which false prophets held the souls of men in bondage. His restless spirit led him to the Syrian deserts and to the chapel of the Holy Sepulchre. Thence he wandered back to the farthest West, and astonished the convents of Spain and the schools of France by his penances and vigils. The same lively imagination, which had been employed in picturing the tumult of unreal battles and the charms of unreal queens, now peopled his solitude with saints and angels. The Holy Virgin descended to commune with him. He saw the Saviour face to face with the eye of flesh. Even those mysteries of religion which are the hardest trial of faith were in his case palpable to sight. It is difficult to relate without a pitying smile that, in the sacrifice of the mass, he saw transubstantiation take place, and that as he stood praying on the steps of the Church of St. Dominic, he saw the Trinity in Unity, and wept aloud with joy and wonder. Such was the celebrated Ignatius Loyola, who in the great Catholic reaction bore the same part which Luther bore in the great Protestant movement.

Dissatisfied with the system of the Theatines, the enthusiastic Spaniard turned his face towards Rome. Poor, obscure, without a patron, without recommendations, he entered the city where now two princely temples, rich with painting and many-coloured marble, commemorate his great services to the Church; where his form stands sculptured in massive silver; where his bones, enshrined amidst jewels, are placed beneath the altar of God. His activity and zeal bore down all opposition; and under his rule the order of Jesuits began to exist and grew rapidly to the full measure of its gigantic powers. With what vehemence, with what policy, with what exact discipline, with what dauntless courage, with what self-denial, with what forgetfulness of the dearest private ties, with what intense and stubborn devotion to a single end, with what unscrupulous laxity and versatility in the choice of means the Jesuits fought the battle of their church is written in every page of the annals of Europe during several generations. In the order of Jesus was concentrated the quintessence of the Catholic spirit; and the history of the order of Jesus is the history of the great Catholic reaction. That order possessed itself at once of all the strongholds which command the public mind—of the pulpit, of the press, of the confessional, of the academies. Wherever the Jesuit preached, the church was too small for the audience. The name of Jesuit on a title-page secured the circulation of a book. It was in the ears of the Jesuit that the powerful, the noble and the beautiful breathed the secret history of their lives. It was at the feet of the Jesuit that the youth of the higher and middle classes were brought up from the first rudiments to the courses of rhetoric and philosophy. Literature and science, lately associated with infidelity or with heresy, now became the allies of orthodoxy. Dominant in the South of Europe, the great order soon went forth conquering and to conquer. In spite of oceans and deserts, of hunger and pestilence, of spies and penal laws, of dungeons and racks, of gibbets and quartering-blocks, Jesuits were to be found under every disguise and in every country—scholars, physicians, merchants, serving-men; in the hostile court of Sweden, in the old manor-houses of Cheshire, among the hovels of Connaught; arguing, instructing, consoling, stealing away the hearts of the young, animating the courage of the timid, holding up the crucifix before the eyes of the dying. Nor was it less their office to plot against the thrones and lives of apostate kings, to spread evil rumours, to raise tumults, to inflame civil wars, to arm the hand of the assassin. Inflexible in nothing but in their fidelity to the Church, they were equally ready to appeal in her cause to the spirit of loyalty and to the spirit of freedom. Extreme doctrines of obedience and extreme doctrines of liberty—the right of rulers to misgovern the people, the right of every one of the people to plunge his knife in the heart of a bad ruler—were inculcated by the same man, according as he addressed himself to the subject of Philip or to the subject of Elizabeth. Some described these men as the most rigid, others as the most indulgent of spiritual directors. And both descriptions were correct. The truly devout listened with awe to the high and saintly morality of the Jesuit. The gay cavalier who had run his rival through the body, the frail beauty who had forgotten her marriage vow, found in the Jesuit an easy, well-bred man of the world, tolerant of the little irregularities of people of fashion. The confessor was strict or lax, according to the temper of the penitent. His first object was to drive no person out of the pale of the Church. Since there were bad people, it was better that they should be bad Catholics than bad Protestants. If a person was so unfortunate as to be a bravo, a libertine or a gambler, that was no reason for making him a heretic too.

The Old World was not wide enough for this strange activity. The Jesuits invaded all the countries which the great maritime discoveries of the preceding age had laid open to European enterprise. In the depths of the Peruvian mines, at the marts of the African slave-caravans, on the shores of the Spice Islands, in the observatories of China, they were to be found. They made converts in regions which neither avarice nor curiosity had tempted any of their countrymen to enter; and preached and disputed in tongues of which no other native of the West understood a word.

The spirit which appeared so eminently in this order animated the whole Catholic world. The Court of Rome itself was purified. During the generation which preceded the Reformation, that court had been a scandal to the Christian name. Its annals are black with treason, murder and incest. Even its more respectable members were utterly unfit to be ministers of religion. They were men like Leo X.; men who, with the Latinity of the Augustan age, had acquired its atheistical and scoffing spirit. They regarded those Christian mysteries, of which they were stewards, just as the Augur Cicero and the Pontifa Maximus Cæsar regarded the Sibylline books and the pecking of the sacred chickens. Among themselves they spoke of the Incarnation, the Eucharist and the Trinity in the same tone in which Cotta and Velleius talked of the oracle of Delphi or the voice of Faunus in the mountains. Their years glided by in a soft dream of sensual and intellectual voluptuousness. Choice cookery, delicious wines, lovely women, hounds, falcons, horses, newly-discovered manuscripts of the classics, sonnets and burlesque romances in the sweetest Tuscan—just as licentious as a fine sense of the graceful would permit;

plate from the hand of Benvenuto, designs for palaces by Michael Angelo, frescoes by Raphael, busts, mosaics and gems just dug up from among the ruins of ancient temples and villas—these things were the delight and even the serious business of their lives. Letters and the fine arts undoubtedly owe much to this not inelegant sloth. But when the great stirring of the mind of Europe began—when doctrine after doctrine was assailed—when nation after nation withdrew from communion with the successor of St. Peter—it was felt that the Church could not be safely confided to chiefs whose highest praise was that they were good judges of Latin compositions, of paintings and of statues, whose severest studies had a pagan character, and who were suspected of laughing in secret at the sacraments which they administered and of believing no more of the Gospel than of the Morgante Maggiore. Men of a very different class now rose to the direction of ecclesiastical affairs—men whose spirit resembled that of Dunstan and of Becket. The Roman Pontiffs exhibited in their own persons all the austerity of the early anchorites of Syria. Paul IV. brought to the Papal throne the same fervent zeal which had carried him into the Theatine convent. Pius V., under his gorgeous vestments, wore day and night the hair shirt of a simple friar; walked barefoot in the streets at the head of processions; found, even in the midst of his most pressing avocations, time for private prayer; often regretted that the public duties of his station were unfavourable to growth in holiness; and edified his flock by innumerable instances of humility, charity and forgiveness of personal injuries; while, at the same time, he upheld the authority of his see and the unadulterated doctrines of his Church with all the stubbornness and vehemence of Hildebrand. Gregory XIII. exerted himself not only to imitate but to surpass Pius in the severe virtues of his sacred profession. As was the head, such were the members. The change in the spirit of the Catholic world may be traced in every walk of literature and of art. It will be at once perceived by every person who compares the poem of Tasso with that of Ariosto, or the monuments of Sixtus V. with those of Leo X.

But it was not on moral influence alone that the Catholic Church relied. The civil sword in Spain and Italy was unsparingly employed in her support. The Inquisition was armed with new powers and inspired with a new energy. If Protestantism, or the semblance of Protestantism, showed itself in any quarter, it was instantly met, not by petty, teasing persecution, but by persecution of that sort which bows down and crushes all but a very few select spirits. Whoever was suspected of heresy, whatever his rank, his learning or his reputation, was to purge himself to the satisfaction of a severe and vigilant tribunal or die by fire. Heretical books were sought out and destroyed with the same unsparing rigour. Works which were once in every house were so effectually suppressed that no copy of them is now to be found in the most extensive libraries. One book in particular, entitled "Of the Benefits of the Death of Christ," had this fate. It was written in Tuscan, was many times reprinted, and was eagerly read in every part of Italy. But the Inquisitors detected in it the Lutheran doctrine of justification by faith alone. They proscribed it; and it is now as utterly lost as the second decade of Livy.

Thus, while the Protestant reformation proceeded rapidly at one extremity of Europe, the Catholic revival went on as rapidly at the other. About half a century after the great separation, there were, throughout the North, Protestant governments and Protestant nations. In the South were governments and nations actuated by the most intense zeal for the ancient Church. Between these two hostile regions lay, morally as well as geographically, a great debatable land. In France, Belgium, Southern Germany, Hungary and Poland, the contest was still undecided. The governments of those countries had not renounced their connection with Rome; but the Protestants were numerous, powerful, bold and active. In France, they formed a commonwealth within the realm, held fortresses, were able to bring great armies into the field, and had treated with their sovereign on terms of equality. In Poland, the King was still a Catholic; but the Protestants had the upper hand in the Diet, filled the chief offices in the administration, and, in the large towns, took possession of the parish churches. "It appeared," says the Papal nuncio, "that in Poland Protestantism would completely supersede Catholicism." In Bavaria, the state of things was nearly the same. The Protestants had a majority in the Assembly of the States, and demanded from the duke concessions in favour of their religion as the price of their subsidies. In Transylvania, the House of Austria was unable to prevent the Diet from confiscating, by one sweeping decree, the states of the Church. In Austria Proper, it was generally said that only one-thirtieth part of the population could be counted on as good Catholics. In Belgium, the adherents of the new opinions were reckoned by hundreds of thousands.

The history of the two succeeding generations is the history of the great struggle between Protestantism possessed of the North of Europe and Catholicism possessed of the South for the doubtful territory which lay between. All the weapons of carnal and of spiritual warfare were employed. Both sides may boast of great talents and of great virtues. Both have to blush for many follies and crimes. At first, the chances seemed to be decidedly in favour of Protestantism; but the victory remained with the Church of Rome. On every point she was successful. If we overleap another half century, we find her victorious and dominant in France, Belgium, Bavaria, Bohemia, Austria, Poland and Hungary. Nor has Protestantism, in the course of two hundred years, been able to reconquer any portion of what was then lost.

It is, moreover, not to be dissembled that this wonderful triumph of the Papacy is to be chiefly attributed, not to the force of arms, but to a great reflux in public opinion. During the first half century after the commencement of the Reformation, the current of feeling in the countries on this side of the Alps and of the Pyrenees ran impetuously towards the new doctrines. Then the tide turned and rushed as fiercely in the opposite direction. Neither during the one period, nor during the other, did much depend upon the event of battles or sieges. The Protestant movement was hardly checked for an instant by the defeat at Muhlberg. The Catholic reaction went on at full speed in spite of the destruction of the Armada. It is difficult to say whether the violence of the first blow or of the recoil was the greater. Fifty years after the Lutheran separation, Catholicism could scarcely maintain itself on the shores of the Mediterranean. A hundred years after the separation, Protestantism could scarcely maintain itself on the shores of the Baltic. The causes of this memorable turn in human affairs well deserve to be investigated.

The contest between the two parties bore some resemblance to the fencing-match in Shakspeare, "Laertes wounds Hamlet; then, in scuffling, they change rapiers, and Hamlet wounds Laertes." The war between Luther and Leo was a war between firm faith and unbelief, between zeal and apathy, between energy and indolence, between seriousness and frivolity, between a pure morality and vice. Very different was the war which degenerate Protestantism had to wage against regenerate Catholicism. To the debauchee, the poisoners, the atheists, who had worn the tiara during the generation which preceded the Reformation, had succeeded Popes who, in religious fervour and severe sanctity of manners, might bear a comparison with Cyprian or Ambrose. The order of Jesuits alone could show many men not inferior in sincerity, constancy, courage and austerity of life to the apostles of the Reformation. But, while danger had thus called forth in the bosom of the Church of Rome many of the highest qualities of the Reformers, the Reformed Church had contracted some of the corruptions which had been justly censured in the Church of Rome. They had become lukewarm and worldly. Their great old leaders had been borne to the grave and had left no successors. Among the Protestant princes there was little or no hearty Protestant feeling. Elizabeth herself was a Protestant rather from policy than from firm conviction. James I., in order to effect his favourite object of marrying his son into one of the great continental houses, was ready to make immense concessions to Rome, and even to admit a modified primacy in the Pope. Henry IV. twice abjured the reformed doctrines from interested motives. The Elector of Saxony, the natural head of the Protestant party in Germany, submitted to become, at the most important crisis of the struggle, a tool in the hands of the Papists. Among the Catholic sovereigns, on the other hand, we find a religious zeal often amounting to fanaticism. Philip II. was a Papist in a very different sense from that in which Elizabeth was a Protestant. Maximilian of Bavaria, brought up under the teaching of the Jesuits, was a fervent missionary wielding the powers of a prince. The Emperor Ferdinand II. deliberately put his throne to hazard over and over again, rather than make the smallest concession to the spirit of religious innovation. Sigismund of Sweden lost a crown which he might have preserved if he would have renounced the Catholic faith. In short, everywhere on the Protestant side we see languor; everywhere on the Catholic side we see ardour and devotion.

Not only was there, at this time, a much more intense zeal among the Catholics than among the Protestants, but the whole zeal of the Catholics was directed against the Protestants, while almost the whole zeal of the Protestants was directed against each other. Within the Catholic Church there were no serious disputes on points of doctrine. The decisions of the Council of Trent were received, and the Jansenian controversy had not yet arisen. The whole force of Rome was, therefore, effective for the purpose of carrying on the war against the Reformation. On the other hand, the force which ought to have fought the battle of the Reformation was exhausted in civil conflict. While Jesuit preachers, Jesuit confessors, Jesuit teachers of youth overspread Europe, eager to expend every faculty of their minds and every drop of their blood in the cause of their Church, Protestant doctors were confuting and Protestant rulers were punishing sectaries who were just as good Protestants as themselves.

"Cumque superba foret BABYLON spolianda tropæis,
Bella geri placuit nullos habitura triumphos."

In the Palatinate, a Calvinistic prince persecuted the Lutherans. In Saxony, a Lutheran prince persecuted the Calvinists. In Sweden, everybody who objected to any of the articles of the Confession of Augsburg was banished. In Scotland, Melville was disputing with other Protestants on questions of ecclesiastical government. In England, the gaols were filled with men who, though zealous for the Reformation, did not exactly agree with the Court on all points of discipline and doctrine. Some were in ward for denying the tenet of reprobation; some for not wearing surplices. The Irish people might at that time have been, in all probability, reclaimed from Popery at the expense of half the zeal and activity which Whitgift employed in oppressing Puritans and Martin Marprelate in reviling bishops.

As the Catholics in zeal and in union had a great advantage over the Protestants, so had they also an infinitely superior organisation. In truth, Protestantism, for aggressive purposes, had no organisation at all. The Reformed Churches were mere national Churches. The Church of England existed for England alone. It was an institution as purely local as the Court of Common Pleas, and was utterly without any machinery for foreign operations. The Church of Scotland, in the same manner, existed for Scotland alone. The operations of the Catholic Church, on the other hand, took in the whole world. Nobody at Lambeth or at Edinburgh troubled himself about what was doing in Poland or Bavaria. But at Rome, Cracow and Munich were objects of as much interest as the purlieus of St. John Lateran. Our island, the head of the Protestant interest, did not send out a single missionary or a single instructor of youth to the scene of the great spiritual war. Not a single seminary was established here for the purpose of furnishing a supply of such persons to foreign countries. On the other hand, Germany, Hungary and Poland were filled with able and active Catholic emissaries of Spanish or Italian birth; and colleges for the instruction of the northern youth were founded at Rome. The spiritual force of Protestantism was a mere local militia, which might be useful in case of an invasion, but could not be sent abroad, and could therefore make no conquests. Rome had such a local militia; but she had also a force disposable at a moment's notice for foreign service, however dangerous or disagreeable. If it was thought at head-quarters that a Jesuit at Palermo was qualified by his talents and character to withstand the Reformers in Lithuania, the order was instantly given and instantly obeyed. In a month, the faithful servant of the Church was preaching, catechising, confessing beyond the Niemen.

It is impossible to deny that the polity of the Church of Rome is the very masterpiece of human wisdom. In truth, nothing but such a polity could, against such assaults, have borne up such doctrines. The experience of twelve hundred eventful years, the ingenuity and patient care of forty generations of statesmen have improved it to such perfection that, among the contrivances of political ability, it occupies the highest place. The stronger our conviction that reason and scripture were decidedly on the side of Protestantism, the greater is the reluctant admiration with which we regard that system of tactics against which reason and scripture were arrayed in vain.

If we went at large into this most interesting subject, we should fill volumes. We will, therefore, at present advert to only one important part of the policy of the Church of Rome. She thoroughly understands, what no other Church has ever understood, how to deal with enthusiasts. In some sects—particularly in infant sects—enthusiasm is suffered to be rampant. In other sects—particularly in sects long established and richly endowed—it is regarded with aversion. The Catholic Church neither submits to enthusiasm nor proscribes it, but uses it. She considers it as a great moving force which in itself, like the muscular power of a fine horse, is neither good nor evil, but which may be so directed as to produce great good or great evil; and she assumes the direction to herself. It would be absurd to run down a horse like a wolf. It would be still more absurd to let him run wild, breaking fences and trampling down passengers. The rational course is to subjugate his will without impairing his vigour— to teach him to obey the rein and then to urge him to full speed. When once he knows his master, he is valuable in proportion to his strength and spirit. Just such has been the system of the Church of Rome with regard to enthusiasts. She knows that when religious feelings have obtained the complete empire of the mind they impart a strange energy, that they raise men above the dominion of pain and pleasure, that obloquy becomes glory, that death itself is contemplated only as the beginning of a higher and happier life. She knows that a person in this state is no object of contempt. He may be vulgar, ignorant, visionary, extravagant; but he will do and suffer things which it is for her interest that somebody should do and suffer, yet from which calm and sober-minded men would shrink. She accordingly enlists him in her service, assigns to him some forlorn hope, in which intrepidity and impetuosity are more wanted than judgment and self-command, and sends him forth with her benedictions and her applause.

In England it not unfrequently happens that a tinker or coalheaver hears a sermon or falls in with a tract which alarms him about the state of his soul. If he be a man of excitable nerves and strong imagination, he thinks himself given over to the Evil Power. He doubts whether he has not committed the unpardonable sin. He imputes every wild fancy that springs up in his mind to the whisper of a fiend. His sleep is broken by dreams of the great judgment-seat, the open books and the unquenchable fire. If, in order to escape from these vexing thoughts, he flies to amusement or to licentious indulgence, the delusive relief only makes his misery darker and more hopeless. At length a turn takes place. He is reconciled to his offended Maker. To borrow the fine imagery of one who had himself been thus tried, he emerges from the Valley of the Shadow of Death, from the dark land of gins and snares, of quagmires and precipices, of evil spirits and ravenous beasts. The sunshine is on his path. He ascends the Delectable Mountains, and catches from their summit a distant view of the shining city which is the end of his pilgrimage. Then arises in his mind a natural and surely not a censurable desire, to impart to others the thoughts of which his own heart is full—to warn the careless, to comfort those who are troubled in spirit. The impulse which urges him to devote his whole life to the teaching of religion is a strong passion in the guise of a duty. He exhorts his neighbours; and, if he be a man of strong parts, he often does so with great effect. He pleads as if he were pleading for his life, with tears and pathetic gestures and burning words; and he soon finds with delight, not perhaps wholly unmixed with the alloy of human infirmity, that his rude eloquence rouses and melts hearers who sleep very composedly while the rector preaches on the apostolical succession. Zeal for God, love for his fellow-creatures, pleasure in the exercise of his newly discovered powers, impel him to become a preacher. He has no quarrel with the establishment, no objection to its formularies, its government or its vestments. He would gladly be admitted among its humblest ministers, but, admitted or rejected, his vocation is determined. His orders have come down to him, not through a long and doubtful series of Arian and Popish bishops, but direct from on high. His commission is the same that on the Mountain of Ascension was given to the Eleven. Nor will he, for lack of human credentials, spare to deliver the glorious message with which he is charged by the true Head of the Church. For a man thus minded, there is within the pale of the establishment no place. He has been at no college; he cannot construe a Greek author, nor write a Latin theme; and he is told that, if he remains in the communion of the Church, he must do so as a hearer, and that if he is resolved to be a teacher, he must begin by being a schismatic. His choice is soon made. He harangues on Tower Hill or in Smithfield. A congregation is formed. A license is obtained. A plain brick building, with a desk and benches, is run up, and named Ebenezer or Bethel. In a few weeks the Church has lost for ever a hundred families, not one of which entertained the least scruple about her articles, her liturgy, her government or her ceremonies.

Far different is the policy of Rome. The ignorant enthusiast whom the Anglican Church makes an enemy, and whatever the polite and learned may think, a most dangerous enemy, the Catholic Church makes a champion. She bids him curse his beard, covers him with a gown and hood of coarse dark stuff, ties a rope round his waist and sends him forth to teach in her name. He costs her nothing. He takes not a ducat away from the revenues of her beneficed clergy. He lives by the alms of those who respect his spiritual character and are grateful for his instructions. He preaches, not exactly in the style of Massillon, but in a way which moves the passions of uneducated hearers ; and all his influence is employed to strengthen the Church of which he is a minister. To that church he becomes as strongly attached as any of the cardinals whose scarlet carriages and liveries crowd the entrance of the palace on the Quirinal. In this way the Church of Rome unites in herself all the strength of establishment and all the strength of dissent. With the utmost pomp of a dominant hierarchy above, she has all the energy of the voluntary system below. It would be easy to mention very recent instances in which the hearts of hundreds of thousands, estranged from her by the selfishness, sloth and cowardice of the beneficed clergy, have been brought back by the zeal of the begging friars.

Even for female agency there is a place in her system. To devout women she assigns spiritual functions, dignities and magistracies. In our country, if a noble lady is moved by more than ordinary zeal for the propagation of religion, the chance is that, though she may disapprove of no doctrine or ceremony of the Established Church, she will end by giving her name to a new schism. If a pious and benevolent woman enters the cells of a prison to pray with the most unhappy and degraded of her own sex, she does so without any authority from the Church. No line of action is traced out for her ; and it is well if the Ordinary does not complain of her intrusion and if the Bishop does not shake his head at such irregular benevolence. At Rome, the Countess of Huntingdon would have a place in the calendar as St. Selina and Mrs. Fry would be foundress and first Superior of the Blessed Order of Sisters of the Gaols.

Place Ignatius Loyola at Oxford. He is certain to become the head of a formidable secession. Place John Wesley at Rome. He is certain to be the first General of a new society devoted to the interest and honour of the Church. Place St. Theresa in London. Her restless enthusiasm ferments into madness, not untinctured with craft. She becomes the prophetess, the mother of the faithful, holds disputations with the devil, issues sealed pardons to her adorers, and lies in of the Shiloh. Place Joanna Southcote at Rome. She founds an order of barefooted Carmelites, every one of whom is ready to suffer martyrdom for the Church—a solemn service is consecrated to her memory—and her statue, placed over the holy water, strikes the eye of every stranger who enters St. Peter's.

We have dwelt long on this subject, because we believe that, of the many causes to which the Church of Rome owed her safety and her triumph at the close of the sixteenth century, the chief was the profound policy with which she used the fanaticism of such persons as St. Ignatius and St. Theresa.

The Protestant party was now, indeed, vanquished and humbled. In France, so strong had been the Catholic reaction that Henry IV. found it necessary to choose between his religion and his crown. In spite of his clear hereditary right, in spite of his eminent personal qualities, he saw that, unless he reconciled himself to the Church of Rome, he could not count on the fidelity even of those gallant gentlemen whose impetuous valour turned the tide of battle at Ivry. In Belgium, Poland and South Germany, Catholicism had obtained complete ascendency. The resistance of Bohemia was put down. The Palatinate was conquered. Upper and Lower Saxony were overflowed by Catholic invaders. The King of Denmark stood forth as the Protector of the Reformed Churches : he was defeated, driven out of the empire and attacked in his own possessions. The armies of the House of Austria pressed on, subjugated Pomerania, and were stopped in their progress only by the ramparts of Stralsund.

And now again the tide turned. Two violent outbreaks of religious feeling in opposite directions had given a character to the whole history of a whole century. Protestantism had at first driven back Catholicism to the Alps and the Pyrenees. Catholicism had rallied and had driven back Protestantism even to the German Ocean. Then the great southern reaction began to slacken, as the great northern movement had slackened before. The zeal of the Catholics became cool; their union was dissolved. The paroxysm of religious excitement was over on both sides. The one party had degenerated as far from the spirit of Loyola, as the other from the spirit of Luther. During three generations, religion had been the mainspring of politics. The revolutions and civil wars of France, Scotland, Holland, Sweden, the long struggle between Philip and Elizabeth, the bloody competition for the Bohemian crown, had all originated in theological disputes. But a great change now took place. The contest which was raging in Germany lost its religious character. It was now, on one side, less a contest for the spiritual ascendency of the Church of Rome than for the temporal ascendency of the House of Austria. On the other, it was less a contest for the reformed doctrines than for national independence. Governments began to form themselves into new combinations, in which community of political interest was far more regarded than community of religious belief. Even at Rome, the progress of the Catholic arms was observed with very mixed feelings. The Supreme Pontiff was a sovereign prince of the second rank, and was anxious about the balance of power as well as about the propagation of truth. It was known that he dreaded the rise of an universal monarchy even more than he desired the prosperity of the Universal Church. At length a great event announced to the world that the war of sects had ceased and that the war of states had succeeded. A coalition, including Calvinists, Lutherans and Catholics, was formed against the House of Austria. At the head of that coalition were the first statesman and the first warrior of the age; the former a prince of the Catholic Church, distinguished by the vigour and success with which he had put down the Huguenots—the latter a Protestant king who owed his throne to a revolution caused by hatred of Popery. The alliance of Richelieu and Gustavus marks the time at which the great religious struggle terminated. The war which followed was a war for the equilibrium of Europe. When, at length, the peace of Westphalia was concluded, it appeared that the Church of Rome remained in full possession of a vast dominion, which, in the middle of the preceding century, she seemed to be on the point of losing. No part of Europe remained Protestant except that part which had become thoroughly Protestant before the generation which heard Luther preach had passed away.

Since that time there has been no religious war between Catholics and Protestants as such. In the time of Cromwell, Protestant England was united with Catholic France, then governed by a priest, against Catholic Spain. William III., the eminently Protestant hero, was at the head of a coalition which included many Catholic powers, and which was secretly favoured even by Rome against the Catholic Louis. In the time of Anne, Protestant England and Protestant Holland joined with Catholic Savoy and Catholic Portugal for the purpose of transferring the crown of Spain from one bigoted Catholic to another.

The geographical frontier between the two religions has continued to run almost precisely where it ran at the close of the Thirty Years' War; nor has Protestantism given any proofs of that "expansive power" which has been ascribed to it. But the Protestant boasts, and boasts most justly, that wealth, civilisation and intelligence have increased far more on the northern than on the southern side of the boundary; that countries so little favoured by nature as Scotland and Prussia are now among the most flourishing and best governed portions of the world—while the marble palaces of Genoa are deserted, while banditti infest the beautiful shores of Campania, while the fertile sea-coast of the Pontifical State is abandoned to buffaloes and wild boars. It cannot be doubted that, since the sixteenth century, the Protestant nations have made decidedly greater progress than their neighbours. The progress made by those nations in which Protestantism, though not finally successful, yet maintained a long struggle and left permanent traces, has generally been considerable. But when we come to the Catholic Land, to the part of Europe in which the first spark of reformation was trodden out as soon as it appeared, and from which proceeded the impulse which drove Protestantism back, we find, at best, a very slow progress, and, on the whole, a retrogression. Compare Denmark and Portugal. When Luther began to preach, the superiority of the Portuguese was unquestionable. At present, the superiority of the Danes is no less so. Compare Edinburgh and Florence. Edinburgh has owed less to climate, to soil and to the fostering care of rulers than any capital, Protestant or Catholic. In all these respects, Florence has been singularly happy. Yet whoever knows what Florence and Edinburgh were in the generation preceding the Reformation and what they are now will acknowledge that some great cause has, during the last three centuries, operated to raise one part of the European family and to depress the other. Compare the history of England and that of Spain during the last century. In arms, arts, sciences, letters, commerce, agriculture, the contrast is most striking. The distinction is not confined to this side of the Atlantic. The colonies, planted by England in America, have immeasurably outgrown in power those planted by Spain. Yet we have no reason to believe that at the beginning of the sixteenth century the Castilian was in any respect inferior to the Englishman. Our firm belief is, that the North owes its great civilisation and prosperity chiefly to the moral effect of the Protestant Reformation; and that the decay of the southern countries of Europe is to be mainly ascribed to the great Catholic revival.

About a hundred years after the final settlement of the boundary line between Protestantism and Catholicism began to appear the signs of the fourth great peril of the Church of Rome. The storm which was now rising against her was of a very different kind from those which had preceded it. Those who had formerly attacked her had questioned only a part of her doctrines. A school was now growing up which rejected the whole. The Albigenses, the Lollards, the Lutherans, the Calvanists had a positive religious system and were strongly attached to it. The creed of the new sectaries was altogether negative. They took one of their premises from the Protestants and one from the Catholics. From the former they borrowed the principle that Catholicism was the only pure and genuine Christianity. With the latter they held that some parts of the Catholic system were contrary to reason. The conclusion was obvious. Two propositions, each of which separately is compatible with the most exalted piety, formed, when held in conjunction, the groundwork of a system of irreligion. The doctrine of Bossuet, that transubstantiation is affirmed in the Gospel, and the doctrine of Tillotson, that transubstantiation is an absurdity, when put together, produced by logical necessity the inferences of Voltaire.

Had the sect which was rising at Paris been a sect of mere scoffers, it is very improbable that it would have left deep traces of its existence in the institutions and manners of Europe. Mere negation—mere Epicurean infidelity, as Lord Bacon most justly observes—has never disturbed the peace of the world. It furnishes no motive for action. It inspires no enthusiasm. It has no missionaries, no crusaders, no martyrs. If the Patriarch of the Holy Philosophical Church had contented himself with making jokes about Saul's asses and David's wives and with criticising the poetry of Ezekiel in the same narrow spirit in which he criticised that of Shakespeare, the Church would have had little to fear. But it is due to him and to his compeers to say that the real secret of their strength lay in the truth which was mingled with their errors and in the generous enthusiasm which was hidden under their flippancy. They were men who, with all their faults, moral and intellectual, sincerely and earnestly desired the improvement of the condition of the human race—whose blood boiled at the sight of cruelty and injustice—who made manful war, with every faculty which they possessed, on what they considered as abuses—and who on many signal occasions placed themselves gallantly between the powerful and the oppressed. While they assailed Christianity with a rancour and an unfairness disgraceful to men who called themselves philosophers, they yet had, in far greater measure than their opponents, that charity towards men of all classes and races which Christianity enjoins. Religious persecution, judicial torture, arbitrary imprisonment, the unnecessary multiplication of capital punishments, the delay and chicanery of tribunals, the exactions of farmers of the revenue, slavery, the slave trade, were the constant subjects of their lively satire and eloquent disquisitions. When an innocent man was broken on the wheel at Toulouse—when a youth, guilty only of an indiscretion, was burned at Abbeville—when a brave officer, borne down by public injustice, was dragged, with a gag in his mouth, to die on the Place de Grève—a voice instantly went forth from the banks of Lake Leman, which made itself heard from Moscow to Cadiz, and which sentenced the unjust judges to the contempt and detestation of all Europe. The really efficient weapons with which the philosophers assailed the evangelical faith were borrowed from the evangelical morality. The ethical and dogmatical arts of the Gospel were unhappily turned against each other. On the one side was a Church boasting of the purity of a doctrine derived from the Apostles, but disgraced by the massacre of St. Bartholomew, by the murder of the best of kings, by the war of Cevennes, by the destruction of Port-Royal. On the other side was a sect laughing at the Scriptures, shooting out the tongue at the sacraments, but ready to encounter principalities and powers in the cause of justice, mercy and toleration.

Irreligion, accidentally associated with philanthropy, triumphed for a time over religion accidentally associated with political and social abuses. Everything gave way to the zeal and activity of the new reformers. In France, every man distinguished in letters was found in their ranks. Every year gave birth to works in which the fundamental principles of the Church were attacked with argument, invective and ridicule. The Church made no defence, except by acts of power. Censures were pronounced, editions were seized, insults were offered to the remains of infidel writers; but no Bossuet, no Pascal came forth to encounter Voltaire. There appeared not a single defence of the Catholic doctrine which produced any considerable effect or which is now even remembered. A bloody and unsparing persecution, like that which put down the Albigenses, might have put down the philosophers. But the time for De Montforts and Dominics had gone by. The punishments which the priests were still able to inflict were sufficient to irritate, but not sufficient to destroy. The war was between power on one side and wit on the other; and the power was under far more restraint than the wit. Orthodoxy soon became a badge of ignorance and stupidity. It was as necessary to the character of an accomplished man that he should despise the religion of his country as that he should know his letters. The new doctrines spread rapidly through Christendom. Paris was the capital of the whole continent. French was everywhere the language of polite circles. The literary glory of Italy and Spain had departed. That of Germany had not yet dawned. The teachers of France were the teachers of Europe. The Parisian opinions spread fast among the educated classes beyond the Alps; nor could the vigilance of the Inquisition prevent the contraband importation of the new heresy into Castile and Portugal. Governments—even arbitrary governments—saw with pleasure the progress of this philosophy. Numerous reforms, generally laudable, sometimes, hurried on without sufficient regard to time, to place and to public feeling, showed the extent of its influence. The rulers of Prussia, of Russia, of Austria, and of many smaller states, were supposed to be among the initiated.

The Church of Rome was still, in outward show, as stately and splendid as ever; but her foundation was undermined. No state had quitted her communion or confiscated her revenues; but the reverence of the people was everywhere departing from her.

The first great warning stroke was the fall of that society which, in the conflict with Protestantism, had saved the Catholic Church from destruction. The order of Jesus had never recovered from the injury received in the struggle with Port-Royal. It was now still more rudely assailed by the philosophers. Its spirit was broken; its reputation was tainted. Insulted by all the men of genius in Europe, condemned by the civil magistrate, feebly defended by the chiefs of the hierarchy, it fell—and great was the fall of it.

The movement went on with increasing speed. The first generation of the new sect passed away. The doctrines of Voltaire were inherited and exaggerated by successors, who bore to him the same relation which the Anabaptists bore to Luther or the Fifth-Monarchy men to Pym. At length the Revolution came. Down went the old Church of France, with all its pomp and wealth. Some of its priests purchased a maintenance by separating themselves from Rome and by becoming the authors of a fresh schism. Some, rejoicing in the new license, flung away their sacred vestments, proclaimed that their whole life had been an imposture, insulted and persecuted the religion of which they had been ministers, and distinguished themselves, even in the Jacobin Club and the Commune of Paris, by the excess of their impudence and ferocity. Others, more faithful to their principles, were butchered by scores without a trial, drowned, shot, hung on lamp-posts. Thousands fled from their country to take sanctuary under the shade of hostile altars. The churches were closed; the bells were silent; the shrines were plundered; the silver crucifixes were melted down. Buffoons, dressed in copes and surplices, came dancing the *carmagnole* even to the bar of the Convention. The bust of Marat was substituted for the statues of the martyrs of Christianity. A prostitute, seated in state in the chancel of Nôtre Dame, received the adoration of thousands, who exclaimed that at length, for the first time, those ancient Gothic arches had resounded with the accents of truth. The new unbelief was as intolerant as the old superstition. To show reverence for religion was to incur the suspicion of disaffection. It was not without imminent danger that the priest baptised the infant, joined the hands of lovers, or listened to the confession of the dying. The absurd worship of the Goddess of Reason was, indeed, of short duration; but the deism of Robespierre and Lepaux was not less hostile to the Catholic faith than the atheism of Clootz and Chaumette.

Nor were the calamities of the Church confined to France. The revolutionary spirit, attacked by all Europe, beat all Europe back, became conqueror in its turn; and, not satisfied with the Belgian cities and the rich domains of the spiritual electors, went raging over the Rhine and through the passes of the Alps. Throughout the whole of the great war against Protestantism, Italy and Spain had been the base of the Catholic operations. Spain was now the obsequious vassal of the infidels. Italy was subjugated by them. To her ancient principalities succeeded the Cisalpine republic, and the Ligurian republic, and the Parthenopean republic. The shrine of Loretto was stripped of the treasures piled up by the devotion of six hundred years. The convents of Rome were pillaged. The tricoloured flag floated on the top of the Castle of St. Angelo. The successor of St. Peter was carried away captive by the unbelievers. He died a prisoner in their hands; and even the honours of sepulture were long withheld from his remains.

It is not strange that, in the year 1799, even sagacious observers should have thought that, at length, the hour of the Church of Rome was come. An infidel power ascendant, the Pope dying in captivity, the most illustrious prelates of France living in a foreign country on Protestant alms, the noblest edifices, which the munificence of former ages had consecrated to the worship of God, turned into temples of Victory, or into banqueting-houses for political societies, or into Theophilanthropic chapels—such signs might well be supposed to indicate the approaching end of that long domination.

But the end was not yet. Again doomed to death, the milk-white hind was still fated not to die. Even before the funeral rites had been performed over the ashes of Pius the Sixth, a great reaction had commenced, which, after the lapse of more than forty years, appears to be still in progress. Anarchy had had its day. A new order of things rose out of the confusion, new dynasties, new laws, new titles; and amidst them emerged the ancient religion. The Arabs have a fable that the Great Pyramid was built by antediluvian kings, and alone, of all the works of men, bore the weight of the flood. Such as this was the fate of the Papacy. It had been buried under the great inundation; but its deep foundations had remained unshaken; and, when the waters abated, it appeared alone amidst the ruins of a world which had passed away. The republic of Holland was gone, and the empire of Germany, and the great Council of Venice, and the old Helvetian League, and the House of Bourbon, and the parliaments and aristocracy of France. Europe was full of young creations, a French empire, a kingdom of Italy, a Confederation of the Rhine. Nor had the late events affected only territorial limits and political institutions. The distribution of property, the composition and spirit of society, had, through great part of Catholic Europe, undergone a complete change? But the unchangeable Church was still there.

Some future historian, as able and temperate as Professor Ranke, will, we hope, trace the progress of the Catholic revival of the nineteenth century. We feel that we are drawing too near our own time, and that, if we go on, we shall be in danger of saying much which may be supposed to indicate, and which will certainly excite, angry feelings. We will, therefore, make only one more observation, which, in our opinion, is deserving of serious attention.

During the eighteenth century, the influence of the Church of Rome was constantly on the decline. Unbelief made extensive conquests in all the Catholic countries of Europe, and in some countries obtained a complete ascendency. The Papacy was at length brought so low as to be an object of derision to infidels and of pity, rather than of hatred, to Protestants. During the nineteenth century, this fallen Church has been gradually rising from her depressed state and reconquering her old dominion. No person who calmly reflects on what, within the last few years, has passed in Spain, in Italy, in South America, in Ireland, in the Netherlands, in Prussia, even in France, can doubt that her power over the hearts and minds of men is now greater far than it was when the "Encyclopædia" and the "Philosophical Dictionary" appeared. It is surely remarkable that neither the moral revolution of the eighteenth century, nor the moral counter-revolution of the nineteenth, should, in any perceptible degree, have added to the domain of Protestanism. During the former period, whatever was lost to Catholicism was lost also to Christianity; during the latter, whatever was regained by Christianity in Catholic countries was regained also by Catholicism. We should naturally have expected that many minds, on the way from superstition to infidelity, or on the way back from infidelity to superstition, would have stopped at an intermediate point. Between the doctrines taught in the schools of the Jesuits and those which were maintained at the little supper parties of the Baron Holbach, there is a vast interval, in which the human mind, it should seem, might find for itself some resting-place more satisfactory than either of the two extremes. And at the time of the Reformation millions found such a resting-place. Whole nations then renounced Popery without ceasing to believe in a first cause, in a future life, or in the Divine authority of Christianity. In the last century, on the other hand, when a Catholic renounced his belief in the real presence, it was a thousand to one that he renounced his belief in the Gospel too; and, when the reaction took place, with belief in the Gospel came back belief in the real presence.

We by no means venture to deduce from these phenomena any general law; but we think it a most remarkable fact that no Christian nation, which did not adopt the principles of the Reformation before the end of the sixteenth century, should ever have adopted them. Catholic communities have, since that time, become infidel and become Catholic again; but none has become Protestant.

Here we close this hasty sketch of one of the most important portions of the history of mankind. Our readers will have great reason to feel obliged to us if we have interested them sufficiently to induce them to peruse Professor Ranke's book. We will only caution them against the French translation—a performance which, in our opinion, is just as discreditable to the moral character of the person from whom it proceeds as a false affidavit or a forged bill of exchange would have been; and advise them to study either the original or the English version, in which the sense and spirit of the original are admirably preserved.

LEIGH HUNT. (JANUARY, 1841.)

The Dramatic Works of WYCHERLEY, CONGREVE, VANBRUGH *and* FARQUHAR, *with Biographical and Critical Notices.* By LEIGH HUNT. 8vo. London, 1840.

WE have a kindness for Mr. Leigh Hunt. We form our judgment of him, indeed, only from events of universal notoriety, from his own works and from the works of other writers, who have generally abused him in the most rancorous manner. But, unless we are greatly mistaken, he is a very clever, a very honest and a very good-natured man. We can clearly discern, together with many merits, many serious faults both in his writings and in his conduct. But we really think that there is hardly a man living whose merits have been so grudgingly allowed and whose faults have been so cruelly expiated.

In some respects, Mr. Leigh Hunt is excellently qualified for the task which he has now undertaken. His style, in spite of its mannerism—nay, partly by reason of its mannerism—is well suited for light, garrulous, desultory *ana*, half critical, half biographical. We do not always agree with his literary judgments; but we find in him what is very rare in our time, the power of justly appreciating and heartily enjoying good things of very different kinds. He can adore Shakspeare and Spenser without denying poetical genius to the author of "Alexander's Feast," or fine observation, rich fancy and exquisite humour to him who imagined "Will Honeycomb" and "Sir Roger de Coverley." He has paid particular attention to the history of the English drama from the age of Elizabeth down to our own time, and has every right to be heard with respect on that subject.

The plays to which he now acts as introducer are, with few exceptions, such as, in the opinion of many very respectable people, ought not to be reprinted. In this opinion we can by no means concur. We cannot wish that any work or class of works which has exercised a great influence on the human mind, and which illustrates the character of an important epoch in letters, politics and morals, should disappear from the world. If we err in this matter, we err with the gravest men and bodies of men in the empire, and especially with the Church of England and with the great schools of learning which are connected with her. The whole liberal education of our countrymen is conducted on the principle that no book which is valuable, either by reason of the excellence of its style or by reason of the light which it throws on the history, polity and manners of nations, should be withheld from the student on account of its impurity. The Athenian Comedies, in which there are scarcely a hundred lines together without some passage of which Rochester would have been ashamed, have been reprinted at the Pitt Press and the Clarendon Press under the direction of Syndics and delegates appointed by the Universities, and have been illustrated with notes by reverend, very reverend and right reverend commentators. Every year the most distinguished young men in the kingdom are examined by bishops and professors of divinity on the "Lysistrata" of Aristophanes and the Sixth Satire of Juvenal. There is certainly something a little ludicrous in the idea of a conclave of venerable fathers of the Church rewarding a lad for his intimate acquaintance with writings compared with which the loosest tale in Prior is modest. But, for our own part, we have no doubt that the greatest societies which direct the education of the English gentry have herein judged wisely. It is unquestionable that an extensive acquaintance with ancient literature enlarges and enriches the mind. It is unquestionable that a man, whose mind has been thus enlarged and enriched, is likely to be far more useful to the state and to the Church than one who is unskilled, or little skilled, in classical learning. On the other hand, we find it difficult to believe that, in a world so full of temptation as this, any gentleman, whose life would have been virtuous if he had not read Aristophanes and Juvenal, will be made vicious by reading them. A man who, exposed to all the influences of such a state of society as that in which we live, is yet afraid of exposing himself to the influences of a few Greek or Latin verses, acts, we think, much like the felon who begged the sheriffs to let him have an umbrella held over his head from the door of Newgate to the gallows because it was a drizzling morning and he was apt to take cold. The virtue which the world wants is a healthful virtue, not a valetudinarian virtue—a virtue which can expose itself to the risks inseparable from all spirited exertion—not a virtue which keeps out of the common air for fear of infection and eschews the common food as too stimulating. It would be indeed absurd to attempt to keep men from acquiring those qualifications which fit them to play their part in life with honour to themselves and advantage to their country, for the sake of preserving a delicacy which cannot be preserved—a delicacy which a walk from Westminster to the Temple is sufficient to destroy.

But we should be justly chargeable with gross inconsistency if, while we defend the policy which invites the youth of our country to study such writers as Theocritus and Catullus, we were to set up a cry against a new edition of the "Country Wife" or the "Way of the World." The immoral English writers of the seventeenth century are indeed much less excusable than those of Greece and Rome. But the worst English writings of the seventeenth century are decent compared with much that has been bequeathed to us by Greece and Rome. Plato, we have little doubt, was a much better man than Sir George Etherege. But Plato has written things at which Sir George Etherege would have shuddered. Buckhurst and Sedley, even in those wild orgies at the Cock in Bow-street, for which they were pelted by the rabble and fined by the Court of King's Bench, would never have dared to hold such discourse as passed between Socrates and Phædrus on that fine summer day under the plane-tree, while the fountain warbled at their feet and the cicadas chirped overhead. If it be, as we think it is, desirable that an English gentleman should be well informed touching the government and the manners of little commonwealths which, both in place and time, are far removed from us—whose independence has been more than two thousand years extinguished—whose language has not been spoken for ages—and whose ancient magnificence is attested only by a few broken columns and friezes—much more must it be desirable that he should be intimately acquainted with the history of the public mind of his own country, and with the causes, the nature and the extent of those revolutions of opinion and feeling which, during the last two centuries, have alternately raised and depressed the standard of our national morality. And knowledge of this sort is to be very sparingly gleaned from Parliamentary debates, from state papers and from the works of grave historians. It must either not be acquired at all, or it must be acquired by the perusal of the light literature which has at various periods been fashionable. We are therefore by no means disposed to condemn this publication, though we certainly cannot recommend the handsome volume* before us as an appropriate Christmas present for young ladies.

We have said that we think the present publication perfectly justifiable. But we can by no means agree with Mr. Leigh Hunt, who seems to hold that there is little or no ground for the charge of immorality so often brought against the literature of the Restoration. We do not blame him for not bringing to the judgment-seat the merciless rigour of Lord Angelo; but we really think that such flagitious and impudent offenders, as those who are now at the bar, deserved at least the gentle rebuke of Escalus. Mr. Leigh Hunt treats the whole matter a little too much in the easy style of Lucio; and perhaps his exceeding lenity disposes us to be somewhat too severe.

And yet it is not easy to be too severe. For in truth this part of our literature is a disgrace to our language and our national character. It is clever, indeed, and very entertaining; but it is, in the most emphatic sense of the words, "earthly, sensual, devilish." Its indecency,* though perpetually such as is condemned, not less by the rules of good taste than by those of morality, is not, in our opinion, so disgraceful a fault as its singularly inhuman spirit. We have here Belial, not as when he inspired Ovid and Ariosto, "graceful and humane," but with the iron eye and cruel sneer of Mephistophiles. We find ourselves in a world in which the ladies are like very profligate, impudent and unfeeling men, and in which the men are too bad for any place but

---

* Mr. Moxon, its publisher, is well entitled to commendation and support for having—by a series of corresponding Reprints (comprising the works of the elder Dramatists), executed in a compendious but very comely form, and accompanied with useful prolegomena—put it in the power of anyone desirous of such an acquisition, to procure, at a comparatively small cost, the noblest Dramatic Library in the world.

Pandæmonium or Norfolk Island. We are surrounded by foreheads of bronze, hearts like the nether millstone and tongues set on fire of hell.

Dryden defended or excused his own offences and those of his contemporaries by pleading the example of the earlier English dramatists; and Mr. Leigh Hunt seems to think that there is force in the plea. We altogether differ from this opinion. The crime charged is not mere coarseness of expression. The terms which are delicate in one age become gross in the next. The diction of the English version of the Pentateuch is sometimes such as Addison would not have ventured to imitate; and Addison, the standard of moral purity in his own age, used many phrases which are now proscribed. Whether a thing shall be designated by a plain noun-substantive or by a circumlocution is mere matter of fashion. Morality is not at all interested in the question. But morality is deeply interested in this—that what is immoral shall not be presented to the imagination of the young and susceptible in constant connection with what is attractive. For every person who has observed the operation of the law of association in his own mind and in the minds of others, knows that whatever is constantly presented to the imagination in connection with what is attractive will commonly itself become attractive. There is undoubtedly a great deal of indelicate writing in Fletcher and Massinger, and more than might be wished even in Ben Jonson and Shakspeare, who are comparatively pure. But it is impossible to trace in their plays any systematic attempt to associate vice with those things which men value most and desire most and virtue with everything ridiculous and degrading. And such a systematic attempt we find in the whole dramatic literature of the generation which followed the return of Charles the Second. We will take, as an instance of what we mean, a single subject of the highest importance to the happiness of mankind—conjugal fidelity. We can at present hardly call to mind a single English play, written before the civil war, in which the character of a seducer of married women is represented in a favourable light. We remember many plays in which such persons are baffled, exposed, covered with derision and insulted by triumphant husbands. Such is the fate of Falstaff, with all his wit and knowledge of the world. Such is the fate of Brisac in Fletcher's "Elder Brother," and of Ricardo and Ubaldo in Massinger's "Picture." Sometimes, as in the "Fatal Dowry" and "Love's Cruelty," the outraged honour of families is repaired by a bloody revenge. If now and then the lover is represented as an accomplished man and the husband as a person of weak or odious character, this only makes the triumph of female virtue the more signal, as in Jonson's Celia and Mrs. Fitzdottrel, and in Fletcher's Maria. In general, we will venture to say, that the dramatists of the age of Elizabeth and James the First either treat the breach of the marriage-vow as a serious crime, or, if they treat it as matter for laughter, turn the laugh against the gallant.

On the contrary, during the forty years which followed the Restoration, the whole body of the dramatists invariably represent adultery—we do not say as a peccadillo—we do not say as an error which the violence of passion may excuse—but as the calling of a fine gentleman—as a grace without which his character would be imperfect. It is as essential to his breeding and to his place in society that he should make love to the wives of his neighbours, as that he should know French, or that he should have a sword at his side. In all this, there is no passion and scarcely anything that can be called preference. The hero intrigues just as he wears a wig; because, if he did not, he would be a queer fellow, a city prig, perhaps a Puritan. All the agreeable qualities are always given to the gallant. All the contempt and aversion are the portion of the unfortunate husband. Take Dryden for example; and compare Woodall with Brainsick, or Lorenzo with Gomez. Take Wycherley; and compare Horner with Pinchwife. Take Vanbrugh; and compare Constant with Sir John Brute. Take Farquhar; and compare Archer with Squire Sullen. Take Congreve; and compare Bellmore with Fondlewife, Careless with Sir Paul Plyant, or Scandal with Foresight. In all these cases, and in many more which might be named, the dramatist evidently does his best to make the person who commits the injury graceful, sensible and spirited, and the person who suffers it a fool, or a tyrant, or both.

Mr. Charles Lamb, indeed, attempted to set up a defence for this way of writing. The dramatists of the latter part of the seventeenth century are not, according to him, to be tried by the standard of morality which exists, and ought to exist, in real life. Their world is a conventional world. Their heroes and heroines belong, not to England, not to Christendom, but to an Utopia of gallantry, to a Fairyland where the Bible and Burn's Justice are unknown— where a prank, which on this earth would be rewarded with the pillory, is merely matter for a peal of elvish laughter. A real Horner, a real Careless, would, it is admitted, be exceedingly bad men. But to predicate morality or immorality of the Horner of Wycherley and the Careless of Congreve, is as absurd as it would be to arraign a sleeper for his dreams. "They belong to the regions of pure comedy, where no cold moral reigns. When we are amongst them, we are amongst a chaotic people. We are not to judge them by our usages. No reverend institutions are insulted by their proceedings, for they have none among them. No peace of families is violated, for no family ties exist amongst them. There is neither right nor wrong—gratitude or its opposite—claim or duty, paternity or sonship."

This is, we believe, a fair summary of Mr. Lamb's doctrine. We are sure that we do not wish to represent him unfairly. For we admire his genius; we love the kind nature which appears in all his writing; and we cherish his memory as much as if we had known him personally. But we must plainly say that his argument, though ingenious, is altogether sophistical.

Of course we perfectly understand that it is possible for a writer to create a conventional world in which things forbidden by the Decalogue and the Statute Book shall be lawful, and yet that the exhibition may be harmless, or even edifying. For example, we suppose that the most austere critics would not accuse Fenelon of impiety and immorality on account of his "Telemachus" and his "Dialogues of the Dead." In "Telemachus" and the "Dialogues of the Dead" we have a false religion, and consequently a morality which is in some points incorrect. We have a right and a wrong, differing from the right and the wrong of real life. It s represented as the first duty of men to pay honour to Jove and Minerva. Philocles, who employs his leisure in making graven images of these deities is extolled for his piety in a way which contrasts singularly with the expressions of Isaiah on the same subject. The dead are judged by Minos, and rewarded with lasting happiness for actions which Fenelon would have been the first to pronounce splendid sins. The same may be said of Mr. Southey's Mahommedan and Hindoo heroes and heroines. In Thalaba, to speak in derogation of the Arabian impostor is blasphemy—to drink wine is a crime—to perform ablutions and to pay honour to the holy cities are works of merit. In the "Curse of Kehama," Kailyal is commended for her devotion to the statue of Mariataly, the goddess of the poor. But certainly no person will accuse Mr. Southey of having promoted or intended to promote either Islamism or Brahminism.

It is easy to see why the conventional worlds of Fenelon and Mr. Southey are unobjectionable. In the first place they are utterly unlike the real world in which we live. The state of society, the laws even of the physical world, are so different from those with which we are familiar, that we cannot be shocked at finding the morality also very different. But in truth the morality of these conventional worlds differs from the morality of the real world only in points where there is no danger that the real world will ever go wrong. The generosity and docility of Telemachus, the fortitude, the modesty, the filial tenderness of Kailyal, are virtues of all ages and nations. And there was very little danger that the Dauphin would worship Minerva, or that an English damsel would dance, with a bucket on her head, before the statue of Mariataly.

The case is widely different with what Mr. Charles Lamb calls the conventional world of Wycherley and Congreve. Here the costume, the manners, the topics of conversation are those of the real town and of the passing day. The hero is in all superficial accomplishments exactly the fine gentleman, whom every youth in the pit would gladly resemble. The heroine is the fine lady whom every youth in the pit would gladly marry. The scene is laid in some place which is as well known to the audience as their own houses, in St. James's Park, or Hyde Park, or Westminster Hall. The lawyer bustles about with his bag between the Common Pleas and the Exchequer. The Peer calls for his carriage to go to the House of Lords on a private bill. A hundred little touches are employed to make the fictitious world appear like the actual world. And the immorality is of a sort which never can be out of date, and which all the force of religion, law and public opinion united can but imperfectly restrain.

In the name of art, as well as in the name of virtue, we protest against the principle that the world of pure comedy is one into which no moral enters. If comedy be an imitation, under whatever conventions, of real life, how is it possible that it can have no reference to the great rule which directs life, and to feelings which are called forth by every incident of life? If what Mr. Charles Lamb says were correct, the inference would be that these dramatists did not in the least understand the very first principles of their craft. Pure landscape-painting into which no light or shade enters, pure portrait-painting into which no expression enters, are phrases less at variance with sound criticism than pure comedy into which no moral enters.

But it is not the fact that the world of these dramatists is a world into which no moral enters. Morality constantly enters into that world, a sound morality and an unsound morality; the sound morality to be insulted, derided, associated with everything mean and hateful; the unsound morality to be set off to every advantage and inculcated by all methods, direct and indirect. It is not the fact that none of the inhabitants of this conventional world feel reverence for sacred institutions and family ties. Fondlewife, Pinchwife, every person, in short, of narrow understanding and disgusting manners, expresses that reverence strongly. The heroes and heroines, too, have a moral code of their own, an exceedingly bad one, but not as Mr. Charles Lamb seems to think, a code existing only in the imagination of dramatists. It is, on the contrary, a code actually received and obeyed by great numbers of people. We need not go to Utopia or Fairyland to find them. They are near at hand. Every night some of them play at the "hells" in the Quadrant and others pace the Piazza in Covent-Garden. Without flying to Nephelococcygia or to the Court of Queen Mab, we can meet with sharpers, bullies, hard-hearted impudent debauchees and women worthy of such paramours. The morality of the "Country Wife" and the "Old Bachelor" is the morality, not, as Mr. Charles Lamb maintains, of an unreal world, but of a world which is a great deal too real. It is the morality, not of a chaotic people, but of low town-rakes and of those ladies whom the newspapers call "dashing Cyprians." And the question is simply whether a man of genius, who constantly and systematically endeavours to make this sort of character attractive by uniting it with beauty, grace, dignity, spirit, a high social position, popularity, literature, wit, taste, knowledge of the world, brilliant success in every undertaking, does or does not make an ill use of his powers. We own that we are unable to understand how this question can be answered in any way but one.

It must, indeed, be acknowledged, in justice to the writers of whom we have spoken thus severely, that they were, to a great extent, the creatures of their age. And if it be asked why that age encouraged immorality which no other age would have tolerated, we have no hesitation in answering that this great depravation of the national taste was the effect of the prevalence of Puritanism under the Commonwealth.

To punish public outrages on morals and religion is unquestionably within the competence of rulers. But when a government, not content with requiring decency, requires sanctity, it oversteps the bound which mark its proper functions. And it may be laid down as an universal rule, that a government which attempts more than it ought will perform less. A lawgiver, who, in order to protect distressed borrowers, limits the rate of interest, either makes it impossible for the objects of his care to borrow at all, or places them at the mercy of the worst class of usurers. A lawgiver, who, from tenderness for labouring men, fixes the hours of their work and the amount of their wages, is certain to make them far more wretched than he found them. And so a government, which, not content with repressing scandalous excesses, demands from its subjects fervent and austere piety, will soon discover that, while attempting to render an impossible service to the cause of virtue, it has in truth only promoted vice.

For what are the means by which a government can effect it ends? Two only, rewards and punishments—powerful means, indeed, for influencing the exterior act, but altogether impotent for the purpose of touching the heart. A public functionary, who is told that he will be advanced if he is a devout Catholic and turned out of his place if he is not, will probably go to mass every morning, exclude meat from his table on Fridays, shrive himself regularly, and perhaps let his superiors know that he wears a hair shirt nex this skin. Under a Puritan government, a person who is apprised that piety is essential to thriving in the world, will be strict in the observance of the Sunday, or, as he will call it, Sabbath, and will avoid a theatre as if it were plague-stricken. Such a show of religion as this, the hope of gain and the fear of loss will produce, at a week's notice, in any abundance which a government may require. But under this show, sensuality, ambition, avarice and hatred retain unimpaired power; and the seeming convert has only added to the vices of a man of the world all the still darker vices which are engendered by the constant practice of dissimulation. The truth cannot be long concealed. The public discovers that the grave persons, who are proposed to it as patterns, are more utterly destitute of moral principle and of moral sensibility than avowed libertines. It sees that these Pharisees are farther removed from real goodness that publicans and harlots. And, as usual, it rushes to the extreme opposite to that which it quits. It considers a high religious profession as a sure mark of meanness and depravity. On the very first day on which the restraint of fear is taken away and on which men can venture to say what they feel, a frightful peel of blasphemy and ribaldry proclaims that the short-sighted policy which aimed at making a nation of saints has made a nation of scoffers.

It was thus in France about the beginning of the eighteenth century. Louis the Fourteenth in his old age became religious, and determined that his subjects should be religious too—shrugged his shoulders and knitted his brows if he observed at his levee or near his dinner-table any gentleman who neglected the duties enjoined by the church—and rewarded piety with blue ribands, invitations to Marli, governments, pensions and regiments. Forthwith Versailles became, in everything but dress, a convent. The pulpits and confessionals were surrounded by swords and embroidery. The Marshals of France were much in prayer; and there was hardly one among the Dukes and Peers who did not carry good little books in his pocket, fast during Lent and communicate at Easter. Madame de Maintenon, who had a great share in the blessed work, boasted that devotion had become quite the fashion. A fashion indeed it was; and like a fashion it passed away. No sooner had the old king been carried to St. Denis than the whole court unmasked. Every man hastened to indemnify himself by the excess of licentiousness and impudence, for years of mortification. The same persons, who, a few months before, with meek voices and demure looks, had consulted divines about the state of their souls, now surrounded the midnight table where, amidst the bounding of champagne corks, a drunken prince, enthroned between Dubois and Madame de Parabère, hiccoughed out atheistical arguments and obscene jests. The early part of the reign of Louis the Fourteenth had been a time of license; but the most dissolute men of that generation would have blushed at the orgies of the Regency.

It was the same with our fathers in the time of the Great Civil War. We are by no means unmindful of the great debt which mankind owes to the Puritans of that time; the deliverers of England, the founders of the Great American Commonwealths. But, in the day of their power, they committed one great fault, which left deep and lasting traces in the national character and manners. They mistook the end and overrated the force of government. They determined, not merely to protect religion and public morals from insult, an object for which the civil sword, in discreet hands, may be beneficially employed—but to make the people committed to their rule truly devout. Yet, if they had only reflected on events which they had themselves witnessed, and in which they had themselves borne a great part, they would have seen what was likely to be the result of their enterprise. They had lived under a government which, during a long course of years, did all that could be done, by lavish bounty and by rigorous punishment, to enforce conformity to the doctrine and discipline of the Church of England. No person suspected of hostility to that church had the smallest chance of obtaining favour at the court of Charles. Avowed dissent was punished by imprisonment, by ignominious exposure, by cruel mutilations and by ruinous fines. And the event had been that the Church had fallen, and had, in its fall, dragged down with it a monarchy which had stood six hundred years. The Puritan might have learned, if from nothing else, yet from his own recent victory, that governments which attempt things beyond their reach are likely, not merely to fail, but to produce an effect directly the opposite of that which they contemplate as desirable.

All this was overlooked. The saints were to inherit the earth. The theatres were closed. The fine arts were placed under absurd restraints. Vices which had never before been even misdemeanors were made capital felonies. It was solemnly resolved by Parliament, "that no person shall be employed but such as the House shall be satisfied of his real godliness." The pious assembly had a Bible lying on the table for reference. If they had consulted it they might have learned that the wheat and the tares grow together inseparably, and must either be spared together or rooted up together. To know whether a man was really godly was impossible. But it was easy to know whether he had a plain dress, lank hair, no starch in his linen, no gay furniture in his house; whether he talked through his nose and showed the whites of his eyes; whether he named his children Assurance, Tribulation and Maharshalat-hash-baz; whether he avoided Spring Garden when in town and abstained from hunting and hawking when in the country—whether he expounded hard scriptures to his troop of dragoons—and talked in a committee of ways and means about seeking the Lord. These were tests which could easily be applied. The misfortune was that they were tests which proved nothing. Such as they were, they were employed by the dominant party. And the consequence was, that a crowd of impostors, in every walk of life, began to mimic and to caricature what were then regarded as the outward signs of sanctity. The nation was not duped. The restraints of that gloomy time were such as would have been impatiently borne if imposed by men who were universally believed to be saints. Those restraints became altogether insupportable when they were known to be kept up for the profit of hypocrites. It is quite certain that, even if the royal family had never returned—even if Richard Cromwell or Henry Cromwell had been at the head of the administration—there would have been a great relaxation of manners. Before the Revolution many signs indicated that a period of license was at hand. The Restoration crushed for a time the Puritan party and placed supreme power in the hands of a libertine. The political counter-revolution assisted the moral counter-revolution and was in turn assisted by it. A period of wild and desperate dissoluteness followed. Even in remote manor-houses and hamlets, the change was in some degree felt; but in London the outbreak of debauchery was appalling. And in London the places most deeply infected were the Palace, the quarters inhabited by the aristocracy and the Inns of Court. It was on the support of these parts of the town that the playhouses depended. The character of the drama became conformed to the character of its patrons. The comic poet was the mouthpiece of the most deeply corrupted part of a corrupted society. And in the plays before us we find, distilled and condensed, the essential spirit of the fashionable world during the Anti-puritan reaction.

The Puritan had affected formality; the comic poet laughed at decorum. The Puritan had frowned at innocent diversions; the comic poet took under his patronage the most flagitious excesses. The Puritan had canted; the comic poet blasphemed. The Puritan had made an affair of gallantry felony without benefit of clergy; the comic poet represented it as an honourable distinction. The Puritan spoke with disdain of the low standard of popular morality; his life was regulated by a far more rigid code; his virtue was sustained by motives unknown to men of the world. Unhappily, it had been amply proved in many cases, and might well be suspected in many more, that these high pretensions were unfounded. Accordingly, the fashionable circles, and the comic poets who were the spokesmen of those circles, took up the notion that all professions of piety and integrity were to be construed by the rule of contrary; that it might well be doubted whether there was such a thing as virtue in the world; but that, at all events, a person who affected to be better than his neighbours was sure to be a knave.

In the old drama there had been much that was reprehensible. But whoever compares even the least decorous plays of Fletcher with those contained in the volume before us will see how much the profligacy which follows a period of overstrained austerity goes beyond the profligacy which precedes such a period. The nation resembled the demoniac in the New Testament. The Puritans boasted that the unclean spirit was cast out. The house was empty, swept and garnished: and for a time the expelled tenant wandered through dry places seeking rest and finding none. But the force of the exorcism was spent. The fiend returned to his abode and returned not alone. He took to him seven other spirits more wicked than himself.

They entered in and dwelt together; and the second possession was worse than the first.

We will now, as far as our limits will permit, pass in review the writers to whom Mr. Leigh Hunt has introduced us. Of the four, Wycherley stands, we think, last in literary merit, but first in order of time, and first, beyond all doubt, in immorality.

WILLIAM WYCHERLEY was born in 1640. He was the son of a Shropshire gentleman of old family, and of what was then accounted a good estate. The property was estimated at £600 a year, a fortune which, among the fortunes at that time, probably ranked as a fortune of £2,000 a year would rank in our days.

William was an infant when the civil war broke out; and, while he was still in his rudiments, a Presbyterian hierarchy and a republican government were established on the ruins of the ancient church and throne. Old Mr. Wycherley was attached to the royal cause, and was not disposed to intrust the education of his heir to the solemn Puritans who now ruled the universities and public schools. Accordingly, the young gentleman was sent at fifteen to France. He resided some time in the neighbourhood of the Duke of Montausier, chief of one of the noblest families of Touraine. The Duke's wife, a daughter of the house of Rambouillet, was a finished specimen of those talents and accomplishments for which her house was celebrated. The young foreigner was introduced to the splendid circle which surrounded the duchess, and there he appears to have learned some good and some evil. In a few years he returned to this country a fine gentleman and a Papist: His conversion, it may safely be affirmed, was the effect not of any strong impression on his understanding or feelings, but partly of intercourse with an agreeable society in which the Church of Rome was the fashion, and partly of that aversion to Calvinistic austerities which was then almost universal among young Englishmen of parts and spirit, and which, at one time, seemed likely to make one half of them Catholics and the other half Atheists.

But the Restoration came. The universities were again in loyal hands, and there was reason to hope that there would be again a national church fit for a gentleman. Wycherley became a member of Queen's College, Oxford, and abjured the errors of the Church of Rome. The somewhat equivocal glory of turning, for a short time, a good-for-nothing Papist into a very good-for-nothing Protestant is ascribed to Bishop Barlow.

Wycherley left Oxford without taking a degree and entered at the Temple, where he lived gaily for some years, observing the humours of the town, enjoying its pleasures. and picking up just as much law as was necessary to make the character of a pettifogging attorney or of a litigious client entertaining in a comedy.

From an early age, he had been in the habit of amusing himself by writing. Some wretched lines of his on the Restoration are still extant. Had he devoted himself to the making of verses he would have been nearly as far below Tate and Blackmore as Tate and Blackmore are below Dryden. His only chance for renown would have been that he might have occupied a niche in a satire between Flecknoe and Settle. There was, however, another kind of composition in which his talents and acquirements qualified him to succeed; and to that he judiciously betook himself.

In his old age he used to say that he wrote "Love in a Wood" at nineteen, the "Gentleman Dancing-Master" at twenty-one, the "Plain Dealer" at twenty-five and the "Country Wife" at one or two and thirty. We are incredulous, we own, as to the truth of this story. Nothing that we know of

Wycherley leads us to think him incapable of sacrificing truth to vanity. And his memory in the decline of his life played him such strange tricks that we might question the correctness of his assertion without throwing any imputation on his veracity. It is certain that none of his plays was acted till 1672, when he gave "Love in a Wood" to the public. It seems improbable that he should resolve, on so important an occasion as that of a first appearance before the world, to run his chance with a feeble piece, written before his talents, were ripe before his style was formed, before he had looked abroad into the world; and this when he had actually in his desk two highly finished plays, the fruit of his matured powers. When we look minutely at the pieces themselves, we find in every part of them reason to suspect the accuracy of Wycherley's statement. In the first scene of "Love in a Wood," to go no further, we find many passages which he could not have written when he was nineteen. There is an allusion to gentlemen's periwigs, which first came into fashion in 1663; an allusion to guineas, which were first struck in 1663; an allusion to the vests which Charles ordered to be worn at court in 1666; an allusion to the fire of 1666; and several allusions to political and ecclesiastical affairs which must be assigned to times later than the year of the Restoration—to times when the government and the city were opposed to each other, and when the Presbyterian ministers had been driven from the parish churches to the conventicles. But it is needless to dwell on particular expressions. The whole air and spirit of the piece belong to a period subsequent to that mentioned by Wycherley. As to the "Plain Dealer," which is said to have been written when he was twenty-five, it contains one scene unquestionably written after 1675, several which are later than 1668, and scarcely a line which can have been composed before the end of 1666.

Whatever may have been the age at which Wycherley composed his plays, it is certain that he did not bring them before the public till he was upwards of thirty. In 1672, "Love in a Wood" was acted with more success than it deserved, and this event produced a great change in the fortunes of the author. The Duchess of Cleveland cast her eyes upon him and was pleased with his appearance. This abandoned woman, not content with her complaisant husband and her royal keeper, lavished her fondness on a crowd of paramours of all ranks, from dukes to rope-dancers. In the time of the commonwealth she commenced her career of gallantry, and terminated it under Anne, by marrying, when a great-grandmother, that worthless fop, Beau Fielding. It is not strange that she should have regarded Wycherley with favour. His figure was commanding, his countenance strikingly handsome, his look and deportment full of grace and dignity. He had, as Pope said long after, "the true nobleman look," the look which seems to indicate superiority, and a not unbecoming consciousness of superiority. His hair indeed, as he says in one of his poems, was prematurely grey. But in that age of periwigs this misfortune was of little importance. The Duchess admired him, and proceeded to make love to him after the fashion of the coarse-minded and shameless circle to which she belonged. In the Ring, when the crowd of beauties and fine gentlemen was thickest, she put her head out of her coach-window and bawled to him—"Sir, you are a rascal; you are a villain;" and, if she is not belied, she added another phrase of abuse which we will not quote, but of which we may say that it might most justly have been applied to her own children. Wycherley called on her Grace the next day, and with great humility begged to know in what way he had been so unfortunate as to disoblige her. Thus began an intimacy from which the poet probably expected wealth and honours. Nor were such expectations unreasonable. A handsome young fellow about the court, known by the name of Jack Churchill, was, about the same time, so lucky as to become the object of a short-lived fancy of the Duchess. She had presented him with £4,500, the price, in all probability, of some title or some pardon. The prudent youth had lent the money on high interest and on landed security; and this judicious investment was the beginning of the most splendid private fortune in Europe. Wycherley was not so lucky. The partiality with which the great lady regarded him was indeed the talk of the whole town; and, sixty years later, old men who remembered those days told Voltaire that she often stole from the court to her lover's chambers in the Temple, disguised like a country girl, with a straw hat on her head, pattens on her feet and a basket in her hand. The poet was indeed too happy and proud to be discreet. He dedicated to the Duchess the play which had led to their acquaintance, and in the dedication expressed himself in terms which could not but confirm the reports which had gone abroad. But at Whitehall such an affair was regarded in no serious light. The lady was not afraid to bring Wycherley to court and to introduce him to a splendid society, with which, as far as appears, he had never before mixed. The easy king, who allowed to his mistresses the same liberty which he claimed for himself, was pleased with the conversation and manners of his new rival. So high did Wycherley stand in the royal favour that once, when he was confined by a fever to his lodgings in Bow Street, Charles, who, with all his faults, was certainly a man of social and affable disposition, called on him, sat by his bed, advised him to try change of air, and gave him a handsome sum of money to defray the expense of a journey. Buckingham, then Master of the Horse and one of that infamous ministry known by the name of the Cabal, had been one of the Duchess's innumerable paramours. He at first showed some symptoms of jealousy, but he soon, after his fashion, veered round from anger to fondness, and gave Wycherley a commission in his own regiment and a place in the royal household.

It would be unjust to Wycherley's memory not to mention here the only good action, as far as we know, of his whole life. He is said to have made great exertions to obtain the patronage of Buckingham for the illustrious author of "Hudibras," who was now sinking into an obscure grave, neglected by a nation proud of his genius and by a court which he had served too well. His Grace consented to see poor Butler; and an appointment was made. But unhappily two pretty women passed by; the volatile Duke ran after them; the opportunity was lost and could never be regained.

The second Dutch war, the most disgraceful war in the whole history of England, was now raging. It was not in that age considered as by any means necessary that a naval officer should receive a professional education. Young men of rank, who were hardly able to keep their feet in a breeze, served on board the King's ships, sometimes with commissions and sometimes as volunteers. Mulgrave, Dorset, Rochester and many others left the playhouses and the Mall for hammocks and salt pork; and, ignorant as they were of the rudiments of naval service, showed, at least, on the day of battle, the courage which is seldom wanting in an English gentleman. All good judges of maritime affairs complained that, under this system, the ships were grossly mismanaged, and that the tarpaulins contracted the vices, without acquiring the graces, of the court. But on this subject, as on every other, the government of Charles was deaf to all remonstrances where the interests or whims of favourites were concerned. Wycherley did not choose to be out of the fashion. He embarked, was present at a battle, and celebrated it, on his return, in a copy of verses too bad for the bellman.*

About the same time he brought on the stage his second piece, the "Gentleman Dancing-Master." The biographers say nothing, as far as we remember, about the fate of this play. There is, however, reason to believe that, though certainly far superior to "Love in a Wood," it was not equally successful. It was first tried at the west end of the town, and, as the poet confessed, "would scarce do there." It was then performed in Salisbury Court, but, as it should seem, with no better event. For, in the prologue to the "Country Wife," Wycherley described himself as "the late so baffled scribbler."

In 1675, the "Country Wife" was performed with brilliant success, which, in a literary point of view, was not wholly unmerited. For, though one of the most profligate and heartless of human compositions, it is the elaborate production of a mind, not indeed rich, original or imaginative, but ingenious, observant, quick to seize hints and patient of the toil of polishing.

The "Plain Dealer," equally immoral and equally well written, appeared in 1677. At first this piece pleased the people less than the critics ; but after a time its unquestionable merits and the zealous support of Lord Dorset, whose influence in literary and fashionable society was unbounded, established it in the public favour.

The fortune of Wycherley was now in the zenith and began to decline. A long life was still before him. But it was destined to be filled with nothing but shame and wretchedness, domestic dissensions, literary failures and pecuniary embarrassments.

The King, who was looking about for an accomplished man to conduct the education of his natural son, the young Duke of Richmond, at length fixed on Wycherley. The poet, exulting in his good luck, went down to amuse himself at Tunbridge, looked into a bookseller's shop on the Pantiles, and, to his great delight, heard a handsome woman ask for the "Plain Dealer," which had just been published. He made acquaintance with the lady, who proved to be the Countess of Drogheda, a gay young widow with an ample jointure. She was charmed with his person and his wit, and, after a short flirtation, agreed to become his wife. Wycherley seems to have been apprehensive that this connection might not suit well with the King's plans respecting the Duke of Richmond. He accordingly prevailed on the lady to consent to a private marriage. All came out. Charles thought the conduct of Wycherley both disrespectful and disingenuous. Other causes probably assisted to alienate the sovereign from the subject who had lately been so highly favoured. Buckingham was now in opposition and had been committed to the Tower ; not, as Mr. Leigh Hunt supposes, on a charge of treason, but by an order of the House of Lords for some expressions which he had used in

---

* Mr. Leigh Hunt supposes that the battle at which Wycherley was present was that which the Duke of York gained over Opdam, in 1665. We believe that it was one of the battles between Rupert and De Ruyter, in 1673.

The point is of no importance; and there cannot be said to be much evidence either way. We offer, however, to Mr. Leigh Hunt's consideration three arguments—of no great weight certainly—yet such as ought, we think, to prevail in the absence of better. First, it is not very likely that a young Templar, quite unknown in the world—and Wycherley was such in 1665—should have quitted his chambers to go to sea. On the other hand, it would have been in the regular course of things that, when a courtier and an equerry, he should offer his services. Secondly, his verses appear to have been written after a drawn battle, like those of 1673, and not after a complete victory, like that of 1665. Thirdly, in the epilogue to the Gentleman Dancing-Master, written in 1673, he says that "all gentlemen must pack to sea;" an expression which makes it probable that he did not himself mean to stay behind.

debate. Wycherley wrote some bad lines in praise of his imprisoned patron, which, if they came to the knowledge of the King, would certainly have made his majesty very angry. The favour of the court was completely withdrawn from the poet. An amiable woman with a large fortune might indeed have been an ample compensation for the loss. But Lady Drogheda was ill-tempered, imperious and extravagantly jealous. She had herself been a maid of honour at Whitehall. She well knew in what estimation conjugal fidelity was held among the fine gentlemen there, and watched her town husband as assiduously as Mr. Pinchwife watched his country wife. The unfortunate wit was, indeed, allowed to meet his friends at a tavern opposite to his own house. But on such occasions the windows were always open, in order that her ladyship, who was posted on the other side of the street, might be satisfied that no woman was of the party.

The death of Lady Drogheda released the poet from this distress; but a series of disasters in rapid succession broke down his health, his spirits and his fortune. His wife meant to leave him a good property and left him only a lawsuit. His father could not or would not assist him. He was at length thrown into the Fleet, and languished there during seven years, utterly forgotten, as it should seem, by the gay and lively circle of which he had been a distinguished ornament. In the extremity of his distress, he implored the publisher who had been enriched by the sale of his works to lend him twenty pounds, and was refused. His comedies, however, still kept possession of the stage and drew great audiences, which troubled themselves little about the situation of the author. At length, James the Second, who had now succeeded to the throne, happened to go to the theatre on an evening when the "Plain Dealer" was acted. He was pleased with the performance, and touched by the fate of the writer, whom he probably remembered as one of the gayest and handsomest of his brother's courtiers. The King determined to pay Wycherley's debts and to settle on the unfortunate poet a pension of £200 a-year. This munificence on the part of a prince who was little in the habit of rewarding literary merit, and whose whole soul was devoted to the interests of his Church, raises in us a surmise which Mr. Leigh Hunt will, we fear, pronounce very uncharitable. We cannot help suspecting that it was at this time that Wycherley returned to the communion of the Church of Rome. That he did return to the communion of the Church of Rome is certain. The date of his reconversion, as far as we know, has never been mentioned by any biographer. We believe that, if we place it at this time, we do no injustice to the character either of Wycherley or James.

Not long after, old Mr. Wycherley died; and his son, now past the middle of life, came to the family estate. Still, however, he was not at his ease. His embarrassments were great; his property was strictly tied up; and he was on very bad terms with the heir-at-law. He appears to have led, during a long course of years, that most wretched life, the life of an old boy about town. Expensive tastes with little money and licentious appetites with declining vigour, were the just penance for his early irregularities. A severe illness had produced a singular effect on his intellect. His memory played him pranks stranger than almost any that are to be found in the history of that strange faculty. It seemed to be at once preternaturally strong and preternaturally weak. If a book was read to him before he went to bed, he would wake the next morning with his mind full of the thoughts and expressions which he had heard over night; and he would write them down, without in the least suspecting that they were not his own. In his verses the same ideas, and even the same words, came over and over again several times in a short composition. His fine person bore the marks of age, sickness and sorrow; and he mourned for his departed beauty with an effeminate regret. He could not look without a sigh at the portrait which Lely had painted of him when he was only twenty-eight, and often murmured, *Quantum mutatas ab illo*. He was still nervously anxious about his literary reputation, and, not content with the fame which he still possessed as a dramatist, was determined to be renowned as a satirist and an amatory poet. In 1704, after twenty-seven years of silence, he again appeared as an author. He put forth a large folio of miscellaneous verses, which, we believe, has never been reprinted. Some of these pieces had probably circulated through the town in manuscript. For, before the volume appeared, the critics at the coffee-houses very confidently predicted that it would be utterly worthless, and were in consequence bitterly reviled by the poet in an ill-written, foolish and egotistical preface. The book amply vindicated the most unfavourable prophecies that had been hazarded. The style and versification are beneath criticism ; the morals are those of Rochester. For Rochester, indeed, there was some excuse. When his offences against decorum were committed, he was a very young man, misled by a prevailing fashion. Wycherley was sixty-four. He had long outlived the times when libertinism was regarded as essential to the character of a wit and a gentleman. Most of the rising poets, Addison, for example, John Philips and Rowe, were studious of decency. We can hardly conceive anything more miserable than the figure which the ribald old man makes in the midst of so many sober and well-conducted youths.

In the very year in which this bulky volume of obscene doggerel was published, Wycherley formed an acquaintance of a very singular kind. A little, pale, crooked, sickly, bright-eyed urchin, just turned of sixteen, had written some copies of verses in which discerning judges could detect the promise of future eminence. There was, indeed, as yet nothing very striking or original in the conceptions of the young poet. But he was already skilled in the art of metrical composition. His diction and his music were not those of the great old masters ; but that which his ablest contemporaries were labouring to do he already did best. His style was not richly poetical; but it was always neat, compact and pointed. His verse wanted variety of pause, of swell and of cadence, but never grated harshly on the ear or disappointed it by a feeble close. The youth was already free of the company of wits, and was greatly elated at being introduced to the author of the "Plain Dealer" and the "Country Wife."

It is curious to trace the history of the intercourse which took place between Wycherley and Pope—between the representative of the age that was going out and the representative of the age that was coming in—between the friend of Rochester and Buckingham and the friend of Lyttleton and Mansfield. At first the boy was enchanted by the kindness and condescension of his new friend, haunted his door and followed him about like a spaniel from coffee-house to coffee-house. Letters full of affection, humility and fulsome flattery were interchanged between the friends. But the first ardour of affection could not last. Pope, though at no time scrupulously delicate in his writings or fastidious as to the morals of his associates, was shocked by the indecency of a rake who, at seventy, was still the representative of the monstrous profligacy of the Restoration. As the youth grew older, as his mind expanded and his fame rose, he appreciated both himself and Wycherley more correctly. He felt a well founded contempt for the old gentleman's verses, and was at no great pains to conceal his opinion. Wycherley, on the other hand, though blinded by self-love to the imperfections of what he called his poetry, could not but see that there was an immense difference between his young companion's rhymes and his own. He was divided between two feelings. He wished to have the assistance of so skilful a hand to polish his lines; and yet he shrank from the humiliation of being beholden for literary assistance to a lad who might have been his grandson. Pope was willing to give assistance, but was by no means disposed to give assistance and flattery too. He took the trouble to retouch whole reams of feeble, stumbling verses, and inserted many vigorous lines, which the least skilful reader will distinguish in an instant. But he thought that by these services he acquired a right to express himself in terms which would not, under ordinary circumstances, become one who was addressing a man of four times his age. In one letter, he tells Wycherley that "the worst pieces are such as, to render them very good, would require almost the entire new writing of them." In another, he gives the following account of his corrections: "Though the whole be as short again as at first, there is not one thought omitted but what is a repetition of something in your first volume or in this very paper; and the versification throughout is, I believe, such as nobody can be shocked at. The repeated permission you give me of dealing freely with you, will, I hope, excuse what I have done; for, if I have not spared you when I thought severity would do you a kindness, I have not mangled you where I thought there was no absolute need of amputation." Wycherley continued to return thanks for all this hacking and hewing, which was, indeed, of inestimable service to his compositions. But by degrees his thanks began to sound very like reproaches. In private, he is said to have described Pope as a person who could not cut out a suit, but who had some skill in turning old coats. In his letters to Pope, while he acknowledged that the versification of the poems had been greatly improved, he spoke of the whole art of versification with scorn, and sneered at those who preferred sound to sense. Pope revenged himself for this outbreak of spleen by return of post. He had in his hands a volume of Wycherley's rhymes, and he wrote to say that this volume was so full of faults that he could not correct it without completely defacing the manuscript. "I am," he said, "equally afraid of sparing you and of offending you by too impudent a correction." This was more than flesh and blood could bear. Wycherley reclaimed his papers in a letter in which resentment shows itself plainly through the thin disguise of civility. Pope, glad to be rid of a troublesome and inglorious task, sent back the deposit, and, by way of a parting courtesy, advised the old man to turn his poetry into prose, and assured him that the public would like thoughts much better without his versification. Thus ended this memorable correspondence.

Wycherley lived some years after the termination of the strange friendship which we have described. The last scene of his life was, perhaps, the most scandalous. Ten days before his death, at seventy-five, he married a young girl, merely in order to injure his nephew, an act which proves that neither years nor adversity, nor what he called his philosophy, nor either of the religions which he had at different times professed, had taught him the rudiments of morality. He died in December, 1715, and lies in the vault under the church of St. Paul in Covent Garden.

His bride soon after married a Captain Shrimpton, who thus became possessed of a large collection of manuscripts. These were sold to a bookseller. They were so full of erasures and interlineations that no printer could decipher them. It was necessary to call in the aid of a professed critic; and Theobald, the editor of Shakspeare and the hero of the first Dunciad, was employed to ascertain the true reading. In this way, a volume of miscellanies in verse and prose was got up for the market. The collection derives all its value from the traces of Pope's hand, which are everywhere discernible.

Of the moral character of Wycherley it can hardly be necessary for us to say more. His fame as a writer rests wholly on his comedies, and chiefly on the last two. Even as a comic writer, he was neither of the best school, nor highest in his school. He was in truth a worse Congreve. His chief merit, like Congreve's, lies in the style of his dialogue. But the wit which lights up the "Plain Dealer" and the "Country Wife" is pale and flickering when compared with the gorgeous blaze which dazzles us almost to blindness in "Love for Love" and the "Way of the World." Like Congreve, and, indeed, even more than Congreve, Wycherley is ready to sacrifice dramatic propriety to the liveliness of his dialogue. The poet speaks out of the mouths of all his dunces and coxcombs, and makes them describe themselves with a good sense and acuteness which puts them on a level with the wits and heroes. We will give two instances, the first which occur to us, from the "Country Wife." There are in the world fools who find the society of old friends insipid and who are always running after new companions. Such a character is a fair subject for comedy. But nothing can be more absurd than to introduce a man of this sort saying to his comrade, "I can deny you nothing: for though I have known thee a great while, never go if I do not love thee as well as a new acquaintance." That town-wits, again, have always been rather a heartless class, is true. But none of them, we will answer for it, ever said to a young lady to whom he was making love, "We wits rail and make love often but to show our parts: as we have no affections, so we have no malice."

Wycherley's plays are said to have been the produce of long and patient labour. The epithet of "slow" was early given to him by Rochester, and was frequently repeated. In truth, his mind, unless we are greatly mistaken, was naturally a very meagre soil, and was forced only by great labour and outlay to bear fruit which, after all, was not of the highest flavour. He has scarcely more claim to originality than Terence. It is not too much to say that there is hardly anything of the least value in his plays of which the hint is not to be found elsewhere. The best scenes in the "Gentleman Dancing-Master" were suggested by Calderon's "Maestro de Danzar," not by any means one of the happiest comedies of the great Castilian poet. The "Country Wife" is borrowed from the "Ecole des Maris" and the "Ecole des Femmes." The groundwork of the "Plain Dealer" is taken from the "Misanthrope" of Molière. One whole scene is almost translated from the "Critique de l'Ecole des Femmes." Fidelia is Shakspeare's Viola stolen, and marred in the stealing; and the Widow Blackacre, beyond comparison Wycherley's best comic character, is the Countess in Racine's "Plaideurs," talking the jargon of English chicane instead of that of French chicane.

The only thing original about Wycherley, the only thing which he could furnish from his own mind in inexhaustible abundance, was profligacy. It is curious to observe how everything that he touched, however pure and noble, took in an instant the colour of his own mind. Compare the "Ecole des Femmes" with the "Country Wife." Agnes is a simple and amiable girl, whose heart is indeed full of love, but of love sanctioned by honour, morality and religion. Her natural talents are great. They have been hidden and, as it might appear, destroyed by an education elaborately bad. But they are called forth into full energy by a virtuous passion. Her lover, while he adores her beauty, is too honest a man to abuse the confiding tenderness of a creature so charming and inexperienced. Wycherley takes this plot into his hands; and forthwith this sweet and graceful courtship becomes a licentious intrigue of the lowest and least sentimental kind, between an impudent London rake and the idiot wife of a country squire. We will not go into details. In truth, Wycherley's indecency is protected against the critics as a skunk is protected against the hunters. It is safe, because it is too filthy to handle and too noisome even to approach.

x

It is the same with the "Plain Dealer." How careful has Shakspeare been in "Twelfth Night" to preserve the dignity and delicacy of Viola under her disguise! Even when wearing a page's doublet and hose, she is never mixed up with any transaction which the most fastidious mind could regard as leaving a stain on her. She is employed by the Duke on an embassy of love to Olivia, but on an embassy of the most honourable kind. Wycherley borrows Viola—and Viola forthwith becomes a pandar of the basest sort. But the character of Manly is the best illustration of our meaning. Molière exhibited in his misanthrope a pure and noble mind which had been sorely vexed by the sight of perfidy and malevolence disguised under the forms of politeness. As every extreme naturally generates its contrary, Alceste adopts a standard of good and evil directly opposed to that of the society which surrounds him. Courtesy seems to him a vice; and those stern virtues which are neglected by the fops and coquettes of Paris become too exclusively the objects of his veneration. He is often to blame; he is often ridiculous: but he is always a good man; and the feeling which he inspires is regret that a person so estimable should be so unamiable. Wycherley borrowed Alceste, and turned him—we quote the words of so lenient a critic as Mr. Leigh Hunt—into "a ferocious sensualist, who believed himself as great a rascal as he thought everybody else." The surliness of Molière's hero is copied and caricatured. But the most nauseous libertinism and the most dastardly fraud are substituted for the purity and integrity of the original. And, to make the whole complete, Wycherley does not seem to have been aware that he was not drawing the portrait of an eminently honest man. So depraved was his moral taste, that, while he firmly believed that he was producing a picture of virtue too exalted for the commerce of this world, he was really delineating the greatest rascal that is to be found even in his own writings.

We pass a very severe censure on Wycherley when we say that it is a relief to turn from him to Congreve. Congreve's writings, indeed, are by no means pure: nor was he, as far as are able to judge, a warm-hearted or high-minded man. Yet, in coming to him, we feel that the worst is over—that we are one remove further from the Restoration—that we are past the Nadir of national taste and morality.

WILLIAM CONGREVE was born in 1670,* at Bardsey, in the neighbourhood of Leeds. His father, a younger son of a very ancient Staffordshire family, had distinguished himself among the cavaliers in the civil war, was set down after the Restoration for the Order of the Royal Oak, and subsequently settled in Ireland, under the patronage of the Earl of Burlington.

Congreve passed his childhood and youth in Ireland. He was sent to school at Kilkenny, and thence went to the University of Dublin. His learning does great honour to his instructors. From his writings it appears not only that he was well acquainted with Latin literature, but that his knowledge of the Greek poets was such as was not, in his time, common even in a college.

When he had completed his academical studies, he was sent to London to study the law, and was entered of the Middle Temple. He troubled himself, however, very little about pleading or conveyancing, and gave himself up to literature and society. Two kinds of ambition early took possession of his mind, and often pulled it in opposite directions. He was conscious of great fertility of thought and power of ingenious combination. His lively conversation, his polished manners and his highly respectable connections had obtained for him ready access to the best company. He longed to be a great writer.

---

* Mr. Leigh Hunt says 1669. But the old style has misled him.

He longed to be a man of fashion. Either object was within his reach. But could he secure both? Was there not something vulgar in letters—something inconsistent with the easy apathetic graces of a man of the mode? Was it aristocratical to be confounded with creatures who lived in the cocklofts of Grub Street, to bargain with publishers, to hurry printers' devils, to squabble with managers, to be applauded or hissed by pit, boxes and galleries? Could he forego the renown of being the first wit of his age? Could he attain that renown without sullying, what he valued quite as much, his character for gentility? The history of his life is the history of a conflict between these two impulses. In his youth, the desire of literary fame had the mastery; but soon the meaner ambition overpowered the higher and obtained supreme dominion over his mind.

His first work, a novel of no great value, he published under the assumed name of Cleophil. His second was the "Old Bachelor," acted in 1693, a play inferior indeed to his other comedies, but, in its own line, inferior to them alone. The plot is equally destitute of interest and of probability. The characters are either not distinguishable, or are distinguished only by peculiarities of the most glaring kind. But the dialogue is resplendent with wit and eloquence—which indeed are so abundant that the fool comes in for an ample share—and yet preserves a certain colloquial air, a certain indescribable ease, of which Wycherley had given no example and which Sheridan in vain attempted to imitate. The author, divided between pride and shame—pride at having written a good play and shame at having done an ungentlemanlike thing—pretended that he had merely scribbled a few scenes for his own amusement, and affected to yield unwillingly to the importunities of those who pressed him to try his fortune on the stage. The "Old Bachelor" was seen in manuscript by Dryden, one of whose best qualities was a hearty and generous admiration for the talents of others. He declared that he had never seen such a first play, and lent his services to bring it into a form fit for representation. Nothing was wanted to the success of the piece. It was so cast as to bring into play all the comic talent, and to exhibit on the boards in one view all the beauty which Drury Lane Theatre, then the only theatre in London, could assemble. The result was a complete triumph; and the author was gratified with rewards more substantial than the applauses of the pit. Montagu, then a lord of the Treasury, immediately gave him a place, and, in a short time, added the reversion of another place of much greater value, which, however, did not become vacant till many years had elapsed.

In 1694, Congreve brought out the "Double Dealer," a comedy in which all the powers which had produced the "Old Bachelor" showed themselves matured by time and improved by exercise. But the audience was shocked by the characters of Maskwell and Lady Touchwood. And, indeed, there is something strangely revolting in the way in which a group that seems to belong to the house of Laius or of Pelops is introduced into the midst of the Brisks, Froths, Carelesses and Plyants. The play was unfavourably received. Yet, if the praise of distinguished men could compensate an author for the disapprobation of the multitude, Congreve had no reason to repine. Dryden, in one of the most ingenious, magnificent and pathetic pieces that he ever wrote, extolled the author of the "Double Dealer" in terms which now appear extravagantly hyperbolical. Till Congreve came forth—so ran this exquisite flattery—the superiority of the poets who preceded the civil wars was acknowledged.

"Theirs was the giant race before the flood."

Since the return of the Royal House, much art and ability had been exerted, but the old masters had been still unrivalled.

> "Our builders were with want of genius curst,
> The second temple was not like the first."

At length a writer had arisen who, just emerging from boyhood, had surpassed the authors of the "Knight of the Burning Pestle" and of the "Silent Woman," and who had only one rival left to contend with.

> "Heaven, that but once was prodigal before,
> To Shakspeare gave as much, he could not give him more."

Some lines near the end of the poem are singularly graceful and touching, and sank deep into the heart of Congreve.

> "Already am I worn with cares and age,
> And just abandoning the ungrateful stage;
> But you, whom every Muse and Grace adorn,
> Whom I foresee to better fortune born,
> Be kind to my remains; and, oh, defend
> Against your judgment your departed friend.
> Let not the insulting foe my fame pursue,
> But guard those laurels which descend to you."

The crowd, as usual, gradually came over to the opinion of the men of note; and the "Double Dealer" was before long quite as much admired, though perhaps never so much liked, as the "Old Bachelor."

In 1695 appeared "Love for Love," superior both in wit and in scenic effect to either of the preceding plays. It was performed at a new theatre which Betterton and some other actors, disgusted by the treatment which they had received in Drury Lane, had just opened in a tennis-court near Lincoln's Inn. Scarcely any comedy within the memory of the oldest man had been equally successful. The actors were so elated that they gave Congreve a share in their theatre, and he promised in return to furnish them with a play every year, if his health would permit. Two years passed, however, before he produced the "Mourning Bride," a play which, paltry as it is when compared, we do not say, with "Lear" or "Macbeth," but with the best dramas of Massinger and Ford, stands very high among the tragedies of the age in which it was written. To find anything so good we must go twelve years back to "Venice Preserved," or six years forward to the "Fair Penitent." The noble passage, which Johnson, both in writing and in conversation, extolled above any other in the English drama, has suffered greatly in the public estimation from the extravagance of his praise. Had he contented himself with saying that it was finer than anything in the tragedies of Dryden, Otway, Lee, Rowe, Southern, Hughes and Addison, than anything, in short, that had been written for the stage since the days of Charles I., he would not have been in the wrong.

The success of the "Mourning Bride" was even greater than that of "Love for Love." Congreve was now allowed to be the first tragic as well as the first comic dramatist of his time; and all this at twenty-seven. We believe that no English writer except Lord Byron has, at so early an age, stood so high in the estimation of his contemporaries.

At this time took place an event which deserves, in our opinion, a very different sort of notice from that which has been bestowed on it by Mr. Leigh Hunt. The nation had now nearly recovered from the demoralising effect of the Puritan austerity. The gloomy follies of the reign of the Saints were but faintly remembered. The evils produced by profaneness and debauchery were recent and glaring. The Court, since the Revolution, had ceased to patronise licentiousness. Mary was strictly pious, and the vices of the cold, stern and silent William were not obtruded on the public eye. Discountenanced by the government and falling in the favour of the people, the profligacy of the Restoration still maintained its ground in some parts of society. Its strongholds were the places where men of wit and fashion congregated, and, above all, the theatres. At this conjuncture arose a great reformer, whom, widely as we differ from him in many important points, we can never mention without respect.

Jeremy Collier was a clergyman of the Church of England, bred at Cambridge. His talents and attainments were such as might have been expected to raise him to the highest honours of his profession. He had an extensive knowledge of books, and yet he had mingled much with polite society, and is said not to have wanted either grace or vivacity in conversation. There were few branches of literature to which he had not paid some attention. But ecclesiastical antiquity was his favourite study. In religious opinions, he belonged to that section of the Church of England which lies furthest from Geneva and nearest to Rome. His notions touching Episcopal government, holy orders, the efficacy of the sacraments, the authority of the Fathers, the guilt of schism, the importance of vestments, ceremonies and solemn days, differed little from those which are now held by Dr. Pusey and Mr. Newman. Towards the close of his life, indeed, Collier took some steps which brought him still nearer to Popery—mixed water with the wine in the Eucharist, made the sign of the cross in confirmation, employed oil in the visitation of the sick, and offered up prayers for the dead. His politics were of a piece with his divinity. He was a Tory of the highest sort, such as in the cant of his age was called a Tantivy. Not even the tyranny of James, not even the persecution of the bishops and the spoliation of the universities could shake his steady loyalty. While the Convention was sitting, Collier wrote with vehemence in defence of the fugitive king, and was in consequence arrested. But his dauntless spirit was not to be so tamed. He refused to take the oaths, renounced all his preferments, and, in a succession of pamphlets written with much violence and with some ability, attempted to excite the nation against its new masters. In 1692, he was again arrested on suspicion of having been concerned in a treasonable plot. So unbending were his principles that his friends could hardly persuade him to let them bail him; and he afterwards expressed his remorse for having been induced thus to acknowledge, by implication, the authority of an usurping government. He was soon in trouble again. Sir John Friend and Sir William Parkins were tried and convicted of high treason for planning the murder of King William. Collier administered spiritual consolation to them, attended them to Tyburn, and, just before the execution, laid his hands on their heads, and, by the authority which he derived from Christ, solemnly absolved them. This scene gave indescribable scandal. Tories joined with Whigs in blaming the conduct of the daring priest. There are some acts, it was said, which fall under the definition of treason, into which a good man may, in troubled times, be led even by his virtues. It may be necessary for the protection of society to punish such a man. But even in punishing him we consider him as legally rather than morally guilty, and hope that his honest error, though it cannot be pardoned here, will not be counted to him for sin hereafter. But such was not the case of Collier's penitents. They were concerned in a plot for waylaying and butchering, in an hour of security, one who, whether he were or were not their king, was at all events their fellow-creature. Whether the Jacobite theory about the rights of governments and the duties of subjects were or were not well founded, assassination must always be considered as a great crime. It is condemned even by the maxims of worldly honour and morality. Much more must it be an object of abhorrence to the pure Spouse of Christ. The Church cannot surely, without the saddest and most mournful forebodings, see one of her children, who has been guilty of this great wickedness, pass into eternity without any sign of repentance. That these traitors had given any sign of repentance was not alleged. It might be that they had privately declared their contrition; and, if so, the minister of religion might be justified in privately assuring them of the Divine forgiveness. But a public remission ought to have been preceded by a public atonement. The regret of these men, if expressed at all, had been expressed in secret. The hands of Collier had been laid on them in the presence of thousands. The inference which his enemies drew from his conduct was that he did not consider the conspiracy against the life of William as sinful. But this inference he very vehemently and, we doubt not, very sincerely denied.

The storm raged. The bishops put forth a solemn censure of the absolution. The Attorney-General brought the matter before the Court of King's Bench. Collier had now made up his mind not to give bail for his appearance before any court which derived its authority from the usurper. He accordingly absconded and was outlawed. He survived these events about thirty years. The prosecution was not pressed, and he was soon suffered to resume his literary pursuits in quiet. At a later period, many attempts were made to shake his perverse integrity by offers of wealth and dignity, but in vain. When he died, towards the end of the reign of George I., he was still under the ban of the law.

We shall not be suspected of regarding either the politics or the theology of Collier with partiality; but we believe him to have been as honest and courageous a man as ever lived. We will go further, and say that, though passionate and often wrongheaded, he was a singularly fair controversialist—candid, generous, too high-spirited to take mean advantages even in the most exciting disputes, and pure from all taint of personal malevolence. It must also be admitted that his opinions on ecclesiastical and political affairs, though in themselves absurd and pernicious, eminently qualified him to be the reformer of our lighter literature. The libertinism of the press and of the stage was, as we have said, the effect of a reaction against the Puritan strictness. Profligacy was, like the oak leaf of the twenty-ninth of May, the badge of a cavalier and a high churchman. Decency was associated with conventicles and calves' heads. Grave prelates were too much disposed to wink at the excesses of a body of zealous and able allies who covered Roundheads and Presbyterians with ridicule. If a Whig raised his voice against the impiety and licentiousness of the fashionable writers, his mouth was instantly stopped by the retort, You are one of those who groan at a light quotation from Scripture and raise estates out of the plunder of the Church—who shudder at a *double entendre* and chop off the heads of kings. A Baxter, a Burnet, even a Tillotson, would have done little to purify our literature. But when a man, fanatical in the cause of episcopacy and actually under outlawry for his attachment to hereditary right, came forward as the champion of decency, the battle was already half won.

In 1698, Collier published his "Short View of the Profaneness and Immorality of the English Stage," a book which threw the whole literary world into commotion, but which is now much less read than it deserves. The faults of the work, indeed, are neither few nor small. The dissertations on the Greek and Latin drama do not at all help the argument, and, whatever may have been thought of them by the generation which fancied that Christ Church had refuted Bentley, are such as, in the present day, a scholar of very humble pretensions may venture to pronounce boyish, or, rather, babyish. The censures are not sufficiently discriminating. The authors whom Collier accused had been guilty of such gross sins against decency that he was certain to weaken instead of strengthening his case by introducing into his charge against them any matter about which there could be the smallest dispute. He was, however, so injudicious as to place among the outrageous offences which he justly arraigned, some things which are really quite innocent, and some slight instances of levity which, though not strictly correct, could easily be paralleled from the works of writers who had rendered great services to morality and religion. Thus he blames Congreve, the number and gravity of whose real transgressions made it quite unnecessary to tax him with any that were not real, for using the words " martyr" and "inspiration": in a light sense; as if an archbishop might not say that a speech was inspired by claret, or that an alderman was a martyr to the gout. Sometimes, again, Collier does not sufficiently distinguish between the dramatist and the persons of the drama. Thus he blames Vanbrugh for putting into Lord Foppington's mouth some contemptuous expressions respecting the Church service; though it is obvious that Vanbrugh could not better express reverence than by making Lord Foppington express contempt. There is also throughout the "Short View" too strong a display of professional feeling. Collier is not content with claiming for his order an immunity from indiscriminate scurrility; he will not allow that, in any case, any word or act of a divine can be a proper subject for ridicule. Nor does he confine this benefit of clergy to the Ministers of the Established Church. He extends the privilege to Catholic priests and, what in him is more surprising, to Dissenting preachers. This, however, is a mere trifle. Imaums, Brahmins, priests of Jupiter, priests of Baal are all held to be sacred. Dryden is blamed for making the Mufti in "Don Sebastian" talk nonsense. Lee is called to a severe account for his incivility to Tiresias. But the most curious passage is that in which Collier resents some uncivil reflections thrown by Cassandra, in "Cleomenes," on the calf Apis and his hierophants. The words "grass-eating, foddered god," words which really are much in the style of several passages in the Old Testament, give as much offence to this Christian divine as they could have given to the priests of Memphis.

But, when all deductions have been made, great merit must be allowed to this work. There is hardly any book of that time from which it would be possible to select specimens of writing so excellent and so various. To compare Collier with Pascal would indeed be absurd. Yet we hardly know where, except in the "Provincial Letters," we can find mirth so harmoniously and becomingly blended with solemnity as in the "Short View." In truth, all the modes of ridicule, from broad fun to polished and antithetical sarcasm, were at Collier's command. On the other hand, he was complete master of the rhetoric of honest indignation. We scarcely know any volume which contains so many bursts of that peculiar eloquence which comes from the heart and goes to the heart. Indeed, the spirit of the book is truly heroic. In order fairly, appreciate it, we must remember the situation in which the writer stood. He was under the frown of power. His name was already a mark for the invectives of one half of the writers of the age when, in the cause of good taste, good sense and good morals, he gave battle to the other half. Strong as his political prejudices were, he seems on this occasion to have entirely laid them aside. He has forgotten that he is a Jacobite and remembers only that he is a citizen and a Christian. Some of his sharpest censures are directed against poetry which had been hailed with delight by the Tory party and had inflicted a deep wound on the Whigs. It is really inspiriting to see how gallantly the solitary outlaw advances to attack enemies, formidable separately, and it might have been thought, irresistible when combined—distributes his swashing blows right and left among Wycherley, Congreve and Vanbrugh—treads the wretched D'Urfey down in the dirt beneath his feet—and strikes with all his strength full at the towering crest of Dryden.

The effect produced by the "Short View" was immense. The nation was on the side of Collier. But it could not be doubted that, in the great host which he had defied, some champion would be found to lift the gauntlet. The general belief was that Dryden would take the field; and all the wits anticipated a sharp contest between two well-paired combatants. The great poet had been singled out in the most marked manner. It was well known that he was deeply hurt, that much smaller provocations had formerly roused him to violent resentment, and that there was no literary weapon, offensive or defensive, of which he was not master. But his conscience smote him; he stood abashed, like the fallen archangel at the rebuke of Zephon,

"And felt how awful goodness is, and saw
Virtue in her shape how lovely; saw and pined
His loss."

At a later period he mentioned the "Short View" in the preface to his "Fables." He complained, with some asperity, of the harshness with which he had been treated, and urged some matters in mitigation. But, on the whole, he frankly acknowledged that he had been justly reproved. "If," said he, "Mr. Collier be my enemy, let him triumph. If he be my friend, as I have given him no personal occasion to be otherwise, he will be glad of my repentance."

It would have been wise in Congreve to follow his master's example. He was precisely in that situation in which it is madness to attempt a vindication; for his guilt was so clear that no address or eloquence could obtain an acquittal. On the other hand, there were in his case many extenuating circumstances which, if he had acknowledged his error and promised amendment, would have procured his pardon. The most rigid censor could not but make great allowances for the faults into which so young a man had been seduced by evil example, by the luxuriance of a vigorous fancy, and by the inebriating effect of popular applause. The esteem, as well as the admiration of the public, was still within his reach. He might easily have effaced all memory of his transgressions, and have shared with Addison the glory of showing that the most brilliant wit may be the ally of virtue. But, in any case, prudence should have restrained him from encountering Collier. The non-juror was a man thoroughly fitted by nature, education and habit for polemical dispute. Congreve's mind, though one of no common fertility and vigour, was of a different class. No man understood so well the art of polishing epigrams and repartees into the clearest effulgence, and setting them neatly in easy and familiar dialogue. In this sort of jewellery, he attained to a mastery unprecedented and inimitable. But he was altogether rude in the art of controversy; and he had a cause to defend which scarcely any art could have rendered victorious.

The event was such as might have been foreseen. Congreve's answer was a complete failure. He was angry, obscure and dull. Even the Green Room and Will's Coffee-House were compelled to acknowledge that in wit, as well as in argument, the parson had a decided advantage over the poet. Not only was Congreve unable to make any show of a case where he was in the wrong; but he succeeded in putting himself completely in the wrong where he was in the right. Collier had taxed him with profaneness for calling a clergyman Mr. Prig and for introducing a coachman named Jehu, in allusion to the King of Israel who was known at a distance by his furious driving. Had there been nothing worse in the "Old Bachelor" and "Double Dealer," Congreve might pass for as pure a writer as Cowper himself, who, in poems revised by so austere a censor as John Newton, calls a fox-hunting squire Nimrod and gives to a chaplin the disrespectful name of Smug. Congreve might with good effect have appealed to the public whether it might not be fairly presumed that, when such frivolous charges were made, there were no very serious charges to make. Instead of doing this, he pretended that he meant no allusion to the Bible by the name of Jehu and no reflection by the name of Prig. Strange, that a man of such parts should, in order to defend himself against imputations which nobody could regard as important, tell untruths which it was certain that nobody would believe.

One of the pleas which Congreve set up for himself and his brethren was that, though they might be guilty of a little levity here and there, they were careful to inculcate a moral, packed closed into two or three lines, at the end of every play. Had the fact been as he stated it, the defence would be worth very little. For no man acquainted with human nature could think that a sententious couplet would undo all the mischief that five profligate acts had done. But it would have been wise in Congreve to have looked again at his own comedies before he used this argument. Collier did so; and found that the moral of the "Old Batchelor"—the grave apophthegm which is to be a set-off against all the libertinism of the piece—is contained in the following triplet:

"What rugged ways attend the noon of life!
Our sun declines, and with what anxious strife,
What pain, we tug that galling load—a wife."

"Love for Love," says Collier, "may have a somewhat better farewell, but it would do a man little service should he remember it to his dying day:"

"The miracle to-day is, that we find
A lover true, not that a woman's kind."

Collier's reply was severe and triumphant. One of his repartees we will quote, not as a favourable specimen of his manner, but because it was called forth by Congreve's characteristic affectation. The poet spoke of the "Old Bachelor" as a trifle to which he attached no value and which had become public by a sort of accident. "I wrote it," he said, "to amuse myself in a slow recovery from a fit of sickness." "What his disease was," replied Collier, "I am not to inquire: but it must be a very ill one to be worse than the remedy."

All that Congreve gained by coming forward on this occasion was that he completely deprived himself of the excuse which he might with justice have pleaded for his early offences. "Why," asked Collier, "should the man laugh at the mischief of the boy and make the disorders of his nonage his own by an after approbation?"

Congreve was not Collier's only opponent. Vanbrugh, Dennis and Settle took the field. And from a passage in a contemporary satire, we are inclined to think that among the answers to the "Short View" was one written, or supposed to be written, by Wycherley. The victory remained with Collier. A great and rapid reform in all the departments of our lighter literature was the effect of his labours. A new race of wits and poets arose, who generally treated with reverence the great ties which bind society together, and whose very indecencies were decent when compared with those of the school which flourished during the last forty years of the seventeenth century.

This controversy probably prevented Congreve from fulfilling the engagements into which he had entered with the actors. It was not till 1700 that he produced the "Way of the World," the most deeply meditated and the most brilliantly written of all his works. It wants, perhaps, the constant movement, the effervescence of animal spirits, which we find in "Love for Love." But the hysterical rants of Lady Wishfort, the meeting of Witwould and his brother, the country knight's courtship and his subsequent revel, and, above all, the chase and surrender of Millamant, are superior to anything that is to be found in the whole range of English comedy from the civil war downwards. It is quite inexplicable to us that this play should have failed on the stage. Yet so it was; and the author, already sore with the wounds which Collier had inflicted, was galled past endurance by this new stroke. He resolved never again to expose himself to the rudeness of a tasteless audience, and took leave of the theatre for ever.

He lived twenty-eight years longer without adding to the high literary reputation which he had attained. He read much while he retained his eyesight, and now and then wrote a short essay or an idle tale in verse, but appears never to have planned any considerable work. The miscellaneous pieces which he published in 1710 are of little value and have long been forgotten. The stock of fame which he had acquired by his comedies was sufficient, assisted by the graces of his manner and conversation, to secure for him a high place in the estimation of the world. During the winter, he lived among the most distinguished and agreeable people in London. His summers were passed at the splendid country-seats of ministers and peers. Literary envy and political faction, which in that age respected nothing else, respected his repose. He professed to be one of the party of which his patron Montagu, now Lord Halifax, was the head. But he had civil words and small good offices for men of every shade of opinion. And men of every shade of opinion spoke well of him in return.

His means were for a long time scanty. The place which he had in possession barely enabled him to live with comfort. And, when the Tories came into power, some thought that he would lose even this moderate provision. But Harley, who was by no means disposed to adopt the exterminating policy of the October club, and who, with all his faults of understanding and temper, had a sincere kindness for men of genius, reassured the anxious poet by quoting very gracefully and happily the lines of Virgil:

"Non obtusa adeo gestamus pectora Poeni,
Nec tam aversus equos Tyria Sol jungit ab urbe."

The indulgence with which Congreve was treated by the Tories was not purchased by any concession on his part which could justly offend the Whigs. It was his rare good fortune to share the triumph of his friends without having shared their proscription. When the House of Hanover came to the throne, his fortunes began to flourish. The reversion, to which he had been nominated twenty years before, fell in. He was made secretary to the island of Jamaica, and his whole income amounted to £1,200 a year—a fortune which, for a single man, was in that age not only easy but splendid. He continued, however, to practise the frugality which he had learned when he could scarce spare, as Swift tells us, a shilling to pay the chairman who carried him to Lord Halifax's. Though he had nobody to save for, he laid up at least as much as he spent.

The infirmities of age came early upon him. His habits had been intemperate; he suffered much from gout; and, when confined to his chamber, he had no longer the solace of literature. Blindness, the most cruel misfortune that can befall the lonely student, made his books useless to him. He was thrown on society for all his amusement; and, in society, his good breeding and vivacity made him always welcome.

By the rising men of letters, he was considered not as a rival, but as a classic. He had left their arena; he never measured his strength with them; and he was always loud in applause of their exertions. They could, therefore, entertain no jealousy of him, and thought no more of detracting from his fame than of carping at the great men who had been lying a hundred years in Poet's

Corner. Even the inmates of Grub Street, even the heroes of the "Dunciad," were for once just to living merit. There can be no stronger illustration of the estimation in which Congreve was held than the fact that Pope's "Iliad," a work which appeared with more splendid auspices than any other in our language, was dedicated to him. There was not a Duke in the kingdom who would not have been proud of such a compliment. Dr. Johnson expresses great admiration for the independence of spirit which Pope showed on this occasion, and some surprise at his choice. "He passed over peers and statesmen to inscribe his "Iliad" to Congreve, with a magnanimity of which the praise had been complete had his friend's virtue been equal to his wit. Why he was chosen for so great an honour it is not now possible to know." It is certainly impossible to know; yet we think it is possible to guess. The translation of the "Iliad" had been zealously befriended by men of all political opinions. The poet, who, at an early age, had been raised to affluence by the emulous liberality of Whigs and Tories, could not with propriety inscribe to a chief of either party a work which had been munificently patronised by both. It was necessary to find some person who was at once eminent and neutral. It was therefore necessary to pass over peers and statesmen. Congreve had a high name in letters. He had a high name in aristocratic circles. He lived on terms of civility with men of all parties. By a courtesy paid to him, neither the ministers nor the leaders of the opposition could be offended.

The singular affectation, which had from the first been characteristic of Congreve, grew stronger and stronger as he advanced in life. At last it became disagreeable to him to hear his own comedies praised. Voltaire, whose soul was burned up by the raging desire for literary renown, was half puzzled and half disgusted by what he saw, during his visit to England, of this extraordinary whim. Congreve disclaimed the character of a poet—declared that his plays were trifles produced in an idle hour, and begged that Voltaire would consider him merely as a gentleman. "If you had been merely a gentleman," said Voltaire, "I should not have come to see you."

Congreve was not a man of warm affections. Domestic ties he had none; and in the temporary connections which he formed with a succession of beauties from the green-room his heart does not appear to have been interested. Of all his attachments, that to Mrs. Bracegirdle lasted the longest and was the most celebrated. This charming actress, who was, during many years, the idol of all London, whose face caused the fatal broil in which Mountfort fell and for which Lord Mohun was tried by the Peers, and to whom the Earl of Scarsdale was said to have made honourable addresses, had conducted herself, in very trying circumstances, with extraordinary discretion. Congreve at length became her confidential friend. They constantly rode out together and dined together. Some people said that she was his mistress and others that she would soon be his wife. He was at last drawn away from her by the influence of a wealthier and haughtier beauty. Henrietta, daughter of the great Marlborough, and wife of the Earl of Godolphin, had, on her father's death, succeeded to his dukedom and to the greater part of his immense property. Her husband was an insignificant man, of whom Lord Chesterfield said that he came to the House of Peers only to sleep, and that he might as well sleep on the right as on the left of the woolsack. Between the Duchess and Congreve sprang up a most eccentric friendship. He had a seat every day at her table, and assisted in the direction of her concerts. That malignant old hag, the Dowager Duchess Sarah, who had quarrelled with her daughter as she had quarrelled with everybody else, affected to suspect that there was something wrong. But the world in general appears to have thought that a great lady might, without any imputation on her character, pay attention to a man of eminent genius who was nearly sixty years old, who was still older in appearance and in constitution, who was confined to his chair by gout and was unable to read from blindness.

In the summer of 1728, Congreve was ordered to try the Bath waters. During his excursion he was overturned in his chariot and received some severe internal injury from which he never recovered. He came back to London in a dangerous state, complained constantly of a pain in his side, and continued to sink till, in the following January, he expired.

He left £10,000, saved out of the emoluments of his lucrative places. Johnson says that this money ought to have gone to the Congreve family, which was then in great distress. Doctor Young and Mr. Leigh Hunt, two gentlemen who seldom agree with each other, but with whom, on this occasion, we are happy to agree, think that it ought to have gone to Mrs. Bracegirdle. Congreve bequeathed two hundred pounds to Mrs. Bracegirdle and an equal sum to a certain Mrs. Jellat; but the bulk of his accumulations went to the Duchess of Marlborough, in whose immense wealth such a legacy was as a drop in the bucket. It might have raised the fallen fortunes of a Staffordshire squire; it might have enabled a retired actress to enjoy every comfort and, in her sense, every luxury—but it was hardly sufficient to defray the Duchess's establishment for two months.

The great lady buried her friend with a pomp seldom seen at the funeral of poets. The corpse lay in state under the ancient roof of the Jerusalem Chamber, and was interred in Westminster Abbey. The pall was borne by the Duke of Bridgewater, Lord Cobham, the Earl of Wilmington, who had been Speaker and was afterwards First Lord of the Treasury, and other men of high consideration. Her Grace laid out her friend's bequest in a superb diamond necklace, which she wore in honour of him, and, if report is to be believed, showed her regard in ways much more extraordinary. It is said that she had a statue of him in ivory, which moved by clockwork, and was placed daily at her table; that she had a wax doll made in imitation of him, and that the feet of the doll were regularly blistered and anointed by the doctors as poor Congreve's feet had been when he suffered from the gout. A monument was erected to the poet in Westminster Abbey with an inscription written by the Duchess; and Lord Cobham honoured him with a cenotaph, which seems to us, though that is a bold word, the ugliest and most absurd of the buildings at Stowe.

We have said that Wycherley was a worse Congreve. There was, indeed, a remarkable analogy between the writings and lives of these two men. Both were gentlemen liberally educated. Both led town lives, and knew human nature only as it appears between Hyde Park and the Tower. Both were men of wit. Neither had much imagination. Both at an early age produced lively and profligate comedies. Both retired from the field while still in early manhood, and owed to their youthful achievements in literature the consideration which they enjoyed in later life. Both, after they had ceased to write for the stage, published volumes of miscellanies which did little credit either to their talents or to their morals. Both, during their declining years, hung loose upon society; and both, in their last moments, made eccentric and unjustifiable dispositions of their estates.

But in every point Congreve maintained his superiority to Wycherley. Wycherley had wit; but the wit of Congreve far outshines that of every comic writer, except Sheridan, who has arisen within the last two centuries. Congreve had not, in a large measure, the poetical faculty; but compared with Wycherley he might be called a great poet. Wycherley had some knowledge of books; but Congreve was a man of real learning. Congreve's offences against decorum, though highly culpable, were not so gross as those of Wycherley; nor did Congreve, like Wycherley, exhibit to the world the deplorable spectacle of a licentious dotage. Congreve died in the enjoyment of high consideration; Wycherley forgotten or despised. Congreve's will was absurd and capricious; but Wycherley's last actions appear to have been prompted by obdurate malignity.

Here, at least for the present, we must stop. Vanbrugh and Farquhar are not men to be hastily dismissed, and we have not left ourselves space to do them justice.

LORD HOLLAND. (JULY, 1841.)

The Opinions of Lord Holland, as Recorded in the Journals of the House of Lords from 1797 to 1841. Collected and edited by D. C. MOYLAN, of Lincoln's Inn, Barrister-at-Law. 8vo. London, 1841.

MANY reasons make it impossible for us to lay before our readers, at the present moment, a complete view of the character and public career of the late Lord Holland. But we feel that we have already deferred too long the duty of paying some tribute to his memory. We feel that it is more becoming to bring without further delay an offering, though intrinsically of little value, than to leave his tomb longer without some token of our reverence and love.

We shall say very little of the book which lies on our table. And yet it is a book which, even if it had been the work of a less distinguished man or had appeared under circumstances less interesting, would have well repaid an attentive perusal. It is valuable, both as a record of principles and as a model of composition. We find in it all the great maxims which, during more than forty years, guided Lord Holland's public conduct, and the chief reasons on which those maxims rest, condensed into the smallest possible space and set forth with admirable perspicuity, dignity and precision. To his opinions on Foreign Policy, we for the most part cordially assent; but, now and then, we are inclined to think them imprudently generous. We could not have signed the Protest against the detention of Napoleon. The Protest respecting the course which England pursued at the congress of Verona, though it contains much that is excellent, contains also positions which, we are inclined to think, Lord Holland would, at a later period, have admitted to be unsound. But to all his doctrines on Constitutional Questions, we give our hearty approbation; and we firmly believe that no British government has ever deviated from that line of internal policy which he has traced without detriment to the public.

We will give, as a specimen of this little volume, a single passage, in which a chief article of the political creed of the Whigs is stated and explained with singular clearness, force and brevity. Our readers will remember that, in 1825, the Catholic Association agitated for emancipation with most formidable effect. The Tories acted after their kind. Instead of removing the grievance, they tried to put down the agitation, and brought in a law, apparently sharp and stringent, but, in truth, utterly impotent for restraining the right of petition. Lord Holland's Protest on that occasion is excellent.

"We are," says he, "well aware that the privileges of the people, the rights of free discussion, and the spirit and letter of our popular institutions must render—and they are intended to render—the continuance of an extensive grievance, and of the dissatisfaction consequent thereupon, dangerous to the tranquillity of the country, and ultimately subversive of the authority of the state. Experience and theory alike forbid us to deny that effect of a free constitution; a sense of justice and a love of liberty equally deter us from lamenting it. But we have always been taught to look for the remedy of such disorders in the redress of the grievances which justify them, and in the removal of the dissatisfaction from which they flow—not in restraints on ancient privileges, not in inroads on the right of public discussion, nor in violations of the principles of a free government. If, therefore, the legal method of seeking redress, which has been resorted to by persons labouring under grievous disabilities, be fraught with immediate or remote danger to the state, we draw from that circumstance a conclusion long since foretold by great authority—namely, that the British constitution and large exclusions cannot subsist together; that the constitution must destroy them, or they will destroy the constitution."

It was not, however, of this little book, valuable and interesting as it is, but of the author, that we meant to speak; and we will try to do so with calmness and impartiality.

In order to fully appreciate the character of Lord Holland, it is necessary to go far back into the history of his family; for he had inherited something more than a coronet and an estate. To the House of which he was the head belongs one distinction which we believe to be without a parallel in our annals. During more than a century, there has never been a time at which a Fox has not stood in a prominent station among public men. Scarcely had the chequered career of the first Lord Holland closed, when his son, Charles, rose to the head of the Opposition and to the first rank among English debaters. And before Charles was borne to Westminster Abbey a third Fox had already become one of the most conspicuous politicians in the kingdom.

It is impossible not to be struck by the strong family likeness which, in spite of diversities arising from education and position, appears in these three distinguished persons. In their faces and figures there was a resemblance, such as is common enough in novels, where one picture is good for ten generations, but such as in real life is seldom found. The ample person, the massy and thoughtful forehead, the large eyebrows, the full cheek and lip, the expression so singularly compounded of sense, humour, courage, openness, a strong will and a sweet temper, were common to all. But the features of the founder of the House, as the pencil of Reynolds and the chisel of Nollekens have handed them down to us, were disagreeably harsh and exaggerated. In his descendants, the aspect was preserved, but it was softened, till it became, in the late lord, the most gracious and interesting countenance that was ever lighted up by the mingled lustre of intelligence and benevolence.

As it was with the faces of the men of this noble family, so was it also with their minds. Nature had done much for them all. She had moulded them all of that clay of which she is most sparing. To all she had given strong reason and sharp wit; a quick relish for every physical and intellectual enjoyment; constitutional intrepidity, and that frankness by which constitutional intrepidity is generally accompanied; spirits which nothing could depress; tempers easy, generous and placable; and that genial courtesy which has its seat in the heart, and of which artificial politeness is only a faint and cold imitation. Such a disposition is the richest inheritance that ever was entailed on any family.

But training and situation greatly modified the fine qualities which nature lavished with such profusion on three generations of the house of Fox. The first Lord Holland was a needy political adventurer. He entered public life at a time when the standard of integrity among statesmen was low. He started as the adherent of a minister who had indeed many titles to respect, who possessed eminent talents both for administration and for debate, who understood the public interest well, and who meant fairly by the country; but who had seen so much perfidy and meanness that he had become sceptical as to the existence of probity. Weary of the cant of patriotism, Walpole had learned to talk a cant of a different kind. Disgusted by that sort of hypocrisy which is at least a homage to virtue, he was too much in the habit of practising the less respectable hypocrisy which ostentatiously displays, and sometimes even simulates, vice. To Walpole, Fox attached himself, politically and personally, with the ardour which belonged to his temperament. And it is not to be denied that in the school of Walpole he contracted faults which destroyed the value of his many great endowments. He raised himself, indeed, to the first consideration in the House of Commons; he became a consummate master of the art of debate; he attained honours and immense wealth; but the public esteem and confidence were withheld from him. His private friends, indeed, justly extolled his generosity and good nature. They maintained that in those parts of his conduct which they could least defend, there was nothing sordid; and that, if he was misled, he was misled by amiable feelings—by a desire to serve his friends and by anxious tenderness for his children. But by the nation he was regarded as a man of insatiable rapacity and desperate ambition; as a man ready to adopt, without scruple, the most immoral and the most unconstitutional measures; as a man perfectly fitted, by all his opinions and feelings, for the work of managing the Parliament by means of secret-service money and of keeping down the people with the bayonet. Many of his contemporaries had a morality quite as lax as his; but very few among them had his talents, and none had his hardihood and energy. He could not, like Sandys and Doddington, find safety in contempt. He therefore became an object of such general aversion as no statesman since the fall of Strafford has incurred—of such general aversion as was probably never in any country incurred by a man of so kind and cordial a disposition. A weak mind would have sunk under such a load of unpopularity. But that resolute spirit seemed to derive new firmness from the public hatred. The only effect which reproaches appeared to produce on him was to sour, in some degree, his naturally sweet temper. The last acts of his public life were marked, not only by that audacity which he had derived from nature—not only by that immorality which he had learned in the school of Walpole—but by a harshness which almost amounted to cruelty, and which had never been supposed to belong to his character. His severity increased the unpopularity from which it had sprung. The well-known lampoon of Gray may serve as a specimen of the feeling of the country. All the images are taken from shipwrecks, quicksands and cormorants. Lord Holland is represented as complaining that the cowardice of his accomplices had prevented him from putting down the free spirit of the City of London by sword and fire, and as pining for the time when birds of prey should make their nests in Westminster Abbey and unclean beasts burrow in St. Paul's.

Within a few months after the death of this remarkable man, his second son, Charles, appeared at the head of the party opposed to the American War. Charles had inherited the bodily and mental constitution of his father, and had been much—far too much—under his father's influence. It was indeed impossible that a son of so affectionate and noble a spirit should not have been warmly attached to a parent who possessed many fine qualities and who carried his indulgence and liberality towards his children even to a culpable extent. The young man saw that the person to whom he was bound by the strongest ties was in the highest degree odious to the nation; and the effect was what might have been expected from his strong passions and constitutional boldness. He cast in his lot with his father and took, while still a boy, a deep part in the most unjustifiable and unpopular measures that had been adopted since the reign of James the Second. In the debates on the Middlesex Election, he distinguished himself, not only by his precocious powers of eloquence, but by the vehement and scornful manner in which he bade defiance to public opinion. He was at that time regarded as a man likely to be the most formidable champion of arbitrary government that had appeared since the Revolution—to be a Bute with far greater powers—a Mansfield with far greater courage. Happily his father's death liberated him early from the pernicious influence by which he had been misled. His mind expanded. His range of observation became wider. His genius broke through early prejudices. His natural benevolence and magnanimity had fair play. In a very short time he appeared in a situation worthy of his understanding and of his heart. From a family whose name was associated in the public mind with tyranny and corruption—from a party of which the theory and the practice were equally servile—from the midst of the Luttrells, the Dysons, the Barringtons—came forth the greatest parliamentary defender of civil and religious liberty.

The late Lord Holland succeeded to the talents and to the fine natural dispositions of his house. But his situation was very different from that of the two eminent men of whom we have spoken. In some important respects it was better; in some it was worse than theirs. He had one great advantage over them. He received a good political education. The first lord was educated by Sir Robert Walpole. Mr. Fox was educated by his father. The late lord was educated by Mr. Fox. The pernicious maxims early imbibed by the first Lord Holland made his great talents useless, and worse than useless, to the state. The pernicious maxims early imbibed by Mr. Fox led him, at the commencement of his public life, into great faults which, though afterwards nobly expiated, were never forgotten. To the very end of his career, small men, when they had nothing else to say in defence of their own tyranny, bigotry and imbecility, could always raise a cheer by some paltry taunt about the election of Colonel Luttrell, the imprisonment of the lord mayor, and other measures in which the great Whig leader had borne a part at the age of one or two and twenty. On Lord Holland, no such slur could be thrown. Those who most dissent from his opinions must acknowledge that a public life more consistent is not to be found in our annals. Every part of it is in perfect harmony with every other part; and the whole is in perfect harmony with the great principles of toleration and civil freedom. This rare felicity is in a great measure to be attributed to the influence of Mr. Fox. Lord Holland, as was natural in a person of his talents and expectations, began at a very early age to take the keenest interest in politics; and Mr. Fox found the greatest pleasure in forming the mind of so hopeful a pupil. They corresponded largely on political subjects when the young lord was only sixteen; and their friendship and mutual confidence continued to the day of that mournful separation at Chiswick. Under such training, such a man as Lord Holland was in no danger of falling into those faults which threw a dark shade over the whole career of his grandfather and from which the youth of his uncle was not wholly free.

On the other hand, the late Lord Holland, as compared with his grandfather and his uncle, laboured under one great disadvantage. They were members of the House of Commons. He became a Peer while still an infant. When he entered public life, the House of Lords was a very small and a very decorous assembly. The minority to which he belonged was scarcely able to muster five or six votes on the most important nights, when eighty or ninety lords were present. Debate had accordingly become a mere form, as it was in the Irish House of Peers before the Union. This was a great misfortune to a man like Lord Holland. It was not by occasionally addressing fifteen or twenty solemn and unfriendly auditors that his grandfather and his uncle attained their unrivalled parliamentary skill. The former had learned his art in "the great Walpolean battles," on nights when Onslow was in the chair seventeen hours without intermission, when the thick ranks on both sides kept unbroken order till long after the winter sun had risen upon them, when the blind were led out by the hand into the lobby and the paralytic laid down in their bedclothes on the benches. The powers of Charles Fox were, from the first, exercised in conflicts not less exciting. The great talents of the late Lord Holland had no such advantage. This was the more unfortunate because the peculiar species of eloquence which belonged to him, in common with his family, required much practice to develope it. With strong sense and the greatest readiness of wit, a certain tendency to hesitation was hereditary in the line of Fox. This hesitation arose, not from the poverty, but from the wealth of their vocabulary. They paused, not from the difficulty of finding one expression, but from the difficulty of choosing between several. It was only by slow degrees and constant exercise that the first Lord Holland and his son overcame the defect. Indeed, neither of them overcame it completely.

In statement, the late Lord Holland was not successful; his chief excellence lay in reply. He had the quick eye of his house for the unsound parts of an argument and a great felicity in exposing them. He was decidedly more distinguished in debate than any peer of his time who had not sat in the House of Commons. Nay, to find his equal among persons similarly situated, we must go back eighty years—to Earl Granville. For Mansfield, Thurlow, Loughborough, Grey, Grenville, Brougham, Plunket and other eminent men, living and dead, whom we will not stop to enumerate, carried to the Upper House an eloquence formed and matured in the Lower. The opinion of the most discerning judges was that Lord Holland's oratorical performances, though sometimes most successful, afforded no fair measure of his oratorical powers, and that, in an assembly of which the debates were frequent and animated, he would have attained a very high order of excellence. It was, indeed, impossible to converse with him without seeing that he was born a debater. To him, as to his uncle, the exercise of the mind in discussion was a positive pleasure. With the greatest good nature and good breeding, he was the very opposite to an assenter. The word "disputatious" is generally used as a word of reproach; but we can express our meaning only by saying that Lord Holland was most courteously and pleasantly disputatious. In truth, his quickness in discovering and apprehending distinctions and analogies was such as a veteran judge might envy. The lawyers of the Duchy of Lancaster were astonished to find in an unprofessional man so strong a relish for the esoteric parts of their science, and complained that as soon as they had split a hair, Lord Holland proceeded to split the filaments into filaments still finer. In a mind less happily constituted, there might have been a risk that this turn for subtilty would have produced serious evil. But in the heart and understanding of Lord Holland there was ample security against all such danger. He was not a man to be the dupe of his own ingenuity. He put his logic to its proper use; and in him the dialectician was always subordinate to the statesman.

His political life is written in the chronicles of his country. Perhaps, as we have already intimated, his opinions on two or three great questions of Foreign Policy were open to just objection. Yet even his errors, if he erred, were amiable and respectable. We are not sure that we do not love and admire him the more because he was now and then seduced from what we regard as a wise policy, by sympathy with the oppressed, by generosity towards the fallen, by a philanthropy so enlarged that it took in all nations, by love of peace, which in him was second only to the love of freedom, by the magnanimous credulity of a mind which was as incapable of suspecting as of devising mischief.

To his views on questions of Domestic Policy, the voice of his countrymen does ample justice. They revere the memory of the man who was, during forty years, the constant protector of all oppressed races, of all persecuted sects—of the man, whom neither the prejudices nor the interests belonging to his station could seduce from the path of right—of the noble, who in every great crisis cast in his lot with the commons—of the planter, who made manful war on the slave trade—of the landowner, whose whole heart was in the struggle against the corn-laws.

We have hitherto touched almost exclusively on those parts of Lord Holland's character which were open to the observation of millions. How shall we express the feelings with which his memory is cherished by those who were honoured with his friendship. Or in what language shall we speak of that House, once celebrated for its rare attractions to the furthest ends of the civilised world and now silent and desolate as the grave? That House was a hundred and twenty years ago apostrophised by a poet in tender and graceful lines, which have now acquired a new meaning not less sad than that which they originally bore:

> "Thou hill, whose brow the antique structures grace,
> Reared by bold chiefs of Warwick's noble race,
> Why, once so loved, whene'er thy bower appears,
> O'er my dim eyeballs glance the sudden tears?
> How sweet were once thy prospects fresh and fair,
> Thy sloping walks and unpolluted air!
> How sweet the glooms beneath thine aged trees,
> Thy noon-tide shadow and thine evening breeze!
> His image thy forsaken bowers restore;
> Thy walks and airy prospects charm no more:
> No more the summer in thy glooms allayed,
> Thine evening breezes and thy noon-day shade."

Yet a few years and the shades and structures may follow their illustrious masters. The wonderful city which, ancient and gigantic as it is, still continues to grow as fast as a young town of logwood by a water-privilege in Michigan, may soon displace those turrets and gardens which are associated with so much that is interesting and noble—which the courtly magnificence of Rich—with the loves of Ormond—with the counsels of Cromwell—with the death of Addison. The time is coming when, perhaps a few old men, the last survivors of our generation, will in vain seek, amidst new streets and squares and railway stations, for the site of that dwelling which was in their youth the favourite resort of wits and beauties—of painters and poets—of scholars, philosophers and statesmen. They will then remember, with strange tenderness, many objects once familiar to them—the avenue and the terrace, the busts and the paintings, the carving, the grotesque gilding and the enigmatical mottoes. With peculiar fondness they will recall that venerable chamber, in which all the antique gravity of a college library was so singularly blended with all that female grace and wit could devise to embellish a drawing-room. They will recollect, not unmoved, those shelves loaded with the varied learning of many lands and many ages; those portraits in which were preserved the features of the best and wisest Englishmen of two generations. They will recollect how many men who have guided the politics of Europe—who have moved great assemblies by reason and eloquence—who have put life into bronze and canvas, or who have left to posterity things so written as it shall not willingly let them die—were there mixed with all that was loveliest and gayest in the society of the most splendid of capitals. They will remember the singular character which belonged to that circle, in which every talent and accomplishment, every art and science had its place. They will remember how the last debate was discussed in one corner and the last comedy of Scribe in another; while Wilkie gazed with modest admiration on Reynold's Baretti; while Mackintosh turned over Thomas Aquinas to verify a quotation; while Talleyrand related his conversations with Barras at the Luxembourg, or his ride with Lannes over the field of Austerlitz. They will remember, above all, the grace—and the kindness, far more admirable than grace—with which the princely hospitality of that ancient mansion was dispensed. They will remember the venerable and benignant countenance and the cordial voice of him who bade them welcome. They will remember that temper, which years of pain, of sickness, of lameness, of confinement seemed only to make sweeter and sweeter; and that frank politeness, which at once relieved all the embarrassment of the youngest and most timid writer or artist who found himself for the first time among Ambassadors and Earls. They will remember that constant flow of conversation, so natural, so animated, so various, so rich with observation and anecdote; that wit which never gave a wound; that exquisite mimicry which ennobled instead of degrading; that goodness of heart which appeared in every look and accent and gave additional value to every talent and acquirement. They will remember, too, that he whose name they hold in reverence was not less distinguished by the inflexible uprightness of his political conduct than by his loving disposition and his winning manners. They will remember that, in the last lines which he traced, he expressed his joy that he had done nothing unworthy of the friend of Fox and Grey; and they will have reason to feel similar joy if, in looking back on many troubled years, they cannot accuse themselves of having done anything unworthy of men who were distinguished by the friendship of Lord Holland.

WARREN HASTINGS. (OCTOBER, 1841.)

Memoirs of the Life of Warren Hastings, first Governor-General of Bengal. Compiled from Original Papers by the Rev. G. R. GLEIG, M.A. 3 vols. 8vo. London, 1841.

THIS book seems to have been manufactured in pursuance of a contract, by which the representatives of Warren Hastings, on the one part, bound themselves to furnish papers, and Mr. Gleig, on the other part, bound himself to furnish praise. It is but just to say that the covenants on both sides have been most faithfully kept; and the result is before us in the form of three big bad volumes, full of undigested correspondence and undiscerning panegyric.

If it were worth while to examine this performance in detail, we could easily make a long article by merely pointing out inaccurate statements, inelegant expressions and immoral doctrines. But it would be idle to waste criticism on a bookmaker; and, whatever credit Mr. Gleig may have justly earned by former works, it is as a bookmaker, and nothing more, that he now comes before us. More eminent men than Mr. Gleig have written nearly as ill as he, when they have stooped to similar drudgery. It would be unjust to estimate Goldsmith by the "Vicar of Wakefield" or Scott by the "Life of Napoleon." Mr. Gleig is neither a Goldsmith nor a Scott; but it would be unjust to deny that he is capable of something better than these Memoirs. It would also, we hope and believe, be unjust to charge any Christian minister with the guilt of deliberately maintaining some propositions which we find in this book. It is not too much to say that Mr. Gleig has written several passages which bear the same relation to the "Prince" of Machiavelli that the "Prince" of Machiavelli bears to the "Whole Duty of Man," and which would excite amazement in a den of robbers or on board of a schooner of pirates. But we are willing to attribute these offences to haste, to thoughtlessness, and to that disease of the understanding which may be called the *Furor Biographicus*, and which is to writers of lives what the *goitre* is to an Alpine shepherd or dirt-eating to a Negro slave.

We are inclined to think that we shall best meet the wishes of our readers if, instead of dwelling on the faults of this book, we attempt to give, in a way necessarily hasty and imperfect, our own view of the life and character of Mr. Hastings. Our feeling towards him is not exactly that of the House of Commons which impeached him in 1787 ; neither is it that of the House of Commons which uncovered and stood up to receive him in 1813. He had great qualities and he rendered great services to the state. But to represent him as a man of stainless virtue is to make him ridiculous ; and from regard for his memory, if from no other feeling, his friends would have done well to lend no countenance to such adulation. We believe that, if he were now living, he would have sufficient judgment and sufficient greatness of mind to wish to be shown as he was. He must have known that there were dark spots on his fame. He might also have felt with pride that the splendour of his fame would bear many spots. He would have wished posterity to have a likeness of him, though an unfavourable likeness, rather than a daub at once insipid and unnatural, resembling neither him nor anybody else. "Paint me as I am," said Oliver Cromwell, while sitting to young Lely. "If you leave out the scars and wrinkles, I will not pay you a shilling." Even in such a trifle the great Protector showed both his good sense and his magnanimity. He did not wish all that was characteristic in his countenance to be lost in the vain attempt to give him the regular features and smooth blooming cheeks of the curl-pated minions of James I. He was content that his face should go forth marked with all the blemishes which had been put on it by time, by war, by sleepless nights, by anxiety, perhaps by remorse ; but with valour, policy, authority and public care written in all its princely lines. If men truly great knew their own interest, it is thus that they would wish their minds to be portrayed.

Warren Hastings sprung from an ancient and illustrious race. It has been affirmed that his pedigree can be traced back to the great Danish sea-king whose sails were long the terror of both coasts of the British Channel, and who, after many fierce and doubtful struggles, yielded at last to the valour and genius of Alfred. But the undoubted splendour of the line of Hastings needs no illustration from fable. One branch of that line wore, in the fourteenth century, the coronet of Pembroke. From another branch sprang the renowned Chamberlain, the faithful adherent of the White Rose, whose fate has furnished so striking a theme both to poets and to historians. His family received from the Tudors the earldom of Huntingdon, which, after long dispossession, was regained in our time by a series of events scarcely paralleled in romance.

The lords of the manor of Daylesford, in Worcestershire, claimed to be considered as the heads of this distinguished family. The main stock, indeed, prospered less than some of the younger shoots. But the Daylesford family, though not ennobled, was wealthy and highly considered till, about two hundred years ago, it was overwhelmed by the great ruin of the civil war. The Hastings of that time was a zealous cavalier. He raised money on his lands, sent his plate to the mint at Oxford, joined the royal army, and, after spending half his property in the cause of King Charles, was glad to ransom himself by making over most of the remaining half to Speaker Lenthal. The old seat at Daylesford still remained in the family; but it could no longer be kept up, and in the following generation it was sold to a merchant of London.

Before this transfer took place, the last Hastings of Daylesford had presented his second son to the rectory of the parish in which the ancient residence of the family stood. The living was of little value; and the situation of the poor clergyman, after the sale of the estate, was deplorable. He was constantly engaged in lawsuits about his tithes with the new lord of the manor, and was at length utterly ruined. His eldest son, Howard, a well-conducted young man, obtained a place in the Customs. The second son, Pynaston, an idle, worthless boy, married before he was sixteen, lost his wife in two years, and went to the West Indies, where he died, leaving to the care of his unfortunate father a little orphan, destined to strange and memorable vicissitudes of fortune.

Warren, the son of Pynaston, was born on the sixth of December, 1732. His mother died a few days later, and he was left dependent on his distressed grandfather. The child was early sent to the village school, where he learned his letters on the same bench with the sons of the peasantry; nor did anything in his garb or face indicate that his life was to take a widely different course from that of the young rustics with whom he studied and played. But no cloud could overcast the dawn of so much genius and so much ambition. The very ploughmen observed, and long remembered, how kindly little Warren took to his book. The daily sight of the lands which his ancestors had possessed, and which had passed into the hands of strangers, filled his young brain with wild fancies and projects. He loved to hear stories of the wealth and greatness of his progenitors, of their splendid housekeeping, their loyalty and their valour. On one bright summer day, the boy, then just seven years old, lay on the bank of the rivulet which flows through the old domain of his house to join the Isis. There, as threescore and ten years later he told the tale, rose in his mind a scheme which, through all the turns of his eventful career, was never abandoned. He would recover the estate which had belonged to his fathers. He would be Hastings of Daylesford. This purpose, formed in infancy and poverty, grew stronger as his intellect expanded and as his fortune rose. He pursued his plan with that calm but indomitable force of will which was the most striking peculiarity of his character. When, under a tropical sun, he ruled fifty millions of Asiatics, his hopes, amidst all the cares of war, finance and legislation, still pointed to Daylesford. And when his long public life, so singularly chequered with good and evil, with glory and obloquy, had at length closed for ever, it was to Daylesford that he retired to die.

When he was eight years old, his uncle Howard determined to take charge of him and to give him a liberal education. The boy went up to London, and was sent to a school at Newington, where he was well taught but ill fed. He always attributed the smallness of his stature to the hard and scanty fare of this seminary. At ten he was removed to Westminster school, then flourishing under the care of Dr. Nichols. Vinny Bourne, as his pupils affectionately called him, was one of the masters. Churchill, Colman, Lloyd, Cumberland, Cowper, were among the students. With Cowper, Hastings formed a friendship, which neither the lapse of time nor a wide dissimilarity of opinions and pursuits could wholly dissolve. It does not appear that they ever met after they had grown to manhood. But forty years later, when the voices of many great orators were crying for vengeance on the oppressor of India, the shy and secluded poet could image to himself Hastings the Governor-General only as the Hastings with whom he had rowed on the Thames and played in the cloister, and refused to believe that so good-tempered a fellow could have done anything very wrong. His own life had been spent in praying, musing and rhyming among the water-lilies of the Ouse. He had preserved in no common measure the innocence of childhood. His spirit had indeed been severely tried, but not by temptations which impelled him to any gross violation of the rules of social morality. He had never been attacked by combinations of powerful and deadly enemies. He had never been compelled to make a choice between innocence and greatness, between crime and ruin. Firmly as he held in theory the doctrine of human depravity, his habits were such that he was unable to conceive how far from the path of right even kind and noble natures may be hurried by the rage of conflict and the lust of dominion.

Hastings had another associate at Westminster of whom we shall have occasion to make frequent mention—Elijah Impey. We know little about their school days. But, we think, we may safely venture to guess that, whenever Hastings wished to play any trick more than usually naughty, he hired Impey with a tart or a ball to act as fag in the worst part of the prank.

Warren was distinguished among his comrades as an excellent swimmer, boatman and scholar. At fourteen he was first in the examination for the foundation. His name in gilded letters on the walls of the dormitory still attests his victory over many older competitors. He stayed two years longer at the school and was looking forward to a studentship at Christ Church, when an event happened which changed the whole course of his life. Howard Hastings died, bequeathing his nephew to the care of a friend and distant relation named Chiswick. This gentleman, though he did not absolutely refuse the charge, was desirous to rid himself of it as soon as possible. Dr. Nichols made strong remonstrances against the cruelty of interrupting the studies of a youth who seemed likely to be one of the first scholars of the age. He even offered to bear the expense of sending his favourite pupil to Oxford. But Mr. Chiswick was inflexible. He thought the years which had already been wasted on hexameters and pentameters quite sufficient. He had it in his power to obtain for the lad a writership in the service of the East India Company. Whether the young adventurer, when once shipped off, made a fortune or died of a liver complaint, he equally ceased to be a burden to anybody. Warren was accordingly removed from Westminster school and placed for a few months at a commercial academy to study arithmetic and book-keeping. In January, 1750, a few days after he had completed his seventeenth year, he sailed for Bengal, and arrived at his destination in the October following.

He was immediately placed at a desk in the Secretary's office at Calcutta, and laboured there during two years. Fort William was then a purely commercial settlement. In the south of India, the encroaching policy of Dupleix had transformed the servants of the English Company, against their will, into diplomatists and generals. The war of the succession was raging in the Carnatic; and the tide had been suddenly turned against the French by the genius of young Robert Clive. But in Bengal the European settlers, at peace with the natives and with each other, were wholly occupied with ledgers and bills of lading.

After two years passed in keeping accounts at Calcutta, Hastings was sent up the country to Cossimbazar, a town which lies on the Hoogley, about a mile from Moorshedabad, and which then bore to Moorshedabad a relation, if we may compare small things with great, such as the city of London bears to Westminster. Moorshedabad was the abode of the prince who, by an authority ostensibly derived from the Mogul, but really independent, ruled the three great provinces of Bengal, Orissa and Bahar. At Moorshedab were the court, the harem and the public offices. Cossimbazar was a port and a place of trade, renowned for the quantity and excellence of the silks which were sold in its marts, and constantly receiving and sending forth fleets of richly laden barges. At this important point, the Company had established a small factory subordinate to that of Fort William. Here, during several years, Hastings was employed in making bargains for stuffs with native brokers. While he was thus engaged, Surajah Dowlah succeeded to the government, and declared war against the English. The defenceless settlement of Cossimbazar, lying close to the tyrant's capital, was instantly seized. Hastings was sent a prisoner to Moorshedabad, but, in consequence of the humane intervention of the servants of the Dutch Company, was treated with indulgence. Meanwhile the Nabob marched on Calcutta; the governor and the commandant fled; the town and citadel were taken, and most of the English prisoners perished in the Black Hole.

In these events originated the greatness of Warren Hastings. The fugitive governor and his companions had taken refuge on the dreary islet of Fulda, near the mouth of the Hoogley. They were naturally desirous to obtain full information respecting the proceedings of the Nabob; and no person seemed so likely to furnish it as Hastings, who was a prisoner at large in the immediate neighbourhood of the court. He thus became a diplomatic agent, and soon established a high character for ability and resolution. The treason which at a later period was fatal to Surajah Dowlah was already in progress; and Hastings was admitted to the deliberations of the conspirators. But the time for striking had not arrived. It was necessary to postpone the execution of the design; and Hastings, who was now in extreme peril, fled to Fulda.

Soon after his arrival at Fulda, the expedition from Madras, commanded by Clive, appeared in the Hoogley. Warren, young, intrepid and excited probably by the example of the Commander of the Forces, who, having like himself been a mercantile agent of the Company, had been turned by public calamities into a soldier, determined to serve in the ranks. During the early operations of the war he carried a musket. But the quick eye of Clive soon perceived that the head of the young volunteer would be more useful than his arm. When, after the battle of Plassey, Meer Jaffier was proclaimed Nabob of Bengal, Hastings was appointed to reside at the court of the new prince as agent for the Company.

He remained at Moorshedabad till the year 1761, when he became a Member of Council, and was consequently forced to reside at Calcutta. This was during the interval between Clive's first and second administration—an interval which has left on the face of the East India Company a stain not wholly effaced by many years of just and humane government. Mr. Vansittart, the Governor, was at the head of a new and anomalous empire. On one side was a band of English functionaries, daring, intelligent, eager to be rich. On the other side was a great native population, helpless, timid, accustomed to crouch under oppression. To keep the stronger race from preying on the weaker was an undertaking which tasked to the utmost the talents and energy of Clive. Vansittart, with fair intentions, was a feeble and inefficient ruler. The master caste, as was natural, broke loose from all restraint; and then was seen what we believe to be the most frightful of all spectacles, the strength of civilisation without its mercy. To all other despotism there is a check, imperfect, indeed, and liable to gross abuse, but still sufficient to preserve society from the last extreme of misery. A time comes when the evils of submission are obviously greater than those of resistance, when fear itself begets a sort of courage, when a convulsive burst of popular rage and despair warns tyrants not to presume too far on the patience of mankind. But against misgovernment such as then afflicted Bengal it was impossible to struggle. The superior intelligence and energy of the dominant class made their power irresistible. A war of Bengalees against Englishmen was like a war of sheep against wolves, of men against dæmons. The only protection which the conquered could find was in the moderation, the clemency, the enlarged policy of the conquerors. That protection, at a later period, they found. But at first English power came among them unaccompanied by English morality. There was an interval between the time at which they became our subjects and the time at which we began to reflect that we were bound to discharge towards them the duties of rulers. During that interval the business of a servant of the Company was simply to wring out of the natives a hundred or two hundred thousand pounds as speedily as possible, that he might return home before his constitution had suffered from the heat, to marry a peer's daughter, to buy rotten boroughs in Cornwall and to give balls in St. James's Square. Of the conduct of Hastings at this time little is known; but the little that is known, and the circumstance that little is known, must be considered as honourable to him. He could not protect the natives: all that he could do was to abstain from plundering and oppressing them; and this he appears to have done. It is certain that at this time he continued poor; and it is equally certain that by cruelty and dishonesty he might easily have become rich. It is certain that he was never charged with having borne a share in the abuses which then prevailed; and it is almost equally certain that, if he had borne a share in those abuses, the able and bitter enemies who afterwards persecuted him would not have failed to discover and to proclaim his guilt. The keen, severe and even malevolent scrutiny to which his whole public life was subjected—a scrutiny unparalleled, as we believe, in the history of mankind—is in one respect advantageous to his reputation. It brought many lamentable blemishes to light; but it entitles him to be considered pure from every blemish which has not been brought to light.

The truth is that the temptations to which so many English functionaries yielded in the time of Mr. Vansittart were not temptations addressed to the ruling passions of Warren Hastings. He was not squeamish in pecuniary transactions; but he was neither sordid nor rapacious. He was far too enlightened a man to look on a great empire merely as a buccaneer would look on a galleon. Had his heart been much worse than it was, his understanding would have preserved him from that extremity of baseness. He was an unscrupulous, perhaps an unprincipled, statesman; but still he was a statesman and not a freebooter.

In 1764 Hastings returned to England. He had realised only a very moderate fortune; and that moderate fortune was soon reduced to nothing, partly by his praiseworthy liberality and partly by his mismanagement. Towards his relations he appears to have acted very generously. The greater part of his savings he left in Bengal, hoping probably to obtain the high usury of India. But high usury and bad security generally go together; and Hastings lost both interest and principal.

He remained four years in England. Of his life at this time very little is known. But it has been asserted, and is highly probable, that liberal studies and the society of men of letters occupied a great part of his time. It is to be remembered to his honour that, in days when the languages of the East were regarded by other servants of the Company merely as the means of communicating with weavers and money-changers, his enlarged and accomplished mind sought in Asiatic learning for new forms of intellectual enjoyment and for new views of government and society. Perhaps, like most persons who have paid much attention to departments of knowledge which lie out of the common track, he was inclined to overrate the value of his favourite studies. He conceived that the cultivation of Persian literature might with advantage be made a part of the liberal education of an English gentleman; and he drew up a plan with that view. It is said that the University of Oxford, in which Oriental learning had never, since the revival of letters, been wholly neglected, was to be the seat of the institution which he contemplated. An endowment was expected from the munificence of the Company: and professors thoroughly competent to interpret Hafiz and Ferdusi were to be engaged in the East. Hastings called on Johnson, with the hope, as it should seem, of interesting in this project a man who enjoyed the highest literary reputation, and who was particularly connected with Oxford. The interview appears to have left on Johnson's mind a most favourable impression of the talents and attainments of his visitor. Long after, when Hastings was ruling the immense population of British India, the old philosopher wrote to him, and referred in the most courtly terms, though with great dignity, to their short but agreeable intercourse.

Hastings soon began to look again towards India. He had little to attach him to England; and his pecuniary embarrassments were great. He solicited his old masters the Directors for employment. They acceded to his request, with high compliments both to his abilities and to his integrity, and appointed him a Member of Council at Madras. It would be unjust not to mention that, though forced to borrow money for his outfit, he did not withdraw any portion of the sum which he had appropriated to the relief of his distressed relations. In the spring of 1769 he embarked on board of the *Duke of Grafton*, and commenced a voyage distinguished by incidents which might furnish matter for a novel.

Among the passengers in the *Duke of Grafton* was a German of the name of Imhoff. He called himself a Baron; but he was in distressed circumstances and was going out to Madras as a portrait-painter, in the hope of picking up some of the pagodas which were then lightly got and as lightly spent by the English in India. The Baron was accompanied by his wife, a native, we have somewhere read, of Archangel. This young woman, who, born under the Arctic circle, was destined to play the part of a Queen under the tropic of Cancer, had an agreeable person, a cultivated mind, and manners in the highest degree engaging. She despised her husband heartily, and, as the story which we have to tell sufficiently proves, not without reason. She was interested by the conversation and flattered by the attentions of Hastings. The situation was indeed perilous. No place is so propitious to the formation either of close friendships or of deadly enmities as an Indiaman. There are very few people who do not find a voyage which lasted several months insupportably dull. Anything is welcome which may break that long monotony, a sail, a shark, an albatross, a man overboard. Most passengers find some resource in eating twice as many meals as on land. But the great devices for killing the time are quarrelling and flirting. The facilities for both these exciting pursuits are great. The inmates of the ship are thrown together far more than in any country-seat or boarding-house. None can escape from the rest except by imprisoning himself in a cell in which he can hardly turn. All food, all exercise is taken in company. Ceremony is to a great extent banished. It is every day in the power of a mischievous person to inflict innumerable annoyances; it is every day in the power of an amiable person to confer little services. It not seldom happens that serious distress and danger call forth, in genuine beauty and deformity, heroic virtues and abject vices which, in the ordinary intercourse of good society, might remain during many years unknown even to intimate associates. Under such circumstances met Warren Hastings and the Baroness Imhoff; two persons whose accomplishments would have attracted notice in any court of Europe. The gentleman had no domestic ties. The lady was tied to a husband for whom she had no regard and who had no regard for his own honour. An attachment sprang up, which was soon strengthened by events such as could hardly have occurred on land. Hastings fell ill. The Baroness nursed him with womanly tenderness, gave him his medicines with her own hand, and even sat up in his cabin while he slept. Long before the *Duke of Grafton* reached Madras, Hastings was in love. But his love was of a most characteristic description. Like his hatred, like his ambition, like all his passions, it was strong, but not impetuous. It was calm, deep, earnest, patient of delay, unconquerable by time. Imhoff was called into council by his wife and his wife's lover. It was arranged that the Baroness should institute a suit for a divorce in the courts of Franconia; that the Baron should afford every facility to the proceeding; and that during the years which might elapse before the sentence should be pronounced they should continue to live together. It was also agreed that Hastings should bestow some very substantial marks of gratitude on the complaisant husband, and should, when the marriage was dissolved, make the lady his wife and adopt the children whom she had already born to Imhoff.

We are not inclined to judge either Hastings or the Baroness severely. There was undoubtedly much to extenuate their fault. But we can by no means concur with the Rev. Mr. Gleig, who carries his partiality to so injudicious an extreme as to describe the conduct of Imhoff—conduct the baseness of which is the best excuse for the lovers—as "wise and judicious."

At Madras, Hastings found the trade of the Company in a very disorganised state. His own tastes would have led him rather to political than to commercial pursuits; but he knew that the favour of his employers depended chiefly on their dividends, and their dividends depended chiefly on the investment. He therefore, with great judgment, determined to apply his vigorous mind for a time to this department of business, which had been much neglected since the servants of the Company had ceased to be clerks and had become warriors and negotiators.

In a very few months he effected an important reform. The Directors notified to him their high approbation, and were so much pleased with his conduct that they determined to place him at the head of the government of Bengal. Early in 1772 he quitted Fort St. George for his new post. The Imhoffs, who were still man and wife, accompanied him, and lived at Calcutta "on the same wise and judicious plan" (we quote the words of Mr. Gleig) which they had already followed during more than two years.

When Hastings took his seat at the head of the council board, Bengal was still governed according to the system which Clive had devised—a system which was, perhaps, skilfully contrived for the purpose of facilitating and concealing a great revolution, but which, when that revolution was complete and irrevocable, could produce nothing but inconvenience. There were two governments, the real and the ostensible. The supreme power belonged to the Company, and was in truth the most despotic power that can be conceived. The only restraint on the English masters of the country was that which their own justice and humanity imposed on them. There was no constitutional check on their will, and resistance to them was utterly hopeless.

But though thus absolute in reality, the English had not yet assumed the style of sovereignty. They held their territories as vassals of the throne of Delhi; they raised their revenues as collectors appointed by the imperial commission; their public seal was inscribed with the imperial titles; and their mint struck only the imperial coin.

There was still a nabob of Bengal, who stood in the English rulers of his country in the same relation in which Augustulus stood to Odoacer, or the last Merovingians to Charles Martel and Pepin. He lived at Moorshedabad, surrounded by princely magnificence. He was approached with outward marks of reverence, and his name was used in public instruments. But in the government of the country he had less real share than the youngest writer or cadet in the Company's service.

The English council which represented the Company at Calcutta was constituted on a very different plan from that which has since been adopted. At present the Governor is, as to all executive measures, absolute. He can declare war, conclude peace, appoint public functionaries or remove them, in opposition to the unanimous sense of those who sit with him in council. They are, indeed, entitled to know all that is done, to discuss all that is done, to advise, to remonstrate, to send home protests. But it is with the Governor that the supreme power resides, and on him that the whole responsibility rests. This system, which was introduced by Mr. Pitt and Mr. Dundas in spite of the strenuous opposition of Mr. Burke, we conceive to be on the whole the best that was ever devised for the government of a country where no materials can be found for a representative constitution. In the time of Hastings, the Governor had only one vote in council, and, in case of an equal division, a casting vote. It therefore happened not unfrequently that he was overruled on the gravest questions; and it was possible that he might be wholly excluded, for years together, from the real direction of public affairs.

The English functionaries at Fort William had as yet paid little or no attention to the internal government of Bengal. The only branch of politics about which they much busied themselves was negotiation with the native princes. The police, the administration of justice, the details of the collection of revenue were almost entirely neglected. We may remark that the phraseology of the Company's servants still bears the trace of this state of things. To this day they always use the word "political" as synonymous with "diplomatic." We could name a gentleman still living, who was described by the highest authority as an invaluable public servant, eminently fit to be at the head of the departments of finance, revenue and justice, but unfortunately quite ignorant of all political business.

The internal government of Bengal, the English rulers delegated to a great native minister, who was stationed at Moorshedabad. All military affairs and, with the exception of what pertains to mere ceremonial, all foreign affairs were withdrawn from his control; but the other departments of the administration were entirely confided to him. His own stipend amounted to near a hundred thousand pounds sterling a-year. The civil list of the nabob, amounting to more than three hundred thousand pounds a-year, passed through the minister's hands and was to a great extent at his disposal. The collection of the revenue, the superintendence of the household of the Prince, the administration of justice, the maintenance of order were left to this high functionary; and for the exercise of his immense power he was responsible to none but the British masters of the country.

A situation so important, lucrative and splendid was naturally an object of ambition to the ablest and most powerful natives. Clive had found it difficult to decide between conflicting pretensions. Two candidates stood out prominently from the crowd, each of them the representative of a race and of a religion.

One of these was Mahommed Reza Khan, a Mussulman of Persian extraction, able, active, religious after the fashion of his people, and highly esteemed by them. In England he might perhaps have been regarded as a corrupt and greedy politician. But, tried by the lower standard of Indian morality, he might be considered as a man of integrity and honour.

His competitor was a Hindoo Brahmin whose name has, by a terrible and melancholy event, been inseparably associated with that of Warren Hastings— the Maharajar Nuncomar. This man had played an important part in all the revolutions which, since the time of Surajah Dowlah, had taken place in Bengal. To the consideration which in that country belongs to high and pure caste, he added the weight which is derived from wealth, talents and experience. Of his moral character it is difficult to give a notion to those who are acquainted with human nature only as it appears in our island. What the Italian is to Englishman, what the Hindoo is to the Italian, what the Bengalee is to other Hindoos, that was Nuncomar to other Bengalees. The physical organisation of the Bengalee is feeble even to effeminacy. He lives in a constant vapour bath. His pursuits are sedentary, his limbs delicate, his movements languid. During many ages he has been trampled upon by men of bolder and more hardy breeds. Courage, independence, veracity, are qualities to which his constitution and his situation are equally unfavourable. His mind bears a singular analogy to his body. It is weak even to helplessness for purposes of manly resistance; but its suppleness and its tact move the children of sterner climates to admiration not unmingled with contempt. All those arts which are the natural defence of the weak are more familiar to this subtle race than to the Ionian of the time of Juvenal or to the Jew of the dark ages. What the horns are to the buffalo, what the paw is to the tiger, what the sting is to the bee, what beauty, according to the old Greek song, is to woman, deceit is to the Bengalee. Large promises, smooth excuses, elaborate tissues of circumstantial falsehood, chicanery, perjury, forgery, are the weapons offensive and defensive of the people of the Lower Ganges. All those millions do not furnish one sepoy to the armies of the Company. But as usurers, as moneychangers, as sharp legal practitioners, no class of human beings can bear a comparison with them. With all his softness, the Bengalee is by no means placable in his enmities or prone to pity. The pertinacity with which he adheres to his purposes yields only to the immediate pressure of fear. Nor does he lack a certain kind of courage which is often wanting to his masters. To inevitable evils he is sometimes found to oppose a passive fortitude such as the Stoics attributed to their ideal sage. An European warrior, who rushes on a battery of cannon with a loud hurrah, will shriek under the surgeon's knife and fall into an agony of despair at the sentence of death. But the Bengalee, who would see his country overrun, his house laid in ashes, his children murdered or dishonoured, without having the spirit to strike one blow, has yet been known to endure torture with the firmness of Mucius and to mount the scaffold with the steady step and even pulse of Algernon Sidney.

In Nuncomar, the national character was strongly and with exaggeration personified. The company's servants had repeatedly detected him in the most criminal intrigues. On one occasion he brought a false charge against another Hindoo and tried to substantiate it by producing forged documents. On another occasion it was discovered that, while professing the strongest attachment to the English, he was engaged in several conspiracies against them, and in particular that he was the medium of a correspondence between the court of Delhi and the French authorities in the Carnatic. For these and similar practices he had been long detained in confinement. But his talents and influence had not only procured his liberation, but had obtained for him a certain degree of consideration even among the British rulers of his country.

Clive was extremely unwilling to place a Mussulman at the head of the administration of Bengal. On the other hand, he could not bring himself to confer immense power on a man to whom every sort of villany had repeatedly been brought home. Therefore, though the Nabob, over whom Nuncomar had by intrigue acquired great influence, begged that the artful Hindoo might be intrusted with the government, Clive, after some hesitation, decided honestly and wisely in favour of Mahommed Reza Khan, who, when Hastings became governor, had held his high office seven years. An infant son of Meer Jaffier was now nabob; and the guardianship of the young prince's person had been confided to the minister.

Nuncomar, stimulated at once by cupidity and malice, had been constantly attempting to undermine his successful rival. This was not difficult. The revenues of Bengal, under the administration established by Clive, did not yield such a surplus as had been anticipated by the Company; for, at that time, the most absurd notions were entertained in England respecting the wealth of India. Palaces of porphyry, hung with the richest brocade, heaps of pearls and diamonds, vaults from which pagodas and gold mohurs were measured out by the bushel, filled the imagination even of men of business. Nobody seemed to be aware of what nevertheless was most undoubtedly the truth, that India was a much poorer country than countries which in Europe are reckoned poor, than Ireland, for example, than Portugal, than Sweden. It was confidently believed by Lords of the Treasury and members for the city that Bengal would not only defray its own charges, but would afford an increased dividend to the proprietors of India stock and large relief to the English finances. These absurd expectations were disappointed; and the Directors, naturally enough, chose to attribute the disappointment rather to the mismanagement of Mahommed Reza Khan than to their own ignorance of the country intrusted to their care. They were confirmed in their error by the agents of Nuncomar; for Nurcomar had agents even in Leadenhall Street. Soon after Hastings reached Calcutta, he received a letter addressed by the Court of Directors, not to the Council generally, but to himself in particular. He was directed to remove Mahommed Reza Khan, to arrest him, together with all his family and all his partisans, and to institute a strict inquiry into the whole administration of the province. It was added that the Governor would do well to avail himself of the assistance of Nuncomar in the investigation. The vices of Nuncomar were acknowledged. But even from his vices, it was said, much advantage might at such a conjuncture be derived; and, though he could not safely be trusted, it might still be proper to encourage him by hopes of reward.

The Governor bore no good will to Nuncomar. Many years before, they had known each other at Moorshedabad; and then a quarrel had arisen between them which all the authority of their superiors could hardly compose. Widely as they differed in most points, they resembled each other in this, that both were men of unforgiving natures. To Mahommed Reza Khan, on the other hand, Hastings had no feelings of hostility. Nevertheless he proceeded to execute the instructions of the Company with an alacrity which he never showed, except when instructions were in perfect conformity with his own views. He had, wisely as we think, determined to get rid of the system of double government in Bengal. The orders of the Directors furnished him with the means of effecting his purpose and dispensed him from the necessity of discussing the matter with his Council. He took his measures with his usual vigour and dexterity. At midnight, the palace of Mahommed Reza Khan at Moorshedabad was surrounded by a battalion of Sepoys. The Minister was roused from his slumbers and informed that he was a prisoner. With the Mussulman gravity, he bent his head and submitted himself to the will of God. He fell not alone. A chief named Schitab Roy had been intrusted with the government of Bahar. His valor and his attachment to the English had more than once been signally proved. On that memorable day on which the people of Patna saw from their walls the whole army of the Mogul scattered by the little band of Captain Knox, the voice of the British conquerors assigned the palm of gallantry to the brave Asiatic. "I never," said Knox, when he introduced Schitab Roy, covered with blood and dust, to the English functionaries assembled in the factory, "I never saw a native fight so before." Schitab Roy was involved in the ruin of Mahommed Reza Khan, was deprived of his government and was placed under arrest. The members of the Council received no intimation of these measures till the prisoners were on their road to Calcutta.

The inquiry into the conduct of the minister was postponed on different pretences. He was detained in an easy confinement during many months. In the meantime, the great revolution which Hastings had planned was carried into effect. The office of minister was abolished. The internal administration was transferred to the servants of the Company. A system—a very imperfect system, it is true—of civil and criminal justice, under English superintendence, was established. The Nabob was no longer to have even an ostensible share in the government; but he was still to receive a considerable annual allowance and to be surrounded with the state of sovereignty. As he was an infant, it was necessary to provide guardians for his person and property. His person was intrusted to a lady of his father's harem, known by the name of the Munny Begum. The office of treasurer of the household was bestowed on a son of Nuncomar named Goordas. Nuncomar's services were wanted; yet he could not safely be trusted with power; and Hastings thought it a masterstroke of policy to reward the able and unprincipled parent by promoting the inoffensive child.

The revolution completed, the double government dissolved, the Company installed in the full sovereignty of Bengal, Hastings had no motive to treat the late ministers with rigour. Their trial had been put off on various pleas till the new organisation was complete. They were then brought before a committee, over which the Governor presided. Schitab Roy was speedily acquitted with honour. A formal apology was made to him for the restraint to which he had been subjected. All the Eastern marks of respect were bestowed on him. He was clothed in a robe of state, presented with jewels and with a richly-harnessed elephant, and sent back to his government at Patna. But his health had suffered from confinement; his high spirit had been cruelly wounded; and soon after his liberation he died of a broken heart.

The innocence of Mahommed Reza Khan was not so clearly established. But the Governor was not disposed to deal harshly. After a long hearing, in which Nuncomar appeared as the accuser, and displayed both the art and the inveterate rancour which distinguished him, Hastings pronounced that the charges had not been made out, and ordered the fallen minister to be set at liberty.

Nuncomar had purposed to destroy the Mussulman administration and to rise on its ruin. Both his malevolence and his cupidity had been disappointed. Hastings had made him a tool—had used him for the purpose of accomplishing the transfer of the government from Moorshedabad to Calcutta, from native to European hands. The rival, the enemy, so long envied, so implacably persecuted, had been dismissed unhurt. The situation so long and ardently desired had been abolished. It was natural that the Governor should be from that time an object of the most intense hatred to the vindictive Brahmin. As yet, however, it was necessary to suppress such feelings. The time was coming when that long animosity was to end in a desperate and deadly struggle.

In the meantime, Hastings was compelled to turn his attention to foreign affairs. The object of his diplomacy was at this time simply to get money. The finances of his government were in an embarrassed state, and this embarrassment he was determined to relieve by some means, fair or foul. The principle which directed all his dealings with his neighbours is fully expressed by the old motto of one of the great predatory families of Teviotdale, "Thou shalt want ere I want." He seems to have laid it down, as a fundamental proposition which could not be disputed, that, when he had not as many lacs of rupees as the public service required, he was to take them from anybody who had. One thing, indeed, is to be said in excuse for him. The pressure applied to him by his employers at home was such as only the highest virtue could have withstood—such as left him no choice except to commit great wrongs or to resign his high post, and with that post all his hopes of fortune and distinction. It is perfectly true that the Directors never enjoined or applauded any crime. Far from it. Whoever examines their letters at that time will find there many just and humane sentiments, many excellent precepts—in short, an admirable code of political ethics. But every exhortation is modified or nullified by a demand for money. "Govern leniently and send more money; practise strict justice and moderation towards neighbouring powers and send more money;" this is, in truth, the sum of almost all the instructions that Hastings ever received from home. Now these instructions, being interpreted, mean simply, "Be the father and the oppressor of the people; be just and unjust, moderate and rapacious." The Directors dealt with India as the Church in the good old times dealt with a heretic. They delivered the victim over to the executioners with an earnest request that all possible tenderness might be shown. We by no means accuse or suspect those who framed these despatches of hypocrisy. It is probable that, writing fifteen thousand miles from the place where their orders were to be carried into effect, they never perceived the gross inconsistency of which they were guilty. But the inconsistency was at once manifest to their lieutenant at Calcutta, who, with an empty treasury, with an unpaid army, with his own salary often in arrear, with deficient crops, with government tenants daily running away, was called upon to remit home another half million without fail. Hastings saw that it was absolutely necessary for him to disregard either the moral discourses or the pecuniary requisitions of his employers. Being forced to disobey them in something, he had to consider what kind of disobedience they would most readily pardon; and he correctly judged that the safest course would be to neglect the Sermons and find the Rupees.

A mind so fertile as his, and so little restrained by conscientious scruples, speedily discovered several modes of relieving the financial embarrassments of the government. The allowance of the Nabob of Bengal was reduced at a stroke from £320,000 a-year to half that sum. The Company had bound itself to pay near £300,000 a-year to the Great Mogul as a mark of homage for the provinces which he had intrusted to their care, and they had ceded to him the districts of Corah and Allahabad. On the plea that the Mogul was not really independent, but merely a tool in the hands of others, Hastings determined to retract these concessions. He accordingly declared that the English would pay no more tribute, and sent troops to occupy Allahabad and Corah. The situation of these places were such that there would be little advantage and great expense in retaining them. Hastings, who wanted money and not territory, determined to sell them. A purchaser was not wanting. The rich province of Oude had, in the general dissolution of the Mogul empire, fallen to the share of the great Mussulman house by which it is still governed. About twenty years ago, this house, by the permission of the British government, assumed the royal title; but in the time of Warren Hastings such an assumption would have been considered by the Mahommedans of India as a monstrous impiety. The Prince of Oude, though he held the power, did not venture to use the style of sovereignty. To the appellation of Nabob or Viceroy he added that of Vizier of the monarchy of Hindostan, just as in the last century the Electors of Saxony and Brandenburg, though independent of the Emperor and often in arms against him, were proud to style themselves his Grand Chamberlain and Grand Marshal. Sujah Dowlah, then Nabob Vizier, was on excellent terms with the English. He had a large treasure. Allahabad and Corah were so situated that they might be of use to him and could be of none to the Company. The buyer and seller soon came to an understanding; and the provinces which had been torn from the Mogul were made over to the government of Oude for about half a million sterling.

But there was another matter still more important to be settled by the Vizier and the Governor. The fate of a brave people was to be decided. It was decided in a manner which has left a lasting stain on the fame of Hastings and of England.

The people of Central Asia had always been to the inhabitants of India what the warriors of the German forests were to the subjects of the decaying monarchy of Rome. The dark, slender and timid Hindoo shrank from a conflict with the strong muscle and resolute spirit of the fair race which dwelt beyond the passes. There is reason to believe that, at a period anterior to the dawn of regular history, the people who spoke the rich and flexible Sanscrit came from regions lying far beyond the Hyphasis and the Hystaspes and imposed their yoke on the children of the soil. It is certain that, during the last ten centuries, a succession of invaders descended from the west on Hindostan; nor was the course of conquest ever turned back towards the setting sun till that memorable campaign in which the Cross of Saint George was planted on the walls of Ghizni.

The Emperors of Hindostan themselves came from the other side of the great mountain ridge; and it had always been their practice to recruit their army from the hardy and valiant race from which their own illustrious house sprang. Among the military adventurers who were allured to the Mogul standards from the neighbourhood of Cabul and Candahar, were conspicuous several gallant bands, known by the name of Rohillas. Their services had been rewarded with large tracts of land—fiefs of the spear, if we may use an expression drawn from an analogous state of things—in that fertile plain through which the Ramgunga flows from the snowy heights of Kumaon to join the Ganges. In the general confusion which followed the death of Aurungzebe, the warlike colony became virtually independent. The Rohillas were distinguished from the other inhabitants of India by a peculiarly fair complexion. They were more honourably distinguished by valour in war and by skill in the arts of peace. While anarchy raged from Lahore to Cape Comorin, their little territory enjoyed the blessings of repose under the guardianship of courage. Agriculture and commerce flourished among them; nor were they negligent of rhetoric and poetry. Many persons now living have heard aged men talk with regret of the golden days when the Afghan princes ruled in the vale of Rohilcund.

Sujah Dowlah had set his heart on adding this rich district to his own principality. Right, or show of right, he had absolutely none. His claim was in no respect better founded than that of Catherine to Poland, or that of the Bonaparte family to Spain. The Rohillas held their country by exactly the same title by which he held his, and had governed their country far better than his had ever been governed. Nor were they a people whom it was perfectly safe to attack. Their land was indeed an open plain destitute of natural defences; but their veins were full of the high blood of Afghanistan. As soldiers they had not the steadiness which is seldom found except in company with strict discipline; but their impetuous valour had been proved on many fields of battle. It was said that their chiefs, when united by common peril, could bring eighty thousand men into the field. Sujah Dowlah had himself seen them fight, and wisely shrank from a conflict with them. There was in India one army, and only one, against which even those proud Causican tribes could not stand. It had been abundantly proved that neither tenfold odds nor the martial ardour of the boldest Asiatic nations could avail aught against English science and resolution. Was it possible to induce the Governor of Bengal to let out to hire the irresistible energies of the imperial people, the skill against which the ablest chiefs of Hindostan were helpless as infants—the discipline which so often triumphed over the frantic struggles of fanaticism and despair—the unconquerable British courage which is never so sedate and stubborn as towards the close of a doubtful and murderous day?

This was what the Nabob Vizier asked, and what Hastings granted. A bargain was soon struck. Each of the negotiators had what the other wanted. Hastings was in need of funds to carry on the Government of Bengal and to send remittances to London; and Sujah Dowlah had an ample revenue. Sujah Dowlah was bent on subjugating the Rohillas; and Hastings had at his disposal the only force by which the Rohillas could be subjugated. It was agreed that an English army should be lent to the Nabob Vizier, and that for the loan he should pay £400,000 sterling, besides defraying all the charge of the troops while employed in his service.

"I really cannot see," says the Rev. Mr. Gleig, "upon what grounds, either of political or moral justice, this proposition deserves to be stigmatised as infamous." If we understand the meaning of words, it is infamous to commit a wicked action for hire, and it is wicked to engage in war without provocation. In this particular war, scarcely one aggravating circumstance was wanting. The object of the Rohilla war was this—to deprive a large population, who had never done us the least harm, of a good government, and to place them, against their will, under an execrably bad one. Nay, even this is not all. England now descended far below the level even of those petty German princes who about the same time sold us troops to fight the Americans. The hussar-mongers of Hesse and Anspach had at least the assurance that the expeditions on which their soldiers were to be employed would be conducted in conformity with the humane rules of civilised warfare. Was the Rohilla war likely to be so conducted? He well knew what Indian warfare was. He well knew that the power which he covenanted to put into Sujah Dowlah's hands would, in all probability, be atrociously abused, and he required no guarantee, no promise, that it should not be so abused. He did not even reserve to himself the right of withdrawing his aid in case of abuse, however gross. Mr. Gleig repeats Major Scott's absurd plea, that Hastings was justified in letting out English troops to slaughter the Rohillas because the Rohillas were not of Indian race, but a colony from a distant country. What were the English themselves? Was it for them to proclaim a crusade for the expulsion of all intruders from the countries watered by the Ganges? Did it lie in their mouths to contend that a foreign settler who establishes an Empire in India is a *caput lupinum*? What would they have said if any other power had, on such a ground, attacked Madras or Calcutta without the slightest provocation? Such a defence was wanting to make the infamy of the transaction complete. The atrocity of the crime and the hypocrisy of the apology are worthy of each other.

One of the three brigades of which the Bengal army consisted was sent under Colonel Champion to join Sujah Dowlah's forces. The Rohillas expostulated, entreated, offered a large ransom, but in vain. They then resolved to defend themselves to the last. A bloody battle was fought. "The enemy," says Colonel Champion, "gave proof of a good share of military knowledge; and it is impossible to describe a more obstinate firmness of resolution than they displayed. The dastardly sovereign of Oude fled from the field. The English were left unsupported; but their fire and their charge were irresistible. It was not, however, till the most distinguished chiefs had fallen, fighting bravely at the head of their troops, that the Rohilla ranks gave way. Then the Nabob Vizier and his rabble made their appearance, and hastened to plunder the camp of the valiant enemies whom they had never dared to look in the face. The soldiers of the Company, trained in an exact discipline, kept unbroken order while the tents were pillaged by these worthless allies. But many voices were heard to exclaim, "We have had all the fighting and those rogues are to have all the profit."

Then the horrors of Indian war were let loose on the fair valleys and cities of Rohilcund. The whole country was in a blaze. More than a hundred thousand people fled from their homes to pestilential jungles, preferring famine, and fever, and the haunts of tigers to the tyranny of him to whom an English and a Christian Government had, for shameful lucre, sold their substance, and their blood, and the honour of their wives and daughters. Colonel Champion remonstrated with the Nabob Vizier, and sent strong representations to Fort William; but the Governor had made no conditions as to the mode in which the war was to be carried on. He had troubled himself about nothing but his forty lacs; and, though he might disapprove of Sujah Dowlah's wanton barbarity, he did not think himself entitled to interfere except by offering advice. This delicacy excites the admiration of the Reverend biographer. "Mr. Hastings," he says, "could not himself dictate to the Nabob, nor permit the commander of the Company's troops to dictate how the war was to be carried on." No, to be sure, Mr. Hastings had only to put down by main force the brave struggles of innocent men fighting for their liberty. Their military resistance crushed, his duties ended; and he had then only to fold his arms and look on while their villages were burned, their children butchered and their women violated. Will Mr. Gleig seriously maintain this opinion? Is any rule more plain than this, that whoever voluntarily gives to another irresistible power over human beings is bound to take order that such power shall not be barbarously abused? But we beg pardon of our readers for arguing a point so clear.

We hasten to the end of this sad and disgraceful story. The war ceased. The finest population in India was subjected to a greedy, cowardly, cruel tyrant. Commerce and agriculture languished. The rich province which had tempted the cupidity of Sujah Dowlah became the most miserable part even of his miserable dominions. Yet is the injured nation not yet extinct. At long intervals gleams of its ancient spirit have flashed forth; and even at this day, valour, and self-respect, and a chivalrous feeling rare among Asiatics, and a bitter remembrance of the great crime of England distinguish that noble Afghan face. To this day they are regarded as the best of all sepoys at the cold steel; and it was very recently remarked, by one who had enjoyed great opportunities of observation, that the only natives of India to whom the word "gentleman" can with perfect propriety be applied are to be found among the Rohillas.

Whatever we may think of the morality of Hastings, it cannot be denied that the financial results of his policy did honour to his talents. In less than two years after he assumed the government, he had, without imposing any additional burdens on the people subject to his authority, added about £450,000 to the annual income of the Company, besides procuring about a million in ready money. He had also relieved the finances of Bengal from military expenditure, amounting to near £250,000 a year, and had thrown that charge on the Nabob of Oude. There can be no doubt that this was a result which, if it had been obtained by honest means, would have entitled him to the warmest gratitude of his country, and which, by whatever means obtained, proved that he possessed great talents for administration.

In the meantime, Parliament had been engaged in long and grave discussions on Asiatic affairs. The ministry of Lord North, in the session of 1773, introduced a measure which made a considerable change in the constitution of the Indian government. This law, known by the name of the Regulating Act, provided that the presidency of Bengal should exercise a control over the other possessions of the Company; that the chief of that presidency should be styled Governor-General; that he should be assisted by four Councillors; and that a supreme court of judicature, consisting of a chief justice and three inferior judges, should be established at Calcutta. This court was made independent of the Governor-General and Council, and was intrusted with a civil and criminal jurisdiction of immense and, at the same time, of undefined extent.

The Governor-General and Councillors were named in the act, and were to hold their situations for five years. Hastings was to be the first Governor-General. One of the four new Councillors, Mr. Barwell, an experienced servant of the Company, was then in India. The other three, General Clavering, Mr. Monson and Mr. Francis, were sent out from England.

The ablest of the new Councillors was, beyond all doubt, Philip Francis. His acknowledged compositions prove that he possessed considerable eloquence and information. Several years passed in the public offices had formed him to habits of business. His enemies had never denied that he had a fearless and manly spirit; and his friends, we are afraid, must acknowledge that his estimate of himself was extravagantly high, that his temper was irritable, that his deportment was often rude and petulant, and that his hatred was of intense bitterness and long duration.

It is scarcely possible to mention this eminent man without adverting for a moment to the question which his name at once suggests to every mind. Was he the author of the Letters of Junius? Our own firm belief is that he was. The external evidence is, we think, such as would support a verdict in a civil, nay, in a criminal, proceeding. The handwriting of Junius is the very peculiar handwriting of Francis, slightly disguised. As to the position, pursuits and connections of Junius, the following are the most important facts which can be considered as clearly proved: first, that he was acquainted with the technical forms of the secretary of state's office; secondly, that he was intimately acquainted with the business of the war office; thirdly, that he, during the year 1770, attended debates in the House of Lords and took notes of speeches particularly of the speeches of Lord Chatham; fourthly, that he bitterly resented the appointment of Mr. Chamier to the place of deputy secretary-at-war; fifthly, that he was bound by some strong tie to the first Lord Holland. Now, Francis passed some years in the secretary of state's office. He was subsequently chief clerk of the war-office. He repeatedly mentioned that he had himself, in 1770, heard speeches of Lord Chatham; and some of the speeches were actually printed from his notes. He resigned his clerkship at the war-office from resentment at the appointment of Mr. Chamier. It was by Lord Holland that he was first introduced into the public service. Now, here are five marks, all of which ought to be found in Junius. They are all five found in Francis. We do not believe that more than two of them can be found in any other person whatever; if this argument does not settle the question, there is an end of all reasoning on circumstantial evidence.

The internal evidence seems to us to point the same way. The style of Francis bears a strong resemblance to that of Junius; nor are we disposed to admit, what is generally taken for granted, that the acknowledged compositions of Francis are very decidedly inferior to the anonymous letters. The argument from inferiority, at all events, is one which may be urged with at least equal force against every claimant that has ever been mentioned, with the single exception of Burke, who certainly was not Junius. And what conclusion, after all, can be drawn from mere inferiority? Every writer must produce his best work; and the interval between his best work and his second best work may be very wide indeed. Nobody will say that the best letters of Junius are more decidedly superior to the acknowledged works of Francis than three or four of Corneille's tragedies to the rest, than three or four of Ben Jonson's comedies to the rest, than the "Pilgrim's Progress" to any other works of Bunyan, than "Don Quixote" to the other works of Cervantes. Nay, it is certain that the Man in the Mask, whoever he may have been, was a most unequal writer. To go no further than the letters which have the signature of Junius—the letter to the king and the letters to Horne Tooke have little in common, except the asperity; and asperity was an ingredient seldom wanting either in the writings or in the speeches of Francis.

Indeed, one of the strongest reasons for believing that Francis was Junius is the moral resemblance between the two men. It is not difficult, from the letters which, under various signatures, are known to have been written by Junius and from his dealings with Woodfall and others, to form a tolerably correct notion of his character. He was clearly a man not destitute of real patriotism and magnanimity—a man whose vices were not of a sordid kind. But he must also have been a man in the highest degree arrogant and insolent; a man prone to malevolence, and prone to the error of mistaking his malevolence for public virtue. "Doest thou well to be angry?" was the question asked in old time by the Hebrew prophet. And he answered, "I do well." This was evidently the temper of Junius; and to this cause we attribute the savage cruelty which disgraces several of his letters. No man is so merciless as he who, under a strong self-delusion, confounds his antipathies with his duties. It may be added that Junius, though allied with the democratic party by common enmities, was the very opposite of a democratic politician. While attacking individuals with a ferocity which perpetually violated all the laws of literary warfare, he regarded the most defective parts of old institutions with a respect amounting to pedantry—pleaded the cause of Old Sarum with fervour, and contemptuously told the capitalists of Manchester and Leeds that, if they wanted votes, they might buy land and become freeholders of Lancashire and Yorkshire. All this, we believe, might stand, with scarcely any change, for a character of Philip Francis.

It is not strange that the great anonymous writer should have been willing at that time to leave the country which had been so powerfully stirred by his eloquence. Everything had gone against him. That party which he clearly preferred to any other, the party of George Grenville, had been scattered by the death of its chief; and Lord Suffolk had led the greater part of it over to the ministerial benches. The ferment produced by the Middlesex election had gone down. Every faction must have been alike an object of aversion to Junius. His opinions on domestic affairs separated him from the ministry; his opinions on colonial affairs from the opposition. Under such circumstances, he had thrown down his pen in misanthropical despair. His farewell letter to Woodfall bears date the 19th of January, 1773. In that letter, he declared that he must be an idiot to write again; that he had meant well by the cause and the public; that both were given up; that there were not ten men who would act steadily together on any question. "But it is all alike," he added, "vile and contemptible. You have never flinched that I know of; and I shall always rejoice to hear of your prosperity." These were the last words of Junius. In a year from that time, Philip Francis was on his voyage to Bengal.

With the three new Councillors came out the judges of the Supreme Court. The chief justice was Sir Elijah Impey. He was an old acquaintance of Hastings; and it is probable that the Governor-General, if he had searched through all the inns of court, could not have found an equally serviceable tool. But the members of Council were by no means in an obsequious mood. Hastings greatly disliked the new form of government and had no very high opinion of his coadjutors. They had heard of this, and were disposed to be suspicious and punctilious. When men are in such a frame of mind, any trifle is sufficient to give occasion for dispute. The members of Council expected a salute of twenty-one guns from the batteries of Fort William. Hastings allowed them only seventeen. They landed in ill-humour. The first civilities were exchanged with cold reserve. On the morrow commenced that long quarrel which, after distracting British India, was renewed in England, and in which all the most eminent statesmen and orators of the age took active part on one or the other side.

Hastings was supported by Barwell. They had not always been friends. But the arrival of the new members of Council from England naturally had the effect of uniting the old servants of the Company. Clavering, Monson and Francis formed the majority. They instantly wrested the government out of the hands of Hasting; condemned, certainly not without justice, his late dealings with the Nabob Vizier; recalled the English agent from Oude and sent thither a creature of their own; ordered the brigade which had conquered the unhappy Rohillas to return to the Company's territories; and instituted a severe inquiry into the conduct of the war. Next, in spite of the Governor-General's remonstrances, they proceeded to exercise, in the most indiscreet manner, their new authority over the subordinate presidencies; threw all the affairs of Bombay into confusion; and interfered, with an incredible union of rashness and feebleness, in the intestine disputes of the Mahratta government. At the same time, they fell on the internal administration of Bengal, and attacked the whole fiscal and judicial system—a system which was undoubtedly defective, but which it was very improbable that gentlemen fresh from England would be competent to amend. The effect of their reforms was that all protection to life and property was withdrawn; and that gangs of robbers plundered and slaughtered with impunity in the very suburbs of Calcutta. Hastings continued to live in the Government House and to draw the salary of Governor-General. He continued even to take the lead at the council-board in the transaction of ordinary business; for his opponents could not but feel that he knew much of which they were ignorant, and that he decided, both surely and speedily, many questions which to them would have been hopelessly puzzling. But the higher powers of government and the most valuable patronage had been taken from him.

The natives soon found this out. They considered him as a fallen man; and they acted after their kind. Some of our readers may have seen, in India, a cloud of crows pecking a sick vulture to death—no bad type of what happens in that country as often as fortune deserts one who has been great and dreaded. In an instant, all the sycophants, who had lately been ready to lie for him, to forge for him, to pander for him, to poison for him, hasten to purchase the favour of his victorious enemies by accusing him. An Indian government has only to let it be understood that it wishes a particular man to be ruined, and in twenty-four hours it will be furnished with grave charges, supported by depositions so full and circumstantial, that any person unaccustomed to Asiatic mendacity would regard them as decisive. It is well if the signature of the destined victim is not counterfeited at the foot of some illegal compact, and if some treasonable paper is not slipped into a hiding-place in his house. Hastings was now regarded as helpless. The power to make or mar the fortune of every man in Bengal had passed, as it seemed, into the hands of his opponents. Immediately charges against the Governor-General began to pour in. They were eagerly welcomed by the majority, who, to do them justice, were men of too much honour knowingly to countenance false accusations, but who were not sufficiently acquainted with the East to be aware that, in that part of the world, a very little encouragement from power will call forth, in a week, more Oateses, and Bedloes, and Dangerfields, than Westminster Hall sees in a century.

It would have been strange indeed if, at such a juncture, Nuncomar had remained quiet. That bad man was stimulated at once by malignity, by avarice and by ambition. Now was the time to be avenged on his old enemy, to wreak a grudge of seventeen years, to establish himself in the favour of the majority of the Council, to become the greatest native in Bengal. From the time of the arrival of the new Councillors, he had paid the most marked court to them, and had in consequence been excluded with all indignity from the Government House. He now put into the hands of Francis, with great ceremony, a paper containing several charges of the most serious description. By this document, Hastings was accused of putting offices up to sale and of receiving bribes for suffering offenders to escape. In particular, it was alleged that Mahommed Reza Khan had been dismissed with impunity in consideration of a great sum paid to the Governor-General.

Francis read the paper in Council. A violent altercation followed. Hastings complained in bitter terms of the way in which he was treated, spoke with contempt of Nuncomar and of Nuncomar's accusation, and denied the right of the Council to sit in judgment on the Governor. At the next meeting of the Board another communication from Nuncomar was produced. He requested that he might be permitted to attend the Council, and that he might be heard in support of his assertions. Another tempestuous debate took place. The Governor-General maintained that the council-room was not a proper place for such an investigation; that from persons who were heated by daily conflict with him he could not expect the fairness of judges; and that he could not, without betraying the dignity of his post, submit to be confronted with such a man as Nuncomar. The majority, however, resolved to go into the charges. Hastings rose, declared the sitting at an end, and left the room, followed by Barwell. The other members kept their seats, voted themselves a council, put Clavering in the chair, and ordered Nuncomar to be called in. Nuncomar not only adhered to the original charges, but, after the fashion of the East, produced a large supplement. He stated that Hastings had received a great sum for appointing Rajah Goordas treasurer of the Nabob's household and for committing the care of his Highness's person to the Munny Begum. He put in a letter, purporting to bear the seal of the Munny Begum, for the purpose of establishing the truth of his story. The seal, whether forged, as Hastings affirmed, or genuine, as we are rather inclined to believe, proved nothing. Nuncomar, as everybody knows who knows India, had only to tell the Munny Begum that such a letter would give pleasure to the majority of the Council in order to procure her attestation. The majority, however, voted that the charge was made out; that Hastings had corruptly received between thirty and forty thousand pounds; and that he ought to be compelled to refund.

The general feeling among the English in Bengal was strongly in favour of the Governor-General. In talents for business, in knowledge of the country, in general courtesy of demeanour, he was decidedly superior to his persecutors. The servants of the Company were naturally disposed to side with the most distinguished member of their own body against a war office clerk, who, profoundly ignorant of the native languages and of the native character, took on himself to regulate every department of the administration. Hastings, however, in spite of the general sympathy of his countrymen, was in a most painful situation. There was still an appeal to higher authority in England. If that authority took part with his enemies, nothing was left to him but to throw up his office. He accordingly placed his resignation in the hands of his agent in London, Colonel Macleane. But Macleane was instructed not to produce the resignation unless it should be fully ascertained that the feeling at the India House was adverse to the Governor-General.

The triumph of Nuncomar seemed to be complete. He held a daily levee, to which his countrymen resorted in crowds, and to which, on one occasion, the majority of the Council condescended to repair. His house was an office for the purpose of receiving charges against the Governor-General. It was said that, partly by threats and partly by wheedling, he had induced many of the wealthiest men of the province to send in complaints. But he was playing a desperate game. It was not safe to drive to despair a man of such resources and of such determination as Hastings. Nuncomar, with all his acuteness, did not understand the nature of the institutions under which he lived. He saw that he had with him the majority of the body which made treaties, gave places, raised taxes. The separation between political and judicial functions was a thing of which he had no conception. It had probably never occurred to him that there was in Bengal an authority perfectly independent of the Council—an authority which could protect one whom the Council wished to destroy and send to the gibbet one whom the Council wished to protect. Yet such was the fact. The Supreme Court was, within the sphere of its own duties, altogether independent of the Government. Hastings, with his usual sagacity, had seen how much advantage he might derive from possessing himself of this stronghold; and he had acted accordingly. The Judges, especially the Chief Justice, were hostile to the majority of the Council. The time had now come for putting this formidable machinery into action.

On a sudden, Calcutta was astounded by the news that Nuncomar had been taken up on a charge of felony, committed, and thrown into the common gaol. The crime imputed to him was, that six years before he had forged a bond. The ostensible prosecutor was a native. But it was then, and still is, the opinion of everybody—idiots and biographers excepted—that Hastings was the real mover in the business.

The rage of the majority rose to the highest point. They protested against the proceedings of the Supreme Court, and sent several urgent messages to the Judges demanding that Nuncomar should be admitted to bail. The Judges returned haughty and resolute answers. All that the Council could do was to heap honours and emoluments on the family of Nuncomar; and this they did. In the meantime, the assizes commenced; a true bill was found, and Nuncomar was brought before Sir Elijah Impey and a jury composed of Englishmen. A great quantity of contradictory swearing and the necessity of having every word of the evidence interpreted, protracted the trial to a most unusual length. At last a verdict of guilty was returned, and the Chief Justice pronounced sentence of death on the prisoner.

Mr. Gleig is so strangely ignorant as to imagine that the Judges had no further discretion in the case; and that the power of extending mercy to Nuncomar resided with the Council. He therefore throws on Francis and Francis's party the whole blame of what followed. We should have thought that a gentleman who has published five or six bulky volumes on Indian affairs might have taken the trouble to inform himself as to the fundamental principles of the Indian Government. The Supreme Court had, under the Regulating Act, the power to respite criminals till the pleasure of the Crown should be known. The Council had, at that time, no power to interfere.

That Impey ought to have respited Nuncomar, we hold to be perfectly clear. Whether the whole proceeding was not illegal, is a question. But it is certain that whatever may have been, according to technical rules of construction, the effect of the statute under which the trial took place, it was most unjust to hang a Hindoo for forgery. The law which made forgery capital in England was passed without the smallest reference to the state of society in India. It was unknown to the natives of India. It had never been put in execution among them, certainly not for want of delinquents. It was in the highest degree shocking to all their notions. They were not accustomed to the distinction which many circumstances, peculiar to our own state, of society, have led us to make between forgery and other kinds of cheating. The counterfeiting of a seal was, in their estimation, a common act of swindling; nor had it ever crossed their minds that it was to be punished as severely as gang-robbery or assassination. A just judge would beyond all doubt, have reserved the case for the consideration of the sovereign. But Impey would not hear of mercy or delay.

The excitement among all classes was great. Francis and Francis's few English adherents described the Governor-General and the Chief Justice as the worst of murderers. Clavering, it was said, swore that even at the foot of the gallows Nuncomar should be rescued. The bulk of the European society, though strongly attached to the Governor-General, could not but feel compassion for a man who, with all his crimes, had so long filled so large a space in their sight—who had been great and powerful before the British empire in India began to exist—and to whom, in the old times, governors and members of council, then mere commercial factors, had paid court for protection. The feeling of the Hindoos was infinitely stronger. They were, indeed, not a people to strike one blow for their countryman. But his sentence filled them with sorrow and dismay. Tried even by their low standard of morality, he was a bad man. But, bad as he was, he was the head of their race and religion—a Brahmin of the Brahmins. He had inherited the purest and highest caste. He had practised, with the greatest punctuality, all those ceremonies to which the superstitious Bengalees ascribe far more importance than to the correct discharge of the social duties. They felt, therefore, as a devout Catholic in the dark ages would have felt at seeing a prelate of the highest dignity sent to the gallows by a secular tribunal. According to their old national laws, a Brahmin could not be put to death for any crime whatever. And the crime for which Nuncomar was about to die was regarded by them in much the same light in which the selling of an unsound horse for a sound price is regarded by a Yorkshire jockey.

The Mahommedans alone appear to have seen with exultation the fate of the powerful Hindoo who had attempted to rise by means of the ruin of Mahommed Reza Khan. The Mussulman historian of those times takes delight in aggravating the charge. He assures us, that in Nuncomar's house, a casket was found containing counterfeits of the seals of all the richest men of the province. We have never fallen in with any other authority for this story, which, in itself, is by no means improbable.

The day drew near; and Nuncomar prepared himself to die with that quiet fortitude with which the Bengalee, so effeminately timid in personal conflict, often encounters calamities for which there is no remedy. The sheriff, with the humanity which is seldom wanting in an English gentleman, visited the prisoner on the eve of the execution and assured him that no indulgence, consistent with the law, should be refused to him. Nuncomar expressed his gratitude with great politeness and unaltered composure. Not a muscle of his face moved. Not a sigh broke from him. He put his finger to his forehead and calmly said that fate would have its way and that there was no resisting the pleasure of God. He sent his compliments to Francis, Clavering and Monson, and charged them to protect Rajah Goordas, who was about to become the head of the Brahmins of Bengal. The sheriff withdrew, greatly agitated by what had passed, and Nuncomar sat composedly down to write notes and examine accounts.

The next morning, before the sun was in his power, an immense concourse assembled round the place where the gallows had been set up. Grief and sorrow were on every face; yet, to the last the multitude could hardly believe that the English really purposed to take the life of the great Brahmin. At length the mournful procession came through the crowd. Nuncomar sat up in his palanquin and looked round him with unaltered serenity. He had just parted from those who were most nearly connected with him. Their cries and contortions had appalled the European ministers of justice, but had not produced the smallest effect on the iron stoicism of the prisoner. The only anxiety which he expressed was, that men of his own priestly caste might be in attendance to take charge of his corpse. He again desired to be remembered to his friends in the Council, mounted the scaffold with firmness and gave the signal to the executioner. The moment that the drop fell, a howl of sorrow and despair rose from the innumerable spectators. Hundreds turned away their faces from the polluting sight, fled with loud wailings towards the Hoogley and plunged into its holy waters, as if to purify themselves from the guilt of having looked on such a crime. These feelings were not confined to Calcutta. The whole province was greatly excited, and the population of Decca, in particular, gave strong signs of grief and dismay.

Of Impey's conduct, it is impossible to speak too severely. We have already said that, in our opinion, he acted unjustly in refusing to respite Nuncomar. No rational man can doubt that he took this course in order to gratify the Governor-General. If we had ever had any doubts on that point, they would have been dispelled by a letter which Mr. Gleig has published. Hastings, three or four years later, described Impey as the man "to whose support he was at one time indebted for the safety of his fortune, honour and reputation." These strong words can refer only to the case of Nuncomar, and they must mean that Impey hanged Nuncomar in order to support Hastings. It is, therefore, our deliberate opinion that Impey, sitting as a judge, put a man unjustly to death in order to serve a political purpose.

But we look on the conduct of Hastings in a somewhat different light. He was struggling for fortune, honour, liberty—all that makes life valuable. He was beset by rancorous and unprincipled enemies. From his colleagues he could expect no justice. He cannot be blamed for wishing to crush his accusers. He was indeed bound to use only legitimate means for that end. But it was not strange that he should have thought any means legitimate which were pronounced legitimate by the sages of the law—by men whose peculiar duty it was to deal justly between adversaries, and whose education might be supposed to have peculiarly qualified them for the discharge of that duty. Nobody demands from a party the unbending equity of a judge. The reason that judges are appointed is, that even good men cannot be trusted to decide causes in they are themselves concerned. Not a day passes on which an honest prosecutor does not ask for what none but a dishonest tribunal would grant. It is too much to expect that any man, when his dearest interests are at stake and his strongest passions excited, will, as against himself, be more just than the sworn dispensers of justice. To take an analogous case from the history of our own island. Suppose that Lord Stafford, when in the Tower on suspicion of being concerned in the Popish plot, had done something which might, by a questionable construction, be brought under the head of felony. Should we severely blame Lord Stafford, in the supposed case, for causing a prosecution to be instituted, for furnishing funds, for using all his influence to intercept the mercy of the Crown? We think not. If a judge, indeed, from favour to the Catholic lords, were to strain the law in order to hang Oates, such a judge would richly deserve impeachment. But it does not appear to us that the Catholic lord, by bringing the case before the judge for decision, would materially overstep the limits of a just self-defence.

While, therefore, we have not the least doubt that this memorable execution is to be attributed to Hastings, we doubt whether it can with justice be reckoned among his crimes. That his conduct was dictated by a profound policy is evident. He was in a minority in Council. It was possible that he might long be in a minority. He knew the native character well. He knew in what abundance accusations are certain to flow in against the most innocent inhabitant of India who is under the frown of power. There was not in the whole black population of Bengal a place-holder, a place-hunter, a government tenant, who did not think that he might better himself by sending up a deposition against the Governor-General. Under these circumstances, the persecuted statesman resolved to teach the whole crew of accusers and witnesses that, though in a minority at the council-board, he was still to be feared. The lesson which he gave them was indeed a lesson not to be forgotten. The head of the combination which had been formed against him, the richest, the most powerful, the most artful of the Hindoos, distinguished by the favour of those who then held the government, fenced round by the superstitious reverence of millions, was hanged in broad day before many thousands of people. Everything that could make the warning impressive—dignity in the sufferer, solemnity in the proceeding—was found in this case. The helpless rage and vain struggles of the Council made the triumph more signal. From that moment, the conviction of every native was that it was safer to take the part of Hastings in a minority than that of Francis in a majority, and that he who was so venturous as to join in running down the Governor-General might chance, in the phrase of the Eastern poet, to find a tiger while beating the jungle for a deer. The voices of a thousand informers were silenced in an instant. From that time, whatever difficulties Hastings might have to encounter, he was never molested by accusations from natives of India.

It is a remarkable circumstance that one of the letters of Hastings to Dr. Johnson bears date a very few hours after the death of Nuncomar. While the whole settlement was in commotion, while a mighty and ancient priesthood were weeping over the remains of their chief, the conqueror in that deadly grapple sat down, with characteristic self-possession, to write about the "Tour to the Hebrides," Jones's "Persian Grammar," and the history, traditions, arts and natural productions of India.

In the meantime, intelligence of the Rohilla war and of the first disputes between Hastings and his colleagues had reached London. The Directors took part with the majority, and sent out a letter filled with severe reflections on the conduct of Hastings. They condemned, in strong but just terms, the iniquity of undertaking offensive wars merely for the sake of pecuniary advantage. But they utterly forgot that, if Hastings had by illicit means obtained pecuniary advantages, he had done so, not for his own benefit, but in order to meet their demands. To enjoin honesty and to insist on having what could not be honestly got was then the constant practice of the Company. As Lady Macbeth says of her husband, they " would not play false and yet would wrongly win."

The Regulating Act, by which Hastings had been appointed Governor-

General for five years, empowered the Crown to remove him on an address from the Company. Lord North was desirous to procure such an address. The three members of Council who had been sent out from England were men of his own choice. General Clavering, in particular, was supported by a large parliamentary connection such as no cabinet could be inclined to disoblige. The wish of the minister was to displace Hastings and to put Clavering at the head of the government. In the Court of Directors, parties were very nearly balanced. Eleven voted against Hastings—ten for him. The Court of Proprietors was then convened. The great sale-room presented a singular appearance. Letters had been sent by the Secretary of the Treasury exhorting all the supporters of government who held India stock to be in attendance. Lord Sandwich marshalled the friends of the administration with his usual dexterity and alertness. Fifty peers and privy councillors, seldom seen so far eastward, were counted in the crowd. The debate lasted till midnight. The opponents of Hastings had a small superiority on the division; but a ballot was demanded; and the result was that the Governor-General triumphed by a majority of above a hundred votes over the combined efforts of the Directors and the Cabinet. The ministers were greatly exasperated by this defeat. Even Lord North lost his temper—no ordinary occurrence with him—and threatened to convoke parliament before Christmas, and to bring in a bill for depriving the Company of all political power and for restricting it to its old business of trading in silks and teas.

Colonel Macleane, who through all this conflict had zealously supported the cause of Hastings, now thought that his employer was in imminent danger of being turned out, branded with parliamentary censure, perhaps prosecuted. The opinion of the crown lawyers had already been taken respecting some parts of the Governor-General's conduct. It seemed to be high time to think of securing an honourable retreat. Under these circumstances, Macleane thought himself justified in producing the resignation with which he had been intrusted. The instrument was not in very accurate form; but the Directors were too eager to be scrupulous. They accepted the resignation, fixed on Mr. Wheler, one of their own body, to succeed Hastings, and sent out orders that General Clavering, as senior member of the Council, should exercise the functions of Governor-General till Mr. Wheler should arrive.

But, while these things were passing in England, a great change had taken place in Bengal. Monson was no more. Only four members of the government were left. Clavering and Francis were on one side, Barwell and the Governor-General on the other; and the Governor-General had the casting vote. Hastings, who had been during two years destitute of all power and patronage, became at once absolute. He instantly proceeded to retaliate on his adversaries. Their measures were reversed: their creatures were displaced. A new valuation of the lands of Bengal, for the purposes of taxation, was ordered; and it was provided that the whole inquiry should be conducted by the Governor-General, and that all the letters relating to it should run in his name. He began, at the same time, to revolve vast plans of conquest and dominion, plans which he lived to see realised—though not by himself. His project was to form subsidiary alliances with the native princes, particularly with those of Oude and Berar, and thus to make Britain the paramount power in India. While he was meditating these great designs, arrived the intelligence that he had ceased to be Governor-General, that his resignation had been accepted, that Wheler was coming out immediately, and that, till Wheler arrived, the chair was to be filled by Clavering.

Had Hastings still been in a minority he would probably have retired without a struggle; but he was now the real master of British India, and he was not disposed to quit his high place. He asserted that he had never given any instructions which could warrant the steps taken at home. What his instructions had been, he owned he had forgotten. If he had kept a copy of them, he had mislaid it. But he was certain that he had repeatedly declared to the Directors that he would not resign. He could not see how the court possessed of that declaration from himself could receive his resignation from the doubtful hands of an agent. If the resignation were invalid, all the proceedings which were founded on that resignation were null and Hastings was still Governor-General.

He afterwards affirmed that, though his agents had not acted in conformity with his instructions, he would nevertheless have held himself bound by their acts if Clavering had not attempted to seize the supreme power by violence. Whether this assertion were or were not true, it cannot be doubted that the imprudence of Clavering gave Hastings an advantage. The General sent for the keys of the fort and of the treasury, took possession of the records, and held a council at which Francis attended. Hastings took the chair in another apartment, and Barwell sat with him. Each of the two parties had a plausible show of right. There was no authority entitled to their obedience within fifteen thousand miles. It seemed that there remained no way of settling the dispute except an appeal to arms; and from such an appeal Hastings, confident of his influence over his countrymen in India, was not inclined to shrink. He directed the officers of the garrison at Fort William and of all the neighbouring stations to obey no orders but his. At the same time, with admirable judgment, he offered to submit the case to the Supreme Court and to abide by its decision. By making this proposition, he risked nothing; yet it was a proposition which his opponents could hardly reject. Nobody could be treated as a criminal for obeying what the judges should solemnly pronounce to be the lawful government. The boldest man would shrink from taking arms in defence of what the judges should pronounce to be usurpation. Clavering and Francis, after some delay, unwillingly consented to abide by the award of the court. The court pronounced that the resignation was invalid, and that, therefore, Hastings was still Governor-General under the Regulating Act; and the defeated members of the Council, finding that the sense of the whole settlement was against them, acquiesced in the decision.

About this time arrived the news that, after a suit which had lasted several years, the Franconian courts had decreed a divorce between Imhoff and his wife. The Baron left Calcutta, carrying with him the means of buying an estate in Saxony. The lady became Mrs. Hastings. The event was celebrated by great festivities; and all the most conspicuous persons at Calcutta, without distinction of parties, were invited to the Government House. Clavering, as the Mahommedan chronicler tells the story, was sick in mind and body, and excused himself from joining the splendid assembly. But Hastings, whom, as it should seem, success in ambition and in love had put into high good-humour, would take no denial. He went himself to the General's house, and at length brought his vanquished rival in triumph to the gay circle which surrounded the bride. The exertion was too much for a frame broken by mortification as well as by disease. Clavering died a few days later.

Wheler, who came out expecting to be Governor-General and was forced to content himself with a seat at the council-board, generally voted with Francis. But the Governor-General, with Barwell's help and his own casting vote, was still the master. Some change took place at this time in the feeling both of the Court of Directors and of the Ministers of the Crown. All designs against Hastings were dropped; and, when his original term of five years expired, he was quietly reappointed. The truth is, that the fearful dangers to which the public interests in every quarter were now exposed made both Lord North and the Company unwilling to part with a Governor whose talents, experience and resolution, enmity itself was compelled to acknowledge.

The crisis was indeed formidable. The great and victorious empire, on the throne of which George the Third had taken his seat eighteen years before with brighter hopes than had attended the accession of any of the long line of English sovereigns, had, by the most senseless misgovernment, been brought to the verge of ruin. In America millions of Englishmen were at war with the country from which their blood, their language, their religion and their institutions were derived, and to which, but a short time before, they had been as strongly attached as the inhabitants of Norfolk and Leicestershire. The great powers of Europe, humbled to the dust by the vigour and genius which had guided the councils of George the Second, now rejoiced in the prospect of a signal revenge. The time was approaching when our island, while struggling to keep down the United States of America and pressed with a still nearer danger by the too just discontents of Ireland, was to be assailed by France, Spain and Holland, and to be threatened by the armed neutrality of the Baltic; when even our maritime supremacy was to be in jeopardy; when hostile fleets were to command the Straits of Calpe and the Mexican Sea; when the British flag was to be scarcely able to protect the British Channel. Great as were the faults of Hastings, it was happy for our country that at that conjuncture, the most terrible through which she has ever passed, he was the ruler of her Indian dominions.

An attack by sea on Bengal was little to be apprehended. The danger was that the European enemies of England might form an alliance with some native power, might furnish that power with troops, arms and ammunition, and might thus assail our possessions on the side of the land. It was chiefly from the Mahrattas that Hastings anticipated danger. The original seat of that singular people was the wild range of hills which runs along the western coast of India. In the reign of Aurungzebe, the inhabitants of those regions, led by the great Sevajee, began to descend on the possessions of their wealthier and less war-like neighbours. The energy, ferocity and cunning of the Mahrattas soon made them the most conspicuous among the new powers which were generated by the corruption of the decaying monarchy. At first they were only robbers. They soon rose to the dignity of conquerors. Half the provinces of the empire were turned into Mahratta principalities. Freebooters, sprung from low castes and accustomed to menial employments, became mighty Rajahs. The Bonslas, at the head of a band of plunderers, occupied the vast region of Berar. The Guicowar, which is, being interpreted, the Herdsman, founded that dynasty which still reigns in Guzerat. The houses of Scindia and Holkar waxed great in Malwa. One adventurous captain made his nest on the impregnable rock of Gooti. Another became the lord of the thousand villages which are scattered among the green rice-fields of Tanjore.

That was the time throughout India of double government. The form and the power were everywhere separated. The Mussulman nabobs, who had become sovereign princes, the Vizier in Oude and the Nizam at Hyderabad still called themselves the viceroys of the house of Tamerlane. In the same manner, the Mahratta states, though really independent of each other, pretended to be members of one empire; and acknowledged, by words and ceremonies, the supremacy of the heir of Sevajee—a *roi fainéant* who chewed bang and toyed with dancing girls in a state-prison at Sattara—and of his Peshwa, or mayor of the palace, a great hereditary magistrate, who kept a court with kingly state at Poonah, and whose authority was obeyed in the spacious provinces of Aurungabad and Bejapoor.

Some months before war was declared in Europe, the government of Bengal was alarmed by the news that a French adventurer, who passed for a man of quality, had arrived at Poonah. It was said that he had been received there with great distinction—that he had delivered to the Peshwa letters and presents from Louis the Sixteenth—and that a treaty, hostile to England, had been concluded between France and the Mahrattas.

Hastings immediately resolved to strike the first blow. The title of the Peshwa was not undisputed. A portion of the Mahratta nation was favourable to a pretender. The Governor-General determined to espouse this pretender's interest, to move an army across the peninsula of India, and to form a close alliance with the chief of the house of Bonsla, who ruled Berar, and who, in power and dignity, was inferior to none of the Mahratta princes.

The army had marched, and the negotiations with Berar were in progress, when a letter from the English consul at Cairo brought the news that war had been proclaimed both in London and Paris. All the measures which the crisis required were adopted by Hastings without a moment of delay. The French factories in Bengal were seized. Orders were sent to Madras that Pondicherry should instantly be occupied. Near Calcutta works were thrown up which were thought to render the approach of a hostile force impossible. A maritime establishment was formed for the defence of the river. Nine new battalions of sepoys were raised, and a corps of native artillery was formed out of the hardy Lascars of the Bay of Bengal. Having made these arrangements, the Governor-General, with calm confidence, pronounced his presidency secure from all attack unless the Mahratta should march against it in conjunction with the French.

The expedition which Hastings had sent westward was not so speedily or completely successful as most of his undertakings. The commanding officer procrastinated. The authorities at Bombay blundered. But the Governor-General persevered. A new commander repaired the errors of his predecessor. Several brilliant actions spread the military renown of the English through regions where no European flag had ever been seen. It is probable that if a new and more formidable danger had not compelled Hastings to change his whole policy, his plans respecting the Mahratta empire would have been carried into complete effect.

The authorities in England had wisely sent out to Bengal, as commander of the forces and member of the Council, one of the most distinguished soldiers of that time. Sir Eyre Coote had, many years before, been conspicuous among the founders of the British empire in the East. At the council of war which preceded the battle of Plassey, he earnestly recommended, in opposition to the majority, that daring course which, after some hesitation, was adopted, and which was crowned with such splendid success. He subsequently commanded in the south of India against the brave and unfortunate Lally; gained the decisive battle of Wandewash over the French and their native allies, took Pondicherry, and made the English power supreme in the Carnatic. Since those great exploits near twenty years had elapsed. Coote had no longer the bodily activity which he had shown in earlier days; nor was the vigour of his mind altogether unimpaired. He was capricious and fretful and required much coaxing to keep him in good humour. It must, we fear, be added that the love of money had grown upon him, and that he thought more about his allowances and less about his duties than might have been expected from so eminent a member of so noble a profession. Still he was perhaps the ablest officer that was then to be found in the British army. Among the native soldiers his name was great and his influence unrivalled. Nor is he yet forgotten by them. Now and then a white-bearded old sepoy may still be found, who loves to talk of Porto Novo and Pollilore. It is but a short time since one of these aged men came to present a memorial to an English officer who holds one of the highest employments in India. A print of Coote hung in the room. The veteran recognised at once that face and figure which he had not seen for more than half a century, and, forgetting his salam to the living, halted, drew himself up, lifted his hand, and, with solemn reverence, paid his military obeisance to the dead.

Coote, though he did not, like Barwell, vote constantly with the Governor-General, was by no means inclined to join in systematic opposition; and on most questions concurred with Hastings, who did his best, by assiduous courtship and by readily granting the most exorbitant allowances, to gratify the strongest passions of the old soldier.

It seemed likely at this time that a general reconciliation would put an end to the quarrels which had, during some years, weakened and disgraced the government of Bengal. The dangers of the empire might well induce men of patriotic feeling—and of patriotic feeling neither Hastings nor Francis was destitute—to forget private enmities and to co-operate heartily for the general good. Coote had never been concerned in factions. Wheler was thoroughly tired of it. Barwell had made an ample fortune, and, though he had promised that he would not leave Calcutta while Hastings wanted his help, was most desirous to return to England, and exerted himself to promote an arrangement which would set him at liberty. A compact was made by which Francis agreed to desist from opposition, and Hastings engaged that the friends of Francis should be admitted to a fair share of the honours and emoluments of the service. During a few months after this treaty there was apparent harmony at the council-board.

Harmony, indeed, was never more necessary; for at this moment internal calamities, more formidable than war itself, menaced Bengal. The authors of the Regulating Act of 1773 had established two independent powers, the one judicial and the other political; and, with a carelessness scandalously common in English legislation, had omitted to define the limits of either. The judges took advantage of the indistinctness and attempted to draw to themselves supreme authority, not only within Calcutta, but through the whole of the great territory subject to the Presidency of Fort William. There are few Englishmen who will not admit that the English law, in spite of modern improvements, is neither so cheap nor so speedy as might be wished. Still, it is a system which has grown up among us. In some points it has been fashioned to suit our feelings; in others it has gradually fashioned our feelings to suit itself. Even to its worst evils we are accustomed; and, therefore, though we may complain of them, they do not strike us with the horror and dismay which would be produced by a new grievance of smaller severity. In India the case is widely different. English law, transplanted to that country, has all the vices from which we suffer here; it has them all in a far higher degree; and it has other vices compared with which the worst vices from which we suffer are trifles. Dilatory here, it is far more dilatory in a land where the help of an interpreter is needed by every judge and by every advocate. Costly here, it is far more costly in a land into which the legal practitioners must be imported from an immense distance. All English labour in India, from the labour of the Governor-General and the Commander-in-Chief down to that of a groom or a watchmaker, must be paid for at higher rate than at home. No man will be banished, and banished to the torrid zone, for nothing. The rule holds good with respect to the legal profession. No English barrister will work, fifteen thousand miles from all his friends, with the thermometer at ninety-six in the shade, for the emoluments which will content him in chambers that overlook the Thames.

Accordingly, the fees at Calcutta are about three times as great as the fees of Westminster Hall; and this, though the people of India are, beyond all comparison, poorer than the people of England. Yet the delay and the expense, grievous as they are, form the smallest part of the evil which English law, imported without modifications into India, could not fail to produce. The strongest feelings of our nature, honour, religion, female modesty, rose up against the innovation. Arrest on mesne process was the first step in most civil proceedings; and to a native of rank arrest was not merely a restraint, but a foul personal indignity. Oaths were required in every stage of every suit; and the feeling of a Quaker about an oath is hardly stronger than that of a respectable native. That the apartments of a woman of quality should be entered by strange men or that her face should be seen by them, are, in the East, intolerable outrages—outrages which are more dreaded than death, and which can be expiated only by the shedding of blood. To these outrages the most distinguished families of Bengal, Bahar and Orissa were now exposed. Imagine what the state of our own country would be if a jurisprudence were on a sudden introduced among us which should be to us what our jurisprudence was to our Asiatic subjects. Imagine what the state of our country would be if it were enacted that any man, by merely swearing that a debt was due to him, should acquire a right to insult the persons of men of the most honourable and sacred callings and of women of the most shrinking delicacy, to horse-whip a general officer, to put a bishop in the stocks, to treat ladies in the way which called forth the blow of Wat Tyler. Something like this was the effect of the attempt which the Supreme Court made to extend its jurisdiction over the whole of the Company's territory.

A reign of terror began—of terror heightened by mystery; for even that which was endured was less horrible than that which was anticipated. No man knew what was next to be expected from this strange tribunal. It came from beyond the black water, as the people of India, with mysterious horror, call the sea. It consisted of judges, not one of whom spoke the language or was familiar with the usages of the millions over whom they claimed boundless authority. Its records were kept in unknown characters; its sentences were pronounced in unknown sounds. It had already collected round itself an army of the worst part of the native population—informers, and false witnesses, and common barrators, and agents of chicane, and, above all, a banditti of bailiff's followers, compared with whom the retainers of the worst English sponging-houses, in the worst times, might be considered as upright and tender-hearted. Many natives, highly considered among their countrymen, were seized, hurried up to Calcutta, flung into the common gaol, not for any crime even imputed, not for any debt that had been proved, but merely as a precaution till their cause should come to trial. There were instances in which men of the most venerable dignity, persecuted without a cause by extortioners, died of rage and shame in the gripe of the vile alguazils of Impey. The harems of noble Mahommedans—sanctuaries respected in the East by governments which respected nothing else—were burst open by gangs of bailiffs. The Mussulmans, braver and less accustomed to submission than the Hindoos, sometimes stood on their defence; and there were instances in which they shed their blood in the doorway, while defending, sword in hand, the sacred apartments of their women. Nay, it seemed as if even the faint-hearted Bengalee, who had crouched at the feet of Surajah Dowlah, who had been mute during the administration of Vansittart, would at length find courage in despair. No Mahratta invasion had ever spread through the province such dismay as this inroad of English lawyers. All the injustice of former oppressors,

Asiatic and European, appeared as a blessing when compared with the justice of the Supreme Court.

Every class of the population, English and native, with the exception of the ravenous pettifoggers who fattened on the misery and terror of an immense community, cried out loudly against this fearful oppression. But the judges were immovable. If a bailiff was resisted, they ordered the soldiers to be called out. If a servant of the Company, in conformity with the orders of the government, withstood the miserable catchpoles who, with Impey's writs in their hands, exceeded the insolence and rapacity of gang-robbers, he was flung into prison for a contempt. The lapse of sixty years—the virtue and wisdom of many eminent magistrates who have during that time administered justice in the Supreme Court—have not effaced from the minds of the people of Bengal the recollection of those evil days.

The members of the government were, on this subject, united as one man. Hastings had courted the judges; he had found them useful instruments; but he was not disposed to make them his own masters or the masters of India. His mind was large; his knowledge of the native character most accurate. He saw that the system pursued by the Supreme Court was degrading to the government and ruinous to the people; and he resolved to oppose it manfully. The consequence was, that the friendship—if that be the proper word for such a connection,—which had existed between him and Impey, was for a time completely dissolved. The government placed itself firmly between the tyrannical tribunal and the people. The Chief Justice proceeded to the wildest excesses. The Governor-General and all the members of Council were served with summonses calling on them to appear before the King's justices and to answer for their public acts. This was too much. Hastings, with just scorn, refused to obey the call, set at liberty the persons wrongfully detained by the Court and took measures for resisting the outrageous proceedings of the sheriff's officers, if necessary, by the sword. But he had in view another device which might prevent the necessity of an appeal to arms. He was seldom at a loss for an expedient; and he knew Impey well. The expedient, in this case, was a very simple one—neither more nor less than a bribe. Impey was, by act of parliament, a judge, independent of the government of Bengal and entitled to a salary of £8,000 a-year. Hastings proposed to make him also a judge in the Company's service, removable at the pleasure of the government of Bengal, and to give him, in that capacity, about £8,000 a-year more. It was understood that, in consideration of this new salary, Impey would desist from urging the high pretensions of his court. If he did urge these pretensions, the government could, at a moment's notice, eject him from the new place which had been created for him. The bargain was struck; Bengal was saved; an appeal to force was averted: and the Chief Justice was rich, quiet and infamous.

Of Impey's conduct, it is unnecessary to speak. It was of a piece with almost every part of his conduct that comes under the notice of history. No other such judge has dishonoured the English ermine since Jefferies drank himself to death in the Tower. But we cannot agree with those who have blamed Hastings for this transaction. The case stood thus. The negligent manner in which the Regulating Act had been framed put it in the power of the Chief Justice to throw a great country into the most dreadful confusion. He was determined to use his power to the utmost unless he was paid to be still; and Hastings consented to pay him. The necessity was to be deplored. It is also to be deplored that pirates should be able to exact ransom by threatening to make their captives walk the plank. But to ransom a captive from pirates has always been held a humane and Christian act; and it would be absurd to charge the payer of the ransom with corrupting the virtue of the corsair. This, we seriously think, is a not unfair illustration of the relative position of Impey, Hastings and the people of India. Whether it was right in Impey to demand or to accept a price for powers which, if they really belonged to him, he could not abdicate—which, if they did not belong to him, he ought never to have usurped—and which in neither case he could honestly sell—is one question. It is quite another question whether Hastings was not right to give any sum, however large, to any man, however worthless, rather than either surrender millions of human beings to pillage or rescue them by civil war.

Francis strongly opposed this arrangement. It may, indeed, be suspected that personal aversion to Impey was as strong a motive with Francis as regard for the welfare of the province. To a mind burning with resentment, it might seem better to leave Bengal to the oppressors than to redeem it by enriching them. It is not improbable, on the other hand, that Hastings may have been the more willing to resort to an expedient agreeable to the Chief Justice, because that high functionary had already been so serviceable, and might, when existing dissensions were composed, be serviceable again.

But it was not on this point alone that Francis was now opposed to Hastings. The peace between them proved to be only a short and hollow truce, during which their mutual aversion was constantly becoming stronger. At length an explosion took place. Hastings publicly charged Francis with having deceived him and induced Barwell to quit the service by insincere promises. Then came a dispute such as frequently arises even between honourable men when they make important agreements by mere verbal communication. An impartial historian will probably be of opinion that they had misunderstood each other; but their minds were so much embittered that they imputed to each other nothing less than deliberate villany. "I do not," said Hastings, in a minute recorded on the Consultations of the Government—"I do not trust to Mr. Francis's promises of candour, convinced that he is incapable of it. I judge of his public conduct by his private, which I have found to be void of truth and honour!" After the Council had risen, Francis put a challenge into the Governor-General's hand. It was instantly accepted. They met, and fired. Francis was shot through the body. He was carried to a neighbouring house, where it appeared that the wound, though severe, was not mortal. Hastings inquired repeatedly after his enemy's health and proposed to call on him; but Francis coldly declined the visit. He had a proper sense, he said, of the Governor-General's politeness, but could not consent to any private interview. They could meet only at the Council-Board.

In a very short time it was made signally manifest to how great a danger the Governor-General had, on this occasion, exposed his country. A crisis arrived with which he, and he alone, was competent to deal. It was not too much to say that, if he had been taken from the head of affairs, the years 1780 and 1781 would have been as fatal to our power in Asia as to our power in America.

The Mahrattas had been the chief objects of apprehension to Hastings. The measures which he had adopted for the purpose of breaking their power had at first been frustrated by the errors of those whom he was compelled to employ; but his perseverance and ability seemed likely to be crowned with success when a far more formidable danger showed itself in a distant quarter.

About thirty years before this time, a Mahommedan soldier had begun to distinguish himself in the wars of Southern India. His education had been neglected; his extraction was mean. His father had been a petty officer of revenue; his grandfather a wandering dervise. But though thus meanly descended—though ignorant even of the alphabet—the adventurer had no sooner been placed at the head of a body of troops than he approved himself a man born for conquest and command. Among the crowd of chiefs who were struggling for a share of India, none could compare with him in the qualities of the captain and the statesman. He became a general—he became a prince. Out of the fragments of old principalities, which had gone to pieces in the general wreck, he formed for himself a great, compact and vigorous empire. That empire he ruled with the ability, severity and vigilance of Louis the Eleventh. Licentious in his pleasures, implacable in his revenge, he had yet enlargement of mind enough to perceive how much the prosperity of subjects adds to the strength of governments. He was an oppressor; but he had at least the merit of protecting his people against all oppression except his own. He was now in extreme old age; but his intellect was as clear and his spirit as high as in the prime of manhood. Such was the great Hyder Ali, the founder of the Mahommedan kingdom of Mysore and the most formidable enemy with whom the English conquerors of India have ever had to contend.

Had Hastings been governor of Madras, Hyder would have been either made a friend, or vigorously encountered as an enemy. Unhappily, the English authorities in the south provoked their powerful neighbour's hostility without being prepared to repel it. On a sudden, an army of ninety thousand men, far superior in discipline and efficiency to any other native force that could be found in India, came pouring through those wild passes which, worn by mountain torrents and dark with jungle, lead down from the table-land of Mysore to the plains of the Carnatic. This great army was accompanied by a hundred pieces of cannon; and its movements were guided by many French officers, trained in the best military schools of Europe.

Hyder was everywhere triumphant. The sepoys in many British garrisons flung down their arms. Some forts were surrendered by treachery and some by despair. In a few days, the whole open country north of the Coleroon had submitted. The English inhabitants of Madras could already see by night, from the top of Mount St. Thomas, the eastern sky reddened by a vast semi-circle of blazing villages. The white villas—to which our countrymen retire after the daily labours of government and of trade, when the cool evening breeze springs up from the sea—were now left without inhabitants; for bands of the fierce horsemen of Mysore had already been seen prowling near those gay verandas. Even the town was not thought secure; and the British merchants and public functionaries made haste to crowd themselves behind the cannon of Fort St. George.

There were the means, indeed, of forming an army which might have defended the presidency and even driven the invader back to his mountains. Sir Hector Munro was at the head of one considerable force; Baillie was advancing with another. United, they might have presented a formidable front even to such an enemy as Hyder. But the English commanders, neglecting those fundamental rules of military art, of which the propriety is obvious even to men who had never received a military education, deferred their junction and were separately attacked. Baillie's detachment was destroyed. Munro was forced to abandon his baggage, to fling his guns into the tanks and to save himself by a retreat which might be called a flight. In three weeks from the commencement of the war, the British empire in Southern India had been brought to the verge of ruin. Only a few fortified places remained to us. The glory of our arms had departed. It was known that a great French expedition might soon be expected on the coast of Coromandel. England, beset by enemies on every side, was in no condition to protect such remote dependencies.

Then it was that the fertile genius and serene courage of Hastings achieved their most signal triumph. A swift ship, flying before the south-west monsoon, brought the evil tidings in few days to Calcutta. In twenty-four hours the

Governor-General had framed a complete plan of policy adapted to the altered state of affairs. The struggle with Hyder was a struggle for life and death. All minor objects must be sacrificed to the preservation of the Carnatic. The disputes with the Mahrattas must be accommodated. A large military force and a supply of money must be instantly sent to Madras. But even these measures would be insufficient unless the war, hitherto so grossly mismanaged, were placed under the direction of a vigorous mind. It was no time for trifling. Hastings determined to resort to an extreme exercise of power; to suspend the incapable governor of Fort St. George, to send Sir Eyre Coote to oppose Hyder, and to intrust that distinguished general with the whole administration of the war.

In spite of the sullen opposition of Francis, who had now recovered from his wound and had returned to the Council, the Governor-General's wise and firm policy was approved by the majority of the board. The reinforcements were sent off with great expedition, and reached Madras before the French armament arrived in the Indian seas. Coote, broken by age and disease, was no longer the Coote of Wandewash; but he was still a resolute and skilful commander. The progress of Hyder was arrested; and in a few months the great victory of Porto Novo retrieved the honour of English arms.

In the meantime, Francis had returned to England, and Hastings was now left perfectly unfettered. Wheler had gradually been relaxing in his opposition, and, after the departure of his vehement and implacable colleague, co-operated heartily with the Governor-General, whose influence over the British in India, always great, had, by the vigour and success of his recent measures, been considerably increased.

But, though the difficulties arising from factions within the Council were at an end, another class of difficulties had become more pressing than ever. The financial embarrassment was extreme. Hastings had to find the means, not only of carrying on the Government of Bengal, but of maintaining a most costly war against both Indian and European enemies in the Carnatic and of making remittances to England; A few years before this time, he had obtained relief by plundering the Mogul and enslaving the Rohillas; nor were the resources of his fruitful mind by any means exhausted.

His first design was on Benares, a city which in wealth, population, dignity, and sanctity was among the foremost of Asia. It was commonly believed that half a million of human beings was crowded into that labyrinth of lofty alleys, rich with shrines, and minarets, and balconies, and carved oriels, to which the sacred apes clung by hundreds. The traveller could scarcely make his way through the press of holy mendicants and not less holy bulls. The broad and stately flights of steps which descended from these swarming haunts to the bathing-places along the Ganges were worn every day by the footsteps of an innumerable multitude of worshippers. The schools and temples drew crowds of pious Hindoos from every province where the Brahminical faith was known. Hundreds of devotees came thither every month to die—for it was believed that a peculiarly happy fate awaited the man who should pass from the sacred city into the sacred river. Nor was superstition the only motive which allured strangers to that great metropolis. Commerce had as many pilgrims as religion. All along the shores of the venerable stream lay great fleets of vessels laden with rich merchandise. From the looms of Benares went forth the most delicate silks that adorned the balls of St. James's and of the Petit Trianon; and in the bazaars the muslins of Bengal and the sabres of Oude were mingled with the jewels of Golconda and the shawls of Cashmere. This rich capital and the surrounding tract had long been under the immediate rule of a Hindoo prince who rendered homage to the Mogul emperors. During the great anarchy of India, the lords of Benares became independent of the court of Delhi, but were compelled to submit to the authority of the Nabob of Oude. Oppressed by this formidable neighbour, they invoked the protection of the English. The English protection was given; and at length the Nabob Vizier, by a solemn treaty, ceded all his rights over Benares to the Company. From that time the Rajah was the vassal of the government of Bengal, acknowledged its supremacy and sent an annual tribute to Fort William. This tribute Cheyte Sing, the reigning prince, had paid with strict punctuality.

About the precise nature of the legal relation between the Company and the Rajah of Benares, there has been much warm and acute controversy. On the one side, it has been maintained that Cheyte Sing was merely a great subject on whom the superior power had a right to call for aid in the necessities of the empire. On the other side, it has been contended that he was an independent prince, that the only claim which the Company had upon him was for a fixed tribute, and that while the fixed tribute was regularly paid, as it assuredly was, the English had no more right to exact any further contributions from him than to demand subsidies from Holland or Denmark. Nothing is easier than to find precedents and analogies in favour of either view.

Our own impression is that neither view is correct. It was too much the habit of English politicians to take it for granted that there was in India a known and definite constitution by which questions of this kind were to be decided. The truth is that, during the interval which elapsed between the fall of the house of Tamerlane and the establishment of the British ascendency, there was no such constitution. The old order of things had passed away; the new order of things was not yet formed. All was transition, confusion, obscurity. Everybody kept his head as he best might, and scrambled for whatever he could get. There have been similar seasons in Europe. The time of the dissolution of the Carlovingian empire is an instance. Who would think of seriously discussing the question, what extent of pecuniary aid and of obedience Hugh Capet had a constitutional right to demand from the Duke of Britanny or the Duke of Normandy? The words, "constitutional right" had, in that state of society, no meaning. If Hugh Capet laid hands on all the possessions of the Duke of Normandy, this might be unjust and immoral; but it would not be illegal, in the sense in which the ordinances of Charles the Tenth were illegal. If, on the other hand, the Duke of Normandy made war on Hugh Capet, this might be unjust and immoral; but it would not be illegal, in the sense in which the expedition of Prince Louis Bonaparte was illegal.

Very similar to this was the state of India sixty years ago. Of the existing governments, not a single one could lay claim to legitimacy or plead any other title than recent occupation. There was scarcely a province in which the real sovereignty and the nominal sovereignty were not disjoined. Titles and forms were still retained which implied that the heir of Tamerlane was an absolute ruler and that the Nabobs of the provinces were his lieutenants. In reality, he was a captive. The Nabobs were in some places independent princes. In other places, as in Bengal and the Carnatic, they had, like their master, become mere phantoms, and the Company was supreme. Among the Mahrattas, again, the heir of Sevajee still kept the title of Rajah; but he was a prisoner, and his prime minister, the Peshwa, had become the hereditary chief of the state. The Peshwa, in his turn, was fast sinking into the same degraded situation into which he had reduced the Rajah. It was, we believe, impossible to find, from the Himalayas to Mysore, a single government which was at once *de facto* and *de jure*—which possessed the physical means of making itself feared by its neighbours and subjects, and which had at the same time the authority derived from law and long prescription.

Hastings clearly discerned what was hidden from most of his contemporaries, that such a state of things gave immense advantages to a ruler of great talents and few scruples. In every international question that could arise, he had his option between the *de facto* ground and the *de jure* ground; and the probability was that one of those grounds would sustain any claim that it might be convenient for him to make and enable him to resist any claim made by others. In every controversy, accordingly, he resorted to the plea which suited his immediate purpose, without troubling himself in the least about consistency; and thus he scarcely ever failed to find what, to persons of short memories and scanty information, seemed to be a justification for what he wanted to do. Sometimes the Nabob of Bengal is a shadow, sometimes a monarch. Sometimes the Vizier is a mere deputy, sometimes an independent potentate. If it is expedient for the Company to show some legal title to the revenues of Bengal, the grant under the seal of the Mogul is brought forward as an instrument of the highest authority. When the Mogul asks for the rents which were reserved to him by that very grant, he is told that he is a mere pageant; that the English power rests on a very different foundation from a charter given by him; that he is welcome to play at royalty as long as he likes, but that he must expect no tribute from the real masters of India.

It is true that it was in the power of others, as well as of Hastings, to practise this legerdemain; but in the controversies of governments, sophistry is of little use unless it be backed by power. There is a principle which Hastings was fond of asserting in the strongest terms and on which he acted with undeviating steadiness. It is a principle which, we must own, can hardly be disputed in the present state of public law. It is this—that where an ambiguous question arises between two governments, there is, if they cannot agree, no appeal except to force, and that the opinion of the strongest must prevail. Almost every question was ambiguous in India. The English government was the strongest in India. The consequences are obvious. The English government might do exactly what it chose.

The English government now chose to wring money out of Cheyte Sing. It had formerly been convenient to treat him as a sovereign prince; it was now convenient to treat him as a subject. Dexterity inferior to that of Hastings could easily find, in the general chaos of laws and customs, arguments for either course. Hastings wanted a great supply. It was known that Cheyte Sing had a large revenue, and it was suspected that he had accumulated a treasure. Nor was he a favourite at Calcutta. He had, when the Governor-General was in great difficulties, courted the favour of Francis and Clavering. Hastings, who, less perhaps from evil passions than from policy, seldom left an injury unpunished, was not sorry that the fate of Cheyte Sing should teach neighbouring princes the same lesson which the fate of Nuncomar had already impressed on the inhabitants of Bengal.

In 1778, on the first breaking out of the war with France, Cheyte Sing was called upon to pay, in addition to his fixed tribute, an extraordinary contribution of £50,000. In 1779, an equal sum was exacted. In 1780, the demand was renewed. Cheyte Sing, in the hope of obtaining some indulgence, secretly offered the Governor-General a bribe of £20,000. Hastings took the money; and his enemies have maintained that he took it intending to keep it. He certainly concealed the transaction, for a time, both from the Council in Bengal and from the Directors at home; nor did he ever give any satisfactory reason for the concealment. Public spirit or the fear of detection, however, determined him to withstand the temptation. He paid over the bribe to the Company's treasury, and insisted that the Rajah should instantly comply with the demands of the English government. The Rajah, after the fashion of his countrymen, shuffled, solicited and pleaded poverty. The grasp of Hastings was not to be so eluded. He added to the requisition another £10,000, as a fine for delay, and sent troops to exact the money.

The money was paid. But this was not enough. The late events in the south of India had increased the financial embarrassments of the Company. Hastings was determined to plunder Cheyte Sing, and, for that end, to fasten a quarrel on him. Accordingly, the Rajah was now required to keep a body of cavalry for the service of the British government. He objected and evaded. This was exactly what the Governor-General wanted. He had now a pretext for treating the wealthiest of his vassals as a criminal. "I resolved"—these are the words of Hastings himself—"to draw from his guilt the means of relief of the Company's distresses—to make him pay largely for his pardon, or to exact a severe vengeance for past delinquency." The plan was simply this, to demand larger and larger contributions till the Rajah should be driven to remonstrance; then to call his remonstrance a crime and to punish him by confiscating all his possessions.

Cheyte Sing was in the greatest dismay. He offered £200,000 to propitiate the British government. But Hastings replied that nothing less than half a million would be accepted. Nay, he began to think of selling Benares to Oude, as he had formerly sold Allahabad and Rohilcund. The matter was one which could not be well managed at a distance, and Hastings resolved to visit Benares.

Cheyte Sing received his liege lord with every mark of reverence, came near sixty miles, with his guards, to meet and escort the illustrious visitor, and expressed his deep concern at the displeasure of the English. He even took off his turban and laid it in the lap of Hastings—a gesture which in India marks the most profound submission and devotion. Hastings behaved with cold and repulsive severity. Having arrived at Benares, he sent to the Rajah a paper containing the demands of the government of Bengal. The Rajah, in reply, attempted to clear himself from the accusations brought against him. Hastings, who wanted money and not excuses, was not to be put off by the ordinary artifices of Eastern negotiation. He instantly ordered the Rajah to be arrested and placed under the custody of two companies of sepoys.

In taking these strong measures, Hastings scarcely showed his usual judgment. It is possible that, having had little opportunity of personally observing any part of the population of India except the Bengalees, he was not fully aware of the difference between their character and that of the tribes which inhabit the upper provinces. He was now in a land far more favourable to the vigour of the human frame than the Delta of the Ganges; in a land fruitful of soldiers who have been found worthy to follow English battalions to the charge and into the breach. The Rajah was popular among his subjects. His administration had been mild; and the prosperity of the district which he governed presented a striking contrast to the depressed state of Bahar under our rule—and a still more striking contrast to the misery of the provinces which were cursed by the tyranny of the Nabob Vizier. The national and religious prejudices with which the English were regarded throughout India were peculiarly intense in the metropolis of the Brahminical superstition. It can therefore scarcely be doubted that the Governor-General, before he outraged the dignity of Cheyte Sing by an arrest, ought to have assembled a force capable of bearing down all opposition. This had not been done. The handful of sepoys who attended Hastings would probably have been sufficient to overawe Moorshedabad or the Black Town of Calcutta. But they were unequal to a conflict with the hardy rabble of Benares. The streets surrounding the palace were filled by an immense multitude, of whom a large proportion, as is usual in Upper India, wore arms. The tumult became a fight, and the fight a massacre. The English officers defended themselves with desperate courage against overwhelming numbers, and fell, as became them, sword in hand. The sepoys were butchered. The gates were forced. The captive prince, neglected by his gaolers during the confusion, discovered an outlet which opened on the precipitous bank of the Ganges, let himself down to the water by a string made of the turbans of his attendants, found a boat, and escaped to the opposite shore.

If Hastings had, by indiscreet violence, brought himself into a difficult and perilous situation, it is only just to acknowledge that he extricated himself with even more than his usual ability and presence of mind. He had only fifty men with him. The building in which he had taken up his residence was on every side blockaded by the insurgents. But his fortitude remained unshaken. The Rajah, from the other side of the river, sent apologies and liberal offers. They were not even answered. Some subtle and enterprising men were found who undertook to pass through the throng of enemies and to convey the intelligence of the late events to the English cantonments. It is the fashion of the natives of India to wear large earrings of gold. When they travel, the rings are laid aside lest they should tempt some gang of robbers, and, in place of the ring, a quill or a roll of paper is inserted in the orifice to prevent it from closing. Hastings placed in the ears of his messengers letters rolled up in the smallest compass. Some of these letters were addressed to the commanders of English troops. One was written to assure his wife of his safety. One was to the envoy whom he had sent to negotiate with the Mahrattas. Instructions for the negotiations were needed, and the Governor-General framed them in that situation of extreme danger with as much composure as if he had been writing in his palace at Calcutta.

Things, however, were not yet at the worst. An English officer of more spirit than judgment, eager to distinguish himself, made a premature attack on the insurgents beyond the river. His troops were entangled in narrow streets and assailed by a furious population. He fell, with many of his men, and the survivors were forced to retire.

This event produced the effect which has never failed to follow every check, however slight, sustained in India by the English arms. For hundreds of miles round, the whole country was in commotion. The entire population of the district of Benares took arms. The fields were abandoned by the husbandmen, who thronged to defend their prince. The infection spread to Oude. The oppressed people of that province rose up against the Nabob Vizier, refused to pay their imposts and put the revenue officers to flight. Even Bahar was ripe for revolt. The hopes of Cheyte Sing began to rise. Instead of imploring mercy in the humble style of a vassal, he began to talk the language of a conqueror, and threatened, it was said, to sweep the white usurpers out of the land. But the English troops were now assembling fast. The officers, and even the private men, regarded the Governor-General with enthusiastic attachment, and flew to his aid with an alacrity which, as he boasted, had never been shown on any other occasion. Major Popham, a brave and skilful soldier, who had highly distinguished himself in the Mahratta war, and in whom the Governor-General reposed the greatest confidence, took the command. The tumultuary army of the Rajah was put to rout. His fastnesses were stormed. In a few hours, above thirty thousand men left his standard and returned to their ordinary avocations. The unhappy prince fled from his country for ever. His fair domain was added to the British dominions. One of his relations indeed was appointed Rajah; but the Rajah of Benares was henceforth to be, like the Nabob of Bengal, a mere pensioner.

By this revolution, an addition of £400,000 a-year was made to the revenues of the Company. But the immediate relief was not as great as had been expected. The treasure laid up by Cheyte Sing had been popularly estimated at a million sterling. It turned out to be about a fourth part of that sum; and, such as it was, it was seized and divided by the army as prize-money.

Disappointed in his expectations from Benares, Hastings was more violent than he would otherwise have been in his dealings with Oude. Sujah Dowlah had long been dead. His son and successor, Asaph-ul-Dowlah, was one of the weakest and most vicious even of Eastern princes. His life was divided between torpid repose and the most odious forms of sensuality. In his court there was boundless waste; throughout his dominions wretchedness and disorder. He had been, under the skilful management of the English government, gradually sinking from the rank of an independent prince to that of a vassal of the Company. It was only by the help of a British brigade that he could be secure from the aggressions of neighbours who despised his weakness, and from the vengeance of subjects who detested his tyranny. A brigade was furnished; and he engaged to defray the charge of paying and maintaining it. From that time his independence was at an end. Hastings was not a man to lose the advantage which he had thus gained. The Nabob soon began to complain of the burden which he had undertaken to bear. His revenues, he said, were falling off; his servants were unpaid; he could no longer support the expense of the arrangement which he had sanctioned. Hastings would not listen to these representations. The Vizier, he said, had invited the government of Bengal to send him troops and had promised to pay for them. The troops had been sent. How long the troops were to remain in Oude was a matter not settled by the treaty. It remained, therefore, to be settled between the contracting parties. But the contracting parties differed. Who then must decide? The strongest.

Hastings also argued that, if the English force was withdrawn, Oude would certainly become a prey to anarchy and would probably be overrun by a Mahratta army. That the finances of Oude were embarrassed he admitted. But he contended, not without reason, that the embarrassment was to be attributed to the incapacity and vices of Asaph-ul-Dowlah himself, and that if less were spent on the troops, the only effect would be that more would be squandered on worthless favourites.

Hastings had intended, after settling the affairs of Benares, to visit Lucknow and there to confer with Asaph-ul-Dowlah. But the obsequious courtesy of the Nabob Vizier prevented this visit. With a small train, he hastened to meet the Governor-General. An interview took place in the fortress which, from the crest of the precipitous rock of Chunar, looks down on the waters of the Ganges.

At first sight it might appear impossible that the negotiation should come to an amicable close. Hastings wanted an extraordinary supply of money. Asaph-ul-Dowlah wanted to obtain a remission of what he already owed. Such a difference seemed to admit of no compromise. There was, however, one course satisfactory to both sides—one course by which it was possible to relieve the finances both of Oude and of Bengal; and that course was adopted. It was simply this—that the Governor-General and the Nabob Vizier should join to rob a third party; and the third party whom they determined to rob was the parent of one of the robbers.

The mother of the late Nabob, and his wife, who was the mother of the present Nabob, were known as the Begums or Princesses of Oude. They had possessed great influence over Sujah Dowlah, and had, at his death, been left in possession of a splendid dotation. The domains of which they received the rents and administered the government were of wide extent. The treasure hoarded by the late Nabob—a treasure which was popularly estimated at near three millions sterling—was in their hands. They continued to occupy his favourite palace at Fyzabad, the Beautiful Dwelling; while Asaph-ul-Dowlah held his court in the stately Lucknow, which he had built for himself on the shores of the Goomti, and had adorned with noble mosques and colleges.

Asaph-ul-Dowlah had already extorted considerable sums from his mother. She had at length appealed to the English, and the English had interfered. A solemn compact had been made, by which she consented to give her son some pecuniary assistance and he in his turn promised never to commit any further invasion of her rights. This compact was formally guaranteed by the government of Bengal. But times had changed; money was wanted; and the power which had given the guarantee was not ashamed to instigate the spoiler.

It was necessary to find some pretext for a confiscation inconsistent, not merely with plighted faith,—not merely with the ordinary rules of humanity and justice—but also with that great law of filial piety which, even in the wildest tribes of savages—even in those more degraded communities which wither under the influence of a corrupt half-civilisation—retains a certain authority over the human mind. A pretext was the last thing that Hastings was likely to want. The insurrection at Benares had produced disturbances in Oude. These disturbances it was convenient to impute to the Princesses. Evidence for the imputation there was scarcely any; unless reports wandering from one mouth to another and gaining something by every transmission may be called evidence. The accused were furnished with no charge; they were permitted to make no defence; for the Governor-General wisely considered that, if he tried them, he might not be able to find a ground for plundering them. It was agreed between him and the Nabob Vizier that the noble ladies should, by a sweeping act of confiscation, be stripped of their domains and treasures for the benefit of the Company, and that the sums thus obtained should be accepted by the government of Bengal in satisfaction of its claims on the government of Oude.

While Asaph-ul-Dowlah was at Chunar, he was completely subjugated by the clear and commanding intellect of the English statesman. But, when they had separated, he began to reflect with uneasiness on the engagements into which he had entered. His mother and grandmother protested and implored. His heart, deeply corrupted by absolute power and licentious pleasures, yet not naturally unfeeling, failed him in this crisis. Even the English resident at Lucknow though hitherto devoted to Hastings, shrank from extreme measures. But the Governor-General was inexorable. He wrote to the resident in terms of the greatest severity, and declared that, if the spoliation which had been agreed upon were not instantly carried into effect, he would himself go to Lucknow and do that from which feebler minds recoiled with dismay. The resident, thus menaced, waited on his Highness and insisted that the treaty of Chunar should be carried into full and immediate effect. Asaph-ul-Dowlah yielded—making, at the same time a solemn protestation, that he yielded to compulsion. The lands were resumed; but the treasure was not so easily obtained. It was necessary to use force. A body of the Company's troops marched to Fyzabad and forced the gates of the palace. The Princesses were confined to their own apartments. But still they refused to submit. Some more stringent mode of coercion was to be found. A mode was found of which, even at this distance of time, we cannot speak without shame and sorrow.

There were at Fyzabad two ancient men, belonging to that unhappy class which a practice, of immemorial antiquity in the East, has excluded from the pleasures of love and from the hope of posterity. It has always been held in Asiatic courts that beings thus estranged from sympathy with their kind are those whom princes may most safely trust. Sujah Dowlah had been of this opinion. He had given his entire confidence to the two eunuchs; and after his death they remained at the head of the household of his widow.

These men were, by the orders of the British government, seized, imprisoned, ironed, starved almost to death, in order to extort money from the Princesses. After they had been two months in confinement, their health gave way. They implored permission to take a little exercise in the garden of their prison. The officer who was in charge of them stated that, if they were allowed this indulgence, there was not the smallest chance of their escaping, and that their irons really added nothing to the security of the custody in which they were kept. He did not understand the plan of his superiors. Their object in these inflictions was not security but torture; and all mitigation was refused. Yet this was not the worst. It was resolved by an English government that these two infirm old men should be delivered to the tormentors. For that purpose they were removed to Lucknow. What horrors their dungeon there witnessed can only be guessed. But there remains on the records of Parliament this letter, written by a British resident to a British soldier.

"Sir, the Nabob having determined to inflict corporal punishment upon the prisoners under your guard, this is to desire that his officers, when they shall come, may have free access to the prisoners, and be permitted to do with them as they shall see proper."

While these barbarities were perpetrated at Lucknow, the Princesses were still under duress at Fyzabad. Food was allowed to enter their apartments only in such scanty quantities that their female attendants were in danger of perishing with hunger. Month after month this cruelty continued, till at length, after twelve hundred thousand pounds had been wrung out of the Princesses, Hastings began to think that he had really got to the bottom of their revenue, and that no rigour could extort more. Then at length the wretched men who were detained at Lucknow regained their liberty. When their irons were knocked off and the doors of their prison opened, their quivering lips, the tears which ran down their cheeks and the thanksgivings which they poured forth to the common Father of Mussulmans and Christians, melted even the stout hearts of the English warriors who stood by.

There is a man to whom the conduct of Hastings, through the whole of these proceedings, appears not only excusable but laudable. There is a man who tells us that he "must really be pardoned if he ventures to characterise as something pre-eminently ridiculous and wicked the sensibility which would balance against the preservation of British India a little personal suffering, which was applied only so long as the sufferers refused to deliver up a portion of that wealth, the whole of which their own and their mistresses' treason had forfeited." We cannot, we must own, envy the reverend biographer either his singular notion of what constitutes pre-eminent wickedness or his equally singular perception of the pre-eminently ridiculous. Is this the generosity of an English soldier? Is this the charity of a Christian priest? Could neither of Mr. Gleig's professions teach him the very rudiments of morality? Or is morality a thing which may be well enough in sermons, but which has nothing to do with biography?

But we must not forget to do justice to Sir Elijah Impey's conduct on this occasion. It was not indeed easy for him to intrude himself into a business so entirely alien from all his official duties. But there was something inexpressibly alluring, we must suppose, in the peculiar rankness of the infamy which was then to be got at Lucknow. He hurried thither as fast as relays of palanquin-bearers could carry him. A crowd of people came before him with affidavits against the Begums ready drawn in their hands. Those affidavits he did not read. The greater part, indeed, he could not read; for they were in Persian and Hindoostanee, and no interpreter was employed. He administered the oath to the deponents with all possible expedition, and asked not a single question, not even whether they had perused the statements to which they swore. This work performed, he got again into his palanquin and posted back to Calcutta, to be in time for the opening of term. The cause was one which, by his own confession, lay altogether out of his jurisdiction. Under the charter of justice, he had no more right to inquire into crimes committed by natives in Oude than the Lord President of the Court of Session of Scotland to hold an assize at Exeter. He had no right to try the Begums, nor did he pretend to try them. With what object, then, did he undertake so long a journey? Evidently in order that he might give, in an irregular manner, that sanction which, in a regular manner, he could not give to the crimes of those who had recently hired him; and in order that a confused mass of testimony, which he did not sift, which he did not even read, might acquire an authority not properly belonging to it from the signature of the highest judicial functionary in India.

The time was approaching, however, when he was to be stripped of that robe which has never, since the Revolution, been disgraced so foully as by him. The state of India had for some time occupied much of the attention of the British Parliament. Towards the close of the American war, two committees of the Commons sat on Eastern affairs. In the one Edmund Burke took the lead. The other was under the presidency of the able and versatile Henry Dundas, then Lord Advocate of Scotland. Great as are the changes which, during the last sixty years, have taken place in our Asiatic dominions, the reports which those committees laid on the table of the House will still be found most interesting and instructive.

There was as yet no connection between the Company and either of the great parties in the state. The ministers had no motive to defend Indian abuses. On the contrary, it was for their interest to show, if possible, that the government and patronage of our Oriental empire might, with advantage, be transferred to themselves. The votes, therefore, which, in consequence of the reports made by the two committees, were passed by the Commons, breathed the spirit of stern and indignant justice. The severest epithets were applied to several of the measures of Hastings, especially to the Rohilla war; and it was resolved, on the motion of Mr. Dundas, that the Company ought to recall a Governor-General who had brought such calamities on the Indian people and such dishonour on the British name. An act was passed for limiting the jurisdiction of the Supreme Court. The bargain which Hastings had made with the Chief Justice was condemned in the strongest terms: and an address was presented to the king, praying that Impey might be ordered home to answer for his misdeeds.

Impey was recalled by a letter from the Secretary of State. But the proprietors of India Stock resolutely refused to dismiss Hastings from their service; and passed a resolution affirming, what was undeniably true, that they were intrusted by law with the right of naming and removing their Governor-General, and that they were not bound to obey the directions of a single branch of the legislature with respect to such nomination or removal.

Thus supported by his employers, Hastings remained at the head of the government of Bengal till the spring of 1785. His administration, so eventful and stormy, closed in almost perfect quiet. In the Council, there was no regular opposition to his measures. Peace was restored to India. The Mahratta war had ceased. Hyder was no more. A treaty had been concluded with his son Tippoo; and the Carnatic had been evacuated by the armies of Mysore. Since the termination of the American war, England had no European enemy or rival in the Eastern seas.

On a general review of the long administration of Hastings, it is impossible to deny that, against the great crimes by which it is blemished, we have to set off great public services. England had passed through a perilous crisis. She still, indeed, maintained her place in the foremost rank of European powers; and the manner in which she had defended herself against fearful odds had inspired surrounding nations with a high opinion both of her spirit and of her strength. Nevertheless, in every part of the world, except one, she had been a loser. Not only had she been compelled to acknowledge the independence of thirteen colonies peopled by her children and to conciliate the Irish by giving up the right of legislating for them, but, in the Mediterranean, in the Gulf of Mexico, on the coast of Africa, on the continent of America, she had been compelled to cede the fruits of her victories in former wars. Spain regained Minorca and Florida; France regained Senegal, Goree and several West Indian Islands. The only quarter of the world in which Britain had lost nothing was the quarter in which her interests had been committed to the care of Hastings. In spite of the utmost exertions both of European and Asiatic enemies, the power of our country in the East had been greatly augmented. Benares was subjected; the Nabob Vizier reduced to vassalage. That our influence had been thus extended, nay, that Fort William and Fort St. George had not been occupied by hostile armies, was owing, if we may trust the general voice of the English in India, to the skill and resolution of Hastings.

His internal administration, with all its blemishes, gives him a title to be considered as one of the most remarkable men in our history. He dissolved the double government. He transferred the direction of affairs to English hands. Out of a frightful anarchy, he educed at least a rude and imperfect order. The whole organisation by which justice was dispensed, revenue collected, peace maintained throughout a territory not inferior in population to the dominions of Louis the Sixteenth or the Emperor Joseph, was created and superintended by him. He boasted that every public office, without exception, which existed when he left Bengal was his work. It is quite true that this system, after all the improvements suggested by the experience of sixty years, still needs improvement, and that it was at first far more defective than it now is. But whoever seriously considers what it is to construct from the beginning the whole of the machine so vast and complex as a government, will allow that what Hastings effected deserves high admiration. To compare the most celebrated European ministers to him seems to us as unjust as it would be to compare the best baker in London with Robinson Crusoe, who, before he could bake a single loaf, had to make his plough and his harrow, his fences and his scarecrows, his sickle and his flail, his mill and his oven.

The just fame of Hastings rises still higher when we reflect that he was not bred a statesman; that he was sent from school to a counting-house; and that he was employed during the prime of his manhood as a commercial agent, far from all intellectual society.

Nor must we forget that all, or almost all, to whom, when placed at the head of affairs, he could apply for assistance, were persons who owed as little as himself, or less than himself, to education. A minister in Europe finds himself, on the first day on which he commences his functions, surrounded by experienced public servants, the depositories of official traditions. Hastings had no such help. His own reflection, his own energy, were to supply the place of all

Downing Street and Somerset House. Having had no facilities for learning, he was forced to teach. He had first to form himself and then to form his instruments, and this not in a single department, but in all the departments of the administration.

It must be added that, while engaged in this most arduous task, he was constantly trammelled by orders from home and frequently borne down by a majority in council. The preservation of an Empire from a formidable combination of foreign enemies, the construction of a government in all its parts, were accomplished by him, while every ship brought out bales of censure from his employers and while the records of every consultation were filled with acrimonious minutes by his colleagues. We believe that there never was a public man whose temper was so severely tried—not Marlborough when thwarted by the Dutch Deputies—not Wellington when he had to deal at once with the Portuguese Regency, the Spanish Juntas and Mr. Percival. But the temper of Hastings was equal to almost any trial. It was not sweet; but it was calm. Quick and vigorous as his intellect was, the patience with which he endured the most cruel vexations, till a remedy could be found, resembled the patience of stupidity. He seems to have been capable of resentment, bitter and long enduring; yet his resentment so seldom hurried him into any blunder that it may be doubted whether what appeared to be revenge was anything but policy.

The effect of this singular equanimity was that he always had the full command of all the resources of one of the most fertile minds that ever existed. Accordingly, no complication of perils and embarrassments could perplex him. For every difficulty he had a contrivance ready; and whatever may be thought of the justice and humanity of some of his contrivances, it is certain that they seldom failed to serve the purpose for which they were designed.

Together with this extraordinary talent for devising expedients, Hastings possessed, in a very high degree, another talent scarcely less necessary to a man in his situation—we mean the talent for conducting political controversy. It is as necessary to an English statesman in the East that he should be able to write as it is to a minister in this country that he should be able to speak. It is chiefly by the oratory of a public man here that the nation judges of his powers. It is from the letters and reports of a public man in India that the dispensers of patronage form their estimate of him. In each case the talent which receives peculiar encouragement is developed, perhaps at the expense of the other powers. In this country we sometimes hear men speak above their abilities. It is not very unusual to find gentlemen in the Indian service who write above their abilities. The English politician is a little too much of a debater; the Indian politician a little too much of an essayist.

Of the numerous servants of the Company, who have distinguished themselves as framers of minutes and despatches, Hastings stands at the head. He was indeed the person who gave to the official writing of the Indian governments the character which it still retains. He was matched against no common antagonist. But even Francis was forced to acknowledge, with sullen and resentful candour, that there was no contending against the pen of Hastings. And, in truth, the Governor-General's power of making out a case—of perplexing what it was inconvenient that people should understand—and of setting in the clearest point of view whatever would bear the light—was incomparable. His style must be praised with some reservation. It was in general forcible, pure and polished; but it was sometimes, though not often, turgid, and, on one or two occasions, even bombastic. Perhaps the fondness of Hastings for Persian literature may have tended to corrupt his taste.

And, since we have referred to his literary tastes, it would be most unjust not to praise the judicious encouragement which, as a ruler, he gave to liberal studies and curious researches. His patronage was extended, with prudent generosity, to voyages, travels, experiments, publications. He did little, it is true, towards introducing into India the learning of the West— to make the young natives of Bengal familiar with Milton and Adam Smith— to substitute the geography, astronomy and surgery of Europe for the dotages of the Brahminical superstition, or for the imperfect science of ancient Greece transfused through Arabian expositions—this was a scheme reserved to crown the beneficent administration of a far more virtuous ruler. Still, it is impossible to refuse high commendation to a man who, taken from a ledger to govern an empire, overwhelmed by public business, surrounded by men as busy as himself and separated by thousands of leagues from almost all literary society, gave, both by his example and by his munificence, a great impulse to learning. In Persian and Arabic literature, he was deeply skilled. With the Sanscrit, he was not himself acquainted; but those who first brought that language to the knowledge of European students owed much to his encouragement. It was under his protection that the Asiatic Society commenced its honourable career. That distinguished body selected him to be its first president; but with excellent taste and feeling, he declined the honour in favour of Sir William Jones. But the chief advantage which the students of Oriental letters derived from his patronage remains to be mentioned. The Pundits of Bengal had always looked with great jealousy on the attempts of foreigners to pry into those mysteries which were locked up in the sacred dialect. Their religion had been persecuted by the Mahommedans. What they knew of the spirit of the Portuguese government might warrant them in apprehending persecution from Christians. That apprehension, the wisdom and moderation of Hastings removed. He was the first foreign ruler who succeeded in gaining the confidence of the hereditary priests of India and who induced them to lay open to English scholars the secrets of the old Brahminical theology and jurisprudence.

It is indeed impossible to deny that, in the great art of inspiring large masses of human beings with confidence and attachment, no ruler ever surpassed Hastings. If he had made himself popular with the English by giving up the Bengalees to extortion and oppression, or if, on the other hand, he had conciliated the Bengalees and alienated the English, there would have been no cause for wonder. What is peculiar to him is that, being the chief of a small band of strangers who exercised boundless power over a great indigenous population, he made himself beloved both by the subject many and by the dominant few. The affection felt for him by the civil service was singularly ardent and constant. Through all his disasters and perils, his brethren stood by him with steadfast loyalty. The army, at the same time, loved him as armies have seldom loved any but the greatest chiefs who have led them to victory. Even in his disputes with distinguished military men, he could always count on the support of the military profession. While such was his empire over the hearts of his countrymen, he enjoyed among the natives a popularity such as other governors have perhaps better merited, but such as no other governor has been able to attain. He spoke their vernacular dialects with facility and precision. He was intimately acquainted with their feelings and usages. On one or two occasions, for great ends, he deliberately acted in defiance of their opinions; but on such occasions he gained more in their respect than he lost in their love. In general, he carefully avoided all that could shock their national or religious prejudices. His administration was indeed in many respects faulty; but the Bengalee standard of good government was not high. Under the Nabobs, the hurricane of Mahratta cavalry had passed annually over the rich alluvial plain. But even the Mahratta shrank from a conflict with the mighty children of the sea; and the immense rice harvests of the Lower Ganges were safely gathered in under the protection of the English sword. The first English conquerors had been more rapacious and merciless even then the Mahrattas; but that generation had passed away. Defective as was the police, heavy as were the public burdens, it is probable that the oldest man in Bengal could not recollect a season of equal security and prosperity. For the first time within living memory, the province was placed under a government strong enough to prevent others from robbing and not inclined to play the robber itself. These things inspired good-will. At the same time, the constant success of Hastings and the manner in which he extricated himself from every difficulty made him an object of superstitious admiration; and the more than regal splendour which he sometimes displayed dazzled a people who have much in common with children. Even now, after the lapse of more than fifty years, the natives of India still talk of him as the greatest of the English; and nurses sing children to sleep with a jingling ballad about the fleet horses and richly caparisoned elephants of Sahib Warren Hostein.

The gravest offence of which Hastings was guilty did not affect his popularity with the people of Bengal; for those offences were committed against neighbouring states. Those offences, as our readers must have perceived, we are not disposed to vindicate; yet, in order that the censure may be justly apportioned to the transgression, it is fit that the motive of the criminal should be taken into consideration. The motive which prompted the worst acts of Hastings was misdirected and ill-regulated public spirit. The rules of justice, the sentiments of humanity, the plighted faith of treaties, were in his view as nothing when opposed to the immediate interest of the state. This is no justification according to the principles either of morality, or, what we believe to be identical with morality, namely, far-sighted policy. Nevertheless, the common sense of mankind, which in questions of this sort seldom goes far wrong, will always recognise a distinction between crimes which originate in an inordinate zeal for the commonwealth and crimes which originate in selfish cupidity. To the benefit of this distinction Hastings is fairly entitled. There is, we conceive, no reason to suspect that the Rohilla war, the revolution of Benares or the spoliation of the Princesses of Oude added a rupee to his fortune. We will not affirm that, in all pecuniary dealings, he showed that punctilious integrity, that dread of the faintest appearance of evil, which is now the glory of the Indian civil service. But when the school in which he had been trained and the temptations to which he was exposed are considered, we are more inclined to praise him for his general uprightness with respect to money than rigidly to blame him for a few transactions which would now be called indelicate and irregular, but which even now would hardly be designated as corrupt. A rapacious man he certainly was not. Had he been so, he would infallibly have returned to his country the richest subject in Europe. We speak within compass when we say that, without applying any extraordinary pressure, he might easily have obtained from the zemindars of the Company's provinces and from neighbouring princes, in the course of thirteen years, more than three millions sterling, and might have outshone the splendour of Carlton House and of the Palais Royal. He brought home a fortune such as a Governor-General, fond of state and careless of thrift, might easily, during so long a tenure of office, save out of his legal salary. Mrs. Hastings, we are afraid, was less scrupulous. It was generally believed that she accepted presents with great alacrity, and that she thus formed, without the connivance of her husband, a private hoard amounting to several lacs of rupees. We are the more inclined to give credit to this story because Mr. Gleig, who cannot but have heard it, does not, as far as we have observed, notice or contradict it.

The influence of Mrs. Hastings over her husband was indeed such that she might easily have obtained much larger sums than she was ever accused of receiving. At length her health began to give way; and the Governor-General, much against his will, was compelled to send her to England. He seems to have loved her with that love which is peculiar to men of strong minds, to men whose affection is not easily won or widely diffused. The talk of Calcutta ran for some time on the luxurious manner in which he fitted up the round-house of an Indiaman for her accommodation—on the profusion of sandal-wood and carved ivory which adorned her cabin—and on the thousands which had been expended in order to procure for her the society of an agreeable female companion during the voyage. We may remark here, that the letters of Hastings to his wife are exceedingly characteristic—tender, and full of indications of esteem and confidence; but, at the same time, a little more ceremonious than is usual in so intimate a relation. The solemn courtesy with which he compliments "his elegant Marian" reminds us now and then of the dignified air with which Sir Charles Grandison bowed over Miss Byron's hand in the cedar parlour.

After some months, Hastings prepared to follow his wife to England. When it was announced that he was about to quit his office, the feeling of the society which he had so long governed manifested itself by many signs. Addresses poured in from Europeans and Asiatics, from civil functionaries, soldiers and traders. On the day on which he delivered up the keys of office, a crowd of friends and admirers formed a lane to the quay where he embarked. Several barges escorted him far down the river; and some attached friends refused to quit him till the low coast of Bengal was fading from the view and till the pilot was leaving the ship.

Of his voyage, little is known except that he amused himself with books and with his pen; and that, among the compositions by which he beguiled the tediousness of that long leisure, was a pleasing imitation of Horace's "Otium Divos Rogat." This little poem was inscribed to Mr. Shore, afterwards Lord Teignmouth—a man of whose integrity, humanity and honour, it is impossible to speak too highly, but who, like some other excellent members of the civil service, extended to the conduct of his friend Hastings an indulgence of which his own conduct never stood in need.

The voyage was, for those times, very speedy. Hastings was little more than four months on the sea. In June, 1785, he landed at Plymouth, posted to London, appeared at Court, paid his respects in Leadenhall Street, and then retired with his wife to Cheltenham.

He was greatly pleased with his reception. The King treated him with marked distinction. The Queen, who had already incurred much censure on account of the favour which, in spite of the ordinary severity of her virtue, she had shown to the "elegant Marian," was not less gracious to Hastings. The Directors received him in a solemn sitting, and their chairman read to him a vote of thanks which they had passed without one dissentient voice. "I find myself," said Hastings, in a letter written about a quarter of a year after his arrival in England, "I find myself everywhere, and universally, treated with evidences, apparent even to my own observation, that I possess the good opinion of my country."

The confident and exulting tone of his correspondence about this time is the more remarkable because he had already received ample notice of the attack which was in preparation. Within a week after he landed at Plymouth, Burke gave notice in the House of Commons of a motion seriously affecting a gentleman lately returned from India. The session, however, was then so far advanced that it was impossible to enter on so extensive and important a subject.

Hastings, it is clear, was not sensible of the danger of his position. Indeed, that sagacity, that judgment, that readiness in devising expedients, which had distinguished him in the East, seemed now to have forsaken him; not that his abilities were at all impaired, not that he was not still the same man who had triumphed over Francis and Nuncomar, who had made the Chief Justice and the Nabob Vizier his tools, who had deposed Cheyte Sing and repelled Hyder Ali—but an oak, as Mr. Grattan finely said, should not be transplanted at fifty. A man, who, having left England when a boy, returns to it after thirty or forty years passed in India, will find, be his talents what they may, that he has much both to learn and to unlearn before he can take a place among English statesmen. The working of a representative system, the war of parties, the arts of debate, the influence of the press, are startling novelties to him. Surrounded on every side by new machines and new tactics, he is as much bewildered as Hannibal would have been at Waterloo or Themistocles at Trafalgar. His very acuteness deludes him. His very vigour causes him to stumble. The more correct his maxims, when applied to the state of society to which he is accustomed, the more certain they are to lead him astray. This was strikingly the case with Hastings. In India he had a bad hand; but he was master of the game and he won every stake. In England he held excellent cards if he had known how to play them; and it was chiefly by his own errors that he was brought to the verge of ruin.

Of all his errors, the most serious was perhaps the choice of a champion. Clive, in similar circumstances, had made a singularly happy selection. He put himself into the hands of Wedderburn, afterwards Lord Loughborough, one of the few great advocates who have also been great in the House of Commons. To the defence of Clive, therefore, nothing was wanting, neither learning nor knowledge of the world, neither forensic acuteness nor that eloquence which charms political assemblies. Hastings intrusted his interests to a very different person, a Major in the Bengal army named Scott. This gentleman had been sent over from India some time before as the agent of the Governor-General. It was rumoured that his services were rewarded with Oriental munificence; and we believe that he received much more than Hastings could conveniently spare. The Major obtained a seat in Parliament, and was there regarded as the organ of his employer. It was evidently impossible that a gentleman so situated could speak with the authority which belongs to an independent position. Nor had the agent of Hastings the talents necessary for obtaining the ear of an assembly which, accustomed to listen to great orators, had naturally become fastidious. He was always on his legs; he was very tedious; and he had only one topic, the merits and wrongs of Hastings. Everybody who knows the House of Commons will easily guess what followed. The Major was soon considered as the greatest *bore* of his time. His exertions were not confined to Parliament. There was hardly a day on which the newspapers did not contain some puff upon Hastings signed *Asiaticus* or *Bengalensis*, but known to the written by the indefatigable Scott; and hardly a month in which some bulky pamphlet on the same subject, and from the same pen, did not pass to the trunkmakers and the pastrycooks. As to this gentleman's capacity for conducting a delicate question through Parliament, our readers will want no evidence beyond that which they will find in letters preserved in these volumes. We will give a single specimen of his temper and judgment. He designated the greatest man then living as "that reptile Mr. Burke."

In spite, however, of this unfortunate choice, the general aspect of affairs was favourable to Hastings. The King was on his side. The Company and its servants were zealous in his cause. Among public men he had many ardent friends. Such were Lord Mansfield, who had outlived the vigour of his body, but not that of his mind; and Lord Lansdowne, who, though unconnected with any party, retained the importance which belongs to great talents and knowledge. The ministers were generally believed to be favourable to the late Governor-General. They owed their power to the clamour which had been raised against Mr. Fox's East India Bill. The authors of that bill, when accused of invading vested rights and of setting up powers unknown to the constitution, had defended themselves by pointing to the crimes of Hastings, and by arguing that abuses so extraordinary justified extraordinary measures. Those who, by opposing that bill had raised themselves to the head of affairs, would naturally be inclined to extenuate the evils which had been made the plea for administering so violent a remedy; and such, in fact, was their general disposition. The Lord Chancellor Thurlow, in particular, whose great place and force of intellect gave him a weight in the government inferior only to that of Mr. Pitt, espoused the cause of Hastings with indecorous violence. Mr. Pitt, though he had censured many parts of the Indian system, had studiously abstained from saying a word against the late chief of the Indian Government. To Major Scott, indeed, the young minister had in private extolled Hastings as a great, a wonderful man, who had the highest claims on the government. There was only one objection to granting all that so eminent a servant of the public could ask: The resolution of censure still remained on the journals of the House of Commons. That resolution was, indeed, unjust; but, till it was rescinded, could the minister advise the King to bestow any mark of approbation on the person censured? If Major Scott is to be trusted, Mr. Pitt declared that this was the only reason which prevented the advisers of the Crown from conferring a peerage on the late Governor-General. Mr. Dundas was the only important member of the administration who was deeply committed to a different view of the subject. He had moved the resolution which created the difficulty; but even from him little was to be apprehended. Since he had presided over the committee on Eastern affairs, great changes had taken place. He was surrounded by new allies; he had fixed his hopes on new objects; and whatever may have been his good qualities—and he had many—flattery itself never reckoned rigid consistency in the number.

From the Ministry, therefore, Hastings had every reason to expect support; and the Ministry was very powerful. The Opposition was loud and vehement against him. But the Opposition, though formidable from the wealth and influence of some of its members and from the admirable talents and eloquence of others, was outnumbered in parliament and odious throughout the country. Nor, as far as we can judge, was the Opposition generally desirous to engage in so serious an undertaking as the impeachment of an Indian Governor. Such an impeachment must last for years. It must impose on the chiefs of the party an immense load of labour. Yet it could scarcely in any manner affect the event of the great political game. The followers of the coalition were therefore more inclined to revile Hastings than to prosecute him. They lost no opportunity of coupling his name with the names of the most hateful tyrants of whom history makes mention. The wits of Brooks's aimed their keenest sarcasms both at his public and at his domestic life. Some fine diamonds, which he had presented, as it was rumoured, to the royal family, and a certain richly carved ivory bed, which the Queen had done him the honour to accept from him, were favourite subjects of ridicule. One lively poet proposed that the great acts of the fair Marian's present husband should be immortalised by the pencil of his predecessor; and that Imhoff should be employed to embellish the House of Commons with paintings of the bleeding Rohillas, of Nuncomar swinging, of Cheyte Sing letting himself down to the Ganges. Another, in exquisitely humourous parody of Virgil's third eclogue, propounded the question—what that mineral could be of which the rays had power to make the most austere of princesses the friend of a wanton? A third described, with gay malevolence, the gorgeous appearance of Mrs. Hastings at St. James's, the galaxy of jewels, torn from Begums, which adorned her head-dress, her necklace gleaming with future votes, and the depending questions that shone upon her ears. Satirical attacks of this description, and perhaps a motion for a vote of censure, would have satisfied the great body of the Opposition. But there were two men whose indignation was not to be so appeased, Philip Francis and Edmund Burke.

Francis had recently entered the House of Commons, and had already established a character there for industry and ability. He laboured indeed under one most unfortunate defect, want of fluency. But he occasionally expressed himself with a dignity and energy worthy of the greatest orators. Before he had been many days in Parliament, he incurred the bitter dislike of Pitt, who constantly treated him with as much asperity as the laws of debate would allow. Neither lapse of years nor change of scene had mitigated the enmities which Francis had brought back from the East. After his usual fashion, he mistook his malevolence for virtue; nursed it, as preachers tell us that we ought to nurse our good dispositions; and paraded it, on all occasions, with Pharisaical ostentation.

The zeal of Burke was still fiercer; but it was far purer. Men, unable to understand the elevation of his mind, have tried to find out some discreditable motive for the vehemence and pertinacity which he showed on this occasion. But they have altogether failed. The idle story, that he had some private slight to revenge, has long been given up, even by the advocates of Hastings. Mr. Gleig supposes that Burke was actuated by party spirit, that he retained a bitter remembrance of the fall of the coalition, that he attributed that fall to the exertions of the East India interest, and that he considered Hastings as the head and the personification of that interest. This explanation seems to be sufficiently refuted by a reference to dates. The hostility of Burke to Hastings commenced long before the coalition, and lasted long after Burke had become a strenuous supporter of those by whom the coalition had been defeated. It began when Burke and Fox, closely allied together, were attacking the influence of the crown and calling for peace with the American republic. It continued till Burke, alienated from Fox and loaded with the favours of the Crown, died; preaching a crusade against the French republic. We surely cannot attribute to the events of 1784 an enmity which began in 1781, and which retained undiminished force long after persons far more deeply implicated than Hastings in the events of 1784 had been cordially forgiven. And why should we look for any other explanation of Burke's conduct than that which we find on the surface? The plain truth is that Hastings had committed some great crimes, and that the thought of those crimes made the blood of Burke boil in his veins. For Burke was a man in whom compassion for suffering and hatred of injustice and tyranny were as strong as in Las Casas or Clarkson. And although in him, as in Las Casas and in Clarkson, these noble feelings were alloyed with the infirmity which belongs to human nature, he is, like them, entitled to this great praise, that he devoted years of intense labour to the service of a people with whom he had neither blood nor language, neither religion nor manners in common; and from whom no requital, no thanks, no applause could be expected.

His knowledge of India was such as few, even of those Europeans who have passed many years in that country, have attained, and such as certainly was never attained by any public man who had not quitted Europe. He had studied the history, the laws and the usages of the East with an industry such as is seldom found united to so much genius and so much sensibility. Others have perhaps been equally laborious and have collected an equal mass of materials. But the manner in which Burke brought his higher powers of intellect to work on statements of facts and on tables of figures was peculiar to himself. In every part of those huge bales of Indian information which repelled almost all other readers, his mind, at once philosophical and poetical, found something to instruct or to delight. His reason analysed and digested those vast and shapeless masses; his imagination animated and coloured them. Out of darkness and dullness and confusion, he drew a rich abundance of ingenious theories and vivid pictures. He had, in the highest degree, that noble faculty whereby man is able to live in the past and in the future, in the distant and in the unreal. India and its inhabitants were not to him, as to most Englishmen, mere names and abstractions, but a real country and a real people. The burning sun, the strange vegetation of the palm and the cocoa tree, the rice field, the tank; the huge trees, older than the Mogul empire, under which the village crowds assemble; the thatched roof of the peasant's hut and the rich tracery of the mosque, where the imaun prayed with his face to Mecca; the drums, and banners and gaudy idols; the devotee swinging in the air, the graceful maiden, with the pitcher on her head, descending the steps to the river side; the black faces, the long beards, the yellow streaks of sect; the turbans and the flowing robes; the spears and the silver maces; the elephants with their canopies of state; the gorgeous palanquin of the prince and the close litter of the noble lady—all these things were to him as the objects amidst which his own life had been passed, as the objects which lay on the road between Beaconsfield and St. James's Street. All India was present to the eye of his mind, from the halls where suitors laid gold and perfumes at the feet of sovereigns to the wild moor where the gipsy camp was pitched—from the bazaar, humming like a beehive with the crowd of buyers and sellers, to the jungle where the lonely courier shakes his bunch of iron rings to scare away the hyænas. He had just as lively an idea of the insurrection at Benares as of Lord George Gordon's riots, and of the execution of Nuncomar as of the execution of Dr. Dodd. Oppression in Bengal was to him the same thing as oppression in the streets of London.

He saw that Hastings had been guilty of some most unjustifiable acts. All that followed was natural and necessary in a mind like Burke's. His imagination and his passions, once excited, hurried him beyond the bounds of justice and good sense. His reason, powerful as it was, was reduced to be the slave of feelings which it should have controlled. His indignation, virtuous in its origin, acquired too much of the character of personal aversion. He could see no mitigating circumstances, no redeeming merit. His temper, which, though generous and affectionate, had always been irritable, had now been made almost savage by bodily infirmities and mental vexations. Conscious of great powers and great virtues, he found himself, in age and poverty, a mark for the hatred of a perfidious court and a deluded people. In Parliament his eloquence was out of date. A young generation, which knew him not, had filled the House. Whenever he rose to speak, his voice was drowned by the unseemly interruption of lads who were in their cradles when his orations on the Stamp Act called forth the applause of the great Earl of Chatham. These things had produced on his proud and sensitive spirit an effect at which we cannot wonder. He could no longer discuss any question with calmness, or make allowances for honest differences of opinion. Those who think that he was more violent and acrimonious in debates about India than on other occasions are ill-informed respecting the last years of his life. In the discussions on the Commercial Treaty with the Court of Versailles, on the Regency, on the French Revolution, he showed even more virulence than in conducting the impeachment. Indeed, it may be remarked that the very persons who represented him as a mischievous maniac, for condemning in burning words the Rohilla war and the spoliation of the Begums, exalted him into a prophet as soon as he began to declaim, with greater vehemence, and not with greater reason, against the taking of the Bastile and the insults offered to Marie Antoinette. To us he appears to have been neither a maniac in the former case nor a prophet in the latter, but in both cases a great and good man, led into extravagance by a tempestuous sensibility which domineered over all his faculties.

It may be doubted whether the personal antipathy of Francis or the nobler indignation of Burke would have led their party to adopt extreme measures against Hastings if his own conduct had been judicious. He should have felt that, great as his public services had been, he was not faultless; and should have been content to make his escape without aspiring to the honours of a triumph. He and his agent took a different view. They were impatient for the rewards which, as they conceived, were deferred only till Burke's attack should be over. They accordingly resolved to force on a decisive action with an enemy for whom, if they had been wise, they would have made a bridge of gold. On the first day of the session of 1786, Major Scott reminded Burke of the notice given in the preceding year, and asked whether it was seriously intended to bring any charge against the late Governor-General. This challenge left no course open to the Opposition except to come forward as accusers or to acknowledge themselves calumniators. The administration of Hastings had not been so blameless, nor was the great party of Fox and North so feeble, that it could be prudent to venture on so bold a defiance. The leaders of the Opposition instantly returned the only answer which they could with honour return, and the whole party was irrevocably pledged to a prosecution.

Burke began his operations by applying for Papers. Some of the documents for which he asked were refused by the ministers, who, in the debate, held language such as strongly confirmed the prevailing opinion that they intended to support Hastings. In April, the charges were laid on the table. They had been drawn by Burke with great ability, though in a form too much resembling that of a pamphlet. Hastings was furnished with a copy of the accusation, and it was intimated to him that he might, if he thought fit, be heard in his own defence at the bar of the Commons.

Here again Hastings was pursued by the same fatality which had attended him ever since the day when he set foot on English ground. It seemed to be decreed that this man, so politic and so successful in the East, should commit nothing but blunders in Europe. Any judicious adviser would have told him that he best thing which he could do would be to make an eloquent, forcible and affecting oration at the bar of the House; but that, if he could not trust himself to speak, and found it necessary to read, he ought to be as concise as possible. Audiences accustomed to extemporaneous debating of the highest excellence are always impatient of long, written compositions. Hastings, however, sat down as he would have done at the Government House in Bengal and prepared a paper of immense length. This paper, if recorded on the consultations of an Indian administration, would have been justly praised as a very able minute. But it was now out of place. It fell flat, as the best written defence must have fallen flat, on an assembly accustomed to the animated and strenuous conflicts of Pitt and Fox. The members, as soon as their curiosity about the face and demeanour of so eminent a stranger was satisfied, walked away to dinner and left Hastings to tell his story till midnight to the clerks and the Serjeant-at-arms.

All preliminary steps having been duly taken, Burke, in the beginning of June, brought forward the charge relating to the Rohilla war. He acted discreetly in placing this accusation in the van; for Dundas had formerly moved, and the House had adopted, a resolution condemning, in the most severe terms, the policy followed by Hastings with regard to Rohilcund. Dundas had little, or rather nothing, to say in defence of his own consistency; but he put a bold face on the matter and opposed the motion. Among other things, he declared that, though he still thought the Rohilla war unjustifiable, he considered the services which Hastings had subsequently rendered to the state as sufficient to atone even for so great an offence. Pitt did not speak, but voted with Dundas; and Hastings was absolved by a hundred and nineteen votes against sixty-seven.

Hastings was now confident of victory. It seemed, indeed, that he had reason to be so. The Rohilla war was, of all his measures, that which his accusers might with greatest advantage assail. It had been condemned by the Court of Directors. It had been condemned by the House of Commons. It had been condemned by Mr. Dundas, who had since become the chief minister of the Crown for Indian affairs. Yet Burke, having chosen this strong ground, had been completely defeated on it. That, having failed here, he should succeed on any point, was generally thought impossible. It was rumoured at the clubs and coffee-houses that one or perhaps two more charges would be brought forward, that if, on those charges, the sense of the House of Commons should be against impeachment, the Opposition would let the matter drop; that Hastings would be immediately raised to the peerage, decorated with the star of the Bath, sworn of the privy council, and invited to lend the assistance of his talents and experience to the India board. Lord Thurlow, indeed, some months before, had spoken with contempt of the scruples which prevented Pitt from calling Hastings to the House of Lords; and had even said that, if the Chancellor of the Exchequer was afraid of the Commons, there was nothing to prevent the Keeper of the Great Seal from taking the royal pleasure about a patent of peerage. The very title was chosen. Hastings was to be Lord Daylesford. For, through all changes of scene and changes of fortune, remained unchanged his attachment to the spot which had witnessed the greatness and the fall of his family, and which had borne so great a part in the first dreams of his young ambition.

But in a very few days these fair prospects were overcast. On the 13th of June, Mr. Fox brought forward, with great ability and eloquence, the charge respecting the treatment of Cheyte Sing. Francis followed on the same side. The friends of Hastings were in high spirits when Pitt rose. With his usual abundance and felicity of language, the Minister gave his opinion on the case. He maintained that the Governor-General was justified in calling on the Rajah of Benares for pecuniary assistance and in imposing a fine when that assistance was contumaciously withheld. He also thought that the conduct of the Governor-General during the insurrection had been distinguished by ability and presence of mind. He censured, with great bitterness, the conduct of Francis, both in India and in Parliament, as most dishonest and malignant. The necessary inference from Pitt's argument seemed to be that Hastings ought to be honourably acquitted; and both the friends and the opponents of the Minister expected from him a declaration to that effect. To the astonishment of all parties, he concluded by saying that, though he thought it right in

Hastings to fine Cheyte Sing for contumacy, yet the amount of the fine was too great for the occasion. On this ground, and on this ground alone, did Mr. Pitt, applauding every other part of the conduct of Hastings with regard to Benares, declare that he should vote in favour of Mr. Fox's motion.

The House was thunderstruck; and it well might be so. For the wrong done to Cheyte Sing, even had it been as flagitious as Fox and Francis contended, was a trifle when compared to the horrors which had been inflicted on Rohilcund. But if Mr. Pitt's view of the case of Cheyte Sing were correct, there was no ground for an impeachment or even for a vote of censure. If the offence of Hastings was really no more than this, that, having a right to impose a mulct, the amount of which mulct was not defined, but was left to be settled by his discretion, he had, not for his own advantage, but for that of the state, demanded too much, was this an offence which required a criminal proceeding of the highest solemnity: a criminal proceeding to which, during sixty years, no public functionary had been subjected? We can see, we think, in what way a man of sense and integrity might have been induced to take any course respecting Hastings except the course which Mr. Pitt took. Such a man might have thought a great example necessary for the preventing of injustice and for the vindicating of the national honour, and might, on that ground, have voted for impeachment both on the Rohilla charge and on the Benares charge. Such a man might have thought that the offences of Hastings had been atoned for by great services, and might, on that ground, have voted against the impeachment on both charges. With great diffidence, we give it as our opinion that the most correct course would, on the whole, have been to impeach on the Rohilla charge and to acquit on the Benares charge. Had the Benares charge appeared to us in the same light in which it appeared to Mr. Pitt, we should, without hesitation, have voted for acquittal on that charge. The one course which it is inconceivable that any man of a tenth part of Mr. Pitt's abilities can have honestly taken was the course which he took. He acquitted Hastings on the Rohilla charge. He softened down the Benares charge till it became no charge at all; and then he pronounced that it contained matter for impeachment.

Nor must it be forgotten that the principal reason assigned by the ministry for not impeaching Hastings on account of the Rohilla war was this, that the delinquencies of the early part of his administration had been atoned for by the excellence of the later part. Was it not most extraordinary that men who had held this language could afterwards vote that the later part of his administration furnished matter for no less than twenty articles of impeachment? They first contended that the conduct of Hastings in 1780 and 1781 was so highly meritorious that, like works of supererogation in the Catholic theology, it ought to be efficacious for the cancelling of former offences; and they then prosecuted him for his conduct in 1780 and 1781.

The general astonishment was the greater, because, only twenty-four hours before, the members on whom the minister could depend had received the usual notes from the Treasury, begging them to be in their places and to vote against Mr. Fox's motion. It was asserted by Mr. Hastings that, early on the morning of the very day on which the debate took place, Dundas called on Pitt, woke him, and was closeted with him many hours. The result of this conference was a determination to give up the late Governor-General to the vengeance of the Opposition. It was impossible even for the most powerful minister to carry all his followers with him in so strange a course. Several persons high in office, the Attorney-General, Mr. Grenville and Lord Mulgrave, divided against Mr. Pitt. But the devoted adherents who stood by the head of the government without asking questions were sufficiently numerous to turn the scale. A hundred and nineteen members voted for Mr. Fox's motion; seventy-nine against it. Dundas silently followed Pitt.

That good and great man, the late William Wilberforce, often related the events of this remarkable night. He described the amazement of the House, and the bitter reflections which were muttered against the Prime Minister by some of the habitual supporters of government. Pitt himself appeared to feel that his conduct required some explanation. He left the treasury bench, sat for some time next to Mr. Wilberforce, and very earnestly declared that he had found it impossible, as a man of conscience, to stand any longer by Hastings. The business, he said, was too bad. Mr. Wilberforce, we are bound to add, fully believed that his friend was sincere, and that the suspicions to which this mysterious affair gave rise were altogether unfounded.

Those suspicions, indeed, were such as it is painful to mention. The friends of Hastings, most of whom, it is to be observed, generally supported the administration, affirmed that the motive of Pitt and Dundas was jealousy. Hastings was personally a favourite with the King. He was the idol of the East India Company and of its servants. If he were absolved by the Commons, seated among the Lords, admitted to the Board of Control, closely allied with the strong-minded and imperious Thurlow, was it not almost certain that he would soon draw to himself the entire management of Eastern affairs? Was it not possible that he might become a formidable rival in the cabinet? It had probably got abroad that very singular communications had taken place between Thurlow and Major Scott, and that, if the First Lord of the Treasury was afraid to recommend Hastings for a peerage, the Chancellor was ready to take the responsibility of that step on himself. Of all ministers, Pitt was the least likely to submit with patience to such an encroachment on his functions. If the Commons impeached Hastings, all danger was at an end. The proceeding, however it might terminate, would probably last some years. In the meantime, the accused person would be excluded from honours and public employments, and could scarcely venture even to pay his duty at court. Such were the motives attributed by a great part of the public to the young minister, whose ruling passion was generally believed to be avarice of power.

The prorogation soon interrupted the discussions respecting Hastings. In the following year, those discussions were resumed. The charge touching the spoliation of the Begums was brought forward by Sheridan in a speech which was so imperfectly reported that it may be said to be wholly lost, but which was, without doubt, the most elaborately brilliant of all the productions of his ingenious mind. The impression which it produced was such as has never been equalled. He sat down, not merely amidst cheering, but amidst the loud clapping of hands, in which the Lords below the bar and the strangers in the gallery joined. The excitement of the House was such that no other speaker could obtain a hearing; and the debate was adjourned. The impression made by this remarkable display of eloquence on severe and experienced critics, whose discernment may be supposed to have been quickened by emulation, was deep and permanent. Mr. Windham, twenty years later, said that the speech deserved all its fame, and was, in spite of some faults of taste such as were seldom wanting either in the literary or in the parliamentary performances of Sheridan, the finest that had been delivered within the memory of man. Mr. Fox, about the same time, being asked by the late Lord Holland what was the best speech ever made in the House of Commons, assigned the first place, without hesitation, to the great oration of Sheridan on the Oude charge.

When the debate was resumed, the tide ran so strongly against the accused that his friends were coughed and scraped down. Pitt declared himself for

Sheridan's motion; and the question was carried by a hundred and seventy-five votes against sixty-eight.

The Opposition, flushed with victory and strongly supported by the public sympathy, proceeded to bring forward a succession of charges relating chiefly to pecuniary transactions. The friends of Hastings were discouraged, and, having now no hope of being able to avert an impeachment, were not very strenuous in their exertions. At length the House, having agreed to twenty articles of charge, directed Burke to go before the Lords and to impeach the late Governor-General of High Crimes and Misdemeanours. Hastings was at the same time arrested by the Serjeant-at-arms and carried to the bar of the Peers.

The session was now within ten days of its close. It was, therefore, impossible that any progress could be made in the trial till the next year. Hastings was admitted to bail; and further proceedings were postponed till the Houses should re-assemble.

When Parliament met in the following winter, the Commons proceeded to elect a committee for managing the impeachment. Burke stood at the head; and with him were associated most of the leading members of the Opposition. But when the name of Francis was read, a fierce contention arose. It was said that Francis and Hastings were notoriously on bad terms, that they had been at feud during many years, that on one occasion their mutual aversion had impelled them to seek each other's lives, and that it would be improper and indelicate to select a private enemy to be a public accuser. It was urged on the other side with great force, particularly by Mr. Windham, that impartiality, though the first duty of a judge, had never been reckoned among the qualities of an advocate; that in the ordinary administration of criminal justice among the English, the aggrieved party, the very last person who ought to be admitted into the jury-box, is the prosecutor; that what was wanted in a manager was, not that he should be free from bias, but that he should be energetic, able, well-informed and active. The ability and information of Francis were admitted; and the very animosity with which he was reproached, whether a virtue or a vice, was at least a pledge for his energy and activity. It seems difficult to refute these a guments. But the inveterate hatred borne by Francis to Hastings had excited general disgust. The House decided that Francis should not be a manager. Pitt voted with the majority, Dundas with the minority.

In the meantime, the preparations for the trial had proceeded rapidly; and on the 13th of February, 1788, the sittings of the Court commenced. There have been spectacles more dazzling to the eye, more gorgeous with jewellery and cloth of gold, more attractive to grown-up children, than that which was then exhibited at Westminster; but, perhaps, there never was a spectacle so well calculated to strike a highly cultivated, a reflecting, an imaginative mind. All the various kinds of interest which belong to the near and to the distant, to the present and to the past, were collected on one spot and in one hour. All the talents and all the accomplishments which are developed by liberty and civilisation were now displayed with every advantage that could be derived both from co-operation and from contrast. Every step in the proceedings carried the mind either backward, through many troubled centuries, to the days when the foundations of our constitution were laid; or far away, over boundless seas and deserts, to dusky nations living under strange stars, worshipping strange gods, and writing strange characters from right to left. The High Court of Parliament was to sit, according to forms handed down from the days of the Plantagenets, on an Englishman accused of exercising tyranny over the lord of the holy city of Benares and over the ladies of the princely house of Oude.

The place was worthy of such a trial. It was the great hall of William Rufus, the hall which had resounded with acclamations at the inauguration of thirty kings, the hall which had witnessed the just sentence of Bacon and the just absolution of Somers, the hall where the eloquence of Strafford had for a moment awed and melted a victorious party inflamed with just resentment, the hall where Charles had confronted the High Court of Justice with the placid courage which has half redeemed his fame. Neither military nor civil pomp was wanting. The avenues were lined with grenadiers. The streets were kept clear by cavalry. The peers, robed in gold and ermine, were marshalled by the heralds under Garter King-at-arms. The judges in their vestments of state attended to give advice on points of law. Near a hundred and seventy lords, three-fourths of the Upper House as the Upper House then was, walked in solemn order from their usual place of assembling to the tribunal. The junior Baron present led the way, Lord Heathfield, recently ennobled for his memorable defence of Gibraltar against the fleets and armies of France and Spain. The long procession was closed by the Duke of Norfolk, Earl Marshal of the realm, by the great dignitaries, and by the brothers and sons of the King. Last of all came the Prince of Wales, conspicuous by his fine person and noble bearing. The grey old walls were hung with scarlet. The long galleries were crowded by an audience such as has rarely excited the fears or the emulation of an orator. There were gathered together, from all parts of a great, free, enlightened and prosperous empire, grace and female loveliness, wit and learning, the representatives of every science and of every art. There were seated round the Queen the fair-haired young daughters of the house of Brunswick. There the Ambassadors of great Kings and Commonwealths gazed with admiration on a spectacle which no other country in the world could present. There Siddons, in the prime of her majestic beauty, looked with emotion on a scene surpassing all the imitations of the stage. There the historian of the Roman Empire thought of the days when Cicero pleaded the cause of Sicily against Verres, and when, before a senate which still retained some show of freedom, Tacitus thundered against the oppressor of Africa. There were seen, side by side, the greatest painter and the greatest scholar of the age. The spectacle had allured Reynolds from that easel which has preserved to us the thoughtful foreheads of so many writers and statesmen and the sweet smiles of so many noble matrons. It had induced Parr to suspend his labours in that dark and profound mine from which he had extracted a vast treasure of erudition—a treasure too often buried in the earth, too often paraded with injudicious and inelegant ostentation; but still precious, massive and splendid. There appeared the voluptuous charms of her to whom the heir of the throne had in secret plighted his faith. There too was she, the beautiful mother of a beautiful race, the Saint Cecilia, whose delicate features, lighted up by love and music, art has rescued from the common decay. There were the members of that brilliant society which quoted, criticised and exchanged repartees under the rich peacock hangings of Mrs. Montague. And there the ladies, whose lips, more persuasive than those of Fox himself, had carried the Westminster election against palace and treasury, shone round Georgiana, Duchess of Devonshire.

The Serjeants made proclamation. Hastings advanced to the bar and bent his knee. The culprit was indeed not unworthy of that great presence. He had ruled an extensive and populous country, had made laws and treaties, had sent forth armies, had set up and pulled down princes. And in his high place he had so borne himself that all had feared him, that most had loved him, and that hatred itself could deny him no title to glory except virtue. He looked like a great man and not like a bad man. A person small and emaciated, yet deriving dignity from a carriage which, while it indicated deference to the court, indicated also habitual self-possession and self-respect; a high and intellectual forehead; a brow, pensive, but not gloomy; a mouth of inflexible decision; a face, pale and worn, but serene, on which was written, as legibly as under the picture in the council-chamber at Calcutta, *Mens æqua in arduis;* such was the aspect with which the great Proconsul presented himself to his judges.

His counsel accompanied him, men all of whom were afterwards raised by their talents and learning to the highest posts in their profession—the bold and strong-minded Law, afterwards Chief Justice of the King's Bench; the more humane and eloquent Dallas, afterwards Chief Justice of the Common Pleas; and Plomer who, near twenty years later, successfully conducted in the same high court the defence of Lord Melville, and subsequently became Vice-chancellor and Master of the Rolls.

But neither the culprit nor his advocates attracted so much notice as the accusers. In the midst of the blaze of red drapery, a space had been fitted up with green benches and tables for the Commons. The managers, with Burke at their head, appeared in full dress. The collectors of gossip did not fail to remark that even Fox, generally so regardless of his appearance, had paid to the illustrious tribunal the compliment of wearing a bag and sword. Pitt had refused to be one of the conductors of the impeachment; and his commanding, copious and sonorous eloquence was wanting to that great muster of various talents. Age and blindness had unfitted Lord North for the duties of a public prosecutor; and his friends were left without the help of his excellent sense, his tact and his urbanity. But in spite of the absence of these two distinguished members of the Lower House, the box in which the managers stood contained an array of speakers such as perhaps had not appeared together since the great age of Athenian eloquence. There stood Fox and Sheridan, the English Demosthenes and the English Hyperides. There was Burke, ignorant, indeed, or negligent of the art of adapting his reasonings and his style to the capacity and taste of his hearers, but in amplitude of comprehension and richness of imagination superior to every orator, ancient or modern. There, with eyes reverentially fixed on Burke, appeared the finest gentleman of the age—his form developed by every manly exercise—his face beaming with intelligence and spirit—the ingenious, the chivalrous, the high-souled Windham. Nor, though surrounded by such men, did the youngest manager pass unnoticed. At an age when most of those who distinguish themselves in life are still contending for prizes and fellowships at college, he had won for himself a conspicuous place in parliament. No advantage of fortune or connection was wanting that could set off to the height his splendid talents and his unblemished honour. At twenty-three he had been thought worthy to be ranked with the veteran statesmen who appeared as the delegates of the British Commons at the bar of the British nobility. All who stood at that bar, save him alone, are gone—culprit, advocates, accusers. To the generation which is now in the vigour of life, he is the sole representative of a great age which has passed away. But those who, within the last ten years, have listened with delight, till the morning sun shone on the tapestries of the House of Lords, to the lofty and animated eloquence of Charles, Earl Grey, are able to form some estimate of the powers of a race of men among whom he was not the foremost.

The charges, and the answers of Hastings, were first read. The ceremony occupied two whole days, and was rendered less tedious than it would otherwise have been by the silver voice and just emphasis of Cowper, the clerk of the court, a near relation of the amiable poet. On the third day Burke rose

Four sittings of the court were occupied by his opening speech, which was intended to be a general introduction to all the charges. With an exuberance of thought and a splendour of diction which more than satisfied the highly raised expectation of the audience, he described the character and institutions of the natives of India; recounted the circumstances in which the Asiatic empire of Britain had originated; and set forth the constitution of the Company and of the English Presidencies. Having thus attempted to communicate to his hearers an idea of Eastern society, as vivid as that which existed in his own mind, he proceeded to arraign the administration of Hastings, as systematically conducted in defiance of morality and public law. The energy and pathos of the great orator extorted expressions of unwonted admiration from the stern and hostile Chancellor, and, for a moment, seemed to pierce even the resolute heart of the defendant. The ladies in the galleries, unaccustomed to such displays of eloquence, excited by the solemnity of the occasion, and perhaps not unwilling to display their taste and sensibility, were in a state of uncontrollable emotion. Handkerchiefs were pulled out; smelling bottles were handed round; hysterical sobs and screams were heard: and Mrs. Sheridan was carried out in a fit. At length the orator concluded. Raising his voice till the old arches of Irish oak resounded, "Therefore," said he, "hath it with all confidence been ordered, by the Commons of Great Britain, that I impeach Warren Hastings of high crimes and misdemeanours. I impeach him in the name of the Commons' House of Parliament, whose trust he has betrayed. I impeach him in the name of the English nation, whose ancient honour he has sullied. I impeach him in the name of the people of India, whose rights he has trodden under foot and whose country he has turned into a desert. Lastly, in the name of human nature itself, in the name of both sexes, in the name of every age, in the name of every rank, I impeach the common enemy and oppressor of all!"

When the deep murmur of various emotions had subsided, Mr. Fox rose to address the Lords respecting the course of proceeding to be followed. The wish of the accusers was that the Court would bring to a close the investigation of the first charge before the second was opened. The wish of Hastings and of his counsel was that the managers should open all the charges and produce all the evidence for the prosecution before the defence began. The Lords retired to their own House to consider the question. The Chancellor took the side of Hastings. Lord Loughborough, who was now in opposition, supported the demand of the managers. The division showed which way the inclination of the tribunal leaned. A majority of near three to one decided in favour of the course for which Hastings contended.

When the Court sat again, Mr. Fox, assisted by Mr. Grey, opened the charge respecting Cheyte Sing, and several days were spent in reading papers and hearing witnesses. The next article was that relating to the Princesses of Oude. The conduct of this part of the case was intrusted to Sheridan. The curiosity of the public to hear him was unbounded. His sparkling and highly-finished declamation lasted two days; but the Hall was crowded to suffocation during the whole time. It was said that fifty guineas had been paid for a single ticket. Sheridan, when he concluded, contrived, with a knowledge of stage effect which his father might have envied, to sink back, as if exhausted, into the arms of Burke, who hugged him with the energy of generous admiration.

June was now far advanced. The session could not last much longer; and the progress which had been made in the impeachment was not very satisfactory. There were twenty charges. On two only of these had even the case for the prosecution been heard; and it was now a year since Hastings had been admitted to bail.

The interest taken by the public in the trial was great when the Court began to sit, and rose to the height when Sheridan spoke on the charge relating to the Begums. From that time the excitement went down fast. The spectacle had lost the attraction of novelty. The great displays of rhetoric were over. What was behind was not of a nature to entice men of letters from their books in the morning, or to tempt ladies who had left the masquerade at two to be out of bed before eight. There remained examinations and cross-examinations. There remained statements of accounts. There remained the reading of papers, filled with words unintelligible to English ears—with lacs and crores, zemindars and aumils, sunnuds and perwannahs, jaghires and nuzzurs. There remained bickerings, not always carried on with the best taste or with the best temper, between the managers of the impeachment and the counsel for the defence, particularly between Mr. Burke and Mr. Law. There remained the endless marches and counter-marches of the Peers between their House and the Hall: for as often as a point of law was to be discussed, their Lordships retired to discuss it apart; and the consequence was, as a Peer wittily said, that the judges walked and the trial stood still.

It is to be added that, in the spring of 1788, when the trial commenced, no important question, either of domestic or foreign policy, occupied the public mind. The proceeding in Westminster Hall, therefore, naturally attracted most of the attention of Parliament and of the country. It was the one great event of that season. But in the following year, the King's illness, the debates on the Regency, the expectation of a change of ministry, completely diverted public attention from Indian affairs; and within a fortnight after George the Third had returned thanks in St. Paul's for his recovery, the States-General of France met at Versailles. In the midst of the agitation produced by these events, the impeachment was for a time almost forgotten.

The trial in the Hall went on languidly. In the session of 1788, when the proceedings had the interest of novelty and when the Peers had little other business before them, only thirty-five days were given to the impeachment. In 1789, the Regency Bill occupied the Upper House till the session was far advanced. When the King recovered, the circuits were beginning. The judges left town; the Lords waited for the return of the oracles of jurisprudence; and the consequence was that during the whole year only seventeen days were given to the case of Hastings. It was clear that the matter would be protracted to a length unprecedented in the annals of criminal law.

In truth, it is impossible to deny that impeachment, though it is a fine ceremony, and though it may have been useful in the seventeenth century, is not a proceeding from which much good can now be expected. Whatever confidence may be placed in the decision of the Peers on an appeal arising out of ordinary litigation, it is certain that no man has the least confidence in their impartiality when a great public functionary, charged with a great state crime, is brought to their bar. They are all politicians. There is hardly one among them whose vote on an impeachment may not be confidently predicted before a witness has been examined; and, even if it were possible to rely on their justice, they would still be quite unfit to try such a cause as that of Hastings. They sit only during half the year. They have to transact much legislative and much judicial business. The law-lords, whose advice is required to guide the unlearned majority, are employed daily in administering justice elsewhere. It is impossible, therefore, that during a busy session the Upper House should give more than a few days to an impeachment. To expect that their Lordships would give up partridge-shooting in order to bring the greatest delinquent to speedy justice, or to relieve accused innocence by speedy acquittal, would be unreasonable indeed. A well constituted tribunal, sitting regularly six days in the week and nine hours in the day, would have brought the trial of Hastings to a close in less than three months. The Lords had not finished their work in seven years.

The result ceased to be matter of doubt from the time when the Lords resolved that they would be guided by the rules of evidence which are received in the inferior courts of the realm. Those rules, it is well known, exclude much information which would be quite sufficient to determine the conduct of any reasonable man in the most important transactions of private life. These rules, at every assizes, save scores of culprits whom judges, jury and spectators firmly believe to be guilty. But, when those rules were rigidly applied to offences committed many years before, at the distance of many thousands of miles, conviction was, of course, out of the question. We do not blame the accused and his counsel for availing themselves of every legal advantage in order to obtain an acquittal. But it is clear that an acquittal so obtained cannot be pleaded in bar of the judgment of history.

Several attempts were made by the friends of Hastings to put a stop to the trial. In 1789 they proposed a vote of censure upon Burke for some violent language which he had used respecting the death of Nuncomar and the connection between Hastings and Impey. Burke was then unpopular in the last degree both with the House and with the country. The asperity and indecency of some expressions which he had used during the debates on the Regency had annoyed even his warmest friends. The vote of censure was carried; and those who had moved it hoped that the managers would resign in disgust. Burke was deeply hurt. But his zeal for what he considered as the cause of justice and mercy triumphed over his personal feelings. He received the censure of the House with dignity and meekness, and declared that no personal mortification or humiliation should induce him to flinch from the sacred duty which he had undertaken.

In the following year, the Parliament was dissolved; and the friends of Hastings entertained a hope that the new House of Commons might not be disposed to go on with the impeachment. They began by maintaining that the whole proceeding was terminated by the dissolution. Defeated on this point, they made a direct motion that the impeachment should be dropped; but they were defeated by the combined forces of the Government and the Opposition. It was, however, resolved that, for the sake of expedition, many of the articles should be withdrawn. In truth, had not some such measure been adopted, the trial would have lasted till the defendant was in his grave.

At length, in the spring of 1795, the decision was pronounced, nearly eight years after Hastings had been brought by the Serjeant-at-arms of the Commons to the bar of the Lords. On the last day of this great procedure, the public curiosity, long suspended, seemed to be revived. Anxiety about the judgment there could be none; for it had been fully ascertained that there was a great majority for the defendant. But many wished to see the pageant, and the Hall was as much crowded as on the first day. But those who, having been present on the first day, now bore a part in the proceedings of the last were few; and most of those few were altered men.

As Hastings himself said, the arraignment had taken place before one generation and the judgment was pronounced by another. The spectator could not look at the woolsack, or at the red benches of the Peers, or at the green benches of the Commons, without seeing something that reminded him of the instability of all human things; of the instability of power and fame and life, of the more lamentable instability of friendship. The great seal was borne before Lord Loughborough, who, when the trial commenced, was a fierce opponent of Mr. Pitt's government, and who was now a member of that government, while Thurlow, who presided in the court when it first sat, estranged from all his old allies, sat scowling among the junior barons. Of about a hundred and sixty nobles who walked in the procession on the first day, sixty had been laid in their family vaults. Still more affecting must have been the sight of the manager's box. What had become of that fair fellowship, so closely bound together by public and private ties, so resplendent with every talent and accomplishment? It had been scattered by calamities more bitter than the bitterness of death. The great chiefs were still living and still in the full vigour of their genius. But their friendship was at an end. It had been violently and publicly dissolved, with tears and stormy reproaches. If those men, once so dear to each other, were now compelled to meet for the purpose of managing the impeachment, they met as strangers whom public business had brought together, and behaved to each other with cold and distant civility. Burke had in his vortex whirled away Windham. Fox had been followed by Sheridan and Grey.

Only twenty-nine Peers voted. Of these only six found Hastings guilty on the charges relating to Cheyte Sing and to the Begums. On other charges, the majority in his favour was still greater. On some he was unanimously absolved. He was then called to the bar, was informed from the woolsack that the Lords had acquitted him, and was solemnly discharged. He bowed respectfully and retired.

We have said that the decision had been fully expected. It was also generally approved. At the commencement of the trial, there had been a strong and indeed unreasonable feeling against Hastings. At the close of the trial, there was a feeling equally strong and equally unreasonable in his favour. One cause of the change was, no doubt, what is commonly called the fickleness of the multitude, but what seems to us to be merely the general law of human nature. Both in individuals and in masses violent excitement is always followed by remission, and often by reaction. We are all inclined to depreciate whatever we have overpraised, and, on the other hand, to show undue indulgence where we have shown undue rigour. It was thus in the case of Hastings. The length of the trial, moreover, made him an object of compassion. It was thought, and not without reason, that, even if he was guilty, he was still an ill-used man, and that an impeachment of eight years was more than a sufficient punishment. It was also felt that, though, in the ordinary course of criminal law, a defendant is not allowed to set off his good actions against his crimes, a great political cause should be tried on different principles; and that a man who had governed a great country during thirteen years might have done some very reprehensible thing and yet might be on the whole deserving of rewards and honours rather than of fine and imprisonment. The press, an instrument neglected by the prosecutors, was used by Hastings and his friends with great effect. Every ship too, that arrived from Madras or Bengal, brought a cuddy full of his admirers. Every gentleman from India spoke of the late Governor-General as having deserved better, and having been treated worse, than any man living. The effect of this testimony, unanimously given by all persons who knew the East, was naturally very great. Retired members of the Indian services, civil and military, were settled in all corners of the kingdom. Each of them was, of course, in his own little circle, regarded as an oracle on an Indian question; and they were, with scarcely one exception, the zealous advocates of Hastings. It is to be added, that the numerous addresses to the late Governor-General, which his friends in Bengal obtained from the natives and transmitted to England, made a considerable impression. To these addresses we attach little or no importance. That Hastings was beloved by the people whom he governed is true; but the eulogies of pundits, zemindars,

Mahommedan doctors, do not prove it to be true. For an English collector or judge would have found it easy to induce any native who could write to sign a panegyric on the most odious ruler that ever was in India. It is said that at Benares, the very place at which the acts set forth in the first article of impeachment had been committed, the natives had erected a temple to Hastings; and this story excited a strong sensation in England. Burke's observations on the apotheosis were admirable. He saw no reason for astonishment, he said, in the incident which had been represented as so striking. He knew something of the mythology of the Brahmins. He knew that as they worshipped some gods from love, so they worshipped others from fear. He knew that they erected shrines, not only to the benignant deities of light and plenty, but also to the fiends who preside over smallpox and murder; nor did he at all dispute the claim of Mr. Hastings to be admitted into such a Pantheon. This reply has always struck us as one of the finest that ever was made in Parliament. It is a grave and forcible argument, decorated by the most brilliant wit and fancy.

Hastings was, however, safe. But in everything except character, he would have been far better off if, when first impeached, he had at once pleaded guilty and paid a fine of fifty thousand pounds. He was a ruined man. The legal expenses of his defence had been enormous. The expenses which did not appear in his attorney's bill were perhaps larger still. Great sums had been paid to Major Scott. Great sums had been laid out in bribing newspapers, rewarding pamphleteers and circulating tracts. Burke, so early as 1790, declared in the House of Commons that twenty thousand pounds had been employed in corrupting the press. It is certain that no controversial weapon, from the gravest reasoning to the coarsest ribaldry, was left unemployed. Logan in prose defended the accused Governor with great ability. For the lovers of verse, the speeches of the managers were burlesqued in Simpkin's letters. It is, we are afraid, indisputable that Hastings stooped so low as to court the aid of that malignant and filthy baboon John Williams, who called himself Anthony Pasquin. It was necessary to subsidise such allies largely. The private hoards of Mrs. Hastings had disappeared. It is said that the banker to whom they had been intrusted had failed. Still if Hastings had practised strict economy, he would, after all his losses, have had a moderate competence; but in the management of his private affairs he was imprudent. The dearest wish of his heart had always been to regain Daylesford. At length, in the very year in which his trial commenced, the wish was accomplished, and the domain, alienated more than seventy years before, returned to the descendant of its old lords. But the manor house was a ruin, and the grounds round it had, during many years, been utterly neglected. Hastings proceeded to build, to plant, to form a sheet of water, to excavate a grotto, and, before he was dismissed from the bar of the House of Lords, he had expended more than forty thousand pounds in adorning his seat.

The general feeling both of the Directors and of the proprietors of the East India Company was that he had great claims on them, that his services to them had been eminent, and that his misfortunes had been the effect of his zeal for their interest. His friends in Leadenhall Street proposed to reimburse him the costs of his trial, and to settle on him an annuity of five thousand pounds a-year. But the consent of the Board of Control was necessary; and at the head of the Board of Control was Mr. Dundas, who had himself been a party to the impeachment, who had, on that account, been reviled with great bitterness by the adherents of Hastings, and who, therefore, was not in a very complying mood. He refused to consent to what the Directors suggested. The Directors remonstrated. A long controversy followed. Hastings, in the mean time, was reduced to such distress that he could hardly pay his weekly bills. At length a compromise was made. An annuity of four thousand a-year was settled on Hastings; and in order to enable him to meet pressing demands, he was to receive ten years' annuity in advance. The Company was also permitted to lend him fifty thousand pounds, to be repaid by instalments without interest. This relief, though given in the most absurd manner, was sufficient to enable the retired Governor to live in comfort, and even in luxury, if he had been a skilful manager. But he was careless and profuse, and was more than once under the necessity of applying to the Company for assistance, which was liberally given.

He had security and affluence, but not the power and dignity which, when he landed from India, he had reason to expect. He had then looked forward to a coronet, a red riband, a seat at the Council Board, an office at Whitehall. He was then only fifty-two, and might hope for many years of bodily and mental vigour. The case was widely different when he left the bar of the Lords. He was now too old a man to turn his mind to a new class of studies and duties. He had no chance of receiving any mark of royal favour while Mr. Pitt remained in power; and, when Mr. Pitt retired, Hastings was approaching his seventieth year.

Once, and only once, after his acquittal, he interfered in politics; and that interference was not much to his honour. In 1804 he exerted himself strenuously to prevent Mr. Addington, against whom Fox and Pitt had combined, from resigning the Treasury. It is difficult to believe that a man, so able and energetic as Hastings, can have thought that, when Bonaparte was at Boulogne with a great army, the defence of our island could safely be entrusted to a ministry which did not contain a single person whom flattery could describe as a great statesman. It is also certain that, on the important question which had raised Mr. Addington to power and on which he differed from both Fox and Pitt, Hastings, as might have been expected, agreed with Fox and Pitt and was decidely opposed to Addington. Religious intolerance has never been the vice of the Indian service, and certainly was not the vice of Hastings. But Mr. Addington had treated him with marked favour. Fox had been a principal manager of the impeachment. To Pitt it was owing that there had been an impeachment; and Hastings, we fear, was on this occasion guided by personal considerations rather than by a regard to the public interest.

The last twenty-four years of his life were chiefly passed at Daylesford. He amused himself with embellishing his grounds, riding fine Arab horses, fattening prize-cattle, and trying to rear Indian animals and vegetables in England. He sent for seeds of a very fine custard apple, from the garden of what had once been his own villa, among the green hedgerows of Allipore. He tried also to naturalise in Worcestershire the delicious leechee, almost the only fruit of Bengal which deserves to be regretted even amidst the plenty of Covent Garden. The Mogul emperors, in the time of their greatness, had in vain attempted to introduce into Hindostan the goat of the table-land of Thibet, whose down supplies the looms of Cashmere with the materials of the finest shawls. Hastings tried, with no better fortune, to rear a breed at Daylesford; nor does he seem to have succeeded better with the cattle of Bootan, whose tails are in high esteem as the best fans for brushing away the mosquitoes.

Literature divided his attention with his conservatories and his menagerie. He had always loved books, and they were now necessary to him. Though not a poet, in any high sense of the word, he wrote neat and polished lines with great facility, and was fond of exercising this talent. Indeed, if we must speak out, he seems to have been more of a Trissotin than was to be expected from the powers of his mind and from the great part which he had played in life. We are assured, in these "Memoirs," that the first thing which he did in the morning was to compose a copy of verses. When the family and guests assembled, the poem made its appearance as regularly as the eggs and rolls ; and Mr. Gleig requires us to believe that, if from any accident Hastings came to the breakfast-table without one of his charming performances in his hand, the omission was felt by all as a grievous disappointment. Tastes differ widely. For ourselves, we must say that, however good the breakfasts at Daylesford may have been—and we are assured that the tea was of the most aromatic flavour, and that neither tongue nor venison-pasty was wanting—we should have thought the reckoning high if we had been forced to earn our repast by listening every day to a new madrigal or sonnet composed by our host. We are glad, however, that Mr. Gleig has preserved this little feature of character, though we think it by no means a beauty. It is good to be often reminded of the inconsistency of human nature, and to learn to look without wonder or disgust on the weaknesses which are found in the strongest minds. Dionysius in old times, Frederic in the last century, with capacity and vigour equal to the conduct of the greatest affairs, united all the little vanities and affectations of provincial blue-stockings. These great examples may console the admirers of Hastings for the affliction of seeing him reduced to the level of the Hayleys and Sewards.

When Hastings had passed many years in retirement and had long outlived the common age of men, he again became for a short time an object of general attention. In 1813, the charter of the East India Company was renewed ; and much discussion about Indian affairs took place in Parliament. It was determined to examine witnesses at the bar of the Commons ; and Hastings was ordered to attend. He had appeared at that bar once before. It was when he read his answer to the charges which Burke had laid on the table. Since that time twenty-seven years had elapsed ; public feeling had undergone a complete change ; the nation had now forgotten his faults and remembered only his services. The reappearance, too, of a man who had been among the most distinguished of a generation that had passed away, who now belonged to history, and who seemed to have risen from the dead, could not but produce a solemn and pathetic effect. The Commons received him with acclamations, ordered a chair to be set for him, and, when he retired, rose and uncovered. There were, indeed, a few who did not sympathise with the general feeling. One or two of the managers of the impeachment were present. They sat in the same seats which they had occupied when they had been thanked for the services which they had rendered in Westminster Hall : for, by the courtesy of the House, a member who has been thanked in his place is considered as having a right always to occupy that place. These gentlemen were not disposed to admit that they had employed several of the best years of their lives in persecuting an innocent man. They accordingly kept their seats and pulled their hats over their brows ; but the exceptions only made the prevailing enthusiasm more remarkable. The Lords received the old man with similar tokens of respect. The University of Oxford conferred on him the degree of Doctor of Laws ; and, in the Sheldonian Theatre, the undergraduates welcomed him with tumultuous cheering.

These marks of public esteem were soon followed by marks of the favour of the Crown. Hastings was sworn of the Privy Council, and was admitted to a long private audience of the Prince Regent, who treated him very graciously. When the Emperor of Russia and the King of Prussia visited England, Hastings appeared in their train both at Oxford and in the Guildhall of London, and, though surrounded by a crowd of princes and great warriors, was everywhere received by the public with marks of respect and admiration.

He was presented by the Prince Regent both to Alexander and to Frederic William; and his Royal Highness went so far as to declare in public that honours far higher than a seat in the Privy Council were due, and would soon be paid, to the man who had saved the British dominions in Asia. Hastings now confidently expected a peerage; but, from some unexplained cause, he was again disappointed.

He lived about four years longer, in the enjoyment of good spirits, of faculties not impaired to any painful or degrading extent, and of health such as is rarely enjoyed by those who attain such an age. At length, on the 22nd of August, 1818, in the eighty-sixth year of his age, he met death with the same tranquil and decorous fortitude which he had opposed to all the trials of his various and eventful life.

With all his faults—and they were neither few nor small—only one cemetery was worthy to contain his remains. In that temple of silence and reconciliation where the enmities of twenty generations lie buried, in the Great Abbey which has during many ages afforded a quiet resting-place to those whose minds and bodies have been shattered by the contentions of the Great Hall, the dust of the illustrious accused should have mingled with the dust of the illustrious accusers. This was not to be. Yet the place of interment was not ill-chosen. Behind the chancel of the parish church of Daylesford, in earth which already held the bones of many chiefs of the house of Hastings, was laid the coffin of the greatest man who has ever borne that ancient and widely extended name. On the very spot, probably, fourscore years before, the little Warren, meanly clad and scantily fed, had played with the children of ploughmen. Even then his young mind had revolved plans which might be called romantic. Yet, however romantic, it is not likely that they had been so strange as the truth. Not only had the poor orphan retrieved the fallen fortunes of his line. Not only had he repurchased the old lands and rebuilt the old dwelling—he had preserved and extended an empire. He had founded a polity. He had administered government and war with more than the capacity of Richelieu. He had patronised learning with the judicious liberality of Cosmo. He had been attacked by the most formidable combination of enemies that ever sought the destruction of a single victim; and over that combination, after a struggle of ten years, he had triumphed. He had at length gone down to his grave in the fulness of age—in peace, after so many troubles, in honour, after so much obloquy.

Those who look on his character without favour or malevolence, will pronounce that, in the two great elements of all social virtue—in respect for the rights of others and in sympathy for the sufferings of others—he was deficient. His principles were somewhat lax. His heart was somewhat hard. But though we cannot with truth describe him either as a righteous or as a merciful ruler, we cannot regard without admiration and amplitude the fertility of his intellect—his rare talents for command, for administration and for controversy—his dauntless courage, his honourable poverty, his fervent zeal for the interests of the state, his noble equanimity—tried by both extremes of fortune and never disturbed by either.

FREDERIC THE GREAT. (APRIL, 1842.)

Frederic the Great and his Times. Edited, with an Introduction, by THOMAS CAMPBELL, Esq. 2 vols. 8vo. London, 1842.

THIS work, which has the high honour of being introduced to the world by the author of "Lochiel" and "Hohenlinden," is not wholly unworthy of so distinguished a *chaperon*. It professes, indeed, to be no more than a compilation; but it is an exceedingly amusing compilation, and we shall be glad to have more of it. The narrative comes down at present only to the commencement of the Seven Years' War, and therefore does not comprise the most interesting portion of Frederic's reign.

It may not be unacceptable to our readers that we should take this opportunity of presenting them with a slight sketch of the life of the greatest king that has, in modern times, succeeded by right of birth to a throne. It may, we fear, be impossible to compress so long and eventful a story within the limits which we must prescribe to ourselves. Should we be compelled to break off, we shall, when the continuation of this work appears, return to the subject.

The Prussian monarchy, the youngest of the great European states, but in population and revenue the fifth among them, and in art, science and civilisation entitled to the third, if not to the second place, sprang from a humble origin. About the beginning of the fifteenth century, the Marquisate of Brandenburg was bestowed by the Emperor Sigismund on the noble family of Hohenzollern. In the sixteenth century that family embraced the Lutheran doctrines. Early in the seventeenth century, it obtained from the King of Poland the investiture of the duchy of Prussia. Even after this accession of territory, the chiefs of the house of Hohenzollern hardly ranked with the Electors of Saxony and Bavaria. The soil of Brandenburg was for the most part sterile. Even round Berlin, the capital of the province, and round Potsdam, the favourite residence of the Margraves, the country was a desert. In some tracts the deep sand could with difficulty be forced by assiduous tillage to yield thin crops of rye and oats. In other places the ancient forests, from which the conquerors of the Roman empire had descended on the Danube, remained untouched by the hand of man. Where the soil was rich it was generally marshy, and its insalubrity repelled the cultivators whom its fertility attracted. Frederic William, called the Great Elector, was the prince to whose policy his successors have agreed to ascribe their greatness. He acquired by the peace of Westphalia several valuable possessions, and among them the rich city and district of Magdeburg; and he left to his son Frederic a principality as considerable as any which was not called a kingdom.

Frederic aspired to the style of royalty. Ostentatious and profuse, negligent of his true interests and of his high duties, insatiably eager for frivolous distinctions, he added nothing to the real weight of the state which he governed: perhaps he transmitted his inheritance to his children impaired rather than augmented in value; but he succeeded in gaining the great object of his life, the title of King. In the year 1700, he assumed this new dignity. He had on that occasion to undergo all the mortifications which fall to the lot of ambitious upstarts. Compared with the other crowned heads of Europe, he made a figure resembling that which a Nabob or a Commissary, who had bought a title, would make in the company of Peers whose ancestors had been attainted for treason against the Plantagenets. The envy of the class which he quitted, and the civil scorn of the class into which he intruded himself, were marked in very significant ways. The Elector of Saxony at first refused to acknowledge the new Majesty. Louis the Fourteenth looked down on his brother King with an air not unlike that with which the Count in Molière's play regards Monsieur Jourdain, just fresh from the mummery of being made a gentleman. Austria exacted large sacrifices in return for her recognition, and at last gave it ungraciously.

Frederic was succeeded by his son, Frederic William, a prince who must be allowed to have possessed some talents for administration, but whose character was disfigured by the most odious vices, and whose eccentricities were such as had never been seen out of a madhouse. He was exact and diligent in the transacting of business, and he was the first who formed the design of obtaining for Prussia a place among the European powers, altogether out of proportion to her extent and population, by means of a strong military organisation. Strict economy enabled him to keep up a peace establishment of sixty thousand troops. These troops were disciplined in such a manner that, placed beside them, the household regiments of Versailles and St. James's would have appeared an awkward squad. The master of such a force could not but be regarded by all his neighbours as a formidable enemy and a valuable ally.

But the mind of Frederic William was so ill-regulated that his inclinations became passions and all his passions partook of the character of moral and intellectual disease. His parsimony degenerated into sordid avarice. His taste for military pomp and order became a mania, like that of a Dutch burgomaster for tulips, or that of a member of the Roxburghe Club for Caxtons. While the envoys of the Court of Berlin were in a state of such squalid poverty as moved the laughter of foreign capitals, while the food placed before the princes and princesses of the blood-royal of Prussia was too scanty to appease hunger and so bad that even hunger loathed it—no price was thought too extravagant for tall recruits. The ambition of the King was to form a brigade of giants, and every country was ransacked by his agents for men above the ordinary stature. These researches were not confined to Europe. No head that towered above the crowd in the bazaars of Aleppo, of Cairo, or of Surat could escape the crimps of Frederic William. One Irishman more than seven feet high, who was picked up in London by the Prussian ambassador, received a bounty of near £1,300 sterling—very much more than the ambassador's salary. This extravagance was the more absurd, because a stout youth of five feet eight, who might have been procured for a few dollars, would in all probability have been a much more valuable soldier. But to Frederic William this huge Irishman was what a brass Otho or a Vinegar Bible is to a collector of a different kind.

It is remarkable, that though the main end of Frederic William's administration was to have a great military force, though his reign forms an important epoch in the history of military discipline, and though his dominant passion was the love of military display, he was yet one of the most pacific of princes. We are afraid that his aversion to war was not the effect of humanity, but was merely one of his thousand whims. His feeling about his troops seems to have resembled a miser's feeling about his money. He loved to collect them, to count them, to see them increase; but he could not find it in his heart to break in upon the precious hoard. He looked forward to some future time when his Patagonian battalions were to drive hostile infantry before them like sheep. But this future time was always receding; and it is probable that, if his life had been prolonged thirty years, his superb army would never have seen any harder service than a sham fight in the fields near Berlin. But the great military means which he had collected were destined to be employed by a spirit far more daring and inventive than his own.

Frederic, surnamed the Great, son of Frederic William, was born in January, 1712. It may safely be pronounced that he had received from nature a strong and sharp understanding and a rare firmness of temper and intensity of will. As to the other parts of his character, it is difficult to say whether they are to be ascribed to nature or to the strange training which he underwent. The history of his boyhood is painfully interesting. Oliver Twist in the parish workhouse, Smike at Dotheboys Hall, were petted children when compared with this wretched heir apparent of a crown. The nature of Frederic William was hard and bad, and the habit of exercising arbitrary power had made him frightfully savage. His rage constantly vented itself to right and left in curses and blows. When his Majesty took a walk, every human being fled before him, as if a tiger had broken loose from a menagerie. If he met a lady in the street, he gave her a kick and told her to go home and mind her brats. If he saw a clergyman staring at the soldiers, he admonished the reverend gentleman to betake himself to study and prayer, and enforced this pious advice by a sound caning administered on the spot. But it was in his own house that he was most unreasonable and ferocious. His palace was hell and he the most execrable of fiends—a cross between Moloch and Puck. His son Frederic and his daughter Wilhelmina, afterwards Margravine of Bareuth, were in an especial manner objects of his aversion. His own mind was uncultivated. He despised literature. He hated infidels, papists and metaphysicians, and did not very well understand in what they differed from each other. The business of life, according to him, was to drill and to be drilled. The recreations suited to a prince were to sit in a cloud of tobacco-smoke, to sip Swedish beer between the puffs of the pipe, to play backgammon for three-halfpence a rubber, to kill wild hogs and to shoot partridges by the thousand. The Prince-Royal showed little inclination either for the serious employments or for the amusements of his father. He shirked the duties of the parade ; he detested the fume of tobacco; he had no taste either for backgammon or for field sports. He had an exquisite ear, and performed skilfully on the flute. His earliest instructors had been French refugees, and they had awakened in him a strong passion for French literature and French society. Frederic William regarded these tastes as effeminate and contemptible, and, by abuse and persecution, made them still stronger. Things became worse when the Prince-Royal attained that time of life at which the great revolution in the human mind and body takes place. He was guilty of some youthful indiscretions which no good and wise parent would regard with severity. At a later period he was accused, truly or falsely, of vices from which History averts her eyes, and which even Satire blushes to name—vices such that, to borrow the energetic language of Lord Keeper Coventry, "the depraved nature of man, which of itself carrieth man to all other sin, abhorreth them." But the offences of his youth were not characterised by any peculiar turpitude. They excited, however, transports of rage in the King, who hated all faults except those to which he was himself inclined, and who conceived that he made ample atonement to Heaven for his brutality by holding the softer passions in detestation. The Prince-Royal, too, was not one of those who are content to take their religion on trust. He asked puzzling questions, and brought forward arguments which seemed to savour of something different from pure Lutheranism. The King suspected that his son was inclined to be a heretic of some sort or other, whether Calvinist or Atheist his Majesty did not very well know. The ordinary malignity of Frederic William was bad enough. He now thought malignity a part of his duty as a Christian man and all the conscience that he had stimulated his hatred. The flute was broken—the French books were sent out of the palace—the Prince was kicked and cudgelled and pulled by the hair. At dinner the plates were hurled at his head—sometimes he was restricted to bread and water—sometimes he was forced to swallow food so nauseous that he could not keep it on his stomach. Once his father knocked him down, dragged him along the floor to a window, and was with difficulty prevented from strangling him with the cord of the curtain. The Queen, for the crime of not wishing to see her son murdered, was subjected to the grossest indignities. The Princess Wilhelmina, who took her brother's part, was treated almost as ill as Mrs. Brownrigg's apprentices. Driven to despair, the unhappy youth tried to run away; then the fury of the old tyrant rose to madness. The Prince was an officer in the army; his flight was therefore desertion; and, in the moral code of Frederic William, desertion was the highest of all crimes—" Desertion," says this royal theologian, in one of his half crazy letters, "is from hell. It is a work of the children of the Devil. No child of God could possibly be guilty of it." An accomplice of the Prince, in spite of the recommendation of a court-martial, was mercilessly put to death. It seemed probable that the Prince himself would suffer the same fate. It was with difficulty that the intercession of the States of Holland, of the Kings of Sweden and Poland, and of the Emperor of Germany, saved the House of Brandenburg from the stain of an unnatural murder. After months of cruel suspense, Frederic learned that his life would be spared. He remained, however, long a prisoner; but he was not on that account to be pitied. He found in his gaolers a tenderness which he had never found in his father; his table was not sumptuous, but he had wholesome food in sufficient quantity to appease hunger; he could read the "Henriade" without being kicked and could play on his flute without having it broken over his head.

When his confinement terminated, he was a man. He had nearly completed his twenty-first year, and could scarcely even by such a parent as Frederic William be kept much longer under the restraints which had made his boyhood miserable. Suffering had matured his understanding while it had hardened his heart and soured his temper. He had learnt self-command and dissimulation: he affected to conform to some of his father's views; and submissively accepted a wife, who was a wife only in name, from his father's hand. He also served with credit, though without any opportunity of acquiring brilliant distinction, under the command of Prince Eugene, during a campaign marked by no extraordinary events. He was now permitted to keep a separate establishment, and was therefore able to indulge with caution his own tastes. Partly in order to conciliate the King and partly, no doubt, from inclination, he gave up a portion of his time to military and political business, and thus gradually acquired such an aptitude for affairs as his most intimate associates were not aware that he possessed.

His favourite abode was at Rheinsberg, near the frontier which separates the Prussian dominions from the Duchy of Mecklenburg. Rheinsberg is a fertile and smiling spot in the midst of the sandy waste of the Marquisate. The mansion, surrounded by woods of oak and beech, looks out upon a spacious lake. There Frederic amused himself by laying out gardens in regular alleys and intricate mazes, by building obelisks, temples and conservatories, and by collecting rare fruits and flowers. His retirement was enlivened by a few companions, among whom he seems to have preferred those who, by birth or extraction, were French. With these inmates, he dined and supped well, drank freely, and amused himself sometimes with concerts and sometimes with holding chapters of a fraternity which he called the Order of Bayard; but literature was his chief resource.

His education had been entirely French. The long ascendency which Louis XIV. had enjoyed, and the eminent merit of the tragic and comic dramatists, of the satirists and of the preachers who had flourished under that magnificent prince, had made the French language predominant in Europe. Even in countries which had a national literature and which could boast of names greater than those of Racine, of Molière and of Massillon—in the country of Dante, in the country of Cervantes, in the country of Shakspeare and Milton—the intellectual fashions of Paris had been to a great extent adopted. Germany had not yet produced a single masterpiece of poetry or eloquence. In Germany, therefore, the French taste reigned without rival and without limit. Every youth of rank was taught to speak and write French. That he should speak and write his own tongue with politeness, or even with accuracy and facility, was regarded as comparatively an unimportant object. Even Frederic William, with all his rugged Saxon prejudices, thought it necessary that his children should know French and quite unnecessary that they should be well versed in German. The Latin was positively interdicted. "My son," his Majesty wrote, "shall not learn Latin; and, more than that, I will not suffer anybody even to mention such a thing to me." One of the preceptors ventured to read the "Golden Bull" in the original with the Prince-Royal. Frederic William entered the room, and broke out in his usual kingly style.

"Rascal, what are you at there?"

"Please your Majesty," answered the preceptor, "I was explaining the "Golden Bull" to his Royal Highness."

"I'll Golden Bull you, you rascal!" roared the Majesty of Prussia. Up went the King's cane; away ran the terrified instructor; and Frederic's classical studies ended for ever. He now and then affected to quote Latin sentences, and produced such exquisitely Ciceronian phrases as these: "Stante pede morire;" "De gustibus non est disputandus;" "Tot verbas, tot spondera." Of Italian, he had not enough to read a page of Metastasio with ease; and of the Spanish and English, he did not, as far as we are aware, understand a single word.

As the highest human compositions to which he had access were those of the French writers, it is not strange that his admiration for those writers should have been unbounded. His ambitious and eager temper early prompted him to imitate what he admired. The wish, perhaps, dearest to his heart was, that he might rank among the masters of French rhetoric and poetry. He wrote prose and verse as indefatigably as if he had been a starving hack of Cave or Osborn; but Nature, which had bestowed on him, in a large measure, the talents of a captain and of an administrator, had withheld from him those higher and rarer gifts without which industry labours in vain to produce immortal eloquence and song. And, indeed, had he been blessed with more imagination, wit and fertility of thought than he appears to have had, he would still have been subject to one great disadvantage, which would, in all probability, have for ever prevented him him from taking a high place among men of letters. He had not the full command of any language. There was no machine of thought which he could employ with perfect ease, confidence and freedom. He had German enough to scold his servants or to give the word of command to his grenadiers, but his grammar and pronunciation were extremely bad. He found it difficult to make out the meaning even of the simplest German poetry. On one occasion, a version of Racine's "Iphigénie" was read to him. He held the French original in his hand; but was forced to own that, even with such help, he could not understand the translation. Yet, though he had neglected his mother tongue in order to bestow all his attention on French, his French was, after all, the French of a foreigner. It was necessary for him to have always at his beck some men of letters from Paris to point out the solecisms and false rhymes of which, to the last, he was frequently guilty. Even had he possessed the poetic faculty—of which, as far as we can judge, he was utterly destitute—the want of a language would have prevented him from being a great poet. No noble work of imagination, as far as we recollect, was ever composed by any man, except in a dialect which he had learned without remembering how or when, and which he had spoken with perfect ease before he had ever analysed its structure. Romans of great talent wrote Greek verses; but how many of those verses have deserved to live? Many men of eminent genius have, in modern times, written Latin poems; but, as far as we are aware, none of those poems, not even Milton's, can be ranked in the first class of art, or even very high in the second. It is not strange, therefore, that, in the French verses of Frederic, we can find nothing beyond the reach of any man of good parts and industry, nothing above the level of Newdigate and Seatonian poetry. His best pieces may perhaps rank with the worst in Dodsley's collection. In history, he succeeded better. We do not, indeed, find, in any part of his voluminous "Memoirs," either deep reflection or vivid painting. But the narrative is distinguished by clearness, conciseness, good sense and a certain air of truth and simplicity, which is singularly graceful in a man who, having done great things, sits down to relate them. On the whole, however, none of his writings are so agreeable to us as his "Letters," particularly those which are written with earnestness and are not embroidered with verses.

It is not strange that a young man devoted to literature, and acquainted only with the literature of France, should have looked with profound veneration on the genius of Voltaire, nor is it just to condemn him for this feeling. "A man who has never seen the sun," says Calderon, in one of his charming comedies, "cannot be blamed for thinking that no glory can exceed that of the moon. A man who has seen neither moon nor sun, cannot be blamed for talking of the unrivalled brightness of the morning star." Had Frederic been able to read Homer and Milton, or even Virgil and Tasso, his admiration of the "Henriade" would prove that he was utterly destitute of the power of discerning what is excellent in art. Had he been familiar with Sophocles or Shakspeare, we should have expected him to appreciate "Zaire" more justly. Had he been able to study Thucydides and Tacitus in the original Greek and Latin, he would have known that there were heights in the eloquence of history far beyond the reach of the author of the "Life of Charles the Twelfth." But the finest heroic poem, several of the most powerful tragedies, and the most brilliant and picturesque historical work that Frederic had ever read, were Voltaire's. Such high and various excellence moved the young Prince almost to adoration. The opinions of Voltaire on religious and philosophical questions had not yet been fully exhibited to the public. At a later period, when an exile from his country and at open war with the Church, he spoke out. But when Frederic was at Rheinsberg, Voltaire was still a courtier; and, though he could not always curb his petulant wit, he had as yet published nothing that could exclude him from Versailles, and little that a divine of the mild and generous school of Grotius and Tillotson might not read with pleasure. In the "Henriade," in "Zaire" and in "Alzire," Christian piety is exhibited in the most amiable form; and, some years after the period of which we are writing, a Pope condescended to accept the dedication of "Mahomet." The real sentiments of the poet, however, might be clearly perceived by a keen eye through the decent disguise with which he veiled them, and could not escape the sagacity of Frederic, who held similar opinions and had been accustomed to practise similar dissimulation.

The Prince wrote to his idol in the style of a worshipper; and Voltaire replied with exquisite grace and address. A correspondence followed, which may be studied with advantage by those who wish to become proficients in the ignoble art of flattery. No man ever paid compliments better than Voltaire. His sweetest confectionery had always a delicate yet stimulating flavour which was delightful to palates wearied by the coarse preparations of inferior artists. It was only from his hand that so much sugar could be swallowed without making the swallower sick. Copies of verses, writing desks, trinkets of amber, were exchanged between the friends. Frederic confided his writings to Voltaire; and Voltaire applauded as if Frederic had been Racine and Bossuet in one. One of his Royal Highness's performances was a refutation of the "Principe" of Machiavelli. Voltaire undertook to convey it to the press. It was entitled the "Anti-Machiavel," and was an edifying homily against rapacity, perfidy, arbitrary government, unjust war—in short, against almost everything for which its author is now remembered among men.

The old King uttered now and then a ferocious growl at the diversions of Rheinsberg. But his health was broken; his end was approaching; and his vigour was impaired. He had only one pleasure left, that of seeing tall soldiers. He could always be propitiated by a present of a grenadier of six feet four or six feet five; and such presents were from time to time judiciously offered by his son.

Early in the year 1740, Frederic William met death with a firmness and dignity worthy of a better and wiser man; and Frederic, who had just completed his twenty-eighth year, became King of Prussia. His character was little understood. That he had good abilities, indeed, no person who had talked with him or corresponded with him, could doubt. But the easy Epicurean life which he had lead, his love of good cookery and good wine, of music, of conversation, of light literature, led many to regard him as a sensual and intellectual voluptuary. His habit of canting about moderation, peace, liberty and the happiness which a good mind derives from the happiness of others, had imposed on some who should have known better. Those who thought best of him expected a Telemachus after Fénélon's pattern. Others predicted the approach of a Medicean age—an age propitious to learning and art and not unpropitious to pleasure. Nobody had the least suspicion that a tyrant, of extraordinary military and political talents, of industry more extraordinary still, without fear, without faith and without mercy, had ascended the throne.

The disappointment of Falstaff at his old boon-companion's coronation was not more bitter than that which awaited some of the inmates of Rheinsberg. They had long looked forward to the accession of their patron as to the day from which their own prosperity and greatness was to date. They had at last reached the promised land, the land which they had figured to themselves as flowing with milk and honey; and they found it a desert. "No more of these fooleries," was the short, sharp admonition given by Frederic to one of them. It soon became plain that, in the most important points, the new sovereign bore a strong family likeness to his predecessor. There was indeed a wide difference between the father and the son as respected extent and vigour of intellect, speculative opinions, amusements, studies, outward demeanour. But the groundwork of the character was the same in both. To both were common the love of order, the love of business, the military taste, the parsimony, the imperious spirit, the temper, irritable even to ferocity, the pleasure in the pain and humiliation of others. But these propensities had in Frederic William partaken of the general unsoundness of his mind, and wore a very different aspect when found in company with the strong and cultivated understanding of his successor. Thus, for example, Frederic was as anxious as any prince could be about the efficacy of his army. But this anxiety never degenerated into a monomania like that which led his father to pay fancy-prices for giants. Frederic was as thrifty about money as any prince or any private man ought to be. But he did not conceive, like his father, that it was worth while to eat unwholesome cabbages for the sake of saving four or five rixdollars in the year. Frederic was, we fear, as malevolent as his father; but Frederic's wit enabled him often to show his malevolence in ways more decent than those to which his father resorted, and to inflict misery and degradation by a taunt instead of a blow. Frederic, it is true, by no means relinquished his hereditary privilege of kicking and cudgelling. His practice, however, as to that matter, differed in some important respects from his father's. To Frederick William, the mere circumstance that any person whatever, men, women or children, Prussians or foreigners, were within reach of his toes and of his cane, appeared to be a sufficient reason for proceeding to belabour them. Frederic required provocation as well as vivacity; nor was he ever known to inflict this paternal species of correction on any but his born subjects, though on one occasion M. Thiébault had reason, during a few seconds, to anticipate the high honour of being an exception to this general rule.

The character of Frederic was still very imperfectly understood either by his subjects or by his neighbours, when events occurred which exhibited it in a strong light. A few months after his accession died Charles VI., Emperor of Germany, the last descendant, in the male line, of the house of Austria.

Charles left no son, and had, long before his death, relinquished all hopes of male issue. During the latter part of his life, his principal object had been to secure to his descendants in the female line the many crowns of the house of Hapsburg. With this view, he had promulgated a new law of succession, widely celebrated throughout Europe under the name of the Pragmatic Sanction. By virtue of this law, his daughter, the Archduchess Maria Theresa, wife of Francis of Loraine, succeeded to the dominions of her ancestors.

No sovereign has ever taken possession of a throne by a clearer title. All the politics of the Austrian cabinet had, during twenty years, been directed to one single end—the settlement of the succession. From every person whose rights could be considered as injuriously affected, renunciations in the most solemn form had been obtained. The new law had been ratified by the Estates of all the kingdoms and principalities which made up the great Austrian monarchy. England, France, Spain, Russia, Poland, Prussia, Sweden, Denmark, the Germanic body, had bound themselves by treaty to maintain the Pragmatic Sanction. That instrument was placed under the protection of the public faith of the whole civilised world.

Even if no positive stipulations on this subject had existed, the arrangement was one which no good man would have been willing to disturb. It was a peaceable arrangement. It was an arrangement acceptable to the great population whose happiness was chiefly concerned. It was an arrangement which made no change in the distribution of power among the states of Christendom. It was an arrangement which could be set aside only by means of a general war; and, if it were set aside, the effect would be that the equilibrium of Europe would be deranged, that the loyal and patriotic feelings of millions would be cruelly outraged, and that great provinces which had been united for centuries would be torn from each other by main force.

The sovereigns of Europe were, therefore, bound by every obligation which those who are intrusted with power over their fellow-creatures ought to hold most sacred, to respect and defend the rights of the Archduchess. Her situation and her personal qualities were such as might be expected to move the mind of any generous man to pity, admiration and chivalrous tenderness. She was in her twenty-fourth year. Her form was majestic, her features beautiful, her countenance sweet and animated, her voice musical, her deportment gracious and dignified. In all domestic relations she was without reproach. She was married to a husband whom she loved, and was on the point of giving birth to a child when death deprived her of her father. The loss of a parent and the new cares of empire were too much for her in the delicate state of her health. Her spirits were depressed and her cheek lost its bloom. Yet it seemed that she had little cause for anxiety. It seemed that justice, humanity and the faith of treaties would have their due weight, and that the settlement so solemnly guaranteed would be quietly carried into effect. England, Russia, Poland and Holland declared in form their intention to adhere to their engagements. The French ministers made a verbal declaration to the same effect. But from no quarter did the young Queen of Hungary receive stronger assurances of friendship and support than from the King of Prussia.

Yet the King of Prussia, the Anti-Machiavel, had already fully determined to commit the great crime of violating his plighted faith, of robbing the ally whom he was bound to defend, and of plunging all Europe into a long, bloody and desolating war; and all this for no end whatever, except that he might extend his dominions and see his name in the gazettes. He determined to assemble a great army with speed and secrecy, to invade Silesia before Maria Theresa should be apprised of his design, and to add that rich province to his kingdom.

We will not condescend to refute at length the pleas which the compiler of the "Memoirs" before us has copied from Doctor Preuss. They amount to this, that the house of Brandenburg had some ancient pretensions to Silesia, and had in the previous century been compelled, by hard usage on the part of the Court of Vienna, to waive those pretensions. It is certain that, whoever might originally have been in the right, Prussia had submitted. Prince after prince of the house of Brandenburg had acquiesced in the existing arrangement. Nay, the Court of Berlin had recently been allied with that of Vienna and had guaranteed the integrity of the Austrian states. Is it not perfectly clear that, if antiquated claims are to be set up against recent treaties and long possession, the world can never be at peace for a day? The laws of all nations have wisely established a time of limitation, after which titles, however illegitimate in their origin, cannot be questioned. It is felt by everybody that to eject a person from his estate on the ground of some injustice committed in the time of the Tudors would produce all the evils which result from arbitrary confiscation and would make all property insecure. It concerns the commonwealth —so runs the legal maxim—that there be an end of litigation. And surely this maxim is at least equally applicable to the great commonwealth of states; for in that commonwealth litigation means the devastation of provinces, the suspension of trade and industry, sieges like those of Badajoz and St. Sebastian, pitched fields like those of Eylau and Borodino. We hold that the transfer of Norway from Denmark to Sweden was an unjustifiable proceeding; but would the King of Denmark be therefore justified in landing, without any new provocation in Norway, and commencing military operations there? The King of Holland thinks, no doubt, that he was unjustly deprived of the Belgian provinces. Grant that it were so. Would he, therefore, be justified in marching with an army on Brussels? The case against Frederic was still stronger, inasmuch as the injustice of which he complained had been committed more than a century before. Nor must it be forgotten that he owed the highest personal obligations to the house of Austria. It may be doubted whether his life had not been preserved by the intercession of the prince whose daughter he was about to plunder.

To do the King justice, he pretended to no more virtue than he had. In manifestoes he might, for form's sake, insert some idle stories about his antiquated claim on Silesia; but in his conversations and "Memoirs" he took a very different tone. To quote his own words: "Ambition, interest, the desire of making people talk about me, carried the day; and I decided for war."

Having resolved on his course, he acted with ability and vigour. It was impossible wholly to conceal his preparations; for throughout the Prussian territories regiments, guns and baggage were in motion. The Austrian envoy at Berlin apprised his court of these facts and expressed a suspicion of Frederic's designs; but the ministers of Maria Theresa refused to give credit to so black an imputation on a young prince who was known chiefly by his high professions of integrity and philanthropy. "We will not," they wrote—"we cannot believe it."

In the meantime, the Prussian forces had been assembled. Without any declaration of war, without any demand for reparation, in the very act of pouring forth compliments and assurances of good will, Frederic commenced hostilities. Many thousands of his troops were actually in Silesia before the Queen of Hungary knew that he had set up any claim to any part of her territories. At length he sent her a message which could be regarded only as an insult. If she would but let him have Silesia, he would, he said, stand by her against any power which should try to deprive her of her other dominions: as if he was not already bound to stand by her, or as if his new promise could be of more value than the old one!

It was the depth of winter. The cold was severe and the roads deep in mire. But the Prussians pressed on. Resistance was impossible. The Austrian army was then neither numerous nor efficient. The small portion of that army which lay in Silesia was unprepared for hostilities. Glogau was blockaded; Breslau opened its gates; Ohlau was evacuated. A few scattered garrisons still held out; but the whole open country was subjugated; no enemy ventured to encounter the King in the field; and, before the end of January, 1741, he returned to receive the congratulations of his subjects at Berlin.

Had the Silesian question been merely a question between Frederic and Maria Theresa, it would be impossible to acquit the Prussian King of gross perfidy. But when we consider the effects which his policy produced, and could not fail to produce, on the whole community of civilised nations, we are compelled to pronounce a condemnation still more severe. Till he began the war, it seemed possible, even probable, that the peace of the world would be preserved. The plunder of the great Austrian heritage was indeed a strong temptation; and in more than one cabinet ambitious schemes were already meditated. But the treaties by which the Pragmatic Sanction had been guaranteed were express and recent. To throw all Europe into confusion for a purpose clearly unjust was no light matter. England was true to her engagements. The voice of Fleury had always been for peace. He had a conscience. He was now in extreme old age and was unwilling, after a life which, when his situation was considered, must be pronounced singularly pure, to carry the fresh stain of a great crime before the tribunal of his God. Even the vain and unprincipled Belle Isle, whose whole life was one wild day-dream of conquest and spoliation, could not, without disgrace, make a direct attack on the Austrian dominions. Charles, Elector of Bavaria, pretended that he had a right to a large part of the inheritance which the Pragmatic Sanction gave to the Queen of Hungary; but he was not sufficiently powerful to move without support. It might, therefore, not unreasonably be expected that, after a short period of restlessness, all the potentates of Christendom would acquiesce in the arrangements made by the late Emperor. But the selfish rapacity of the King of Prussia gave the signal to his neighbours. His example quieted their sense of shame. His success led them to underrate the difficulty of dismembering the Austrian monarchy. The whole world sprang to arms. On the head of Frederic is all the blood which was shed in a war which raged during many years and in every quarter of the globe—the blood of the column of Fontenoy, the blood of the brave mountaineers who were slaughtered at Culloden. The evils produced by his wickedness were felt in lands where the name of Prussia was unknown; and, in order that he might rob a neighbour whom he had promised to defend, black men fought on the coast of Coromandel and red men scalped each other by the Great Lakes of North America.

Silesia had been occupied without a battle; but the Austrian troops were advancing to the relief of the fortresses which still held out. In the spring, Frederic rejoined his army. He had seen little of war and had never commanded any great body of men in the field. It is not, therefore, strange that his first military operations showed little of that skill which, at a later period, was the admiration of Europe. What connoisseurs say of some pictures painted by Raphael in his youth may be said of this campaign. It was in Frederic's early, bad manner. Fortunately for him, the generals to whom he was opposed were men of small capacity. The discipline of his own troops, particularly of the infantry, was unequalled in that age; and some able and experienced officers were at hand to assist him with their advice. Of these, the most distinguished was Field-Marshal Schwerin, a brave adventurer of Pomeranian extraction, who had served half the governments in Europe, had borne the commissions of the States-General of Holland and of the Duke of Mecklenburg, had fought under Marlborough at Blenheim and had been with Charles the Twelfth at Bender.

Frederic's first battle was fought at Molwitz; and never did the career of a great commander open in a more inauspicious manner. His army was victorious. Not only, however, did he not establish his title to the character of an able general, but he was so unfortunate as to make it doubtful whether he possessed the vulgar courage of a soldier. The cavalry, which he commanded in person, was put to flight. Unaccustomed to the tumult and carnage of a field of battle, he lost his self-possession and listened too readily to those who urged him to save himself. His English grey carried him many miles from the field, while Schwerin, though wounded in two places, manfully upheld the day. The skill of the old Field-Marshal and the steadiness of the Prussian battalions prevailed; and the Austrian army was driven from the field with the loss of eight thousand men.

The news was carried late at night to a mill in which the King had taken shelter. It gave him a bitter pang. He was successful; but he owed his success to dispositions which others had made and to the valour of men who had fought while he was flying. So unpromising was the first appearance of the greatest warrior of that age!

The battle of Molwitz was the signal for a general explosion throughout Europe. Bavaria took up arms. France, not yet declaring herself a principal in the war, took part in it as an ally of Bavaria. The two great statesmen to whom mankind had owed many years of tranquility disappeared about this time from the scene, but not till they had both been guilty of the weakness of sacrificing their sense of justice and their love of peace to the vain hope of preserving their power. Fleury, sinking under age and infirmity, was borne down by the impetuosity of Belle Isle. Walpole retired from the service of his ungrateful country to his woods and paintings at Houghton; and his power devolved on the daring and eccentric Carteret. As were the ministers, so were the nations. Thirty years, during which Europe had, with few interruptions, enjoyed repose, had prepared the public mind for great military efforts. A new generation had grown up which could not remember the siege of Turin or the slaughter of Malplaquet; which knew war by nothing but its trophies; and which, while it looked with pride on the tapestries at Blenheim or the statue in the Place of Victories, little thought by what privations, by what waste of private fortunes, by how many bitter tears, conquests must be purchased.

For a time fortune seemed adverse to the Queen of Hungary. Frederic invaded Moravia. The French and Bavarians penetrated into Bohemia and were there joined by the Saxons. Prague was taken. The Elector of Bavaria was raised by the suffrages of his colleagues to the Imperial throne, a throne which the practice of centuries had almost entitled the House of Austria to regard as a hereditary possession.

Yet was the spirit of the haughty daughter of the Cæsars unbroken. Hungary was still hers by an unquestionable title; and, although her ancestors had found Hungary the most mutinous of all their kingdoms, she resolved to trust herself to the fidelity of a people, rude indeed, turbulent and impatient of oppression, but brave, generous and simple-hearted. In the midst of distress and peril, she had given birth to a son, afterwards the Emperor Joseph the Second. Scarcely had she risen from her couch when she hastened to Presburg. There, in the sight of an innumerable multitude, she was crowned with the crown and robed with the robe of St. Stephen. No spectator could restrain his tears when the beautiful young mother, still weak from child-bearing, rode, after the fashion of her fathers, up the Mount of Defiance, unsheathed the ancient sword of state, shook it towards north 'and south, east and west, and, with a glow on her pale face, challenged the four corners of the world to dispute her rights and those of her boy. At the first sitting of the Diet, she appeared clad in deep mourning for her father; and in pathetic and dignified words implored her people to support her just cause. Magnates and deputies sprang up, half drew their sabres, and with eager voices vowed to stand by her with their lives and fortunes. Till then, her firmness had never once forsaken her before the public eye; but at that shout she sank down upon her throne and wept aloud. Still more touching was the sight when, a few days later, she came again before the Estates of her realm, and held up before them the little Archduke in her arms. Then it was that the enthusiasm of Hungary broke forth into that war-cry which soon resounded throughout Europe, "Let us die for our King, Maria Theresa!"

In the meantime, Frederic was meditating a change of policy. He had no wish to raise France to supreme power on the Continent at the expense of the house of Hapsburg. His first object was to rob the Queen of Hungary. His second was that, if possible, nobody should rob her but himself. He had entered into engagements with the powers leagued against Austria; but these engagements were in his estimation of no more force than the guarantee formerly given to the Pragmatic Sanction. His game now was to secure his share of the plunder by betraying his accomplices. Maria Theresa was little inclined to listen to any such compromise; but the English government represented to her so strongly the necessity of buying off so formidable an enemy as Frederic that she agreed to negotiate. The negotiation would not, however, have ended in a treaty had not the arms of Frederic been crowned with a second victory. Prince Charles of Loraine, brother-in-law to Maria Theresa, a bold and active, though unfortunate, general, gave battle to the Prussians at Chotusitz and was defeated. The King was still only a learner of the military art. He acknowledged, at a later period, that his success on this occasion was to be attributed, not at all to his own generalship, but solely to the valour and steadiness of his troops. He completely effaced, however, by his courage and energy, the stain which Molwitz had left on his reputation.

A peace, concluded under the English mediation, was the fruit of this battle. Maria Theresa ceded Silesia; Frederic abandoned his allies; Saxony followed his example; and the Queen was left at liberty to turn her whole force against

France and Bavaria. She was everywhere triumphant. The French were compelled to evacuate Bohemia, and with difficulty effected their escape. The whole line of their retreat might be tracked by the corpses of thousands who had died of cold, fatigue and hunger. Many of those who reached their country carried with them the seeds of death. Bavaria was overrun by bands of ferocious warriors from that bloody "debatable land" which lies on the frontier between Christendom and Islam. The terrible names of the Pandoor, the Croat and the Hussar, then first became familiar to western Europe. The unfortunate Charles of Bavaria, vanquished by Austria, betrayed by Prussia, driven from his hereditary states and neglected by his allies, was hurried by shame and remorse to an untimely end. An English army appeared in the heart of Germany and defeated the French at Dettingen. The Austrian captains already began to talk of completing the work of Marlborough and Eugene, and of compelling France to relinquish Alsace and the three Bishoprics.

The Court of Versailles, in this peril, looked to Frederic for help. He had been guilty of two great treasons—perhaps he might be induced to commit a third. The Duchess of Chateauroux then held the chief influence over the feeble Louis. She determined to send an agent to Berlin; and Voltaire was selected for the mission. He eagerly undertook the task; for, while his literary fame filled all Europe, he was troubled with a childish craving for political distinction. He was vain, and not without reason, of his address and of his insinuating eloquence; and he flattered himself that he possessed boundless influence over the King of Prussia. The truth was, that he knew, as yet, only one corner of Frederic's character. He was well acquainted with all the petty vanities and affectations of the poetaster, but was not aware that these foibles were united with all the talents and vices which lead to success in active life, and that the unlucky versifier who bored him with reams of middling Alexandrines, was the most vigilant, suspicious and severe of politicians.

Voltaire was received with every mark of respect and friendship, was lodged in the palace and had a seat daily at the royal table. The negotiation was of an extraordinary description. Nothing can be conceived more whimsical than the conferences which took place between the first literary man and the first practical man of the age, whom a strange weakness had induced to exchange their parts. The great poet would talk of nothing but treaties and guarantees and the great King of nothing but metaphors and rhymes. On one occasion, Voltaire put into his Majesty's hands a paper on the state of Europe, and received it back with verses scrawled on the margin. In secret they both laughed at each other. Voltaire did not spare the King's poems; and the King has left on record his opinion of Voltaire's diplomacy. "He had no credentials," says Frederic, "and the whole mission was a joke, a mere farce."

But what the influence of Voltaire could not effect, the rapid progress of the Austrian arms effected. If it should be in the power of Maria Theresa and George the Second to dictate terms of peace to France, what chance was there that Prussia would long retain Silesia? Frederic's conscience told him that he had acted perfidiously and inhumanly towards the Queen of Hungary. That her resentment was strong, she had given ample proof; and of her respect for treaties he judged by his own. Guarantees, he said, were mere filigree, pretty to look at, but too brittle to bear the slightest pressure. He thought it his safest course to ally himself closely to France and again to attack the Empress Queen. Accordingly, in the autumn of 1744, without notice, without any decent pretext, he recommenced hostilities, marched through the electorate of Saxony without troubling himself about the permission of the Elector, invaded Bohemia, took Prague and even menaced Vienna.

It was now that, for the first time, he experienced the inconstancy of fortune.

A A

An Austrian army under Charles of Loraine threatened his communications with Silesia. Saxony was all in arms behind him. He found it necessary to save himself by a retreat. He afterwards owned that his failure was the natural effect of his own blunders. No general, he said, had ever committed greater faults. It must be added, that to the reverses of this campaign he always ascribed his subsequent successes. It was in the midst of difficulty and disgrace that he caught the first clear glimpse of the principles of the military art.

The memorable year 1745 followed. The war raged by sea and land, in Italy, in Germany and in Flanders; and even England, after many years of profound internal quiet, saw, for the last time, hostile armies set in battle array against each other. This year is memorable in the life of Frederic as the date at which his noviciate in the art of war may be said to have terminated. There have been great captains whose precocious and self-taught military skill resembled intuition—Condé, Clive and Napoleon are examples. But Frederic was not one of these brilliant portents. His proficiency in military science was simply the proficiency which a man of vigorous faculties makes in any science to which he applies his mind with earnestess and industry. It was at Hohenfriedberg that he first proved how much he had profited by his errors and by their consequences. His victory on that day was chiefly due to his skilful dispositions, and convinced Europe that the prince who, a few years before, had stood aghast in the rout of Molwitz, had attained in the military art a mastery equalled by none of his contemporaries or equalled by Saxe alone. The victory of Hohenfriedberg was speedily followed by that of Sorr.

In the meantime, the arms of France had been victorious in the Low Countries. Frederic had no longer reason to fear that Maria Theresa would be able to give law to Europe, and he began to meditate a fourth breach of his engagements. The Court of Versailles was alarmed and mortified. A letter of earnest expostulation, in the handwriting of Louis, was sent to Berlin; but in vain. In the autumn of 1745, Frederick made peace with England and, before the close of the year, with Austria also. The pretensions of Charles of Bavaria could present no obstacle to an accommodation. That unhappy prince was no more; and Francis of Loraine, the husband of Maria Theresa, was raised, with the general assent of the Germanic body, to the Imperial throne.

Prussia was again at peace; but the European war lasted till, in the year 1748, it was terminated by the treaty of Aix-la-Chapelle. Of all the powers that had taken part in it, the only gainer was Frederic. Not only had he added to his patrimony the fine province of Silesia: he had, by his unprincipled dexterity, succeeded so well in alternately depressing the scale of Austria and that of France, that he was generally regarded as holding the balance of Europe, a high dignity for one who ranked lowest among kings and whose great-grandfather had been no more than a Margrave. By the public, the king of Prussia was considered as a politician destitute alike of morality and decency, insatiably rapacious and shamelessly false; nor was the public much in the wrong. He was at the same time allowed to be a man of parts, a rising general, a shrewd negotiator and administrator. Those qualities wherein he surpassed all mankind were as yet unknown to others or to himself, for they were qualities which shine out only on a dark ground. His careeer had hitherto, with little interruption, been prosperous; and it was only in adversity, in adversity which seemed without hope or resource, in adversity which would have overwhelmed even men celebrated for strength of mind, that his real greatness could be shown.

He had, from the commencement of his reign, applied himself to public business after a fashion unknown among kings. Louis XIV., indeed, had been his own prime minister and had exercised a general superintendence over all the departments of the government; but this was not sufficient for Frederic. He was not content with being his own prime minister—he would be his own sole minister. Under him there was no room, not merely for a Richelieu or a Mazarin, but for a Colbert, a Louvois or a Torcy. A love of labour for its own sake, a restless and insatiable longing to dictate, to intermeddle, to make his power felt, a profound scorn and distrust of his fellow-creatures, indisposed him to ask counsel, to confide important secrets, to delegate ample powers. The highest functionaries under his government were mere clerks, and were not so much trusted by him as valuable clerks are often trusted by the heads of departments. He was his own treasurer, his own commander-in-chief, his own intendant of public works, his own minister for trade and justice, for home affairs and foreign affairs, his own master of the horse, steward and chamberlain. Matters of which no chief of an office in any other government would ever hear were, in this singular monarchy, decided by the King in person. If a traveller wished for a good place to see a review, he had to write to Frederic, and received next day, from a royal messenger, Frederic's answer signed by Frederic's own hand. This was an extravagant, a morbid activity. The public business would assuredly have been better done if each department had been put under a man of talents and integrity and if the King had contented himself with a general control. In this manner, the advantages which belong to unity of design and the advantages which belong to the division of labour would have been to a great extent combined. But such a system would not have suited the peculiar temper of Frederic. He could tolerate no will, no reason, in the state, save his own. He wished for no abler assistance than that of penmen who had just understanding enough to translate, to transcribe, to make out his scrawls and to put his concise Yes and No into an official form. Of the higher intellectual faculties, there is as much in a copying machine or a lithographic press as he required from the secretary of the cabinet.

His own exertions were such as were hardly to be expected from a human body or a human mind. At Potsdam, his ordinary residence, he rose at three in summer and four in winter. A page soon appeared with a large basketful of all the letters which had arrived for the King by the last courier—despatches from ambassadors, reports from officers of revenue, plans of buildings, proposals for draining marshes, complaints from persons who thought themselves aggrieved, applications from persons who wanted titles, military commission and civil situations. He examined the seals with a keen eye; for he was never for a moment free from the suspicion that some fraud might be practised on him. Then he read the letters, divided them into several packets, and signified his pleasure generally by a mark, often by two or three words, now and then by some cutting epigram. By eight he had generally finished this part of his task. The adjutant-general was then in attendance, and received instructions for the day as to all the military arrangements of the kingdom. Then the King went to review his guards, not as kings ordinarily review their guards, but with the minute attention and severity of an old drill-sergeant. In the meantime, the four cabinet secretaries had been employed in answering the letters on which the King had that morning signified his will. These unhappy men were forced to work all the year round like negro slaves in the time of the sugar-crop. They never had a holiday. They never knew what it was to dine. It was necessary that before they stirred they should finish the whole of their work. The King, always on his guard against treachery, took from the heap a handful at random, and looked into them to see whether his instructions had been exactly followed. This was no bad security against foul play on the part of the secretaries; for if one of them were detected in a trick, he might think himself fortunate if he escaped with five years of imprisonment in a dungeon. Frederic then signed the replies; and all were sent off the same evening.

The general principles on which this strange government was conducted, deserve attention. The policy of Frederic was essentially the same as his father's; but Frederic, while he carried that policy to lengths to which his father never thought of carrying it, cleared it at the same time from the absurdities with which his father had encumbered it. The King's first object was to have a great, efficient and well-trained army. He had a kingdom which in extent and population was hardly in the second rank of European powers; and yet he aspired to a place not inferior to that of the sovereigns of England, France and Austria. For that end, it was necessary that Prussia should be all sting. Louis XV., with five times as many subjects as Frederic, and more than five times as large a revenue, had not a more formidable army. The proportion which the soldiers in Prussia bore to the people seems hardly credible. Of the males in the vigour of life, a seventh part were probably under arms; and this great force had, by drilling, by reviewing and by the unsparing use of cane and scourge, been taught to perform all evolutions with a rapidity and a precision which would have astonished Villars or Eugene. The elevated feelings which are necessary to the best kind of army were then wanting to the Prussian service. In those ranks were not found the religious and political enthusiasm which inspired the pikemen of Cromwell— the patriotic ardour, the thirst of glory, the devotion to a great leader, which inflamed the Old Guard of Napoleon. But in all the mechanical parts of the military calling, the Prussians were as superior to the English and French troops of that day as the English and French troops to a rustic militia.

Though the pay of the Prussian soldier was small, though every rixdollar of extraordinary charge was scrutinised by Frederic with a vigilance and suspicion such as Mr. Joseph Hume never brought to the examination of an army estimate, the expense of such an establishment was, for the means of the country, enormous. In order that it might not be utterly ruinous, it was necessary that every other expense should be cut down to the lowest possible point. Accordingly, Frederic, though his dominions bordered on the sea, had no navy. He neither had nor wished to have colonies. His judges, his fiscal officers, were meanly paid. His ministers at foreign courts walked on foot, or drove shabby old carriages till the axle-trees gave way. Even to his highest diplomatic agents, who resided at London and Paris, he allowed less than a thousand pounds sterling a-year. The royal household was managed with a frugality unusual in the establishments of opulent subjects—unexampled in any other palace. The King loved good eating and drinking, and during great part of his life took pleasure in seeing his table surrounded by guests; yet the whole charge of his kitchen was brought within the sum of two thousand pounds sterling a-year. He examined every extraordinary item with a care which might be thought to suit the mistress of a boarding-house better than a great prince. When more than four rixdollars were asked of him for a hundred oysters, he stormed as if he had heard that one of his generals had sold a fortress to the Empress Queen. Not a bottle of Champagne was uncorked without his express order. The game of the royal parks and forests, a serious head of expenditure in most kingdoms, was to him a source of profit. The whole was farmed out; and though the farmers were almost ruined by their contract, the King would grant them no remission. His wardrobe consisted of one fine gala dress, which lasted him all his life; of two or three old coats fit for Monmouth Street, of yellow waistcoats soiled with snuff and of huge boots embrowned by time. One taste alone sometimes allured him beyond the limits of parsimony, nay, even beyond the limits of prudence, the taste for building. In all other things his economy was such as we might call by a harsher name if we did not reflect that his funds were drawn from a heavily taxed people, and that it was impossible for him, without excessive tyranny, to keep up at once a formidable army and a splendid court.

Considered as an administrator, Frederic had undoubtedly many titles to praise. Order was strictly maintained throughout his dominions. Property was secure. A great liberty of speaking and of writing was allowed. Confident in the irresistible strength derived from a great army, the King looked down on malcontents and libellers with a wise disdain; and gave little encouragement to spies and informers. When he was told of the disaffection of one of his subjects, he merely asked, "how many thousand men can he bring into the field?" He once saw a crowd staring at something on a wall. He rode up and found that the object of curiosity was a scurrilous placard against himself. The placard had been posted up so high that it was not easy to read it. Frederic ordered his attendants to take it down and put it lower. "My people and I," he said, "have come to an agreement which satisfies us both. They are to say what they please and I am to do what I please." No person would have dared to publish in London satires on George II. approaching to the atrocity of those satires on Frederic, which the booksellers at Berlin sold with impunity. One bookseller sent to the palace a copy of the most stinging lampoon that perhaps was ever written in the world as the "Memoirs of Voltaire," published by Beaumarchais, and asked for his Majesty's orders. "Do not advertise it in an offensive manner," said the King; "but sell it by all means. I hope it will pay you well." Even among statesmen accustomed to the license of a free press, such steadfastness of mind as this is not very common.

It is due also to the memory of Frederic to say that he earnestly laboured to secure to his people the great blessing of cheap and speedy justice. He was one of the first rulers who abolished the cruel and absurd practice of torture. No sentence of death, pronounced by the ordinary tribunals, was executed without his sanction; and his sanction, except in cases of murder, was rarely given. Towards his troops he acted in a very different manner. Military offences were punished with such barbarous scourging that to be shot was considered by the Prussian soldier as a secondary punishment. Indeed, the principle which pervaded Frederic's whole policy was this—that the more severely the army is governed, the safer it is to treat the rest of the community with lenity.

Religious persecution was unknown under his government—unless some foolish and unjust restrictions which lay upon the Jews may be regarded as forming an exception. His policy with respect to the Catholics of Silesia presented an honourable contrast to the policy which, under very similar circumstances, England long followed with respect to the Catholics of Ireland. Every form of religion and irreligion found an asylum in his states. The scoffer whom the Parliaments of France had sentenced to a cruel death was consoled by a commission in the Prussian service. The Jesuit who could show his face nowhere else—who in Britain was still subject to penal laws, who was prescribed by France, Spain, Portugal and Naples, who had been given up even by the Vatican—found safety and the means of subsistence in the Prussian dominions.

Most of the vices of Frederic's administration resolve themselves into one vice—the spirit of meddling. The indefatigable activity of his intellect, his dictatorial temper, his military habits, all inclined him to this great fault. He drilled his people as he drilled his grenadiers. Capital and industry were diverted from their natural direction by a crowd of preposterous regulations. There was a monopoly of coffee, a monopoly of tobacco, a monopoly of refined sugar. The public money, of which the King was generally so sparing, was lavishly spent in ploughing bogs, in planting mulberry trees amidst the sand, in bringing sheep from Spain to improve the Saxon wool, in bestowing prizes for fine yarn, in building manufactories of porcelain, manufactories of carpets, manufactories of hardware, manufactories of lace. Neither the experience of other rulers, nor his own, could ever teach him that something more than an edict and a grant of public money was required to create a Lyons, a Brussels or a Birmingham.

For his commercial policy, however, there is some excuse. He had on his side illustrious examples and popular prejudice. Grievously as he erred, he erred in company with his age. In other departments, his meddling was altogether without apology. He interfered with the course of justice as well as with the course of trade, and set up his own crude notions of equity against the law as expounded by the unanimous voice of the gravest magistrates. It never occurred to him that a body of men whose lives were passed in adjudicating on questions of civil right were more likely to form correct opinions on such questions than a prince whose attention was divided among a thousand objects and who had probably never read a law book through. The resistance opposed to him by the tribunals inflamed him to fury. He reviled his Chancellor. He kicked the shins of his Judges. He did not, it is true, intend to act unjustly. He firmly believed that he was doing right and defending the cause of the poor against the wealthy. Yet this well-meant meddling probably did far more harm than all the explosions of his evil passions during the whole of his long reign. We could make shift to live under a debauchee or a tyrant; but to be ruled by a busybody is more than human nature can bear.

The same passion for directing and regulating appeared in every part of the King's policy. Every lad of a certain station in life was forced to go to certain schools within the Prussian dominions. If a young Prussian repaired, though but for a few weeks, to Leyden or Gottingen, for the purpose of study, the offence was punished with civil disabilities and sometimes with the confiscation of property. Nobody was to travel without the royal permission. If the permission were granted, the pocket money of the tourist was fixed by royal ordinance. A merchant might take with him two hundred and fifty rixdollars in gold, a noble was allowed to take four hundred; for it may be observed, in passing, that Frederic studiously kept up the old distinction between the nobles and the community. In speculation, he was a French philosopher; but in action, a German prince. He talked and wrote about the privileges of blood in the style of Siêyes; but in practice no chapter in the empire looked with a keener eye to genealogies and quarterings.

Such was Frederic the Ruler. But there was another Frederic, the Frederic of Rheinsberg, the fiddler and flute-player, the poetaster and metaphysician. Amidst the cares of state, the King had retained his passion for music, for reading, for writing, for literary society. To these amusements he devoted all the time that he could snatch from the business of war and government; and perhaps more light is thrown on his character by what passed during his hours of relaxation than by his battles or his laws.

It was the just boast of Schiller that, in his country, no Augustus, no Lorenzo had watched over the infancy of art. The rich and energetic language of Luther, driven by the Latin from the schools of pedants and by the French from the palaces of kings, had taken refuge among the people. Of the powers of that language, Frederic had no notion. He generally spoke of it, and of those who used it, with the contempt of ignorance. His library consisted of French books; at his table nothing was heard but French conversation.

The associates of his hours of relaxation were, for the most part, foreigners. Britain furnished to the royal circle two distinguished men, born in the highest rank and driven by civil dissensions from the land to which, under happier circumstances, their talents and virtues might have been a source of strength and glory. George Keith, Earl Marischal of Scotland, had taken arms for the house of Stuart in 1715, and his younger brother James, then only seventeen years old, had fought gallantly by his side. When all was lost, they retired together to the Continent, roved from country to country, served under many standards, and so bore themselves as to win the respect and goodwill of many who had no love for the Jacobite cause. Their long wanderings terminated at Potsdam; nor had Frederic any associates who deserved or obtained so large a share of his esteem. They were not only accomplished men, but nobles and warriors, capable of serving him in war and diplomacy as well as of amusing him at supper. Alone of all his companions, they appear never to have had reason to complain of his demeanour towards them. Some of those who knew the palace best pronounced that Lord Marischal was the only human being whom Frederic ever really loved.

Italy sent to the parties at Potsdam the ingenious and amiable Algarotti and Bastiani, the most crafty, cautious and servile of Abbés. But the greater part of the society which Frederic had assembled round him was drawn from France. Maupertuis had acquired some celebrity by the journey which he had made to Lapland for the purpose of ascertaining, by actual measurement, the shape of our planet. He was placed in the chair of the Academy of Berlin, a humble imitation of the renowned academy of Paris. Baculard D'Arnaud, a young poet, who was thought to have given promise of great things, had been induced to quit his country and to reside at the Prussian Court. The Marquess D'Argens was among the King's favourite companions, on account, as it should seem, of the strong opposition between their characters. The parts of D'Argens were good and his manners those of a finished French gentleman; but his whole soul was dissolved in sloth, timidity and self-indulgence. His was one of that abject class of minds which are superstitious without being religious. Hating Christianity with a rancour which made him incapable of rational inquiry, unable to see in the harmony and beauty of the universe the traces of divine power and wisdom, he was the slave of dreams and omens—would not sit down to table with thirteen in company, turned pale if the salt fell towards him, begged his guests not to cross their knives and forks on their plates, and would not for the world commence a journey on Friday. His health was a subject of constant anxiety to him. Whenever his head ached or his pulse beat quick, his dastardly fears and effeminate precautions were the jest of all Berlin. All this suited the King's purpose admirably. He wanted somebody by whom he might be amused and whom he might despise. When he wished to pass half an hour in easy, polished conversation, D'Argens was an excellent companion; when he wanted to vent his spleen and contempt, D'Argens was an excellent butt.

With these associates and others of the same class, Frederic loved to spend the time which he could steal from public cares. He wished his supper parties to be gay and easy, and invited his guests to lay aside all restraint and to forget that he was at the head of a hundred and sixty thousand soldiers and was absolute master of the life and liberty of all who sat at meat with him. There was, therefore, at these parties, the outward show of ease. The wit and learning of the company were ostentatiously displayed. The discussions on history and literature were often highly interesting. But the absurdity of all the religions known among men was the chief topic of conversation ; and the audacity with which doctrines and names venerated throughout Christendom were treated on these occasions startled even persons accustomed to the society of French and English freethinkers. Real liberty, however, or real affection, was in this brilliant society not to be found. Absolute kings seldom have friends ; and Frederic's faults were such as, even where perfect equality exists, make friendship exceedingly precarious. He had indeed many qualities which, on a first acquaintance, were captivating. His conversation was lively ; his manners, to those whom he desired to please, were even caressing. No man could flatter with more delicacy. No man succeeded more completely in inspiring those who approached him with vague hopes of some great advantage from his kindness. But under this fair exterior he was a tyrant—suspicious, disdainful and malevolent. He had one taste which may be pardoned in a boy, but which, when habitually and deliberately indulged by a man of mature age and strong understanding, is almost invariably the sign of a bad heart—a taste for severe practical jokes. If a courtier was fond of dress, oil was flung over his richest suit. If he was fond of money, some prank was invented to make him disburse more than he could spare. If he was hypochondriacal, he was made to believe that he had the dropsy. If he had particularly set his heart on visiting a place, a letter was forged to frighten him from going thither. These things, it may be said, are trifles. They are so ; but they are indications, not to be mistaken, of a nature to which the sight of human suffering and human degradation is an agreeable excitement.

Frederic had a keen eye for the foibles of others, and loved to communicate his discoveries. He had some talent for sarcasm and considerable skill in detecting the sore places where sarcasm would be most acutely felt. His vanity, as well as his malignity, found gratification in the vexation and confusion of those who smarted under his caustic jests. Yet, in truth, his success on these occasions belonged quite as much to the king as to the wit. We read that Commodus descended, sword in hand, into the arena against a wretched gladiator, armed only with a foil of lead, and, after shedding the blood of the helpless victim, struck medals to commemorate the inglorious victory. The triumphs of Frederic in the war of repartee were of much the same kind. How to deal with him was the most puzzling of questions. To appear constrained in his presence was to disobey his commands and to spoil his amusement. Yet, if his associates were enticed by his graciousness to indulge in the familiarity of a cordial intimacy, he was certain to make them repent of their presumption by some cruel humiliation. To resent his affronts was perilous ; yet not to resent them was to deserve and to invite them. In his view, those who mutinied were insolent and ungrateful ; those who submitted were curs made to receive bones and kickings with the same fawning patience. It is, indeed, difficult to conceive how anything short of the rage of hunger should have induced men to bear the misery of being the associates of the Great King. It was no lucrative post. His Majesty was as severe and economical in his friendships as in the other charges of his establishment, and as unlikely to give a rixdollar too much for his guests as for his dinners. The sum which he allowed to a poet or a philosopher was the very smallest sum for which such poet or philosopher could be induced to sell himself into slavery ; and the bondsman might think himself fortunate, if what had been so grudgingly given was not, after years of suffering, rudely and arbitrarily withdrawn.

Potsdam was, in truth, what it was called by one of its most illustrious inmates, the Palace of Alcina. At the first glance, it seemed to be a delightful spot, where every intellectual and physical enjoyment awaited the happy adventurer. Every new comer was received with eager hospitality, intoxicated with flattery, encouraged to expect prosperity and greatness. It was in vain that a long succession of favourites, who had entered that abode with delight and hope, and who, after a short term of delusive happiness, had been doomed to expiate their folly by years of wretchedness and degradation, raised their voices to warn the aspirant who approached the charmed threshold. Some had wisdom enough to discover the truth early and spirit enough to fly without looking back; others lingered on to a cheerless and unhonoured old age. We have no hesitation in saying that the poorest author of that time in London, sleeping on a bulk, dining in a cellar, with a cravat of paper and a skewer for a shirt-pin, was a happier man than any of the literary inmates of Frederic's court.

But of all who entered the enchanted garden in the inebriation of delight and quitted it in agonies of rage and shame, the most remarkable was Voltaire. Many circumstances had made him desirous of finding a home at a distance from his country. His fame had raised him up enemies. His sensibility gave them a formidable advantage over him. They were, indeed, contemptible assailants. Of all that they wrote against him, nothing has survived except what he has himself preserved. But the constitution of his mind resembled the constitution of those bodies in which the slightest scratch of a bramble, or the bite of a gnat, never fails to fester. Though his reputation was rather raised than lowered by the abuse of such writers as Fréron and Desfontaines— though the vengeance which he took on Fréron and Desfontaines was such, that scourging, branding, pillorying, would have been a trifle to it—there is reason to believe that they gave him far more pain than he ever gave them. Though he enjoyed during his own lifetime the reputation of a classic—though he was extolled by his contemporaries above all poets, philosophers and historians, though his works were read with as much delight and admiration at Moscow and Westminster, at Florence and Stockholm as at Paris itself, he was yet tormented by that restless jealousy which should seem to belong only to minds burning with the desire of fame and yet conscious of impotence. To men of letters, who could by no possibility be his rivals, he was, if they behaved well to him, not merely just, not merely courteous, but often a hearty friend and a munificent benefactor. But to every writer who rose to a celebrity approaching his own, he became either a disguised or an avowed enemy. He slyly depreciated Montesquieu and Buffon. He publicly and with violent outrage made war on Rousseau. Nor had he the art of hiding his feelings under the semblance of good humour or of contempt. With all his great talents and all his long experience of the world, he had no more self-command than a petted child or a hysterical woman. Whenever he was mortified, he exhausted the whole rhetoric of anger and sorrow to express his mortification. His torrents of bitter words—his stamping and cursing—his grimaces and his tears of rage— were a rich feast to those abject natures whose delight is in the agonies of powerful spirits and in the abasement of immortal names. These creatures had now found out a way of galling him to the very quick. In one walk, at least, it had been admitted by envy itself that he was without a living competitor. Since Racine had been laid among the great men whose dust made the holy precinct of Port Royal holier, no tragic poet had appeared who could contest the palm with the author of "Zaire," of "Alzire" and of "Merope." At length a rival was announced. Old Crébillon, who, many years before, had obtained some theatrical success, and who had long been forgotten, came forth from his garret in one of the meanest lanes near the Rue St. Antoine and was welcomed by the acclamations of envious men of letters and of a capricious populace. A thing called "Catiline," which he had written in his retirement, was acted with boundless applause. Of this execrable piece it is sufficient to say that the plot turns on a love affair, carried on in all the forms of Scudery, between Catiline, whose confidant is the Prætor Lentulus, and Tullia, the daughter of Cicero. The theatre resounded with acclamations. The King pensioned the successful poet ; and the coffee-houses pronounced that Voltaire was a clever man, but that the real tragic inspiration, the celestial fire which had glowed in Corneille and Racine was to be found in Crébillon alone.

The blow went to Voltaire's heart. Had his wisdom and fortitude been in proportion to the fertility of his intellect and to the brilliancy of his wit, he would have seen that it was out of the power of all the puffers and detractors in Europe to put "Catiline" above "Zaire;" but he had none of the magnanimous patience with which Milton and Bentley left their claims to the unerring judgment of time. He eagerly engaged in an undignified competition with Crébillon ; and produced a series of plays on the same subjects which his rival had treated. These pieces were coolly received. Angry with the court, angry with the capital, Voltaire began to find pleasure in the prospect of exile. His attachment for Madame de Châtelet long prevented him from executing his purpose. Her death set him at liberty ; and he determined to take refuge at Berlin.

To Berlin he was invited by a series of letters, couched in terms of the most enthusiastic friendship and admiration. For once the rigid parsimony of Frederic seemed to have relaxed. Orders, honourable offices, a liberal pension, a well-served table, stately apartments under a royal roof, were offered in return for the pleasure and honour which were expected from the society of the first wit of the age. A thousand louis were remitted for the charges of the journey. No ambassador, setting out from Berlin for a court of the first rank, had ever been more amply supplied. But Voltaire was not satisfied. At a later period, when he possessed an ample fortune, he was one of the most liberal of men ; but till his means had become equal to his wishes, his greediness for lucre was unrestrained either by justice or by shame. He had the effrontery to ask for a thousand louis more, in order to enable him to bring his niece, Madame Denis, the ugliest of coquettes, in his company. The indelicate rapacity of the poet produced its natural effect on the severe and frugal King. The answer was a dry refusal. "I did not," said his Majesty, "solicit the honour of the lady's society." On this, Voltaire went off into a paroxysm of childish rage. "Was there ever such avarice? He has hundreds of tubs full of dollars in his vaults and haggles with me about a poor thousand louis." It seemed that the negotiation would be broken off ; but Frederic, with great dexterity, affected indifference, and seemed inclined to transfer his idolatry to Baculard D'Arnaud. His Majesty even wrote some bad verses, of which the sense was that Voltaire was a setting sun and that D'Arnaud was rising. Good-natured friends soon carried the lines to Voltaire. He was in his bed. He jumped out in his shirt, danced about the room with rage, and sent for his passport and his post-horses. It was not difficult to foresee the end of a connection which had such a beginning.

It was in the year 1750 that Voltaire left the great capital, which he was not to see again till, after the lapse of near thirty years, he returned bowed down by extreme old age to die in the midst of a splendid and ghastly triumph. His reception in Prussia was such as might well have elated a less vain and excitable mind. He wrote to his friends at Paris, that the kindness and the attention with which he had been welcomed surpassed description— that the King was the most amiable of men—that Potsdam was the paradise of philosophers. He was created chamberlain, and received, together with his gold key, the cross of an order and a patent ensuring to him a pension of eight hundred pounds sterling a-year for life. A hundred and sixty pounds a-year were promised to his niece if she survived him. The royal cooks and coachmen were put at his disposal. He was lodged in the same apartments in which Saxe had lived when, at the height of power and glory, he visited Prussia. Frederic, indeed, stooped for a time even to use the language of adulation. He pressed to his lips the meagre hand of the little grinning skeleton, whom he regarded as the dispenser of immortal renown. He would add, he said, to the titles which he owed to his ancestors and his sword, another title, derived from his last and proudest acquisition. His style should run thus: Frederic, King of Prussia, Margrave of Brandenburg, Sovereign Duke of Silesia, Possessor of Voltaire. But even amidst the delights of the honeymoon, Voltaire's sensitive vanity began to take alarm. A few days after his arrival, he could not help telling his niece that the amiable King had a trick of giving a sly scratch with one hand while patting and stroking with the other. Soon came hints not the less alarming because mysterious. "The supper parties are delicious. The King is the life of the company. But—I have operas and comedies, reviews and concerts, my studies and books. But—but—Berlin is fine, the princesses charming, the maids of honour handsome. But——"

This eccentric friendship was fast cooling. Never had there met two persons so exquisitely fitted to plague each other. Each of them had exactly the fault of which the other was most impatient; and they were, in different ways, the most impatient of mankind. Frederic was frugal, almost niggardly. When he had secured his plaything, he began to think that he had bought it too dear. Voltaire, on the other hand, was greedy, even to the extent of imprudence and knavery; and conceived that the favourite of a monarch, who had barrels full of gold and silver laid up in cellars, ought to make a fortune which a receiver-general might envy. They soon discovered each other's feelings. Both were angry; and a war began in which Frederic stooped to the part of Harpagon and Voltaire to that of Scapin. It is humiliating to relate, that the great warrior and statesmen gave orders that his guest's allowance of sugar and chocolate should be curtailed. It is, if possible, a still more humiliating fact that Voltaire indemnified himself by pocketing the wax-candles in the royal antechamber. Disputes about money, however, were not the most serious disputes of these extraordinary associates. The sarcasms of the King soon galled the sensitive temper of the poet. D'Arnaud and D'Argens, Guichard and La Métrie, might, for the sake of a morsel of bread, be willing to bear the insolence of a master; but Voltaire was of another order. He knew that he was a potentate as well as Frederic, that his European reputation and his incomparable power of covering whatever he hated with ridicule, made him an object of dread even to the leaders of armies and the rulers of nations. In truth, of all the intellectual weapons which have ever been wielded by man, the most terrible was the mockery of Voltaire. Bigots and tyrants, who had never been moved by the wailing and cursing of millions, turned pale at his name. Principles unassailable by reason, principles which had withstood the fiercest attacks of power, the most valuable truths, the most generous sentiments, the noblest and most graceful images, the purest reputations, the most august institutions, began to look mean and loathsome as soon as that withering smile was turned upon them. *⁎ ⁎ ⁎ ⁎ ⁎* and his talents, in his station *⁎ ⁎ ⁎ ⁎ ⁎* greater scoffer, might be *⁎ ⁎ ⁎ ⁎ ⁎* r. stood to the Archangel:

⁎ ⁎ ⁎ ⁎ ⁎ee, shun
His *⁎ ⁎ ⁎ ⁎ ⁎* neither vainly hope

> To be invulnerable in those bright arms,
> Though temper'd heavenly; for that fatal dint,
> Save Him who reigns above, none can resist."

We cannot pause to recount how often that rare talent was exercised against rivals worthy of esteem—how often it was used to crush and torture enemies worthy only of silent disdain—how often it was perverted to the more noxious purpose of destroying the last solace of earthly misery and the last restraint on earthly power. Neither can we pause to tell how often it was used to vindicate justice, humanity and toleration—the principles of sound philosophy, the principles of free government. This is not the place for a full character of Voltaire.

Causes of quarrel multiplied fast. Voltaire, who, partly from love of money and partly from love of excitement, was always fond of stockjobbing, became implicated in transactions of at least a dubious character. The King was delighted at having such an opportunity to humble his guest; and bitter reproaches and complaints were exchanged. Voltaire, too, was soon at war with the other men of letters who surrounded the King; and this irritated Frederic, who, however, had himself chiefly to blame, for, from that love of tormenting which was in him a ruling passion, he perpetually lavished extravagant praises on small men and bad books, merely in order that he might enjoy the mortification and rage which on such occasions Voltaire took no pains to conceal. His Majesty, however, soon had reason to regret the pains which he had taken to kindle jealousy among the members of his household. The whole palace was in a ferment with literary intrigues and cabals. It was to no purpose that the imperial voice, which kept a hundred and sixty thousand soldiers in order, was raised to quiet the contention of the exasperated wits. It was far easier to stir up such a storm than to lull it. Nor was Frederic, in his capacity of wit, by any means without his own share of vexations. He had sent a large quantity of verses to Voltaire and requested that they might be returned with remarks and corrections. "See," exclaimed Voltaire, "what a quantity of his dirty linen the King has sent me to wash!" Talebearers were not wanting to carry the sarcasm to the royal ear; and Frederic was as much incensed as a Grub Street writer who had found his name in the "Dunciad."

This could not last. A circumstance which, when the mutual regard of the friends was in its first glow, would merely have been matter for laughter, produced a violent explosion. Maupertuis enjoyed as much of Frederic's goodwill as any man of letters. He was President of the Academy of Berlin; and he stood second to Voltaire, though at an immense distance, in the literary society which had been assembled at the Prussian court. Frederic had, by playing for his own amusement on the feelings of the two jealous and vainglorious Frenchmen, succeeded in producing a bitter enmity between them. Voltaire resolved to set his mark, a mark never to be effaced, on the forehead of Maupertuis, and wrote the exquisitely ludicrous diatribe of "Doctor Akakia." He showed this little piece to Frederic, who had too much taste and too much malice not to relish such delicious pleasantry. In truth, even at this time of day, it is not easy for any person who has the least perception of the ridiculous to read the jokes on the Latin city, the Patagonians and the hole to the centre of the earth, without laughing till he cries. But though Frederic was diverted by this charming pasquinade, he was unwilling that it should get abroad. His self-love was interested. He had selected Maupertuis to fill the chair of his Academy. If all Europe were taught to laugh at Maupertuis, would not the reputation of the Academy, would not even the dignity of its royal patron, be in some degree compromised? The King, therefore, begged

Voltaire to suppress this performance. Voltaire promised to do so, and broke his word. The diatribe was published, and received with shouts of merriment and applause by all who could read the French language. The King stormed. Voltaire, with his usual disregard of truth, asserted his innocence, and made up some lie about a printer or an amanuensis. The King was not to be so imposed upon. He ordered the phamphlet to be burned by the common hangman, and insisted upon having an apology from Voltaire couched in the most abject terms. Voltaire sent back to the King his cross, his key and the patent of his pension. After this burst of rage, the strange pair began to be ashamed of their violence and went through the forms of reconciliation. But the breach was irreparable; and Voltaire took his leave of Frederic for ever. They parted with cold civility; but their hearts were big with resentment. Voltaire had in his keeping a volume of the King's poetry, and forgot to return it. This was, we believe, merely one of the oversights which men setting out upon a journey often commit. That Voltaire could have meditated plagiarism is quite incredible. He would not, we are confident, for the half of Frederic's kingdom, have consented to father Frederic's verses. The king, however, who rated his own writings much above their value, and who was inclined to see all Voltaire's actions in the worst light, was enraged to think that his favourite compositions were in the hands of an enemy as thievish as a daw and as mischievous as a monkey. In the anger excited by this thought, he lost sight of reason and decency and determined on committing an outrage at once odious and ridiculous.

Voltaire had reached Frankfort. His niece, Madame Denis, came thither to meet him. He conceived himself secure from the power of his late master, when he was arrested by order of the Prussian resident. The precious volume was delivered up. But the Prussian agents had, no doubt, been instructed not to let Voltaire escape without some gross indignity. He was confined twelve days in a wretched hovel. Sentinels with fixed bayonets kept guard over him. His niece was dragged through the mire by the soldiers. Sixteen hundred dollars were extorted from him by his insolent gaolers. It is absurd to say that this outrage is not to be attributed to the King. Was anybody punished for it? Was anybody called in question for it? Was it not consistent with Frederic's character? Was it not of a piece with his conduct on other similar occasions? Is it not notorious that he repeatedly gave private directions to his officers to pillage and demolish the houses of persons against whom he had a grudge, charging them at the same time to take their measures in such a way that his name might not be compromised? He acted thus towards Count Bruhl in the Seven Years' War. Why should we believe that he would have been more scrupulous with regard to Voltaire?

When at length the illustrious prisoner regained his liberty, the prospect before him was but dreary. He was an exile both from the country of his birth and from the country of his adoption. The French Government had taken offence at his journey to Prussia and would not permit him to return to Paris; and in the vicinity of Prussia it was not safe for him to remain.

He took refuge on the beautiful shores of Lake Leman. There, loosed from every tie which had hitherto restrained him and having little to hope or to fear from courts and churches, he began his long war against all that, whether for good or evil, had authority over man; for what Burke said of the Constituent Assembly was eminently true of this, its great forerunner. He could not build—he could only pull down—he was the very Vitruvius of ruin. He has bequeathed to us not a single doctrine to be called by his name—not a single addition to the stock of our positive knowledge. But no human teacher ever left behind him so vast and terrible a wreck of truths and falsehoods—of things noble and things base—of things useful and things pernicious. From the time when his sojourn beneath the Alps commenced, the dramatist, the wit, the historian, was merged in a more important character. He was now the patriarch, the founder of a sect, the chief of a conspiracy, the prince of a wide intellectual commonwealth. He often enjoyed a pleasure dear to the better part of his nature, the pleasure of vindicating innocence which had no other helper—of repairing cruel wrongs—of punishing tyranny in high places. He had also the satisfaction, not less acceptable to his ravenous vanity, of hearing terrified Capuchins call him the Antichrist. But whether employed in works of benevolence or in works of mischief, he never forgot Potsdam and Frankfort; and he listened anxiously to every murmur which indicated that a tempest was gathering in Europe and that his vengeance was at hand.

He soon had his wish. Maria Theresa had never for a moment forgotten the great wrong which she had received at the hand of Frederic. Young and delicate, just left an orphan, just about to be a mother, she had been compelled to fly from the ancient capital of her race, she had seen her fair inheritance dismembered by robbers; and of those robbers he had been the foremost. Without a pretext, without a provocation, in defiance of the most sacred engagements, he had attacked the helpless ally whom he was bound to defend. The Empress Queen had the faults as well as the virtues which are connected with quick sensibility and a high spirit. There was no peril which she was not ready to brave, no calamity which she was not ready to bring on her subjects, or on the whole human race, if only she might once taste the sweetness of a complete revenge. Revenge, too, presented itself to her narrow and superstitious mind in the guise of duty. Silesia had been wrested not only from the House of Austria, but from the Church of Rome. The conqueror had indeed permitted his new subjects to worship God after their own fashion; but this was not enough. To bigotry it seemed an intolerable hardship that the Catholic Church, having long enjoyed ascendency, should be compelled to content itself with equality. Nor was this the only circumstance which led Maria Theresa to regard her enemy as the enemy of God. The profaneness of Frederic's writings and conversation, and the frightful rumours which were circulated respecting the immorality of his private life, naturally shocked a woman who believed with the firmest faith all that her confessor told her, and who, though surrounded by temptations, though young and beautiful, though ardent in all her passions, though possessed of absolute power, had preserved her fame unsullied even by the breath of slander.

To recover Silesia, to humble the dynasty of Hohenzollern to the dust, was the great object of her life. She toiled during many years for this end with zeal as indefatigable as that which the poet ascribes to the stately goddess who tired out her immortal horses in the work of raising the nations against Troy, and who offered to give up to destruction her darling Sparta and Mycenæ if only she might once see the smoke going up from the palace of Priam. With even such a spirit did the proud Austrian Juno strive to array against her foe a coalition such as Europe had never seen. Nothing would content her but that the whole civilised world, from the White Sea to the Adriatic, from the Bay of Biscay to the pastures of the wild horses of the Tanais, should be combined in arms against one petty state.

She early succeeded by various arts in obtaining the adhesion of Russia. An ample share of spoil was promised to the King of Poland; and that prince, governed by his favourite, Count Bruhl, readily promised the assistance of the Saxon forces. The great difficulty was with France. That the Houses of Bourbon and of Hapsburg should ever cordially co-operate in any great scheme of European policy had long been thought, to use the strong expression of

Frederic, just as impossible as that fire and water should amalgamate. The whole history of the Continent, during two centuries and a half, had been the history of the mutual jealousies and enmities of France and Austria. Since the adminstration of Richelieu, above all, it had been considered as the plain policy of the Most Christian King to thwart on all occasions the Court of Vienna and to protect every member of the Germanic body who stood up against the dictation of the Cæsars. Common sentiments of religion had been unable to mitigate this strong antipathy. The rulers of France, even while clothed in the Roman purple, even while persecuting the heretics of Rochelle and Auvergne, had still looked with favour on the Lutheran and Calvanistic princes who were struggling against the chief of the empire. If the French ministers paid any respect to the traditional rules handed down to them through many generations, they would have acted towards Frederic as the greatest of their predecessors acted towards Gustavus Adolphus. That there was deadly enmity between Prussia and Austria was of itself sufficient reason for close friendship between Prussia and France. With France, Frederic could never have any serious controversy. His territories were so situated that his ambition, greedy and unscrupulous as it was, could never impel him to attack her of his own accord. He was more than half a Frenchman: he wrote, spoke, read nothing but French: he delighted in French society: the admiration of the French he proposed to himself as the best reward of all his exploits. It seemed incredible that any French government, however notorious for levity or stupidity, could spurn away such an ally.

The Court of Vienna, however, did not despair. The Austrian diplomatists propounded a new scheme of politics, which, it must be owned, was not altogether without plausibility. The great powers, according to this theory, had long been under a delusion. They had looked on each other as natural enemies while in truth they were natural allies. A succession of cruel wars had devastated Europe, had thinned the population, had exhausted the public resources, had loaded governments with an immense burden of debt; and when, after two hundred years of murderous hostility or of hollow truce, the illustrious Houses whose enmity had distracted the world sat down to count their gains, to what did the real advantage on either side amount? Simply to this, that they had kept each other from thriving. It was not the King of France, it was not the Emperor, who had reaped the fruits of the Thirty Years' War, of the War of the Grand Alliance, of the War of the Pragmatic Sanction. Those fruits had been pilfered by states of the second and third rank, which, secured against jealousy by their insignificance, had dexterously aggrandised themselves while pretending to serve the animosity of the great chiefs of Christendom. While the lion and tiger were tearing each other, the jackal had run off into the jungle with the prey. The real gainer by the Thirty Years' War had been neither France nor Austria, but Sweden. The real gainer by the war of the Grand Alliance had been neither France nor Austria, but Savoy. The real gainer by the war of the Pragmatic Sanction had been neither France nor Austria, but the upstart Brandenburg. Of all these instances, the last was the most striking. France had made great efforts, had added largely to her military glory and largely to her public burdens; and for what end? Merely that Frederic might rule Silesia. For this, and this alone, one French army, wasted by sword and famine, had perished in Bohemia; and another had purchased, with floods of the noblest blood, the barren glory of Fontenoy. And this prince, for whom France had suffered so much, was he a grateful, was he even an honest, ally? Had he not been as false to the Court of Versailles as to the Court of Vienna? Had he no played, on a large scale, the same part which, in private life, is played by the vile agent of chicane, who sets his neighbours quarrelling, involves them in costly and interminable litigation, and betrays them to each other all round, certain that, whoever may be ruined, he shall be enriched? Surely the true wisdom of the great powers was to attack, not each other, but this common barrator, who, by inflaming the passions of both, by pretending to serve both, and by deserting both, had raised himself above the station to which he was born. The great object of Austria was to regain Silesia; the great object of France was to obtain an accession of territory on the side of Flanders. If they took opposite sides, the result would probably be that, after a war of many years, after the slaughter of many thousands of brave men, after the waste of many millions of crowns, they would lay down their arms without having achieved either object; but, if they came to an understanding there would be no risk and no difficulty. Austria would willingly make in Belgium such cessions as France could not expect to obtain by ten pitched battles. Silesia would easily be annexed to the monarchy of which it had long been a part. The union of two such powerful governments would at once overawe the King of Prussia. If he resisted, one short campaign would settle his fate. France and Austria, long accustomed to rise from the game of war both loosers, would, for the first time, both be gainers. There could be no room for jealousy between them. The power of both would be increased at once; the equilibrium between them would be preserved; and the only sufferer would be a mischievous and unprincipled buccaneer who deserved no tenderness from either.

These doctrines, attractive from their novelty and ingenuity, soon became fashionable at the supper-parties and in the coffee-houses of Paris, and were espoused by every gay marquis and every facetious abbé who was admitted to see Madame de Pompadour's hair curled and powdered. It was not, however, to any political theory that the strange coalition between France and Austria owed its origin. The real motive which induced the great continental powers to forget their old animosities and their old state maxims was personal aversion to the King of Prussia. This feeling was strongest in Maria Theresa; but it was by no means confined to her. Frederic, in some respects a good master, was emphatically a bad neighbour. That he was hard in all dealings, and quick to take all advantages, was not his most odious fault. His bitter and scoffing speech had inflicted keener wounds than his ambition. In his character of wit, he was under less restraint than even in his character of ruler. Satirical verses against all the princes and ministers of Europe were ascribed to his pen. In his letters and conservation, he alluded to the greatest potentates of the age in terms which would have better suited Collé in a war of repartee with young Crébillon at Pelletier's table than a great sovereign speaking of great sovereigns. About women, he was in the habit of expressing himself in a manner which it was impossible for the meekest of women to forgive; and, unfortunately for him, almost the whole Continent was then governed by women who were by no means conspicuous for meekness. Maria Theresa herself had not escaped his scurrilous jests. The Empress Elizabeth of Russia knew that her gallantries afforded him a favourite theme for ribaldry and invective. Madame de Pompadour, who was really the head of the French government, had been even more keenly galled. She had attempted, by the most delicate flattery, to propitiate the King of Prussia; but her messages had drawn from him only dry and sarcastic replies. The Empress Queen took a very different course. Though the haughtiest of princesses, though the most austere of matrons, she forget in her thirst for revenge both the dignity of her race and the purity of her character, and condescended to flatter the low-born and low-minded concubine, who, having acquired influence by prostituting herself, retained it by prostituting others. Maria Theresa actually wrote with her own hand a note, full of expressions of esteem and friendship, to her dear cousin, the daughter of the butcher Poisson, the wife of the publican D'Etioles, the kidnapper of young girls for the Parc-aux-cerfs—a strange cousin for the descendant of so many Emperors of the West! The mistress was completely gained over, and easily carried her point with Louis, who had, indeed, wrongs of his own to resent. His feelings were not quick; but contempt, says the eastern proverb, pierces even through the shell of the tortoise; and neither prudence nor decorum had ever restrained Frederic from expressing his measureless contempt for the sloth, the imbecility and the baseness of Louis. France was thus induced to join the coalition; and the example of France determined the conduct of Sweden, then completely subject to French influence.

The enemies of Frederic were surely strong enough to attack him openly; but they were desirous to add to all their other advantages the advantage of a surprise. He was not, however, a man to be taken off his guard. He had tools in every court; and he now received from Vienna, from Dresden and from Paris accounts so circumstantial and so consistent that ne could not doubt of his danger. He learnt that he was to be assailed at once by France, Austria, Russia, Saxony, Sweden and the Germanic body; that the greater part of his dominions was to be portioned out among his enemies; that France, which from her geographical position could not directly share in his spoils, was to receive an equivalent in the Netherlands; that Austria was to have Silesia; and the Czarina East Prussia; that Augustus of Saxony expected Magdeburg; and that Sweden would be rewarded with part of Pomerania. If these designs succeeded, the house of Brandenburg would at once sink in the European system to a place lower than that of the Duke of Wurtemburg or the Margrave of Baden.

And what hope was there that these designs would fail. No such union of the continental powers had been seen for ages. A less formidable confederacy had in a week conquered all the provinces of Venice when Venice was at the height of power, wealth and glory. A less formidable confederacy had compelled Louis the Fourteenth to bow down his haughty head to the very earth. A less formidable confederacy has, within our own memory, subjugated a still mightier empire and abased a still prouder name. Such odds had never been heard of in war. The people whom Frederic ruled were not five millions. The population of the countries which were leagued against him amounted to a hundred millions. The disproportion in wealth was at least equally great. Small communities, actuated by strong sentiments of patriotism or loyalty, have sometimes made head against great monarchies weakened by factions and discontents. But small as was Frederic's kingdom, it probably contained a greater number of disaffected subjects than were to be found in all the states of his enemies. Silesia formed a fourth part of his dominions; and from the Silesians, borne under Austrian princes, the utmost that he could expect was apathy. From the Silesian Catholics, he could hardly expect anything but resistance.

Some states have been enabled, by their geographical position, to defend themselves with advantage against immense force. The sea has repeatedly protected England against the fury of the whole Continent. The Venetian government, driven from its possessions on the land, could still bid defiance to the confederates of Cambray from the Arsenal amidst the lagoons. More than one great and well-appointed army, which regarded the shepherds of Switzerland as an easy prey, has perished in the passes of the Alps. Frederic had no such advantage. The form of his states, their situation, the nature of the ground, all were against him. His long, scattered, straggling territory seemed to have been shaped with an express view to the convenience of invaders, and was protected by no sea, by no chain of hills. Scarcely any corner of it was a week's march from the territory of the enemy. The capital itself, in the event of war, would be constantly exposed to insult. In truth, there was hardly a politician or a soldier in Europe who doubted that the conflict would be terminated in a very few days by the prostration of the house of Brandenburg.

Nor was Frederic's own opinion very different. He anticipated nothing short of his own ruin and of the ruin of his family. Yet there was still a chance, a slender chance, of escape. His states had at least the advantage of a central position; his enemies were widely separated from each other and could not conveniently unite their overwhelming forces on one point. They inhabited different climates, and it was probable that the season of the year which would be best suited to the military operations of one portion of the league would be unfavourable to those of another portion. The Prussian monarchy, too, was free from some infirmities which were found in empires far more extensive and magnificent. Its effective strength for a desperate struggle was not to be measured merely by the number of square miles or the number of people. In that spare, but well-knit and well-exercised body, there was nothing but sinew, and muscle, and bone. No public creditors looked for dividends. No distant colonies required defence. No court, filled with flatterers and mistresses, devoured the pay of fifty battalions. The Prussian army, though far inferior in number to the troops which were about to be opposed to it, was yet strong out of all proportion to the extent of the Prussian dominions. It was also admirably trained and admirably officered, accustomed to obey and accustomed to conquer. The revenue was not only unincumbered by debt, but exceeded the ordinary outlay in time of peace. Alone of all the European princes, Frederic had a treasure laid up for a day of difficulty. Above all, he was one and his enemies were many. In their camps would certainly be found the jealousy, the dissension, the slackness inseparable from coalitions; on his side was the energy, the unity, the secrecy of a strong dictatorship. To a certain extent the deficiency of military means might be supplied by the resources of military art. Small as the King's army was, when compared with the six hundred thousand men whom the confederates could bring into the field, celerity of movement might in some degree compensate for deficiency of bulk. It was thus just possible that genius, judgment, resolution and good luck united might protract the struggle during a campaign or two; and to gain even a month was of importance. It could not be long before the vices which are found in all extensive confederacies would begin to show themselves. Every member of the league would think his own share of the war too large and his own share of the spoils too small. Complaints and recriminations would abound. The Turk might stir on the Danube; the statesmen of France might discover the error which they had committed in abandoning the fundamental principles of their national policy. Above all, death might rid Prussia of its most formidable enemies. The war was the effect of the personal aversion with which three or four sovereigns regarded Frederic; and the decease of any one of those sovereigns might produce a complete revolution in the state of Europe.

In the midst of a horizon generally dark and stormy, Frederic could discern one bright spot. The peace, which had been concluded between England and France in 1748, had been in Europe no more than an armistice; and had not even been an armistice in the other quarters of the globe. In India, the sovereignty of the Carnatic was disputed between two great Mussulman houses;

Fort Saint George had taken one side, Pondicherry the other; and in a series of battles and sieges, the troops of Lawrence and Clive had been opposed to those of Dupleix. A struggle less important in its consequences, but not less likely to produce irritation, was carried on between those French and English adventurers who kidnapped negroes and collected gold dust on the coast of Guinea. But it was in North America that the emulation and mutual aversion of the two nations were most conspicuous. The French attempted to hem in the English colonists by a chain of military posts extending from the Great Lakes to the mouth of the Mississippi. The English took arms. The wild aboriginal tribes appeared on each side mingled with the Pale Faces. Battles were fought; forts were stormed; and hideous stories about stakes, scalpings and death-songs reached Europe and inflamed that national animosity which the rivalry of ages had produced. The disputes between France and England came to a crisis at the very time when the tempest which had been gathering was about to burst on Prussia. The tastes and interests of Frederic would have led him, if he had been allowed an option, to side with the house of Bourbon. But the folly of the Court of Versailles left him no choice. France became the tool of Austria; and Frederic was forced to become the ally of England. He could not, indeed, expect that a power which covered the sea with its fleets, and which had to make war at once on the Ohio and the Ganges, would be able to spare a large number of troops for operations in Germany. But England, though poor compared with the England of our time, was far richer than any country on the Continent. The amount of her revenue and the resources which she found in her credit, though they may be thought small by a generation which has seen her raise a hundred and thirty millions in a single year, appeared miraculous to the politicians of that age. A very moderate portion of her wealth, expended by an able and economical prince, in a country where prices were low, would be sufficient to equip and maintain a formidable army.

Such was the situation in which Frederic found himself. He saw the whole extent of his peril. He saw that there was still a faint possibility of escape; and, with prudent temerity, he determined to strike the first blow. It was in the month of August, 1756, that the great war of the Seven Years commenced. The King demanded of the Empress Queen a distinct explanation of her intentions, and plainly told her that he should consider a refusal as a declaration of war. "I want," he said, "no answer in the style of an oracle." He received an answer at once haughty and evasive. In an instant, the rich electorate of Saxony was overflowed by sixty thousand Prussian troops. Augustus with his army occupied a strong position at Pirna. The Queen of Poland was at Dresden. In a few days Pirna was blockaded and Dresden was taken. The first object of Frederic was to obtain possession of the Saxon State papers; for those papers, he well knew, contained ample proofs that, though apparently an aggressor, he was really acting in self-defence. The Queen of Poland, as well acquainted as Frederic with the importance of those documents, had packed them up, had concealed them in her bed-chamber, and was about to send them off to Warsaw when a Prussian officer made his appearance. In the hope that no soldier would venture to outrage a lady, a queen, the daughter of an emperor, the mother-in-law of a dauphin, she placed herself before the trunk, and at length sat down on it. But all resistance was vain. The papers were carried to Frederic, who found in them, as he expected, abundant evidence of the designs of the coalition. The most important documents were instantly published, and the effect of the publication was great. It was clear that, of whatever sins the King of Prussia might formerly have been guilty, he was now the injured party and had merely anticipated a blow intended to destroy him.

The Saxon camp at Pirna was in the meantime closely invested ; but the besieged were not without hopes of succour. A great Austrian army under Marshal Brown was about to pour through the passes which separate Bohemia from Saxony. Frederic left at Pirna a force sufficient to deal with the Saxons, hastened into Bohemia, encountered Brown at Lowositz, and defeated him. This battle decided the fate of Saxony. Augustus and his favourite Bruhl fled to Poland. The whole army of the electorate capitulated. From that time till the end of the war, Frederic treated Saxony as a part of his dominions, or, rather, he acted towards the Saxons in a manner which may serve to illustrate the whole meaning of that tremendous sentence, "*subjectos tanquam suos, viles tanquam alienos.*" Saxony was as much in his power as Brandenburg ; and he had no such interest in the welfare of Saxony as he had in the welfare of Brandenburg. He accordingly levied troops and exacted contributions throughout the enslaved province with far more rigour than in any part of his own dominions. Seventeen thousand men, who had been in the camp at Pirna, were half compelled, half persuaded to enlist under their conqueror. Thu, within a few weeks from the commencement of hostilities, one of the confederates had been disarmed and his weapons pointed against the rest.

The winter put a stop to military operations. All had hitherto gone well. But the real tug of war was still to come. It was easy to foresee that the year 1757 would be a memorable era in the history of Europe.

The scheme for the campaign was simple, bold and judicious. The Duke of Cumberland, with an English and Hanoverian army, was in Western Germany, and might be able to prevent the French troops from attacking Prussia. The Russians, confined by their snows, would probably not stir till the spring was far advanced. Saxony was prostrated. Sweden could do nothing very important. During a few months, Frederic would have to deal with Austria alone. Even thus the odds were against him. But ability and courage have often triumphed against odds still more formidable.

Early in 1757, the Prussian army in Saxony began to move. Through four defiles in the mountains they came pouring into Bohemia. Prague was the King's first mark ; but the ulterior object was probably Vienna. At Prague lay Marshal Brown with one great army. Daun, the most cautious and fortunate of the Austrian captains, was advancing with another. Frederic determined to overwhelm Brown before Daun should arrive. On the sixth of May was fought, under those walls, which, a hundred and thirty years before, had witnessed the victory of the Catholic league and the flight of the unhappy Palatine, a battle more bloody than any which Europe saw during the long interval between Malplaquet and Eylau. The King and Prince Ferdinand of Brunswick were distinguished on that day by their valour and exertions. But the chief glory was with Schwerin. When the Prussian infantry wavered, the stout old marshal snatched the colours from an ensign and, waving them in the air, led back his regiment to the charge. Thus, at seventy-two years of age, he fell in the thickest battle, still grasping the standard which bears the black eagle on the field argent. The victory remained with the King ; but it had been dearly purchased. Whole columns of his bravest warriors had fallen. He admitted that he had lost eighteen thousand men. Of the enemy, twenty-four thousand had been killed, wounded or taken.

Part of the defeated army was shut up in Prague. Part fled to join the troops which, under the command of Daun, were now close at hand. Frederic determined to play over the same game which had succeeded at Lowositz. He left a large force to besiege Prague, and, at the head of thirty thousand men, he marched against Daun. The cautious Marshal, though he had a great superiority in numbers, would risk nothing. He occupied at Kolin a position almost impregnable, and awaited the attack of the King.

It was the 18th of June, a day, which, if the Greek superstition still retained its influence, would be held sacred to Nemesis; a day on which the two greatest princes of modern times were taught by a terrible experience that neither skill nor valour can fix the inconstancy of fortune. The battle began before noon, and part of the Prussian army maintained the contest till after the midsummer sun had gone down. But at length the King found that his troops, having been repeatedly driven back with frightful carnage, could no longer be led to the charge. He was with difficulty persuaded to quit the field. The officers of his personal staff were under the necessity of expostulating with him, and one of them took the liberty to say, "Does your Majesty mean to storm the batteries alone?" Thirteen thousand of his bravest followers had perished. Nothing remained for him but to retreat in good order, to raise the siege of Prague, and to hurry his army by different routes out of Bohemia.

This stroke seemed to be final. Frederic's situation had at best been such that only an uninterrupted run of good luck could save him, as it seemed, from ruin. And now almost in the outset of the contest, he had met with a check, which, even in a war between equal powers, would have been felt as serious. He had owed much to the opinion which all Europe entertained of his army. Since his accession, his soldiers had in many successive battles been victorious over the Austrians. But the glory had departed from his arms. All whom his malevolent sarcasms had wounded made haste to avenge themselves by scoffing at the scoffer. His soldiers had ceased to confide in his star. In every part of his camp his dispositions were severely criticised. Even in his own family he had detractors. His next brother, William, heir-presumptive, or rather, in truth, heir-apparent to the throne, and great-grandfather of the present king, could not refrain from lamenting his own fate and that of the house of Hohenzollern, once so great and so prosperous, but now, by the rash ambition of its chief, made a by-word to all nations. These complaints, and some blunders which William committed during the retreat from Bohemia, called forth the bitter displeasure of the inexorable King. The prince's heart was broken by the cutting reproaches of his brother; he quitted the army, retired to a country seat, and in a short time died of shame and vexation.

It seemed that the King's distress could hardly be increased. Yet at this moment another blow not less terrible than that of Kolin fell upon. The French under Marshal D'Estrées had invaded Germany. The Duke of Cumberland had given them battle at Hastembeck, and had been defeated. In order to save the Electorate of Hanover from entire subjugation, he had made, at Closter Seven, an arrangement with the French Generals, which left them at liberty to turn their arms against the Prussian dominions.

That nothing might be wanting to Frederic's distress, he lost his mother just at this time, and he appears to have felt the loss more than was to be expected from the hardness and severity of his character. In truth, his misfortunes had now cut to the quick. The mocker, the tyrant, the most rigorous, the most imperious, the most cynical of men, was very unhappy. His face was so haggard and his form so thin, that, when on his return from Bohemia he passed through Liepsic, the people hardly knew him again. His sleep was broken; the tears, in spite of himself, often started into his eyes; and the grave began to present itself to his agitated mind as the best refuge from misery and dishonour. His resolution was fixed never to be taken alive and never to make peace on condition of descending from his place among the powers of Europe. He saw nothing left for him except to die; and he deliberately chose his mode of death. He always carried about with him a sure and speedy poison in a small glass case; and to the few in whom he placed confidence, he made no mystery of his resolution.

But we should very imperfectly describe the state of Frederic's mind if we left out of view the laughable peculiarities which contrasted so singularly with the gravity, energy and harshness of his character. It is difficult to say whether the tragic or the comic predominated in the strange scene which was then acting. In the midst of all the great King's calamities, his passion for writing indifferent poetry grew stronger and stronger. Enemies all round him, despair in his heart, pills of corrosive sublimate hidden in his clothes, he poured forth hundreds upon hundreds of lines, hateful to gods and men – the insipid dregs of Voltaire's "Hippocrene"—the faint echo of the lyre of Chaulieu. It is amusing to compare what he did during the last months of 1757 with what he wrote during the same time. It may be doubted whether any equal portion of the life of Hannibal, of Cæsar or of Napoleon, will bear a comparison with that short period, the most brilliant in the history of Prussia and of Frederic. Yet, at this very time, the scanty leisure of the illustrious warrior was employed in producing odes and epistles, a little better than Cibber's and a little worse than Hayley's. Here and there a manly sentiment, which deserves to be in prose, makes its appearance in company with Prometheus and Orpheus, Elysium and Acheron, the plaintive Philomel, the poppies of Morpheus, and all the other frippery, which, like a robe tossed by a proud beauty to her waiting-woman, has long been contemptuously abandoned by genius to mediocrity. We hardly know any instance of the strength and weakness of human nature so striking and so grotesque as the character of this haughty, vigilant, resolute, sagacious blue stocking, half Mithridates and half Trissotin, bearing up against a world in arms with an ounce of poison in one pocket and a quire of bad verses in the other.

Frederic had some time before made advances toward a reconciliation with Voltaire; and some civil letters had passed between them. After the battle of Kolin, their epistolary intercourse became, at least in seeming, friendly and confidential. We do not know any collection of Letters which throws so much light on the darkest and most intricate parts of human nature as the correspondence of these strange beings after they had exchanged forgiveness. Both felt that the quarrel had lowered them in the public estimation. They admired each other. They stood in need of each other. The great King wished to be handed down to posterity by the great Writer. The great Writer felt himself exhalted by the homage of the great King. Yet the wounds which they had inflicted on each other were too deep to be effaced or even perfectly healed. Not only did the scars remain, the sore places often festered and bled afresh. The letters consisted for the most part of compliments, thanks, offers of service, assurances of attachment. But if anything brought back to Frederic's recollection the cunning and mischievous pranks by which Voltaire had provoked him, some expression of contempt and displeasure broke forth in the midst of eulogy. It was much worse when Voltaire recalled to the mind of Voltaire the outrages which he and his kinswoman had suffered at Frankfort. All at once his flowing panegyric was turned into invective. " Remember how you behaved to me. For your sake I have lost the favour of my native king. For your sake I am an exile from my country. I loved you. I trusted myself to you. I had no wish but to end my life in your service. And what was my reward? Stripped of all that you had bestowed on me, the key, the order, the pension, I was forced to fly from your territories. I was hunted as if I had been a deserter from your grenadiers. I was arrested, insulted, plundered. My niece was dragged through the mud of Frankfort by your soldiers as if she had been some wretched follower of your camp. You have great talents. You have good qualities. But you have one odious vice. You delight in the abasement of your fellow-creatures. You have brought disgrace on the name of philosopher. You have given some colour to the slanders of the bigots who say that no confidence can be placed in the justice or humanity of those who reject the Christian faith." Then the King answers, with less heat but equal severity— "You know that you behaved shamefully in Prussia. It was well for you that you had to deal with a man so indulgent to the infirmities of genius as I am. You richly deserved to see the inside of a dungeon. Your talents are not more widely known than your faithlessness and your malevolence. The grave itself is no asylum from your spite. Maupertuis is dead; but you still go on calumniating and deriding him as if you had not made him miserable enough while he was living. Let us have no more of this. And, above all, let me hear no more of your niece. I am sick to death of her name. I can bear with your faults for the sake of your merits; but she has not written 'Mahomet' or 'Merope.'"

An explosion of this kind, it might be supposed, would necessarily put an end to all amicable communication. But it was not so. After every outbreak of ill-humour, this extraordinary pair became more loving than before, and exchanged compliments and assurances of mutual regard with a wonderful air of sincerity.

It may well be supposed that men who wrote thus to each other were not very guarded in what they said to each other. The English ambassador, Mitchell, who knew that the King of Prussia was constantly writing to Voltaire with the greatest freedom on the most important subjects, was amazed to hear his Majesty designate this highly-favoured correspondent as a bad hearted fellow, the greatest rascal on the face of the earth. And the language which the poet held about the King was not much more respectful.

It would probably have puzzled Voltaire himself to say what was his real feeling towards Frederic. It was compounded of all sentiments, from enmity to friendship, and from scorn to admiration; and the proportions in which these elements were mixed changed every moment. The old patriarch resembled the spoiled child who screams, stamps, cuffs, laughs, kisses and cuddles within one-quarter of an hour. His resentment was not extinguished; yet he was not without sympathy for his old friend. As a Frenchman, he wished success to the arms of his country. As a philosopher, he was anxious for the stability of a throne on which a philosopher sat. He longed both to save and to humble Frederic. There was one way, and only one, in which all his conflicting feelings could at once be gratified. If Frederic were preserved by the interference of France, if it were known that for that interference he was indebted to the mediation of Voltaire, this would indeed be delicious revenge, this would indeed be to heap coals of fire on that haughty head. Nor did the vain and restless poet think it impossible that he might, from his hermitage near the Alps, dictate peace to Europe. D'Estrées had quitted Hanover, and the command of the French army had been intrusted to the Duke of Richelieu, a man whose chief distinction was derived from his success in gallantry. Richelieu was in truth the most eminent of that race of seducers by profession who furnished Crébillon the younger and La Clos with models for their heroes. In his earlier days, the royal house itself had not been secure from his presumptuous love. He was believed to have carried his conquests into the family of Orleans; and some suspected that he was not unconcerned in the mysterious remorse which embittered the last hours of the charming mother of Louis the Fifteenth. But the Duke was now sixty years old. With a heart deeply corrupted by vice, a head long accustomed to think only on trifles, an impaired constitution, an impaired fortune, and, worst of all, a very red nose, he was entering on a dull, frivolous and unrespected old age. Without one qualification for military command, except that personal courage which was common between him and the whole nobility of France, he had been placed at the head of the army of Hanover; and in that situation he did his best to repair, by extortion and corruption, the injury which he had done to his property by a life of dissolute profusion.

The Duke of Richelieu to the end of his life hated the philosophers as a sect —not for those parts of their system which a good and wise man would have condemned—but for their virtues, for their spirit of free inquiry and for their hatred of those social abuses of which he was himself the personification. But he, like many of those who thought with him, excepted Voltaire from the list of proscribed writers. He frequently sent flattering letters to Ferney. He did the patriarch the honour to borrow money of him, and even carried this condescending friendship so far as to forget to pay interest. Voltaire thought that it might be in his power to bring the Duke and the King of Prussia into communication with each other. He wrote earnestly to both; and he so far succeeded that a correspondence between them was commenced.

But it was to very different means that Frederic was to owe his deliverance. At the beginning of November, the net seemed to have closed completely round him. The Russians were in the field, and were spreading devastation through his eastern provinces. Silesia was overrun by the Austrians. A great French army was advancing from the west under the command of Marshall Soubise, a prince of the great Armorican house of Rohan. Berlin itself had been taken and plundered by the Croatians. Such was the situation from which Frederic extricated himself, with dazzling glory, in the short space of thirty days.

He marched first against Soubise. On the fifth of November, the armies met at Rosbach. The French were two to one; but they were ill-disciplined, and their general was a dunce. The tactics of Frederic and the well-regulated valour of the Prussian troops obtained a complete victory. Seven thousand of the invaders were made prisoners. Their guns, their colours, their baggage fell into the hands of the conquerors. Those who escaped fled as confusedly as a mob scattered by cavalry. Victorious in the West, the King turned his arms towards Silesia. In that quarter everything seemed to be lost. Breslau had fallen; and Charles of Loraine, with a mighty power, held the whole province. On the fifth of December, exactly one month after the battle of Rosbach, Frederic, with forty thousand men, and Prince Charles, at the head of not less than sixty thousand, met at Leuthen, hard by Breslau. The King, who was, in general, perhaps too much inclined to consider the common soldier as a mere machine, resorted, on this great day, to means resembling those which Bonaparte afterwards employed with such signal success for the purpose of stimulating military enthusiasm. The principal officers were convoked. Frederic addressed them with great force and pathos; and directed them to speak to their men as he had spoken to them. When the armies were set in battle array, the Prussian troops were in a state of fierce excitement; but their excitement showed itself after the fashion of a grave people. The columns advanced to the attack chanting, to the sound of drums and fifes, the rude hymns of the old Saxon Sternholds. They had never fought so well, nor had the genius of their chief ever been so conspicuous. "That battle," said Napoleon, "was a masterpiece. Of itself it is sufficient to entitle Frederic to a place in the first rank among generals." The victory was complete. Twenty-seven thousand Austrians were killed, wounded or taken; fifty stand of colours, a hundred guns, four thousand waggons fell into the hands of the Prussians. Breslau opened its gates; Silesia was reconquered;

Charles of Loraine retired to hide his shame and sorrow at Brussels; and Frederic allowed his troops to take some repose in winter quarters, after a campaign to the vicissitudes of which it will be difficult to find any parallel in ancient or modern history.

The King's fame filled all the world. He had, during the last year, maintained a contest, on terms of advantage, against three powers, the weakest of which had more than three times his resources. He had fought four great pitched battles against superior forces. Three of these battles he had gained; and the defeat of Kolin, repaired as it had been, rather raised than lowered his military renown. The victory of Leuthen is, to this day, the proudest on the roll of Prussian fame. Leipsic, indeed, and Waterloo produced consequences more important to mankind. But the glory of Leipsic must be shared by the Prussians with the Austrians and Russians; and at Waterloo the British infantry bore the burden and heat of the day. The victory of Rosbach was, in a military point of view, less honourable than that of Leuthen; for it was gained over an incapable general and a disorganised army; but the moral effect which it produced was immense. All the preceding triumphs of Frederic had been triumphs over Germans, and could excite no emotions of national pride among the German people. It was impossible that a Hessian or a Hanoverian could feel any patriotic exultation at hearing that Pomeranians had slaughtered Moravians, or that Saxon banners had been hung in the churches of Berlin. Indeed, though the military character of the Germans justly stood high throughout the world, they could boast of no great day which belonged to them as a people—of no Agincourt, of no Bannockburn. Most of their victories had been gained over each other; and their most splendid exploits against foreigners had been achieved under the command of Eugene, who was himself a foreigner. The news of the battle of Rosbach stirred the blood of the whole of the mighty population from the Alps to the Baltic, and from the borders of Courland to those of Loraine. Westphalia and Lower Saxony had been deluged by a great host of strangers whose speech was unintelligible, and whose petulant and licentious manners had excited the strongest feelings of disgust and hatred. That great host had been put to flight by a small band of German warriors, led by a prince of German blood on the side of father and mother, and marked by the fair hair and the clear blue eye of Germany. Never since the dissolution of the empire of Charlemagne had the Teutonic race won such a field against the French. The tidings called forth a general burst of delight and pride from the whole of the great family which spoke the various dialects of the ancient language of Arminius. The fame of Frederic began to supply, in some degree, the place of a common government and of a common capital. It became a rallying point for all true Germans—a subject of mutual congratulation to the Bavarian and the Westphalian, to the citizen of Frankfort and the citizen of Nuremburg. Then first it was manifested that the Germans were truly a nation. Then first was discernible that patriotic spirit which, in 1813, achieved the great deliverance of central Europe, and which still guards, and long will guard, against foreign ambition the old freedom of the Rhine.

Nor were the effects produced by that celebrated day merely political. The greatest masters of German poetry and eloquence have admitted that, though the great King neither valued nor understood his native language, though he looked on France as the only seat of taste and philosophy, yet, in his own despite, he did much to emancipate the genius of his countrymen from the foreign yoke; and that, in the act of vanquishing Soubise, he was, unintentionally, rousing the spirit which soon began to question the literary precedence of Boileau and Voltaire. So strangely do events confound all the plans of man. A prince who read only French, who wrote only French, who aspired to rank as a French classic, became, quite unconsciously, the means of liberating half the Continent from the dominion of that French criticism of which he was himself, to the end of his life, a slave. Yet even the enthusiasm of Germany in favour of Frederic hardly equalled the enthusiasm of England. The birthday of our ally was celebrated with as much enthusiasm as that of our own sovereign; and at night the streets of London were in a blaze with illuminations. Portraits of the Hero of Rosbach, with his cocked hat and long pigtail, were in every house. An attentive observer will, at this day, find in the parlours of old-fashioned inns and in the portfolios of print-sellers, twenty portraits of Frederic for one of George the Second. The sign-painters were everywhere employed in touching up Admiral Vernon into the King of Prussia. Some young Englishmen of rank proposed to visit Germany as volunteers, for the purpose of learning the art of war under the greatest of commanders. This last proof of British attachment and admiration, Frederic politely but firmly declined. His camp was no place for amateur students of military science. The Prussian discipline was rigorous even to cruelty. The officers, while in the field, were expected to practice an abstemiousness and self-denial such as was hardly surpassed by the most rigid monastic orders. However noble their birth, however high their rank in the service, they were not permitted to eat from anything better than pewter. It was a high crime even in a count and field-marshal to have a single silver spoon among his baggage. Gay young Englishmen of twenty thousand a-year, accustomed to liberty and to luxury, would not easily submit to these Spartan restraints. The King could not venture to keep them in order as he kept his own subjects in order. Situated as he was with respect to England, he could not well imprison or shoot refractory Howards and Cavendishes. On the other hand, the example of a few fine gentlemen, attended by chariots and livery servants, eating in plate and drinking champagne and Tokay, was enough to corrupt his whole army. He thought it best to make a stand at first, and civilly refused to admit such dangerous companions among his troops.

The help of England was bestowed in a manner far more useful and more acceptable. An annual subsidy of near seven hundred thousand pounds enabled the King to add probably more than fifty thousand men to his army. Pitt, now at the height of power and popularity, undertook the task of defending Western Germany against France, and asked Frederic only for the loan of a general. The general selected was Prince Ferdinand of Brunswick, who had attained high distinction in the Prussian service. He was put at the head of an army, partly English, partly Hanoverian, partly composed of mercenaries hired from the petty princes of the empire. He soon vindicated the choice of the two allied courts, and proved himself the second general of the age.

Frederic passed the winter at Breslau, in reading, writing and preparing for the next campaign. The havoc which the war had made among his troops was rapidly repaired; and in the spring of 1758 he was again ready for the conflict. Prince Ferdinand kept the French in check. The King in the meantime, after attempting some operations against the Austrians which led to no very important result, marched to encounter the Russians, who, slaying, burning and wasting wherever they turned, had penetrated into the heart of his realm. He gave them battle at Zorndorf, near Frankfort on the Oder. The fight was long and bloody. Quarter was neither given nor taken; for the Germans and Scythians regarded each other with bitter aversion, and the sight of the ravages committed by the half savage invaders had incensed the King and his army. The Russians were overthrown with great slaughter; and for a few months no further danger was to be apprehended from the East.

A day of thanksgiving was proclaimed by the King, and was celebrated with pride and delight by his people. The rejoicings in England were not less enthusiastic or less sincere. This may be selected as the point of time at which the military glory of Frederic reached the zenith. In the short space of three quarters of a year he had won three great battles over the armies of three mighty and warlike monarchies—France, Austria and Russia.

But it was decreed that the temper of that strong mind should be tried by both extremes of fortune in rapid succession. Close upon this bright series of triumphs came a series of disasters such as would have blighted the fame and broken the heart of almost any other commander. Yet Frederic, in the midst of his calamities, was still an object of admiration to his subjects, his allies and his enemies. Overwhelmed by adversity, sick of life, he still maintained the contest—greater in defeat, in flight and in what seemed hopeless ruin than on the fields of his proudest victories.

Having vanquished the Russians, he hastened into Saxony to oppose the troops of the Empress Queen, commanded by Daun, the most cautious, and Laudohn, the most inventive and enterprising of her generals. These two celebrated commanders agreed on a scheme, in which the prudence of the one and the vigour of the other seem to have been happily combined. At dead of night they surprised the King in his camp at Hochkirchen. His presence of mind saved his troops from destruction; but nothing could save them from defeat and severe loss. Marshal Keith was among the slain. The first roar of the guns roused the noble exile from his rest, and he was instantly in the front of the battle. He received a dangerous wound, but refused to quit the field, and was in the act of rallying his broken troops when an Austrian bullet terminated his chequered and eventful life.

The misfortune was serious. But of all generals, Frederic understood best how to repair defeat and Daun understood least how to improve victory. In a few days, the Prussian army was as formidable as before the battle. The prospect was, however, gloomy. An Austrian army under General Harsch had invaded Silesia and invested the fortress of Neisse. Daun, after his success at Hochkirchen, had written to Harsch in very confident terms: "Go on with your operations against Neisse. Be quite at ease as to the King, I will give a good account of him." In truth, the position of the Prussians was full of difficulties. Between them and Silesia lay the victorious army of Daun. It was not easy for them to reach Silesia at all. If they did reach it, they left Saxony exposed to the Austrians. But the vigour and activity of Frederic surmounted every obstacle. He made a circuitous march of extraordinary rapidity, passed Daun, hastened into Silesia, raised the siege of Neisse and drove Harsch into Bohemia. Daun availed himself of the King's absence to attack Dresden. The Prussians defended it desperately. The inhabitants of that wealthy and polished capital begged in vain for mercy from the garrison within and from the besiegers without. The beautiful suburbs were burned to he ground. It was clear that the town, if won at all, would be won street by street by the bayonet. At this conjuncture came news that Frederic, having cleared Silesia of his enemies, was returning by forced marches into Saxony. Daun retired from before Dresden and fell back into the Austrian territories. The King, over heaps of ruins, made his triumphant entry into the unhappy metropolis, which had so cruelly expiated the weak and perfidious policy of its sovereign. It was now the twentieth of November. The cold weather suspended military operations; and the King again took up his winter quarters at Breslau.

The third of the seven terrible years was over; and Frederic still stood his ground. He had been recently tried by domestic as well as by military disasters. On the fourteenth of October, the day on which he was defeated at

Hochkirchen, the day on the anniversary of which, forty-eight years later, a defeat far more tremendous laid the Prussian monarchy in the dust, died Wilhelmina, Margravine of Bareuth. From the accounts which we have of her, by her own hand and by the hands of the most discerning of her contemporaries, we should pronounce her to have been coarse, indelicate and a good hater, but not destitute of kind and generous feelings. Her mind, naturally strong and observant, had been highly cultivated; and she was, and deserved to be, Frederic's favourite sister. He felt the loss as much as it was in his iron nature to feel the loss of anything but a province or a battle.

At Breslau, during the winter, he was indefatigable in his poetical labours. The most spirited lines, perhaps, that he ever wrote, are to be found in a bitter lampoon on Louis and Madame de Pompadour, which he composed at this time, and sent to Voltaire. The verses were, indeed, so good, that Voltaire was afraid that he might himself be suspected of having written them, or at least of having corrected them; and partly from fright—partly, we fear, from love of mischief—sent them to the Duke of Choiseul, then prime minister of France. Choiseul very wisely determined to encounter Frederic at Frederic's own weapons, and applied for assistance to Palissot, who had some skill as a versifier, and who, though he had not yet made himself famous by bringing Rosseau and Helvetius on the stage, was known to possess some little talent for satire. Palissot produced some very stinging lines on the moral and literary character of Frederic, and these lines the Duke sent to Voltaire. This war of couplets, following close on the carnage of Zorndorf and the conflagration of Dresden, illustrates well the strangely compounded character of the King of Prussia.

At this moment, he was assailed by a new enemy. Benedict XIV., the best and wisest of the two hundred and fifty successors of St. Peter, was no more. During the short interval between his reign and that of his disciple Ganganelli, the chief seat in the Church of Rome was filled by Rezzonico, who took the name of Clement XIII. This absurd priest determined to try what the weight of his authority could effect in favour of the orthodox Maria Theresa against a heretic king. At the high mass on Christmas day, a sword with a rich belt and scabbard, a hat of crimson velvet lined with ermine, and a dove of pearls, the mystic symbol of the Divine Comforter, were solemnly blessed by the supreme pontiff, and were sent with great ceremony to Marshal Daun, the conqueror of Kolin and Hochkirchen. This mark of favour had more than once been bestowed by the Popes on the great champions of the faith. Similar honours had been paid, more than six centuries earlier, by Urban II. to Godfrey of Bouillon. Similar honours had been conferred on Alba for destroying the liberties of the Low Countries, and on John Sobiesky after the deliverance of Vienna. But the presents, which were received with profound reverence by the Baron of the Holy Sepulchre in the eleventh century, and which had not wholly lost their value in the seventeenth century, appeared inexpressibly ridiculous to a generation which read Montesquieu and Voltaire. Frederic wrote sarcastic verses on the gifts, the giver and the receiver. But the public wanted no prompter; and an universal roar of laughter from Petersburg to Lisbon reminded the Vatican that the age of crusades was over.

The fourth campaign, the most disastrous of all the campaigns of this fearful war, had now opened. The Austrians filled Saxony and menaced Berlin. The Russians defeated the King's generals on the Oder, threatened Silesia, effected a junction with Laudohn, and intrenched themselves strongly at Kunersdorf. Frederic hastened to attack them. A great battle was fought. During the earlier part of the day, everything yielded to the impetuosity of the Prussians and to the skill of their chief. The lines were forced. Half the

Russian guns were taken. The King sent off a courier to Berlin with two lines, announcing a complete victory. But, in the meantime, the stubborn Russians, defeated yet unbroken, had taken up their stand in an almost impregnable position, on an eminence where the Jews of Frankfort were wont to bury their dead. Here the battle recommenced. The Prussian infantry, exhausted by six hours of hard fighting under a sun which equalled the tropical heat, were yet brought up repeatedly to the attack, but in vain. The King led three charges in person. Two horses were killed under him. The officers of his staff fell all round him. His coat was pierced by several bullets. All was in vain. His infantry was driven back with frightful slaughter. Terror began to spread fast from man to man. At that moment, the fiery cavalry of Laudohn, still fresh, rushed on the wavering ranks. Then followed an universal rout. Frederic himself was on the point of falling into the hands of the conquerors, and was with difficulty saved by a gallant officer, who, at the head of a handful of Hussars, made good a diversion of a few minutes. Shattered in body, shattered in mind, the King reached that night a village which the Cossacks had plundered; and there, in a ruined and deserted farm-house, flung himself on a heap of straw. He had sent to Berlin a second despatch very different from the first: "Let the royal family leave Berlin. Send the archives to Potsdam. The town may make terms with the enemy."

The defeat was, in truth, overwhelming. Of fifty thousand men who had that morning marched under the black eagles, not three thousand remained together. The King bethought him again of his corrosive sublimate, and wrote to bid adieu to his friends and to give directions as to the measures to be taken in the event of his death: "I have no resource left," such is the language of one of his letters, "all is lost. I will not survive the ruin of my country. Farewell for ever."

But the mutual jealousies of the confederates prevented them from following up their victory. They lost a few days in loitering and squabbling; and a few days, improved by Frederic, were worth more than the years of other men. On the morning after the battle, he had got together eighteen thousand of his troops. Very soon his force amounted to thirty thousand. Guns were procured from the neighbouring fortresses; and there was again an army. Berlin was for the present safe; but calamities came pouring on the King in uninterrupted succession. One of his generals, with a large body of troops, was taken at Maxen; another was defeated at Meissen; and when at length the campaign of 1759 closed, in the midst of a rigorous winter, the situation of Prussia appeared desperate. The only consoling circumstance was that, in the West, Ferdinand of Brunswick had been more fortunate than his master; and, by a series of exploits of which the battle of Minden was the most glorious, had removed all apprehension of danger on the side of France.

The fifth year was now about to commence. It seemed impossible that the Prussian territories, repeatedly devastated by hundreds of thousands of invaders, could longer support the contest. But the King carried on war as no European power has ever carried on war, except the Committee of Public Safety during the great agony of the French Revolution. He governed his kingdom as he would have governed a besieged town, not caring to what extent property was destroyed or the pursuits of civil life suspended, so that he did but make head against the enemy. As long as there was a man left in Prussia, that man might carry a musket; as long as there was a horse left, that horse might draw artillery. The coin was debased, the civil functionaries were left unpaid; in some provinces civil government altogether ceased to exist. But there were still rye-bread and potatoes; there were still lead and gunpowder; and, while the means of sustaining and destroying life remained, Frederic was determined to fight it out to the very last.

The earlier part of the campaign of 1760 was unfavourable to him. Berlin was again occupied by the enemy. Great contributions were levied on the inhabitants, and the royal palace was plundered. But at length, after two years of calamity, victory came back to his arms. At Lignitz he gained a great battle over Laudohn; at Torgau, after a day of horrible carnage, he triumphed over Daun. The fifth year closed, and still the event was in suspense. In the countries where the war had raged, the misery and exhaustion were more appalling than ever; but still there were left men and beasts, arms and food, and still Frederic fought on. In truth he had now been baited into savageness. His heart was ulcerated with hatred. The implacable resentment with which his enemies persecuted him, though originally provoked by his own unprincipled ambition, excited in him a thirst for vengeance which he did not even attempt to conceal. "It is hard," he says in one of his letters, "for man to bear what I bear. I begin to feel that, as the Italians say, revenge is a pleasure for the gods. My philosophy is worn out by suffering. I am no saint like those of whom we read in the legends; and I will own that I should die content if only I could first inflict a portion of the misery which I endure."

Borne up by such feelings, he struggled with various success, but constant glory, through the campaign of 1761. On the whole, the result of this campaign was disastrous to Prussia. No great battle was gained by the enemy; but, in spite of the desperate bounds of the hunted tiger, the circle of pursuers was fast closing round him. Laudohn had surprised the important fortress of Schweidnitz. With that fortress, half of Silesia and the command of the most important defiles through the mountains had been transferred to the Austrians. The Russians had overpowered the King's generals in Pomerania. The country was so completely desolated that he began, by his own confession, to look round him with blank despair, unable to imagine where recruits, horses or provisions were to be found.

Just at this time, two great events brought on a complete change in the relations of almost all the powers of Europe. One of those events was the retirement of Mr. Pitt from office; the other was the death of the Empress Elizabeth of Russia.

The retirement of Pitt seemed to be an omen of utter ruin to the House of Brandenburg. His proud and vehement nature was incapable of anything that looked like either fear or treachery. He had often declared that while he was in power, England should never make a peace of Utrecht; should never, for any selfish object, abandon an ally even in the last extremity of distress. The Continental war was his own war. He had been bold enough—he who in former times had attacked, with irresistible powers of oratory, the Hanoverian policy of Carteret and the German subsidies of Newcastle—to declare that Hanover ought to be as dear to us as Hampshire, and that he would conquer America in Germany. He had fallen; and the power which he had exercised, not always with descretion, but always with vigour and genius, had devolved on a favourite who was the representative of the Tory party, of the party which had thwarted William, which had persecuted Marlborough and which had given up the Catalans to the vengeance of Philip of Anjou. To make peace with France, to shake off with all, or more than all, the speed compatible with decency every Continental connection, these were among the chief objects of the new Minister. The policy then followed inspired Frederic with an unjust, but deep and bitter, aversion to the English name, and produced effects which are still felt throughout the civilised world. To that policy it was owing that, some years later, England could not find on the whole Continent a single ally to stand by her, in her extreme need, against the House of Bourbon. To that policy it was owing that Frederic, alienated from England, was compelled to connect himself closely during his latter years with Russia, and was induced reluctantly to assist in that great crime, the fruitful parent of other great crimes, the first partition of Poland.

Scarcely had the retreat of Mr. Pitt deprived Prussia of her only friend, when the death of Elizabeth produced an entire revolution in the politics of the North. The Grand Duke Peter, her nephew, who now ascended the Russian throne, was not merely free from the prejudices which his aunt had entertained against Frederic, but was a worshipper, a servile imitator of the Great King. The days of the new Czar's government were few and evil, but sufficient to produce a change in the whole state of Christendom. He set the Prussian prisoners at liberty, fitted them out decently and sent them back to their master; he withdrew his troops from the provinces which Elizabeth had decided on incorporating with her dominions; and absolved all those Prussian subjects who had been compelled to swear fealty to Russia from their engagements.

Not content with concluding peace on terms favourable to Prussia, he solicited rank in the Prussian service, dressed himself in a Prussian uniform, wore the Black Eagle of Prussia on his breast, made preparations for visiting Prussia, in order to have an interview with the object of his idolatry, and actually sent fifteen thousand excellent troops to reinforce the shattered army of Frederic. Thus strengthened, the King speedily repaired the losses of the preceeding year, reconquered Silesia, defeated Daun at Buckersdorf, invested and retook Schweidnitz, and, at the close of the year, presented to the forces of Maria Theresa a front as formidable as before the great reverses of 1759. Before the end of the campaign, his friend, the Emperor Peter, having, by a series of absurd insults to the institutions, manners and feelings of his people, united them in hostility to his person and government, was deposed and murdered. The Empress, who, under the title of Catherine the Second, now assumed the supreme power, was, at the commencement of her administration, by no means partial to Frederic, and refused to permit her troops to remain under his command. But she observed the peace made by her husband; and Prussia was no longer threatened by danger from the East.

England and France at the same time paired off together. They concluded a treaty, by which they bound themselves to observe neutrality with respect to the German war. Thus the coalitions on both sides were dissolved; and the original enemies, Austria and Prussia, remained alone confronting each other.

Austria had undoubtedly far greater means than Prussia and was less exhausted by hostilities; yet it seemed hardly possible that Austria could effect alone what she had in vain attempted to effect when supported by France on the one side and by Russia on the other. Danger also began to menace the Imperial house from another quarter. The Ottoman Porte held threatening language, and a hundred thousand Turks were mustered on the frontiers of Hungary. The proud and revengeful spirit of the Empress Queen at length gave way; and, in February 1763, the peace of Hubertsburg put an end to the conflict which had, during seven years, devastated Germany. The King ceded nothing. The whole Continent in arms had proved unable to tear Silesia from that iron grasp.

The war was over. Frederic was safe. His glory was beyond the reach of envy. If he had not made conquests as vast as those of Alexander, of Cæsar and of Napoleon, if he had not, on fields of battle, enjoyed the constant success of Marlborough and Wellington—he had yet given an example unrivalled in history of what capacity and resolution can effect against the greatest superiority of power and the utmost spite of fortune. He entered Berlin in

.ter an absence of more than six years. The streets were brilliantly
 ; and, as he passed along in an open carriage, with Ferdinand of
 ck at his side, the multitude saluted him with loud praises and bless-
He was moved by those marks of attachment, and repeatedly exclaimed
 ong live my dear people !—Long live my children !" Yet, even in the
 st of that gay spectacle, he could not but perceive everywhere the traces
oi destruction and decay. The city had been more than once plundered.
The population had considerably diminished. Berlin, however, had suffered
little when compared with most parts of the kingdom. The ruin of private
fortunes, tne distress of all ranks, was such as might appal the firmest mind.
Almost every province had been the seat of war, and of war conducted with
merciless ferocity. Clouds of Croatians had descended on Silesia. Tens of
thousands of Cossacks had been let loose on Pomerania and Brandenburg.
The mere contributions levied by the invaders amounted, it was said, to more
than a hundred millions of dollars ; and the value of what they extorted was
probably much less than the value of what they destroyed. The fields lay
uncultivated. The very seed-corn had been devoured in the madness of hunger. Famine, and contagious maladies, the effect of famine, had swept away
the herbs and flocks; and there was reason to fear that a great pestilence
among the human race was likely to follow in the train of that tremendous
war, Near fifteen thousand houses had been burned to the ground. The population of the kingdom had in seven years decreased to the frightful extent
of ten per cent. A sixth of the males capable of bearing arms had actually
perished on the field of battle. In some districts, no labourers, except
women, were seen in the fields at harvest-time. In others, the traveller
passed shuddering through a succession of silent villages in which not a single
inhabitant remained. The currency had been debased ; the authority of
laws and magistrates had been suspended; the whole social system was
deranged. For, during that convulsive struggle, everything that was not military violence was anarchy. Even the army was disorganised. Some great
generals and a crowd of excellent officers had fallen, and it had been
impossible to supply their place. The difficulty of finding recruits had,
towards the close of the war, been so great that selection and rejection were
impossible. Whole battalions were composed of deserters or of prisoners.
It was hardly to be hoped that thirty years of repose and industry would
repair the ruin produced by seven years of havoc. One consolatary circumstance, indeed, there was. No debt had been incurred. The burdens of
the war had been terrible, almost insupportable ; but no arrear was left to
embarrass the finances in time of peace.

Here, for the present, we must pause. We have accompanied Frederic to the
close of his career as a warrior. Possibly, when these " Memoirs " are completed,
we may resume the consideration of his character, and give some account
of his domestic and foreign policy, and of his private habits during the many
years of tranquillity which followed the Seven Years' War.

MADAME D'ARBLAY. (JANUARY, 1843.)

Diary and Letters of Madame D'Arblay. 2 vols., 8vo. London, 1842.

THOUGH the world saw and heard little of Madame D'Arblay during the last
forty years of her life, and though that little did not add to her fame, there
were thousands, we believe, who felt a singular emotion when they learned
that she was no longer among us. The news of her death carried the minds of

men back at one leap clear over two generations, to the time when her first literary triumphs were won. All those whom we had been accustomed to revere as intellectual patriarchs seemed children when compared with her; for Burke had sat up all night to read her writings and Johnson had pronounced her superior to Fielding, when Rogers was still a schoolboy and Southey still in petticoats. Yet more strange did it seem that we should just have lost one whose name had been widely celebrated before anybody had heard of some illustrious men who, twenty, thirty or forty years ago, were, after a long and splendid career, borne with honour to the grave. Yet so it was. Frances Burney was at the height of fame and popularity before Cowper had published his first volume, before Porson had gone up to college, before Pitt had taken his seat in the House of Commons, before the voice of Erskine had been once heard in Westminster Hall. Since the appearance of her first work, sixty-two years had passed; and this interval had been crowded, not only with political, but also with intellectual revolutions. Thousands of reputations had, during that period, sprung up, bloomed, withered and disappeared. New kinds of composition had come into fashion, had gone out of fashion, had been derided, had been forgotten. The fooleries of Della Crusca and the fooleries of Kotzebue had for a time bewitched the multitude, but had left no trace behind them; nor had misdirected genius been able to save from decay the once flourishing schools of Godwin, of Darwin and of Radcliffe. Many books, written for temporary effect, had run through six or seven editions and had then been gathered to the novels of Afra Behn and the epic poems of Sir Richard Blackmore. Yet the early works of Madame D'Arblay, in spite of the lapse of years, in spite of the change of manners, in spite of the popularity deservedly obtained by some of her rivals, continued to hold a high place in the public esteem. She lived to be a classic. Time set on her fame, before she went hence, that seal which is seldom set except on the fame of the departed. Like Sir Condy Rackrent in the tale, she survived her own wake and overheard the judgment of posterity.

Having always felt a warm and sincere, though not a blind, admiration for her talents, we rejoiced to learn that her "Diary" was about to be made public. Our hopes, it is true, were not unmixed with fears. We could not forget the fate of the "Memoirs of Dr. Burney," which were published ten years ago. That unfortunate book contained much that was curious and interesting. Yet it was received with a cry of disgust, and was speedily consigned to oblivion. The truth is that it deserved its doom. It was written in Madame D'Arblay's later style, the worst style that has ever been known among men. No genius, no information, could save from proscription a book so written. We, therefore, opened the "Diary" with no small anxiety, trembling lest we should light upon some of that peculiar rhetoric which deforms almost every page of the "Memoirs," and which it is impossible to read without a sensation made up of mirth, shame and loathing. We soon, however, discovered to our great delight that this "Diary" was kept before Madame D'Arblay became eloquent. It is, for the most part, written in her earliest and best manner, in true woman's English, clear, natural and lively. The two works are lying side by side before us; and we never turn from the "Memoirs" to the "Diary" without a sense of relief. The difference is as great as the difference between the atmosphere of a perfumer's shop, fetid with lavender water and jasmine soap, and the air of a heath on a fine morning in May. Both works ought to be consulted by every person who wishes to be well acquainted with the history of our literature and our manners. But to read the "Diary" is a pleasure; to read the "Memoirs" will always be a task.

We may, perhaps, afford some harmless amusement to our readers if we attempt, with the help of these two books, to give them an account of the most important years of Madame D'Arblay's life.

She was descended from a family which bore the name of Macburney, and which, though probably of Irish origin, had been long settled in Shropshire and was possessed of considerable estates in that county. Unhappily, many years before her birth, the Macburneys began, as if of set purpose and in a spirit of determined rivalry, to expose and ruin themselves. The heir apparent, Mr. James Macburney, offended his father by making a runaway match with an actress from Goodman's Fields. The old gentleman could devise no more judicious mode of wreaking vengeance on his undutiful boy than by marrying the cook. The cook gave birth to a son, named Joseph, who succeeded to all the lands of the family, while James was cut off with a shilling. The favourite son, however, was so extravagant that he soon became as poor as his disinherited brother. Both were forced to earn their bread by their labour. Joseph turned dancing-master and settled in Norfolk. James struck off the Mac from the beginning of his name and set up as a portrait painter at Chester. Here he had a son, named Charles, well known as the author of the "History of Music" and as the father of two remarkable children, of a son distinguished by learning and of a daughter still more honourably distinguished by genius.

Charles early showed a taste for that art of which, at a later period, he became the historian. He was apprenticed to a celebrated musician in London, and applied himself to study with vigour and success. He early found a kind and munificent patron in Fulk Greville, a highborn and highbred man, who seems to have had in large measure all the accomplishments and all the follies, all the virtues and all the vices, which, a hundred years ago, were considered as making up the character of a fine gentleman. Under such protection, the young artist had every prospect of a brilliant career in the capital. But his health failed. It became necessary for him to retreat from the smoke and river fog of London to the pure air of the coast. He accepted the place of organist at Lynn, and settled at that town with a young lady who had recently become his wife.

At Lynn, in June, 1752, Frances Burney was born. Nothing in her childhood indicated that she would, while still a young woman, have secured for herself an honourable and permanent place among English writers. She was shy and silent. Her brothers and sisters called her a dunce, and not altogether without some show of reason; for at eight years old she did not know her letters.

In 1760, Mr. Burney quitted Lynn for London, and took a house in Poland Street; a situation which had been fashionable in the reign of Queen Anne, but which, since that time, had been deserted by most of its wealthy and noble inhabitants. He afterwards resided in St. Martin's Street, on the south side of Leicester Square. His house there is still well known, and will continue to be well known as long as our island retains any trace of civilisation; for it was the dwelling of Newton, and the square turret which distinguishes it from all the surrounding buildings was Newton's observatory.

Mr. Burney at once obtained as many pupils of the most respectable description as he had time to attend, and was thus enabled to support his family, modestly indeed, and frugally, but in comfort and independence. His professional merit obtained for him the degree of Doctor of Music from the University of Oxford; and his works on subjects connected with his art gained for him a place, respectable, though certainly not eminent, among men of letters.

The progress of the mind of Frances Burney, from her ninth to her twenty-fifth year, well deserves to be recorded. When her education had proceeded no further than the hornbook, she lost her mother, and thenceforward she educated herself. Her father appears to have been as bad a father as a very honest, affectionate and sweet-tempered man can well be. He loved his daughter dearly; but it never seems to have occurred to him that a parent has other duties to perform to children than that of fondling them. It would indeed have been impossible for him to superintend their education himself. His professional engagements occupied him all day. At seven in the morning, he began to attend his pupils, and, when London was full, was sometimes employed in teaching till eleven at night. He was often forced to carry in his pocket a tin box of sandwiches and a bottle of wine and water, on which he dined in a hackney coach while hurrying from one scholar to another. Two of his daughters he sent to a seminary at Paris; but he imagined that Frances would run some risk of being perverted from the Protestant faith if she were educated in a Catholic country, and he therefore kept her at home. No governess, no teacher of any art or of any language was provided for her. But one of her sisters showed her how to write; and, before she was fourteen, she began to find pleasure in reading.

It was not, however, by reading that her intellect was formed. Indeed, when her best novels were produced, her knowledge of books was very small. When at the height of her fame, she was unacquainted with the most celebrated works of Voltaire and Molière; and, what seems still more extraordinary, had never heard or seen a line of Churchill, who, when she was a girl, was the most popular of living poets. It is particularly deserving of observation that she appears to have been by no means a novel reader. Her father's library was large, and he had admitted into it so many books which rigid moralists generally exclude that he felt uneasy, as he afterwards owned, when Johnson began to examine the shelves. But in the whole collection there was only a single novel, Fielding's "Amelia."

An education, however, which to most girls would have been useless, but which suited Fanny's mind better than elaborate culture, was in constant progress during her passage from childhood to womanhood. The great book of human nature was turned over before her. Her father's social position was very peculiar. He belonged in fortune and station to the middle class. His daughters seemed to have been suffered to mix freely with those whom butlers and waiting-maids call vulgar. We are told that they were in the habit of playing with the children of a wig-maker who lived in the adjoining house. Yet few nobles could assemble in the most stately mansions of Grosvenor Square or St. James's Square a society so various and so brilliant as was sometimes to be found in Dr. Burney's cabin. His mind, though not very powerful or capacious, was restlessly active; and, in the intervals of his professional pursuits, he had contrived to lay up much miscellaneous information. His attainments, the suavity of his temper and the gentle simplicity of his manners had obtained for him ready admission to the first literary circles. While he was still at Lynn, he had won Johnson's heart by sounding with honest zeal the praises of the "English Dictionary." In London, the two friends met frequently and agreed most harmoniously. One tie, indeed, was wanting to their mutual attachment. Burney loved his own art passionately, and Johnson just knew the bell of Saint Clement's church from the organ. They had, however, many topics in common; and on winter nights their conversations were sometimes prolonged till the fire had gone out and the candles had burned away to the wicks. Burney's admiration of the powers which had produced "Rasselas" and "The Rambler" bordered on idolatry. He gave a singular proof of this at his first visit to Johnson's ill-furnished garret. The master of the apartment was not at home. The enthusiastic visitor looked about for some relic which he could carry away, but he could see nothing lighter than the chairs and the fireirons. At last he discovered an old broom, tore some bristles from the stump, wrapped them in silver paper, and departed as happy as Louis IX. when the holy nail of St. Denis was found. Johnson, on the other hand, condescended to growl out that Burney was an honest fellow, a man whom it was impossible not to like.

Garrick, too, was a frequent visitor in Poland Street and Saint Martin's Lane. That wonderful actor loved the society of children, partly from good nature and partly from vanity. The ecstasies of mirth and terror, which his gestures and play of countenance never failed to produce in a nursery, flattered him quite as much as the applause of mature critics. He often exhibited all his powers of mimicry for the amusement of the little Burneys, awed them by shuddering and crouching as if he saw a ghost, scared them by raving like a maniac in Saint Luke's, and then at once became an auctioneer, a chimney-sweeper or an old woman, and made them laugh till the tears ran down their cheeks.

But it would be tedious to recount the names of all the men of letters and artists whom Frances Burney had an opportunity of seeing and hearing. Colman, Twining, Harris, Baretti, Hawkesworth, Reynolds, Barry, were among those who occasionally surrounded the tea table and supper tray at her father's modest dwelling. This was not all. The distinction which Dr. Burney had acquired as a musician and as the historian of music, attracted to his house the most eminent musical performers of that age. The greatest Italian singers who visited England regarded him as the dispenser of fame in their art, and exerted themselves to obtain his suffrage. Pachierotti became his intimate friend. The rapacious Agujari, who sang for nobody else under fifty pounds an air, sang her best for Dr. Burney without a fee ; and in the company of Dr. Burney even the haughty and eccentric Gabrielli constrained herself to behave with civility. It was thus in his power to give, with scarcely any expense, concerts equal to those of the aristocracy. On such occasions, the quiet street in which he lived was blocked up by coroneted chariots, and his little drawing-room was crowded with peers, peeresses, ministers and ambassadors. On one evening, of which we happen to have a full account, there were present Lord Mulgrave, Lord Bruce, Lord and Lady Edgecumbe, Lord Barrington from the War Office, Lord Sandwich from the Admiralty, Lord Ashburnham, with his gold key dangling from his pocket, and the French ambassador, M. De Guignes, renowned for his fine person and for his success in gallantry. But the great show of the night was the Russian ambassador, Count Orloff, whose gigantic figure was all in a blaze with jewels, and in whose demeanour the untamed ferocity of the Scythian might be discerned through a thin varnish of French politeness. As he stalked about the small parlour, brushing the ceiling with his toupee, the girls whispered to each other, with mingled admiration and horror, that he was the favoured lover of his august mistress ; that he had borne the chief part in the revolution to which she owed her throne ; and that his huge hands, now glittering with diamond rings, had given the last squeeze to the windpipe of her unfortunate husband.

With such illustrious guests as these were mingled all the most remarkable specimens of the race of lions, a kind of game which is hunted in London every spring with more than Meltonian ardour and perseverance. Bruce, who had washed down steaks cut from living oxen with water from the fountains of the Nile, came to swagger and talk about his travels. Omai lisped broken English, and made all the assembled musicians hold their ears by howling Otaheitean love-songs, such as those with which Oberea charmed her Opano.

With the literary and fashionable society which occasionally met under Dr. Burney's roof, Frances can scarcely be said to have mingled. She was not a musician, and could therefore bear no part in the concerts. She was shy almost to awkwardness, and scarcely ever joined in the conversation. The slightest remark from a stranger disconcerted her, and even the old friends of her father who tried to draw her out could seldom extract more than a Yes or a No. Her figure was small, her face not distinguished by beauty. She was therefore suffered to withdraw quietly to the background, and, unobserved herself, to observe all that passed. Her nearest relations were aware that she had good sense; but seem not to have suspected that under her demure and bashful deportment were concealed a fertile invention and a keen sense of the ridiculous. She had not, it is true, an eye for the fine shades of character. But every marked peculiarity instantly caught her notice and remained engraven on her imagination. Thus while still a girl she had laid up such a store of materials for fiction as few of those who mix much in the world are able to accumulate during a long life. She had watched and listened to people of every class, from princes and great officers of state down to artists living in garrets and poets familiar with subterranean cookshops. Hundreds of remarkable persons had passed in review before her, English, French, German, Italian, lords and fiddlers, deans of cathedrals and managers of theatres, travellers leading about newly caught savages, and singing women escorted by deputy husbands.

So strong was the impression made on the mind of Frances by the society which she was in the habit of seeing and hearing, that she began to write little fictitious narratives as soon as she could use her pen with ease, which, as we have said, was not very early. Her sisters were amused by her stories. But Dr. Burney knew nothing of their existence; and in another quarter her literary propensities met with serious discouragement. When she was fifteen, her father took a second wife. The new Mrs. Burney soon found out that her daughter-in-law was fond of scribbling, and delivered several good-natured lectures on the subject. The advice no doubt was well meant, and might have been given by the most judicious friend; for at that time, from causes to which we may hereafter advert, nothing could be more disadvantageous to a young lady than to be known as a novel writer. Frances yielded, relinquished her favourite pursuit, and made a bonfire of all her manuscripts.*

She now hemmed and stitched from breakfast to dinner with scrupulous regularity. But the dinners of that time were early; and the afternoon was her own. Though she had given up novel-writing, she was still fond of using her pen. She began to keep a diary, and she corresponded largely with a person who seems to have had the chief share in the formation of her mind. This was Samuel Crisp, an old friend of her father. His name, well known, near a century ago, in the most splendid circles of London, has long been forgotten. His history is, however, so interesting and instructive, that it tempts us to venture on a digression.

Long before Frances Burney was born, Mr. Crisp had made his entrance into the world, with every advantage. He was well connected and well educated. His face and figure were conspicuously handsome; his manners were polished; his fortune was easy; his character was without stain; he lived in the best society; he had read much; he talked well; his taste in literature, music, painting, architecture, sculpture, was held in high esteem. Nothing that the world can give seemed to be wanting to his happiness and respectability, except that he should understand the limits of his powers, and should

---

* There is some difficulty here as to the chronology. "This sacrifice," says the editor of the Diary, "was made in the young authoress's fifteenth year." This could not be; for the sacrifice was the effect, according to the editor's own showing, of the remonstrances of the second Mrs. Burney; and Frances was in her sixteenth year when her father's second marriage took place.

not throw away distinctions which were within his reach in the pursuit of distinctions which were unattainable.

"It is an uncontrolled truth," says Swift, "that no man ever made an ill figure who understood his own talents, nor a good one who mistook them." Every day brings with it fresh illustrations of this weighty saying; but the best commentary that we remember is the history of Samuel Crisp. Men like him have their proper place, and it is a most important one, in the Commonwealth of Letters. It is by the judgment of such men that the rank of authors is finally determined. It is neither to the multitude, nor to the few who are gifted with great creative genius, that we are to look for sound critical decisions. The multitude, unacquainted with the best models, are captivated by whatever stuns and dazzles them. They deserted Mrs. Siddons to run after Master Betty; and they now prefer, we have no doubt, Jack Sheppard to Von Artevelde. A man of great original genius, on the other hand, a man who has attained to mastery in some high walk of art, is by no means to be implicitly trusted as a judge of the performances of others. The erroneous decisions pronounced by such men are without number. It is commonly supposed that jealousy makes them unjust. But a more creditable explanation may easily be found. The very excellence of a work shows that some of the faculties of the author have been developed at the expense of the rest; for it is not given to the human intellect to expand itself widely in all directions at once and to be at the same time gigantic and well-proportioned. Whoever becomes pre-eminent in any art, nay, in any style of art, generally does so by devoting himself with intense and exclusive enthusiasm to the pursuit of one kind of excellence. His perception of other kinds of excellence is therefore too often impaired. Out of his own department, he praises and blames at random, and is far less to be trusted than the mere connoisseur, who produces nothing, and whose business is only to judge and enjoy. One painter is distinguished by his exquisite finishing. He toils day after day to bring the veins of a cabbage leaf, the folds of a lace veil, the wrinkles of an old woman's face, nearer and nearer to perfection. In the time which he employs on a square foot of canvass, a master of a different order covers the walls of a palace with gods burying giants under mountains, or makes the cupola of a church alive with seraphim and martyrs. The more fervent the passion of each of these artists for his art, the higher the merit of each in his own line, the more unlikely it is that they will justly appreciate each other. Many persons, who never handled a pencil, probably do far more justice to Michael Angelo than would have been done by Gerard Douw, and far more justice to Gerard Douw than would have been done by Michael Angelo.

It is the same with literature. Thousands, who have no spark of the genius of Dryden or Wordsworth, do to Dryden the justice which has never been done by Wordsworth, and to Wordsworth the justice which, we suspect, would never have been done by Dryden. Gray, Johnson, Richardson, Fielding, are all highly esteemed by the great body of intelligent and well informed men. But Gray could see no merit in "Rasselas," and Johnson could see no merit in "The Bard." Fielding thought Richardson a solemn prig, and Richardson perpetually expressed contempt and disgust for Fielding's lowness.

Mr. Crisp seems, as far as we can judge, to have been a man eminently qualified for the useful office of a connoisseur. His talents and knowledge fitted him to appreciate justly almost every species of intellectual superiority. As an adviser he was inestimable. Nay, he might probably have held a respectable rank as a writer if he would have confined himself to some department of literature in which nothing more than sense, taste and reading was required. Unhappily, he set his heart on being a great poet, wrote a tragedy in five acts on the death of Virginia, and offered it to Garrick, who was his personal friend. Garrick read, shook his head, and expressed a doubt whether it would be wise in Mr. Crisp to stake a reputation, which stood high, on the success of such a piece. But the author, blinded by self-love, set in motion a machinery such as none could long resist. His intercessors were the most eloquent man and the most lovely woman of that generation. Pitt was induced to read "Virginia" and to pronounce it excellent. Lady Coventry, with fingers which might have furnished a model to sculptors, forced the manuscript into the reluctant hand of the manager; and, in the year 1754, the play was brought forward.

Nothing that skill or friendship could do was omitted. Garrick wrote both prologue and epilogue. The zealous friends of the author filled every box; and, by their strenuous exertions, the life of the play was prolonged during ten nights. But, though there was no clamorous reprobation, it was universally felt that the attempt had failed. When "Virginia" was printed, the public disappointment was even greater than at the representation. The critics, the Monthly Reviewers in particular, fell on plot, characters and diction without mercy, but, we fear, not without justice. We have never met with a copy of the play; but if we may judge from the lines which are extracted in the *Gentleman's Magazine*, and which do not appear to have been malevolently selected, we should say that nothing but the acting of Garrick and the partiality of the audience could have saved so feeble and unnatural a drama from instant damnation.

The ambition of the poet was still unsubdued. When the London season closed, he applied himself vigorously to the work of removing blemishes. He does not seem to have suspected, what we are strongly inclined to suspect, that the whole piece was one blemish, and that the passages which were meant to be fine were, in truth, bursts of that tame extravagance into which writers fall when they set themselves to be sublime and pathetic in spite of nature. He omitted, added, retouched, and flattered himself with hopes of a complete success in the following year; but, in the following year, Garrick showed no disposition to bring the amended tragedy on the stage. Solicitation and remonstrance were tried in vain. Lady Coventry, drooping under that malady which seems ever to select what is loveliest for its prey, could render no assistance. The manager's language was civilly evasive; but his resolution was inflexible.

Crisp had committed a great error; but he had escaped with a very slight penance. His play had not been hooted from the boards. It had, on the contrary, been better received than many very estimable performances have been—than Johnson's "Irene," for example, or Goldsmith's "Good-natured Man." Had Crisp been wise, he would have thought himself happy in having purchased self-knowledge so cheap. He would have relinquished, without vain repinings, the hope of poetical distinction, and would have turned to the many sources of happiness which he still possessed. Had he been, on the other hand, an unfeeling and unblushing dunce, he would have gone on writing scores of bad tragedies in defiance of censure and derision. But he had too much sense to risk a second defeat, yet too little to bear his first defeat like a man. The fatal delusion that he was a great dramatist had taken firm possession of his mind. His failure he attributed to every cause except the true one. He complained of the ill-will of Garrick, who appears to have done everything that ability and zeal could do, and who, from selfish motives, would of course, have been well pleased if "Virginia" had been as successful as the "Beggar's Opera." Nay, Crisp complained of the languor of the friends whose partiality had given him three benefit nights to which he had no claim.

He complained of the injustice of the spectators, when, in truth, he ought to have been grateful for their unexampled patience. He lost his temper and spirits, and became a cynic and a hater of mankind. From London he retired to Hampton, and from Hampton to a solitary and long-deserted mansion, built on a common in one of the wildest tracts of Surrey. No road, not even a sheepwalk, connected his lonely dwelling with the abodes of men. The place of his retreat was strictly concealed from his old associates. In the spring, he sometimes emerged, and was seen at exhibitions and concerts in London. But he soon disappeared and hid himself, with no society but his books, in his dreary hermitage. He survived his failure about thirty years. A new generation sprang up around him. No memory of his bad verses remained among men. His very name was forgotten. How completely the world had lost sight of him will appear from a single circumstance. We looked for his name in a copious Dictionary of Dramatic Authors published while he was still alive, and we found only that Mr. Samuel Crisp, of the Custom House, had written a play called "Virginia," acted in 1754. To the last, however, the unhappy man continued to brood over the injustice of the manager and the pit, and tried to convince himself and others that he had missed the highest literary honours only because he had omitted some fine passages in compliance with Garrick's judgment. Alas for human nature, that the wounds of vanity should smart and bleed so much longer than the wounds of affection! Few people, we believe, whose nearest friends and relations died in 1754, had any acute feeling of the loss in 1782. Dear sisters, and favourite daughters, and brides snatched away before the honeymoon was passed, had been forgotten, or were remembered only with a tranquil regret. But Samuel Crisp was still mourning for his tragedy, like Rachel weeping for her children, and would not be comforted. "Never," such was his language twenty-eight years after his disaster, "never give up or alter a tittle unless it perfectly coincides with your inward feelings. I can say this to my sorrow and my cost. But mum!" Soon after these words were written, his life—a life which might have been eminently useful and happy—ended in the same gloom in which, during more than a quarter of a century, it had been passed. We have thought it worth while to rescue from oblivion this curious fragment of literary history. It seems to us at once ludicrous, melancholy and full of instruction.

Crisp was an old and very intimate friend of the Burneys. To them alone was confided the name of the desolate old hall in which he hid himself like a wild beast in a den. For them were reserved such remains of his humanity as had survived the failure of his play. Frances Burney he regarded as his daughter. He called her his Fannikin; and she in return called him her dear Daddy. In truth, he seems to have done much more than her real father for the development of her intellect; for though he was a bad poet, he was a scholar, a thinker and an excellent counsellor. He was particularly fond of Dr. Burney's concerts. They had, indeed, been commenced at his suggestion, and when he visited London he constantly attended them. But when he grew old, and when gout, brought on partly by mental irritation, confined him to his retreat, he was desirous of having a glimpse of that gay and brilliant world from which he was exiled, and he pressed Fannikin to send him full accounts of her father's evening parties. A few of her letters to him have been published; and it is impossible to read them without discerning in them all the powers which afterwards produced "Evelina" and "Cecilia"; the quickness in catching every odd peculiarity of character and manner; the skill in grouping; the humour, often richly comic, sometimes even farcical.

Fanny's propensity to novel-writing had for a time been kept down. It now rose up stronger than ever. The heroes and heroines of the tales which had perished in the flames were still present to the eye of her mind. One favourite story, in particular, haunted her imagination. It was about a certain Caroline Evelyn, a beautiful damsel who made an unfortunate love match and died, leaving an infant daughter. Frances began to image to herself the various scenes, tragic and comic, through which the poor motherless girl, highly connected on one side, meanly connected on the other, might have to pass. A crowd of unreal beings, good and bad, grave and ludicrous, surrounded the pretty, timid young orphan; a coarse sea captain; an ugly, insolent fop, blazing in a superb court dress; another fop, as ugly and as insolent, but lodged on Snow Hill and tricked out in second-hand finery for the Hampstead ball; an old woman, all wrinkles and rouge, flirting her fan with the air of a miss of seventeen and screaming in a dialect made up of vulgar French and vulgar English; a poet, lean and ragged, with a broad Scotch accent. By degrees these shadows acquired stronger and stronger consistence; the impulse which urged Frances to write became irresistible; and the result was the "History of Evelina."

Then came, naturally enough, a wish, mingled with many fears, to appear before the public; for, timid as Frances was, and bashful, and altogether unaccustomed to hear her own praises, it is clear that she wanted neither a strong passion for distinction nor a just confidence in her own powers. Her scheme was to become, if possible, a candidate for fame without running any risk of disgrace. She had not money to bear the expense of printing. It was therefore necessary that some bookseller should be induced to take the risk; and such a bookseller was not readily found. Dodsley refused even to look at the manuscript unless he were intrusted with the name of the author. A publisher in Fleet Street, named Lowndes, was more complaisant. Some correspondence took place between this person and Miss Burney, who took the name of Grafton, and desired that the letters addressed to her might be left at the Orange Coffee-house. But, before the bargain was finally struck, Fanny thought it her duty to obtain her father's consent. She told him that she had written a book, that she wished to have his permission to publish it anonymously, but that she hoped that he would not insist upon seeing it. What followed may serve to illustrate what we meant when we said that Dr. Burney was as bad a father as so goodhearted a man could possibly be. It never seems to have crossed his mind that Fanny was about to take a step on which the whole happiness of her life might depend, a step which might raise her to an honourable eminence or cover her with ridicule and contempt. Several people had already been trusted, and strict concealment was therefore not to be expected. On so grave an occasion, it was surely his duty to give his best counsel to his daughter, to win her confidence, to prevent her from exposing herself if her book were a bad one, and, if it were a good one, to see that the terms which she made with the publisher were likely to be beneficial to her. Instead of this, he only stared, burst out a-laughing, kissed her, gave her leave to do as she liked, and never even asked the name of her work. The contract with Lowndes was speedily concluded. Twenty pounds were given for the copyright, and were accepted by Fanny with delight. Her father's inexcusable neglect of his duty happily caused her no worse evil than the loss of twelve or fifteen hundred pounds.

After many delays, "Evelina" appeared in January, 1778. Poor Fanny was sick with terror, and durst hardly stir out of doors. Some days passed before anything was heard of the book. It had, indeed, nothing but its own merits to push it into public favour. Its author was unknown. The house by which it was published, was not, we believe, held high in estimation. No body of partisans had been engaged to applaud. The better class of readers expected little from a novel about a young lady's entrance into the world. There was, indeed, at that time a disposition among the most respectable people to condemn novels generally: nor was this disposition by any means without excuse; for works of that sort were then almost always silly and very frequently wicked.

Soon, however, the first faint accents of praise began to be heard. The keepers of the circulating libraries reported that everybody was asking for "Evelina," and that some person had guessed Anstey to be the author. Then came a favourable notice in the *London Review;* then another still more favourable in the *Monthly*. And now the book found its way to tables which had seldom been polluted by marble-covered volumes. Scholars and statesmen, who contemptuously abandoned the crowd of romances to Miss Lydia Languish and Miss Sukey Saunter, were not ashamed to own that they could not tear themselves away from "Evelina." Fine carriages and rich liveries, not often seen east of Temple Bar, were attracted to the publisher's shop in Fleet Street. Lowndes was daily questioned about the author, but was himself as much in the dark as any of the questioners. The mystery, however, could not remain a mystery long. It was known to brothers and sisters, aunts and cousins: and they were far too proud and too happy to be discreet. Dr. Burney wept over the book in rapture. Daddy Crisp shook his fist at his Fannikin in affectionate anger at not having been admitted to her confidence. The truth was whispered to Mrs. Thrale: and then it began to spread fast.

The book had been admired while it had been ascribed to men of letters long conversant with the world and accustomed to composition. But when it was known that a reserved, silent young woman had produced the best work of fiction that had appeared since the death of Smollett, the acclamations were redoubled. What she had done was, indeed, extraordinary. But, as usual, various reports improved the story till it became miraculous. "Evelina," it was said, was the work of a girl of seventeen. Incredible as this tale was, it continued to be repeated down to our own time. Francis was too honest to confirm it. Probably she was too much a woman to contradict it; and it was long before any of her detractors thought of this mode of annoyance. Yet there was no want of low minds and bad hearts in the generation which witnessed her first appearance. There was the envious Kenrick and the savage Wolcot, the asp George Steevens and the polecat John Williams. It did not, however, occur to them to search the parish register of Lynn, in order that they might be able to twit a lady with having concealed her age. That truly chivalrous exploit was reserved for a bad writer of our own time, whose spite she had provoked by not furnishing him with materials for a worthless edition of Boswell's "Life of Johnson," some sheets of which our readers have doubtless seen round parcels of better books.

But we must return to our story. The triumph was complete. The timid and obscure girl found herself on the highest pinnacle of fame. Great men, on whom she had gazed at a distance with humble reverence, addressed her with admiration, tempered by the tenderness due to her sex and age. Burke, Windham, Gibbon, Reynolds, Sheridan, were among her most ardent eulogists. Cumberland acknowledged her merit, after his fashion, by biting his lips and wriggling in his chair whenever her name was mentioned. But it was at Streatham that she tasted, in the highest perfection, the sweets of flattery mingled with the sweets of friendship. Mrs. Thrale, then at the height of prosperity and popularity—with gay spirits, quick wit, showy, though superficial, acquirements, pleasing, though not refined, manners, a singularly amiable temper and a loving heart—felt towards Fanny as towards a younger sister. With the Thrales, Johnson was domesticated. He was an old friend of Dr. Burney; but he had probably taken little notice of Dr. Burney's daughters; and Fanny, we imagine, had never in her life dared to speak to him, unless to ask whether he wanted a nineteenth or a twentieth cup of tea. He was charmed by her tale, and preferred it to the novels of Fielding, to whom, indeed, he had always been grossly unjust. He did not, indeed, carry his partiality so far as to place "Evelina" by the side of "Clarissa" and "Sir Charles Grandison"; yet he said that his little favourite had done enough to have made even Richardson feel uneasy. With Johnson's cordial approbation of the book was mingled a fondness, half gallant, half paternal, for the writer; and this fondness his age and character entitled him to show without restraint. He began by putting her hand to his lips. But he soon clasped her in his huge arms, and immediately implored her to be a good girl. She was his pet, his dear love, his dear little Burney, his little character-monger. At one time, he broke forth in praise of the good taste of her caps. At another time, he insisted on teaching her Latin. That, with all his coarseness and irritability, he was a man of sterling benevolence, has long been acknowledged. But how gentle and endearing his deportment could be, was not known till the "Recollections of Madame D'Arblay" were published.

We have mentioned a few of the most eminent of those who paid their homage to the author of "Evelina." The crowd of inferior admirers would require a catalogue as long as that in the second book of the "Iliad." In that catalogue would be Mrs. Cholmondeley, the sayer of odd things; and Seward, much given to yawning; and Baretti, who slew the man in the Haymarket; and Paoli, talking broken English; and Langton, taller by the head than any other member of the club; and Lady Millar, who kept a vase wherein fools were wont to put bad verses; and Jerningham, who wrote verses fit to be put into the vase of Lady Millar; and Dr. Franklin—not, as some have dreamed, the great Pennsylvanian Dr. Franklin, who could not then have paid his respects to Miss Burney without much risk of being hanged, drawn and quartered, but Dr. Franklin the less.

Αἴας
μείων, οὔτι τόσος γε ὅσος Τελαμώνιος Αἴας,
ἀλλὰ πολὺ μείων.

It would not have been surprising if such success had turned even a strong head and corrupted even a generous and affectionate nature. But, in the "Diary," we can find no trace of any feeling inconsistent with a truly modest and amiable disposition. There is, indeed, abundant proof that Frances enjoyed with an intense, though a troubled, joy, the honours which her genius had won; but it is equally clear that her happiness sprang from the happiness of her father, her sister and her dear Daddy Crisp. While flattered by the great, the opulent and the learned, while followed along the Steyne at Brighton and the Pantiles at Tunbridge Wells by the gaze of admiring crowds, her heart seems to have been still with the little domestic circle in Saint Martin's Street. If she recorded with minute diligence all the compliments, delicate and coarse, which she heard wherever she turned, she recorded them for the eyes of two or three persons who had loved her from infancy, who had loved her in obscurity, and to whom her fame gave the purest and most exquisite delight. Nothing can be more unjust than to confound these outpourings of a kind heart, sure of perfect sympathy, with the egotism of a bluestocking who prates to all who come near her about her own novel or her own volume of sonnets.

It was natural that the triumphant issue of Miss Burney's first venture should tempt her to try a second. "Evelina," though it had raised her fame, had added nothing to her fortune. Some of her friends urged her to write for the stage. Johnson promised to give her his advice as to the composition. Murphy, who was supposed to understand the temper of the pit as well as any man of his time, undertook to instruct her as to stage effect. Sheridan declared that he would accept a play from her without even reading it. Thus encouraged, she wrote a comedy named "The Witlings." Fortunately, it was never acted or printed. We can, we think, easily perceive, from the little which is said on the subject in the "Diary," that "The Witlings" would have been damned, and that Murphy and Sheridan thought so, though they were too polite to say so. Happily Frances had a friend who was not afraid to give her pain. Crisp, wiser for her than he had been for himself, read the manuscript in his lonely retreat and manfully told her that she had failed, and that to remove blemishes here and there would be useless; that the piece had abundance of wit but no interest, that it was bad as a whole; that it would remind every reader of the "Femmes Savantes," which, strange to say, she had never read, and that she could not sustain so close a comparison with Moliere. This opinion, in which Dr. Burney concurred, was sent to Frances in what she called "a hissing, groaning, catcalling epistle." But she had too much sense not to know that it was better to be hissed and catcalled by her Daddy than by a whole sea of heads in the pit of Drury Lane Theatre; and she had too good a heart not to be grateful for so rare an act of friendship. She returned an answer which shows how well she deserved to have a judicious, faithful and affectionate adviser. "I intend," she wrote, "to console myself for your censure by this greatest proof I have received of the sincerity, candour and, let me add, esteem of my dear daddy. And, as I happen to love myself more than my play, this consolation is not a very trifling one. This, however, seriously I do believe, that when my two daddies put their heads together to concert that hissing, groaning, catcalling epistle they sent me, they felt as sorry for poor little Miss Bayes as she could possibly do for herself. You see I do not attempt to repay your frankness with an air of pretended carelessness. But, though somewhat disconcerted just now, I will promise not to let my vexation live out another day. Adieu, my dear daddy; I won't be mortified and I won't be *downed;* but I will be proud to find I have, out of my own family, as well as in it, a friend who loves me well enough to speak plain truth to me."

Frances now turned from her dramatic schemes to an undertaking far better suited to her talents. She determined to write a new tale on a plan excellently contrived for the display of the powers in which her superiority to other writers lay. It was, in truth, a grand and various picture gallery, which presented to the eye a long series of men and women, each marked by some strong peculiar feature. There were avarice and prodigality, the pride of blood and the pride of money, morbid restlessness and morbid apathy, frivolous garrulity, supercilious silence, a Democritus to laugh at everything and a Heraclitus to lament over everything. The work proceeded fast, and in twelve months was completed. It wanted something of the simplicity which had been among the most attractive charms of "Evelina"; but it furnished ample proof that the four years, which had elapsed since "Evelina" appeared, had not been unprofitably spent. Those who saw "Cecilia" in manuscript pronounced it the best novel of the age. Mrs. Thrale laughed and wept over it. Crisp was even vehement in applause, and offered to insure the rapid and complete success of the book for half-a-crown. What Miss Burney received for the copyright is not mentioned in the "Diary;" but we have observed several expressions from which we infer that the sum was considerable. That the sale would be great, nobody could doubt; and Frances now had shrewd and experienced advisers, who would not suffer her to wrong herself. We have been told that the publishers gave her two thousand pounds, and we have no doubt that they might have given a still larger sum without being losers.

"Cecilia" was published in the summer of 1782. The curiosity of the town was intense. We have been informed by persons who remember those days, that no romance of Sir Walter Scott was more impatiently awaited or more eagerly snatched from the counters of the booksellers. High as public expectation was, it was amply satisfied; and "Cecilia" was placed, by general acclamation, among the classical novels of England.

Miss Burney was now thirty. Her youth had been singularly prosperous; but clouds soon began to gather over that clear and radiant dawn. Events deeply painful to a heart so kind as that of Frances followed each other in rapid succession. She was first called upon to attend the deathbed of her best friend, Samuel Crisp. When she returned to Saint Martin's Street after performing this melancholy duty, she was appalled by hearing that Johnson had been struck with paralysis, and, not many months later, she parted from him for the last time with solemn tenderness. He wished to look on her once more; and on the day before his death she long remained in tears on the stairs leading to his bedroom, in the hope that she might be called in to receive his blessing. But he was then sinking fast and, though he sent her an affectionate message, was unable to see her. But this was not the worst. There are separations far more cruel than those which are made by death. Frances might weep with proud affection for Crisp and Johnson. She had to blush as well as to weep for Mrs. Thrale.

Life, however, still smiled upon her. Domestic happiness, friendship, independence, leisure, letters, all these things were hers; and she flung them all away.

Among the distinguished persons to whom Miss Burney had been introduced, none appears to have stood higher in her regard than Mrs. Delany. This lady was an interesting and venerable relic of a past age. She was the niece of George Granville, Lord Lansdowne, who, in his youth, exchanged verses and compliments with Edmund Waller, and who was among the first to applaud the opening talents of Pope. She had married Dr. Delany, a man known to his contemporaries as a profound scholar and eloquent preacher, but remembered in our time chiefly as one of that small circle in which the fierce spirit of Swift, tortured by disappointed ambition, by remorse and by the approaches of madness, sought for amusement and repose. Doctor Delany had long been dead. His widow, nobly descended, eminently accomplished, and retaining, in spite of the infirmities of advanced age, the vigour of her faculties and the serenity of her temper, enjoyed and deserved the favour of the royal family. She had a pension of three hundred a-year; and a house at Windsor, belonging to the crown, had been fitted up for her accommodation. At this house, the King and Queen sometimes called, and found a very natural pleasure in thus catching an occasional glimpse of the private life of English families.

In December, 1785, Miss Burney was on a visit to Mrs. Delany at Windsor. The dinner was over. The old lady was taking a nap. Her grandniece, a little girl of seven, was playing at some Christmas game with the visitors, when the door opened, and a stout gentleman entered unannounced, with a star on his breast and "What? what? what?" in his mouth. A cry of "The King!" was set up. A general scampering followed. Miss Burney owns that she could not have been more terrified if she had seen a ghost. But Mrs. Delany came forward to pay her duty to her royal friend, and the disturbance was quieted. Frances was then presented, and underwent a long examination and cross-examination about all that she had written and all that she meant to write. The Queen soon made her appearance, and his Majesty repeated, for the benefit of his consort, the information which he had extracted from Miss Burney. The good nature of the royal pair might have softened even the authors of the "Probationary Odes," and could not but be delightful to a young lady who had been brought up a Tory. In a few days the visit was repeated. Miss Burney was more at ease than before. His Majesty, instead of seeking for information, condescended to impart it, and passed sentence on many great writers, English and foreign. Voltaire he pronounced a monster. Rosseau he liked rather better. "But was there ever," he cried, "such stuff as great part of Shakspeare? Only one must not say so. But what think you? What? Is there not sad stuff? What? What?"

The next day Frances enjoyed the privilege of listening to some equally valuable criticism uttered by the Queen touching Goethe and Klopstock, and might have learned an important lesson of economy from the mode in which her Majesty's library had been formed. "I picked the book up on a stall," said the Queen. "Oh, it is amazing what good books there are on stalls!" Mrs. Delany, who seems to have understood from these words that her Majesty was in the habit of exploring the booths of Moorfields and Holywell Street in person, could not suppress an exclamation of surprise. "Why," said the Queen, "I don't pick them up myself. But I have a servant very clever; and if they are not to be had at the booksellers, they are not for me more than for another." Miss Burney describes this conversation as delightful; and, indeed, we cannot wonder that, with her literary tastes, she should be delighted at hearing in how magnificent a manner the greatest lady in the land encouraged literature.

The truth is, that Frances was fascinated by the condescending kindness of the two great personages to whom she had been presented. Her father was even more infatuated than herself. The result was a step of which we cannot think with patience, but which, recorded as it is with all its consequences in these volumes, deserves at least this praise, that it has furnished a most impressive warning.

A German lady of the name of Haggerdorn, one of the keepers of the Queen's robes, retired about this time, and her Majesty offered the vacant post to Miss Burney. When we consider that Miss Burney was decidedly the most popular writer of fictitious narrative then living, that competence, if not opulence, was within her reach, and that she was more than usually happy in her domestic circle, and when we compare the sacrifice which she was invited to make with the remuneration which was held out to her, we are divided between laughter and indignation.

What was demanded of her was that she should consent to be almost as completely separated from her family and friends as if she had gone to Calcutta, and almost as close a prisoner as if she had been sent to gaol for a libel; that with talents which had instructed and delighted the highest living minds, she should now be employed only in mixing snuff and sticking pins; that she should be summoned by a waiting-woman's bell to a waiting-woman's duties; that she should pass her whole life under the restraints of a paltry etiquette, should sometimes fast till she was ready to swoon with hunger, should sometimes stand till her knees gave way with fatigue; that she should not dare to speak or move without considering how her mistress might like her words and gestures. Instead of those distinguished men and women, the flower of all political parties, with whom she had been in the habit of mixing on terms of equal friendship, she was to have for her perpetual companion the chief keeper of the robes, an old hag from Germany, of mean understanding, of insolent manners, and of temper which, naturally savage, had now been exasperated by disease. Now and then, indeed, poor Frances might console herself for the loss of Burke's and Windham's society by joining in the "celestial colloquy sublime" of his Majesty's Equerries.

And what was the consideration for which she was to sell herself to this slavery? A peerage in her own right? A pension of two thousand a-year for life? A seventy-four for her brother in the navy? A deanery for her brother in the church? Not so. The price at which she was valued was her board, her lodging, the attendance of a man-servant and two hundred pounds a-year.

The man, who, even when hard pressed by hunger, sells his birthright for a mess of pottage, is unwise. But what shall we say of him who parts with his birthright and does not get even the pottage in return? It is not necessary to inquire whether oppulence be an adequate compensation for the sacrifice of bodily and mental freedom; for Frances Burney paid for leave to be a prisoner and a menial. It was evidently understood as one of the terms of her engagement, that, while she was a member of the royal household, she was not to appear before the public as an author; and, even had there been no such understanding, her avocations were such as left her no leisure for any considerable intellectual effort. That her place was incompatible with her literary pursuits was indeed frankly acknowledged by the King when she resigned. "She had given up," he said, "five years of her pen." That during those five years she might, without painful exertion, without any exertion that would not have been a pleasure, have earned enough to buy an annuity for life much larger than the precarious salary which she received at court, is quite certain. The same income, too, which in Saint Martin's Street would have afforded her every comfort, must have been found scanty at St. James's. We cannot venture to speak confidently of the price of millinery and jewellery; but we are greatly deceived if a lady, who had to attend Queen Charlotte on many public occasions, could possibly save a farthing out of a salary of two hundred a-year. The principle of the arrangement was, in short, simply this, that Frances Burney should become a slave and should be rewarded by being made a beggar.

With what object their Majesties brought her to their palace, we must own ourselves unable to conceive. Their object could not be to encourage her literary exertions; for they took her from a situation in which it was almost certain that she would write and put her into a situation in which it was impossible for her to write. Their object could not be to promote her pecuniary interest; for they took her from a situation where she was likely to become rich and put her into a situation in which she could not but continue poor. Their object could not be to obtain an eminently useful waiting-maid; for it is clear that, though Miss Burney was the only woman of her time who could have described the death of Harrel, thousands might have been found more expert in tying ribands and filling snuff-boxes. To grant her a pension on the civil list would have been an act of judicious liberality honourable to the court. If this was impracticable the next best thing was to let her alone. That the King and Queen meant her nothing but kindness, we do not in the least doubt. But their kindness was the kindness of persons raised high above the mass of mankind, accustomed to be addressed with profound deference, accustomed to see all who approach them mortified by their coldness and elated by their smiles. They fancied that to be noticed by them, to be near them, to serve them, was in itself a kind of happiness; and that Frances Burney ought to be full of gratitude for being permitted to purchase, by the surrender of health, wealth, freedom, domestic affection and literary fame, the privilege of standing behind a royal chair and holding a pair of royal gloves.

And who can blame them? Who can wonder that princes should be under such a delusion when they are encouraged in it by the very persons who suffer from it most cruelly? Was it to be expected that George III. and Queen Charlotte should understand the interest of Frances Burney better, or promote it with more zeal, than herself and her father? No deception was practised,

The conditions of the house of bondage were set forth with all simplicity. The hook was presented without a bait; the net was spread in sight of the bird, and the naked hook was greedily swallowed and the silly bird made haste to entangle herself in the net.

It is not strange indeed that an invitation to court should have caused a fluttering in the bosom of an inexperienced woman. But it was the duty of the parent to watch over the child, and to show her that on one side were only infantine vanities and chimerical hopes, on the other, liberty, peace of mind, affluence, social enjoyments, honourable distinctions. Strange to say, the only hesitation was on the part of Frances. Dr. Burney was transported out of himself with delight. Not such are the raptures of a Circassian father who has sold his pretty daughter well to a Turkish slave merchant. Yet Dr. Burney was an amiable man, a man of good abilities, a man who had seen much of the world. But he seems to have thought that going to court was like going to heaven; that to see princes and princesses was a kind of beatific vision; that the exquisite felicity enjoyed by royal persons was not confined to themselves, but was communicated by some mysterious efflux or reflection to all who were suffered to stand at their toilettes or to bear their trains. He overruled all his daughter's objections, and himself escorted her to prison. The door closed. The key was turned. She, looking back with tender regret on all she had left, and forward with anxiety and terror to the new life on which she was entering, was unable to speak or stand; and he went on his way homeward rejoicing in her marvellous prosperity.

And now began a slavery of five years, of five years taken from the best part of life and wasted in menial drudgery or in recreations duller than even menial drudgery, under galling restraints and amidst unfriendly or uninteresting companions. The history of an ordinary day was this: Miss Burney had to rise and dress herself early, that she might be ready to answer the royal bell, which rang at half after seven. Till about eight she attended in the Queen's dressing-room, and had the honour of lacing her august mistress's stays, and of putting on the hoop, gown and neckhandkerchief. The morning was chiefly spent in rummaging drawers and laying fine clothes in their proper places. Then the Queen was to be powdered and dressed for the day. Twice a week her Majesty's hair was curled and craped; and this operation appears to have added a full hour to the business of the toilette. It was generally three before Miss Burney was at liberty. Then she had two hours at her own disposal. To these hours we owe great part of her "Diary." At five she had to attend her colleague, Madame Schwellenberg, a hateful old toadeater, as illiterate as a chambermaid, as proud as a whole German Chapter, rude, peevish, unable to bear solitude, unable to conduct herself with common decency in society. With this delightful associate, Frances Burney had to dine and pass the evening. The pair generally remained together from five to eleven, and often had no other company the whole time, except during the hour from eight to nine, when the equerries came to tea. If poor Frances attempted to escape to her own apartment, and to forget her wretchedness over a book, the execrable old woman railed and stormed, and complained that she was neglected. Yet, when Frances stayed, she was constantly assailed with insolent reproaches. Literary fame was, in the eyes of the German crone, a blemish, a proof that the person who enjoyed it was meanly born and out of the pale of good society. All her scanty stock of broken English was employed to express the contempt with which she regarded the author of "Evelina" and "Cecilia." Frances detested cards, and indeed knew nothing about them; but she soon found that the least miserable way of passing an evening with Madame Schwellenberg was at the card-table, and consented, with patient sadness, to give hours which might have called forth the laughter and the tears of many generations to the king of clubs and the knave of spades. Between eleven and twelve, the bell rang again. Miss Burney had to pass twenty minutes or half an hour in undressing the Queen, and was then at liberty to retire and to dream that she was chatting with her brother by the quiet hearth in Saint Martin's Street, that she was the centre of an admiring assembly at Mrs. Crewe's, that Burke was calling her the first woman of the age, or that Dilly was giving her a cheque for two thousand guineas.

Men, we must suppose, are less patient than women; for we are utterly at a loss to conceive how any human being could endure such a life while there remained a vacant garrett in Grub Street, a crossing in want of a sweeper, a parish workhouse or a parish vault. And it was for such a life that Frances Burney had given up liberty and peace, a happy fireside, attached friends, a wide and splendid circle of acquaintance, intellectual pursuits, in which she was qualified to excel, and the sure hope of what to her would have been affluence.

There is nothing new under the sun. The last great master of Attic eloquence and Attic wit has left us a forcible and touching description of the misery of a man of letters, who, lulled by hopes similar to those of Frances, had entered the service of one of the magnates of Rome. "Unhappy that I am," cries the victim of his own childish ambition: "would nothing content me but that I must leave mine old pursuits and mine old companions, and the life which was without care, and the sleep which had no limit save mine own pleasure, and the walks which I was free to take where I listed, and fling myself into the lowest pit of a dungeon like this? And, O God! for what? Is this the bait which enticed me? Was there no way by which I might have enjoyed in freedom comforts even greater than those which I now earn by servitude? Like a lion which has been made so tame that men may lead him about by a thread, I am dragged up and down, with broken and humbled spirit, at the heels of those to whom, in my own domain, I should have been an object of awe and wonder. And, worst of all, I feel that here I gain no credit, that here I give no pleasure. The talents and accomplishments, which charmed a far different circle, are here out of place. I am rude in the arts of palaces, and can ill bear comparison with those whose calling from their youth up has been to flatter and to sue. Have I then, two lives, that, after I have wasted one in the service of others, there may yet remain to me a second, which I may live unto myself?"

Now and then, indeed, events occurred which disturbed the wretched monotony of Frances Burney's life. The court moved from Kew to Windsor, and from Windsor back to Kew. One dull colonel went out of waiting, and another dull colonel came into waiting. An impertinent servant made a blunder about tea, and caused a misunderstanding between the gentlemen and the ladies. A half-witted French Protestant minister talked oddly about conjugal fidelity. An unlucky member of the household mentioned a passage in the *Morning Herald* reflecting on the Queen; and forthwith Madame Schwellenberg began to storm in bad English, and told him that he had made her "what you call perspire!"

A more important occurrence was the royal visit to Oxford. Miss Burney went in the Queen's train to Nuneham, was utterly neglected there in the crowd, and could with difficulty find a servant to show the way to her bedroom or a hairdresser to arrange her curls. She had the honour of entering Oxford in the last of a long string of carriages which formed the royal procession, of walking after the Queen all day through refectories and chapels, and of standing, half dead with fatigue and hunger, while her august mistress was seated at an excellent cold collation. At Magdalene College, Frances was left for a moment in a parlour, where she sank down on a chair. A good-natured equerry saw that she was exhausted, and shared with her some apricots and bread which he had wisely put into his pockets. At that moment, the door opened; the Queen entered; the wearied attendants sprang up; the bread and fruit were hastily concealed. "I found," says poor Miss Burney, "that our appetites were to be supposed annihilated at the same moment that our strength was to be invincible."

Yet Oxford, seen even under such disadvantages, "revived in her," to use her own words, a "consciousness to pleasure which had long lain nearly dormant." She forgot, during one moment, that she was a waiting-maid, and felt as a woman of true genius might be expected to feel amidst venerable remains of antiquity, beautiful works of art, vast repositories of knowledge, and memorials of the illustrious dead. Had she still been what she was before her father induced her to take the most fatal step of her life, we can easily imagine what pleasure she would have derived from a visit to the noblest of English cities. She might, indeed, have been forced to travel in a hack chaise, and might not have worn so fine a gown of Chambery gauze as that in which she tottered after the royal party; but with what delight would she have then paced the cloisters of Magdalene, compared the antique gloom of Merton with the splendour of Christ Church, and looked down from the dome of the Radcliffe Library on the magnificent sea of turrets and battlements below! How gladly would learned men have laid aside for a few hours Pindar's "Odes" and Aristotle's "Ethics," to escort the author of "Cecilia" from college to college! What neat little banquets would she have found set out in their monastic cells! With what eagerness would pictures, medals and illuminated missals have been brought forth from the most mysterious cabinets for her amusement! How much she would have had to hear and to tell about Johnson, as she walked over Pembroke, and about Reynolds, in the antechapel of New College. But these indulgences were not for one who had sold herself into bondage.

About eighteen months after the visit to Oxford, another event diversified the wearisome life which Frances led at Court. Warren Hastings was brought to the bar of the House of Peers. The Queen and Princesses were present when the trial commenced, and Miss Burney was permitted to attend. During the subsequent proceedings, a day rule for the same purpose was occasionally granted to her; for the Queen took the strongest interest in the trial, and, when she could not go herself to Westminster Hall, liked to receive a report of what passed from a person who had singular powers of observation, and who was, moreover, personally acquainted with some of the most distinguished managers. The portion of the "Diary" which relates to this celebrated proceeding is lively and picturesque. Yet we read it, we own, with pain; for it seems to us to prove that the fine understanding of Frances Burney was beginning to feel the pernicious influence of a mode of life which is as incompatible with health of mind as the air of the Pomptine marshes with health of body. From the first day, she espouses the cause of Hastings with a presumptuous vehemence and acrimony quite inconsistent with the modesty and suavity of her ordinary deportment. She shudders when Burke enters the Hall at the head of the Commons. She pronounces him the cruel oppressor of an innocent man. She is at a loss to conceive how the managers can look at the defendant and not blush. Windham comes to her from the manager's box, to offer her refreshment. "But," says she, "I could not break bread with him." Then again, she exclaims, "Ah, Mr. Windham, how come you ever engaged in so cruel, so unjust a cause?" "Mr. Burke saw me," she says, "and he bowed with the most marked civility of manner." This, be it observed, was just after his opening speech, a speech which had produced a mighty effect, and which, certainly, no other orator that ever lived could have made. "My curtsy," she continues, "was the most ungrateful, distant and cold; I could not do otherwise; so hurt I felt to see him the head of such a cause." Now, not only had Burke treated her with constant kindness, but the very last act which he performed on the day on which he was turned out of the Pay Office, about four years before this trial, was to make Dr. Burney organist of Chelsea Hospital. When, at the Westminster election, Dr. Burney was divided between his gratitude for this favour and his Tory opinions, Burke in the noblest manner disclaimed all right to exact a sacrifice of principle. "You have little or no obligations to me," he wrote; "but if you had as many as I really wish it were in my power, as it is certainly in my desire, to lay on you, I hope you do not think me capable of conferring them in order to subject your mind or your affairs to a painful and mischievous servitude." Was this a man to be uncivilly treated by a daughter of Dr. Burney because she choose to differ from him respecting a vast and most complicated question which he had studied deeply during many years and which she had never studied at all? It is clear, from Miss Burney's own statement, that when she behaved so unkindly to Mr. Burke, she did not even know of what Hastings was accused. One thing, however, she must have known, that Burke had been able to convince a House of Commons, bitterly prejudiced against him, that the charges were well founded, and that Pitt and Dundas had concurred with Fox and Sheridan in supporting the impeachment. Surely a woman of far inferior abilities to Miss Burney might have been expected to see that this never could have happened unless there had been a strong case against the late Governor General. And there was, as all reasonable men now admit, a strong case against him. That there were great public services to be set off against his great crimes is perfectly true. But his services and his crimes were equally unknown to the lady who so confidently asserted his perfect innocence, and imputed to his accusers—that is to say, to all the greatest men of all parties in the state—not merely error, but gross injustice and barbarity.

She had, it is true, occasionally seen Mr. Hastings, and had found his manners and conversation agreeable. But surely she could not be so weak as to infer from the gentleness of his deportment in a drawing-room that he was incapable of committing a great state crime under the influence of ambition and revenge. A silly Miss, fresh from a boarding school, might fall into such a mistake; but the woman who had drawn the character of Mr. Monckton should have known better.

The truth is that she had been too long at Court. She was sinking into a slavery worse than that of the body. The iron was beginning to enter into the soul. Accustomed during many months to watch the eye of a mistress, to receive with boundless gratitude the slightest mark of royal condescension, to feel wretched at every symptom of royal displeasure, to associate only with spirits long tamed and broken in, she was degenerating into something fit for her place. Queen Charlotte was a violent partisan of Hastings, had received presents from him, and had so far departed from the severity of her virtue as to lend her countenance to his wife, whose conduct had certainly been as reprehensible as that of any of the frail beauties who were then rigidly excluded from the English Court. The King, it was well known, took the same side. To the King and Queen, all the members of the household looked submissively for guidance. The impeachment, therefore, was an atrocious persecution; the managers were rascals; the defendant was the most deserving and the worst used man in the kingdom. This was the cant of the whole palace, from Gold Stick in Waiting down to the Table-Deckers and

Yeoman of the Silver Scullery; and Miss Burney canted like the rest, though in livelier tones and with less bitter feelings.

The account which she has given of the King's illness contains much excellent narrative and description, and will, we think, be more valued by the historians of a future age than any equal portion of Pepys' or Evelyn's "Diaries." That account shows also how affectionate and compassionate her nature was. But it shows also, we must say, that her way of life was rapidly impairing her powers of reasoning and her sense of justice. We do not mean to discuss, in this place, the question, whether the views of Mr. Pitt or those of Mr. Fox respecting the regency were the more correct. It is, indeed, quite needless to discuss that question; for the censure of Miss Burney falls alike on Pitt and Fox, on majority and minority. She is angry with the House of Commons for presuming to inquire whether the King was mad or not, and whether there was a chance of his recovering his senses. "A melancholy day," she writes; "news bad both at home and abroad. At home the dear unhappy king still worse: abroad new examinations voted of the physicians. Good heavens! what an insult does this seem from Parliamentary power, to investigate and bring forth to the world every circumstance of such a malady as is ever held sacred to secresy in the most private families! How indignant we all feel here, no words can say." It is proper to observe that the motion which roused the indignation at Kew was made by Mr. Pitt himself, and that if withstood by Mr Pitt, it would certainly have been rejected. We see, therefore, that the loyalty of the minister, who was then generally regarded as the most heroic champion of his Prince, was lukewarm indeed when compared with the boiling zeal which filled the pages of the backstairs and the women of the bedchamber. Of the Regency Bill, Pitt's own bill, Miss Burney speaks with horror. "I shuddered," she says "to hear it named." And again, "Oh, how dreadful will be the day when that unhappy bill takes place! I cannot approve the plan of it." The truth is that Mr. Pitt, whether a wise and upright statesman or not, was a statesman, and, whatever motives he might have for imposing restrictions on the regent, felt that in some way or other there must be some provision made for the execution of some part of the kingly office or that no government would be left in the country. But this was a matter of which the household never thought. It never occurred, as far as we can see, to the Exons and Keepers of the Robes, that it was necessary that there should be somewhere or other a power in the state to pass laws, to observe order, to pardon criminals, to fill up offices, to negotiate with foreign governments, to command the army and navy. Nay, these enlightened politicians, and Miss Burney among the rest, seem to have thought that any person who considered the subject with reference to the public interest showed himself to be a badhearted man. Nobody wonders at this in a gentleman usher, but it is melancholy to see genius sinking into such debasement.

During more than two years after the King's recovery, Frances dragged on a miserable existence at the palace. The consolations which had for a time mitigated the wretchedness of servitude were one by one withdrawn. Mrs. Delany, whose society had been a great resource when the Court was at Windsor, was now dead. One of the gentlemen of the royal establishment, Colonel Digby, appears to have been a man of sense, of taste, of some reading, and of prepossessing manners. Agreeable associates were scarce in the prison house, and he and Miss Burney therefore naturally were attached to each other. She owns that she valued him as a friend, and it would not have been strange if his attentions had led her to entertain for him a sentiment warmer than friendship. He quitted the Court, and married in a way which astonished Miss Burney greatly, and which evidently wounded her feelings and lowered him in her esteem. The palace grew duller and duller; Madame Schwellenberg became more and more savage and insolent; and now the health of poor Frances began to give way; and all who saw her pale face, her emaciated figure and her feeble walk predicted that her sufferings would soon be over.

Frances uniformly speaks of her royal mistress and of the princesses with respect and affection. The princesses seem to have well deserved all the praise which is bestowed on them in the "Diary." They were, we doubt not, most amiable women. But "the sweet Queen," as she is constantly called in these volumes, is not by any means an object of admiration to us. She had, undoubtedly, sense enough to know what kind of deportment suited her high station and self-command enough to maintain that deportment invariably. She was, in her intercourse with Miss Burney, generally gracious and affable, sometimes, when displeased, cold and reserved, but never, under any circumstances, rude, peevish or violent. She knew how to dispense, gracefully and skilfully, those little civilities which, when paid by a sovereign, are prized at many times their intrinsic value; how to pay a compliment; how to lend a book; how to ask after a relation. But she seems to have been utterly regardless of the comfort, the health, the life of her attendants, when her own convenience was concerned. Weak, feverish, hardly able to stand, Frances had still to rise before seven, in order to dress "the sweet Queen," and to sit up till midnight, in order to undress "the sweet Queen." The indisposition of the handmaid could not, and did not, escape the notice of her royal mistress. But the established doctrine of the Court was that all sickness was to be considered as a pretence until it proved fatal. The only way in which the invalid could clear herself from the suspicion of malingering, as it is called in the army, was to go on lacing and unlacing, till she fell down dead at the royal feet. "This," Miss Burney wrote, when she was suffering cruelly from sickness, watching and labour, "is by no means from hardness of heart; far otherwise. There is no hardness of heart in any one of them; but it is prejudice and want of personal experience."

Many strangers sympathised with the bodily and mental sufferings of this distinguished woman. All who saw her saw that her frame was sinking, that her heart was breaking. The last, it should seem, to observe the change was her father. At length, in spite of himself, his eyes were opened. In May, 1790, his daughter had an interview of three hours with him, the only long interview which they had had since he took her to Windsor in 1786. She told him that she was miserable, that she was worn with attendance and want of sleep, that she had no comfort in life, nothing to love, nothing to hope, that her family and friends were to her as though they were not, and were remembered by her as men remember the dead. From daybreak to midnight the same killing labour, the same recreations, more hateful than labour itself, followed each other without variety, without any interval of liberty and repose.

The Doctor was greatly dejected by this news; but was too goodnatured a man not to say that, if she wished to resign, his house and arms were open to her. Still, however, he could not bear to remove her from the Court. His veneration for royalty amounted in truth to idolatry. It can be compared only to the grovelling superstition of those Syrian devotees who made their children pass through the fire to Moloch. When he induced his daughter to accept the place of Keeper of the Robes, he entertained, as she tells us, a hope that some worldly advantage or other, not set down in the contract of service, would be the result of her connection with the Court. What advantage he expected we do not know, nor did he probably know himself. But, whatever he expected, he certainly got nothing. Miss Burney had been hired for board, lodging and two hundred a-year. Board, lodging and two hundred a-year she had duly received. We have looked carefully through the "Diary", in the hope of finding some trace of those extraordinary benefactions on which the Doctor reckoned. But we can discover only a promise, never performed, of a gown: and for this promise Miss Burney was expected to return thanks, such as might have suited the beggar with whom Saint Martin, in the legend, divided his cloak. The experience of four years was, however, insufficient to dispel the illusion which had taken possession of the Doctor's mind; and between the dear father and "the sweet Queen" there seemed to be little doubt that some day or other Frances would drop down a corpse. Six months had elapsed since the interview between the parent and the daughter. The resignation was not sent in. The sufferer grew worse and worse. She took bark; but it soon ceased to produce a beneficial effect. She was stimulated with wine; she was soothed with opium; but in vain. Her breath began to fail. The whisper that she was in a decline spread through the Court. The pains in her side became so severe that she was forced to crawl from the card-table of the old Fury to whom she was tethered three or four times in an evening for the purpose of taking hartshorn. Had she been a negro slave, a humane planter would have excused her from work. But her Majesty showed no mercy. Thrice a day the accursed bell still rang; the Queen was still to be dressed for the morning at seven, and to be dressed for the day at noon, and to be undressed at eleven at night.

But there had arisen, in literary and fashionable society, a general feeling of compassion for Miss Burney, and of indignation against both her father and the Queen. "Is it possible," said a great French lady to the Doctor, "that your daughter is in a situation where she is never allowed a holiday?" Horace Walpole wrote to Frances to express his sympathy. Boswell, boiling over with good-natured rage, almost forced an entrance into the palace to see her. "My dear ma'am, why do you stay? It won't do, ma'am; you must resign. We can put up with it no longer. Some very violent measures, I assure you, will be taken. We shall address Dr. Burney in a body." Burke and Reynolds, though less noisy, were zealous in the same cause. Windham spoke to Dr. Burney; but found him still irresolute. "I will set the club upon him," cried Windham; "Miss Burney has some very true admirers there, and I am sure they will eagerly assist." Indeed, the Burney family seem to have been apprehensive that some public affront, such as the Doctor's unpardonable folly, to use the mildest term, had richly deserved, would be put upon him. The medical men spoke out, and plainly told him that his daughter must resign or die.

At last paternal affection, medical authority, and the voice of all London crying shame, triumphed over Dr. Burney's love of courts. He determined that Frances should write a letter of resignation. It was with difficulty that, though her life was at stake, she mustered spirit to put the paper into the Queen's hands. "I could not," so runs the "Diary," "summon courage to present my memorial—my heart always failed me from seeing the Queen's entire freedom from such an expectation. For though I was frequently so ill in her presence that I could hardly stand, I saw she concluded me, while life remained, inevitably hers."

At last, with a trembling hand, the paper was delivered. Then came the storm. Juno, as in the Æneid, delegated the work of vengeance to Alecto. The Queen was calm and gentle; but Madame Schwellenberg raved like a maniac in the incurable ward of Bedlam! Such insolence! Such ingratitude! Such folly! Would Miss Burney bring utter destruction on herself and her family? Would she throw away the inestimable advantages of royal protection? Would she part with privileges which, once relinquished, could never be regained? It was idle to talk of health and life. If people could not live in the palace, the best thing that could befall them was to die in it. The resignation was not accepted. The language of the medical men became stronger and stronger. Dr. Burney's parental fears were fully roused; and he explicitly declared, in a letter meant to be shown to the Queen, that his daughter must retire. The Schwellenberg raged like a wild cat. "A scene almost horrible ensued," says Miss Burney. "She was too much enraged for disguise, and uttered the most furious expressions of indignant contempt at our proceedings. I am sure she would gladly have confined us both in the Bastille, had England such a misery, as a fit place to bring us to ourselves, from a daring so outrageous against imperial wishes." This passage deserves notice, as being the only one in the "Diary," as far as we have observed, which shows Miss Burney to have been aware that she was a native of a free country, that she could not be pressed for a waiting-maid against her will, and that she had just as good a right to live, if she chose, in Saint Martin's Street as Queen Charlotte had to live at St. James's.

The Queen promised that, after the next birthday, Miss Burney should be set at liberty. But the promise was ill kept; and her Majesty showed displeasure at being reminded of it. At length Frances was informed that in a fortnight her attendance should cease. "I heard this," she says, "with a fearful presentiment I should surely never go through another fortnight in so weak and languishing and painful a state of health. . . . As the time of separation approached, the Queen's cordiality rather diminished, and traces of internal displeasure appeared sometimes, arising from an opinion I ought rather to have struggled on, live or die, than to quit her. Yet I am sure she saw how poor was my own chance, except by a change in the mode of life, and at least ceased to wonder, though she could not approve." Sweet Queen! What noble candour, to admit that the undutifulness of people who did not think the honour of adjusting her tuckers worth the sacrifice of their own lives, was, though highly criminal, not altogether unnatural!

We perfectly understand her Majesty's contempt for the lives of others where her own pleasure was concerned. But what pleasure she can have found in having Miss Burney about her, it is not so easy to comprehend. That Miss Burney was an eminently skilful keeper of the robes is not very probable. Few women, indeed, had paid less attention to dress. Now and then, in the course of five years, she had been asked to read aloud or to write a copy of verses. But better readers might easily have been found: and her verses were worse than even the Poet Laureate's Birthday Odes. Perhaps that economy, which was among her Majesty's most conspicuous virtues, had something to do with her conduct on this occasion. Miss Burney had never hinted that she expected a retiring pension; and, indeed, would gladly have given the little that she had for freedom. But her Majesty knew what the public thought, and what became her own dignity. She could not for very shame suffer a woman of distinguished genius, who had quitted a lucrative career to wait on her, who had served her faithfully for a pittance during five years, and whose constitution had been impaired by labour and watching, to leave the Court without some mark of royal liberality. George the Third, who, on all occasions where Miss Burney was concerned, seems to have behaved like an honest, good-natured gentleman, felt this, and said plainly that she was entitled to a provision. At length, in return for all the misery which she had undergone, and for the health which she had sacrificed, an annuity of one hundred pounds was granted to her, dependent on the Queen's pleasure.

Then the prison was opened, and Frances was free once more. Johnson, as Burke observed, might have added a striking page to his poem on the Vanity of Human Wishes, if he had lived to see his little Burney as she went into the palace and as she came out of it.

The pleasures, so long untasted, of liberty, of friendship, of domestic affection, were almost too acute for her shattered frame. But happy days and tranquil nights soon restored the health which the Queen's toilette and Madame Schwellenberg's card-table had impaired. Kind and anxious faces surrounded the invalid. Conversation the most polished and brilliant revived her spirits. Travelling was recommended to her; and she rambled by easy journeys from cathedral to cathedral, and from watering place to watering place. She crossed the New Forest, and visited Stonehenge and Wilton, the cliffs of Lyme, and the beautiful valley of Sidmouth. Thence she journeyed by Powderham Castle, and by the ruins of Glastonbury Abbey to Bath, and from Bath, when the winter was approaching, returned well and cheerful to London. There she visited her old dungeon, and found her successor already far on the way to the grave, and kept to strict duty, from morning till midnight, with a sprained ankle and a nervous fever.

At this time England swarmed with French exiles, driven from their country by the Revolution. A colony of these refugees settled at Juniper Hall, in Surrey, not far from Norbury Park, where Mr. Lock, an intimate friend of the Burney family, resided. Frances visited Norbury, and was introduced to the strangers. She had strong prejudices against them ; for her Toryism was far beyond, we do not say that of Mr. Pitt, but that of Mr. Reeves ; and the inmates of Juniper Hall were all attached to the constitution of 1791, and were, therefore, more detested by the royalists of the first emigration than Petion or Marat. But such a woman as Miss Burney could not long resist the fascination of that remarkable society. She had lived with Johnson and Windham, with Mrs. Montague and Mrs. Thrale. Yet she was forced to own that she had never heard conversation before. The most animated eloquence, the keenest observation, the most sparkling wit, the most courtly grace, were united to charm her. For Madame de Staël was there, and M. de Talleyrand. There, too, was M. de Narbonne, a noble representative of French aristocracy ; and with M. de Narbonne was his friend and follower General D'Arblay, an honourable and amiable man, with a handsome person, frank soldierlike manners, and some taste for letters.

The prejudices which Frances had conceived against the constitutional royalists of France rapidly vanished. She listened with rapture to Talleyrand and Madame de Staël, joined with M. D'Arblay in execrating the Jacobins and in weeping for the unhappy Bourbons, took French lessons from him, fell in love with him, and married him on no better provision than a precarious annuity of one hundred pounds.

Here the "Diary" stops for the present. We will, therefore, bring our narrative to a speedy close, by rapidly recounting the most important events which we know to have befallen Madame D'Arblay during the latter part of her life.

M. D'Arblay's fortune had perished in the general wreck of the French Revolution ; and in a foreign country his talents, whatever they may have been, could scarcely make him rich. The task of providing for the family devolved on his wife. In the year 1796, she published by subscription her third novel, "Camila." It was impatiently expected by the public; and the sum which she obtained for it was, we believe, greater than had ever at that time been received for a novel. We have heard that she had cleared more than three thousand guineas. But we give this merely as a rumour. "Camilla," however, never attained popularity like that which "Evelina" and "Cecilia" had enjoyed; and it must be allowed that there was a perceptible falling off, not, indeed, in humour or in power or portraying character, but in grace and in purity of style.

We have heard that, about this time, a tragedy by Madame D'Arblay was performed without success. We do not know whether it was ever printed; nor, indeed, have we had time to make any researches into its history or merits.

During the short truce which followed the treaty of Amiens, M. D'Arblay visited France. Lauriston and La Fayette represented his claims to the French government, and obtained a promise that he should be reinstated in his military rank. M. D'Arblay, however, insisted that he should never be required to serve against the countrymen of his wife. The First Consul, of course, would not hear of such a condition, and ordered the general's commission to be instantly revoked.

Madame D'Arblay joined her husband at Paris, a short time before the war of 1803 broke out, and remained in France ten years, cut off from almost all intercourse with the land of her birth. At length, when Napoleon was on his march to Moscow, she with great difficulty obtained from his ministers permission to visit her own country, in company with her son, who was a native of England. She returned in time to receive the last blessing of her father, who died in his eighty-seventh year. In 1814 she published her last novel, "The Wanderer," a book which no judicious friend to her memory will attempt to draw from the oblivion into which it has justly fallen. In the same year her son Alexander was sent to Cambridge. He obtained an honourable place among the wranglers of his year, and was elected a fellow of Christ's College. But his reputation at the University was higher than might be inferred from his success in academical contests. His French education had not fitted him for the examinations of the Senate House; but, in pure mathematics, we have been assured by some of his competitors that he had very few equals. He went into the Church, and it was thought likely that he would attain high eminence as a preacher; but he died before his mother. All that we have heard of him leads us to believe that he was such a son as such a mother deserved to have. In 1832, Madame D'Arblay published the "Memoirs of her Father;" and on the sixth of January, 1840, she died in her eighty-eighth year.

We now turn from the life of Madame D'Arblay to her writings. There can, we apprehend, be little difference of opinion as to the nature of her merit, whatever differences may exist as to its degree. She was emphatically what Johnson called her, a character-monger. It was in the exhibition of human passions and whims that her strength lay; and in this department of art she had, we think, very distinguished skill.

But, in order that we may, according to our duty as kings at arms, versed in the laws of literary precedence, marshal her to the exact seat to which she is entitled, we must carry our examination somewhat further.

There is, in one respect, a remarkable analogy between the faces and the minds of men. No two faces are alike; and yet very few faces deviate very widely from the common standard. Among the eighteen hundred thousand human beings who inhabit London, there is not one who could be taken by his acquaintance for another; yet we may walk from Paddington to Mile End without seeing one person in whom any feature is so overcharged that we turn round to stare at it. An infinite number of varieties lies between limits which are not very far asunder. The specimens which pass those limits on either side, form a very small minority.

It is the same with the characters of men. Here, too, the variety passes all enumeration. But the cases in which the deviation from the common standard is striking and grotesque, are very few. In one mind avarice predominates; in another pride; in a third, love of pleasure—just as in one countenance, the nose is the most marked feature, while in others the chief expression lies in the brow, or in the lines of the mouth. But there are very few countenances in which nose, brow and mouth do not contribute, though in unequal degrees, to the general effect; and so there are very few characters in which one overgrown propensity makes all others utterly insignificant.

It is evident that a portrait painter, who was able only to represent faces and figures such as those which we pay money to see at fairs, would not, however spirited his execution might be, take rank among the highest artists. He must always be placed below those who have skill to seize peculiarities which do not amount to deformity. The slighter those peculiarities, the greater is the merit of the limner who can catch them and transfer them to his canvass. To paint Daniel Lambert or the living skeleton, the pig-faced lady or the Siamese twins, so that nobody can mistake them, is an exploit within the reach of a sign painter. A third-rate artist might give us the squint of Wilkes, and the depressed nose and protuberent cheeks of Gibbon. It would require a much higher degree of skill to paint two such men as Mr. Canning and Sir Thomas Lawrence, so that nobody who had ever seen them could for a moment hesitate to assign each picture to its original. Here the mere caricaturist would be quite at fault. He would find in neither face anything on which he could lay hold for the purpose of making a distinction. Two ample bald foreheads, two regular profiles, two full faces of the same oval form, would baffle his art; and he would be reduced to the miserable shift of writing their names at the foot of his picture. Yet there was a great difference; and a person who had seen them once would no more have mistaken one of them for the other than he would have mistaken Mr. Pitt for Mr. Fox. But the difference lay in delicate lineaments and shades, reserved for pencils of a rare order.

This distinction runs through all the imitative arts. Foote's mimicry was exquisitely ludicrous, but it was all caricature. He could take off only some strange peculiarity, a stammer or a lisp, a Northumbrian burr or an Irish brogue, a stoop or a shuffle. "If a man," said Johnson, "hops on one leg, Foote can hop on one leg." Garrick, on the other hand, could seize those differences of manner and pronunciation, which, though highly characteristic, are yet too slight to be described. Foote, we have no doubt, could have made the Haymarket theatre shake with laughter by imitating a conversation between a Scotchman and a Somersetshire man. But Garrick could have imitated a dialogue between two fashionable men, both models of the best breeding, Lord Chesterfield, for example, and Lord Albemarle, so that no person could doubt which was which, although no person could say that, in any point, either Lord Chesterfield or Lord Albemarle spoke or moved otherwise than in conformity with the usages of the best society.

The same distinction is found in the drama and in fictitious narrative. Highest among those who have exhibited human nature by means of dialogue, stands Shakspeare. His variety is like the variety of nature, endless diversity, scarcely any monstrosity. The characters of which he has given us an impression as vivid as that which we receive from the characters of our own associates, are to be reckoned by scores. Yet in all these scores hardly one character is to be found which deviates widely from the common standard, and which we should call very eccentric if we met it in real life. The silly notion that every man has one ruling passion, and that this clue, once known, unravels all the mysteries of his conduct, finds no countenance in the plays of Shakspeare. There man appears as he is, made up of a crowd of passions, which contend for the mastery over him, and govern him in turn. What is Hamlet's ruling passion? Or Othello's? Or Harry the Fifth's? Or Wolsey's? Or Lear's? Or Shylock's? Or Benedick's? Or Macbeth's? Or that of Cassius? Or that of Falconbridge? But we might go on for ever. Take a single example—Shylock. Is he so eager for money as to be indifferent to revenge? Or so eager for revenge as to be indifferent to money? Or so bent on both together as to be indifferent to the honour of his nation and the law of Moses? All his propensities are mingled with each other, so that, in trying to apportion to each its proper part, we find the same difficulty which constantly meets us in real life. A superficial critic may say that hatred is Shylock's ruling passion. But how many passions have amalgamated to form that hatred? It is partly the result of wounded pride: Antonio has called him dog. It is partly the result of covetousness: Antonio has hindered him of half a million; and, when Antonio is gone, there will be no limit to the gains of usury. It is partly the result of national and religious feeling; Antonio has spit on the Jewish gaberdine; and the oath of revenge has been sworn by the Jewish Sabbath. We might go through all the characters which we have mentioned, and through fifty more in the same way; for it is the constant manner of Shakspeare to represent the human mind as lying, not under the absolute dominion of one despotic propensity, but under a mixed government, in which a hundred powers balance each other. Admirable as he was in all parts of his art, we most admire him for this, that while he has left us a greater number of striking portraits than all other dramatists put together, he has scarcely left us a single caricature.

Shakspeare has had neither equal nor second. But among the writers who, in the point which we have noticed, have approached nearest to the manner of the great master, we have no hesitation in placing Jane Austen, a woman of whom England is justly proud. She has given us a multitude of characters, all, in a certain sense, common place, all such as we meet every day. Yet they are all as perfectly discriminated from each other as if they were the most eccentric of human beings. There are, for example, four clergymen, none of whom we should be surprised to find in any parsonage in the kingdom, Mr. Edward Ferrars, Mr. Henry Tilney, Mr. Edmund Bertram, and Mr. Elton. They are all specimens of the upper part of the middle class. They have all been liberally educated. They all lie under the restraints of the same sacred profession. They are all young. They are all in love. Not one of them has any hobbyhorse, to use the phrase of Sterne. Not one has a ruling passion, such as we read of in Pope. Who would not have expected them to be insipid likenesses of each other? No such thing. Harpagon is not more unlike to Jourdain, Joseph Surface is not more unlike to Sir Lucius O'Trigger, than every one of Miss Austen's young divines to all his reverend brethren. And almost all this is done by touches so delicate that they elude analysis, that they defy the powers of description, and that we know them to exist only by the general effect to which they have contributed.

A line must be drawn, we conceive, between artists of this class and those poets and novelists whose skill lies in the exhibiting of what Ben Jonson called humours. The words of Ben are so much to the purpose that we will quote them:—

> "When some one peculiar quality
> Doth so possess a man, that it doth draw
> All his affects, his spirits and his powers,
> In their confluxions all to run one way,
> This may be truly said to be a humour."

There are undoubtedly persons in whom humours such as Ben describes have attained a complete ascendency. The avarice of Elwes, the insane desire of Sir Egerton Brydges for a barony, to which he had no more right than to the crown of Spain, the malevolence which long meditation on imaginary wrongs generated in the gloomy mind of Bellingham, are instances. The feeling which animated Clarkson and other virtuous men against the slave trade and slavery, is an instance of a more honourable kind.

Seeing that such humours exist, we cannot deny that they are proper subjects for the imitations of art. But we conceive that the imitation of such humours, however skilful and amusing, is not an achievement of the highest order; and, as such humours are rare in real life, they ought, we conceive, to be sparingly introduced into works which profess to be pictures of real life. Nevertheless, a writer may show so much genius in the exhibition of these humours as to be fairly entitled to a distinguished and permanent rank among classics. The chief seats of all, however, the places on the dais and under the canopy, are reserved for the few who have excelled in the difficult art of portraying characters in which no single feature is extravagantly over-charged.

If we have expounded the law soundly, we can have no difficulty in applying it to the particular case before us. Madame D'Arblay has left us scarcely anything but humours. Almost every one of her men and women has some one propensity developed to a morbid degree. In "Cecilia," for example, Mr. Delville never open his lips without some allusion to his own birth and station; or Mr. Briggs, without some allusion to the hoarding of money; or Mr. Hobson, without betraying the self-indulgence and self-importance of a purse-proud upstart; or Mr. Simkins, without uttering some sneaking remark for the purpose of currying favour with his customers; or Mr. Meadows, without expressing apathy and weariness of life; or Mr. Albany, without declaiming about the vices of the rich and the misery of the poor; or Mrs. Belfield, without some indelicate eulogy on her son; or Lady Margaret, without indicating jealousy of her husband. Morrice is all skipping, officious impertinence, Mr. Gosport all sarcasm, Lady Honoria all lively prattle, Miss Larolles all silly prattle. If ever Madame D'Arblay aimed at more, as in the character of Monckton, we do not think that she succeeded well.

We are, therefore, forced to refuse to Madame D'Arblay a place in the highest rank of art; but we cannot deny that, in the rank to which she belonged, she had few equals and scarcely any superior. The variety of humours which is to be found in her novels is immense; and though the talk of each person separately is monotonous, the general effect is not monotony, but a very lively and agreeable diversity. Her plots are rudely constructed and improbable, if we consider them in themselves. But they are admirably framed for the purpose of exhibiting striking groups of eccentric characters, each governed by his own peculiar whim, each talking his own peculiar jargon, and each bringing out by opposition the oddities of all the rest. We will give one example out of many which occur to us. All probability is violated in order to bring Mr. Delville, Mr. Briggs, Mr. Hobson and Mr. Albany into a room together. But when we have them there, we soon forget probability in the exquisitely ludicrous effect which is produced by the conflict of four old fools, each raging with a monomania of his own, each talking a dialect of his own, and each inflaming all the others anew every time he opens his mouth.

Madame D'Arblay was most successful in comedy, and, indeed, in comedy which bordered on farce. But we are inclined to infer from some passages, both in "Cecilia" and "Camilla," that she might have attained equal distinction in the pathetic. We have formed this judgment, less from those ambitious scenes of distress which lie near the catastrophe of each of those novels, than from some exquisite strokes of natural tenderness which take us, here and there, by surprise. We would mention as examples, Mrs. Hill's account of her little boy's death in "Cecilia," and the parting of Sir Hugh Tyrold and Camilla, when the honest baronet thinks himself dying.

It is melancholy to think that the whole fame of Madame D'Arblay rests on what she did during the earlier part of her life, and that everything which she published during the forty-three years which preceded her death, lowered her reputation. Yet we have no reason to think that at the time when her faculties ought to have been in their maturity, they were smitten with any blight. In "The Wanderer," we catch now and then a gleam of her genius. Even in the Memoirs of her father, there is no trace of dotage. They are very bad; but they are so, as it seems to us, not from a decay of power, but from a total perversion of power.

The truth is, that Madame D'Arblay's style underwent a gradual and most pernicious change—a change which, in degree at least, we believe to be unexampled in literary history, and of which it may be useful to trace the progress. When she wrote her letters to Mr. Crisp, her early journals and her first novel, her style was not, indeed, brilliant or energetic; but it was easy, clear and free from all offensive faults. When she wrote "Cecilia" she aimed higher. She had then lived much in a circle of which Johnson was the centre; and she was herself one of his most submissive worshippers. It seems never to have crossed her mind that the style even of his best writings was by no means faultless, and that even had it been faultless, it might not be wise in her to imitate it. Phraseology which is proper in a disquisition on the Unities or in a preface to a dictionary, may be quite out of place in a tale of fashionable life. Old gentlemen do not criticise the reigning modes, nor do young gentlemen make love, with the balanced epithets and sonorous cadences which, on occasions of great dignity, a skilful writer may use with happy effect.

In an evil hour the author of "Evelina" took the "Rambler" for her model. This would not have been wise even if she could have imitated her pattern as well as Hawkesworth did. But such imitation was beyond her power. She had her own style. It was a tolerably good one; and might, without any violent change, have been improved into a very good one. She determined to throw it away, and to adopt a style in which she could attain excellence only by achieving an almost miraculous victory over nature and over habit. She could cease to be Fanny Burney; it was not so easy to become Samuel Johnson.

In "Cecilia" the change of manner began to appear. But in "Cecilia" the imitation of Johnson, though not always in the best taste, is sometimes eminently happy; and the passages which are so verbose as to be positively offensive, are few. There were people who whispered that Johnson had assisted his young friend, and that the novel owed all its finest passages to his hand. This was merely the fabrication of envy. Miss Burney's real excellences were as much beyond the reach of Johnson as his real excellences were beyond her reach. He could no more have written the Masquerade scene or the Vauxhall scene, than she could have written the life of Cowley or the Review of Soame Jenyns. But we have not the smallest doubt that he revised "Cecilia," and that he re-touched the style of many passages. We know that he was in the habit of giving assistance of this kind most freely. Goldsmith, Hawkesworth, Boswell, Lord Hailes, Mrs. Williams, were among those who obtained his help. Nay, he even corrected the poetry of Mr. Crabbe, whom, we believe, he had never seen. When Miss Burney thought of writing a comedy, he promised to give her his best counsel, though he owned that he was not particularly well qualified to advise on matters relating to the stage. We therefore think it in the highest degree improbable that his little Fanny, when living in habits of the most affectionate intercourse with him, would have brought out an important work without consulting him; and, when we look into "Cecilia," we see such traces of his hand in the grave and elevated passages as it is impossible to mistake. Before we conclude this article, we will give two or three examples.

When next Madame D'Arblay appeared before the world as a writer, she was in a very different situation. She would not content herself with the simple English in which "Evelina" had been written. She had no longer the friend who, we are confident, had polished and strengthened the style of "Cecilia." She had to write in Johnson's manner without Johnson's aid. The consequence was, that in "Camilla" every passage which she meant to be fine is detestable; and that the book has been saved from condemnation only by the admirable spirit and force of those scenes in which she was content to be familiar.

But there was to be a still deeper descent. After the publication of "Camilla" Madame D'Arblay resided ten years at Paris. During those years there was scarcely any intercourse between France and England. It was with difficulty that a short letter could occasionally be transmitted. All Madame D'Arblay's companions were French. She must have written, spoken, thought in French. Ovid expressed his fear that a shorter exile might have affected the purity of his Latin. During a shorter exile Gibbon unlearned his native English. Madame D'Arblay had carried a bad style to France. She brought back a style which we are really at a loss to describe. It is a sort of broken Johnsonese, a barbarous *patois*, bearing the same relation to the language of "Rasselas" which the gibberish of the Negroes of Jamaica bears to the English of the House of Lords. Sometimes it reminds us of the finest, that is to say the vilest, parts of Mr. Galt's novels; sometimes of the perorations of Exeter Hall; sometimes of the leading articles of the *Morning Post*. But it most resembles the puffs of Mr. Rowland and Dr. Goss. It matters not what ideas are clothed in such a style. The genius of Shakspeare and Bacon united would not save a work so written from general derision.

It is only by means of specimens that we can enable our readers to judge how widely Madame D'Arblay's three styles differed from each other.

The following passage was written before she became intimate with Johnson. It is from "Evelina."

"His son seems weaker in his understanding and more gay in his temper; but his gaiety is that of a foolish, overgrown schoolboy, whose mirth consists in noise and disturbance. He disdains his father for his close attention to business and love of money, though he seems himself to have no talents, spirit or generosity to make him superior to either. His chief delight appears to be in tormenting and ridiculing his sisters, who in return most cordially despise him. Miss Braughton, the eldest daughter, is by no means ugly; but looks proud, ill-tempered and conceited. She hates the city, though without knowing why; for it is easy to discover she has lived nowhere else. Miss Polly Braughton is rather pretty, very foolish, very ignorant, very giddy and, I believe, very goodnatured."

This is not a fine style, but simple, perspicuous and agreeable. We now come to "Cecilia," written during Miss Burney's intimacy with Johnson; and we leave it to our readers to judge whether the following passage was not at least corrected by his hand.

"It is rather an imaginary than an actual evil and, though a deep wound to pride, no offence to morality. Thus have I laid open to you my whole heart, confessed my perplexities, acknowledged my vain glory and exposed, with equal sincerity, the sources of my doubts and the motives of my decision. But now, indeed, how to proceed I know not. The difficulties which are yet to encounter I fear to enumerate, and the petition I have to urge I have scarce courage to mention. My family, mistaking ambition for honour and rank for dignity, have long planned a splendid connection for me, to which, though my invariable repugnance has stopped any advances, their wishes and their views immoveably adhere. I am but too certain they will now listen to no other. I dread, therefore, to make a trial where I despair of success. I know not how to risk a prayer with those who may silence me by a command."

Take now a specimen of Madame D'Arblay's later style. This is the way in which she tells us that her father, on his journey back from the Continent, caught the rheumatism.

"He was assaulted, during his precipitate return, by the rudest fierceness of wintry elemental strife; through which, with bad accommodations and innumerable accidents, he became a prey to the merciless pangs of the acutest spasmodic rheumatism, which barely suffered him to reach his home ere, long and piteously, it confined him, a tortured prisoner, to his bed. Such was the check that almost instantly curbed, though it could not subdue, the rising pleasure of his hopes of entering upon a new species of existence— that of an approved man of letters; for it was on the bed of sickness, exchanging the light wines of France, Italy and Germany, for the black and loathsome potions of the Apothecaries' Hall, writhed by darting stitches and burning with fiery fever, that he felt the full force of that sublunary equipoise that seems evermore to hang suspended over the attainment of long-sought and uncommon felicity, just as it is ripening to burst forth with enjoyment!"

Here is a second passage from "Evelina."

"Mrs. Selwyn is very kind and attentive to me. She is extremely clever. Her understanding, indeed, may be called masculine; but unfortunately her manners deserve the same epithet; for, in studying to acquire the knowledge of the other sex, she has lost all the softness of her own. In regard to myself, however, as I have neither courage nor inclination to argue with her, I have never been personally hurt at her want of gentleness—a virtue which nevertheless seems so essential a part of the female character, that I find myself more awkward and less at ease with a woman who wants it than I do with a man."

This is a good style of its kind, and the following passage from "Cecilia" is also in a good style, though not in a faultless one. We say with confidence— either Sam Johnson or the Devil.

"Even the imperious Mr. Delvile was more supportable here than in London. Secure in his own castle, he looked round him with a pride of power and possession which softened while it swelled him. His superiority was undisputed: his will was without control. He was not, as in the great capital of the kingdom, surrounded by competitors. No rivalry disturbed his peace; no equality mortified his greatness. All he saw were either vassals of his power, or guests bending to his pleasure. He abated, therefore, considerably the stern gloom of his haughtiness and soothed his proud mind by the courtesy of condescension."

We will stake our reputation for critical sagacity on this, that no such paragraph as that which we have last quoted can be found in any of Madame D'Arblay's works except "Cecilia." Compare with it the following sample of her later style.

"If beneficence be judged by the happiness which it diffuses, whose claim, by that proof, shall stand higher than that of Mrs. Montagu, from the munificence with which she celebrated her annual festival for those hapless artificers who perform the most abject offices of any authorised calling in being the active guardians of our blazing hearths? Not to vain glory, then, but to kindness of heart, should be adjudged the publicity of that superb charity which made its jetty objects, for one bright morning, cease to consider themselves as degraded outcasts from all society."

We add one or two shorter samples. Sheridan refused to permit his lovely wife to sing in public, and was warmly praised on this account by Johnson.

"The last of men," says Madame D'Arblay, "was Doctor Johnson to have abetted squandering the delicacy of integrity by nullifying the labours of talents."

The Club, Johnson's Club, did itself no honour by rejecting, on political grounds, two distinguished men—one a Tory, the other a Whig. Madame D'Arblay tells the story thus :—"A similar ebullition of political rancour with that which so difficultly had been conquered for Mr. Canning foamed over the ballot box to the exclusion of Mr. Rogers."

An offence punishable with imprisonment is, in this language, an offence "which produces incarceration." To be starved to death is "to sink from inanition into nonentity." Sir Isaac Newton is "the developer of the skies in their embodied movements;" and Mrs. Thrale, when a party of clever people sat silent, is said to have been "provoked by the dulness of a taciturnity that in the midst of such renowned interlocutors, produced as narcotic a torpor as could have been caused by a dearth the most barren of all human faculties."

In truth, it is impossible to look at any page of Madame D'Arblay's later works without finding flowers of rhetoric like these. Nothing in the language of those jargonists at whom Mr. Gosport laughed, nothing in the language of Sir Sedley Clarendel approaches this new Euphuism.

It is from no unfriendly feeling to Madame D'Arblay's memory that we have expressed ourselves so strongly on the subject of her style. On the contrary, we conceive that we have really rendered a service to her reputation. That her later works were complete failures is a fact too notorious to be dissembled, and some persons, we believe, have consequently taken up a notion that she was from the first an overrated writer, and that she had not the powers which were necessary to maintain her on the eminence on which good luck and fashion had placed her. We believe, on the contrary, that her early popularity was no more than the just reward of distinguished merit, and would never have undergone an eclipse if she had only been content to go on writing in her mother tongue. If she failed when she quitted her own province and attempted to occupy one in which she had neither part nor lot, this reproach is common to her with a crowd of distinguished men. Newton failed when he turned from the courses of the stars and the ebb and flow of the ocean to apocalyptic seals and vials. Bentley failed when he turned from Homer and Aristophanes to edit the "Paradise Lost." Inigo failed when he attempted to rival the Gothic churches of the fourteenth century. Wilkie failed when he took it into his head that the "Blind Fiddler" and the "Rent Day" were unworthy of his powers, and challenged competition with Lawrence as a portrait painter. Such failures should be noted for the instruction of posterity, but they detract little from the permanent reputation of those who have really done great things.

Yet one word more. It is not only on account of the intrinsic merit of Madame D'Arblay's early works that she is entitled to honourable mention. Her appearance is an important epoch in our literary history. "Evelina" was the first tale written by a woman, and purporting to be a picture of life and manners, that lived or deserved to live. The female Quixote is no exception. That work has undoubtedly great merit, when considered as a wild, satirical harlequinade; but if we consider it as a picture of life and manners, we must pronounce it more absurd than any of the romances which it was designed to ridicule.

Indeed, most of the popular novels which preceded "Evelina" were such as no lady would have written; and many of them were such as no lady could without confusion own that she had read. The very name of novel was held in horror among religious people. In decent families, which did not profess extraordinary sanctity, there was a strong feeling against all such works. Sir Anthony Absolute, two or three years before "Evelina" appeared, spoke the sense of the great body of fathers and husbands, when he pronounced the circulating library an evergreen tree of diabolical knowledge. This feeling on the part of the grave and reflecting increased the evil from which it had sprung. The novelist having little character to lose, and having few readers among serious people, took without scruple liberties which in our generation seem almost incredible.

Miss Burney did for the English novel what Jeremy Collier did for the English drama; and she did it in a better way. She first showed that a tale might be written in which both the fashionable and the vulgar life of London might be exhibited with great force and with broad comic humour, and which yet should not contain a single line inconsistent with rigid morality or even with virgin delicacy. She took away the reproach which lay on a most useful and delightful species of composition. She vindicated the right of her sex to an equal share in a fair and noble province of letters. Several accomplished women have followed in her track. At present, the novels which we owe to

English ladies form no small part of the literary glory of our country. No class of works is more honourably distinguished by fine observation, by grace, by delicate wit, by pure moral feeling. Several among the successors of Madame D'Arblay have equalled her; two, we think, have surpassed her. But the fact that she has been surpassed gives her an additional claim to our respect and gratitude; for, in truth, we owe to her not only "Evelina," "Cecilia" and "Camilla," but also "Mansfield Park" and the "Absentee."

THE LIFE AND WRITINGS OF ADDISON. (JULY, 1843.)

The Life of Joseph Addison. By LUCY AIKIN. 2 vols., 8vo. London. 1843.

SOME reviewers are of opinion that a lady who dares to publish a book renounces by that act the franchises appertaining to her sex and can claim no exemption from the utmost rigour of critical procedure. From that opinion we dissent. We admit, indeed, that in a country which boasts of many female writers, eminently qualified by their talents and acquirements to influence the public mind, it would be of most pernicious consequence that inaccurate history or unsound philosophy should be suffered to pass uncensured, merely because the offender chanced to be a lady. But we conceive that, on such occasions, a critic would do well to imitate that courteous knight who found himself compelled by duty to keep the lists against Bradamante. He, we are told, defended successfully the cause of which he was the champion; but, before the fight began, exchanged Balisarda for a less deadly sword, of which he carefully blunted the point and edge.*

Nor are the immunities of sex the only immunities which Miss Aikin may rightfully plead. Several of her works, and especially the very pleasing "Memoirs of the Reign of James the First," have fully entitled her to the privileges enjoyed by good writers. One of those privileges we bold to be this, that such writers, when, either from the unlucky choice of a subject, or from the indolence too often produced by success, they happen to fail, shall not be subjected to the severe discipline which it is sometimes necessary to inflict upon dunces and impostors, but shall merely be reminded by a gentle touch, like that with which the Laputan flapper roused his dreaming lord, that it is high time to wake.

Our readers will probably infer from what we have said that Miss Aikin's book has disappointed us. The truth is, that she is not well acquainted with her subject. No person who is not familiar with the political and literary history of England during the reigns of William the Third, of Anne and of George the First, can possibly write a good life of Addison. Now, we mean no reproach to Miss Aikin, and many will think that we pay her a compliment, when we say that her studies have taken a different direction. She is better acquainted with Shakspeare and Raleigh than with Congreve and Prior; and is far more at home among the ruffs and peaked beards of Theobald's than among the Steenkirks and flowing periwigs which surrounded Queen Anne's tea-table at Hampton. She seems to have written about the Elizabethan age because she had read much about it; she seems, on the other hand, to have read a little about the age of Addison because she had determined to write about it. The consequence is that she has had to describe men and things without having either a correct or a vivid idea of them, and that she has often fallen into errors of a very serious kind. The reputation which Miss Aikin has

---

* Orlando Furioso, xlv. 68.

justly earned stands so high and the charm of Addison's letters is so great, that a second edition of this work may probably be required. If so, we hope that every paragraph will be revised and that every date and fact about which there can be the smallest doubt will be carefully verified.

To Addison himself we are bound by a sentiment as much like affection as any sentiment can be which is inspired by one who has been sleeping a hundred and twenty years in Westminster Abbey. We trust, however, that this feeling will not betray us into that abject idolatry which we have often had occasion to reprehend in others, and which seldom fails to make both the idolater and the idol ridiculous. A man of genius and virtue is but a man. All his powers cannot be equally developed; nor can we expect from him perfect self-knowledge. We need not, therefore, hesitate to admit that Addison has left us some compositions which do not rise above mediocrity, some heroic poems hardly equal to Parnell's, some criticism as superficial as Dr. Blair's, and a tragedy not very much better than Dr. Johnson's. It is praise enough to say of a writer that, in a high department of literature, in which many eminent writers have distinguished themselves, he has had no equal; and this may, with strict justice, be said of Addison.

As a man, he may not have deserved the adoration which he received from those who, bewitched by his fascinating society, and indebted for all the comforts of life to his generous and delicate friendship, worshipped him nightly in his favourite temple at Button's. But, after full inquiry and impartial reflection, we have long been convinced that he deserved as much love and esteem as can be justly claimed by any of our infirm and erring race. Some blemishes may undoubtedly be detected in his character; but the more carefully it is examined, the more will it appear, to use the phrase of the old anatomists, sound in the noble parts—free from all taint of perfidy, of cowardice, of cruelty, of ingratitude, of envy. Men may easily be named, in whom some particular good disposition has been more conspicuous than in Addison. But the just harmony of qualities, the exact temper between the stern and the humane virtues, the habitual observance of every law, not only of moral rectitude, but of moral grace and dignity, distinguish him from all men who have been tried by equally strong temptations, and about whose conduct we possess equally full information.

His father was the Reverend Lancelot Addison, who, though eclipsed by his more celebrated son, made some figure in the world, and occupies with credit two folio pages in the "Biographia Britannica." Lancelot was sent up, as a poor scholar, from Westmoreland to Queen's College, Oxford, in the time of the Commonwealth, made some progress in learning, became, like most of his fellow students, a violent Royalist; lampooned the heads of the University, and was forced to ask pardon on his bended knees. When he had left college, he earned a humble subsistence by reading the liturgy of the fallen Church to the families of those sturdy squires whose manor houses were scattered over the Wild of Sussex. After the Restoration, his loyalty was rewarded with the post of chaplain to the garrison of Dunkirk. When Dunkirk was sold to France he lost his employment. But Tangier had been ceded by Portugal to England as part of the marriage portion of the Infanta Catharine, and to Tangier Lancelot Addison was sent. A more miserable situation can hardly be conceived. It was difficult to say whether the unfortunate settlers were more tormented by the heats or by the rains, by the soldiers within the wall or by the Moors without. One advantage the chaplain had. He enjoyed an excellent opportunity of studying the history and manners of Jews and Mahometans; and of this opportunity he appears to have made excellent use. On his return to England, after some years of banishment, he published an interesting volume on the Polity and Religion of Barbary, and another on the Hebrew Customs and the

State of Rabbinical Learning. He rose to eminence in his profession, and became one of the royal chaplains, a Doctor of Divinity, Archdeacon of Salisbury and Dean of Lichfield. It is said that he would have been made a bishop after the Revolution if he had not given offence to the government by strenuously opposing, in the Convocation of 1689, the liberal policy of William and Tillotson.

In 1672, not long after Dr. Addison's return from Tangier, his son Joseph was born. Of Joseph's childhood we know little. He learned his rudiments at schools in his father's neighbourhood, and was then sent to the Charter House. The anecdotes which are popularly related about his boyish tricks do not harmonize very well with what we know of his riper years. There remains a tradition that he was the ringleader in a barring-out; and another tradition that he ran away from school and hid himself in a wood, where he fed on berries and slept in a hollow tree, till, after a long search, he was discovered and brought home. If these stories be true, it would be curious to know by what moral discipline so mutinous and enterprising a lad was transformed into the gentlest and most modest of men.

We have abundant proof that, whatever Joseph's pranks may have been, he pursued his studies vigorously and successfully. At fifteen he was not only fit for the university, but carried thither a classical taste and a stock of learning which would have done honour to a Master of Arts. He was entered at Queen's College, Oxford; but he had not been many months there, when some of his Latin verses fell by accident into the hands of Dr. Lancaster, Dean of Magdalene College. The young scholar's diction and versification were already such as veteran professors might envy. Dr. Lancaster was desirous to serve a boy of such promise; nor was an opportunity long wanting. The Revolution had just taken place; and nowhere had it been hailed with more delight than at Magdalene College. That great and opulent corporation had been treated by James and by his Chancellor with an insolence and injustice which, even in such a Prince and in such a Minister, may justly excite amazement, and which had done more than even the prosecution of the Bishops to alienate the Church of England from the throne. A president, duly elected, had been violently expelled from his dwelling; a Papist had been set over the society by a royal mandate; the Fellows who, in conformity with their oaths, had refused to submit to this usurper, had been driven forth from their quiet cloisters and gardens to die of want or to live on charity. But the day of redress and retribution speedily came. The intruders were ejected; the venerable House was again inhabited by its old inmates; learning flourished under the rule of the wise and virtuous Hough; and with learning was united a mild and liberal spirit too often wanting in the princely colleges of Oxford. In consequence of the troubles through which the society had passed, there had been no valid election of new members during the year 1688. In 1689, therefore, there was twice the ordinary number of vacancies; and thus Dr. Lancaster found it easy to procure for his young friend admittance to the advantages of a foundation then generally esteemed the wealthiest in Europe.

At Magdalene Addison resided during ten years. He was, at first, one of those scholars who are called *Demies*, but was subsequently elected a Fellow. His college is still proud of his name; his portrait still hangs in the hall; and strangers are still told that his favourite walk was under the elms which fringe the meadow on the banks of the Cherwell. It is said, and is highly probable, that he was distinguished among his fellow students by the delicacy of his feelings, by the shyness of his manners and by the assiduity with which he often prolonged his studies far into the night. It is certain that his reputation for ability and learning stood high. Many years later, the ancient doctors of Magdalene continued to talk in their common room of his boyish compositions, and expressed their sorrow that no copy of exercises so remarkable had been preserved.

It is proper, however, to remark that Miss Aikin has committed the error, very pardonable in a lady, of overrating Addison's classical attainments. In one department of learning, indeed, his proficiency was such as it is hardly possible to overrate. His knowledge of the Latin poets, from Lucretius and Catullus down to Claudian and Prudentius, was singularly exact and profound. He understood them thoroughly, entered into their spirit, and had the finest and most discriminating perception of all their peculiarities of style and melody; nay, he copied their manner with admirable skill, and surpassed, we think, all their British imitators who had preceded him, Buchanan and Milton alone excepted. This is high praise; and beyond this we cannot with justice go. It is clear that Addison's serious attention during his residence at the university was almost entirely concentrated on Latin poetry, and that, if he did not wholly neglect other provinces of ancient literature, he vouchsafed to them only a cursory glance. He does not appear to have attained more than an ordinary acquaintance with the political and moral writers of Rome; nor was his own Latin prose by any means equal to his Latin verse. His knowledge of Greek, though doubtless such as was, in his time, thought respectable at Oxford, was evidently less than that which many lads now carry away every year from Eton and Rugby. A minute examination of his works, if we had time to make such an examination, would fully bear out these remarks. We will briefly advert to a few of the facts on which our judgment is grounded.

Great praise is due to the notes which Addison appended to his version of the second and third books of the Metamorphoses. Yet those notes, while they show him to have been, in his own domain, an accomplished scholar, show also how confined that domain was. They are rich in apposite references to Virgil, Statius and Claudian; but they contain not a single illustration drawn from the Greek poets. Now, if in the whole compass of Latin literature, there be a passage which stands in need of illustration drawn from the Greek poets, it is the story of Pentheus in the third book of the Metamorphoses. Ovid was indebted for that story to Euripides and Theocritus, both of whom he has sometimes followed minutely. But neither to Euripides nor to Theocritus does Addison make the faintest allusion; and we, therefore, believe that we do not wrong him by supposing that he had little or no knowledge of their works.

His travels in Italy, again, abound with classical quotations happily introduced; but scarcely one of those quotations is in prose. He draws more illustrations from Ausonius and Manilius than from Cicero. Even his notions of the political and military affairs of the Romans seem to be derived from poets and poetasters. Spots made memorable by events which have changed the destinies of the world, and which have been worthily recorded by great historians, bring to his mind only scraps of some ancient Pye or Hayley. In the gorge of the Apennines he naturally remembers the hardships which Hannibal's army endured, and proceeds to cite, not the authentic narrative of Polybius, not the picturesque narrative of Livy, but the languid hexameters of Silius Italicus. On the banks of the Rubicon he never thinks of Plutarch's lively description; or of the stern conciseness of the Commentaries; or of those letters to Atticus which so forcibly express the alternations of hope and fear in a sensitive mind at a great crisis. His only authority for the events of the civil war is Lucan.

All the best ancient works of art at Rome and Florence are Greek. Addison saw them, however, without recalling one single verse of Pindar, of Callimachus, or of the Attic dramatists; but they brought to his recollection innumerable passages of Horace, Juvenal, Statius and Ovid.

The same may be said of the "Treatise on Medals." In that pleasing work we find about three hundred passages extracted with great judgment from the Roman Poets; but we do not recollect a single passage taken from any Roman orator or historian; and we are confident that not a line is quoted from any Greek writer. No person, who had derived all his information on the subject of medals from Addison, would suspect that the Greek coins were in historical interest equal, and in beauty of execution far superior, to those of Rome.

If it were necessary to find any further proof that Addison's classical knowledge was confined within narrow limits, that proof would be furnished by his Essay on the "Evidences of Christianity." The Roman poets throw little or no light on the literary and historical questions which he is under the necessity of examining in that Essay. He is, therefore, left completely in the dark; and it is melancholy to see how helplessly he gropes his way from blunder to blunder. He assigns, as grounds for his religious belief, stories as absurd as that of the Cock-Lane ghost, and forgeries as rank as Ireland's "Vortigern," puts faith in the lie about the "Thundering Legion," is convinced that Tiberius moved the senate to admit Jesus among the gods and pronounces the letter of Agbarus, King of Edessa, to be a record of great authority. Nor were these errors the effects of superstition; for to superstition Addison was by no means prone. The truth is that he was writing about what he did not understand.

Miss Aikin has discovered a letter, from which it appears that, while Addison resided at Oxford, he was one of several writers whom the booksellers engaged to make an English version of Herodotus; and she infers that he must have been a good Greek scholar. We can allow very little weight to this argument when we consider that his fellow-labourers were to have been Boyle and Blackmore. Boyle is remembered chiefly as the nominal author of the worst book on Greek history and phylology that ever was printed; and this book, bad as it is, Boyle was unable to produce without help. Of Blackmore's attainments in the ancient tongues, it may be sufficient to say that, in his prose, he has confounded an aphorism with an apophthegm, and that when, in his verse, he treats of classical subjects, his habit is to regale his readers with four false quantities to a page.

It is probable that the classical acquirements of Addison were of as much service to him as if they had been more extensive. The world generally gives its admiration, not to the man who does what nobody else even attempts to do, but to the man who does best what multitudes do well. Bentley was so immeasurably superior to all the other scholars of his time, that very few among them could discover his superiority. But the accomplishment in which Addison excelled his contemporaries was then, as it is now, highly valued and assiduously cultivated at all English seats of learning. Everybody who had been at a public school had written Latin verses; many had written such verses with tolerable success, and were quite able to appreciate, though by no means able to rival the skill with which Addison imitated Virgil. His lines on the Barometer and the Bowling Green were applauded by hundreds, to whom the "Dissertation on the Epistles of Phalaris," was as unintelligible as the hieroglyphics on an obelisk.

Purity of style, and an easy flow of numbers, are common to all Addison's Latin poems. Our favourite piece is the "Battle of the Cranes and Pygmies;" for in that piece we discern a gleam of the fancy and humour which many years later enlivened thousands of breakfast tables. Swift boasted that he was never known to steal a hint; and he certainly owed as little to his predecessors as any modern writer. Yet we cannot help suspecting that he borrowed, perhaps unconsciously, one of the happiest touches in his "Voyage to Lilliput" from Addison's verses. Let our readers judge.

"The Emperor," says Gulliver, "is taller by about the breadth of my nail than any of his court, which alone is enough to strike an awe into the beholders."

About thirty years before "Gulliver's Travels" appeared, Addison wrote these lines:

> "Jamque acies inter medias sese arduus infert
> Pygmeadum ductor, qui, majestate verendus,
> Incessuque gravis, reliquos supereminet omnes
> Mole gigantea, mediamque exsurgit in ulnam."

The Latin poems of Addison were greatly and justly admired, both at Oxford and Cambridge, before his name had ever been heard by the wits who thronged the coffee-houses round Drury Lane Theatre. In his twenty-second year, he ventured to appear before the public as a writer of English verse. He addressed some complimentary lines to Dryden, who, after many triumphs and many reverses, had at length reached a secure and lonely eminence among the literary men of that age. Dryden appears to have been much gratified by the young scholar's praise; and an interchange of civilities and good offices followed. Addison was probably introduced by Dryden to Congreve, and was certainly presented by Congreve to Charles Montagu, who was then Chancellor of the Exchequer and leader of the Whig party in the House of Commons.

At this time Addison seemed inclined to devote himself to poetry. He published a translation of part of the fourth "Georgic," "Lines to King William," and other performances of equal value, that is to say, of no value at all. But in those days, the public was in the habit of receiving with applause pieces which would now have little chance of obtaining the Newdigate prize or the Seatonian prize. And the reason is obvious. The heroic couplet was then the favourite measure. The art of arranging words in that measure, so that the lines may flow smoothly, that the accents may fall correctly, that the rhymes may strike the ear strongly, and that there may be a pause at the end of every distich, is an art as mechanical as that of mending a kettle or shoeing a horse, and may be learned by any human being who has sense enough to learn anything. But like other mechanical arts, it was gradually improved by means of many experiments and many failures. It was reserved for Pope to discover the trick, to make himself complete master of it, and to teach it to everybody else. From the time when his "Pastorals" appeared, heroic versification became matter of rule and compass; and, before long, all artists were on a level. Hundreds of dunces who never blundered on one happy thought or expression were able to write reams of couplets which, as far as euphony was concerned, could not be distinguished from those of Pope himself, and which very clever writers of the reign of Charles the Second—Rochester, for example, or Marvel, or Oldham—would have contemplated with admiring despair.

Ben Jonson was a great man, Hoole a very small man. But Hoole, coming after Pope, had learned how to manufacture decasyllable verses, and poured them forth by thousands and tens of thousands, all as well turned, as smooth and as like each other as the blocks which have passed through Mr. Brunel's mill in the dockyard at Portsmouth. Ben's heroic couplets resemble blocks rudely hewn out by an unpractised hand, with a blunt hatchet. Take as a specimen his translation of a celebrated passage in the "Æneid":

> "This child out parent earth, stirr'd up with spite
> Of all the gods, brought forth, and, as some write,
> She was last sister of that giant race
> That sought to scale Jove's court, right swift of pace,
> And swifter far of wing, a monster vast
> And dreadful. Look, how many plumes are placed
> On her huge corpse, so many waking eyes
> Stick underneath, and, which may stranger rise
> In the report, as many tongues she wears."

Compare with these jagged misshapen distichs the neat fabric which Hoole's machine produces in unlimited abundance. We take the first lines on which we open in his version of Tasso. They are neither better no worse than the rest :

> "O thou, whoe'er thou art, whose steps are led,
> By choice or fate, these lonely shores to tread,
> No greater wonders east or west can boast
> Than yon small island on the pleasing coast.
> If e'er thy sight would blissful scenes explore,
> The current pass, and seek the further shore."

Ever since the time of Pope there had been a glut of lines of this sort ; and we are now as little disposed to admire a man for being able to write them, as for being able to write his name. But in the days of William the Third such versification was rare ; and a rhymer who had any skill in it passed for a great poet, just as in the dark ages a person who could write his name passed for a great clerk. Accordingly, Duke, Stepney, Granville, Walsh, and others whose only title to fame was that they said in tolerable metre what might have been as well said in prose, or what was not worth saying at all, were honoured with marks of distinction which ought to be reserved for genius. With these Addison must have ranked, if he had not earned true and lasting glory by performances which very little resembled his juvenile poems.

Dryden was now busied with Virgil, and obtained from Addison a critical preface to the "Georgics." In return for this service, and for other services of the same kind, the veteran poet, in the postscript to the translation of the "Æneid," complimented his young friend with great liberality, and indeed with more liberality than sincerity. He affected to be afraid that his own performance would not sustain a comparison with the version of the fourth " Georgic," by " the most ingenious Mr. Addison of Oxford." ". After his bees," added Dryden, " my latter swarm is scarcely worth the hiving."*

The time had now arrived when it was necessary for Addison to choose a calling. Everything seemed to point his course towards the clerical profession. His habits were regular, his opinions orthodox. His college had large ecclesiastical preferment in its gift, and boasts that it has given at least one bishop to almost every see in England. Dr. Lancelot Addison held an honourable place in the Church and had set his heart on seeing his son a clergyman. It is clear, from some expressions in the young man's rhymes, that his intention was to take orders. But Charles Montagu interfered. Montagu had first brought himself into notice by verses, well timed and not contemptibly written, but never, we think, rising above mediocrity. Fortunately for himself and for his country, he early quitted poetry, in which he could never have attained a rank as high as that of Dorset or Rochester, and turned his mind to official and parliamentary business. It is written that the ingenious person who undertook to instruct Rasselas, prince of Abyssinia, in the art of flying, ascended an eminence, waved his wings, sprang into the air, and instantly dropped into the lake. But it is added that the wings, which were unable to support him through the sky, bore him up effectually as soon as he was in the water. This is no bad type of the fate of Charles Montagu and of men like him. When he attempted to sore into the regions of poetical invention, he altogether failed ; but, as soon as he had descended from that ethereal elevation into a lower and grosser element, his talents instantly raised him above the mass. He became a distinguished financier, debater, courtier and party leader. He still retained his fondness for the pursuits of his early days ; but he showed that fondness not by wearying the public with his own feeble performances, but by discovering and encouraging literary excellence in others.

---

* Miss Aikin makes this compliment altogether unmeaning, by saying that it was paid to a translation of the second Georgic (l. 30).

A crowd of wits and poets, who would easily have vanquished him as a competitor, revered him as a judge and a patron. In his plans for the encouragement of learning, he was cordially supported by the ablest and most virtuous of his colleagues, the Lord Keeper Somers. Though both these great statesmen had a sincere love of letters, it was not solely from a love of letters that they were desirous to enlist youths of high intellectual qualifications in the public service. The Revolution had altered the whole system of government. Before that event the press had been controlled by censors and the Parliament had sat only two months in eight years. Now the press was free and had begun to exercise unprecedented influence on the public mind. Parliament met annually and sat long. The chief power in the state had passed to the House of Commons. At such a conjuncture, it was natural that literary and oratorical talents should rise in value. There was danger that a Government which neglected such talents might be subverted by them. It was, therefore, a profound and enlightened policy which led Montagu and Somers to attach such talents to the Whig party by the strongest ties both of interest and of gratitude.

It is remarkable that in a neighbouring country, we have recently seen similar effects follow from similar causes. The revolution of July, 1830, established representative government in France. The men of letters instantly rose to the highest importance in the state. At the present moment most of the persons whom we see at the head both of the Administration and of the Opposition have been Professors, Historians, Journalists, Poets. The influence of the literary class in England, during the generation which followed the Revolution, was great, but by no means so great as it has lately been in France. For, in England, the aristocracy of intellect had to contend with a powerful and deeply rooted aristocracy of a very different kind. France had no Somersets and Shrewsburys to keep down her Addisons and Priors.

It was in the year 1699, when Addison had just completed his twenty-seventh year, that the course of his life was finally determined. Both the great chiefs of the Ministry were kindly disposed towards him. In political opinions he already was what he continued to be through life, a firm, though a moderate Whig. He had addressed the most polished and vigorous of his early English lines to Somers, and had dedicated to Montagu a Latin poem, truly Virgilian, both in style and rhythm, on the peace of Ryswick. The wish of the young poet's great friends was, it should seem, to employ him in the service of the Crown abroad. But an intimate knowledge of the French language was a qualification indispensable to a diplomatist; and this qualification Addison had not acquired. It was, therefore, thought desirable that he should pass some time on the continent in preparing himself for official employment. His own means were not such as would enable him to travel: but a pension of £300 a-year was procured for him by the interest of the Lord Keeper. It seems to have been apprehended that some difficulty might be started by the rulers of Magdalene College. But the Chancellor of the Exchequer wrote in the strongest terms to Hough. The State—such was the purport of Montagu's letter—could not, at that time, spare to the Church such a man as Addison. Too many high civil posts were already occupied by adventurers, who, destitute of every liberal art and sentiment, at once pillaged and disgraced the country which they pretended to serve. It had become necessary to recruit for the public service from a very different class: from that class of which Addison was the representative. The close of the Minister's letter was remarkable. "I am called," he said, "an enemy of the Church: but I will never do it any other injury than keeping Mr. Addison out of it."

This interference was successful: and, in the summer of 1699, Addison, made a rich man by his pension, and still retaining his fellowship, quitted his beloved Oxford and set out on his travels. He crossed from Dover to Calais, proceeded to Paris, and was received there with great kindness and politeness by a kinsman of his friend Montagu—Charles, Earl of Manchester, who had just been appointed Ambassador to the Court of France. The Countess, a Whig and a toast, was probably as gracious as her lord, for Addison long retained an agreeable recollection of the impression which she at this time made on him, and in some lively lines written on the glasses of the Kit Cat Club, described the envy which her cheeks, glowing with the genuine bloom of England, had excited among the painted beauties of Versailles.

Louis XIV. was at this time expiating the vices of his youth by a devotion which had no root in reason and bore no fruit of charity. The servile literature of France had changed its character to suit the changed character of the prince. No book appeared that had not an air of sanctity. Racine, who was just dead, had passed the close of his life in writing sacred dramas; and Dacier was seeking for the Athanasian mysteries in Plato. Addison described this state of things in a short but lively and graceful letter to Montagu. Another letter, written about the same time to the Lord Keeper, conveyed the strongest assurances of gratitude and attachment. "The only return I can make to your Lordship," said Addison, "will be to apply myself entirely to my business." With this view he quitted Paris and repaired to Blois, a place where it was supposed that the French language was spoken in its highest purity and where not a single Englishman could be found. Here he passed some months pleasantly and profitably. Of his way of life at Blois, one of his associates, an Abbé named Philippeaux, gave an account to Joseph Spence. If this account is to be trusted, Addison studied much, mused much, talked little, had fits of absence, and either had no love affairs, or was too discreet to confide them to the Abbé. A man who, even when surrounded by fellow countrymen and fellow students, had always been remarkably shy and silent, was not likely to be loquacious in a foreign tongue and among foreign companions. But it is clear from Addison's letters, some of which were long after published in the *Guardian*, that, while he appeared to be absorbed in his own meditations, he was really observing French society with that keen and sly, yet not illnatured side-glance, which was peculiarly his own.

From Blois he returned to Paris; and having now mastered the French language, found great pleasure in the society of French philosophers and poets. He gave an account, in a letter to Bishop Hough, of two highly interesting conversations, one with Malbranche, the other with Boileau. Malbranche expressed great partiality for the English, and extolled the genius of Newton, but shook his head when Hobbes was mentioned, and was indeed so unjust as to call the author of the "Leviathan" a poor silly creature. Addison's modesty restrained him from fully relating in his letter the circumstances of his introduction to Boileau. Boileau, having survived the friends and rivals of his youth, old, deaf and melancholy, lived in retirement, seldom went either to Court or to the Academy, and was almost inaccessible to strangers. Of the English and of English literature he knew nothing. He had hardly heard the name of Dryden. Some of our countrymen in the warmth of their patriotism have asserted that this ignorance must have been affected. We own that we see no ground for such a supposition. English literature was to the French of the age of Louis XIV. what German literature was to our own grandfathers. Very few, we suspect, of the accomplished men who, sixty or seventy years ago, used to dine in Leicester Square with Sir Joshua, or at Streatham with Mrs. Thrale, had the slightest notion that Wieland was one of the first wits and poets, and Lessing, beyond all dispute, the first critic in Europe. Boileau knew just as little about the "Paradise Lost," and about "Absolom and Ahitophel;" but he had read Addison's Latin poems and admired them greatly. They had given him, he said, quite a new notion of the state of learning and taste among the English. Johnson will have it that these praises were insincere. "Nothing," says he, "is better known of Boileau than that he had an injudicious and peevish contempt of modern Latin; and, therefore, his profession of regard was probably the effect of his civility rather than approbation." Now, nothing is better known of Boileau than that he was singularly sparing of compliments. We do not remember that either friendship or fear ever induced him to bestow praise on any composition which he did not approve. On literary questions, his caustic, disdainful and self-confident spirit rebelled against that authority to which everything else in France bowed down. He had the spirit to tell Louis XIV., firmly and even rudely, that his Majesty knew nothing about poetry, and admired verses which were detestable. What was there in Addison's position that could induce the satirist, whose stern and fastidious temper had been the dread of two generations, to turn sycophant for the first and last time? Nor was Boileau's contempt of modern Latin either injudicious or peevish. He thought, indeed, that no poem of the first order would ever be written in a dead language. And did he think amiss? Has not the experience of centuries confirmed his opinion? Boileau also thought it probable that in the best modern Latin, a writer in the Augustan age would have detected ludicrous improprieties. And who can think otherwise? What modern scholar can honestly declare that he sees the smallest impurity in the style of Livy? Yet is it not certain that, in the style of Livy, Pollio, whose taste had been formed on the banks of the Tiber, detected the inelegant idiom of the Po? Has any modern scholar understood Latin better than Frederic the Great understood French? Yet it is not notorious that Frederic the Great after reading, speaking, writing French, and nothing but French, during more than half a century, after unlearning his mother tongue in order to learn French, after living familiarly during many years with French associates, could not, to the last, compose in French, without imminent risk of committing some mistake which would have moved a smile in the literary circles of Paris? Do we believe that Erasmus and Fracastorius wrote Latin as well as Dr. Robertson and Sir Walter Scott wrote English? And are there not in the "Dissertation on India" (the last of Dr. Robertson's works), in "Waverley," in "Marmion," Scotticisms at which a London apprentice would laugh? But does it follow, because we think thus, that we can find nothing to admire in the noble alcaics of Gray, or in the playful elegiacs of Vincent Bourne? Surely not. Nor was Boileau so ignorant or tasteless as to be incapable of appreciating good modern Latin. In the very letter to which Johnson alludes, Boileau says: "Ne croyez pas pourtant que je veuille par là blâmer les vers Latins que vous m'avez envoyés d'un de vos illustres académiciens. Je les ai trouvés fort beaux, et dignes de Vida et de Sannazar, mais non pas d'Horace et de Virgile." Several poems, in modern Latin, have been praised by Boileau quite as liberally as it was his habit to praise anything. He says, for example, of the Père Fraguier's epigrams, that Catullus seems to have come to life again. But the best proof that Boileau did not feel the undiscerning contempt for modern Latin verses which has been imputed to him, is that he wrote and published Latin verses in several metres. Indeed, it happens, curiously enough, that the most severe censure ever pronounced by him on modern Latin is conveyed in Latin hexameters. We allude to the fragment which begins—

"Quid numerus iterum me balbutire Latinis,
Longe Alpes citra natum de patre Sicambro,
Musa, jubes?"

For these reasons we feel assured that the praise which Boileau bestowed on the *Machinæ Gesticulantes* and the *Gerano-Pygmæomachia* was sincere. He certainly opened himself to Addison with a freedom which was a sure indication of esteem. Literature was the chief subject of conversation. The old man talked on his favourite theme much and well, indeed, as his young hearer thought, incomparably well. Boileau had undoubtedly some of the qualities of a great critic. He wanted imagination; but he had strong sense. His literary code was formed on narrow principles; but in applying it, he showed great judgment and penetration. In mere style, abstracted from the ideas of which style is the garb, his taste was excellent. He was well acquainted with the great Greek writers; and, though unable fully to appreciate their creative genius, admired the majestic simplicity of their manner, and had learned from them to despise bombast and tinsel. It is easy, we think, to discover in the *Spectator* and the *Guardian*, traces of the influence, in part salutary and in part pernicious, which the mind of Boileau had on the mind of Addison.

While Addison was at Paris, an event took place which made that capital a disagreeable residence for an Englishman and a Whig. Charles, second of the name, King of Spain, died, and bequeathed his dominions to Philip, Duke of Anjou, a younger son of the Dauphin. The King of France, in direct violation of his engagements both with Great Britain and with the States General, accepted the bequest on behalf of his grandson. The House of Bourbon was at the summit of human grandeur. England had been outwitted, and found herself in a situation at once degrading and perilous. The people of France, not presaging the calamities by which they were destined to expiate the perfidy of their sovereign, went mad with pride and delight. Every man looked as if a great estate had just been left him. "The French conversation," said Addison, "begins to grow insupportable; that which was before the vainest nation in the world is now worse than ever." Sick of the arrogant exultation of the Parisians, and probably foreseeing that the peace between France and England could not be of long duration he set off for Italy.

In December, 1700,* he embarked at Marseilles. As he glided along the Ligurian coast, he was delighted by the sight of myrtles and olive trees, which retained their verdure under the winter solstice. Soon, however, he encountered one of the black storms of the Mediterranean. The captain of the ship gave up all for lost, and confessed himself to a capuchin who happened to be on board. The English heretic, in the meantime, fortified himself against the terrors of death with devotions of a very different kind. How strong an impression this perilous voyage made on him appears from the ode, "How are Thy servants blest, O Lord!" which was long after published in the *Spectator*. After some days of discomfort and danger, Addison was glad to land at Savona, and to make his way, over mountains where no road had yet been hewn out by art, to the city of Genoa.

At Genoa, still ruled by her own Doge, and by the nobles whose names were inscribed on her "Book of Gold," Addison made a short stay. He admired the narrow streets overhung by long lines of towering palaces, the walls rich with frescoes, the gorgeous temple of the Annunciation, and the tapestries whereon were recorded the long glories of the house of Doria. Thence he hastened to Milan, where he contemplated the Gothic magnificence of the cathedral with more wonder than pleasure. He passed Lake Benacus while a gale was blowing, and saw the waves raging as they raged when Virgil looked upon them. At Venice, then the gayest spot in Europe, the traveller

---

* It is strange that Addison should, in the first line of his travels, have misdated his departure from Marseilles by a whole year, and still more strange that this slip of the pen, which throws the whole narrative into inextricable confusion, should have been repeated in a succession of editions, and never detected by Tickell or by Hurd.

spent the Carnival, the gayest season of the year, in the midst of masques, dances and serenades. Here he was at once diverted and provoked by the absurd dramatic pieces which then disgraced the Italian stage. To one of those pieces, however, he was indebted for a valuable hint. He was present when a ridiculous play on the death of Cato was performed. Cato, it seems, was in love with a daughter of Scipio. The lady had given her heart to Cæsar. The rejected lover determined to destroy himself. He appeared seated in his library, a dagger in his hand, a Plutarch and a Tasso before him; and, in this position, he pronounced a soliloquy before he struck the blow. We are surprised that so remarkable a circumstance as this should have escaped the notice of all Addison's biographers. There cannot, we conceive, be the smallest doubt that this scene, in spite of its absurdities and anachronisms, struck the traveller's imagination and suggested to him the thought of bringing Cato on the English stage. It is well known that about this time he began his tragedy, and that he finished the first four acts before he returned to England.

On his way from Venice to Rome he was drawn some miles out of the beaten road by a wish to see the smallest independent state in Europe. On a rock where the snow still lay, though the Italian spring was now far advanced, was perched the little fortress of San Marino. The roads which led to the secluded town were so bad that few travellers had ever visited it, and none had ever published an account of it. Addison could not suppress a good-natured smile at the simple manners and institutions of this singular community. But he observed, with the exultation of a Whig, that the rude mountain tract which formed the territory of the republic swarmed with an honest, healthy and contented peasantry, while the rich plain which surrounded the metropolis of civil and spiritual tyranny was scarcely less desolate than the uncleared wilds of America.

At Rome Addison remained on his first visit only long enough to catch a glimpse of St. Peter's and of the Pantheon. His haste is the more extraordinary because the Holy Week was close at hand. He has given no hint which can enable us to pronounce why he chose to fly from a spectacle which every year allures from distant regions persons of far less taste and sensibility than his. Possibly, travelling, as he did, at the charge of a Government distinguished by its enmity to the Church of Rome, he may have thought that it would be imprudent in him to assist at the most magnificent rite of that Church. Many eyes would be upon him; and he might find it difficult to behave in such a manner as to give offence neither to his patrons in England nor to those among whom he resided. Whatever his motives may have been, he turned his back on the most august and affecting ceremony which is known among men and posted along the Appian way to Naples.

Naples was then destitute of what are now, perhaps, its chief attractions. The lovely bay and the awful mountain were indeed there. But a farmhouse stood on the theatre of Herculaneum, and rows of vines grew over the streets of Pompeii. The temples of Pæstum had not, indeed, been hidden from the eye of man by any great convulsion of nature; but, strange to say, their existence was a secret even to artists and antiquaries. Though situated within a few hours' journey of a great capital, where Salvator had not long before painted and where Vico was then lecturing, those noble remains were as little known to Europe as the ruined cities overgrown by the forests of Yucatan. What was to be seen at Naples, Addison saw. He climbed Vesuvius, explored the tunnel of Posilipo, and wandered among the vines and almond trees of Capreæ. But neither the wonders of nature nor those of art could so occupy his attention as to prevent him from noticing, though cursorily, the abuses of the government and the misery of the people. The great kingdom which had just descended to Philip the Fifth, was in a state of paralytic dotage. Even Castile and Aragon were sunk in wretchedness. Yet, compared with the Italian dependencies of the Spanish crown, Castile and Aragon might be called prosperous. It is clear that all the observations which Addison made in Italy tended to confirm him in the political opinions which he had adopted at home. To the last he always spoke of foreign travel as the best cure for Jacobitism. In his "Freeholder," the Tory Foxhunter asks what travelling is good for, except to teach a man to jabber French and to talk against passive obedience.

From Naples Addison returned to Rome by sea, along the coast which his favourite Virgil had celebrated. The felucca passed the headland where the oar and trumpet were placed by the Trojan adventurers on the tomb of Misenus, and anchored at night under the shelter of the fabled promontory of Circe. The voyage ended in the Tiber, still overhung with dark verdure, and still turbid with yellow sand, as when it met the eyes of Æneas. From the ruined port of Ostia the stranger hurried to Rome; and at Rome he remained during those hot and sickly months when, even in the Augustan age, all who could make their escape fled from mad dogs, and from streets black with funerals, to gather the first figs of the season in the country. It is probable that when he, long after, poured forth in verse his gratitude to the Providence which had enabled him to breathe unhurt in tainted air, he was thinking of the August and September which he passed at Rome.

It was not till the latter end of October that he tore himself away from the masterpieces of ancient and modern art which are collected in the city so long the mistress of the world. He then journeyed northward, passed through Sienna, and for a moment forgot his prejudices in favour of classic architecture as he looked on the magnificent cathedral. At Florence he spent some days with the Duke of Shrewsbury, who, cloyed with the pleasures of ambition and impatient of its pains, fearing both parties and loving neither, had determined to hide in an Italian retreat talents and accomplishments which, if they had been united with fixed principles and civil courage, might have made him the foremost man of his age. These days, we are told, passed pleasantly; and we can easily believe it. For Addison was a delightful companion when he was at his ease; and the Duke, though he seldom forgot that he was a Talbot, had the invaluable art of putting at ease all who came near him.

Addison gave some time to Florence, and especially to the sculptures in the museum, which he preferred even to those of the Vatican. He then pursued his journey through a country in which the ravages of the last war were still discernible, and in which all men were looking forward with dread to a still fiercer conflict. Eugene had already descended from the Rhætian Alps to dispute with Catinat the rich plain of Lombardy. The faithless ruler of Savoy was still reckoned among the allies of Louis. England had not yet actually declared war against France, but Manchester had left Paris; and the negotiations which produced the Grand Alliance against the House of Bourbon were in progress. Under such circumstances it was desirable for an English traveller to reach neutral ground without delay. Addison resolved to cross Mont Cenis. It was December, and the road was very different from that which now reminds the stranger of the power and genius of Napoleon. The winter, however, was mild, and the passage was, for those times, easy. To this journey Addison alluded when, in the ode which we have already quoted, he said that for him the Divine goodness had "warmed the hoary Alpine hills.".

It was in the midst of the eternal snow that he composed his Epistle to his friend Montagu, now Lord Halifax. That Epistle, once widely renowned, is now known only to curious readers, and will hardly be considered by those to whom it is known as in any perceptible degree heightening Addison's fame.

It is, however, decidedly superior to any English composition which he had previously published. Nay, we think it quite as good as any poem in heroic metre which appeared during the interval between the death of Dryden and the publication of the "Essay on Criticism." It contains passages as good as the second-rate passages of Pope, and would have added to the reputation of Parnell or Prior.

But, whatever be the literary merits or defects of the "Epistle," it undoubtedly does honour to the principles and spirit of the author. Halifax had now nothing to give. He had fallen from power, had been held up to obloquy, had been impeached by the House of Commons, and, though his Peers had dismissed the impeachment,* had, as it seemed, little chance of ever again filling high office. The "Epistle," written at such a time, is one among many proofs that there was no mixture of cowardice or meanness in the suavity and moderation which distinguished Addison from all the other public men of those stormy times.

At Geneva the traveller learned that a partial change of ministry had taken place in England, and that the Earl of Manchester had become Secretary of State.† Manchester exerted himself to serve his young friend. It was thought advisable that an English agent should be near the person of Eugene in Italy; and Addison, whose diplomatic education was now finished, was the man selected. He was preparing to enter on his honourable functions when all his prospects were for a time darkened by the death of William III.

Anne had long felt a strong aversion, personal, political and religious, to the Whig party. That aversion appeared in the first measures of her reign. Manchester was deprived of the seals, after he had held them only a few weeks. Neither Somers nor Halifax was sworn of the Privy Council. Addison shared the fate of his three patrons. His hopes of employment in the public service were at an end; his pension was stopped, and it was necessary for him to support himself by his own exertions. He became tutor to a young English traveller, and appears to have rambled with his pupil over great part of Switzerland and Germany. At this time he wrote his pleasing treatise on "Medals." It was not published till after his death; but several distinguished scholars saw the manuscript and gave just praise to the grace of the style and to the learning and ingenuity evinced by the quotations.

From Germany Addison repaired to Holland, where he learned the melancholy news of his father's death. After passing some months in the United Provinces, he returned about the close of the year 1703 to England. He was there cordially received by his friends, and introduced by them into the Kit-Cat Club—a society in which were collected all the various talents and accomplishments which then gave lustre to the Whig party.

Addison was, during some months after his return from the Continent, hard pressed by pecuniary difficulties. But it was soon in the power of his noble patrons to serve him effectually. A political change, silent and gradual, but of the highest importance, was in daily progress.‡ The accession of Anne had

---

* Miss Aikin says (i. 121) that the epistle was written long before Halifax was justified by the Lords. This is a mistake. The epistle was written in December, 1701; the impeachment had been dismissed in the preceding June.

† Miss Aikin misdates this event by a year (i. 93).

‡ We are sorry to say that, in the account which Miss Aikin gives of the politics of this period there are more errors than sentences. Rochester was the Queen's uncle; Miss Aikin calls him the Queen's cousin. The battle of Blenheim was fought in Marlborough's third campaign; Miss Aikin says that it was fought in Marlborough's second campaign. She confounds the dispute which arose in 1703, between the two Houses, about Lord Halifax, with the dispute about the Aylesbury men, which was determined by the dissolution of 1705. These mistakes and four or five others will be found within the space of about two pages (i. 165, 165, 167).

been hailed by the Tories with transports of joy and hope; and, for a time, it seemed that the Whigs had fallen never to rise again. The throne was surrounded by men supposed to be attached to the prerogative and to the Church; and among these none stood so high in the favour of the sovereign as the Lord Treasurer Godolphin and the Captain General Marlborough.

The country gentlemen and country clergymen fully expected that the policy of these ministers would be directly opposed to that which had been almost constantly followed by William; that the landed interest would be favoured at the expense of trade; that no addition would be made to the funded debt; that the privileges conceded to Dissenters by the late King would be curtailed, if not withdrawn; that the war with France, if there must be such a war, would, on our part, be almost entirely naval; and that the Government with avoid close connection with foreign powers, and, above all, with Holland.

But the country gentlemen and country clergymen were fated to be deceived, not for the last time. The prejudices and passions which raged without control in vicarages, in cathedral closes, and in the manor-houses of fox-hunting squires, were not shared by the chiefs of the ministry. Those statesmen saw that it was both for the public interest, and for their own interest, to adopt a Whig policy, at least as respected the alliances of the country and the conduct of the war. But, if the foreign policy of the Whigs were adopted, it was impossible to abstain from adopting also their financial policy. The natural consequences followed. The rigid Tories were alienated from the Government. The votes of the Whigs became necessary to it. The votes of the Whigs could be secured only by further concessions; and further concessions the Queen was induced to make.

At the beginning of the year 1704, the state of parties bore a close analogy to the state of parties in 1826. In 1826, as in 1704, there was a Tory ministry divided into two hostile sections. The position of Mr. Canning and his friends in 1826 corresponded to that which Marlborough and Godolphin occupied in 1704. Nottingham and Jersey were, in 1704, what Lord Eldon and Lord Westmoreland were in 1826. The Whigs of 1704 were in a situation resembling that in which the Whigs of 1826 stood. In 1704, Somers, Halifax, Sunderland, Cowper were not in office. There was no avowed coalition between them and the moderate Tories. It is probable that no direct communication tending to such a coalition had yet taken place; yet all men saw that such a coalition was inevitable, nay, that it was already half formed. Such, or nearly such, was the state of things when tidings arrived of the great battle fought at Blenheim on the 13th August, 1704. By the Whigs the news was hailed with transports of joy and pride. No fault, no cause of quarrel, could be remembered by them against the Commander whose genius had, in one day, changed the face of Europe, saved the Imperial throne, humbled the House of Bourbon, and secured the Act of Settlement against foreign hostility. The feeling of the Tories was very different. They could not, indeed, without imprudence, openly express regret at an event so glorious to their country; but their congratulations were so cold and sullen as to give deep disgust to the victorious general and his friends.

Godolphin was not a reading man. Whatever time he could spare from business he was in the habit of spending at Newmarket or at the card-table. But he was not absolutely indifferent to poetry; and he was too intelligent an observer not to perceive that literature was a formidable engine of political warfare, and that the great Whig leaders had strengthened their party and raised their character by extending a liberal and judicious patronage to good writers. He was mortified, and not without reason, by the exceeding badness of the poems which appeared in honour of the battle of Blenheim. One of these poems has been rescued from oblivion by the exquisite absurdity of three lines.

> "Think of two thousand gentlemen at least,
> And each man mounted on his capering beast;
> Into the Danube they were pushed by shoals."

Where to procure better verses the Treasurer did not know. He understood how to negotiate a loan or remit a subsidy: he was also well versed in the history of running horses and fighting cocks; but his acquaintance among the poets was very small. He consulted Halifax, but Halifax affected to decline the office of adviser. He had, he said, done his best, when he had power, to encourage men whose abilities and acquirements might do honour to their country. Those times were over. Other maxims had prevailed. Merit was suffered to pine in obscurity; and the public money was squandered on the undeserving. "I do know," he added, "a gentleman who would celebrate the battle in a manner worthy of the subject; but I will not name him." Godolphin, who was expert at the soft answer which turneth away wrath, and who was under the necessity of paying court to the Whigs, gently replied that there was too much ground for Halifax's complaints, but that what was amiss should in time be rectified; and that in the meantime the services of a man such as Halifax had described should be liberally rewarded. Halifax then mentioned Addison, but, mindful of the dignity as well as of the pecuniary interest of his friend, insisted that the Minister should apply in the most courteous manner to Addison himself; and this Godolphin promised to do.

Addison then occupied a garret up three pair of stairs, over a small shop in the Haymarket. In this humble lodging he was surprised, on the morning which followed the conversation between Godolphin and Halifax, by a visit from no less a person than the Right Honourable Henry Boyle, then Chancellor of the Exchequer, and afterwards Lord Carleton.* This high-born minister had been sent by the Lord Treasurer as ambassador to the needy poet. Addison readily undertook the proposed task, a task which, to so good a Whig, was probably a pleasure. When the poem was little more than half finished, he showed it to Godolphin, who was delighted with it, and particularly with the famous similitude of the Angel. Addison was instantly appointed to a Commissionership, with about two hundred pounds a-year, and was assured that this appointment was only an earnest of greater favours.

The "Campaign" came forth, and was as much admired by the public as by the Minister. It pleases us less on the whole than the "Epistle to Halifax." Yet it undoubtedly ranks high among the poems which appeared during the interval between the death of Dryden and the dawn of Pope's genius. The chief merit of the "Campaign," we think, is that which was noticed by Johnson—the manly and rational rejection of fiction. The first great poet whose works have come down to us sang of war long before war became a science or a trade. If, in his time, there was enmity between two little Greek towns, each poured forth its crowd of citizens, ignorant of discipline, and armed with implements of labour rudely turned into weapons. On each side appeared conspicuous a few chiefs, whose wealth had enabled them to procure good armour, horses and chariots, and whose leisure had enabled them to practice military exercises. One such chief, if he were a man of great strength, agility and courage, would probably be more formidable than twenty common men; and the force and dexterity with which he flung his spear might have no inconsiderable share in deciding the event of the day. Such were probably the battles with which Homer was familiar. But Homer related the actions of men of a former generation— of men who sprang from the gods, and communed with the gods face to face—

. .* Miss Aikin says that he was afterwards Lord Orrery. This is a mistake (l. 1701.

of men, one of whom could with ease hurl rocks which two sturdy hinds of a later period would be unable even to lift. He, therefore, naturally represented their martial exploits as resembling in kind, but far surpassing in magnitude, those of the stoutest and most expert combatants of his own age. Achilles, clad in celestial armour, drawn by celestial coursers, grasping the spear which none but himself could raise, driving all Troy and Lycia before him, and choking Scamander with dead, was only a magnificent exaggeration of the real hero, who, strong, fearless, accustomed to the use of weapons, guarded by a shield and helmet of the best Sidonian fabric and whirled along by horses of Thessalian breed, struck down with his own right arm foe after foe. In all rude societies similar notions are found. There are at this day countries where the Lifeguardsman Shaw would be considered as a much greater warrior than the Duke of Wellington. Buonaparte loved to describe the astonishment with which the Mamelukes looked at his diminutive figure. Mourad Bey, distinguished above all his fellows by his bodily strength and by the skill with which he managed his horse and his sabre, could not believe that a man who was scarcely five feet high and rode like a butcher could be the greatest soldier in Europe.

Homer's descriptions of war had, therefore, as much truth as poetry requires. But truth was altogether wanting to the performances of those who, writing about battles which had scarcely anything in common with the battles of his times, servilely imitated his manner. The folly of Silius Italicus, in particular, is positively nauseous. He undertook to record in verse the vicissitudes of a great struggle between generals of the first order, and his narrative is made up of the hideous wounds which these generals inflicted with their own hands. Asdrubal flings a spear which grazes the shoulder of the consul Nero; but Nero sends his spear into Asdrubal's side. Fabius slays Thuris, and Butes, and Maris, and Arses, and the long-haired Adherbes, and the gigantic Thylis, and Sapharus, and Monæsus, and the trumpeter Morinus. Hannibal runs Perusinus through the groin with a stake and breaks the backbone of Telesinus with a huge stone. This detestable fashion was copied in modern times, and continued to prevail down to the age of Addison. Several versifiers had described William turning thousands to flight by his single prowess and dyeing the Boyne with Irish blood. Nay, so estimable a writer as John Philips, the author of the "Splendid Shilling," represented Marlborough as having won the battle of Blenheim merely by strength of muscle and skill in fence. The following lines may serve as an example:—

> "Churchill viewing where
> The violence of Tallard most prevailed,
> Came to oppose his slaughtering arm. With speed
> Precipitate he rode, urging his way
> O'er hills of gasping heroes and fallen steeds
> Rolling in death. Destruction, grim with blood,
> Attends his furious course. Around his head
> The glowing balls play innocent, while he
> With dire impetuous sway deals fatal blows
> Among the flying Gauls. In Gallic blood
> He dyes his reeking sword, and strews the ground
> With headless ranks. What can they do? Or how
> Withstand his wide-destroying sword?"

Addison, with excellent sense and taste, departed from this ridiculous fashion. He reserved his praise for the qualities which made Marlborough truly great—energy, sagacity, military science. But, above all, the poet extolled the firmness of that mind which, in the midst of confusion, uproar and slaughter, examined and disposed everything with the serene wisdom of a higher intelligence.

Here it was that he introduced the famous comparison of Marlborough to an angel guiding the whirlwind. We will not dispute the general justice of Johnson's remarks on this passage. But we must point out one circumstance which appears to have escaped all the critics. The extraordinary effect which the simile produced when it first appeared, and which to the following generations seemed inexplicable, is doubtless to be chiefly attributed to a line which most readers now regard as a feeble parenthesis—

"Such as, of late, o'er pale Britannia passed."

Addison spoke, not of a storm, but of *the* storm. The great tempest of November, 1703, the only tempest which in our latitude has equalled the rage of a tropical hurricane, had left a dreadful recollection in the minds of all men. No other tempest was ever in this country the occasion of a parliamentary address or of a public fast. Whole fleets had been cast away. Large mansions had been blown down. One prelate had been buried beneath the ruins of his palace. London and Bristol had presented the appearance of cities just sacked. Hundreds of families were still in mourning. The prostrate trunks of large trees and the ruins of houses still attested, in all the southern counties, the fury of the blast. The popularity which the simile of the angel enjoyed among Addison's contemporaries has always seemed to us to be a remarkable instance of the advantage which, in rhetoric and poetry, the particular has over the general.

Soon after the "Campaign" was published Addison's "Narrative of his Travels in Italy." The first effect produced by this "Narrative" was disappointment. The crowd of readers who expected politics and scandal, speculations on the projects of Victor Amadeus, and anecdotes about the jollities of convents and the amours of cardinals and nuns, were confounded by finding that the writer's mind was much more occupied by the war between the Trojans and Rutulians than by the war between France and Austria, and that he seemed to have heard no scandal of later date than the gallantries of the Empress Faustina. In time, however, the judgment of the many was overruled by that of the few; and, before the book was reprinted, it was so eagerly sought that it sold for five times the original price. It is still read with pleasure: the style is pure and flowing, the classical quotations and allusions are numerous and happy, and we are now and then charmed by that singularly humane and delicate humour in which Addison excelled all men. Yet this agreeable work, even when considered merely as the history of a literary tour, may justly be censured on account of its faults of omission. We have already said that, though rich in extracts from the Latin poets, it contains scarcely any references to the Latin orators and historians. We must add that it contains little or rather no information respecting the history and literature of modern Italy. To the best of our remembrance Addison does not mention Dante, Petrarch, Boccaccio, Boiardo, Berni, Lorenzo de Medici or Machiavelli. He coldly tells us that at Ferrara he saw the tomb of Ariosto, and that at Venice he heard the gondoliers sing verses of Tasso. But for Tasso and Ariosto he cared far less than for Valerius Flaccus and Sidonius Apollinaris. The gentle flow of the Ticin brings a line of Silius to his mind. The sulphurous steam of Albula suggests to him several passages of Martial. But he has not a word to say of the illustrious dead of Santa Croce, he crosses the wood of Ravenna without recollecting the Spectre Huntsman, and wanders up and down Rimini without one thought of Francesca. At Paris he had eagerly sought an introduction to Boileau; but he seems not to have been at all aware that at Florence he was in the vicinity of a poet with whom Boileau could not sustain a comparison, of the greatest lyric poet of modern times, Vincenzio Filicaja. This is the more remarkable because Filicaja was the favourite poet of the all-accomplished Somers, under whose protection Addison travelled, and to whom the account of the Travels is dedicated. The truth is that Addison knew little and cared less about the literature of modern Italy. His favourite models were Latin; his favourite critics were French. Half the Tuscan poetry that he had read seemed to him monstrous and the other half tawdry.

His "Travels" were followed by the lively Opera of "Rosamond." This piece was ill set to music, and therefore failed on the stage, but it completely succeeded in print, and is, indeed, excellent in its kind. The smoothness with which the verses glide, and the elasticity with which they bound, is to our ears, at least, very pleasing. We are inclined to think that if Addison had left heroic couplets to Pope and blank verse to Rowe, and had employed himself in writing airy and spirited songs, his reputation as a poet would have stood far higher than it now does. Some years after his death, "Rosamond" was set to new music by Dr. Arne; and was performed with complete success. Several passages long retained their popularity, and were daily sung, during the latter part of George the Second's reign, at all the harpsichords in England.

While Addison thus amused himself, his prospects, and the prospects of his party, were constantly becoming brighter and brighter. In the spring of 1705 the ministers were freed from the restraint imposed by a House of Commons in which Tories of the most perverse class had the ascendency. The elections were favourable to the Whigs. The coalition which had been tacitly and gradually formed was now openly avowed. The Great Seal was given to Cowper. Somers and Halifax were sworn of the Council. Halifax was sent in the following year to carry the decorations of the order of the garter to the Electoral Prince of Hanover, and was accompanied on this honourable mission by Addison, who had just been made Under Secretary of State. The Secretary of State under whom Addison first served was Sir Charles Hedges, a Tory. But Hedges was soon dismissed, to make room for the most vehement of Whigs, Charles, Earl of Sunderland. In every department of the state, indeed, the High Churchmen were compelled to give place to their opponents. At the close of 1707, the Tories who still remained in office strove to rally, with Harley at their head. But the attempt, though favoured by the Queen, who had always been a Tory at heart, and who had now quarrelled with the Duchess of Marlborough, was unsuccessful. The time was not yet. The Captain General was at the height of popularity and glory. The Low Church party had a majority in Parliament. The country squires and rectors, though occasionally uttering a savage growl, were for the most part in a state of torpor, which lasted till they were roused into activity, and, indeed, into madness, by the prosecution of Sacheverell. Harley and his adherents were compelled to retire. The victory of the Whigs was complete. At the general election of 1708, their strength in the House of Commons became irresistible; and, before the end of that year, Somers was made Lord President of the Council and Wharton Lord Lieutenant of Ireland.[*]

Addison sat for Malmesbury in the House of Commons which was elected in 1708. But the House of Commons was not the field for him. The bashful,

---

[*] Miss Aikin has not informed herself accurately as to the politics of that time. We give a single specimen. We could easily give many. "The Earl of Sunderland" she says, "was not suffered long to retain his hard-won secretaryship. In the last month of 1708 he was dismissed to make room for Lord Dartmouth, who ranked with the Tories. Just at this time the Earl of Wharton, being appointed Lord Lieutenant of Ireland, named Mr. Addison his chief secretary." (1235). Sunderland was not dismissed to make room for Dartmouth till June, 1710; and most certainly Wharton would never have been appointed Lord Lieutenant at all if he had not been appointed long before Sunderland's dismissal. Miss Aikin's mistake exactly resembles that of a person who should relate the history of our times as follows; "Lord John Russell was dismissed in 1839 from the Home office, to make room for Sir James Graham, who ranked with the Tories, but just at this time, Earl Fortescue was appointed Lord Lieutenant of Ireland with Lord Morpeth for his secretary." Such a narrative would give to posterity rather a strange notion of the ministerial revolutions of Queen Victoria's days.

ness of his nature made his wit and eloquence useless in debate. He once rose, but could not overcome his diffidence, and ever after remained silent. Nobody can think it strange that a great writer should fail as a speaker. But many, probably, will think it strange that Addison's failure as a speaker should have had no unfavourable effect on his success as a politician. In our time, a man of high rank and great fortune might, though speaking very little and very ill, hold a considerable post. But it would now be inconceivable that a mere adventurer, a man who, when out of office, must live by his pen, should in a few years become successively Under Secretary of State, Chief Secretary for Ireland, and Secretary of State, without some oratorical talent. Addison, without high birth, and with little property, rose to a post which Dukes, the heads of the great houses of Talbot, Russell and Bentick, have thought it an honour to fill. Without opening his lips in debate, he rose to a post, the highest that Chatham or Fox ever reached. And this he did before he had been nine years in Parliament. We must look for the explanation of this seeming miracle to the peculiar circumstances in which that generation was placed. During the interval which elapsed between the time when the censorship of the Press ceased and the time when parliamentary proceedings began to be freely reported, literary talents were, to a public man, of much more importance, and oratorical talents of much less importance, than in our time. At present the best way of giving rapid and wide publicity to a fact or an argument is to introduce that fact or argument into a speech made in Parliament. If a political tract were to appear superior to the "Conduct of the Allies," or to the best numbers of the *Freeholder*, the circulation of such a tract would be languid indeed when compared with the circulation of every remarkable word uttered in the deliberations of the legislature. A speech made in the House of Commons at four in the morning is on thirty thousand tables before ten. A speech made on the Monday is read on the Wednesday by multitudes in Antrim and Aberdeenshire. The orator, by the help of the shorthand writer, has to a great extent superseded the pamphleteer. It was not so in the reign of Anne. The best speech could then produce no effect except on those who heard it. It was only by means of the Press that the opinion of the public without doors could be influenced; and the opinion of the public without doors could not but be of the highest importance in a country governed by parliaments; and, indeed, at that time governed by triennial parliaments. The pen was, therefore, a more formidable political engine than the tongue. Mr. Pitt and Mr. Fox contended only in Parliament. But Walpole and Pulteney, the Pitt and Fox of an earlier period, had not done half of what was necessary when they sat down amidst the acclamations of the House of Commons. They had still to plead their cause before the country, and this they could do only by means of the press. Their works are now forgotten. But it is certain that there were in Grub Street few more assiduous scribblers of thoughts, letters, answers, remarks, than these two great chiefs of parties. Pulteney, when leader of the Opposition, and possessed of £30,000 a year, edited the *Craftsman*. Walpole, though not a man of literary habits, was the author of at least ten pamphlets, and retouched and corrected many more. These facts sufficiently show of how great importance literary assistance then was to the contending parties. St. John was, certainly, in Anne's reign, the best Tory speaker; Cowper was probably the best Whig speaker. But it may well be doubted whether St. John did so much for the Tories as Swift, and whether Cowper did so much for the Whigs as Addison. When these things are duly considered, it will not be thought strange that Addison should have climbed higher in the state than any other Englishman has ever, by means merely of literary talents, been able to climb. Swift would, in all probability, have climbed as high, if he had not been encumbered by his cassock and his pudding sleeves. As far as the homage of the great went, Swift had as much of it as if he had been Lord Treasurer.

To the influence which Addison derived from his literary talents was added all the influence which arises from character. The world, always ready to think the worst of needy political adventurers, was forced to make one exception. Restlessness, violence, audacity, laxity of principle, are the vices ordinarily attributed to that class of men. But faction itself could not deny that Addison had, through all changes of fortune, been strictly faithful to his early opinions and to his early friends; that his integrity was without stain; that his whole deportment indicated a fine sense of the becoming; that, in the utmost heat of controversy, his zeal was tempered by a regard for truth, humanity and social decorum; that no outrage could ever provoke him to retaliation unworthy of a Christian and a gentleman; and that his only faults were a too sensitive delicacy and a modesty which amounted to bashfulness.

He was undoubtedly one of the most popular men of his time; and much of his popularity he owed, we believe, to that very timidity which his friends lamented. That timidity often prevented him from exhibiting his talents to the best advantage. But it propitiated Nemesis. It averted that envy which would otherwise have been excited by fame so splendid, and by so rapid an elevation. No man is so great a favourite with the public as he who is at once an object of admiration, of respect and of pity; and such were the feelings which Addison inspired. Those who enjoyed the privilege of hearing his familiar conversation, declared with one voice that it was superior even to his writings. The brilliant Mary Montagu said, that she had known all the wits, and that Addison was the best company in the world. The malignant Pope was forced to own that there was a charm in Addison's talk which could be found nowhere else. Swift, when burning with animosity against the Whigs, could not but confess to Stella that, after all, he had never known any associate so agreeable as Addison. Steele, an excellent judge of lively conversation, said, that the conversation of Addison was at once the most polite and the most mirthful that could be imagined—that it was Terence and Catullus in one, heightened by an exquisite something which was neither Terence nor Catullus, but Addison alone. Young, an excellent judge of serious conversation, said, that when Addison was at his ease, he went on in a noble strain of thought and language, so as to chain the attention of every hearer. Nor were his great colloquial powers more admirable than the courtesy and softness of heart which appeared in his conversation. At the same time, it would be too much to say that he was wholly devoid of the malice which is, perhaps, inseparable from a keen sense of the ludicrous. He had one habit which both Swift and Stella applauded, and which he hardly knew how to blame. If his first attempts to set a presuming dunce right were ill received, he changed his tone, "assented with civil leer," and lured the flattered coxcomb deeper and deeper into absurdity. That such was his practice, we should, we think, have guessed from his works. The *Tatler's* criticisms on Mr. Softly's sonnet, and the Spectator's dialogue with the politician who is so zealous for the honour of Lady Q—p—t—s, are excellent specimens of this innocent mischief.

Such were Addison's talents for conversation. But his rare gifts were not exhibited to crowds or to strangers. As soon as he entered a large company, as soon as he saw an unknown face, his lips were sealed and his manners became constrained. None who met him only in great assemblies would have been able to believe that he was the same man who had often kept a few friends listening and laughing round a table, from the time when the play ended, till the clock of St. Paul's in Covent Garden struck four. Yet, even at such a table, he was not seen to the best advantage. To enjoy his conversation in the highest perfection, it was necessary to be alone with him, and to hear him, in his own phrase, think aloud. "There is no such thing," he used to say, "as real conversation, but between two persons."

This timidity, a timidity surely neither ungraceful nor unamiable, led Addison into the two most serious faults which can with justice be imputed to him. He found that wine broke the spell which lay on his fine intellect, and was, therefore, too easily seduced into convivial excess. Such excess was in that age regarded, even by grave men, as the most venial of all peccadilloes; and was so far from being a mark of ill-breeding, that it was almost essential to the character of a fine gentleman. But the smallest speck is seen on a white ground; and almost all the biographers of Addison have said something about this failing. Of any other statesman or writer of Queen Anne's reign, we should no more think of saying that he sometimes took too much wine, than that he wore a long wig and a sword.

To the excessive modesty of Addison's nature, we must ascribe another fault which generally arises from a very different cause. He became a little too fond of seeing himself surrounded by a small circle of admirers, to whom he was as a King or rather as a God. All these men were far inferior to him in ability, and some of them had very serious faults. Nor did those faults escape his observation; for, if ever there was an eye which saw through and through men, it was the eye of Addison. But, with the keenest observation, and the finest sense of the ridiculous, he had a large charity. The feeling with which he looked on most of his humble companions was one of benevolence, slightly tinctured with contempt. He was at perfect ease in their company; he was grateful for their devoted attachment; and he loaded them with benefits. Their veneration for him appears to have exceeded that with which Johnson was regarded by Boswell, or Warburton by Hurd. It was not in the power of adulation to turn such a head or deprave such a heart as Addison's. But it must in candour be admitted that he contracted some of the faults which can scarcely be avoided by any person who is so unfortunate as to be the oracle of a small literary coterie.

One member of this little society was Eustace Budgell, a young Templar of some literature, and a distant relation of Addison. There was at this time no stain on the character of Budgell, and it is not improbable that his career would have been prosperous and honourable if the life of his cousin had been prolonged. But when the master was laid in the grave, the disciple broke loose from all restraint, descended rapidly from one degree of vice and misery to another, ruined his fortune by follies, attempted to repair it by crimes, and at length closed a wicked and unhappy life by self-murder. Yet, to the last, the wretched man, gambler, lampooner, cheat, forger, as he was, retained his affection and veneration for Addison, and recorded those feelings in the last lines which he traced before he hid himself from infamy under London Bridge.

Another of Addison's favourite companions was Ambrose Phillipps, a good Whig and a middling poet, who had the honour of bringing into fashion a species of composition which has been called, after his name, *Namby-Pamby*. But the most remarkable members of the little senate, as Pope long afterwards called it, were Richard Steele and Thomas Tickell.

Steele had known Addison from childhood. They had been together at the Charter House and at Oxford; but circumstances had then, for a time, separated them widely. Steele had left college without taking a degree, had been disinherited by a rich relation, had led a vagrant life, had served in the army, had tried to find the philosopher's stone and had written a religious treatise and several comedies. He was one of those people whom it is impossible either to hate or to respect. His temper was sweet, his affections warm, his spirits lively, his passions strong, and his principles weak. His life was spent in sinning and repenting; in inculcating what was right and doing what was wrong. In speculation, he was a man of piety and honour; in practice, he was much of the rake and a little of the swindler. He was, however, so goodnatured that it was not easy to be seriously angry with him, and that even rigid moralists felt more inclined to pity than to blame him, when he diced himself into a spunging house or drank himself into a fever. Addison regarded Steele with kindness not unmingled with scorn—tried, with little success, to keep him out of scrapes, introduced him to the great, procured a good place for him, corrected his plays and, though by no means rich, lent him large sums of money. One of these loans appears, from a letter dated in August, 1708, to have amounted to a thousand pounds. These pecuniary transactions probably led to frequent bickerings. It is said that, on one occasion, Steele's negligence, or dishonesty, provoked Addison to repay himself by the help of a bailiff. We cannot join with Miss Aikin in rejecting this story. Johnson heard it from Savage, who heard it from Steele. Few private transactions which took place a hundred and twenty years ago are proved by stronger evidence than this. But we can by no means agree with those who condemn Addison's severity. The most amiable of mankind may well be moved to indignation, when what he has earned hardly, and lent with great inconvenience to himself, for the purpose of relieving a friend in distress, is squandered with insane profusion. We will illustrate our meaning by an example, which is not the less striking because it is taken from fiction. Dr. Harrison, in Fielding's "Amelia," is represented as the most benevolent of human beings; yet he takes in execution, not only the goods, but the person of his friend Booth. Dr. Harrison resorts to this strong measure because he has been informed that Booth, while pleading poverty as an excuse for not paying just debts, has been buying fine jewellery and setting up a coach. No person who is well acquainted with Steele's life and correspondence can doubt that he behaved quite as ill to Addison as Booth was accused of behaving to Dr. Harrison. The real history, we have little doubt, was something like this:—A letter comes to Addison, imploring help in pathetic terms, and promising reformation and speedy repayment. Poor Dick declares that he has not an inch of candle, or a bushel of coals, or credit with the butcher for a shoulder of mutton. Addison is moved. He determines to deny himself some medals which are wanting to his series of the twelve "Cæsars;" to put off buying the new edition of "Bayle's Dictionary;" and to wear his old sword and buckles another year. In this way he manages to send a hundred pounds to his friend. The next day he calls on Steele and finds scores of gentlemen and ladies assembled. The fiddles are playing. The table is groaning under Champagne, Burgundy and pyramids of sweetmeats. Is it strange that a man whose kindness is thus abused, should send sheriff's officers to reclaim what is due to him?

Tickell was a young man, fresh from Oxford, who had introduced himself to public notice by writing a most ingenious and graceful little poem in praise of the opera of "Rosamond." He deserved, and at length attained, the first place in Addison's friendship. For a time Steele and Tickell were on good terms. But they loved Addison too much to love each other, and at length became as bitter enemies as the rival bulls in Virgil.

At the close of 1708 Wharton became Lord Lieutenant of Ireland, and appointed Addison Chief Secretary. Addison was consequently under the necessity of quitting London for Dublin. Besides the chief secretaryship, which was then worth about two thousand pounds a year, he obtained a patent appointing him keeper of the Irish Records for life, with a salary of three or four hundred a year. Budgell accompanied his cousin in the capacity of private Secretary.

Wharton and Addison had nothing in common but Whiggism. The Lord Lieutenant was not only licentious and corrupt, but was distinguished from other libertines and jobbers by a callous impudence which presented the strongest contrast to the Secretary's gentleness and delicacy. Many parts of the Irish administration at this time appear to have deserved serious blame. But against Addison there was not a murmur. He long afterwards asserted— what all the evidence which we have ever seen tends to prove—that his diligence and integrity gained the friendship of all the most considerable persons in Ireland.

The parliamentary career of Addison in Ireland has, we think, wholly escaped the notice of all his biographers. He was elected member for the borough of Cavan in the summer of 1709; and in the journals of two sessions his name frequently occurs. Some of the entries appear to indicate that he so far overcame his timidity as to make speeches. Nor is this by any means improbable; for the Irish House of Commons was a far less formidable audience than the English House; and many tongues which were tied by fear in the greater assembly became fluent in the smaller. Gerard Hamilton, for example, who, from fear of losing the fame gained by his "single speech," sat mute at Westminster during forty years, spoke with great effect at Dublin when he was Secretary to Lord Halifax.

While Addison was in Ireland, an event occurred to which he owes his high and permanent rank among British writers. As yet his fame rested on performances which, though highly respectable, were not built for duration, and which would, if he had produced nothing else, have now been almost forgotten: on some excellent Latin verses, on some English verses which occasionally rose above mediocrity, and on a book of travels, agreeably written, but not indicating any extraordinary powers of mind. These works showed him to be a man of taste, sense and learning. The time had come when he was to prove himself a man of genius, and to enrich our literature with compositions which will live as long as the English language.

In the spring of 1709 Steele formed a literary project, of which he was far indeed from forseeing the consequences. Periodical papers had during many years been published in London. Most of these were political; but in some of them questions of morality, taste and love-casuistry had been discussed. The literary merit of these works was small indeed; and even their names are now known only to the curious.

Steele had been appointed Gazetteer by Sunderland, at the request, it is said, of Addison, and thus had access to foreign intelligence earlier and more authentic than was in those times within the reach of an ordinary news-writer. This circumstance seems to have suggested to him the scheme of publishing a periodical paper on a new plan. It was to appear on the days on which the post left London for the country, which were, in that generation, the Tuesdays, Thursdays and Saturdays. It was to contain the foreign news, accounts of theatrical representations, and the literary gossip of Will's and of the Grecian. It was also to contain remarks on the fashionable topics of the day, compliments to beauties, pasquinades on noted sharpers, and criticisms on popular preachers. The aim of Steele does not appear to have been at first higher than this. He was not ill qualified to conduct the work which he had planned. His public intelligence he drew from the best sources. He knew the town, and had paid dear for his knowledge. He had read much more than the dissipated men of that time were in the habit of reading. He was a rake among scholars and a scholar among rakes. His style was easy and not incorrect; and, though his wit and humour were of no high order, his gay animal spirits imparted to his compositions an air of vivacity which ordinary readers could hardly distinguish from comic genius. His writings have been well compared to those light wines which, though deficient in body and flavour, are yet a pleasant small drink, if not kept too long or carried too far.

Isaac Bickerstaff, Esquire, Astrologer, was an imaginary person, almost as well known in that age as Mr. Paul Pry or Mr. Samuel Pickwick in ours. Swift had assumed the name of Bickerstaff in a satirical pamphlet against Partridge, the almanack-maker. Partridge had been fool enough to publish a furious reply. Bickerstaff had rejoined in a second pamphlet still more diverting than the first. All the wits had combined to keep up the joke, and the town was long in convulsions of laughter. Steele determined to employ the name which this controversy had made popular; and, in 1709, it was announced that Isaac Bickerstaff, Esquire, Astrologer, was about to publish a paper called the *Tatler*.

Addison had not been consulted about this scheme; but as soon as he heard of it, he determined to give it his assistance. The effect of that assistance cannot be better described than in Steele's own words. "I fared," he said, "like a distressed prince who calls in a powerful neighbour to his aid. I was undone by my auxiliary. When I had once called him in, I could not subsist without dependence on him." "The paper," he says elsewhere, "was advanced indeed. It was raised to a greater thing than I intended it."

It is probable that Addison, when he sent across St. George's Channel his first contribution to the *Tatler*, had no notion of the extent and variety of his own powers. He was the possessor of a vast mine, rich with a hundred ores. But he had been acquainted only with the least precious part of his treasures, and had hitherto contented himself with producing sometimes copper and sometimes lead, intermingled with a little silver. All at once, and by mere accident, he had lighted on an inexhaustible vein of the finest gold.

The mere choice and arrangement of his words would have sufficed to make his essays classical. For never, not even by Dryden, not even by Temple, had the English language been written with such sweetness, grace and facility. But this was the smallest part of Addison's praise. Had he clothed his thoughts in the half French style of Horace Walpole, or in the half Latin style of Dr. Johnson, or in the half German jargon of the present day, his genius would have triumphed over all faults of manner. As a moral satirist he stands unrivalled. If ever the best *Tatlers* and *Spectators* were equalled in their own kind, we should be inclined to guess that it must have been by the lost comedies of Menander.

In wit, properly so called, Addison was not inferior to Cowley or Butler. No single ode of Cowley contains so many happy analogies as are crowded into the lines to Sir Godfrey Kneller; and we would undertake to collect from the *Spectator* as great a number of ingenious illustrations as can be found in "Hudibras." The still higher faculty of invention Addison possessed in still larger measure. The numerous fictions, generally original, often wild and grotesque, but always singularly graceful and happy, which are found in his essays, fully entitle him to the rank of a great poet—a rank to which his metrical compositions give him no claim. As an observer of life, of manners, of all the shades of human character, he stands in the first class. And what he observed he had the art of communicating in two widely different ways. He could describe virtues, vices, habits, whims, as well as Clarendon. But he could do something better. He could call human beings into existence and make them exhibit themselves. If we wish to find anything more vivid than Addison's best portraits, we must go either to Shakspeare or to Cervantes.

But what shall we say of Addison's humour, of his sense of the ludicrous, of his power of awakening that sense in others, and of drawing mirth from incidents which occur every day, and from little peculiarities of temper and manner, such as may be found in every man? We feel the charm: we give ourselves up to it: but we strive in vain to analyse it.

Perhaps the best way of describing Addison's peculiar pleasantry is to compare it with the pleasantry of some other great satirists. The three most eminent masters of the art of ridicule, during the eighteenth century, were, we conceive, Addison, Swift and Voltaire. Which of the three had the greatest power of moving laughter may be questioned. But each of them, within his own domain, was supreme. Voltaire is the prince of buffoons. His merriment is without disguise or restraint. He gambols; he grins; he shakes his sides; he points the finger; he turns up the nose; he shoots out the tongue. The manner of Swift is the very opposite to this. He moves laughter, but never joins in it. He appears in his works such as he appeared in society. All the company are convulsed with merriment, while the Dean, the author of all the mirth, preserves an invincible gravity and even sourness of aspect, and gives utterance to the most eccentric and ludicrous fancies, with the air of a man reading the commination-service.

The manner of Addison is as remote from that of Swift as from that of Voltaire. He neither laughs out like the French wit nor, like the Irish wit, throws a double portion of severity into his countenance while laughing inly; but preserves a look peculiarly his own, a look of demure serenity, disturbed only by an arch sparkle of the eye, an almost imperceptible elevation of the brow, an almost imperceptible curl of the lip. His tone is never that either of a Jack Pudding or of a Cynic. It is that of a gentleman, in whom the quickest sense of the ridiculous is constantly tempered by good nature and good breeding.

We own that the humour of Addison is, in our opinion, of a more delicious flavour than the humour of either Swift or Voltaire. Thus much, at least, is certain, that both Swift and Voltaire have been successfully mimicked, and that no man has yet been able to mimic Addison. The letter of the Abbé Coyer to Pansophe is Voltaire all over, and imposed, during a long time, on the Academicians of Paris. There are passages in Arbuthnot's satirical works which we, at least, cannot distinguish from Swift's best writing. But of the many eminent men who have made Addison their model, though several have copied his mere diction with happy effect, none has been able to catch the tone of his pleasantry. In the *World*, in the *Connoisseur*, in the *Mirror*, in the *Lounger*, there are numerous papers written in obvious imitation of his *Tatlers* and *Spectators*. Most of those papers have some merit; many are very lively and amusing; but there is not a single one which could be passed off as Addison's on a critic of the smallest perspicacity.

But that which chiefly distinguishes Addison from Swift, from Voltaire, from almost all the other great masters of ridicule, is the grace, the nobleness, the moral purity, which we find even in his merriment. Severity, gradually hardening and darkening into misanthropy, characterises the works of Swift. The nature of Voltaire was, indeed, not inhuman; but he venerated nothing. Neither in the masterpieces of art nor in the purest examples of virtue, neither in the Great First Cause nor in the awful enigma of the grave, could he see anything but subjects for drollery. The more solemn and august the theme, the more monkey-like was his grimacing and chattering. The mirth of Swift is the mirth of Mephistophiles; the mirth of Voltaire is the mirth of Puck. If, as Soame Jenyns oddly imagined, a portion of the happiness of Seraphim and just men made perfect be derived from an exquisite perception of the ludicrous, their mirth must surely be none other than the mirth of Addison; a mirth consistent with tender compassion for all that is frail, and with profound reverence for all that is sublime. Nothing great, nothing amiable, no moral duty, no doctrine of natural or revealed religion, has ever been associated by

Addison with any degrading idea. His humanity is without a parallel in literary history. The highest proof of virtue is to possess boundless power without abusing it. No kind of power is more formidable than the power of making men ridiculous; and that power Addison possessed in boundless measure. How grossly that power was abused by Swift and by Voltaire is well known. But of Addison it may be confidently affirmed that he has blackened no man's character, nay, that it would be difficult, if not impossible, to find in all the volumes which he has left us a single taunt which can be called ungenerous or unkind. Yet he had detractors, whose malignity might have seemed to justify as terrible a revenge as that which men, not superior to him in genius, wreaked on Bettesworth and on Franc de Pompignan. He was a politician; he was the best writer of his party; he lived in times of fierce excitement—in times when persons of high character and station stooped to scurrility such as is now practised only by the basest of mankind. Yet no provocation and no example could induce him to return railing for railing.

Of the service which his Essays rendered to morality it is difficult to speak too highly. It is true that, when the *Tatler* appeared, that age of outrageous profaneness and licentiousness which followed the Restoration had passed away. Jeremy Collier had shamed the theatres into something which, compared with the excesses of Etherege and Wycherley, might be called decency. Yet there still lingered in the public mind a pernicious notion that there was some connection between genius and profligacy—between the domestic virtues and the sullen formality of the Puritans. That error it is the glory of Addison to have dispelled. He taught the nation that the faith and the morality of Hale and Tillotson might be found in company with wit more sparkling than the wit of Congreve and with humour richer than the humour of Vanbrugh. So effectually, indeed, did he retort on vice the mockery which had recently been directed against virtue, that, since his time, the open violation of decency has always been considered among us as the mark of a fool. And this revolution, the greatest and most salutary ever effected by any satirist, he accomplished, be it remembered, without writing one personal lampoon.

In the early contributions of Addison to the *Tatler* his peculiar powers were not fully exhibited. Yet from the first, his superiority to all his coadjutors was evident. Some of his later *Tatlers* are fully equal to anything that he ever wrote. Among the portraits we most admire Tom Folio, Ned Softly and the Political Upholsterer. The proceedings of the Court of Honour, the Thermometer of Zeal, the story of the Frozen Words, the Memoirs of the Shilling, are excellent specimens of that ingenious and lively species of fiction in which Addison excelled all men. There is one still better paper of the same class. But though that paper, a hundred and thirty-three years ago, was probably thought as edifying as one of Smalridge's sermons, we dare not indicate to the squeamish readers of the nineteenth century.

During the session of Parliament which commenced in November, 1709, and which the impeachment of Sacheverell has made memorable, Addison appears to have resided in London. The *Tatler* was now more popular than any periodical paper had ever been; and his connection with it was generally known. It was not known, however, that almost everything good in the *Tatler* was his. The truth is, that the fifty or sixty numbers which we owe to him were not merely the best, but so decidedly the best that any five of them are more valuable than all the two hundred numbers in which he had no share.

He required, at this time, all the solace which he could derive from literary success. The Queen had always disliked the Whigs. She had during some years disliked the Marlborough family. But, reigning by a disputed title, she could not venture directly to oppose herself to a majority of both Houses of

Parliament; and, engaged as she was in a war on the event of which her own Crown was staked, she could not venture to disgrace a great and successful general. But at length, in the year 1710, the causes which had restrained her from showing her aversion to the Low Church party ceased to operate. The trial of Sacheverell produced an outbreak of public feeling scarcely less violent than the outbreaks which we can ourselves remember in 1820 and in 1831. The country gentlemen, the country clergymen, the rabble of the towns, were all, for once, on the same side. It was clear that, if a general election took place before the excitement abated, the Tories would have a majority. The services of Marlborough had been so splendid that they were no longer necessary. The Queen's throne was secure from all attack on the part of Louis. Indeed, it seemed much more likely that the English and German armies would divide the spoils of Versailles and Marli than that a Marshal of France would bring back the Pretender to St. James's. The Queen, acting by the advice of Harley, determined to dismiss her servants. In June the change commenced. Sunderland was the first who fell. The Tories exulted over his fall. The Whigs tried, during a few weeks, to persuade themselves that her Majesty had acted only from personal dislike to the Secretary, and that she meditated no further alteration. But early in August, Godolphin was surprised by a letter from Anne, which directed him to break his white staff. Even after this event, the irresolution or dissimulation of Harley kept up the hopes of the Whigs during another month; and then the ruin became rapid and violent. The Parliament was dissolved. The Ministers were turned out. The Tories were called to office. The tide of popularity ran violently in favour of the High Church party. That party, feeble in the the late House of Commons, was now irresistible. The power which the Tories had thus suddenly acquired, they used with blind and stupid ferocity. The howl which the whole pack set up for prey and for blood appalled even him who had roused and unchained them. When, at this distance of time, we calmly review the conduct of the discarded ministers, we cannot but feel a movement of indignation at the injustice with which they were treated. No body of men had ever administered the government with more energy, ability and moderation; and their success had been proportioned to their wisdom. They had saved Holland and Germany. They had humbled France. They had, as it seemed, all but torn Spain from the House of Bourbon. They had made England the first power in Europe. At home they had united England and Scotland. They had respected the rights of conscience and the liberty of the subject. They retired, leaving their country at the height of prosperity and glory.* And yet they were pursued to their retreat by such a roar of obloquy as was never raised against the government which threw away thirteen colonies, or against the government which sent a gallant army to perish in the ditches of Walcheren.

None of the Whigs suffered more in the general wreck than Addison. He had just sustained some heavy pecuniary losses, of the nature of which we are imperfectly informed, when his Secretaryship was taken from him. He had reason to believe that he should also be deprived of the small Irish office which he held by patent. He had just resigned his Fellowship. It seems probable that he had already ventured to raise his eyes to a great lady, and that, while his political friends were in power, and while his own fortunes were rising, he had been, in the phrase of the romances which were then fashionable, permitted to hope. But Mr. Addison the ingenious writer, and Mr. Addison the chief Secretary, were, in her ladyship's opinion, two very different persons.

---

* Miss Aikin attributes the unpopularity of the Whigs and the change of government to the surrender of Stanhope's army (ii. 13). The fact is, that the Ministry was changed and the new House of Commons elected, before that surrender took p'ace.

All these calamities united, however, could not disturb the serene cheerfulness of a mind conscious of innocence, and rich in its own wealth. He told his friends, with smiling resignation, that they ought to admire his philosophy, that he had lost at once his fortune, his place, his Fellowship and his mistress, that he must think of turning tutor again, and yet that his spirits were as good as ever.

He had one consolation. Of the unpopularity which his friends had incurred, he had no share. Such was the esteem with which he was regarded that, while the most violent measures were taken for the purpose of forcing Tory members on Whig corporations, he was returned to Parliament without even a contest. Swift, who was now in London, and who had already determined on quitting the Whigs, wrote to Stella in these remarkable words: "The Tories carry it among the new members six to one. Mr. Addison's election has passed easy and undisputed; and I believe if he had a mind to be king he would hardly be refused."

The good will with which the Tories regarded Addison is the more honourable to him, because it had not been purchased by any concession on his part. During the general election he published a political Journal, entitled the *Whig Examiner*. Of that Journal it may be sufficient to say that Johnson, in spite of his strong political prejudices, pronounced it to be superior in wit to any of Swift's writings on the other side. When it ceased to appear, Swift, in a letter to Stella, expressed his exultation at the death of so formidable an antagonist. "He might well rejoice." says Johnson, "at the death of that which he could not have killed." "On no occasion," he adds, "was the genius of Addison more vigorously exerted, and on none did the superiority of his powers more evidently appear."

The only use which Addison appears to have made of the favour with which he was regarded by the Tories was to save some of his friends from the general ruin of the Whig party. He felt himself to be in a situation which made it his duty to take a decided part in politics. But the case of Steele and of Ambrose Phillipps was different. For Phillipps, Addison even condescended to solicit, with what success we have not ascertained.* Steele held two places. He was Gazetteer, and he was also a Commissioner of Stamps. The *Gazette* was taken from him. But he was suffered to retain his place in the Stamp Office, on an implied understanding that he should not be active against the new government; and he was, during more than two years, induced by Addison to observe this armistice with tolerable fidelity.

Isaac Bickerstaff accordingly became silent upon politics, and the article of News, which had once formed about one-third of his paper, altogether disappeared. The *Tatler* had completely changed its character. It was now nothing but a series of essays on books, morals and manners. Steele, therefore, resolved to bring it to a close and commence a new work on an improved plan. It was announced that this new work would be published daily. The undertaking was generally regarded as bold, or rather rash; but the event amply justified the confidence with which Steele relied on the fertility of Addison's genius. On the second of January, 1711, appeared the last *Tatler*. At the begin of March following appeared the first of an incomparable series of papers, containing observations on life and literature by an imaginary Spectator.

---

* Miss Aikin mentions the exertions which Addison made in 1710, before the change of Ministry, to serve Phillipps, and adds that " Phillipps some time afterwards appears to have obtained a mission to Copenhagen, which enabled him to gratify the world with his poetical description of a frozen shower." (ii. 14). This is all wrong. The poem was written in March, 1709, and printed in the *Tatler* of the 6th of May, following.

The Spectator himself was conceived and drawn by Addison; and it is not easy to doubt that the portrait was meant to be in some features a likeness of the painter. The Spectator is a gentleman who, after passing a studious youth at the university, has travelled on classic ground and has bestowed much attention on curious points of antiquity. He has, on his return, fixed his residence, in London, and has observed all the forms of life which are to be found in that great city; has daily listened to the wits of Will's, has smoked with the philosophers of the Grecian, and has mingled with the parsons at Child's and with the politicians at the St. James's. In the morning he often listens to the hum of the Exchange; in the evening his face is constantly to be seen in the pit of Drury Lane Theatre. But an insurmountable bashfulness prevents him from opening his mouth, except in a small circle of intimate friends.

These friends were first sketched by Steele. Four of the club, the templar, the clergyman, the soldier and the merchant were uninteresting figures, fit only for a background. But the other two, an old country baronet and an old town rake, though not delineated with a very delicate pencil, had some good strokes. Addison took the rude outlines into his own hands, retouched them, coloured them, and is in truth the creator of the Sir Roger de Coverley and the Will Honeycomb with whom we are all familiar.

The plan of the *Spectator* must be allowed to be both original and eminently happy. Every valuable essay in the series may be read with pleasure separately; yet the five or six hundred essays form a whole, and a whole which has the interest of a novel. It must be remembered, too, that at that time no novel, giving a lively and powerful picture of the common life and manners of England, had appeared. Richardson was working as a compositor. Fielding was robbing birds' nests. Smollett was not yet born. The narrative, therefore, which connects together the Spectator's Essays, gave to our ancestors their first taste of an exquisite and untried pleasure. That narrative was indeed constructed with no art or labour. The events were such events as occur every day. Sir Roger comes up to town to see Eugenio, as the worthy baronet always calls Prince Eugene, goes with the Spectator on the water to Spring Gardens, walks among the tombs in the Abbey, and is frightened by the Mohawks, but conquers his apprehension so far as to go to the theatre when the "Distressed Mother" is acted. The Spectator pays a visit in the summer to Coverley Hall, is charmed with the old house, the old butler and the old chaplain, eats a jack caught by Will Wimble, rides to the assizes and hears a point of law discussed by Tom Touchy. At last a letter from the honest butler brings to the club the news that Sir Roger is dead. Will Honeycomb marries and reforms at sixty. The club breaks up; and the Spectator resigns his functions. Such events can hardly be said to form a plot; yet they are related with such truth, such grace, such wit, such humour, such pathos, such knowledge of the human heart, such knowledge of the ways of the world, that they charm us on the hundredth perusal. We have not the least doubt that if Addison had written a novel on an extensive plan, it would have been superior to any that we possess. As it is, he is entitled to be considered, not only as the greatest of the English essayists, but as the forerunner of the great English novelists.

We say this of Addison alone: for Addison is the *Spectator*. About three-sevenths of the work are his; and it is no exaggeration to say that his worst essay is as good as the best essay of any of his coadjutors. His best essays approach near to absolute perfection; nor is their excellence more wonderful than their variety. His invention never seems to flag; nor is he ever under the necessity of repeating himself, or of wearing out a subject. There are no dregs in his wine. He regales us after the fashion of that prodigal nabob who held that there was only one good-glass in a bottle. As soon as we have tasted the first sparkling foam of a jest it is withdrawn, and a fresh draught of nectar is at our lips. On the Monday we have an allegory as lively and ingenious as Lucian's "Auction of Lives"; on the Tuesday an Eastern apologue, as richly coloured as the "Tales of Scherezade"; on the Wednesday, a character described with the skill of La Bruyere; on the Thursday, a scene from common life, equal to the best chapters in the "Vicar of Wakefield"; on the Friday, some sly Horatian pleasantry on fashionable follies—on hoops, patches or puppet shows; and on the Saturday a religious meditation, which will bear a comparison with the finest passages in Massillon.

It is dangerous to select where there is so much that deserves the highest praise. We will venture, however, to say that any person who wishes to form a just notion of the extent and variety of Addison's powers, will do well to read at one sitting the following papers:—the two Visits to the Abbey, the Visit to the Exchange, the Journal of the Retired Citizen, the Vision of Mirza, the Transmigrations of Pug the Monkey, and the death of Sir Roger de Coverley.*

The least valuable of Addison's contributions to the *Spectator* are, in the judgment of our age, his critical papers. Yet his critical papers are always luminous and often ingenious. The very worst of them must be regarded as creditable to him, when the character of the school in which he had been trained is fairly considered. The best of them were much too good for his readers. In truth, he was not so far behind our generation as he was before his own. No essays in the *Spectator* were more censured and derided than those in which he raised his voice against the contempt with which our fine old ballads were regarded, and showed the scoffers that the same gold which, burnished and polished, gives lustre to the "Æneid" and the "Odes of Horace," is mingled with the rude dross of "Chevy Chace."

It is not strange that the success of the *Spectator* should have been such as no similar work has ever obtained. The number of copies daily distributed was at first three thousand. It subsequently increased, and had risen to near four thousand when the stamp tax was imposed. That tax was fatal to a crowd of journals. The *Spectator*, however, stood its ground, doubled its price, and, though its circulation fell off, still yielded a large revenue both to the state and to the authors. For particular papers the demand was immense; of some, it is said, twenty thousand copies were required. But this was not all. To have the *Spectator* served up every morning with the bohea and rolls was a luxury for the few. The majority were content to wait till essays enough had appeared to form a volume. Ten thousand copies of each volume were immediately taken off, and new editions were called for. It must be remembered that the population of England was then hardly a third of what it now is. The number of Englishmen who were in the habit of reading, was probably not a sixth of what it now is. A shopkeeper or a farmer who found any pleasure in literature was a rarity. Nay, there was doubtless more than one knight of the shire whose country seat did not contain ten books—receipt books and books on farriery included. In these circumstances, the sale of the *Spectator* must be considered as indicating a popularity quite as great as that of the most successful works of Sir Walter Scott and Mr. Dickens in our own time.

At the close of 1712 the *Spectator* ceased to appear. It was probably felt that the short-faced gentleman and his club had been long enough before the town, and that it was time to withdraw them, and to replace them by a new set of characters. In a few weeks the first number of the *Guardian*

---

* Nos. 26, 329, 69, 317, 159, 343, 517. These papers are all in the first seven volumes. The eighth must be considered as a separate work.

was published.* But the *Guardian* was unfortunate both in its birth and in its death. It began in dulness and disappeared in a tempest of faction. The original plan was bad. Addison contributed nothing till sixty-six numbers had appeared, and it was then impossible even for him to make the *Guardian* what the *Spectator* had been. Nestor Ironside and the Miss Lizards were people to whom even he could impart no interest. He could only furnish some excellent little essays, both serious and comic, and this he did.

Why Addison gave no assistance to the *Guardian* during the first two months of its existence, is a question which has puzzled the editors and biographers, but which seems to us to admit of a very easy solution. He was then engaged in bringing his "Cato" on the stage.

The first four acts of this drama had been lying in his desk since his return from Italy. His modest and sensitive nature shrank from the risk of a public and shameful failure; and, though all who saw the manuscript were loud in praise, some thought it possible that an audience might become impatient even of very good rhetoric, and advised Addison to print the play without hazarding a representation. At length, after many fits of apprehension, the poet yielded to the urgency of his political friends, who hoped that the public would discover some analogy between the followers of Cæsar and the Tories, between Sempronius and the apostate Whigs, between Cato, struggling to the last for the liberties of Rome, and the band of patriots who still stood firm round Halifax and Wharton.

Addison gave the play to the managers of Drury Lane Theatre, without stipulating for any advantage to himself. They, therefore, thought themselves bound to spare no cost in scenery and dresses. The decorations, it is true, would not have pleased the skilful eye of Mr. Macready. Juba's waistcoat blazed with gold lace; Marcia's hoop was worthy of a duchess on the birthday, and Cato wore a wig worth fifty guineas. The prologue was written by Pope, and is undoubtedly a dignified and spirited composition. The part of the hero was excellently played by Booth. Steele undertook to pack a house. The boxes were in a blaze with the stars of the Peers in opposition. The pit was crowded with attentive and friendly listeners from the Inns of Court and the literary coffee houses. Sir Gilbert Heathcote, Governor of the Bank of England, was at the head of a powerful body of auxiliaries from the City—warm men and true Whigs, but better known at Jonathan's and Garraway's than in the haunts of wits and critics.

These precautions were quite superfluous. The Tories, as a body, regarded Addison with no unkind feelings. Nor was it for their interest—professing, as they did, profound reverence for law and prescription, and abhorrence both of popular insurrections and of standing armies—to appropriate to themselves reflections thrown on the great military chief and demagogue, who, with the support of the legions and of the common people, subverted all the ancient institutions of his country. Accordingly, every shout that was raised by the members of the Kit-Cat was echoed by the High Churchmen of the October, and the curtain at length fell amidst thunders of unanimous applause.

The delight and admiration of the town were described by the *Guardian* in terms which we might attribute to partiality, were it not that the *Examiner*, the organ of the ministry, held similar language. The Tories, indeed, found much to sneer at in the conduct of their opponents. Steele had on this, as on other occasions, shown more zeal than taste or judgment. The honest citizens who marched under the orders of Sir Gibby, as he was facetiously called, probably knew better when to buy and when to sell stock than when to clap

---

* Miss Aikin says that the *Guardian* was launched in November, 1713 (ii. 106). It was launched in March, 1713, and was given over in the following September.

and when to hiss at a play, and incurred some ridicule by making the hypocritical Sempronius their favourite, and by giving to his insincere rants louder plaudits than they bestowed on the temperate eloquence of Cato. Wharton, too, who had the incredible effrontery to applaud the lines about flying from prosperous vice and from the power of impious men to a private station, did not escape the sarcasms of those who justly thought that he could fly from nothing more vicious or impious than himself. The epilogue, which was written by Garth, a zealous Whig, was severely and not unreasonably censured as ignoble and out of place. But Addison was described, even by the bitterest Tory writers, as a gentleman of wit and virtue, in whose friendship many persons of both parties were happy, and whose name ought not to be mixed up with factious squabbles.

Of the jests by which the triumph of the Whig party was disturbed, the most severe and happy was Bolingbroke's. Between two acts he sent for Booth to his box, and presented him, before the whole theatre, with a purse of fifty guineas, for defending the cause of liberty so well against the perpetual Dictator.*

It was April; and in April, a hundred and thirty years ago, the London season was thought to be far advanced. During a whole month, however, "Cato" was performed to overflowing houses, and brought into the treasury of the theatre twice the gains of an ordinary spring. In the summer the Drury Lane Company went down to the Act at Oxford, and there, before an audience which retained an affectionate remembrance of Addison's accomplishments and virtues, his tragedy was acted during several days. The gownsmen began to besiege the theatre in the forenoon, and by one in the afternoon all the seats were filled.

About the merits of the piece which had so extraordinary an effect, the public, we suppose, has made up its mind. To compare it with the masterpieces of the Attic stage, with the great English dramas of the time of Elizabeth, or even with the productions of Schiller's manhood, would be absurd indeed. Yet it contains excellent dialogue and declamation, and among plays fashioned on the French model, must be allowed to rank high; not, indeed, with "Athalie," "Zaire," or "Saul;" but, we think, not below "Cinna," and certainly above any other English tragedy of the same school, above many of the plays of Corneille, above many of the plays of Voltaire and Alfieri, and above some plays of Racine. Be this as it may, we have little doubt that "Cato" did as much as the *Tatlers*, *Spectators* and *Freeholders* united, to raise Addison's fame among his contemporaries.

The modesty and good nature of the successful dramatist had tamed even the malignity of faction. But literary envy, it should seem, is a fiercer passion than party spirit. It was by a zealous Whig that the fiercest attack on the Whig tragedy was made. John Dennis published remarks on "Cato," which were written with some acuteness and with much coarseness and asperity. Addison neither defended himself nor retaliated. On many points he had an excellent defence, and nothing would have been easier than to retaliate; for Dennis had written bad odes, bad tragedies, bad comedies; he had, moreover, a larger share than most men of those infirmities and eccentricities which excite laughter; and Addison's power of turning either an absurd book or an absurd man into ridicule was unrivalled. Addison, however, serenely conscious of his superiority, looked with pity on his assailant, whose temper, naturally irritable and gloomy, had been soured by want, by controversy, and by literary failures.

But among the young candidates for Addison's favour there was one distinguished by talents from the rest, and distinguished, we fear, not less by

---

* "The long sway of the Duke of Marlborough," says Miss Aikin, "was here glanced at." Under favour, if Bolingbroke had meant no more than this, his sarcasm would have been pointless. The allusion was to the attempt which Marlborough had made to convert the Captain-Generalship into a patent office, to be held by himself for life. The patent was stopped by Lord Cowper.

malignity and insincerity. Pope was only twenty-five. But his powers had expanded to their full maturity; and his best poem, the "Rape of the Lock," had recently been published. Of his genius, Addison had always expressed high admiration. But Addison had early discerned, what might indeed have been discerned by an eye less penetrating than his, that the diminutive, crooked, sickly boy was eager to revenge himself on society for the unkindness of nature. In the *Spectator*, the "Essay on Criticism" had been praised with cordial warmth; but a gentle hint had been added, that the writer of so excellent a poem would have done well to avoid ill-natured personalities. Pope, though evidently more galled by the censure than gratified by the praise, returned thanks for the admonition and promised to profit by it. The two writers continued to exchange civilities, counsel and small good offices. Addison publicly extolled Pope's miscellaneous pieces; and Pope furnished Addison with a prologue. This did not last long. Pope hated Dennis, whom he had injured without provocation. The appearance of the "Remarks on Cato" gave the irritable poet an opportunity of venting his malice under the show of friendship; and such an opportunity could not but be welcome to a nature which was implacable in enmity, and which always preferred the tortuous to the straight path. He published, accordingly, the "Narrative of the Frenzy of John Dennis." But Pope had mistaken his powers. He was a great master of invective and sarcasm: he could dissect a character in terse and sonorous couplets, brilliant with antithesis: but of dramatic talent he was altogether destitute. If he had written a lampoon on Dennis, such as that on Atticus, or that on Sporus, the old grumbler would have been crushed. But Pope writing dialogue resembled—to borrow Horace's imagery and his own —a wolf, which, instead of biting, should take to kicking, or a monkey which should try to sting. The "Narrative" is utterly contemptible. Of argument there is not even the show; and the jests are such as, if they were introduced into a farce, would call forth the hisses of the shilling gallery. Dennis raves about the drama; and the nurse thinks that he is calling for a dram. "There is," he cries, "no peripetia in the tragedy, no change of fortune, no change at all.". "Pray, good sir, be not angry," says the old woman, "I'll fetch change." This is not exactly the pleasantry of Addison.

There can be no doubt that Addison saw through this officious zeal, and felt himself deeply aggrieved by it. So foolish and spiteful a pamphlet could do him no good, and if he were thought to have any hand in it, must do him harm. Gifted with incomparable powers of ridicule; he had never, even in self-defence, used those powers inhumanly or uncourteously; and he was not disposed to let others make his fame and his interests a pretext under which they might commit outrages from which he had himself constantly abstained. He accordingly declared that he had no concern in the "Narrative," that he disapproved of it, and that if he answered the "Remarks," he would answer them like a gentleman; and he took care to communicate this to Dennis. Pope was bitterly mortified; and to this transaction we are inclined to ascribe the hatred with which he ever after regarded Addison.

In September, 1713, the *Guardian* ceased to appear. Steele had gone mad about politics. A general election had just taken place: he had been chosen member for Stockbridge; and fully expected to play a first part in Parliament. The immense success of the *Tatler* and *Spectator* had turned his head. He had been the editor of both those papers and was not aware how entirely they owed their influence and popularity to the genius of his friend. His spirits, always violent, were now excited by vanity, ambition and faction, to such a pitch that he every day committed some offence against good sense and good taste. All the discreet and moderate members of his own party regretted and condemned his folly. "I am in a thousand troubles," Addison wrote, "about poor Dick, and wish that his zeal for the public may not be ruinous to himself.

But he has sent me word that he is determined to go on, and that any advice I may give him in this particular will have no weight with him."

Steel set up a political paper called the *Englishman*, which, as it was not supported by contributions from Addison, completely failed. By this work, by some other writings of the same kind, and by the airs which he gave himself at the first meeting of the new Parliament, he made the Tories so angry that they determined to expel him. The Whigs stood by him gallantly, but were unable to save him. The vote of expulsion was regarded by all dispassionate men as a tyrannical exercise of the power of the majority. But Steele's violence and folly, though they by no means justified the steps which his enemies took, had completelely disgusted his friends; nor did he ever regain the place which he had held in the public estimation.

Addison, about this time, conceived the design of adding an eighth volume to the *Spectator*. In June, 1714, the first number of the new series appeared, and during about six months three papers were published weekly. Nothing can be more striking than the contrast between the *Englishman* and the eighth volume of the *Spectator*—between Steele without Addison, and Addison without Steele. The *Englishman* is forgotten; the eighth volume of the *Spectator* contains, perhaps, the finest essays, both serious and playful, in the English language.

Before this volume was completed, the death of Anne produced an entire change in the administration of public affairs. The blow fell suddenly. It found the Tory party distracted by internal feuds and unprepared for any great effort. Harley had just been disgraced. Bolingbroke, it was supposed, would be the chief minister. But the Queen was on her death-bed before the white staff had been given, and her last public act was to deliver it with a feeble hand to the Duke of Shrewsbury. The emergency produced a coalition between all sections of public men who were attached to the Protestant succession. George I. was proclaimed without opposition. A Council, in which the leading Whigs had seats, took the direction of affairs till the new King should arrive. The first act of the Lords Justices was to appoint Addison their secretary.

There is an idle tradition that he was directed to prepare a letter to the King, that he could not satisfy himself as to the style of this composition, and that the Lords Justices called in a clerk who at once did what was wanted. It is not strange that a story so flattering to mediocrity should be popular; and we are sorry to deprive dunces of their consolation. But the truth must be told. It was well observed by Sir James Mackintosh, whose knowledge of these times was unequalled, that Addison never, in any official document, affected wit or eloquence, and that his despatches are, without exception, remarkable for unpretending simplicity. Everybody who knows with what ease Addison's finest essays were produced must be convinced that, if well turned phrases had been wanted, he would have had no difficulty in finding them. We are, however, inclined to believe, that the story is not absolutely without a foundation. It may well be that Addison did not know, till he had consulted experienced clerks who remembered the times when William III. was absent on the Continent, in what form a letter from the Council of Regency to the King ought to be drawn. We think it very likely that the ablest statesmen of our time, Lord John Russell, Sir Robert Peel, Lord Palmerston, for example, would, in similar circumstances, be found quite as ignorant. Every office has some little mysteries which the dullest man may learn with a little attention, and which the greatest man cannot possibly know by intuition. One paper must be signed by the chief of the department, another by his deputy. To a third the royal sign-manual is necessary. One communication is to be registered and another is not. One sentence must be in black ink and another in red ink. If the ablest Secretary for Ireland were moved to the India Board, if the ablest President of the India Board were moved to the War Office, he would require instruction on points like these; and we do not doubt that Addison required such instruction when he became, for the first time, Secretary to the Lords Justices.

George I. took possession of his kingdom without opposition. A new ministry was formed and a new Parliament, favourable to the Whigs, chosen. Sunderland was appointed Lord Lieutenant of Ireland, and Addison again went to Dublin as Chief Secretary.

At Dublin Swift resided, and there was much speculation about the way in which the Dean and the Secretary would behave towards each other. The relations which existed between these remarkable men form an interesting and pleasing portion of literary history. They had early attached themselves to the same political party and to the same patrons. While Anne's Whig ministry was in power, the visits of Swift to London and the official residence of Addison in Ireland had given them opportunities of knowing each other. They were the two shrewdest observers of their age. But their observations on each other had led them to favourable conclusions. Swift did full justice to the rare powers of conversation which were latent under the bashful deportment of Addison. Addison, on the other hand, discerned much good nature under the severe look and manner of Swift; and, indeed, the Swift of 1708 and the Swift of 1738 were two very different men.

But the paths of the two friends diverged widely. The Whig statesmen loaded Addison with solid benefits. They praised Swift, asked him to dinner, and did nothing more for him. His profession laid them under a difficulty. In the State they could not promote him; and they had reason to fear that, by bestowing preferment in the Church on the author of the "Tale of a Tub," they might give scandal to the public, which had no high opinion of their orthodoxy. He did not make fair allowance for the difficulties which prevented Halifax and Somers from serving him, thought himself an ill-used man, sacrificed honour and consistency to revenge, joined the Tories, and became their most formidable champion. He soon found, however, that his old friends were less to blame than he had supposed. The dislike with which the Queen and the heads of the Church regarded him was insurmountable, and it was with the greatest difficulty that he obtained an ecclesiastical dignity of no great value, on condition of fixing his residence in a country which he detested.

Difference of political opinion had produced, not indeed a quarrel, but a coolness between Swift and Addison. They at length ceased altogether to see each other. Yet there was between them a tacit compact like that between the hereditary guests in the "Iliad."

1.
'Εγχεα δ' αλληλων αλεώμεθα και δι' ομίλου.
Πολλοί μέν γάρ έμοι Τρώες κλειτοί τ' επίκουροι,
Κτείνειν, όν κε θεος γε πόρη και ποσσί κιχείω,
Πολλοι δ' αυ σοι Αχαιοι, εναιρεμεν, όν κε δύνηαι.

It is not strange that Addison, who calumniated and insulted nobody, should not have calumniated or insulted Swift. But it is remarkable that Swift, to whom neither genius nor virtue was sacred, and who generally seemed to find, like most other renegades, a peculiar pleasure in attacking old friends, should have shown so much respect and tenderness to Addison.

Fortune had now changed. The accession of the House of Hanover had secured in England the liberties of the people and in Ireland the dominion of the Protestant caste. To that caste Swift was more odious than any other man. He was hooted and even pelted in the streets of Dublin, and could not venture to ride along the strand for his health without the attendance of armed servants. Many whom he had formerly served now libelled and insulted him. At this time Addison arrived. He had been advised not to show the smallest civility to the Dean of St. Patrick's. He had answered, with admirable spirit, that it might be necessary for men whose fidelity to their party was suspected, to hold no intercourse with political opponents; but that one who had been a steady Whig in the worst times might venture, when the good cause was triumphant, to shake hands with an old friend who was one of the vanquished Tories. His kindness was soothing to the proud and cruelly wounded spirit of Swift, and the two great satirists resumed their habits of friendly intercourse.

Those associates of Addison whose political opinions agreed with his shared his good fortune. He took Tickell with him to Ireland. He procured for Budgell a lucrative place in the same kingdom. Ambrose Phillipps was provided for in England. Steele had injured himself so much by his eccentricity and perverseness that he obtained but a very small part of what he thought his due. He was, however, knighted, he had a place in the household, and he subsequently received other marks of favour from the Court.

Addison did not remain long in Ireland. In 1715 he quitted his secretaryship for a seat at the Board of Trade. In the same year his comedy of " The Drummer" was brought on the stage. The name of the author was not announced, the piece was coldly received, and some critics have expressed a doubt whether it were really Addison's. To us the evidence, both external and internal, seems decisive. It is not in Addison's best manner, but it contains numerous passages which no other writer known to us could have produced. It was again performed after Addison's death, and, being known to be his, was loudly applauded.

Towards the close of the year 1715, while the Rebellion was still raging in Scotland,* Addison published the first number of a paper called the *Freeholder*. Among his political works the *Freeholder* is entitled to the first place. Even in the *Spectator* there are few serious papers nobler than the character of his friend Lord Somers, and certainly no satirical papers superior to those in which the Tory fox-hunter is introduced. This character is the original of Squire Western, and is drawn with all Fielding's force and with a delicacy of which Fielding was altogether destitute. As none of Addison's works exhibit stronger marks of his genius than the *Freeholder*, so none does more honour to his moral character. It is difficult to extol too highly the candour and humanity of a political writer whom even the excitement of civil war cannot hurry into unseemly violence. Oxford, it is well known, was then the stronghold of Toryism. The High Street had been repeatedly lined with bayonets in order to keep down the disaffected gownsmen, and traitors pursued by the messengers of the Government had been concealed in the garrets of several colleges. Yet the admonition which, even under such circumstances, Addison addressed to the University is singularly gentle, respectful and even affectionate. Indeed, he could not find it in his heart to deal harshly even with imaginary persons. His fox-hunter, though ignorant, stupid and violent, is at heart a good fellow, and is at last reclaimed by the clemency of the King. Steele was dissatisfied with his friend's moderation, and, though he acknowledged that the *Freeholder*, was excellently written, complained that the ministry played on a lute when it was necessary to blow the trumpet. He accordingly determined to execute a flourish after his own fashion, and tried to rouse the public spirit of the nation by means of a paper called the *Town Talk*, which is now as utterly forgotten as his *Englishman*, as his "Crisis," as his "Letter to the Bailiff of Stockbridge," as his "Reader," in short, as everything that he wrote without the help of Addison.

In the same year in which the "Drummer" was acted, and in which the first numbers of the *Freeholder* appeared, the estrangement of Pope and Addison became complete. Addison had from the first seen that Pope was

* Miss Aikin has been most unfortunate in her account of this Rebellion. We will notice only two errors which occur in one page. She says that the Rebellion was under taken in favour of James II., who had been fourteen years dead, and that it was headed by Charles Edward. who was not born (ii. 172).

false and malevolent. Pope had discovered that Addison was jealous. The discovery was made in a strange manner. Pope had written the "Rape of the Lock," in two cantos, without supernatural machinery. These two cantos had been loudly applauded, and by none more loudly than by Addison. Then Pope thought of the Sylphs and Gnomes, Ariel, Momentilla, Crispassa and Umbriel; and resolved to interweave the Rosicrucian mythology with the original fabric. He asked Addison's advice. Addison said that the poem as it stood was a delicious little thing, and entreated Pope not to run the risk of marring what was so excellent in trying to mend it. Pope afterwards declared that this insidious counsel first opened his eyes to the baseness of him who gave it.

Now there can be no doubt that Pope's plan was most ingenious, and that he afterwards executed it with great skill and success. But does it necessarily follow that Addison's advice was bad? And if Addison's advice was bad, does it necessarily follow that it was given from bad motives? If a friend were to ask us whether we would advise him to risk his all in a lottery of which the chances were ten to one against him, we should do our best to dissuade him from running such a risk. Even if he were so lucky as to get the £30,000 prize, we should not admit that we had counselled him ill; and we should certainly think it the height of injustice in him to accuse us of having been actuated by malice. We think Addison's advice good advice. It rested on a sound principle, the result of long and wide experience. The general rule undoubtedly is that, when a successful work of imagination has been produced, it should not be recast. We cannot at this moment call to mind a single instance in which this rule has been transgressed with happy effect, except the instance of the "Rape of the Lock." Tasso recast his "Jerusalem;" Akenside recast his "Pleasure of the Imagination," and his "Epistle to Curio." Pope himself, emboldened no doubt by the success with which he had expanded and remodelled the "Rape of the Lock," made the same experiment on the "Dunciad." All these attempts failed. Who was to forsee that Pope would, once in his life, be able to do what he could not himself do twice, and what nobody else has ever done?

Addison's advice was good. But had it been bad, why should we pronounce it dishonest? Scott tells us that one of his best friends predicted the failure of "Waverley." Herder adjured Goethe not to take so unpromising a subject as "Faust." Hume tried to dissuade Robertson from writing the "History of Charles the Fifth." Nay, Pope, himself was one of those who prophesied that "Cato" would never succeed on the stage, and advised Addison to print it without risking a representation. But Scott, Geothe, Robertson, Addison, had the good sense and generosity to give their advisers credit for the best intentions. Pope's heart was not of the same kind with theirs.

In 1715, while he was engaged in translating the "Iliad," he met Addison at a coffee-house. Phillips and Budgell were there; but their sovereign got rid of them, and asked Pope to dine with him alone. After dinner, Addison said that he lay under a difficulty which he wished to explain. "Tickell," he said, "translated some time ago the first book of the 'Iliad.' I have promised to look it over and correct it. I cannot therefore ask to see yours; for that would would be double dealing." Pope made a civil reply, and begged that his second book might have the advantage of Addison's revision. Addison readily agreed, looked over the second book, and sent it back with warm commendations.

Tickell's version of the first book appeared soon after this conversation. In the preface, all rivalry was earnestly disclaimed. Tickell declared that he should not go on with the "Iliad." That enterprise he should leave to powers which he admitted to be superior to his own. His only view, he said, in publishing this specimen was to bespeak the favour of the public to a translation of the "Odyssey," in which he had made some progress.

Addison, and Addison's devoted followers, pronounced both the versions good, but maintained that Tickell's had more of the original. The town gave a decided preference to Pope's. We do not think it worth while to settle such a question of precedence. Neither of the rivals can be said to have translated the "Iliad," unless, indeed, the word translation be used in the sense which it bears in the "Midsummer Night's Dream." When Bottom makes his appearance with an ass's head instead of his own, Peter Quince exclaims, "Bless thee! Bottom, bless thee! thou art translated." In this sense, undoubtedly, the readers of either Pope or Tickell may very properly exclaim, "Bless thee! Homer; thou art translated indeed."

Our readers will, we hope agree with us in thinking that no man in Addison's situation could have acted more fairly and kindly, both towards Pope, and towards Tickell, than he appears to have done. But an odious suspicion had sprung up in the mind of Pope. He fancied, and he soon firmly believed, that there was a deep conspiracy against his fame and his fortunes. The work on which he had staked his reputation was to be depreciated. The subscription, on which rested his hopes of a competence, was to be defeated. With this view Addison had made a rival translation; Tickell had consented to father it; and the wits of Button's had united to puff it.

Is there any external evidence to support this grave accusation? The answer is short. There is absolutely none.

Was there any internal evidence which proved Addison to be the author of this version? Was it a work which Tickell was incapable of producing? Surely not. Tickell was a Fellow of a College at Oxford, and must be supposed to have been able to construe the "Iliad;" and he was a better versifier than his friend. We are not aware that Pope pretended to have discovered any turns of expression peculiar to Addison. Had such turns of expression been discovered, they would be sufficiently accounted for by supposing Addison to have corrected his friend's lines, as he owned that he had done.

Is there anything in the character of the accused persons which makes the accusation probable? We answer confidently—nothing. Tickell was long after this time described by Pope himself as a very fair and worthy man. Addison had been, during many years, before the public. Literary rivals, political opponents, had kept their eyes on him. But neither envy nor faction in their utmost rage, had ever imputed to him a single deviation from the laws of honour and of social morality. Had he been indeed a man meanly jealous of fame and capable of stooping to base and wicked arts for the purpose of injuring his competitors, would his vices have remained latent so long? He was a writer of tragedy; had he ever injured Rowe? He was a writer of comedy; had he not done ample justice to Congreve and given valuable help to Steele? He was a pamphleteer; have not his good nature and generosity been acknowledged by Swift, his rival in fame and his adversary in politics?

That Tickell should have been guilty of a villainy seems to us highly improbable. That Addison should have been guilty of villainy seems to us highly improbable. But that these two men should have conspired together to commit a villainy seems to us improbable in a tenfold degree. All that is known to us of their intercourse tends to prove, that it was not the intercourse of two accomplices in crime. These are some of the lines in which Tickell poured forth his sorrow over the coffin of Addison:

> "Or dost thou warn poor mortals left behind,
> A task well suited to thy gentle mind?
> Oh, if sometimes thy spotless form descend,
> To me thine aid, thou guardian genius, lend.
> When rage misguides me, or when fear alarms,
> When pain distresses, or when pleasure charms,
> In silent whisperings purer thoughts impart,
> And turn from ill a frail and feeble heart;
> Lead through the paths thy virtue trod before,
> Till bliss shall join, nor death can part us more."

In what words, we should like to know, did this guardian genius invite his pupil to join in a plan such as the Editor of the *Satirist* would hardly dare to propose to the Editor of the *Age*.

We do not accuse Pope of bringing an accusation which he knew to be false. We have not the smallest doubt that he believed it to be true ; and the evidence on which he believed it he found in his own bad heart. His own life was one long series of tricks, as mean and as malicious as that of which he suspected Addison and Tickell. He was all stiletto and mask. To injure, to insult, and to save himself from the consequences of injury and insult by lying and equivocating, was the habit of his life. He published a lampoon on the Duke of Chandos ; he was taxed with it ; and he lied and equivocated. He published a lampoon on Aaron Hill ; he was taxed with it ; and he lied and equivocated. He published a still fouler lampoon on Lady Mary Wortley Montagu ; he was taxed with it ; and he lied with more than usual effrontery and vehemence. He puffed himself and abused his enemies under feigned names. He robbed himself of his own letters and then raised the hue and cry after them. Besides his frauds of malignity, of fear, of interest and of vanity, there were frauds which he seems to have committed from love of fraud alone. He had a habit of stratagem—a pleasure in outwitting all who came near him. Whatever his object might be, the indirect road to it was that which he preferred. For Bolingbroke, Pope undoubtedly felt as much love and veneration as it was in his nature to feel for any human being. Yet Pope was scarcely dead when it was discovered that, from no motive except the mere love of artifice, he had been guilty of an act of gross perfidy to Bolingbroke.

Nothing was more natural than that such a man as this should attribute to others that which he felt within himself. A plain, probable, coherent explanation is frankly given to him. He is certain that it is all a romance. A line of conduct scrupulously fair, and even friendly, is pursued towards him. He is convinced that it is merely a cover for a vile intrigue by which he is to be disgraced and ruined. It is vain to ask him for proofs. He has none and wants none, except those which he carries in his own bosom.

Whether Pope's malignity at length provoked Addison to retaliate for the first and last time, cannot now be known with certainty. We have only Pope's story, which runs thus. A pamphlet appeared containing some reflections which stung Pope to the quick. What those reflections were, and whether they were reflections of which he had a right to complain, we have now no means of deciding. The Earl of Warwick, a foolish and vicious lad, who regarded Addison with the feelings with which such lads generally regard their best friends, told Pope, truly or falsely, that this pamphlet had been written by Addison's direction. When we consider what a tendency stories have to grow, in passing even from one honest man to another honest man, and when we consider that to the name of honest man neither Pope nor the Earl of Warwick had a claim, we are not disposed to attach much importance to this anecdote.

It is certain, however, that Pope was furious. He had already sketched the character of Atticus in prose. In his anger he turned this prose into the brilliant and energetic lines which everybody knows by heart, or ought to know by heart, and sent them to Addison. One charge which Pope has enforced with great skill is probably not without foundation. Addison was, we are inclined to believe, too fond of presiding over a circle of humble friends. Of the other imputations which these famous lines are intended to convey, scarcely one has ever been proved to be just, and some are certainly false. That Addison was not in the habit of " damning with faint praise " appears from innumerable passages in his writings, and from none more than from those in which he mentions Pope. And it is not merely unjust, but ridiculous, to describe a man who made the fortune of almost every one of his intimate friends, as "so obliging that he ne'er obliged."

That Addison felt the sting of Pope's satire keenly, we cannot doubt. That he was conscious of one of the weaknesses with which he was reproached, is highly probable. But his heart, we firmly believe, acquitted him of the gravest part of the accusation. He acted like himself. As a satirist he was, at his own weapons, more than Pope's match; and he would have been at no loss for topics. A distorted and diseased body, tenanted by a yet more distorted and diseased mind—spite and envy thinly disguised by sentiments as benevolent and noble as those which Sir Peter Teazle admired in Mr. Joseph Surface; a feeble sickly licentiousness—an odious love of filthy and noisome images—these were things which a genius less powerful than that to which we owe the *Spectator* could easily have held up to the mirth and hatred of mankind. Addison had, moreover, at his command, other means of vengeance which a bad man would not have scrupled to use. He was powerful in the state. Pope was a Catholic; and, in those times, a minister would have found it easy to harass the most innocent Catholic by innumerable petty vexations. Pope, near twenty years later, said that "through the lenity of the government alone he could live with comfort." "Consider," he exclaimed, "the injury that a man of high rank and credit may do to a private person, under penal laws and many other disadvantages." It is pleasing to reflect that the only revenge which Addison took was to insert in the *Freeholder* a warm encomium on the translation of the "Iliad," and to exhort all lovers of learning to put down their names as subscribers. There could be no doubt, he said, from the specimens already published, that the masterly hand of Pope would do as much for Homer as Dryden had done for Virgil. From that time to the end of his life, he always treated Pope, by Pope's own acknowledgement, with justice. Friendship was, of course, at an end.

One reason which induced the Earl of Warwick to play the ignominious part of talebearer on this occasion, may have been his dislike of the marriage which was about to take place between his mother and Addison. The Countess Dowager, a daughter of the old and honourable family of the Middletons of Chirk, a family which, in any country but ours, would be called noble, resided at Holland House. Addison had, during some years, occupied at Chelsea a small dwelling, once the abode of Nell Gwynn. Chelsea is now a district of London, and Holland House may be called a town residence. But, in the days of Anne and George the First, milkmaids and sportsmen wandered between green hedges and over fields bright with daisies, from Kensington almost to the shore of the Thames. Addison and Lady Warwick were country neighbours and became intimate friends. The great wit and scholar tried to allure the young Lord from the fashionable amusements of beating watchmen, breaking windows and rolling women in hogsheads down Holborn Hill, to the study of letters and the practice of virtue. These well-meant exertions did little good, however, either to the disciple or to the master. Lord Warwick grew up a rake; and Addison fell in love. The mature beauty of the Countess has been celebrated by poets in language which, after a very large allowance has been made for flattery, would lead us to believe that she was a fine woman; and her rank doubtless heightened her attractions. The courtship was long. The hopes of the lover appear to have risen and fallen with the fortunes of his party. His attachment was at length a matter of such notoriety that, when he visited Ireland for the last time, Rowe addressed some consolatory verses to the Chloe of Holland House. It strikes us as a little strange that, in these verses, Addison should be called Lycidas; a name of singularly evil omen for a swain just about to cross St. George's Channel.

At length Chloe capitulated. Addison was, indeed, able to treat with her on equal terms. He had reason to expect preferment even higher than that which he had attained. He had inherited the fortune of a brother who died Governor of Madras. He had purchased an estate in Warwickshire, and had been welcomed to his domain in very tolerable verse by one of the neighbouring squires, the poetical fox-hunter, William Somerville. In August 1716, the newspapers announced that Joseph Addison, Esquire, famous for many excellent works both in verse and prose, had espoused the Countess Dowager of Warwick.

He now fixed his abode at Holland House—a house which can boast of a greater number of inmates distinguished in political and literary history than any other private dwelling in England. His portrait now hangs there. The features are pleasing; the complexion is remarkably fair; but in the expression we trace rather the gentleness of his disposition than the force and keenness of his intellect.

Not long after his marriage he reached the height of civil greatness. The Whig Government had, during some time, been torn by internal dissensions. Lord Townshend led one section of the Cabinet, Lord Sunderland the other. At length, in the spring of 1717, Sunderland triumphed. Townshend retired from office, and was accompanied by Walpole and Cowper. Sunderland proceeded to reconstruct the Ministry, and Addison was appointed Secretary of State. It is certain that the Seals were pressed upon him, and were at first declined by him. Men equally versed in official business might easily have been found, and his colleagues knew that they could not expect assistance from him in debate. He owed his elevation to his popularity, to his stainless probity and to his literary fame.

But scarcely had Addison entered the Cabinet when his health began to fail. From one serious attack he recovered in the autumn, and his recovery was celebrated in Latin verses, worthy of his own pen, by Vincent Bourne, who was then at Trinity College, Cambridge. A relapse soon took place, and in the following spring Addison was prevented by a severe asthma from discharging the duties of his post. He resigned it, and was succeeded by his friend Craggs, a young man whose natural parts, though little improved by cultivation, were quick and showy, whose graceful person and winning manners had made him generally acceptable in society, and who, if he had lived, would probably have been the most formidable of all the rivals of Walpole.

As yet there was no Joseph Hume. The Ministers therefore were able to bestow on Addison a retiring pension £1,500 a year. In what form this pension was given we are not told by the biographers, and have not time to inquire. But it is certain that Addison did not vacate his seat in the House of Commons.

Rest of mind and body seem to have re-established his health, and he thanked God with cheerful piety for having set him free both from his office and from his asthma. Many years seemed to be before him, and he meditated many works—a tragedy on the death of Socrates, a translation of the Psalms, a treatise on the evidences of Christianity. Of this last performance a part, which we could well spare, has come down to us.

But the fatal complaint soon returned and gradually prevailed against all the resources of medicine. It is melancholy to think that the last moments of such a life should have been overclouded both by domestic and by political vexations. A tradition which began early, which has been generally received, and to which we have nothing to oppose, has represented his wife as an arrogant and imperious woman. It is said that, till his health failed him, he was glad to escape from the Countess-Dowager and her magnificent dining room, blazing with the gilded devices of the House of Rich, to some tavern where he could enjoy a laugh, a talk about Virgil and Boileau, and a bottle of claret, with the friends of his happier days. All those friends, however, were not left to him.

Sir Richard Steele had been gradually estranged by various causes. He considered himself as one who, in evil times, had braved martyrdom for his political principles, and demanded, when the Whig party was triumphant, a large compensation for what he had suffered when it was militant. The Whig leaders took a very different view of his claims. They thought that he had, by his own petulance and folly, brought them as well as well as himself into trouble, and though they did not absolutely neglect him, doled out favours to him with a sparing hand. It was natural that he should be angry with them, and especially angry with Addison. But what above all seems to have disturbed Sir Richard was the elevation of Tickell, who, at thirty, was made by Addison Under-Secretary of State, while the editor of the *Tatler* and *Spectator*, the author of the "Crisis," the member for Stockbridge, who had been persecuted for firm adherence to the House of Hanover, was, at near fifty, forced, after many solicitations and complaints, to content himself with a share in the patent of Drury Lane Theatre. Steele himself says, in his celebrated letter to Congreve, that Addison, by his preference of Tickell, "incurred the warmest resentment of other gentlemen," and everything seems to indicate that, of those resentful gentlemen, Steele was himself one.

While poor Sir Richard was brooding over what he considered as Addison's unkindness, a new cause of quarrel arose. The Whig party, already divided against itself, was rent by a new schism. The celebrated Bill for limiting the number of Peers had been brought in. The proud Duke of Somerset, first in rank of all the nobles whose religion permitted them to sit in Parliament, was the ostensible author of the measure. But it was supported, and in truth devised by the Prime Minister.

We are satisfied that the Bill was most pernicious, and we fear that the motives which induced Sunderland to frame it were not honourable to him. But we cannot deny that it was supported by many of the best and wisest men of that age. Nor was this strange. The royal prerogative had, within the memory of the generation then in the vigour of life, been so grossly abused that it was still regarded with a jealousy which, when the peculiar situation of the House of Brunswick is considered, may perhaps be called immoderate. The prerogative of creating Peers had, in the opinion of the Whigs, been grossly abused by Queen Anne's last ministry, and even the Tories admitted that her Majesty, in swamping, as it has since been called, the Upper House, had done what only an extreme case could justify. The theory of the English constitution, according to many high authorities, was that three independent powers, the sovereign, the nobility and the commons, ought constantly to act as checks on each other. If this theory were sound, it seemed to follow that to put one of these powers under the absolute control of the other two, was absurd. But if the number of peers were unlimited, it could not be denied that the Upper House was under the absolute control of the Crown and the Commons, and was indebted only to their moderation for any power which it might be suffered to retain.

Steele took part with the Opposition, Addison with the Ministers. Steele, in a paper called the *Plebian*, vehemently attacked the Bill. Sunderland called for help on Addison, and Addison obeyed the call. In a paper called the *Old Whig*, he answered, and indeed refuted, Steele's arguments. It seems to us that the premises of both the controversialists were unsound, that on those premises Addison reasoned well and Steele ill; and that consequently Addison brought out a false conclusion while Steele blundered upon the truth. In style, in wit and in politeness, Addison maintained his superiority, though the *Old Whig* is by no means one of his happiest performances.*

---

* Miss Aikin says that these pieces, never having been reprinted are now of extreme rarity. This is a mistake. They have been reprinted, and may be obtained without the smallest difficulty. The copy now lying before us bears the date of 1789.

At first both the anonymous opponents observed the laws of propriety; but at length Steele so far forgot himself as to throw an odious imputation on the morals of the chiefs of the administration. Addison replied with severity, but, in our opinion, with less severity than was due to so grave an offence against morality and decorum; nor did he, in his just anger, forget for a moment the laws of good taste and good breeding. One calumny which has been often repeated, and never yet contradicted, it is our duty to expose. It is asserted in the "Biographia Britannica," that Addison designated Steele as "little Dicky." This assertion was repeated by Johnson, who had never seen the *Old Whig*, and was therefore excusable. It has also been repeated by Miss Aikin, who has seen the *Old Whig*, and for whom therefore there is less excuse. Now it is true that the words "little Dicky" occur in the *Old Whig*, and that Steele's name was Richard. It is equally true that the words "little Isaac" occur in the "Duenna," and that Newton's name was Isaac. But we confidently affirm that Addison's little Dicky had no more to do with Steele, than Sheridan's little Isaac with Newton. If we apply the words "little Dicky" to Steele, we deprive a very lively and ingenious passage, not only of all its wit but of all its meaning. Little Dicky was the nickname of Henry Norris, an actor of remarkably small stature, but of great humour, who played the usurer Gomez, then a most popular part, in Dryden's "Spanish Friar."*

The merited reproof which Steele had received, though softened by some kind and courteous expressions, galled him bitterly. He replied with little force and great acrimony; but no rejoinder appeared. Addison was fast hastening to his grave; and had, we may well suppose, little disposition to prosecute a quarrel with an old friend. His complaint had terminated in dropsy. He bore up long and manfully. But at length he abandoned all hope, dismissed his physicians and calmly prepared himself to die.

His works he entrusted to the care of Tickell, and dedicated them a very few days before his death to Craggs, in a letter written with the sweet and graceful eloquence of a Saturday's *Spectator*. In this, his last composition, he alluded to his approaching end in words so manly, so cheerful and so tender, that it is difficult to read them without tears. At the same time he earnestly recommended the interest of Tickell to the care of Craggs.

Within a few hours of the time at which this dedication was written, Addison sent to beg Gay, who was then living by his wits about town, to come to Holland House. Gay went, and was received with great kindness. To his amazement his forgiveness was implored by the dying man. Poor Gay, the the most good-natured and simple of mankind, could not imagine what he had to forgive. There was, however, some wrong, the remembrance of which weighed on Addison's mind, and which he declared himself anxious to repair. He was in a state of extreme exhaustion; and the parting was doubtless a friendly one on both sides. Gay supposed that some plan to serve him had been in agitation at Court, and had been frustrated by Addison's influence. Nor is this improbable. Gay had paid assiduous court to the royal family. But

---

* We will transcribe the whole paragraph. How it can ever have been misunderstood is unintelligible to us:
"But our author's chief concern is for the poor House of Commons, whom he represents as naked and defenceless, when the Crown, by losing this prerogative, would be less able to protect them against the power of a House of Lords. Who forbears laughing when the Spanish Friar represents little Dicky, under the person of Gomez, insulting the Colonel that was able to fright him out of his wits with a single frown? This Gomez, says he, flew upon him like a dragon, got him down, the Devil being strong in him, and gave him bastinado on bastinado, and buffet on buffet, which the poor Colonel, being prostrate, suffered with a most Christian patience. The improbability of the fact nevers fails to raise mirth in the audience; and one may venture to answer for a British House of Commons, if we may guess from its conduct hitherto, that it will scarce be either so tame or so weak as our author supposes."

in the Queen's days he had been the eulogist of Bolingbroke, and was still connected with many Tories. It is not strange that Addison, while heated by conflict, should have thought himself justified in obstructing the preferment of one whom he might regard as a political enemy. Neither is it strange that, when reviewing his whole life, and earnestly scrutinising all his motives, he should think that he had acted an unkind an ungenerous part, in using his power against a distressed man of letters, who was as harmless and as helpless as a child.

One inference may be drawn from this anecdote. It appears that Addison, on his death-bed, called himself to a strict account, and was not at ease till he had asked pardon for an injury which it was not even suspected that he had committed—for an injury which would have caused disquiet only to a very tender conscience. Is it not then reasonable to infer that, if he had really been guilty of forming a base conspiracy against the fame and fortunes of a rival, he would have expressed some remorse for so serious a crime? But it is unnecessary to multiply arguments and evidence for the Defence, when there is neither argument nor evidence for the Accusation.

The last moments of Addison were perfectly serene. His interview with his step-son is universally known. "See," he said, "how a Christian can die." The piety of Addison was, in truth, of a singularly cheerful character. The feeling which predominates in all his devotional writings, is gratitude. God was to him the allwise and allpowerful friend who had watched over his cradle with more than maternal tenderness; who had listened to his cries before they could form themselves in prayer; who had preserved his youth from the snares of vice; who had made his cup run over with worldly blessings; who had doubled the value of those blessings by bestowing a thankful heart to enjoy them, and dear friends to partake them; who had rebuked the waves of the Ligurian gulf, who had purified the autumnal air of the Campagna, and had restrained the avalanches of Mont Cenis. Of the Psalms, his favourite was that which represents the Ruler of all things under the endearing image of a shepherd, whose crook guides the flock safe, through gloomy and desolate glens, to meadows well-watered and rich with herbage. On that goodness to which he ascribed all the happiness of his life, he relied in the hour of death with the love which casteth out fear. He died on the seventeenth of June, 1719. He had just entered on his forty-eighth year.

His body lay in state in the Jerusalem Chamber, and was borne thence to the Abbey at dead of night. The choir sang a funeral hymn. Bishop Atterbury, one of those Tories who had loved and honoured the most accomplished of the Whigs, met the corpse, and led the procession by torchlight, round the shrine of Saint Edward and the graves of the Plantagenets, to the Chapel of Henry the Seventh. On the north side of that Chapel, in the vault of the House of Albemarle, the coffin of Addison lies next to the coffin of Montagu. Yet a few months; and the same mourners passed again along the same aisle. The same sad anthem was again chanted. The same vault was again opened; and the coffin of Craggs was placed close to the coffin of Addison.

Many tributes were paid to the memory of Addison; but one alone is now remembered. Tickell bewailed his friend in an elegy which would do honour to the greatest name in our literature, and which unites the energy and magnificence of Dryden to the tenderness and purity of Cowper. This fine poem was prefixed to a superb edition of Addison's works, which was published in 1721, by subscription. The names of the subscribers proved how widely his fame had been spread. That his countrymen should be eager to possess his writings, even in a costly form, is not wonderful. But it is wonderful that, though English literature was then little studied on the continent, Spanish Grandees, Italian Prelates, Marshals of France, should be found in the list. Among the most remarkable names are those of the Queen of Sweden, of

Prince Eugene, of the Grand Duke of Tuscany, of the Dukes of Parma, Modena and Guastalla, of the Doge of Genoa, of the Regent Orleans and of Cardinal Dubois. We ought to add that this edition, though eminently beautiful, is in some important points defective; nor, indeed, do we yet possess a complete collection of Addison's writings.

It is strange that neither his opulent and noble widow, nor any of his powerful and attached friends should have thought of placing even a simple tablet, inscribed with his name, on the walls of the Abbey. It was not till three generations had laughed and wept over his pages that the omission was supplied by the public veneration. At length, in our own time, his image, skilfully graven, appeared in Poet's Corner. It represents him, as we can conceive him, clad in his dressing-gown and freed from his wig, stepping from his parlour at Chelsea into his trim little garden, with the account of the "Everlasting Club," or the "Loves of Hilpa and Shalum," just finished for the next day's *Spectator*, in his hand. Such a mark of national respect was due to the unsullied statesman, to the accomplished scholar, to the master of pure English eloquence, to the consummate painter of life and manners. It was due, above all, to the great satirist, who alone knew how to use ridicule without abusing it, who, without inflicting a wound, effected a great social reform, and who reconciled wit and virtue, after a long and disastrous separation, during which wit had been led astray by profligacy and virtue by fanaticism.

THE EARL OF CHATHAM. (OCTOBER, 1844.)

1. *Correspondence of William Pitt, Earl of Chatham.* 4 vols., 8vo. London, 1840.
2. *Letters of Horace Walpole, Earl of Orford, to Horace Mann.* 4 vols., 8vo. London, 1843-44.

MORE than ten years ago we commenced a sketch of the political life of the great Lord Chatham.* We then stopped at the death of George the Second with the intention of speedily resuming our task. Circumstances, which it would be tedious to explain, long prevented us from carrying this intention into effect. Nor can we regret the delay. For the materials which were within our reach in 1834 were scanty and unsatisfactory when compared with those which we at present possess. Even now, though we have had access to some valuable sources of information which have not yet been opened to the public, who cannot but feel that the history of the first ten years of the reign of George III. is but imperfectly known to us. Nevertheless, we are inclined to think that we are in a condition to lay before our readers a narrative neither uninstructive nor uninteresting. We therefore return with pleasure to our long interrupted labour.

We left Pitt in the zenith of prosperity and glory, the idol of England, the terror of France, the admiration of the whole civilized world. The wind, from whatever quarter it blew, carried to England tidings of battles won, fortresses taken, provinces added to the empire. At home factions had sunk into a lethargy such has had never been known since the great religious schism of the sixteenth century had roused the public mind from repose.

In order that the events which we have to relate may be clearly understood, it may be desirable that we should advert to the causes which had for a time suspended the animation of both the great English parties.

If, rejecting all that is merely accidental, we look at the essential characteristics of the Whig and the Tory, we may consider each of them as the representative of a great principle, essential to the welfare of nations. One is, in an especial manner, the guardian of liberty, and the other of order. One is the moving power and the other the steadying power of the state. One is the

* No. cxviii.

sail, without which society would make no progress; the other the ballast, without which there would be small safety in a tempest. But, during the forty-six years which followed the accession of the House of Hanover, these distinctive peculiarities seemed to be effaced. The Whig conceived that he could not better serve the cause of civil and religious freedom than by strenuously supporting the Protestant dynasty. The Tory conceived that he could not better prove his hatred of revolutions than by attacking a government to which a revolution had given birth. Both came by degrees to attach more importance to the means than to the end. Both were thrown into unnatural situations; and both, like animals transported to an uncongenial climate, languished and degenerated. The Tory, removed from the sunshine of the Court, was as a camel in the snows of Lapland. The Whig, basking in the rays of royal favour, was as a reindeer in the sands of Arabia.

Dante tells us that he saw, in Malebolge, a strange encounter between a human form and a serpent. The enemies, after cruel wounds inflicted, stood for a time glaring on each other. A great cloud surrounded them, and then a wonderful metamorphosis began. Each creature was transfigured into the likeness of its antagonist. The serpent's tail divided itself into two legs; the man's legs intertwined themselves into a tail. The body of the serpent put forth arms; the arms of the man shrank into his body. At length the serpent stood up a man, and spake; the man sank down a serpent, and glided hissing away. Something like this was the transformation which, during the reign of George the First, befel the two English parties. Each gradually took the shape and colour of its foe, till at length the Tory rose up erect, the zealot of freedom, and the Whig crawled and licked the dust at the feet of power.

It is true that when these degenerate politicians discussed questions merely speculative, and, above all, when they discussed questions relating to the conduct of their own grandfathers, they still seemed to differ as their grandfathers had differed. The Whig, who, during three Parliaments, had never given one vote against the court, and who was ready to sell his soul for the Comptroller's Staff or for the Great Wardrobe, still professed to draw his political doctrines from Locke and Milton, still worshipped the memory of Pym and Hampden, and would still, on the thirtieth of January, take his glass, first to the man in the mask and then to the man who would do it without a mask. The Tory, on the other hand, while he reviled the mild and temperate Walpole as a deadly enemy of liberty, could see nothing to reprobrate in the iron tyranny of Strafford and Laud. But whatever judgment the Whig or the Tory of that age might pronounce on transactions long past, there can be no doubt that, as respected the practical questions then pending, the Tory was a reformer, and indeed an intemperate and indiscreet reformer, while the Whig was conservative even to bigotry. We have ouselves seen similar effects produced in a neighbouring country by similar causes. Who would have believed, fifteen years ago, that M. Guizot and M. Villemain would have to defend property and social order against the Jacobinical attacks of such enemies as M. Genoude and M. de La Roche Jaquelin?

Thus the successors of the old Cavaliers had turned demagogues; the successors of the old Roundheads had turned courtiers. Yet was it long before their mutual animosity began to abate; for it is the nature of parties to retain their original enmities far more firmly than their original principles. During many years, a generation of Whigs, whom Sidney would have spurned as slaves, continued to wage deadly war with a generation of Tories whom Jeffreys would have hanged for republicans.

Through the whole reign of George the First, and through nearly half of the reign of George the Second, a Tory was regarded as an enemy of the reigning house, and was excluded from all the favours of the crown. Though most of the country gentlemen were Tories, none but Whigs were created peers and baronets. Though most of the clergy were Tories, none but Whigs were appointed deans and bishops. In every county, opulent and well-descended Tory squires complained that their names were left out of the commission of the peace, while men of small estate and mean birth, who were for toleration and excise, septennial parliaments and standing armies, presided at quarter sessions, and became deputy lieutenants.

By degrees some approaches were made towards a reconciliation. While Walpole was at the head of affairs, enmity to his power induced a large and powerful body of Whigs, headed by the heir apparent of the throne, to make an alliance with the Tories and a truce even with the Jacobites. After Sir Robert's fall, the ban which lay on the Tory party was taken off. The chief places in the administration continued to be filled by Whigs, and, indeed, could scarcely have been filled otherwise; for the Tory nobility and gentry, though strong in numbers and in property, had among them scarcely a single man distinguished by talents, either for business or for debate. A few of them, however, were admitted to subordinate offices; and this indulgence produced a softening effect on the temper of the whole body. The first levee of George the Second after Walpole's resignation was a remarkable spectacle. Mingled with the constant supporters of the House of Brunswick, with the Russells, the Cavendishes and the Pelhams, appeared a crowd of faces utterly unknown to the pages and gentlemen ushers, lords of rural manors, whose ale and foxhounds were renowned in the neighbourhood of the Mendip hills, or round the Wrekin, but who had never crossed the threshold of the palace since the days when Oxford, with the white staff in his hand, stood behind Queen Anne.

During the eighteen years which followed this day, both factions were gradually sinking deeper and deeper into repose. The apathy of the public mind is partly to be ascribed to the unjust violence with which the administration of Walpole had been assailed. In the body politic, as in the natural body, morbid languor generally succeeds to morbid excitement. The people had been maddened by sophistry, by calumny, by rhetoric, by stimulants applied to the national pride. In the fulness of bread, they had raved as if famine had been in the land. While enjoying such a measure of civil and religious freedom as, till then, no great society had ever known, they had cried out for a Timoleon or a Brutus to stab their oppressor to the heart. They were in this frame of mind when the change of administration took place; and they soon found that there was to be no change whatever in the system of government. The natural consequences followed. To frantic zeal succeeded sullen indifference. The cant of patriotism had not merely ceased to charm the public ear, but had become as nauseous as the cant of Puritanism after the downfall of the Rump. The hot fit was over, the cold fit had begun; and it was long before seditious arts, or even real grievances, could bring back the fiery paroxysm which had run its course and reached its termination.

Two attempts were made to disturb this tranquility. The banished heir of the House of Stuart headed a rebellion; the discontented heir of the House of Brunswick headed an opposition. Both the rebellion and the opposition came to nothing. The battle of Culloden annihilated the Jacobite party. The death of Prince Frederic dissolved the faction which, under his guidance, had feebly striven to annoy his father's government. His chief followers hastened to make their peace with the ministry; and the political torpor became complete.

Five years after the death of Prince Frederic, the public mind was for a time violently excited. But this excitement had nothing to do with the old disputes between Whigs and Tories. England was at war with France. The war had been feebly conducted. Minorca had been torn from us. Our fleet had retired before the white flag of the House of Bourbon. A bitter sense of humiliation, new to the proudest and bravest of nations, superseded every other feeling. The cry of all the counties and great towns of the realm was for a government which would retrieve the honour of the English arms. The two most powerful men in the country were the Duke of Newcastle and Pitt. Alternate victories and defeats had made them sensible that neither of them could stand alone. The interest of the state, and the interest of their own ambition, impelled them to coalesce. By their coalition was formed the ministry which was in power when George the Third ascended the throne.

The more carefully the structure of this celebrated ministry is examined, the more shall we see reason to marvel at the skill or the luck which had combined in one harmonious whole such various and, as it seemed, incompatible elements of force. The influence which is derived from stainless integrity, the influence which is derived from the vilest arts of corruption, the strength of aristocratical connection, the strength of democratical enthusiasm, all these things were for the first time found together. Newcastle brought to the coalition a vast mass of power, which had descended to him from Walpole and Pelham. The public offices, the church, the courts of law, the army, the navy, the diplomatic service, swarmed with his creatures. The boroughs, which long afterwards made up the memorable schedules A and B, were represented by his nominees. The great Whig families, which, during several generations, had been trained in the discipline of party warfare, and were accustomed to stand together in a firm phalanx, acknowledged him as their captain. Pitt, on the other hand, had what Newcastle wanted, an eloquence which stirred the passions and charmed the imagination, a high reputation for purity, and the confidence and ardent love of millions.

The partition which the two ministers made of the powers of government was singularly happy. Each occupied a province for which he was well qualified; and neither had any inclination to intrude himself into the province of the other. Newcastle took the treasury, the civil and ecclesiastical patronage, and the disposal of that part of the secret service money which was then employed in bribing members of Parliament. Pitt was Secretary of State, with the direction of the war and of foreign affairs. Thus the filth of all the noisome and pestilential sewers of government was poured into one channel. Through the other passed only what was bright and stainless. Mean and selfish politicians, pining for commissionerships, gold sticks and ribands, flocked to the great house at the corner of Lincoln's Inn Fields. There at every levee, appeared eighteen or twenty pair of lawn sleeves; for there was not, it was said, a single prelate who had not owed either his first elevation or some subsequent translation to Newcastle. There appeared those members of the House of Commons in whose silent votes the main strength of the government lay. One wanted a place in the excise for his butler. Another came about a prebend for his son. A third whispered that he had always stood by his Grace and the Protestant succession; that his last election had been very expensive; that potwallopers had now no conscience; and that he had been forced to take up money on mortgage; and that he hardly knew where to turn for five hundred pounds. The Duke pressed all their hands, passed his arms round all their shoulders, patted all their backs, and sent away, some with wages and some with promises. From this traffic Pitt stood haughtily aloof. Not only was he himself incorruptible, but he shrank from the loathsome drudgery of corrupting others. He had not, however, been twenty years in Parliament, and ten in office, without discovering how the government was carried on. He was perfectly aware that bribery was practised on a large scale by his colleagues. Hating the practice, yet despairing of putting it down, and doubting, whether in those times, any ministry could stand without it, he determined to be blind to it. He would see nothing, know nothing, believe nothing. People who came to talk to him about shares in lucrative contracts or about the means of securing a Cornish corporation, were soon put out of countenance by his arrogant humility. They did him too much honour. Such matters were beyond his capacity. It was true that his poor advice about expeditions and treaties was listened to with indulgence by a gracious sovereign. If the question were, who should command in North America, or who should be ambassador at Berlin, his colleagues would probably condescend to take his opinion. But he had not the smallest influence with the Secretary of the Treasury, and could not venture to ask even for a tidewaiter's place.

It may be doubted whether he did not owe as much of his popularity to his ostentatious purity as to his eloquence, or to his talents for the administration of war. It was everywhere said with delight and admiration that the great Commoner, without any advantages of birth or fortune, had, in spite of the dislike of the Court and of the aristocracy, made himself the first man in England, and made England the first country in the world; that his name was mentioned with awe in every palace from Lisbon to Moscow; that his trophies were in all the four quarters of the globe; yet that he was still plain William Pitt, without title or riband, without pension or sinecure place. Whenever he should retire, after saving the state, he must sell his coach horses and his silver candlesticks. Widely as the taint of corruption had spread, his hands were clean. They had never received, they had never given, the price of infamy. Thus the coalition gathered to itself support from all the high and all the low parts of human nature, and was strong with the whole united strength of virtue and of Mammon.

Pitt and Newcastle were co-ordinate chief ministers. The subordinate places had been filled on the principle of including in the government every party and shade of party, the avowed Jacobites alone excepted, nay, every public man who, from his abilities or from his situation, seemed likely to be either useful in office or formidable in opposition.

The Whigs, according to what was then considered as their prescriptive right, held by far the largest share of power. The main support of the administration was what may be called the great Whig connection—a connection which, during near half a century, had generally had the chief sway in the country, and which derived an immense authority from rank, wealth, borough interest and firm union. To this connection, of which Newcastle was the head, belonged the houses of Cavendish, Lennox, Fitzroy, Bentinck, Manners, Conway, Wentworth, and many others of high note.

There were two other powerful Whig connections, either of which might have been a nucleus for a strong opposition. But room had been found in the government for both. They were known as the Grenvilles and the Bedfords.

The head of the Grenvilles was Richard, Earl Temple. His talents for administration and debate were of no high order. But his great possessions, his turbulent and unscrupulous character, his restless activity and his skill in the most ignoble tactics of faction, made him one of the most formidable enemies that a ministry could have. He was keeper of the privy seal. His brother George was treasurer of the navy. They were supposed to be on terms of close friendship with Pitt, who had married their sister, and was the most uxorious of husbands.

The Bedfords, or, as they were called by their enemies, the Bloomsbury gang, professed to be led by John, Duke of Bedford, but in truth led him wherever they chose, and very often led him where he never would have gone of his own accord. He had many good qualities of head and heart, and would have been certainly a respectable, and possibly a distinguished, man, if he had been less under the influence of his friends, or more fortunate in choosing them. Some of them were indeed, to do them justice, men of parts. But here, we are afraid, eulogy must end. Sandwich and Rigby were able debaters, pleasant boon companions, dexterous intriguers, masters of all the arts of jobbing and electioneering, and both in public and private life, shamelessly immoral. Weymouth had a natural eloquence, which sometimes astonished those who knew how little he owed to study. But he was indolent and dissolute, and had early impaired a fine estate with the dice-box and a fine constitution with the bottle. The wealth and power of the Duke, and the talents and audacity of some of his retainers, might have seriously annoyed the strongest ministry. But his assistance had been secured. He was Lord Lieutenant of Ireland; Rigby was his secretary, and the whole party dutifully supported the measures of the Government.

Two men had, a short time before, been thought likely to contest with Pitt the lead of the House of Commons, William Murray and Henry Fox. But Murray had been removed to the Lords, and was Chief Justice of the King's Bench. Fox was, indeed, still in the Commons; but means had been found to secure, if not his strenuous support, at least his silent acquiescence. He was a poor man; he was a doting father. The office of Paymaster-General during an expensive war was, in that age, perhaps the most lucrative situation in the gift of the government. This office was bestowed on Fox. The prospect of making a noble fortune in a few years, and of providing amply for his darling boy Charles, was irresistibly tempting. To hold a subordinate place, however profitable, after having led the House of Commons, and having been intrusted with the business of forming a ministry, was indeed a great descent. But a punctilious sense of personal dignity was no part of the character of Henry Fox.

We have not time to enumerate all the other men of weight who were, by some tie or other, attached to the government. We may mention Hardwicke, reputed the first lawyer of the age; Legge, reputed the first financier of the age; the acute and ready Oswald; the bold and humorous Nugent; Charles Townshend, the most brilliant and versatile of mankind; Elliot, Barrington, North, Pratt. Indeed, as far as we recollect, there were in the whole House of Commons only two men of distinguished abilities who were not connected with the government; and those two men stood so low in public estimation, that the only service which they could have rendered to any government would have been to oppose it. We speak of Lord George Sackville and Bubb Dodington.

Though most of the official men, and all the members of the cabinet, were reputed Whigs, the Tories were by no means excluded from employment. Pitt had gratified many of them with commands in the militia, which increased both their income and their importance in their own counties; and they were therefore in better humour than at any time since the death of Anne. Some of the party still continued to grumble over their punch at the "Cocoa Tree;" but in the House of Commons not a single one of the malcontents durst lift his eyes above the buckle of Pitt's shoe.

Thus there was absolutely no opposition. Nay, there was no sign from which it could be guessed in what quarter opposition was likely to arise. Several years passed during which Parliament seemed to have abdicated its chief functions. The Journals of the House of Commons, during four sessions, contain no trace of a division on a party question. The supplies, though beyond precedent great, were voted without discussion. The most animated debates of that period were on road bills and inclosure bills.

The old King was content; and it mattered little whether he were content or not. It would have been impossible for him to emancipate himself from a ministry so powerful, even if he had been inclined to do so. But he had no such inclination. He had once, indeed, been strongly prejudiced against Pitt, and had repeatedly been ill-used by Newcastle; but the vigour and success with which the war had been waged in Germany, and the smoothness with which all public business was carried on, had produced a favourable change in the royal mind.

Such was the posture of affairs when, on the twenty-fifth of October, 1760, George the Second suddenly died, and George the Third, then twenty-two years old, became King. The situation of George the Third differed widely from that of his grandfather and that of his great-grandfather. Many years had elapsed since a sovereign of England had been an object of affection to any part of his people. The first two Kings of the House of Hanover had neither those hereditary rights which have often supplied the defect of merit, nor those personal qualities which have often supplied the defect of title. A prince may be popular with little virtue or capacity, if he reigns by birthright derived from a long line of illustrious predecessors. An usurper may be popular, if his genius has saved or aggrandised the nation which he governs. Perhaps no rulers have in our time had a stronger hold on the affection of subjects than the Emperor Francis, and his son-in law the Emperor Napoleon. But imagine a ruler with no better title than Napoleon, and no better understanding than Francis. Richard Cromwell was such a ruler; and, as soon as an arm was lifted up against him, he fell without a struggle, amidst universal derision. George the First and George the Second were in a situation which bore some resemblance to that of Richard Cromwell. They were saved from the fate of Richard Cromwell by the strenuous and able exertions of the Whig party, and by the general conviction that the nation had no choice but between the House of Brunswick and popery. But by no class were the Guelphs regarded with that devoted affection, of which Charles the First, Charles the Second and James the Second, in spite of the greatest faults, and in the midst of the greatest misfortunes, received innumerable proofs. Those Whigs who stood by the new dynasty so manfully with purse and sword did so on principles independent of, and, indeed, almost incompatible with, the sentiment of devoted loyalty. The moderate Tories regarded the foreign dynasty as a great evil, which must be endured for fear of a greater evil. In the eyes of the high Tories, the Elector was the most hateful of robbers and tyrants. The crown of another was on his head; the blood of the brave and loyal was on his hands. Thus, during many years, the Kings of England were objects of strong personal aversion to many of their subjects, and of strong personal attachment to none. They found, indeed, firm and cordial support against the pretender to their throne; but this support was given, not at all for their sake, but for the sake of a religious and political system which would have been endangered by their fall. This support, too, they were compelled to purchase by perpetually sacrificing their private inclinations to the party which had set them on the throne, and which maintained them there.

At the close of the reign of George the Second, the feeling of aversion with which the House of Brunswick had long been regarded by half the nation had died away; but no feeling of affection to that house had yet sprung up. There was little, indeed, in the old King's character to inspire esteem or tenderness. He was not our countryman. He never set foot on our soil till he was more than thirty years old. His speech betrayed his foreign origin and breeding. His love for his native land, though the most amiable part of his character, was not likely to endear him to his British subjects. He was never so happy as when he could exchange St. James's for Hernhausen; that year after year, our fleets were employed to convoy him to the Continent; that the interests of his kingdom were as nothing to him when compared with the interests of his Electorate, could scarcely be denied. As to the rest, he had neither the qualities which make dulness respectable, nor the qualities which make libertinism attractive. He had been a bad son and a worse father, an unfaithful husband and an ungraceful lover. Not one magnanimous or humane action is recorded of him; but many instances of meanness, and of a harshness which, but for the strong constitutional restraints under which he was placed, might have made the misery of his people.

He died; and at once a new world opened. The young King was a born

Englishman. All his tastes and habits, good or bad, were English. No portion of his subjects had anything to reproach him with. Even the remaining adherents of the House of Stuart could scarcely impute to him the guilt of usurpation. He was not responsible for the Revolution, for the Act of Settlement, for the suppression of the risings of 1715 and of 1745. He was innocent of the blood of Derwentwater and of Kilmarnock, of Balmerino and Cameron. Born fifty years after the old line had been expelled, fourth in descent and third in succession of the Hanoverian dynasty, he might plead some show of hereditary right. His age, his appearance, and all that was known of his character, conciliated public favour. He was in the bloom of youth; his person and address were pleasing. Scandal imputed to him no vice; and flattery might, without any glaring absurdity, ascribe to him many princely virtues.

It is not strange, therefore, that the sentiment of loyalty, a sentiment which had lately seemed to be as much out of date as the belief in witches or the practice of pilgrimage, should, from the day of his accession, have begun to revive. The Tories in particular, who had always been inclined to King-worship, and who had long felt with pain the want of an idol before whom they could bow themselves down, were as joyful as the priests of Apis, when, after a long interval, they had found a new calf to adore. It was soon clear that George the Third was regarded by a portion of the nation with a very different feeling from that which his two predecessors had inspired. They had been merely First Magistrates, Doges, Stadtholders; he was emphatically a King, the anointed of heaven, the breath of his people's nostrils. The years of the widowhood and mourning of the Tory party were over. Dido had kept faith long enough to the cold ashes of a former lord; she had at last found a comforter, and recognised the vestiges of the old flame. The golden days of Harley would return. The Somersets, the Lees and the Wyndhams would again surround the throne. The latitudinarian Prelates, who had not been ashamed to correspond with Doddridge and to shake hands with Whiston, would be succeeded by divines of the temper of South and Atterbury. The devotion which had been so signally shown to the House of Stuart—which had been proof against defeats, confiscations and proscriptions, which perfidy, oppression, ingratitude could not weary out, was now transferred entire to the House of Brunswick. If George the Third would but accept the homage of the Cavaliers and High Churchmen, he should be to them all that Charles the First and Charles the Second had been.

The Prince, whose accession was thus hailed by a great party long estranged from his house, had received from nature a strong will, a firmness of temper to which a harsher name might perhaps be given, and an understanding not, indeed, acute or enlarged, but such as qualified him to be a good man of business. But his character had not yet fully developed itself. He had been brought up in strict seclusion. The detractors of the Princess Dowager of Wales affirmed that she had kept her children from commerce with society, in order that she might hold an undivided empire over their minds. She gave a very different explanation of her conduct. She would gladly, she said, see her sons and daughters mix in the world, if they could do so without risk to their morals. But the profligacy of the people of quality alarmed her. The young men were all rakes; the young women made love, instead of waiting till it was made to them. She could not bear to expose those whom she loved best to the contaminating influence of such society. The moral advantages of the system of education which formed the Duke of York, the Duke of Cumberland and the Queen of Denmark, may perhaps be questioned. George the Third was indeed no libertine; but he brought to the throne a mind only half opened, and was for some time entirely under the influence of his mother and of his groom of the Stole, John Stuart, Earl of Bute.

The Earl of Bute was scarcely known, even by name, to the country which he was soon to govern. He had, indeed, a short time after he came of age, been chosen to fill a vacancy, which, in the middle of a parliament, had taken place among the Scotch representative peers. He had disobliged the Whig ministers by giving some silent votes with the Tories, had consequently lost his seat at the next dissolution, and had never been re-elected. Near twenty years had elapsed since he had borne any part in politics. He had passed some of those years at his seat in one of the Hebrides, and from that retirement he had emerged as one of the household of Prince Frederic. Lord Bute, excluded from public life, had found out many ways of amusing his leisure. He was a tolerable actor in private theatricals, and was particularly successful in the part of Lothario. A handsome leg, to which both painters and satirists took care to give prominence, was among his chief qualifications for the stage. He devised quaint dresses for masquerades. He dabbled in geometry, mechanics and botany. He paid some attention to antiquities and works of art, and was considered in his own circle as a judge of painting, architecture and poetry. It is said that his spelling was incorrect. But though, in our time, incorrect spelling is justly considered as a proof of sordid ignorance, it would be unjust to apply the same rule to people who lived a century ago. The novel of Sir Charles Grandison was published about the time at which Lord Bute made his appearance at Leicester House. Our readers may, perhaps, remember the account which Charlotte Grandison gives of her two lovers. One of them, a fashionable baronet who talks French and Italian fluently, cannot write a line in his own language without some sin against orthography; the other, who is represented as a most respectable specimen of the young aristocracy, and something of a virtuoso, is described as spelling pretty well for a lord. On the whole, the Earl of Bute might fairly be called a man of cultivated mind. He was also a man of undoubted honour. But his understanding was narrow, and his manners cold and haughty. His qualifications for the part of a statesman were best described by Frederic, who often indulged in the unprincely luxury of sneering at his dependents. " Bute," said his Royal Highness, " you are the very man to be envoy at some small, proud German court where there is nothing to do."

Scandal represented the Groom of the Stole as the favoured lover of the Princess Dowager. He was undoubtedly her confidential friend. The influence which the two united exercised over the mind of the King was for a time unbounded. The Princess, a woman and a foreigner, was not likely to be a judicious adviser about affairs of state. The Earl could scarcely be said to have served even a noviciate in politics. His notions of government had been acquired in the society which had been in the habit of assembling round Frederic at Kew and Leicester House. That society consisted principally of Tories, who had been reconciled to the House of Hanover by the civility with which the Prince had treated them, and by the hope of obtaining high preferment when he should come to the throne. Their political creed was a peculiar modification of Toryism. It was the creed neither of the Tories of the seventeenth nor of the Tories of the nineteenth century. It was the creed, not of Filmer and Sacheverell, not of Perceval and Eldon, but of the sect of which Bolingbroke may be considered as the chief doctor. This sect deserves commendation for having pointed out and justly reprobated some great abuses which sprang up during the long domination of the Whigs. But it is far easier to point out and reprobate abuses than to propose reforms; and the reforms which Bolingbroke proposed would either have been utterly inefficient, or would have produced much more mischief than they would have removed.

The Revolution had saved the nation from one class of evils, but had at the same time—such is the imperfection of all things human—engendered or aggravated another class of evils which required new remedies. Liberty and property were secure from the attacks of prerogative. Conscience was respected. No government ventured to infringe any of the rights solemnly recognised by the instrument which had called William and Mary to the throne. But it cannot be denied that, under the new system, the public interests and the public morals were seriously endangered by corruption and faction. During the long struggle against the Stuarts, the chief object of the most enlightened statesmen had been to strengthen the House of Commons. The struggle was over; the victory was won; the House of Commons was supreme in the state; and all the vices which had till then been latent in the representative system were rapidly developed by prosperity and power. Scarcely had the executive government become really responsible to the House of Commons, when it began to appear that the House of Commons was not really responsible to the nation. Many of the constituent bodies were under the absolute control of individuals; many were notoriously at the command of the highest bidder. The debates were not published. It was very seldom known out of doors how a gentleman had voted. Thus, while the ministry was accountable to the Parliament, the majority of the Parliament was accountable to nobody. Under such circumstances, nothing could be more natural than that the members should insist on being paid for their votes, should form themselves into combinations for the purpose of raising th eprice of their votes, and should, at critical conjunctures, extort large wages by threatening a strike. Thus the Whig Ministers of George the First and George the Second were compelled to reduce corruption to a system, and to practise it on a gigantic scale.

If we are right as to the cause of these abuses, we can scarcely be wrong as to the remedy. The remedy was surely not to deprive the House of Commons of its weight in the state. Such a course would undoubtedly have put an end to parliamentary corruption and to parliamentary factions; for, when votes cease to be of importance, they will cease to be bought; and, when knaves can get nothing by combining, they will cease to combine. But to destroy corruption and faction by introducing despotism would have been to cure bad by worse. The proper remedy evidently was, to make the House of Commons responsible to the nation; and this was to be effected in two ways—first, by giving publicity to parliamentary proceedings, and thus placing every member on his trial before the tribunal of public opinion; and secondly, by so reforming the constitution of the House that no man should be able to sit in it who had not been returned by a respectable and independent body of constituents.

Bolingbroke and Bolingbroke's disciples recommended a very different mode of treating the diseases of the state. Their doctrine was that a vigorous use of the prerogative by a patriot King would at once break all factious combinations and supersede the pretended necessity of bribing members of Parliament. The King had only to resolve that he would be master, that he would not be held in thraldom by any set of men, that he would take for ministers any persons in whom he had confidence, without distinction of party, and that he would restrain his servants from influencing by immoral means either the constituent bodies or the representative body. This childish scheme proved that those who proposed it knew nothing of the nature of the evil with which they pretended to deal. The real cause of the prevalence of corruption and faction was that a House of Commons, not accountable to the people, was more powerful than the King. Bolingbroke's remedy could be applied only by a King more powerful than the House of Commons. How was the patriot Prince to govern in defiance of the body without whose consent he could not equip a sloop, keep a battalion under arms, send an embassy, or defray even the charges of his own household? Was he to dissolve the Parliament? And what was he likely to gain by appealing to Sudbury and Old Sarum against the venality of their representatives? Was he to send out privy seals? Was he to levy ship-money? If so, this boasted reform must commence in all probability by civil war, and, if consummated, must be consummated by the establishment of absolute monarchy. Or was the patriot King to carry the House of Commons with him in his upright designs? By what means? Interdicting himself from the use of corrupt influence, what motive was he to address to the Dodingtons and Winningtons? Was cupidity, strengthened by habit, to be laid asleep by a few fine sentences about virtue and union.

Absurd as this theory was, it had many admirers, particularly among men of letters. It was now to be reduced to practice; and the result was, as any man of sagacity must have foreseen, the most piteous and ridiculous of failures.

On the very day of the young King's accession, appeared some signs which indicated the approach of a great change. The speech which he made to his council was not submitted to the cabinet. It was drawn up by Bute, and contained some expressions which might be construed into reflections on the conduct of affairs during the late reign. Pitt remonstrated, and begged that these expressions might be softened down in the printed copy; but it was not till after some hours of altercation that Bute yielded; and, even after Bute had yielded, the King affected to hold out till the following afternoon. On the same day on which this singular contest took place, Bute was not only sworn of the privy council, but introduced into the cabinet.

Soon after this Lord Holdernesse, one of the Secretaries of State, in pursuance of a plan concerted with the court, resigned the seals. Bute was instantly appointed to the vacant place. A general election speedily followed, and the new Secretary entered parliament in the only way in which he then could enter it, as one of the sixteen representative peers of Scotland.*

Had the ministers been firmly united, it can scarcely be doubted that they would have been able to withstand the Court. The parliamentary influence of the Whig aristocracy, combined with the genius, the virtue and the fame of Pitt, would have been irresistible. But there had been in the Cabinet of George the Second latent jealousies and enmities, which now began to show themselves. Pitt had been estranged from his old ally Legge, the Chancellor of the Exchequer. Some of the ministers were envious of Pitt's popularity; others were, not altogether without cause, disgusted by his imperious and haughty demeanour: others, again, were honestly opposed to some parts of his policy. They admitted that he had found the country in the depths of humiliation and had raised it to the height of glory; they admitted he had conducted the war with energy, ability and splendid success. But they began to hint that the drain on the resources of the state was unexampled, and that the public debt was increasing with a speed at which Montagu or Godolphin would have stood aghast. Some of the acquisitions made by our fleets and armies were, it was acknowledged, profitable as well as honourable; but, now that George the Second was dead, a courtier might venture to ask why England was to become a party in a dispute between two German powers. What was it to her whether the House of Hapsburg or the House of Brandenburg ruled in Silesia? Why were the best English regiments fighting on the Main? Why were the Prussian battalions paid with English gold? The great minister seemed to think it beneath him to calculate the price of victory. As long as the Tower guns were fired, as the streets were illuminated, as French banners were carried in triumph through the streets of London, it was to him matter of indifference to what extent the public burdens were augmented. Nay, he seemed to glory in the magnitude of those sacrifices which the people, fascinated by his eloquence and success, had too readily made and would long and bitterly regret. There was no check on waste or embezzlement. Our commissaries returned from the camp of Prince Ferdinand to buy boroughs, to rear palaces, to rival the magni-

* In the reign of Anne, the House of Lords had resolved that, under the 23rd article of Union, no Scotch peer could be created a peer of Great Britain. This resolution was not annulled till the year 1782.

ficence of the old aristocracy of the realm. Already had we borrowed, in four years of war, more than the most skilful and economical government would pay in forty years of peace. But the prospect of peace was as remote as ever. It could not be doubted that France, smarting and prostrate, would consent to fair terms of accommodation; but this was not what Pitt wanted. War had made him powerful and popular; with war, all that was brightest in his life was associated; for war his talents were peculiarly fitted. He had at length begun to love war for its own sake, and was more disposed to quarrel with neutrals than to make peace with enemies.

Such were the views of the Duke of Bedford and of the Earl of Hardwicke; but no member of the government held these opinions so strongly as George Grenville, the Treasurer of the Navy. George Grenville was brother-in-law of Pitt, and had always been reckoned one of Pitt's personal and political friends. But it is difficult to conceive two men of talents and integrity more utterly unlike each other. Pitt, as his sister often said, knew nothing accurately except Spenser's "Fairy Queen." He had never applied himself steadily to any branch of knowledge. He was a wretched financier. He never became familiar even with the rules of that House of which he was the brightest ornament. He had never studied public law as a system; and was, indeed, so ignorant of the whole subject, that George the Second, on one occasion, complained bitterly that a man who had never read Vattel should presume to undertake the direction of Foreign affairs. But these defects were more than redeemed by high and rare gifts; by a strange power of inspiring great masses of men with confidence and affection; by an eloquence which not only delighted the ear, but stirred the blood, and brought tears into the eyes; by originality in devising plans; by vigour in executing them. Grenville, on the other hand, was by nature and habit a man of details. He had been bred a lawyer; and he had brought the industry and acuteness of the Temple into official and parliamentary life. He was supposed to be intimately acquainted with the whole fiscal system of the country. He had paid special attention to the law of Parliament, and was so learned in all things relating to the privileges and orders of the House of Commons, that those who loved him least pronounced him the only person competent to succeed Onslow in the Chair. His speeches were generally instructive, and sometimes, from the gravity and earnestness with which he spoke, even impressive, but never brilliant, and generally tedious. Indeed, even when he was at the head of affairs, he sometimes found it difficult to obtain the ear of the House. In dis position as well as in intellect, he differed widely from his brother-in-law. Pitt was utterly regardless of money. He would scarcely stretch out his hand to take it; and, when it came, he threw it away with childish profusion. Grenville, though strictly upright, was grasping and parsimonious. Pitt was a man of excitable nerves, sanguine in hope, easily elated by success and popularity, keenly sensible of injury, but prompt to forgive; Grenville's character was stern, melancholy and pertinacious. Nothing was more remarkable in him than his inclination always to look on the dark side of things. He was the raven of the House of Commons, always croaking defeat in the midst of triumphs, and bankruptcy with an overflowing exchequer. Burke, with general applause, compared Grenville, in a time of quiet and plenty, to the evil spirit whom Ovid described looking down on the stately temples and wealthy haven of Athens, and scarce able to refrain from weeping because she could find nothing at which to weep. Such a man was not likely to be popular. But to unpopularity Grenville opposed a dogged determination, which sometimes forced even those who hated him to respect him.

It was natural that Pitt and Grenville, being such as they were, should take very different views of the situation of affairs. Pitt could see nothing but the trophies; Grenville could see nothing but the bill. Pitt boasted that England was victorious at once in America, in India and in Germany—the umpire of the

Continent, the mistress of the sea. Grenville cast up the subsidies, sighed over the army extraordinaries, and groaned in spirit to think that the nation had borrowed eight millions in one year.

With a ministry thus divided it was not difficult for Bute to deal. Legge was the first who fell. He had given offence to the young King in the late reign, by refusing to support a creature of Bute at a Hampshire election. He was now not only turned out, but in the closet, when he delivered up his seal of office, was treated with gross incivility.

Pitt, who did not love Legge, saw this event with indifference. But the danger was now fast approaching himself. Charles the Third of Spain had early conceived a deadly hatred of England. Twenty years before, when he was King of the Two Sicilies, he had been eager to join the coalition against Maria Theresa. But an English fleet had suddenly appeared in the Bay of Naples. An English Captain had landed, had proceeded to the palace, had laid a watch on the table, and had told his majesty that, within an hour, a treaty of neutrality must be signed, or a bombardment would commence. The treaty was signed; the squadron sailed out of the bay twenty-four hours after it had sailed in; and from that day the ruling passion of the humbled Prince was aversion to the English name. He was at length in a situation in which he might hope to gratify that passion. He had recently become King of Spain and the Indies. He saw, with envy and apprehension, the triumphs of our navy and the rapid extension of our colonial Empire. He was a Bourbon, and sympathised with the distress of the house from which he sprang. He was a Spaniard; and no Spaniard could bear to see Gibraltar and Minorca in the possession of a foreign power. Impelled by such feelings, Charles concluded a secret treaty with France. By this treaty, known as the Family Compact, the two powers bound themselves, not in express words, but by the clearest implication, to make war on England in common. Spain postponed the declaration of hostilities only till her fleet, laden with the treasures of America, should have arrived.

The existence of the treaty could not be kept a secret from Pitt. He acted as a man of his capacity and energy might be expected to act. He at once proposed to declare war against Spain and to intercept the American fleet. He had determined, it is said, to attack without delay both Havanna and the Philippines.

His wise and resolute counsel was rejected. Bute was foremost in opposing it, and was supported by almost the whole cabinet. Some of the ministers doubted, or affected to doubt, the correctness of Pitt's intelligence; some shrank from the responsibility of advising a course so bold and decided as that which he proposed; some were weary of his ascendancy, and were glad to be rid of him on any pretext. One only of his colleagues agreed with him, his brother-in-law, Earl Temple.

Pitt and Temple resigned their offices. To Pitt the young King behaved at parting in the most gracious manner. Pitt, who, proud and fiery everywhere else, was always meek and humble in the closet, was moved even to tears. The King and the favourite urged him to accept some substantial mark of royal gratitude. Would he like to be appointed governor of Canada? A salary of £5,000 a-year should be annexed to the office. Residence would not be required. It was true that the governor of Canada, as the law then stood, could not be a member of the House of Commons. But a bill should be brought in, authorising Pitt to hold his government together with a seat in Parliament, and in the preamble should be set forth his claims to the gratitude of his country. Pitt answered, with all delicacy, that his anxieties were rather for his wife and family than for himself, and that nothing would be so acceptable to him as a mark of royal goodness which might be beneficial to those who were dearest to him. The hint was taken. The same *Gazette* which announced the retirement of the Secretary of State announced also that, in consideration of his great public services, his wife had been created a peeress in her own right, and that a pension of three thousand pounds a-year, for three lives, had been bestowed on himself. It was doubtless thought that the rewards and honours conferred on the great minister would have a conciliatory effect on the public mind. Perhaps, too, it was thought that his popularity, which had partly arisen from the contempt which he had always shown for money, would be damaged by a pension; and, indeed, a crowd of libels instantly appeared, in which he was accused of having sold his country. Many of his true friends thought that he would have best consulted the dignity of his character by refusing to accept any pecuniary reward from the Court. Nevertheless, the general opinion of his talents, virtues and services remained unaltered. Addresses were presented to him from several large towns. London showed its admiration and affection in a still more marked manner. Soon after his resignation came the Lord Mayor's day. The King and the royal family dined at Guildhall. Pitt was one of the guests. The young Sovereign, seated by his bride in his state coach, received a remarkable lesson. He was scarcely noticed. All eyes were fixed on the fallen minister; all acclamations directed to him. The streets, the balconies, the chimney tops, burst into a roar of delight as his chariot passed by. The ladies waved their handkerchiefs from the windows. The common people clung to the wheels, shook hands with the footmen, and even kissed the horses. Cries of "No Bute!" "No Newcastle salmon!" were mingled with the shouts of "Pitt for ever!" when Pitt entered Guildhall, he was welcomed by loud huzzas and clapping of hands, in which the very magistrates of the city joined. Lord Bute, in the meantime, was hooted and pelted through Cheapside, and would, it was thought, have been in some danger, if he had not taken the precaution of surrounding his carriage with a strong body guard of boxers. Many persons blamed the conduct of Pitt on this occasion as disrespectful to the King. Indeed, Pitt himself afterwards owned that he had done wrong. He was led into this error, as he was afterwards led into more serious errors, by the influence of his turbulent and mischievious brother-in-law, Temple.

The events which immediately followed Pitt's retirement raised his fame higher than ever. War with Spain proved to be, as he had predicted, inevitable. News came from the West Indies that Martinique had been taken by an expedition which he had sent forth. Havanna fell; and it was known that he had planned an attack on Havanna. Manilla capitulated; and it was believed that he had meditated a blow against Manilla. The American fleet, which he had proposed to intercept, had unloaded an immense cargo of bullion in the haven of Cadiz, before Bute could be convinced that the Court of Madrid really entertained hostile intentions.

The session of Parliament which followed Pitt's retirement passed over without any violent storm. Lord Bute took on himself the most prominent part in the House of Lords. He had become Secretary of State, and, indeed, Prime Minister, without having once opened his lips in public except as an actor. There was, therefore, no small curiosity to know how he would acquit himself. Members of the House of Commons crowded the bar of the Lords and covered the steps of the throne. It was generally expected that the orator would break down; but his most malicious hearers were forced to own that he had made a better figure than they expected. They, indeed, ridiculed his action as theatrical and his style as tumid. They were especially amused by the long pauses which, not from hesitation, but from affectation, he made at all the emphatic words, and Charles Townshend cried out, "Minute guns!" The general opinion however was, that, if Bute had been early practised in debate, he might have become an impressive speaker.

In the Commons, George Grenville had been intrusted with the lead. The task was not, as yet, a very difficult one: for Pitt did not think fit to raise the standard of opposition. His speeches at this time were distinguished, not only by that eloquence in which he excelled all his rivals, but also by a temperance and a modesty which had too often been wanting to his character. When war was declared against Spain, he justly laid claim to the merit of having foreseen what had at length become manifest to all, but he carefully abstained from arrogant and acrimonious expressions; and this abstainence was the more honourable to him, because his temper, never very placid, was now severely tried, both by gout and by calumny. The courtiers had adopted a mode of warfare which was soon turned with far more formidable effect against themselves. Half the inhabitants of the Grub Street garrets paid their milk scores and got their shirts out of pawn by abusing Pitt. His German war, his subsidies, his pension, his wife's peerage, were shin of-beef and gin, blankets and baskets of small coal, to the starving poetasters of the Fleet. Even in the House of Commons he was, on one occasion during this session, assailed with an insolence and malice which called forth the indignation of men of all parties; but he endured the outrage with majestic patience. In his younger days he had been but too prompt to retaliate on those who attacked him; but now, conscious of his great services, and of the space which he filled in the eyes of all mankind, he would not stoop to personal squabbles. "This is no season," he said, in the debate on the Spanish war, "for altercation and recrimination. A day has arrived when every Englishman should stand forth for his country. Arm the whole; be one people; forgot everything but the public. I set you the example. Harrassed by slanderers, sinking under pain and disease, for the public I forget both my wrongs and my infirmities!" On a general review of his life, we are inclined to think that his genius and virtue never shone with so pure an effulgence as during the session of 1762.

The session drew towards the close; and Bute, emboldened by the acquiescence of the Houses, resolved to strike another great blow, and to become first minister in name as well as in reality. That coalition, which a few months before had seemed all powerful, had been dissolved. The retreat of Pitt had deprived the government of popularity. Newcastle had exulted in the fall of the illustrious colleague whom he envied and dreaded, and had not foreseen that his own doom was at hand. He still tried to flatter himself that he was at the head of the government; but insults heaped on insults at length undeceived him. Places which had always been considered as in his gift, were bestowed without any reference to him. His expostulations only called forth significant hints that it was time for him to retire. One day he pressed on Bute the claims of a Whig Prelate to the archbishopric of York. "If your grace thinks so highly of him," answered Bute, "I wonder that you did not promote him when you had the power." Still the old man clung with a desperate grasp to the wreck. Seldom, indeed, have Christian meekness and Christian humility equalled the meekness and humility of his patient and abject ambition. At length he was forced to understand that all was over. He quitted that Court where he had held high office during forty-five years, and hid his shame and regret among the cedars of Claremont. Bute became First Lord of the Treasury.

The favourite had undoubtedly committed a great error. It is impossible to imagine a tool better suited to his purposes than that which he thus threw away, or rather put into the hands of his enemies. If Newcastle had been suffered to play at being first minister, Bute might securely and quietly have enjoyed the substance of power. The gradual introduction of Tories into all the departments of the government might have been effected without any violent clamour, if the chief of the great Whig connection had been ostensibly at the head of affairs. This was strongly represented to Bute by Lord Mansfield, a man who may justly be called the father of modern Toryism, of Toryism modified to suit an order of things under which the House of Commons is the most powerful body in the state. The theories which had dazzled

Bute could not impose on the fine intellect of Mansfield. The temerity with which Bute provoked the hostility of powerful and deeply rooted interests, was displeasing to Mansfield's cold and timid nature. Expostulation, however, was vain. Bute was impatient of advice, drunk with success, eager to be, in show as well as in reality, the head of the government. He had engaged in an undertaking in which a screen was absolutely necessary to his success, and even to his safety. He found an excellent screen ready in the very place where it was most needed; and he rudely pushed it away.

And now the new system of government came into full operation. For the first time since the accession of the House of Hanover, the Tory party was in the ascendant. The Prime Minister himself was a Tory. Lord Egremont, who had succeeded Pitt as Secretary of State, was a Tory and the son of a Tory. Sir Francis Dashwood, a man of slender parts, of small experience, and of notoriously immoral character, was made Chancellor of the Exchequer, for no reason that could be imagined, except that he was a Tory and had been a Jacobite. The royal household was filled with men whose favourite toast, a few years before, had been the "King over the water." The relative position of the two great national seats of learning was suddenly changed. The University of Oxford had long been the chief seat of disaffection. In troubled times the High Street had been lined with bayonets; the colleges had been searched by the King's messengers. Grave doctors were in the habit of talking very Ciceronian treason in the theatre; and the undergraduates drank bumpers to Jacobite toasts and chanted Jacobite airs. Of four successive Chancellors of the University, one had notoriously been in the Pretender's service; the other three were fully believed to be in secret correspondence with the exiled family. Cambridge had, therefore, been especially favoured by the Hanoverian Princes, and had shown herself grateful for their patronage. George the First had enriched her library; George the Second had contributed munificently to her Senate House. Bishoprics and deaneries were showered on her children. Her Chancellor was Newcastle, the chief of the Whig aristocracy; her High Steward was Hardwicke, the Whig head of the law. Both her burgesses had held office under the Whig ministry. Times had now changed. The University of Cambridge was received at St. James's with comparative coldness. The answers to the addresses of Oxford were all graciousness and warmth.

The watchwords of the new government were prerogative and purity. The sovereign was no longer to be a puppet in the hands of any subject, or of any combination of subjects. George the Third would not be forced to take ministers whom he disliked, as his grandfather had been forced to take Pitt. George the Third would not be forced to part with any whom he delighted to honour, as his grandfather had been forced to part with Carteret. At the same time, the system of bribery which had grown up during the late reigns was to cease. It was ostentatiously proclaimed that, since the accession of the young King, neither constituents nor representatives had been bought with the secret service money. To free Britain from corruption and oligarchical cabals, to detach her from continental connections, to bring the bloody and expensive war with France and Spain to a close, such were the specious objects which Bute professed to procure.

Some of these objects he attained. England withdrew, at the cost of a deep stain on her faith, from her German connections. The war with France and Spain was terminated by a peace, honourable, indeed, and advantageous to our country, yet less honourable and less advantageous than might have been expected from a long and almost unbroken series of victories, by land and sea, in very part of the world. But the only effect of Bute's domestic administration was to make faction wilder and corruption fouler than ever.

The mutual animosity of the Whig and Tory parties had begun to languish after the fall of Walpole and had seemed to be almost extinct at the close of the reign of George the Second. It now revived in all its force. Many Whigs, it is true, were still in office. The Duke of Bedford had signed the treaty with France. The Duke of Devonshire, though much out of humour, still continued to be Lord Chamberlain. Grenville, who led the House of Commons, and Fox, who still enjoyed in silence the immense gains of the Pay Office, had always been regarded as strong Whigs. But the bulk of the party throughout the country regarded the new minister with abhorrence. There was, indeed, no want of popular themes for invective against his character. He was a favourite; and favourites have always been odious in this country. No mere favourite had been at the head of the government since the dagger of Felton had reached the heart of the Duke of Buckingham. After that event the most arbitrary and the most frivolous of the Stuarts had felt the necessity of confiding the chief direction of affairs to men who had given some proof of parliamentary or official talent. Strafford, Falkland, Clarendon, Clifford, Shaftesbury, Lauderdale, Danby, Temple, Halifax, Rochester, Sunderland, whatever their faults mights be, were all men of acknowledged ability. They did not owe their eminence merely to the favour of the sovereign. On the contrary, they owed the favour of the sovereign to their eminence. Most of them, indeed, had first attracted the notice of the court by the capacity and vigour which they had shown in opposition. The Revolution seemed to have for ever secured the state against the domination of a Carr or a Villiers. Now, however, the personal regard of the King had at once raised a man who had seen nothing of public business, who had never opened his lips in Parliament, over the heads of a crowd of eminent orators, financiers, diplomatists. From a private gentleman, this fortunate minion had at once been turned into a Secretary of State. He had made his maiden speech when at the head of the administration. The vulgar resorted to a simple explanation of the phenomenon, and the coarsest ribaldry against the Princess Mother was scrawled on every wall and sung in every alley.

This was not all. The spirit of party, roused by impolitic provocation from its long sleep, roused in turn a still fiercer and more malignant Fury, the spirit of national animosity. The grudge of Whig against Tory was mingled with the grudge of Englishman against Scot. The two sections of the great British people had not yet been indissolubly blended together. The events of 1715 and of 1745 had left painful and enduring traces. The tradesmen of Cornhill had been in dread of seeing their tills and warehouses plundered by bare-legged mountaineers from the Grampians. They still recollected that Black Friday, when the news came that the rebels were at Derby, when all the shops in the city were closed, and when the Bank of England began to pay in sixpences. The Scots, on the other hand, remembered, with natural resentment, the severity with which the insurgents had been chastised, the military outrages, the humiliating laws, the heads fixed on Temple Bar, the fires and quartering blocks on Kennington Common. The favourite did not suffer the English to forget from what part of the island he came. The cry of all the south was that the public offices, the army, the navy, were filled with high-cheeked Drummonds and Erskines, Macdonalds and Macgillivrays, who could not talk a Christian tongue, and some of whom had but lately begun to wear Christian breeches. All the old jokes on hills without trees, girls without stockings, men eating the food of horses, pails emptied from the fourteenth storey, were pointed against these lucky adventurers. To the honour of the Scots it must be said, that their prudence and their pride restrained them from retaliation. Like the princess in the Arabian tale, they stopped their ears tight, and, unmoved by the shrillest notes of abuse, walked on, without once looking round, straight towards the Golden Fountain.

Bute, who had always been considered as a man of taste and reading, affected, from the moment of his elevation, the character of a Mæcenas. If he expected to conciliate the public by encouraging literature and art, he was grievously mistaken. Indeed, none of the objects of his munificence, with the single exception of Johnson, can be said to have been well selected; and the public, not unnaturally, ascribed the selection of Johnson rather to the Doctor's political prejudices than to his literary merits. For a wretched scribbler named Shebbeare, who had nothing in common with Johnson except violent Jacobitism, and who had stood in the pillory for a libel on the Revolution, was honoured with a mark of royal approbation, similar to that which was bestowed on the author of the "English Dictionary," and of the "Vanity of Human Wishes." It was remarked that Adam, a Scotchman, was the court architect, and that Ramsay, a Scotchman, was the court painter, and was preferred to Reynolds. Mallet, a Scotchman, of no high literary fame, and of infamous character, partook largely of the liberality of the government. John Home, a Scotchman, was rewarded for the tragedy of "Douglas," both with a pension and with a sinecure place. But, when the author of the "Bard," and of the "Elegy in a Country Churchyard," ventured to ask for a Professorship, the emoluments of which he much needed, and for the duties of which he was, in many respects, better qualified than any man living, he was refused; and the post was bestowed on the pedagogue under whose care the favourite's son-in-law, Sir James Lowther, had made such signal proficiency in the graces and in the humane virtues.

Thus, the First Lord of the Treasury was detested by many as a Tory, by many as a favourite and by many as a Scot. All the hatred which flowed from these various sources soon mingled, and was directed in one torrent of obloquy against the treaty of peace. The Duke of Bedford, who had negotiated that treaty, was hooted through the streets. Bute was attacked in his chair, and was with difficulty rescued by a troop of the guards. He could hardly walk the streets in safety without disguising himself. A gentleman who died not many years ago used to say that he once recognised the favourite Earl in the piazza of Covent Garden, muffled in a large coat and with a hat and wig drawn down over his brows. His lordship's established type with the mob was a jack boot, a wretched pun on his Christian name and title. A jack boot, generally accompanied by a petticoat, was sometimes fastened on a gallows and sometimes committed to the flames. Libels on the court, exceeding in audacity and rancour any that had been published for many years, now appeared daily in prose and verse. Wilkes, with lively insolence, compared the mother of George the Third to the mother of Edward the Third, and the Scotch minister to the gentle Mortimer. Churchill, with all the energy of hatred, deplored the fate of his country, invaded by a new race of savages, more cruel and ravenous than the Picts or the Danes, the poor, proud children of Leprosy and Hunger. It is a slight circumstance, but deserves to be recorded, that in this year pamphleteers first ventured to print at length the names of the great men whom they lampooned. George the Second had always been the K——. His ministers had been Sir R—— W——, Mr. P—— and the Duke of N——. But the libellers of George the Third, of the Princess Mother and of Lord Bute did not give quarter to a single vowel.

It was supposed that Lord Temple secretly encouraged the most scurrilous assailants of the government. In truth, those who knew his habits tracked him as men track a mole. It was his nature to grub underground. Whenever a heap of dirt was flung up it might well be suspected that he was at work in some foul, crooked labyrinth below. Pitt turned away from the filthy work of opposition with the same scorn with which he had turned away from the filthy work of government. He had the magnanimity to proclaim everywhere the disgust which he felt at the insults offered by his own adherents to the Scottish nation, and missed no opportunity of extolling the courage and fidelity which the Highland regiments had displayed through the whole war.

But, though he disdained to use any but lawful and honourable weapons, it was well known that his fair blows were likely to be far more formidable than the privy thrusts of his brother-in-law's stiletto.

Bute's heart began to fail him. The Houses were about to meet. The treaty would instantly be the subject of discussion. It was probable that Pitt, the great Whig connection and the multitude would all be on the same side. The favourite had professed to hold in abhorrence those means by which preceding ministers had kept the House of Commons in good humour. He now began to think that he had been too scrupulous. His Utopian visions were at an end. It was necessary, not only to bribe, but to bribe more shamelessly and flagitiously than his predecessors, in order to make up for lost time. A majority must be secured, no matter by what means. Could Grenville do this? Would he do it? His firmness and ability had not yet been tried in any perilous crisis. He had been generally regarded as a humble follower of his brother Temple and of his brother-in-law Pitt, and was supposed, though with little reason, to be still favourably inclined towards them. Other aid must be called in. And where was other aid to be found?

There was one man, whose sharp and manly logic had often in debate been found a match for the lofty and impassioned rhetoric of Pitt, whose talents for jobbing were not inferior to his talents for debate, whose dauntless spirit shrank from no difficulty or danger, and who was as little troubled with scruples as with fears. Henry Fox, or nobody, could weather the storm which was about to burst. Yet was he a person to whom the Court, even in that extremity, was unwilling to have recourse. He had always been regarded as a Whig of the Whigs. He had been the friend and disciple of Walpole. He had long been connected by close ties with William, Duke of Cumberland. By the Tories he was more hated than any man living. So strong was their aversion to him that when, in the late reign, he had attempted to form a party against the Duke of Newcastle, they had thrown all their weight into Newcastle's scale. By the Scots, Fox was abhorred as the confidential friend of the conqueror of Culloden. He was, on personal grounds, most obnoxious to the Princess Mother. For he had, immediately after her husband's death, advised the late King to take the education of her son, the heir apparent, entirely out of her hands. He had recently given, if possible, still deeper offence; for he had indulged, not without some ground, the ambitious hope that his beautiful sister-in-law, the Lady Sarah Lennox, might be queen of England. It had been observed that the King at one time rode every morning by the grounds of Holland House, and that on such occasions, Lady Sarah, dressed like a shepherdess at a masquerade, was making hay close to the road, which was then separated by no wall from the lawn. On account of the part which Fox had taken in this singular love affair, he was the only member of the Privy Council who was not summoned to the meeting at which his Majesty announced his intended marriage with the Princess of Mecklenburg. Of all the statesmen of the age, therefore, it seemed that Fox was the last with whom Bute, the Tory, the Scot, the favourite of the Princess Mother, could, under any circumstances, act. Yet to Fox Bute was now compelled to apply.

Fox had many noble and amiable qualities, which in private life shone forth in full lustre, and made him dear to his children, to his dependents and to his friends; but as a public man he had no title to esteem. In him the vices which were common to the whole school of Walpole appeared, not, perhaps, in their worst, but certainly in their most prominent form; for his parliamentary and official talents made all his faults conspicuous. His courage, his vehement temper, his contempt for appearances, led him to display much that others, quite as unscrupulous as himself, covered with a decent veil. He was the most unpopular of the statesmen of his time, not because he sinned more than many of them, but because he canted less.

He felt his unpopularity; but he felt it after the fashion of strong minds. He became, not cautious, but reckless, and faced the rage of the whole nation with a scowl of inflexible defiance. He was born with a sweet and generous temper; but he had been goaded and baited into a savageness which was not natural to him, and which amazed and shocked those who knew him best. Such was the man to whom Bute, in extreme need, applied for succour.

That succour Fox was not unwilling to afford. Though by no means of an envious temper, he had undoubtedly contemplated the success and popularity of Pitt with bitter mortification. He thought himself Pitt's match as a debater and Pitt's superior as a man of business. They had long been regarded as well-paired rivals. They had started fair in the career of ambition. They had long run side by side. At length Fox had taken the lead and Pitt had fallen behind. Then had come a sudden turn of fortune, like that in Virgil's footrace. Fox had stumbled in the mire, and had not only been defeated, but befouled. Pitt had reached the goal and received the prize. The emoluments of the Pay Office might induce the defeated statesman to submit in silence to the ascendancy of his competitor, but could not satisfy a mind conscious of great powers and sore from great vexations. As soon, therefore, as a party arose adverse to the war and to the supremacy of the great war minister, the hopes of Fox began to revive. His feuds with the Princess Mother, with the Scots, with the Tories, he was ready to forget, if, by the help of his old enemies, he could now regain the importance which he had lost, and confront Pitt on equal terms.

The alliance was, therefore, soon concluded. Fox was assured that, if he would pilot the government out of its embarrassing situation, he should be rewarded with a peerage, of which he had long been desirous. He undertook on his side to obtain, by fair or foul means, a vote in favour of the peace. In consequence of this arrangement he became leader of the House of Commons; and Grenville stifling his vexation as well as he could, sullenly acquiesced in the change.

Fox had expected that his influence would secure to the Court the cordial support of some eminent Whigs who were his personal friends, particularly of the Duke of Cumberland and of the Duke of Devonshire. He was disappointed, and soon found that, in addition to all his other difficulties, he must reckon on the opposition of the ablest prince of the blood and of the great house of Cavendish.

But he had pledged himself to win the battle; and he was not a man to go back. It was no time for squeamishness. Bute was made to comprehend that the ministry could be saved only by practising the tactics of Walpole to an extent at which Walpole himself would have stared. The Pay Office was turned into a mart for votes. Hundreds of members were closeted there with Fox, and, as there is too much reason to believe, departed carrying with them the wages of infamy. It was affirmed by persons who had the best opportunities of obtaining information, that twenty-five thousand pounds were thus paid away in a single morning. The lowest bribe given, it was said, was a banknote for two hundred pounds.

Intimidation was joined with corruption. All ranks, from the highest to the lowest, were to be taught that the King would be obeyed. The Lords Lieutenants of several counties were dismissed. The Duke of Devonshire was especially singled out as the victim by whose fate the magnates of England were to take warning. His wealth, rank and influence, his stainless private character, and the constant attachment of his family to the House of Hanover did not secure him from gross personal indignity. It was known that he disapproved of the course which the government had taken; and it was accordingly determined to humble the Prince of the Whigs, as he had been nicknamed by the Princess Mother. He went to the palace to pay his duty. "Tell him," said the King to a page, "that I will not see him." The page hesitated. "Go to him," said the King, "and tell him those very words."

The message was delivered. The Duke tore off his gold key, and went away boiling with anger. His relations who were in office instantly resigned. A few days later, the King called for the list of Privy Councillors, and with his own hand struck out the Duke's name.

In this step there was at least courage, though little wisdom or good nature. But, as nothing was too high for the revenge of the Court, so also was nothing too low. A persecution, such as had never been known before, and has never been known since, raged in every public department. Great numbers of humble and laborious clerks were deprived of their bread, not because they had neglected their duties, not because they had taken an active part against the ministry, but merely because they had owed their situations to the recommendation of some nobleman or gentleman who was against the peace. The proscription extended to tidewaiters, to gaugers, to doorkeepers. One poor man to whom a pension had been given for his gallantry in a fight with smugglers, was deprived of it because he had been befriended by the Duke of Grafton. An aged widow, who, on account of her husband's services in the navy, had, many years before, been made housekeeper to a public office, was dismissed from her situation, because it was imagined that she was distantly connected by marriage with the Cavendish family. The public clamour, as may well be supposed, grew daily louder and louder. But the louder it grew, the more resolutely did Fox go on with the work which he had begun. His old friends could not conceive what had possessed him. "I could forgive," said the Duke of Cumberland, " Fox's political vagaries; but I am quite confounded by his inhumanity. Surely he used to be the best-natured of men."

At last Fox went so far as to take a legal opinion on the question, whether the patents granted by George the Second were binding on George the Third. It is said, that, if his colleagues had not flinched, he would at once have turned out the Tellers of the Exchequer and Justices in Eyre.

Meanwhile the Parliament met. The ministers, more hated by the people than ever, were secure of a majority, and they had also reason to hope that they would have the advantage in the debates as well as in the divisions; for Pitt was confined to his chamber by a severe attack of gout. His friends moved to defer the consideration of the treaty till he should be able to attend: but the motion was rejected. The great day arrived. The discussion had lasted some time, when a loud huzza was heard in Palace Yard. The noise came nearer and nearer, up the stairs, through the lobby. The door opened, and from the midst of a shouting multitude came forth Pitt, borne in the arms of his attendants. His face was thin and ghastly, his limbs swathed in flannel, his crutch in his hand. The bearers set him down within the bar. His friends instantly surrounded him, and with their help he crawled to his seat near the table. In this condition he spoke three hours and a half against the peace. During that time he was repeatedly forced to sit down and to use cordials. It may well be supposed that his voice was faint, that his action was languid, and that his speech, though occasionally brilliant and impressive, was feeble when compared with his best oratorical performances. But those who remembered what he had done, and who saw what he suffered, listened to him with emotions stronger than any that mere eloquence can produce. He was unable to stay for the division, and was carried away from the House amidst shouts as loud as those which had announced his arrival.

A large majority approved the peace. The exultation of the Court was boundless. "Now," exclaimed the Princess Mother, "my son is really King." The young sovereign spoke of himself as freed from the bondage in which his grandfather had been held. On one point, it was announced, his mind was unalterably made up. Under no circumstances whatever should those Whig grandees, who had enslaved his predecessors and endeavoured to enslave himself, be restored to power.

This vaunting was premature. The real strength of the favourite was by no means proportioned to the number of votes which he had, on one particular division, been able to command. He was soon again in difficulties. The most important part of his budget was a tax on cider. The measure was opposed, not only by those who were generally hostile to his administration, but also by many of his supporters. The name of excise had always been hateful to the Tories. One of the chief crimes of Walpole, in their eyes, had been his partiality for this mode of raising money. The Tory Johnson had in his "Dictionary" given so scurrilous a definition of the word "Excise," that the Commissioners of Excise had seriously thought of prosecuting him. The counties which the new impost particularly affected had always been Tory counties. It was the boast of John Philips, the poet of the English vintage, that the Ciderland had ever been faithful to the throne, and that all the pruning-hooks of her thousand orchards had been beaten into swords for the service of the ill-fated Stuarts. The effect of Bute's fiscal scheme was to produce an union between the gentry and the yeomanry of the Cider-land and the Whigs of the capital. Herefordshire and Worcestershire were in a flame. The city of London, though not so directly interested, was, if possible, still more excited. The debates on this question irreparably damaged the government. Dashwood's financial statement had been confused and absurd beyond belief, and had been received by the House with roars of laughter. He had sense enough to be conscious of his unfitness for the high situation which he held, and exclaimed in a comical fit of despair, "What shall I do? The boys will point at me in the street, and cry, 'There goes the worst Chancellor of the Exchequer that ever was.'" George Grenville came to the rescue, and spoke strongly on his favourite theme, the profusion with which the late war had been carried on. That profusion, he said had made taxes necessary. He called on the gentlemen opposite to him to say where they would have a tax laid, and dwelt on this topic with his usual prolixity. "Let them tell me where," he repeated, in a monotonous and somewhat fretful tone. "I say, sir, let them tell me where. I repeat it, sir; I am entitled to say to them, Tell me where." Unluckily for him, Pitt had come down to the House that night, and had been bitterly provoked by the reflections thrown on the war. He revenged himself by murmuring in a whine resembling Grenville's, a line of a well-known song, "Gentle Shepherd, tell me where." "If," cried Grenville, "gentlemen are to be treated in this way——" Pitt, as was his fashion when he meant to mark extreme contempt, rose deliberately, made his bow, and walked out of the House, leaving his brother-in-law in convulsions of rage, and everybody else in convulsions of laughter. It was long before Grenville lost the nickname of the Gentle Shepherd.

But the ministry had vexations still more serious to endure. The hatred which the Tories and Scots bore to Fox was implacable. In a moment of extreme peril they had consented to put themselves under his guidance. But the aversion with which they regarded him broke forth as soon as the crisis seemed to be over. Some of them attacked him about the accounts of the Pay Office. Some of them rudely interrupted him when speaking, by laughter and ironical cheers. He was naturally desirous to escape from so disagreeable a situation, and demanded the peerage which had been promised as the reward of his services.

It was clear that there must be some change in the composition of the ministry. But scarcely any, even of those who, from their situation, might be supposed to be in all the secrets of the government, anticipated what really took place. To the amazement of the Parliament and the nation, it was suddenly announced that Bute had resigned.

Twenty different explanations of this strange step were suggested. Some attributed it to profound design, and some to sudden panic. Some said that the lampoons of the opposition had driven the Earl from the field; some that he had taken office only in order to bring the war to a close, and had always meant to retire when that object had been accomplished. He publicly assigned ill health as his reason for quitting business, and privately complained that he was not cordially seconded by his colleagues, and that Lord Mansfield, in particular, whom he had himself brought into the cabinet, gave him no support in the House of Peers. Mansfield was, indeed, far too sagacious not to perceive that Bute's situation was one of great peril, and far too timorous to thrust himself into peril for the sake of another. The probability, however, is that Bute's conduct on this occasion, like the conduct of most men on most occasions, was determined by mixed motives. We suspect that he was sick of office; for this is a feeling much more common among ministers than persons who see public life from a distance are disposed to believe; and nothing could be more natural than that this feeling should take possession of the mind of Bute. In general, a statesman climbs by slow degrees. Many laborious years elapse before he reaches the topmost pinnacle of preferment. In the earlier part of his career, therefore, he is constantly lured on by seeing something above him. During his ascent he gradually becomes inured to the annoyances which belong to a life of ambition. By the time that he has attained the highest point, he has become patient of labour and callous to abuse. He is kept constant to his vocation, in spite of all its discomforts, at first by hope, and at last by habit. It was not so with Bute. His whole public life lasted little more than two years. On the day on which he became a politician he became a cabinet minister. In a few months he was, both in name and in show, chief of the administration. Greater than he had been he could not be. If what he already possessed was vanity and vexation of spirit, no delusion remained to entice him onward. He had been cloyed with the pleasures of ambition before he had been seasoned to its pains. His habits had not been such as were likely to fortify his mind against obloquy and public hatred. He had reached his forty-eighth year in dignified ease, without knowing, by personal experience, what it was to be ridiculed and slandered. All at once, without any previous initiation, he had found himself exposed to such a storm of invective and satire as had never burst on the head of any statesman. The emoluments of office were now nothing to him; for he had just succeeded to a princely property by the death of his father-in-law. All the honours which could be bestowed on him he had already secured. He had obtained the Garter for himself and a British peerage for his son. He seems also to have imagined that by quitting the treasury he should escape from danger and abuse without really resigning power, and should still be able to exercise in private supreme influence over the royal mind.

Whatever may have been his motives, he retired. Fox at the same time took refuge in the House of Lords; and George Grenville became First Lord of the Treasury and Chancellor of the Exchequer.

We believe that those who made this arrangement fully intended that Grenville should be a mere puppet in the hands of Bute; for Grenville was as yet very imperfectly known even to those who had observed him long. He passed for a mere official drudge; and he had all the industry, the minute accuracy, the formality, the tediousness, which belong to the character. But he had other qualities which had not yet shown themselves: devouring ambition, dauntless courage, self-confidence amounting to presumption, and a temper which could not endure opposition. He was not disposed to be anybody's tool; and he had no attachment, political or personal, to Bute. The two men had, indeed, nothing in common, except a strong propensity towards harsh and unpopular courses. Their principles were fundamentally different.

Bute was a Tory. Grenville would have been very angry with any person who should have denied his claim to be a Whig. He was more prone to tyrannical measures than Bute; but he loved tyranny only when disguised under the forms of constitutional liberty. He mixed up, after a fashion then not very unusual, the theories of the republicans of the seventeenth century with the technical maxims of English law, and thus succeeded in combining anarchical speculation with arbitrary practice. The voice of the people was the voice of God; but the only legitimate organ through which the voice of the people could be uttered was the Parliament. All power was from the people; but to the Parliament the whole power of the people had been delegated. No Oxonian divine had ever, even in the years which immediately followed the Restoration, demanded for the King so abject, so unreasoning a homage, as Grenville, on what he considered as the purest Whig principles, demanded for the Parliament. As he wished to see the Parliament despotic over the nation, so he wished to see it also despotic over the Court. In his view the Prime Minister, possessed of the confidence of the House of Commons, ought to be Mayor of the Palace. The king was a mere Childeric or Chilperic, who might well think himself lucky in being permitted to enjoy such handsome apartments at Saint James's and so fine a park at Windsor.

Thus the opinions of Bute and those of Grenville were diametrically opposed. Nor was there any private friendship between the two statesmen. Grenville's nature was not forgiving; and he well remembered how, a few months before, he had been compelled to yield the lead of the House of Commons to Fox.

We are inclined to think, on the whole, that the worst administration which has governed England since the Revolution was that of George Grenville. His public acts may be classed under two heads, outrages on the liberty of the people and outrages on the dignity of the crown.

He began by making war on the press. John Wilkes, member of Parliament for Aylesbury, was singled out for persecution. Wilkes had, till very lately, been known chiefly as one of the most profane, licentious and agreeable rakes about town. He was a man of taste, reading and engaging manners. His sprightly conversation was the delight of green-rooms and taverns, and pleased even grave hearers when he was sufficiently under restraint to abstain from detailing the particulars of his amours, and from breaking jests on the New Testament. His expensive débaucheries forced him to have recourse to the Jews. He was soon a ruined man, and determined to try his chance as a political adventurer. In parliament he did not succeed. His speaking, though pert, was feeble, and by no means interested his hearers so much as to make them forget his face, which was so hideous that the Caricaturists were forced, in their own despite, to flatter. As a writer he made a better figure. He set up a weekly paper called the *North Briton*. This journal, written with some pleasantry and great audacity and impudence, had a considerable number of readers. Forty-four numbers had been published when Bute resigned; and, though almost every number had contained matter grossly libellous, no prosecution had been instituted. The forty-fifth number was innocent when compared with the majority of those which had preceded it, and, indeed, contained nothing so strong as may in our time be found daily in the leading articles of the *Times* and *Morning Chronicle*. But Grenville was now at the head of affairs. A new spirit had been infused into the administration. Authority was to be upheld. The government was no longer to be braved with impunity. Wilkes was arrested under a general warrant, conveyed to the Tower, and confined there with circumstances of unusual severity. His papers were seized and carried to the Secretary of State. These harsh and illegal measures produced a violent outbreak of popular rage, which was soon changed to delight and exultation. The arrest was pronounced unlawful by the Court of Common Pleas, in which Chief Justice Pratt presided, and the prisoner was discharged. This victory over the government was celebrated with enthusiasm both in London and in the cider counties.

While the ministers were daily becoming more odious to the nation, they were doing their best to make themselves also odious to the Court. They gave the King plainly to understand that they were determined not to be Lord Bute's creatures, and exacted a promise that no secret adviser should have access to the royal ear. They soon found reason to suspect that this promise had not been observed. They remonstrated in terms less respectful than their master had been accustomed to hear, and gave him a fortnight to make his choice between his favourite and his cabinet.

George the Third was greatly disturbed. He had but a few weeks before exulted in his deliverance from the yoke of the great Whig connection. He had even declared that his honour would not permit him ever again to admit the members of that connection into his service. He now found that he had only exchanged one set of masters for another set still harsher and more imperious. In his distress he thought on Pitt. From Pitt it was possible that better terms might be obtained than either from Grenville or from the party of which Newcastle was the head.

Grenville, on his return from an excursion into the country, repaired to Buckingham House. He was astonished to find at the entrance a chair, the shape of which was well known to him and, indeed, to all London. It was distinguished by a large boot, made for the purpose of accommodating the great Commoner's gouty leg. Grenville guessed the whole. His brother-in-law was closeted with the King. Bute, provoked by what he considered as the unfriendly and ungrateful conduct of his successors, had himself proposed that Pitt should be summoned to the palace.

Pitt had two audiences on two successive days. What passed at the first interview led him to expect that the negotiation would be brought to a satisfactory close; but on the morrow he found the King less complying. The best account, indeed the only trustworthy account of the conference, is that which was taken from Pitt's own mouth by Lord Hardwicke. It appears that Pitt strongly represented the importance of conciliating those chiefs of the Whig party who had been so unhappy as to incur the royal displeasure. They had, he said, been the most constant friends of the House of Hanover. Their power was great; they had been long versed in public business. If they were to be under sentence of exclusion, a solid administration could not be formed. His Majesty could not bear to think of putting himself into the hands of those whom he had recently chased from his Court with the strongest marks of anger. "I am sorry, Mr. Pitt," he said, "but I see this will not do. My honour is concerned. I must support my honour." How his Majesty succeeded in supporting his honour, we shall soon see.

Pitt retired, and the King was reduced to request the ministers, whom he had been on the point of discarding, to remain in office. During the two years which followed, Grenville, now closely leagued with the Bedfords, was the master of the Court; and a hard master he proved. He knew that he was kept in place only because there was no choice except between himself and the Whigs. That under any circumstances the Whigs would be forgiven, he thought impossible. The late attempt to get rid of him had roused his resentment; the failure of that attempt had liberated him from all fear. He had never been very courtly. He now began to hold a language, to which, since the days of Cornet Joyce and President Bradshaw, no English King had been compelled to listen.

In one matter, indeed, Grenville, at the expense of justice and liberty, gratified the passions of the Court while gratifying his own. The persecution of Wilkes was eagerly pressed. He had written a parody on "Pope's Essay on Man," entitled "The Essay on Woman," and had appended to it notes, in ridicule of Warburton's famous "Commentary."

This composition was exceedingly profligate, but not more so, we think than some of Pope's own works—the imitation of the second satire of the "First book of Horace," for example; and, to do Wilkes justice, he had not; like Pope, given his ribaldry to the world. He had merely printed at a private press a very small number of copies, which he meant to present to some of his boon companions, whose morals were in no more danger of being corrupted by a loose book than a negro of being tanned by a warm sun. A tool of the government, by giving a bribe to the printer, procured a copy of this trash and placed it in the hands of the ministers. The ministers resolved to visit Wilkes's offence against decorum with the utmost rigour of the law. What share piety and respect for morals had in dictating this resolution, our readers may judge from the fact that no person was more eager for bringing the libertine poet to punishment than Lord March, afterwards Duke of Queensbury. On the first day of the session of Parliament, the book, thus disgracefully obtained, was laid on the table of the Lords by the Earl of Sandwich, whom the Duke of Bedford's interest had made Secretary of State. The unfortunate author had not the slightest suspicion that his licentious poem had ever been seen, except by his printer and by a few of his dissipated companions, till it was produced in full Parliament. Though he was a man of easy temper, averse from danger, and not very susceptible of shame, the surprise, the disgrace, the prospect of utter ruin, put him beside himself. He picked a quarrel with one of Lord Bute's dependents, fought a duel, was seriously wounded, and when half recovered, fled to France. His enemies had now their own way both in the Parliament and in the King's Bench. He was censured, expelled from the House of Commons, outlawed. His works were ordered to be burned by the common hangman. Yet was the multitude still true to him. In the minds even of many moral and religious men, his crime seemed light when compared with the crime of his accusers. The conduct of Sandwich, in particular, excited universal disgust. His own vices were notorious; and only a fortnight before he laid the "Essay on Woman" before the House of Lords, he had been drinking and singing loose catches with Wilkes at one of the most dissolute clubs in London. Shortly after the meeting of Parliament, the "Beggar's Opera" was acted at Covent Garden Theatre. When Macheath uttered the words:—"That Jemmy Twitcher should peach me I own surprised me,"—pit, boxes and galleries burst into a roar which seemed likely to bring the roof down. From that day Sandwich was universally known by the nickname of Jemmy Twitcher. The ceremony of burning the *North Briton* was interrupted by a riot. The constables were beaten; the paper was rescued, and, instead of it, a jack boot and a petticoat were committed to the flames. Wilkes had instituted an action for the seizure of his papers against the Under-secretary of State. The jury gave a thousand pounds damages. But neither these nor any other indications of public feeling had power to move Grenville. He had the Parliament with him; and, according to his political creed, the sense of the nation was to be collected from the Parliament alone.

Soon, however, he found reason to fear that even the Parliament might fail him. On the question of the legality of general warrants, the Opposition, having on its side all sound principles, all constitutional authorities, and the voice of the whole nation, mustered in great force, and was joined by many who did not ordinarily vote against the government. On one occasion the ministry, in a very full House, had a majority of only fourteen votes. The storm, however, blew over. The spirit of the Opposition, from whatever cause, began to flag at the moment when success seemed almost certain. The session ended without any change. Pitt, whose eloquence had shone with its usual lustre in all the principal debates, and whose popularity was greater than ever, was still a private man. Grenville, detested alike by the Court and by the people, was still minister.

As soon as the Houses had risen, Grenville took a step which proved, even more signally than that of his past acts, how despotic, how acrimonious and how fearless his nature was. Among the gentlemen not ordinarily opposed to the government, who, on the great constitutional question of general warrants, had voted with the minority, was Henry Conway, brother of the Earl of Hertford, a brave soldier, a tolerable speaker, and a well-meaning, though not a wise or vigorous politician. He was now deprived of his regiment, the merited reward of faithful and gallant service in two wars. It was confidently asserted that in this violent measure the King heartily concurred.

But whatever pleasure the persecution of Wilkes or the dismissal of Conway may have given to the royal mind, it is certain that his Majesty's aversion to his ministers increased day by day. Grenville was as frugal of the public money as of his own, and morosely refused to accede to the King's request that a few thousand pounds might be expended in buying some open fields to the west of the gardens of Buckingham House. In consequence of this refusal, the fields were soon covered with buildings, and the King and Queen were overlooked in their most private walks by the upper windows of a hundred houses. Nor was this the worst. Grenville was as liberal of words as he was sparing of guineas. Instead of explaining himself in that clear, concise and lively manner which alone could win the attention of a young mind new to business, he spoke in the closet just as he spoke in the House of Commons. When he had harangued two hours, he looked at his watch, as he had been in the habit of looking at the clock opposite the Speaker's chair, apologised for the length of his discourse, and then went on for an hour more. The members of the House of Commons can cough an orator down, or can walk away to dinner; and they were by no means sparing in the use of these privileges when Grenville was on his legs. But the poor young King had to endure all this eloquence with mournful civility. To the end of his life he continued to talk with horror of Grenville's orations.

About this time took place one of the most singular events in Pitt's life. There was a certain Sir William Pynsent, a Somersetshire baronet of Whig politics, who had been a member of the House of Commons in the days of Queen Anne, and had retired to rural privacy when the Tory party, towards the end of her reign, obtained the ascendancy in her councils. His manners were eccentric. His morals lay under very odious imputations. But his fidelity to his political opinions was unalterable. During fifty years of seclusion he continued to brood over the circumstances which had driven him from public life, the dismissal of the Whigs, the peace of Utrecht, the desertion of our allies. He now thought that he perceived a close analogy between the well remembered events of his youth and the events which he had witnessed in extreme old age; between the disgrace of Marlborough and the disgrace of Pitt; between the elevation of Harley and the elevation of Bute; between the treaty negotiated by St. John and the treaty negotiated by Bedford; between the wrongs of the House of Austria in 1712 and the wrongs of the House of Brandenburgh in 1762. This fancy took such possession of the old man's mind that he determined to leave his whole property to Pitt. In this way, Pitt unexpectedly came into possession of near three thousand pounds a-year. Nor could all the malice of his enemies find any ground for reproach in the transaction. Nobody could call him a legacy-hunter. Nobody could accuse him of seizing that to which others had a better claim. For he had never in his life seen Sir William; and Sir William had left no relation so near as to be entitled to form any expectations respecting the estate.

The fortunes of Pitt seemed to flourish; but his health was worse than ever. We cannot find that, during the session which began in January, 1765, he once appeared in parliament. He remained some months in profound retirement at Hayes, his favourite villa, scarcely moving except from his armchair to his bed, and from his bed to his armchair, and often employing his wife as his amanuensis in his most confidential correspondence. Some of his detractors whispered that his invisibility was to be ascribed quite as much to affectation as to gout. In truth, his character, high and splendid as it was, wanted simplicity. With genius which did not need the aid of stage tricks, and with a spirit which should have been far above them, he had yet been, through life, in the habit of practising them. It was, therefore, now surmised that, having acquired all the consideration which could be derived from eloquence and from great services to the state, he had determined not to make himself cheap by often appearing in public, but, under the pretext of ill health, to surround himself with mystery, to emerge only at long intervals and on momentous occasions, and at other times to deliver his oracles only to a few favoured votaries, who were suffered to make pilgrimages to his shrine. If such were his object, it was for a time fully attained. Never was the magic of his name so powerful, never was he regarded by his country with such superstitious veneration, as during this year of silence and seclusion.

While Pitt was thus absent from Parliament, Grenville proposed a measure destined to produce a great revolution, the effects of which will long be felt by the whole human race. We speak of the act for imposing stamp duties on the North American colonies. The plan was eminently characteristic of its author. Every feature of the parent was found in the child. A timid statesman would have shrunk from a step, of which Walpole, at a time when the colonies were far less powerful, had said—"He who shall propose it will be a much bolder man than I." But the nature of Grenville was insensible to fear. A statesman of large views would have felt that to lay taxes at Westminster on New England and New York, was a course opposed, not indeed to the letter of the "Statute Book," or to any decision contained in the "Term Reports," but to the principles of good government, and to the spirit of the constitution. A statesman of large views would also have felt that ten times the estimated produce of the American stamps would have been dearly purchased by even a transient quarrel between the mother country and the colonies. But Grenville knew of no spirit of the constitution distinct from the letter of the law, and of no national interests except those which are expressed by pounds, shillings and pence. That his policy might give birth to deep discontents in all the provinces, from the shore of the Great Lakes to the Mexican sea: that France and Spain might seize the opportunity of revenge; that the empire might be dismembered; that the debt, that debt with the amount of which he perpetually reproached Pitt, might, in consequence of his own policy, be doubled; these were possibilities which never occurred to that small, sharp mind.

The Stamp Act will be remembered as long as the globe lasts. But, at the time, it attracted much less notice in this country than another Act which is now almost utterly forgotten. The King fell ill, and was thought to be in a dangerous state. His complaint, we believe, was the same which at a later period, repeatedly incapacitated him for the performance of his regal functions. The heir-apparent was only two years old. It was clearly proper to make provision for the administration of the government, in case of a minority. The discussions on this point brought the quarrel between the Court and the ministry to a crisis. The King wished to be intrusted with the power of naming a regent by will. The ministers feared, or affected to fear, that if this power were conceded to him, he would name the Princess Mother, nay, possibly the Earl of Bute. They, therefore, insisted on introducing into the bill words confining the King's choice to the royal family. Having thus excluded Bute, they urged the King to let them, in the most marked manner, exclude the Princess Dowager also. They assured him that the House of Commons would undoubtedly strike her name out, and by this threat they wrung from him a reluctant assent. In a few days, it appeared that the representations by which they had induced the King to put this gross and public affront on his mother were unfounded. The friends of the Princess in the House of Commons moved that her name should be inserted. The ministers could not decently attack the parent of their master. They hoped that the Opposition would come to their help, and put on them a force to which they would gladly have yielded. But the majority of the opposition, though hating the Princess, hated Grenville more, beheld his embarrassment with delight, and would do nothing to extricate him from it. The Princess's name was accordingly placed in the list of persons qualified to hold the regency.

The King's resentment was now at the height. The present evil seemed to him more intolerable than any other. Even the junta of Whig grandees could not treat him worse than he had been treated by his present ministers. In his distress, he poured out his whole heart to his uncle, the Duke of Cumberland. The Duke was not a man to be loved; but he was eminently a man to be trusted. He had an intrepid temper, a strong understanding, and a high sense of honour and duty. As a general, he belonged to a remarkable class of captains—captains, we mean, whose fate it has been to lose almost all the battles which they have fought, and yet to be reputed stout and skilful soldiers. Such Captains were Coligni and William the Third. We might, perhaps, add Marshal Soult to the list. The bravery of the Duke of Cumberland was such as distinguished him even among the princes of his brave house. The indifference with which he rode about amidst musket balls and cannon balls was not the highest proof of his fortitude. Hopeless maladies, horrible surgical operations, far from unmanning him, did not even discompose him. With courage, he had the virtues which are akin to courage. He spoke the truth, was open in enmity and friendship, and upright in all his dealings. But his nature was hard; and what seemed to him justice was rarely tempered with mercy. He was, therefore, during many years one of the most unpopular men in England. The severity with which he had treated the rebels after the battle of Culloden, had gained for him the name of the Butcher. His attempts to introduce into the army of England, then in a most disorderly state, the rigorous discipline of Potsdam, had excited still stronger disgust. Nothing was too bad to be believed of him. Many honest people were so absurd as to fancy that, if he were left Regent during the minority of his nephews, there would be another smothering in the Tower. These feelings, however, had passed away. The Duke had been living, during some years, in retirement. The English, full of animosity against the Scots, now blamed his Royal Highness only for having left so many Camerons and Macphersons to be made gaugers and custom-house officers. He was, therefore, at present, a favourite with his countrymen, and especially with the inhabitants of London.

He had little reason to love the King, and had shown clearly, though not obtrusively, his dislike of the system which had lately been pursued. But he had high and almost romantic notions of the duty which, as a prince of the blood, he owed to the head of his house. He determined to extricate his nephew from bondage, and to effect a reconciliation between the Whig party and the throne, on terms honourable to both.

In this mind he set off for Hayes, and was admitted to Pitt's sick room; for Pitt would not leave his chamber and would not communicate with any messenger of inferior dignity. And now began a long series of errors on the part of the illustrious statesman, errors which involved his country in difficulties and distresses more serious even than those from which his genius had formerly rescued her. His language was haughty, unreasonable, almost unintelligible. The only thing which could be discerned through a cloud of vague and not very gracious phrases, was that he would not at that moment take office. The truth, we believe, was this. Lord Temple, who was Pitt's evil genius, had just formed a new scheme of politics. Hatred of Bute and of the Princess had, it should seem, taken entire possession of Temple's soul. He had quarrelled with his brother George, because George had been connected with Bute and the Princess. Now that George appeared to be the enemy of Bute and of the Princess, Temple was eager to bring about a general family reconciliation. The three brothers, as Temple, Grenville and Pitt were popularly called, might make a ministry, without leaning for aid either on Bute or on the Whig connection. With such views, Temple used all his influence to dissuade Pitt from acceding to the propositions of the Duke of Cumberland. Pitt was not convinced. But Temple had an influence over him such as no other person had ever possessed. They were very old friends, very near relations. If Pitt's talents and fame had been useful to Temple, Temple's purse had formerly, in times of great need been useful to Pitt. They had never been parted in politics. Twice they had come into the cabinet together, twice they had left it together. Pitt could not bear to think of taking office without his chief ally. Yet he felt that he was doing wrong, that he was throwing away a great opportunity of serving his country. The obscure and unconciliatory style of the answers which he returned to the overtures of the Duke of Cumberland, may be ascribed to the embarrassment and vexation of a mind not at peace with itself. It is said that he mournfully exclaimed to Temple,

"Extinxti te meque, soror, populumque, patresque
Sidonios, urbemque tuam."

The prediction was but too just.

Finding Pitt impracticable, the Duke of Cumberland advised the King to submit to necessity, and to keep Grenville and the Bedfords. It was, indeed, not a time at which offices could safely be left vacant. The unsettled state of the government had produced a general relaxation through all the departments of the public service. Meetings, which at another time would have been harmless, now turned to riots, and rapidly rose almost to the dignity of rebellions. The Houses of Parliament were blockaded by the Spitalfields weavers. Bedford house was assailed on all sides by a furious rabble, and was strongly garrisoned with horse and foot. Some people attributed these disturbances to the friends of Bute, and some to the friends of Wilkes. But, whatever might be the cause, the effect was general insecurity. Under such circumstances the King had no choice. With bitter feelings of mortification, he informed the ministers that he meant to retain them.

They answered by demanding from him a promise on his royal word never more to consult Lord Bute. The promise was given. They then demanded something more. Lord Bute's brother, Mr. Mackenzie, held a lucrative office in Scotland. Mr. Mackenzie must be dismissed. The King replied that the office had been given under very peculiar circumstances, and that he had promised never to take it away while he lived. Grenville was obstinate; and the King, with a very bad grace, yielded.

The session of Parliament was over. The triumph of the ministers was complete. The King was almost as much a prisoner as Charles the First had been, when in the Isle of Wight. Such were the fruits of the policy which, only a few months before, was represented as having for ever secured the throne against the dictation of insolent subjects.

His Majesty's natural resentment showed itself in every look and word. In his extremity he looked wistfully towards that Whig connection, once the object of his dread and hatred. The Duke of Devonshire, who had been treated with such unjustifiable harshness, had lately died, and had been succeeded by his son, who was still a boy. The King condescended to express his regret for what had passed, and to invite the young Duke to Court. The noble youth came, attended by his uncles, and was received with marked graciousness.

This and many other symptoms of the same kind irritated the ministers. They had still in store for their sovereign an insult which would have provoked his grandfather to kick them out of the room. Grenville and Bedford demanded an audience of him, and read him a remonstrance of many pages, which they had drawn up with great care. His Majesty was accused of breaking his word and of treating his advisers with gross unfairness. The Princess was mentioned in language by no means eulogistic. Hints were thrown out that Bute's head was in danger. The King was plainly told that he must not continue to show, as he had done, that he disliked the situation in which he was placed, that he must frown upon the Opposition, that he must carry it fair towards his ministers in public. He several times interrupted the reading by declaring that he had ceased to hold any communication with Bute. But the ministers, disregarding his denial, went on, and the King listened in silence, almost choked by rage. When they ceased to read, he merely made a gesture expressive of his wish to be left alone. He afterwards owned that he thought he should have gone into a fit.

Driven to despair, he again had recourse to the Duke of Cumberland; and the Duke of Cumberland again had recourse to Pitt. Pitt was really desirious to undertake the direction of affairs, and owned, with many dutiful expressions, that the terms offered by the King were all that any subject could desire. But Temple was impracticable; and Pitt, with great regret, declared that he could not, without the concurrence of his brother-in-law, undertake the administration.

The Duke now saw only one way of delivering his nephew. An administration must be formed of the Whigs in opposition, without Pitt's help. The difficulties seemed almost insuperable. Death and desertion had grievously thinned the ranks of the party lately supreme in the state. Those among whom the Duke's choice lay might be divided into two classes, men too old for important offices and men who had never been in any important office before. The cabinet must be composed of broken invalids or of raw recruits.

This was an evil, yet not an unmixed evil. If the new Whig statesmen had little experience in business and debate, they were, on the other hand, pure from the taint of that political immorality which had deeply infected their predecessors. Long prosperity had corrupted that great party which had expelled the Stuarts, limited the prerogotives of the Crown, and curbed the intolerance of the Hierarchy. Adversity had already produced a salutary effect. On the day of the accession of George the Third, the ascendency of the Whig party terminated; and on that day the purification of the Whig party began. The rising chiefs of that party were men of a very different sort from Sandys and Winnington, from Sir William Yonge and Henry Fox. They were men worthy to have charged by the side of Hampden at Chalgrove, or to have exchanged the last embrace with Russell on the scaffold in Lincoln's Inn Fields. They carried into politics the same high principles of virtue which regulated their private dealings, nor would they stoop to promote even the noblest and most salutary ends by means which honour and probity condemn. Such men were Lord John Cavendish, Sir George Savile, and others whom we hold in honour as the second founders of the Whig party, as the restorers of its pristine health and energy after half a century of degeneracy.

The chief of this respectable band was the Marquess of Rockingham, a man of splendid fortune, excellent sense and stainless character. He was, indeed, nervous to such a degree that, to the very close of his life, he never rose without great reluctance and embarrassment to address the

House of Lords. But, though not a great orator, he had in a high degree some of the qualities of a statesman. He chose his friends well; and he had, in an extraordinary degree, the art of attaching them to him by ties of the most honourable kind. The cheerful fidelity with which they adhered to him through many years of almost hopeless opposition was less admirable than the disinterestedness and delicacy which they showed when he rose to power.

We are inclined to think that the use and the abuse of party cannot be better illustrated than by a parallel between two powerful connections of that time, the Rockinghams and the Bedfords. The Rockingham party was, in our view, exactly what a party should be. It consisted of men bound together by common opinions, by common public objects, by mutual esteem. That they desired to obtain, by honest and constitutional means, the direction of affairs, they openly avowed. But, though often invited to accept the honours and emoluments of office, they steadily refused to do so on any conditions inconsistent with their principles. The Bedford party, as a party, had, as far as we can discover, no principle whatever. Rigby and Sandwich wanted public money, and thought that they should fetch a higher price jointly than singly. They therefore acted in concert, and prevailed on a much more important and a much better man than themselves to act with them.

It was to Rockingham that the Duke of Cumberland now had recourse. The Marquess consented to take the Treasury. Newcastle so long the recognized chief of the Whigs could not well be excluded from the ministry. He was appointed Keeper of the Privy Seal. A very honest clear-headed country gentleman, of the name of Dowdeswell, became Chancellor of the Exchequer. General Conway, who had served under the Duke of Cumberland, and was strongly attached to his royal highness, was made Secretary of State, with the lead in the House of Commons. A great Whig nobleman, in the prime of manhood, from whom much was at that time expected, Augustus, Duke of Grafton, was the other Secretary.

The oldest man living could remember no government so weak in oratorical talents and in official experience. The general opinion was, that the ministers might hold office during the recess, but that the first day of debate in Parliament would be the last day of their power. Charles Townshend was asked what he thought of the new administration. "It is," said he, "mere lutestring; pretty summer wear. It will never do for the winter."

At this conjuncture Lord Rockingham had the wisdom to discern the value, and secure the aid, of an ally, who, to eloquence surpassing the eloquence of Pitt, and to industry which shamed the industry of Grenville, united an amplitude of comprehension to which neither Pitt nor Grenville could lay claim. A young Irishman had some time before, come over to push his fortune in London. He had written much for the booksellers; but he was best known by a little treatise, in which the style and reasoning of Bolingbroke were mimicked with exquisite skill, and by a theory, of more ingenuity than soundness, touching the pleasures which we receive from the objects of taste. He had also attained a high reputation as a talker, and was regarded by the men of letters who supped together at the Turk's Head, as the only match in conversation for Dr. Johnson. He now became private secretary to Lord Rockingham, and was brought into Parliament by his patron's influence. These arrangements, indeed, were not made without some difficulty. The Duke of Newcastle, who was always meddling and chattering, adjured the First Lord of the Treasury to be on his guard against this adventurer, whose real name was O'Bourke, and whom his Grace knew to be a wild Irishman, a Jacobite, a Papist, a concealed Jesuit. Lord Rockingham treated the calumny as it deserved; and the Whig party was strengthened and adorned by the accession of Edmund Burke.

The party, indeed, stood in need of accessions; for it sustained about this time an almost irreparable loss. The Duke of Cumberland had formed the government, and was its main support. His exalted rank and great name in some degree balanced the fame of Pitt. As mediator between the Whigs and the Court, he held a place which no other person could fill. The strength of his character supplied that which was the chief defect of the new ministry. Conway, in particular, who, with excellent intentions and respectable talents, was the most dependent and irresolute of human beings, drew from the counsels of that masculine mind a determination not his own. Before the meeting of Parliament the Duke suddenly died. His death was generally regarded as the signal of great troubles, and on this account, as well as from respect for his personal qualities, was greatly lamented. It was remarked that the mourning in London was the most general ever known, and was both deeper and longer than the *Gazette* had prescribed.

In the meantime, every mail from America brought alarming tidings. The crop which Grenville had sown his successors had now to reap. The colonies were in a state bordering on rebellion. The stamps were burned, the revenue officers were tarred and feathered. All traffic between the discontented provinces and the mother country was interrupted. The Exchange of London was in dismay. Half the firms of Bristol and Liverpool were threatened with bankruptcy. In Leeds, Manchester, Nottingham, it was said that three artisans out of every ten had been turned adrift. Civil war seemed to be at hand; and it could not be doubted that, if once the British nation were divided against itself, France and Spain would soon take part in the quarrel.

Three courses were open to the ministers. The first was to enforce the Stamp Act by the sword. This was the course on which the King and Grenville, whom the King hated beyond all living men, were alike bent. The natures of both were arbitrary and stubborn. They resembled each other so much that they could never be friends; but they resembled each other also so much that they saw almost all important practical questions in the same point of view. Neither of them would bear to be governed by the other; but they were perfectly agreed as to the best way of governing the people.

Another course was that which Pitt recommended. He held that the British Parliament was not constitutionally competent to pass a law for taxing the colonies. He therefore considered the Stamp Act as a nullity, as a document of no more validity than Charles's writ of shipmoney, or James's proclamation dispensing with the penal laws. This doctrine seems to us, we must own, to be altogether untenable.

Between these extreme courses lay a third way. The opinion of the most judicious and temperate statesmen of those times was that the British constitution had set no limit whatever to the legislative power of the British King, Lords and Commons, over the whole British Empire. Parliament, they held, was legally competent to tax America, as Parliament was legally competent to commit any other act of folly or wickedness, to confiscate the property of all the merchants in Lombart Street, or to attaint any man in the kingdom of high treason, without examining witnesses against him, or hearing him in his own defence. The most atrocious act of confiscation or of attainder is just as valid an act as the Toleration Act or the Habeas Corpus Act. But from acts of confiscation and acts of attainder lawgivers are bound, by every obligation of morality, systematically to refrain. In the same manner ought the British legislature to refrain from taxing the American Colonies. The Stamp Act was indefensible, not because it was beyond the constitutional competence of Parliament, but because it was unjust and impolitic, sterile of revenue and fertile of discontents. These sound doctrines were adopted by Lord Rockingham and his colleagues, and were, during a long course of years, inculcated by Burke, in orations, some of which will last as long as the English language.

The winter came; the Parliament met; and the state of the colonies instantly became the subject of fierce contention. Pitt, whose health had been somewhat restored by the waters of Bath, reappeared in the House of Commons, and, with ardent and pathetic eloquence, not only condemned the Stamp Act, but applauded the resistance of Massachusetts and Virginia, and vehemently maintained, in defiance, we must say, of all reason and of all authority, that, according to the British constitution, the supreme legislative power does not include the power to tax. The language of Grenville, on the other hand, was such as Strafford might have used at the council table of Charles the First, when news came of the resistance to the liturgy at Edinburgh. The colonists were traitors; those who excused them were little better. Frigates, mortars, bayonets, sabres, were the proper remedies for such distempers.

The ministers occupied an intermediate position; they proposed to declare that the legislative authority of the British Parliament over the whole Empire was in all cases supreme; and they proposed, at the same time, to repeal the Stamp Act. To the former measure Pitt objected; but it was carried with scarcely a dissentient voice. The repeal of the Stamp Act Pitt strongly supported; but against the Government was arrayed a formidable assemblage of opponents. Grenville and the Bedfords were furious. Temple, who had now allied himself closely with his brother, and separated himself from Pitt, was no despicable enemy. This, however, was not the worst. The ministry was without its natural strength. It had to struggle, not only against its avowed enemies, but against the insidious hostility of the King, and of a set of persons who, about this time, began to be designated as the King's friends.

The character of this faction has been drawn by Burke with even more than his usual force and vivacity. Those who know how strongly, through his whole life, his judgment was biassed by his passions, may not unnaturally suspect that he has left us rather a caricature than a likeness; and yet there is scarcely, in the whole portrait, a single touch of which the fidelity is not proved by facts of unquestionable authenticity.

The public generally regarded the King's friends as a body of which Bute was the directing soul. It was to no purpose that the Earl professed to have done with politics, that he absented himself year after year from the levee and the drawing-room, that he went to the North, that he went to Rome. The notion that, in some inexplicable manner, he dictated all the measures of the Court, was fixed in the minds, not only of the multitude, but of some who had good opportunities of obtaining information and who ought to have been superior to vulgar prejudices. Our own belief is that these suspicions were unfounded, and that he ceased to have any communication with the King on political matters some time before the dismissal of George Grenville. The supposition of Bute's influence is, indeed, by no means necessary to explain the phenomena. The King, in 1765, was no longer the ignorant and inexperienced boy who had, in 1760, been managed by his mother and his Groom of the Stole. He had, during several years, observed the struggles of parties, and conferred daily on high questions of state with able and experienced politicians. His way of life had developed his understanding and character. He was now no longer a puppet, but had very decided opinions both of men and things. Nothing could be more natural than that he should have high notions of his own prerogatives, should be impatient of opposition, and should wish all public men to be detached from each other and dependent on himself alone; nor could anything be more natural than that, in the state in which the political world then was, he should find instruments fit for his purpose.

Thus sprang into existence and into note a reptile species of politicians never before and never since known in our country. These men disclaimed all political ties, except those which bound them to the throne. They were willing to coalesce with any party, to abandon any party, to undermine any party, to assault any party, at a moment's notice. To them, all administrations, and all oppositions were the same. They regarded Bute, Grenville, Rockingham, Pitt, without one sentiment either of predilection or of aversion. They were the King's friends. It is to be observed that this friendship implied no personal intimacy. These people had never lived with their master as Dodington at one time lived with his father, or as Sheridan afterwards lived with his son. They never hunted with him in the morning or played cards with him in the evening, never shared his mutton or walked with him among his turnips. Only one or two of them ever saw his face, except on public days. The whole band, however, always had early and accurate information as to his personal inclinations. None of these people were high in the administration. They were generally to be found in places of much emolument, little labour and no responsibility; and these places they continued to occupy securely while the cabinet was six or seven times reconstructed. Their peculiar business was not to support the ministry against the opposition, but to support the King against the ministry. Whenever his Majesty was induced to give a reluctant assent to the introduction of some bill which his constitutional advisers regarded as necessary, his friends in the House of Commons were sure to speak against it, to vote against it, to throw in its way every obstruction compatible with the forms of Parliament. If his Majesty found it necessary to admit into his closet a Secretary of State or a First Lord of the Treasury whom he disliked, his friends were sure to miss no opportunity of thwarting and humbling the obnoxious minister. In return for these services, the King covered them with his protection. It was to no purpose that his responsible servants complained to him that they were daily betrayed and impeded by men who were eating the bread of the government. He sometimes justified the offenders, sometimes excused them, sometimes owned that they were to blame, but said that he must take time to consider whether he could part with them. He never would turn them out; and, while every thing else in the state was constantly changing, these sycophants seemed to have a life estate in their offices.

It was well known to the King's friends that, though his Majesty had consented to the repeal of the Stamp Act, he had consented with a very bad grace, and that though he had eagerly welcomed the Whigs, when, in his extreme need and at his earnest entreaty, they had undertaken to free him from an insupportable yoke, he had by no means got over his early prejudices against his deliverers. The ministers soon found that while they were encountered in front by the whole force of a strong opposition, their rear was assailed by a large body of those whom they had regarded as auxiliaries.

Nevertheless, Lord Rockingham and his adherents went on resolutely with the bill for repealing the Stamp Act. They had on their side all the manufacturing and commercial interests of the realm. In the debates the government was powerfully supported. Two great orators and statesmen, belonging to two different generations, repeatedly put forth all their powers in defence of the bill. The House of Commons heard Pitt for the last time and Burke for the first time, and was in doubt to which of them the palm of eloquence should be assigned. It was indeed a splendid sunset and a splendid dawn.

For a time the event seemed doubtful. In several divisions the ministers were hard pressed. On one occasion not less than twelve of the King's friends, all men in office, voted against the government. It was to no purpose that Lord Rockingham remonstrated with the King. His Majesty confessed that there was ground for complaint, but hoped that gentle means would bring the mutineers to a better mind. If they persisted in their misconduct he would dismiss them.

At length the decisive day arrived. The gallery, the lobby, the Court of Requests, the staircases, were crowded with merchants from all the great ports of the island. The debate lasted till long after midnight. On the division the ministers had a great majority. The dread of civil war, and the outcry of all the trading towns of the kingdom, had been too strong for the combined strength of the Court and the Opposition.

It was in the first dim twilight of a February morning that the doors were thrown open, and that the chiefs of the hostile parties showed themselves to the multitude. Conway was received with loud applause. But, when Pitt appeared all eyes were fixed on him alone. All hats were in the air. Loud and long huzzars accompanied him to his chair and a train of admirers escorted him all the way to his home. Then came forth Grenville. As soon as he was recognised a storm of hisses and curses broke forth. He turned fiercely on the crowds and caught one man by the throat. The bystanders were in great alarm. If a scuffle began none could say how it might end. Fortunately the person who had been collared only said, "If I may not hiss sir, I hope I may laugh," and laughed in Grenville's face.

The majority had been so decisive, that all the opponents of the ministry, save one, were disposed to let the bill pass without any further contention. But solicitation and expostulation were thrown away on Grenville. His indomitable spirit rose up stronger and stronger under the load of public hatred. He fought out the battle obstinately to the end. On the last reading he had a sharp altercation with his brother-in-law, the last of their many sharp altercations. Pitt thundered in his loftiest tones against the man who had wished to dip the ermine of a British King in the blood of the British people. Grenville replied with his wonted intrepidity and asperity. "If the tax," he said, "were still to be laid on, I would lay it on. For the evils which it may produce my accuser is answerable. His profusion made it necessary. His declarations against the constitutional powers of Kings, Lords and Commons, have made it doubly necessary. I do not envy him the huzza. I glory in the hiss. If it were to be done again I would do it."

The repeal of the Stamp Act was the chief measure of Lord Rockingham's government. But that government is entitled to the praise of having put a stop to two oppressive practices, which, in Wilkes' case, had attracted the notice and excited the just indignation of the public. The House of Commons was induced by the ministers to pass a resolution condemning the use of general warrants and another resolution condemning the seizure of papers in cases of libel.

It must be added, to the lasting honour of Lord Rockingham, that his administration was the first which, during a long course of years, had the courage and the virtue to refrain from bribing members of Parliament. His enemies accused him and his friends of weakness, of haughtiness, of party spirit; but calumny itself never dared to couple his name with corruption.

Unhappily his government, though one of the best that has ever existed in our country, was also one of the weakest. The King's friends assailed and obstructed the ministers at every turn. To appeal to the King was only to draw forth new promises and new evasions. His Majesty was sure that there must be some misunderstanding. Lord Rockingham had better speak to the gentlemen. They should be dismissed on the next fault. The next fault was soon committed, and his Majesty still continued to shuffle. It was too bad. It was quite abominable; but it mattered less as the prorogation was at hand. He would give the delinquents one more chance. If they did not alter their conduct next session, he should not have one word to say for them. He had already resolved that, long before the commencement of the next session, Lord Rockingham should cease to be minister.

We have now come to a part of our story which, admiring as we do the genius and the many noble qualities of Pitt, we cannot relate without much pain. We believe that, at this conjuncture, he had it in his power to give the victory either to the Whigs or to the King's friends. If he had allied himself closely with Lord Rockingham, what could the Court have done? There would have been only one alternative, the Whigs or Grenville; and there could be no doubt what the King's choice would be. He still remembered, as well he might, with the uttermost bitterness, the thraldom from which his uncle had freed him, and said about this time, with great vehemence, that he would sooner see the Devil come into his closet than Grenville.

And what was there to prevent Pitt from allying himself with Lord Rockingham? On all the most important questions their views were the same. They had agreed in condemning the peace, the Stamp Act, the general warrant, the seizure of papers. The points on which they differed were few and unimportant. In integrity, in disinterestedness, in hatred of corruption, they resembled each other. Their personal interests could not clash. They sat in different Houses, and Pitt had always declared that nothing should induce him to be First Lord of the Treasury.

If the opportunity of forming a coalition beneficial to the state and honourable to all concerned was suffered to escape, the fault was not with the Whig ministers. They behaved towards Pitt with an obsequiousness which, had it not been the effect of sincere admiration and of anxiety for the public interests, might have been justly called servile. They repeatedly gave him to understand that if he chose to join their ranks, they were ready to receive him, not as an associate, but as a leader. They had proved their respect for him by bestowing a peerage on the person who at that time enjoyed the largest share of his confidence, Chief Justice Pratt. What then was there to divide Pitt from the Whigs? What, on the other hand, was there in common between him and the King's friends, that he should lend himself to their purposes—he who had never owed anything to flattery or intrigue, he whose eloquence and independent spirit had overawed two generations of slaves and jobbers, he who had twice been forced by the enthusiasm of an admiring nation on a reluctant Prince?

Unhappily the Court had gained Pitt, not, it is true, by those ignoble means which were employed when such men as Rigby and Wedderburn were to be won, but by allurements suited to a nature noble even in its aberrations. The King set himself to seduce the one man who could turn the Whigs out without letting Grenville in. Praise, caresses, promises, were lavished on the idol of the nation. He, and he alone, could put an end to faction, could bid defiance to all the powerful connections in the land united, Whigs and Tories, Rockinghams, Bedfords and Grenvilles. These blandishments produced a great effect. For though Pitt's spirit was high and manly, though his eloquence was often exerted with formidable effect against the Court, and though his theory of government had been learned in the school of Locke and Sydney, he had always regarded the person of the sovereign with profound veneration. As soon as he was brought face to face with royalty, his imagination and sensibility became too strong for his principles. His Whiggism thawed and disappeared; and he became, for the time, a Tory of the old Ormond pattern. Nor was he by any means unwilling to assist in the work of dissolving all political connections. His own weight in the state was wholly independent of such connections. He was, therefore, inclined to look on them with dislike, and made far too little distinction between gangs of knaves associated for the mere purpose of robbing the public, and confederacies of honourable men for the promotion of great public objects. Nor had he the sagacity to perceive that the strenuous efforts which he made to annihilate all parties tended only to establish the ascendency of one party, and that the basest and most hateful of all.

It may be doubted whether he would have been thus misled if his mind had been in full health and vigour. But the truth is that he had for some time been in an unnatural state of excitement. No suspicion of this sort had yet got abroad. His eloquence had never shone with more splendour than during the recent debates. But people afterwards called to mind many things which ought to have roused their apprehensions. His habits were gradually becoming more and more eccentric. A horror of all loud sounds, such as is said to have been one of the many oddities of Wallenstein, grew upon him. Though the most affectionate of fathers, he could not at this time bear to hear the voices of his own children, and laid out great sums at Hayes in buying up houses contiguous to his own, merely that he might have no neighbours to disturb him with their noise. He then sold Hayes, and took possession of a villa at Hampstead, where he again began to purchase houses to right and left. In expense, indeed, he vied, during this part of his life, with the wealthiest of the conquerors of Bengal and Tanjore. At Burton Pynsent, he ordered a great extent of ground to be planted with cedars. Cedars enough for the purpose were not to be found in Somersetshire. They were therefore collected in London, and sent down by land carriage. Relays of labourers were hired; and the work went on all night by torchlight. No man could be more abstemious than Pitt; yet the profusion of his kitchen was a wonder even to epicures. Several dinners were always dressing; for his appetite was capricious and fanciful; and at whatever moment he felt inclined to eat, he expected a meal to be instantly on the table. Other circumstances might be mentioned, such as separately are of little moment, but such as, when taken together and when viewed in connection with the strange events which followed, justify us in believing that his mind was already in a morbid state.

Soon after the close of the session of Parliament Lord Rockingham received his dismissal. He retired, accompanied by a firm body of friends, whose consistency and uprightness enmity itself was forced to admit. None of them had asked or obtained any pension or any sinecure, either in possession or in reversion. Such disinterestedness was then rare among politicians. Their chief, though not a man of brilliant talents, had won for himself an honourable fame, which he kept pure to the last. He had, in spite of difficulties which seemed almost insurmountable, removed great abuses and averted a civil war. Sixteen years later, in a dark and terrible day, he was again called upon to save the state, brought to the very brink of ruin by the same perfidy and obstinacy which had embarrassed, and at length overthrown, his first administration.

Pitt was planting in Somersetshire when he was summoned to Court by a letter written by the royal hand. He instantly hastened to London. The irritability of his mind and body were increased by the rapidity with which he travelled; and when he reached his journey's end he was suffering from fever. Ill as he was, he saw the King at Richmond, and undertook to form an administration.

Pitt was scarcely in a state in which a man should be who has to conduct delicate and arduous negotiations. In his letters to his wife he complained that the conferences in which it was necessary for him to bear a part heated his blood and accelerated his pulse. From other sources of information we learn that his language, even to those whose co-operation he wished to engage, was strangely peremptory and despotic. Some of his notes written at this time have been preserved, and are in a style which Louis the Fourteenth would have been too well bred to employ in addressing any French gentleman.

In the attempt to dissolve all parties, Pitt met with some difficulties. Some Whigs, whom the Court would gladly have detached from Lord Rockingham, rejected all offers. The Bedfords were perfectly willing to break with Grenville; but Pitt would not come up to their terms. Temple, whom Pitt at first meant to place at the head of the treasury, proved intractible. A coldness, indeed, had, during some months, been fast growing between the brothers-in-law, so long and so closely allied in politics. Pitt was angry with Temple for opposing the repeal of the Stamp Act. Temple was angry with Pitt for refusing to accede to that family league which was now the favourite plan at Stowe. At length the Earl proposed an equal partition of power and patronage, and offered, on this condition, to give up his brother George. Pitt thought the demand exorbitant, and positively refused compliance. A bitter quarrel followed. Each of the kinsmen was true to his character. Temple's soul festered with spite, and Pitt's swelled into contempt. Temple represented Pitt as the most odious of hypocrites and traitors. Pitt held a different and, perhaps, a more provoking tone. Temple was a good sort of man enough, whose single title to distinction was, that he had a large garden, with a large piece of water, and a great many pavilions and summer-houses. To his fortunate connection with a great orator and statesman he was indebted for an importance in the state which his own talents could never have gained for him. That importance had turned his head. He had begun to fancy that he could form administrations and govern empires. It was piteous to see a well-meaning man under such a delusion.

In spite of all these difficulties, a ministry was made such as the King wished to see, a ministry in which all his Majesty's friends were comfortably accommodated, and which, with the exception of his Majesty's friends, contained no four persons who had ever in their lives been in the habit of acting together. Men who had never concurred in a single vote found themselves seated at the same board. The office of Paymaster was divided between two persons who had never exchanged a word. Most of the chief posts were filled either by personal adherents of Pitt, or by members of the late ministry, who had been induced to remain in place after the dismissal of Lord Rockingham. To the former class belonged Pratt, now Lord Camden, who accepted the great seal, and Lord Shelburne, who was made one of the Secretaries of State. To the latter class belonged the Duke of Grafton, who became First Lord of the Treasury, and Conway, who kept his old position both in the government and in the House of Commons. Charles Townshend, who had belonged to every party, and cared for none, was Chancellor of the Exchequer. Pitt himself was declared Prime Minister, but refused to take any laborious office. He was created Earl of Chatham, and the privy seal was delivered to him.

It is scarcely necessary to say, that the failure, the complete and disgraceful failure, of this arrangement, is not to be ascribed to any want of talents in the persons whom we have named. None of them were deficient in abilities ; and four of them, Pitt himself, Shelburne, Camden and Townshend, were men of high intellectual eminence. The fault was not in the materials, but in the principle on which the materials were put together. Pitt had mixed up these conflicting elements, in the full confidence that he should be able to keep them all in perfect subordination to himself and in perfect harmony with each other. We shall soon see how the experiment succeeded.

On the very day on which the new Prime Minister kissed hands, three-fourths of that popularity which he had long enjoyed without a rival, and to which he owed the greater party of his authority, departed from him. A violent outcry was raised, not against that part of his conduct which really deserved severe condemnation, but against a step in which we can see nothing to censure. His acceptance of a peerage produced a general burst of indignation. Yet surely no peerage had ever been better earned ; nor was there ever a statesman who more needed the repose of the Upper house. Pitt was now growing old. He was much older in constitution than in years. It was with imminent risk to his life that he had, on some important occasions, attended his duty in Parliament. During the session of 1764, he had not been able to take part in a single debate. It was impossible that he should go through the nightly labour of conducting the business of the government in the House of Commons. His wish to be transferred, under such circumstances, to a less busy and less turbulent assembly, was natural and reasonable.

The nation, however, overlooked all these considerations. Those who had most loved and honoured the great Commoner were loudest in invective against the new made Lord. London had hitherto been true to him through every vicissitude. When the citizens learned that he had been sent for from Somersetshire, that he had been closeted with the King at Richmond, and that he was to be first minister, they had been in transports of joy. Preparations were made for a grand entertainment and for a general illumination. The lamps had actually been placed round the Monument, when the *Gazette* announced that the object of all this enthusiasm was an Earl. Instantly the feast was countermanded. The lamps were taken down. The newspapers raised the roar of obloquy. Pamphlets, made up of calumny and scurrility, filled the shops of all the booksellers; and of those pamphlets, the most galling were written under the direction of the malignant Temple. It was now the fashion to compare the two Williams, William Pulteney and William Pitt. Both, it was said, had, by eloquence and simulated patriotism, acquired a great ascendency in the House of Commons and in the country. Both had been intrusted with the office of reforming the government. Both had, when at the heighth of power and popularity, been seduced by the splendour of the coronet. Both had been made Earls, and both had at once become objects of aversion and scorn to the nation which a few hours before had regarded them with affection and veneration.

The clamour against Pitt appears to have had a serious effect on the foreign relations of the country. His name had till now, acted like a spell at Versailles and Saint Ildefonso. English travellers on the Continent had remarked that nothing more was necessary to silence a whole room full of boasting Frenchmen than to drop a hint of the probability that Mr. Pitt would return to power. In an instant there was deep silence: all shoulders rose and all faces were lengthened. Now, unhappily, every foreign court, in learning that he was recalled to office, learned also that he no longer possessed the hearts of his countrymen. Ceasing to be loved at home, he ceased to be feared abroad. The name of Pitt had been a charmed name. Our envoys tried in vain to conjure with the name of Chatham.

The difficulties which beset Chatham were daily increased by the despotic manner in which he treated all around him. Lord Rockingham had, at the time of the change of ministry, acted with great moderation, had expressed a hope that the new government would act on the principles of the late government, and had even interfered to prevent many of his friends from quitting office. Thus Saunders and Keppel, two naval commanders of great eminence, had been induced to remain at the Admiralty, where their services were much needed. The Duke of Portland was still Lord Chamberlain, and Lord Besborough Postmaster. But within a quarter of a year, Lord Chatham had so effectually disgusted these men, that they all retired in disgust. In truth, his tone, submissive in the closet, was at this time insupportably tyrannical in the cabinet. His colleagues were merely his clerks for naval, financial and diplomatic business. Conway, meek as he was, was on one occasion provoked into declaring that such language as Lord Chatham's had never been heard west of Constantinople, and was with difficulty prevented by Horace Walpole from resigning, and rejoining the standard of Lord Rockingham.

The breach which had been made in the government by the defection of so many of the Rockinghams, Chatham hoped to supply by the help cf the Bedfords. But with the Bedfords he could not deal as he had dealt with other parties. It was to no purpose that he bade high for one or two members of the faction, in the hope of detaching them from the rest. They were to be had; but they were to be had only in the lot. There was, indeed, for a moment, some wavering and some disputing among them. But at length the counsels of the shrewd and resolute Rigby prevailed. They determined to stand firmly together, and plainly intimated to Chatham that he must take them all, or that he should get none of them. The event proved that they were wiser in their generation than any other connection in the state. In a few months they were able to dictate their own terms.

The most important public measure of Lord Chatham's administration was his celebrated interference with the corn trade. The harvest had been bad; the price of food was high; and he thought it necessary to take on himself the responsibility of laying an embargo on the exportation of grain. When Parliament met, this proceeding was attacked by the opposition as unconstitutional and defended by the ministers as indispensably necessary. At last an act was passed to indemnify all who had been concerned in the embargo.

The first words uttered by Chatham, in the House of Lords, were in defence of his conduct on this occasion. He spoke with a calmness, sobriety and dignity, well suited to the audience which he was addressing. A subsequent speech which he made on the same subject was less successful. He bade defiance to aristocratical connections, with a superciliousness to which the Peers were not accustomed, and with tones and gestures better suited to a large and stormy assembly than to the body of which he was now a member. A short altercation followed, and he was told very plainly that he should not be suffered to browbeat the old nobility of England.

It gradually became clearer and clearer that he was in a distempered state of mind. His attention had been drawn to the territorial acquisitions of the East India Company, and he determined to bring the whole of that great subject before Parliament. He would not, however, confer on the subject with any of his colleagues. It was in vain that Conway, who was charged with the conduct of business in the House of Commons, and Charles Townshend, who was responsible for the direction of the finances, begged for some glimpse of light as to what was in contemplation. Chatham's answers were sullen and mysterious. He must decline any discussion with them; he did not want their assistance; he had fixed on a person to take charge of his measure in the House of Commons. This person was a member who was not connected with the government, and who neither had, nor deserved to have, the ear of the House—a noisy, purse-proud, illiterate demagogue, whose Cockney English and scraps of mispronounced Latin were the jest of the newspapers—Alderman Beckford. It may well be supposed that these strange proceedings produced a ferment through the whole political world. The city was in commotion. The East India Company invoked the faith of charters. Burke thundered against the ministers. The ministers looked at each other, and knew not what to say. In the midst of the confusion, Lord Chatham proclaimed himself gouty, and retired to Bath. It was announced, after some time, that he was better, that he would shortly return, that he would soon put everything in order. A day was fixed for his arrival in London. But when he reached the Castle Inn, at Marlborough, he stopped, shut himself up in his room, and remained there some weeks. Everybody who travelled that road was amazed by the number of his attendants. Footmen and grooms, dressed in his family livery, filled the whole inn, though one of the largest in England, and swarmed in the streets of the little town. The truth was, that the invalid had insisted that, during his stay, all the waiters and stable-boys of the Castle should wear his livery.

His colleagues were in despair. The Duke of Grafton proposed to go down to Marlborough in order to consult the oracle. But he was informed that Lord Chatham must decline all conversation on business. In the mean time, all the parties which were out of office, Bedfords, Grenvilles and Rockinghams, joined to oppose the distracted government on the vote for the land tax. They were reinforced by almost all the county members, and had a considerable majority. This was the first time that a ministry had been beaten on an important division in the House of Commons since the fall of Sir Robert Walpole. The administration, thus furiously assailed from without, was torn by internal dissensions. It had been formed on no principle whatever. From the very first, nothing but Chatham's authority had prevented the hostile contingents which made up his ranks from going to blows with each other. That authority was now withdrawn, and everything was in commotion. Conway, a brave soldier, but in civil affairs the most timid and irresolute of men, afraid of disobliging the King, afraid of being abused in the newspapers, afraid of being thought factious if he went out, afraid of being thought interested if he stayed in, afraid of everything, and afraid of being known to be afraid of anything, was beaten backwards and forwards like a shuttlecock, between Horace Walpole, who wished to make him Prime Minister, and Lord John Cavendish, who wished to draw him into opposition. Charles Townshend, a man of splendid talents, of lax principles and of boundless vanity and presumption, would submit to no control. The full extent of his parts, of his ambition and of his arrogance, had not yet been made manifest ; for he had always quailed before the genius and the lofty character of Pitt. But now that Pitt had quitted the House of Commons, and seemed to have abdicated the part of chief minister, Townshend broke loose from all restraint.

While things were in this state, Chatham at length returned to London. He might as well have remained at Marlborough. He would see nobody; he would give no opinion on any public matter. The Duke of Grafton begged piteously for an interview, for an hour, for half-an-hour, for five minutes. The answer was that it was impossible. The King himself repeatedly condescended to expostulate and implore: "Your duty," he wrote, "your own honour, require you to make an effort." The answers to these appeals were commonly written in Lady Chatham's hand, from her lord's dictation; for he had not energy even to use a pen. He flings himself at the King's feet ; he is penetrated by the royal goodness so signally shown to the most unhappy of men ; he implores a little more indulgence ; he cannot as yet transact business ; he cannot see his colleagues ; least of all can he bear the excitement of an interview with majesty.

Some were half inclined to suspect that he was, to use a military phrase, malingering. He had made, they said, a great blunder, and had found it out. His immense popularity, his high reputation for statesmanship, were gone for ever. Intoxicated by pride, he had undertaken a task beyond his abilities. He now saw nothing before him but distresses and humiliations ; and he had therefore simulated illness, in order to escape from vexations which he had not fortitude to meet. This suspicion, though it derived some colour from that weakness which was the most striking blemish of his character, was certainly unfounded. His mind, before he became first minister, had been, as we have said, in an unsound state ; and physical and moral causes now concurred to make the derangement of his faculties complete. The gout, which had been the torment of his whole life, had been suppressed by strong remedies. For the first time since he was a boy at Oxford, he had passed several months without a twinge. But his hand and foot had been relieved at the expense of his nerves. He became melancholy, fanciful, irritable. The embarrassing state of public affairs, the grave responsibility which lay on him, the consciousness of his errors, the disputes of his colleagues, the savage clamours raised by his detractors, bewildered his enfeebled mind. One thing alone, he said, could save him. He must repurchase Hayes. The unwilling consent of the new occupant was extorted by Lady Chatham's entreaties and tears ; and her lord was somewhat easier. But if business were mentioned to him, he, once the proudest and boldest of mankind, behaved like a hysterical girl, trembled from head to foot and burst into a flood of tears.

His colleagues for a time continued to entertain the expectation that his health would soon be restored, and that he would emerge from his retirement. But month followed month, and still he remained hidden in mysterious seclusion and sunk, as far as they could learn, in the deepest dejection of spirits. They at length ceased to hope or to fear anything from him; and though he was still nominally Prime Minister, took without scruple steps which they knew to be diametrically opposed to all his opinions and feelings, allied themselves with those whom he had proscribed, disgraced those whom he most esteemed, and laid taxes on the colonies, in the face of the strong declarations which he had recently made.

When he had passed about a year and three quarters in gloomy privacy, the King received a few lines in Lady Chatham's hand. They contained a request, dictated by her lord, that he might be permitted to resign the Privy Seal. After some civil show of reluctance, the resignation was accepted. Indeed Chatham was, by this time, almost as much forgotten as if he had already been lying in Westminster Abbey.

At length the clouds which had gathered over his mind broke and passed away. His gout returned, and freed him from a more cruel malady. His nerves were newly braced. His spirits became buoyant. He woke as from a sickly dream. It was a strange recovery. Men had been in the habit of talking of him as of one dead, and, when he first showed himself at the King's levee, started as if they had seen a ghost. It was more than two years and a half since he had appeared in public.

He, too, had cause for wonder. The world which he now entered was not the world which he had quitted. The administration which he had formed had never been, at any one moment, entirely changed. But there had been so many losses and so many accessions that he could scarcely recognise his own work. Charles Townshend was dead. Lord Shelburne had been dismissed. Conway had sunk into utter insignificance. The Duke of Grafton had fallen into the hands of the Bedfords. The Bedfords had deserted Grenville, had made their peace with the King and the King's friends, and had been admitted to office. Lord North was Chancellor of the Exchequer, and was rising fast in importance. Corsica had been given up to France without a struggle. The disputes with the American colonies had been revived. A general election had taken place. Wilkes had returned from exile, and, outlaw as he was, had been chosen knight of the shire for Middlesex. The multitude was on his side. The Court was obstinately bent on ruining him, and was prepared to shake the very foundations of the constitution for the sake of a paltry revenge. The House of Commons, assuming to itself an authority which of right belongs only to the whole legislature, had declared Wilkes incapable of sitting in Parliament. Nor had it been thought sufficient to keep him out. Another must be brought in. Since the freeholders of Middlesex had obstinately refused to choose a member acceptable to the Court, the House had chosen a member for them. This was the only instance, perhaps not the most disgraceful instance, of the inveterate malignity of the Court. Exasperated by the steady opposition of the Rockingham party, the King's friends had tried to rob a distinguished Whig nobleman of his private estate, and had persisted in their mean wickedness till their own servile majority had revolted from mere disgust and shame. Discontent had spread throughout the nation, and was kept up by stimulants such as had rarely been applied to the public mind. Junius had taken the field, had trampled Sir William Draper in the dust, had well nigh broken the heart of Blackstone, and had so mangled the reputation of the Duke of Grafton, that his grace had become sick of office, and was beginning to look wistfully towards the shades of Euston. Every principle of foreign, domestic and colonial policy which was dear to the heart of Chatham had, during the eclipse of his genius, been violated by the government which he had formed.

The remaining years of his life were spent in vainly struggling against that fatal policy which, at the moment when he might have given it a death blow, he had been induced to take under his protection. His exertions redeemed his own fame, but they effected little for his country,

He found two parties arrayed against the government, the party of his own brothers-in-law, the Grenvilles and the party of Lord Rockingham. On the question of the Middlesex election these parties were agreed. But on many other important questions they differed widely; and they were, in truth, not less hostile to each other than to the Court. The Grenvilles had, during several years, annoyed the Rockinghams with a succession of acrimonious pamphlets. It was long before the Rockinghams could be induced to retaliate. But an ill-natured tract, written under Grenville's direction and entitled "A State of the Nation," was too much for their patience. Burke undertook to defend and avenge his friends, and executed the task with admirable skill and vigour. On every point he was victorious, and nowhere more completely victorious than when he joined issue on those dry and minute questions of statistical and financial detail in which the main strength of Grenville lay. The official drudge, even on his own chosen ground, was utterly unable to maintain the fight against the great orator and philosopher. When Chatham reappeared, Grenville was still writhing with the recent shame and smart of this well merited chastisement. Cordial co-operation between the two sections of the Opposition was impossible. Nor could Chatham easily connect himself with either. His feelings, in spite of many affronts given and received, drew him towards the Grenvilles. For he had strong domestic affections; and his nature, which, though haughty, was by no means obdurate, had been softened by affliction. But from his kinsmen he was separated by a wide difference of opinion on the question of colonial taxation. A reconciliation, however, took place. He visited Stowe: he shook hands with George Grenville; and the Whig freeholders of Buckinghamshire, at their public dinners, drank many bumpers to the union of the three brothers.

In opinions, Chatham was much nearer to the Rockinghams than to his own relatives. But between him and the Rockinghams there was a gulf not easily to be passed. He had deeply injured them, and in injuring them had deeply injured his country. When the balance was trembling between them and the Court, he had thrown the whole weight of his genius, of his renown, of his popularity, into the scale of misgovernment. It must be added, that many eminent members of the party still retained a bitter recollection of the asperity and disdain with which they had been treated by him at the time when he assumed the direction of affairs. It is clear from Burke's pamphlets and speeches, and still more clear from his private letters, and from the language which he held in conversation, that he long regarded Chatham with a feeling not far removed from dislike. Chatham was undoubtedly conscious of his error and desirous to atone for it. But his overtures of friendship, though made with earnestness, and even with unwonted humility, were at first received by Lord Rockingham with cold and austere reserve. Gradually the intercourse of the two statesmen became courteous and even amicable. But the past was never wholly forgotten.

Chatham did not, however, stand alone. Round him gathered a party, small in number, but strong in great and various talents. Lord Camden, Lord Shelburne, Colonel Barre, and Dunning, afterwards Lord Ashburton, were the principal members of this connection.

There is no reason to believe that, from this time till within a few weeks of Chatham's death, his intellect suffered any decay. His eloquence was almost to the last heard with delight. But it was not exactly the eloquence of the House of Lords. That lofty and passionate, but somewhat desultory declamation, in which he excelled all men, and which was set off by looks, tones and gesture, worthy of Garrick or Talma, was out of place in a small apartment where the audience often consisted of three or four drowsy prelates, three or four old judges, accustomed during many years to disregard rhetoric, and to look only at facts and arguments, and three or four listless and supercilious men of fashion, whom anything like enthusiasm moved to a sneer. In the House of Commons a flash of his eye, a wave of his arm, had sometimes cowed Murray. But in the House of Peers his utmost vehemence and pathos produced less effect than the moderation, the reasonableness, the luminous order and the serene dignity which characterised the speeches of Lord Mansfield.

On the question of the Middlesex election, all the three divisions of the Opposition acted in concert. No orator in either House defended what is now universally admitted to have been the constitutional cause with more ardour or eloquence than Chatham. Before this subject had ceased to occupy the public mind George Grenville died. His party rapidly melted away; and in a short time most of his adherents appeared on the ministerial benches.

Had George Grenville lived many months longer the friendly ties which, after years of estrangement and hostility, had been renewed between him and his brother-in-law, would, in all probability, have been a second time violently dissolved. For now the quarrel between England and the North American Colonies took a gloomy and terrible aspect. Oppression provoked resistance: resistance was made the pretext for fresh oppression. The warnings of all the greatest statesmen of the age were lost on an imperious Court and a deluded nation. Soon a colonial senate confronted the British Parliament. Then the colonial militia crossed bayonets with the British regiments. At length the commonwealth was torn asunder. Two millions of Englishmen, who, fifteen years before, had been as loyal to their prince and as proud of their country as the people of Kent or Yorkshire, separated themselves by a solemn act from the Empire. For a time it seemed that the insurgents would struggle to small purpose against the vast financial and military means of the mother country. But disasters, following one another in rapid succession, rapidly dispelled the illusions of national vanity. At length a great British force, exhausted, famished, harassed on every side by hostile peasantry, was compelled to deliver up its arms. Those governments which England had, in the late war so signally humbled, and which had during many years been sullenly brooding over the recollections of Quebec, of Minden and of the Moro, now saw with exultation that the day of revenge was at hand. France recognised the independence of the United States; and there could be little doubt that the example would soon be followed by Spain.

Chatham and Rockingham had cordially concurred in opposing every part of the fatal policy which had brought the state into this dangerous situation. But their paths now diverged. Lord Rockingham thought, and, as the event proved, thought most justly, that the revolted colonies were separated from the Empire for ever, and that the only effect of prolonging the war on the American continent would be to divide resources which it was desirable to concentrate. If the hopeless attempt to subjugate Pennsylvania and Virginia were abandoned, war against the House of Bourbon might possibly be avoided, or, if inevitable, might be carried on with success and glory. We might even indemify ourselves for part of what we had lost, at the expense of those foreign enemies who had hoped to profit by our domestic dissensions. Lord Rockingham, therefore, and those who acted with him, conceived that the wisest course now open to England was to acknowledge the independence of the United States, and to turn her whole force against her European enemies.

Chatham, it should seem, ought to have taken the same side. Before France had taken any part in our quarrel with the colonies, he had repeatedly, and with great energy of language, declared that it was impossible to conquer

America, and he could not without absurdity maintain that it was easier to conquer France and America together than America alone. But his passions overpowered his judgment, and made him blind to his own inconsistency. The very circumstances which made the separation of the colonies inevitable made it to him altogether insupportable. The dismemberment of the Empire seemed to him less ruinous and humiliating, when produced by domestic dissensions, than when produced by foreign interference. His blood boiled at the degredation of his country. Whatever lowered her among the nations of the earth, he felt as a personal outrage to himself. And the feeling was natural. He had made her so great. He had been so proud of her; and she had been so proud of him. He remembered how, more than twenty years before, in a day of gloom and dismay, when her possessions were torn from her, when her flag was dishonoured, she had called on him to save her. He remembered the sudden and gloriouschange which his energy had wrought, the long series of triumphs, the days of thanksgiving, the nights of illumination. Fired by such recollections, he determined to separate himself from those who advised that the independence of the colonies should be acknowledged. That he was in error will scarcely, we think, be disputed by his warmest admirers. Indeed, the treaty, by which, a few years later, the Republic of the United States was recognised, was the work of his most attached adherents and of his favourite son.

The Duke of Richmond had given notice of an address to the throne, against the further prosecution of hostilities with America. Chatham had, during some time, absented himself from Parliament, in consequence of his growing infirmities. He determined to appear in his place on this occasion, and to declare that his opinions were decidedly at variance with those of the Rockingham party. He was in a state of great excitement. His medical attendants were uneasy, and strongly advised him to calm himself, and to remain at home. But he was not to be controlled. His son William and his son-in-law Lord Mahon, accompanied him to Westminster. He rested himself in the Chancellor's room till the debate commenced, and then, leaning on his two young relations, limped to his seat. The slightest particular of that day were remembered, and have been carefully recorded. He bowed, it was remarked, with great courtliness to those Peers who rose to make way for him and his supporters. His crutch was in his hand. He wore, as was his fashion, a rich velvet coat. His legs were swathed in flannel. His wig was so large and his face so emaciated that none of his features could be discerned, except the high curve of his nose and his eyes, which still retained a gleam of the old fire.

When the Duke of Richmond had spoken, Chatham rose. For some time his voice was inaudible. At length his tones became distinct and his action animated. Here and there his hearers caught a thought or an expression which reminded them of William Pitt. But it was clear that he was not himself. He lost the thread of his discourse, hesitated, repeated the same words several times, and was so confused that, in speaking of the Act of Settlement, he could not recall the name of the Electress Sophia. The House listened in solemn silence, and with the aspect of profound respect and compassion. The stillness was so deep that the dropping of a handkerchief would have been heard. The Duke of Richmond replied with great tenderness and courtesy; but while he spoke, the old man was observed to be restless and irritable. The Duke sat down. Chatham stood up again, pressed his hand on his breast, and sank down in an apoplectic fit. Three or four lords who sat near him caught him in his fall. The House broke up in confusion. The dying man was carried to the residence of one of the officers of Parliament, and was so far restored as to be able to bear a journey to Hayes. At Hayes, after lingering a few weeks, he expired in his seventieth year. His bed was watched to the last, with anxious tenderness, by his wife and children;

and he well deserved their care. Too often haughty and wayward to others, to them he had been almost effeminately kind. He had through life been dreaded by his political opponents, and regarded with more awe than love even by his political associates. But no fear seems to have mingled with the affections which his fondness, constantly overflowing in a thousand endearing forms, had inspired in the little circle at Hayes.

Chatham, at the time of his decease, had not, in both Houses of Parliament, ten personal adherents. Half the public men of the age had been estranged from him by his errors, and the other half by the exertions which he had made to repair his errors. His last speech had been an attack at once on the policy pursued by the government and on the policy recommended by the opposition. But death at once restored him to his old place in the affection of his country. Who could hear unmoved of the fall of that which had been so great and which had stood so long? The circumstances, too, seemed rather to belong to the tragic stage than real life. A great statesman, full of years and honours, led forth to the Senate House by a son of rare hopes, and stricken down in full council while straining his feeble voice to rouse the drooping spirit of his country, could not but be remembered with peculiar veneration and tenderness. Detraction was overawed. The voice even of just and temperate censure was mute, nothing was remembered but the lofty genius, the unsullied probity, the undisputed services of him who was no more. For once, the chiefs of all all parties were agreed. A public funeral, a public monument, were eagerly voted. The debts of the deceased were paid. A provision was made for his family. The City of London requested that the remains of the great man whom she had so long loved and honoured might rest under the dome of her magnificent cathedral. But the petition came too late. Everything was already prepared for the interment in Westminster Abbey.

Though men of all parties had concurred in decreeing posthumous honours to Chatham, his corpse was attended to the grave almost exclusively by opponents of the government. The banner of the lordship of Chatham was borne by Colonel Barré, attended by the Duke of Richmond and Lord Rockingham. Burke, Saville and Dunning upheld the pall. Lord Camden was conspicuous in the procession. The chief mourner was young William Pitt. After the lapse of more than twenty-seven years, in a season as dark and perilous, his own shattered frame and broken heart were laid, with the same pomp, in the same consecrated mould.

Chatham sleeps near the northern door of the Church, in a spot which has ever since been appropriated to statesmen, as the other end of the same transept has long been to poets. Mansfield rest there, and the second William Pitt, and Fox, and Grattan, and Canning, and Wilberforce. In no other cemetery do so many great citizens lie within so narrow a space. High over those venerable graves towers the stately monument of Chatham, and from above, his own effigy, graven by a cunning hand, seems still, with eagle face and outstretched arm, to bid England be of good cheer, and to hurl defiance at her foes. The generation which reared that memorial of him has disappeared. The time has come when the rash and indiscriminate judgments which his contemporaries passed on his character may be calmly revised by history. And history, while, for the warning of vehement, high and daring natures, she notes his many errors, will yet deliberately pronounce, that among the eminent men whose bones lie near his, scarcely one has left a more stainless, and none a more splendid name.

LAYS OF ANCIENT ROME.

PREFACE.

THAT what is called the history of the Kings and early Consuls of Rome is to a great extent fabulous, few scholars have, since the time of Beaufort, ventured to deny. It is certain that, more than three hundred and sixty years after the date ordinarily assigned for the foundation of the city, the public records were, with scarcely an exception, destroyed by the Gauls. It is certain that the oldest annals of the commonwealth were compiled more than a century and a half after the destruction of the records. It is certain, therefore, that the great Latin writers of the Augustan age did not possess those materials, without which a trustworthy account of the infancy of the Republic could not possibly be framed. Those writers own, indeed, that the chronicles to which they had access were filled with battles that were never fought and Consuls that were never inaugurated; and we have abundant proof that in these chronicles events of the greatest importance, such as the issue of the war with Porsena, and the issue of the war with Brennus, were grossly misrepresented. Under these circumstances a wise man will look with great suspicion on the legend which has come down to us. He will, perhaps, be inclined to regard the princes who are said to have founded the civil and religious institutions of Rome, the son of Mars, and the husband of Egeria, as mere mythological personages, of the same class with Perseus and Ixion. As he draws nearer and nearer to the confines of authentic history, he will become less and less hard of belief. He will admit that the most important parts of the narrative have some foundation in truth. But he will distrust almost all the details, not only because they seldom rest on any solid evidence, but also because he will constantly detect in them, even when they are within the limits of physical possibility, that peculiar character, more easily understood than defined, which distinguishes the creations of the imagination from the realities of the world in which we live.

The early history of Rome is indeed far more poetical than anything else in Latin literature. The loves of the Vestal and the God of War, the cradle laid among the reeds of Tiber, the fig-tree, the she-wolf, the shepherd's cabin, the recognition, the fratricide, the rape of the Sabines, the death of Tarpeia, the fall of Hostus Hostilius, the struggle of Mettus Curtius through the marsh, the women rushing with torn raiment and dishevelled hair between their fathers and their husbands, the nightly meetings of Numa and the Nymph by the well in the sacred grove, the fight of the three Romans and the three Albans, the purchase of the Sibylline books, the crime of Tullia, the simulated madness of Brutus, the ambiguous reply of the Delphian oracle to the Tarquins, the wrongs of Lucretia, the heroic actions of Horatius Cocles, of Scævola and of Clœlia, the battle of Regillus won by the aid of Castor and Pollux, the defence of Cremera, the touching story of Coriolanus, the still more touching story of Virginia, the wild legend about the draining of the Alban lake, the combat between Valerius Corvus and the gigantic Gaul are among the many instances which will at once suggest themselves to every reader.

In the narrative of Livy, who was a man of fine imagination, these stories retain much of their genuine character. Nor could even the tasteless Dionysius distort and mutilate them into mere prose. The poetry shines, in spite of him, through the dreary pedantry of his eleven books. It is discernible in the most tedious and in the most superficial modern works on the early times of Rome. It enlivens the dulness of the Universal History, and gives a charm to the most meagre abridgments of Goldsmith.

Even in the age of Plutarch there were discerning men who rejected the popular account of the foundation of Rome, because that account appeared to them to have the air, not of a history, but of a romance or a drama. Plutarch, who was displeased at their incredulity, had nothing better to say in reply to their arguments than that chance sometimes turns poet, and produces trains of events not to be distinguished from the most elaborate plots which are constructed by art.* But though the existence of a poetical element in the early history of the Great City was detected so many years ago, the first critic who distinctly saw from what source that poetical element had been derived was James Perizonius, one of the most acute and learned antiquaries of the seventeenth century. His theory, which, in his own days, attracted little or no notice, was revived in the present generation by Niebuhr, a man who would have been the first writer of his time, if his talent for communicating truths had borne any proportion to his talent for investigating them. It has been adopted by several eminent scholars of our own country, particularly by the Bishop of St. David's, by Professor Malden, and by the lamented Arnold. It appears to be now generally received by men conversant with classical antiquity; and indeed it rests on such strong proofs, both internal and external, that it will not be easily subverted. A popular exposition of this theory, and of the evidence by which it is supported, may not be without interest even for readers who are unacquainted with the ancient languages.

The Latin literature which has come down to us is of later date than the commencement of the Second Punic War, and consists almost exclusively of works fashioned on Greek models. The Latin metres, heroic, elegiac, lyric, and dramatic, are of Greek origin. The best Latin epic poetry is the feeble echo of the Iliad and Odyssey. The best Latin eclogues are imitations of Theocritus. The plan of the most finished didactic poem in the Latin tongue was taken from Hesiod. The Latin tragedies are bad copies of the masterpieces of Sophocles and Euripides. The Latin comedies are free translations from Demophilus, Menander and Apollodorus. The Latin philosophy was borrowed, without alteration, from the Portico and the Academy; and the great Latin orators constantly proposed to themselves as patterns the speeches of Demosthenes and Lysias.

But there was an earlier Latin literature, a literature truly Latin, which has wholly perished, which had, indeed, almost wholly perished long before those whom we are in the habit of regarding as the greatest Latin writers were born. That literature abounded with metrical romances, such as are found in every country where there is much curiosity and intelligence, but little reading and writing. All human beings, not utterly savage, long for some information about past times, and are delighted by narratives which present pictures to the

---

* Ὕποπτον μὲν ἐνίοις ἐστὶ τὸ δραματικὸν καὶ πλασματῶδες· οὐ δεῖ δὲ ἀπιστεῖν, τὴν τύχην ὁρῶντας, οἵων ποιημάτων δημιουργός ἐστι.—*Plut. Rom,* viii. This remarkable passage has been more grossly misinterpreted than any other in the Greek language, where the sense was so obvious. The Latin version of Cruserius, the French version of Amyot, the old English version by several hands, and the later English version by Langhorne, are all equally destitute of every trace of the meaning of the original. None of the translators saw even that ποίημα is a poem. They all render it an event.

eye of the mind. But it is only in very enlightened communities that books are readily accessible. Metrical composition, therefore, which, in a highly civilised nation, is a mere luxury, is, in nations imperfectly civilised, almost a necessary of life, and is valued less on account of the pleasure which it gives to the ear than on account of the help which it gives to the memory. A man who can invent or embellish an interesting story, and put it into a form which others may easily retain in their recollection, will always be highly esteemed by a people eager for amusement and information, but destitute of libraries. Such is the origin of ballad-poetry, a species of composition which scarcely ever fails to spring up and flourish in every society, at a certain point in the progress towards refinement. Tacitus informs us that songs were the only memorials of the past which the ancient Germans possessed. We learn from Lucan and from Ammianus Marcellinus that the brave actions of the ancient Gauls were commemorated in the verses of Bards. During many ages, and through many revolutions, minstrelsy retained its influence over both the Teutonic and the Celtic race. The vengeance exacted by the spouse of Attila for the murder of Siegfried was celebrated in rhymes, of which Germany is still justly proud. The exploits of Athelstane were commemorated by the Anglo-Saxons, and those of Canute by the Danes, in rude poems, of which a few fragments have come down to us. The chants of the Welsh harpers preserved, through ages of darkness, a faint and doubtful memory of Arthur. In the Highlands of Scotland may still be gleaned some relics of the old songs about Cuthullin and Fingal. The long struggle of the Servians against the Ottoman power was recorded in lays full of martial spirit. We learn from Herrera that, when a Peruvian Inca died, men of skill were appointed to celebrate him in verses, which all the people learned by heart, and sang in public on days of festival. The feats of Kurroglou, the great-freebooter of Turkistan, recounted in ballads composed by himself, are known in every village of Northern Persia. Captain Beechey heard the bards of the Sandwich Islands recite the heroic achievements of Tamehameha, the most illustrious of their kings. Mungo Park found in the heart of Africa a class of singing men, the only annalists of their rude tribes, and heard them tell the story of the victory which Damel, the Negro prince of the Jaloffs, won over Abdulkader, the Mussulman tyrant off Foota Torra. This species of poetry attained a high degree of excellence among the Castilians, before they began to copy Tuscan patterns. It attained a still higher degree of excellence among the English and the Lowland Scotch during the fourteenth, fifteenth and sixteenth centuries. But it reached its full perfection in ancient Greece; for there can be no doubt that the great Homeric poems are generically ballads, though widely distinguished from all other ballads, and indeed, from almost all other human compositions, by transcendent merit.

As it is agreeable to general experience that, at a certain stage in the progress of society, ballad-poetry should flourish, so is it also agreeable to general experience that, at a subsequent stage in the progress of society, ballad-poetry should be undervalued and neglected. Knowledge advances: manners change: great foreign models of composition are studied and imitated. The phraseology of the old minstrels becomes obsolete. Their versification, which, having received its laws only from the ear, abound in irregularities, seems licentious and uncouth. Their simplicity appears beggarly when compared with the quaint forms and gaudy colouring of such artists as Cowley and Gongora. The ancient lays, unjustly despised by the learned and polite, linger for a time in the memory of the vulgar, and are at length too often irretrievably lost. We cannot wonder that the ballads of Rome should have altogether disappeared, when we remember how very narrowly, in spite of the invention of printing, those of our own country and those of Spain escaped the same fate. There is, indeed, little doubt that oblivion covers many English songs equal to any that were published by Bishop Percy, and many Spanish songs as good as the best of those which have been so happily translated by Mr. Lockhart. Eighty years ago England possessed only one tattered copy of Childe Waters and Sir Cauline, and Spain only one tattered copy of the noble poem of the Cid. The snuff of a candle, or a mischievous dog, might in a moment have deprived the world for ever of any of those fine compositions. Sir Walter Scott, who united to the fire of a great poet the minute curiosity and patient diligence of a great antiquary, was but just in time to save the precious relics of the Minstrelsy of the Border. In Germany, the lay of the Nibelungs had been long utterly forgotten, when, in the eighteenth century, it was, for the first time, printed from a manuscript in the old library of a noble family. In truth, the only people who, through their whole passage from simplicity to the highest civilisation, never for a moment ceased to love and admire their old ballads were the Greeks.

That the early Romans should have had ballad-poetry, and that this poetry should have perished, is, therefore, not strange. It would, on the contrary, have been strange if these things had not come to pass; and we should be justified in pronouncing them highly probable, even if we had no direct evidence on the subject. But we have direct evidence of unquestionable authority.

Ennius, who flourished in the time of the Second Punic War, was regarded in the Augustan age as the father of Latin poetry. He was, in truth, the father of the second school of Latin poetry, the only school of which the works have descended to us. But from Ennius himself we learn that there were poets who stood to him in the same relation in which the author of the romance of Count Alarcos stood to Garcilaso, or the author of the "Lytell Geste of Robyn Hode" to Lord Surrey. Ennius speaks of verses which the Fauns and the Bards were wont to chant in the old time, when none had yet studied the graces of speech, when none had yet climbed the peaks sacred to the goddesses of Grecian song. "Where," Cicero mournfully asks, "are those old verses now?"*

Contemporary with Ennius was Quintus Fabius Pictor, the earliest of the Roman annalists. His account of the infancy and youth of Romulus and Remus has been preserved by Dionysius, and contains a very remarkable reference to the ancient Latin poetry. Fabius says that, in his time, his countrymen were still in the habit of singing ballads about the Twins. "Even in the hut of Faustulus"—so these old lays appear to have run—"the children of Rhea and Mars were, in port and in spirit, not like unto swineherds or

---

* " Quid ? Nostri veteres versus ubi sunt ?
. . . . 'Quos olim Fauni vatesque canebant,
Cum neque Musarum scopulos quisquam superârat,
Nec dicti studiosus erat.' "
         Cic. in *Bruto*, cap. xviii.

The Muses, it should be observed, are Greek divinities. The Italian goddesses of verse were the Camœnæ. At a later period, the appellations were used indiscriminately; but in the age of Ennius there was probably a distinction. In the epitaph of Nævius, who was the representative of the old Italian school of poetry, the Camœnæ, not the Muses, are represented as grieving for the loss of their votary. The " Musarum scopuli " are evidently the peaks of Parnassus.

Scaliger, in a note on Varro (*De Lingua Latina*, lib. vii), suggests, with great ingenuity, that the Fauns, who were represented by the superstition of later ages as a race of monsters, half gods and half brutes, may really have been a class of men who exercised in Latium, at a very remote period, the same functions which belonged to the Magians in Persia and to the Bards in Gaul.

cowherds, but such that men might well guess them to be of the blood of kings and gods." *

Cato the Censor, who also lived in the days of the Second Punic War, mentioned this lost literature in his lost work on the antiquities of his country. Many ages, he said, before his time, there were ballads in praise of illustrious men ; and these ballads it was the fashion for the guests at banquets to sing in turn while the piper played. "Would," exclaims Cicero, "that we still had the old ballads of which Cato speaks!" †

Valerius Maximus gives us exactly similar information, without mentioning his authority, and observes that the ancient Roman ballads were probably of

---

* Οἱ δὲ ἀνδρωθέντες γίνονται, κατά τε ἀξίωσιν μορφῆς καὶ φρονήματος ὄγκον, οὐ συοφορβοῖς καὶ βουκόλοις ἐοικότες, ἀλλ', οἵους ἄν τις ἀξιώσειε τοὺς ἐκ βασιλείου τε φύντας γένους, καὶ ἀπὸ δαιμόνων σπορᾶς γενέσθαι νομιζομένους, ὡς ἐν τοῖς πατρίοις ὕμνοις ὑπὸ Ῥωμαίων ἔτι καὶ νῦν ᾄδεται.—*Dion. Hal.* i. 79. This passage has sometimes been cited as if Dionysius had been speaking in his own person, and had, Greek as he was, been so industrious or so fortunate as to discover some valuable remains of that early Latin poetry which the greatest Latin writers of his age regretted as hopelessly lost. Such a supposition is highly improbable ; and indeed it seems clear from the context that Dionysius, as Reiske and other editors evidently thought, was merely quoting from Fabius Pictor. The whole passage has the air of an extract from an ancient chronicle, and is introduced by the words, Κάιντος μὲν Φάβιος, ὁ Πίκτωρ λεγόμενος, τῇδε γράφει.

Another argument may be urged which seems to deserve consideration. The author of the passage in question mentions a thatched hut which, in his time, stood between the summit of Mount Palatine and the Circus. This hut, he says, was built by Romulus, and was constantly kept in repair at the public charge, but never in any respect embellished. Now, in the age of Dionysius there certainly was at Rome a thatched hut, said to have been that of Romulus. But this hut, as we learn from Vitruvius, stood, not near the Circus, but in the Capitol. (*Vit.* ii. 1.) If, therefore, we understand Dionysius to speak in his own person, we can reconcile his statement with that of Vitruvius only by supposing that there were at Rome in the Augustan age two thatched huts, both believed to have been built by Romulus, and both carefully repaired and held in high honour. The objections to such a supposition seem to be strong. Neither Dionysius nor Vitruvius speak of more than one such hut. Dio Cassius informs us that twice, during the long administration of Augustus, the hut of Romulus caught fire. (xlviii. 43, liv. 29.) Had there been two such huts, would he not have told us of which he spoke? An English historian would hardly give an account of a fire at Queen's College without saying whether it was at Queen's College, Oxford, or at Queen's College, Cambridge. Marcus Seneca, Macrobius, and Conon, a Greek writer from whom Photius has made large extracts, mention only one hut of Romulus, that in the Capitol... (*M. Seneca, Contr.* i. 6; *Macrobius, Sat.* i. 15; *Photius, Bibl.* 186.) Ovid, Livy, Petronius, Valerius Maximus, Lucius Seneca, and St. Jerome mention only one hut of Romulus, without specifying the site. (*Ovid, Fasti,* iii. 183; *Liv.* v. 53; *Petronius, Fragm.*; *Val. Max.* iv. 4; *L. Seneca, Consolatio ad Helviam*; *D. Hieron. ad Paulinianum de Didymo.*)

The whole difficulty is removed if we suppose that Dionysius was merely quoting Fabius Pictor. Nothing is more probable than that the cabin, which in the time of Fabius stood near the Circus, might, long before the age of Augustus, have been transported to the Capitol, as the place fittest, by reason both of its safety and of its sanctity, to contain so precious a relic.

The language of Plutarch confirms this hypothesis. He describes, with great precision, the spot where Romulus dwelt, on the slope of Mount Palatine leading to the Circus; but he says not a word implying that the dwelling was still to be seen there. Indeed, his expressions imply that it was no longer there. The evidence of Solinus is still more to the point. He, like Plutarch, describes the spot where Romulus had resided, and says expressly that the hut had been there, but that in his time it was there no longer. The site, it is certain, was well remembered ; and probably retained its old name, as Charing Cross and the Haymarket have done. This is probably the explanation of the words "casa Romuli," in Victor's description of the Tenth Region of Rome, under Valentinian.

† Cicero refers twice to this important passage in Cato's Antiquities :—" Gravissimus auctor in 'Originibus' dixit Cato, morem apud majores hunc epularum fuisse, ut deinceps, qui accubarent, canerent ad tibiam clarorum virorum laudes atque virtutes. Ex quo perspicuum est, et cantus tum fuisse rescriptos vocum sonis, et carmina."—*Tusc. Quæst.* iv. 2. Again : " Utinam exstarent illa carmina, quæ, multis sæculis ante suam ætatem, in epulis esse cantitata a singulis convivis de clarorum virorum laudibus, in 'Originibus' scriptum reliquit Cato.'—*Brutus,* cap. xix.

more benefit to the young than all the lectures of the Athenian schools, and that to the influence of the national poetry were to be ascribed the virtues of such men as Camillus and Fabricius.*

Varro, whose authority on all questions connected with the antiquities of his country is entitled to the greatest respect, tells us that at banquets it was once the fashion for boys to sing, sometimes with and sometimes without instrumental music, ancient ballads in praise of men of former times. These young performers, he observes, were of unblemished character, a circumstance which he probably mentioned because, among the Greeks, and indeed in his time among the Romans also, the morals of singing boys were in no high repute. †

The testimony of Horace, though given incidentally, confirms the statements of Cato, Valerius Maximus, and Varro. The poet predicts that, under the peaceful administration of Augustus, the Romans will, over their full goblets, sing to the pipe, after the fashion of their fathers, the deeds of brave captains, and the ancient legends touching the origin of the city. ‡

The proposition, then, that Rome had ballad-poetry is not merely in itself highly probable, but is fully proved by direct evidence of the greatest weight.

This proposition being established, it becomes easy to understand why the early history of the city is, unlike almost everything else in Latin literature, native where almost everything else is borrowed, imaginative where almost everything else is prosaic. We can scarcely hesitate to pronounce that the magnificent, pathetic, and truly national legends, which present so striking a contrast to all that surrounds them, are broken and defaced fragments of that early poetry, which, even in the age of Cato the Censor, had become antiquated, and of which Tully had never heard a line.

That this poetry should have been suffered to perish will not appear strange when we consider how complete was the triumph of the Greek Genius over the public mind of Italy. It is probable that, at an early period, Homer, Archilochus, and Herodotus, furnished some hints to the Latin minstrels ;§ but it was not till after the war with Pyrrhus that the poetry of Rome began to put off its old Ausonian character. The transformation was soon consumated. The conquered, says Horace, led captive the conquerors. It was precisely at the time at which the Roman People rose to unrivalled political ascendancy that they stooped to pass under the intellectual yoke. It was precisely at the time at which the sceptre departed from Greece that the empire of her language and of her arts became universal and despotic. The revolution, indeed, was not effected without a struggle. Nævius seems to have been the last of the ancient line of poets. Ennius was the founder of a new dynasty. Nævius celebrated the First Punic War in Saturnian verse, the old

---

* " Majores natu in conviviis ad tibias egregia superiorum opera carmine comprehensa pangebant, quo ad ea imitanda juventutem alacriorem redderent. . . . Quas Athenas, quam scholam, quæ alienigena studia huic domesticæ disciplinæ prætulerim? Inde oriebantur Camilli, Scipiones, Fabricii, Marcelli, Fabii."—*Val. Max.* ii. 1.

† "In conviviis pueri modesti, ut cantarent carmina antiqua, in quibus laudes eran*t* majorum, et assa voce, et cum tibicine."—Nonius, *Assa voce pro sola*.

‡ " Nosque et profestis lucibus et sacris,
  Inter jocosi munera Liberi,
   Cum prole matronisque nostris,
   Rite Deos prius apprecati,
  Virtute functos, MORE PATRUM, duces,
  Lydis remixto carmine tibiis,
   Trojamque, et Anchisen, et almæ
   Progeniem Veneris canemus."
                  Carm. iv. 15.

§ See the Preface to the Lay of the Battle of Regillus.

national verse of Italy.* Ennius sang the Second Punic War in numbers borrowed from the Iliad. The elder poet, in the epitaph which he wrote for himself, and which is a fine specimen of the early Roman diction and versifica-

* Cicero speaks highly in more than one place of this poem of Nævius; Ennius sneered at it and stole from it.
As to the Saturnian measure, see Hermann's Elementa Doctrinæ, Metricæ, iii. 9. The Saturnian line, according to the grammarians, consisted of two parts. The first was a catalectic dimeter iambic; the second was composed of three trochees. But the license taken by the early Latin poets seems to have been almost boundless. The most perfect Saturnian line which has been preserved was the work, not of a professional artist, but of an amateur: "Dabunt malum Metelli Nævio poetæ."
There has been much difference of opinion among learned men respecting the history of this measure. That it is the same with a Greek measure used by Archilochus is indisputable. (*Bentley, Phalaris*, xi.) But in spite of the authority of Terentianus Maurus, and of the still higher authority of Bentley, we may venture to doubt whether the coincidence was not fortuitous. We constantly find the same rude and simple numbers in different countries, under circumstances which make it impossible to suspect that there has been imitation on either side. Bishop Heber heard the children of a village in Bengal singing "Radha, Radha," to the tune of "My Boy Billy." Neither the Castilian nor the German minstrels of the Middle Ages owed anything to Paros or to ancient Rome. Yet both the poem of the Cid and the poem of the Nibelungs contain many Saturnian verses; as,—
  "Estas nuevas a mio Cid eran venidas."
  "A mi lo dicen; a ti dan las orejadas,"
  "Man möhte michel wunder von Sifride sagen;"
  "Wa ich den Künic vinde daz sol man mir sagen."
Indeed, there cannot be a more perfect Saturnian line than one which is sung in every English nursery—
  "The queen was in her parlour eating bread and honey;"
yet the author of this line, we may be assured, borrowed nothing from either Nævius or Archilochus.
On the other hand, it is by no means improbable that, two or three hundred years before the time of Ennius, some Latin minstrel may have visited Sybaris or Cortona, may have heard some verses of Archilochus sung, may have been pleased with the metre, and may have introduced it at Rome. This much is certain, that the Saturnian measure, if not a native of Italy, was at least so early and so completely naturalised there that its foreign origin was forgotten.
Bentley says, indeed, that the Saturnian measure was first brought from Greece into Italy by Nævius. But this is merely *obiter dictum*, to use a phrase common in our courts of law, and would not have been deliberately maintained by that incomparable critic, whose memory is held in reverence by all lovers of learning. The arguments which might be brought against Bentley's assertion—for it is mere assertion, supported by no evidence—are innumerable. A few will suffice.
1. Bentley's assertion is opposed to the testimony of Ennius. Ennius sneered at Nævius for writing on the First Punic War in verses such as the old Italian bards used before Greek literature had been studied. Now the poem of Nævius was in Saturnian verse. Is it possible that Ennius could have used such expressions if the Saturnian verse had been just imported from Greece for the first time?
2. Bentley's assertion is opposed to the testimony of Horace. "When Greece," says Horace, "introduced her arts into our uncivilised country, those rugged Saturnian numbers passed away." Would Horace have said this if the Saturnian numbers had been imported from Greece just before the hexameter?
3. Bentley's assertion is opposed to the testimony of Festus and of Aurelius Victor, both of whom positively say that the most ancient prophecies attributed to the Fauns were in Saturnian verse.
4. Bentley's assertion is opposed to the testimony of Terentianus Maurus, to whom he has himself appealed. Terentianus Maurus does indeed say that the Saturnian measure, though believed by the Romans from a very early period ("Creditit vetustas") to be of Italian invention, was really borrowed from the Greeks. But Terentianus Maurus does not say that it was first borrowed by Nævius. Nay, the expressions used by Terentianus Maurus clearly imply the contrary: for how could the Romans have believed, from a very early period, that this measure was the indigenous production of Latium, if it was really brought over from Greece in an age of intelligence and liberal curiosity—in the age which gave birth to Ennius, Plautus, Cato the Censor, and other distinguished writers? If Bentley's assertion were correct, there could have been no more doubt at Rome about the Greek origin of the Saturnian measure than about the Greek origin of hexametres of Sapphics.

tion, plaintively boasted that the Latin language had died with him.* Thus what to Horace appeared to be the first faint dawn of Roman literature appeared to Nævius to be its hopeless setting. In truth, one literature was setting, and another dawning.

The victory of the foreign taste was decisive: and, indeed, we can hardly blame the Romans for turning away with contempt from the rude lays which had delighted their fathers, and giving their whole admiration to the immortal productions of Greece. The national romances, neglected by the great and the refined, whose education had been finished at Rhodes or Athens, continued, it may be supposed, during some generations, to delight the vulgar. While Virgil, in hexameters of exquisite modulation, described the sports of rustics, those rustics were still singing their wild Saturnian ballads.† It is not improbable that, at the time when Cicero lamented the irreparable loss of the poems mentioned by Cato, a search among the nooks of the Apennines, as active as the search which Sir Walter Scott made among the descendants of the moss-troopers of Liddesdale, might have brought to light many fine remains of ancient minstrelsy. No such search was made. The Latin ballads perished for ever. Yet discerning critics have thought that they could still perceive in the early history of Rome numerous fragments of this lost poetry, as the traveller on classic ground sometimes finds, built into the heavy wall of a fort or convent, a pillar rich with acanthus leaves, or a frieze where the Amazons and Bacchanals seem to live. The theatres and temples of the Greek and the Roman were degraded into the quarries of the Turk and the Goth. Even so did the ancient Saturnian poetry become the quarry in which a crowd of orators and annalists found the materials for their prose.

It is not difficult to trace the process by which the old songs were transmuted into the form which they now wear. Funeral panegyric and chronicle appear to have been the intermediate links which connected the lost ballad with the histories now extant. From a very early period it was the usage that an oration should be pronounced over the remains of a noble Roman. The orator, as we learn from Polybius, was expected, on such an occasion, to recapitulate all the services which the ancestors of the deceased had, from the earliest time, rendered to the commonwealth. There can be little doubt that the speaker on whom this duty was imposed would make use of all the stories suited to his purpose which were to be found in the popular lays. There can be as little doubt that the family of an eminent man would preserve a copy of the speech which had been pronounced over his corpse. The compilers of the early chronicles would have recourse to these speeches; and the great historians of a later period would have recourse to the chronicles.

It may be worth while to select a particular story, and to trace its probable progress through these stages. The description of the migration of the Fabian house to Cremera is one of the finest of the many fine passages which lie thick in the earlier books of Livy. The Consul, clad in his military garb, stands in the vestibule of his house, marshalling his clan, three hundred and six fighting men, all of the same proud patrician blood, all worthy to be attended by the fasces and to command the legions. A sad and anxious retinue of friends accompanies the adventurers through the streets; but the voice of lamentation is drowned by the shouts of admiring thousands. As the procession passes the Capitol, prayers and vows are poured forth, but in vain. The devoted band, leaving Janus on the right, marches to its doom through the Gate of Evil Luck. After achieving high deeds of valour against overwhelming numbers, all

---

* Aulus Gellius, *Noctes Atticæ*, i. 24.
† See Servius, in Georg. ii. 385.

perish save one child, the stock from which the great Fabian race was destined again to spring, for the safety and glory of the commonwealth. That this fine romance, the details of which are so full of poetical truth, and so utterly destitute of all show of historical truth, came originally from some lay which had often been sung with great applause at banquets, is in the highest degree probable. Nor is it difficult to imagine a mode in which the transmission might have taken place. The celebrated Quintus Fabius Maximus, who died about twenty years before the First Punic War, and more than forty years before Ennius was born, is said to have been interred with extraordinary pomp. In the eulogy pronounced over his body all the great exploits of his ancestors were doubtless recounted and exaggerated. If there were then extant songs which gave a vivid and touching description of an event, the saddest and the most glorious in the long history of the Fabian house, nothing could be more natural than that the panegyrist should borrow from such songs their finest touches, in order to adorn his speech. A few generations later the songs would perhaps be forgotten, or remembered only by shepherds and vine-dressers. But the speech would certainly be preserved in the archives of Fabian nobles. Fabius Pictor would be well acquainted with a document so interesting to his personal feelings, and would insert large extracts from it in his rude chronicle. That chronicle, as we know, was the oldest to which Livy had access. Livy would at a glance distinguish the bold strokes of the forgotten poet from the dull and feeble narrative by which they were surrounded, would retouch them with a delicate and powerful pencil, and would make them immortal.

That this might happen at Rome can scarcely be doubted ; for something very like this has happened in several countries, and among others, in our own. Perhaps the theory of Perizonius cannot be better illustrated than by showing that what he supposes to have taken place in ancient times has, beyond all doubt, taken place in modern times.

"History," says Hume with the utmost gravity, "has preserved some instances of Edgar's amours, from which, as from a specimen, we may form a conjecture of the rest." He then tells very agreeably the stories of Elfleda and Elfrida ; two stories which have a most suspicious air of romance, and which, indeed, greatly resemble, in their general character, some of the legends of early Rome. He cites, as his authority for these two tales, the chronicle of William of Malmesbury, who lived in the time of King Stephen. The great majority of readers suppose that the device by which Elfleda was substituted for her young mistress, the artifice by which Athelwold obtained the hand of Elfrida, the detection of that artifice, the hunting party, and the vengeance of the amorous king, are things about which there is no more doubt than about the execution of Anne Boleyn or the slitting of Sir John Coventry's nose. But when we turn to William of Malmesbury, we find that Hume, in his eagerness to relate these pleasant fables, has overlooked one very important circumstance. William does in iced tell both the stories ; but he gives us distinct notice that he does not warrant their truth, and that they rest on no better authority than that of ballads.*

Such is the way in which these two well-known tales have been handed down. They originally appeared in a poetical form. They found their way from ballads into an old chronicle. The ballads perished ; the chronicle remained. A great historian, some centuries after the ballads had been alto-

* "Infamias quas post dicam magis respererunt cantilenæ." Edgar appears to have been most mercilessly treated in the Anglo-Saxon ballads. He was the favourite of the monks ; and the monks and minstrels were at deadly feud.

gether forgotten, consulted the chronicle. He was struck by the lively colouring of these ancient fictions: he transferred them to his pages; and thus we find inserted, as unquestionable facts, in a narrative which is likely to last as long as the English tongue, the inventions of some minstrel whose works were probably never committed to writing, whose name is buried in oblivion, and whose dialect has become obsolete. It must, then, be admitted to be possible, or rather highly probable, that the stories of Romulus and Remus, and of the Horatii and Curiatii, may have had a similar origin.

Castilian literature will furnish us with another parallel case. Mariana, the classical historian of Spain, tells the story of the ill-starred marriage which the King, Don Alonso, brought about between the heirs of Carrion and the two daughters of the Cid. The Cid bestowed a princely dower on his sons-in-law. But the young men were base and proud, cowardly and cruel. They were tried in danger and found wanting. They fled before the Moors, and once, when a lion broke out of his den, they ran and crouched in an unseemly hiding-place. They knew that they were despised, and took council how they might be avenged. They parted from their father-in-law with many signs of love, and set forth on a journey with Dona Elvira and Dona Sol. In a solitary place the bridegrooms seized their brides, stripped them, scourged them, and departed, leaving them for dead. But one of the house of Bivar, suspecting foul play, had followed them in disguise. The ladies were brought back safe to the house of their father. Complaint was made to the king. It was adjudged by the Cortes that the dower given by the Cid should be returned, and that the heirs of Carrion, together with one of their kindred, should do battle against three knights of the party of the Cid. The guilty youths would have declined the combat; but all their shifts were vain. They were vanquished in the lists, and for ever disgraced, while their injured wives were sought in marriage by great princes.*

Some Spanish writers have laboured to show, by an examination of dates and circumstances, that this story is untrue. Such confutation was surely not needed; for the narrative is on the face of it a romance. How it found its way into Mariana's history is quite clear. He acknowledges his obligations to the ancient chronicles; and had doubtless before him the "Cronica del famoso Cavallero Cid Ruy Diez Campeador," which had been printed as early as the year 1552. He little suspected that all the most striking passages in this chronicle were copied from a poem of the twelfth century, a poem of which the language and versification had long been obsolete, but which glowed with no common portion of the fire of the Iliad. Yet such was the fact. More than a century and a half after the death of Mariana, this venerable ballad, of which one imperfect copy on parchment, four hundred year old, had been preserved at Bivar, was for the first time printed. Then it was found that every interesting circumstance of the story of the heirs of Carrion was derived by the eloquent Jesuit from a song of which he had never heard, and which was composed by a minstrel whose very name had long been forgotten.†

Such, or nearly such, appears to have been the process by which the lost ballad-poetry of Rome was transformed into history. To reverse that process, to transform some portions of early Roman history back into the poetry out of which they were made, is the object of this work.

In the following poems the author speaks, not in his own person, but in the

---

* Mariana, lib. x. cap. 4.
† See the account which Sanchez gives of the Bivar manuscript in the first volume of the *Colleccion de Poesias Castellanas anteriores al Siglo XV*. Part of the story of the lords of Carrion, in the poem of the Cid, has been translated by Mr. Frere is a manner above all praise.

persons of ancient minstrels who know only what a Roman citizen, born three or four hundred years before the Christian æra, may be supposed to have known, and who are in nowise above the passions and prejudices of their age and nation. To these imaginary poets must be ascribed some blunders which are so obvious that it is unnecessary to point them out. The real blunder would have been to represent these old poets as deeply versed in general history, and studious of chronological accuracy. To them must also be attributed the illiberal sneers at the Greeks, the furious party spirit, the contempt for the arts of peace, the love of war for its own sake, the ungenerous exultation over the vanquished, which the reader will sometimes observe. To portray a Roman of the age of Camillus or Curius as superior to national antipathies, as mourning over the devastation and slaughter by which empire and triumphs were to be won, as looking on human suffering with the sympathy of Howard, or as treating conquered enemies with the delicacy of the Black Prince, would be to violate all dramatic propriety. The old Romans had some great virtues —fortitude, temperance, veracity, spirit to resist oppression, respect for legitimate authority, fidelity in the observing of contracts, disinterestedness, ardent patriotism ; but Christian charity and chivalrous generosity were alike unknown to them.

It would have been obviously improper to mimic the manner of any particular age or country. Something has been borrowed, however, from our own old ballads, and more from Sir Walter Scott, the great restorer of our ballad-poetry. To the Iliad still greater obligations are due ; and those obligations have been contracted with the less hesitation because there is reason to believe that some of the old Latin minstrels really had recourse to that inexhaustible store of poetical images.

It would have been easy to swell this little volume to a very considerable bulk by appending notes filled with quotations ; but to a learned reader such notes are not necessary ; for an unlearned reader they would have little interest ; and the judgment passed both by the learned and by the unlearned on a work of the imagination will always depend much more on the general character and spirit of such a work than on minute details.

HORATIUS.

THERE can be little doubt that among those parts of early Roman history which had a poetical origin was the legend of Horatius Cocles. We have several versions of the story, and these versions differ from each other in points of no small importance. Polybius, there is reason to believe, heard the tale recited over the remains of some Consul or Prætor descended from the old Horatian patricians ; for he evidently introduces it as a specimen of the narratives with which the Romans were in the habit of embellishing their funeral oratory. It is remarkable that, according to his description, Horatius defended the bridge alone, and perished in the waters. Acccording to the chronicles which Livy and Dionysius followed, Horatius had two companions, swam safe to shore, and was loaded with honours and rewards.

These discrepancies are easily explained. Our own literature, indeed, will furnish an exact parallel to what may have taken place at Rome. It is highly probable that the memory of the war of Porsena was preserved by compositions much resembling the two ballads which stand first in the *Relics of Ancient English Poetry*. In both those ballads the English, commanded by the Percy, fight with the Scots, commanded by the Douglas. In one of the ballads the

Douglas is killed by a nameless English archer, and the Percy by a Scottish spearman: in the other, the Percy slays the Douglas in single combat, and is himself made prisoner. In the former, Sir Hugh Montgomery is shot through the heart by a Northumbrian bowman: in the latter, he is taken and exchanged for the Percy. Yet both the ballads relate to the same event, and that an event which probably took place within the memory of persons who were alive when both the ballads were made. One of the minstrels says:

"Old men that knowen the grounde well yenoughe
Call it the battell of Otterburn:
At Otterburn began this spurne
Upon a monnyn day.
Ther was the douggbte Doglas slean:
The Perse never went away."

The other poet sums up the event in the following lines:

"Thys fraye bygan at Otterborne
Bytwene the nyghte and the day:
Ther the Dowglas lost hys lyfe,
And the Percy was lede away."

It is by no means unlikely that there were two old Roman lays about the defence of the bridge; and that, while the story which Livy has transmitted to us was preferred by the multitude, the other, which ascribed the whole glory to Horatius alone, may have been the favourite with the Horatian house.

The following ballad is supposed to have been made about a hundred and twenty years after the war which it celebrates, and just before the taking of Rome by the Gauls. The author seems to have been an honest citizen, proud of the military glory of his country, sick of the disputes of factions, and much given to pining after good old times which had never really existed. The allusion, however, to the partial manner in which the public lands were allotted could proceed only from a plebeian; and the allusion to the fraudulent sale of spoils marks the date of the poem, and shows that the poet shared in the general discontent with which the proceedings of Camillus, after the taking of Veii, were regarded.

The penultimate syllable of the name Porsena has been shortened in spite of the authority of Niebuhr, who pronounces, without assigning any ground for his opinion, that Martial was guilty of a decided blunder in the line,

"Hanc spectare manum Porsena non potuit."

It is not easy to understand how any modern scholar, whatever his attainments may be—and those of Niebuhr were undoubtedly immense—can venture to pronounce that Martial did not know the quantity of a word which he must have uttered and heard uttered a hundred times before he left school. Niebuhr seems also to have forgotten that Martial has fellow-culprits to keep him in countenance. Horace has committed the same decided blunder; for he gives us, as a pure iambic line,

"Minacis aut Etrusca Porsenæ manus."

Silius Italicus has repeatedly offended in the same way, as when he says,

"Cernitur effugiens ardentem Porsena dextram:"

and again,

"Clusinum vulgus, cum, Porsena magne, jubebas."

A modern writer may be content to err in such company.

Niebuhr's supposition that each of the three defenders of the bridge was the representative of one of the three patrician tribes is both ingenious and probable, and has been adopted in the following poem.

HORATIUS.

A Lay Made about the Year of the City ccclx.

1.

Lars Porsena of Clusium
  By the Nine Gods he swore
That the great house of Tarquin
  Should suffer wrong no more.
By the Nine Gods he swore it,
  And named a trysting day,
And bade his messengers ride forth,
East and west and south and north,
  To summon his array.

2.

East and west and south and north
  The messengers ride fast,
And tower and town and cottage
  Have heard the trumpet's blast.
Shame on the false Etruscan
  Who lingers in his home,
When Porsena of Clusium
  Is on the march for Rome.

3.

The horsemen and the footmen
  Are pouring in amain
From many a stately market place,
  From many a fruitful plain ;
From many a lonely hamlet,
  Which, hid by beech and pine,
Like an eagle's nest, hangs on the crest
  Of purple Apennine ; ·

4.

From lordly Volaterræ,
  Where scowls the far-famed hold
Piled by the hands of giants
  For godlike kings of old ;
From seagirt Populonia,
  Whose sentinels descry
Sardinia's snowy mountain-tops
  Fringing the southern sky ;

5.

From the proud mart of Pisæ,
  Queen of the western waves,
Where ride Massilia's triremes
  Heavy with fair-haired slaves ;
From where sweet Clanis wanders
  Through corn and vines and flowers;
From where Cortona lifts to heaven
  Her diadem of towers.

6.

Tall are the oaks whose acorns
  Drop in dark Auser's rill ;
Fat are the stags that champ the boughs
  Of the Ciminian hill ;
Beyond all streams Clitumnus
  Is to the herdsman dear ;
Best of all pools the fowler loves
  The great Volsinian mere.

7.

But now no stroke of woodman
  Is heard by Auser's rill ;
No hunter tracks the stag's green path
  Up the Ciminian hill ;
Unwatched along Clitumnus
  Grazes the milk-white steer ; ·
Unharmed the water-fowl may dip
  In the Volsinian mere.

8.

The harvests of Arretium,
  This year, old men shall reap ;
This year, young boys in Umbro
  Shall plunge the struggling sheep ;
And in the vats of Luna,
  This year, the must shall foam
Round the white feet of laughing girls,
  Whose sires have marched to Rome.

9.

There be thirty chosen prophets,
  The wisest of the land,
Who alway by Lars Porsena
  Both morn and evening stand :
Evening and morn the Thirty
  Have turned the verses o'er,
Traced from the right on linen white
  By mighty seers of yore.

10.

And with one voice the Thirty
  Have their glad answer given :
" Go forth, go forth, Lars Porsena ;
  Go forth, beloved of Heaven ;
Go, and return in glory
  To Clusium's royal dome ;
And hang round Nurscia's altars
  The golden shields of Rome."

11.

And now hath every city
  Sent up her tale of men;
The foot are fourscore thousand,
  The horse are thousands ten.
Before the gates of Sutrium
  Is met the great array.
A proud man was Lars Porsena
  Upon the trysting day.

12.

For all the Etruscan armies
  Were ranged beneath his eye,
And many a banished Roman,
  And many a stout ally;
And with a mighty following
  To join the muster came
The Tusculan Mamilius,
  Prince of the Latian name.

13.

But by the yellow Tiber
  Was tumult and affright;
From all the spacious champaign
  To Rome men took their flight.
A mile around the city,
  The throng stopped up the ways;
A fearful sight it was to see
  Through two long nights and days.

14.

For aged folk on crutches,
  And women great with child,
And mothers sobbing over babes
  That clung to them and smiled,
And sick men borne in litters
  High on the necks of slaves,
And troops of sun-burned husbandmen
  With reaping-hooks and staves.

15.

And droves of mules and asses
  Laden with skins of wine,
And endless flocks of goats and sheep,
  And endless herds of kine,
And endless trains of waggons
  That creaked beneath the weight
Of corn-sacks and of household goods,
  Choked every roaring gate.

16.

Now, from the rock Tarpeian,
  Could the wan burghers spy
The line of blazing villages
  Red in the midnight sky.
The Fathers of the City,
  They sat all night and day,
For every hour some horseman came
  With tidings of dismay.

17.

To eastward and to westward
  Have spread the Tuscan bands;
Nor house, nor fence, nor dovecote
  In Crustumerium stands.
Verbenna down to Ostia
  Hath wasted all the plain;
Astur hath stormed Janiculum,
  And the stout guards are slain.

18.

I wis, in all the Senate,
  There was no heart so bold,
But sore it ached, and fast it beat,
  When that ill news was told.
Forwith up rose the Consul,
  Up rose the Fathers all;
In haste they girded up their gowns,
  And hied them to the wall.

19.

They held a council standing
  Before the River-Gate;
Short time was there, ye well may guess,
  For musing or debate.
Out spake the Consul roundly:
  "The bridge must straight go down;
For, since Janiculum is lost,
  Nought else can save the town."

20.

Just then a scout came flying,
  All wild with haste and fear:
"To arms! to arms! Sir Consul:
  Lars Porsena is here."
On the low hills to westward
  The Consul fixed his eye,
And saw the swarthy storm of dust
  Rise fast along the sky.

21.

And nearer fast and nearer
  Doth the red whirlwind come;
And louder still and still more loud,
From underneath that rolling cloud,
Is heard the trumpet's war-note proud,
  The trampling, and the hum,

And plainly and more plainly
  Now through the gloom appears,
Far to left and far to right,
In broken gleams of dark-blue light,
  The long array of helmets bright,
  The long array of spears.

22.

And plainly and more plainly,
  Above that glimmering line,
Now might ye see the banners
  Of twelve fair cities shine ;
But the banner of proud Clusium
  Was highest of them all,
The terror of the Umbrian,
  The terror of the Gaul.

23.

And plainly and more plainly
  Now might the burghers know,
By port and vest, by horse and crest,
  Each warlike Lucomo.
There Cilnius of Arretium
  On his fleet roan was seen ;
And Astur of the four-fold shield,
Girt with the brand none else may wield,
Tolumnius with the belt of gold,
And dark Verbenna from the hold
  By reedy Thrasymene.

24.

Fast by the royal standard
  O'erlooking all the war,
Lars Porsena of Clusium
  Sate in his ivory car.
By the right wheel rode Mamilius,
  Prince of the Latian name ;
And by the left false Sextus,
  That wrought the deed of shame.

25.

But when the face of Sextus
  Was seen among the foes,
A yell that rent the firmament
  From all the town arose.
On the house-tops was no woman
  But spat towards him and hissed ;
No child but screamed out curses,
  And shook its little fist.

26.

But the Consul's brow was sad,
  And the Consul's speech was low,
And darkly looked he at the wall,
  And darkly at the foe.
" Their van will be upon us
  Before the bridge goes down ;
And if they once may win the bridge,
  What hope to save the town ? "

27.

Then out spake brave Horatius,
  The Captain of the gate :
" To every man upon this earth
  Death cometh soon or late ;
And how can man die better
  Than facing fearful odds,
For the ashes of his fathers
  And the temples of his gods,

28.

" And for the tender mother
  Who dandled him to rest,
And for the wife who nurses
  His baby at her breast,
And for the holy maidens
  Who feed the eternal flame,
To save them from false Sextus
  That wrought the deed of shame ?

29.

" Hew down the bridge, Sir Consul,
  With all the speed ye may ;
I, with two more to help me,
  Will hold the foe in play.
In yon strait path a thousand
  May well be stopped by three.
Now who will stand on either hand,
  And keep the bridge with me ? "

30.

Then out spake Spurius Lartius ;
  A Ramnian proud was he :
" Lo, I will stand at thy right hand,
  And keep the bridge with thee.".
And out spake strong Herminius ;
  Of Titian blood was he :
" I will abide on thy left side,
  And keep the bridge with thee."

31.

" Horatius," quoth the Consul,
  " As thou sayest, so let it be."
And straight against that great array
  Forth went the dauntless Three.
For Romans in Rome's quarrel
  Spared neither land nor gold,
Nor son nor wife, nor limb nor life,
  In the brave days of old.

32.

Then none was for a party;
  Then all were for the state;
Then the great men helped the poor,
  And the poor man loved the great:
Then lands were fairly portioned;
  Then spoils were fairly sold:
The Romans were like brothers
  In the brave days of old.

33.

Now Roman is to Roman
  More hateful than a foe,
And the Tribunes beard the high,
  And the Fathers grind the low.
As we wax hot in faction,
  In battle we wax cold:
Wherefore men fight not as they fought
  In the brave days of old.

34.

Now while the Three were tightening
  Their harness on their backs,
The Consul was the foremost man
  To take in hand an axe:
And Fathers mixed with Commons
  Seized hatchet, bar, and crow,
And smote upon the planks above,
  And loosed the props below.

35.

Meanwhile the Tuscan army,
  Right glorious to behold,
Came flashing back the noonday light,
Rank behind rank, like surges bright
  Of a broad sea of gold.
Four hundred trumpets sounded
  A peal of warlike glee,
As that great host, with measured tread,
And spears advanced, and ensigns spread,
Rolled slowly towards the bridge's head,
  Where stood the dauntless Three.

36.

The Three stood calm and silent
  And looked upon the foes,
And a great shout of laughter
  From all the vanguard rose:
And forth three chiefs came spurring
  Before that deep array;
To earth they sprang, their swords they drew,
And lifted high their shields, and flew
  To win the narrow way;

37.

Aunus from green Tifernum,
  Lord of the Hill of Vines;
And Seius, whose eight hundred slaves
  Sicken in Ilva's mines;
And Picus, long to Clusium
  Vassal in peace and war,
Who led to fight his Umbrian powers
From that grey crag where, girt with towers,
The fortress of Nequinum lowers
  O'er the pale waves of Nar.

38.

Stout Lartius hurled down Aunus
  Into the stream beneath:
Herminius struck at Seius,
  And clove him to the teeth:
At Picus brave Horatius
  Darted one fiery thrust;
And the proud Umbrian's gilded arms
  Clashed in the bloody dust.

39.

Then Ocnus of Falerii
  Rushed on the Roman Three;
And Lausulus of Urgo,
  The rover of the sea;
And Aruns of Volsinium,
  Who slew the great wild boar,
The great wild boar that had his den
Amidst the reeds of Cosa's fen,
And wasted fields, and slaughtered men,
  Along Albinia's shore.

40.

Herminius smote down Aruns:
  Lartius laid Ocnus low:
Right to the heart of Lausulus
  Horatius sent a blow.
"Lie there," he cried, "fell pirate!
  No more, aghast and pale,
From Ostia's walls the crowd shall mark
The track of thy destroying bark.
No more Campania's hinds shall fly
To woods and caverns when they spy
  Thy thrice accursed sail."

41.

But now no sound of laughter
　Was heard amongst the foes.
A wild and wrathful clamour
　From all the vanguard rose.
Six spears' lengths from the entrance
　Halted that deep array,
And for a space no man came forth
　To win the narrow way.

42.

But hark! the cry is Astur:
　And lo! the ranks divide;
And the great Lord of Luna
　Comes with his stately stride.
Upon his ample shoulders
　Clangs loud the fourfold shield,
And in his hand he shakes the brand
　Which none but he can wield.

43.

He smiled on those bold Romans
　A smile serene and high;
He eyed the flinching Tuscans,
　And scorn was in his eye.
Quoth he, "The she-wolf's litter
　Stand savagely at bay:
But will ye dare to follow,
　If Astur clears the way?"

44.

Then, whirling up his broadsword
　With both hands to the height,
He rushed against Horatius,
　And smote with all his might.
With shield and blade Horatius
　Right deftly turned the blow.
The blow, though turned, came yet
　　too nigh;
It missed his helm, but gashed his
　　thigh:
The Tuscans raised a joyful cry
　To see the red blood flow.

45.

He reeled, and on Herminius
　He leaned one. breathing-space;
Then, like a wild cat mad with
　　wounds,
　Sprang right at Astur's face.
Through teeth, and skull, and helmet,
　So fierce a thrust he sped,
The good sword stood a hand-breadth
　　out
　Behind the Tuscan's head.

46.

And the great Lord of Luna
　Fell at that deadly stroke,
As falls on Mount Alvernus
　A thunder-smitten oak.
Far o'er the crashing forest
　The giant arms lie spread;
And the pale augurs, muttering low,
　Gaze on the blasted head.

47.

On Astur's throat Horatius
　Right firmly pressed his heel,
And thrice and four times tugged
　　amain,
　Ere he wrenched out the steel.
"And see," he cried, "the welcome,
　Fair guests, that waits you here!
What noble Lucumo comes next
　To taste our Roman cheer?"

48.

But at this haughty challenge
　A sullen murmur ran, [dread,
Mingled of wrath, and shame, and
　Along that glittering van.
There lacked not men of prowess,
　Nor men of lordly race;
For all Etruria's noblest
　Were round the fatal place.

49.

But all Etruria's noblest
　Felt their hearts sink to see
On the earth the bloody corpses,
　In the path the dauntless Three:
And, from the ghastly entrance
　Where those bold Romans stood,
All shrank, like boys who unaware,
　Ranging the woods to start a hare,
Come to the mouth of the dark lair
Where, growling low, a fierce old bear
　Lies amidst bones and blood.

50.

Was none who would be foremost
　To lead such dire attack;
But those behind cried "Forward!"
　And those before cried "Back!"
And backward now and forward
　Wavers the deep array;
And on the tossing sea of steel,
　To and fro the standards reel;
And the victorious trumpet-peal
　Dies fitfully away.

51.

Yet one man for one moment
  Strode out before the crowd;
Well known was he to all the Three,
  And they gave him greeting loud.
"Now welcome, welcome, Sextus!
  Now welcome to thy home!
Why dost thou stay, and turn away?
  Here lies the road to Rome."

52.

Thrice looked he at the city;
  Thrice looked he at the dead;
And thrice came on in fury,
  And thrice turned back in dread:
And, white with fear and hatred,
  Scowled at the narrow way,
Where, wallowing in a pool of blood,
  The bravest Tuscans lay.

53.

But meanwhile axe and lever
  Have manfully been plied;
And now the bridge hangs tottering
  Above the boiling tide.
"Come back, come back, Horatius!"
  Loud cried the Fathers all.
"Back, Lartius! back, Herminius!
  Back, ere the ruin fall!"

54.

Back darted Spurius Lartius;
  Herminius darted back:
And, as they passed, beneath their feet
  They felt the timbers crack.
But when they turned their faces,
  And on the farther shore
Saw brave Horatius stand alone,
  They would have crossed once more.

55.

But with a crash like thunder
  Fell every loosened beam,
And, like a dam, the mighty wreck
  Lay right athwart the stream:
And a long shout of triumph
  Rose from the walls of Rome,
As to the highest turret-tops
  Was splashed the yellow foam.

56.

And, like a horse unbroken
  When first he feels the rein,
The furious river struggled hard,
  And tossed his tawny mane;
And burst the curb, and bounded,
  Rejoicing to be free;
And whirling down, in fierce career,
  Battlement, and plank, and pier,
  Rushed headlong to the sea.

57.

Alone stood brave Horatius,
  But constant still in mind;
Thrice thirty thousand foes before,
  And the broad flood behind.
"Down with him!" cried false Sextus,
  With a smile on his pale face.
"Now yield thee," cried Lars Porsena,
  "Now yield thee to our grace."

58.

Round turned he, as not deigning
  Those craven ranks to see;
Nought spake he to Lars Porsena,
  To Sextus nought spake he;
But he saw on Palatinus
  The white porch of his home;
And he spake to the noble river
  That rolls by the towers of Rome.

59.

"O Tiber! father Tiber!
  To whom the Romans pray,
A Roman's life, a Roman's arms,
  Take thou in charge this day!"
So he spake, and speaking sheathed
  The good sword by his side,
And with his harness on his back,
  Plunged headlong in the tide.

60.

No sound of joy or sorrow
  Was heard from either bank;
But friends and foes in dumb surprise
  With parted lips and straining eyes,
  Stood gazing where he sank;
And when above the surges
  They saw his crest appear,
All Rome sent forth a rapturous cry,
  And even the ranks of Tuscany
  Could scarce forbear to cheer.

61.

But fiercely ran the current,
  Swollen high by months of rain:
And fast his blood was flowing;
  And he was sore in pain,
And heavy with his armour,
  And spent with changing blows:
And oft they thought him sinking,
  But still again he rose.

62.

Never, I ween, did swimmer,
  In such an evil case,
Struggle through such a raging flood
  Safe to the landing-place :
But his limbs were borne up bravely
  By the brave heart within,
And our good father Tiber
  Bare bravely up his chin.*

63.

"Curse on him !" quoth false Sextus ;
  "Will not the villain drown ?
But for this stay, ere close of day
  We should have sacked the town !"
"Heaven help him !" quoth Lars Porsena,
  "And bring him safe to shore ;
For such a gallant feat of arms
  Was never seen before."

64.

And now he feels the bottom ;
  Now on dry earth he stands ;
Now round him throng the Fathers
  To press his gory hands ;
And now, with shouts and clapping,
  And noise of weeping loud,
He enters through the River-Gate,
  Borne by the joyous crowd.

65.

They gave him of the corn-land,
  That was of public right,
As much as two strong oxen
  Could plough from morn till night ;
And they made a molten image,
  And set it up on high,
And there it stands unto this day
  To witness if I lie.

---

* "Our ladye bare upp ber chinae."
  Ballad of Childe Waters.

"Never heavier man and horse
  Stemmed a midnight torrent's force ;
Yet, through good heart and our Lady's grace,
At length he gained the landing-place."
  Lay of the Last Minstrel, I.

66.

It stands in the Comitium,
  Plain for all folk to see ;
Horatius in his harness,
  Halting upon one knee :
And underneath is written,
  In letters all of gold,
How valiantly he kept the bridge
  In the brave days of old.

67.

And still his name sounds stirring
  Unto the men of Rome,
As the trumpet blast that cries to them
  To charge the Volscian home ;
And wives still pray to Juno
  For boys with hearts as bold
As his who kept the bridge so well
  In the brave days of old.

68.

And in the nights of winter,
  When the cold north winds blow,
And the long howling of the wolves
  Is heard amidst the snow ;
When round the lonely cottage
  Roars loud the tempest's din,
And the good logs of Algidus
  Roar louder yet within ;

69.

When the oldest cask is opened,
  And the largest lamp is lit,
When the chestnuts glow in the embers,
  And the kid turns on the spit ;
When young and old in circle
  Around the firebrands close ;
When the girls are weaving baskets,
  And the lads are shaping bows ;

70.

When the goodman mends his armour
  And trims his helmet's plume ;
When the goodwife's shuttle merrily
  Goes flashing through the loom ;
With weeping and with laughter
  Still is the story told,
How well Horatius kept the bridge
  In the brave days of old.

THE BATTLE OF THE LAKE REGILLUS.

THE following poem is supposed to have been produced about ninety years after the lay of Horatius. Some persons mentioned in the lay of Horatius make their appearance again, and some appellations and epithets used in the lay of Horatius have been purposely repeated ; for, in an age of ballad-poetry, it scarcely ever fails to happen that certain phrases come to be appropriated to certain men and things, and are regularly applied to those men and things by every minstrel. Thus we find, both in the Homeric poems and in Hesiod, βίη Ἡρακληείη, περικλυτὸς Ἀμφιγυήεις, διάκτορος Ἀργειφόντης, ἑπτάπυλος Θήβη, Ἑλένης ἕνεκ' ἠϋκόμοιο. Thus, too, in our own national songs, Douglas is almost always the doughty Douglas : England is Merry England : all the gold is red ; and all the ladies are gay.

The principal distinction between the lay of Horatius and the lay of the Lake Regillus is that the former is meant to be purely Roman, while the latter, though national in its general spirit, has a slight tincture of Greek learning and of Greek superstition. The story of the Tarquins, as it has come down to us, appears to have been compiled from the works of several popular poets ; and one, at least, of those poets appears to have visited the Greek colonies in Italy, if not Greece itself, and to have had some acquaintance with the works of Homer and Herodotus. Many of the most striking adventures of the house of Tarquin, before Lucretia makes her appearance, have a Greek character. The Tarquins themselves are represented as Corinthian nobles of the great house of the Bacchiadæ, driven from their country by the tyranny of that Cypselus, the tale of whose strange escape Herodotus has related with incomparable simplicity and liveliness.* Livy and Dionysius tell us that, when Tarquin the Proud was asked what was the best mode of governing a conquered city, he replied only by beating down with his staff all the tallest poppies in his garden.† This is exactly what Herodotus, in the passage to which reference has already been made, relates of the counsel given to Periander, the son of Cypselus. The stratagem by which the town of Gabii is brought under the power of the Tarquins is, again, obviously copied from Herodotus.‡ The embassy of the young Tarquins to the oracle at Delphi is just such a story as would be told by a poet whose head was full of the Greek mythology ; and the ambiguous answer returned by Apollo is in the exact style of the prophecies which, according to Herodotus, lured Crœsus to destruction. Then the character of the narrative changes. From the first mention of Lucretia to the retreat of Porsena nothing seems to be borrowed from foreign sources. The villany of Sextus, the suicide of his victim, the revolution, the death of the sons of Brutus, the defence of the bridge, Mucius burning his hand,§ Clœlia swimming through Tiber, seem to be all strictly Roman. But when we have done with the Tuscan war, and enter upon the war with the Latines, we are again struck by the Greek air of the story. The battle of the Lake Regillus is in all respects a Homeric battle, except that the combatants ride astride on their horses, instead of driving chariots. The mass of fighting men is hardly mentioned. The leaders single each other out, and engage hand to hand. The great object of the warriors on both sides is, as in the Iliad, to obtain possession of the spoils and bodies of the slain ; and several circumstances are related which forcibly remind us of the great slaughter round the corpses of Sarpedon and Patroclus.

---
* Herodotus, v. 92. Livy, i. 34. Dionysius, iii. 46.
† Livy, i. 54. Dionysius, iv. 56. ‡ Herodotus, iii. 154. Livy, L 53.
§ M. de Pouilly attempted, a hundred and twenty years ago, to prove that the story of Mucius was of Greek origin ; but he was signally confuted by the Abbé Sallier. See the *Mémoires de l'Académie des Inscriptions*, vi. 27, 66.

But there is one circumstance which deserves especial notice. Both the war of Troy and the war of Regillus were caused by the licentious passions of young princes, who were therefore peculiarly bound not to be sparing of their own persons in the day of battle. Now the conduct of Sextus at Regillus, as described by Livy, so exactly resembles that of Paris, as described at the beginning of the third book of Iliad, that it is difficult to believe the resemblance accidental. Paris appears before the Trojan ranks defying the bravest Greek to encounter him:

Τρωσὶν μὲν προμάχιζεν Ἀλέξανδρος θεοειδής,
. . . Ἀργείων προκαλίζετο πάντας ἀρίστους,
ἀντίβιον μαχέσασθαι ἐν αἰνῇ δηϊοτῆτι.

Livy introduces Sextus to a similar manner: "Ferocem juvenem Tarquinium, ostentantem se in prima exsulum acie." Menelaus rushes to meet Paris. A Roman noble, eager for vengeance, spurs his horse towards Sextus. Both the guilty princes are instantly terror-stricken:

Τὸν δ' ὡς οὖν ἐνόησεν Ἀλέξανδρος θεοειδής
ἐν προμάχοισι φανέντα, κατεπλήγη φίλον ἦτορ·
ἂψ δ' ἑτάρων εἰς ἔθνος ἐχάζετο κῆρ' ἀλεείνων.

"Tarquinius," says Livy, "retro in agmen suorum infenso cessit hosti." If this be a fortuitous coincidence, it is one of the most extraordinary in literature.

In the following poem, therefore, images and incidents have been borrowed, not merely without scruple, but on principle, from the incomparable battle-pieces of Homer.

The popular belief at Rome, from an early period, seems to have been that the event of the great day of Regillus was decided by supernatural agency. Castor and Pollux, it was said, had fought, armed and mounted, at the head of the legions of the Commonwealth, and had afterwards carried the news of the victory with incredible speed to the city. The well in the Forum at which they had alighted was pointed out. Near the well rose their ancient temple. A great festival was kept to their honour on the Ides of Quintilis, supposed to be the anniversary of the battle; and on that day sumptuous sacrifices were offered to them at the public charge. One spot on the margin of Lake Regillus was regarded during many ages with superstitious awe. A mark, resembling in shape a horse's hoof, was discernible in the volcanic rock; and this mark was believed to have been made by one of the celestial chargers.

How the legend originated cannot now be ascertained; but we may easily imagine several ways in which it might have originated: nor is it at all necessary to suppose, with Julius Frontinus, that two young men were dressed up by the Dictator to personate the sons of Leda. It is probable that Livy is correct when he says that the Roman general, in the hour of peril, vowed a temple to Castor. If so, nothing could be more natural than that the multitude should ascribe the victory to the favour of the Twin Gods. When such was the prevailing sentiment, any man who chose to declare that, in the midst of the confusion and slaughter, he had seen two godlike forms on white horses scattering the Latines, would find ready credence. We know, indeed, that, in modern times, a very similar story actually found credence among a people much more civilised than the Romans of the fifth century before Christ. A chaplain of Cortes, writing about thirty years after the conquest of Mexico, in an age of printing-presses, libraries, universities, scholars, logicians, jurists, and statesmen, had the face to assert that, in one engagement against the Indians, St. James had appeared on a grey horse at the head of the Castilian adventurers. Many of those adventurers were living when this lie was printed. One of them, honest Bernal Diaz, wrote an account of the expedition. He had the evidence of his own senses against the chaplain's legend; but he seems to have distrusted even the evidence of his own senses. He says that he was in the battle, and that he saw a grey horse with a man on his back, but that the man was, to his thinking, Francesco de Morla, and not the ever-blessed Apostle St. James. "Nevertheless," he adds, "it may be that the person on the grey horse was the glorious Apostle St. James, and that I, sinner that I am, was unworthy to see him." The Romans of the age of Cincinnatus were probably quite as credulous as the Spanish subjects of Charles the Fifth. It is therefore conceivable that the appearance of Castor and Pollux may have become an article of faith before the generation which had fought at Regillus had passed away. Nor could anything be more natural than that the poets of the next age should embellish this story, and make the celestial horsemen bear the tidings of victory to Rome.

Many years after the temple of the Twin Gods had been built in the Forum, an important addition was made to the ceremonial by which the state annually testified its gratitude for their protection. Quintus Fabius and Publius Decius were elected Censors at a momentous crisis. It had become absolutely necessary that the classification of the citizens should be revised. On that classification depended the distribution of political power. Party spirit ran high; and the Republic seemed to be in danger of falling under the dominion either of a narrow oligarchy or of an ignorant and headstrong rabble. Under such circumstances, the most illustrious patrician and the most illustrious plebeian of the age were intrusted with the office of arbitrating between the angry factions; and they performed their arduous task to the satisfaction of all honest and reasonable men.

One of their reforms was a remodelling of the equestrian order; and, having effected this reform, they determined to give to their work a sanction derived from religion. In the chivalrous societies of modern times, societies which have much more than may at first sight appear in common with the equestrian order of Rome, it has been usual to invoke the special protection of some Saint, and to observe his day with peculiar solemnity. Thus the Companions of the Garter wear the image of St. George depending from their collars, and meet, on great occasions, in St. George's Chapel. Thus, when Louis the Fourteenth instituted a new order of chivalry for the rewarding of military merit, he commended it to the favour of his own glorified ancestor and patron, and decreed that all the members of the fraternity should meet at the royal palace on the Feast of St. Louis, should attend the king to chapel, should hear mass, and should subsequently hold their great annual assembly. There is a considerable resemblance between this rule of the Order of St. Louis and the rule which Fabius and Decius made respecting the Roman knights. It was ordained that a grand muster and inspection of the equestrian body should be part of the ceremonial performed, on the anniversary of the battle of Regillus, in honour of Castor and Pollux, the two equestrian gods. All the knights, clad in purple and crowned with olive, were to meet at a temple of Mars in the suburbs. Thence they were to ride in state to the Forum, where the temple of the Twins stood. This pageant was, during several centuries, considered as one of the most splendid sights of Rome. In the time of Dionysius the calvalcade sometimes consisted of five thousand horsemen, all persons of fair repute and easy fortune.*

---

* See Livy, ix. 46. Val. Max. ii. 2. Aurel. Vict. De Viris Illustribus, 32. Dionysius, vi. 13. Plin. Hist. Nat. xv. 5. See also the singularly ingenious chapter in Niebuhr's posthumous volume, *Die Censur des Q. Fabius und P. Decius*.

There can be no doubt that the Censors who instituted this august ceremony acted in concert with the Pontiffs, to whom, by the constitution of Rome, the superintendence of the public worship belonged ; and it is probable that those high religious functionaries were; as usual, fortunate enough to find in their books or traditions some warrant for the innovation.

The following poem is supposed to have been made for this great occasion. Songs, we know, were chaunted at the religious festivals of Rome from an early period, indeed from so early a period that some of the sacred verses were popularly ascribed to Numa, and were utterly unintelligible in the age of Augustus. In the Second Punic War a great feast was held in honour of Juno, and a song was sung in her praise. This song was extant when Livy wrote ; and, though exceedingly rugged and uncouth, seemed to him not wholly destitute of merit.* A song, as we learn from Horace, was part of the established ritual at the great Secular Jubilee.† It is therefore likely that the Censors and Pontiffs, when they had resolved to add a grand procession of knights to the other solemnities annually performed on the Ides of Quintilis, would call in the aid of a poet. Such a poet would naturally take for his subject the battle of Regillus, the appearance of the Twin Gods, and the institution of their festival. He would find abundant materials in the ballads of his predecessors ; and he would make free use of the scanty stock of Greek learning which he had himself acquired. He would probably introduce some wise and holy Pontiff enjoining the magnificent ceremonial, which, after a long interval, had at length been adopted. If the poem succeeded, many persons would commit it to memory. Parts of it would be sung to the pipe at banquets. It would be peculiarly interesting to the great Posthumian House, which numbered among its many images that of the Dictator Aulus, the hero of Regillus. The orator who, in the following generation, pronounced the funeral panegyric over the remains of Lucius Posthumius Megellus, thrice Consul, would borrow largely from the lay ; and thus some passages, much disfigured, would probably find their way into the chronicles which were afterwards in the hands of Dionysius and Livy.

Antiquaries differ widely as to the situation of the field of battle. The opinion of those who suppose that the armies met near Cornufelle, between Frascati and the Monte Porzio, is at least plausible, and has been followed in the poem.

As to the details of the battle, it has not been thought desirable to adhere minutely to the accounts which have come down to us. Those accounts, indeed, differ widely from each other, and, in all probability, differ as widely from the ancient poem from which they were originally derived.

It is unnecessary to point out the obvious imitations of the Iliad, which have been purposely introduced.

THE BATTLE OF THE LAKE REGILLUS.

A Lay Sung at the Feast of Castor and Pollux on the Ides of Quintilis, in the Year of the City ccccli.

I.

Ho, trumpets, sound a war-note !
Ho, lictors, clear the way !
The Knights will ride, in all their pride,
Along the streets to-day.
To-day the doors and windows
Are hung with garlands all,
From Castor in the Forum,
To Mars without the wall.
Each Knight is robed in purple,
With olive each is crown'd ;
A gallant war-horse under each
Paws haughtily the ground.
While flows the Yellow River,
While stands the Sacred Hill,

---

* Livy, xxvii. 37.   † Hor. Carmen Seculare.

The proud Ides of Quintilis
  Shall have such honour still.
Gay are the Martian Kalends:
  December's notes are gay;
But the proud Ides, when the squadron rides,
  Shall be Rome's whitest day.

2.

Unto the Great Twin Brethren
  We keep this solemn feast.
Swift, swift, the Great Twin Brethren
  Came spurring from the East.
They came o'er wild Parthenius
  Tossing in waves of pine,
O'er Cirrha's dome, o'er Adria's foam,
  O'er purple Apennine,
From where with flutes and dances
  Their ancient mansion rings,
In lordly Lacedæmon,
  The city of two kings,
To where, by Lake Regillus,
  Under the Porcian height,
All in the lands of Tusculum,
  Was fought the glorious fight.

3.

Now on the place of slaughter
  Are cots and sheepfolds seen,
And rows of vines, and fields of wheat,
  And apple-orchards green:
The swine crush the big acorns
  That fall from Corne's oaks.
Upon the turf by the Fair Fount
  The reaper's cottage smokes.
The fisher baits his angle;
  The hunter twangs his bow;
Little they think on those strong limbs
  That moulder deep below:
Little they think how sternly
  That day the trumpets pealed;
How in the slippery swamp of blood
  Warrior and war-horse reeled;
How wolves came with fierce gallop,
  And crows on eager wings,
To tear the flesh of captains
  And peck the eyes of kings;
How thick the dead lay scattered
  Under the Porcian height;
How through the gates of Tusculum
  Raved the wild stream of flight;
And how the Lake Regillus
  Bubbled with crimson foam,
What time the Thirty Cities
  Came forth to war with Rome.

4.

But, Roman, when thou standest
  Upon that holy ground,
Look thou with heed on the dark rock
  That girds the dark lake round.
So shalt thou see a hoof-mark
  Stamped deep into the flint:
It was no hoof of mortal steed
  That made so strange a dint:
There to the great Twin Brethren
  Vow thou thy vows, and pray
That they, in tempest and in fight,
  Will keep thy head alway.

5.

Since last the Great Twin Brethren
  Of mortal eyes were seen,
Have years gone by an hundred
  And fourscore and thirteen.
That summer, a Virginius
  Was Consul first in place;
The second was stout Aulus,
  Of the Posthumian race.
The Herald of the Latines
  From Gabii came in state:
The Herald of the Latines [Gate
  Passed through Rome's Eastern
The Herald of the Latines
  Did in our Forum stand;
And there he did his office,
  A sceptre in his hand.

6.

"Hear, Senators and people
  Of the good town of Rome:
The Thirty Cities charge you
  To bring the Tarquins home:
And if ye still be stubborn
  To work the Tarquins wrong,
The Thirty Cities warn you,
  Look that your walls be strong.

7.

Then spake the Consul Aulus,
  He spake a bitter jest:
"Once the jays sent a message
  Unto the eagle's nest:—
Now yield thou up thine eyrie
  Unto the carrion-kite,
Or come forth valiantly, and face
  The jays in deadly fight.—
Forth looked in wrath the eagle;
  And carrion-kite and jay,
Soon as they saw his beak and claw,
  Fled screaming far away."

8.

The Herald of the Latines
  Hath hied him back in state :
The Fathers of the City
  Are met in high debate.
Then spake the elder Consul,
  An ancient man and wise :
" Now hearken, Conscript Fathers,
  To that which I advise.
In seasons of great peril
  'Tis good that one bear sway,
Then choose we a Dictator,
  Whom all men shall obey.
Camerium knows how deeply
  The sword of Aulus bites ;
And all our city calls him
  The man of seventy fights.
Then let him be Dictator
  For six months and no more.
And have a Master of the Knights,
  And axes twenty-four."

9.

So Aulus was Dictator,
  The man of seventy fights ;
He made Æbutius Elva
  His Master of the Knights.
On the third morn thereafter,
  At dawning of the day,
Did Aulus and Æbutius
  Set forth with their array.
Sempronious Atratinus
  Was left in charge at home
With boys and with grey-headed men,
  To keep the walls of Rome.
Hard by the Lake Regillus
  Our camp was pitched at night :
Eastward a mile the Latines lay,
  Under the Porcian height.
Far over hill and valley
  Their mighty host was spread ;
And with their thousand watch-fires
  The Midnight sky was red.

10

Up rose the golden morning
  Over the Porcian height,
The proud Ides of Quintilis,
  Marked evermore with white.
Not without secret trouble
  Our bravest saw the foes,
For girt by threescore thousand spears
  The thirty standards rose.
From every warlike city
  That boasts the Latian name,
Foredoomed to dogs and vultures,
  That gallant army came ;
From Setia's purple vineyards,
  From Norba's ancient wall,
From the white streets of Tusculum,
  The proudest town of all ;
From where the witch's fortress
  O'erhangs the dark-blue seas,
From the still glassy lake that sleeps
  Beneath Aricia's trees—
Those trees in whose dim shadow
  The ghastly priest doth reign,
The priest who slew the slayer,
  And shall himself be slain ;—
From the drear banks of Ufens,
  Where flights of marsh-fowl play,
And buffaloes lie wallowing
  Through the hot summer's day ;
From the gigantic watch-towers,
  No work of earthly men,
Whence Cora's sentinels o'erlook
  The never-ending fen ;
From the Laurentian jungle,
  The wild hog's reedy home ;
From the green steeps whence Anio leaps
  In floods of snow-white foam.

11

Aricia, Cora, Norba,
  Velitræ, with the might
Of Setia and of Tusculum,
  Were marshalled on their right :
There leader was Mamilius,
  Prince of the Latian name ;
Upon his head a helmet
  Of red gold shone like flame :
High on a gallant charger
  Of dark-grey hue he rode ;
Over his gilded armour
  A vest of purple flowed,
Woven in the land of sunrise
  By Syria's dark-browed daughters,
And by the sails of Carthage brought
  Far o'er the southern waters.

12

Lavinium and Laurentum
  Had on their left their post,
With all the banners of the marsh,
  And banners of the coast.
Their leader was false Sextus,
  That wrought the deed of shame.
With restless pace and haggard face,
  To his last field he came.

Men said he saw strange visions,
  Which none beside might see;
And that strange sounds were in his ears
  Which none might hear but he.
A woman fair and stately,
  But pale as are the dead,
Oft through the watches of the night
  Sate spinning by his bed.
And as she plied the distaff,
  In a sweet voice and low,
She sang of great old houses,
  And fights fought long ago.
So spun she, and so sang she,
  Until the east was grey;
Then pointed to her bleeding breast,
  And shrieked and fled away.

13

But in the centre thickest
  Were ranged the shields of foes,
And from the centre loudest
  The cry of battle rose.
There Tiber marched and Pedum
  Beneath proud Tarquin's rule,
And Ferentinum of the rock,
  And Gabii of the pool.
There rode the Volscian succours:
  There, in a dark stern ring,
The Roman exiles gathered close
  Around the ancient king.
Though white as mount Soracte
  When winter nights are long, [belt,
His beard flowed down o'er mail and
  His heart and hand were strong:
Under his hoary eyebrows
  Still flashed forth quenchless rage;
And, if the lance shook in his gripe,
  'Twas more with hate than age.
Close at his side was Titus
  On an Apulian steed,
Titus, the yougest Tarquin
  Too good for such a breed.

14

Now on each side the leaders
  Gave signal for the charge;
And on each side the footmen
  Strode on with lance and targe;
And on each side the horsemen
  Struck their spurs deep in gore,
And front to front the armies
  Met with a mighty roar:
And under that great battle
  The earth with blood was red;
And, like the Pomptine fog at morn,
  The dust hung overhead;
And louder still and louder,
  Rose from the darkened field
The braying of the war-horns,
  The clang of sword and shield,
The rush of squadrons sweeping
  Like whirlwinds o'er the plain,
The shouting of the slayers,
  And screeching of the slain.

15

False Sextus rode out foremost:
  His look was high and bold;
His corslet was of bison's hide,
  Plated with steel and gold.
As glares the famished eagle
  From the Digentian rock,
On the choice lamb that bounds alone
  Before Bandusias flock,
Herminius glared on Sextus
  And came with eagle speed;
Herminius on black Auster,
  Brave champion on brave steed:
In his right hand the broadsword
  That kept the bridge so well,
And on his helm the crown he won
  When proud Fidenæ fell.
Woe to the maid whose lover
  Shall cross his path to-day!
False Sextus saw and trembled,
  And turned and fled away.
As turns, as flies the woodman
  In the Calabrian brake,
When through the reeds gleams the round eye
  Of that fell painted snake;
So turned, so fled, false Sextus,
  And hid him in the rear,
Behind the dark Lavinian ranks,
  Bristling with crest and spear,

16

Then far to north Æbutius,
  The Master of the Knights,
Gave Tubero of Norba
  To feed the Porcian kites.
Next under those red horse-hoofs
  Flaccus of Setia lay;
Better had he been pruning
  Among his elms that day.
Mamilius saw the slaughter,
  And tossed his golden crest,
And towards the Master of the Knights
  Through the thick battle pressed.

Æbutius smote Mamilius
  So fiercely on the shield,
That the great lord of Tusculum
  Well nigh rolled on the field.
Mamilius smote Æbutius,
  With a good aim and true,
Just where the neck and shoulder join,
    And pierced him through and through;
And brave Æbutius Elva
  Fell swooning to the ground;
But a thick wall of bucklers
  Encompassed him around.
His clients from the battle
  Bare him some little space;
And filled a helm from the dark lake,
  And bathed his brow and face;
And when at last he opened
  His swimming eyes to light,
Men say the earliest word he spake
  Was, " Friends, how goes the fight?".

17.

But meanwhile in the centre
  Great deeds of arms were wrought;
There Aulus the Dictator,
  And there Valerius fought.
Aulus, with his good broadsword,
  A bloody passage cleared
To where, amidst the thickest foes,
  He saw the long white beard.
Flat lighted that good broadsword
  Upon proud Tarquin's head.
He dropped the lance: he dropped the reins:
  He fell as fall the dead.
Down Aulus springs to slay him,
  With eyes like coals of fire;
But faster Titus hath sprung down,
  And hath bestrode his sire.
Latian captains, Roman knights,
  Fast down to earth they spring,
And hand to hand they fight on foot
  Around the ancient king.
First Titus gave tall Cæso
  A death-wound in the face;
Tall Cæso was the bravest man
  Of the brave Fabian race:
Aulus slew Rex of Gabii,
  The priest of Juno's shrine:
Valerius smote down Julius,
  Of Rome's great Julian line;
Julius, who left his mansion
  High on the Velian hill,
And through all turns of weal and woe
  Followed proud Tarquin still.
Now right across proud Tarquin
  A corpse was Julius laid;
And Titus groaned with rage and grief,
  And at Valerius made.
Valerius struck at Titus,
  And lopped off half his crest;
But Titus stabbed Valerius
  A span deep in the breast.
Like a mast snapped by the tempest,
  Valerius reeled and fell.
Ah! woe is me for the good house
  That loves the people well!
Then shouted loud the Latines;
  And with one rush they bore
The struggling Romans backward
  Three lances' length and more:
And up they took proud Tarquin,
  And laid him on a shield,
And four strong yeomen bare him,
  Still senseless, from the field.

18.

But fiercer grew the fighting
  Around Valerius dead;
For Titus dragged him by the foot,
  And Aulus by the head.
" On, Latines, on!" quoth Titus,
  " See how the rebels fly!"
" Romans stand firm!" quoth Aulus,
  " And win this fight or die!
They must not give Valerius
  To raven and to kite;
For aye Valerius loathed the wrong
  And aye upheld the right:
And for your wives and babies
  In the front rank he fell.
Now play the men for the good house
  That loves the people well!"

19.

Then tenfold round the body
  The roar of battle rose,
Like the roar of a burning forest
  When a strong north wind blows.
Now backward and now forward
  Rocked furiously the fray,
Till none could see Valerius,
  And none wist where he lay.
For shivered arms and ensigns
  Were heaped there in a mound,
And corpses stiff, and dying men
  That writhed and gnawed the ground;

And wounded horses kicking,
  And snorting purple foam :
Right well did such a couch befit
  A Consular of Rome.

20.

But north looked the Dictator ;
  North looked he long and hard ;
And spake to Caius Cossus.
  The Captain of his guard :
" Caius, of all the Romans
  Thou hast the keenest sight ; [dust
Say, what through yonder storm of
  Comes from the Latian right ? "

21.

Then answered Caius Cossus
  " I see an evil sight ;
The banner of proud Tusculum
  Comes from the Latian right ;
I see the plumed horsemen ;
  And far before the rest
I see the dark-grey charger,
  I see the purple vest ;
I see the golden helmet
  That shines far off like flame ;
So ever rides Mamilius,
  Prince of the Latian name."

22.

" Now hearken, Caius Cossus :
  Spring on thy horse's back ;
Ride as the wolves of Apennine
  Were all upon thy track ;
Haste to our southward battle ;
  And never draw thy rein
Until thou find Herminius,
  And bid him come amain."

23.

So Aulus spake, and turned him
  Again to that fierce strife ;
And Caius Cossus mounted,
  And rode for death and life.
Loud clanged beneath his horse-hoofs
  The helmets of the dead,
And many a curdling pool of blood
  Splashed him from heel to head.
So came he far to southward,
  Where fought the Roman host,
Against the banners of the marsh
  And banners of the coast.
Like corn before the sickle
  The stout Lavinians fell,
Beneath the edge of the true sword
  That kept the bridge so well.

24.

" Herminius ! Aulus greets thee ;
  He bids thee come with speed,
To help our central battle ;
  For sore is there our need.
There wars the youngest Tarquin,
  And there the Crest of Flame,
The Tusculan Mamilius,
  Prince of the Latian name.
Valerius hath fallen fighting
  In front of our array ;
And Aulus of the seventy fields
  Alone upholds the day."

25.

Herminius beat his bosom ;
  But never a word he spake.
He clapped his hand on Auster's
  mane ;
He gave the reins a shake,
Away, away, went Auster,
  Like an arrow from the bow :
Black Auster was the fleetest steed
  From Aufidus to Po.

26.

Right glad were all the Romans
  Who, in that hour of dread,
Against great odds bear up the war
  Around Valerius dead,
When from the South the cheering
  Rose with a mighty swell :
" Herminius comes, Herminius,
  Who kept the bridge so well ! "

27.

Mamilius spied Herminius,
  And dashed across the way.
" Herminius ! I have sought thee
  Through many a bloody day.
One of us two, Herminius,
  Shall never more go home.
I will lay on for Tusculum,
  And lay thou on for Rome ! "

28.

All round them paused the battle,
  While met in mortal fray
The Roman and Tusculan,
  The horses black and grey.
Herminius smote Mamilius
  Through breast-plate and through
    breast ;
And fast flowed out the purple blood
  Over the purple vest.

Mamilius smote Herminius
  Through head-piece and through head;
And side by side those chiefs of pride
  Together fell down dead.
Down fell they dead together
  In a great lake of gore;
And still stood all who saw them fall
  While men might count a score.

29.

Fast, fast, with heels wild spurning,
  The dark-grey charger fled:
He burst through ranks of fighting men,
  He sprang o'er heaps of dead:
His bridle far out-streaming,
  His flanks all blood and foam,
He sought the southern mountains,
  The mountains of his home.
The pass was steep and rugged,
  The wolves they howled and whined;
But he ran like a whirlwind up the pass,
  And he left the wolves behind.
Through many a startled hamlet
  Thundered his flying feet:
He rushed through the gate of Tusculum,
  He rushed up the long white street;
He rushed by tower and temple,
  And paused not from his race
Till he stood before his master's door
  In the stately market-place.
And straightway round him gathered,
  A pale and trembling crowd,
And when they knew him, cries of rage
  Brake forth, and wailing loud:
And women rent their tresses
  For their great prince's fall;
And old men girt on their old swords,
  And went to man the wall.

30.

But, like a graven image,
  Black Auster kept his place,
And ever wistfully he looked
  Into his master's face.
The raven-mane that daily,
  With pats and fond caresses,
The young Herminia washed and combed,
  And twined in even tresses,
And decked with coloured ribands
  From her own gay attire,
Hung sadly o'er her father's corpse
  In carnage and in mire.
Forth with a shout sprang Titus,
  And seized black Auster's rein.
Then Aulus sware a fearful oath,
  And ran at him amain.
"The furies of thy brother
  With me and mine abide,
If one of your accursed house
  Upon black Auster ride!"
As on an Alpine watch-tower
  From Heaven comes down the flame,
Full on the neck of Titus
  The blade of Aulus came:
And out the red blood spouted,
  In a wide arch and tall,
As spouts a fountain in the court,
  Of some rich Capuan's hall.
The knees of all the Latines
  Were loosened with dismay
When dead, on dead Herminius,
  The bravest Tarquin lay.

31.

And Aulus the Dictator
  Stroked Auster's raven mane,
With heed he looked into the girths,
  With heed unto the rein.
"Now bear me well, black Auster,
  Into yon thick array;
And thou and I will have revenge
  For thy good lord this day."

32.

So spake he; and was buckling
  Tighter black Auster's band,
When he was aware of a princely pair
  That rode at his right hand.
So like they were, no mortal
  Might one from other know:
White as snow their armour was;
  Their steeds were white as snow.
Never on earthly anvil
  Did such rare armour gleam;
And never did such gallant steeds
  Drink of an earthly stream.

33.

And all who saw them trembled,
  And pale grew every cheek;
And Aulus the Dictator
  Scarce gathered voice to speak.

"Say by what name men call you?
 What City is your home?
And wherefore ride ye in such guise
 Before the ranks of Rome!"

34.

"By many names men call us;
 In many lands we dwell;
Well Samothracia knows us;
 Cyrene knows us well.
Our house in gay Tarentum
 Is hung each morn with flowers:
High o'er the masts of Syracuse
 Our marble portal towers;
But by the proud Eurotas
 Is our dear native home;
And for the right we come to fight
 Before the ranks of Rome."

35.

So answered those strange horsemen,
 And each couched low his spear;
And forthwith all the ranks of Rome
 Were bold and of good cheer:
And on the thirty armies
 Came wonder and affright,
And Ardea wavered on the left,
 And Cora on the right.
"Rome to the charge!" cried Aulus;
 "The foe begins to yield!
Charge for the hearth of Vesta!
 Charge for the Golden Shield!
Let no man stop to plunder,
 But slay, and slay, and slay;
The Gods who live for ever
 Are on our side to-day."

36.

Then the fierce trumpet flourish
 From earth to heaven arose;
The kites know well the long stern swell
 That bids the Romans close.
Then the good sword of Aulus
 Was lifted up to slay:
Then, like a crag down Apennine
 Rushed Austur through the fray.
But under those strange horsemen
 Still thicker lay the slain;
And after those strange horses
 Black Auster toiled in vain.
Behind them Rome's long battle
 Came rolling on the foe,
Ensigns dancing wild above,
 Blades all in line below.

So comes the Po in flood-time
 Upon the Celtic plain:
So comes the squall, blacker than night,
 Upon the Adrian main.
Now, by our sire Quirinus,
 It was a goodly sight
To see the thirty standards
 Swept down the tide of flight,
So flies the spray of Adria
 When the black squall doth blow;
So corn-sheaves in the flood-time
 Spin down the whirling Po.
False Sextus to the mountains
 Turned first his horse's head;
And fast fled Ferentinum,
 And fast Lanuvium fled.
The horsemen of Nomentum
 Spurred hard out of the fray;
The footmen of Velitræ
 Threw shield and spear away.
And underfoot was trampled,
 Amidst the mud and gore,
The banner of proud Tusculum,
 That never stooped before:
And down went Flavius Faustus,
 Who led his stately ranks
From where the apple blossoms wave
 On Anio's echoing banks,
And Tullus of Arpinum,
 Chief of the Volscian aids,
And Mertus with the long fair curls,
 The love of Anxur's maids,
And the white head of Vulso,
 The great Arician seer,
And Nepos of Laurentum,
 The hunter of the deer;
And in the back false Sextus
 Felt the good Roman steel,
And wriggling in the dust he died,
 Like a worm beneath the wheel:
And fliers and pursuers
 Were mingled in a mass;
And far away the battle
 Went roaring through the pass.

37.

Sempronius Atratinus
 Sat in the Eastern Gate.
Beside him were three Fathers,
 Each in his chair of state;
Fabius, whose nine stout grandsons
 That day were in the field,

And Manlius, eldest of the Twelve
  Who keep the Golden Shield ;
And Sergius, the High Pontiff,
  For wisdom far renowned ;
In all Etruria's colleges
  Was no such Pontiff found.
And all around the portal,
  And high above the wall,
Stood a great throng of people,
  But sad and silent all ;
Young lads, and stooping elders
  That might not bear the mail,
Matrons with lips that quivered,
  And maids with faces pale.
Since the first gleam of daylight
  Sempronius had not ceased
To listen for the rushing
  Of horse-hoofs from the east.
The mist of eve was rising,
  The sun was hastening down,
When he was aware of a princely pair
  Fast pricking towards the town.
So like they were, man never
  Saw twins so like before ;
Red with gore their armour was,
  Their steeds were red with gore.

38.

" Hail to the great Asylum !
  Hail to the hill-tops seven !
Hail to the fire that burns for aye,
  And the shield that fell from heaven!
This day, by Lake Regillus,
  Under the Porcian height,
All in the lands of Tusculum
  Was fought a glorious fight.
To-morrow your Dictator
  Shall bring in triumph home
The spoils of thirty cities
  To deck the shrines of Rome ! "

39.

Then burst from that great concourse
  A shout that shook the towers,
And some ran north, and some ran south,
  Crying, " The day is ours ! "
But on rode these strange horsemen,
  With slow and lordly pace ;
And none who saw their bearing
  Durst ask their name or race.
On rode they to the Forum,
  While laurel-boughs and flowers, .
From house-tops and from windows,
  Fell on their crests in showers.

When they drew nigh to Vesta,
  They vaulted down amain,
And washed their horses in the well
  That springs by Vesta's fane.
And straight again they mounted,
  And rode to Vesta's door ;
Then, like a blast, away they passed,
  And no man saw them more.

40.

And all the people trembled,
  And pale grew every cheek ;
And Sergius the High Pontiff
  Alone found voice to speak :
" The Gods who live for ever
  Have fought for Rome to-day !
These be the Great Twin Brethren
  To whom the Dorians pray.
Back comes the chief in triumph,
  Who in the hour of fight,
Hath seen the Great Twin-Brethren
  In harness on his right.
Safe comes the ship to haven
  Through billows and through gales,
If once the Great Twin Brethren
  Sit shining on the sails.
Wherefore they washed their horses
  In Vesta's holy well,
Wherefore they rode to Vesta's door,
  I know, but may not tell.
Here, hard by Vesta's temple,
  Build we a stately dome
Unto the Great Twin Brethren
  Who fought so well for Rome.
And when the months returning
  Bring back this day of fight
The proud Ides of Quintilis,
  Marked evermore with white,
Unto the Great Twin Brethren
  Let all the people throng,
With chaplets and with offerings,
  With music and with song ;
And let the doors and windows
  Be hung with garlands all,
And let the Knights be summoned
  To Mars without the wall !
Thence let them ride in purple
  With joyous trumpet-sound,
Each mounted on his war-horse,
  And each with olive crowned ;
And pass in solemn order
  Before the sacred dome
Where dwell the Great Twin Brethren
  Who fought so well for Rome."

VIRGINIA.

A collection consisting exclusively of war-songs would give an imperfect, or rather an erroneous, notion of the spirit of the old Latin ballads. The Patricians, during more than a century after the expulsion of the Kings, held all the high military commands. A Plebeian, even though, like Lucius Siccius, he were distinguished by his valour and knowledge of war, could serve only in subordinate posts. A minstrel, therefore, who wished to celebrate the early triumphs of his country, could hardly take any but Patricians for his heroes. The warriors who are mentioned in the two preceding lays, Horatius, Lartius, Herminius, Aulus Posthumius, Æbutius Elva, Sempronius Atratinus, Valerius Poplicola, were all members of the dominant order; and a poet who was singing their praises, whatever his own political opinions might be, would naturally abstain from insulting the class to which they belonged, and from reflecting on the system which had placed such men at the head of the legions of the Commonwealth.

But there was a class of compositions in which the great families were by no means so courteously treated. No parts of early Roman history are richer with poetical colouring than those which relate to the long contest between the privileged houses and the commonalty. The population of Rome was, from a very early period, divided into hereditary castes, which, indeed, readily united to repel foreign enemies, but which regarded each other, during many years, with bitter animosity. Between those castes there was a barrier hardly less strong than that which, at Venice, parted the members of the Great Council from their countrymen. In some respects, indeed, the line which separated an Icilius or a Duilius from a Posthumius or a Fabius was even more deeply marked than that which separated the rower of a Gondola from a Contarini or a Morosini. At Venice the distinction was merely civil. At Rome it was both civil and religious. Among the grievances under which the Plebeians suffered, three were felt as peculiarly severe. They were excluded from the highest magistracies! they were excluded from all share in the public lands; and they were ground down to the dust by partial and barbarous legislation touching pecuniary contracts. The ruling class in Rome was a monied class; and it made and admintstered the laws with a view solely to its own interest. Thus the relation between lender and borrower was mixed up with the relation between sovereign and subject. The great men held a large portion of the community in dependence by means of advances at enormous usury. The law of debt, framed by creditors, and for the protection of creditors, was the most horrible that has ever been known among men. The liberty, and even the life, of the insolvent were at the mercy of the Patrician money-lenders. Children often became slaves in consequence of the misfortunes of their parents. The debtor was imprisoned, not in a public gaol under the care of impartial public functionaries, but in a private workhouse belonging to the creditor. Frightful stories were told respecting these dungeons. It was said that torture and brutal violation were common; that tight stocks, heavy chains, scanty measures of food, were used to punish wretches guilty of nothing but poverty; and that brave soldiers, whose breasts were covered with honourable scars, were often marked still more deeply on the back by the scourges of high-born usurers.

The Plebeians were, however, not wholly without constitutional rights. From an early period they had been admitted to some share of political power. They were enrolled in the centuries, and were allowed a share, considerable though not proportioned to their numerical strength, in the disposal of those high dignities from which they were themselves excluded. Thus their position bore some resemblance to that of the Irish Catholics during the interval between the year 1792 and the year 1829. The Plebeians had also the privilege of annually appointing officers, named Tribunes, who had no active share in the government of the Commonwealth, but who, by degrees, acquired a power which made them formidable even to the ablest and most resolute Consuls and Dictators. The person of the Tribune was inviolable; and, though he could directly effect little, he could obstruct everything.

During more than a century after the institution of the Tribuneship, the Commons struggled manfully for the removal of the grievances under which they laboured; and, in spite of many checks and reverses, succeeded in wringing concession after concession from the stubborn aristocracy. At length, in the year of the city 378, both parties mustered their whole strength for their last and most desperate conflict. The popular and active Tribune, Caius Licinius, proposed the three memorable laws which are called by his name, and which were intended to redress the three great evils of which the Plebeians complained. He was supported, with eminent ability and firmness, by his colleague, Lucius Sextius. The struggle appears to have been the fiercest that ever in any community terminated without an appeal to arms. If such a contest had raged in any Greek city, the streets would have run with blood. But, even in the paroxysms of faction, the Roman retained his gravity, his respect for law, and his tenderness for the lives of his fellow-citizens. Year after year Licinius and Sextius were re-elected Tribunes. Year after year, if the narrative which has come down to us is to be trusted, they continued to exert, to the full extent, the r power of stopping the whole machine of government. No curule magistrates could be chosen; no military muster could be held. We know too little of the state of Rome in those days to be able to conjecture how, during that long anarchy, the peace was kept, and ordinary justice administered between man and man. The animosity of both parties rose to the greatest height. The excitement, we may well suppose, would have been peculiarly intense at the annual election of Tribunes. On such occasions there can be little doubt that the great families did all that could be done, by threats and caresses, to break the union of the Plebeians. That union, however, proved indissoluble. At length the good cause triumphed. The Licinian laws were carried. Lucius Sextius was the first Plebian Consul. Caius Licinius the third.

The results of this great change were singularly happy and glorious. Two centuries of prosperity, harmony and victory followed the reconciliation of the orders. Men who remembered Rome engaged in waging petty wars almost within sight of the Capitol lived to see her the mistress of Italy. While the disabilities of the Plebians continued, she was scarcely able to maintain her ground against the Volscians and Hernicans. When those disabilities were removed, she rapidly became more than a match for Carthage and Macedon.

During the great Licinian contest the Plebeian poets were, doubtless, not silent. Even in modern times songs have been by no means without influence on public affairs; and we may therefore infer that, in a society where printing was unknown, and where books were rare, a pathetic or humorous party-ballad must have produced effects such as we can but faintly conceive. It is certain that satirical poems were common at Rome from a very early period. The rustics, who lived at a distance from the seat of government, and took little part in the strife of factions, gave vent to their petty local animosities in coarse Fescennine verse. The lampoons of the city were doubtless of a higher order; and their sting was early felt by the nobility. For in the Twelve Tables, long before the time of the Licinian laws, a severe punishment was denounced against the citizen who should compose or recite verses reflecting on another.* Satire is, indeed, the only sort of composition in which the Latin poets, whose works have come down to us, were not mere imitators of foreign models; and it is therefore the only sort of composition in which they have never been rivalled. It was not, like their tragedy, their comedy, their epic and lyric poetry, a hot-house plant which, in return for assiduous and skilful culture, gave only scanty and sickly fruits. It was hardy, and full of sap; and in all the various juices which it yielded might be distinguished the flavour of the Ausonian soil. "Satire," said Quintilian, with just pride, "is all our own." It sprang, in truth, naturally from the constitution of the Roman government and from the spirit of the Roman people; and, though it submitted to metrical rules derived from Greece, it retained to the last its essentially Roman character. Lucilius was the earliest satirist whose works were held in esteem under the Cæsars. But, many years before Lucilius was born, Nævius had been flung into a dungeon, and guarded there with circumstances of unusual rigour till the tribunes interfered in his behalf, on account of the bitter lines in which he had attacked the great Cæcilian family.† The genius and spirit of the Roman satirists survived the liberties of their country, and were not extinguished by the cruel despotism of the Julian and Flavian Emperors. The great poet who told the story of Domitian's turbot was the legitimate successor of those forgotten minstrels whose songs animated the factions of the infant Republic.

Those minstrels, as Niebuhr has remarked, appear to have generally taken the popular side. We can hardly be mistaken in supposing that, at the great crisis of the civil conflict, they employed themselves in versifying all the most powerful and virulent speeches of the Tribunes, and in heaping abuse on the chiefs of the aristocracy. Every personal defect, every domestic scandal, every tradition dishonourable to a noble house, would be sought out, brought into notice and exaggerated. The illustrious head of the aristocratical party, Marcus Furius Camillus, might perhaps be, in some measure, protected by his venerable age and by the memory of his great services to the State. But Appius Claudius Crassus enjoyed no such immunity. He was descended from a long line of ancestors distinguished by their haughty demeanour, and by the inflexibility with which they had withstood all the demands of the Plebeian order. While the political conduct and the deportment of the Claudian nobles drew upon them the fiercest public hatred, they were wanting, if any credit is due to the early history of Rome, in a class of qualities which, in a military Commonwealth, is sufficient to cover a multitude of offences. Several of them appear to have been eloquent, versed in civil business, and learned after the fashion of their age; but in war they were not distinguished by skill or valour. Some of them, as if conscious where their weakness lay, had, when filling the highest magistracies, taken internal administration as their department of public business, and left the military command to their colleagues.‡ One of them had been intrusted with an army, and had failed ignominiously.§ None of them had been honoured with a triumph. None of them had achieved any martial exploit, such as those by which Lucius Quinctius Cincinnatus, Titus Quinctius Capitolinus, Aulus Cornelius Cossus, and, above all, the great Camillus, had extorted the reluctant esteem of the multitude. During the Licinian conflict, Appius Claudius Crassus signalised himself by the ability and

---

* Cicero justly infers from this law, that there had been early Latin poets whose works had been lost before his time. "Quamquam id quidem etiam xii tabulæ declarant, condi jam tum solitum esse carmen, quod ne liceret fieri ad alterius injuriam lege sanxerunt."— *Tusc.* iv. 2.
† Plautus, Miles, Gloriosus. Aulus Gellius, iii. 3.'
‡ In the years of the city 260, 304, and 330. § In the year of the city 282.

severity with which he harangued against the two great agitators. He would naturally, therefore, be the favourite mark of the Plebeian satirists; nor would they have been at a loss to find a point on which he was open to attack.

His grandfather, called, like himself, Appius Claudius, had left a name as much detested as that of Sextus Tarquinius. This elder Appius had been Consul more than seventy years before the introduction of the Licinian laws. By availing himself of a singular crisis in public feeling, he had obtained the consent of the Commons to the abolition of the Tribuneship, and had been the Chief of that Council of Ten to which the whole direction of the State had been committed. In a few months his administration had become universally odious. It had been swept away by an irresistible outbreak of popular fury; and its memory was still held in abhorrence by the whole city. The immediate cause of the downfall of this execrable government was said to have been an attempt made by Appius Claudius on the chastity of a beautiful young girl of humble birth. The story ran, that the Decemvir, unable to succeed by bribes and solicitations, resorted to an outrageous act of tyranny. A vile dependant of the Claudian house laid claim to the damsel as his slave. The cause was brought before the tribunal of Appius. The wicked magistrate, in defiance of the clearest proofs, gave judgment for the claimant. But the girl's father, a brave soldier, saved her from servitude and dishonour by stabbing her to the heart in the sight of the whole Forum That blow was the signal for a general explosion. Camp and city rose at once; the Ten were pulled down; the Tribuneship was re-established; and Appius escaped the hands of the executioner only by a voluntary death.

It can hardly be doubted that a story so admirably adapted to the purposes both of the poet and of the demagogue would be eagerly seized upon by minstrels burning with hatred against the Patrician order, against the Claudian house, and especially against the grandson and namesake of the infamous Decemvir.

In order that the reader may judge fairly of these fragments of the lay of Virginia, he must imagine himself a Plebeian who has just voted for the re-election of Sextius and Licinius. All the power of the Patricians has been exerted to throw out the two great champions of the Commons. Every Posthumius, Æmilius and Cornelius has used his influence to the utmost. Debtors have been let out of the workhouses on condition of voting against the men of the people; clients have been posted to hiss and interrupt the favourite candidates; Appius Claudius Crassus has spoken with more than his usual eloquence and asperity: all has been in vain; Licinius and Sextius have a fifth time carried all the tribes; work is suspended; the booths are closed; the Plebeians bear on their shoulders the two champions of liberty through the Forum. Just at this moment it is announced that a popular poet, a zealous adherent of the Tribunes, has made a new song which will cut the Claudian family to the heart. The [crowd gathers round him, and calls on him to recite it. He takes his stand on the spot where, according to tradition, Virginia, more than seventy years ago, was seized by the pander of Appius, and he begins his story.

VIRGINIA.

Fragments of a Lay Sung in the Forum on the Day whereon Lucius Sextius Sextinus Lateranus and Caius Licinius Calvus Stolo were Elected Tribunes of the Commons the Fifth Time, in the Year of the City ccclxxxii.

Ye good men of the Commons, with loving hearts and true,
Who stand by the bold Tribunes that still have stood by you,
Come, make a circle round me, and mark my tale with care,
A tale of what Rome once hath borne, of what Rome yet may bear.

This is no Grecian fable, of fountains
  running wine,
Of maids with snaky tresses, or sailors
  turned to swine.
Here, in this very Forum, under the
  noonday sun,
In sight of all the people, the bloody
  deed was done.
Old men still creep among us who
  saw that fearful day,
Just seventy years and seven ago,
  when the wicked Ten bare sway.

Of all the wicked Ten still the names
  are held accursed,
And of all the wicked Ten Appius
  Claudius was the worst.
He stalked along the Forum like King
  Tarquin in his pride:
Twelve axes waited on him, six
  marching on a side ;
The townsmen shrank to right and
  left, and eyed askance with fear
His lowering brow, his curling mouth,
  which always seemed to sneer :
That brow of hate, that mouth of
  scorn, marks all the kindred still ;
For never was there Claudius yet but
  wished the Commons ill :
Nor lacks he fit attendance ; for close
  behind his heels,
With outstretched chin and crouching
  pace, the client Marcus steals,
His loins girt up to run with speed,
  be the errand what it may,
And the smile flickering on his cheek,
  for aught his lord may say.
Such varlets pimp and jest for hire
  among the lying Greeks :
Such varlets still are paid to hoot
  when brave Licinius speaks.
Where'er ye shed the honey, the
  buzzing flies will crowd ;
Where'er ye fling the carrion, the
  raven's croak is loud ;
Where'er down Tiber garbage flows,
  the greedy pike ye see ;
And wheresoe'er such lord is found,
  such client still will be.
Just then, as through one cloudless
  chink in a black stormy sky
Shines out the dewy morning-star, a
  fair young girl came by.
With her small tablets in her hand,
  and her satchel on her arm,
Home she went bounding from the
  school, nor dreamed of shame or harm
And past those dreaded axes she
  innocently ran,
With bright, frank brow, that had not
  learned to blush at gaze of man ;
And up the Sacred Street she turned,
  and, as she danced along,
She warbled gaily to herself lines of
  the good old song,
How for sport the princes came
  spurring from the camp,
And found Lucrece, combing the
  fleece, under the midnight lamp.
The maiden sang as sings the lark,
  when up he darts his flight,
From his nest in the green April corn,
  to meet the morning light ;
And Appius heard her sweet young
  voice, and saw her sweet young face,
And loved her with the accursed love
  of his accursed race,
And all along the Forum, and up the
  Sacred Street,
His vulture eye pursued the trip of
  those small glancing feet.
  *   *   *   *   *
Over the Alban mountains the light of
  morning broke ;
From all the roofs of the Seven Hills
  curled the thin wreathes of smoke :
The city gates were opened ; the
  Forum, all alive
With buyers and with sellers, was
  humming like a hive :
Blithely on brass and timber the
  craftsman's stroke was ringing,
And blithely o'er her panniers the
  market-girl was singing,
And blithely young Virginia came
  smiling from her home :
Ah! woe for young Virginia, the
  sweetest maid in Rome !
With her small tablets in her hand,
  and her satchel on her arm,
Forth she went bounding to the
  school, nor dreamed of shame or
  harm.
She crossed the Forum shining with
  stalls in alleys gay,
And just had reached the very spot
  whereon I stand this day,

When up the varlet Marcus came;
    not such as when erewhile
He crouched behind his patron's heels
    with the true client smile:
He came with lowering forehead,
    swollen features, and clenched fist,
And strode across Virginia's path,
    and caught her by the wrist.
Hard strove the frighted maiden, and
    screamed with look aghast;
And at her scream from right and left
    the folk came running fast;
The money-changer, Crispus, with his
    thin silver hairs,
And Hanno from the stately booth
    glittering with Punic wares,
And the strong smith Muræna, grasp-
    ing a half-forged brand,
And Volero, the flesher, his cleaver in
    his hand.
All came in wrath and wonder; for
    all knew that fair child;
And, as she passed them twice a day,
    all kissed their hands and smiled;
And the strong smith, Muræna, gave
    Marcus such a blow,
The caitiff reeled three paces back,
    and let the maiden go.
Yet glared he fiercely round him, and
    growled in harsh, fell tone,
"She's mine, and I will have her:
    I seek but for mine own:
She is my slave, born in my house,
    and stolen away and sold,
The year of the sore sickness, ere she
    was twelve hours old.
'Twas in the sad September, the
    month of wail and fright,
Two augurs were borne forth that
    morn; the Consul died ere night.
I wait on Appius Claudius; I waited
    on his sire:
Let him who works the client wrong
    beware the patron's ire!"

So spake the varlet Marcus; and
    dread and silence came
On all the people at the sound of the
    great Claudian name.
For then there was no Tribune to
    speak the word of might,
Which makes the rich man tremble,
    and guards the poor man's right

There was no brave Licinius, no
    honest Sextius then;
But all the city, in great fear,
    obeyed the wicked Ten.
Yet ere the varlet Marcus again might
    seize the maid,
Who clung tight to Muræna's skirt,
    and sobbed, and shrieked for aid,
Forth through the throng of gazers
    the young Icilius pressed,
And stamped his foot, and rent his
    gown, and smote upon his breast,
And sprang upon that column, by
    many a minstrel sung,
Whereon three mouldering helmets,
    three rusting swords, are hung,
And beckoned to the people, and in
    bold voice and clear
Poured thick and fast the burning
    words which tyrants quake to hear.

"Now, by your children's cradles,
    now, by your father's graves,
Be men to-day, Quirites, or be for
    ever slaves!
For this did Servius give us law?
    For this did Lucrece bleed?.
For this was the great vengeance
    wrought on Tarquin's evil seed?
For this did those false sons make
    red the axes of their sire?
For this did Scævola's right hand hiss
    in the Tuscan fire?
Shall the vile fox-earth awe the race
    that stormed the lion's den?
Shall we, who could not brook one
    lord, crouch to the wicked Ten?
Oh for that ancient spirit which
    curbed the Senate's will!
Oh for the tents which in old time
    whitened the Sacred Hill!
In those brave days our fathers stood
    firmly side by side;
They faced the Marcian fury; they
    tamed the Fabian pride:
They drove the fiercest Quinctius an
    outcast forth from Rome;
They sent the haughtiest Claudius
    with shivered fasces home.
But what their care bequeathed us
    our madness flung away:
All the ripe fruit of threescore years
    was blighted in a day.

G G

Exult, ye proud Patricians! The hard-fought fight is o'er.
We strove for honours—'twas in vain: for freedom—'tis no more.
No crier to the polling summons the eager throng;
No Tribune breathes the word of might that guards the weak from wrong.
Our very hearts, that were so high, sink down beneath your will.
Riches, and lands, and power, and state—ye have them:—keep them still.
Still keep the holy fillets; still keep the purple gown,
The axes, and the curule chair, the car, and laurel crown:
Still press us for your cohorts, and, when the fight is done,
Still fill your garners from the soil which our good swords have won.
Still, like a spreading ulcer, which leech-craft may not cure,
Let your foul usance eat away the substance of the poor.
Still let your haggard debtors bear all their fathers bore;
Still let your dens of torment be noisome as of yore;
No fire when Tiber freezes; no air in dog-star heat;
And store of rods for free-born backs, and holes for free-born feet.
Heap heavier still the fetters; bar closer still the grate;
Patient as sheep we yield us up unto your cruel hate.
But, by the Shades beneath us, and by the Gods above,
Add not unto your cruel hate your yet more cruel love!
Have ye not graceful ladies, whose spotless lineage springs
From Consuls, and High Pontifis, and ancient Alban kings?
Ladies, who deign not on our paths to set their tender feet,
Who from their cars look down with scorn upon the wondering street,
Who in Corinthian mirrors their own proud smiles behold,
And breathe of Capuan odours, and shine with Spanish gold

Then leave the poor Plebeian his single tie to life—
The sweet, sweet love of daughter, of sister, and of wife,
The gentle speech, the balm for all that his vexed soul endures,
The kiss, in which he half forgets even such a yoke as yours.
Still let the maiden's beauty swell the father's breast with pride;
Still let the bridegroom's arms infold an unpolluted bride.
Spare us the inexpiable wrong, the unutterable shame,
That turns the coward's heart to steel, the sluggard's blood to flame,
Lest, when our latest hope is fled, ye taste of our despair,
And learn by proof, in some wild hour, how much the wretched dare."

* * * *

Straightway Virginius led the maid a little space aside,
To where the reeking shambles stood, piled up with horn and hide,
Close to yon low dark archway, where, in a crimson flood,
Leaps down to the great sewer the gurgling stream of blood.
Hard by, a flesher on a block had laid his whittle down:
Virginius caught the whittle up, and hid it in his gown.
And then his eyes grew very dim, and his throat began to swell,
And in a hoarse, changed voice he spake, "Farewell, sweet child! Farewell!
Oh! how I loved my darling! Though stern I sometimes be,
To thee, thou know'st, I was not so. Who could be so to thee?
And how my darling loved me! How glad she was to hear
My footstep on the threshold when I came back last year!
And how she danced with pleasure to see my civic crown,
And took my sword, and hung it up, and brought me forth my gown!
Now, all those things are over—yes, all thy pretty ways,
Thy needlework, thy prattle, thy snatches of old lays;

And none will grieve when I go forth,
  or smile when I return,
Or watch beside the old man's bed,
  or weep upon his urn.
The house that was the happiest
  within the Roman walls,
The house that envied not the wealth
  of Capua's marble halls,
Now, for the brightness of thy smile,
  must have eternal gloom,
And for the music of thy voice, the
  silence of the tomb.
The time is come. See how he points
  his eager hand this way!
See how his eyes gloat on thy grief,
  like a kite's upon the prey!
With all his wit, he little deems, that,
  spurned, betrayed, bereft,
The father hath in his despair one
  fearful refuge left.
He little deems that in this hand I
  clutch what still can save
Thy gentle youth from taunts and
  blows, the portion of the slave;
Yea, and from nameless evil, that
  passeth taunt and blow—
Foul outrage which thou know'st not,
  which thou shalt never know.
Then clasp me round the neck once
  more, and give me one more
  kiss;
And now, mine own dear little girl,
  there is no way but this."
With that he lifted high the steel, and
  smote her in the side,
And in her blood she sank to earth,
  and with one sob she died.

Then, for a little moment, all people
  held their breath;
And through the crowded Forum was
  stillness as of death;
And in another moment brake forth
  from one and all
A cry as if the Volscians were coming
  o'er the wall.
Some with averted faces shrieking fled
  home amain;
Some ran to call a leech; and some
  ran to lift the slain:
Some felt her lips and little wrist, if
  life might there be found;
And some tore up their garments fast,
  and strove to stanch the wound.

In vain they ran, and felt, and
  stanched; for never truer blow
That good right arm had dealt in fight
  against a Volscian foe.

When Appius Claudius saw that deed,
  he shuddered and sank down,
And hid his face some little space
  with the corner of his gown,
Till, with white lips and bloodshot
  eyes, Virginius tottered nigh,
And stood before the judgment-seat,
  and held the knife on high.
"Oh! dwellers in the nether gloom,
  avengers of the slain,
By this dear blood I cry to you, do
  right between us twain;
And even as Appius Claudius hath
  dealt by me and mine,
Deal you by Appius Claudius and all
  the Claudian line!"
So spake the slayer of his child, and
  turned, and went his way;
But first he cast one haggard glance
  to where the body lay,
And writhed, and groaned a fearful
  groan, and then, with steadfast
  feet,
Strode right across the market-place
  unto the Sacred Street.

Then up sprang Appius Claudius:
  "Stop him; alive or dead!
Ten thousand pounds of copper to
  the man who brings his head."
He looked upon his clients; but
  none would work his will.
He looked upon his lictors; but they
  trembled and stood still.
And, as Virginius through the press
  his way in silence cleft,
Even the mighty multitude fell back
  to right and left.
And he hath passed in safety unto
  his woeful home.
And there ta'en horse to tell the camp
  what deeds are done in Rome.

By this the flood of people was
  swollen from every side,
And streets and porches round were
  filled with o'erflowing tide;
And close around the body gathered
  a little train

Of them that were the nearest and
  dearest to the slain.
They brought a bier, and hung it with
  many a cypress crown,
And gently they uplifted her, and
  gently laid her down.
The face of Appius Claudius wore the
  Claudian scowl and sneer,
And in the Claudian note he cried,
  "What doth this rabble here?
Have they no crafts to mind at home,
  that hitherward they stray?
Ho! lictors, clear the market-place,
  and fetch the corpse away!"
Till then the voice of pity and fury
  was not loud;
But a deep sullen murmur wandered
  among the crowd,
Like the moaning noise that goes
  before the whirlwind on the deep,
Or the growl of a fierce watch-dog but
  half aroused from sleep.
But when the lictors at that word, tall
  yeomen all and strong,
Each with his axe and sheaf of twigs,
  went down into the throng,
Those old men say, who saw that day
  of sorrow and of sin,
That in the Roman Forum was never
  such a din.
The wailing, hooting, cursing, the
  howls of grief and hate,
Were heard beyond the Pincian Hill,
  beyond the Latin Gate.
But close around the body, where
  stood the little train
Of them that were the nearest and
  dearest to the slain,
No cries were there, but teeth set fast,
  low whispers, and black frowns,
And breaking up of benches, and
  girding up of gowns.
'Twas well the lictors might not pierce
  to where the maiden lay,
Else surely had they been all twelve
  torn limb from limb that day.
Right glad they were to struggle back,
  blood streaming from their heads,
With axes all in splinters, and raiment
  all in shreds.
Then Appius Claudius gnawed his lip,
  and the blood left his cheek;
And thrice he beckoned with his hand,
  and thrice he strove to speak;
And thrice the tossing Forum set up
  a frightful yell;
"See, see thou dog! what thou hast
  done; and hide thy shame in hell!
Thou that would'st make our maidens
  slaves must first make slaves of men.
Tribunes! Hurrah for Tribunes! Down
  with the wicked Ten!"
And straightway, thick as hailstones,
  came whizzing through the air
Pebbles, and bricks, and potsherds,
  all round the curule chair:
And upon Appius Claudius great fear
  and trembling came;
For never was a Claudius yet brave
  against aught but shame.
Though the great houses love us not,
  we own, to do them right,
That the great houses, all save one,
  have borne them well in fight.
Still Caius of Corioli, his triumphs,
  and his wrongs,
His vengeance, and his mercy, live in
  our camp-fire songs.
Beneath the yoke of Furius oft have
  Gaul and Tuscan bowed;
And Rome may bear the pride of him
  of whom herself is proud.
But evermore a Claudius shrinks from
  a stricken field.
And changes colour like a maid at
  sight of sword and shield.
The Claudian triumphs all were won
  within the city towers;
The Claudian yoke was never pressed
  on any necks but ours.
A Cossus, like a wild cat, springs ever
  at the face;
A Fabius rushes like a boar against
  the shouting chase;
But the vile Claudian litter, raging
  with currish spite,
Still yelps and snaps at those who run,
  still runs from those who smite.
So now 't was seen of Appius. When
  stones began to fly,
He shook, and crouched, and wrung
  his hands, and smote upon his thigh.
"Kind clients, honest lictors, stand
  by me in this fray!
Must I be torn in pieces? Home,
  home, the nearest way!"
While yet he spake, and looked around
  with a bewildered stare;

Four sturdy lictors put their necks
   beneath the curule chair;
And fourscore clients on the left, and
   fourscore on the right,
Arrayed themselves with swords and
   staves, and loins girt up for fight.
But, though without or staff or sword,
   so furious was the throng,
That scarce the train with might and
   main could bring their lord along.
Twelve times the crowd made at him;
   five time they seized his gown;
Small chance was his to rise again, if
   once they got him down:
And sharper came the pelting; and
   evermore the yell—
"Tribunes! we will have Tribunes!"
   —rose with a louder swell:
And the chair tossed as tosses a bark
   with tattered sail
When raves the Adriatic beneath an
   eastern gale,
When the Calabrian sea-marks are
   lost in clouds of spume,
And the great Thunder-Cape has
   donned his veil of inky g'oom.
One stone hit Appius in the mouth,
   and one beneath the ear;
And ere he reached Mount Palatine,
   he swooned with pain and fear.
His cursed head, that he was wont to
   hold so high with pride,
Now, like a drunken man's, hung
   down, and swayed from side to
   side;
And when his stout retainers had
   brought him to his door,
His face and neck were all one cake
   of filth and clotted gore.
As Appius Claudius was that day, so
   may his grandson be.
God send Rome one such other sight,
   and send me there to see!

THE PROPHECY OF CAPYS.

It can hardly be necessary to remind any reader that, according to the popular tradition, Romulus, after he had slain his grand-uncle Amulius, and restored his grandfather Numitor, determined to quit Alba, the hereditary domain of the Sylvian princes, and to found a new city. The Gods, it was added, vouchsafed the clearest signs of the favour with which they regarded the enterprise, and of the high destinies reserved for the young colony.

This event was likely to be a favourite theme of the old Latin minstrels. They would naturally attribute the project of Romulus to some divine intimation of the power and prosperity which it was decreed that his city should attain. They would probably introduce seers foretelling the victories of unborn Consuls and Dictators, and the last great victory would generally occupy the most conspicuous place in the prediction. There is nothing strange in the supposition that the poet who was employed to celebrate the first great triumph of the Romans over the Greeks might throw his song of exultation into this form.

The occasion was one likely to excite the strongest feelings of national pride. A great outrage had been followed by a great retribution. Seven years before this time, Lucius Posthumius Megellus, who sprang from one of the noblest houses of Rome, and had been thrice Consul, was sent ambassador to Tarentum, with charge to demand reparation for grievous injuries. The Tarentines gave him audience in their theatre, where he addressed them in such Greek as he could command, which, we may well believe, was not exactly such as Cineas would have spoken. An exquisite sense of the ridiculous belonged to the Greek character; and closely connected with this faculty was a strong propensity to flippancy and impertinence. When Posthumius placed an accent wrong, his hearers burst into a laugh. When he remonstrated, they hooted him, and called him barbarian; and at length hissed him off the stage as if he had been a bad actor. As the grave Roman retired, a buffoon, who, from his constant drunkenness, was nicknamed the Pint-pot, came up with gestures of the grossest indecency, and bespattered the senatorial gown with filth. Posthumius turned round to the multitude, and held up the gown, as if appealing to the universal law of nations. The sight only increased the insolence of the Tarentines. They clapped their hands, and set up a shout of laughter which shook the theatre. "Men of Tarentum," said Posthumius, "it will take not a little blood to wash this gown." *

Rome, in consequence of this insult, declared war against the Tarentines. The Tarentines sought for allies beyond the Ionian Sea. Pyrrhus, king of Epirus, came to their help with a large army; and, for the first time the two great nations of antiquity were fairly matched against each other.

The fame of Greece in arms, as well as in arts, was then at the height. Half a century earlier, the career of Alexander had excited the admiration and terror of all nations from the Ganges to the Pillars of Hercules. Royal houses, founded by Macedonian captains, still reigned at Antioch and Alexandria. That barbarian warriors, led by barbarian chiefs, should win a pitched battle against Greek valour guided by Greek science, seemed as incredible as it would now seem that the Burmese or the Siamese should, in the open plain, put to flight an equal number of the best English troops. The Tarentines were convinced that their countrymen were irresistible in war; and this conviction had emboldened them to treat with the grossest indignity one whom they regarded as the representative of an inferior race. Of the Greek generals then living, Pyrrhus was indisputably the first. Among the troops who were trained in the Greek discipline, his Epirotes ranked high. His expedition to Italy was a turning-point in the history of the world. He found there a people who, far inferior to the Athenians and Corinthians in the fine arts, in the speculative sciences, and in all the refinements of life, were the best soldiers on the face of the earth. Their arms, their graduations of rank, their order of battle, their method of intrenchment, were all of Latian origin, and had all been gradually brought near to perfection, not by the study of foreign models, but by the genius and experience of many generations of great native commanders. The first words which broke from the king, when his practised eye had surveyed the Roman encampment, were full of meaning:—"These barbarians," he said, "have nothing barbarous in their military arrrangements." He was at first victorious; for his own talents were superior to those of the captains who were opposed to him; and the Romans were not prepared for the onset of the elephants of the East, which were then for the first time seen in Italy—moving mountains, with long snakes for hands.† But the victories of the Epirotes were fiercely disputed, dearly purchased, and altogether unprofitable. At length, Manius Curius Dentatus, who had in his first consulship won two triumphs, was again placed at the head of the Roman Commonwealth, and sent to encounter the invaders. A great battle was fought near Beneventum. Pyrrhus was completely defeated. He re-passed the sea; and the world learned with amazement, that a people had been discovered, who, in fair fighting, were superior to the best troops that had been drilled on the system of Parmenio and Antigonus.

The conquerors had a good right to exult in their success; for their glory was all their own. They had not learned from their enemy how to conquer him. It was with their own national arms, and in their own national battle-array, that they had overcome weapons and tactics long believed to be invincible. The pilum and the broadsword had vanquished the Macedonian spear. The legion had broken the Mocedonian phalanx. Even the elephants,

---

* Dion. Hal. De Legationibus.
† *Anguimanus* is the old Latin epithet for an elephant. Lucretius, ii. 538, v. 1302.

when the surprise produced by their first appearance was over, could cause no disorder in the steady yet flexible battalions of Rome.

It is said by Florus, and may easily be believed, that the triumph far surpassed in magnificence any that Rome had previously seen. The only spoils which Papirius Cursor and Fabius Maximus could exhibit were flocks and herds, waggons of rude structure, and heaps of spears and helmets. But now, for the first time, the riches of Asia and the arts of Greece adorned a Roman pageant. Plate, fine stuffs, costly furniture, rare animals, exquisite paintings and sculptures, formed part of the procession. At the banquet would be assembled a crowd of warriors and statesmen, among whom Manius Curius Dentatus would take the highest room. Caius Fabricius Luscinus, then, after two Consulships and two triumphs, Censor of the Commonwealth, would doubtless occupy a place of honour at the board. In situations less conspicuous probably lay some of those who were, a few years later, the terror of Carthage; Caius Duilius, the founder of the maritime greatness of his country; Marcus Atilius Regulus, who owned to defeat a renown far higher than that which he had derived from his victories; and Caius Lutatius Catulus, who, while suffering from a grievous wound, fought the great battle of the Ægates, and brought the first Punic war to a triumphant close. It is impossible to recount the names of these eminent citizens, without reflecting that they were all, without exception, Plebeians, and would, but for the ever-memorable struggle maintained by Caius Licinius and Lucius Sextius, have been doomed to hide in obscurity, or to waste in civil broils the capacity and energy which prevailed against Pyrrhus and Hamilcar.

On such a day we may suppose that the patriotic enthusiasm of a Latin poet would vent itself in reiterated shouts of *Io triumphe*, such as were uttered by Horace on a far less exciting occasion, and in boasts resembling those which Virgil, two hundred and fifty years later, put into the mouth of Anchises. The superiority of some foreign nations, and especially of the Greeks, in the lazy arts of peace, would be admitted with disdainful candour; but preeminence in all the qualities which fit a people to subdue and govern mankind would be claimed for the Romans.

The following lay belongs to the latest age of Latin ballad-poetry. Nævius and Livius Andronicus were probably among the children whose mothers held them up to see the chariot of Curius go by. The minstrel who sang on that day might possibly have lived to read the first hexameters of Ennius, and to see the first comedies of Plautus. His poem, as might be expected, shows a much wider acquaintance with the geography, manners, and productions of remote nations, than would have been found in compositions of the age of Camillus. But he troubles himself little about dates; and having heard travellers talk with admiration of the Colossus of Rhodes, and of the structures and gardens with which the Macedonian kings of Syria had embellished their residence on the banks of the Orontes, he has never thought of inquiring whether these things existed in the age of Romulus.

THE PROPHECY OF CAPYS.

A Lay Sung at the Banquet in the Capitol, on the Day whereon Manius Curius Dentatus, a Second Time Consul, Triumphed over King Pyrrhus and the Tarentines, in the Year of the City cccclxxix.

I.

Now slain is King Amulius,
  Of the great Sylvian line,
Who reigned in Alba Longa,
  On the throne of Aventine.
Slain is the Pontiff Camers,
  Who spake the words of doom
"The children to the Tiber,
  The mother to the tomb."

2.

In Alba's lake no fisher
　His net to-day is flinging:
On the dark rind of Alba's oaks
　To-day no axe is ringing:
The yoke hangs o'er the manger:
　The scythe lies in the hay:
Through all the Alban villages
　No work is done to-day.

3.

And every Alban burgher
　Hath donned his whitest gown;
And every head in Alba
　Weareth a poplar crown:
And every Alban door-post
　With boughs and flowers is gay:
For to-day the dead are living;
　The lost are found to-day.

4.

They were doomed by a bloody king;
　They were doomed by a lying priest:
They were cast on the raging flood:
　They were tracked by the raging beast;
Raging beast and raging flood
　Alike have spared the prey;
And to-day the dead are living:
　The lost are found to-day.

5.

The troubled river knew them,
　And smoothed his yellow foam,
And gently rocked the cradle
　That bore the fate of Rome.
The ravening she-wolf knew them,
　And licked them o'er and o'er,
And gave them of her own fierce milk,
　Rich with raw flesh and gore.
Twenty winters, twenty springs,
　Since then have rolled away;
And to-day the dead are living:
　The lost are found to-day.

6.

Blithe it was to see the twins,
　Right goodly youths and tall,
Marching from Alba Longa
　To their old grandsire's hall.
Along their path fresh garlands
　Are hung from tree to tree:
Before them stride the pipers,
　Piping a note of glee.

7.

On the right goes Romulus,
　With arms to the elbows red,
And in his hand a broadsword,
　And on the blade a head—
A head in an iron helmet,
　With horse-hair hanging down,
A shaggy head, a swarthy head,
　Fixed in a ghastly frown—
The head of King Amulius
　Of the great Sylvian line,
Who reigned in Alba Longa,
　On the throne of Aventine.

8.

On the left side goes Remus,
　With wrist and fingers red,
And in his hand a boar-spear,
　And on the point a head—
A wrinkled head and aged,
　With silver beard and hair,
And holy fillets round it,
　Such as the pontiffs wear—
The head of ancient Camers,
　Who spake the words of doom:
"The children to the Tiber;
　The mother to the tomb."

9.

Two and two behind the twins
　Their trusty comrades go,
Four and forty valiant men,
　With club, and axe, and bow.
On each side every hamlet
　Pours fourth its joyous crowd,
Shouting lads and baying dogs,
　And children laughing loud,
And old men weeping fondly
　As Rhea's boys go by,
And maids who shriek to see the heads,
　Yet shrieking, press more nigh.

10.

So they marched along the lake;
　They marched by fold and stall,
By corn-field and by vineyard,
　Unto the old man's hall.

11.

In the hall-gate sate Capys,
　Capys, the sightless seer;
From head to foot he trembled
　As Romulus drew near.

And up stood stiff his thin white hair,
  And his blind eyes flashed fire :
"Hail ! foster child of the wonderous
    nurse !
  Hail ! son of the wonderous sire !

12.

"But thou—what dost thou here
  In the old man's peaceful hall?
What doth the eagle in the coop,
  The bison in the stall?
Our corn fills many a garner ;
  Our vines clasp many a tree ;
Our flocks are white on many a hill ;
  But these are not for thee.

13.

"For thee no treasure ripens
  In the Tartessian mine :
For thee no ship brings precious bales
  Across the Libyan brine :
Thou shalt not drink from amber ;
  Thou shalt not rest on down ;
Arabia shall not steep thy locks,
  Nor Sidon tinge thy gown.

14.

"Leave gold and myrrh and jewels,
  Rich table and soft bed,
To them who of man's seed are born,
  Whom woman's milk hath fed.
Thou wast not made for lucre,
  For pleasure, nor for rest ;
Thou, that art sprung from the War-
    god's loins,   [breast.
  And hast tugged at the she wolf's

15.

"From sunrise unto sunset
  All earth shall hear thy fame :
A glorious city thou shalt build,
  And name it by thy name :
And there, unquenched through ages,
  Like Vesta's sacred fire,
Shall live the spirit of thy nurse,
  The spirit of thy sire.

16.

"The ox toils through the furrow,
  Obedient to the goad ;
The patient ass, up flinty paths,
  Plods with his weary load :
With whine and bound the spaniel
  His master's whistle hears ;
And the sheep yields her patiently
  To the loud clashing shears.

17.

"But thy nurse will hear no master,
  Thy nurse will bear no load ;
And woe to them that shear her,
  And woe to them that goad !
When all the pack, loud baying,
  Her bloody lair surrounds,
She dies in silence, biting hard,
  Amidst the dying hounds.

18.

"Pomona loves the orchard ;
  And Liber loves the vine ;
And Pales loves the straw-built shed
  Warm with the breath of kine ;
And Venus loves the whispers
  Of plighted youth and maid,
In April's ivory moonlight
  Beneath the chestnut shade.

19.

"But thy father loves the clashing
  Of broadsword and of shield :
He loves to drink the stream that reeks
  From the fresh battle-field :
He smiles a smile more dreadful
  Than his own dreadful frown,
When he sees the thick black cloud
  of smoke
Go up from the conquered town.

20.

"And such as is the War-god,
  The author of thy line,
And such as she who suckles thee,
  Even such be thou and thine.
Leave to the soft Campanian
  His baths and his perfumes ;
Leave to the sordid race of Tyre
  Their dyeing-vats and looms :
Leave to the sons of Carthage
  The rudder and the oar :
Leave to the Greek his marble
    Nymphs
  And scrolls of worthy lore.

21.

"Thine, Roman, is the pilum :
  Roman, the sword is thine,
The even trench, the bristling mound,
  The legion's ordered line ;
And thine the wheels of triumph,
  Which with their laurelled train
Move slowly up the shouting streets
  To Jove's eternal fane.

22.

"Beneath thy yoke the Volscian
  Shall vail his lofty brow:
Soft Capua's curled revellers
  Before thy chairs shall bow:
The Lucumoes of Arnus
  Shall quake thy rods to see; [steel
And the proud Samnite's heart of
  Shall yield to only thee.

23.

"The Gaul shall come against thee
  From the land of snow and night;
Thou shalt give his fair-haired armies
  To the raven and the kite.

24.

"The Greek shall come against thee,
  The conqueror of the East.
Beside him stalks to battle
  The huge earth-shaking beast,
The beast on whom the castle
  With all its guards doth stand,
The beast who hath between his eyes
  The serpent for a hand.
First march the bold Epirotes,
  Wedged close with shield and spear;
And the ranks of false Tarentum
  Are glittering in the rear.

25.

"The ranks of false Tarentum
  Like hunted sheep shall fly:
In vain the bold Epirotes
  Shall round their standards die:
And Apennine's grey vultures
  Shall have a noble feast
On the fat and the eyes
  Of the huge earth-shaking beast.

26.

"Hurrah! for the good weapons
  That keep the War-god's land.
Hurrah! for Rome's stout pilum
  In a stout Roman hand.
Hurrah! for Rome's short broadsword,
  That through the thick array
Of levelled spears and serried shields
  Hews deep its gory way.

27.

"Hurrah! for the great triumph
  That stretches many a mile.
Hurrah! for the wan captives
  That pass in endless file.
Ho! bold Epirotes, whither
  Hath the Red King ta'en flight?
Ho! dogs of false Tarentum,
  Is not the gown washed white?

28.

"Hurrah! for the great triumph
  That stretches many a mile.
"Hurrah! for the rich dye of Tyre,
  And the fine web of Nile,
The helmets gay with plumage
  Torn from the pheasant's wings,
The belts set thick with starry gems
  That shone on Indian kings,
The urns of massy silver,
  The goblets rough with gold,
The many-coloured tablets bright
  With loves and wars of old,
The stone that breathes and struggles,
  The Brass that seems to speak;—
Such cunning they who dwell on high
  Have given unto the Greek.

29.

"Hurrah! for Manius Curius,
  The bravest son of Rome,
Thrice in utmost need sent forth,
  Thrice drawn in triumph home.
Weave, weave, for Manius Curius
  The third embroidered gown:
Make ready the third lofty car,
  And twine the third green crown;
And yoke the steeds of Rosea
  With necks like a bended bow;
And deck the bull, Mevania's bull,
  The bull as white as snow.

30.

"Blest and thrice blest the Roman
  Who sees Rome's brightest day,
Who sees that long victorious pomp
  Wind down the Sacred Way,
And through the bellowing Forum,
  And round the Suppliant's Grove,
Up to the everlasting gates
  Of Capitolian Jove.

31.

"Then where, o'er two bright havens,
  The towers of Corinth frown;
Where the gigantic King of Day
  On his own Rhodes look down;
Where soft Orontes murmurs
  Beneath the laurel shades;
Where Nile reflects the endless length
  Of dark-red colonnades;

Where in the still deep water,
  Sheltered from waves and blasts,
Bristles the dusky forest
  Of Byrsa's thousand masts;
Where fur-clad hunters wander
  Amidst the northern ice;
Where through the sand of morning-
  The camel bears the spice;   [land
Where Atlas flings his shadow
  Far o'er the western foam,
Shall be great fear on all who hear
  The mighty name of Rome."

IVRY:
A Song of the Huguenots.

Now glory to the Lord of Hosts,
  from whom all glories are!
And glory to our Sovereign Liege,
  King Henry of Navarre!
Now let there be the merry sound of
  music and of dance,
Through thy corn-fields green, and
  sunny vines, oh pleasant land of
  France!
And thou, Rochelle, our own Rochelle,
  proud city of the waters,
Again let rapture light the eyes of all
  thy mourning daughters.
As thou wert constant in our ills, be
  joyous in our joy,
For cold, and stiff, and still are they
  who wrought thy walls annoy.
Hurrah! Hurrah! a single field hath
  turned the chance of war,
Hurrah! Hurrah! for Ivry, and
  Henry of Navarre.

Oh! how our hearts were beating,
  when, at the dawn of day,
We saw the army of the League
  drawn out in long array;
With all its priest-led citizens, and
  all its rebel peers,
And Appenzel's stout infantry, and
  Egmont's Flemish spears.
There rode the brood of false Lorraine,
  the curses of our land;
And dark Mayenne was in the midst,
  a truncheon in his hand:
And, as we looked on them, we
  thought of Seine's empurpled flood.
And good Coligni's hoary hair all
  dabbled with his blood;
And we cried unto the living God,
  who rules the fate of war,
To fight for His own holy name, and
  Henry of Navarre.

The King is come to marshal us, in
  all his armour drest,
And he has bound a snow white plume
  upon his gallant crest.
He looked upon his people, and a
  tear was in his eye;
He looked upon the traitors, and his
  glance was stern and high.
Right graciously he smiled on us, as
  rolled from wing to wing,
Down all our line, a deafening shout,
  "God save our Lord the King!"
" And if my standard-bearer fall, as
  fall full well he may, [bloody fray,
For never saw I promise yet of such a
Press where ye see my white plume
  shine, amidst the ranks of war,
And be your oriflamme to-day the
  helmet of Navarre."

Hurrah! the foes are moving. Hark
  to the mingled din
Of fife, and steed, and trump, and
  drum, and roaring culverin.
The fiery Duke is pricking fast across
  Saint André's plain,
With all the hireling chivalry of
  Guelders and Almayne.
Now by the lips of those ye love, fair
  gentlemen of France,
Charge for the golden lilies— upon
  them with the lance.
A thousand spurs are striking deep, a
  thousand spears in rest,
A thousand knights are pressing close
  behind the snow-white crest;
And in they burst, and on they rushed,
  while like a guiding star,
Amidst the thickest carnage blazed
  the helmet of Navarre.

Now, God be praised, the day is ours.
  Mayenne hath turned his rein.
D'Aumale hath cried for quarter The
  Flemish count is slain.
Their ranks are breaking like thin
  clouds before a Biscay gale;

The field is heaped with bleeding
  steeds, and flags, and c'oven mail.
And then we thought on vengeance,
  and, all along our van,
"Remember St. Bartholomew," was
  passed from man to man.
But out spake gentle Henry, "No
  Frenchman is my foe :
Down, down with every foreigner,
  but let your brethren go."
Oh! was there ever such a knight in
  friendship or in war,
As our Sovereign Lord, King Henry,
  the soldier of Navarre?
Right well fought all the Frenchmen
  who fought for France to-day ;
And many a lordly banner God gave
  them for a prey.   [best in fight ;
But we of the religion have borne us
And the good Lord of Rosny has
  ta'en the cornet white.
Our own true Maximilian the cornet
  white hath ta'en,
The cornet white with crosses black,
  the flag of false Lorraine.
Up with it high ; unfurl it wide ; that
  all the host may know

How God hath humbled the proud
  house which wrought His church
  such woe.
Then on the ground, while trumpets
  sound their loudest point of war,
Fling the red shreds, a footcloth meet
  for Henry of Navarre.

Ho! maidens of Vienna ; Ho! ma-
  trons of Lucerne ;
Weep, weep, and rend your hair for
  those who never shall return.
Ho! Philip, send, for charity, thy
  Mexican pistoles,
That Antwerp monks may sing a
  mass for thy poor spearmen's souls.
Ho! gallant nobles of the League,
  look that your arms be bright ;
Ho! burghers of Saint Genevieve,
  keep watch and ward to-night.
For our God hath crushed the tyrant,
  our God hath raised the slave,
And mocked the counsel of the wise,
  and the valour of the brave.
Then glory to His holy name, from
  whom all glories are ;
And glory to our Sovereign Lord,
  King Henry of Navarre.   1824.

THE ARMADA.
A Fragment.

ATTEND, all ye who list to hear our
  noble England's praise ;
I tell of the thrice famous deeds she
  wrought in ancient days,
When that great fleet invincible
  against her bore in vain
The richest spoils of Mexico, the
  stoutest hearts of Spain.

It was about the lovely close of a
  warm summer day,
There came a gallant merchant-ship
  full sail to Plymouth Bay ;
Her crew hath seen Castile's black
  fleet, beyond Aurigny's isle,
At earliest twilight, on the waves lie
  heaving many a mile.
At sunrise she escaped their van, by
  God's especial grace ;
And the tall Pinta, till the noon, had
  held her close in chase.
Forthwith a guard at every gun was
  placed along the wall ;

The beacon blazed upon the roof of
  Edgecumbe's lofty hall ;
Many a light fishing-bark put out to
  pry along the coast,
And with loose rein and bloody spur
  rode inland many a post.
With his white hair unbonneted, the
  stout old sheriff comes ;
Behind him march the halberdiers ;
  before him sound the drums ;
His yeomen round the market cross
  make clear an ample space ;
For there behoves him to set up the
  standard of Her Grace.
And haughtily the trumpets peal, and
  gaily dance the bells,
As slow upon the labouring wind the
  royal blazon swells.
Look how the Lion of the sea lifts up
  his ancient crown,
And underneath his deadly paw treads
  the gay lilies down.

THE ARMADA.

So stalked he when he turned to flight,
  on that famed Picard field,
Bohemia's plume, and Genoa's bow,
  and Cæsar's eagle shield.
So glared he when at Agincourt in
  wrath he turned to bay,
And crushed and torn beneath his
  claws the princely hunters lay.
Ho! strike the flagstaff deep Sir Knight:
  ho! scatter flowers, fair maids:
Ho! gunners, fire a loud salute: ho!
  gallants, draw your blades:
Thou sun, shine on her joyously; ye
  breezes, waft her wide;
Our glorious SEMPER EADEM, the
  banner of our pride.

The freshening breeze of eve unfurled
  that banner's massy fold;
The parting gleam of sunshine kissed
  that haughty scroll of gold;
Night sank upon the dusky beach,
  and on the purple sea,
Such night in England ne'er had been,
  nor e'er again shall be.
From Eddystone to Berwick bounds,
  from Lynn to Milford Bay,
That time of slumber was as bright
  and busy as the day;
For swift to east and swift to west the
  ghastly war-flame spread,
High on St. Michael's Mount it shone:
  it shone on Beachy Head.
Far on the deep the Spaniard saw,
  along each southern shire,
Cape beyond cape, in endless range,
  those twinkling points of fire.
The fisher left his skiff to rock on
  Tamar's glittering waves:
The rugged miners poured to war from
  Mendip's sunless caves!
O'er Longleat's towers, o'er Cran-
  bourne's oaks, the fiery herald
  flew:
He roused the shepherds of Stone-
  henge, the rangers of Beaulieu.
Right sharp and quick the bells all
  night rang out from Bristol town,
And ere the day three hundred horse
  had met on Clifton down;
The sentinel on Whitehall gate looked
  forth into the night,
And saw o'erhanging Richmond Hill
  the streak of blood-red light,
Then bugle's note and cannon's roar
  the deathlike silence broke,
And with one start, and with one cry,
  the royal city woke.
At once on all her stately gates arose
  the answering fires;
At once the wild alarum clashed from
  all her reeling spires;
From all the batteries of the Tower
  pealed loud the voice of fear;
And all the thousand masts of Thames
  sent back a louder cheer;
And from the furthest wards was heard
  the rush of hurrying feet,
And the broad streams of pikes and flags
  rushed down each roaring street;
And broader still became the blaze,
  and louder still the din,
As fast from every village round the
  horse came spurring in:
And eastward straight from wild Black-
  heath the warlike errand went,
And roused in many an ancient hall
  the gallant squires of Kent.
Southward from Surrey's pleasant hills
  flew those bright couriers forth;
High on bleak Hampstead's swarthy
  moor they started for the north;
And on, and on, without a pause, un-
  tired they bounded still:
All night from tower to tower they
  sprang; they sprang from hill to hill:
Till the proud peak unfurled the flag
  o'er Darwin's rocky dales,
Till like volcanoes flared to heaven
  the stormy hills of Wales,
Till twelve fair counties saw the blaze
  on Malvern's lonely height,
Till streamed in crimson on the wind
  the Wrekin's crest of light,
Till broad and fierce the star came
  forth on Ely's stately fane,
And tower and hamlet rose in arms
  o'er all the boundless plain;
Till Belvoir's lordly terraces the sign
  to Lincoln sent,
And Lincoln sped the message on o'er
  the wide vale of Trent;
Till Skiddaw saw the fire that burned
  on Gaunt's embattled pile,
And the red glare on Skiddaw roused
  the burghers of Carlisle.

1832.

INDEX TO ESSAYS.

Abbé and abbot, difference between, 251.
Academy, character of its doctrines, 414.
Adam, Robert, court architect to George III., 831.
Addison, Joseph, review of Miss Aikin's life of, 769-814; his character, 770; his birth and early life, 771; appointed to a scholarship in Magdalene College, Oxford, 771; his Essay on the Evidences of Christianity, 773; his intention to take orders frustrated, 775; sent by the Government to the Continent, 777; his introduction to Boileau, 779; composes his Epistle to Montague (then Lord Halifax) 781; becomes tutor to a young English traveller, 782; writes his Treatise on Medals, 782; engaged by Godolphin to write a poem in honour of Marlborough's exploits, 784; is appointed to a Commissionership, 784; merits of his "Campaign," 784; criticism of his Travels in Italy, 786; his opera of Rosamond, 787; is made Under-Secretary of State, 788; his election to the House of Commons, 788; his failure as a speaker, 788; his popularity and talents for conversation, 789; his timidity and constraint among strangers, 789; becomes Chief Secretary for Ireland under Wharton, 791; origination of the Tatler, 793; his characteristics as a writer, 793; compared with Swift and Voltaire as a master of the art of ridicule, 794; his pecuniary losses, 796; loss of his Secretaryship, 796; resignation of his Fellowship, 796; returned to Parliament without a contest, 797; his Whig Examiner, 797; his discontinuance of the Tatler and commencement of the Spectator, 797; his commencement and discontinuance of the Guardian, 799; his Cato, 800; his intercourse with Pope, 802; his concern for Steele, 802; begins a new series of the Spectator, 803; appointed Secretary to the Lords Justices of the Council on the death of Queen Anne, 803; relations with Swift and Tickell, 805; removed to the Board of Trade, 805; production of his Drummer, 805; his Freeholder, 805; his long courtship of the Countess Dowager of Warwick and union with her, 809; appointed Secretary of State by Sunderland, 810; resigns his post, 810; receives a pension, 810; his estrangement from Steele and other friends, 811; advocates the bill for limiting the number of Peers, 811; refutation of a calumny upon him, 812; his death and funeral, 813; Tickell's elegy on his death, 813; superb edition of his works, 813; his monument, 814.

Adiaphorists, a sect of German Protestants, 238.
Adultery, how represented by the dramatists of the Restoration, 596.
Advancement of Learning, by Bacon, 391.
Æschylus and the Greek drama, 8-12.
Afghanistān, the monarchy of, analogous to that of England in the 16th century, 243; bravery of its inhabitants, 640.
Agricultural and manufacturing labourers, comparison of their conditions, 113.
Agujari, the singer, 740.
Aix, its capture, 326.
Akenside, his Epistle to Curio, 298.
Alexander the Great, compared with Clive, 570.
Alfieri and Cowper, comparison between them, 162.
Allahabad, 639.
Allegories of Johnson and Addison, 197.
Alphabetical writing, views of its value by Plato and Bacon, 420.
America, acquisitions of the Catholic Church in, 572; its capabilities, 572.
American colonies, British, war with them, 653; act for imposing stamp duties upon them, 841; their disaffection, 846; revival of the dispute with them, 856.
Angria, his fortress of Gheriah reduced by Clive, 540.
Anne, Queen, her political and religious inclinations, 275; relative estimation by the Whigs and the Tories of her reign, 276-278, 280; state of parties at her accession, 783; dismisses the Whigs, 796.
Apostolical succession, Mr. Gladstone claims it for the Church of England, 512-524.
Aquinas, Thomas, 431.
Arbuthnot's Satirical Works, 794.
Arcot, Nabob of, his relations with England, 532-535, 570.
Argyle, Duke of, secedes from Walpole's administration, 309.
Arithmetic, comparative estimate of, by Plato and by Bacon, 418, 419.
Arlington, Lord, 451.
Armies in the middle ages, how constituted, 36, 37, 75; a powerful restraint on the regal power, 75; subsequent change in this respect, 75.
Army, The, control of, by Charles I. or by Parliament, 79; its triumph over both, 83; danger of a standing army becoming an instrument of despotism, 230, 231.
Arne, Dr., 787.
Arragon and Castile, their old institutions favourable to public liberty, 256.
Arundel, Earl of, 411.

INDEX TO ESSAYS.

Asiatic Society, commencement of its career under Warren Hastings, 671.
Astronomy, comparative estimate of, by Socrates and by Bacon, 419.
Athenian comedies, their impurity, 594; reprinted at the two Universities, 594.
Atterbury, Bishop, his reply to Bentley to prove the genuineness of the Letters of Phalaris, 486, 487.
Attila, 572.
Aubrey, his charge of corruption against Bacon, 402; Bacon's decision against him after his present, 409.
Augustin, St., 571.
Austen, Jane, notice of, 763.

B.

Bacon, Lord, review of Basil Montagu's new edition of the works of, 368-439; his early years, 375; his services refused by government, 376, 377; his admission at Gray's Inn, 377; sat in Parliament in 1593, 378; his conduct to Essex, 384-388; influence of King James on his fortunes, 388; his servility to Lord Southampton, 389; his distinction in Parliament and in the courts of law, 390; his works, 391; his work of reducing and recompiling the laws of England, 391; his tampering with the judges on the trial of Peacham, 391; his appointment as Lord Keeper, 396; his share in the vices of the administration, 396; his animosity towards Sir Edward Coke, 399; his titles of Baron Verulam and Viscount St. Albans, 400; report against him of the Committee on the Courts of Justice, 402; his admission of his guilt, 403; his sentence, 404; chief peculiarity of his philosophy, 412-417; his views compared with those of Plato, 417-422; his views as a theologian, 427; contemplation of his life, 438.
Bacon, Sir Nicholas, his character, 370-373.
Baconian philosophy, 412.
Baillie, Gen., destruction of his detachment by Hyder Ali, 659.
Balance of power, interest of the Popes in preserving it, 588.
Bar, The, its degraded condition in the time of James II., 95.
Barcelona, capture of, by Peterborough, 270.
Barillon, M., his pithy words on the new council proposed by Temple, 468, 472.
Barlow, Bishop, 602.
Bavaria, its contest between Protestantism and Catholicism, 583-588.
Bayle, Peter, 574.
Bedford, Duke of, 818; his views of the policy of Chatham, 825, 831; presents remonstrance to George III., 844.
Bedfords, The, 818; their opposition to the Rockingham ministry on the Stamp Act, 847.
Bedford House assailed by a rabble, 843.
Begums of Oude, 666; their spoliation charged against Hastings, 681.
Belgium, its contest between Protestantism and Catholicism, 583-588.

Belial, 595.
Bell, Peter, Byron's spleen against, 163.
Benares, its grandeur, 660; its annexation to the British dominions, 665.
Benevolences, Oliver St. John's opposition to, and Bacon's support of, 391.
Bentham, his language on the French Revolution, 335.
Bentham and Dumont, 285.
Bentivoglio, Cardinal, on the state of religion in England in the 16th century, 246.
Bentley, Richard, his quarrel with Boyle, and remarks on Temple's Essay on the Letters of Phalaris, 487; his edition of Milton, 488, 768; his notes on Horace, 488; his reconciliation with Boyle and Atterbury, 489.
Bickerstaff, Isaac, astrologer, 793.
Bishops, claims of those of the Church of England to apostolical succession, 512-515.
Black Hole of Calcutta described, 541-542.
Blackmore, Sir Richard, his attainments in the ancient languages, 773.
Blackstone, 366.
Blasphemous publications, policy of Government in respect to, 143.
Blenheim, battle of, 783.
Blois, Addison's retirement to, 777.
"Bloomsbury gang," the denomination of the Bedfords, 818.
Bodley, Sir Thomas, founder of the Bodleian library, 391, 411.
Boileau, Addison's intercourse with, 777.
Bolingbroke, Lord, the liberal patron of literature, 184; proposed to strengthen the royal prerogative, 293; his pretence of philosophy in his exile, 426; his remedy for the diseases of the state, 823, 824.
Book of the Church, Southey's, 107.
Books, puffing of, 133-135.
Boroughs, rotten, the abolition of, a necessary reform in the time of George I., 297.
Boswell's Life of Johnson, by Croker, review of, 170-196; character of the work, 180.
Bourne, Vincent, 810.
Boyle, Charles, his nominal editorship of the Letters of Phalaris, 487; his book on Greek history and philology, 773.
Boyle, Rt. Hon. Henry, 784.
"Boys, The," in opposition to Sir R. Walpole, 295.
Bracegirdle, Mrs., her celebrity as an actress, 619.
Bribery, foreign, in the time of Charles I., 97.
"Broad Bottom Administration, The," 315.
Brunswick, the House of, 820.
Brydges, Sir Egerton, 763.
Buckingham, Duke of, the "Steenie" of James I., 210, 394, 402.
Buckingham, Duke of, one of the Cabal ministry, 604; anecdote of his volatility, 604.
Bunyan, John, his history and character, 200-202; his style, 203.
Bunyan's Pilgrim's Progress, review of Southey's edition of, 196.
Buonaparte, 86, 322, 785. See also Napoleon.
Burke, Edmund, his characteristics, 106.

not the author of Letters of Junius, 648; his charges against Hastings, 673, 688; his kindness to Miss Burney, 755; his early political career, 845; his opposition to Chatham's measures relating to India, 854; his defence of his party against Grenville's attacks, 857.

Burleigh and his Times, review of Rev. Dr. Nares's, 235; his early life and character, 236-239; his death, 239; importance of the times in which he lived, 239; the great stain on his character, 248; his conduct towards Bacon, 376-380; his apology for having resorted to torture, 393.

Burnet, Bishop, 489.

Burney, Dr., his social position, 736-740; his conduct relative to his daughter's first publication, 745.

Bute, Earl of, his character and education; 822; appointed Secretary of State, 824; opposes the proposal of war with Spain on account of the family compact, 826; becomes Prime Minister, 827; becomes First Lord of the Treasury, 829; his resignation, 835; continues to advise the king privately, 838, 843, 847.

Byng, Admiral, his failure at Minorca, 320; his trial, 322; opinion of his conduct, 322; Chatham's defence of him, 323.

Byron, Lord, his epistolary style, 151; his character, 152; his early life, 152; his quarrel with and separation from his wife, 153; his expatriation, 155; decline of his intellectual powers, 155; his attachment to Italy and Greece, 155; his sickness and death, 156; remarks on his dramatic works, 165-169; his egotism, 169; cause of his influence, 169.

C.

Cabal, The, their proceedings and designs, 459, 460, 463.

Calcutta, scene of the Black Hole of, 541; resentment of the English at its fall, 542; again threatened by Surajah Dowlah, 543; revival of its prosperity, 550; its sufferings during the famine, 565; its capture, 690.

Cambridge, University of, its superiority to Oxford in intellectual activity, 371; disturbances produced in by the Civil War, 445.

Camilla, Madame D'Arblay's, 765.

Canada, subjugation of, by the British, 328.

Canning, Mr., 762.

Carnatic, The, its resources, 532, 539; its invasion by Hyder Ali, 658.

Carteret, Lord, his ascendancy after the fall of Walpole, 299; his defection from Sir Robert Walpole, 307; succeeds Walpole, 314; created Earl Granville, 315.

Carthagena, surrender of the arsenal and ships of, to the Allies, 271.

Catholic Association, attempt of the Tories to put it down, 621.

Catholics and Jews, the same reasoning employed against both, 146.

Cato, its first representation, 800; its performance at Oxford, 801.

Cavaliers, their successors in the reign of George I. turned demagogues, 815.

Cecil. See Burleigh.

Cecil, Robert, his rivalry with Francis Bacon, 376, 381; his interference to obtain knighthood for Bacon, 389.

Cecilia, Madame D'Arblay's, 764.

Censorship, existed in some form from Henry VIII. to the Revolution, 364.

Chalmers, Dr., Mr. Gladstone's opinion of his defence of the Church, 493.

Charles, Archduke, his claim to the Spanish crown, 257; is proclaimed king at Madrid, 270; his reverses and retreat, 272; his re-entry into Madrid, 274.

Charles I., lawfulness of the resistance to, 16-19; Milton's defence of his execution, 21; his treatment of the Parliament of 1640, 65; his treatment of Strafford, 70; estimate of his character, 71-83, 211; his fall, 83; his condemnation and its consequences, 84; resistance of the Scots to him, 219; his increasing difficulties, 219; his conduct towards the House of Commons, 226; his flight, 229; review of his conduct and treatment, 229-231.

Charles I. and Cromwell, choice between, 83.

Charles II., his foreign subsidies, 96; his situation in 1660 contrasted with that of Louis XVIII., 344; his position towards the king of France, 349; consequences of his levity and apathy, 351; his extravagance, 453; his subserviency to France, 453-465; his renunciation of the dispensing power, 463; his system of bribery of the Commons, 469-471; his social disposition, 604.

Charles II., of Spain, his difficulties in respect to the succession, 257-261.

Charles V., 578.

Charles VIII., 433.

Charles XII., compared with Clive, 570.

Chatham, Earl of, character of his public life, 303; his early life, 305; his travels, 305; enters the army, 305; obtains a seat in Parliament, 305; attaches himself to the Whigs in opposition, 309; dismissed from the army, 312; declaims against the ministers, 314; his opposition to Carteret, 314; supports the Pelham ministry, 315; appointed Vice-Treasurer of Ireland, 315; made Secretary of State, 320; defends Admiral Byng, 323; coalesces with the Duke of Newcastle, 325; review of his Correspondence, 813; his coalition with Newcastle, 817; his strength in Parliament, 819; proposes to declare war against Spain on account of the family compact, 826; his resignation, 826; his speech against peace with France and Spain, 834; his unsuccessful audiences with George III. to form an administration, 838; his condemnation of the American Stamp Act, 847; is induced by the king to assist in ousting Rockingham, 850; undertakes to form an administration, 851; is created Earl of Chatham, 851; failure of his ministerial arrangements, 852-855; lays an embargo on the exporta-

tion of corn, 854; his retirement from office, 854; his policy violated, 855; resigns the privy seal, 856; state of parties and of public affairs on his recovery, 856; opposed the recognition of the independence of the United States, 858; his last appearance in the House of Lords, 859; his death, 859.
Cherbourg, guns taken from, 326.
Chesterfield, Lord, his dismissal by Walpole, 308.
Cheyte Sing, 661; his treatment made the successful charge against Hastings, 680.
Chivalry, its form in Languedoc in the 12th century, 575.
Cholmondely, Mrs., 747.
Christianity, its alliance with the ancient philosophy, 415; light in which it was regarded by the Italians at the Reformation, 578.
Church, The, Southey's Book of, 107.
Church, The English, persecutions in her name, 60; High and Low Church parties, 787.
Church of England, its origin and connection with the State, 64, 523; its condition in the time of Charles I., 122-124; endeavour of the leading Whigs at the Revolution to alter its Liturgy and Articles, 361, 518; its contest with the Scotch nation, 361; Mr. Gladstone's work in defence of it, 492, 493; his arguments for its being the pure Catholic Church of Christ, 510, 512; its claims to apostolic succession discussed, 512-519; views respecting its alliance with the State, 519-524; contrast of its operations during the two generations succeeding the Reformation, with those of the Church of Rome, 584, 585.
Church of Rome, its alliance with ancient philosophy, 416; causes of its success and vitality, 571, 572; sketch of its history, 575-593.
Churchill, Charles, 94, 831.
Cicero, the most eloquent and skilful of advocates, 370.
Cider, proposal of a tax on, 835.
Civil privileges and political power identical, 145.
Civil war, its evils the price of our liberty, 19; conduct of the Long Parliament in reference to it, 71, 72, 83.
Clarendon, Lord, his character, 95; his position at the head of affairs, 451-455; his opposition to the growing power of the Commons, 471.
Clarke, Dr. Samuel, 573.
Clarkson, Thomas, 764.
Clifford, Lord, his character, 459; his retirement, 463; his talent for debate, 470.
Clive, Lord, review of Sir John Malcolm's Life of, 524-571; his attack, capture, and defence of Arcot, 533-535; his marriage and return to England, 538; enters Parliament, 539; returns to India, 539; appointed Governor of the Company's possessions in Bengal, 551; his dispersion of Shah Alum's army, 552; nominated Governor of the British possessions in Bengal, 558; suppresses a conspiracy, 558-560; success of his foreign policy, 561; his speech in his defence, and its consequence, 568; his life in retirement, 569; his death, 570.
Club-room, Johnson's, 195.
Coke, Sir E., his conduct towards Bacon, 377, 399; his removal from the Bench, 398; his reconciliation with Bacon, 399; his behaviour to Bacon at his trial, 408.
Coleridge, relative "correctness" of his poetry, 157; Byron's opinion of him, 163.
Collier, Jeremy, his publication on the profaneness of the English stage, 614-617.
Colloquies on Society, Southey's, 105-131.
Colonies, 254; question of the competency of Parliament to tax them, 846.
Comic Dramatists of the Restoration, 593-621.
Commons, House of, increase of its power, 100; increase of its power by and since the Revolution, 362.
Commonwealth, 600.
Congreve, sketch of his career at the Temple, 610; success of his Love for Love, 612; his Mourning Bride, 612; his controversy with Collier, 616; his Way of the World, 617; his death and capricious will, 620.
Congreve and Sheridan, effect of their works upon the comedy of England, 43; contrasted with Shakspeare, 44.
Constance, Council of, put an end to the Wickliffe schism, 577.
Constitution, The, of England, in the 15th and 18th centuries, compared with those of other European States, 74; its theory in respect to the three branches of the legislature, 811.
Constitutional History of England, review of Hallam's, 55-105.
Cooke, Sir Anthony, his learning, 373.
Coote, Sir Eyre, 654.
"Correctness" in the fine arts and in the sciences, 157-160; in painting, 159; what is meant by it in poetry, 158.
Corruption, Parliamentary, not necessary to the Tudors, 292; its extent in the reigns of George I. and II., 823.
Council of York, its abolition, 222.
Courtenay, Rt. Hon. T. P., review of his Memoirs of Sir William Temple, 439-490.
Covenant, the Scotch, 219.
Covenanters, The, their conclusion of a treaty with Charles I., 219.
Coventry, Lady, 743.
Cowley, 289, 437.
Cowper, Earl, Keeper of the Great Seal, 787.
Cowper, William, 162; his friendship with Warren Hastings, 629.
Coyer, Abbé, his imitation of Voltaire, 794.
Cranmer, Archbishop, estimate of his character, 61.
Crebillon the Younger, 286.
Crisis, Steele's, 805.
Crisp, Samuel, his early career, 741; his tragedy of Virginia, 743; his retirement and seclusion, 744.
Criticism, remarks on Johnson's code of, 191.
Croker, Mr., his edition of Boswell's Life of Dr. Johnson, reviewed, 170-196.

Cromwell, Oliver, 86; embarked with Hampden for America, but not suffered to proceed, 218; his administration, 345; his abilities displayed in Ireland, 449.
Crown, The, veto by, on Acts of Parliament, 79; its control over the army, 79; its power in the 16th century, 241; curtailment of its prerogatives, 292; its power predominant at the beginning of the 17th century, 468; decline of its power during the Pensionary Parliament, 470; its long contest with the Parliament put an end to by the Revolution, 473. *See also* Prerogative.
Crusades, The, their beneficial effect upon Italy, 34.
Cumberland, Duke of, 554; his character, 842.

D.

Dacier, Madame, 777.
Danby, Earl, 292; impeached and sent to the Tower, 466.
Danger, public, a certain amount of, will warrant a retrospective law, 223.
Dante, his Divine Comedy, 9, 35; comparison of him with Milton, 9 *et seq.*
D'Arblay, Madame, review of her Diary and Letters, 736–769; her Diary, 737; her first literary efforts, 741; publication of her Evelina, 745; her comedy, The Witlings, 748; her second novel, Cecilia, 748; accepts the situation of keeper of the robes, 750; her espousal of the cause of Hastings, 754; her incivility to Windham and Burke, 754; her sufferings during her keepership, 751, 755, 759; her marriage and close of the Diary, 760.
Dashwood, Sir Francis, Chancellor of the Exchequer under Bute, 829.
Davies, Tom, 177.
De Augmentis Scientiarum, by Bacon, 391, 411.
Debt, the national, effect of its abrogation, 115.
Declaration of Right, 359.
Declaration of the Practices and Treasons attempted and committed by Robert, Earl of Essex, by Lord Bacon, 387.
Delany, Dr., his connection with Swift, 749.
Delium, battle of, 447.
Democracy, violence in its advocates induces reaction, 239.
Demosthenes, 408.
Dennis, John, Pope's narrative of his frenzy, 802; his attack upon Addison's Cato, 801.
Devonshire, Duchess of, 683.
Devonshire, Duke of, forms an administration after the resignation of Newcastle, 321; Lord Chamberlain under Bute, 830; dismissed from his Lord-lieutenancy, 833.
Diary and Letters of Madame D'Arblay, reviewed, 736–769.
Discussion, free, its tendency, 122.
Dissent, cause of, in England, 586; avoidance of, in the Church of Rome, 586; its extent in the time of Charles I, 121.

Dissenters, The, examination of the reasoning of Mr. Gladstone for their exclusion from civil offices, 503–506.
Divine right, 17.
Division of Labour, its necessity, 493.
Dodington, Bubb, 819.
Donne, John, comparison of his wit with Horace Walpole's, 289.
Dover, Lord, review of his edition of Horace Walpole's Letters to Sir Horace Mann, 281–303. *See* Walpole, Sir Horace.
Drama, The, its origin in Greece, 7; causes of its dissolute character soon after the Restoration, 600.
Dramas, Greek, compared with the English plays of the age of Elizabeth, 157.
Dramatic Art, the unities violated in all the great masterpieces of, 157.
Dramatic Works, The, of Wycherley, Congreve, Vanburgh and Farquhar, review of Leigh Hunt's edition of, 593–621.
Dryden, his merits not adequately appreciated in his day, 132; his poetical genius, 594; his excuse for the indecency and immorality of his writings, 596; censure on him by Collier for his language regarding heathen divinities, 615.
Dublin, Archbishop of, his work on logic, 430.
Dumont, M., the interpreter of Bentham, 285.
Dupleix, governor of Pondicherry, 528 *et seq.*

E.

East India Company, its absolute authority in India, 326; its condition when Clive first went to India, 526; its war with the French East India Company, 528; increase of its power, 540; its factories in Bengal, 540; fortunes made by its servants in Bengal, 555; its servants transformed into diplomatists and generals, 630; nature of its government and power, 634–635; rights of the Nabob of Oude over Benares ceded to it, 661; its financial embarrassments, 663.
Ecclesiastical commission, The, 242.
Education in England in the 16th century, 376; duty of the government in promoting it, 520; in Italy, 34.
Egerton, his charge of corruption against Bacon, 402; Bacon's decision against him after receiving his present, 409.
Elephants, use of, in war in India, 535.
Eliot, Sir John, 212–215.
Elizabeth, Queen, fallacy entertained respecting the persecutions under her, 57; her penal laws, 58; condition of the working-classes in her reign, 125, 208; her favour towards Essex, 379; factions at the close of her reign, 379, 388.
Ellenborough, Lord (Law), one of the counsel for Hastings on his trial, 684.
Elphinstone, Lord, 571.
Emigration from England to Ireland under Cromwell, 450.
England, her progress in civilisation due to the people, 131; her physical and moral

condition in the 15th century, 207; never so rich and powerful as since the loss of her American colonies, 254; conduct of, in reference to the Spanish succession, 262; successive steps of her progress, 342; her situation in 1678, 347-351; character of her public men at the latter part of the 17th century, 442; difference in her situation under Charles II. and under the Protectorate, 452.
English, The, in the 16th century a free people, 242-244; their character, 348-351.
English plays of the age of Elizabeth, 158.
Enthusiasts, dealings of the Church of Rome and the Church of England with them, 585-587.
Essay on Government, Sir William Temple's, 461.
Essex, Earl of, 250; his character, popularity and favour with Elizabeth, 379-381, 395; his political conduct, 380; his friendship for Bacon, 380, 381, 384, 395; his expedition to Spain, 382; his faults, 382, 394; decline of his fortunes, 382; his administration in Ireland, 383; his trial and execution, 383.
Essex, Earl of (*temp.* Ch. I.), 232, 233.
Evelina, Madame D'Arblay's, specimens of her style from, 766.
Evelyn, 452, 459.
Exchequer, fraud of the Cabal ministry in closing it, 462.

F.

Falkland, Lord, his conduct in respect to the bill of attainder against Strafford, 70; at the head of the Constitutional Royalists, 226.
Family Compact, The, between France and Spain, 278, 279, 826.
Female Quixote, The, 768.
Fénélon, standard of morality in his Telemachus, 597, 598.
Ferdinand II., his devotion to Catholicism, 584.
Fictions, literary, 30.
Fidelity, touching instance of, in the Sepoys towards Clive, 534.
Fielding, his contempt for Richardson, 742; case from his Amelia analogous to Addison's treatment of Steele, 791.
Finance, Southey's theory of, 115-117.
Fine Arts, The, encouragement of in Italy in the 14th century, 35; causes of their decline in England after the civil war, 287.
Fletcher, the dramatist, 596, 601.
Foote, Charles, his stage character of an Anglo-Indian grandee, 563; his mimicry, 762; his inferiority to Garrick, 762.
Fox, Charles James, comparison of his History of James II. with Mackintosh's History of the Revolution, 330; clamour raised against his India Bill, and his defence of it, 675; his alliance with Burke, and call for peace with the American republic, 676; his rupture with Burke, 685.
Fox, Henry, accepts office, 320; directed to form an administration in concert with Chatham, 321, 325; applied to by Bute to manage the House of Commons, 832; became leader of the House of Commons, 833; obtained his promised peerage, 836.
France, her condition in 1712 and in 1832, 277; her state at the restoration of Louis XVIII., 344; enters into a compact with Spain against England, 826; her recognition of the independence of the United States, 858.
Francis, Sir Philip, councillor under the Regulating Act for India, 643; probability of his being the author of the Letters of Junius, 643; his opposition to Hastings, 645, 652, his patriotic feeling, and reconciliation with Hastings, 655; renewal of his quarrel with Hastings, 658; duel with Hastings, 658; his speech on Mr. Fox's motion relating to Cheyte Sing, 679; his exclusion from the committee selected to conduct the impeachment of Hastings, 682.
Franklin, Benjamin, 573.
Frederic the Great, his birth, 694; his father, 695; his father's cruelty to him, 695; his education, 696; his accession to the throne, 699; death of Charles VI., 700; Maria Theresa, 700; war with Austria, 702; occupation of Silesia, 703; peace, 704; Frederic's associates at Potsdam, 711; Voltaire, 713; the Seven Years' War, 723; frightful state of the kingdom, 736.

G.

Galileo, 573.
Garrick, David, his acquaintance with Johnson, 184; his power of amusing children, 740; his power of imitation, 762.
Genoa, its decay owing to Catholicism, 589.
"Gentleman Dancing-Master," its production on the stage, 605.
George I., his accession, 278.
George II., his resentment against Chatham for his opposition to the payment of Hanoverian troops, 314; compelled to admit him to office, 315; his efforts for the protection of Hanover, 319; his death, 819; his character, 820.
George III., cause of the discontents in the early part of his reign, 101; his partiality to Clive, 568; bright prospects at his accession, 653, 814, 820; his interview with Miss Burney, 749; his opinions of Voltaire, Rousseau and Shakspeare, 750; his partisanship for Hastings, 755, his illness, and the view taken of it in the palace, 756; his characteristics, 821; his favour to Lord Bute, 822; slighted for Chatham at the Lord Mayor's dinner, 827; his treatment by Grenville, 838; increase of h's aversion to his ministers, 840; his illness, 841; disputes between him and his ministry on the regency question, 841; inclined to enforce the American Stamp Act by the sword, 846; the faction of the "King's friends," 847; his unwilling consent to the repeal of the Stamp Act, 845.
George IV., 683.

Ghosts, Johnson's belief in, 189.
Gibbon, his alleged conversion to Mahommedanism, 173; his success as a historian, 329.
Gibraltar, capture of, by Sir George Rooke, 266.
Gifford, Byron's admiration of, 163.
Gladstone, W. E., review of "The State in its Relations with the Church," 490-524; quality of his mind, 491; grounds on which he rests his case for the defence of the Church, 493; his doctrine that the duties of government are paternal, 494; specimen of his arguments, 495; his argument that the profession of a national religion is imperative, 497; the consequence of his reasoning, 502-505.
Gleig, Rev., G. R., review of his Life of Warren Hastings, 627-692.
Godolphin and Marlborough, their policy soon after the accession of Queen Anne, 783.
Goldsmith, 181.
Goordas, son of Nuncomar, his appointment as treasurer of the household, 638.
Goree, conquest of, 326.
Government, various forms of, 190; the science of, experimental and progressive, 276, 338; its conduct in relation to infidel publications, 123; its proper functions, 599.
Grafton, Duke of, Secretary of State under Lord Rockingham, 845; First Lord of the Treasury under Chatham, 852; joined the Bedfords, 856.
Grand Alliance, The, against the Bourbons, 263.
Grand Remonstrance, debate on and passing of it, 225.
Greece, its history compared with that of Italy, 36; instances of the corruption of judges in the ancient commonwealths of, 405; its literature, 575.
Greek drama, its origin, 7; compared with English plays of the age of Elizabeth, 158.
Gregory XIII., his austerity and zeal, 582.
Grenville, George, his character, 825; entrusted with the lead in the Commons under the Bute administration, 827; his support of the proposed tax on cider, 835; his nickname of "Gentle Shepherd," 835; appointed prime minister, 836; proposed the imposition of stamp duties on the North American colonies, 841; his embarrassment on the question of a regency, 841; his triumph over the king, 844; superseded by Lord Rockingham and his friends, 845; popular demonstration against him on the repeal of the Stamp Act, 848; his reconciliation with Chatham, 857; his death, 858.
Grenvilles, The, 818; Richard Lord Temple at their head, 818.
Grey, Earl, 684, 688.
Grey, Lady Jane, her high classical acquirements, 373.
"Grievances," popular, on occasion of Walpole's fall, 296, 298.
Grubb Street, 187.
Guardian, The, its birth, 799; its discontinuance, 802.

Guelfs, The, their success greatly promoted by the ecclesiastical power, 33.
Guicowar, its interpretation, 653.
Guise, Henry, Duke of, his conduct on the day of the barricades at Paris, 384.
Gustavus Adolphus, 588.

H.

Habeas Corpus Act, 475, 479.
Hale, Sir Matthew, his integrity, 235, 392.
Halifax, Lord, a trimmer both by intellect and by constitution, 477; his political tracts, 478; his recommendation of Addison to Godolphin, 784.
Hallam, Mr., review of his Constitutional History of England, 55-105.
Hamilton, Gerard, his celebrated single speech, 320.
Hampden, John, his conduct in the shipmoney affair approved by the Royalists, 66; effect of his loss on the Parliamentary cause, 83, 234; review of Lord Nugent's Memorial of him, 204-235; his origin and early history, 205; took his seat in the House of Commons in 1621, 206; joined the opposition to the Court, 206; his first appearance as a public man, 210; his first stand for the fundamental principle of the Constitution, 211; committed to prison, 211; set at liberty and re-elected for Wendover, 212; Clarendon's character of him as a debater, 213, 222; his acquirements, 204; his resistance to the assessment for ship-money, 217; Strafford's hatred for him, 218; his intention to leave England, 218; his election by two constituencies to the Long Parliament, 220; his opinion on the bill for the attainder of Strafford, 224; his mission to Scotland, 224; his conduct in the House of Commons on the passing of the Grand Remonstrance, 225; his impeachment ordered by the king, 226; returns in triumph to the House, 229; his resolution, 229; raised a regiment in Buckinghamshire, 232; his encounter with Rupert at Chalgrove, 234; his death and burial, 234.
Harcourt, French ambassador to the court of Charles II. of Spain, 259.
Hardwicke, Earl of, 819.
Harley, Robert, 184; his accession to power in 1710, 275; his unsuccessful attempt to rally the Tories in 1707, 787; his advice to the queen to dismiss the Whigs, 796.
Hastings, Warren, review of Mr. Gleig's Memoirs of his Life, 627-692; sent to Westminster school, 629; sent as a writer to Bengal, 630; events which originated his greatness, 631; becomes a member of council at Calcutta, 631; his return to England, and loss of his moderate fortune, 632; his appointment as member of council at Madras, and voyage to India, 633; his attachment to the Baroness Imhoff, 633; his nomination to the head of the government at Bengal, 634; his relation with Nuncomar, 635; his embarrassed finances and means to relieve them, 638,

660; his proceedings towards the Nabob and the Great Mogul, 639; his sale of territory to the Nabob of Oude, 639; his refusal to interfere to stop the barbarities of Sujah Dowlah, 642; his measures reversed, and the powers of government taken from him, 645; charges preferred against him, 646; his condemnation by the directors, 651; his resignation, 651; his reappointment, 652; his duel with Francis, 658; his great influence, 659; his transactions with and measures against Cheyte Sing, 661; his perilous situation in Benares, 664; his treatment of the Nabob Vizier, 665; his treatment of the Begums of Oude, 666-668; close of his administration, 668; his impeachment, 674-678; his defence at the bar of the House, 678; brought to the bar of the Peers, 682; his arraignment by Burke, 684; narrative of the proceedings against him, 684-688; his reception at Oxford, 691; sworn of the Privy Council, and gracious reception by the Prince Regent, 691; his presentation to the Emperor of Russia and King of Prussia, 691; his death, 692.
Hatton, Lady, 382.
Hawke, Admiral, his victory over the French fleet under Conflans, 326.
"Heathens," The, of Cromwell's time, 26.
Heathfield, Lord, 683.
Hebrides, The, Johnson's visit to, 193; his letters from, 194.
Henry IV. of France, 500; twice abjured Protestantism from interested motives, 587.
Henry VIII., 63; his position between the Catholic and Protestant parties, 247.
Hesse Darmstadt, Prince of, commanded the land forces sent against Gibraltar in 1704, 266.
High Commission Court, its abolition, 223.
Hindoos, their mendacity and perjury, 645; their view of forgery, 646; importance attached by them to ceremonial practices, 648; their feelings against English law, 655.
History of the Popes of Rome during the 16th and 17th centuries, review of Ranke's, 571-593.
Hobbes, Thomas, 400.
Holdernesse, Earl of, his resignation of office, 824.
Holkar, origin of the House of, 653.
Holland, governed by John de Witt, 452; its defensive alliance with England and Sweden, 458.
Holland House, 626.
Holland, Lord, review of his opinions as recorded in the journals of the House of Lords, 621-627; his family, 622; his philanthropy, 625; his hospitality at Holland House, 626.
Hollis, Mr., committed to prison by Charles I., 212; his impeachment, 222.
Holwell, Mr., his presence of mind in the Black Hole, 542.
Homer, 6, 157.
Hoole, specimen of his heroic couplets, 774.

House of Commons, The, increase of its power, 100; change in public feeling in respect to its privileges, 102; its responsibility, 103; commencement of the practice of buying of votes in, 292; increase of its influence after the Revolution, 292.
Hunt, Leigh, review of his edition of the Dramatic Works of Wycherley, Congreve, Vanbrugh and Farquhar, 593-621.
Huntingdon, Countess of, 587.
Hutchinson, Mrs., 449.
Hyde, Mr., at the head of the Constitutional Royalists, 225; voted for Strafford's attainder, 224.
Hyder Ali, his invasion of the Carnatic, and triumphant success, 659; his progress arrested by Sir Eyre Coote, 660.

I.

Idolatry, 11.
Illustrations of Bunyan and Milton by Martin, 196.
Impey, Sir Elijah, 630; Chief Justice of the Supreme Court at Calcutta, 644; his hostility to the Council, 646; remarks on his trial of Nuncomar, 648; dissolution of his friendship with Hastings, 649; his interference in the proceedings against the Begums, 667.
Indemnity, bill of, to protect witnesses against Walpole, 314.
India, foundation of the English empire in, 326; high civilisation of its people, 525.
Induction, method of, 427.
Indulgences, 577.
Infidelity, on the treatment of, 123.
Inquisition instituted on the suppression of the Albigensian heresy, 576; armed with powers to suppress the Reformation, 582.
Intolerance, religious, effects of, 123.
Ireland, rebellion in, in 1640, 224; Essex's Administration in, 383; its condition under Cromwell's government, 449; its state contrasted with that of Scotland, 509; reason of it not joining in favour of the Reformation, 578.
Italians, their character in the middle ages, 39.
Italy, progress of civilisation and refinement in, 32 et seq.; its temper at the Reformation, 578 et seq.; its slow progress owing to Catholicism, 589; revival of the power of the Church in, 592.

J.

"Jackboot," a popular pun on Bute's name, 831.
Jacobin Club, its excesses, 591.
Jacobins, their origin, 240.
James I., 65; his folly and weakness, 209; his twofold character, 388; his anxiety for the union of England and Scotland, 390; his employment of Bacon in perverting the laws, 391; absoluteness of his government, 398; his political blunders, 401; his readiness to make concessions to Rome, 584.
James II., the causes of his expulsion, 17 administration of the law in his time, 95 his misgovernment, 353; his claims as

supporter of toleration, 353; his union with Louis XIV., 355; his confidential advisers, 355.
Jeffreys, Judge, his cruelty, 353.
Jesuits, order of, instituted by Loyola, 580; their policy and proceedings, 580.
Jews, The, review of the Civil Disabilities of 143-151.
Johnson, Dr. Samuel, review of Croker's edition of Boswell's Life of, 170-196; his peculiarities, 183; condition of literary men at the time of his settling in London, 184-186; his difficulties, 186; his elevation, 186; his opinion on forms of government, 190; his judgments on books, 190; his visit to the Hebrides, 193; his club-room, 195; singularity of his destiny, 196; his bigotry, 366; his definitions of Excise and Pensioner, 366; his ignorance of music, 739; his position with the Thrales, 746; his irritability, 747; his benevolence, 747; his death, 749.
Jones, Inigo, 703.
Jones, Sir William, 177.
Jonson, Ben, 45; his Hermogenes, 166; his description of humours in character, 763; specimen of his heroic couplets, 774.
Judges, The, condition of their tenure of office, 79; formerly accustomed to receive gifts from suitors, 404-407; how their corruption is generally detected, 409; integrity required from them, 649.
Judgment, private, Milton's defence of the right of, 28.
Junius, Letters of, 643.
Juvenal's Satires, 175; their impurity, 594.

K.

Kimbolton, Lord, his impeachment, 226.
"King's Friends," the faction of the, 847.
Kit-Cat Club, Addison's introduction to the, 782.
Kneller, Sir Godfrey, 287.
Knights, comedy of the, 447.
Knowledge, advancement of society in, 276.

L.

Labour, division of, 493; effects of attempts by government to limit the hours of, 599.
Labouring classes, The, their condition in England and on the Continent, 127; in the United States, 128.
La Fontaine, allusion to, 181.
Lally, Governor, his treatment by the French government, 569.
Lamb, Charles, his defence of the dramatists of the Restoration, 597.
Lampoons, Pope's, 808.
Languedoc, description of it in the 12th century, 575.
Latimer, Hugh, his popularity in London, 407.
Laud, Archbishop, his treatment by the Parliament, 81; his impeachment and imprisonment, 215; his rigour against the Puritans, and tenderness towards the Catholics, 224.
Lawrence, Major, his early notice of Clive, 528, 530; his abilities, 528.

Lawrence, Sir Thomas, 762.
Laws, penal, of Elizabeth, 58.
Learning in Italy, revival of, 34; causes of its decline, 36.
Lemon, Mr., his discovery of Milton's Treatise on Christian Doctrine, 1.
Leo X., 582.
Letters of Phalaris, 487.
Libels on the court of George III. in Bute's time, 831.
Liberty, public, Milton's support of, 21.
Lingard, Dr., 354-457.
Literary men more independent than formerly, 132; their influence, 135; abjectness of their condition during the reign of George II., 184; their importance to contending parties in the reign of Queen Anne, 787.
Literature of the Roundheads, 14; of the Royalists, 15; of Italy in the 14th century, 34; of the Elizabethan age, 250; of Spain in the 16th century, 253.
Locke, 573.
Logan, Mr., his ability in defending Hastings, 689.
Lollardism in England, 247.
London in the 17th century, 227; devoted to the national cause, 228; its public spirit, 242; its prosperity during the ministry of Lord Chatham, 327; conduct of, at the Restoration, 346; effects of the Great Plague upon, 452.
Long Parliament, The, its first meeting, 66, 221; its early proceedings, 71; its nineteen propositions, 78; treatment of it by the army, 83; recapitulation of its acts, 222; its attainder of Strafford defended, 223; sent Hampden to Edinburgh to watch the king, 224; refuses to surrender the members ordered to be impeached, 226; openly defies the king, 228; its conditions of reconciliation, 230.
Lords, the House of, its position previous to the Restoration, 345; its condition as a debating assembly in 1770, 624.
Louis XIV., his conduct in respect to the Spanish succession, 157 et seq.; his proceedings in support of his grandson, Philip, 266; his reverses in Germany, Italy and the Netherlands, 275; his military exploits, 441; his ill-humour at the Triple Alliance, 457; his conquest of Franche Comté, 457; his treaty with Charles, 462; the early part of his reign a time of licence, 599.
Louis XV., his government, 569.
Louisburg, fall of, 326.
Luther, sketch of the contest which began with his preaching against the Indulgences and terminated with the treaty of Westphalia, 577-587.

M.

Machiavelli, his Works, by Périer, review of, 30-54.
Mackenzie, Henry, his ridicule of the Nabob class, 564.
Mackintosh, Sir James, review of his History of the Revolution in England, 329-367.

INDEX TO ESSAYS. 919

Madras, description of it, 526; its capitulation to the French, 528; restored to the English, 529.
Madrid, capture of, by the English army, in 1705, 270.
Magdalen College, 771.
Mahommed Reza Khan, his character, 635; selected by Clive, 636; his capture, confinement at Calcutta, and release, 637.
Mahon, Lord, Review of his History of the War of the Succession in Spain, 251-280.
Mahrattas, sketch of their History, 530, 653; expedition against them, 654.
Malcolm, Sir John, review of his Life of Lord Clive, 524-571; value of his work, 525; his partiality for Clive, 543; his defence of Clive's conduct towards Omichund, 543.
Manchester, Countess of, 777.
Manilla, capitulation of, 827.
Mansfield, Lord, 828; his character and talents, 316; his rejection of the overtures of Newcastle, 320; his elevation, 321.
Manufacturing system, The, Southey's opinion upon, 113.
Marat, his bust substituted for the statues of the martyrs of Christianity, 591.
Marlborough, Duchess of, her friendship with Congreve, 619; her inscription on his monument, 620; her death, 314.
Marlborough, Duke of, 99; his conversion to Whiggism, 276; notice of Addison's poem in his honour, 785.
Marlborough and Godolphin, their policy, 783.
Martinique, capture of, 827.
Mary, Queen, 249.
Massinger, his fondness for the Roman Catholic Church, 248; indelicate writing in his dramas, 596.
Maynooth, Mr. Gladstone's objection to the vote of money for, 513.
Medals, Addison's Treatise on, 772, 782.
Meer Cossim, his talents, 556.
Meer Jaffier, his conspiracy, 545 *et seq.*
Melancthon, 233.
Menander, the lost comedies of, 793.
Mercenaries, employment of, in Italy, 37.
Methodists, their early object, 579.
Middlesex election, the constitutional question in relation to it, 857.
Middleton, Dr., 369.
Militia, The, control of, by Charles I. or by the Parliament, 79.
Mill, James, his merits as a historian, 341; defects of his History of British India, 525; his unfairness towards Clive's character, 543.
Milton, review of his Treatise on Christian Doctrine, 1; his theological opinions, 2; his poetry his great passport to general remembrance, 2 *et seq.*; his public conduct, 15; his defence of the execution of Charles I., 21; his conduct under the Protector, 22; his defence of the freedom of the press, 28.
Minden, Battle of, 327.
Mines, Spanish-American, 255.
Minorca, capture of, by the French, 320.
Missionaries, Catholic, their zeal and spirit, 571.

Mogul, the Great, 639; plundered by Hastings, 660.
Molière, 609, 610.
Mompesson, Sir Giles, conduct of Bacon in regard to his patent, 396; abandoned to the vengeance of the Commons, 401.
Monarchy, absolute, establishment of, in Continental states, 75.
Monarchy, the English, in the 16th century, 241, 244.
Monmouth, Duke of, 351; his supplication for life, 482.
Monopolies, English, during the latter end of Elizabeth's reign, 380; multiplied under James, 396; connived at by Bacon, 397.
Monson, Mr., 645; his death, and its important consequences, 651.
Montagu, Basil, review of his edition of Lord Bacon's works, 368-439.
Montagu, Charles, notice of him, 775. *See also* Halifax.
Montagu, Mary, her testimony to Addison's colloquial powers, 789.
Montague, Lord, 184.
Montague, Mrs., 683.
Montgomery, Mr. Robert, his Omnipresence of the Deity reviewed, 136-143.
Montreal, capture of, by the British, in 1760, 326.
Moore's Life of Lord Byron, review of, 151-170; similes in his Lalla Rookh, 434.
More, Sir Thomas, 574.
"Mountain of Light," 530.
Moylan, Mr., review of his Collection of the Opinions of Lord Holland as recorded in the Journals of the House of Lords, 621-627.
Mussulmans, their resistance to the practices of English law, 655.

N.

Nabobs, class of Englishmen to whom the name was applied, 552.
Napoleon, his early proof of talents for war, 570; protest of Lord Holland against his detention, 621; his hold on the affections of his subjects, 820. *See also* Buonaparte.
Nares, Rev. Dr., review of his "Burleigh and his Times," 235-251.
National debt, Southey's notions of, 115; England's capabilities in respect to it, 128.
Navy, its mismanagement in the reign of Charles II., 604.
Newcastle, Duke of, his appointment as head of the administration, 318; his negotiations with Fox, 318; attacked in Parliament by Chatham, 319; his intrigues, 321; his resignation of office, 321; sent for by the king on Chatham's dismissal, 323; leader of the Whig aristocracy, 324; his strong government with Chatham, 325; his contests with Henry Fox, 539; his unpopularity after the resignation of Chatham, 828; he quits office, 828.
Niagara, conquest of, 326.
Nimeguen, congress at, 465; hollow and unsatisfactory treaty of, 465.
Normans, their warfare against the Albigenses, 576.

North, Lord, his change in the constitution of the Indian government, 643; Chancellor of the Exchequer, 856.
Novels, popular, character of those which preceded Miss Burney's Evelina, 769.
Novum Organum, contrast between its doctrine and the ancient philosophy, 413, 425.
Noy, Attorney-General to Charles I., 217.
Nugent, Lord, review of his Memorials of John Hampden and his party, 204-235.
Nuncomar, his part in the revolutions in Bengal, 636; his committal for felony, trial and sentence, 647; his death, 649.

O.

Oates, Titus, remarks on his plot, 349.
Old Whig, Addison's, 811.
Omichund, 544.
Omnipresence of the Deity, Robert Montgomery's, reviewed, 127.
Opinion, public, its power, 136.
Opposition, parliamentary, when it began to take a regular form, 206.
Orange, the Prince of, 458; his success against the French, 461; his marriage with the Lady Mary, 465.
Overbury, Sir Thomas, 407.
Oxford, Earl of. See Harley, Robert.
Oxford, 754.
Oxford, University of, its inferiority to Cambridge in intellectual activity, 371; its disaffection to the House of Hanover, 805-829.

P.

Papacy, its influence, 577.
Papists and Puritans, persecution of, 57.
Parker, Archbishop, 248.
Parliament of James I., 210; Charles I., his first, 211; his second, 212; its dissolution, 212; his fifth, 219.
Parliament, effect of the publication of its proceedings, 292, 297.
Parliamentary opposition, its origin, 206.
Parties, analogy in the state of, in 1704 and 1826, 783; state of, in the time of Milton, 26; in England in 1710, 275; mixture of, at George II.'s first levée after Walpole's resignation, 816.
Party, power of, during the Reformation and the French Revolution, 239.
Pascal, Blaise, 485, 486, 574.
"Patriots," The, in opposition to Sir R. Walpole, 295; their remedies for state evils, 297.
Paulet, Sir Amias, 376.
Paulician theology, its doctrines and prevalence among the Albigenses, 575.
Peers, new creations of, 79; impolicy of limiting the number of, 811.
Pelhams, The, their ascendancy, 301; their accession to power, 315. See also Newcastle, Duke of.
Peninsular War, Southey's, 107.
People, The, comparison of their condition, in the 16th and 19th centuries, 125 et seq.; their welfare not considered in partition treaties, 258.
Périer, M., translator of the works of Machiavelli, 30.

Persecution, religious, in the reign of Elizabeth, 58; its reactionary effects upon churches and thrones, 65; in England during the progress of the Reformation, 241.
Peterborough, Earl of, his expedition to Spain, 266; his recall to England, 272.
Petition of Right, 212.
Petrarch, 5.
Philip II. of Spain, 252 et seq.
Philip III. of Spain, his accession, 261; is obliged to fly from Madrid, 270; surrender of his arsenal and ships at Carthagena, 271; defeated at Almenara, and again driven from Madrid, 273; forms a close alliance with his late competitor, 279; quarrels with France, 279.
Philip le Bel, 576.
Philips, John, author of the Splendid Shilling, 785; the poet of the English vintage, 835.
Philosophy, ancient, its characteristics, 412; its stationary character, 415; its alliance with Christianity, 415; its fall, 416; its merits compared with the Baconian, 423-425.
Pitt, William (the Second), his admiration for Hastings, 675, 680; his asperity towards Francis, 676.
Plassey, battle of, 546; its effects in England, 551.
Plays, English, of the age of Elizabeth, 158.
Poetry, definition of, 4; Robert Montgomery's, 136 et seq.; laws of, 158, 160; Dr. Johnson's standard of, 191.
Poland, contest between Protestantism and Catholicism in, 582, 587.
Pole, Cardinal, 238.
Pondicherry, 534; its occupation by the English, 654.
Poor, The, their condition in the 16th and 19th centuries, 125 et seq.
Pope, his independence of spirit, 132; Byron's admiration of him, 163; the originator of the heroic couplet, 774; his Rape of the Lock his best poem, 802; his essay on Criticism warmly praised in the Spectator, 802; his suspicious nature, 808.
Popes, review of Ranke's History of the, 571-593.
Popish Plot, circumstances which assisted the belief in, 349.
Portico, the doctrines of the School so called, 414.
Port Nati, the great case in the Exchequer Chamber, conducted by Bacon, 390.
Port Royal, 590.
Pratt, Charles, 819; Chief Justice, 850; created Lord Camden, 852.
Predestination, doctrine of, 148.
Prerogative, royal, its advance, 78; in the 16th century, 241, 244; its curtailment by the Revolution, 291. See also Crown.
Press, Milton's defence of its freedom, 28; its emancipation after the Revolution, 99; censorship of in the reign of Elizabeth, 242; its influence on the public mind after the Revolution, 777.
Prince, The, of Machiavelli, 31.
Private judgment, Mr. Gladstone's notions of the rights and abuses of, 512.

Privy Council, 467.
Progress of mankind in the political and physical sciences, 338-342; in intellectual freedom, 379.
Protestant nonconformists in the reign of Charles I., their intolerance, 224.
Protestantism, its early history, 240; its doctrine touching the right of private judgment, 512; light which Ranke has thrown upon its movements, 571; its victory in the northern parts of Europe, 577; its failure in Italy, 578; effect of its outbreak in any one part of Christendom, 579; its contest with Catholicism in France, Poland and Germany, 583; its stationary character, 592.
Prussia, king of, subsidised by the Pitt and Newcastle ministry, 326.
Prynne, 215-218.
Public spirit an antidote against bad government, 243; a safeguard against oppression, 243.
Publicity, The, of Parliamentary proceedings, influence of, 292; a remedy for corruption, 823.
Pulteney, William, his opposition to Walpole, 306; accepts a peerage, 314.
Pundits of Bengal, their jealousy of foreigners, 671.
Puritans, The, character and estimate of them, 24-26; their persecution by Charles I., 215; settlement of, in America, 218; their position at the close of the reign of Elizabeth, 379; their faults in the day of their power, and their consequences, 600.
Puritans and Papists, persecution of, by Elizabeth, 57.
Pym, John, his influence, 222; his impeachment, 226.

Q.

Quebec, conquest of, by Wolfe, 328.
Quince, Peter, sense in which he uses the word "translated," 807.

R.

Raleigh, Sir Walter, 251; his varied acquirements, 251; his position at court at the close of the reign of Elizabeth, 380; his execution, 396.
Ranke, Leopold, review of his History of the Popes, 571-593; his qualifications as an historian, 571.
Rebellion in Ireland in 1640, 224.
Reform in Parliament before the Revolution, 103; public desire for, 104; policy of it, 104, 822.
Reform Bill, 322; conduct of its opponents, 356.
Reformation, The, its history, much misrepresented, 58, 60; party divisions caused by it, 101; their consequences, 101; its immediate effect upon political liberty in England, 207; its social and political consequences, 239, 241; its effect upon the Church of Rome, 256; auspices under which it commenced, 577; its effect upon the Roman court, 581.
Reformers, always unpopular in their own age, 339.

Regicides of Charles I., 21.
Regulating Act, its introduction by Lord North, 643, 650, 655.
Religion, national establishment of, 118; the religion of the English in the 16th century, 247; what system of, should be taught by a government, 521.
Representative government, decline of, 76.
Restoration, The, degenerated character of our statesmen and politicians in the times succeeding it, 91; violence of party and low state of national feeling after it, 97; its effects upon the morals and manners of the nation, 601.
Retrospective law warranted by a certain amount of public danger, 223.
Revolution, The, its principles often grossly misrepresented, 16; its effect on the character of public men, 98; freedom of the press after it, 99; review of Mackintosh's History of, 329-367.
Revolution, the French, its social and political consequences, 239, 335; warnings which preceded it, 590.
Reynolds, Sir Joshua, 683.
Richardson, 742.
Richmond, Duke of, 859.
Riots, public, during Grenville's administration, 843.
Robespierre, 591.
Robinson, Sir Thomas, 319.
Rochester, Earl of, 355, 489, 774.
Rockingham, Marquess of, his characteristics, 844; accepts the treasury, 845; proposals of his administration on the American Stamp Act, 846, 849; his dismissal, 851; advocated the independence of the United States, 858.
Rockinghams and Bedfords, parallel between them, 845.
Roe, Sir Thomas, 559.
Rohillas, 640.
Romans and Greeks, difference between, 39.
Rome, Church of, effect of the Reformation on it, 256.
Rooke, Sir George, his capture of Gibraltar, 266.
Roundheads, The, their literature, 16.
Rousseau, his sufferings, 169.
Royalists, The, of the time of Charles I., 26; many of them true friends to the Constitution, 77; some of the most eminent formerly in opposition to the court, 225.
Rupert, Prince, 233.
Russell, Lord, 97; his conduct in the new council, 481; his death, 482.
Rutland, Earl of, his character, 401.

S.

Sacheverell, Dr., his impeachment and conviction, 275, 787.
St. John, Henry, his accession to power in 1712, 275, 280. *See also* Bolinbroke, Lord.
St. Louis, his persecution of heretics, 405.
St. Patrick, 515.
Salvator Rosa, 780.
Sandwich, Lord, 839.
"Satan," Robert Montgomery's, 141.
Saxony, its elector the natural head of the Protestant party in Germany, 584.

Schwellenberg, Madame, her position and character, 752, 757.
Science, political progress of, 337, 342, 366.
Scindia, origin of the House of, 653.
Scotland, establishment of the Kirk in, 361, 509; her progress in wealth and intelligence owing to Protestantism, 589.
Scots, The, effects of their resistance to Charles I., 219 *et seq.*; ill feeling excited against them by Bute's elevation to power, 850.
Scott, Sir Walter, 56; his Duke of Buckingham (in "Peveril,") 166; Scotticisms in his works, 778.
Sedley, Sir Charles, 595.
Self-denying ordinance, The, 83.
Seneca, his work On Anger, 413; his work on natural philosophy, 415.
Sevajee, founder of the Mahratta empire, 653.
Seward, Mr., 747.
Shaftesbury, Lord, allusion to, 3, 444; his character, 474.
Shakspeare, allusion to, 3, 250; contrasted with Byron, 166; Johnson's observations on, 192.
Shelburne, Lord, Secretary of State in Chatham's second Administration, 852; his dismissal, 856.
Shelley, Percy Bysshe, 199.
Sheridan, Richard Brinsley, 611; his speech against Hastings, 681.
Sheridan and Congreve, effect of their works upon the Comedy of England, 13.
Ship-money, question of its legality, 217 *et seq.*
Shrewsbury, Duke of, 803.
Sidmouth, Lord, 690.
Sigismund of Sweden, 584.
Sismondi, M., 52.
Smith, Adam, 565.
Smollett, T., 301.
Socrates, the first martyr of intellectual liberty, 374; his reasoning exactly the reasoning of Paley's Natural Theology, 573.
Somers, Lord Chancellor, his encouragement of literature, 776; made Lord President of the Council, 787.
Somerset, the Protector, as a promoter of the English Reformation, 63; his fall, 394.
Sophocles and the Greek drama, 7.
Southampton, Earl of, notice of, 389.
Southcote, Johanna, 587.
Southey, Robert, review of his Colloquies on Society, 105; review of his edition of Bunyan's Pilgrim's Progress, 196. *See also* Bunyan.
South Sea bubble, 306.
Spain, 231; review of Lord Mahon's War of the Succession in, 251; her state under Philip, 252; her literature during the 16th century, 253; her state a century later, 254; effect produced on her by the Reformation, 256; her disputed succession, 257; the Partition treaty, 258; designation of the War of the Spanish Succession, 259; no conversions to Protestantism in, 592.
Spectator, The, notices of it, 798, 803.
Spenser, 197.

Stafford, Lord, incident at his execution, 351.
Stamp Act, disaffection of the American colonies on account of it, 846; its repeal, 848.
Stanhope, Earl of, 306.
Stanhope, General, 269; commands in Spain, 1707, 273.
Steele, 789; his character, 790; Addison's treatment of him, 791; his origination of the Tatler, 793; his subsequent career, 797, 800, 805.
Steevens, George, 746.
Strafford, Earl of, 66; his character as a statesman, 67; bill of attainder against him, 68; his character, 216; his impeachment, attainder and execution, 222; defence of the proceedings against him, 223.
Strawberry Hill, 282, 289.
Subsidies, foreign, in the time of Charles II., 96.
Succession in Spain, War of the, 251. *See also* Spain.
Sujah Dowlah, Nabob Vizier of Oude, 639; his flight, 642; his death, 665.
Sumner, Rev. C. R., 11.
Sunderland, Earl of, 306; Secretary of State, 787; appointed Lord Lieutenant of Ireland, 804; constructs the ministry in 1717, 810.
Sorajah Dowlah, Viceroy of Bengal, his character, 541; the monster of the "Black Hole," 541; his flight and death, 547-549.
Sweden, her part in the Triple Alliance, 456.
Swift, Jonathan, his position at Sir William Temple's, 483; instance of his imitation of Addison, 773; joins the Tories, 804.
Sydney, Sir Philip, 250.

T.

Talleyrand, 92.
Tasso, 164; difference of the spirit of his poem from that of Ariosto, 582.
Tatler, The, its origination, 793; its discontinuance, 797.
Teignmouth, Lord, his high character and regard for Hastings, 673.
Temple, Lord, First Lord of the Admiralty, 322; his parallel between Byng's behaviour at Minorca and the king's behaviour at Oudenarde, 323; his resignation of office, 826; dissuades Pitt from supplanting Grenville, 842; prevents Pitt's acceptance of George III.'s offer of the administration, 844; his opposition to Rockingham's ministry on the question of the Stamp Act, 846; quarrel between him and Pitt, 851.
Temple, Sir William, review of Courtenay's Memoirs of, 439-490; his character as a statesman, 440; his family, 444, 445; his early life, 445; his courtship of Dorothy Osborne, 446, 447; historical interest of his love letters, 447, 448; his marriage, 449; his residence in Ireland, 449; his feelings towards Ireland, 450; attaches himself to Arlington, 451; his embassy to Munster, 453; appointed resident at the court of Brussels, 453; danger of his posi-

tion, 453; his interview with De Witt, 454; his negotiation of the Triple Alliance, 455-457; his fame at home and abroad, 458; his recall, and farewell of De Witt, 459; his cold reception and dismissal, 459; style and character of his compositions, 461; charged to conclude a separate peace with the Dutch, 463, 464; offered the Secretaryship of State, 465; his audiences of the king, 464-466; his share in bringing about the marriage of the Pricce of Orange with the Lady Mary, 465; required to sign the treaty of Nimeguen, 465; recalled to England, 465; his plan of a new privy council, 467, 473; his alienation from his colleagues, 480; his conduct on the Exclusion Question, 481; leaves public life, and retires to the country, 482; his literary pursuits, 484; his amanuensis, Swift, 484; his Essay on Ancient and Modern Learning, 485, 486; his Essay on the Letters of Phuleris, 486; his death and character, 489, 490.

Thackeray, Rev. Francis, review of his Life of the Rt. Hon. William Pitt, Earl of Chatham, &c., 303.

Thrale, Mrs., 178; her character, 188.

Thurlow, Lord, 568, 675, 685.

Tickell, Thomas, Addison's chief favourite, 791; his translation of the first book of the Iliad, 806; appointed by Addison Under-secretary of State, 811; Addison entrusts his works to him, 812.

Tindal, his character of the Earl of Chatham's maiden speech, 310.

Toleration, religious, the safest policy for governments, 64; conduct of James II. as a professed supporter of it, 353.

Tories, their popularity and ascendancy in 1710, 275; description of them during the sixty years following the Revolution, 180; of Walpole's time, 308; mistaken reliance by James II. upon them, 359; their principles and conduct after the Revolution, 366; contempt into which they had fallen (1754), 538; Clive unseated by their vote, 539; their joy on the accession of Anne, 783; analogy between their divisions in 1704 and in 1826, 783; their attempt to rally in 1707, 787; called to office by Queen Anne in 1710, 796; their conduct on occasion of the first representation of Addison's Cato, 800; their expulsion of Steele from the House of Commons, 803; possessed none of the public patronage in the reign of George I., 815; their hatred of the House of Hanover, 815, 820.

Torture, its use forbidden by Elizabeth, 393.

Tory, a modern, 276; his points of resemblance and of difference to a Whig of Queen Anne's time, 277.

Townshend, Lord, his quarrel with Walpole and retirement from public life, 307.

Townshend, Charles, 819; Chancellor of the Exchequer, 852; his death, 856.

Travel, its uses, 194.

Treason, high, law passed at the Revolution respecting trials for, 364.

Trial of the legality of Charles I.'s writ for ship-money, 216; of Strafford, 222; of Warren Hastings, 683.

Triple Alliance, circumstances which led to it, 453-455; its speedy conclusion and importance, 456-458; its abandonment by the English government, 460.

Tudors, The, their government popular though despotic, 242; dependent on the public favour, 244; corruption not necessary to them, 292.

Turkey-carpet style of poetry, 136.

U.

Union of England with Scotland, its happy results, 510; of England with Ireland, its unsatisfactory results, 509.

Universities, their principle of not withholding from the student works containing impurity, 594.

Utrecht, the treaty of, exasperation of parties on account of it, 278.

V.

Vansittart, Mr., Governor of Bengal, his position, 606, 607.

Verona, protest of Lord Holland against the course pursued by England at the Congress of, 621.

Voltaire the connecting link of the literary schools of Louis XIV. and Louis XVI., 165; his partiality to England, 569; his character and that of his compeers, 590.

Villiers, Sir Edward, 401.

Vision of Judgment, Southey's, 111.

W.

Wages, effect of attempts by government to limit the amount of, 599.

Waldegrave, Lord, made First Lord of the Treasury by George II., 325.

Wales, Frederick Prince of, joined the opposition to Walpole, 309; his marriage, 310; makes Pitt his groom of the bedchamber, 313; his death, 316.

Walpole, Lord, 184.

Walpole, Sir Horace, review of Lord Dover's edition of his Letters to Sir Horace Mann, 281-303.

Walpole, Sir Robert, his retaliation on the Tories for their treatment of him, 278; the "glory of the Whigs," 290; his character, 291 et seq.; the charge against him of corrupting the Parliament, 293; his conduct in regard to the Spanish war, 294; his last struggle, 296; outcry for his impeachment, 296; found it necessary to resign, 313; bill of indemnity for witnesses brought against him, 314.

Walpolean battle, the great, 290.

Walsingham, the Earl of (16th century), 250.

Wanderer, Madame D'Arblay's, 765.

War, the Art of, by Machiavelli, 49.

War of the Succession in Spain, Lord Mahon's review of, 251-280. See Spain.

War, civil. See Civil War.

Warburton, Bishop, his views on the ends of government, 519; his social contract a fiction, 519; his opinion as to the religion to be taught by government, 521.

Warning, not the only end of punishment, 69.

Warwick, Countess Dowager of, 809.
Wealth, tangible and intangible, 115; national and private, 116, 117; its increase among all classes in England, 128-129; its accumulation and diffusion in England and Continental states, 128.
Wedderburne, Alexander, his able defence of Lord Clive, 568, 674.
Wellesley, Marquis, his eminence as a statesman, 467; his opinion as to the expediency of reducing the numbers of the Privy Council, 467.
Wendover, his recovery of the elective franchise, 211.
Wesley, John, Southey's Life of, 107; his dislike to the doctrine of predestination, 517.
Westphalia, the treaty of, 577, 588.
Wharton, Earl of, lord lieutenant of Ireland, 791.
Wheler, Mr., his appointment as Governor-General of India, 651; his conduct in the council, 652, 660.
Whigs, The, their unpopularity and loss of power in 1710, 275; their position in Walpole's time, 308; doctrines and literature they patronised during the seventy years they were in power, 365; exclamations of George II. against them, 325; their violence in 1679, 349; the king's revenge on them, 352; revival of their strength, 353; their conduct at the Revolution, 359; after that event, 365; their fall on the accession of Anne, 782; in the ascendant in 1705, 787; Queen Anne's dislike of them, 795; their dismissal by her, 796; their success in the administration of the government, 706; dissensions and reconstruction of the Whig government in 1717, 810; enjoyed all the public patronage in the reign of George I., 815; division of them into two classes, old and young, 844; superior character of the young Whig school, 844. See Tories.
Whig and Tory, inversion of the meaning of, 276.
Whigs and Tories after the Revolution, 99; their relative condition in 1710, 275; their essential characteristics, 815; their transformation in the reign of George I., 815; analogy presented by France, 815; their relative progress, 276; subsidence of party spirit between them, 815; revival under Bute's administration of the animosity between them, 830.
Whitgift, his character, 375; his Calvanistic doctrines, 516.
Wickliffe, John, juncture at which he rose, 577; his influence in England, Germany and Bohemia, 577.

Wilberforce, William, 681.
Wilkes, John, 831 et seq.
Wilkie, David, 627.
William III., 768; low state of national prosperity and national character in his reign, 99; unpopularity of his person and measures, 262; suffered under a complication of diseases, 263; his death, 263; limitation of his prerogatives, 292; compact with the Convention, 360; his vices not obtruded on the public eye, 612; his assassination planned, 613.
Williams, Dean of Westminster, 402-403.
Williams, John, 689, 746.
Windham, Mr., his opinion of Sheridan's speech against Hastings, 681.
Wine, excess in, not a sign of ill-breeding in the reign of Queen Anne, 790.
Witt, John de, power with which he governed Holland, 452; his interview with Temple, 454; his violent death, 461.
Wolcot, 746.
Wolfe, General, his conquest of Quebec, and death, 326.
Woodfall, Mr., his dealings with Junius, 644.
Wordsworth, Byron's distaste for, 163; characteristics of his poems, 165-168.
Works, public, employment of the public wealth in, 116; public and private, comparative value of, 117.
Writing, grand canon of, 251.
Wycherley, William, his literary merits and faults, 602; age at which he wrote his plays, 602, 603; his favour with the Duchess of Cleveland, 603; his marriage, 605; his embarrassments, 606; his character as a writer, 608-610; his severe handling by Collier, 615; analogy between him and Congreve, 620.

X.

Xenophon, his report of the reasoning of Socrates in confutation of Aristodemus, 573.

Y.

York, Duke of, 466; anxiety excited by his sudden return from Holland, 480; detestation of him, 480; revival of the question of his exclusion, 481.
York House, the London residence of Bacon and of his father, 400, 410.
Youge, Sir William, 308.
Young, Dr., his testimony to Addison's colloquial powers, 789, 790.

Z.

Zohak, King, Persian fable of, 510.

FLORIN NOVELS, Cloth—*continued.*

DICKENS, Charles.

Sketches by "Boz."
Nicholas Nickleby.
Oliver Twist.
Barnaby Rudge.
Old Curiosity Shop.
Dombey and Son.
Grimaldi the Clown, with CRUIKSHANK'S Illustrations.
Martin Chuzzlewit.
Pickwick Papers.
David Copperfield. (Copyright.)
Pictures from Italy and American Notes.

DUMAS, Alexandre.

The Three Musketeers.
Twenty Years After.
Monte Cristo.
Marguerite de Valois.
Chicot, the Jester.
Forty-five Guardsmen.
Taking the Bastile.
The Queen's Necklace.
The Conspirators.
The Regent's Daughter.
Memoirs of a Physician.
The Countess of Charny.
The Vicomte de Bragelonne, Vol. 1.
———— Vol. 2.

FERRIER, Miss.

Marriage.
The Inheritance.
Destiny.

FIELDING, Henry.

Tom Jones.
Joseph Andrews.
Amelia.

GRANT, James.

The Romance of War.
The Aide de Camp.
The Scottish Cavalier.
Bothwell.
Philip Rollo.
Legends of the Black Watch.
Jane Seton.
The Yellow Frigate.

LAWRENCE, George.

Guy Livingstone.
Sword and Gown.
Barren Honour.

LEVER, Charles.

Harry Lorrequer.
Charles O'Malley.
Jack Hinton.
Arthur O'Leary.
Con Cregan.
Horace Templeton.

LOVER, Samuel.

Handy Andy.
Rory O'More.

LYTTON, Lord.

Author's Copyright Revised Editions containing Prefaces to be found in no other Edition.

Pelham.
Paul Clifford.
Eugene Aram.
Last Days of Pompeii.
Rienzi.
Ernest Maltravers.
Alice; or, The Mysteries.
Night and Morning.
Disowned.
Devereux.
Godolphin.
Last of the Barons.
Leila; Pilgrims of the Rhine.

FLORIN NOVELS, Cloth—*continued*.

LYTTON, Lord—*continued*.
   Falkland; Zicci.
   Zanoni.
   The Caxtons.
   Harold.
   Lucretia.
   The Coming Race.
   A Strange Story.
   Kenelm Chillingly.
   Pausanias: and The Haunted and the Haunters.
   My Novel, Vol. 1.
   ——— Vol. 2.
   What will He Do with It? Vol. 1
   ——————————Vol. 2.
   The Parisians, Vol. 1.
   ——— Vol. 2.

MARRYAT, *Captain*.
   Frank Mildmay.
   Midshipman Easy.
   Phantom Ship.
   Peter Simple.
   The King's Own.
   Newton Forster.
   Jacob Faithful.
   The Pacha of Many Tales.
   Japhet in Search of a Father.
   Dog Fiend.
   Poacher.
   Percival Keene.
   Monsieur Violet.
   Rattlin, the Reefer.
   Valerie.
   Pirate; Three Cutters.
   Poor Jack.
   Masterman Ready.
   Olla Podrida.
   Settlers in Canada.
   The Mission; or, Scenes in Africa.
   The Privateersman.
   Children of the New Forest.
   The Little Savage.

NEALE, *W. J. N*.
   The Pride of the Mess.

PORTER, *Jane*.
   The Scottish Chiefs.
   The Pastor's Fireside.

RADCLIFFE, *Mrs*.
   The Romance of the Forest.
   The Mysteries of Udolpho.

REID, *Captain Mayne*.
   The Scalp Hunters.
   The Rifle Rangers.
   The War Trail.
   The White Chief.
   The Quadroon.
   The White Gauntlet.
   Lost Lenore.
   The Hunter's Feast.
   The Boy Slaves.
   The Cliff Climbers.
   The Giraffe Hunters.
   The Ocean Waifs.
   The Half Blood.
   The Wild Huntress.
   The Tiger Hunter.
   The White Squaw.
   The Headless Horseman.
   The Guerilla Chief.
   The Maroon.
   Wood Rangers.
   The Desert Home.
   The Bush Boys.
   The Plant Hunters.
   The Boy Hunters.

RICHARDSON, *Samuel*.
   Clarissa Harlowe
   Pamela.
   Sir Charles Grandison.

SCOTT, *Michael*.
   Tom Cringle's Log.
   The Cruise of the "Midge."

Lightning Source UK Ltd.
Milton Keynes UK
UKHW021037271220
375924UK00003B/219